EUGENE O'NEILL

EUGENE O'NEILL

COMPLETE PLAYS
1913–1920

THE LIBRARY OF AMERICA

PS
3529
.N5
1988
V.1

Volume arrangement, notes, and chronology copyright © 1988 by
Literary Classics of the United States, Inc., New York, N.Y.
All rights reserved.
No part of this book may be reproduced commercially
by offset-lithographic or equivalent copying devices without
the permission of the publisher.

Bound East for Cardiff, *In the Zone*, *Ile*, *The Long Voyage Home*, *The
Moon of the Caribbees*, *The Rope*, *Where the Cross Is Made* © 1919,
renewed 1946; *Beyond the Horizon*, *The Dreamy Kid* © 1920, renewed 1947; *The Straw* © 1921, renewed 1947; *Gold* © 1920, renewed 1948; *"Anna Christie"* © 1922, renewed 1949; *The Emperor
Jones* © 1921, renewed 1948. Published by arrangement with
Random House, Inc.

The Personal Equation © 1988; *Chris Christophersen* © 1919, renewed
1946. Published by arrangement with Yale University.

The paper used in this publication meets the
minimum requirements of the American National Standard
for Information Sciences—Permanence of Paper for
Printed Library Materials, ANSI Z39.48—1984.

Distributed to the trade in the United States
and Canada by the Viking Press.

Library of Congress Catalog Card Number: 88-50685
For cataloging information, see end of *Notes* section.
ISBN 0-940450-48-8

First Printing
The Library of America—40

Manufactured in the United States of America

TRAVIS BOGARD
WROTE THE NOTES AND SELECTED
THE TEXTS FOR THIS VOLUME

CONCORDIA COLLEGE LIBRARY
2811 N. E. HOLMAN ST.
PORT   OREGON 97211

CONCORDIA COLLEGE LIBRARY
BRONXVILLE, N. Y.

Grateful acknowledgment is made to the National Endowment for the Humanities, the Ford Foundation, and the Andrew W. Mellon Foundation for their generous support of this series.

Contents

A WIFE FOR A LIFE

A Play in One Act

CHARACTERS

THE OLDER MAN
JACK, *The Younger Man*
OLD PETE, *a miner*

A Wife for a Life

SCENE—*The edge of the Arizona desert; a plain dotted in the foreground with clumps of sagebrush. On the horizon a lonely butte is outlined, black and sinister against the lighter darkness of a sky with stars. The time is in the early hours of the night. In the foreground stands a ragged tent the flap of which is open. Leaning against it are some shovels and a pick or two. Two saddles are on the ground nearby. Before the tent is a smouldering camp fire at which an elderly man of about fifty is seated. He is dressed in miner's costume; flannel shirt, khaki trousers, high boots etc.—all patched and showing evidences of long wear and tear. His wide-brimmed Stetson hat lies on the ground beside him. His hair is turning gray and his face is the face of one who has wandered far, lived hard, seen life in the rough, and is a little weary of it all. Withal his air and speech are those of an educated man whose native refinement has clung to him in spite of many hard knocks.*

On one side of the tent stands a rough stool and a gold-miner's panning tub—a square box half filled with water.

THE OLDER MAN—(*stirring the fire in a futile attempt to start it into flame*) I wonder what can be keeping him so long? (*hears noise of someone approaching*) Hello Jack, I was just beginning to think you were lost.

(*Old Pete enters. He is an old man dressed in rough miner's costume but he wears spurs and carries a quirt in his hand. He is covered with dust and has evidently been riding hard.*)

OLD PETE—It aint Jack. It's me.

THE OLDER MAN—(*disappointed*) Hello Pete. What brings you around at this time of the night?

OLD PETE—(*taking telegram from his pocket*) I was just leaving Lawson when the operator stopped me and give me this for Jack. I seen your camp fire burning and reckoned I'd bring it right over.

THE OLDER MAN—(*taking telegram*) Many thanks Pete. Won't you sit down and rest a bit?

OLD PETE—Much obliged but I reckon I'll travel along. I ain't slept none to speak of in the past few nights and I got to be up at sunrise. (*grinning sheepishly*) That fool town of

Lawson sure does keep you up nights. (*He starts to go, then stops.*) Claim panning out as good as ever?

THE OLDER MAN—Better every day. This morning we took a sample from the upper end which we haven't touched so far. It looks good but we haven't panned it yet.

OLD PETE—You-alls ought to get rich. You know how to keep money. Now me and money never could get on no-way. (*pulls out pockets ruefully*) They cleaned me out in Lawson this time and I reckon they'll clean me again the next time. (*shaking his head*) Cities is sure hell that-a-way. Adios. (*exits*)

THE OLDER MAN—Good night. Poor Pete. Same old story. Been bucking the faro bank again I suppose. (*looks at telegram*) Hmm. Wonder what this is? Jack has had no correspondence in the five years I've been with him. May be something important in connection with the mine. I guess I'd better open it. He won't mind anyway. (*He opens the telegram and reads aloud*) "I am waiting. Come." No name signed. It comes from New York too. Well it's too many for me. I give it up. (*puts telegram in pocket*) Must be that fool operator got mixed up in his names. I wouldn't like to see Jack obey any summons like that. He's about all I've got now and I'd hate to see him leave just when we've struck it rich. (*dismissing the subject*) I guess this wire is all a mistake anyway. (*He looks around yawning and his eye lights on the panning tub.*) Now if only the upper part of the claim is as rich as that we've been working— (*The noise of someone approaching is heard.*) Here he comes now. Welcome wanderer! Where have you been all this time?

(*Jack enters. He is dressed about the same as the Older Man but is much younger—in the early thirties.*)

JACK—One of the horses slipt his hobbles and I had quite a hunt for him. I finally found him down by the spring wallowing around as if water were the commonest thing in this section of Arizona. Fool beast!

THE OLDER MAN—(*forgetting all about the telegram*) It's a strange thing we should run into water out here where the maps say there isn't any. It's the one blessing we've found in this land God forgot. We're fools for luck for once.

JACK—(*nodding*) Yes. (*then rather exultantly*) But we have small cause to kick about this lonely hole after all. Any place is God's country to a man if there's gold in it and he finds it. There's gold here and *(taking a small bag from his pocket and shaking it)* we've found it. So long live the desert say I.

THE OLDER MAN—Those are my sentiments. *(He rolls a cigarette paper and setting it afire in the flame lights his pipe.)* It sure looks as if our ship had come in at last here on the rim of the world. The luck was due to change. We've had our share of the bad variety; just missing a strike in every jumping-off place from South Africa to Alaska. We've taken our hard knocks with the imitation of a laugh at any rate and *(stretching out his hand to the younger man who grasps it heartily)* we've been good pals ever since that day in the Transvaal five years ago when you hauled me out of the river, saved my life, and our friendship began. *(as the younger man starts to speak)* No you needn't try to stop me expressing my gratitude. I haven't forgotten that day and I never will.

JACK—*(to change the subject)* I'm going to see what that prospect we took at the other end of the claim looks like. *(He goes into the tent and returns with a gold pan heaped with dirt under his arm and sitting down in front of the panning tub proceeds to test the prospect. He washes the heap of dirt down until there is but a handful of gravel left. The Older Man comes over and stands behind him looking over his shoulder. Finally after one quick flip of the pan Jack points to the sediment left in the bottom in which a small heap of bright yellow particles can be seen.)* What do you think of that?

THE OLDER MAN—*(reaching over and feeling them with his fingers)* O'course gold; just as I expected. The upper end of the claim is just as rich as it is down here.

JACK—*(with growing excitement)* There's over a quarter of an ounce here at least. That's five dollars a pan—better than we've ever panned down here at any time since we made the strike four months ago. *(lays the pan aside)* I tell you this claim is too much for us to handle alone. One of us ought to go East and organize a company.

THE OLDER MAN—Then it will have to be you. I'm too old. *(Jack smiles and makes a deprecating gesture.)* Anyway I never could get along with civilization and *(laughing)* civilization never cared overmuch for me. *(goes over and sits down by the fire*)—(*after a pause*) You've seemed to be hankering after the East quite a lot in the last month or so. (*smiling*) Getting tired of the company here eh?

JACK—(*quickly*) No you know that isn't so after all the years we've been pals and all we've been through together.

THE OLDER MAN—(*jokingly*) Then what is the attraction the effete East has to offer? (*mockingly*) It's a woman I suppose?

JACK—(*with dignity*) An angel rather.

THE OLDER MAN—(*cynically*) They're all angels—at first. The only trouble is their angelic attributes lack staying qualities. (*then half bitterly*) At any rate you'd find them hard to prove by my experiences.

JACK—(*shrugging his shoulders a little impatiently*) You're a disgusting cynic and I refuse to argue. You know we've never been able to agree on that subject. I'm going to hunt out that bottle we've carried about so long and we'll drink to the mine and future prosperity. (*He goes into tent.*) Here it is. (*He returns with a quart of whiskey, opens it with a knife and pours out two drinks in the tin cups.*) (*laughing*) I think this is a proper occasion for celebration—the two Prodigals welcome the fatted calf. Let's make it a christening also. Here's to the Yvette mine!

THE OLDER MAN—(*who has been laughing turns suddenly grim. His hand trembles as he clinks cups and he almost spills some of the whiskey. He speaks in harsh jerky tones.*) Why the Yvette?

JACK—(*not noticing his agitation*) I know it sounds like rather a frivolous name for a mine but I have a hunch. There's a romance back of it—my romance. That was her name. One rarely speaks of such things. I've never told you but I will now if you care to hear it. It was over a year before I met you. I had just been out of mining school a short time and was prospecting around in the mountains of Peru hoping to hit a bonanza there. At the time I speak of I had returned to reoutfit at a small mining camp near the frontier of Ecuador. It was there I met her. She was the wife of a broken-down mining engineer from the States, over twenty years her senior. (*The Older Man who has been listening intently is poking the fire nervously and his face becomes harsher and harsher.*) According to all accounts he was a drunken brute who left her alone most of the time and only lived from one drunk to another. Personally I never saw him. It was probably better that I did not. You see I fell in love with her on the spot and the thought of how he treated her made my blood boil.

THE OLDER MAN—(*in stifled tones*) What was the name of the mining town you mention? I've been in that country myself—many years ago.

JACK—San Sebastien. Do you know it?

(*At the words "San Sebastien" the Older Man seems to crumple up. Nothing seems alive about him but his eyes, staring horribly, and his right hand which nervously fingers the gun in the belt around his waist.*)

THE OLDER MAN—(*in a hoarse whisper*) Yes. I know it. Go on.

JACK—(*dreamily, absorbed in his own thoughts*) I loved her. In the corrupt environment of a mining camp she seemed like a lily growing in a field of rank weeds. I longed to take her away from all that atmosphere of sordid sin and suffering; away from her beast of a husband who was steadily ruining that beautiful young life and driving her to desperation. I over-stayed my time. I should have been back in the mountains. I went to see her often. He was always away it seemed. Finally people began to talk. Then I realized that the time had come and I told her that I loved her. I shall never forget her face. She looked at me with great calm eyes but her lips trembled as she said: "I know you love me and I—I love you; but you must go away and we must never see each other again. I am his wife and I must keep my pledge."

THE OLDER MAN—(*starting to his feet and half drawing the pistol from the holster*) You lie!

JACK—(*rudely awakened from his dream also springs to his feet, his face angry and perplexed*) Why what do you mean? What is it?

THE OLDER MAN—(*controlling his rage with a mighty effort and sitting down again*) Nothing. Nerves I guess. It's my sore spot—the virtue of women. I've seen but little of it in my mining camp experiences and your heroine seems to me too impossible. (*Wonderingly Jack sits down beside him again.*)

JACK—(*eagerly*) You wouldn't think so if you could have seen her. (*The Older Man covers his face in his hands and groans.*) Here's a picture of her she sent me a year ago. (*takes small photo out of pocket of his shirt*) Look at it. (*handing him the photo*) Do you think a woman with a face like that could be the regular mining camp kind? (*feels in pocket again and goes into tent as if searching for something*)

THE OLDER MAN—(*looks at the photo with haggard eyes for a moment, then whispers in a half sob*) My wife! (*Then staring into vacancy he speaks to himself, unconsciously aloud.*) She has not changed.

JACK—(*who has come back from the tent with a soiled envelope in his hand in time to hear the last sentence*) (*astonished*) Changed? Who? Do you know her?

THE OLDER MAN—(*quickly mastering his emotion and lying bravely*) No. Of course not. But she reminds me of a girl I knew here in the States a long time ago. But the girl I speak of must be an old woman by this time. I forget my grey hairs.

JACK—Yvette is only twenty-five. Her parents were poor French people. In a fit of mistaken zeal for her welfare they forced her to marry this man when she was too young to know her own mind. They thought they were making an excellent match. Immediately after the marriage he dragged her off to San Sebastien where he was half owner of a small mine. It seems the devil broke out in him before they were hardly settled there. (*after a pause*) I'd like to be fair to him. Maybe he realized that she could never love him and was trying to drown the memory of the mistake he had made. He certainly loved her—in his fashion.

THE OLDER MAN—(*in a pathetic whisper*) Yes. He must have loved her—in his fashion.

JACK—(*looking at the letter in his hand which he had forgotten*) Ah, I forgot. I have proof positive of her innocence and noble-mindedness. Here is a letter which she wrote and sent to me the morning I was leaving. It's only a few words. Read it Mr. Doubting Thomas. (*hands letter to the Older Man*)

THE OLDER MAN—(*His hands tremble.*) (*aside*) Her writing. (*reading aloud*) "I must keep my oath. He needs me and I must stay. To be true to myself I must be true to him. (*aside "My God I was wrong after all"*) Sometime I may send for you. Good-bye" signed Yvette. (*He folds the letter up slowly, puts it back in the envelope and hands it to Jack. Suddenly he turns to him with quick suspicion.*) What does she mean by that last sentence?

JACK—When I left I gave her my address in the States and she promised to let me know if she changed her mind or if conditions changed.

THE OLDER MAN—(*with grim irony*) You mean if the drunken husband died.

JACK—(*his face growing hard*) Yes. That's what I mean.

THE OLDER MAN—Well how do you know he hasn't? Have you ever heard from her since?

JACK—Only the one time when she sent the picture I showed you. I received the letter from her in Cape Town a year ago. It had been forwarded from the States. She said her husband had disappeared soon after I left. No one knew where he had gone but the rumor was that he had set out on my trail for vengeance, refusing to believe in her innocence. (*grimly patting his gun*) I'm sorry he didn't find me.

THE OLDER MAN—(*He has by this time regained control of himself and speaks quite calmly.*) Where is she now?

JACK—Living with her parents in New York. She wrote to say that she would wait a year longer. If he did not return to her by then she would become legally free of him and would send for me. The year is up today but (*hopelessly*) I have received no word. (*walks back and looks into the darkness as if hoping to see someone coming*)

THE OLDER MAN—(*suddenly remembers the telegram he has. He takes it from his pocket as if to give it to Jack; then hesitates and says in agony*) My God I cannot! (*as he realizes the full significance of what the telegram says. Mastered by a contrary impulse he goes to burn it in the camp fire but again hesitates. Finally as Jack returns slowly to the camp fire he turns quickly and hands the telegram to him.*) Cheer up! Here's a surprise for you. Read this. Old Pete brought it from Lawson before you returned and I forgot all about it. I opened it by mistake thinking it might have something to do with the mine. (*He turns quickly away as if unable to bear the sight of Jack's elation.*)

(*Jack feverishly opens the yellow envelope. His face lights up and he gives an exclamation of joy and rushes to the Older Man.*)

JACK—It's too good to be true. Tell me I am not dreaming.

THE OLDER MAN—(*He looks at Jack steadily for a moment, then tries hard to smile and mutters*) Congratulations. (*He is suffering horribly.*)

JACK—(*misunderstanding the cause of his emotion*) Never mind Old Pal I won't be gone long and when I come back I'll bring her with me.

THE OLDER MAN—(*hastily*) No. I'll manage all right. Better stay East for a while. We'll need someone there when the work really starts.

JACK—When can I get a train?

THE OLDER MAN—If you ride hard and start right away you can get to Lawson in time for the Limited at three in the morning.

JACK—(*rushing off with saddle under arm*) My horse is hobbled at the mouth of the canyon.

THE OLDER MAN—(*stands in front of tent*) So I have found him after all these years and I cannot even hate him. What tricks Fate plays with us. When he told me his name that first day I noticed that it was the same as the man's I was looking for. But he seemed such a boy to me and my heart went out to him so strongly that I never for an instant harbored the idea that he could be the John Sloan I was after. Of course he never knew my right name. I wonder what he would say if he knew. I've half a mind to tell him. But no, what's the use? Why should I mar his happiness? In this affair I alone am to blame and I must pay. As I listened to his story this evening until no doubt remained that he was the John Sloan I had sworn to kill, my hand reached for my gun and all the old hate flared up in my heart. And then I remembered his face as he looked that day in the Transvaal when he bent over me after saving my life at the risk of his own. I could almost hear his words as he spoke that day when death was so near: "All right, old pal, you're all right." Then my hand left my gun and the old hatred died out forever. I could not do it. (*He pauses and a bitter smile comes over his face as at some new thought.*) O what a fool I have been. She was true to me in spite of what I was. God bless him for telling me so. God grant they may both be happy—the only two beings I have ever loved. And I—must keep wandering on. I cannot be the ghost at their feast.

JACK—(*entering hurriedly, putting on spurs, hat, etc.*) Good-bye Old Pal. I'm sorry to leave you this way but I have waited so long for this. You understand don't you?

THE OLDER MAN—(*slowly*) Yes. (*grasping his hand and looking deep into his eyes*) Good-bye and God bless you both.

JACK—(*feelingly*) Good-bye. (*exits*)

THE OLDER MAN—(*sits down by the camp fire and buries face in his hands. Finally he rouses himself with an effort, stirs the camp fire and smiling with a whimsical sadness softly quotes:*) Greater love hath no man than this that he giveth his wife for his friend.

(*The Curtain Falls*)

THE WEB

A Play in One Act

CHARACTERS

Rose Thomas
Steve, *a "Cadet"*
Tim Moran, *a Yeggman*
A Policeman
Two Plain Clothes Men

The Web

SCENE—*A squalid bedroom on the top floor of a rooming house on the lower East Side, New York. The wall paper is dirty and torn in places showing the plaster beneath. There is an open window in back looking out on a fire escape on which a bottle of milk can be seen. On the right is a door leading to the hallway. On the left a wash-stand with a bowl and pitcher, and some meager articles of a woman's toilet-set scattered on it. Above the wash-stand a cracked mirror hangs from a nail in the wall. In the middle of the room stands a rickety table and a chair. In the left hand corner near the window is a bed in which a baby is lying asleep. A gas jet near the mirror furnishes the only light.*

Rose Thomas, a dark-haired young woman looking thirty but really only twenty-two, is discovered sitting on the chair smoking a cheap Virginia cigarette. An empty beer bottle and a dirty glass stand on the table beside her. Her hat, a gaudy, cheap affair with a scraggy, imitation plume, is also on the table. Rose is dressed in the tawdry extreme of fashion. She has earrings in her ears, bracelets on both wrists, and a quantity of rings—none of them genuine. Her face is that of a person in an advanced stage of consumption—deathly pale with hollows in under the eyes, which are wild and feverish. Her attitude is one of the deepest dejection. When she glances over at the bed, however, her expression grows tenderly maternal. From time to time she coughs—a harsh, hacking cough that shakes her whole body. After these spells she raises her handkerchief to her lips—then glances at it fearfully.

The time is in the early hours of a rainy summer night. The monotonous sound of the rain falling on the flags of the court below is heard.

ROSE—(*listening to the rain—throws the cigarette wearily on the table*) Gawd! What a night! (*laughing bitterly*) What a chance I got! (*She has a sudden fit of coughing; then gets up and goes over to the bed and bending down gently kisses the sleeping child on the forehead. She turns away with a sob and murmurs*) What a life! Poor kid! (*She goes over to the mirror and makes up her eyes and cheeks. The effect is ghastly. Her blackened eyes look enormous and the dabs of rouge on each cheek serve to heighten her aspect of feverish illness. Just as she has completed her toilet and is putting on her hat in front of the mirror, the door is flung open and Steve lurches in and bolts the door after him. He has very evidently been drinking. In appearance he is a typical "cadet," flashily dressed, rat-eyed, weak of mouth, undersized, and showing on his face the effects of drink and drugs.*)

ROSE—(*hurriedly putting her hat down on the wash-stand—half frightened*) Hello, Steve.

STEVE—(*looking her up and down with a sneer*) Yuh're a fine lookin' mess! (*He walks over and sits down in the chair.*) Yuh look like a dead one. Put on some paint and cheer up! Yuh give me the willies standin' there like a ghost.

ROSE—(*rushes over to mirror and plasters on more rouge—then turns around*) Look, Steve! Ain't that better?

STEVE—Better? Naw, but it'll do. (*seeing empty beer bottle*) Gimme a drink!

ROSE—Yuh know there ain't any. That's the bottle yuh brought up last night.

STEVE—(*with peevish anger*) Yuh lie! I'll bet yuh got some burried around here some place. Yuh're always holdin' out on me and yuh got to quit it, see?

ROSE—I never hold out on yuh and yuh know it. That's all the thanks I get. (*angrily*) What'ud yuh do if I was like Bessie with your friend Jack? Then yuh might have some chance to kick. She's got enough salted to leave him any time she wants to—and he knows it and sticks to her like glue. Yuh don't notice him runnin' after every doll he sees like some guys I know. He's afraid of losin' her—while *you* don't care.

STEVE—(*flattered—in a conciliating tone*) Aw, shut up! Yuh make me sick with dat line of bull. Who said I was chasin' any dolls? (*then venomously*) I'm not so sure Jack is wise to Bessie holdin' out on him; but I'll tell him, and if he isn't wise to it, Bessie'll be in for a good beatin'.

ROSE—Aw, don't do that! What 'cha got against her? She ain't done nothin' to you, has she?

STEVE—Naw; but she oughta be learned a lesson dat's all. She oughta be on the level with him. Us guys has got to stand together. What'ud we do if all youse dolls got holdin' out on the side?

ROSE—(*dejectedly*) Don't ask me. I dunno. It's a bum game all round. (*She has a fit of horrible coughing.*)

STEVE—(*his nerves shattered*) Dammit! Stop that barkin'. It goes right trou me. Git some medicine for it, why don't yuh?

ROSE—(*wiping her lips with her handkerchief*) I did but it ain't no good.

STEVE—Then git somethin' else. I told yuh months ago to go and see a doctor. Did yuh?

ROSE—(*nervously, after a pause*) No.

STEVE—Well den, yuh can't blame me. It's up to you.

ROSE—(*speaking eagerly and beseechingly, almost in tears*) Listen, Steve! Let me stay in to-night and go to the Doc's. I'm sick. (*pointing to breast*) I got pains here and it seems as if I was on fire inside. Sometimes I git dizzy and everythin' goes round and round. Anyway it's rainin' and my shoes are full of holes. There won't be no one out to-night, and even if there was they're all afraid of me on account of this cough. Gimme a couple of dollars and let me go to the Doc's and git some medicine. Please, Steve, for Gawd's sake! I'll make it up to yuh when I'm well. I'll be makin' lots of coin then and yuh kin have it all. (*goes off into a paroxysm of coughing*) I'm so sick!

STEVE—(*in indignant amazement*) A couple of beans! What'd'yuh think I am—the mint?

ROSE—But yuh had lots of coin this mornin'. Didn't I give yuh all I had?

STEVE—(*sullenly*) Well, I ain't got it now, see? I got into a game at Tony's place and they cleaned me. I ain't got a nick. (*with sudden anger*) And I wouldn't give it to yuh if I had it. D'yuh think I'm a simp to be gittin' yuh protection and keepin' the bulls from runnin' yuh in when all yuh do is to stick at home and play dead? If yuh want any coin git out and make it. That's all I got to say.

ROSE—(*furiously*) So that's all yuh got to say, is it? Well, I'll hand yuh a tip right here. I'm gittin' sick of givin' yuh my roll and gittin' nothin' but abuse in retoin. Yuh're half drunk now. And yuh been hittin' the pipe too; I kin tell by the way your eyes look. D'yuh think I'm goin' to stand for a guy that's always full of booze and hop? Not so yuh could notice it! There's too many others I kin get.

STEVE—(*His eyes narrow and his voice becomes loud and threatening.*) Can that chatter, d'yuh hear me? If yuh ever t'row me down—look out! I'll get yuh!

ROSE—(*in a frenzy*) Get me? Wha'd I care? D'yuh think I'm so stuck on this life I wanta go on livin'? Kill me! Wha'd I care?

STEVE—(*jumps up from the table and raises his hand as if to strike her. He shouts*) Fur Chris' sake, shut up! (*The baby, awakened by the loud voices, commences to cry.*)

ROSE—(*her anger gone in a flash*) Sssshhh! There, we woke her up. Keep still, Steve. I'll go out, yuh needn't worry. Jest don't make so much noise, that's all. (*She goes over to the bed and cuddles the child. It soon falls asleep again. She begins to cough and rising to her feet walks away from the bed keeping her face turned away from the baby.*)

STEVE—(*who has been watching her with a malignant sneer*) Yuh'll have to take that kid out of the bed. I gotta git some sleep.

ROSE—But, Steve, where'll I put her? There's no place else.

STEVE—On the floor—any place. Wha'd I care where yuh put it?

ROSE—(*supplicatingly*) Aw please, Steve! Be a good guy! She won't bother yuh none. She's fast asleep. Yuh got three-quarters of the bed to lie on. Let her stay there.

STEVE—Nix! Yuh heard what I said, didn't yuh? Git busy, then. Git her out of there.

ROSE—(*with cold fury*) I won't do it.

STEVE—Yuh won't, eh? Den I will. (*He makes a move toward the bed.*)

ROSE—(*standing between him and the bed in a resolute attitude, speaks slowly and threateningly*) I've stood about enough from you. Don't yuh dare touch her or I'll—

STEVE—(*blusteringly, a bit shaken in his coward soul however*) What'll yuh do? Don't try and bluff me. And now we're talkin' about it I wanta tell yuh that kid has got to go. I've stood fur it as long as I kin with its ballin' and whinin'. Yuh gotta git rid of it, that's all. Give it to some orphan asylum. They'll take good care of it. I know what I'm talkin' about cause I was brung up in one myself. (*with a sneer*) What'd *you* want with a kid? (*Rose winces.*) A fine mother *you* are and dis is a swell dump to bring up a family in.

ROSE—Please, Steve for the love of Gawd lemme keep her! She's all I got to live for. If yuh take her away I'll die. I'll kill myself.

STEVE—(*contemptuously*) Dat's what they all say. But she's got to go. All yuh do now is fuss over dat kid, comin' home every ten minutes to see if it's hungry or somethin'! Dat's why we're broke all the time. I've stood fur it long enough.

ROSE—(*on her knees—weeping*) Please, Steve, for Gawd's sake lemme keep her!

STEVE—(*coldly*) Stop dat blubberin'. It won't do no good. I give yuh a week. If yuh don't git dat brat outa here in a week den I will.

ROSE—Wha'd'yuh mean? What'll yuh do?

STEVE—I'll have yuh pinched and sent to the Island. The kid'll be took away from yuh then.

ROSE—(*in anguish*) Yuh're jest tryin' to scare me, ain't yuh, Steve? They wouldn't do that, would they?

STEVE—Yuh'll soon know whether dey would or not.

ROSE—But yuh wouldn't have me pinched, would yuh, Steve? Yuh wouldn't do me dirt like that?

STEVE—I wouldn't, wouldn't I? Yuh jest wait and see!

ROSE—Aw, Steve, I always been good to *you*.

STEVE—Git dat kid outa here or I'll put yuh in the cooler as sure as hell!

ROSE—(*maddened, rushing at him with outstretched hands*) Yuh dirty dog! (*There is a struggle during which the table is overturned. Finally Steve frees himself and hits her in the face with his fist, knocking her down. At the same instant the door from the hallway is forced open and Tim Moran pushes his way in. He is short and thick set, with a bullet head, close-cropped black hair, a bull neck, and small blue eyes set close together. Although distinctly a criminal type his face is in part redeemed by its look of manliness. He is dressed in dark ill-fitting clothes, and has an automatic revolver in his hand which he keeps pointed at Steve.*)

TIM—(*pointing to the door, speaks to Steve with cold contempt*) Git outa here, yuh lousy skunk, and stay out! (*as Steve's hand goes to his hip*) Take yer hand away from that gat or I'll fill yuh full of holes. (*Steve is cowed and obeys.*) Now git out and don't come back. If yuh bother this goil again I'll fix yuh and fix yuh right. D'yuh get me?

STEVE—(*snarling, and slinking toward door*) Yuh think yuh're some smart, dontcha, buttin' in dis way on a guy? It ain't none of your business. She's my goil.

TIM—D'yuh think I'm goin' to stand by and let yuh beat her up jest cause she wants to keep her kid? D'yuh think I'm as low as you are, yuh dirty mut? Git outa here before I croak yuh.

STEVE—(*standing in the doorway and looking back*) Yuh got the drop on me now; but I'll get yuh, yuh wait and see! (*to Rose*) And *you* too. (*He goes out and can be heard descending the stairs. Rose hurries over to the door and tries to lock it, but the lock is shattered, so she puts the chair against it to keep it shut. She then goes over to the baby, who has been whimpering unnoticed during the quarrel, and soothes her to sleep again. Tim, looking embarrassed, puts the revolver back in his pocket and picking up the table sets it to rights again and sits on the edge of it. Rose looks up at him from the bed, half bewildered at seeing him still there. Then she breaks into convulsive sobbing.*)

TIM—(*making a clumsy attempt at consolation*) There, there, Kid, cut the cryin'. He won't bother yuh no more. I know his kind. He's got a streak of yellow a yard wide, and beatin' up women is all he's game for. But he won't hurt *you* no more—not if I know it.

ROSE—Yuh don't know him. When he's full of booze and hop he's liable to do anythin'. I don't care what he does to me. I might as well be dead anyway. But there's the kid. I got to look after her. And (*looking at him gratefully*) I don't want you to git in no mix-ups on account of me. I ain't worth it.

TIM—(*quickly*) Nix on that stuff about your not bein' worth it!

ROSE—(*smiling*) Thanks. And I'm mighty glad yuh came in when yuh did. Gawd knows what he'd'a done to the kid and me not able to stop him.

TIM—Don't yuh worry about my gettin' into no mix-ups. I c'n take care of myself.

ROSE—How did yuh happen to blow in when yuh did?

There usually ain't no one around in this dump at this time of the night.

TIM—I got the room next to yuh. I heard every word the both of yuh said—tonight and every other night since I come here a week ago. I know the way he's treated yuh. I'd'a butted in sooner only I didn't want to mix in other people's business. But tonight when he started in about the kid there I couldn't stand fur it no longer. I was jest wantin' to hand him a call and I let him have it. Why d'yuh stand fur him anyway? Why don't yuh take the kid and beat it away from him?

ROSE—(despondently) It's easy to say: "Why don't I beat it?" I can't.

TIM—Wha'd'yuh mean? Why can't yuh?

ROSE—I never have enough coin to make a good break and git out of town. He takes it all away from me. And if I went to some other part of this burg he'd find me and kill me. Even if he didn't kill me he'd have me pinched and where'ud the kid be then? (grimly) Oh, he's got me where he wants me all right, all right.

TIM—I don't get yuh? How could he have yuh pinched if yuh ain't done nothin'?

ROSE—Oh, he's got a drag somewhere. He squares it with the cops so they don't hold me up for walkin' the streets. Yuh ought to be wise enough to know all of his kind stand in. If he tipped them off to do it they'd pinch me before I'd gone a block. Then it'ud be the Island fur mine.

TIM—Then why don't yuh cut this life and be on the level? Why don't yuh git a job some place? He couldn't touch yuh then.

ROSE—(scornfully) Oh, couldn't he? D'yuh suppose they'd keep me any place if they knew what I was? And d'yuh suppose he wouldn't tell them or have some one else tell them? Yuh don't know the game I'm up against. (bitterly) I've tried that job thing. I've looked fur decent work and I've starved at it. A year after I first hit this town I quit and tried to be on the level. I got a job at housework—workin' twelve hours a day for twenty-five dollars a month. And I worked like a dog, too, and never left the house I was so scared of seein' some one who knew me. But what was the use? One night they have a guy to dinner who's seen me some place when I was on the town. He tells the lady—his duty he said it was—and she fires me right off the reel. I tried the same thing a lot of times. But there was always some one who'd drag me back. And then I quit tryin'. There didn't seem to be no use. They—all the good people—they got me where I am and they're goin' to keep me there. Reform? Take it from me it can't be done. They won't let yuh do it, and that's Gawd's truth.

TIM—Give it another trial any way. Yuh never know your luck. Yuh might be able to stick this time.

ROSE—(*wearily*) Talk is cheap. Yuh don't know what yuh're talkin' about. What job c'n I git? What am I fit fur? Housework is the only thing I know about and I don't know much about that. Where else could I make enough to live on? That's the trouble with all us girls. Most all of us ud like to come back but we jest can't and that's all there's to it. We can't work out of this life because we don't know how to work. We was never taught how. (*She shakes with a horrible fit of coughing, wipes her lips, and smiles pitifully.*) Who d'yuh think would take a chance on hiring me the way I look and with this cough? Besides, there's the kid. (*sarcastically*) Yuh may not know it but people ain't strong for hirin' girls with babies—especially when the girls ain't married.

TIM—But yuh could send the kid away some place.

ROSE—(*fiercely*) No. She's all I got. I won't give her up. (*She coughs again.*)

TIM—(*kindly*) That's a bad cough yuh got, Kid. I heard yuh tellin' him tonight yuh hadn't seen a doctor. (*putting hand in his pocket*) I'll stake yuh and yuh c'n run around and see one now.

ROSE—Thanks jest the same but it ain't no use. I lied to Steve. I went to a doc about a month ago. He told me I had the "con" and had it bad. (*with grim humor*) He said the only hope fur me was to git out in the country, sleep in the open air, and eat a lot of good food. He might jest as well 'uv told me to go to Heaven and I told him so. Then he said I could go out to some dump where yuh don't have to pay nothin', but he said I'd have to leave the kid behind. I told him I'd rather die than do that, and he said I'd have to be careful or the kid 'ud catch it from me. And I have been careful. (*She sobs.*) I don't even kiss her on the mouth no more.

TIM—Yuh sure are up against it, Kid. (*He appears deeply moved.*) Gee, I thought I was in bad, but yuh got me skinned to death.

ROSE—(*interested*) You in bad? Yuh don't look it.

TIM—Listen! Yuh talk about tryin' to be good and not bein' able to— Well, I been up against the same thing. When I was a kid I was sent to the Reform school fur stealin'; and it wasn't my fault. I was mixed up with a gang older than me and wasn't wise to what I was doin'. They made me the goat; and in the Reform school they made a crook outa me. When I come out I tried to be straight and hold down a job, but as soon as any one got wise I'd been in a Reform school they canned me same as they did you. Then I stole again—to keep from starvin'. They got me and this time I went to the coop fur five years. Then I give up. I seen it was no use. When I got out again I got in with a gang of yeggmen and learned how to be a yegg—and I've been one ever since. I've spent most of my life in jail but I'm free now.

ROSE—What are yuh goin' to do?

TIM—(*fiercely*) What am I goin' to do? They made a yegg outa me! Let 'em look out!

ROSE—When did yuh get out?

TIM—(*suspiciously*) What's it to you? (*then suddenly*) Nix, I didn't mean that. Yuh're a good kid and maybe yuh c'n help me.

ROSE—I'd sure like to.

TIM—Then listen! (*looking at her fixedly*) Yuh swear yuh won't squeal on me?

ROSE—I won't, so help me Gawd!

TIM—Well, I'm Tim Moran. I jest broke out two weeks ago.

ROSE—(*staring at him with a fascinated wonder*) You! Tim Moran! The guy that robbed that bank a week ago! The guy they're all lookin' fur!

TIM—Sssshhh! Yuh never c'n tell who's got an ear glued to the wall in a dump like this.

ROSE—(*lowering her voice*) I read about yuh in the papers. (*She looks at him as if she were half afraid.*)

TIM—Yuh're not afraid of me, are yuh? I ain't the kind of crook Steve is, yuh know.

ROSE—(*calmly*) No, I ain't afraid of yuh, Tim; but I'm afraid they may find yuh here and take yuh away again. (*anxiously*) D'yuh think Steve knew yuh? He'd squeal sure if he did—to git the reward.

TIM—No, I could tell by his eyes he didn't know me.

ROSE—How long have yuh been here?

TIM—A week—ever since I cracked that safe. I wanted to give the noise time to blow over. I ain't left that room except when I had to git a bite to eat, and then I got enough fur a couple of days. But when I come in tonight I seen a guy on the corner give me a long look. He looked bad to me and I wanta git out of here before they git wise.

ROSE—Yuh think he was a cop?

TIM—Yes, I got a hunch. He looked bad to me.

ROSE—(*wonderingly*) And yuh come in here tonight knowin' he was liable to spot yuh! Yuh took that chance fur me when yuh didn't even know me! (*impulsively going over to him and taking his hand which he tries to hold back*) Gee, yuh're a regular guy, all right.

TIM—(*in great confusion*) Aw, that's nothin'. Any one would'a done it.

ROSE—No one would'a done it in your place. (*A slight noise is heard from the hallway. Rose looks around startled and speaks hurriedly almost in a whisper.*) Supposin' that guy was a cop? Supposin' he had a hunch who you was? How're yuh goin' to make a getaway? Can't I help yuh outa this? Can't I do somethin' fur yuh?

TIM—(*points to window*) That's a fire escape, ain't it?

ROSE—Yes.

TIM—Where does it lead to?

ROSE—Down to the yard and up to the roof.

TIM—To hell with the yard. I'll try the roofs if it comes to a showdown. I'll stick in here with you so's if they come I c'n make a quick getaway. Yuh tell 'em yuh don't know anything about me, see? Give 'em a bum steer if you kin. Try and hold 'em so's I c'n get a good start.

ROSE—(*resolutely*) I'll hold 'em as long as I c'n, don't worry. I'll tell 'em I seen yuh goin' down stairs an hour ago.

Tim—Good Kid! (*They are standing in the middle of the room with their backs to the window. Steve's face appears peering around the edge of the window-frame. He is crouched on the fire-escape outside. His eyes glare with hatred as he watches the two persons in the room. Rose starts to cough, is frightened by the noise she makes, and holds her handkerchief over her mouth to stifle the sound.*)

Tim—Ssssshhh! Poor Kid! (*He turns to her and speaks rapidly in low tones.*) Here, Kid. (*He takes a large roll of money out of his pocket and forces it into her hand—as she starts to remonstrate*) Shut up! I ain't got time to listen to your beefin'. Take it. It ain't much but it's all I got with me. I don't need it. There's plenty more waitin' fur me outside. This'll be enough to git you and the kid out of town away from that dirty coward. (*Steve's face is convulsed with fury.*) Go some place out in the mountains and git rid of that cough.

Rose—(*sobbing*) I can't take it. Yuh been too good to me already. Yuh don't know how rotten I am.

Tim—(*suddenly taking her in his arms and kissing her roughly*) That's how rotten I think yuh are. Yuh're the whitest kid I've ever met, see? (*They look into each other's eyes. All the hardness of Rose's expression has vanished. Her face is soft, transfigured by a new emotion. Steve moves his hand into the room. He holds a revolver which he tries to aim at Tim but he is afraid to fire.*)

Rose—(*throwing her arms around his neck*) Tim, Tim, yuh been too good to me.

Tim—(*kissing her again*) Lemme know where yuh are and when it's safe I'll come to yuh. (*releases her and takes a small folded paper from pocket*) This'll find me. (*She takes it, her eyes full of happy tears.*) Maybe after a time we c'n start over again—together! (*A sound like the creaking of a floor board is heard from the hallway.*) What's that? (*They both stand looking fixedly at the door. Steve noiselessly disappears from the window.*) Gee, Kid, I got a feelin' in my bones they're after me. It's only a hunch but it's never gone wrong yet. (*He pulls a cap out of his pocket and puts it on.*) I'm goin' to blow.

Rose—(*goes over to the door and listens*) Sounds as if somebody was sneakin' up the stairs. (*She tiptoes quickly over to him and kisses him.*) Go, go while yuh got a chance. Don't let 'em git yuh! I love yuh, Tim.

TIM—Good-bye, Kid. I'll come as soon as I c'n. (*He kisses her again and goes quickly to the window. Steve stretches his hand around the side of the window and fires, the muzzle of the gun almost on Tim's chest. There is a loud report and a little smoke. Tim staggers back and falls on the floor. Steve throws the gun into the room, then quietly pulls down the window and disappears. The child in the bed wakes up and cries feebly.*)

ROSE—(*rushes to Tim and kneels beside him, holding his head on her breast*) Tim! Tim! Speak to me, Tim! (*She kisses him frantically.*)

TIM—(*his eyes glazing*) Good Kid—mountains—git rid of that cough. (*He dies.*)

ROSE—(*letting his head fall back on the floor sinks to a sitting position beside him. The money is still clutched in her right hand. She stares straight before her and repeats in tones of horrible monotony*) Dead. Oh Gawd, Gawd, Gawd! (*The sound of people running up the stairs in the hall is heard. A voice shouts:* "Must be in here." *The door is pushed open and three men enter. One is a policeman in uniform and the other two are evidently plain clothes men. The landlady and several roomers stand in the doorway looking in with frightened faces.*)

THE POLICEMAN—(*goes to Rose and, taking her arm, hauls her to her feet*) Come, get up outa that! (*The two plain clothes men take one look at the dead man and both exclaim together*) Tim Moran!

FIRST PLAIN CLOTHES MAN—I told yuh it was him I seen comin' in here tonight. I never forget a face.

SECOND PLAIN CLOTHES MAN—(*picking revolver off the floor and examining it*) I didn't think he'd be fool enough to stick around here. (*turning suddenly to Rose*) What did yuh croak him for? (*ironically*) A little love spat, eh? (*sees the roll of money in her hand and grabs her quickly by the wrist*) Pipe the roll! Little sister here attends to business, all right. Gave him a frisk before we had a chance to get here. (*to Rose in loud, rough tones*) Why did yuh kill him? It was for this coin, wasn't it? (*During the detective's remarks Rose gradually realizes the position she is in. Her expression becomes one of amazed pain as she sees they think she is guilty of the murder. She speaks brokenly, trying to hold herself in control.*)

ROSE—Honest to Gawd, I didn't do it. He gave me this money. Some one shot him from the window. (*then quite simply as if that explained it all away*) Why, I loved him.

SECOND PLAIN CLOTHES MAN—Stop that noise! Wha'-d'yuh take us for—boobs? The window ain't even open and the glass ain't broken. He gave yuh the money, eh? And then shot himself, I suppose? Aw say, Kid, wha'd'yuh take us for?

ROSE—(*losing all control, frenziedly breaks from the Policeman's grasp and throws herself beside body*) Tim! Tim! For the love of Gawd speak to them. Tell 'em I didn't do it, Tim! Tell 'em yuh gave that money to me. Yuh know what yuh said— "Take the kid into the mountains and git rid of that cough." Tell 'em yuh said that, Tim! Speak to 'em! Tell 'em I loved yuh, Tim—that I wanted to help yuh git away. Tell 'em yuh kissed me. They think I shot yuh. They don't know I loved yuh. For the love of Gawd speak to 'em. (*weeping and sobbing bitterly*) Oh Gawd, why don't yuh speak, why don't yuh speak?

FIRST PLAIN CLOTHES MAN—(*sneeringly*) That's good stuff but it won't get yuh anything. (*turning to his two companions*) Looks to me as if this doll was full of coke or something. You two better take her to the station and make a report. I'll stay here and keep cases on the room. I'm sick of listenin' to that sob stuff.

ROSE—(*The Policeman taps her on the shoulder and she rises to her feet with a spring, wildly protesting*) But I tell yuh I didn't do it! It was from the window. Can't yuh believe me? I swear I— (*She stops appalled by the unbelieving sneers of the policemen, by the white faces in the doorway gazing at her with fascinated horror. She reads her own guilt in every eye. She realizes the futility of all protest, the maddening hopelessness of it all. The child is still crying. She notices it for the first time and goes over to the bed to soothe it. The Policeman keeps a tight hold of one of her arms. She speaks words of tenderness to the child in dull, mechanical tones. It stops crying. All are looking at her in silence with a trace of compassionate pity on their faces. Rose seems in a trance. Her eyes are like the eyes of a blind woman. She seems to be aware of something in the room which none of the others can see—perhaps the personification of the ironic life force that has crushed her.*)

FIRST PLAIN CLOTHES MAN—Your kid?

ROSE—(*to the unseen presence in the room*) Yes. I suppose yuh'll take her too?

FIRST PLAIN CLOTHES MAN—(*misunderstanding her, good naturedly*) I'll take care of her for the time bein'.

ROSE—(*to the air*) That's right. Make a good job of me. (*Suddenly she stretches both arms above her head and cries bitterly, mournfully, out of the depths of her desolation*) Gawd! Gawd! Why d'yuh hate me so?

THE POLICEMAN—(*shocked*) Here, here, no rough talk like that. Come along now! (*Rose leans against him weakly and he supports her to the door where the group of horrified lodgers silently make way for them. The Second Plain Clothes Man follows them. A moment later Rose's hollow cough echoes in the dark hallway. The child wakes up and cries fitfully. The First Plain Clothes Man goes over to the bed and cuddles her on his lap with elephantine playfullness.*)

THE CHILD—(*feebly*) Maamaaaa!

THE FIRST PLAIN CLOTHES MAN—Mama's gone. I'm your Mama now.

(*Curtain*)

THIRST

A Play in One Act

CHARACTERS

A GENTLEMAN

A DANCER

A WEST INDIAN MULATTO SAILOR

Thirst

SCENE—*A steamer's life raft rising and falling slowly on the long ground-swell of a glassy tropic sea. The sky above is pitilessly clear, of a steel blue color merging into black shadow on the horizon's rim. The sun glares down from straight overhead like a great angry eye of God. The heat is terrific. Writhing, fantastic heat-waves rise from the white deck of the raft. Here and there on the still surface of the sea the fins of sharks may be seen slowly cutting the surface of the water in lazy circles.*

Two men and a woman are on the raft. Seated at one end is a West Indian mulatto dressed in the blue uniform of a sailor. Across his jersey may be seen the words "Union Mail Line" in red letters. He has on rough sailor shoes. His head is bare. When he speaks it is in drawling sing-song tones as if he were troubled by some strange impediment of speech. He croons a monotonous negro song to himself as his round eyes follow the shark fins in their everlasting circles.

At the other end of the raft sits a middle-aged white man in what was once an evening dress; but sun and salt water have reduced it to the mere caricature of such a garment. His white shirt is stained and rumpled; his collar a formless pulp about his neck; his black tie a withered ribbon. Evidently he had been a first-class passenger. Just now he cuts a sorry and pitiful figure as he sits staring stupidly at the water with unseeing eyes. His scanty black hair is disheveled, revealing a bald spot burnt crimson by the sun. A mustache droops over his lips, and some of the dye has run off it making a black line down the side of his lean face, blistered with sunburn, haggard with hunger and thirst. From time to time he licks his swollen lips with his blackened tongue.

Between the two men a young woman lies with arms out-stretched, face downward on the raft. She is even a more bizarre figure than the man in evening clothes, for she is dressed in a complete short-skirted dancer's costume of black velvet covered with spangles. Her long blond hair streams down over her bare, unprotected shoulders. Her silk stockings are baggy and wrinkled and her dancing shoes swollen and misshapen. When she lifts her head a diamond necklace can be seen glittering coldly on the protruding collar-bones of her emaciated shoulders. Continuous weeping has made a blurred smudge of her rouge and the black make-up of her eyes but one can still see that she must have been very beautiful before hunger and thirst had transformed her into a mocking spectre of a dancer. She is sobbing endlessly, hopelessly.

In the eyes of all three the light of a dawning madness is shining.

THE DANCER—(*raising herself to a sitting posture and turning piteously to the Gentleman*) My God! My God! This silence is driving me mad! Why do you not speak to me? Is there no ship in sight yet?

THE GENTLEMAN—(*dully*) No. I do not think so. At least I cannot see any. (*He tries to rise to his feet but finds himself too weak and sits down again with a groan.*) If I could only stand up I could tell better. I cannot see far from this position. I am so near the water. And then my eyes are like two balls of fire. They burn and burn until they feel as if they were boring into my brain.

THE DANCER—I know! I know! Everywhere I look I see great crimson spots. It is as if the sky were raining drops of blood. Do you see them too?

THE GENTLEMAN—Yesterday I did—or some day—I no longer remember days. But to-day everything is red. The very sea itself seems changed to blood. (*He licks his swollen, cracked lips—then laughs—the shrill cackle of madness.*) Perhaps it is the blood of all those who were drowned that night rising to the surface.

THE DANCER—Do not say such things. You are horrible. I do not care to listen to you. (*She turns away from him with a shudder.*)

THE GENTLEMAN—(*sulkily*) Very well. I will not speak. (*He covers his face with his hands.*) God! God! How my eyes ache! How my throat burns! (*He sobs heavily—there is a pause—suddenly he turns to the Dancer angrily.*) Why did you ask me to speak if you do not care to listen to me?

THE DANCER—I did not ask you to speak of blood. I did not ask you to mention that night.

THE GENTLEMAN—Well, I will say no more then. You may talk to him if you wish. (*He points to the Sailor with a sneer.*

The negro does not hear. He is crooning to himself and watching the sharks. There is a long pause. The raft slowly rises and falls on the long swells. The sun blazes down.)

THE DANCER—(*almost shrieking*) Oh, this silence! I cannot bear this silence. Talk to me about anything you please but, for God sake, talk to me! I must not think! I must not think!

THE GENTLEMAN—(*remorsefully*) Your pardon, dear lady! I am afraid I spoke harshly. I am not myself. I think I am a little out of my head. There is so much sun and so much sea. Everything gets vague at times. I am very weak. We have not eaten in so long—we have not even had a drink of water in so long. (*then in tones of great anguish*) Oh, if we only had some water!

THE DANCER—(*flinging herself on the raft and beating it with clenched fists*) *Please* do not speak of water!

THE SAILOR—(*stopping his song abruptly and turning quickly around*) Water? Who's got water? (*His swollen tongue shows between his dry lips.*)

THE GENTLEMAN—(*turning to the Sailor*) You know no one here has any water. You stole the last drop we had yourself. (*irritably*) Why do you ask such questions? (*The Sailor turns his back again and watches the shark fins. He does not answer nor does he sing any longer. There is a silence, profound and breathless.*)

THE DANCER—(*creeping over to the Gentleman and seizing his arm*) Do you not notice how deep the silence is? The world seems emptier than ever. I am afraid. Tell me why it is.

THE GENTLEMAN—I, too, notice it. But I do not know why it is.

THE DANCER—Ah! I know now. He is silent. Do you not remember he was singing? A queer monotonous song it was—more of a dirge than a song. I have heard many songs in many languages in the places I have played, but never a song like that before. Why did he stop, do you think? Maybe something frightened him.

THE GENTLEMAN—I do not know. But I will ask him. (*to the Sailor*) Why have you stopped singing? (*The Sailor looks at him with a strange expression in his eyes. He does not answer but turns to the circling fins again and takes up his song, dully, droningly, as if from some place he had left off. The Dancer and the Gentleman listen in attitudes of strained attention for a long time.*)

THE DANCER—(*laughing hysterically*) What a song! There is no tune to it and I can understand no words. I wonder what it means.

THE GENTLEMAN—Who knows? It is doubtless some folk song of his people which he is singing.

THE DANCER—But I wish to find out. Sailor! Will you tell me what it means—that song you are singing? (*The negro stares at her uneasily for a moment.*)

THE SAILOR—(*drawlingly*) It is a song of my people.

THE DANCER—Yes. But what do the words mean?

THE SAILOR—(*pointing to the shark fins*) I am singing to them. It is a charm. I have been told it is very strong. If I sing long enough they will not eat us.

THE DANCER—(*terrified*) Eat us? What will eat us?

THE GENTLEMAN—(*pointing to the moving fins in the still water*) He means the sharks. Those pointed black things you see moving through the water are their fins. Have you not noticed them before?

THE DANCER—Yes, yes. I have seen them. But I did not know they were sharks. (*sobbing*) Oh it is horrible, all this!

THE GENTLEMAN—(*to the negro, harshly*) Why do you tell her such things? Do you not know you will frighten her?

THE SAILOR—(*dully*) She asked me what I was singing.

THE GENTLEMAN—(*trying to comfort the Dancer who is still sobbing*) At least tell her the truth about the sharks. That is all a children's tale about them eating people. (*raising his voice*) You know they never eat anyone. And I know it. (*The negro looks at him and his lips contract grotesquely. Perhaps he is trying to smile.*)

THE DANCER—(*raising her head and drying her eyes*) You are sure of what you say?

THE GENTLEMAN—(*confused by the negro's stare*) Of course I am sure. Everyone knows that sharks are afraid to touch a person. They are all cowards. (*to the negro*) You were just trying to frighten the lady, were you not? (*The negro turns away from them and stares at the sea. He commences to sing again.*)

THE DANCER—I no longer like his song. It makes me dream of horrible things. Tell him to stop.

THE GENTLEMAN—Bah! You are nervous. Anything is better than dead silence.

THE DANCER—Yes. Anything is better than silence—even a song like that.

THE GENTLEMAN—He is strange—that sailor. I do not know what to think of him.

THE DANCER—It is a strange song he sings.

THE GENTLEMAN—He does not seem to want to speak to us.

THE DANCER—I have noticed that, too. When I asked him about the song he did not want to answer at all.

THE GENTLEMAN—Yet he speaks good English. It cannot be that he does not understand us.

THE DANCER—When he does speak it is as if he had some impediment in his throat.

THE GENTLEMAN—Perhaps he has. If so, he is much to be pitied and we are wrong to speak of him so.

THE DANCER—I do not pity him. I am afraid of him.

THE GENTLEMAN—That is foolish. It is the sun which beats down so fiercely which makes you have such thoughts. I, also, have been afraid of him at times, but I know now that I had been gazing at the sea too long and listening to the great silence. Such things distort your brain.

THE DANCER—Then you no longer fear him?

THE GENTLEMAN—I no longer fear him now that I am quite sane. It clears my brain to talk to you. We must talk to each other all the time.

THE DANCER—Yes, we must talk to each other. I do not dream when I talk to you.

THE GENTLEMAN—I think at one time I was going mad. I dreamed he had a knife in his hand and looked at me. But it was all madness; I can see that now. He is only a poor negro sailor—our companion in misfortune. God knows we are all in the same pitiful plight. We should not grow suspicious of one another.

THE DANCER—All the same, I am afraid of him. There is something in his eyes when he looks at me, which makes me tremble.

THE GENTLEMAN—There is nothing I tell you. It is all your imagination. (*There is a long pause.*)

THE DANCER—Good God! Is there no ship in sight yet?

THE GENTLEMAN—(*attempting to rise but falling back weakly*) I can see none. And I cannot stand to get a wider view.

THE DANCER—(*pointing to the negro*) Ask him. He is stronger than we are. He may be able to see one.

THE GENTLEMAN—Sailor! (*The negro ceases his chant and turns to him with expressionless eyes.*) You are stronger than we are and can see farther. Stand up and tell me if there is any ship in sight.

THE SAILOR—(*rising slowly to his feet and looking at all points of the horizon*) No. There is none. (*He sits down again and croons his dreary melody.*)

THE DANCER—(*weeping hopelessly*) My God, this is horrible. To wait and wait for something that never comes.

THE GENTLEMAN—It is indeed horrible. But it is to be expected.

THE DANCER—Why do you say it is to be expected? Have you no hopes, then, of being rescued?

THE GENTLEMAN—(*wearily*) I have hoped for many things in my life. Always I have hoped in vain. We are far out of the beaten track of steamers. I know little of navigation, yet I heard those on board say that we were following a course but little used. Why we did so, I do not know. I suppose the Captain wished to make a quicker passage. He alone knows what was in his mind and he will probably never tell.

THE DANCER—No, he will never tell.

THE GENTLEMAN—Why do you speak so decidedly? He might have been among those who escaped in the boats.

THE DANCER—He did not escape. He is dead!

THE GENTLEMAN—Dead?

THE DANCER—Yes. He was on the bridge. I can remember seeing his face as he stood in under a lamp. It was pale and drawn like the face of a dead man. His eyes, too, seemed dead. He shouted some orders in a thin trembling voice. No one paid any attention to him. And then he shot himself. I saw the flash, and heard the report above all the screams of the drowning. Some one grasped me by the arm and I heard a hoarse voice shouting in my ear. Then I fainted.

THE GENTLEMAN—Poor Captain! It is evident, then, that he felt himself guilty—since he killed himself. It must be terrible to hear the screams of the dying and know oneself to blame. I do not wonder that he killed himself.

THE DANCER—He was so kind and good-natured—the Captain. It was only that afternoon on the promenade deck that he stopped beside my chair. "I hear you are to entertain us this evening" he said. "That will be delightful, and it is very kind of you. I had promised myself the pleasure of seeing you in New York, but you have forestalled me." (*after a pause*) How handsome and broad-shouldered he was—the Captain.

THE GENTLEMAN—I would have liked to have seen his soul.

THE DANCER—You would have found it no better and no worse than the souls of other men. If he was guilty he has paid with his life.

THE GENTLEMAN—No. He has avoided payment by taking his life. The dead do not pay.

THE DANCER—And the dead cannot answer when we speak evil of them. All we can know is that he is dead. Let us talk of other things. (*There is a pause.*)

THE GENTLEMAN—(*fumbles in the inside pocket of his dress coat and pulls out a black object that looks like a large card case. He opens it and stares at it with perplexed eyes. Then, giving a hollow laugh, he holds it over for the Dancer to see.*) Oh, the damned irony of it!

THE DANCER—What is it? I cannot read very well. My eyes ache so.

THE GENTLEMAN—(*still laughing mockingly*) Bend closer! Bend closer! It is worth while understanding—the joke that has been played on me.

THE DANCER—(*reading slowly, her face almost touching the case*) United States Club of Buenos Aires! I do not understand what the joke is.

THE GENTLEMAN—(*impatiently snatching the case from her hand*) I will explain the joke to you then. Listen! M-e-n-u— menu. That is the joke. This is a souvenir menu of a banquet given in my honor by this Club. (*reading*) "Martini cocktails,

soup, sherry, fish, Burgundy, chicken, champagne"—and
here we are dying for a crust of bread, for a drink of water!
(*His mad laughter suddenly ceases and in a frenzy of rage he
shakes his fist at the sky and screams*) God! God! What a joke
to play on us! (*After this outburst he sinks back dejectedly, his
trembling hand still clutching the menu.*)

THE DANCER—(*sobbing*) This is too horrible. What have
we done that we should suffer so? It is as if one misfortune
after another happened to make our agony more terrible.
Throw that thing away! The very sight of it is a mockery.
(*The Gentleman throws the menu into the sea where it floats, a
black spot on the glassy water.*) How do you happen to have
that thing with you? It is ghastly for you to torment me by
reading it.

THE GENTLEMAN—I am sorry to have hurt you. The jest
was so grotesque I could not keep it to myself. You ask how
I happen to have it with me? I will tell you. It gives the joke
an even bitterer flavor. You remember when the crash came?
We were all in the salon. You were singing—a Cockney song
I think?

THE DANCER—Yes. It is one I first sang at the Palace in
London.

THE GENTLEMAN—It was in the salon. You were singing.
You were very beautiful. I remember a woman on my right
saying: "How pretty she is! I wonder if she is married?"
Strange how some idiotic remark like that will stick in one's
brain when all else is vague and confused. A tragedy happens—we are in the midst of it—and one of our clearest
remembrances afterwards is a remark that might have been
overheard in any subway train.

THE DANCER—It is so with me. There was a fat, bald-
headed, little man. It was on deck after the crash. Everywhere
they were fighting to get into the boats. This poor little man
stood by himself. His moon face was convulsed with rage. He
kept repeating in loud angry tones: "I shall be late. I must
cable! I can never make it!" He was still bewailing his broken
appointment when a rush of the crowd swept him off his feet
and into the sea. I can see him now. He is the only person
besides the Captain I remember clearly.

THE GENTLEMAN—(*continuing his story in a dead voice*)

You were very beautiful. I was looking at you and wondering what kind of a woman you were. You know I had never met you personally—only seen you in my walks around the deck. Then came the crash—that horrible dull crash. We were all thrown forward on the floor of the salon; then screams, oaths, fainting women, the hollow boom of a bulkhead giving way. I vaguely remember rushing to my stateroom and picking up my wallet. It must have been that menu that I took instead. Then I was on deck fighting in the midst of the crowd. Somehow I got into a boat—but it was overloaded and was swamped immediately. I swam to another boat. They beat me off with the oars. That boat too was swamped a moment later. And then the gurgling, choking cries of the drowning! Something huge rushed by me in the water leaving a gleaming trail of phosphorescence. A woman near me with a life belt around her gave a cry of agony and disappeared—then I realized—sharks! I became frenzied with terror. I swam. I beat the water with my hands. The ship had gone down. I swam and swam with but one idea—to put all that horror behind me. I saw something white on the water before me. I clutched it—climbed on it. It was this raft. You and he were on it. I fainted. The whole thing is a horrible nightmare in my brain—but I remember clearly that idiotic remark of the woman in the salon. What pitiful creatures we are!

THE DANCER—When the crash came I also rushed to my stateroom. I took this, (*pointing to the diamond necklace*) clasped it round my neck and ran on deck; the rest I have told you.

THE GENTLEMAN—Do you not remember how you came on this raft? It is strange that you and he should be on a raft alone when so many died for lack of a place. Were there ever any others on the raft with you?

THE DANCER—No, I am sure there were not. Everything in my memory is blurred. But I feel sure we were always the only ones—until you came. I was afraid of you—your face was livid with fear. You were moaning to yourself.

THE GENTLEMAN—It was the sharks. Until they came I kept a half-control over myself. But when I saw them even my soul quivered with terror.

THE DANCER—(*horror-stricken, looking at the circling fins*) Sharks! Why they are all around us now. (*frenziedly*) You lied to me. You said they would not touch us. Oh, I am afraid, I am afraid! (*She covers her face with her hands.*)

THE GENTLEMAN—If I lied to you it was because I wished to spare you. Be brave! We are safe from them as long as we stay on the raft. These things must be faced. (*then in tones of utter despondency*) Besides, what does it matter?—sharks or no sharks—the end is the same.

THE DANCER—(*taking her hands away from her eyes and looking dully at the water*) You are right. What does it matter?

THE GENTLEMAN—God! How still the sea is! How still the sky is! One would say the world was dead. I think the accursed humming of that nigger only makes one feel the silence more keenly. There is nothing—but the sharks—that seems to live.

THE DANCER—How the sun burns into me! (*piteously*) My poor skin that I was once so proud of!

THE GENTLEMAN—(*rousing himself with an effort*) Come! Let us not think about it. It is madness to think about it so. How do you account for your being on the raft alone with this nigger? You have not yet told me.

THE DANCER—How can I tell? The last thing I remember was that harsh voice in my ear shouting something—what, I cannot recollect.

THE GENTLEMAN—There was nothing else?

THE DANCER—Nothing. (*pause*) Stop! Yes, there was something I had forgotten. I think that someone kissed me. Yes, I am sure that someone kissed me. But no, I am not sure. It may have all been a dream I dreamed. I have had so many dreams during these awful days and nights—so many mad, mad dreams. (*Her eyes begin to glaze, her lips to twitch. She murmurs to herself*) Mad, mad dreams.

THE GENTLEMAN—(*reaching over and shaking her by the shoulder*) Come! You said someone kissed you. You must be mistaken. I surely did not, and it could hardly have been that sailor.

THE DANCER—Yet I am sure someone did. It was not since I have been on this raft. It was on the deck of the ship just as I was fainting.

THE GENTLEMAN—Who could it have been, do you think?

THE DANCER—I hardly dare to say what I think. I might be wrong. You remember the Second Officer—the young Englishman with the great dark eyes who was so tall and handsome? All the women loved him. I, too, I loved him—a little bit. He loved me—very much—so he said. Yes, I know he loved me very much. I think it was he who kissed me. I am almost sure it was he.

THE GENTLEMAN—Yes, he must have been the one. That would explain it all. He must have sent away the raft when only you and this sailor were on it. He probably did not let the others know of the existence of this raft. Indeed he must have loved you to disregard his duty so. I will ask the sailor about it. Maybe he can clear away our doubts. (*to the negro*) Sailor! (*The negro stops singing and looks at them with wide, blood-shot eyes.*) Did the Second Officer order you to take this lady away from the ship?

THE SAILOR—(*sullenly*) I do not know.

THE GENTLEMAN—Did he tell you to take no one else with you but this lady—and perhaps himself afterwards?

THE SAILOR—(*angrily*) I do not know. (*He turns away again and commences to sing.*)

THE DANCER—Do not speak to him any more. He is angry at something. He will not answer.

THE GENTLEMAN—He is going mad I think. However it seems certain that it was the Second Officer who kissed you and saved your life.

THE DANCER—He was kind and brave to me. He meant well. Yet I wish now he had let me die. I would have been way down in the cold green water. I would have been sleeping, coldly sleeping. While now my brain is scorched with sun-fire and dream-fire. And I am going mad. We are all going mad. Your eyes shine with a wild flame at times—and that Sailor's are horrible with strangeness—and mine see great drops of blood that dance upon the sea. Yes we are all mad. (*pause*) God! Oh God! Must this be the end of all? I was coming home, home after years of struggling, home to success and fame and money. And I must die out here on a raft like a mad dog. (*She weeps despairingly.*)

THE GENTLEMAN—Be still! You must not despair so. I, too, might whine a prayer of protest: "Oh God, God! After twenty years of incessant grind, day after weary day, I started on my first vacation. I was going home. And here I sit dying by slow degrees, desolate and forsaken. Is this the meaning of all my years of labor? Is this the end, oh God?" So I might wail with equal justice. But the blind sky will not answer your appeals or mine. Nor will the cruel sea grow merciful for any prayer of ours.

THE DANCER—Have you no hope that one of the ship's boats may have reached land and reported the disaster. They would surely send steamers out to search for the other survivors.

THE GENTLEMAN—We have drifted far, very far, in these long weary days. I am afraid no steamer would find us.

THE DANCER—We are lost then! (*She falls face downward on the raft. A great sob shakes her thin bare shoulders.*)

THE GENTLEMAN—I have not given up hope. These seas, I have heard, are full of coral islands and we surely ought to drift near one of them soon. It was probably an uncharted coral reef that our steamer hit. I heard someone say "derelict" but I saw no sign of one in the water. With us it is only a question of whether we can hold out until we sight land. (*His voice quivers; he licks his blackened lips. His eyes have grown very mad and he is shaking spasmodically from head to foot.*) Water would save us—just a little water—even a few drops would be enough. (*intensely*) God, if we only had a little water!

THE DANCER—Perhaps there will be water on the island. Look; look hard! An island or a ship may have come in sight while we were talking. (*There is a pause. Suddenly she rises to her knees and pointing straight in front of her shouts*) See! An island!

THE GENTLEMAN—(*shading his eyes with a trembling hand and peering wildly around him*) I see nothing—nothing but a red sea and a red sky.

THE DANCER—(*still looking at some point far out over the water, speaks in disappointed tones*) It is gone. Yet I am quite sure I saw one. It was right out there quite near to us. It was all green and clean looking with a clear stream that ran into the sea. I could hear the water running over the stones. You do not believe me. You, Sailor, you must have seen it too, did you not? (*The negro does not answer.*) I cannot see it any more. Yet I must see it. I *will* see it!

THE GENTLEMAN—(*shaking her by the shoulder*) What you say is nonsense. There is no island there I tell you. There is nothing but sun and sky and sea around us. There are no green trees. There is no water. (*The Sailor has stopped singing and turns and looks at them.*)

THE DANCER—(*angrily*) Do you mean to tell me I lie? Can I not believe my own eyes, then? I tell you I saw it—cool clear water. I heard it bubbling over the stones. But now I hear nothing, nothing at all. (*turning suddenly to the Sailor*) Why have you stopped singing? Is not everything awful enough already that you should make it worse?

THE SAILOR—(*sticking out his swollen tongue and pointing to it with a long, brown finger*) Water! I want water! Give me some water and I will sing.

THE GENTLEMAN—(*furiously*) We have no water, fool! It is your fault we have none. Why did you drink all that was left in the cask when you thought we were asleep? I would not give you any even if we had some. You deserve to suffer, you pig! If anyone of the three of us has any water it is you who have hidden some out of what you stole. (*with a laugh of mad cunning*) But you will get no chance to drink it, I promise you that. I am watching you. (*The negro sullenly turns away from them.*)

THE DANCER—(*taking hold of the Gentleman's arm and almost hissing into his ear. She is terribly excited and he is still chuckling crazily to himself.*) Do you really think he has some?

THE GENTLEMAN—(*chuckling*) He may have. He may have.

THE DANCER—Why do you say that?

THE GENTLEMAN—He has been acting strangely. He has looked as if he wished to hide something. I was wondering what it could be. Then suddenly I thought to myself: "What if it should be some of the water?" Then I knew I had found him out. I will not let him get the best of me. I will watch him. He will not drink while I am watching him. I will watch him as long as I can see.

THE DANCER—What could he have put the water in? He

has nothing that I can discover. (*She is rapidly falling in with this mad fixed idea of his.*)

THE GENTLEMAN—Who knows? He may have a flask hidden in under his jersey. But he has something, that I am sure of. Why is it he is so much stronger than we are? He can stand up without effort and we can scarcely move. Why is that, I ask you?

THE DANCER—It is true. He stood up and looked for a ship as easily as if he had never known hunger and thirst. You are right. He must have something hidden—food or water.

THE GENTLEMAN—(*with mad eagerness to prove his fixed idea*) No, he has no food. There has never been any food. But there has been water. There was a whole small cask full of it on the raft when I came. On the second or third night, I do not remember which, I awoke and saw him draining the cask. When I reached it, it was empty. (*furiously shaking his fist at the negro's back*) Oh you pig! You rotten pig! (*The negro does not seem to hear.*)

THE DANCER—That water would have saved our lives. He is no better than a murderer.

THE GENTLEMAN—(*with insane shrewdness*) Listen. I think he must have poured some of the water into his flask. There was quite a little there. He could not have drunk it all. Oh, he is a cunning one! That song of his—it was only a blind. He drinks when we are not looking. But he will drink no more for I will watch him. I will watch him!

THE DANCER—You will watch him? And what good will that do either of us? Will we die any the less soon for your watching? No! Let us get the water away from him in some way. That is the only thing to do.

THE GENTLEMAN—He will not give it to us.

THE DANCER—We will steal it while he sleeps.

THE GENTLEMAN—I do not think he sleeps. I have never seen him sleep. Besides we should wake him.

THE DANCER—(*violently*) We will kill him then. He deserves to be killed.

THE GENTLEMAN—He is stronger than we are—and he has a knife. No, we cannot do that. I would willingly kill him. As you say, he deserves it. But I cannot even stand. I have no strength left. I have no weapons. He would laugh at me.

THE DANCER—There must be some way. You would think even the most heartless savage would share at a time like this. We must get that water. It is horrible to be dying of thirst with water so near. Think! Think! Is there no way?

THE GENTLEMAN—You might buy it from him with that necklace of yours. I have heard his people are very fond of such things.

THE DANCER—This necklace? It is worth a thousand pounds. An English duke gave it to me. I will not part with it. Do you think I am a fool?

THE GENTLEMAN—Think of a drink of water! (*They both lick their dry lips feverishly.*) If we do not drink soon we will die. (*laughing harshly*) You will take your necklace to the sharks with you? Very well then, I will say no more. For my part, I would sell my soul for a *drop* of water.

THE DANCER—(*Shuddering with horror she glances instinctively at the moving shark fins.*) You are horrible. I had almost forgotten those monsters. It is not kind of you to be always bringing them back to my memory.

THE GENTLEMAN—It is well that you should not forget them. You will value your Duke's present less when you look at them. (*impatiently pounding the deck with one boney hand*) Come, come, we shall both die of thirst while you are dreaming. Offer it to him! Offer it to him!

THE DANCER—(*She takes off the necklace and, musing vacantly, turns it over in her hands watching it sparkle in the sun.*) It is beautiful, is it not? I hate to part with it. He was very much in love with me—the old Duke. I think he would even have married me in the end. I did not like him. He was old, very old. Something came up—I forget what. I never saw him again. This is the only gift of his that I have left.

THE GENTLEMAN—(*in a frenzy of impatience—the vision of the water clear before his glaring eyes*) Damn it, why are you chattering so? Think of the water he has got. Offer it to him! Offer it to him!

THE DANCER—Yes, yes, my throat is burning up; my eyes are on fire. I must have the water. (*She drags herself on hands and knees across the raft to where the negro is sitting. He does not notice her approach. She reaches out a trembling hand and touches him on the back. He turns slowly and looks at her, his round, animal eyes dull and lusterless. She holds the necklace out in her right hand before his face and speaks hurriedly in a husky voice.*) Look, you have stolen our water. You deserve to be killed. We will forget all that. Look at this necklace. It was given to me by an English Duke—a nobleman. It is worth a thousand pounds—five thousand dollars. It will provide for you for the rest of your life. You need not be a sailor any more. You need never work at all any more. Do you understand what that means? (*The negro does not answer. The Dancer hurries on how-ever, her words pouring out in a sing-song jumble.*) That water that you stole—well, I will give you this necklace—they are all real diamonds, you know—five thousand dollars—for that water. You need not give me all of it. I am not unreasonable. You may keep some for yourself. I would not have you die. I want just enough for myself and my friend—to keep us alive until we reach some island. My lips are cracked with heat! My head is bursting! Here, take the necklace. It is yours. (*She tries to force it into his hand. He pushes her hand away and the neck-lace falls to the deck of the raft where it lies glittering among the heat waves.*)

THE DANCER—(*her voice raised stridently*) Give me the water! I have given you the necklace. Give me the water!

THE GENTLEMAN—(*who has been watching her with anxious eyes, also cries*) Yes. Give her the water!

THE SAILOR—(*his voice drawling and without expression*) I have no water.

THE DANCER—Oh, you are cruel! Why do you lie? You see me suffering so and yet you lie to me. I have given you the necklace. It is worth five thousand dollars, do you under-stand? Surely for five thousand dollars you will give me a drink of water!

THE SAILOR—I have no water, I tell you. (*He turns his back to her. She crawls over to the Gentleman and lies beside him, sobbing brokenly.*)

THE GENTLEMAN—(*his face convulsed with rage, shaking both fists in the air*) The pig! The pig! The black dog!

THE DANCER—(*sitting up and wiping her eyes*) Well, you have heard him. He will not give it to us. Maybe he only has a little and is afraid to share it. What shall we do now? What can we do?

THE GENTLEMAN—(*despondently*) Nothing. He is stronger than we are. There is no wind. We will never reach an island. We can die, that is all. (*He sinks back and buries his head in his hands. A great dry sob shakes his shoulders.*)

THE DANCER—(*her eyes flaming with a sudden resolution*) Ah, who is the coward now? You have given up hope, it seems. Well, I have not. I have still one chance. It has never failed me yet.

THE GENTLEMAN—(*raising his head and looking at her in amazement*) You are going to offer him more money?

THE DANCER—(*with a strange smile*) No. Not that. I will offer more than money. We shall get our water. (*She tears a piece of crumpled lace off the front of her costume and carefully wipes her face with it as if she were using a powder-puff.*)

THE GENTLEMAN—(*watching her stupidly*) I do not understand.

THE DANCER—(*She pulls up her stockings—tries to smooth the wrinkles out of her dress—then takes her long hair and having braided it, winds it into a coil around her head. She pinches her cheeks, already crimson with sunburn. Then turning coquettishly to the Gentleman, she says*) There! Do I not look better? How do I look?

THE GENTLEMAN—(*bursting into a mad guffaw*) You look terrible! You are hideous!

THE DANCER—You lie! I am beautiful. Everyone knows I am beautiful. You yourself have said so. It is you who are hideous. You are jealous of me. I will not give you any water.

THE GENTLEMAN—You will get no water. You are frightful. What is it you would do—dance for him? (*mockingly*) Dance! Dance Salome! I will be the orchestra. He will be the gallery. We will both applaud you madly. (*He leans on one elbow and watches her, chuckling to himself.*)

THE DANCER—(*turning from him furiously and crawling on her knees over to the Sailor, calls in her most seductive voice*) Sailor! Sailor! (*He does not seem to hear—she takes his arm and shakes it gently—he turns around and stares wonderingly at her.*) Listen to me, Sailor. What is your name—your first name? (*She smiles enticingly at him. He does not answer.*) You will not tell me then? You are angry at me, are you not? I cannot blame you. I have called you bad names. I am sorry, very sorry. (*indicating the Gentleman who has ceased to notice them and is staring at the horizon with blinking eyes*) It was he who put such ideas into my head. He does not like you. Neither did I, but I see now that you are the better of the two. I hate him! He has said dreadful things which I cannot forgive. (*Putting her hand on his shoulder she bends forward with her golden hair almost in his lap and smiles up into his face.*) I like you, Sailor. You are big and strong. We are going to be great friends, are we not? (*The negro is hardly looking at her. He is watching the sharks.*) Surely you will not refuse me a little sip of your water?

THE SAILOR—I have no water.

THE DANCER—Oh, why will you keep up this subterfuge? Am I not offering you price enough? (*putting her arm around his neck and half whispering in his ear*) Do you not understand? I will love you, Sailor! Noblemen and millionaires and all degrees of gentleman have loved me, have fought for me. I have never loved any of them as I will love you. Look in my eyes, Sailor, look in my eyes! (*Compelled in spite of himself by something in her voice, the negro gazes deep into her eyes. For a second his nostrils dilate—he draws in his breath with a hissing sound—his body grows tense and it seems as if he is about to sweep her into his arms. Then his expression grows apathetic again. He turns to the sharks.*)

THE DANCER—Oh, will you never understand? Are you so stupid that you do not know what I mean? Look! I am offering myself to you! I am kneeling before you—I who always had men kneel to me! I am offering my body to you—my body that men have called so beautiful. I have promised to love *you*—a negro sailor—if you will give me one small drink of water. Is that not humiliation enough that you must keep me waiting so? (*raising her voice*) Answer me! Answer me! Will you give me that water?

THE SAILOR—(*without even turning to look at her*) I have no water.

THE DANCER—(*shaking with fury*) Great God, have I abased myself for this? Have I humbled myself before this black animal only to be spurned like a wench of the streets. It is too much! You lie, you dirty slave! You have water. You have stolen my share of the water. (*In a frenzy she clutches the*

Sailor about the throat with both hands.) Give it to me! Give it to me!

THE SAILOR—(*takes her hands from his neck and pushes her roughly away. She falls face downward in the middle of the raft.*) Let me alone! I have no water.

THE GENTLEMAN—(*aroused from the stupor he has been in*) What is it? I was dreaming I was sitting before great tumblers of ice-water. They were just beyond my reach. I tried and tried to get one of them. It was horrible. But what has happened here? What is the matter? (*No one answers him. The negro is watching the sharks again. The Dancer is lying in a huddled heap, moaning to herself. Suddenly she jumps to her feet. All her former weakness seems quite gone. She stands swaying a little with the roll of the raft. Her eyes have a terrible glare in them. They seem bursting out of her head. She mutters incoherently to herself. The last string has snapped. She is mad.*)

THE DANCER—(*smoothing her dress over her hips and looking before her as if in a mirror*) Quick, Marie! You are so slow tonight. I will be late. Did you not hear the bell? I am the next on. Did he send any flowers to-night, Marie? Good, he will be in a stage box. I will smile at him, the poor old fool. He will marry me some day and I will be a Duchess. Think of that Marie—a real Duchess! Yes, yes I am coming! You need not hold the curtain. (*She drops her head on her breast and mutters to herself. The Gentleman has been watching her, at first in astonishment, then in a sort of crazy appreciation. When she stops talking he claps his hands.*)

THE GENTLEMAN—Go on! Go on! It is as good as a play. (*He bursts into cackling laughter.*)

THE DANCER—They are laughing. It cannot be at me. How hot it is! How the footlights glare! I shall be glad to get away to-night. I am very thirsty. (*passing her hand across her eyes*) There he is in the box—the poor, old duke. I will wave to him. (*She waves her hand in the air.*) He is kind to me. It is a pity he is so old. What song is it I am to sing? Oh yes. (*She sings the last few lines of some music hall ballad in a harsh cracked voice. The negro turns and looks at her wonderingly. The Gentleman claps his hands.*) They are applauding. I must dance for them! (*She commences to dance on the swaying surface of the raft, half-stumbling every now and then. Her hair falls down. She *is like some ghastly marionette jerked by invisible wires. She dances faster and faster. Her arms and legs fly grotesquely around as if beyond control.*) Oh, how hot it is! (*She grasps the front of her bodice in both hands and rips it over her shoulders. It hangs down in back. She is almost naked to the waist. Her breasts are withered and shrunken by starvation. She kicks first one foot and then the other frenziedly in the air.*) Oh it is hot! I am stifling. Bring me a drink of water! I am choking! (*She falls back on the raft. A shudder runs over her whole body. A little crimson foam appears on her lips. Her eyes glaze. The wild stare leaves them. She is dead.*)

THE GENTLEMAN—(*laughing insanely and clapping his hands*) Bravo! Bravo! Give us some more! (*There is no answer. A great stillness hangs over everything. The heat waves rising from the raft near the woman's body seem like her soul departing into the great unknown. A look of fear appears on the Gentleman's face. The negro wears a strange expression. One might say he looked relieved, even glad, as if some perplexing problem has been solved for him.*)

THE GENTLEMAN—She does not answer me. She must be sick. (*He crawls over to her.*) She has fainted. (*He puts his hand on her left breast—then bends and rests his ear over her heart. His face grows livid in spite of the sunburn.*) My God! She is dead! Poor girl! Poor Girl! (*He whimpers weakly to himself, mechanically running her long golden hair through his fingers with a caressing gesture. He is startled when he hears the negro's voice.*)

THE SAILOR—Is she dead?

THE GENTLEMAN—Yes. She is dead, poor girl. Her heart no longer beats.

THE SAILOR—She is better off. She does not suffer now. One of us had to die. (*after a pause*) It is lucky for us she is dead.

THE GENTLEMAN—What do you mean? What good can her death do us?

THE SAILOR—We will live now. (*He takes his sailor's knife from its sheath and sharpens it on the sole of his shoe. While he is doing this he sings—a happy negro melody that mocks the great silence.*)

THE GENTLEMAN—(*in hushed, frightened tones*) I do not understand.

THE SAILOR—(*his swollen lips parting in a grin as he points with his knife to the body of the Dancer*) We shall eat. We shall drink.

THE GENTLEMAN—(*for a moment struck dumb with loathing—then in tones of anguished horror*) No! No! No! Good God, not that! (*With a swift movement he grasps the Dancer's body with both hands and making a tremendous effort, pushes it into the water. There is a swift rush of waiting fins. The sea near the raft is churned into foam. The Dancer's body disappears in a swirling eddy; then all is quiet again. A black stain appears on the surface of the water.*)

The Sailor, who has jumped forward to save the body, gives a harsh cry of disappointed rage and, knife in hand, springs on the Gentleman and drives the knife in his breast. The Gentleman rises to his feet with a shriek of agony. As he falls backward into the sea, one of his clutching hands fastens itself in the neck of the Sailor's jersey. The Sailor tries to force the hand away, stumbles, loses his balance, and plunges headlong after him. There is a great splash. The waiting fins rush in. The water is lashed into foam. The Sailor's black head appears for a moment, his features distorted with terror, his lips torn with a howl of despair. Then he is drawn under.

The black stain on the water widens. The fins circle no longer. The raft floats in the midst of a vast silence. The sun glares down like a great angry eye of God. The eerie heat waves float upward in the still air like the souls of the drowned. On the raft a diamond necklace lies glittering in the blazing sunshine.

(*Curtain*)

RECKLESSNESS

A Play in One Act

CHARACTERS

Arthur Baldwin
Mildred, *his wife*
Fred Burgess, *their chauffeur*
Gene, *Mrs. Baldwin's maid*
Mary, *a housemaid*

Recklessness

SCENE—*The library of Arthur Baldwin's summer home in the Catskills, N. Y. On the left a door and two large French windows opening on the veranda. A bookcase covers the space of wall between the two windows. In the corner is a square wickerwork table. The far side of the room also looks out on the veranda. Two French windows are on each side of a rolltop desk that stands against the wall. Near the desk a small telephone such as is used on estates to connect the house with the outbuildings. On top of the desk a Bell telephone and a small pile of letters. In the right background a divan, then a door leading to the hallway, and a long bookcase. A heavy oak table stands in the center of the room. On it are several magazines and books, an ash receiver, cigar box, etc., and an electric reading lamp wired from the chandelier above. Two Morris-chairs are within reading reach of the lamp and several light rocking chairs are placed about the room. The walls are of light wainscoting. The floor is of polished hard wood with a large darkish colored rug covering the greater part. Several pictures of a sporting nature, principally of racing automobiles, are hung on the walls in the spaces between windows and bookcases.*

The room is the typical sitting-room of a moderately wealthy man who has but little taste and is but little worried by its absence. On this warm August night with the door and all the windows thrown open, and only the reading lamp burning, it presents a cool and comfortable appearance.

It's about eight o'clock in the evening. The time is the present.

Mrs. Baldwin is discovered lying back in one of the Morris-chairs with an unopened book in her lap. She is holding her head on one side in an attitude of strained attention as if she were waiting for someone or something. In appearance she is a tall, strikingly voluptuous-looking young woman of about twenty-eight. Her hair is reddish-gold, almost a red, and her large eyes are of that dark greyish-blue color which is called violet. She is very pale—a clear transparent pallor that serves to accentuate the crimson of the full lips of her rather large mouth. She is dressed in a low-cut evening gown of a grey that matches her eyes. Her shoulders, neck and arms are beautiful.

MRS. BALDWIN—(*rousing herself with a sigh of vexation, goes to the wall on the right and pushes an electric button near the bookcase. After a moment a maid enters.*) I won't wait any longer, Mary. He evidently isn't coming. You may clear the table. I won't eat anything now. I'll have something after a while.

MARY—Very well, ma'am. (*She goes out.*)

MRS. BALDWIN—(*looks around quickly to make sure she is alone, then locks the door to the hallway and, going to the door on the left opening on the verandah, calls in a low voice*) Fred. (*She beckons with her hand to someone who is evidently waiting outside. A moment later Fred Burgess comes quickly into the room. He throws a furtive glance around him—then reassured, takes Mrs. Baldwin in his arms and kisses her passionately on the lips. In appearance he is a tall, clean-shaven, dark-complected young fellow of twenty-five or so with clear-cut, regular features, big brown eyes and black curly hair. He is dressed in a gray chauffeur's uniform with black puttees around the calves of his legs.*)

MRS. BALDWIN—(*putting her arms about his neck and kissing him again and again*) Oh Fred! Fred! I love you so much!

FRED—Ssh! Someone might hear you.

MRS. BALDWIN—There's no one around. They're all in back having dinner. You've had your's? (*He nods.*) They won't expect you then. There's nothing to fear. I've locked the door. (*He is reassured.*) But you do love me, don't you, Fred? (*He kisses her smilingly.*) Oh I know! I know! But say so! I love to hear it.

FRED—(*stroking her hair caressingly with one hand*) Of course I love you. You know I do, Mildred. (*Mrs. Baldwin's maid Gene appears noiselessly in the doorway from the verandah. They are looking raptly into each other's eyes and do not notice her. She glares at them for a moment, vindictive hatred shining in her black eyes. Then she disappears as quietly as she came.*)

MRS. BALDWIN—(*brokenly*) I can't stand this life much longer Fred. These last two weeks while he has been away have been heaven to me but when I think of his coming back tonight—I—I could kill him!

FRED—(*worried by this sudden outbreak*) You mustn't feel so badly about it. You—we have got to make the best of it, that's all.

MRS. BALDWIN—(*reproachfully*) You take it very easily. Think of me.

FRED—(*releasing her and walking nervously up and down the room*) You know, Mildred, I'd like to do something. But how can I help matters? I haven't any money. We can't go away together yet.

MRS. BALDWIN—But I can get money—all the money we need.

FRED—(*scornfully*) His money!

MRS. BALDWIN—I have my jewels. I can sell those.

FRED—He gave you those jewels.

MRS. BALDWIN—Oh, why are you so hard on me? (*She sinks down in one of the Morris-chairs. He comes over and stands before her.*) Why won't you let me help a little?

FRED—I don't want to touch any of his money. (*Kneeling beside her he puts one arm around her—then with sudden passion*) I want you! God, how I want you! But I can't do that! (*He leans over and kisses her bare neck. She gives a long shuddering gasp, her white fingers closing and unclosing in his dark curls. He gets suddenly to his feet.*) We'll have to wait and love when we can for awhile. I promise you it won't be long. I worked my way this far and I don't intend to stop here. As soon as I've passed those engineering examinations—and I will pass them—we'll go away together. I won't be anybody's servant then. (*He glances down at his livery in disgust.*)

MRS. BALDWIN—(*pleading tearfully*) Fred, dearest, please take me away now—tonight—before he comes. What difference does the money make as long as I have you?

FRED—(*with a harsh laugh*) You don't know what you're talking about. You'd never stand it. Being poor doesn't mean anything to you. You've never been poor. Well, I have, and I know. It's hell, that's what it is. You've been used to having everything, and when you found out you were tied to a servant who could give you nothing, you'd soon get tired. And I'd be the last one to blame you for it. I'm working out and I don't want to go back and drag you with me.

MRS. BALDWIN—You don't realize how much I love you or you wouldn't talk like that. I'd rather die of starvation with you than live the way I'm living now.

FRED—(*shaking his head skeptically*) You don't know what

starvation means. Besides, how do you know he'll get a divorce? He might keep you bound to him in name for years—just for spite.

MRS. BALDWIN—No. I'm sure he isn't as mean as all that. To do him justice he's been kind to me—in his way. He has looked upon me as his plaything, the slave of his pleasure, a pretty toy to be exhibited that others might envy him his ownership. But he's given me everything I've ever asked for without a word—more than I ever asked for. He hasn't ever known what the word "husband" ought to mean but he's been a very considerate "owner." Let us give him credit for that. I don't think— (*She hesitates.*)

FRED—Go on! Go on! I expect to hear you love him next.

MRS. BALDWIN—(*smiling*) Don't misunderstand me. I simply can't think him the devil in human form you would make him out to be. (*grimly*) I love him? It was my kind parents who loved his money. He is so much older than I am and we have nothing in common. Well, I simply don't love him—there's an end to it. And so—being his wife—I hate him! (*Her voice is like a snarl as she says these last words—there is a pause.*) But what is your plan?

FRED—When the time comes I shall go to him frankly and tell him we love each other. I shall offer to go quietly away with you without any fuss or scandal. If he's the man you think him—and I don't agree with you on that point—he'll get a divorce so secretly it will never even get into the papers. He'll save his own name and yours. If he tries to be nasty about it I know something that'll bring him around. (*Mrs. Baldwin looks at him in astonishment.*) Oh, I haven't been idle. His past is none too spotless.

MRS. BALDWIN—What have you found out?

FRED—I can't tell you now. It's got nothing to do with you anyway. It was a business deal.

MRS. BALDWIN—A business deal?

FRED—Yes. It happened a long time ago. (*abruptly changing the subject*) What can be keeping him? What time did he say he'd be here?

MRS. BALDWIN—The telegram said "for dinner." (*suddenly with intense feeling*) Oh, if you knew the agony that telegram caused me! I knew it had to come but I kept hoping against hope that something would detain him. After the wire came and I knew he would be here, I kept thinking of how he would claim me—force his loathsome kisses on me. (*Fred groans in impotent rage.*) I was filled with horror. That is why I asked you to take me away tonight—to save me that degradation. (*after a pause—her face brightening with hope*) It's getting late. Maybe he won't come after all. Fred, dear, we may have one more night together. (*He bends over and kisses her. The faint throb of a powerful motor with muffler cut out is heard. Fred listens for a moment—then kisses Mrs. Baldwin hastily.*)

FRED—There he is now! I know the sound of the car. (*He rushes to the open door and disappears in the darkness.*)

MRS. BALDWIN—(*springing tensely to her feet, runs over and unlocks the door to hall and opens it*) Oh God! (*The noise of the motor sounds louder, then seems to grow fainter, and suddenly ceases altogether.*) He's gone to the garage. They're meeting. Oh God! (*She shrinks away from the door—then remains standing stiffly with one hand clenched on the table. Quick footsteps are heard on the gravel, then on the steps of the verandah. A moment later Arthur Baldwin enters from the hall. He comes quickly over to her, takes both of her hands and kisses her. A shudder of disgust runs over her whole body.*)

(*Baldwin is a stocky, undersized man of about fifty. His face is puffy and marked by dissipation and his thick-lipped mouth seems perpetually curled in a smile of cynical scorn. His eyes are small with heavily drooping lids that hide their expression. He talks softly in rather a bored drawl and exhibits enthusiasm on but two subjects—his racing car and his wife—in the order named. He has on a motoring cap with goggles on it and a linen duster, which he takes off on entering the room and throws in a chair. He is rather foppishly dressed in a perfectly fitting dark grey suit of extreme cut.*)

BALDWIN—(*holding his wife at arm's length and throwing an ardent glance at her bare neck and shoulders*) As beautiful as ever I see. Why you're all togged out! (*with a half-sneer*) Is it to welcome the prodigal bridegroom?

MRS. BALDWIN—(*forcing a smile*) Of course!

BALDWIN—And how has the fairest of the fair been while her lord has been on the broad highway?

MRS. BALDWIN—Very well.

BALDWIN—Time hang heavily on your hands in this rural paradise?

MRS. BALDWIN—(*nervously avoiding his eyes*) The limousine has been out of commission—Fred has had to send away for some new part or other. I was rather glad of the opportunity to rest up a bit. You know when you're here we're always on the go. How's the car?

BALDWIN—(*enthusiastically*) Great! (*He drops her hand and takes cigar out of box on table.*) I made eighty-six about a week ago. (*lights cigar*) Ran across eight straight miles of level road—let her out the limit. It's some car all right! (*his enthusiasm suddenly vanishing—with a frown*) By the way, where's Fred?

MRS. BALDWIN—(*startled*) Wasn't he at the garage?

BALDWIN—No. No one was there.

MRS. BALDWIN—He must have gone to dinner. We had all given you up. (*anxiously*) Why do you want to see him?

BALDWIN—Because I was forgetting. The car isn't all right just now. I blew out a tire yesterday and went into a ditch— nothing serious. I backed out all right and everything seemed to be O. K. after I'd put on a new tire. She ran smoothly to-day until I hit the road up here about six o'clock. That's why I'm so late—had the devil of a time making this hill—or mountain I should say. Engine worked fine but something wrong with the steering gear. It was all I could do to hold the road—and you know I'm no slouch at driving. I nearly ran into boulders and trees innumerable. All the people at the summer camp down the line were looking at me—thought I was drunk I guess. I had to just creep up here. If I'd have gone fast your hubby would be draped around some pine tree right now. (*with a laugh*) Sorry! You'd look well in black. (*Mrs. Baldwin starts guiltily.*) I think I'll have to have this house moved into the valley. It's too much of a climb and the roads are devilish. No car, even if it has ninety horse power can stand the gaff long. I've paid enough for tires on account of this road to have it macadamized ten times over. Eaten yet?

MRS. BALDWIN—No. I wasn't hungry enough to eat alone. I'll have something light later on. And you?

BALDWIN—I had something on the way—knew I'd probably be too late up here.

MRS. BALDWIN—Shall I have them get you anything?

BALDWIN—No. I'm not hungry.

MRS. BALDWIN—Then if you don't mind I think I'll go upstairs and take off this dress. I'm rather tired tonight. I'll be with you again in a short time.

BALDWIN—Why the formality of asking? Have I been away as long as that? Make yourself comfortable, of course. (*with his cynical laugh*) I have only to humbly thank you for going to all this trouble. I assure you I appreciate it. You look more than charming.

MRS. BALDWIN—(*with a cold smile*) Thank you. (*moving toward door*) You will find the letters I did not forward on top of the desk. (*She goes out.*)

BALDWIN—(*going to desk and glancing over the letters*) Humph! There's nothing much here except bills. (*He throws them down and walks back to the table again. Gene, Mrs. Baldwin's maid enters from the hall and stands just inside the doorway, looking quickly around the room. Having assured herself that Baldwin is alone, she comes farther into the room and waits nervously for him to speak to her. She is a slight, pretty young woman of twenty-one or so neatly dressed in a black ladies-maid costume. Her hair and eyes are black, her features small and regular, her complexion dark.*)

BALDWIN—(*glancing up and seeing her*) Why, hello Gene! As pretty as ever I see.

GENE—Good evening, sir.

BALDWIN—Are you looking for Mrs. Baldwin? She just went upstairs to change her dress.

GENE—No, sir. I just left Mrs. Baldwin. She said she wished to be alone—that I was to tell you she had a headache but would be down later if she felt better. (*She pauses and clasps her hands nervously together.*)

BALDWIN—(*looking at her curiously*) Anything you wish to see me about?

GENE—(*a look of resolution coming into her face*) Yes, sir.

BALDWIN—(*half-bored*) All right; what is it? Oh, by the way, before you begin can you tell me if Fred has gone down to the village tonight or not?

GENE—I'm quite sure he's over at the garage, sir.

BALDWIN—I must phone to him about fixing the car—if he can. Can't use it the way it is. But what is it that's troubling you?

GENE—I hardly dare to tell you, sir.

BALDWIN—I love to comfort beauty in distress.

GENE—I know you'll be awful angry at me when you hear it.

BALDWIN—You are foolish to think so. It's a love affair, of course.

GENE—Yes, sir.

BALDWIN—Well, who is the fortunate party and what has he done or not done?

GENE—Oh no, you're mistaken, sir. It isn't my love affair. It's someone else's.

BALDWIN—(*impatiently*) You're very mysterious. Whose is it then?

GENE—It's Fred's sir.

BALDWIN—But—I had rather an idea that you and Fred were not altogether indifferent to each other. (*sarcastically*) You don't mean to tell me the handsome young devil has jilted you?

GENE—(*her voice harsh with anger*) He does not love me any more.

BALDWIN—(*mockingly*) I shall have to chide him. His morals are really too corrupt for his station in life. My only advice to you is to find another sweetheart. There is nothing that consoles one so much for the loss of a lover as—another lover.

GENE—(*trembling with rage at his banter*) I am well through with him. It's you and not me who ought to be concerned the most this time.

BALDWIN—(*frowning*) I? And pray tell me why I should be interested in the amours of my chauffeur?

GENE—(*a bit frightened*) There's lots of things happened since you've been away.

BALDWIN—(*irritably*) I am waiting for you to reveal in what way all this concerns me.

GENE—They've been together all the time you've been away—every day and (*hesitating for a moment at the changed look on his face—then resolutely*) every night too. (*vindictively*) I've watched them when they thought no one was around. I've heard their "I love yous" and their kisses. Oh, they thought they were so safe! But I'll teach him to throw me over the way he did. I'll pay her for all her looking down on me and stealing him away. She's a bad woman, is what I say! Let her keep to her husband like she ought to and not go meddling with other people—

BALDWIN—(*interrupting her in a cold, hard voice and holding himself in control by a mighty effort*) It isn't one of the servants? (*Gene shakes her head.*) No. I forget you said she was married. One of the summer people near here? (*Gene shakes her head.*) Someone in this house? (*Gene nods. Baldwin's body grows tense. His heavy lids droop over his eyes, his mouth twitches. He speaks slowly as if the words came with difficulty.*) Be careful! Think what you are saying! There is only one other person in this house. Do—you—mean to—say it is that person? (*Gene is too terrified to reply.*) Answer me, do you hear? Answer me! Is that the person you refer to?

GENE—(*in a frightened whisper*) Yes.

BALDWIN—(*springing at her and clutching her by the throat with both hands*) You lie! You lie! (*He forces her back over the edge of the table. She frantically tries to tear his hands away.*) Tell me you lie, damn you, or I'll choke you to hell! (*She gasps for breath and her face becomes a dark crimson. Baldwin suddenly realizes what he is doing and takes his hands away. Gene falls half across the table, her breath coming in great shuddering sobs. Baldwin stands silently beside her waiting until she can speak again. Finally he leads her to one of the Morris-chairs and pushes her into it. He stands directly in front of her.*)

BALDWIN—You can speak again?

GENE—(*weakly*) Yes—no thanks to you.

BALDWIN—You understand, don't you, that what you have said requires more proof than the mere statement of a jealous servant. (*He pronounces the "servant" with a sneer of contempt.*)

GENE—I've got proof, don't you worry, but I don't know whether I'll show it to you or not. A man that chokes women deserves to be made a fool of.

BALDWIN—(*stung by her scorn*) You will show me, damn

you, or— (*He leans over as if to grab her by the throat again.*)

GENE—(*shrinking back in the chair*) Don't you dare touch me or I'll scream and tell them all about it. I'll prove it to you, but it isn't because I'm afraid of you or your threats but simply because I want to get even with her. (*She reaches in under her belt and pulls out a closely folded piece of paper.*) Do you recognize her writing when you see it?

BALDWIN—Give it to me.

GENE—(*holding it away from him*) Will you promise to tell her—them—just how you found out—after I'm gone. I'm leaving tomorrow morning. I'd like them to know it was me who spoiled their fun. Will you promise?

BALDWIN—Yes! Yes! Anything. Give it to me!

GENE—There! Take it.

BALDWIN—(*He reads the letter slowly and a terrible expression comes over his pale, twitching features. Gene watches him with a smile of triumph. When he speaks his voice is ominously soft and subdued.*) What night was this she speaks of?

GENE—The night before last.

BALDWIN—She says she would come to him at half-past eleven. Did she mean to the garage?

GENE—Yes. When she thought we were all in bed in the back part of the house she would slip down and go out the front door. She kept on the grass and in the shade of the trees so no one would notice her.

BALDWIN—You know all this?

GENE—I followed her on several different nights.

BALDWIN—You *must* hate her.

GENE—I loved Fred.

BALDWIN—Why was she so careless as to write this note? Couldn't she have telephoned or told him?

GENE—The little garage telephone was out of order. It was only fixed this morning. The Lynches were here to dinner and she had no chance to speak to him alone. She sent me to the garage to tell him to come over. When he came she pretended to give him some orders and dropped this at his feet. I suspected something, so I was watching and saw it all.

BALDWIN—How did you get hold of this?

GENE—Yesterday when he went to the village to see if the

new part for the limousine had come I went to the garage and found this in the inside pocket of his other clothes.

BALDWIN—(*his eyes narrowing*) He is very careless.

GENE—Oh, they knew you wouldn't be home until to-day and they felt safe. And I knew you wouldn't believe me without proof.

BALDWIN—Do you think he has missed this?

GENE—No. (*with a sneer*) As you say he is very careless in such matters. If he does miss it he'll think he has forgotten where he hid it.

BALDWIN—(*after a pause—putting the note in his pocket*) You may go. Be sure you do leave in the morning, otherwise—

GENE—You needn't fret. I wouldn't stay another day if you paid me a million. (*She yawns heavily.*) Oh, I'm glad that's off my mind. I'll sleep tonight. I haven't slept a bit, it seems, since you've been away. (*She goes slowly to the hall door—then turns around and looks at him curiously.*) What are you going to do?

BALDWIN—Go! Go!

GENE—(*with a mocking laugh*) I wish you luck! (*She goes out.*)

BALDWIN—(*stares at the rug for a moment—then takes the note out of his pocket and reads it again. In a burst of rage he crumples it up in his hand and curses beneath his breath. His eyes wander to his auto coat and goggles in the chair, then to the garage telephone near his desk. They seem to suggest an idea to him—a way for his vengeance. His face lights up with savage joy and he mutters fiercely to himself*) The dirty cur! By God, I'll do it! (*He ponders for a moment turning over his plan in his mind, then goes over and shuts the door to the hall and striding quickly to the garage telephone, takes off the receiver. After a pause he speaks, making his voice sound as if he were in a state of great anxiety.*) Hello! Fred? You haven't touched the car yet? Good! Take it out immediately! Go to the village and get the doctor—any doctor. Mildred—Mrs. Baldwin has been taken very ill. Hemorrhage I think—blood running from her mouth. She's unconscious—it's matter of life and death. Drive like hell, do you hear? Drive like hell! Her life's in your hands. Turn the car loose! Drive like hell! (*He hangs up the receiver and stands listening intently, with one hand on the desk. A minute later the purr of an engine is heard. It grows to a roar as the car rushes by on the driveway near the house—then gradually fades in the distance. Baldwin's thick lips are narrowed taut in a cruel grin.*) Drive *to* hell, you b——rd!

(*The stage is darkened. Half to three-quarters of an hour are supposed to intervene before the lights go up again.*)

(*Baldwin is discovered sitting in one of the Morris-chairs. He nervously pulls at the cigar he is smoking and glances at the telephone on his desk. There is a ring and he goes quickly over to it. He answers in a very low voice.*) Yes. This is Mr. Baldwin. What? Ran into a boulder you say? He's dead? (*This last question burst out exultingly—then in tones of mocking compassion*) How horrible! They're bringing it up here? That's right. How did you happen to find him?—Quite by accident then?—Yes, come right to the house. It *is* terrible—awful road—Knew something of the kind would happen sometime—ever so much obliged for your trouble. (*He hangs up receiver and opens door into hallway—then pushes the electric bell button in the wall. A moment later the maid enters.*)

THE MAID—Yes, sir?

BALDWIN—Where's Gene?

THE MAID—She's gone to bed, sir. Shall I call her?

BALDWIN—No. You'll do just as well. Will you run up and tell Mrs. Baldwin I'd like very much to see her for a few minutes. Tell her it's something of importance or else I wouldn't disturb her.

THE MAID—Yes, sir. (*She goes out. Baldwin walks over and fixes the two Morris chairs and lamp so that the light will fall on the face of the person sitting in one while the other will be in shadow. He then sits down in the shaded chair and waits. A minute or so elapses before Mrs. Baldwin appears in the doorway. She walks over to him with an expression of wondering curiosity not unmixed with fear. She wears a light blue kimona and bedroom slippers of the same color. Her beautiful hair hangs down her back in a loose braid.*)

MRS. BALDWIN—I'm sorry not to have come down before but my head aches wretchedly. I sent Gene to tell you. Did she?

BALDWIN—(*with curious emphasis*) Yes. She told me. Sit

down, my dear. (*He points to the other Morris chair— she sits in it.*)

MRS. BALDWIN—(*after a pause in which she waits for him to begin and during which he is studying her closely from his position of vantage in the shadow*) I really thought you had gone out again. That was one reason why I didn't come down. I heard the car go out and supposed of course it was you.

BALDWIN—No. It was Fred.

MRS. BALDWIN—You sent him to the village for something?

BALDWIN—No, I simply told him there was something wrong with the steering-gear—something I couldn't discover. I told him to attend to it—if he could—the first thing in the morning. It seems he has gone me one better and is trying to locate the trouble tonight. (*with grim sarcasm*) Really his zeal in my service is astounding.

MRS. BALDWIN—(*trying to conceal her anxiety*) But isn't it very dangerous to go over these roads at night in a car that is practically disabled?

BALDWIN—Fred is very careless—very, very careless in some things. I shall have to teach him a lesson. He is absolutely reckless (*Mrs. Baldwin shudders in spite of herself*) especially with other people's property. You are worrying about Fred; but I am bewailing my car which he is liable to smash from pure over-zealousness. Chauffeurs—even over-zealous ones—are to be had for the asking, but cars like mine are out of the ordinary.

MRS. BALDWIN—(*coldly*) Why do you talk like that? You know you do not mean it.

BALDWIN—I assure you I do—every word of it.

MRS. BALDWIN—You said you wished to see me on something of importance?

BALDWIN—(*dryly*) Exactly, my dear. We are coming to that. (*then softly*) I wanted to ask you, Mildred, if you are perfectly happy up here.

MRS. BALDWIN—(*astonished*) Why—of course—what makes you ask such a question?

BALDWIN—Well you know I have left you so much alone this summer I feel rather conscience-stricken. You must be bored to death on this mountain with none of your old friends around. I was thinking it might be a good plan for us to economize a bit by letting Fred go and getting along with just my car. It would be quite possible then for you to go to some more fashionable resort where things would be livelier for you.

MRS. BALDWIN—(*eagerly*) I assure you I am quite contented where I am. Of course I miss you and feel a trifle lonely at times, but then I have the other car and you know I enjoy motoring so much.

BALDWIN—Do you? You never seemed to care very much about touring round with me.

MRS. BALDWIN—You drive so dreadfully fast I am frightened to death.

BALDWIN—Fred is a careful driver then?

MRS. BALDWIN—Very careful.

BALDWIN—You have no complaint to make against him?

MRS. BALDWIN—None at all. I think he is the best chauffeur we have ever had.

BALDWIN—Why, I am delighted to hear that. I had an idea he was reckless.

MRS. BALDWIN—He is always very careful when he drives me. As for the rest of the help, they are the average with one exception. I think I shall discharge Gene. (*Baldwin smiles.*) She is getting so bold and insolent I can't put up with it any longer. As soon as I can get a new maid I shall let her go.

BALDWIN—You may save yourself the trouble. She is going to leave tomorrow. She gave me notice of her departure when you sent her downstairs.

MRS. BALDWIN—(*flushing angrily*) It's just like her to act that way—another piece of her insolence. I suppose I'll have to make the best of it. It's good riddance at all events.

BALDWIN—(*in the same, soft, half-mocking voice he has used during the whole conversation with his wife*) Do you suppose Fred will stay with us when he finds out?

MRS. BALDWIN—(*puzzled*) Finds out what? Why shouldn't he stay?

BALDWIN—He is Gene's lover—or was.

MRS. BALDWIN—(*growing pale—violently*) That is a lie!

BALDWIN—(*as if astonished*) Why, my dear, as if it mattered.

MRS. BALDWIN—(*forcing a laugh*) How silly of me! It is my anger at Gene breaking out. But I am sure you are mistaken. I know Gene was very much in love with him but I do not think he ever noticed her.

BALDWIN—Now *you* are mistaken. He may not care for her at present but there was a time when—

MRS. BALDWIN—(*biting her lips*) I do not believe it. That was servant's gossip you heard.

BALDWIN—It was not what I heard, my dear Mildred, but what I saw with my own eyes.

MRS. BALDWIN—(*in an agony of jealousy*) You—saw—them?

BALDWIN—(*apparently oblivious to her agitation*) In a very compromising position to say the least. (*Mrs. Baldwin winks back her tears of rage.*) But that was long ago. (*Mrs. Baldwin sighs as if relieved.*) Besides, what have these servant intrigues to do with us? (*Mrs. Baldwin tries to look indifferent.*) I was only joking about Fred leaving. In fact from what Gene said Fred already has some other foolish woman in love with him. Only this time it is no maid, if you please, but the lady of the house herself who has lost her heart at the sight of his dark curls. The fellow is ambitious.

MRS. BALDWIN—(*her face terror-stricken —her words faltering on her lips*) Do—you—know—who—this woman—is?

BALDWIN—(*watching her with grim amusement*) I have one of her letters here. Would you care to read it? (*He takes her note from his pocket and gives it to her.*)

MRS. BALDWIN—(*taking it in her trembling hand and smoothing it out. One glance and her face grows crimson with shame. She seems to crumple up in her chair. After a moment she throws her head back defiantly and looks up at him—a pause.*) Well?

BALDWIN—(*dryly, his voice softly menacing*) Well? You do not know how to play the game, my sweet Mildred. If ever guilt was stamped on a face it was on your's a moment ago.

MRS. BALDWIN—(*her eyes flashing*) Yes. I love him! I acknowledge it.

BALDWIN—You are better at affirming than denying. It takes courage to proclaim oneself the mistress of one's chauffeur—to play second-fiddle to one's maid!

Mrs. Baldwin—(*in a fury*) You lie! He is a man and not the beast you are.

Baldwin—(*softly*) Be calm! You will awaken your rival and she will listen and gloat!

Mrs. Baldwin—(*lowering her voice to a shrill whisper*) Oh, it was she who stole that letter?

Baldwin—Exactly. You are a novice at the game, my dear. Take the advice of a hardened old sinner—in the years and loves to come never write any more letters. Kisses come and kisses go, but letters remain forever—and are often brought into court.

Mrs. Baldwin—(*relieved at the easy way he takes it*) I cannot help this. I love him—that's all. (*pause*) What are you going to do?

Baldwin—It was to tell you that, I sent for you.

Mrs. Baldwin—You will get a divorce?

Baldwin—No.

Mrs. Baldwin—You will keep me tied to you when you know I do not love you?—when you know I love someone else? (*in pleading tones*) You will not be as hard on me as that, will you, Arthur? This is not all my fault. You have never really loved me. We are not the same age. (*Baldwin winces.*) We do not look at things in the same light—we have nothing in common. It would be needless cruelty to both of us to keep up this farce. You will not keep me tied to you for mere spite, will you?

Baldwin—(*in his kindest tone*) No. What I intend to do is to *let you* get a divorce. I will give you all the evidence you need. Could I be fairer than that?

Mrs. Baldwin—(*staring at him as if she could not believe her ears*) You will do that? (*She rushes over and kneels at his feet, kissing his hands and sobbing.*) Oh thank you! Thank you!

Baldwin—(*looking down at her bowed head with a cruel smile*) There! There! It is no more than just. I realize that youth must have it's day. You should have trusted me.

Mrs. Baldwin—(*her voice thrilling with gratitude*) How could I dream that you would be so kind? I did not dare to hope that you would ever forgive me—and he was certain you would think only of revenge. Oh, how unjust we have been to you! (*She takes one of his hands in her's and kisses it.*)

BALDWIN—It is true neither of you have given me due credit for being the man I am, or you would never have acted as you did. I have known from the first it must have been for money you married me— (*with a twisted smile*) An old man like me. Tell me the truth. Wasn't it?

MRS. BALDWIN—(*falteringly*) Yes. I would not lie to you now. My family forced me into it. You must have realized that. I hardly knew you, but they were nagging me night and day until I gave in. It was anything to get away from home. Oh, I am sorry, so sorry! Will you forgive me?

BALDWIN—(*evading her question*) I have done my best to make you happy. I have given you everything you desired, have I not?

MRS. BALDWIN—You have been very good, very kind to me. I have tried to love you but there has always been a gulf separating us. I could never understand you.

BALDWIN—I have trusted you, have I not—always and in everything?

MRS. BALDWIN—(*slowly*) Yes, but you have never loved me. I have been just a plaything with which you amused yourself—or so it has always seemed to me. Perhaps I have been unjust to you—in that too.

BALDWIN—If I have regarded you as a plaything I was only accepting the valuation your parents set upon you when they sold you. But these things are over and done and it is useless to discuss them. Let us talk of the present. You love Fred?

MRS. BALDWIN—Yes, I do.

BALDWIN—I will not stand in your way. You shall have him.

MRS. BALDWIN—(*getting up and putting her arms around his neck*) Oh I do love you now—you are so good to me. (*She kisses him on the lips. He does not move or touch her in any way but looks at her coldly with half-closed eyes, his thick lips curled in a sneering smile. In sudden fear Mrs. Baldwin moves away from him with a shudder. The noise of an automobile is faintly heard. Baldwin springs to his feet, his face transformed with savage exultation.*)

BALDWIN—(*with a hard laugh*) Thanks for that Judas kiss. I hear a machine coming. It is Fred, I know. We will have him in and relieve his mind by telling him of our agreement.

(*The machine is heard coming slowly up the drive toward the house.*)

MRS. BALDWIN—(*frightened by Baldwin's change of manner*) It does not sound like your car.

BALDWIN—It is Fred, I tell you. I know it is Fred. (*The car stops before the house. The horn sounds. Baldwin hurries to the door leading into the hall. Several persons can be heard coming up the steps to the verandah. A door is opened and shut and the hushed murmur of voices comes from the hallway.*)

BALDWIN—In here if you please—in here! (*Mrs. Baldwin moves closer to the door, her face wan with the terror of an unknown fear. Three men, one a chauffeur, the other two servants of some description, enter carrying the dead man. Two are supporting the shoulders and one the feet. A dark robe is wrapped around the whole body. They hurriedly place it on the divan to which Baldwin points and go out quickly, glad to be rid of their gruesome task. Mrs. Baldwin is swaying weakly on her feet, her eyes wildly staring at the figure on the divan. Suddenly she gives a frantic cry and rushing over pulls the covering from the dead man's head. The livid countenance of Fred is revealed. Several crimson streaks run down his cheek from his clotted, curly hair. Mrs. Baldwin shrieks and falls senseless on the floor. Baldwin who has watched her with the same cruel smile on his lips goes slowly over and pushes the button of the electric bell.*)

BALDWIN—(*when the maid appears*) Help me to get Mrs. Baldwin to her room. (*He picks up the prostrate woman in his arms and with the assistance of the maid, carries her out to the hallway. They can be heard stumbling up the stair to the floor above. A moment later Baldwin reappears, breathing heavily from his exertion, his pale face emotionless and cold. He stands looking down at the dead body on the divan—finally shrugs his shoulders disdainfully, comes over to the table, takes a cigar out of the box and lights it. The maid rushes in, all out of breath and flustered.*)

THE MAID—Please go upstairs, sir. Mrs. Baldwin has come to, and she ordered me out of the room. I think she's gone mad, sir. She's pulling out all the drawers looking for something . . . (*A dull report sounds from upstairs. The maid gives a terrified gasp.*)

BALDWIN—(*is startled for a moment and starts as if to run*

out to the hallway. Then his face hardens and he speaks to the trembling maid in even tones.) Mrs. Baldwin has just shot herself. You had better phone for the doctor, Mary.

(Curtain)

WARNINGS

A Play in One Act

CHARACTERS

JAMES KNAPP, *wireless operator of the S. S. "Empress"*

MARY KNAPP, *his wife*

CHARLES, *aged 15*

DOLLY, *aged 14*

LIZZIE, *aged 11*   } *their children*

SUE, *aged 8*

A BABY, *aged 1 yr.*

CAPT. HARDWICK *of the "Empress"*

MASON, *First Officer of the "Empress"*

DICK WHITNEY, *wireless operator of the S. S. "Duchess"
of the same line*

SCENE I—The dining-room of James Knapp's flat
    in the Bronx, New York City.

SCENE II—Section of the boat deck of the S. S.
    "Empress" showing the wireless room. (*About
    two months later.*)

Warnings

SCENE I—*The dining room of James Knapp's flat in the Bronx, N. Y. City. To the left is a door opening into the main hall, farther back a chair, and then a heavy green curtain which screens off an alcove probably used as a bedroom. To the right a doorway leading into the kitchen, another chair, and a window, with some plants in pots on the sill, which opens on a court. Hanging in front of the window is a gilt cage in which a canary chirps sleepily. The walls of the room are papered an impossible green and the floor is covered with a worn carpet of nearly the same color. Several gaudy Sunday-supplement pictures in cheap gilt frames are hung at spaced intervals around the walls. The dining table with its flowered cover is pushed back against the middle wall to allow of more space for free passage between the kitchen and the front part of the flat. On the wall above the table is a mantle piece on the middle of which a black marble clock ticks mournfully. The clock is flanked on both sides by a formidable display of family photographs. Above the mantle hangs a "Home Sweet Home" motto in a black frame. A lamp of the Welsbach type, fixed on the chandelier which hangs from the middle of the ceiling, floods the small room with bright light. It is about half-past eight of an October evening. The time is the present.*

Mrs. Knapp is discovered sitting at the end of the table near the kitchen. She is a pale, thin, peevish-looking woman of about forty, made prematurely old by the thousand worries of a penny-pinching existence. Her originally fine constitution has been broken down by the bearing of many children in conditions under which every new arrival meant a new mouth crying for its share of the already inadequate supply of life's necessities. Her brown hair, thickly streaked with gray, is drawn back tightly over her ears into a knot at the back of her head. Her thin-lipped mouth droops sorrowfully at the corners, and her faded blue eyes have an expression of fretful weariness. She wears a soiled grey wrapper and black carpet slippers. When she speaks, her voice is plaintively querulous and without authority.

Two of the children, Lizzie and Sue, are seated on her left facing the family photos. They are both bent over the table with curly blond heads close together. Under Lizzie's guidance Sue is attempting to write something on the pad before her. Both are dressed in clean looking dark clothes with black shoes and stockings.

LIZZIE—That's not the way to make a "g." Give *me* the pencil and *I'll* show you. (*She tries to take the pencil away from Sue.*)

SUE—(*resisting and commencing to cry*) I don' wanta give you the pencil. Mama-a! Make her stop!

MRS. KNAPP—(*wearily*) For goodness' sake stop that racket, Sue! Give her the pencil, Lizzie! You ought to be ashamed to fight with your little sister—and you so much older than her. I declare a body can't have a moment's peace in this house with you children all the time wranglin' and fightin'.

SUE—(*bawling louder than ever*) Mama-a! She won't give it to me!

MRS. KNAPP—(*with an attempt at firmness*) Lizzie! Did you hear what I said? Give her that pencil this instant!

LIZZIE—(*not impressed*) I wanta show her how to make a "g" and she won't let me. Make her stop, Mama!

SUE—(*screaming*) I did make a "g!" I did make a "g!"

LIZZIE—Ooo! Listen to her tellin' lies, Mama. She didn't make a "g" at all. She don't know how.

SUE—I do! Gimme that pencil.

LIZZIE—You don't. I won't give it to you.

MRS. KNAPP—(*aggravated into action gets quickly from her chair and gives Lizzie a ringing box on the ear*) There, you naughty child! That will teach you to do what I say. Give me that pencil. (*She snatches it from Lizzie's hand and gives it to Sue.*) There's the pencil! For goodness sake hush up your cryin'! (*Sue subsides into sobbing but Lizzie puts her hand over the smarting ear and starts to howl with all her might.*)

SUE—(*whimpering again as she discovers the point of the pencil has been broken off*) Look Mama! She broke the pencil!

MRS. KNAPP—(*distracted*) Be still and I'll sharpen it for you. (*turning to Lizzie and taking her on her lap*) There! There! Stop cryin'! Mama didn't mean to hurt you. (*Lizzie only cries the harder.*) Stop crying and I'll give you a piece of candy. (*Lizzie's anguish vanishes in a flash.*) Kiss mama now and promise not to be naughty any more!

LIZZIE—(*kissing her obediently*) I promise. Where's the candy Mama?

SUE—(*no longer interested in pencils*) I wanta piece of candy too.

MRS. KNAPP—(*goes to the kitchen and returns with two sticky chunks of molasses candy*) Here Lizzie! Here Sue! (*Sue manages with some effort to cram the candy into her small mouth.*) Neither one of you said "thank you." (*Lizzie dutifully mumbles* "thanks" *but Sue is beyond speech.*) I declare I don't know what I'll do with you children. You never seem to learn manners. It's just as if you were brought up on the streets— the way you act. (*The clock strikes 8.30 and Mrs. Knapp looks at it gratefully.*) There, children. It's half-past eight and you must both go to bed right away. Goodness knows I have a hard enough time gettin' you up for school in the morning.

SUE—(*having eaten enough of her candy to allow of her voicing a protest*) I don' wanta go to bed.

LIZZIE—(*sulking*) You said you'd let us stay up to see Papa.

SUE—I wanta see Papa.

MRS. KNAPP—That will do. I won't listen to any more of your talk. You've seen your father all afternoon. That's only an excuse to stay up late. He went to the doctor's and goodness knows when he'll be back. I promised to let you sit up till half-past eight and it's that now. Come now! Kiss me like two good little girls and go straight to bed. (*The two good little girls perform their kissing with an ill grace and depart slowly for bed through the alcove.*)

MRS. KNAPP—Mind you don't wake the baby with your carryings-on or I'll tell your father to spank you good. (*She has an afterthought.*) And don't forget your prayers! (*She sinks back with a deep sigh of relief and taking up an evening paper from the table, commences to read. She has hardly settled back comfortably when shouts and the noise of running steps are heard from the stairs in the hallway. Then a rattling tattoo of knocks shakes the door and a girl's voice laughingly shouts thro' the key hole,* "Open up Ma!")

MRS. KNAPP—(*going quickly to the door and unlocking it*)

Hush up your noise for goodness sakes! Do you want to wake up the baby? I never saw such children. You haven't any feelin' for your mother at all.

(*Charles and Dolly push hurriedly into the room. Mrs. Knapp locks the door again and resumes her seat at the table. Charles is a gawky, skinny youth of fifteen who has outgrown his clothes, and whose arms and legs seem to have outgrown him. His features are large and irregular; his eyes small and watery-blue in color. When he takes off his cap a mop of sandy hair falls over his forehead. He is dressed in a shabby grey Norfolk suit.*

(*Although extremely thin, Dolly is rather pretty with her dark eyes, and brown curls hanging over her shoulders. She is dressed neatly in a dark blue frock with black shoes and stockings and a black felt hat. Her ordinarily sallow city complexion is flushed from the run upstairs.*)

DOLLY—(*rushing over and kissing her mother—mischievously*) What do you think I saw, Ma?

CHARLIE—(*in a loud voice—almost a shout*) What do you think *I* saw, Mom?

MRS. KNAPP—For heaven's sake, Charlie, speak lower. Do you want the people in the next block to hear you? If you wake up the baby I shall certainly tell your father on you. Take off your hat when you're in the house! Whatever is the matter with you? Can't you remember anything? I'm really ashamed of you—the way you act.

CHARLIE—(*taking off his cap*) Aw, what's the matter, Mom? Gee, you're got an awful grouch on tonight.

MRS. KNAPP—Never mind talkin' back to your mother, young man. Why shouldn't I be cranky with you bellowin' around here like a young bull? I just got the baby to sleep and if you wake her up with your noise heaven knows when I'll get any peace again.

DOLLY—(*interrupting her—with a laughing glance at Charlie*) You can't guess what I saw, Ma.

CHARLIE—(*sheepishly*) Aw, all right for you. Go ahead and tell her if you wanta. I don't care. I'll tell her what I saw too.

DOLLY—You didn't see anything.

CHARLIE—I did too.

DOLLY—You didn't.

MRS. KNAPP—For goodness sake stop your quarrelin'!

First it's Lizzie and Sue and then it's you two. I never get time to even read a paper. What was it you saw, Dolly? Tell me if you're going to.

DOLLY—I saw Charlie and that red-headed Harris girl in the corner drug store. He was buying her ice cream soda with that quarter Pop gave him.

CHARLIE—I was no such thing.

DOLLY—Oh, what a lie! You know you were.

MRS. KNAPP—You ought to be ashamed of yourself, you big grump, you, goin' round with girls at your age and spendin' money on them. I'll tell your father how you spend the money he gives you and it'll be a long time before you get another cent.

CHARLIE—(*sullenly*) Aw you needn't think I'm the only one. (*pointing to Dolly*) I saw her down in the hallway with that Dutch kid whose father runs the saloon in the next block. It was dark down there too. I could hardly see them. And he's cross-eyed!

DOLLY—He is not.

CHARLIE—Aw g'wan, of course he is. He can't see straight or he'd never look at you.

DOLLY—He's better than you are.

CHARLIE—(*losing control of his voice and shouting again*) I'll hand him a punch in the eye the first time I see him. That's what I'll do to him, the Dutch boob. And I'll slap you in the nose too if you get too fresh. (*Dolly starts to cry.*)

MRS. KNAPP—(*rising up swiftly and giving him a crack over the ear with her open hand*) That'll teach you, young man! Don't you dare to lay a hand on your sister or your father will whip you good.

CHARLIE—(*backing away with his hand on his ear—in a whimper*) Aw, what are you always pickin' on me for? Why don't you say something to her?

MRS. KNAPP—(*turning to the still tearful Dolly*) And you, Miss! Don't you let me hear of you bein' in any dark hallways with young men again or I'll take you over my knee, so I will. The idea of such a thing! I can't understand you at all. I never was allowed out alone with anyone,—not even with your father, before I was engaged to be married to him. I don't know what's come over you young folks nowadays.

DOLLY—It—wasn't—dark.

MRS. KNAPP—It makes no difference. You heard what I said. Don't let it happen again. (*Dolly wipes her eyes and makes a face at Charlie.*)

CHARLIE—(*his tones loud with triumph*) It was awful dark. She's liein' to you, Mom.

MRS. KNAPP—Hold your tongue! I've heard enough from you. And don't yell at the top of your voice. You don't have to shout. I'm not deaf.

CHARLIE—(*lower*) All right, Mom. But I've got into the habit of talking loud since Pop's been home. He don't seem to hear me when I talk low.

DOLLY—That's right, Ma. I was talking to him this morning and when I got through he didn't know half that I'd told him.

MRS. KNAPP—Your father has a bad cold and his head is all stopped up. *He* says he hasn't got a cold but I know better. I've been that way myself. But he won't believe me. So he's gone to pay five dollars to an ear specialist when all he needs is a dose of quinine—says a wireless operator can't afford to take chances. I told him a wireless operator couldn't afford to pay five dollars for nothin'—specially when he's got a wife and five children. (*peevishly*) I don't know what's come over your father. He don't seem like the same man since this last trip on the "Empress." I think it must be that South American climate that's affectin' him.

DOLLY—He's awful cross since he's been home this time. He yells at Charlie and me for nothing.

MRS. KNAPP—He'd be all right if he could get another job. But he's afraid if he gives up this one he won't be able to get another. Your father ain't as young as he used to be and they all want young men now. He's got to keep on workin' or we'd never be able to even pay the rent. Goodness knows his salary is small enough. If it wasn't for your brother Jim sendin' us a few dollars every month, and Charlie earnin' five a week, and me washin', we'd never be able to get along even *with* your father's salary. But heaven knows what we'd do without it. We'd be put out in the streets.

CHARLIE—Is that where Pop's gone tonight—to the doctor's?

MRS. KNAPP—Yes, and I don't know what can be keepin' him so long. He left after supper right after you did. You'd think he'd spend his last night at home when we won't see him again for three months.

CHARLIE—Shall I go out and see if I can see him?

MRS. KNAPP—Don't go makin' excuses to get out on the street. You better go to bed if you wanta be up on time in the morning—you too, Dolly.

DOLLY—I still got some of my lessons to finish. (*There is a sound from the hallway of someone coming up the stairs with slow, heavy steps.*)

MRS. KNAPP—Here your father comes now! Get into the parlor, Dolly, if you wanta do your lessons. Don't let him see you up so late. Keep the light shaded so you won't wake up the baby. (*The steps stop before the door and a knock is heard.*) Charlie, go open that door. My feet are worn out from standin' up all day. (*Charlie opens the door and James Knapp enters. He is a slight, stoop-shouldered, thin-faced man of about fifty. When he takes off his derby hat he reveals a long narrow head almost completely bald with a thin line of gray hair extending over his large ears around the back of his head. His face has been tanned by the tropic sun—but now it seems a sickly yellow in the white glare of the lamp. His eyes are small, dark, and set close together; his nose stubby and of no particular shape; his mouth large and weak. He is dressed in a faded, brown suit and unshined tan shoes. His expression must be unusually depressed as he stands nervously fingering his drooping, gray moustache, for Mrs. Knapp looks at him sharply for a moment, then gets up quickly and goes over and kisses him.*)

MRS. KNAPP—(*pulling out the arm chair from the other end of the table for him*) Come! Sit down! You look all worn out. You shouldn't walk so much.

KNAPP—(*sinking into the chair and speaking in a slow, dull voice*) I am a bit tired. (*He stares at the flowered patterns of the table cover for a moment—then sighs heavily.*)

MRS. KNAPP—Whatever is the matter with you? You look as if you'd lost your last friend.

KNAPP—(*pulling himself together and smiling feebly*) I guess I've got the blues. I get to thinking about how I've got to sail tomorrow on that long, lonesome trip, and how I won't see any of you for three months, and it sort of makes me feel bad. I wish I could throw up this job. I wish I was young enough to try something else.

CHARLIE—(*who is slouched down in a chair with hands in his pockets speaks in his lowest, nicest voice*) Aw, cheer up, Pop! It won't seem long. I should think you'd be glad to get out of the cold weather. Gee, I wish't I had a chance.

KNAPP—(*looking at him blankly*) Eh? What was that, Charlie? I didn't quite hear what you said.

CHARLIE—(*in his best bellow*) I said: Cheer up! It won't seem long.

KNAPP—(*shaking his head sadly*) It's easy for you to say that. You're young. (*The shrill crying of a baby sounds from behind the green curtain of the alcove.*)

MRS. KNAPP—(*turning on Charlie furiously*) There! You're gone and done it with your big, loud mouth. I told you to speak lower. (*turning to her husband*) James, I wish you'd do something to make him behave. He don't mind what I say at all. Look at him—sprawled all over the chair with his long legs stretched out for everybody to trip over. Is that the way to sit on a chair? Anybody'd think you were brought up in a barn. I declare I'm ashamed to have you go anywhere for fear you'd disgrace me.

CHARLIE—You'd needn't worry. There's no place for me to go—and if there was I wouldn't go there with these old clothes on. Why don't you ball out Pop? He couldn't hear me, so I had to speak louder.

KNAPP—(*with sudden irritation*) Of course I heard you. But I wasn't paying any attention to what you said. I have other things to think about beside your chatter. (*Charlie sulks back in his chair.*)

MRS. KNAPP—That's right James. I knew you'd have to tell him where he belongs. You'd think he owned the house the way he acts. (*A piercing wail comes from behind the curtain and Mrs. Knapp hurries there saying*) Hush! Hush! I'm coming. (*She can be heard soothing the baby.*)

CHARLIE—(*plucking up his courage now that his mother is out of the room*) Say, Pop!

KNAPP—Well, Charlie, what is it?

CHARLIE—Please can I have a new suit of clothes? Gee, I

need 'em bad enough. This one is full of patches and holes and all the other kids down at the store laugh at me 'cause I ain't got long pants on and these don't fit me any more. Please can I have a new suit, Pop?

KNAPP—(*a look of pain crossing his features*) I'm afraid not just now, boy. (*Charlie descends into the depths of gloom.*) You see, I've had to go to this doctor about (*he hesitates*) the—er—trouble I've had with my stomach, and he's very expensive. But when I come back from this trip I'll surely buy you a fine new suit with long pants the very first thing I do. I promise it to you and you know I don't break my promises. Try and get along with that one until I get back.

CHARLIE—(*ruefully*) All right, Pop. I'll try, but I'm afraid it's going to bust if I get any bigger.

KNAPP—That's a good boy. We haven't been having much luck lately and we've all got to stand for our share of doing without things. I may have to do without a lot— (*He turns his face away to hide his emotion from Charlie. A sob shakes his shoulders. Charlie notices it and goes over clumsily and pats his father on the back.*)

CHARLIE—Gee, Pop, what's the matter? I can get along without a suit all right. I wouldn't have asked you if I thought you was so blue.

KNAPP—Never mind me, boy. I'm just not feeling well, that's all—something I must have eaten—or a touch of fever. (*He glances at the clock.*) It's getting pretty late, Charlie, and you've got to be up early in the morning. Better go to bed. Your mother and I have a lot to talk about yet—things which wouldn't interest you.

CHARLIE—All right, Pop. Good night. I'll see you in the morning before I go.

KNAPP—Good night and—remember I'm trying to do the best I know how. (*Charlie disappears behind the green curtain. Knapp stares at the table, his head between his hands, his face full of suffering. Mrs. Knapp comes back into the room. The baby is safely asleep again.*)

MRS. KNAPP—You sent Charlie to bed, didn't you? (*He nods.*) That's right. He stays up altogether too late nights. He's always prowlin' around the streets. I don't know what will become of him I'm sure. Dolly told me tonight she saw him buyin' soda for that red-headed Harris girl with the quarter you gave him. What do you think of that? And he says he saw her talkin' in the dark hallway downstairs with some German bartender's boy. What do you think of that?

KNAPP—(*mildly*) Where's the hurt? They're only kids and they've got to have some fun.

MRS. KNAPP—Fun? I'm glad you call it fun. I think it disgraceful.

KNAPP—Come, come, you exaggerate everything so. I see no harm in it. God knows I have enough to worry about without being bothered with children's pranks.

MRS. KNAPP—(*scornfully*) You have worries? And what are they, I'd like to know? You sail away and have a fine time with nothin' to do but eat the best of food and talk to the pretty women in the First Class. Worries? I wish you'd stay home and change places with me—cookin', scrubbin', takin' care of the children, puttin' off the grocer and the butcher, doin' washin' and savin' every penny. You'd soon find out what worry meant then.

KNAPP—(*placatingly*) I know you have to put up with a lot, Mary, and I wish I could do something to make it easier for you. (*brokenly*) I don't know what's going to become of us—now.

MRS. KNAPP—Oh, we'll manage to get along as we have been doin', I expect.

KNAPP—But—Mary—something terrible has happened. I'm almost afraid to tell you.

MRS. KNAPP—What do you mean? You haven't lost your job, have you?

KNAPP—I went to see that ear specialist and— (*His emotion chokes him; he stops to regain his composure.*)

MRS. KNAPP—Yes?

KNAPP—(*his voice breaking in spite of himself*) He says I'm losing my hearing—that I'm liable to go stone deaf at any moment. (*He lets his head fall on his arms with a sob.*)

MRS. KNAPP—(*coming over and putting her arm around him*) There Jim! Don't take on about it so. All those doctors make things worse than they really are. He's just tryin' to scare you so you'll keep comin' to see him. Why, you can hear just as well as I can.

KNAPP—No, I've noticed how hard it's been for me to catch some of the messages lately. And since I've been home I've had a hard time of it now and then to understand the children. The doctor said I would probably be able to hear for a long time yet but I got to be prepared for a sudden shock which'll leave me stone deaf.

MRS. KNAPP—(*quickly*) Does anyone on the ship know?

KNAPP—Of course not. If they knew my hearing was going back on me I wouldn't hold my job a minute. (*His voice trembles.*) But I've got to tell them now. I've got to give up.

MRS. KNAPP—You didn't tell the specialist what you were, did you?

KNAPP—No. I said I was a mechanist.

MRS. KNAPP—(*getting up from her chair and speaking in a hard voice*) Then why have you got to tell them? If you don't tell them they'll never know. You say yourself the doctor told you your hearin' would hold out for a long time yet.

KNAPP—He said "probably."

MRS. KNAPP—(*an angry flush spreading over her face*) Give up your job? Are you a fool? Are you such a coward that a doctor can scare you like that?

KNAPP—I'm not afraid for myself. I'm not afraid of being deaf if I have to be. You don't understand. You don't know the responsibility of a man in my job.

MRS. KNAPP—Responsibility? You've told me lots of times there was so few messages to send and take you wondered why they had a wireless. What's the matter with you all of a sudden? You're not deaf now and even if that liein' doctor spoke the truth you'll hear for a long time yet. He only told you about that sudden stroke to keep you comin' to him. I know the way they talk.

KNAPP—(*protesting weakly*) But it ain't right. I ought to tell them and give up the job. Maybe I can get work at something else.

MRS. KNAPP—(*furiously*) Right? And I suppose you think it's right to loaf around here until we all get put out in the streets? God knows your salary is small enough but without it we'd starve to death. Can't you think of others besides yourself? How about me and the children? What's goin' to buy them clothes and food? I can't earn enough and what

Charlie gets wouldn't keep *him* alive for a week. Jim sends us a few dollars a month but he don't get much and he ain't workin' regular. We owe the grocer and the butcher now. If they found out you wasn't workin' they wouldn't give us any more credit. And the landlord? How long would he let us stay here? You'll get other work? Remember the last time you tried. We had to pawn everything we had then and we was half-starved when you did land this job. You had to go back to the same old work, didn't you? They didn't want you at any telegraph office, did they? You was too old and slow, wasn't you? Well you're older and slower than ever now and that's the only other job you're fit for. (*with bitter scorn*) You'll get another job! (*She sits down and covers her face with her hands, weeping bitterly.*) And this is all the thanks I get for slavin' and workin' my fingers off! What a father for my poor children! Oh, why did I ever marry such a man? It's been nothin' but worryin' and sufferin' ever since.

KNAPP—(*who has been writhing under the lash of her scorn, is tortured beyond endurance at her last reproaches*) For God's sake let me alone! I'll go! I'll go! But this is going to be my last trip. I got to do the right thing. (*He gets up and pushes aside the green curtain.*) Come on! I'm going to bed. (*He leaves Mrs. Knapp alone. She lifts her tear-stained face from her hands and sighs with relief as she turns out the gas.*)

SCENE II

SCENE—*A section of the boat deck of the S. S. "Empress" just abaft of the bridge. The deck slants sharply downward in the direction of the bow. To the left the officers' cabins with several lighted port holes. Just in back of them and in the middle of the deck is the wireless room with its door wide open revealing James Knapp bent over his instrument on the forward side of the compartment. His face is pale and set, and he is busy sending out calls, pausing every now and then with a strained expression as if he were vainly trying to catch some answer to his messages. Every time he taps on the key the snarl of the wireless sounds above the confused babble of frightened voices that rises from the promenade deck. To the right of the wireless room on the port side a life-raft. Still farther to the right one of the funnels. The background is a tropic sky blazing with stars. The wires running up from the wireless room to the foremast may be seen dimly lined against the sky. The time is about eleven o'clock.*

Captain Hardwick enters hurriedly from the direction of the bridge and walks across to the door of the wireless room where he stands looking in at Knapp. He is a stocky man about fifty dressed in a simple blue uniform. His face is reddened by sun and wind — that is, all of it which is not hidden by his grey beard and mustache. He drums nervously on the door. Knapp pretends not to see him and appears absorbed in his instrument.

CAPT. HARDWICK—No answer yet? (*Knapp does not reply and the Captain leans over impatiently and shakes him by the shoulder.*) I asked you if there was any answer yet?

KNAPP—(*looking at him furtively*) I haven't heard a thing yet, sir.

CAPT. HARDWICK—Damnation! What in hell is the matter with them? Are they all asleep?

KNAPP—I'll try again sir. (*He taps on the key before him and the whine of the wireless shrills out discordantly.*)

CAPT. HARDWICK—(*turning away with a muttered oath*) Well, I've got to get back on the bridge. Let me know the moment you catch anyone.

KNAPP—(*who has been watching his lips move*) Yes, sir. (*His tone is vague as if he were guessing at the answer.*)

CAPT. HARDWICK—Tell 'em we hit a derelict and are sinking. Make it as strong as you can. We need help and we need it right away.

KNAPP—(*more vaguely than ever*) Yes sir.

CAPT. HARDWICK—You surely ought to get the "Verdari." She can't be more than a hundred miles away if my reckoning is correct. (*turning away again*) I've got to go. Keep sending until you get an answer.

KNAPP—Yes sir.

CAPT. HARDWICK—(*in under his breath*) Damn your "yes sirs." I believe you're frightened out of your wits. (*He walks quickly toward the bridge. Half-way across the deck he is met by Mason the First Officer, a tall, clean-shaven, middle-aged man in uniform who hurries in from forward.*) Well, Mason, how do things look below?

MASON—Very bad sir. I'm afraid the bulkhead can't hold out much longer. They're doing all they can to strengthen it but it don't look to me as if it would stand the pressure. I wouldn't give it more than half an hour—an hour at most, sir.

CAPT. HARDWICK—She's listing pretty badly. Guess you're right, Mason. When that bulkhead goes it's only a question of five or ten minutes. Are the crew all ready to man the boats?

MASON—Yes sir.

CAPT. HARDWICK—Good! Passengers all on deck and ready to leave?

MASON—Yes sir.

CAPT. HARDWICK—Good! Lucky there's only a few of them or we'd be in a nice mess. Lucky it's a calm night too. There'll be no panic. (*There is a pause broken only by the confused sound of voices from below.*) Damned funny we get no reply to our calls for help, eh? Don't you think so?

MASON—Very funny, sir. The "Verdari" ought to be right around here about this time. There ought to be four or five vessels we could reach, I should think.

CAPT. HARDWICK—Just what I told Knapp. The poor devil seems scared to death because he can't get an answer. All he says every time I ask him is: (*mimicking Knapp*) Haven't heard a thing yet, sir!

MASON—He's told me the same thing three or four times. I don't like the looks of it, sir. He appears to act queer to me.

CAPT. HARDWICK—You're right. He has been strange all during the trip—didn't seem to want to speak to anyone. I thought he must be sick. Think it's drink?

MASON—No sir. I never saw him touch a drop—even on shore.

CAPT. HARDWICK—Let's see what he's got to say now. By God, we've got to get a message in soon or there'll be the devil to pay. (*They both go over to the wireless room where Knapp is frenziedly sending out call after call. The Captain goes into the compartment and stands beside Knapp. Mason remains outside the door. Knapp looks up and sees them. He glances fearfully from one to the other.*)

CAPT. HARDWICK—Caught the "Verdari" yet?

KNAPP—(*in the uncertain tone he had used before*) I haven't heard a thing yet, sir.

CAPT. HARDWICK—Are you sure there's nothing wrong with this machine of yours?

KNAPP—(*bewilderedly*) No sir. Not a single answer, sir. I can't account for it, sir.

CAPT. HARDWICK—(*angrily*) I know that. You've told me often enough. Answer my question! (*Knapp looks at him with puzzled eyes; then turns to the key of his instrument. Capt. Hardwick grabs him by the shoulder.*) Did you hear what I said? Dammit, answer my question.

KNAPP—(*his lips trembling*) No sir.

CAPT. HARDWICK—(*furiously*) What?

MASON—(*interposing*) Excuse me, sir, but something's wrong with the man. I don't think he heard what you said.

CAPT. HARDWICK—The coward is frightened silly—that's what's the matter. (*Bending down he shouts against the receivers which Knapp has over both his ears.*) Say something, can't you? Are you deaf? (*Knapp shrinks away from him, his face ashy with fear, but does not answer.*)

MASON—Maybe it's those things on his ears, sir.

CAPT. HARDWICK—(*taking hold of the metal loops that go over Knapp's head and jerking the receivers off his ears*) Now! Answer me! What in hell's the matter with you? (*then his voice softening a bit*) If you're sick, why don't you say so?

KNAPP—(*looking at him helplessly for a moment—then hiding his face in his arms and weeping hysterically*) Oh my God! it's come! (*The Captain and Mason look at each other in amazement as Knapp blurts out between his sobs*) I wasn't sure. I was hoping against hope. I can't hear a word you say. I can't hear anything. It's happened just as the doctor said it might. (*looking up at the Captain and clasping and unclasping his hands piteously*) Oh, I should have told you, sir, before we started—but we're so poor and I couldn't get another job. I was just going to make this one more trip. I wanted to give up the job this time but she wouldn't let me. She said I wanted them to starve—and Charlie asked me for a suit. (*His sobs stifle him.*) Oh God, who would have dream't this could have happened—at such a time. I thought it would be all right—just this trip. I'm not a bad man, Captain. And now I'm deaf—

stone deaf. I can't hear what you say. I'm deaf! Oh my God! My God! (*He flings his arms on the instrument in front of him and hides his face on them, sobbing bitterly.*)

CAPT. HARDWICK—(*turning to Mason*) Well, I'll be damned! What do you make of this?

MASON—I guess what he says is true, sir. He's gone deaf. That's why we've had no answer to our calls.

CAPT. HARDWICK—(*fuming helplessly*) What in hell can we do? I must know they're coming for us before I send the boats away. (*He thinks a moment. Suddenly his face lights up and he strikes his fist into his open palm.*) By God, I've got it. You know Dick Whitney? (*Mason nods.*) Operator of the "Duchess"—been laid up in Bahia with fever—came on board there—going home on vacation—he's in the First Cabin—run and get him. (*Mason runs down deck toward bridge.*) Hurry, for God's sake! (*Mason is gone. Captain Hardwick turns to Knapp and lifting him by the arms helps him out of cabin and sits him down on the life-raft. Pats him roughly on back.*) Brace up! Poor beggar! (*Knapp continues to sob brokenly. Mason reappears followed by Dick Whitney, a thin, sallow-faced young fellow of about twenty-five, wearing a light sack suit. He shows the effect of his recent battle with tropical fever but he walks over to the wireless room confidently enough and takes his seat before the instrument.*)

CAPT. HARDWICK—Get some one quick, Whitney. Tell 'em we're just about to launch the boats.

WHITNEY—(*who has put the receivers over his ears*) They're calling us now, sir. (*He sends answering call—a pause.*) It's the "Verdari."

CAPT. HARDWICK—Good! I knew she ought to be near us.

WHITNEY—Operator says they're coming full speed— ought to reach us before daylight—wants to know if we can't keep up till then.

CAPT. HARDWICK—No. Tell them the bulkhead's almost gone. We're due to sink within an hour at most. (*to Mason*) Better go down and see how things are below. (*Mason leaves hurriedly.*)

WHITNEY—All right, sir. (*He taps on the key—the wail of the wireless sounds again—then a pause.*)

CAPT. HARDWICK—What do they say now?

WHITNEY—(*with a slight smile*) "Hard luck."

CAPT. HARDWICK—(*exploding*) Damn their sympathy!

WHITNEY—The operator says he's been trying to communicate with us for a long time. He got our messages all right but we never seemed to get his. (*The Capt. glances at Knapp who is still sitting on the life-raft with his face hidden in his hands.*) He says he got a call from one of the Fruit Co.'s boats. She's rushing to help us too. He wants to know if we've heard anything from her.

CAPT. HARDWICK—No. (*He looks at Knapp again, then speaks dryly.*) Tell him our receiving apparatus has been out of order.

WHITNEY—(*looks up in surprise—then sends the message—there is a pause*) He asks if we're sure it was a derelict we struck—says the "Verdari" sighted one about where we are now yesterday and he sent out warnings to all vessels he could reach—says he tried to get us especially because he knew we passed this way; but if our receiving end was bad that explains it.

CAPT. HARDWICK—(*staring at Knapp*) By God!

WHITNEY—Anything more you want to say, sir?

CAPT. HARDWICK—(*mechanically*) Tell them to hurry, that's all. (*Suddenly in a burst of rage he strides toward Knapp and raises his fist as if to strike him. Mason comes in from astern and steps in between them. Capt. Hardwick glares at him for a moment—then recovers himself.*) You're right, Mason. I won't touch him; but that miserable, cowardly shrimp has lost my ship for me. (*His face plainly shows how much this loss means to him. Mason does not understand what he means. Capt. Hardwick turns to the wireless room again where young Whitney is sitting expectantly awaiting orders.*) Say Whitney! Write out that last message from the "Verdari" about her sending out warnings of that derelict yesterday—warnings which we didn't get. Put down how the operator on the "Verdari" tried especially to warn us because he knew we would pass this way. (*Mason now understands and turns from Knapp with a glance full of scorn. Whitney writes rapidly on the report pad near him and hands the sheet to the Capt. who walks over to Knapp and shaking him, holds the message out. Knapp takes it in a trembling hand.*)

MASON—I've got all the men up from below, sir. The

bulkhead's ready to go any minute. Shall I get some of the boats away, sir?

CAPT. HARDWICK—Yes. (*Mason starts astern.*) Wait a moment. I'm coming with you. Come on Whitney. You can't do any good there any longer. (*He stops in front of Knapp as he walks toward the stern. Knapp is staring at the paper in his hand with wild eyes and pale, twitching features. Capt. Hardwick motions to him to follow them. They go off to right. Knapp sits still with the sheet of paper in his hand. The creaking of blocks is heard and Mason's voice shouting orders.*)

KNAPP—(*in a hoarse whisper*) God! It's my fault then! It's my fault! (*He staggers weakly to his feet.*) What if the ship is lost! (*He looks astern where they are lowering the boats—his face is convulsed with horror—he gives a bitter cry of despair.*) O-o-h! They're lowering the boats! She *is* lost! She *is* lost! (*He stumbles across the deck into the wireless room, pulls out a drawer, and takes out a revolver, which he presses against his temple.*) She *is* lost! (*There is a sharp report and Knapp falls forward on his face on the floor before his instrument. His body twitches for a moment, then is still. The operator Whitney comes running in from the right calling:* "Knapp! They're waiting for you." *He gives one horrified glance at the body in the room; says* "Good God!" *in a stupefied tone, and then, seized with sudden terror, rushes astern again.*)

(*Curtain*)

FOG

A Play in One Act

CHARACTERS

A Poet
A Man of Business
A Polish Peasant Woman
A Dead Child
The Third Officer of a Steamer
Sailors from the Steamer

Time—The Present

Fog

The life-boat of a passenger steamer is drifting helplessly off the Grand Banks of Newfoundland. A dense fog lies heavily upon the still sea. There is no wind and the long swells of the ocean are barely perceptible. The surface of the water is shadowy and unreal in its perfect calmness. A menacing silence, like the genius of the fog, broods over everything.

Three figures in the boat are darkly outlined against the gray background of vapor. Two are seated close together on the thwarts in the middle. The other is huddled stiffly at one end. None of their faces can be distinguished.

Day is just about to break and as the action progresses the vague twilight of dawn creeps over the sea. This, in turn, is succeeded by as bright a semblance of daylight as can sift through the thick screen of fog.

A MAN'S VOICE—(*appallingly brisk and breezy under the circumstances*) Brrr! I wish daylight would come. I'm beginning to feel pretty chilly. How about you? (*He receives no answer and raises his voice, the fear of solitude suddenly alive within him.*) Hello there! You haven't gone to sleep, have you?

ANOTHER MAN'S VOICE—(*more refined than the first, clear and unobtrusively melancholy*) No, I'm not asleep.

FIRST VOICE—(*complacently reassured*) Thought you might have dozed off. I did a while ago—eyes refused to stay open any longer—couldn't imagine where I was when I woke up—had forgotten all about the damned wreck.

SECOND VOICE—You are fortunate to be able to sleep. I wish I could go to sleep and forget—all this—

FIRST VOICE—Oh come now! You mustn't keep thinking about it. That won't do any good. Brace up! We're sure to get out of this mess all right. I've figured it all out. You know how long a time it was between the time we hit the derelict—it was a derelict we hit, wasn't it?

SECOND VOICE—I believe so.

FIRST VOICE—Well, the wireless was going all the time, if you remember, and one of the officers told me we had lots of answers from ships saying they were on the way to help us. One of them is sure to pick us up.

SECOND VOICE—In this fog?

FIRST VOICE—Oh this'll all go away as soon as the sun goes up. I've seen plenty like it at my country place on the Connecticut shore, maybe not as thick as this one but nearly as bad, and when the sun came up they always disappeared before the morning was over.

SECOND VOICE—You forget we are now near the Grand Banks, the home of fog.

FIRST VOICE—(*with a laugh that is a bit troubled*) I must say you aren't a very cheerful companion. Why don't you look at the bright side? (*a pause during which he is evidently thinking over what the other man has told him*) The Grand Banks? Hmm, well, I refuse to be scared.

THE SECOND VOICE—I have no intention of making our situation seem worse than it really is. I have every hope that we will eventually be rescued but it's better not to expect too much. It only makes disappointment more bitter when it comes.

FIRST VOICE—I suppose you're right but I can't help being optimistic.

SECOND VOICE—You remember how downcast you were yesterday when we failed to hear any sound of a ship? Today is liable to be the same unless this fog lifts. So don't hope for too much.

FIRST VOICE—You're forgetting the fact that there was no sun yesterday. That kind of weather can't last forever.

SECOND VOICE—(*dryly*) Perhaps we could not see the sun on account of the fog.

FIRST VOICE—(*after a pause*) I'll admit I did feel pretty dismal yesterday—after that terrible thing happened.

SECOND VOICE—(*softly*) You mean after the child died?

FIRST VOICE—(*gloomily*) Yes. I thought that woman would never stop crying. Ugh! It was awful—her cries, and the fog, and not another sound anywhere.

SECOND VOICE—It was the most horrible thing I have ever seen or even heard of. I never dreamed anything could be so full of tragedy.

FIRST VOICE—It was enough to give anyone the blues, that's sure. Besides my clothes were wet and I was freezing cold and you can imagine how merry I felt. (*grumbling*) Not that they're any dryer now but somehow I feel warmer.

SECOND VOICE—(*after a long pause*) So you think the child's death was a terrible thing?

FIRST VOICE—(*in astonishment*) Of course. Why? Don't you?

SECOND VOICE—No.

FIRST VOICE—But you said just a minute ago that—

SECOND VOICE—I was speaking of the grief and despair of the mother. But death was kind to the child. It saved him many a long year of sordid drudgery.

FIRST VOICE—I don't know as I agree with you there. Everyone has a chance in this world; but we've all got to work hard, of course. That's the way I figure it out.

SECOND VOICE—What chance had that poor child? Naturally sickly and weak from underfeeding, transplanted to the stinking room of a tenement or the filthy hovel of a mining village, what glowing opportunities did life hold out that death should not be regarded as a blessing for him? I mean if he possessed the ordinary amount of ability and intelligence—considering him as the average child of ignorant Polish immigrants. Surely his prospects of ever becoming anything but a beast of burden were not bright, were they?

FIRST VOICE—Well, no, of course not, but—

SECOND VOICE—If you could bring him back to life would you do so? Could you conscientiously drag him away from that fine sleep of his to face what he would have to face? Leaving the joy you would give his mother out of the question, would you do it for him individually?

FIRST VOICE—(*doubtfully*) Perhaps not, looking at it from that standpoint.

SECOND VOICE—There is no other standpoint. The child was diseased at birth, stricken with a hereditary ill that only the most vital men are able to shake off.

FIRST VOICE—You mean?

SECOND VOICE—I mean poverty—the most deadly and prevalent of all diseases.

FIRST VOICE—(*amused*) Oh, that's it, eh? Well, it seems

to be a pretty necessary sickness and you'll hardly find a cure for it. I see you're a bit of a reformer.

SECOND VOICE—Oh no. But there are times when the frightful injustice of it all sickens me with life in general.

FIRST VOICE—I find life pretty good. I don't know as I'd change it even if I could.

SECOND VOICE—Spoken like a successful man. For I'm sure you are a successful man, are you not? I mean in a worldly way.

FIRST VOICE—(*flattered*) Yes, you might call me so, I guess. I've made my little pile but it was no easy time getting it, let me tell you.

SECOND VOICE—You had some advantages, did you not? Education and plenty to eat, and a clean home, and so forth?

FIRST VOICE—I went to high school and of course had the other things you mentioned. My people were not exactly what you could call poor but they were certainly not rich. Why do you ask?

SECOND VOICE—Do you think you would be as successful and satisfied with life if you had started with handicaps like those which that poor dead child would have had to contend with if he had lived?

FIRST VOICE—(*impatiently*) Oh, I don't know! What's the use of talking about what might have happened? I'm not responsible for the way the world is run.

SECOND VOICE—But supposing you are responsible?

FIRST VOICE—What!

SECOND VOICE—I mean supposing we—the self-satisfied, successful members of society—are responsible for the injustice visited upon the heads of our less fortunate "brothers-in-Christ" because of our shameful indifference to it. We see misery all around us and we do not care. We do nothing to prevent it. Are we not then, in part at least, responsible for it? Have you ever thought of that?

FIRST VOICE—(*in tones of annoyance*) No, and I'm not going to start in thinking about it now.

SECOND VOICE—(*quietly*) I see. It's a case of what is Hecuba to you that you should weep for her.

FIRST VOICE—(*blankly*) Hecuba? Oh, you mean the woman. You can't accuse me of any heartlessness there. I never felt so sorry for anyone in my life. Why I was actually crying myself at one time I felt so sorry for her. By the way, she hasn't made a sound since it got dark last evening. Is she asleep? Can you see her? You're nearer to her than I am.

(*It is becoming gradually lighter although the fog is as thick as ever. The faces of the two men in the boat can be dimly distinguished—one round, jowly, and clean-shaven; the other oval with big dark eyes and a black mustache and black hair pushed back from his high forehead. The huddled figure at the end of the boat is clearly that of a woman. One arm is flung over her face concealing it. In the other she clutches something like a bundle of white clothes.*)

THE DARK MAN—(*he of the Second Voice who is seated on the thwart nearer to the woman—turning round and peering in her direction*) She is very still. She must be asleep. I hope so, poor woman!

THE OTHER MAN—Yes, a little sleep will do her a world of good.

THE DARK MAN—She still holds the body of the child close to her breast. (*He returns to his former position facing the Other Man.*) I suppose you—

THE OTHER MAN—(*exultingly*) Excuse my interrupting you but have you noticed how light it's getting? It didn't strike me until you turned around just now. I can see your face plainly and a few minutes ago I couldn't tell whether you were a blond or brunette.

THE DARK MAN—Now if this fog would only lift—

THE OTHER MAN—It's going to lift. You wait and see. You'll find my optimism is justified. But what was it you started to say?

THE DARK MAN—I was saying that I supposed you had never seen this woman on board.

THE OTHER MAN—No. I was in the smoking room playing bridge most of the time. I'm not much of a sailor—don't care much about the water—just went over to Europe because the wife and the girls insisted. I was bored to death—made an excuse to get away as soon as I could. No sir, you can't teach an old dog new tricks. I'm a business man pure and simple and the farther I get away from that business the more dissatisfied I am. I've built that business up from nothing and it's sort of like a child of mine. It gives me pleasure to watch over it and when I'm away I'm uneasy. I don't like to leave it in strange hands. As for travelling, little old New York in the U. S. A. is good enough for me. (*He pauses impressively, waiting for some word of approval for his sterling patriotic principles. The Dark Man is silent and he of the U. S. A. continues, a bit disconcerted.*) But you asked me if I had seen the woman. I don't think so because I never went down into the steerage. I know some of the first class passengers did but I wasn't curious. It's a filthy sort of hole, isn't it?

THE DARK MAN—It's not so bad. I spent quite a good deal of my time down there.

THE BUSINESS MAN—(*for he of the jowly, fat face and the bald spot is such by his own confession*) (*chuckling*) In your role of reformer?

THE DARK MAN—No. Simply because I found the people in the steerage more interesting to talk to than the second class passengers. I am not a reformer—at least not in the professional sense.

THE BUSINESS MAN—Do you mind my asking what particular line you are in?

THE DARK MAN—I am a writer.

THE BUSINESS MAN—I thought it was something of the kind. I knew you weren't in business when I heard those Socialistic ideas of yours. (*condescendingly*) Beautiful idea—Socialism—but too impractical—never come about—just a dream.

THE DARK MAN—I'm not a Socialist—especially—just a humanist, that is all.

THE BUSINESS MAN—What particular kind of writing do you do?

THE DARK MAN—I write poetry.

THE BUSINESS MAN—(*in a tone indicating that in his mind poets and harmless lunatics have more than one point in common*) Oh I see. Well, there's not much money in that, is there?

THE POET—No.

THE BUSINESS MAN—(*after a long pause*) I don't know about you but I'm beginning to feel hungry. Is that box of crackers near you? (*The Poet reaches in under a thwart and pulls out a box of sea-biscuits. The Business Man takes a handful and munches greedily.*) Never thought hard-tack could taste so good. Aren't you going to have any?

THE POET—No. I am not hungry. The thought of that poor woman takes all my hunger away. I used to watch her every day down in the steerage playing with her little son who is now dead. I think he must have been the only child she ever had, the look on her face was so wonderfully tender as she bent over him. What will her life be now that death has robbed her of the only recompense for her slavery? It seems such needless cruelty. Why was I not taken instead?— I, who have no family or friends to weep, and am not afraid to die.

THE BUSINESS MAN—(*his mouth full*) You take things to heart too much. That's just like a poet. She'll forget all about it—probably sooner than you will. One forgets everything in time. What a devil of a world it would be if we didn't. (*He takes another handful of sea-biscuits and continues his munching. The Poet turns away from him in disgust.*) Funny thing when you come to think of it—I mean how we happened to come together in this boat. It's a mystery to me how she ever got in here. And then, how is it there's no oars in this boat and still there's plenty of food? You remember there was no lack of life-boats, and after the women and children were taken off I was ordered into one and we were rowed away. The damned thing must have gotten smashed somehow for it leaked like a sieve and in spite of our bailing we were soon dumped in the water. I heard the noise of voices near us and tried to swim to one of the other boats, but I must have got twisted in the fog for when I did find a boat—and let me tell you I was pretty nearly "all in" about then—it was this one and you and she were in it. Now what I want to know is—

THE POET—It is easily explained. Did you ever become so sick of disappointment and weary of life in general that death appeared to you the only way out?

THE BUSINESS MAN—Hardly. But what has that to do—

THE POET—Listen and you will see. That is the way I felt—sick and weary of soul and longing for sleep. When the ship struck the derelict it seemed to me providential. Here was the solution I had been looking for. I would go down with the ship and that small part of the world which knew me would think my death an accident.

THE BUSINESS MAN—(*forgetting to eat in his amazement*) You mean to say you were going to commit—

THE POET—I was going to die, yes. So I hid in the steerage fearing that some of the ship's officers would insist on saving my life in spite of me. Finally when everyone had gone I came out and walked around the main deck. I heard the sound of voices come from a dark corner and discovered that this woman and her child had been left behind. How that happened I don't know. Probably she hid because she was afraid the child would be crushed by the terror-stricken immigrants. At any rate there she was and I decided she was so happy in her love for her child that it would be wrong to let her die. I looked around and found this life-boat had been lowered down to the main deck and left hanging there. The oars had been taken out—probably for extra rowers in some other boat. I persuaded the woman to climb in and then went up to the boat deck and lowered the boat the rest of the way to the water. This was not much of a task for the steamer was settling lower in the water every minute. I then slid down one of the ropes to the boat and cutting both of the lines that held her, pushed off. There was a faint breeze which blew us slowly away from the sinking ship until she was hidden in the fog. The suspense of waiting for her to go down was terrible. Even as it was we were nearly swamped by the waves when the steamer took her final plunge.

THE BUSINESS MAN—(*edges away from the Poet, firmly convinced that his convictions regarding the similarity of poets and madmen are based upon fact*) I hope you've abandoned that suicide idea.

THE POET—I have—absolutely. I think all that happened to me is an omen sent by the Gods to convince me my past unhappiness is past and my fortune will change for the better.

THE BUSINESS MAN—That's the way to talk! Superstition is a good thing sometimes.

THE POET—But if I had known the sufferings that poor woman was to undergo as a result of my reckless life-saving I would have let her go down with the ship and gone myself.

THE BUSINESS MAN—Don't think of it any longer. You

couldn't help that. I wonder what it was the child died of? I thought it was asleep when I heard it choke and cough—and the next minute *she* commenced to scream. I won't forget those screams for the rest of my life.

THE POET—The child was naturally frail and delicate and I suppose the fright he received and the exposure combined to bring on some kind of convulsion. He was dead when I went over to see what was the matter.

THE BUSINESS MAN—(*peering upward through the fog*) It's getting considerably lighter. It must be about time for the sun to rise—if we're going to have any sun.

THE POET—(*sadly*) It was just about this time yesterday morning when the poor little fellow died.

THE BUSINESS MAN—(*looks apprehensively toward the huddled figure in the end of the boat. Now that it is lighter what appeared before like a bundle of white clothes can be seen to be a child four or five years old with a thin, sallow face and long, black curls. The body is rigid, wrapped in a white shawl, and the eyes are open and glassy.*) Let's not talk any more about it. She might wake up and start screaming again—and I can't stand that.

THE POET—She does not understand English.

THE BUSINESS MAN—(*shaking his head*) She'd know we were talking about the kid just the same. Mothers have an instinct when it comes to that. I've seen that proved in my own family more than once.

THE POET—Have you ever lost any of your children?

THE BUSINESS MAN—No. Thank God!

THE POET—You may well thank God, even if people do, as you claimed a while ago, forget so easily.

THE BUSINESS MAN—You're not married, are you?

THE POET—No.

THE BUSINESS MAN—I didn't think you were. (*jocularly*) You people with artistic temperaments run more to affinities than to wives. I suppose you've lots of those?

THE POET—(*does not hear or will not notice this question. He is staring through the fog and speaks in excited tones.*) Did you hear that?

THE BUSINESS MAN—Hear what?

THE POET—Just now when you were talking. I thought I

heard a sound like a steamer's whistle. (*They both listen intently. After a second or so the sound comes again, faint and far-off, wailing over the water.*)

THE BUSINESS MAN—(*wildly elated*) By God, it is a steamer!

THE POET—It sounded nearer that time. She must be coming this way.

THE BUSINESS MAN—Oh, if only this rotten fog would lift for a minute!

THE POET—Let's hope it will. We run as much risk of being run down as we do of being saved while this continues. They couldn't see us twenty feet away in this.

THE BUSINESS MAN—(*nervously*) Can't we yell or make some kind of a noise?

THE POET—They couldn't hear us now. We can try when they get close to us. (*a pause during which they hear the steamer whistle again*) How cold the air is! Or is it my imagination?

THE BUSINESS MAN—No, I notice it too. I've been freezing to death for the last five minutes. I wish we had the oars so we could row and keep warm.

THE POET—Sssh! Do you hear that?

THE BUSINESS MAN—What? The whistle? I heard it a moment ago.

THE POET—No. This is a sound like running water. There! Don't you hear it now? (*A noise as of water falling over rocks comes clearly through the fog.*)

THE BUSINESS MAN—Yes, I hear it. What can it be? There isn't any water out here except what's under us. (*with a shiver*) Brrr, but it's chilly!

THE POET—That poor woman will be frozen when she wakes up. (*He takes off his ulster and walking carefully to the end of the boat covers the form of the sleeping woman with it.*)

THE BUSINESS MAN—It sounds louder every minute but I can't see anything. Damn this fog! (*The noise of the falling water grows more and more distinct. At regular intervals the steamer's whistle blows and that, too, seems to be drawing nearer.*)

THE POET—(*still bent over the sleeping woman*) Perhaps it may be land but I hardly think we could have drifted that far.

THE BUSINESS MAN—(*in terrified tones*) Good God, what's that? (*The Poet turns quickly around. Something huge and white is looming up through the fog directly beside the boat. The boat drifts up to it sideways and strikes against it with a slight jar. The Business Man shrinks away as far along the thwart as he can get, causing the boat to tip a little to one side. The spattering splash of falling water sounds from all around them.)*

THE POET—(*looking at the white mass towering above them*) An iceberg! (*turning to the Business Man*) Steady there! You will be in the water in a minute if you're not careful. There is nothing to be frightened over. Lucky for us it's calm or we would be smashed to pieces.

THE BUSINESS MAN—(*reassured by finding out that what he took for some horrible phantom of the sea is an ice and water reality, moves over to the center of his thwart and remarks sarcastically*) As it is we'll only freeze to death. Is that what you mean?

THE POET—(*thumping his hands against his sides*) It *is* cold. I wonder how big the berg is. Help me try to push the boat away from it. (*They push against the side of the berg. The boat moves away a little but drifts right back again.*)

THE BUSINESS MAN—Ouch! My hands are freezing.

THE POET—No use wasting effort on that. The boat is too heavy and you can get no grip on the ice. (*A blast of the steamer's whistle shrills thro' the fog. It sounds very close to them.*) Oh God, I never thought of that. (*He sits down dejectedly opposite the Business Man.*)

THE BUSINESS MAN—Never thought of what?

THE POET—(*excitedly*) The steamer, man, the steamer! Think of the danger she is in. If she were ever to hit this mass of ice she would sink before they could lower a boat.

THE BUSINESS MAN—Can't we do something? We'll yell to them when they get nearer.

THE POET—Oh my God, man, don't do that. This may be one of the rescue ships come to pick up the survivors from our boat, and if they heard any shouts they would think they were cries for help and come right in this direction. Not a sound if you have any regard for the lives of those on board.

THE BUSINESS MAN—(*almost whimpering*) But if we don't let them know we're here they are liable to pass by us and never know it.

THE POET—(*sternly*) We can die but we cannot risk the

lives of others to save our own. (*The Business Man does not reply to this but a look of sullen stubbornness comes over his face. There is a long pause. The silence is suddenly shattered by a deafening blast from the steamer's whistle.*)

THE POET—God! She must be right on top of us. (*They both start to their feet and stand straining their eyes to catch some glimpse of the approaching vessel through the blinding mist. The stillness is so intense that the throb of the engines can be plainly heard. This sound slowly recedes and the next whistle indicates by its lack of volume that the steamer has passed and is proceeding on her way.*)

THE BUSINESS MAN—(*furiously*) She's going away. I'm not going to be left here to die on account of your damn fool ideas. (*He turns in the direction he supposes the steamer to be and raises his hands to his mouth, shaping them like a megaphone.*)

THE POET—(*jumping over and forcing his hand over the Business Man's mouth in time to stifle his call for help*) You damned coward! I might have known what to expect. (*The Business Man struggles to free himself, rocking the boat from side to side with his futile twistings, but he is finally forced down to a sitting position on the thwart. The Poet then releases him. He opens his mouth as if to shout but the Poet stands over him with his right fist drawn back threateningly and the Business Man thinks better of it.*)

THE BUSINESS MAN—(*snarling*) I'll get even with you, you loafer, if we ever get on shore. (*The Poet pays no attention to this threat but sits down opposite him. They hear the whistle again, seemingly no farther away than before. The Business Man stirs uneasily. A rending, tearing crash cracks through the silence, followed a moment later by a tremendous splash. Great drops of water fall in the rocking boat.*)

THE BUSINESS MAN—(*trembling with terror*) She must have hit it after all.

THE POET—No. That can't be it. I don't hear any shouts. (*suddenly smiling with relief as he guesses what has happened*) I know what it is. The berg is melting and breaking up. That was a piece that fell in the water.

THE BUSINESS MAN—It almost landed on us. (*He becomes panic-stricken at this thought and jumps to his feet.*) I'm not going to stand this any longer. We'll be crushed like flies. I'll

take a chance and swim for it. You can stay here and be killed
if you want to. (*Insane with fear of this new menace he puts one
foot on the gunwale of the boat and is about to throw himself into
the water when the Poet grabs him by the arm and pulls him
back.*) Let me go! This is all right for you. You want to die.
Do you want to kill me too, you murderer? (*He hides his face
in his hands and weeps like a fat child in a fit of temper.*)

THE POET—You fool! You could not swim for five minutes
in this icy water. (*more kindly*) Come! Be sensible! Act like a
man! (*The Business Man shakes with a combination of sigh and
sob. The whistle blows again and seems once more to be in their
immediate vicinity. The Business Man takes a new lease on life at
this favorable sign and raises his head.*)

THE BUSINESS MAN—She seems to be getting quite near
us again.

THE POET—Yes, and a moment ago I heard something like
oars creaking in the oar-locks and striking the water.

THE BUSINESS MAN—(*hopefully*) Maybe they've lowered a
boat. (*Even as he is speaking the curtain of fog suddenly lifts. The
sun has just risen over the horizon rim and the berg behind them,
its surface carved and fretted by the streams of water from the
melting ice, its whiteness vivid above the blue-gray water, seems
like the facade of some huge Viking temple.*)

THE POET—(*He and the Business Man, their backs turned to
the berg, are looking at something over the water as if they could
hardly believe their good fortune.*) There's the steamer now and
she can hardly be more than a quarter of a mile away. What
luck!

THE BUSINESS MAN—And there's the boat you heard.
Look! They were rowing straight towards us.

THE POET—(*half to himself with a puzzled expression*) I
wonder how they knew we were here.

A VOICE FROM OVER THE WATER—Hello there!

THE BUSINESS MAN—(*waving frantically*) Hello!

THE VOICE—(*nearer—the creak of the oars can be clearly
heard*) Are you people off the "Starland?"

THE BUSINESS MAN—Yes. (*With the return of his courage
he has regained all his self-assured urbanity. He tries to pull his
clothes into some semblance of their former immaculateness, and
his round face with its imposing double chin assumes an expression*

of importance. The Poet's face is drawn and melancholy as if he were uncertain of the outcome of this unexpected return to life.)

THE BUSINESS MAN—(*turning to the Poet with a smile*) You see my optimism was justified after all. (*growing confused before the Poet's steady glance*) I wish you'd—er—forget all about the little unpleasantness between us. I must confess I was a bit—er—rattled and didn't exactly know what I was doing. (*He holds out his hand uncertainly. The Poet takes it with a quiet smile.*)

THE POET—(*simply*) I had forgotten all about it.

THE BUSINESS MAN—Thank you. (*The voice that hailed them is heard giving some orders. The sound of the oars ceases and a moment later a life-boat similar to the one they are in but manned by a full crew of sailors comes along side of them. A young man in uniform, evidently the third officer of the ship, is in the stern steering.*)

THE BUSINESS MAN—(*breezily*) Hello! You certainly are a welcome sight.

THE OFFICER—(*looking up at the towering side of the berg*) You picked out a funny island to land on. What made you cling so close to this berg? Cold, wasn't it?

THE POET—We drifted into it in the fog and having no oars could not get away. It was about the same time we first heard your whistle.

THE OFFICER—(*nodding toward the woman's figure*) Woman sick?

THE POET—She has been asleep, poor woman.

THE OFFICER—Where's the kid?

THE POET—In her arms. (*then wonderingly*) But how did you know?—

THE OFFICER—We'd never have found you but for that. Why didn't you give us a shout or make some kind of a racket?

THE BUSINESS MAN—(*eagerly*) We were afraid you would come in our direction and hit this ice-berg.

THE OFFICER—But we might have passed you and never had an inkling—

THE BUSINESS MAN—(*impressively*) In a case of that kind one has to take chances. (*The Poet smiles quietly. The Officer looks surprised.*)

THE OFFICER—That was very fine of you I must say. Most people would only have thought of themselves. As it was, if it hadn't been for the kid crying we would have missed you. I was on the bridge with the first officer. We had been warned about this berg and when the fog came up we slowed down until we were barely creeping, and stopped altogether every now and then. It was during one of these stops when everything was still, we heard the crying and I said to the first officer: "Sounds like a kid balling, doesn't it?" and he thought it did too. It kept getting plainer and plainer until there was no chance for a mistake—weird too it sounded with everything so quiet and the fog so heavy—I said to him again: "It's a kid sure enough, but how in the devil did it get out here?" And then we both remembered we had been ordered to keep a lookout for any of the survivors of the "Starland" who hadn't been picked up yet, and the first officer said: "It's probably some of the poor devils from the Starland" and told me to have a boat lowered. I grabbed a compass and jumped in. We could hear the kid crying all the time, couldn't we, boys? (*He turns to the crew who all answer:* "Yes sir.") That's how I was able to shape such a direct course for you. I was steering by the sound. It stopped just as the fog rose. (*During the Officer's story the Business Man has been looking at him with an expression of annoyed stupefaction on his face. He is unable to decide whether the Officer is fooling or not and turns to the Poet for enlightenment. But the latter, after listening to the Officer's explanation with intense interest, goes quickly to the side of the woman and, removing his ulster from over her shoulders, attempts to awaken her.*)

THE OFFICER—(*noticing what he is doing*) That's right. Better wake her up. The steamer will be ready to pick us up in a minute, and she must be stiff with the cold. (*He turns to one of his crew.*) Make a line fast to this boat and we'll tow her back to the ship. (*The sailor springs into the "Starland's" boat with a coil of rope in his hand.*)

THE POET—(*Failing to awaken the woman he feels for her pulse and then bends down to listen for a heart beat, his ear against her breast. He straightens up finally and stands looking down at the two bodies and speaks to himself half aloud.*) Poor happy woman. (*The Officer and the Business Man are watching him.*)

THE OFFICER—(*sharply*) Well?

THE POET—(*softly*) The woman is dead.

THE BUSINESS MAN—Dead! (*He casts a horrified glance at the still figures in the end of the boat—then clambers clumsily into the other boat and stands beside the Officer.*)

THE OFFICER—Too bad! But the child is all right, of course?

THE POET—The child has been dead for twenty-four hours. He died at dawn yesterday. (*It is the Officer's turn to be bewildered. He stares at the Poet pityingly and then turns to the Business Man.*)

THE OFFICER—(*indicating the Poet with a nod of his head*) A bit out of his head, isn't he? Exposure affects a lot of them that way.

THE BUSINESS MAN—(*solemnly*) He told you the exact truth of the matter.

THE OFFICER—(*concluding he has two madmen to deal with instead of one*) Of course. (*to the sailor who has made fast the towing rope*) All fast? (*The sailor jumps into his own boat with a brisk:* "Aye, Aye sir.") (*The Officer turns to the Poet.*) Coming in here or going to stay where you are?

THE POET—(*gently*) I think I will stay with the dead. (*He is sitting opposite the two rigid figures looking at their still white faces with eyes full of a great longing.*)

THE OFFICER—(*mutters*) Cheerful beggar! (*He faces the crew.*) Give way all. (*The oars take the water and the two boats glide swiftly away from the ice berg.*

(*The fresh morning breeze ripples over the water bringing back to the attentive ear some words of the Man of Business spoken argumentatively, but in the decided accents of one who is rarely acknowledged to be wrong.*)

—the exact truth. So you see that, if you will pardon my saying so, Officer, what you have just finished telling us is almost unbelievable.

(*Curtain*)

BREAD AND BUTTER

A Play in Four Acts

CHARACTERS

EDWARD BROWN, *hardware merchant of Bridgetown, Conn.*
MRS. BROWN, *his wife*
EDWARD, *a town alderman* ⎫
HARRY   ⎬ *their sons*
JOHN   ⎭
MARY, *a school-teacher*   ⎫ *their daughters*
BESSIE, *a stenographer*   ⎭
RICHARD STEELE, *dry goods merchant of Bridgetown*
MAUD, *his daughter*
STEVE HARRINGTON ⎫
"BABE" CARTER   ⎬ *art students*
TED NELSON, *a writer*
EUGENE GRAMMONT, *Master of the Art School*
HELENE, *a cloak and suit model*

ACT FIRST—The sitting-room of Edward Brown's home
    in Bridgetown, Conn. on a hot evening in August of
    the present day.
ACT SECOND—The studio in New York in which John is
    living—about a year and a half later.
ACT THIRD—The same—four months later.
ACT FOURTH—The living-room of John's home in
    Bridgetown—two years later.
          Period—The Present Day.

Bread and Butter

ACT 1

SCENE—*The sitting-room of Edward Brown's home in Bridgetown, Conn. To the left in the foreground a door leading into the dining room. Farther back a book-case and two windows looking out on the back yard. In the corner an expensive Victrola machine with cabinet for records. In the middle of the far side of the room is a huge old-fashioned fire-place with brass andirons. On either side of the fire-place a window opening on the garden. In the right hand corner near the window a Morris chair. Farther forward a large doorway leading to the parlor with two sliding doors which are tightly drawn together, it being neither Sunday nor a holiday. Still farther in the foreground a smaller door opening on the hallway.*

Above the fire-place a mantel on the center of which is a Mission clock with a bright brass pendulum. The remainder of the mantel is taken up by cigar boxes, a skull-and-cross-bones tobacco jar, a brass match safe, etc. A square table with four or five easy chairs grouped around it stands in the center of the large sober-colored rug which covers all but the edge of the hard-wood floor. On the table a stack of magazines and a newspaper, also an embroidered center-piece, the fringe of which can be seen peeking out from under the shining base of an electric reading lamp wired from the chandelier above. Two stiff looking chairs have been used to fill up floor spaces which must have seemed unduly bare to the mistress of the household. The walls are papered a dull blurred crimson. This monotony of color is at well-regulated intervals monotonously relieved by pretentiously stupid paintings of the "Cattle-at-the-Stream", "Sunrise-on-the-Lake" variety. These daubs are imprisoned in ornate gilt frames.

The room is sufficiently commonplace and ordinary to suit the most fastidious Philistine. Just at present it's ugliness is shamelessly revealed by the full downward glare of the reading lamp and the searching stare of all four bulbs on the chandelier.

It is about eight o'clock on a hot evening in September of the present day. All the windows are open.

Mr. and Mrs. Brown and their eldest son, Edward, are discovered seated by the table. Mrs. Brown is a small grey-haired, tired-

looking woman about fifty years old, neatly dressed in black. Her expression is meek and when she speaks the tone of her voice apologizes for the unseemly indulgence.

Brown himself is a tall, lean old man with a self-satisfied smile forever on his thin lips. He is smooth-shaven, a trifle bald, fifty-eight years old, and dressed as becomes a leading citizen.

Edward is tall and stout, pudgy-faced, dark-haired, small of eye, thick of lip and neck. He is dressed exactly as a small-town alderman should be dressed and is thirty years old.

BROWN—(laying aside the newspaper he has been reading) I don't think much of that "ad" you've got in here, Ed.

EDWARD—(solemnly deferential) What's the matter with it, Father? (with dignity) I wrote it myself.

BROWN—(dryly) I know you did. I can see you sticking out all over it. It's too wordy and solemn—lifeless, in other words.

EDWARD—My desire was to appeal to the better class of people in the town—the people whose patronage is really worth while and—

BROWN—Stop right there. You're running a hardware store, not a cotillion. The people you've got to appeal to are the people who want something we've got and have the money to pay for it. No other distinction goes in our business.

EDWARD—But I thought it would be an asset to get and hold the trade of the best people.

BROWN—It isn't as much of an asset as getting and holding the trade of the working people. They pay cash. While the others—I'd never have to hire a collector if it wasn't for those same best people. Keep your social high-flying out of the store. It's no place for it. (with asperity) Remember I haven't retired yet and, although God knows I've earned it, I never will be able to if you mess things up this way. Please consult me after this before you appeal to the best people.

EDWARD—(sullenly) I'll have the "ad" taken out tomorrow and you can write another yourself.

BROWN—(more kindly) No, write it yourself. You know how to do it when you want to. (with a sly smile) Forget you're an alderman for a few minutes. Keep your speeches for the Board of Common Council. Remember your father was a working man and a farm hand, and all the education he's got beyond grammar school he picked up along the way. Write an "ad" which would appeal to him if he had five dollars and needed some kitchen utensils.

EDWARD—(*shocked—considering his father's acknowledgement of his humble origin a grave social error*) You have risen beyond all such comparisons.

BROWN—Don't be so sure of me. Well, don't forget about that "ad." Anything else new?

EDWARD—N-no; but there is another matter not directly connected with the store which I would like to talk over seriously with you.

BROWN—Fire away. You've got the floor, Alderman.

EDWARD—(*ponderously*) It's about John.

BROWN—What's John done?

EDWARD—Well, it's like this, Father. Harry and I, and I am sure the girls will agree with us, think it is rather hard John should so obviously be made the pet of the family. High school was good enough for any of us but you sent him through four years at Princeton. You have always told us you considered a college education more of a hindrance than a help to a man's success in life, and yet you allowed John to take up a classical course—a gentleman's course, as they call it, which will certainly be of little use to him if he goes into business.

BROWN—(*frowning*) And who said he was to go into business? I always clearly stated I intended John for one of the professions. We've got enough business men in the family already.

EDWARD—I never heard him speak of taking up a profession.

BROWN—(*hesitatingly*) It's been sort of a secret between your mother, John, and myself, but since you bring the matter up I might as well tell you I've decided he shall go to law school. There's plenty of opportunity here for a young lawyer with position and money to back him up—of that I'm certain. Thanks to you and Harry the business I've built up will be well taken care of if anything should happen to me, and I see no reason for placing John in it; especially as his talents seem to run in another direction.

EDWARD—(*suppressing the indignation he feels at this fresh favor shown his younger brother*) Perhaps you are right, sir. I confess I am no judge of what future would best suit John. He never speaks of himself or his plans to me, or, for that matter, to any of us except Bessie, and she seems to treat whatever he tells her as confidential. What appeared strange to Harry and me was the fact that you had never asked John to work during any of his vacations.

(*While he is speaking Harry enters from the hall. He is a tall, dark, pleasant-looking young fellow of twenty-five with the good-natured air and breezy manners of a young-man-about-small-town. A bit of a sport, given to beer drinking, poker parties and kelly pool, if the foppish mode of his light check clothes be any criterion.*)

HARRY—(*who has caught his brother's remark about vacations*) Good evening people. Go to it, Ed. (*He goes over and takes a chair near the table.*)

EDWARD—(*not relishing the interruption*) I was just explaining to Father how we feel about John not helping us in any way.

HARRY—I got part of what you said. On the level, Father, it isn't square for us to toil and sweat while our fair young brother pulls that lily of the field stuff. (*He says this with the air of getting off something clever.*)

BROWN—(*severely*) Keep your vulgar slang for your bar-room companions and don't play the fool when you come home. You perform well enough outside without any rehearsals. If you can't talk sense, don't say anything. (*Harry accepts this reprimand with a smile.*) What was it you were saying, Ed?

EDWARD—I was saying that while Harry and I and the girls, too, have been working at something ever since we left high school, you have never even suggested that John help in any way.

BROWN—I intend to put him in some law office during the summers in which he's in law school.

HARRY—Law school?

EDWARD—(*bitterness in his tones*) Yes, John is going to law school this fall. Father just told me.

HARRY—Why be peeved? Every family in town has a

lawyer in it that can afford the luxury. Why not us? But you'll have a hard time making John approve of your scheme. He doesn't want to be a lawyer. You'll find out he wants to be a painter.

EDWARD—(*stolidly*) There is room for a good painting business in this town with all the new summer homes being built along the shore.

HARRY—(*with a laugh*) Not that kind of a painter, you nut. He's too much high-brow for houses. Portraits of the Four Hundred would be more in his line.

BROWN—I tell you he wants to be a lawyer. His painting's only something to take up spare time.

HARRY—All his time is spare time. (*His father looks at him angrily and Harry hastily changes the subject.*) Where is the subject of this elevating discussion this evening?

MRS. BROWN—(*looking up from her knitting*) You mean John? He's over at the Steele's for dinner. (*Edward looks glum and Harry glances meaningly at him with a tantalizing smile.*)

HARRY—Romeo and Juliet had nothing on those two. Why so pensive, Edward?

EDWARD—I was thinking—

HARRY—You surprise me, Alderman.

EDWARD—You— You,—you're a damned ass, Harry.

HARRY—(*meekly*) Thank you, dear brother. (*He turns to his mother.*) Mother, when are the glad tidings to be made public? You ought to be in the secret.

MRS. BROWN—You mean about Maud and John?

HARRY—Yes; Ed and I are anxious to know in time to dust off the old frock coats and not disgrace ourselves.

MRS. BROWN—I wish I could tell you. I do hope it will come about, I'm sure. Maud is such a nice sensible girl, she would make a lovely wife.

HARRY—Not forgetting the fact that her dear daddy is over-burdened with coin and she's an only child; and remembering that the Steeles are socially spotless. Ask Edward if I speak not truth. He doped it all out for himself once, didn't you, Ed? (*in tones of great sadness*) But that was long, long ago—almost a year. And, alas, she tied the can to him.

EDWARD—(*enraged*) Father, I appeal to you to inform Harry there are feelings he should respect and not make the butts of his vulgar jokes. My—er—former affection for Miss. Steele is one of them. Though I have never told anyone but this (*glaring at Harry*) would-be humorist,—and that in a moment of foolish confidence I shall never cease to regret—

HARRY—(*interrupting him with soft approach*) Oh, Edward! You forced the confidence on me. You were in liquor, Edward. You had been drinking heavily. I can remember vividly to this day how grieved I was to see you in such a state— you—a pillar of the church!

MRS. BROWN—Harry!

BROWN—What!

EDWARD—(*his face red with shame*) I must acknowledge to my shame that what Harry says about my—er—condition at the time is not wholly unwarranted. He exaggerates, greatly exaggerates, but—

HARRY—You were so sad. You wept on my shoulder and ruined a new silk tie I had just bought.

MRS. BROWN—Oh, Harry! (*Brown is smiling.*)

EDWARD—I have to confess I had a great deal too much to drink. (*pompously*) It was the first time in my life such a thing has happened and I promise you it will be the last.

HARRY—That's what they all say. (*Edward glowers at him.*) All right, I'm going. (*He turns round at the door to hurl a parting shot.*) My feelings are too much for me. I cannot bear to hear the harrowing tale of my elder brother's shame a second time. I will go out in the garden and weep a little. (*He goes out. Edward wears an expression of patient martyrdom. Brown with difficulty hides his impulse to laugh outright.*)

BROWN—Tut, tut, don't be so serious. You know Harry. What if you were a bit under the weather? It's a good man's fault—once in a great while. I can remember a good many times in my life when I was three sheets in the wind celebrating one thing or another.

EDWARD—(*stiffly*) I have never approved of intoxicants in any form. It was a shocking deviation from my principles. (*firmly*) It shall never happen again. (*Brown cannot hide a smile. Edward is piqued.*) I beg of you, Father, to believe what I say. My one lapse—er—I was upset, terribly upset, by Miss. Steele's refusal to become my wife and—

BROWN—(*in amazement*) You asked Maud to marry you!

MRS. BROWN—Good gracious!

EDWARD—(*nettled that they should think such a thing strange*) Why do you seem so surprised? I flatter myself I was in a better position to take care of a wife than my brother John is now.

BROWN—I wasn't thinking about that. I was surprised neither your mother nor I had ever suspected anything of the kind. Now that I come to think of it you did used to be over at the Steele's a lot of the time.

MRS. BROWN—(*flabbergasted by this piece of news*) Who'd ever dream of such a thing!

EDWARD—Maud—Miss. Steele did not definitely refuse me. She said she was too young to marry. However she gave me to understand she had already bestowed her affections on someone else.

BROWN—Did old man Steele know anything of all this?

EDWARD—Certainly. I thought it my duty to inform him of my intentions before I spoke to his daughter. He did not seem displeased with the idea but left the matter entirely to Maud—er—Miss. Steele, with the result I have just made known to you.

MRS. BROWN—(*not able to recover from her astonishment*) You're the last one I ever thought would fall in love, Ed.

EDWARD—Please do not harp on that point, Mother. I am quite human though you do not appear to think so.

BROWN—(*thoughtfully*) So that's how the land lies, is it? That explains a lot of things.

EDWARD—I do not understand you.

BROWN—I mean your sudden interest in John and your desire to see him improving his time at the store instead of at the Steele's.

EDWARD—(*flushing*) Do you mean to accuse me of vulgar jealousy because I still take enough interest in Miss. Steele's welfare to be unwilling my brother should compromise her? (*While he is speaking his two sisters, Mary and Bessie, enter from the hall. Mary is a thin, angular woman with a long face and sharp features. She is twenty-eight years old but looks older, wears spectacles, and is primly dressed in a plain, black gown as unfashionable as she considers respectable.*

(*Bessie is as attractive as Mary is plain. Small, plump, with a mass of wavy black hair and great hazel eyes, a red, pouting, laughing mouth, glowing complexion, and small restless hands and feet, Bessie is quite adorable. She is twenty-three years old, one year older than John, but she only looks about nineteen.*)

BROWN—I said nothing about jealousy, Ed. It must have been your conscience you heard. (*Edward grows confused.*)

BESSIE—(*goes over to her mother and kisses her saying*) We walked up to the post-office. (*Mary sits down in one of the straight-backed chairs near Edward and breaks right into the subject in discussion.*)

MARY—(*her voice raspy and monotonous*) I must say I agree with Ed, Father. It's the talk of the town the way John is tagging after Maud Steele.

BROWN—Bosh! The town's always gossiping about something.

MARY—And I do think it's high time John put his education to some use. We all have to work at something—even Bessie is a stenographer—and I don't see why he shouldn't.

BESSIE—Goodness, why don't you leave John alone? He's been working all summer at his painting. (*Edward gives a scornful grunt.*) You don't think that's work because he gets no regular salary for it. I should think you'd be ashamed, Ed, running him down the way you do. Your real reason is just jealousy because Mauds in love with him. You ought to be more of a man.

EDWARD—You are very unjust, Bessie, and you don't know what you're talking about. I merely want to see John do the right thing for all our sakes.

MARY—I don't think Mr. Steele will ever consent to Maud's being married so young. I know if I were he I would never approve of it. A young girl of twenty is altogether too young to think of marriage.

HARRY—(*entering suddenly from the hall—mockingly*) But it's better to be married too soon than not at all, isn't it, Sister? (*Mary favors him with a terrible look. He grins back at her.*) Still holding the inquest? Then allow me to announce that the subject of this debate has just entered the house. (*He turns around and shouts into the hall*) Come on, John! Don't keep the court waiting. (*Bessie giggles.*) Thanks, Bessie. Thank God, I am not wholly unappreciated.

(*John enters, smiling bashfully, his face flushed and excited. They all greet him in embarrassed tones. He is an altogether different type from the other members of the family; a finer, more sensitive organization. In appearance he is of medium height, wiry looking and graceful in his flannel clothes of unmistakable college cut. His naturally dark complexion has been burnt to a gold bronze by the sun. His hair, worn long and brushed straight back from his forehead, is black, as are his abnormally large dreamer's eyes, deep-set and far apart in the oval of his face. His mouth is full lipped and small, almost weak in it's general character; his nose straight and thin with the nostrils of the enthusiast. When he experiences any emotion his whole face lights up with it. In the bosom of his own family and in the atmosphere of their typical New England fireside he seems woefully out of place.*)

HARRY—(*in a nasal drawl*) Prisoner at the bar, you are accused—

BROWN—For God's sake, stop your chatter for a moment. Sit down, John. (*John takes a chair by the table.*)

JOHN—(*in pleasant tones—to Harry*) Well, what am I accused of?

HARRY—Mary and Edward accuse you of being a flagrant member of the Idle Rich Class.

MARY—Oh!
EDWARD—A joke's a joke but—   } (*protests from the court*)
BROWN—Be still, sir!
MRS. BROWN—Harry!

JOHN—(*clasping and unclasping his hands nervously*) I suppose it would be hopeless to enter a plea before this court that trying to express oneself in paint is a praiseworthy occupation which should be encouraged. I have to acknowledge being salaryless and I guess the best thing to do to save the court's time is plead guilty.

EDWARD—(*ponderously*) I think this joke has gone far enough and we ought to explain to John—

HARRY—(*bellowing*) Silence! (*Edward jumps in his chair.*) Alderman, you are liable to fine for contempt.

EDWARD—(*sputtering*) Harry—you *are* a fool!

HARRY—You made that remark once before, Alderman. Don't repeat your statements. You're not running for office now.

EDWARD—I—I—I (*He looks as if he meditated assault and battery.*)

JOHN—(*nervously, not relishing this form of entertainment*) Come back to me, Harry. What else am I accused of?

HARRY—Mother accuses you of contemplated theft. (*John is puzzled and embarrassed. The others raise a storm of protest.*)

BROWN—(*severely*) You shouldn't say such a thing even if you are only joking. Explain what you mean.

HARRY—How can I when you make so much noise? Prisoner, Mother insists that you are planning to purloin from one of our most respected citizens—his only daughter! (*All laugh except Edward. John grows red with confusion and smiles foolishly.*) What have you to say on that charge?

JOHN—I'm afraid I'll have to plead guilty to that, too—not only to the intention but to the actual deed itself.

MARY—(*sharply*) You mean Maud has accepted you?

JOHN—Yes. (*They all crowd around him showering him with congratulations. The women kiss him, Harry claps him on the back, Brown shakes his hand. Edward mutters a few conventional phrases but is unable to hide his mortification.*)

EDWARD—(*coldly, taking his watch out and looking at it*) I am sorry to have to leave all of you on such a joyful occasion but (*importantly*) I have an engagement at the club with Congressman Whitney which I cannot very well ignore. (*swelling out with dignity*) He said he wished to confer with me on a matter of grave importance. So I hope you will excuse me. Good night, everyone. (*He bows gravely and goes toward the door to the hall.*)

HARRY—(*imitating Edward's pose*) I beg of you not to plunge your country into any bloody war, Edward. You have a terrible responsibility on your shoulders. (*Edward glares at him for a moment as if meditating a retort but thinks better of it and goes out.*)

BESSIE—If he isn't the original Mr. Gloom!

MARY—(*intent on finding out all the facts of John's romance*) John, does Mr. Steele know about Maud's accepting you?

JOHN—(*fidgetting*) Yes, we both told him tonight. He seems quite reconciled to our news. Of course, it is under-

stood the engagement will have to be a long one, as I have my way to make and my future—

HARRY—Stop! What has an engaged man to say about his own future? Speaking of futures shall I communicate to you the reverend judge's (*indicating his father*) sentence regarding yours? He has sentenced you to a lifetime of delightful idleness— You are condemned to be a lawyer.

BESSIE—What? You're joking.

MARY—A lawyer?

BROWN—(*gravely*) What Harry says is the truth. I have decided John shall go to law school this fall. He fully agrees with me that the practice of law opens up the land of opportunity to a young man of position. (*John's miserable expression contradicts this sweeping statement.*)

BESSIE—(*impetuously turning to her father*) But John doesn't want to be a lawyer.

HARRY—Just exactly what I said.

BROWN—You hear how cock-sure they are, John. You better tell them the truth.

JOHN—(*falteringly*) I'm afraid what Bessie said is the truth, Father.

BROWN—(*frowning*) What!

JOHN—I don't want to be a lawyer. When you spoke to me about this before you didn't really give me a chance to say what I thought. You decided it all for me. I have been intending to tell you how I felt ever since but you never mentioned it again and I thought you had discovered my unfitness and given up the idea. (*There is a pause during which all eyes are fixed on Brown who is staring at John in angry bewilderment.*)

BROWN—Given up the idea? Why, I supposed the thing settled! That's why I never spoke of it.

JOHN—(*simply*) I'm sorry, Father. It has been a misunderstanding all around.

BESSIE—How could you imagine John a lawyer, Daddy!

BROWN—(*gently*) We're not all gifted with your insight, my dear. (*turning to John rather severely*) Young man, this is a sad blow to all my plans for you. I'm sure this decision of yours is a hasty one and you will reconsider it when you've looked more thoroughly into the matter.

JOHN—I think not, Father. I am certain of my own mind or I wouldn't trouble you so.

BROWN—May I ask what your objections are?

JOHN—Just this, Father: I simply am not fitted for it. The idea is repugnant to me, and it's useless for me to try and live a lie. As a lawyer I would be a failure in every way. In later years you, yourself, would be the first to regret it. My interest in life is different, and if I wish to be a man I must develope the inclinations which God has given me—not attempt to blot them out.

BESSIE—Hear! Hear!

BROWN—Why are you so sure you wouldn't learn to like the law? You know very little about it on which to base such a pronounced dislike.

JOHN—(*in great nervous excitement*) Oh, I have seen and met all the lawyers in town—most of them at any rate—and I don't care for them. I don't understand them or they me. We're of a different breed. How do I know I wouldn't learn to like law? In the same way a man knows he cannot love two women at the same time. I love, really love in the full sense of the word, something else in life. If I took up law I would betray my highest hope, degrade my best ambition.

BROWN—(*staggered by this outburst*) And what is this—er —love of yours?

JOHN—(*his large eyes glowing with enthusiasm*) Art! I am an artist in soul I know. My brain values are Art values. I want to learn how to express in terms of color the dreams in my brain which demand expression. (*Harry gives a comic gasp and winks at Mary who is regarding John as if he were a lunatic. In fact, it is plain there is a suspicion in the minds of all of them except Bessie that perhaps John has been drinking.*)

BROWN—(*stupefied*) Do I understand you to say you wish to make painting pictures the serious aim of your life?

JOHN—(*his fiery ardor smothered under this wet blanket*) I wish to become an artist, yes, if that's what you mean. I want to go to art school instead of law school, if you will permit me to choose my own career.

HARRY—(*triumphantly*) I'm a bad prophet, I guess!

JOHN—A course in art school will be very inexpensive. You remember Babe Carter, my room-mate at Princeton? The fellow who came up here to spend last Thanksgiving holidays with us? (*Brown nods.*)

HARRY—(*mischievously*) Ask Bessie if she remembers. (*Bessie looks confused.*)

JOHN—Well, he's going to art school in New York this Fall; has made arrangements to take a studio with two other fellows and wants me to come in with them. With four in the studio the living expenses would be reduced to almost nothing; while on the other hand the cost of sending me to law school would be pretty heavy, as you know.

BROWN—(*impatiently*) But heavens, boy, what money is there in art? From all I've ever read about artists it seems the only time their pictures sell for a big price is after they're dead.

JOHN—There are plenty of artists in the world today who are painting and making their living at it. (*eagerly*) But money is not the important point. Think of the work they're doing—the beauty and wonder of it! (*He stops realizing the hopelessness of trying to make them understand this side of the question.*)

BROWN—It seems to me a young man who is engaged to be married ought to make money the important point.

MARY—(*severely*) Does Maud know of this craze of your's?

JOHN—Yes, Maud knows of this craze of mine, as you are pleased to call it, and approves of it in every way. She realizes I would not be worthy of her love if I were not true to myself.

MARY—(*sneeringly*) Love must be blind. And I suppose you told Mr. Steele all about your intended career?

JOHN—I talked it all over with him this evening.

MARY—(*sarcastically*) And of course he approved!

JOHN—He certainly did!

BROWN—What!

HARRY—Aw, what'a you giving us!

MARY—I don't believe it.

BESSIE—Bully for old Steele! I never thought he had so much sense.

BROWN—Bessie! I'm not disputing your statement, John, but it seems impossible a practical, hard-headed business man like my friend Steele could approve of this idea of yours. Are

you sure he understood this was to be your whole occupation, not just a side issue? Now I, myself, think you'd be foolish to drop painting altogether when you've such a talent and
liking for it. But as a means of living I can't see it.

JOHN—I laid emphasis on that point in my conversation
with Mr. Steele. I told him quite frankly I was painting my
life work. He said it was a good idea and told me he didn't
think much of your law school plan.

BROWN—Well! (*The others are all equally astonished.*)

JOHN—He'll be here in a few minutes and verify my
statement; he said he'd be over tonight to have a talk with
you.

BROWN—I'll be very glad to hear his views on this matter.
His opinions are always sound and sensible—but in the present case—

MARY—(*rising stiffly from her chair*) Well, if Mr. Steele is
coming over we'd better make ourselves a little more present-
able. Come Bessie! You, too, Mother.

MRS. BROWN—(*going toward hall door with Bessie and
Mary*) Goodness, Johnnie, why couldn't you have told us before? The house is in a nice state. (*They go out with Mrs. Brown
fuming and fretting.*)

HARRY—(*beckoning to John*) A word with you. (*whispering*) Have you got a real cigarette? (*John produces a box.*)
Thanks, I'll take a couple. The week is waning and in the
latter end of weeks I'm usually confined to a diet of self-
mades. (*puts cigarette in mouth*) Stringency of the paternal
money market, you know. (*lights cigarette*) And now I'll say
farewell. I want to get away before old Steele comes. He detests me, and with all due respect to your future father-in-
law I think he's the prize simp of the world. It would only
ruffle his good nature to find me here. (*then seriously*) John, I
didn't get some of that high-brow stuff you pulled. It sort of
soared over my sordid bean—some phrase, that, what?—
but volplaning down from your lofty artistic ozone I want
to say I'm for you. Do what you want to do, that's the only
dope. I can't wish you any better than good luck. (*He holds
out his hand which John clasps heartily, his face lighting up with
gratitude. The door bell rings.*) There he is now. I'll blow out
the back way; be good; s'long, Father. (*He goes out by the*

door to left leading to the dining room, carefully closing it after him.)

BROWN—You better go out and meet him, John. (*John hurries into the hall and returns a moment later with Steele. Steele is a tall, stout, vigorous looking man of about fifty-five, with the imposing air of one who is a figure of importance in the town and takes this importance seriously. He has grey hair and a short-cropped grey mustache; a full florid face with undistinguished features, and small, shrewd, grey eyes. He is carefully dressed in a well-fitting light suit and looks the part of the prosperous small-town merchant. He comes over to Brown, who has risen to greet him, and they shake hands after the manner of old friends.*)

STEELE—Good evening, Ed.

BROWN—Glad to see you, Dick. Sit down and make yourself at home. (*They both take chairs by the table. A confused babble of women's voices and laughter is heard from the hallway.*) Maud come over with you?

STEELE—Yes. (*with a wink at Brown*) And that being the case I guess we can excuse the young man here, don't you think so, Ed?

BROWN—(*laughingly*) Oh, I guess we can manage. (*John gives an embarrassed laugh and hurries out.*)

STEELE—Well, Ed, I hate to think of losing Maud. (*feelingly*) She's all I've got, you know; but if it has to be someone I'm mighty glad it's one of your boys. For a time I sort of thought it would be Edward. He spoke to me once about the matter and I wished him luck. I like Edward very much. He's a good solid business man and bound to succeed; but Maud didn't love him and there you are. I guess she and John were pretty thick even then, although I never suspected what was in the wind until just lately.

BROWN—I can't say I was wholly unprepared for John's announcement. He hasn't much of a faculty for hiding his feelings—too nervous and high-strung. (*with a chuckle*) Of course his mother has known right along. You can't fool a woman on those things.

STEELE—(*sadly*) I wish Maud's mother were alive today. (*briskly*) Well, well, what can't be, can't be. John's an awful likable chap, and Maud says she loves him, so I'm sure I'm satisfied. As long as she's happy I'm contented. She's the boss.

BROWN—John's got his way to make yet, but as long as they're willing to make it a long engagement—

STEELE—(*interrupting him laughingly*) I'm selfish enough to like the idea of the marriage being a long ways off; I'll have Maud so much longer.

BROWN—Speaking of John's future, he told me tonight you fully approved of this artistic notion of his—going to art school and all that. I found it pretty hard to believe, knowing you the way I do.

STEELE—John was perfectly right. I think it's the real thing for him.

BROWN—You know I was intending to send him to law school.

STEELE—Don't be foolish, Ed. The supply of lawyers already is ten times greater than the demand. Take this town for example. Nearly every family I know of any importance has a lawyer in it or is going to have one. Where will they all get cases? Why, do you know, I actually think some families get into suits just to give their sons a job.

BROWN—I'll have to admit there's an abundance of legal talent in Bridgetown; but in a broader field—

STEELE—Same thing all over the country—too many lawyers and doctors. Besides, John would never make a lawyer—too sensitive and retiring. You have to have push and gall to burn. On the other hand he's got an undoubted talent for painting. I've seen sketches he made for Maud and those drawings he did for the college magazine. They're great! And look at those posters he did for the Fair last month—finest things of the kind I ever looked at. John's bound to succeed. I'm sure of it.

BROWN—(*dubiously*) But where does the money end of it come in?

STEELE—Money? Why, Ed, there's loads of money in it. Look at advertising. I know of a young fellow in New York who paints those high-toned fashion plates. He makes between ten and twelve thousand dollars a year; has his own business and everything. He's only been at it a few years, too. (*Brown is evidently impressed but shakes his head doubtfully.*) Look at the magazines. (*He picks one from the table and points to the picture on the outside cover—a girl's head.*) How much do you think that fellow got for that? Not less than a couple of hundred dollars, I'll bet. John could draw a prettier girl than that in half an hour. With new magazines coming out every month the demand for that sort of stuff is tremendous. There's all kinds of opportunity for a young fellow with the goods; and John *has* the goods. I tell you, Ed, you don't appreciate the talent your own son has.

BROWN—But he wants to go to art *school*.

STEELE—Well, let him; he's young; if he thinks he's got any rough edges that need polishing off, why let him have a year or so of schooling. He looks as good to me right now as any of them, but he's a better judge than we are on that point. He can't be too good and while he's studying he can be looking around New York getting the lay of the land. He'll meet a lot of people in the same line who can put him on to the ropes.

BROWN—But listen here! I never heard him mention the advertising or magazine end of it. His ideas on the subject of painting are very lofty. He may consider such things beneath him. You've never seen any of his big oil paintings, have you?

STEELE—No.

BROWN—You'd hardly call those a salable product. (*with a smile*) It's hard to make out what some of them are.

STEELE—(*laughingly*) They must be some of those Impressionistic pictures you hear so much about. But don't worry. John'll get over all that. Give him a year in New York and don't allow him any more money than is absolutely necessary, and I'll guarantee at the end of that time he'll have lost his high-fangled notions. He's just an enthusiastic kid and there's nothing like a year in New York to make him realize the importance of a bank account and settle down to brass tacks. He'll get in with the others who are making money and want to fall in line. But don't let on about this to him. There's no use in offending the young man's dignity. Encourage him to go to the city and paint his head off. He'll come gradually to see the commercial aspects of the case—especially if you keep a tight hand on the pocket-book.

BROWN—(*his face clearing*) You've convinced me, Dick. I'll let the boy go his own road.

STEELE—(*complacently*) That's the idea. Biggest mistake

in the world to force a boy into something he's not interested in.

BROWN—(*in a stage whisper*) And now what do you say to a wee drop to celebrate this joyful occasion?

STEELE—(*in the same tone*) Your proposition tickles me to death.

BROWN—Then follow me. (*They go into the dining room, shutting the door after them. A moment later John appears in the doorway leading to the hall. He looks quickly around to make sure the room is empty; then beckons to someone in the hall behind him, and walks softly over to the table. Maud Steele, giggling and flushed with excitement, tiptoes after him. She is a remarkably pretty girl of twenty with great blue eyes, golden brown hair, and small delicate features. Of medium height her figure is lithe and graceful. She is dressed in a fluffy white summer frock and wears white tennis shoes. Her rather kittenish manner and the continual pout of her small red mouth indicate the spoiled child even before one hears the note of petulance in her soft, all-too-sweet voice.*)

MAUD—I gave them the slip. (*She comes over to John who takes her in his arms and kisses her passionately.*)

JOHN—Oh, Maudie dear, I can't realize it. It all seems too good to be true.

MAUD—Don't. (*He releases her. She speaks with soft reproach.*) You've got my dress all mussed up. What will your sisters think. (*makes a face at him*) Rough thing.

JOHN—(*making a motion as if to take her in his arms again*) Dear!

MAUD—(*moving out of reach—mockingly*) I said just one. Aren't you ever satisfied?

JOHN—With kissing you? Each one is sweeter than the last and I eternally long for the next one.

MAUD—Thank you. You do say such sweet things, Johnnie dear. We'll be caught if we stay in here much longer. Where are the two fathers?

JOHN—In the dining room, I guess. We can hear them coming.

MAUD—Is it all settled—about us?

JOHN—(*trying to catch her*) Yes, dearest girl. (*She evades him.*) Yes, cruel one, it's all settled. All I'm afraid of is father won't let me go to art school. He can't understand. None of them can but you and Bessie.

MAUD—(*stamping her foot*) He must; I won't have you a horrid old lawyer. (*with a confident smile*) Papa'll persuade him. I'm sure of it. He thinks you'll just make oodles and oodles of money in New York when you get started.

JOHN—(*frowning*) The money part will take a long time, I'm afraid. (*turning to her with deep emotion*) But you'll wait for me, won't you, dear? You'll have faith in me, won't you?—no matter what they say? It's going to be a long hard struggle.

MAUD—Of course I will, silly boy! (*She goes to the table. The magazine with the pretty girl cover catches her eye. She holds it up with a flourish.*) Look! Papa says he gets a couple of hundred dollars apiece for those. (*She smiles at him rougishly.*) I know whose name is going to be down in the corner there in a year or so. (*John makes a gesture of annoyance.*) Oh, I'll be so proud then! I'll carry a copy with me all the time and show it to everyone I meet.

JOHN—(*contemplating the picture on the cover with a contemptuous smile reads the title disdainfully*) The September Girl, eh?

MAUD—Isn't she just too sweet for anything?

JOHN—Too sweet for anything human. (*In sudden impatience he takes the magazine from her hand and drops it into the waste-paper basket. Maud looks at him in pained astonishment, her large eyes filling with tears at his rudeness. John takes her in his arms in a passion of repentance.*) Forgive me, Maudie! I only meant I want to do much finer things than that, don't you understand?

MAUDIE—(*winking her tears away and smiling up into his face*) Of course I do! (*He kisses her again as*

The Curtain Falls)

ACT 2

SCENE—*A studio in New York on a cold evening in March, a year and a half later. On the left a black table with a reading lamp and a confused mass of books and pamphlets on it. Farther back a large bay-window looking out over the street, with a comfortable window-seat piled up with faded cushions. In the corner a number of frames for paintings stacked up against the wall. Before them a divan with a dark red cover. The far side of the room is hidden by a profusion of paintings of all sizes and subjects. There are nudes and landscapes, portraits and seascapes; also a number of small prints of old masters filling up the smaller wall spaces. Two long, low book cases, with a piano between them take up all the lower space. On the right of the studio a kitchinette hidden by a partition six feet high covered over with green burlap. In the foreground a doorway leading in to the kitchinette. Over the doorway a curtain of green material. In the front of the partition and helping to conceal it, another book case. In the far, right-hand corner where the partition ends is a small hallway leading to the outer door.*

Two rather disabled-looking Morris-chairs are on either side of the table. Several rocking chairs are placed nearby. The rest of the floor space is occupied by a model stand of dark wood and a huge easel on which a half-finished painting is clamped. There is a large skylight in the middle of the ceiling which sheds the glow from the lights of the city down in a sort of faint half-light. The reading lamp on the table, connected by a tube with a gas-jet on the wall above, and another gas-jet near the piano furnish the only light.

John, Babe Carter, and Steve Harrington are discovered fussing around the studio trying to get things in order. Carter is a broad-shouldered giant with a mop of blond hair and a feeble attempt at a blond mustache. He has large deep-set, blue eyes and fine, handsome features. His voice is a deep bass and his laugh a marvel of heartiness. His coat is off and he appears in a white soft shirt and khaki trousers. Harrington is a tall slender fellow of about twenty-eight, with large, irregular features, light brown hair, and brown eyes set far apart. He is dressed in a black suit and wears a white shirt with a soft collar and a bow tie. His manner is reserved and quiet, but when he does speak his voice is low and pleasing. John has on a heavy, grey overcoat and a green felt hat. He has aged

*considerably, and there are lines of worry about his eyes. His face
has an unhealthy city pallor, and he seems very nervous.*

JOHN—(*going toward door*) Time for me to be going. I've
got to meet him at 7.30 at the hotel. I'll bring him right over.

BABE—And I'll away to Bridgetown by that 8.30 train. It'll
be just as well for you if your father doesn't meet me; and I'll
have a better chance of seeing Bessie now that he's out of
town.

JOHN—Well, you know you've got my best wishes. I hope
you win.

BABE—Thanks. (*laughing*) I wish more of your family
could say the same.

JOHN—Give my love to Maudie if you see her. (*He stops at
the door.*) Remember I won't be long, not more than half an
hour at most, and if you want to get away without meeting
father, you better hurry.

BABE—Don't worry. I won't be here—not on your life!
(*John goes out.*)

BABE—(*picking up a pair of old pants off the nearest divan*)
What'll I do with these?

STEVE—(*carelessly*) Must be Ted's—in under the couch
with them! We'll teach him the first principles of neatness.

BABE—Old man Brown would sure think these neglected
pants a sign of our radical mode of life. In under the couch
with them you say? All right—only they happen to be yours.

STEVE—(*hastily*) Hold! (*goes over to Babe and gets them*)

BABE—First principles of neatness, you know.

STEVE—(*throws the pants over the partition into the kitchinette*) I wouldn't have these pants treated with indignity for
worlds. Have you no respect for old age? (*He looks Babe up
and down with a critical stare.*) Babe, I wonder at you! Are
you going a'courting in those? (*indicates Babes trousers*)
They'll lock you in the Bridgetown jail and throw away the key.

BABE—(*resignedly*) I suppose I'd better change. (*He goes
into the kitchinette and can be heard pulling out the drawers of a
dresser.*) I'll sacrifice my pants to small-town respectability, but
I wish to state right here that my soft shirt stays on. My collars have gotten so small for me I nearly commit suicide every
time I put one on. Look! (*He appears in the doorway with one*

of the offending collars clutched around his neck. His flesh bulges out over it. Steve laughs, and sits down in one of the chairs near the table.)

STEVE—This visit of old Browns promises to be stormy, if his letters to John are any indication.

BABE—(*from inside the partition*) I'm sure glad my folks are located so far out in the wild and wooly they can't come to visit. Although I don't think they'd be shocked any—more liable to be disappointed. From my kid brother's letters I gather he believes we maintain a large harem full of beautiful models with names like Suzette and Mimi. You can judge for yourself how the study of art has begun to fascinate him. He's been reading some Iowa school teachers romance of Paris Latin Quarter life, I guess. I've tried to disillusion him—told him the only naughty models nowadays were cloak and suit models—but whats the use? He thinks I'm stalling—says I shouldn't try to hog all the artistic temperament of the family. (*Steve laughs.*) But I reckon Pop'll keep him out on the ranch. The kid's talents run more to branding cattle than to painting them, and Pop considers one artist in the family enough. (*He comes out of the kitchinette and sits down near Steve.*) They all think I'm going to be the greatest artist in the world, and they're willing to stake me to all they've got. If I didn't have confidence of getting somewhere, I'd have quit long ago. But how do I look? (*He gets up and turns slowly around for inspection. He has changed to creaseless, baggy, dark pants and a wrinkled coat matching them.*)

STEVE—(*solemnly eyeing him*) O feebleness of words!

BABE—Remember the true artist sees beauty even in the commonest things. (*a pause*) Appreciation isn't one of your long points, I see. (*He sits down again.*)

STEVE—Have patience. I was just about to say you resembled an enlarged edition of Beau Brummel.

BABE—Enlarged? You're sure you didn't mean distorted?

STEVE—God forbid! Candidly, you look surprisingly respectable.

BABE—Disgustingly respectable, as Ted would say. By the way, where's Ted?

STEVE—(*surprised*) Don't you know? Then let me tell you the astounding news. You know how despairfully he has wailed about his having to seek a reporting job if something didn't turn up soon. Well, he got a check today—sold one of his stories.

BABE—What!

STEVE—Yea, verily; incredible to relate, it is true. You remember that blood-soaked detective yarn of his—the one where the lady's husband strangles her with a piece of barbwire and hides her head in the piano. (*Babe groans.*) That's the one. The New Magazine bought it and sent Ted a check for fifty large dollars.

BABE—O festive occasion! I suppose he's now out shooting up the town. I think we better prepare the net and straight jacket.

STEVE—He won't be in till God knows when—maybe not at all. (*A knock at the door is heard.*)

BABE—They couldn't have got over that quick. (*He hides in the kitchinette nevertheless.*)

STEVE—Come in! (*Eugene Grammont, Master of the Art School, comes slowly into the room. He is a slight, stoop-shouldered, old man of sixty or more with a mass of wavy white hair and a white mustache and imperial. His keen, black eyes peer kindly out of his lean ascetic face. He is dressed entirely in black with a white shirt and collar and a black Windsor tie. There is a distinct foreign atmosphere about him, but he speaks English without a trace of an accent.*)

GRAMMONT—(*ceremoniously, with a little bow*) Good evening, gentlemen.

STEVE—Good evening.

BABE—(*coming out again*) Won't you sit down?

GRAMMONT—(*taking a chair near them*) Thank you. (*with a slight smile*) Would it be rude of me to remark upon the unusual neatness of the studio?

BABE—And of the occupants of the studio?

GRAMMONT—I did not say that, but since you mention it—

BABE—We're expecting visitors, or, I should say, a visitor, the father of your worthy pupil, John.

GRAMMONT—Indeed. (*with a troubled expression*) What type of a man is his father?

STEVE—I've never met him but Babe knows him quite well.

BABE—I spent several vacations at their home when we were in college together; you know I live so far out West I never could make the trip. Old man Brown is a common enough type, but I'm afraid he's not the kind of man you have much sympathy for. He's a hardware merchant with a large family, moderately rich, self-made, hard-headed, and with absolutely not the faintest appreciation of Art in any form.

GRAMMONT—I thought it would be so.

STEVE—I've read a number of his letters to John and they were impossible. He wanted him to study law, you know. He's sorry now he didn't compel him to do so; says he's wasting time and money down here. As for the family I believe the height of their ambition was to see John making fashion-plates and pretty girls at so much per page, and they're all disappointed because he doesn't move in that direction.

BABE—(*quickly*) All but Bess; she encourages him to go ahead.

GRAMMONT—Ah, it is well he has someone, poor boy. Who is she,—his fiancee?

STEVE—(*with a smile*) No, his sister; but suspected of being another artists fiancee. (*He looks pointedly at Babe whose face reddens.*)

GRAMMONT—(*leaning over and patting Babe's knee with his long white hand*) I am indeed glad to hear it.

BABE—I have hopes—that's all.

GRAMMONT—You have more than hopes or you would not—hope. But have I not heard somewhere that John is engaged to be married?

BABE—Yes; he is.

GRAMMONT—And the girl?

STEVE—You've met her. Don't you remember one Sunday last winter we had sort of a tea here, and John introduced you to a girl,—a very pretty girl with golden-brown hair? The tea was in her honor. You only glanced in for a moment.

GRAMMONT—A moment—I detest teas and never go to one; that is why I remember your's so distinctly; you all looked so out of place. Surely you cannot mean the girl who was so shocked at all your nudes—and said so?

STEVE—(*dryly*) You have guessed it.

GRAMMONT—(*with a comic groan*) That doll-face! How could she understand? Oh, how blind is love!

STEVE—She is evidently very much in love with John. She, at least, tries to understand, and if she can't it's hardly her fault, with all her environment and bringing-up to fight against.

BABE—While his family are determined they won't understand.

GRAMMONT—Mon Dieu, but our friend John seems to have a hard fight before him. It is too bad. Never in my long experience as teacher have I met a young man who gave finer promise of becoming a great artist—and I have taught many who are on the heights today. He has the soul, he has everything. (*passionately*) And behold these worshipers of the golden calf, these muddy souls, will exert all their power to hold him to their own level. (*shakes his head sadly*) And I am afraid they may succeed if, as you say, he loves one of them. He is not one of the strong ones who can fight against discouragement and lack of appreciation through long years of struggle. He is all-too-sensitive and finely-keyed. I have noticed of late how his work has fallen off. It is as if the life and vigour had departed from it. His mind has not been able to joyfully concentrate on the Art he loves.

STEVE—The effect of the girl's letters, no doubt. She urged him to return home and do his painting there.

GRAMMONT—She does not know how much he has yet to learn.

BABE—His people would soon nag all the art out of him up there. But I don't agree with you about John being as weak as you think. He's got the grit. If his old man does stop the money he can get some work here in town,—something to keep him alive, at any rate, while he goes on with his painting.

STEVE—What can he do in a money making way?

BABE—(*after a pause*) I can't think of anything. He's always been so unpractical,—even more so than most of us.

STEVE—There you are! That means the best he can hope for is drudgery. He'll be able to keep alive; but he won't paint. I tried it before my father died, and I know; and I'm a

good deal less sensitive than John and a lot more fit for business and other abominations. In my younger days those
things were forced on me; I had to learn something about
them.

GRAMMONT—You are right. In John's case the thing
would be a tragedy; and he is so worthy of surviving!

BABE—Can't we think of something to do to help him? Of
course, in a money way it's impossible, and even if it weren't
he'd never accept, but—

STEVE—Let's see. It wouldn't be the slightest use for me
to say anything to the old man; but you (*turning to Grammont*) might be able to convince him of John's future and
persuade him to keep his hands off for a while.

GRAMMONT—I will be more than glad to try if you think
it might benefit John in any way; but I fear you overestimate
my ability as mediator. I do not know how to talk to that
class of people.

STEVE—It will do no harm to try.

GRAMMONT—(*with decision*) I will do my utmost.

BABE—That's the stuff! We'll pull him out of the hole yet.

GRAMMONT—When do you expect them?

BABE—They ought to be here in five or ten minutes
now.

GRAMMONT—Then I will leave you. (*He goes toward door.*)
You will let me know when the propitious time comes?

STEVE—I'm coming to your studio as soon as they arrive;
want to give them a chance to argue it all out themselves.
After a time we'll come back and I'll take John away and leave
you alone with the terrible parent.

GRAMMONT—I see. (*He goes out.*)

STEVE—The poor Old Master! He's as much worried as if
John were his own son.

BABE—It would be a God's blessing for John if the Old Master were his father instead of the present incumbent. Why is it
fine things like that never happen? (*He goes into the kitchinette
and returns wearing a dark overcoat and derby hat and carrying
a suit case.*) Even his name,—John Brown! Isn't that the hell
of a name for an artist? Look better at the top of a grocery
store than on the bottom of a painting. The only thing re-

corded in the Book of Fame about a John Brown is that his body lies moldering in the grave,—nice thought, that!

STEVE—(*laughing*) You can't complain of lacking a famous Carter. Everyones heard of Nick.

BABE—Yes, all through college I just escaped that nick-name.

STEVE—What's that! (*picking up a book as if to hurl it at Babe's head*) Was that pun intentional?

BABE—What pun? (*He realizes and bursts into a roar of laughter.*) No, on the level, I never thought of it. I humbly beg your pardon. All the same, that's some pun and I won't forget it.

STEVE—I'll bet you won't; and you'll not let anyone else forget it either.

BABE—It was a toss-up whether Nick should be wished on me or not; but I was so big, fat, ugly, and awkward when at prep. school, they just couldn't resist the temptation of "Babe". So Babe I've been ever since. (*a pause during which he chuckles to himself and Steve grins at him*) Well, I'm off. (*He goes toward door.*) Nick-name, eh? Oh, I guess that's rotten. (*He shakes with laughter.*)

STEVE—Shut up! Oh, but you're the subtle humorist. Look out you don't run into them.

BABE—Trust me to hide if I see old Brown. So long!

STEVE—Good luck! (*Babe goes out. Steve sits for a while reading. Presently a rap on the door is heard. Steve gets up and walks toward it as Brown and John enter. Brown seems a little leaner and his lips are stern and unsmiling. He wears a black derby hat and heavy black overcoat.*)

JOHN—You haven't met Mr. Harrington, have you, Father? He's the only one you don't know. (*Steve and Brown shake hands and murmur conventional nothings.*)

STEVE—You'll excuse me, I hope? I was just going over to Grammonts studio when you came in. I'll be back later.

BROWN—(*perfunctorily*) Hope I'm not driving you away.

STEVE—Oh, not at all. (*He goes out. John takes off coat and hat, helps father off with his things and puts them on the window-seat. He and father take chairs near the table.*)

BROWN—I'm glad that other fellow isn't here.

JOHN—You mean Carter?

BROWN—Yes,—the good-for-nothing!

JOHN—(*quietly*) Babe is my best friend.

BROWN—When you hear what I have to tell you about that same Carter, I think you'll agree with me, the less you have to do with him in future the better.

JOHN—Babe has done nothing dishonorable, I know.

BROWN—It all depends on what you artists understand by honor. Do you know what your so-called friend has been doing? He's been coming to Bridgetown and meeting Bessie on the sly. I found out about it and spoke to her last evening. She as much as told me to mind my own business, and said she intended to marry this Carter. I lost my temper and informed her that if she married that loafer I'd have nothing more to do with her. What do think she did? Packed up her things and left the house,—yes, in spite of all your mother could say—and went to the hotel and got a room.

JOHN—(*impulsively*) Good for Bess!

BROWN—Am I to infer from that remark that you approve of her conduct?

JOHN—Of course, I approve of it. I've known about it all along. Babe told me every time he went up and I wished him luck. If they met secretly, it's all your own fault. You told Bessie you didn't want him in the house. She loves him. What could she do.

BROWN—(*furiously*) Let's have none of that romantic piffle. I've heard enough of it from Bessie.

JOHN—She must be true to herself. Her duty to herself stands before her duty to you.

BROWN—(*losing all control and pounding on the arm of his chair with his fist*) Rot! Damned rot! only believed by a lot of crazy Socialists and Anarchists. What is a father for I'd like to know?

JOHN—(*shrugging his shoulders*) I suppose, when a man is a willing party to bringing children into the world, he takes upon himself the responsibility of doing all in his power to further their happiness.

BROWN—But isn't that what I'm doing?

JOHN—Absolutely not! You consider your children to be

your possessions, your property, to belong to you. You don't think of them as individuals with ideas and desires of their own. It's for you to find out the highest hope of each of them and give it your help and sympathy. Are you doing this in Bessie's case? No, you're trying to substitute a desire of your own which you think would benefit her in a worldly way.

BROWN—Stuff! Bessie has no experience with the world. Would you like me to stand by and see her ruin her life, and not do my best to protect her?

JOHN—Why will you harp on her ruining her life? If she marries Babe, they are both to be congratulated. Bess is a great girl and Babe is as fine and clean a fellow as ever lived. You are angry because you planned to marry her to someone else. Why not be frank about it?

BROWN—(*indignantly*) I don't want her to be tied to a penniless adventurer. It's true Mr. Arnold asked her to marry him, and that I fully approved. I still hope she'll marry him. He's an established man with plenty of money and position and—

JOHN—(*jumping to his feet*) And forty years old,—a fool with a rotten past behind him, as you know.

BROWN—That's all talk. He was a bit wild, that's all; and that was years ago.

JOHN—She'll never marry him.

BROWN—Well, if she marries that scamp Carter, she's left my home for good.

JOHN—If you treat her this way she'll not have many regrets; but let's drop the subject. You didn't come down to consult me about Bess, did you?

BROWN—I should say not. I knew only too well whose side you would take. I came down to tell you we've all decided it's high time you gave up this art foolishness, and came home and settled down to work. I spoke with Mr. Steele about you, and he said there's a good position open for you in his store. He's an old man with no children except Maud, and you'd naturally be at the head of the business after his death. He's willing to give Maud a nice home as a wedding present, and you'll be able to get married right away. (*Brown's manner becomes more and more kindly and persuasive.*) Come, is that no inducement? And I'll do the best I can for you on your wedding day. You ought to consider Maud a little. She's up there waiting for you while you idle away your time on a hobby.

JOHN—Hobby! Good God, can't you understand me better than that? (*frenziedly*) I'm painting, painting, painting, can't you see?

BROWN—Then it's about time you showed some promise of making some money at it if you intend to marry and have children. Look at the future, boy! You can't go on this way forever. Steele and I thought you'd be selling your things long before this or I'd never have let you come. You're wasting time at something you're not fitted for, it seems to me. You've been here a year and a half, and you're right where you started. (*John does not answer but sits down on the window-seat and looks down at the street. Brown gets up, puts on his glasses, and goes to the far wall to look at the paintings. He speaks in tones of wondering disgust.*) Who painted this? (*pointing to an impressionistic painting of a nude dancer*)

JOHN—(*wearily*) I did.

BROWN—You ought to be ashamed to acknowledge it. What decent family would ever hang that up in their house? No wonder you can't sell anything if your fancies run that way. I'm glad to see you didn't finish it.

JOHN—It is finished.

BROWN—You'd never know it. She's an awful rough looking female. That's Impressionism, I suppose. Rot! Damned rot! I suppose she came here and posed—like that?

JOHN—Yes.

BROWN—(*with a chuckle*) I begin to see there may be other attractions in this career of your's besides a lofty ideal.

JOHN—(*furious at the insinuation in his father's voice*) What do you mean?

BROWN—Oh, don't be so indignant. You wouldn't be my son if you were an angel. (*comes back to chair again*) But there's a time for all that and I think you ought to settle down,—for Maud's sake anyway. This atmosphere isn't doing you any good, and you need the clean, Bridgetown air to set you right again, mentally and physically. You've changed a lot since you left, and I'm only telling the truth when I say it hasn't been for the good. This big city game is a tough proposition,—too tough for you when you've got such advantages at home. (*John stares despondently at the floor.*) I saw Maud just before I left. She said to me: "Don't tell John I said so but do try to bring him home."

JOHN—(*miserably*) Don't! You can't understand. (*A sound of singing from the hall. The door is pushed open and Ted Nelson lurches into the studio followed by Helene. Ted is drunk, and Helene shows she has been drinking. Ted is a small, wiry-looking young fellow with long sandy hair, grey eyes with imperceptible brows and lashes, a long, thin nose, and a large, thick-lipped mouth. He is dressed in a shabby, grey suit of an exaggerated cut, and wears black patent-leather shoes with grey spats. He carries a grey overcoat over his arm and a grey felt hat. Helene is a large voluptuous creature of beautiful figure and startling taste in dress. She looks like the fashion-plate of a French magazine. Her slit skirt is a marvel of economy in material; her hat a turban with a thin, reed-like feather waving skywards. For the rest, she is twenty, blond-haired, blue-eyed, rouged, and powdered. By profession she is a cloak and suit model, a renegade from the ranks of artists models, lured away by the brilliant inducement of wearing beautiful clothes instead of wearing none at all.*)

TED—(*pulling Helene toward him and kissing her maudlinly*) Here we are, Light of My Soul, here we are. (*sings*) "Home is the sailor."

HELENE—(*laughing*) Crazy, crazy; you're drunk.

TED—(*bellowing*) What ho, within! (*He suddenly catches sight of John's father sitting by the table, and walks over to him with all the dignity he can command.*) Pardon me, Mr. Brown; I didn't see you. (*He offers his hand which Brown barely touches.*)

BROWN—(*severely*) How do you do, sir.

TED—Oh, I stagger along, I stagger along, (*with a foolish laugh*) "stagger" being the correct word at present writing. (*His eyes suddenly fix themselves on John.*) Why, hello, Old Masterpiece. (*He detaches himself from Brown and lurches over to John.*) Have you heard the glad tidings? (*John throws a worried look at his father, who has turned his back on them. Helene, having satisfied herself that she doesn't know Brown, comes over toward John, whom she doesn't at first recognize in the gloom of the window-seat.*)

JOHN—You mean about your selling that story? Of course, I've heard about it. Congratulations!

HELENE—(*recognizing his voice, rushes over and throws her arms around his neck*) You're a fine piece of cheese! Don't you remember your old friends any more? Oh, look at him blush! (*Brown has turned around and is frowning sternly at them. John twists out of her embrace and walks away, biting his lips with vexation.*)

TED—(*leaning over and speaking to her in what he means to be a whisper*) Sssshhh! Can that stuff! That's his old man.

HELENE—Oho!

TED—(*going over to John and winking at him with drunken cunning*) S'all right. I'll square it for you. (*He walks to Brown, not heeding John's gestures of remonstrance.*) Mr. Brown, I have an apology to make. I must humbly confess I am unduly vivacious this evening. I have looked upon the wine, and all that. (*with a sweeping gesture which threatens to overbalance him*) Let this be my justification. I have sold for fifty shining pesos a story which I had the misfortune to write. (*Brown gives an exclamation of angry impatience.*) You are right. The idea is incredible. Let me say this in my defence, however: It was the first story I ever sold; and it was the rottenest, absurdest, and most totally imbecile story I ever wrote,—And I am a man of many manuscripts. I pity the editor who accepted it. I have pitied him all evening,—toasted him for his generous humanity, and pitied him for his bad taste. (*He stops and stares vaguely at Brown who turns from him in disgust. John signals frantically and points to Helene. She stifles a giggle. Ted has a bright idea.*) Helene, you have not met John's father. (*Helene gazes at him in consternation. Brown turns to her stiffly.*) Mr. Brown, allow me to present my wife.

JOHN—(*tearing his hair*) Good heavens!

HELENE—(*bowing with a loud giggle*) What! Oh,—pleased to meet you.

BROWN—(*indignant at the suspicion that he is being hoaxed*) Your wife? (*Before anyone can say anything more the door opens and Steve comes in followed by Grammont.*)

JOHN—(*turns to them with a look of anguished pleading and whispers hoarsely to Steve*) Take them away for God's sake!

(*Steve takes in the situation at a glance. He grabs Ted by the arm, and with his other hand guides Helene, weak with laughter, to the door. John brings Grammont over to introduce to his father.*)

HELENE—Oh, Steve, I almost died.

STEVE—Come on over to Grammonts and dance.

TED—Dance? That's my middle name.

(as they go out)

JOHN—Father, I'd like you to meet Mr. Grammont, Master of the Art School, whose unworthy pupil I am.

BROWN—(*with a forced smile*) I have heard of Mr. Grammont many times, although I'm not familiar with art matters. I'm glad to meet you, sir.

GRAMMONT—(*taking his hand*) The pleasure is mine. (*They sit down together by the table.*)

STEVE—(*from the door*) Oh, John! I need your moral support. Come over to Grammonts for a moment, will you?

JOHN—All right. Excuse me for a moment, will you, Father. (*He goes out.*)

GRAMMONT—(*after an embarrassed pause*) It gives me great pleasure to be able to tell you that your son, John, is one of the most promising pupils who has ever entered my school. He has all the qualities of a great artist.

BROWN—(*not impressed,—thinking this praise but the business policy of the head of a school with the father of a well-paying pupil*) I have no doubt of it but—

GRAMMONT—(*earnestly*) I have heard that you are not in favor of his continuing his artistic career; that you think it better for him to take up something else? (*Brown nods.*) My dear sir, you will pardon me if I presume on such short acquaintance to say that I think you are making a great mistake. (*Brown frowns.*) In the interest of the Art I love, I implore you not to withdraw your support from John at this crucial moment in his life when he has most need of you and your encouragement. He is just finding himself, becoming conscious of his own powers. Discouragement now would be fatal to his future; and I can unhesitatingly predict a great future for him,—for I know a real artist when I see one.

BROWN—I'm much obliged to you for your frankness, but there are a great many things which influence my decision which you can't possibly know of.

GRAMMONT—(*with grave conviction*) I know your decision will spoil his life.

BROWN—(*rising to his feet to indicate the discussion is closed*) That's a matter of opinion. Our points of view are different. It seems to me his life is more likely to be ruined idling his time away down here with drunken companions, and low women of the type I have just met.

GRAMMONT—But what you have seen is the unfortunate exception—

BROWN—(*pointing to the paintings*) And are all those naked women who come here to pose, are they exceptions? Is this the atmosphere for a young man to live in who's engaged to a decent girl?

GRAMMONT—(*also rising to his feet—to himself, half-aloud, with a shrug of hopelessness*) Alas, the poor boy is lost.

BROWN—(*overhearing him—sarcastically*) Of course, I appreciate the fact that it's your business to keep your pupils as long as possible. (*John enters as his father is speaking.*)

GRAMMONT—(*flushing with anger*) You are insulting, sir! I was only trying to save your son. (*He walks quickly to John and takes his hand.*) Be true to yourself, John, remember! For that no sacrifice is too great. (*He goes out.*)

JOHN—What's the matter?

BROWN—(*picking up his hat and coat*) Matter enough; that old fool was trying to get me to keep paying out money to him for all this nonsense of your's.

JOHN—That's not true! He's above such considerations.

BROWN—(*putting on overcoat*) Rot! I saw through him and I let him know it. He'll mind his own business after this.

JOHN—He's one of the finest men I have ever known.

BROWN—No doubt, no doubt! They are all fine people you live with down here,—drunkards, old lunatics, and women of the streets. (*as John starts to expostulate*) Oh, I've seen one of your models; that's enough.

JOHN—(*with a hysterical laugh*) But she's only a cloak and suit model—now!

BROWN—It makes no difference. I tell you here and now, young man, I've had enough of it. You either come home with me in the morning or you needn't look to me for help in the future. I'll bring you to your senses. Starve awhile, and see how much bread and butter this high art will bring you! No more coming to me for money, do you understand?

JOHN—(*dully*) Yes.

BROWN—(*after a pause*) Well, if you decide to come with me, meet me at that ten-four train. Think it over.

JOHN—I have thought it over. I won't come.

BROWN—(*starting toward door*) You'll change your tune when you see how much help you'll get from these so-called friends of yours. Think it over. I've got to save you in spite of yourself, if there's no other way. (*He stops at the door.*) And remember Steele won't keep that position open for you forever.

JOHN—(*pouring out all his rage*) Oh, to hell with Steele! (*The hall door closes with a slam as*

The Curtain Falls)

ACT 3

SCENE—*The studio about three o'clock on a hot Sunday after-noon in July of the same year. John, Steve, and Ted are discovered. Steve, dressed in his dark suit, is sprawled out in one of the Morris chairs near the table. John is painting at an unfinished portrait clamped on the big easel in under the skylight. His hands are paint-stained and a daub of brown shows on one of his cheeks. He is dressed in a dirty paint-smirched pair of grey flannel trousers, a grey flannel shirt open at the neck, and a pair of "sneaks". His face is haggard and dissipated-looking. Ted is sitting on the win-dow-seat idly watching the street below. He wears a shabby light suit and a pair of tan shoes run down at the heel. A straw hat is perched on the back of his head.*

JOHN—(*throwing down his brush with an exclamation of hopeless irritation*) It's no use; I might as well quit. Nothing seems to take on life any more. (*He goes over and sits by Ted.*)

STEVE—No use trying to work with that feeling. I know; I've had experience with it myself.

JOHN—The sad part of it is, mine seems to be chronic.

STEVE—You'll get over it. You're worrying too much about other things. When they go the emptiness'll go with them. (*John does not answer but stares moodily at the street below.*)

TED—(*after a pause—with a groan of boredom*) What a hell-ish long day Sunday is! On the level, I'd be better satisfied if I had to work. Nothing to do all day and no place to go that's fit to go to.

STEVE—Better advise your editor to get out a Sunday af-ternoon paper. Tell him you're anxious to work more for the same pay; that ought to fetch him.

TED—You don't call that emaciated envelope I drag down every week "pay" do you? I'm getting less now than ever. In fact it's only the devil's tenderness I wasn't fired when they cut down for the summer. Every time my high literary ambi-tions fall to earth for lack of appreciative editors, and I have to hunt a job again, I find out I'm worth less money. They'll have me selling the papers some day, at this rate.

STEVE—How about short-story writing on the Sabbath?

Have you any religious convictions which bar you from that?

TED—I've already written more short stories than Maupassant and O. Henry put together—and I sold *one*. I'll have to wait until some philanthropist endows a college for the higher education of editors before I stand a chance.

STEVE—You mentioned an idea for a play. Play writing is a good, healthy Sabbath exercise.

TED—Oh, my ideas are plentiful enough; but execution doesn't seem to be my long suit. I'm always going to start that play—tomorrow. (*gloomily*) They ought to write on my tombstone: The deceased at last met one thing he couldn't put off till tomorrow. It would be rather an appropriate epitaph.

STEVE—(*with a grin*) What time did you get in last night?

TED—This morning.

STEVE—I thought this was a little morning-after pessimism. I don't want to preach but isn't that the answer, Ted? And you too, John? (*John shrugs his shoulders indifferently.*)

TED—I suppose so; but the helluvit is I never see that side of the argument till afterwards. You can't keep a squirrel on the ground; not unless you cut down all the trees.

JOHN—(*to Ted*) Where did we end up last night?

TED—(*shaking his head sorrowfully*) Ask me not. All I know is I feel like a wet rag today.

STEVE—(*smilingly quotes*) Have drowned my glory in a shallow cup.

TED—Oh, stop that noise, Mr. Ree Morse!

JOHN—(*impatiently to Steve*) It's all right for you to talk. Everything is running smoothly with you; but just try a week or two at my job and see if you won't want to cut loose and forget it all for a while on Saturday night. Checking sugar bags and barrels down on the docks! Oh, it's a nice job, mine is! You'd have to do it yourself for a while to know how bad it is—day after day of monotonous drudgery—life nothing but a panorama of sugar bags! (*with a sudden burst of feeling*) Oh, how I loathe that rotten dock with its noise and smells and its—sugar bags. I can't paint any more—not even *pretty* pictures. I've wanted to do some real work on Sundays but— I don't know how to express it—something is like a dead weight inside me—no more incentive, no more imagination, no more joy in creating,—only a great sickness and lassitude of soul, a desire to drink, to do anything to get out of myself and forget.

STEVE—The trouble with you is you brood too much over the row with your family. Don't take it so seriously. It'll all be over and forgotten before you know it. Those family brawls are part of a lifetime and we all have them and get over them without serious results.

JOHN—It's not my family's antagonism; it's Maud,—her letters to me; every one of them showing she can't understand, although she's trying so hard to; that she thinks I'm throwing my life away, and her's too, on a whim; that she has no faith in my ultimate success; but that her love is so great she will stick to me till the end—to a lost cause, a forlorn hope. (*He hides his face in his hands with a groan.*) Oh, it's hell to love and be loved by a girl who can't understand; who, you know, tries to and cannot; who loves you, and whose life you are making miserable and unhappy by trying to be true to yourself.

STEVE—(*his voice full of sympathetic understanding*) If you feel that way, there's only one thing to do; go back home, get married, save up your money for awhile and then come back again when your mind is free once more. Or else—give up the girl for good and all.

TED—That's the idea!

JOHN—What would life be worth if I gave her up?

STEVE—Then go back to her.

JOHN—I can't go back—now.

TED—Why, look here, at the end of six months or a year at the salary you'll get from father-in-law you ought to save enough to stay down here for an age.

JOHN—You forget Maud.

TED—It'll be different after you're married. She's sure to understand you better then. She'll take a selfish interest in trying to help you become something higher than a small town shop keeper.

STEVE—There! You ought to be convinced now! Listen to the pitiless dissector of women's souls, the author of a thousand and one tales of love, passion, and divorce. If anyone can predict the vagaries of the "female of the species", surely he can.

TED—(*laughing*) I'm a grand little predicter.

JOHN—I'd be proving myself a cowardly weakling by giving in like that—and you know it.

STEVE—You'd be showing more sense than you have in a long time.

TED—Coward? Nonsense! It's just like this: There's no use slaving away at a job that's disgusting to you for the sole purpose of earning enough to live on. You don't have to do it, and you're only ruining your health and accumulating a frame of mind where you think the world hates you. If you had any time or energy to paint, it would be another thing. You'll have plenty of time up there and your mind won't be in such a rut.

JOHN—It's useless for you to try and argue with me. I can't—and I won't—go back. Go back to Maud—a confessed failure! Is that what you advise me to do? Another thing; I know the conditions in Bridgetown, and you don't. You don't consider how I hate the town and how hostile all the surroundings are, when you talk of all the painting I could do. No. I've got to stay here, sink or swim. (*A knock on the door. Babe Carter and Bessie enter. Bessie has matured from a girl into a very pretty woman since the night in Bridgetown when John announced his engagement. Her face has grown seriously thoughtful but her smile is as ready as ever. She looks much slenderer, in her blue tailor-made suit, stylish but severely simple. Babe has on a blue serge suit and carries a straw hat in his hand.*)

BABE—Hello, folks! We were on our way to the Museum and thought we'd drop in.

TED—Welcome to the Newlyweds! (*All exchange greetings. Bessie goes over and sits down by John. Babe takes a chair by the table.*)

BABE—What was all the argument about when we came in?

JOHN—They're trying to persuade me to return to Bridgetown. Think of it!

TED—John was bewailing his rotten job and his having no time or inclination for real work; and he was feeling love-sick and lonely for a certain young lady, so we suggested—

JOHN—That I go back to Bridgetown. A fine remedy, that! Ask Bessie what I'd have to contend with up there. She knows. (*to Bessie*) I told them they didn't understand conditions or they wouldn't give me any such advice. Am I right?

BESSIE—You are—even more so than you realize.

JOHN—What do you mean?

BESSIE—Oh, nothing; only don't go back whatever you do; anything rather than that—even your horrible position on the dock.

JOHN—Thats just what I told them.

STEVE—We weren't thinking so much about Bridgetown. We had an idea that if John were married it would give him back the tranquility of mind he has lost; and since it's impossible for him to get married or paint down here we urged Bridgetown as a necessary evil.

TED—That's it.

BABE—I'm not so sure you're wrong there, myself.

JOHN—(*reproachfully*) What! "Et tu Brute."

BABE—You're not satisfied here; you're brooding and worrying and drudging yourself to death without accomplishing anything. Once married, your whole attitude toward Bridgetown might change; and with an easy mind you can paint there as well as anywhere else.

BESSIE—You're wrong, all of you.

JOHN—Thanks, Bessie.

BESSIE—My advice is: Don't get married.

BABE—Oh, come now, that's pretty hard on me. I hope you're not speaking from experience.

BESSIE—Foolish! Of course, I mean in John's case.

JOHN—(*puzzled*) You don't think it wise for me to marry Maud?

BESSIE—I certainly do not.

JOHN—But why? Because I have no money?

BESSIE—That's one reason; but it wasn't the one I had in mind.

JOHN—What did you have in mind?

BESSIE—I can't explain very well. It's more of a feeling than a real, good reason. I know Maud so well—much better than you do, John, although you'll probably never admit that—and I know you so well—much better than you know yourself; and you won't admit that either—and that's my reason.

JOHN—(*indignantly*) You don't believe we love each other?

BESSIE—Oh, yes I do.

JOHN—Then why shouldn't we marry?

BESSIE—Don't get so excited about it. My opinion is very likely all wrong.

JOHN—I should hope so. You were taking a stand exactly like father's in regard to you and Babe. That isn't like you, Bessie.

BESSIE—It does seem that way, doesn't it? Well, I apologize if I was, for I had no intention of doing anything of the sort. I take back all I said. Do what you want to. Stay here till the last string snaps. And now, let's change the subject. Have you sold any of those drawings of yours?

JOHN—(*despondently*) No. I haven't had much chance to go around with them. The editor at Colpers Weekly seemed a little impressed and promised to consider them further, and bear me in mind for illustrating; but I haven't heard from him since.

BESSIE—If he's going to bear you in mind, that's encouraging, at any rate.

STEVE—I've been trying to convince John those drawings are salable, and all he has to do is push them; but he won't hear of it. (*to Babe*) You saw them, didn't you?

BABE—Yes, he showed them to me.

STEVE—Don't you think I'm right.

BABE—I sure do.

JOHN—(*brightening up*) Well, lets hope you're both right. It would be a great encouragement if I could land them somewhere. They represent the best I've got in me at that sort of work.

BESSIE—Well, Babe, we better be going. (*to Steve*) May I use your mirror?

BABE—O vanity!

STEVE—Go ahead. I don't think there's anything in there that shouldn't be seen. (*Bessie goes across to the kitchinette.*)

BABE—Won't you fellows come over to the Museum with us?

TED—Excuse *me*! Not today. I feel far from well.

BABE—Morning after, eh? Won't you come, John?

BESSIE—(*from inside the kitchinette*) Yes, do come, John.

JOHN—No, I'm going to try and work a bit. (*He gets up and goes over in front of the easel and stands looking at the unfinished painting.*) Besides, I'm not dressed, or shaved, or anything fit to be seen with a lady.

STEVE—Well, if I won't be too much of a number three I'll take a walk over with you. (*Bessie comes out of the kitchinette. Babe goes toward the door. Steve gets his straw hat from the kitchinette and follows Babe.*)

BESSIE—(*going to John*) Come along, John. We'll wait while you change clothes. You look all worn out and the fresh air will do you good.

JOHN—No; this is the only day I have and I must *try* to work at least.

BESSIE—You don't look at all well lately, do you know it?

JOHN—I don't get much sleep.

BESSIE—(*looking at him searchingly*) You're sure you're not letting your troubles drive you to drink, or anything like that?

JOHN—(*irritably*) No no, of course not! What ideas you get into your head.

BESSIE—I knew it wasn't so.

JOHN—What wasn't so?

BABE—(*from the door*) Coming Bess?

BESSIE—Oh, nothing; just something I overheard. (*She kisses him impulsively and walks quickly to door.*) Here I am. (*She goes out with Steve and Babe.*)

JOHN—(*stares at the painting for a moment; then turns away impatiently*) What's the use of this pretence? I don't want to paint. (*He goes and sits down by Ted again.*) Did you hear what Bessie just said?

TED—No.

JOHN—Asked me if I'd been drinking; said she overheard something to that effect.

TED—(*shrugging his shoulders*) They say that about everybody who ever drank one glass of beer. Revengeful people with Brights Disease start those reports. Necessity is an awful virtue breeder.

JOHN—Damned luck! I don't want her to loose faith in me.

TED—I suppose you denied it?

JOHN—Of course; what else could I do?

TED—Confess you drank when you felt like it. Your sister isn't a prude. She'd simply tell you not to overdo it.

JOHN—But that's what she insinuated—that I was overdoing it.

TED—Everyone who drinks overdoes it sometimes. Speaking of this terrible vice reminds me; I think I have a bottle hidden in yonder kitchinette. (*He walks over to the kitchinette.*) You'll have a hair of the dog, won't you?

JOHN—No, I'm going to cut it out.

TED—(*from inside*) Got the R.E.s?

JOHN—(*fidgetting nervously*) Oh, I guess I will have one after all. There's no use playing the Spartan.

TED—Right you are. (*He comes out with three glasses, one full of water, and lays them on the table; then takes a pint of whiskey from his pocket and uncorks it; places it on the table beside glasses.*) My lord, breakfast is served. (*sings*) "Ho, shun the flowing cup!" Better come along, Jonathan. (*John goes to table and pours out a drink. Ted does the same.*)

TED—Top o' the morning! (*raises his glass*)

JOHN—(*with sudden resolution pours his drink back into the bottle*) No, I'll be damned if I do. I've got to quit, that's all there is to it; and it might as well be now as anytime.

TED—As you like, senor. Skoll! (*He tosses down his drink; then makes a wry face.*) Ugh! We must have been down on the water front when we did our shopping last night. (*John laughs; goes over to the easel and picks up his palette and brushes, and stands squinting at the painting critically. Ted takes out a box of cigarettes and lights one.*) Have a cigarette?

JOHN—No thanks.

TED—You're the slave of a fixed idea today. You're going to work whether you feel like it or not.

JOHN—(*laying down his brushes after making a few half-hearted dabs at the canvas*) You're right; I don't feel like eating, or drinking, or smoking—or painting. (*A timid knock on the door is heard.*)

TED—Who can that be?

JOHN—(*pointing to the bottle and glasses on the table*) Get that stuff out of the way. (*Ted hurries into the kitchinette with them and returns. The knock at the door is repeated, this time a little louder.*)

TED—Come in! (*The door is heard slowly opening and a girls voice asks in frightened tones:* "Does John Brown live here?")

JOHN—(*stunned for a moment, rushes to the door*) Maud! (*He disappears behind the corner of the kitchinette.*) You, too, Mother! What in the name of goodness brings you here? Come in, come in! (*Ted hides in the kitchinette as they enter the studio. A moment later the door is heard closing as he makes his escape. John leads his mother to a seat by the table. She is very frightened by her strange surroundings, and keeps her eyes resolutely down cast from the nudes on the walls. She does not seem to have aged or changed a particle—even her dress looks like the same. Maud has grown stouter, more womanly, in the two years which have elapsed. Her face is still full of a spoiled wilfulness, but it is much less marked in character than before. She is stylishly dressed in white and looks very charming.*)

JOHN—(*taking Maud in his arms and kissing her*) Oh, Maudie, it's so good to see you again! You'll pardon us, Mother, I hope?

MRS. BROWN—(*with an embarrassed smile*) Oh, don't mind me.

MAUD—Why, you're all over with paint! Just look at him, Mrs. Brown. Look at your face. You're like an Indian in war-paint. (*carefully examining the front of her dress*) I do hope you haven't got any of it on my dress.

JOHN—No, you're as spotless as when you entered.

MRS. BROWN—Hm— You haven't been working today, have you, John?—Sunday?

JOHN—It's the only day I have free for painting, Mother.

MRS. BROWN—Weren't you afraid someone would come in and see you—dressed like that? Why I do believe you haven't any socks on!

JOHN—The people who call here don't judge you by your clothes.

MAUD—Oh, Mrs. Brown, I think he looks so picturesque—just like the people you read about in the Paris Latin Quarter.

MRS. BROWN—But on a Sunday!

JOHN—Nonsense, Mother, this isn't Bridgetown.

MAUD—(*who is walking around looking at the paintings*) Everything looks the same as the last time I was here: still the same shocking old pictures. (*stops before the picture of an old hag*) Oh! Is this one of yours? Isn't she horrid! How could you ever do it?

JOHN—(*bruskely*) She really looked that way, you know. (*abruptly changing the subject*) But you haven't told me yet what happy chance brings you down here. (*Maud sits down on the window-seat.*)

MRS. BROWN—Hm—, Edward came with us; he's going to call for us here.

JOHN—(*coldly*) Oh, is he? But what are you down for—a shopping trip?

MRS. BROWN—(*nervously*) Yes,—hm, of course we expect to do some shopping tomorrow before we—you know we're going back tomorrow night—hm—but I can hardly say—hm, shopping was not the—hm— (*She becomes miserably confused and turns to Maud beseechingly.*)

MAUD—Perhaps I better tell him?

MRS. BROWN—(*immensely relieved*) Yes, do.

MAUD—Its a long story, John, and you must promise not to interrupt.

JOHN—I promise.

MAUD—Well, your mother has been terribly worried about you; and I've been worried to death about you, too.

JOHN—(*tenderly*) Maudie!

MAUD—Sssshhh! You promised not to interrupt. Your father, too—we've all been so afraid something had happened to you.

JOHN—But my letters to you?

MAUD—No interruptions, you promised. I thought maybe you were telling fibs in your letters just to keep me from worrying; and you were. You said you never felt better or more contented, and I could tell the moment I saw you that wasn't so. You look frightfully worn out and ill; doesn't he, Mrs. Brown?

MRS. BROWN—He doesn't look at all well.

JOHN—(*impatiently*) Its nothing. I've been troubled with insomnia, thats all.

MAUD—Then you see you're not contented and you *were*

telling fibs. Don't look so impatient! I'm coming to the rest of the story. Your mother was making herself ill wondering if you were starving with the army of the unemployed or something of that sort; and I was tearing my hair at the thought that you had fallen in love with some beautiful model and—

JOHN—Maudie!

MAUD—You know your letters have been getting fewer and fewer, and each one shorter than the last. I didn't know what to think.

JOHN—I couldn't write much. It was always the same old story. I didn't want to bore you with my disappointments. I was waiting for good news to tell you; then I'd have written a long letter, you can be sure of that. But what you said about models—most of them aren't beautiful, you know—you don't believe anything like that?

MAUD—Silly boy! Of course I was only joking. Anyway, your mother and I made up this expedition—with your father's permission—got Edward to come with us, and hurried down to this wicked old city—to rescue you!

JOHN—To rescue me!

MAUD—Yes; you've just simply got to stop breaking people's hearts and homes. We're going to take you back to Bridgetown, a prisoner. (*John walks up and down nervously.*) Then we'll be able to keep an eye on you and see that you don't starve or get sick.

JOHN—(*annoyed*) Maudie!

MAUD—Dad told me to tell you he had just the nicest position in the store for you; you can get off at least one afternoon a week if you care to keep up your painting. We can announce our wedding right away, and we'll be married in the fall or (*looking at him shyly*) even sooner, if you like. I've picked out just the most adorable little house and Dad's agreed to give us that for a wedding present. (*John is striding backward and forward his hands clenched tightly behind him. He keeps his head lowered and does not look at Maud.*) And *your* father—he has the dandiest surprise in store for you; only I'm not to tell you about it. Isn't it all fine? (*John groans but does not answer her. Maud is troubled by his silence.*) You'll come with us, won't you?

JOHN—(*brokenly*) Maudie—you know—I can't.

MAUD—(*her lips trembling, her eyes filling with tears*) You won't come!

JOHN—I'd like to, dear; with all my heart and soul I want to do as you ask—I love you so much—you know that—but— Oh, don't you understand! you must realize in your heart—why I can't. (*There is a long pause. Maud turns and stares down at the street below, winking back her tears.*)

MRS. BROWN—(*wiping her eyes with her handkerchief*) Don't decide so soon, Johnnie. Think over it. (*with a desperate attempt to change the subject before the question is irrevocably decided*) Have you seen Bessie lately?

JOHN—Yes; today; just before you came. She stopped in with Babe.

MRS. BROWN—She's well, I hope?

JOHN—Never better, and just as happy as she can be. She and Babe are getting along in fine shape.

MRS. BROWN—That's good news, I'm sure;—hm,—isn't it, Maud?

MAUD—(*coldly*) I'm glad to hear it. (*There is a knock at the door.*)

MRS. BROWN—That must be Edward.

JOHN—(*gruffly*) Come in. (*The door is opened and Edward enters. He seems less pompous and more self-assured than in Act 1. In appearance he is practically unchanged. His clothes are a model of sober immaculateness.*)

EDWARD—Here you are, I see. (*coldly*) How are you, John? (*They shake hands in a perfunctory manner. Edward casts a disapproving glance around the room. His eyes finally rest on John's paint-stained clothes. There is a trace of scorn in his manner.*) I must say you look the part of the artist.

JOHN—(*with a sneer*) I dare say. You can't paint and keep clean. I suppose it's much the same in politics.

EDWARD—(*stiffening*) We will not discuss that. Are you still employed on the dock?

JOHN—Yes.

EDWARD—Have you sold any pictures yet?

JOHN—No.

EDWARD—Is it an artistic custom to work on Sunday?

JOHN—We work when we please, whenever we have an opportunity. As I reminded Mother, you're in New York now, not Bridgetown. (*Edward turns to his mother. She persistently avoids his eyes.*)

EDWARD—(*after a long pause*) Well, Mother, is the purpose of this visit fulfilled?

MRS. BROWN—Hm—; yes—er—you might say,—hm; but no,—you'd hardly call it—

EDWARD—(*turns impatiently to Maud*) Have you told him, Maud?

MAUD—(*dully*) Yes.

EDWARD—And he's coming with us, of course?

MAUD—(*with difficulty*) No; he won't come. (*She raises her handkerchief to her eyes and commences to cry softly.*)

JOHN—(*starting to go to her*) Maudie, please!

EDWARD—(*stopping him*) Is this true?

JOHN—(*defiantly*) Quite true.

EDWARD—Then all I have to say is, you are guilty of the most shameless ingratitude, not only to your own family, but particularly to Maud and her father. Every kindness has been lavished on you and this is the way you repay us.

MRS. BROWN—Edward!

EDWARD—Let me speak, Mother; it's time someone brought John to his senses. He has been riding rough-shod over all of us for years. Its my duty to show him the wreck he is making of his own life.

JOHN—By all means do your duty, Mr. Alderman. Let me hear what you have to say.

EDWARD—Did Maud tell you of her father's offer and of all that will be done for you?

JOHN—Yes.

EDWARD—You have sold no pictures and you have no hope of selling any.

JOHN—Very little, at present.

EDWARD—You still support yourself as a checker on the docks and only get twelve dollars a week?

JOHN—Exactly.

EDWARD—And you refuse to come back! Have you no heart? Can you see Maud weeping with the unhappiness you cause her by your selfish obstinacy and still refuse?

MAUD—(*starting to her feet, her eyes flashing*) Edward! Don't bring—

JOHN—(*wildly excited*) Yes, I *can* refuse, for Maud's sake most of all. Would you have me give up like a craven; be untrue to my highest hope; slink home a self-confessed failure? Would you have Maud married to such a moral coward? You, with your bread and butter viewpoint of life, probably can't appreciate such feelings but—

EDWARD—There is no more to be said. I call upon you to witness, Mother, that I have done all in my power to persuade John to return.

JOHN—Wait a minute; I begin to see things clearly. I begin to see through your canting pose about duty. Don't think you can fool me with your moral platitudes, your drivel about my ingratitude; for I think—no, by God, I'm sure,—you're only too glad I did refuse.

EDWARD—(*in great confusion*) I? I protest, Mother,—

MRS. BROWN AND MAUD—Johnnie! John!

JOHN—Oh, he knows its the truth! Look at him!

EDWARD—(*growing red*) Why should I be glad? It's of no importance to me—

JOHN—Because right down in your heart you think my refusal will end things between Maud and me and give you another chance.

MAUD—Oh, John, how can— (*Mrs. Brown is beyond speech.*)

EDWARD—(*summoning all his dignity*) I will not deny that I want to see Maud happy.

JOHN—(*with a loud forced laugh*) But you don't think she'll be happy with anyone but you! Well spoken, Mr. Platitude! It's the first real manly thing I've ever heard you say—the only time I've ever known you not to play the sanctimonious hypocrite.

EDWARD—(*raging*) How dare you—

MRS. BROWN—Do stop, Edward!

MAUD—John, please—

EDWARD—I will tell you this. I *do not* think you a fit husband for Maud; for I think I know the real reason for your refusal to come home; and Maud shall know it, too.

JOHN—And what is this reason?

EDWARD—You are mixed up with some woman down here and—

JOHN—(*white with fury*) Liar! (*He strikes Edward in the face with his fist almost knocking him down. Maud steps in between them. Mrs. Brown goes to Edward.*)

MRS. BROWN—Now, Edward, for my sake!

MAUD—John, this is disgraceful—your own brother!

EDWARD—All right, Mother, I forgive him for striking me, but I retract nothing. (*He walks toward door.*) Are you coming with me?

MRS. BROWN—Yes, yes. Good'bye Johnnie. I'll be in tomorrow before we go—hm—or you telephone to the hotel, will you?

JOHN—Yes, Mother. (*He kisses her. She joins Edward near the door.*)

EDWARD—Are you coming, Maud?

MAUD—Yes.

JOHN—Maudie!

MAUD—Don't speak to me!

JOHN—(*in desperation*) But you don't—you can't—believe what he said.

MAUD—(*with a sob*) Oh, how can you act so! I don't know what to believe.

JOHN—This is the end, then.

MAUD—Yes. (*She walks past him to the others at the door. They go out. John flings himself face downward on the divan near the piano. His shoulders shake as if he were sobbing. After about a minute the door is flung open and Maud rushes in. John starts up from the divan and she runs into his arms.*)

MAUD—(*between sobs*) You *do* care! You've been crying! Oh, please Johnnie dear, come back with us. Please if you love me. I do love you so much! Won't you please do this for my sake—just this once for my sake—I love you—I don't want you down here—I don't believe what Edward said— but still it might happen if you never saw me. If you love me, won't you please for my sake?

JOHN—(*slowly—his will broken*) All right—I'll come back —for your sake.

MAUD—Promise?

JOHN—I promise. (*He kisses her.*)

MAUD—Oh, I'm so glad. We're just going to be so happy, aren't we, dear? (*John kisses her again.*)

(The Curtain Falls)

ACT 4

SCENE—*The sitting-room of John Brown's home in Bridgetown, a little before one o'clock on a fine July day two years later. In the extreme left foreground a door leading to the dining-room. Farther back a projecting chimney papered over, and an open fire-place with black andirons. Above, a mantle on which is a brass clock flanked by a china vase on either end. Beyond the fireplace an arm chair stands stiffly against the wall. Still farther back a door leading to the hall. The door is pushed back against the far wall. Next to the door a chair, then a window opening on the verandah, a long sofa, another window, and in the corner a wicker-work rocking chair. On the right wall by the rocking chair a window looking out on the street, a piano with a stool placed before it, and a music stand piled with sheets of music. Finally in the extreme right foreground another window with a round table in front and to the left of it. On the table a lace center-piece and a potted maidenhair fern. The hardwood floor is almost completely hidden by a large rug. In the center of the room a table with wicker-work rocking chairs around it. On the table an electric reading-lamp wired from the chandelier, and a Sunday newspaper. The windows are all lace-curtained. The walls are papered in dark green. In startling incongruity with the general commonplace aspect of the room are two paintings in the Impressionist style, a landscape and a seascape, one of which hangs over the mantle and the other over the piano.*

The front door is heard opening and closing and Maud and Edward enter from the hall. Her two years of married life have told on Maud. She is still pretty but has faded, grown prim and hardened, has lines of fretful irritation about her eyes and mouth, and wears the air of one who has been cheated in the game of life and knows it; but will even up the scale by making those around her as wretched as possible. Her Sunday gown is so gay and pretty she looks almost out of place in it. Edward, too, has aged perceptibly, but his general appearance is practically the same. He is dressed after his usual faultlessly-staid fashion.

MAUD—So good of you to walk home with me. You must sit down for a while. It's been ages since we've had a talk together. (*She sits down by the table.*)

EDWARD—(*taking a chair near the table*) Thank you, I will; but only for a moment.

MAUD—How can you rush off so after all the time it's been since you were here before! You aren't very considerate of your friends.

EDWARD—(*gravely*) You know, Maud, you would never have to complain of me in that respect were it not for John's bitter dislike,—I might more truthfully call it hatred. He would surely misinterpret my visits; as he did when he practically put me out of this house six months ago.

MAUD—(*her face hardening*) I told John at that time, and I tell you now, Edward, this is my house and my friends are always welcome in it.

EDWARD—Of course, Maud, of course; but then I like to avoid all such unpleasantness,—for your sake, especially.

MAUD—A little more or less wouldn't make much difference; but let's not talk of that. Why, I haven't even congratulated you yet, Mr. Congressman!

EDWARD—(*flushing with pleasure*) Oh, nothing's decided yet,—definitely. Of course I will take the nomination if it's offered to me,—as I'm quite sure it will be; but getting elected is another matter.

MAUD—How can you have any doubts after your wonderful victory in the election for Mayor last fall? The biggest majority they ever gave anyone in the history of the town, wasn't it?

EDWARD—Oh yes, but this is entirely different,—the whole district, you see; and in some parts of it I'm hardly known at all.

MAUD—I *know* you'll be elected, so there! (*Edward smiles but shakes his head.*) Will you make a bet? A pair of gloves against a box of cigars,—real cigars; you can pick them out yourself. You're afraid! I won't tell on you for gambling.

EDWARD—Oh now, Maud, what difference does—

MAUD—Is it done?

EDWARD—Done.

MAUD—I won't have to buy any gloves then. What will come after the Congressman? Will it be governor or senator?

EDWARD—(*immensely pleased, bows to her smilingly*) You are altogether too flattering, my dear Maud.

MAUD—(*suddenly becoming melancholy*) Oh, it must be fine

to keep going upward step by step and getting somewhere, instead of sticking in one place all the time without hope of advancement. You are known all over the state now and you'll soon be going to Washington, and after that,—who knows? While to us, Bridgetown is the whole world. Promise you won't forget all about us when you leave?

EDWARD—(*earnestly*) You know I could never forget you, Maud.

MAUD—When you go to Washington—

EDWARD—I haven't got there yet.

MAUD—But you will. Then you'll forget all us poor, unhappy small-town people.

EDWARD—Unhappy?

MAUD—Certainly not happy.

EDWARD—No, you are *not* happy. It shows in all your actions. Has John— Where is he now?

MAUD—Still in bed.

EDWARD—What! Is he sick?

MAUD—(*bitterly*) People who don't come in until three in the morning usually are.

EDWARD—You don't mean to say he doesn't—

MAUD—Oh, it's only on Saturday nights when he goes to the club to meet Harry and the other town sports.

EDWARD—Hm— A man at the club was speaking to me about this; said I'd better give John a word of advice. Of course he didn't know of our—er—strained relations. He said John was drinking altogether too much,—getting to be a regular thing with him.

MAUD—He couldn't know about that. John only goes to the club on Saturday nights; but he drinks quite a lot here at home.

EDWARD—Why don't you speak to him?

MAUD—I have; but he only laughs, and then we have another quarrel. That's all it is,—fight, fight, fight. He says he drinks to give life a false interest since it has no real one.

EDWARD—To say that to you! How can you stand it?

MAUD—I don't stand it. My patience is worn out. When he is with me I can't restrain myself. I fight; and he fights back; and there you are.

EDWARD—Too bad, too bad! Such a shocking state of

affairs, for you above all people; your home life with your father was always so ideal.

MAUD—Oh, you haven't heard the worst of it. Do you know, I even heard that John was associating with those low friends of Harry's,—women, I mean.

EDWARD—Good heavens!

MAUD—(*looking at him searchingly*) You have heard something of this; tell me truthfully, haven't you?

EDWARD—(*hesitating*) Oh, mere rumors; you know what the town is.

MAUD—Ah.

EDWARD—(*after a pause*) I cannot tell how it grieves me to see you in this state. I always had fears that John would fail in his duties as a husband. He has no stability, no—er— will power, as you might say. But to insult you in this gross manner is unthinkable.

MAUD—Have you no advice to give me?

EDWARD—You say you have urged him to reform his mode of living and he refuses? That you are continually quarrelling? That all these reports of—er—women keep coming to you.

MAUD—Yes yes, I hear all sorts of things.

EDWARD—Hm—, where there's so much smoke, you know—

MAUD—But what shall I do?

EDWARD—(*with an air of decision*) I advise you to sue for a divorce.

MAUD—(*astonished*) You, Edward, you think I ought—

EDWARD—I know it's quite against my principles. I have always held divorce to be the greatest evil of modern times and a grave danger to the social life of the nation; but there are cases—and yours is one of them—where there seems to be no other solution. Therefore I repeat, I advise you to free yourself from one who has proved himself so unworthy; and you know I have your interests at heart when I say it.

MAUD—Oh, I can't; it's impossible.

EDWARD—Why? You have no children.

MAUD—No, thank God!

EDWARD—You would have the sympathy of everyone. (*a pause*)

MAUD—I couldn't do it.

EDWARD—Surely you no longer care for him after—all you've told me.

MAUD—No,—but,— Oh, I don't know!

EDWARD—Pardon me if the question I am about to ask seems indelicate. It is to your interest to face facts. Are you still living with him—as his wife?

MAUD—Oh, you know I couldn't! How could you think so—after those reports.

EDWARD—Then why do you hesitate? Is it for his sake?

MAUD—(*fiercely*) Indeed not! He'd be only too glad to get rid of me. He'd be married again in a week,—to that horrible, divorced Mrs. Harper or some other of those rich summer people who are always inviting him to their houses and who think he's so fascinating. No, I'll not play into his hands by getting a divorce; you can say what you like.

EDWARD—(*gets up and goes over beside her chair*) Think of yourself, Maud. You are making yourself sick both in mind and body by remaining in such distressing environment. (*He takes one of her hands. She makes no effort to withdraw it.*) Listen to me, Maud. I love you, as you know. I have always loved you ever since I can remember having loved anyone. Let me take care of your future. Do as I have advised and I will protect you from everything that could possibly hurt you. I ask nothing for myself. My love for you has always been an unselfish one. I only want to see you happy, and to do all in my power to make you so. If, in after years, you could come to love me ever so little—you would be free—with such a hope my life would be—

MAUD—(*her face averted*) Don't, don't, I can't bear it.

EDWARD—Will you promise to consider what I have suggested?

MAUD—Yes. (*John appears in the doorway. He has evidently just risen for he is collarless, unshaven, and has on a faded bathrobe and bedroom slippers. He has grown stout and his face is flabby and pasty-complected, his eyes dull and lusterless. He watches his wife and brother with a cynical smile.*)

EDWARD—From the bottom of my heart I thank you. (*He raises Maud's hand to his lips.*)

JOHN—"Thou shalt not covet thy neighbor's wife." (*Maud*

screams. Edward straightens up with a jerk, his face crimson.) You seem to be forgetting the Lord's commandments on his own day, my worthy deacon. (*Edward stutters in confusion.*) Never try to make love, Edward. You look a fearful ass; and remember Maud is expressly forbidden to covet such animals in that same commandment. Sorry to disturb you. I'll cough the next time. (*He turns around and goes out.*)

EDWARD—(*furiously*) The scoundrel!

MAUD—Now you see what he's like.

EDWARD—I must go before he comes back—the good-for-nothing—I really can't contain myself; I wouldn't be responsible— (*He goes to door, then stops and turns to Maud.*) Good'bye; you won't forget your promise, Maud?

MAUD—I won't forget. (*Edward goes out. The outer door slams and he can be seen walking past the windows. Maud throws herself on the sofa and lies sobbing with her face buried in the pillows. John enters.*)

JOHN—Has the Passionate Pilgrim gone? (*He sits down by the table.*) Why all this fuss? You know I was only joking. I just wanted to take some of the moral starch out of that pompous ass. (*He takes up the newspaper and starts to read. It trembles in his shaking hand with an irritating rustling sound. Maud glances sharply at him with keen dislike in her eyes, opens her lips as if to say something, checks herself, taps the floor nervously with her foot, and finally bursts out*)

MAUD—A nice time to be lying around in that state! Don't you know it's Sunday? (*She pulls down shades of windows open on veranda.*)

JOHN—What of it?

MAUD—At least you might put on a collar and shave yourself.

JOHN—I might; but I'm not going to. What's the matter? Do you expect *other* callers?

MAUD—You never know who might come in on a Sunday.

JOHN—(*giving up the attempt to read by putting down his paper, speaks with nervous irritation*) But I know who won't come in—anyone of the slightest interest to me. If anyone comes I'll run and hide and you can tell them I'm out. They'll all be glad to hear it. Say I haven't come back from church yet; that ought to be scandal enough for one day.

MAUD—You mock at everything decent. However they all know where you are when you're out. You aren't fooling anybody and you needn't think you are.

JOHN—Ah.

MAUD—(*with rising anger*) In some bar-room.

JOHN—You forget, my dear, this is the Sabbath and all such dens of iniquity are closed by law of our God-fearing legislature—the front doors at least.

MAUD—Then you'd be up at the club with your drunken friends.

JOHN—(*flushing*) I would be; and I soon will be if you don't give up this constant nagging.

MAUD—Then come home at a decent hour. Act like a respectable man should and there won't be any nagging.

JOHN—You couldn't keep that promise. You've got the habit. You'd pick on me for something else. My drinking is only an excuse. There are plenty of so-called respectable citizens who drink more than I do; and you ought to know it if your gossiping friends ever air their malicious scandal about anyone but me.

MAUD—I have heard of one other.

JOHN—One? There is hope then.

MAUD—Your brother Harry.

JOHN—Harry's open about what he does and makes no pretence of being a saint. He's a lot better than those psalm-singing hypocrites of whom my respected brother Edward is the leader.

MAUD—Edward is a gentleman.

JOHN—Edward is a fool and (*as she is about to retort*) we will talk no more about him. I feel bad enough already without having to sit and listen while you din the praises of that pompous nincompoop into my ears. (*He picks up the paper again and goes through it hurriedly; finally finds page and begins reading. His hand shakes more than ever and the paper rustles until Maud turns to him sharply.*)

MAUD—For goodness sake, don't rustle that paper so.

JOHN—The excitement of quarrelling with my sweet wife has unnerved me.

MAUD—Last night unnerved you, you mean. Why didn't

you phone you weren't coming home to dinner? You knew I would wait.

JOHN—I told you never to wait after seven. Why will you persist in doing so and then blame me for it.

MAUD—You must think I like to eat alone.

JOHN—I very rarely fail to get here.

MAUD—You were at the club, I suppose? You always say that.

JOHN—And where would I be?

MAUD—You needn't look so innocent. I've heard things.

JOHN—You always do. What things?

MAUD—Have you had any breakfast yet?

JOHN—Damn breakfast! What is it you've heard this time from your select circle of the towns finest?

MAUD—They say you don't always spend your evenings at the club; that you've been seen with some of those low women Harry associates with.

JOHN—And you allow them to say such things?

MAUD—I told them there couldn't be any truth in such stories.

JOHN—(*ironically*) I thank you for your trust in me. I expected you to say you did believe them.

MAUD—I don't know what to believe. When a person drinks so much they're liable to do anything.

JOHN—That's all nonsense, Maud.

MAUD—And that trip of yours to New York last month when you went to see Bessie and said she wasn't there.

JOHN—And she wasn't; she and Babe were out of town.

MAUD—Someone said they saw you down there with some woman.

JOHN—Oh, for God's sake, Maud! (*He gets up and strides nervously around the room. A knocking is heard from the rear of the house.*)

MAUD—There's someone at the back door; and Annie's out, of course. (*She hurries out through the door to hall. John looks around furtively for a moment; then walks to dining-room door and goes in. He returns a moment later with a syphon of seltzer and a bottle of whiskey, and placing them on the table, mixes himself a drink. Maud comes back as he is drinking. She stands watching him with an expression of disgust.*)

MAUD—Can't you leave that horrible stuff alone for a moment?

JOHN—(*rather shamefacedly*) Just a little pick-me-up.

MAUD—(*sinking into a chair*) It's terrible.

JOHN—Don't take everything with such deadly seriousness. Plenty of men take a cocktail before breakfast.

MAUD—I don't know what will happen to us if you keep on this way.

JOHN—You forget, my dear, your tongue is calculated to drive anyone to drink; and things aren't as bad as you'd like to pretend. I see lots of people more unfortunate than you. Every little thing that happens you weep and wail as if the world were coming to an end. Why, in God's name, did you ever marry me?

MAUD—If I could have seen how things would be I'd never—

JOHN—Nor I; I gave up a career for you; and you gave up the righteous citizen Edward for me. We were both very foolish.

MAUD—(*stung by this mention of Edward*) Yes, Edward loved me, and in spite of all your superior sneers he's a better man than you are. All the town looks up to him. He got more votes for Mayor than anyone ever did before. That ought to convince anyone but you what people think of him; and everyone knows he's sure of going to Congress.

JOHN—I don't know which to sympathize with—Congress or Edward.

MAUD—(*furiously*) That's right; sneer! Sneer at everything and everyone; all failures do that. Yes, *failure*! I said it and I mean it. If it wasn't for my father we wouldn't even have this house; and if you weren't my husband, you couldn't keep your position in the store a single day longer. Father told me that himself. He said you weren't worth a bit more to the business now than the day you came in. He said you took absolutely no interest in it at all.

JOHN—He's right, there.

MAUD—Then why do you stay in it? (*John shruggs his shoulders but does not answer. He is very pale.*) Because you know you'd never get a job anywhere else. You might at least be grateful to him for what he's done for you; but instead all you do is sneer at him and his business. You pretend to be too artistic to lower yourself to make money; but I see through your high-art pose. You never made a success of that either. Oh, I don't know how I stand it.

JOHN—(*turning to her quickly*) Ah, now you ask the leading question. Why do you stand it?

MAUD—What do you mean?

JOHN—Simply this: You've stated the truth. Our life together is impossible and the sooner we recognize that fact and do what we can to rectify it, the better for both of us. We're young and life may still hold something pleasant if we've only the courage to break our chains. When nothing is left of the old love but wrangling and distrust, it's high time for us to give up this farce of life together.

MAUD—You mean divorce?

JOHN—Yes. Let's be frank. You hate me and I confess I— but no matter. Such being the undeniable case, is there any reason in God's world why we should be confined together like two cats in a bag? Get a divorce! I'll gladly give you all the evidence you need.

MAUD—I don't doubt that for a moment.

JOHN—Remember you're young,—and Edward is still a bachelor. I'm sure he'd provide balm for your woes, even if his political career suffered from his marrying a divorced woman. I give him credit for being red-blooded in that one respect at least. (*a pause during which Maud bites her lips in nervous anger*) Hasn't he spoken to you about a divorce in your conferences together?

MAUD—No— Yes, why should I deny it? He has spoken of it, and I absolutely refused to consider it.

JOHN—And why, if I may ask?

MAUD—(*defiantly*) I will never get a divorce; you understand—never!

JOHN—I can't see why you want to live with me.

MAUD—Can't you? Well, I haven't your loose morals. I was brought up to regard marriage as a sacred thing; not as something to be thrown aside as soon as one gets tired of it. If I were to get a divorce, think of the scandal, think of what people would say.

JOHN—As if one cared!

MAUD—Well, I do care and I won't do it. Do you think I don't know what's behind your talk? You want to get rid of me so you'll have a chance to run after your Mrs. Harpers, your artists models, and creatures of that sort. I tell you right now I'll never give you the chance. Disgrace yourself, if you will, but don't ask me to make your path easy.

JOHN—(*quietly*) Then let's say no more about it. (*He takes up the paper. Maud fumes and bites her lips. Suddenly John's eye catches an item in the paper and he gives an exclamation of excitement.*) Here, listen to this. You knew Babe Carter well in the old days. This is a criticism of the paintings at the Independent Exhibition. It says: (*reads*) "Mr. Carter is without doubt one of the most promising of the younger school. His work is steadily increasing in worth, and some of his seascapes, notably 'The Coral Reef', deserve to rank among the best painted in recent years by any American." (*putting down the paper, his face glowing with enthusiasm*) Great work! Good old Babe! What do you think of that, Maud? Won't Bessie be tickled to death when she reads that.

MAUD—Then she's still living with him?

JOHN—Of course she is. They're as much in love now as the day they were married. What made you think any differently?

MAUD—Things of that sort don't last long, generally.

JOHN—Things of what sort?

MAUD—Marriages of that kind.

JOHN—What kind? I don't know what you're talking about. If ever two people were absolutely fitted for each other, Babe and Bess are.

MAUD—Oh, I don't mean that.

JOHN—What do you mean?

MAUD—(*spitefully*) They say he was forced to marry her on account of their previous intimacy.

JOHN—(*not understanding for a second; then springing to his feet in a furious rage and standing over her, his fists clenched*) How dare you repeat such a damnable lie! How dare you—

MAUD—(*genuinely frightened—shrinking away from him*) That's right; strike me! It only remains for you to do that.

JOHN—(*recovering himself*) Strike you? Are you crazy? Bah! Such pitiful slanders are beneath notice. I'm surprised that you, who pretend to be her friend, should repeat such calumnies. You're letting your temper carry you beyond all bounds.

MAUD—I never approved of her meeting Carter in secret.

JOHN—But you know there's no truth in what you said as well as— (*He is interrupted by a ring of the door-bell.*)

MAUD—There! I knew someone would come; and here you are in that dirty bath-robe and not even shaved. (*She goes cautiously to the window and peeks out.*) I think— (*in tones of great astonishment*) Yes, it's Bessie. What can she be doing here?

JOHN—(*irritably*) Well, why doesn't someone go to the door?

MAUD—I told you Annie was out. (*The bell rings again.*)

JOHN—Then I'll go and, remember, I won't allow her to be insulted by you or anyone else.

MAUD—I refuse to see her. (*She goes out by the door to the dining-room. John strides into the hallway and opens the front door. "Hello, Bessie." Their voices can be heard exchanging greetings. A moment later Bessie enters with John. What little change she has undergone has been decidedly for the better. An atmosphere of hope fulfilled and happiness attained, which is like an affront to John in his state of nervous melancholia, springs from her person. John feels it and glances with sudden shame at the bottle on the table.*)

BESSIE—(*sitting down*) Wheres Maud?

JOHN—(*angry at being forced to lie*) Oh, out somewhere, church or someplace. (*He slouches miserably into his chair.*)

BESSIE—Sorry she's not here. How is she?

JOHN—As usual.

BESSIE—(*giving him a searching glance—quietly*) And you?

JOHN—Oh, I'm all right, I suppose. (*a pause—suddenly he breaks out with angry impatience*) What rot! Why should I lie and keep up this pretence to you? I can at least be frank with you. Nothing is all right. Everything about me has degenerated since you saw me last. My family life is unbearable. Maud hates me and I— So much for the soothing atmosphere of our home.

BESSIE—You're sure it isn't just an attack of Sabbath blues.

JOHN—I wish it were. The truth is Maud and I have

become disillusioned. I know there's nothing so out of the ordinary in that. Most married couples I have no doubt, go through the same thing. The trouble with us is we've gone to the bitter end. There are no veils left to tear off. We're two corpses chained together.

BESSIE—It's too bad. I always thought your marriage would prove a disappointment but I never dreamed it would be as bad as this. I hoped you'd finally grow used to each other and compromise. (*after a pause*—*musingly*) The pity of it is, you're neither of you really to blame. It's simply the conflict of character. You'll grind together until both are worn out.

JOHN—You're right; Death is the only cure for this marriage.

BESSIE—(*smiling*) Or divorce.

JOHN—You forget my wife is a good member of the church. She has principles. She remembers the sacred duty of every God-fearing wife toward her husband—to make him as miserable as possible. She hates me, but she'll not forego her ownership, her power to strangle what little aspiration I have left, simply because she's afraid some other woman might claim me.

BESSIE—Surely she can't have become the terrible creature you describe. You have no children—

JOHN—No, thank God!

BESSIE—And yet you say she refuses to get a divorce?

JOHN—Yes; we had it all out before you came. She absolutely refused to consider it; and for the exact reason I've told you—because, although she doesn't want me, she's determined no other woman shall get me. So you see I didn't exaggerate. I've put the case mildly. There's no way out. (*with bitter irony*) She's such a good woman I could never hope to get a divorce from her.

BESSIE—Why not run away? I think she'd soon grow more reasonable if she felt she'd lost you.

JOHN—You mistake. That would be just what she desires. As the abandoned wife, the martyr, she would glory in the sympathy of the whole town. It would be too dear a pose for her ever willingly to relinquish. (*He stares moodily before him. Bessie looks at him with pitying surprise as if in her state of hap-*

piness she could conceive of his misfortune only as something vague and incredible.) Besides there are other reasons. I have no money. Manna no longer falls from heaven. How would I live? I only keep my present position, as Maud constantly reminds me, because I'm Steele's son-in-law. As a wage-earner I'm a colossal failure. You know the struggle I had to keep alive when my allowance was withdrawn. It would be a million times worse now. (*despondently*) As I said before there's no way out but—the end.

BESSIE—Nonsense! Have you done any painting lately?

JOHN—None at all. I used to go out on Sundays when I first came up, and do a little.

BESSIE—You ought to have kept up your drawing, at least; especially after Colper's Weekly accepted those things of yours.

JOHN—Do you remember me telling you I received their check the day before I was married? Oh, if I'd only had the courage to turn back then! They asked me if I cared to do some illustrating for them,—and I never answered their letter. You see I was determined for Maud's sake to put the old life completely behind me.

BESSIE—But your letters were always so enthusiastic—

JOHN—Oh, I've lied to you and the rest of the world until I guess noone doubts I'm the happiest married man on earth. Why, I've lied even to myself and shut my eyes to the truth. The struggle to appear happy has worn me out. I used to paint a bit, but Maud didn't want me to leave her alone and was bored if she came with me, and I slid deeper and deeper into the rut and gave up altogether. (*He sighs.*) Just plain degeneration, you see.

BESSIE—(*pointing to the bottle on the table with frank disgust*) Don't you think that may be to blame for this degenerating?

JOHN—(*indifferently*) Oh, I suppose so.

BESSIE—I thought you never—

JOHN—I never did—much, until lately. So you can see it isn't the cause but the result of my degeneration. It makes me callous and lets me laugh at my own futility. That's about the best I can hope for.

BESSIE—(*determined to guide the conversation into more*

pleasant channels) Speaking about painting, I suppose you've heard about Harrington?

JOHN—No, I haven't heard from Steve in a long time.

BESSIE—You know he went to Paris. Well, he's been very successful over there—painting in the Salon and I don't know what else. Babe received a letter from him about two weeks ago, and he wants Babe to come over; and the best part of it is we're going. Babe had a streak of unheard-of luck last month and sold three of his paintings. We figure that with this money and what we've saved we ought to be able to remain there a year. Just think of it—a year in Paris! Of course, we'll have to practice the strictest economy; but then we're used to that. We're going to leave within two weeks at the latest. That's why I came up. I wanted to see you and say good'bye to the folks before we left. Isn't it fine?

JOHN—(*trying his best to share in her enthusiasm in spite of the distressing contrast in their fortunes*) I'm awful glad to hear it, Bess. There's noone in the world I'd rather see happy than you and Babe. (*He turns away to hide his emotion.*)

BESSIE—(*seeing that something is wrong—with a sudden intuition runs to him and throws her arms around him*) What a beast I am! Flaunting our measly success in your face as if I were trying to torment you!

JOHN—It's all right—just my damn peevishness. I guess I've got an attack of what you called "Sabbath blues" after all.

BESSIE—Listen; why don't you come with us? You can raise enough money for that. It'll give you a new start. Never mind what anyone thinks. You can come back and square it all later on. It's a shame to see you going to seed in this beastly old town.

JOHN—(*after a pause—firmly*) No. It would only add one more failure to the list. I have no more confidence in myself. The incentive is gone. Besides you and Babe are just becoming reconciled with the family. They would never forgive you if I went away with you.

BESSIE—That doesn't matter.

JOHN—Oh, yes it does matter; or it will later on. I just simply can't go. Let's not talk of it. (*Bessie goes slowly over and sits down again.*) What do you hear from Ted?

BESSIE—He's dramatic critic on a Chicago newspaper; does lots of magazine work, too. He's the same old Ted though and heaven only knows how long he'll stand prosperity. Haven't you seen any of his stuff?

JOHN—I rarely read any more, magazines or anything else.

BESSIE—Don't you hear from any of the old crowd at all?

JOHN—They used to write but I never had anything to tell them but my failures so I was too ashamed to answer. (*Bessie can find nothing to say—a pause.*) I saw that notice about Babe in todays Times.

BESSIE—What notice?

JOHN—Haven't you seen it? (*He finds the item and hands it to her.*) Here. It's the best write-up I've ever seen them give anyone.

BESSIE—(*reads the notice, tries to hide her exultation, and contents herself with saying as she lays down the paper*) Very nice of them.

JOHN—(*gloomily*) They've all come to the top but me. What would Grammont say if he were still alive.

BESSIE—You talk like an old man,—as if life were over and done with.

JOHN—It is.

BESSIE—(*rather weary of his gloom*) Oh, cheer up! Come out and get the air. Take a walk over to the house with me. By the way, how is everybody?

JOHN—They haven't changed a bit, unfortunately. Harry is more human than he used to be, and Edward less human, and Mary more prim; but the changes are hardly noticeable.

BESSIE—I gather from mother's letters Edward is now the hope of the town.

JOHN—He's Mayor—you know that—and he's going to run for Congress.

BESSIE—Oh dear! And I suppose I'll have to kiss him.

JOHN—(*with a faint smile*) He'll deem it your patriotic duty. (*Bessie laughs.*)

BESSIE—Well, I must go.

JOHN—Come over tomorrow night. You'll be here, won't you?

BESSIE—I'll stay a couple of days if I can stand it. Come

on and walk over with me. You're bad company for yourself today.

JOHN—No, I'm not shaved or anything else. I'll drop over tonight. I don't feel equal to a dose of Edward's platitudes this afternoon. (*Bessie walks into the hall followed by John. Their voices can be heard saying* "Good'bye for the present" *etc. The door is heard closing and John comes back into the room. He goes to the table and picks up the bottle as if to pour out a drink; then puts it down again with an exclamation of disgust. He sits down in the chair, his head in his hands, a picture of despondency. Maud enters from the dining room. Her face is twisted with the rage she is holding back only by the most violent effort.*)

MAUD—Your lunch is ready. What made her leave so soon?

JOHN—She hasn't seen the folks yet. She had to go there.

MAUD—She's all dressed up. Carter must be making money. (*John is silent. Maud continues trying to conceal her anger.*) So they're going to Paris?

JOHN—Ah, I might have known it.

MAUD—Known what?

JOHN—Known you'd been listening. I hope you're satisfied with what you heard. Listeners, you know, never hear good of themselves.

MAUD—(*losing control of herself*) Yes, I listened, you—you —you beast, you!—to tell—to talk that way about me— about your wife— I heard you— You said I hated you— Well, I do hate you!—sponging on my father—you drunken good-for-nothing—tell her you wanted to get rid of me— make fun of me to an outsider— What is she I'd like to know—the things I've heard about her—married to poverty-stricken artist who's no good— "Come to Paris with us"— Nice advice to give to a married man— And you— Have you no respect for anything?

JOHN—(*very pale, a wild look of despair in his eyes*) Maud! Stop! Won't you please let me alone for a while.

MAUD—(*panting in her fury; her words jumbled out between gasps*) You loafer you!— I couldn't believe my ears—you, to do such a thing— She'll tell everybody— She'll laugh at us— and I'll be to blame— She'll see to that— She won't blame you—but I'll surprise her— I'll tell your family about her—

"Come to Paris with us"— I'll tell father, too— I know some things about her— And you won't get any divorce—not as long as I live—to throw me aside like an old rag—you drunken beast!—to go and live with some low woman of the streets— That's it— I'm not low enough for you— You don't know what a good woman is— And she— I've been a fool— I've always defended her— I wouldn't believe what they said— and this is the thanks I get—asking you to abandon your wife! But I believe their stories now— I know what she is— She's a bad woman— She lived with Carter before— Oooohh!

JOHN—(*his face livid with rage, springs at her and clutches her by the throat*) You devil of a woman! (*Maud pulls at his arms with her hands, her scream strangled into a shrill wheeze. John realizes what he is doing and pushes her from him. She falls to the floor and lies there sobbing convulsively. John looks around him wildly as if he were seeking some place of escape.*) By God, there's an end to everything! (*He rushes out of the door to hall and can be heard running up the stairs. Then for an instant a great silence broods over the house. It is broken by the muffled report of a revolver sounding from the floor above. Some thing falls heavily in the room overhead. Maud springs to her feet and stands in a tense attitude, listening. Then a look of horrified comprehension passes over her face and, shrieking with terror, she rushes to the hall, and a moment later can be seen running past the front windows, her hair dishevelled, her hands pressed over her ears. Her screams grow gradually fainter.*)

(*The Curtain Falls*)

BOUND EAST FOR CARDIFF

A Play in One Act

CHARACTERS

Yank
Driscoll
Cocky
Davis
Scotty
Olson
Paul
Smitty
Ivan
The Captain
The Second Mate

Bound East for Cardiff

SCENE—*The seamen's forecastle of the British tramp steamer* Glencairn *on a foggy night midway on the voyage between New York and Cardiff. An irregular shaped compartment, the sides of which almost meet at the far end to form a triangle. Sleeping bunks about six feet long, ranged three deep with a space of three feet separating the upper from the lower, are built against the sides. On the right above the bunks three or four portholes can be seen. In front of the bunks, rough wooden benches. Over the bunks on the left, a lamp in a bracket. In the left foreground, a doorway. On the floor near it, a pail with a tin dipper. Oilskins are hanging from a hook near the doorway.*

The far side of the forecastle is so narrow that it contains only one series of bunks.

In under the bunks a glimpse can be had of sea chests, suit cases, seaboots, etc., jammed in indiscriminately.

At regular intervals of a minute or so the blast of the steamer's whistle can be heard above all the other sounds.

Five men are sitting on the benches talking. They are dressed in dirty patched suits of dungaree, flannel shirts, and all are in their stocking feet. Four of the men are pulling on pipes and the air is heavy with rancid tobacco smoke. Sitting on the top bunk in the left foreground, a Norwegian, Paul, is softly playing some folk song on a battered accordion. He stops from time to time to listen to the conversation.

In the lower bunk in the rear a dark-haired, hard-featured man is lying apparently asleep. One of his arms is stretched limply over the side of the bunk. His face is very pale, and drops of clammy perspiration glisten on his forehead.

It is nearing the end of the dog watch—about ten minutes to eight in the evening.

COCKY—(*a weazened runt of a man. He is telling a story. The others are listening with amused, incredulous faces, interrupting him at the end of each sentence with loud derisive guffaws.*) Makin' love to me, she was! It's Gawd's truth! A bloomin' nigger. Greased all over with cocoanut oil, she was. Gawd blimey, I couldn't stand 'er. Bloody old cow, I says; and with that I fetched 'er a biff on the ear wot knocked 'er silly, an'— (*He is interrupted by a roar of laughter from the others.*)

DAVIS—(*a middle-aged man with black hair and mustache*) You're a liar, Cocky.

SCOTTY—(*a dark young fellow*) Ho-ho! Ye werr neverr in New Guinea in yourr life, I'm thinkin'.

OLSON—(*a Swede with a drooping blonde mustache—with ponderous sarcasm*) Yust tink of it! You say she wass a cannibal, Cocky?

DRISCOLL—(*a brawny Irishman with the battered features of a prizefighter*) How cud ye doubt ut, Ollie? A quane av the naygurs she musta been surely. Who else wud think herself aqual to fallin' in love wid a beauthiful, divil-may-care rake av a man the loike av Cocky? (*a burst of laughter from the crowd*)

COCKY—(*indignantly*) Gawd strike me dead if it ain't true, every bleedin' word of it. 'Appened ten year ago come Christmas.

SCOTTY—'Twas a Christmas dinner she had her eyes on.

DAVIS—He'd a been a tough old bird.

DRISCOLL—'Tis lucky for both av ye ye escaped; for the quane av the cannibal isles wad 'a died av the belly ache the day afther Christmas, divil a doubt av ut. (*The laughter at this is long and loud.*)

COCKY—(*sullenly*) Blarsted fat 'eads! (*The sick man in the lower bunk in the rear groans and moves restlessly. There is a hushed silence. All the men turn and stare at him.*)

DRISCOLL—Ssshh! (*in a hushed whisper*) We'd best not be talkin' so loud and him tryin' to have a bit av a sleep. (*He tiptoes softly to the side of the bunk.*) Yank! You'd be wantin' a drink av wather, maybe? (*Yank does not reply. Driscoll bends over and looks at him.*) It's asleep he is, sure enough. His breath is chokin' in his throat loike wather gurglin' in a poipe. (*He comes back quietly and sits down. All are silent, avoiding each other's eyes.*)

COCKY—(*after a pause*) Pore devil! It's over the side for 'im, Gawd 'elp 'im.

DRISCOLL—Stop your croakin'! He's not dead yet and, praise God, he'll have many a long day yet before him.

SCOTTY—(*shaking his head doubtfully*) He's bod, mon, he's verry bod.

DAVIS—Lucky he's alive. Many a man's light woulda gone out after a fall like that.

OLSON—You saw him fall?

DAVIS—Right next to him. He and me was goin' down in number two hold to do some chippin'. He puts his leg over careless-like and misses the ladder and plumps straight down to the bottom. I was scared to look over for a minute, and then I heard him groan and I scuttled down after him. He was hurt bad inside for the blood was drippin' from the side of his mouth. He was groanin' hard, but he never let a word out of him.

COCKY—An' you blokes remember when we 'auled 'im in 'ere? Oh, 'ell, 'e says, oh, 'ell—like that, and nothink else.

OLSON—Did the captain know where he iss hurted?

COCKY—That silly ol' josser! Wot the 'ell would 'e know abaht anythink?

SCOTTY—(scornfully) He fiddles in his mouth wi' a bit of glass.

DRISCOLL—(angrily) The divil's own life ut is to be out on the lonely sea wid nothin' betune you and a grave in the ocean but a spindle-shanked, gray-whiskered auld fool the loike av him. 'Twas enough to make a saint shwear to see him wid his gold watch in his hand, tryin' to look as wise as an owl on a tree, and all the toime he not knowin' whether 'twas cholery or the barber's itch was the matther wid Yank.

SCOTTY—(sardonically) He give him a dose of salts, na doot?

DRISCOLL—Divil a thing he gave him at all, but looked in the book he had wid him, and shook his head, and walked out widout sayin' a word, the second mate afther him no wiser than himself, God's curse on the two av thim!

COCKY—(after a pause) Yank was a good shipmate, pore beggar. Lend me four bob in Noo Yark, 'e did.

DRISCOLL—(warmly) A good shipmate he was and is, none betther. Ye said no more than the truth, Cocky. Five years and more ut is since first I shipped wid him, and we've stuck together iver since through good luck and bad. Fights we've had, God help us, but 'twas only when we'd a bit av drink taken, and we always shook hands the nixt mornin'. Whativer was his was mine, and many's the toime I'd a been on the beach or worse, but for him. And now— (*His voice trembles as he fights to control his emotion.*) Divil take me if I'm not startin' to blubber loike an auld woman, and he not dead at all, but goin' to live many a long year yet, maybe.

DAVIS—The sleep'll do him good. He seems better now.

OLSON—If he wude eat someting—

DRISCOLL—Wud ye have him be eatin' in his condishun? Sure it's hard enough on the rest av us wid nothin' the matther wid our insides to be stomachin' the skoff on this rusty lime-juicer.

SCOTTY—(*indignantly*) It's a starvation ship.

DAVIS—Plenty o' work and no food—and the owners ridin' around in carriages!

OLSON—Hash, hash! Stew, stew! Marmalade, py damn! (*He spits disgustedly.*)

COCKY—Bloody swill! Fit only for swine is wot I say.

DRISCOLL—And the dishwather they disguise wid the name av tea! And the putty they call bread! My belly feels loike I'd swalleyed a dozen rivets at the thought av ut! And sea-biscuit that'd break the teeth av a lion if he had the misfortune to take a bite at one! (*Unconsciously they have all raised their voices, forgetting the sick man in their sailor's delight at finding something to grumble about.*)

PAUL—(*swings his feet over the side of his bunk, stops playing his accordion, and says slowly*) And rot-ten po-tay-toes! (*He starts in playing again. The sick man gives a groan of pain.*)

DRISCOLL—(*holding up his hand*) Shut your mouths, all av you. 'Tis a hell av a thing for us to be complainin' about our guts, and a sick man maybe dyin' listenin' to us. (*gets up and shakes his fist at the Norwegian*) God stiffen you, ye squarehead scut! Put down that organ av yours or I'll break your ugly face for you. Is that banshee schreechin' fit music for a sick man? (*The Norwegian puts his accordion in the bunk and lies back and closes his eyes. Driscoll goes over and stands beside Yank. The steamer's whistle sounds particularly loud in the silence.*)

DAVIS—Damn this fog! (*reaches in under a bunk and yanks out a pair of seaboots, which he pulls on*) My lookout next, too. Must be nearly eight bells, boys. (*With the exception of Olson, all the men sitting up put on oilskins, sou'westers, seaboots, etc., in preparation for the watch on deck. Olson crawls into a lower bunk on the right.*)

SCOTTY—My wheel.

OLSON—(*disgustedly*) Nothin' but yust dirty weather all dis voyage. I yust can't sleep when weestle blow. (*He turns his back to the light and is soon fast asleep and snoring.*)

SCOTTY—If this fog keeps up, I'm tellin' ye, we'll no be in Carrdiff for a week or more.

DRISCOLL—'Twas just such a night as this the auld Dover wint down. Just about this toime ut was, too, and we all sittin' round in the fo'c'stle, Yank beside me, whin all av a suddint we heard a great slitherin' crash, and the ship heeled over till we was all in a heap on wan side. What came afther I disremimber exactly, except 'twas a hard shift to get the boats over the side before the auld teakittle sank. Yank was in the same boat wid me, and sivin morthal days we drifted wid scarcely a drop of wather or a bite to chew on. 'Twas Yank here that held me down whin I wanted to jump into the ocean, roarin' mad wid the thirst. Picked up we were on the same day wid only Yank in his senses, and him steerin' the boat.

COCKY—(*protestingly*) Blimey but you're a cheerful blighter, Driscoll! Talkin' abaht shipwrecks in this 'ere blushin' fog. (*Yank groans and stirs uneasily, opening his eyes. Driscoll hurries to his side.*)

DRISCOLL—Are ye feelin' any betther, Yank?

YANK—(*in a weak voice*) No.

DRISCOLL—Sure, you must be. You look as sthrong as an ox. (*appealing to the others*) Am I tellin' him a lie?

DAVIS—The sleep's done you good.

COCKY—You'll be 'avin your pint of beer in Cardiff this day week.

SCOTTY—And fish and chips, mon!

YANK—(*peevishly*) What're yuh all lyin' fur? D'yuh think I'm scared to— (*He hesitates as if frightened by the word he is about to say.*)

DRISCOLL—Don't be thinkin' such things! (*The ship's bell is heard heavily sounding eight times. From the forecastle head above the voice of the lookout rises in a long wail:* Aaall's welll.

The men look uncertainly at Yank as if undecided whether to say good-by or not.)

YANK—(*in an agony of fear*) Don't leave me, Drisc! I'm dyin', I tell yuh. I won't stay here alone with everyone snorin'. I'll go out on deck. (*He makes a feeble attempt to rise, but sinks back with a sharp groan. His breath comes in wheezy gasps.*) Don't leave me, Drisc! (*His face grows white and his head falls back with a jerk.*)

DRISCOLL—Don't be worryin', Yank. I'll not move a step out av here—and let that divil av a bo'sun curse his black head off. You speak a word to the bo'sun, Cocky. Tell him that Yank is bad took and I'll be stayin' wid him a while yet.

COCKY—Right-o. (*Cocky, Davis and Scotty go out quietly.*)

COCKY—(*from the alleyway*) Gawd blimey, the fog's thick as soup.

DRISCOLL—Are ye satisfied now, Yank? (*Receiving no answer, he bends over the still form.*) He's fainted, God help him! (*He gets a tin dipper from the bucket and bathes Yank's forehead with the water. Yank shudders and opens his eyes.*)

YANK—(*slowly*) I thought I was goin' then. Wha' did yuh wanta wake me up fur?

DRISCOLL—(*with forced gayety*) Is it wishful for heaven ye are?

YANK—(*gloomily*) Hell, I guess.

DRISCOLL—(*crossing himself involuntarily*) For the love av the saints don't be talkin' loike that! You'd give a man the creeps. It's chippin' rust on deck you'll be in a day or two wid the best av us. (*Yank does not answer, but closes his eyes wearily. The seaman who has been on lookout, Smitty, a young Englishman, comes in and takes off his dripping oilskins. While he is doing this the man whose turn at the wheel has been relieved enters. He is a dark burly fellow with a round stupid face. The Englishman steps softly over to Driscoll. The other crawls into a lower bunk.*)

SMITTY—(*whispering*) How's Yank?

DRISCOLL—Betther. Ask him yourself. He's awake.

YANK—I'm all right, Smitty.

SMITTY—Glad to hear it, Yank. (*He crawls to an upper bunk and is soon asleep.*)

IVAN—(*The stupid-faced seaman who came in after Smitty twists his head in the direction of the sick man.*) You feel gude, Jank?

YANK—(*wearily*) Yes, Ivan.

IVAN—Dot's gude. (*He rolls over on his side and falls asleep immediately.*)

YANK—(*after a pause broken only by snores—with a bitter laugh*) Good-by and good luck to the lot of you!

DRISCOLL—Is ut painin' you again?

YANK—It hurts like hell—here. (*He points to the lower part of his chest on the left side.*) I guess my old pump's busted. Ooohh! (*A spasm of pain contracts his pale features. He presses his hand to his side and writhes on the thin mattress of his bunk. The perspiration stands out in beads on his forehead.*)

DRISCOLL—(*terrified*) Yank! Yank! What is ut? (*jumping to his feet*) I'll run for the captain. (*He starts for the doorway.*)

YANK—(*sitting up in his bunk, frantic with fear*) Don't leave me, Drisc! For God's sake, don't leave me alone! (*He leans over the side of his bunk and spits. Driscoll comes back to him.*) Blood! Ugh!

DRISCOLL—Blood again! I'd best be gettin' the captain.

YANK—No, no, don't leave me! If yuh do I'll git up and follow you. I ain't no coward, but I'm scared to stay here with all of them asleep and snorin'. (*Driscoll, not knowing what to do, sits down on the bench beside him. He grows calmer and sinks back on the mattress.*) The captain can't do me no good, yuh know it yourself. The pain ain't so bad now, but I thought it had me then. It was a buzz-saw cuttin' into me.

DRISCOLL—(*fiercely*) God blarst ut!

(*The captain and the second mate of the steamer enter the forecastle. The captain is an old man with gray mustache and whiskers. The mate is clean-shaven and middle-aged. Both are dressed in simple blue uniforms.*)

THE CAPTAIN—(*taking out his watch and feeling Yank's pulse*) How do you feel now?

YANK—(*feebly*) All right, sir.

THE CAPTAIN—And the pain in your chest?

YANK—It still hurts, sir, worse than ever.

THE CAPTAIN—(*taking a thermometer from his pocket and*

putting it into Yank's mouth) Here. Be sure and keep this in under your tongue, not over it.

THE MATE—(*after a pause*) Isn't this your watch on deck, Driscoll?

DRISCOLL—Yes, sorr, but Yank was fearin' to be alone, and—

THE CAPTAIN—That's all right.

DRISCOLL—Thank ye, sorr.

THE CAPTAIN—(*stares at his watch for a moment or so; then takes the thermometer from Yank's mouth and goes to the lamp to read it. His expression grows very grave. He beckons the mate and Driscoll to the corner near the doorway. Yank watches them furtively. The captain speaks in a low voice to the mate.*) Way up, both of them. (*to Driscoll*) Has he been spitting blood again?

DRISCOLL—Not much for the hour just past, sorr, but before that—

THE CAPTAIN—A great deal?

DRISCOLL—Yes, sorr.

THE CAPTAIN—He hasn't eaten anything?

DRISCOLL—No, sorr.

THE CAPTAIN—Did he drink that medicine I sent him?

DRISCOLL—Yes, sorr, but it didn't stay down.

THE CAPTAIN—(*shaking his head*) I can't do anything else for him. It's too serious for me. If this had only happened a week later we'd be in Cardiff in time to—

DRISCOLL—Plaze help him some way, sorr!

THE CAPTAIN—(*impatiently*) But, my good man, I'm not a doctor. (*more kindly as he sees Driscoll's grief*) You and he have been shipmates a long time?

DRISCOLL—Five years and more, sorr.

THE CAPTAIN—I see. Well, don't let him move. Keep him quiet and we'll hope for the best. I'll read the matter up and send him some medicine, something to ease the pain, anyway. (*goes over to Yank*) Keep up your courage! You'll be better tomorrow. (*He breaks down lamely before Yank's steady gaze.*) We'll pull you through all right—and—hm—well—coming, Robinson? Dammit! (*He goes out hurriedly, followed by the mate.*)

DRISCOLL—(*trying to conceal his anxiety*) Didn't I tell you

you wasn't half as sick as you thought you was? The Captain'll have you out on deck cursin' and swearin' loike a trooper before the week is out.

YANK—Don't lie, Drisc. I heard what he said, and if I didn't I c'd tell by the way I feel. I know what's goin' to happen. I'm goin' to— (*He hesitates for a second—then resolutely*) I'm goin' to die, that's what, and the sooner the better!

DRISCOLL—(*wildly*) No, and be damned to you, you're not. I'll not let you.

YANK—It ain't no use, Drisc. I ain't got a chance, but I ain't scared. Gimme a drink of water, will yuh, Drisc? My throat's burnin' up. (*Driscoll brings the dipper full of water and supports his head while he drinks in great gulps.*)

DRISCOLL—(*seeking vainly for some word of comfort*) Are ye feelin' more aisy loike now?

YANK—Yes—now—when I know it's all up. (*a pause*) You mustn't take it so hard, Drisc. I was just thinkin' it ain't as bad as people think—dyin'. I ain't never took much stock in the truck them sky-pilots preach. I ain't never had religion; but I know whatever it is what comes after it can't be no worser'n this. I don't like to leave you, Drisc, but—that's all.

DRISCOLL—(*with a groan*) Lad, lad, don't be talkin'.

YANK—This sailor life ain't much to cry about leavin'— just one ship after another, hard work, small pay, and bum grub; and when we git into port, just a drunk endin' up in a fight, and all your money gone, and then ship away again. Never meetin' no nice people; never gittin' outa sailor town, hardly, in any port; travelin' all over the world and never seein' none of it; without no one to care whether you're alive or dead. (*with a bitter smile*) There ain't much in all that that'd make yuh sorry to lose it, Drisc.

DRISCOLL—(*gloomily*) It's a hell av a life, the sea.

YANK—(*musingly*) It must be great to stay on dry land all your life and have a farm with a house of your own with cows and pigs and chickens, 'way in the middle of the land where yuh'd never smell the sea or see a ship. It must be great to have a wife, and kids to play with at night after supper when your work was done. It must be great to have a home of your own, Drisc.

DRISCOLL—(*with a great sigh*) It must, surely; but what's the use av thinkin' av ut? Such things are not for the loikes av us.

YANK—Sea-farin' is all right when you're young and don't care, but we ain't chickens no more, and somehow, I dunno, this last year has seemed rotten, and I've had a hunch I'd quit—with you, of course—and we'd save our coin, and go to Canada or Argentine or some place and git a farm, just a small one, just enough to live on. I never told yuh this 'cause I thought you'd laugh at me.

DRISCOLL—(*enthusiastically*) Laugh at you, is ut? When I'm havin' the same thoughts myself, toime afther toime. It's a grand idea and we'll be doin' ut sure if you'll stop your crazy notions—about—about bein' so sick.

YANK—(*sadly*) Too late. We shouldn'ta made this trip, and then— How'd all the fog git in here?

DRISCOLL—Fog?

YANK—Everything looks misty. Must be my eyes gittin' weak, I guess. What was we talkin' of a minute ago? Oh, yes, a farm. It's too late. (*his mind wandering*) Argentine, did I say? D'yuh remember the times we've had in Buenos Aires? The moving pictures in Barracas? Some class to them, d'yuh remember?

DRISCOLL—(*with satisfaction*) I do that; and so does the piany player. He'll not be forgettin' the black eye I gave him in a hurry.

YANK—Remember the time we was there on the beach and had to go to Tommy Moore's boarding house to git shipped? And he sold us rotten oilskins and seaboots full of holes, and shipped us on a skys'l yarder round the Horn, and took two months' pay for it. And the days we used to sit on the park benches along the Paseo Colon with the vigilantes lookin' hard at us? And the songs at the Sailor's Opera where the guy played ragtime—d'yuh remember them?

DRISCOLL—I do, surely.

YANK—And La Plata—phew, the stink of the hides! I always liked Argentine—all except that booze, caña. How drunk we used to git on that, remember?

DRISCOLL—Cud I forget ut? My head pains me at the menshun av that divil's brew.

YANK—Remember the night I went crazy with the heat in Singapore? And the time you was pinched by the cops in Port Said? And the time we was both locked up in Sydney for fightin'?

DRISCOLL—I do so.

YANK—And that fight on the dock at Cape Town— (*His voice betrays great inward perturbation.*)

DRISCOLL—(*hastily*) Don't be thinkin' av that now. 'Twas past and gone.

YANK—D'yuh think He'll hold it up agin me?

DRISCOLL—(*mystified*) Who's that?

YANK—God. They say He sees everything. He must know it was done in fair fight, in self-defense, don't yuh think?

DRISCOLL—Av course. Ye stabbed him, and be damned to him, for the skulkin' swine he was, afther him tryin' to stick you in the back, and you not suspectin'. Let your conscience be aisy. I wisht I had nothin' blacker than that on my sowl. I'd not be afraid av the angel Gabriel himself.

YANK—(*with a shudder*) I c'd see him a minute ago with the blood spurtin' out of his neck. Ugh!

DRISCOLL—The fever, ut is, that makes you see such things. Give no heed to ut.

YANK—(*uncertainly*) You don't think He'll hold it up agin me—God, I mean?

DRISCOLL—If there's justice in hiven, no! (*Yank seems comforted by this assurance.*)

YANK—(*after a pause*) We won't reach Cardiff for a week at least. I'll be buried at sea.

DRISCOLL—(*putting his hands over his ears*) Ssshh! I won't listen to you.

YANK—(*as if he had not heard him*) It's as good a place as any other, I s'pose—only I always wanted to be buried on dry land. But what the hell'll I care—then? (*fretfully*) Why should it be a rotten night like this with that damned whistle blowin' and people snorin' all around? I wish the stars was out, and the moon, too; I c'd lie out on deck and look at them, and it'd make it easier to go—somehow.

DRISCOLL—For the love av God don't be talkin' loike that!

YANK—Whatever pay's comin' to me yuh can divvy up

with the rest of the boys; and you take my watch. It ain't worth much, but it's all I've got.

DRISCOLL—But have ye no relations at all to call your own?

YANK—No, not as I know of. One thing I forgot: You know Fanny the barmaid at the Red Stork in Cardiff?

DRISCOLL—Sure, and who doesn't?

YANK—She's been good to me. She tried to lend me half a crown when I was broke there last trip. Buy her the biggest box of candy yuh c'n find in Cardiff. (*breaking down—in a choking voice*) It's hard to ship on this voyage I'm goin' on— alone! (*Driscoll reaches out and grasps his hand. There is a pause, during which both fight to control themselves.*) My throat's like a furnace. (*He gasps for air.*) Gimme a drink of water, will yuh, Drisc? (*Driscoll gets him a dipper of water.*) I wish this was a pint of beer. Oooohh! (*He chokes, his face convulsed with agony, his hands tearing at his shirt front. The dipper falls from his nerveless fingers.*)

DRISCOLL—For the love av God, what is ut, Yank?

YANK—(*speaking with tremendous difficulty*) S'long, Drisc! (*He stares straight in front of him with eyes starting from their sockets.*) Who's that?

DRISCOLL—Who? What?

YANK—(*faintly*) A pretty lady dressed in black. (*His face twitches and his body writhes in a final spasm, then straightens out rigidly.*)

DRISCOLL—(*pale with horror*) Yank! Yank! Say a word to me for the love av hiven! (*He shrinks away from the bunk, making the sign of the cross. Then comes back and puts a trembling hand on Yank's chest and bends closely over the body.*)

COCKY—(*from the alleyway*) Oh, Driscoll! Can you leave Yank for arf a mo' and give me a 'and?

DRISCOLL—(*with a great sob*) Yank! (*He sinks down on his knees beside the bunk, his head on his hands. His lips move in some half-remembered prayer.*)

COCKY—(*enters, his oilskins and sou'wester glistening with drops of water*) The fog's lifted. (*Cocky sees Driscoll and stands staring at him with open mouth. Driscoll makes the sign of the cross again.*)

COCKY—(*mockingly*) Sayin' 'is prayers! (*He catches sight of

the still figure in the bunk and an expression of awed understand-
ing comes over his face. He takes off his dripping sou'wester and
stands, scratching his head.)

COCKY—(*in a hushed whisper*) Gawd blimey!

(*The Curtain Falls*)

ABORTION

A Play in One Act

CHARACTERS

JACK TOWNSEND
JOHN TOWNSEND, *his father*
MRS. TOWNSEND, *his mother*
LUCY TOWNSEND, *his sister*
EVELYN SANDS, *his fiancee*
DONALD (BULL) HERRON, *his room-mate*
JOE MURRAY, *a machinist*
STUDENTS OF THE UNIVERSITY

The action takes place in the study of the suite of rooms occupied by Townsend and Herron on the ground floor of a dormitory in a large eastern university in the United States.

Time—The Present.

Abortion

SCENE—*The study of the suite of rooms occupied by Jack Town-send and Donald Herron on the ground floor of a dormitory in a large eastern university of the United States. The left wall is composed almost entirely of a large bow-window looking out on the campus, and forming a window seat which is piled high with bright colored cushions. In the middle of the far side, a door opening into a hallway of the dormitory. On either side of the door, leather covered divans with leather cushions. In the right corner to the rear, a writing desk with an electric drop-light hanging over it. In the middle of the right wall, a fireplace. In the extreme right foreground, a door opening into a bedroom. In the center of the room, a table with an electric reading-lamp wired from the chandelier above. Books, periodicals, pipes, cigarette boxes, ash-trays, etc., are also on the table. The walls of the room are hung with flags, class banners, framed photographs of baseball and football teams, college posters, etc. Two Morris chairs and several rockers are grouped about the table.*

It is about eight o'clock in the evening of a warm day in June. At first the windows on the left are gray with the dim glow of the dying twilight but as the action progresses this slowly disappears.

A sound of voices comes from the hall. The door in the rear is opened and Mrs. Townsend and Lucy enter, escorted by Herron. Their figures can be vaguely made out in the dusk of the room.

LUCY—(*feeling her way toward the table*) Do put on the lights, Bull! I know I'm going to break my neck in a minute. (*Mrs. Townsend remains standing by the doorway.*)

HERRON—(*cheerfully*) One minute, one minute! (*strikes his shin against the corner of the divan—wrathfully*) Oh— (*bites his tongue just in time*)

LUCY—(*with a gurgling laugh*) Say it! Say it!

HERRON—(*leaning over the divan and feeling on the wall for the electric switch—softly*) Oh darn!

LUCY—Hypocrite! That isn't what you were going to say.

HERRON—Oh gosh, then. (*finds the switch*) There! (*turns on all the lights except the drop-light*) Let there be light!

LUCY—(*She is a small, vivacious blond nineteen years old, gushing with enthusiasm over everything and everybody. She wears an immense bouquet of flowers at the waist of her dark blue dress and carries a flag.*) Don't stand there posing, Bull. (*flings herself into one of the Morris chairs*) You look much more like a God of darkness than one of light.

MRS. TOWNSEND—(*a sweet-faced, soft-spoken, gray-haired lady in her early fifties. She is dressed in dark gray. She turns to Lucy with smiling remonstrance.*) Lucy! (*to Herron who clumsily arranges a cushion at the back of a rocking chair for her*) Thank you, Donald. (*Herron winces at the "Donald."*)

LUCY—(*contemptuously*) Donald!

HERRON—(*chuckling—He is a huge, swarthy six-footer with a bull neck and an omnipresent grin, slow to anger and to understanding but—an All-American tackle. His immense frame is decked out in white flannels which make him look gigantic.*) I don't care much for the "Donald" myself.

LUCY—And I still claim, Mother, that Donald, alias Bull, resembles Pluto more than any other divinity. It is true, judging from the pictures I have seen, that Pluto was not as fat— (*as Herron slouches into a sitting position on the divan*) nor as clumsy, but—

HERRON—(*grinning*) What have I done today? What have I done? Didn't I purchase candy and beautiful flowers? And now I reap nothing but abuse. I appeal to you, Mrs. Townsend. She is breaking me on the wheel.

LUCY—Poor butterfly! (*convulsed with laughter*) Ha ha ha! Poor, delicate fragile butterfly!

HERRON—There you go again! (*appealingly*) You see, Mrs. Townsend? Every word of mine is turned to mockery. (*He sighs explosively.*)

MRS. TOWNSEND—(*smiling*) Never mind, Donald; you ought to hear the nice things she says behind your back.

LUCY—(*indignantly*) Mother!

HERRON—I find it hard to believe.

LUCY—Mother is fibbing so as not to hurt your feelings. (*with a roguish smile*) I never, never in all my life said a good word about you. You don't deserve it.

MRS. TOWNSEND—Why, Lucy, what a thing to say! (*While she is speaking Joe Murray appears in the doorway to the rear. He is a slight, stoop-shouldered, narrow-chested young fellow of eighteen, with large, feverish, black eyes, thin lips, pasty complexion, and the sunken cheeks of a tuberculosis victim. He wears a shabby dark suit. He peers blinkingly around the room and knocks but they do not hear him.*)

LUCY—(*glancing toward the door and seeing him*) Someone to see you, Bull.

HERRON—(*turning to Murray*) Anything you want?

MURRAY—(*aggressively*) I wanta see Townsend, Jack Townsend.

HERRON—He's not here.

MURRAY—D'yuh know when he'll be in?

HERRON—Any minute; but I advise you not to wait. He won't have any time for you tonight. If you want to leave a message I'll give it to him.

MURRAY—(*truculently*) He'll find time for me all right.

HERRON—(*staring at him*) You think so? Suit yourself. (*pointedly*) You can wait for him *outside*. (*Murray's face pales with rage. He starts to say something then turns abruptly and disappears into the hallway.*)

HERRON—Pleasant little man!

LUCY—Don't you know who it was?

HERRON—Never saw him before; probably some fresh "townie" who thinks Jack's indebted to him because he recovered a stolen baseball bat or something, and wants to put the acid on him for a dollar or two. Jack's such a good-natured slob—

LUCY—(*with a giggle*) Listen to who is talking.

MRS. TOWNSEND—(*proudly*) Jack always has been so good-hearted.

HERRON—(*with a smile*) He's only stingy with base-hits. Great game he pitched today. Star players usually fall down when they're captains of teams and it's their last year in college; but not old Jack—only three hits off him.

MRS. TOWNSEND—This game we saw today decides the championship, doesn't it?

LUCY—Certainly, Mother. You don't suppose I'd have yelled my whole voice away if it wasn't, do you? I can hardly speak.

MRS. TOWNSEND—(*with a sly wink at Herron*) I hadn't noticed that, Lucy. (*Herron shakes with suppressed mirth.*)

LUCY—(*pouting*) Oh, Mother, how unkind!

MRS. TOWNSEND—I must confess I'm not much of a fan— Is that what you call it?— I do not understand the game and if it wasn't for Jack playing I'm afraid I would find it rather wearisome.

HERRON—Jack is the big man of the college tonight, all right. The President is a mere nonentity beside him. Add to our list of athletic heroes one Jack Townsend, captain and pitcher.

MRS. TOWNSEND—How they carried him around the field after the game!

LUCY—And cheered him!

HERRON—You bet we did. I had a hold of one leg. But I agree with you Mrs. Townsend. If Jack didn't play I wouldn't take much interest in baseball myself. (*enthusiastically*) Football is the real game.

LUCY—Of course you'd say that.

MRS. TOWNSEND—That's beyond me, too. I've heard it's so rough, that so many players are injured. When John first entered college his father and I made him promise not to go in for it on any account.

HERRON—(*regretfully*) You spoiled a fine player. (*noise of voices from the hall*) Speaking of the—hm—angel. (*Evelyn Sands enters followed by Jack Townsend. Evelyn is a tall, dark-haired, beautiful girl about twenty years old. Her eyes are large and brown; her mouth full-lipped, resolute; her figure lithe and graceful. She is dressed simply but stylishly in white. Jack is a well-built handsome young fellow about twenty-two years old, with blond hair brushed straight back from his forehead, intelligent blue eyes, a good-natured, self-indulgent mouth, and ruddy, tanned complexion. He has the easy confident air of one who has, through his prowess in athletics, become a figure of note in college circles and is accustomed to the deference of those around him. He wears a dark coat, white soft shirt with a bright colored tie, flannel trousers, and white tennis shoes.*)

LUCY—Hail to the hero! (*Evelyn comes over and sits on the arm of Lucy's chair. Jack stands beside his mother.*)

MRS. TOWNSEND—(*smiling fondly up at him*) Where is your father?

JACK—Right outside, talking to Professor Simmons. After dinner as we were following you out of the Inn we ran into the Prof and he walked down with us. Did you think we were lost?

LUCY—(*with a mischievous glance at Evelyn*) We thought you might have forestalled the forthcoming happy event by eloping. (*Evelyn blushes.*)

JACK—(*laughing*) With father for chaperon?

LUCY—Well, don't you dare do it! I'd never forgive you spoiling my chance to wear my gown. I'm going to be just the most stunning bridesmaid. Am I not, Mother?

MRS. TOWNSEND—Of course, dear. (*to Jack*) Why didn't you ask the professor to come in?

JACK—I did, Mother, but he's on his way somewhere or other.

HERRON—By the way, Jack, there was a "townie" in here asking to see you a few minutes ago.

JACK—(*starting nervously*) A "townie"? Did he give any name?

HERRON—No. A fresh little shrimp; said he'd wait. Wasn't he outside?

JACK—(*visibly uneasy*) I didn't see anyone.

HERRON—He'll be back probably; and look out for a touch. (*The singing of a distant quartet sounds faintly from the campus.*)

LUCY—(*springing up*) I hear them singing on the campus. I'm going out. Bull, when does the big P'rade start?

HERRON—Pretty soon; you can hear the clans gathering now.

LUCY—I'm going to march beside them all the way to the lake.

MRS. TOWNSEND—The lake?

LUCY—There's going to be a canoe carnival, and bonfires, and dancing, and everything, Mother. You've simply got to come, all of you, in honor of hero Jack.

JACK—(*embarrassed*) Come, come, Sis, praise from you is rare indeed.

HERRON—(*emphatically*) Indeed!

LUCY—(*archly to Herron*) Indeed?

MRS. TOWNSEND—(*getting quickly from her chair—with a girlish laugh*) I'm going with you. I'll show you young people I can celebrate with the best of you.

JACK—Are you sure it isn't too much for you, Mother?

MRS. TOWNSEND—(*her face flushed with excitement*) Nonsense, Jack!

JACK—(*putting his arm around her affectionately*) Dear old mother—young mother, I should say.

LUCY—Come on everybody!

JACK—You people go on ahead and I'll catch up with you. (*Mrs. Townsend goes out.*)

LUCY—(*to Herron*) Come on, Jumbo.

HERRON—(*groaning*) Jumbo! And Bull! Lucy thinks I'm a menagerie. (*He and Lucy go out. Evelyn starts to follow them but Jack stops her and takes her in his arms.*)

JACK—We won't be alone again for ages. (*kisses her*)

EVELYN—(*smiling up into his face*) I'm so proud of you, Jack, dear.

JACK—(*laughingly puts his fingers across her lips*) Ssshhh! You'll give me an awful attack of exaggerated ego if you go on talking like that.

EVELYN—But it's true, dear.

JACK—Then for the good of my soul don't tell me. Praise from Sis is wonder enough for one day.

EVELYN—(*moving a few steps away from him*) I wish I could tell you how proud I felt when I sat in the grandstand and watched you. (*with a laugh*) It was a horrid sort of selfish pride, too, for I couldn't help saying to myself from time to time: He loves me, *me*! He belongs to *me*; and I thought of how jealous all the girls around me who were singing his praises would be if they knew.

JACK—(*his face suddenly grown serious, as if at some painful memory*) Please Evelyn! You make me feel so mean—and contemptible when you talk like that.

EVELYN—(*astonished*) Mean? Contemptible? How foolish you are, Jack. (*excitedly*) I felt like standing on my seat and shouting to all of them: "What right have you to think of him? He is *mine, mine*!" (*laughing at her own enthusiasm, adds in a matter-of-fact tone*) Or will be in three months.

JACK—(*his voice thrilling with emotion*) In three months!

(*jokingly*) Do you know those three months are going to seem like three years?

EVELYN—(*gaily*) Three centuries; but I was telling you how splendid you were this afternoon.

JACK—(*protestingly*) Sssshh, Evelyn! (*tries to put his arms around her*)

EVELYN—(*backing away and avoiding him*) You were so cool, so brave. It struck me as symbolical of the way you would always play, in the game of life—fairly, squarely, strengthening those around you, refusing to weaken at critical moments, advancing others by sacrifices, fighting the good fight for the cause, the team, and always, always, whether vanquished or victor, reserving a hearty, honest cheer for the other side. (*breaking off breathlessly*) Oh, Jack dear, I loved you so!

JACK—(*a strong note of pain in his voice, puts his hands over his ears, and forces a laugh*) I won't listen any longer. I positively refuse.

EVELYN—(*smiling*) It's all over. I'm through. I simply had to tell you. (*She holds out both hands to him. He draws her into his arms and kisses her.*)

JACK—(*with deep feeling*) I shall try—with all my strength—in the future, Evelyn,—to live as you have said and become worthy of you. Today was nothing. One does one's best for the sake of the game, for the love of the struggle. Our best happened to be luckier, more skillful, perhaps, than the other fellow's—that's all.

EVELYN—It's so like you to say that. You're a dear. (*She kisses him. Jack's father, John Townsend, appears in the doorway. He is a tall, kindly old man of sixty or so with a quantity of white hair. He is erect, well-preserved, energetic, dressed immaculately but soberly. He laughs and shakes a finger at Evelyn.*)

TOWNSEND—Caught in the act. (*Evelyn smiles and blushes.*) Evelyn, they're waiting for you outside and Lucy threatens to come in and drag you out if my persuasive powers have no effect. They want to make a start for the Steps and see the P'rade form. It's due to start shortly. (*While he is speaking he comes forward, puts his straw hat on the table, and sits down in one of the Morris chairs.*)

EVELYN—(*eagerly*) I wouldn't miss it for worlds. (*She goes to the door; then turns and looks at Jack irresolutely.*) Aren't you coming with us, both of you? (*Jack looks at his father uncertainly.*)

TOWNSEND—We'll join you there; or, better still,— (*to Jack*) The P'rade passes right by here, doesn't it? They always used to in the old days.

JACK—Yes, Dad.

TOWNSEND—Then you go ahead with the others, Evelyn, and since Lucy tells me you're going to follow the P'rade, we'll be able to join you when you pass by. (*explanatively*) I've seen and taken part in so many of these affairs that their novelty has sort of worn off for me; and Jack,—if they were to discover the hero of the day at this stage of the game he wouldn't have a rag to his back, eh, Jack?

JACK—(*smiling*) I'm black and blue all over from their fond caresses this afternoon.

EVELYN—(*gaily*) I'm off, then. (*looking at Jack*) You'll surely join us when we pass?

JACK—Sure thing.

EVELYN—(*waving her hand*) Bye-bye. (*She goes out. Jack sits down near his father.*)

TOWNSEND—(*takes out a cigar and lights it. Jack watches him uneasily as if he foresees what his father is going to say and dreads it. Townsend avoids his eyes. There is an uncomfortable silence. Then Townsend begins vaguely*) It certainly removes the burden of the years from my shoulders to come out to the old college in the Spring and live the old days over in memory and hobnob with some of the old-timers who were young-timers with me. It becomes more difficult every year I find. All the old landmarks are disappearing one by one.

JACK—(*perfunctorily*) Yes, even in my time there have been great changes.

TOWNSEND—(*very palpably talking to gain time*) It gives me a painful heart-throb every time I come back and look for some old place and find it renovated or torn down.

JACK—(*shortly*) I can well understand that.

TOWNSEND—You don't realize what this college comes to mean to you in after years; how it becomes inseparably woven into the memories of one's lost youth until the two become identical.

JACK—(*impatiently*) Yes, I suppose so.

TOWNSEND—(*more and more vaguely*) Happiest days of my life, of anyone's life—

JACK—(*abruptly*) Come to the point, Dad.

TOWNSEND—(*confused*) What? Eh?

JACK—(*firmly*) You didn't send Evelyn away in order that you might wax reminiscent; you know that, Dad.

TOWNSEND—(*heaving a sigh of relief*) You are quite right, I did not; but what I ought to speak about is such a deuced painful subject for both of us that I hardly dare speak of it— especially on your day of triumph when I should be the last one to bring up any unpleasantness.

JACK—(*kindly*) Never mind that, Dad.

TOWNSEND—You see I didn't know when I'd have another opportunity of seeing you alone without arousing your mother's suspicions.

JACK—I understand.

TOWNSEND—And the thing has caused me so much worry. I simply had to hear from your own lips that everything was all right.

JACK—Then I will set your mind at rest immediately. Everything *is* all right.

TOWNSEND—(*fervently*) Thank God for that! Why haven't you written to me?

JACK—Until a few days ago I had nothing new to tell you.

TOWNSEND—When was the operation performed?

JACK—Last Monday.

TOWNSEND—And you've heard from her since?

JACK—I received a short note from her that night. It was all over and everything was all right, she said. She told me I needn't worry any longer.

TOWNSEND—That was five days ago. You haven't had any word since then?

JACK—No.

TOWNSEND—That's a favorable sign. If any further complications had cropped up she would surely have let you know, wouldn't she?

JACK—Yes, I think she would. I imagine she's frightened to death and doesn't want any more to do with me. I'm sure

I hope so. And then, you see I never answered her letter or telephoned.

TOWNSEND—(*gravely*) You were wrong there, my boy.

JACK—(*excitedly*) I know it, I know it, Dad; but I had just received a letter from Evelyn telling me she was coming out for Commencement Week and the game, and— Oh, when I thought of her the other affair seemed so horrible and loathsome, I swore I'd never speak or write again. When I was certain she was in no danger I judged it best for both of us to break off once and for all.

TOWNSEND—Listen, my boy; Are you sure—you know one's vanity blinds one in such cases—are you sure, absolutely sure, you were the father of this child which would have been born to her?

JACK—(*emphatically*) Yes, I am certain of it, as certain as one can possibly be. (*wildly*) Oh I wish to God I had grounds for some suspicion of the sort. What a salve it would be for my conscience! But no, no! To even think such is an insult to a sweet girl. (*defiantly*) For she is a sweet, lovely girl in spite of everything, and if I had loved her the least particle, if I had not been in love with Evelyn, I should certainly have married her.

TOWNSEND—Hm,—if you did not love this girl, why did you,—why, in the first place,—?

JACK—(*leaning toward his father and fixing his eyes upon him searchingly*) Why? Why? Who knows why or who, that does know, has the courage to confess it, even to himself. Be frank, Dad! Judging from several anecdotes which your friend Professor Simmons has let slip about your four years here, you were no St. Anthony. Turn your mind back to those days and then answer your own question: "Why, in the first place?"

TOWNSEND—(*stares at the floor in moody retrospection—a pause*) We've retained a large portion of the original mud in our make-up. That's the only answer I can think of.

JACK—(*ironically*) That's it! Do you suppose it was the same man who loves Evelyn who did this other thing? No, a thousand times no, such an idea is abhorrent. It was the male beast who ran gibbering through the forest after its female thousands of years ago.

TOWNSEND—Come, Jack, that is pure evasion. You are

responsible for the Mr. Hyde in you as well as for the Dr. Jekyll. Restraint—

JACK—(*scornfully*) Restraint? Ah, yes, everybody preaches but who practices it? And could they if they wanted to? Some impulses are stronger than we are, have proved themselves so throughout the world's history. Is it not rather our ideals of conduct, of Right and Wrong, our ethics, which are unnatural and monstrously distorted? Is society not suffering from a case of the evil eye which sees evil where there is none? Isn't it our moral laws which force me into evasions like the one which you have just found fault with?

TOWNSEND—You're delving too deep, for me, my boy. Save your radical arguments for the younger generation. I cannot see them in the same light you do (*grumblingly*) and if I could, I wouldn't. What I cannot understand is how you happened to get in with this young woman in the first place. You'll pardon me, Jack, but it seems to me to show a lack of judgment on your part, and—er—good taste.

JACK—(*shrugging his shoulders*) Such things usually are errors in taste.

TOWNSEND—This young woman was hardly of the class you have been accustomed to associate with, I presume.

JACK—She is a working girl, a stenographer.

TOWNSEND—Has she any immediate relations who would be liable to discover the unfortunate termination of your (*sarcastically*) love affair?

JACK—Her father is dead. Her mother is a silly woman who would be the last to suspect anything. She has two sisters, both youngsters under ten, and one brother about eighteen, a machinist or something of the sort who is only home for week-ends.

TOWNSEND—And she and her brother support the others?

JACK—(*avoiding his father's eyes*) So I believe.

TOWNSEND—(*his expression stern and accusing, starts to say something but restrains himself*) Ah.

JACK—(*glancing at his father*) Yes, yes I know it, Dad. I have played the scoundrel all the way through. I realize that now. Why couldn't I have felt this way before, at the start? Then this would never have happened. But at that time the whole thing seemed just a pleasant game we were playing; its serious aspects appeared remote, unreal. I never gave them a thought. I have paid for it since then, I want you to believe that. I have had my glance into the abyss. In loss of confidence and self-respect, in bitter self-abasement I have paid, and I am sure the result of it all will be to make me a better man, a man more worthy to be Evelyn's husband.

TOWNSEND—(*huskily*) God grant it, my boy. (*gets to his feet*) I want to thank you for the confidence you placed in your father by making a frank appeal to me when you got in this trouble. It shows you regard me not only as a father but as a friend; and that is the way I would have it.

JACK—You have always urged me to come to you and be frank about everything; and I always have and always will. I had to have the money and I thought I owed it to you to be open and aboveboard and not start in deceiving you at this late day. I couldn't get it in any other way very well. Two hundred dollars is quite a sum for a college student to raise at a moment's notice.

TOWNSEND—(*restored to good humor*) The wages of sin are rather exorbitant.

JACK—He was the only doctor I could find who would do that sort of thing. He knew I was a college student and probably made inquiries about your financial rating,—and there you are. There was nothing for me to do but grin and pay. But as I said in my letter this money is a loan. It would be unfair for me to make you shoulder my—mistakes.

TOWNSEND—(*cheerfully*) Let's forget all about it. (*He holds out his hand to Jack who clasps it heartily.*) All's well that ends well. You've learned your lesson. (*The sound of a college cheer comes faintly through the open window.*) And now shall we join the others? That cheer wakens the old fever in me. I want to follow the band and get singed by the Roman candles. (*He picks his straw hat from the table.*)

JACK—(*eagerly*) Yes, let's do that. (*They are going toward the door in the rear when Joe Murray appears in the doorway. Jack cannot repress an exclamation of alarm and his face grows pale.*)

MURRAY—(*fixing his eyes on Jack with an expression of furious hatred*) Look here, Townsend, I gotta see yuh for a minute.

JACK—(*unwillingly*) All right, Murray. You join the others, Dad, and I'll catch you in a few minutes. (*Townsend, struck by the change in his son's voice looks questioningly at him, asking an explanation. Jack turns away from him.*)

JACK—Come in, Murray, and have a seat. (*Townsend goes out. Murray slouches to the middle of the room but does not sit down. His fingers fumble nervously at the buttons of his coat. He notices this and plunges his hands into his coat pockets. He seems endeavoring to restrain the hatred and rage which the spasmodic working of his features show to be boiling within him.*)

JACK—(*appears occupied in arranging the things on the table*) Well?

MURRAY—(*chokingly*) Well! (*He can go no further.*)

JACK—(*coldly, without looking at him*) Anything I can do for you?

MURRAY—(*in strangled tones*) Anything you can do for *me*!

JACK—(*hurriedly*) Yes; I'm in rather a hurry and if it's nothing very important I'd be just as well pleased if you'd come some other time.

MURRAY—Important? *You* mayn't think so. It's not important to *you*, yuh— (*He is stopped by a fit of violent coughing which racks his thin body.*)

JACK—(*irritably*) You've come here looking for trouble, Murray. You better wait until you've cooled off. (*then more kindly*) What is it you want to say to me? Out with it!

MURRAY—(*wiping his mouth on his coat sleeve—angrily*) I'll out with it, damn yuh!—standing there so cool—dressed in swell clothes—and all these other goils—(*choking*) and Nellie—and Nellie—

JACK—(*leaning toward him*) Yes, Nellie?

MURRAY—(*sobbing*) She's dead. (*in a transport of rage*) *You* killed her, yuh dirty murderer!

JACK—(*dully, as if he did not understand*) Dead? No, no, you don't mean that. She wrote to me everything was all right. Dead? (*As he speaks he backs away from Murray in horror and stumbles against one of the Morris chairs. He sits down in it mechanically.*)

MURRAY—(*shrilly*) She's dead—Nellie, my sister—she's dead.

JACK—(*half to himself*) No, it's impossible. (*fiercely*) It's a lie! What scheme is this of yours? You're trying to frighten me.

MURRAY—(*raging*) She's dead, I tell yuh, dead! She died this morning.

JACK—(*forced to believe*) She died this morning? (*in a dazed voice*) But why didn't she— I didn't know— (*stares straight before him*) God!

MURRAY—Why didn't she let yuh know, yuh mean? She wrote to yuh, she told me she did; and yuh knew she was sick and never answered it. She might'a lived if she thought yuh cared, if she heard from yuh; but she knew yuh were tryin' to git rid of her.

JACK—(*in agony*) Stop, for God's sake! I know I should have written. I meant to write but—

MURRAY—She kept sayin': "I wanta die. I don't wanta live!" (*furiously*) But I'll fix yuh! I'll make yuh pay.

JACK—(*startled, turns to him quickly*) What do you mean?

MURRAY—Don't give me any of that. Yuh know what I mean. Yuh know how she died. (*fiercely*) Yuh know who killed her.

JACK—(*his voice trembling—not looking at Murray*) How she died? Killed her? I don't understand—

MURRAY—Yuh lie! She was murdered and yuh know it.

JACK—(*horror-struck*) Murdered?

MURRAY—Yes, and *you* murdered her.

JACK—(*shuddering*) I? What? I murdered?—Are you crazy?

MURRAY—You and your dirty skunk of a doctor.

JACK—(*sinks back in his chair with a groan*) Ooh!

MURRAY—(*with fierce scorn*) Yuh thought yuh was safe, didn't yuh, with me away from home? Yuh c'd go out and pitch the champeenship game—and she lyin' dead! Yuh c'd ruin her and throw her down and no one say a word because yuh're a swell college guy and captain of the team, and she ain't good enough for yuh to marry. She's goin' to have a kid, *your* kid, and because yuh're too rotten to act like a man, yuh send her to a faker of a doctor to be killed; and she does what yuh say because she loves yuh; and yuh don't even think enough of her to answer her letter (*sobbing*) when she's dyin' on account of *you*!

JACK—(*speaking with difficulty*) She—told you—all this?

MURRAY—Not a word! (*proudly*) She died game; she wasn't no coward. I tried every way I knew how to git her to tell me but she wouldn't. Not a word outa her against you. (*choking with angry sobs*) And *you*—and *you*—yuh dirty coward!—playin' ball!

JACK—(*dully*) I did what I thought was best for her.

MURRAY—Yuh sneaked out like a coward because yuh thought she wasn't good enough. (*with a sneer*) Yuh think yuh c'n get away with that stuff and then marry some goil of your own kind, I s'pose,—some goil like I seen yuh come in with tonight. (*vindictively*) But yuh won't; not if I have to go to hell for it! (*A pause. Jack is silent, breathing hard. His eyes are haunted, full of despair, as he vainly seeks to escape from the remorse which is torturing him. The faint sound of the college cheer, then of the band, comes from the open window. From this point to the end these sounds are continuous, the band only being silenced to permit the giving of the cheer, and as the action progresses they become more and more distinct.*)

MURRAY—(*continues in the same vindictive tones*) I've always hated yuh since yuh first come to the house. I've always hated all your kind. Yuh come here to school and yuh think yuh c'n do as yuh please with us town people. Yuh treat us like servants, an' what are *you*, I'd like to know?—a lot of lazy no-good dudes spongin' on your old men; and the goils, our goils, think yuh're grand! (*Jack is staring at the floor, his head bowed, and does not seem to hear him.*)

MURRAY—I knew somethin' would happen. I told Nellie to look out, and she laughed. When the old lady sent for me and I come home and saw Nellie and she wouldn't leave me go for a doctor, I had a hunch what was wrong. She wouldn't say nothin' but I got our doc, not the one *you* sent her to, and he told me just what I thought and said she was goin' to die. (*raging*) If I'd seen yuh that minute I'd killed yuh. I knew it was *you* but I couldn't prove it. Then one of the kids got scared and told me Nellie'd sent her to your doc for medicine when she first took sick. I bought a gun and the kid showed me where he was. I shoved the gun in his face and he owned up and told me about you. He offered me money, lots of it, to keep my mouth shut, and I took it—the money he'd got from you—blood money! (*with a savage grin*) An' I'll keep my mouth shut—*maybe!*

JACK—(*his eyes lighting up with a gleam of hope, turns eagerly to Murray*) Listen, Murray! This affair is unspeakably horrible, and I am—everything you say; but I want you—you must believe I honestly thought I was acting for the best in having the operation performed. That it has turned out so tragically is terrible. You cannot realize how I am suffering. I feel as if I were what you called me—a murderer. (*brokenly*) It is horrible, horrible! The thought of it will torture me all my life.

MURRAY—That don't bring her back to life. Yuh're too late!

JACK—(*frenziedly*) Too late! What do you mean? You haven't told anyone? You haven't—

MURRAY—When I left his office I went home and—she was dead. Then I come up here lookin' for *you*. I wanted to kill yuh, but—I been thinkin'—yuh're not worth gittin' hung for. (*with a cruel grin*) I c'n see a better way of fixin' yuh,— one that'll get yuh right.

JACK—(*half to himself*) You haven't told anyone?

MURRAY—What's the difference? There's plenty of time. *I* know.

JACK—(*trying to steady his voice which is trembling with apprehension*) Murray, for your own sake, for your dead sister's good name, for your family's sake you must keep this thing quiet. I do not plead for myself. I am willing to have you punish me individually in any way you see fit; but there are others, innocent ones, who will suffer.

MURRAY—She was innocent, too, before you—

JACK—(*interrupting him*) My mother and father, my sister, Ev— (*bites back the name*) This would kill my mother if she knew. They are innocent. Do not revenge yourself on them.

MURRAY—(*inflexibly*) You killed my sister.

JACK—Why will you keep saying that? You know it was an accident; that I would gladly have given my own life rather than have it happen. And you must keep silent. I will do anything you want, I tell you! (*He goes close to Murray.*) You say the doctor gave you money? I'll give you ten times as much as he did. (*Murray's face grows livid.*) I'll see that you get so much a year for the rest of your life. My father is rich. We'll get you a good position, do everything you wish, (*breaking down*) only do not punish the innocent.

MURRAY—(*slowly*) You want—to pay me—for Nellie! (*With a terrible cry of rage he pulls a revolver from the pocket of his coat. Before he can pull the trigger Jack seizes his wrist. There is a short struggle. Jack takes the revolver away from him and lays it on the table. Murray has a violent attack of coughing. He recovers and is slinking toward the door when Jack suddenly picks up the revolver from the table and holds it out to him.*)

JACK—(*steadily*) Here, take it! I was a fool to stop you. Let the thing end with me and leave the innocent alone.

MURRAY—(*malevolently*) It's too good for yuh. (*He has edged stealthily nearer and nearer the door and with a final spring gains the safety of the dark hallway. He shouts back*) I'm goin' to the p'lice station. D'yuh hear, yuh dirty ba—rd! To the p'lice station! (*His quick footsteps can be heard as he runs out. Jack makes a movement as if to follow him but stops and sits down heavily by the table, laying the revolver on it. He hears the band and the cheers of the paraders who have evidently just invaded that section of the campus. He hurries to the windows, closes them, and pulls down the shades. The band is playing a march song and the students are singing. Jack groans and hides his face in his hands. The parade is about to pass by his windows. The glare of the red fire glows dully on the window shades. Jack springs up and rushes into his bedroom on the right. Several students crowd in the doorway from the hall.*)

ONE STUDENT—He's not here.

ANOTHER STUDENT—He ran away. (*All go out laughing and shouting. The band stops playing. Jack comes out from the bedroom, his face drawn with agony. The cheerleader's voice can be heard shouting* "He ran away but if we give him a cheer, he'll hear us. A long cheer for Townsend, fellows! Hip! Hip!")

JACK—(*staggers toward the window crying brokenly*) No! No! For God's sake! (*The first part of the cheer booms out. He reels to the table and sees the revolver lying there. He snatches it up and presses it to his temple. The report is drowned by the cheering. He falls forward on his face, twitches, is still.*)

THE STUDENTS—(*winding up the nine long rahs*) Rah! Rah! Rah! Townsend! Townsend! Townsend! (*The band* strikes up: "For He's A Jolly Good Fellow." The students commence to sing. The parade moves off again. Evelyn appears in the doorway to the rear.)

EVELYN—Jack! It's all right now, dear. You can come out of hiding. (She blinks for a moment blinded by the light; then comes into the room and sees the body—in terror) Jack! What's the matter? (She rushes over and kneels beside him; then faints as she sees the blood on his temples, the revolver still clutched in his right hand. She falls on the floor beside him.)

THE STUDENTS—(their voices growing gradually fainter) For he's a jolly good fellow, which nobody can·deny.

(The Curtain Falls)

THE MOVIE MAN

A Comedy in One Act

CHARACTERS

HENRY (HEN) ROGERS, *Representative of
    Earth Motion Picture Company*
AL DEVLIN, *Photographer for the same Company*
PANCHO GOMEZ, *Commander-in-Chief of the
    Constitutionalist Army*
LUIS VIRELLA, *General of Division*
ANITA FERNANDEZ
A SENTRY

The Movie Man

SCENE—*The main room of a house in the suburb of a large town in northern Mexico. To the left, a whitewashed wall of adobe with a small black crucifix hanging from a nail. In the rear wall, a doorway opening on the street. On either side of the doorway, an open window. On the right side of the room, another door which is closed. On the wall above it, a faded lithograph of the Virgin. In the left-hand corner several Mauser carbines are stacked, and bandoleers of cartridges are thrown on the dirt floor beside them. In the right-hand corner several saddles are lying. Near the door, another saddle. In the middle of the room a rickety table with a pen, paper, and ink on it. Three or four stiff cane-bottomed chairs are placed about the table.*

Hen Rogers and Al Devlin are sitting by the table. Both are smoking pipes. Both are dressed in khaki shirts, riding breeches, puttees, etc. Their wide-brimmed Stetson hats are on the table beside them. Rogers is tall, blond, clean-shaven, in his early thirties. Devlin is short, dark, with a good-natured irregular face, middle-aged.

A sentry in a filthy, ragged olive-drab uniform lolls in the doorway leaning on his rifle. He wears the wide sombrero of the Mexican peon, and is bare-footed. He is smoking a cigarette and watching the two Americans with an expression of bored indifference.

It is in the early hours of a sultry tropic night.

DEVLIN—(*singing in a cracked falsetto*) Mexico, my nice cool Mexico!

ROGERS—(*mopping the perspiration from his forehead with a bandana handkerchief*) Have a heart, Al, have a heart, and kill the canary-bird stuff. If you see anything to be merry over in this flea-bitten cluster of shanties, you got something on me.

DEVLIN—(*chuckling*) Lovely little spot to spend the summer!

ROGERS—(*dryly*) Ideal is the word. And speaking of fleas, on the level, I never knew what a poor dog has to put up with until I hit this one-horse country.

DEVLIN—They don't bother me any.

ROGERS—No, they've got some class, you gotta hand it to them.

DEVLIN—Is *that* so?

ROGERS—"Discretion is the better part of valor"—any well-bred Mexican flea is hep to that. Those are the first words in the Mexican Constitution and every man and beast in this country swears by them; if they didn't we'd have been in Mexico City months ago; and right now I'd be down at Manhattan Beach in God's Country with a large mint julep, full of ice—

DEVLIN—(*with a groan*) Help! Help! I'm a nut!

ROGERS—When this cruel war is over and on the films I'm going to quit the picture business and go way up north, marry an Esquimau, and start housekeeping on an exclusive, refined, accordion-pleated, little iceberg.

DEVLIN—(*whistles shrilly to the sentry who grabs his rifle in alarm*) Boy, page an iceberg for Mr. Rogers!

THE SENTRY—(*with lazy scorn*) Muy loco!

ROGERS—What's that he said, Al? Look it up in your little book. It sounded almost like real talk.

DEVLIN—(*with a laugh*) I don't have to look that up. He means we're crazy.

ROGERS—(*to the sentry—approvingly*) You said something then, Mike. We sure are as nutty as a fruitcake or we wouldn't be here. Phew, but it's hot! (*after a short pause musingly*) Say, Al, did you ever notice the happy, contented expression on a polar bear's face?

DEVLIN—(*laughing*) Basta! Basta! (*The sentry instinctively springs to attention, then lapses into indifference again as he realizes it is only the crazy American speaking.*)

ROGERS—Say, you're getting to be a regular talker of spigoty! Slip me the answer to that word "basta", will you? I hear friend General pulling it all the time; and just to show you what a fine little guesser I am, I'll bet you a case-note it means "when".

DEVLIN—Come across with that peso. It doesn't mean "when"; it means "enough".

ROGERS—Same thing—I knew it—I never yet heard him say it when I was pouring him out a drink.

DEVLIN—You owe me a peso, don't forget it.

ROGERS—(*grumblingly*) I'm not liable to with you around. (*An excited babble of voices is heard from the door on the right.*) Listen to those boobs, will you! What do you suppose they're framing up in there?

DEVLIN—Who is it—Gomez?

ROGERS—Yes; he and all his little generals are having some sort of a confab. I'll bet you that smack back again he's going to try and capture the town tomorrow.

DEVLIN—What's this you're springing on me—inside information?

ROGERS—Nope; but this afternoon I gave him that case of Scotch I promised him when he signed our contract, and he's feeling some brave this evening.

DEVLIN—Say, Hen, about that contract, I forgot to tell you, you wanta hand a call to this Gomez guy. He is playing the game. You remember the other day when they were going after that fort on the outskirts?

ROGERS—Sure—good stuff—plenty of real live action that day.

DEVLIN—(*indignantly*) It was good stuff all right, but I missed all the first part of it on account of that simp General Virella. He was just waving his sword and ordering 'em to charge when I came up. "Here you!" I said to him, "wait a minute. Can't you see I'm not ready for you yet?" And what do you think that greaser said to me? You know he speaks good English. He says: "Shall my glorious soldiers be massacred waiting for your machine?" And away he runs with all his yellow-bellies after him. What d'you know about that?

ROGERS—(*frowning*) He's a fresh guy, that Virella. I'll have Gomez stick him back in the rear after this. He's a mean little worm, too. He's the one who's nagged Gomez into croaking old Fernandez.

DEVLIN—What! Are they going to shoot Fernandez?

ROGERS—At sunrise tomorrow they stand him against the wall and—curtain.

DEVLIN—It's a damn shame—just because they can't get any more coin out of him. He's a good fellow—Fernandez. Went to school in the States—Cornell or someplace. Can't you get him off?

ROGERS—Nix. Virella has a grudge against him and

Gomez needs Virella. Anyway, I've got no license to butt in
on their little scraps. Besides it'll make a great picture. Be sure
and get it.

DEVLIN—I'll be there. Say, have them hold it till a little
later, will you? The light isn't any good so early.

ROGERS—How'll eight o'clock do?

DEVLIN—Great!

ROGERS—All right, I'll tell Gomez to postpone it till then.
(*A shrill voice is heard shouting:* "Viva" *from the room on the
right.*) That's Virella, now. I'd like to take just one swing at
that guy. They'd carry him home in a white-pine kimona.
(*another cheer from the room next door*) Full of booze and patriotism! Gee, I wish I was a war correspondent. I'd send in
a little notice like this: "The courage and spirits of the troops
were never better. A trainload of rum arrived today. We will
be in Mexico City in two weeks."

DEVLIN—(*picking his hat from the table, gets to his feet*) I
think I'll take a look around and see what's doing.

ROGERS—Oho! I've got your number all right!

DEVLIN—(*laughing*) What do you mean: got my number?

ROGERS—Have a care, little one, have a care! Some one
of these Mexican dolls you're googooing at will carve her ini-
tials on your back with the breadknife some one of these
days.

DEVLIN—I should fret!

ROGERS—(*disgustedly*) What you can see in these skirts,
has got me beat. They're so homely the mules shy at them.

DEVLIN—Is *that* so? Well, let me tell you, there's some
class to some of the dames down here. You ought to have
seen the bear I lamped this afternoon. Some queen, take it
from me.

ROGERS—Load that noise in one of the cannons and fire
it off!

DEVLIN—On the level, Hen, she had the swellest lamps
I've ever seen on a dame; and a figure—my boy! my boy!

ROGERS—Captain Sweeney of the Marines, please listen!
And I suppose you copped her and dated her up?

DEVLIN—Nothing like it, Hen. She was doing a sob act
on one of the benches in that little park out here, and I asked
her in my best Spanish what was the matter. Phew! Talk

about the icy once-over! She looked at me as if I was a wet dog. I turned and beat it like a little man.

ROGERS—You were wise, for once. She'd have operated on you with her stiletto in another second. I wouldn't trust one of these dolls as far as I could hit Walter Johnson's fast one.

DEVLIN—But what d'you suppose she was doing a weep about?

ROGERS—(*dryly*) Maybe one of her husbands got killed in the war.

DEVLIN—What sweet thoughts you have! S'long, Hen. Don't forget to have Gomez postpone that shooting thing. (*He goes to door in rear.*)

ROGERS—I won't; and you come back early—if you're still alive. I want you to scratch my back before I hit the hay. I'd have to be a contortionist or a centipede to follow this flea-game properly.

DEVLIN—(*laughing*) They'll take your mind off your worries. Be good! (*He passes the sentry and disappears in the darkness. Another cheer is heard from the next room. Rogers grunts disgustedly and attempts to scratch the middle of his back. The sentry's head falls forward on his chest as he dozes in the doorway.*

(*Anita Fernandez appears outside the door and creeps stealthily by the sentry into the room. She is a beautiful young Mexican girl with a mass of black hair and great black eyes. She stumbles over the saddle by the door and utters a little cry of pain. The sentry wakes up, rushes over to her and grabs her furiously by the arm. He drags her toward the door. Rogers springs from his chair and yells at the sentry.*)

ROGERS—Hey, you Mike, what are you doing? Let go of that dame! (*The sentry scowls uncertainly at him. Rogers makes a threatening gesture and the sentry releases Anita and returns to his post by the doorway. Anita sinks into a chair by the table and, hiding her face in her hands, commences to sob. Rogers stands beside not knowing what to do.*)

ROGERS—What'll I say to her? (*sees the English-Spanish book of Devlin's on the table*) Here's Al's Spanish book. Let's see. (*turns over the pages*) What do you want?—I wonder how you say it— Oh, here it is. (*He repeats the line to himself, then bends down to Anita.*) Que quere, Senorita? (*He pronounces it "Kwi query, Seenorita?" She raises her head and stares at him with a puzzled expression.*) She doesn't make me at all— Oh Hell!

ANITA—(*haughtily*) Pleese to not swear, senor.

ROGERS—(*confused*) Excuse me—awfully sorry—tongue slipped. (*with a sigh of relief*) Thank Go—heavens, you speak English.

ANITA—But most badly, senor.

ROGERS—(*sitting down across the table from her*) No, very good, just as good as mine. Who was it you wanted to see?

ANITA—El Generalissimo Gomez.

ROGERS—(*shaking his head*) You better wait. He'll be all lit up like a torch tonight.

ANITA—(*mystified*) Senor?

ROGERS—You know what I mean—he's soused, pickled, stewed, boiled—

ANITA—(*in puzzled accents*) Es-stewed? Boiled? (*in horrified tones*) You mean he is cooking—the General? But no, senor, I onderstand Eenglish veree badly. For one year alone, I estudy in the convent in Nueva York—Noo York. Then mi madre—my mothair—die and I must come home to the house of my fathair becose I have more years—I am older than my sisters. (*There is a ringing* "Viva" *from the next room. Anita turns pale.*)

ROGERS—(*making a motion with his hand as if he were taking a drink and nodding toward the room*) You understand now? He's drinking, and—

ANITA—(*shuddering*) Ah, he es drunk, no?

ROGERS—I'm afraid he will be before he leaves that room—if he isn't already.

ANITA—(*the tears starting to her eyes*) Mi padre!

ROGERS—You better wait until tomorrow to see him.

ANITA—Eet ees not possible. I must—tonight!

ROGERS—(*earnestly*) Don't do it, Kid! Don't you know Gomez is a bad guy—man—for a young girl to come and see at night—'specially when he's drunk?

ANITA—(*flushing*) I know, si, senor, but eet must be.

ROGERS—Won't you tell me why?

ANITA—(*her voice trembling*) Si, I will tell you. Eet ees not long to tell, senor. You have heard—you know Ernesto Fernandez?

ROGERS—You mean the Fernandez who is going to be shot tomorrow morning?

ANITA—(*shuddering*) Si, senor, he eet ees I mean. He ees my fathair.

ROGERS—(*astounded*) Your father! Good God!

ANITA—I must see the General Gomez tonight to ask him to save my fathair.

ROGERS—He will not do it.

ANITA—(*faintly*) You know that, senor?

ROGERS—Virella is with him—in there—now!

ANITA—(*terrified*) Virella? He is the most bad enemy of my fathair.

ROGERS—You might buy Gomez off; pay him to set your father free. He'll do anything for money. Have you any money?

ANITA—Alas, no, senor; Gomez has taken from us everything.

ROGERS—Too bad, too bad! Hm— Well, you mustn't stay here any longer. They're liable to come out any minute. Go home now, and I'll see what I can do with Gomez.

ANITA—(*resolutely*) Gracias, I thank you, senor; you are very kind—but I must see Gomez.

ROGERS—(*deliberately,—looking steadily into her eyes*) Don't you know what Gomez will want—the price he will make you pay if he finds you here?

ANITA—(*closing her eyes and swaying weakly on her feet*) For the life—of my fathair— (*sobs softly*)

ROGERS—(*looking at her in admiration*) God!

ANITA—(*fiercely*) I would keel myself to save him!

ROGERS—But even if he said he'd free your father you couldn't believe him. What is Gomez' word worth? No, you must let me fix this for you.

ANITA—(*doubtfully*) But you— Gomez ees veree powerful, senor—ees it possible for you to do?

ROGERS—(*decisively*) I'll save your old man if I have to start a revolution of my own to do it.

ANITA—(*her eyes shining with gratitude*) Ah, thank you, senor—but if you should fail?

ROGERS—(*emphatically*) I won't fail. You just watch me start something! (*He has scarcely finished speaking when the door to the right is thrown open and Gomez and Virella enter the room. They are both in a state of great excitement and show they have been drinking. Virella is an undersized man with shifty, beady black eyes and a black mustache. Gomez is tall and heavily built with a bloated dissipated-looking face and a bristly black mustache. Both are dressed in new uniforms of olive-drab and wear military caps. Cartridge-belts with automatic revolvers in leather holsters are strapped about their waists over their coats.*)

(*Anita stares at them for a moment with horrified loathing; then shrinks away into the far corner of the room. Gomez turns to shout an "Adios" to the officers who are still carousing in the room he has just left; then bangs the door shut behind him. Virella sees Anita and walks toward her with a drunken leer on his flushed face.*)

VIRELLA—Buenos noches, senorita.

ROGERS—(*steps forward and places himself in front of Virella whom he grasps by the shoulders and forcibly turns in the direction of the door*) Now, beat it, Snake-in-the-Grass!

VIRELLA—(*struggling to free himself*) Pig of a Gringo!

ROGERS—General Gomez and I want to have a talk in private, don't we, Gomez? (*He glances at Gomez with a commanding air.*)

GOMEZ—(*uncertainly*) Por cierto, amigo, if you like eet.

VIRELLA—(*frothing at the mouth with rage*) Dog! Pig!

ROGERS—(*calmly*) Those are hard words, my pet—and you hear what your general commands? (*He turns to Gomez.*)

GOMEZ—Si, Virella, I command eet.

ROGERS—(*to Virella, contemptuously*) Now blow before I crown you! (*He draws back his fist threateningly. Virella shrinks away from him, salutes Gomez, and slinks out of the door in rear.*)

GOMEZ—(*forcing a laugh*) Ees thees the way you treat my generals?

ROGERS—You ought to shoot that little scorpion—before he shoots you.

GOMEZ—(*frowning*) Eet ees true, amigo, what you say, and pairhaps soon—but—now he ees to me necessary. (*He notices Anita for the first time and turns to Rogers with a chuckle.*) Excuse me, a senorita! (*takes his cap off and makes her a gallant bow*) Ah, Senor Rogers, you are—how you call eet?—a man of—ladies, no? (*He walks over to Anita who shrinks back to the wall in terror.*) Have you fear of me, chiquita? Of Gomez? But Pancho Gomez, he loav the ladies, that ees well known. Ask el senor Rogers. (*He chucks her under the chin.*)

ROGERS—(*stepping between them—quietly*) This young lady is *my* friend, Gomez.

GOMEZ—(*biting his lips*) I say in fun only. (*He walks back to the table and remarks sullenly to Rogers who is following him*) She ees "muy hermosa", veree preety, your senorita.

ROGERS—She is the daughter of Ernesto Fernandez.

GOMEZ—(*surprised*) Que dice? What you say?

ROGERS—She's the daughter of the man you're going to have shot in the morning. She came to ask you—

GOMEZ—(*emphatically*) No, hombre, no! I know what you will say. I can not do. Eet ees not possible! (*Anita rushes forward and throws herself at his feet.*) No, no, no, senorita, I must go. (*He strides toward the door in the rear. Anita lies where she has thrown herself, sobbing hopelessly.*)

ROGERS—One minute, Gomez! Where are you going?

GOMEZ—To prepare the attack. Ah, I forget! I have not tole you. (*excitedly*) Tonight, amigo, we storm the town. We catch them asleep, no? and before they wake they are—(*he makes a motion across his neck with his forefinger*) dead, how you call eet?—as a nail. (*proudly*) Eet ees a plan sublime, most glorious—eet ees the plan of Gomez! In one small week, hombre, shall we be in Mexico City.

ROGERS—That Scotch is great stuff. One more drink and old Napoleon would be a piker.

GOMEZ—(*puzzled*) What you say?

ROGERS—Nothing, nothing. (*his face lighting up with a ray of hope*) A night attack, eh?

GOMEZ—Si, hombre, at twelve hours—twelve o'clock.

ROGERS—(*calmly*) Who said so?

GOMEZ—I say it, I, Pancho Gomez!

ROGERS—(*emphatically*) Well, you just listen to me, Gomez; I say you can't do it. There'll be no night attacks in this war when I'm around. (*Gomez is stupefied.*) How do you expect us to get pictures at night? You didn't think of that, eh?

GOMEZ—(*bewildered*) But, amigo—

ROGERS—Nix on the night attacks, do you get me? (*pulls a paper out of his pocket*) Here's a copy of your contract giving us rights to all your fights, *all*, do you hear, all! And we got one clause especially for night attacks. (*reads*) The party of the second part hereby agrees to fight no battles at night or on rainy days or at any time whatsoever when the light is so poor as to make the taking of motion pictures impracticable. Failure to comply with these conditions will constitute a breach of contract and free the party of the first part from all the obligations entered into by this contract. (*hands the contract to Gomez*) Here it is, black and white, English and Spanish both, with your signature at the bottom with mine. Read for yourself. (*Gomez glances at the paper mechanically and hands it back.*)

GOMEZ—(*with a defiant snarl*) And if I say: "To hell, you!" Then what you do, eh?

ROGERS—(*mimicking the General's tone*) Who buys and sends you most of your ammunition, eh? Who pays you and the other Generals and the German in charge of your artillery—the only man who savvys how to use the guns right—eh? Who has promised to see that you get siege guns for Mexico City and twenty more machine guns with men, real men, to run them for you, eh? Your soldiers'll desert you if you don't pay them soon, and you know it. Well, who has agreed to loan you the money to give them their back pay, eh? And, above all, who has promised to help you become President when you reach Mexico City? (*impressively*) We have—The Earth Motion Picture Company! Well, you break this contract and all that stops, see? and goes to the other side.

GOMEZ—(*softly—fingering his revolver*) Bueno; but I can also have you shot, hombre.

ROGERS—Nix on that rough stuff! You wouldn't dare. You've got to keep on the right side of the U.S.A. or your revolution isn't worth the powder to blow it to—Mexico.

GOMEZ—(*pleadingly*) But, amigo, permit eet this once. The plan is fine, the town will be ours, my soldiers will steal and no more grumble against Gomez. Tomorrow I will shoot all the prisoners for your pictures, I promise eet.

ROGERS—(*kindly*) I'd like to do you a favor, Gomez, but I don't see my way to do this, unless—

GOMEZ—(*with a smile*) Aha, tell me, hombre, your price.

ROGERS—(*firmly*) The life of Ernesto Fernandez! (*Anita jumps to her feet and stretches out her arms beseechingly to Gomez. He twirls his mustache thoughtfully for a moment.*)

GOMEZ—Bueno, my friend, I accept your terms. (*He goes to the table and hurriedly scratches a few lines which he hands to Anita.*) Su padre de uste—your father, he ees free, senorita. For this thank my fine friend Senor Rogers. (*He claps Rogers jovially on the back.*) Now must I have shot the General Virella who will never forgive me your father should live, senorita. Mexico ees too es-small for those two hombres—both alive. (*pulls a flask from his pocket and offers it to Rogers who refuses with a smile*) Senor Rogers—how you call eet?—here ees looking at you! (*drinks*) And now I must to prepare the attack. (*goes to the door; then turns and remarks grandiloquently*) Should anyone wish me, senor, tell them that een the hour of battle, Pancho Gomez, like the immortal Juarez, will ever be found at the head of his brave soldiers. Adios! (*He makes a sweeping bow and goes out past the saluting sentry.*)

ROGERS—(*with a long whistle of amusement—turning to Anita*) Some bull! Honest, you've got to hand it to that guy, at that.

ANITA—And now I, too, must go—to my poor fathair.

ROGERS—Can't I take you there? You know there's lots of drunken soldiers around and—

ANITA—No, no, senor, you are too kind. Eet ees but two steps to the carcel—the prison. Eet ees not necessary. (*indicating the paper in her hand*) The name of Gomez is most sufficient. (*holding out her hand to him with a shy smile*) Muchissima gracias, senor,—with all my heart do I thank you. My fathair and I—we will be at the home tomorrow—eet ees the first hacienda beyond the hill—you will come, senor? As a brother, my father's son, shall you be to us!

ROGERS—(*holding her hand and looking into her eyes*) Only—a brother?

ANITA—(*drawing her hand away in confusion, runs to the door; then turns*) Quien sabe, senor? Who knows? (*She hurries out.*)

ROGERS—(*does a few Spanish dance steps, snapping his fingers and humming. The sentry grins at him.*) What are you grinning at, Mike?

THE SENTRY—(*with a contemptuous smile makes a gesture of turning a wheel near his head*) Muy loco!

ROGERS—I got you the first time, Mike. Crazy is the right word. (*He commences to sing*) Mexico, My bright-eyed Mexico. (*Devlin appears in the doorway and scowls darkly at him.*)

DEVLIN—Kill it, kill it, you bone! (*Comes in and throws his hat irritably on the table. Rogers looks at him with an amused smile.*) What're you chirping about? Are you soused, too? Where have you hidden the joy-water? Everyone in this bush-league army seems all corned up tonight except me. Say I just got another flash at that dame I was telling you about. She looked right through me at something behind my back. Some nerve to that greaser chicken giving a real white man the foot! (*scornfully*) I got a good slant at her this time. She isn't much to look at after all. Back in God's Country we'd use her photo for a before-taking ad.

ROGERS—(*indignantly*) Al, you always were a simp! (*grumblingly*) Better get a pair of cheaters for those bum lamps of yours. (*cheerfully*) Cheer up, Al, you're all wrong, my son, you're all wrong! (*Devlin gapes at him in open-mouthed amazement, Rogers commences to sing again:* "Mexico, my bright-eyed Mexico." *The sentry grunts contemptuously, as*

The Curtain Falls)

SERVITUDE

A Play in Three Acts

CHARACTERS

DAVID ROYLSTON, *playwright and novelist*
ALICE ROYLSTON, *his wife*
DAVIE ⎫
RUTH ⎭ *their children*
GEORGE FRAZER, *a broker*
ETHEL FRAZER, *his wife*
BENTON, *a man-servant*
WESON, *a gardener*

ACT I: David Roylston's study in his house at Tarryville-on-Hudson, N. Y.—about ten o'clock in the evening.
ACT II: The same—about nine o'clock the following morning.
ACT III: The same—No time elapses between Acts 2 and 3. One is a continuation of the other.

Time: The present day.

Servitude

ACT I

SCENE—*The study in the house of David Roylston at Tarry-ville-on-Hudson, New York. In the middle of the far side of the room, a fireplace. To the right of it, a door. The remaining space of the back wall is covered by book-cases which frame the fireplace and door. In the left foreground, another door. Next to it, a writing desk. Still farther back, a book-case. On the right, a leather sofa and armchairs. On either side of the sofa, an open window looking out on the garden. In the center of the room, a table on which are a heap of books and an electric reading lamp with a green shade. A few framed prints of Old Masters are hung on the walls.*

It is about ten o'clock on a sultry night in early May.

David Roylston is seated at the table, writing. He is a tall, slender, dark-haired man of thirty-five with large handsome features, a strong, ironical mouth half-hidden by a black mustache, and keenly-intelligent dark eyes. He has taken off his coat which hangs from the back of his chair. He wears a white shirt with soft collar and black bow tie, grey trousers, and low tan shoes with rubber soles.

Benton enters from the door at the rear and stands waiting for Roylston to notice his presence. He is fifty-five, clean-shaven, discreetly soft-spoken. One of his eyes is badly crossed giving him a look of sly villainy quite out of keeping with his placid temperament. He wears a livery.

ROYLSTON—(*looking up from his writing*) Well, Benton?

BENTON—Shall I shut the windows, sir? It's started to rain a little.

ROYLSTON—No, I will close them myself when I go to bed.

BENTON—(*reproachfully*) They were open when I came down this morning, sir.

ROYLSTON—Were they? I must have forgotten all about them last night. Never mind; there's nothing much worth the stealing in this house except ideas and the thieves of ideas are not usually housebreakers. But if it will ease your anxiety, you may close them. There's a draft in here.

BENTON—Yes, sir. (*He closes the windows.*)

ROYLSTON—Any telephone calls while I was out?

BENTON—Mrs. Roylston called up, sir; wished me to tell you that she and the children had arrived safely in New York; had a very pleasant trip in the motor; roads were fine all the way down. She said the children were very excited to think they were really going to the theatre.

ROYLSTON—(*abstractedly*) Ah, indeed. No one else called up?

BENTON—No, sir.

ROYLSTON—Not even the young lady who has (*ironically*) asked my advice so frequently of late?

BENTON—No, sir.

ROYLSTON—Well, whenever the young lady in question calls up again you are to tell her I am writing and cannot be disturbed.

BENTON—Yes, sir.

ROYLSTON—(*impatiently*) She is becoming a bore; and I am in the midst of a play and have no time for such foolishness.

BENTON—Very good, sir. Anything else before I go to bed, sir?

ROYLSTON—No, you may go. (*Benton takes Roylston's light overcoat, hat, and stick, which are lying on one of the armchairs, and starts to go out.*) Leave those here. I may take a walk later on to get a breath of the Spring and blow the cobwebs out of my brain, and I don't care to be barking my shins in the dark hall. (*Benton lays them down again. A doorbell is heard ringing somewhere in the house.*) Who can that be at this time of the night? (*as Benton hurries out through the door on the left*) Remember, Benton, I'm busy—too busy to be disturbed.

BENTON—Yes, sir. (*He goes out. Roylston bites his pen nervously, trying to concentrate his thoughts. A minute or so later Benton enters. He is visibly embarrassed and is turning over a card in his fingers.*)

ROYLSTON—Well?

BENTON—It's a lady, sir.

ROYLSTON—Has she gone?

BENTON—No, sir, she—

ROYLSTON—(*frowning*) Did you tell her I was busy?

BENTON—Yes, sir, but she said she must see you on a very important matter; said she wouldn't leave till she saw you. This is her card, sir.

ROYLSTON—(*looking at it*) Mrs. George Frazer—hm—Mrs., eh?; never heard of her. An old crank of some kind, I suppose?

BENTON—Quite the other way, sir; young and pretty, I should say, if I'm any judge.

ROYLSTON—Anyone come with her?

BENTON—I don't think so, sir

ROYLSTON—Alone, at this time of night, and (*sarcastically*) a lady, you say?

BENTON—(*promptly*) No doubt of that, sir; but dressed shabby almost, as if she'd seen better days; you know what I mean, sir.

ROYLSTON—(*cynically*) Ah, then, I had better get my checkbook ready.

BENTON—Beg your pardon, sir, but she doesn't seem that kind either; not like one that'd beg, I mean. I couldn't make her out exactly.

ROYLSTON—Perhaps she's another aspiring playwright who wants me to write her last act for her. At any rate you have aroused my curiosity; so show her in here. (*He takes his coat off the back of the chair and puts it on.*)

BENTON—Very well, sir. (*He goes out through the door on the left. A moment later he shows in Mrs. Frazer. She is a tall, strikingly beautiful woman about twenty-eight years old. Her complexion is pale; her eyes large, expressive, dark; her hair black and wavy; her figure inclining a little toward voluptuousness. There are shadows in under her eyes and her face is drawn. Her manner is troubled, nervous, uncertain. She has on a plain black dress such as is worn by the poorer class of working women.*)

ROYLSTON—(*getting up and staring at her with open admiration*) Ah! (*turning to Benton*) You may go, Benton. I shan't need you again. I will take Mrs.—er (*looking at the card*) Mrs. Frazer to the door myself.

BENTON—Yes, sir. (*He goes out.*)

MRS. FRAZER—(*uncertainly*) I hope you will pardon—

ROYLSTON—(*indicating the armchairs on the left*) Won't

you sit down, Mrs. Frazer? (*She sits down in the one nearest to him.*) And now, what can I do for you?

MRS. FRAZER—I know this intrusion of mine is unpardonable. You must be terribly busy, and I have forced myself on you, interrupted your work—

ROYLSTON—You must not feel conscience-stricken about that. I was only puzzling over a problem in construction. I am glad to have my mind taken off it for a time.

MRS. FRAZER—But my coming here at this time of the night and alone? (*forcing a smile*) What can you think of such a breach of all the conventions!

ROYLSTON—(*dryly*) You are the very first to accuse me of conventionality. I see nothing strange in your coming here when you wanted to, when you were able to. I have lived long enough in this suburb to know the difficulties of getting here at the time one wishes.

MRS. FRAZER—(*looking at him for a moment with a questioning smile*) Can't you remember ever having seen me before?

ROYLSTON—No, I must confess—

MRS. FRAZER—And yet you have met me. I can, at least, plead that much justification for this encroachment on your time.

ROYLSTON—(*trying to remember*) It's no use. My brain is too full of marionettes to recall flesh-and-blood realities. I confess to my shame I will have to ask you where it was.

MRS. FRAZER—Oh, I did not dream of your remembering. We only spoke about two words to each other, and it was at least a year ago. You remember the ball Mr. Coleman, the artist, gave at his studio?

ROYLSTON—So it was there? It would be too trite for me to say I knew I had seen you before; but I really did have that feeling when you came in. One doesn't forget a face like yours. So it was at Coleman's studio? He and I have been friends for years.

MRS. FRAZER—He is a very dear friend of my—of mine, also.

ROYLSTON—Do take off your hat now that we know who's who. To see you sitting there with your hat on gives me the uncomfortable impression that this is a lawyer's office and you are consulting your attorney—and I warn you I am far from being a *legal* adviser.

MRS. FRAZER—(*takes off her hat and puts it on the sofa; leans back in her chair*) I knew it. That is why I came.

ROYLSTON—For advice?

MRS. FRAZER—Advice which I must have or—

ROYLSTON—Or?

MRS. FRAZER—The crowning disillusion.

ROYLSTON—(*smiling*) I hope it is not about me, the illusion.

MRS. FRAZER—(*emphatically*) It is about you but it is not an illusion.

ROYLSTON—Certainty goeth before disappointment.

MRS. FRAZER—In this case it must not. I have borne so much already,—I could not bear it. I must have something firm to stand on.

ROYLSTON—Then it is not a play you come to consult me about? (*seeing her mystified expression*) I beg your pardon, but you know there are so many playwrights-in-embryo who come to me for suggestions about their work—as if I could help them; as if it were not absolutely necessary for them to work out their own salvation!—and I thought when you mentioned advice—

MRS. FRAZER—(*smiling*) I see. No, I almost wish it were. I would like to be able to write a play even if it were only a very bad one. It would at least prove I was capable of creating something; I'm afraid even that is beyond my power.

ROYLSTON—(*perfunctorily*) One never knows till one tries. The thing to do is to make a start; and then, if necessary, realize one's mistake smilingly.

MRS. FRAZER—I intend to try sometime. (*apologetically*) I'm wasting your time and I will come to the point at once; or rather I will have to go back quite a ways to give you a clear idea of my present situation. (*nervously*) Won't you smoke or appear occupied with something? I won't feel such an intruder if you do.

ROYLSTON—(*laughing*) I would have done so before if I had known you didn't object.

MRS. FRAZER—On the contrary, I like it. My hus— I

have always been accustomed to men who smoked. My father was a great smoker.

ROYLSTON—(*who has taken a box of cigarettes from his pocket and lighted one*) There. (*He leans back in his chair in an attitude of attention.*)

MRS. FRAZER—To begin at the beginning; My father was a prominent lawyer with a wide practice. He died five years ago leaving a large estate to my mother who is still alive but in very feeble health. They had only two children, my brother, five years older than I am, and myself. I tell you all this because you lay such stress in all your books and plays on the influence of environment, and I want you to understand thoroughly what mine was. Being the baby and pet of the family you can readily guess how I was brought up—governesses, private tutors, and finally a finishing school. Of course at the end of their elaborate system of education I knew only what a young lady of my position should know—nothing of any value.

ROYLSTON—(*smiling*) Naturally; but you have progressed wonderfully since then.

MRS. FRAZER—If I have, I have paid for it; and whatever progress I have made I owe to you.

ROYLSTON—(*wonderingly*) To me?

MRS. FRAZER—We haven't come to that part of the story yet. When I returned home from the finishing school my life became one long round of receptions, parties, balls, and so forth, until, in spite of the fact that at that time I was only interested in the most superficial things, I became surfeited, bored, and felt a longing to break away and experience something of more interest.

ROYLSTON—You wished to try your wings.

MRS. FRAZER—Yes, that was it. It was about this time I met Mr. Frazer, the man who afterward became my husband. He was then, and still is, a broker on the New York Stock Exchange. He fascinated me. I seemed to see personified in him all I had read about the (*sarcastically*) financial giants, the daring gamblers who fought their battles to the bitter end of ruin. The house he was connected with is one of the largest on the Exchange and some of the so-called Napoleons of finance, whose names were forever in newspaper headlines, did their business through it. I thought of him doing his part in their gigantic enterprises, laboring to effect ever larger combinations in order that this glorious country might thrive and become ever greater and more productive. (*with a short laugh*) You can see what a child I was; but I'm afraid you're not listening.

ROYLSTON—(*eagerly*) I assure you you are mistaken. I am intensely interested. I was simply trying to recall something. Do you know when I watch you and listen to you talk I am forcibly reminded of some other woman. The likeness is so perfect it's uncanny.

MRS. FRAZER—May I ask who it is?

ROYLSTON—That's exactly what I cannot recollect. I am sure it's someone I know intimately and yet, for the life of me, I cannot bring the exact person to my mind.

MRS. FRAZER—How strange.

ROYLSTON—But I'm interrupting you. Please go on with your story.

MRS. FRAZER—Well, the inevitable happened. I fell in love with George—Mr. Frazer—and he with me, and after a short engagement we were married. My family approved of him in every way. I believe they cherished the same illusion about his business, in a modified form, perhaps, as I did.

ROYLSTON—Do you not think your husband also had the same illusions?

MRS. FRAZER—It would be hard to say. In justice to him I must acknowledge he always seemed to idealize it. He never could see his business in all its hideousness as I came to see it, and I don't think he wore a mask just for my benefit; but you never can tell.

ROYLSTON—Most of them can't see the unpleasant side. It becomes so much a part of themselves, you know. And after you were married?

MRS. FRAZER—Oh, the usual honeymoon trip to Europe with it's inevitable visits to Westminster Abbey, the tomb of Napoleon, the Cologne Cathedral, and other points of interest.

ROYLSTON—(*ironically*) How ideal!

MRS. FRAZER—And yet I was very happy, or thought I was happy, which is much the same thing. Of course in the light of what I now know, of what you have taught me, I can see it was merely a stupid happiness, the content of the born blind who have never seen the light.

ROYLSTON—And I am to blame for your enlightenment?

MRS. FRAZER—To blame?

ROYLSTON—Since it has made you unhappy it must be blameworthy.

MRS. FRAZER—(*with fine scorn*) What is such sluggish content worth? When you had opened my eyes to the truth I repudiated it. I felt I must win to a higher plane—or remain unhappy.

ROYLSTON—(*bewildered—running his fingers through his hair—with laughing impatience*) How you do remind me of someone! And yet I cannot remember— But tell me how this great change came about. After your return from your honeymoon I suppose your husband laid aside his rôle of lover and became the business man once more, leaving you to ornament his home, and brood, and read my novels and plays.

MRS. FRAZER—That is what you would naturally think, isn't it? However, you are quite wrong. My husband was as much the lover on the day I left him as he had been when we were married seven years before.

ROYLSTON—Then you have left him?

MRS. FRAZER—Yes, eight months ago.

ROYLSTON—Have you no children?

MRS. FRAZER—No. I used to be very sorry we had not; but now I am glad. It would have made it so much harder for me when the time came to free myself.

ROYLSTON—You fell in love with someone else?

MRS. FRAZER—(*flushing*) If I had ceased to love my husband it is no reason why—

ROYLSTON—(*smiling*) You must not be offended. It usually happens that way you know.

MRS. FRAZER—(*earnestly*) I was in love with an ideal— the ideal of self-realization, of the duty of the individual to assert its supremacy and demand the freedom necessary for its development. You had taught me that ideal and it was that which came in conflict with my marriage. I saw I could never hope to grow in the stifling environment of married life—so I broke away.

ROYLSTON—(*gravely*) Please tell me in what manner I effected this change in you.

MRS. FRAZER—I bought one of your novels one day about two years ago, more out of curiosity than anything else. It was the one about Wall Street.

ROYLSTON—You mean "The Street".

MRS. FRAZER—Yes, that's the one.

ROYLSTON—Then it was that book of mine which disillusioned you about your husband's business?

MRS. FRAZER—Yes. When I first read it I couldn't believe it. I began to ask George questions about his deals and so forth. He was surprised and happy to find me interested in his work and he finally used to explain all his transactions to me—and then I knew.

ROYLSTON—Hm.

MRS. FRAZER—I tried to persuade him to go into something else. He acknowledged there was a lot of truth in your book but said there were two ways of looking at everything. When I pleaded with him he laughed and called me his "dear little muckraker".

ROYLSTON—(*smiling*) So you became disillusioned about the broker—but how about the man?

MRS. FRAZER—Your book made me long to read what you had to say about other things. I bought all your published works, and went to see all your plays, not once but many times. It dawned upon me gradually that the life he and I were living together was the merest sham; that we were contented because he was too busy and I was too lazy to analyze our position, to stop and think. For a long time I was very unhappy. I knew what I must do but I did not have the courage to do it.

ROYLSTON—(*impatiently*) Why didn't you tell him frankly how you felt?

MRS. FRAZER—I couldn't. You see he was so good and kind to me and it seemed such heartless cruelty to hurt him. All the time I felt myself being ground smaller and smaller day by day. I discovered that he and I had not a thought in common. Everything he was interested in was so shallow. He never concerned himself with what lay beneath the surface and I know my thoughts bored him although he was far too kind to ever show it. He observed the change in me and it worried him but the only remedies he could suggest were (*with a short laugh*) Southern California, a trip to Europe, or some other change of air. When I refused to go away he was at a loss what to do. I think toward the end he suspected I was in love with someone else.

ROYLSTON—(*with a cynical smile*) I'll wager he did.

MRS. FRAZER—I resolved not to think. I plunged into all sorts of activities to try and forget myself. I learned shorthand and typewriting—

ROYLSTON—(*interrupting her enthusiastically*) Good! That is your salvation.

MRS. FRAZER—(*wearily*) My soul refused to be lulled to sleep and there came a day when I left a note for my husband and left the house. I had been to see your play "Sacrifice" the night before for the tenth time. It seemed to breathe a message to me over the footlights. You remember when Mrs. Harding in the play leaves her husband with the words: "I have awakened!"?

ROYLSTON—(*his eyes searching hers with keen questioning*) Yes, but Mrs. Harding has a lover to go to.

MRS. FRAZER—(*bearing his scrutiny unflinchingly*) And I have an ideal which I love. When I heard her say those words that night they impressed me as never before. I felt that I, too, had awakened; that the time had come to assert my—

ROYLSTON—(*with a sudden exclamation—interrupting her*) The puzzle is solved. What a dolt I am! It is Mrs. Harding in my play you resemble so much.

MRS. FRAZER—(*surprised*) Oh, is it? I saw the play so many times, you see.

ROYLSTON—And you left your husband the next day?

MRS. FRAZER—Yes. I sold some things which I had a right to call my own and bought a plain black dress. I knew I would have to become a worker, a wage-earner, and I wished to take nothing with me to remind me of the old life.

ROYLSTON—(*sympathetically*) I can imagine the ordeals

you have been through since then. When one is beautiful it is doubly hard.

MRS. FRAZER—(*blushing—hurriedly*) At first I missed all the little comforts and luxuries I had been used to. I never knew till I had to do without them how they had grown into my life. I got bravely over that. I found it very hard to get work and harder still to keep it. The men were all such beasts and the women I had to come in contact with were so unintelligent and ordinary.

ROYLSTON—(*dryly*) You'll find most people are—rather ordinary.

MRS. FRAZER—In my last position I really thought for a time my employer was a gentleman. I discovered he was only playing a part to throw me off my guard and he turned out the worst of all. And then the unspeakably long nights in the dingy hall bedroom of a boarding house with no one to speak to, no money, no place to go; not able even to take a walk alone on the streets for fear of the insults, the smirking groups in the doorways and on the corners. Oh, yes, it has been hard! (*her voice trembling*) It has been almost more than I could endure.

ROYLSTON—(*kindly*) Come; it was your ordeal of fire and you have borne up wonderfully. Have you never received word from your husband?

MRS. FRAZER—That is the worst of all. He has haunted me, waited for me at the doors of boarding houses, at the entrance of office buildings where I worked, pleading with me to come back, offering to do anything I wished, trying to force money on me, even pushing it in under the door of my room. He cannot understand what has come over me. I think he really believes I am the victim of a mad infatuation for a married man; and yet he has had me followed continually, to protect me, as he says, not to spy on me, and he knows I have seen no one. (*putting her hands over her face with a sob*) And he looks so unhappy, so miserable. I feel so guilty whenever I see him.

ROYLSTON—(*gently*) Are you sure you no longer love him?

MRS. FRAZER—(*hysterically*) Oh, love, love, what is love? How can I know? I am certain I could no longer live with him. How can you doubt it after all I have told you? I know that I like him very much and do not want to see him suffer on my account.

ROYLSTON—(*after a pause—frowning*) Have you stopped to think that you might have been followed here?

MRS. FRAZER—I am certain I was not. He has given up hope. I haven't seen him in over a month. Besides, I took special pains to throw anyone off the track. I went down to the office building where I used to work this morning and left by a side entrance. I used the freight elevator to come down in. No one could have seen me.

ROYLSTON—Where have you been all day?

MRS. FRAZER—Sitting on a bench in Central Park.

ROYLSTON—But good heavens, Mrs. Frazer, why didn't you come during the day?

MRS. FRAZER—I was afraid you might be out. You see, I had read in the paper that you always worked at night and I felt pretty sure of finding you. I could not afford more than one trip. To be quite frank with you, it was with the last dollar I had in the world that I came out here.

ROYLSTON—But if I had not been at home?

MRS. FRAZER—(*firmly*) I should have waited until you came. No matter how, I should have waited.

ROYLSTON—(*plainly embarrassed—getting up and walking nervously about the room*) You have been frank with me, Mrs. Frazer. Will you permit me to be the same?

MRS. FRAZER—I wish you to be so.

ROYLSTON—You promise to take no offense at what I am going to ask you?

MRS. FRAZER—I am not afraid. I know you are trying to help me.

ROYLSTON—I am glad of that. What I want to ask is: Will you let me help you in—er—a pecuniary way?

MRS. FRAZER—(*rather indignantly*) How could you think so?

ROYLSTON—I mean as a loan, you know. You really ought to—

MRS. FRAZER—You know I could not.

ROYLSTON—Then you have not freed yourself from all prejudices after all. You will certainly let me see to it that you get a position where you will be well paid and respected?

MRS. FRAZER—Gladly, and be more than grateful for your assistance.

ROYLSTON—(*with a sigh of relief*) Then, that is settled. (*Mrs. Frazer suddenly breaks down and commences to sob. Roylston goes to her and lays his hand on her shoulder.*) There, there, Mrs. Frazer. I know it has been hard. It's bound to be, you know, for a woman in your position. The future will be much easier, you'll find. Please don't break down that way. (*a pause*) I feel as if I were responsible for all this and yet—

MRS. FRAZER—(*wiping her tears away and trying to control herself*) You don't understand. You are only looking at the material side. I don't care about that. What I came here to demand—yes, demand, for I have a right to do so—was certainty, the assurance that I am on the right path. These past few weeks with their sleepless nights have been terrible.

ROYLSTON—How can I—

MRS. FRAZER—Had I the right to do what I did? To cause others so much suffering? Am I realizing the best that is in me or the worst? My will to keep on striving is being broken. I doubt the worth of my action. When I see him so unhappy I say to myself: "Have you the right?" and I find no answer to satisfy me. I can only argue and argue until my brain aches. How can I bear hardship for a cause in which my faith is wavering? That is why I come to you.

ROYLSTON—(*in a troubled voice*) I cannot tell you how deeply grieved I am to have been even the indirect means of causing you pain.

MRS. FRAZER—(*excitedly*) I have the right to come to you, haven't I? Mentally I am your creation. That you had no knowledge of my existence when you wrote does not lessen your responsibility in my eyes. I demand that you restore my peace of mind by justifying me to myself.

ROYLSTON—(*deeply moved*) What I have written cannot apply to every case. (*with conviction*) But it is my sincerest belief that you have found yourself, that as things stand between you, it would be folly for you to go back to your husband; that out of your present distress will spring a higher satisfaction than you have ever before known or believed possible. Therefore I urge you not to give up the battle, for in the end you will achieve a victory well worth the winning.

MRS. FRAZER—(*extending both her hands to him—gratefully*) You have given me new hope, new strength.

ROYLSTON—(*taking her hands and looking into her eyes*) Promise me you will call on me whenever you need help in the future.

MRS. FRAZER—(*withdrawing her hands—simply*) I promise to do so.

ROYLSTON—(*smiling*) You must now, you know. You have charged me with the responsibility. You must let me pay off my debt.

MRS. FRAZER—(*forcing a smile*) Whenever my supply of will-power runs low I'll come a-borrowing, never fear.

ROYLSTON—By the way, I meant to ask you if your mother and brother know anything of all this?

MRS. FRAZER—No. My mother is in Switzerland. Her health is so feeble I have not dared to tell her about it; and I know she would never learn of it through Mr. Frazer. My brother is the manager of a railroad in Brazil and very seldom returns to this country or writes to me. So, of course, he knows nothing.

ROYLSTON—But your husband's family?

MRS. FRAZER—I believe he has told them something about my being in California for my health.

ROYLSTON—You have that in your favor. Family interference always complicates matters. As for the position I promised you, I will see what I can do when I go to the city in the morning. I have many influential friends and I have no doubt a real opportunity will be found for you someplace. In the meantime I have lots of work which should be typewritten and if you care to—

MRS. FRAZER—Oh, how good of you! Your encouragement has made me feel so hopeful, so full of energy, I am ready for anything. A new life of wonderful possibilities seems opening up before me.

ROYLSTON—It will be full of obstacles, too.

MRS. FRAZER—(*spiritedly*) The harder the better. With your help I know I shall overcome them.

ROYLSTON—You are overrating me. Take warning!

MRS. FRAZER—(*picking up her hat from the sofa*) And now I had better be going back to my little hall room.

ROYLSTON—(*looking at his watch—then turning to her with a quizzical smile*) Yes, but how?

MRS. FRAZER—What do you mean?

ROYLSTON—I mean the little hall-room will have to remain empty tonight. You have missed the last train.

MRS. FRAZER—(*apparently greatly astonished*) Surely you don't mean it? And I never looked at the timetable! Why didn't you warn me?

ROYLSTON—I had no idea what time it was.

MRS. FRAZER—How stupid of me! That comes of living in the city where you can always get the Subway or something. I must get back some way.

ROYLSTON—It's impossible, I'm afraid.

MRS. FRAZER—Then what can I do?

ROYLSTON—You must stay here.

MRS. FRAZER—Here—in this house?

ROYLSTON—There is no alternative unless you wish to pass the night in the fields.

MRS. FRAZER—There must be a hotel.

ROYLSTON—There is only a roadhouse, a place of very questionable character, frequented by joy-riders and their—companions. You could not go there; and I know of no other place. You see, there are nothing but summer residences around here and I am hardly acquainted with any of the neighbors. (*gravely*) Think of the time of night, and the rain, of the conclusions which would be drawn. You are beautiful and people have evil minds. Don't you see the impossibility?

MRS. FRAZER—Yes—but, oh—how can I stay here? What will your wife think?

ROYLSTON—She will not think. She will never know.

MRS. FRAZER—I—I don't understand.

ROYLSTON—She is not here. Except for the servants I am all alone.

MRS. FRAZER—(*genuinely alarmed*) Then I must go, even if I do have to spend the night in the fields.

ROYLSTON—Listen; there is rather a strange coincidence, or shall I say fatality in all this. My wife went with the children to see the fairy play in New York, and contrary to her usual custom—she doesn't care for motoring—she went down in the machine. Otherwise I could have had the chauffeur drive you home; but they won't return before tomorrow afternoon at the earliest.

MRS. FRAZER—(*frightened*) This is terrible. How can I— (*hurries to the window and looks out*) It's pouring.

ROYLSTON—Fatality.

MRS. FRAZER—(*imploringly*) Please, please suggest something! You know I can't stay. (*She looks at him pleadingly—her lips tremble.*)

ROYLSTON—Why not? (*slowly*) Don't you believe you would be as safe here in my house as in your dingy hall bedroom?

MRS. FRAZER—(*looking at him searchingly*) Yes—I know I would be—but—

ROYLSTON—(*impatiently*) But you are afraid of appearances, of what people might think if they knew. You never learned that fear from me. Is not the knowledge of your own innocence enough to raise you above such considerations? Or are you afraid I may be a Don Juan in disguise?

MRS. FRAZER—No, I am not afraid of you.

ROYLSTON—And even if you fear appearances? Who is to know?

MRS. FRAZER—(*wavering*) You forget your servant.

ROYLSTON—He has been with me for years, was with my father before me, all his life has been in our service. I flatter myself he's a model of discretion.

MRS. FRAZER—But what will he think of me? (*seeing Roylston's scornful smile*) But it doesn't matter. I will stay.

ROYLSTON—Bravo! It would be foolish and cowardly of you to get soaked with the rain and be insulted, and perhaps worse, in the railroad station for the sake of a worn-out code of ethics.

MRS. FRAZER—(*smiling feebly*) Your wife might not think the ethics worn out.

ROYLSTON—(*carelessly*) Oh, my wife; she would not think anything. If it would ease your conscience, I will tell her the whole thing. I'm sure she'd forget all about it ten minutes later (*contemptuously*) when the butcher came for his order.

MRS. FRAZER—(*impulsively*) You do not love your wife, do you? (*As Roylston looks at her in astonishment, she grows confused.*) What an impertinent question! Forgive me!

ROYLSTON—(*lightly*) So impertinent I never dare ask it of myself. I have always rejected the temptation to analyze my home relations. They are pleasant enough and that is all I care to know.

MRS. FRAZER—(*with a sad smile*) If I had looked at it that way—

ROYLSTON—The family relationship was the most important thing in the world for you at that time. With me it is purely secondary. My work comes first. As long as my home life gives free scope for my creative faculty I will demand nothing further of it. Life is too meager, too stingy with its favors, for us to ask for perfection. So I accept my domestic bliss at its surface value and save my analytical eye for the creations of my brain. (*smiling*) I see you are vainly trying to stifle a yawn, and I know you must be terribly tired and sleepy. Won't you let me direct you to your room? (*He goes to the door on left.*)

MRS. FRAZER—(*forgetting her hat which she leaves lying on the sofa, smilingly walks over to him*) I am dismissed, then?

ROYLSTON—Far from it. I merely wish to save you the embarrassment of falling asleep in the chair. (*pointing*) You see the light at the top of the stairway? Well, turn to your left when you reach the top and boldly enter the first room on your left. You will find everything there you need, I imagine. It is the official number one guest chamber.

MRS. FRAZER—I suppose you won't retire for hours yet?

ROYLSTON—I have some work to finish up.

MRS. FRAZER—(*catching herself in the act of yawning—with a laugh*) I can't deny I'm sleepy—for the first time in months. (*giving him her hand*) If you only knew how grateful I am! How can I ever thank you?

ROYLSTON—(*with sudden passion*) By looking at me like that. How beautiful you are!

MRS. FRAZER—(*withdrawing her hand—a note of warning in her voice*) Remember the Princess in the fairy tales who was as good as—

ROYLSTON—She was beautiful. I understand. Pardon me. Good—but emancipated.

MRS. FRAZER—(*smiling*) Free to be good. (*She turns to go out the door.*)

ROYLSTON—Good night. (*goes toward the table*)

MRS. FRAZER—(*turns to him suddenly, a look of resolution on her face*) I must explain one thing before I go, before I accept your hospitality. I have told you a lie; (*Roylston looks at her in surprise.*) I never met you at the studio ball. I was there but I did not meet you. I knew I had missed the last train. That is the reason I came so late. I wanted to miss it. And I knew there was no hotel for I made inquiries at the station. But I had no idea your wife would be away.

ROYLSTON—(*staring at her in amazement*) But why, why?

MRS. FRAZER—I wanted to put you to the test, to see if you would help me and let me stay. I wanted to get a glimpse of your home life, to see if you were a real man with the courage of your convictions or just a theorist. (*hesitatingly*) You see in my agony of doubt it seemed necessary for me to get back of dry words to a flesh and blood reality. (*with a faint smile*) It all appears such a wild idea now; and the test turned out to be a test of myself after all, didn't it?

ROYLSTON—(*not able to recover from his astonishment*) You tell me this—now—that you purposely missed the last train?

MRS. FRAZER—(*flushing*) I am ashamed to say that is the exact truth. (*avoiding his ardent gaze*) I wish there to be no deception on my part after all your kindness to me.

ROYLSTON—(*intensely*) Do you realize how beautiful you are? Are you not afraid to make such a confession to me—of the conclusions I might be vain enough to draw from it? (*He moves a step toward her.*)

MRS. FRAZER—(*looking straight into his eyes*) No—because I know now you *are* a real man.

ROYLSTON—(*moving still nearer to her*) Take care! The real men are usually the greatest sinners.

MRS. FRAZER—But they protect the helpless. (*with a smile*) So you see how safe I am. Good night. (*She goes out.*)

ROYLSTON—(*going to the door*) Good night. (*He watches her ascend the stairway.*) Good night. (*He comes back and sits down at the table again; starts to look over his manuscript, glances upward in the direction of her room, throws his manuscript down with an exclamation of disgust, goes to the door on the left again and looks up at the top of the stairway, finally comes back to the table again and stands beside it for a moment, frowning thought-*

fully and evidently weighing something in his mind.) Damnation!
(*He takes his hat and light overcoat from the chair, puts them on,
grabs his cane and hurries out through the door at the back as*

The Curtain Falls)

ACT II

SCENE—*The same. It is about nine o'clock on the following morning. Bright sunlight streams in through the two open windows. Benton is arranging the papers and books on the table. Having finished he turns and is going out the door in the rear when he catches sight of Mrs. Frazer's hat which is lying on the sofa. He gives a low whistle of amazement. A shadow falls across the sunlight at one of the windows and a moment later Weson, the gardener, puts his head into the room and peers around near-sightedly. He is an old withered man with a drooping gray mustache stained yellow by tobacco juice.*

BENTON—Good morning, Weson.

WESON—Oh, it's you, is it?

BENTON—Who did you think it was?

WESON—I thought maybe Mr. Roylston—

BENTON—He isn't up yet. Want to see him about anything?

WESON—Nothin' special. When I first come out this mornin' I seen a feller hangin' round the house s'picious like. Soon s'he seen me he turned round and walked off s'fast s'he could go. "D'you think this is a park?" I shouts after him, but he didn't pay no attention. Thinks I: I better tell Mr. Roylston about you. With all them burglaries happenin' near-abouts you can't be too careful.

BENTON—Hm—you're right about that. (*with an involuntary glance at the hat*) Mr. Roylston ought to be more careful.

WESON—Oughter hire a watchman, s'what I say. (*in a whining voice*) T'ain't safe for me sleepin' all alone in that house at the end of the drive. S'me they'd tackle first. I was readin' in the papers t'other day where robbers tortured an old gardener same s'me to make him tell them how to git into the house; burned his bare feet with a red-hot poker! (*with rising inflection*) Ain't that turrible?

BENTON—Oh, I guess you're safe enough. (*meaningly*) It isn't burglars his nibs ought to be frightened of.

WESON—(*eagerly, scenting a scandal*) What's he been up to now?

Benton—(*picks up Mrs. Frazer's hat*) Cast your eye on this.

Weson—Wait till I git my specs. (*reaches into his pocket and pulls out a pair of steel-rimmed spectacles*) I can't see nothin' without 'em no more. (*puts them on and looks at the hat, —in disappointed tones*) What's that? One of the Missus' hats?

Benton—Guess again. She don't wear cheap truck like that. (*throws hat contemptuously on sofa*)

Weson—You don't mean—? (*with an explosive chuckle*) If he don't beat the devil! An' the Missus in Noo York! Makes hay while the sun shines, don't he? Don't the Missus never guess nothin'?

Benton—(*scornfully*) She doesn't know enough; besides usually he chucks 'em before the thing gets serious. He likes to have them crazy about him but when they get too mushy—he doesn't like complications—they interfere with his work, he says; and then when they call up I have to say he's too busy to be disturbed.

Weson—(*admiringly*) Foxy, ain't he?

Benton—I don't know what's wrong with him this time. I don't blame him, though; she's a beauty. But he ought to be more careful. Once caught, twice shy, they say; and he was caught once, good and proper. (*with a short laugh*) It'll do the Missus good to get a dose of her own medicine. It broke the old man's heart when the young fellow married her, and— (*stopping abruptly as he sees how avidly Weson is drinking his words in*) A fine man to work for, the old gentleman; not that I'm complaining of the son at all.

Weson—What was you sayin' about the marriage?

Benton—Nothing that an old scandalmonger like you ought to hear. There's lots of things I could tell if I had a mind to; but I'll keep my mouth shut. It's the best policy, Weson, especially when you're around. You better get out of here. I think I hear someone coming down the stairs. (*Weson hurriedly withdraws. Benton goes to the table and pretends to be arranging the things on it. Mrs. Frazer appears in the doorway on the left. She stops uncertainly when she sees Benton.*)

Benton—(*affably*) Good morning, ma'am.

Mrs. Frazer—(*embarrassed*) Good morning. I believe I left my hat in here.

BENTON—Yes, ma'am. Here it is. (*He picks her hat from the sofa.*)

MRS. FRAZER—(*walking over and taking it from him*) Thank you. (*She goes to the window and stands drinking in the beauty of the Spring morning.*)

BENTON—(*with an admiring glance at her figure framed in the sunlight*) Beautiful morning, ma'am.

MRS. FRAZER—Yes, isn't it? And what a lovely garden.

BENTON—Yes, ma'am, very fine. It has the gardener busy all the time keeping it in shape.

MRS. FRAZER—No doubt; they require a great deal of care. Has Mr. Roylston come down yet?

BENTON—Lord no, ma'am; won't be down for an hour yet, I should say. He's not what you'd call an early bird; stays up so late nights he couldn't be. (*insinuatingly*) But he's been so queer and—hm—different from what he usually does, he might do anything this morning.

MRS. FRAZER—(*crushing him with a look of icy hauteur*) What do you mean?

BENTON—(*confused, fumbling with the books on the table*) Nothing at all, ma'am, only—

MRS. FRAZER—(*her curiosity getting the better of her—more kindly*) Only what?

BENTON—(*accepting her change of manner as a confession which equalizes their position*) Only, begging your pardon, he doesn't usually—he isn't in the habit of—he usually thinks that sort of thing too dangerous. Now, when the others—

MRS. FRAZER—(*horrified*) Others?

BENTON—(*grinning*) Loads of 'em. They're all crazy about him. He likes it, too—phone calls and letters and flowers and all such stuff. He pretends not to care, but it tickles him just the same to have them adoring him, asking for his advice—

MRS. FRAZER—Stop! Is this the way you slander the man who trusts you?

BENTON—(*offended*) It's no secret. He laughs and talks about it himself. I've heard him read parts of the letters to the Missus, Mrs. Roylston. I was only saying it to you because it's never—he's never taken any chances for the others. I thought you'd like to know you were the only one—

MRS. FRAZER—(*her face crimson*) How dare you!

BENTON—(*quickly*) Beg your pardon, ma'am, no offence intended. (*slyly*) Of course I don't mean anything wrong. (*The sound of a door closing is heard from the hallway on the left, then children's voices. Benton turns excitedly to Mrs. Frazer.*) Good Gawd, it must be Mrs. Roylston and the kids. Go in there where she won't see you. (*Mrs. Frazer, too overcome with fear and shame to stop and think, hurries through the door at the rear. Benton closes it after her and is busy with the papers on the table when Mrs. Roylston enters with the children who are talking and laughing together.*

(*Mrs. Roylston is a pretty woman of thirty or so, with a mass of light curly brown hair, big thoughtful eyes, rosy complexion, tiny hands and feet, and a slight girlish figure. She is dressed stylishly but without ostentation.*

(*Davie and Ruth, aged nine and seven respectively, are healthy, noisy, delightful children. Their clothes are simple but of expensive material.*)

MRS. ROYLSTON—Good morning, Benton. Mr. Roylston's not up yet of course?

BENTON—No, ma'am.

MRS. ROYLSTON—Telephone for Dr. Morse at once, will you, Benton? Tell him to come up at once.

BENTON—Yes, ma'am. Nothing serious, I hope ma'am.

MRS. ROYLSTON—Oh no. Ruth was ill last night when we returned from the theatre. Mrs. Dexter sent for her doctor. He said it was nothing but—(*smiling and shaking an accusing finger at Ruth*) too much candy. However, I wanted to make sure. I have no confidence in strange doctors. So I took the first train out this morning and didn't wait for the machine.

RUTH—I did'n eat much, Mother.

DAVIE—I ate more'n she did, and I was'n sick.

MRS. ROYLSTON—But you're a man, dear.

RUTH—I feel puffictly well this morning, Mother.

MRS. ROYLSTON—(*kissing her*) Of course you do, dear. Mother wishes to make sure, that's all. So telephone right away, please, Benton.

BENTON—Yes, ma'am. (*With an apprehensive glance at the door in back he hurries out to the left.*)

DAVIE—Mother, can we go out and play in the sand-pile?

RUTH—I'm goin' to play I'm the Princess in the play last night.

MRS. ROYLSTON—And are you going to be the Prince, Davie?

DAVIE—Nope; I'm goin' to be the dragon.

MRS. ROYLSTON—But the dragon was very, very wicked.

DAVIE—Tha's why I wanta be him.

MRS. ROYLSTON—(*laughing and kissing both of them*) Run along then, and be sure and stay in the sun; and come in when you see Dr. Morse drive up. Try and be as quiet as you can. You know your father isn't up yet. (*The children answer:* "Yes, Mother" *and skip out through the door on the left.*)

BENTON—(*appears in the doorway on the left*) Dr. Morse will be right up, ma'am.

MRS. ROYLSTON—Very well. Thank you, Benton. (*Benton, unwilling to leave the room, and not knowing any excuse for remaining, stands fidgetting nervously in the doorway.*) Anything you wish to see me about, Benton?

BENTON—No, ma'am, nothing at all. So glad to hear it's not serious—Miss Ruth, I mean.

MRS. ROYLSTON—(*smiling at him kindly*) Thank you, Benton. (*She sits down and picking up the manuscript from the table, starts to read. Benton turns reluctantly and leaves. Mrs. Roylston glances over the pages of the manuscript interestedly. The door in the rear is slowly opened and Mrs. Frazer comes into the room. Her face wears an expression of defiant shame. She coughs to attract Mrs. Roylston's attention. Startled by the sound, Mrs. Roylston turns around and sees her. The two women stare at each other in silence for a moment. Mrs. Roylston grows very pale. Her lips tremble and it seems as if she were shrinking up in her chair, becoming small and pitiful. A flush slowly spreads over Mrs. Frazer's face. She drops her eyes.*)

MRS. FRAZER—I beg your pardon.

MRS. ROYLSTON—How did— Who is it you wish to see?

MRS. FRAZER—I am waiting to speak to Mr. Roylston.

MRS. ROYLSTON—How did you get in that room?

MRS. FRAZER—(*defiantly*) I hid there when I heard you coming.

Mrs. Roylston—(*with a sigh that is like a moan*) I knew it! I knew it!

Mrs. Frazer—(*embarrassed*) I lost my head completely for a moment, and I ran away. I was so afraid of what you might think. In there I regained my senses. I had done no wrong. Why should I be afraid of you? So I came back.

Mrs. Roylston—(*slowly*) I am the one who should be afraid.

Mrs. Frazer—I was sure you would misunderstand my presence here.

Mrs. Roylston—(*coldly*) I'm afraid I understand it only too well.

Mrs. Frazer—Mr. Roylston was so positive you would ignore appearances. I knew better. I am a woman. I should never have allowed myself to be persuaded into remaining here against my better judgement.

Mrs. Roylston—(*trying not to understand*) Mr. Roylston? You have seen him? Is he up already?

Mrs. Frazer—(*unflinchingly*) No; I saw him last night.

Mrs. Roylston—Last night? Then you— When did you come here—

Mrs. Frazer—Last night about ten o'clock.

Mrs. Roylston—(*her worst fears realized*) Last night? Ten o'clock? Then you were here in this house—you and he—alone?

Mrs. Frazer—Yes; but you must not draw any conclusions from that until I—

Mrs. Roylston—(*jumping to her feet, her eyes flashing*) Oh!

Mrs. Frazer—You will be sorry if you form a hasty judgement.

Mrs. Roylston—Hasty? As if I had not always a picture of this before my mind! I have known it was coming, dreaded it, for years. Hasty? Oh no! I have prayed this would never happen, but I have seen it drawing nearer every day in spite of my prayers; and I am prepared for it.

Mrs. Frazer—If you will permit me to explain—

Mrs. Roylston—(*with a mocking laugh*) Explain!

Mrs. Frazer—(*firmly*) I came here to ask your husband's advice.

MRS. ROYLSTON—They all want advice—so they say.

MRS. FRAZER—(*flushing angrily but controlling herself*) I was in such desperate straits that only he could help me. I was wild with despair. I formed the mad idea of coming here. I never thought of your being away. And I missed the last train. (*She realizes how improbable this explanation must seem to Mrs. Roylston and continues uncertainly.*) There was no hotel to go to; so your husband kindly—

MRS. ROYLSTON—(*her laughter breaking hysterically*) And you expect me to believe this! Do you think I have no intelligence at all? (*furiously*) Lies! Lies! All lies! (*Throwing herself in the chair by the table she sobs convulsively, her face hidden in her hands.*)

MRS. FRAZER—(*calmly*) I will excuse your insults because I know how you must feel. (*earnestly*) You will regret this when the truth comes out, when you know you have been insulting an innocent woman. You are judging by appearances and letting them deceive you.

MRS. ROYLSTON—Lies, lies! Haven't I read your letters to him?

MRS. FRAZER—(*astonished*) I never wrote to your husband in my life.

MRS. ROYLSTON—(*as if she hadn't heard*) "Will you give me permission to come out and see you sometime?" I suppose you never wrote that? Oh, how well I remember them—those letters!

MRS. FRAZER—Mrs. Roylston, you are mistaken. I never—

MRS. ROYLSTON—To take advantage of my being away with the children; oh, how could he!

MRS. FRAZER—Mrs. Roylston, you must listen to me.

MRS. ROYLSTON—I won't listen to you. What is there to say—now? You love him. I don't blame you for that; but what will become of me? (*She breaks down and sobs unrestrainedly.*)

MRS. FRAZER—(*waiting until Mrs. R. has regained control of herself*) Listen to me, Mrs. Roylston! I do not love your husband.

MRS. ROYLSTON—The more shame, then; for he must love you.

MRS. FRAZER—He never saw me before last night.

MRS. ROYLSTON—(*coldly*) I don't believe you.

MRS. FRAZER—(*angrily*) Ah, there is a limit to everything. Since you persist in insulting me, since you refuse to listen to anything, you may continue to believe whatever you please. I will leave Mr. Roylston to do the explaining. (*She hurries toward the door on the left but Mrs. R. jumps up and reaches it before her, blocking her passage.*)

MRS. ROYLSTON—(*fiercely*) You cannot go now.

MRS. FRAZER—Cannot?

MRS. ROYLSTON—I don't mean that. Please don't go yet, before he comes. There is so much which must be cleared up. I didn't mean to hurt you. If you knew how I am suffering you wouldn't blame me. Please sit down, won't you, until he comes?

MRS. FRAZER—(*on the verge of tears herself*) After the things you have said to me? No, I will not remain in this house a minute longer. Please let me pass.

MRS. ROYLSTON—I am sorry. You are not to blame. No one is to blame. I implore you to stay until he comes. He ought to be down in a few minutes. It won't be long.

MRS. FRAZER—(*after a moment's indecision*) Very well, I will stay; not because you ask me to but because I wish to hear my own justification. (*She sits down in one of the armchairs near the sofa.*)

MRS. ROYLSTON—Thank you. It will help to clear up matters between the three of us once and for all. (*She chokes back a sob and sits down in the chair by the table.*)

MRS. FRAZER—In the meantime, if you please, let us not talk about it. It will only make matters worse—if that were possible.

MRS. ROYLSTON—(*strangely*) How you said that! As if you were giving an order. And why shouldn't you? You have more right in this house than I have. (*She sobs.*)

MRS. FRAZER—(*moved in spite of herself—with great kindness*) Please, Mrs. Roylston, don't make yourself unhappy in this way. If you only knew how wrong you are.

MRS. ROYLSTON—(*more calmly*) I won't break down again. What must be, must be I suppose. I have known this was coming for a long time. The day I was married I could foresee it. I should have had the courage to refuse then; but I didn't. It all seemed such a wonderful dream come true, I just couldn't refuse even when I knew I was wronging him. I was a coward then and I still am, I guess. Eleven years of happiness and now I have to pay and—I am afraid. (*a pause during which Mrs. F. looks at her pityingly*) I've pretended not to see a lot of things in those years. I wanted him to be happy, and I knew he wouldn't be if he thought he had a jealous wife prying into his affairs. All the women who sent him flowers and wrote to him and called him up on the phone—I knew they loved him, and I hated them for it; but I never let him think I suspected anything. Until lately I never thought he considered them seriously.

MRS. FRAZER—(*interrupting her indignantly*) And you think I was one of those fools!

MRS. ROYLSTON—He used to read parts of their letters to me. He never guessed how it hurt. For I could see in spite of the way he joked they pleased him just the same. Then all at once he stopped showing them to me—and they kept coming, all in the same handwriting. I had never read a letter of his before but I brooded until I couldn't resist the temptation any longer. Two of them were lying open on this table one day and I read them. Then I could see the end coming. He had been writing to her, meeting her in New York, and I knew from her letters it was only a question of time.

MRS. FRAZER—And those are the letters you think I wrote?

MRS. ROYLSTON—(*dully*) Yes.

MRS. FRAZER—But when I swear to you I never wrote a line to your husband in my life, never spoke a word to him before last night!

MRS. ROYLSTON—I'd like to believe you. (*intensely*) Oh, I wish I could believe you! But how can I?

MRS. FRAZER—(*desperately*) You will have to. He will tell you the same thing.

MRS. ROYLSTON—(*her voice low and shaken with pain*) What does it matter? You or someone else. She said she had left her home to work out her own salvation; and I thought you looked that way. I thought she would be younger. Her letters sounded girlish. What does it matter? *You* were here—last night.

MRS. FRAZER—(*quietly*) Mrs. Roylston, I really cannot stay and listen to such implications.

MRS. ROYLSTON—I don't blame you or anyone. It's my own sin coming back on me. Marriages like mine are cursed.

MRS. FRAZER—Cursed? It seems to me yours has been a very fortunate one.

MRS. ROYLSTON—Yes, cursed. Sooner or later the curse falls. Retribution finds you out in the end. Forbidden love—you'll find out the curse of it like I have, when you least expect it, when you think you're happy and the future is all smiling.

MRS. FRAZER—(*interested*) I fail to see how all this can apply to your case.

MRS. ROYLSTON—(*continues in a lifeless, monotonous voice as if all the spirit in her had been crushed and broken. Her face wears an expression of dazed, almost stupid, resignation.*) Give him up before it's too late, for your own sake. You'll have to pay. I'll be frank with you. You can't throw any stone. He married me because he had to, or thought he had to. I was his father's stenographer, we loved each other—too well. His father found out and discharged me. Then David asked me to marry him and I couldn't refuse. I loved him so.

MRS. FRAZER—(*bewildered*) Please, Mrs. Roylston, don't—

MRS. ROYLSTON—I want you to understand—whatever happens to me afterwards—it isn't his fault.

MRS. FRAZER—Do you know what you are telling me?

MRS. ROYLSTON—(*hotly*) I wouldn't be ashamed to tell it to the whole world. It shows how good he is. If he no longer loves me it's because I allowed him to make too great a sacrifice. His father cut him off and never spoke to him again. The old gentleman was kind enough generally but he had great plans for his only son, David, and I spoilt them all. He died soon afterward,—of grief over our marriage, they say. I've always thought that perhaps in his heart David has never forgiven me for—killing his father.

MRS. FRAZER—How can you imagine such a thing?

MRS. ROYLSTON—When I married him I resolved that as soon as he was able to take care of himself—

MRS. FRAZER—(*astonished*) Take care of himself?

MRS. ROYLSTON—He wasn't famous in those days. He hadn't even had a book published yet. He used to take positions in offices but he never held them long and I could see how he hated them. He wanted to write, write, write all the time. Every once in a while he sold an article, but not often enough to keep him alive. It must have been terribly hard for him—worrying and fretting how to make two ends meet. He had been accustomed to everything he wanted—and I had dragged him down. He wouldn't have been human if he hadn't had a sort of grudge against me for it.

MRS. FRAZER—He is hardly as mean as that.

MRS. ROYLSTON—I had to stay with him until he got on his feet. I was considered a fine stenographer in those days and my salary was enough to keep us going. Then, too, he had to have someone to typewrite his manuscripts for him.

MRS. FRAZER—(*with wondering admiration*) And you did all that?

MRS. ROYLSTON—I had plenty of time at night to typewrite what he had written during the day. Those were the happiest days of my life. How often since then I've wished that he had never been successful, that we could have gone on like that always. It was selfish of me to feel that way but I couldn't help it sometimes. (*musingly*) We had a small flat all to ourselves.

MRS. FRAZER—And you did all the housekeeping, too?

MRS. ROYLSTON—(*simply*) Of course. I had made a resolve to leave him and let him get a divorce as soon as he was successful and could get along without me. I saw clearly at that time, before the children came, what I see now—that he was never meant for me. I knew he would come to regret his sacrifice and I would become a dead weight holding him back. I knew nothing of what he knew. Whatever I have learned since, he has taught me. We had been married a little over a year when his first play was produced and made a sensation,—and then—

MRS. FRAZER—(*eagerly*) Yes?

Mrs. Roylston—(*softly*) Little Davie came. I couldn't think of going away then. It would have killed me. I wasn't strong enough or brave enough for that. I hoped he would love me more for Davie's sake, and he did for a time. He was so kind to me; and when our little girl was born he was so proud. As he became famous he had less and less time to spend at home, and he hated to be disturbed when he was writing. He met so many people, women, of his own kind outside, who could talk about the things he was interested in, that I guess he commenced to despise me a little because I was so stupid.

Mrs. Frazer—(*with a strange smile, half to herself*) No, no, he has never analyzed his home relations.

Mrs. Roylston—(*as if she had not heard*) Lately he has grown more and more indifferent to me and to the children; so that now I'm afraid he only looks on me as a sort of housekeeper. (*with a pitiful attempt at a smile*) He'll have to acknowledge I'm a good one. I've protected him from all the small worries he detests so much. I don't believe he realizes; he thinks things just run along by themselves.

Mrs. Frazer—(*eagerly*) Why have you never asserted yourself, claimed your right as an individual? Why have you never spoken to him, told him how you felt? You have seen him slipping away and made no attempt to hold him.

Mrs. Roylston—(*fiercely*) I have loved him, loved him, loved him with all my heart and soul; loved him more than you or any other woman will ever love him. If that has no power to hold him,—then I have lost him.

Mrs. Frazer—(*after a pause*) How unhappy you must have been!

Mrs. Roylston—(*scornfully*) Unhappy? So that's what you think! How little you know! I have been happy in serving him, happy in the knowledge that I have had my little part in helping him to success, happy to be able to shield and protect him. In spite of all you other women with your letters and flowers, I have been happy. (*with a sad smile*) However, it's all ended now. As long as I could pretend I didn't know about you others, as long as I was sure he didn't suspect I knew about you, I could remain and love him and still preserve my self-respect. It's different now. I can't pretend to be blind any longer. I know, and you know I know, and he knows I know. Besides I see that his future happiness does not depend on me and (*intensely*) above all else in the world I want him to be happy.

MRS. FRAZER—But he *is* happy—now—with you!

MRS. ROYLSTON—(*shaking her head sadly*) My usefullness is past. I can only thank God for granting the beauty and joy of the past eleven years to a woman who sinned and was too cowardly to pay. The payment was never cancelled, only postponed, I see that now—postponed until I had the courage to pay. I have that courage now. I will pay. I will leave him to his happiness. (*her voice thrilling with pride*) How many of you others love him as much as that? Not many, or one, I think. How many of you would make the sacrifice I will make? How many of you would be willing to give him up to another woman because your love was so great? Not one of you! (*bitterly*) You the least of all—for him or anyone else! I can see it in your face.

MRS. FRAZER—(*slowly*) It is true. Compared to you I am a weakling.

MRS. ROYLSTON—I do not boast of my strength, only of the strength of my love. I thank you just the same. You are the only person who has ever given me credit for being what I must be. Not even he ever saw it in all these eleven years.

MRS. FRAZER—But did you ever lay bare your soul to anyone, even to him, as you have to me?

MRS. ROYLSTON—Yes, to him, every day, every hour; but he never saw it.

MRS. FRAZER—(*after a pause—thoughtfully*) How much you have taught me! Happiness, then, means servitude?

MRS. ROYLSTON—Love means servitude; and *my* love is *my* happiness.

MRS. FRAZER—I should have come to you for advice, not to him.

MRS. ROYLSTON—(*with a scornful smile*) Advice? That word has been my torturer. You women of the flowers and letters have stolen him from me in the name of advice.

MRS. FRAZER—(*hurt*) Even now you have no faith in me.

MRS. ROYLSTON—It isn't possible. How can I? How can I?

Mrs. Frazer—I can't blame you; things are so mixed. It must appear incredible. But can't you see that I, too, have suffered? Even if what you think were true could you not pity me?

Mrs. Roylston—(*excitedly*) No, no, no. I can only hate you. How can the vanquished pity the victor? You ask too much.

Mrs. Frazer—(*rising from her chair*) I cannot wait any longer. I must go out into the fresh air and be alone for a while—to think.

Mrs. Roylston—You are afraid to wait until he comes.

Mrs. Frazer—I will wait outside. In this room the weight of your suspicion is crushing me. I begin to feel guilty.

Mrs. Roylston—(*savagely*) Ah!

Mrs. Frazer—(*weakly*) I will wait outside in the garden if I may. (*She starts to go. The sound of a door slamming is heard. Mrs. Roylston goes to the door on the left and looks out. She gives an exclamation of surprise.*)

Mrs. Roylston—(*slowly*) He has just come in. He must have been out for his morning walk. What could have got him up so early? (*turns impetuously to Mrs. Frazer*) You must have known of this; and you wanted to sneak away before he came. Lies! Lies! Lies everywhere!

Mrs. Frazer—(*distractedly*) No, no, I swear to you—

Mrs. Roylston—Ssshh! Here he comes. (*Roylston enters from the door on the left. He is dressed exactly the same as the night before.*)

Roylston—(*concealing his annoyance*) Hello, Alice, what brings you back at this unearthly hour? Good morning, Mrs. Frazer.

Mrs. Roylston—(*falteringly*) Ruth was sick last night and I didn't wait for the machine this morning but hurried out on the first train. She seems to be all right this morning but I've sent for Dr. Morse to make sure.

Roylston—(*indifferently, shrugging his shoulders*) Stuffed full of candy, probably. I see you and Mrs. Frazer have already made each other's acquaintance.

Mrs. Roylston—(*with a short laugh at what she thinks is his attempt to deceive her in the name*) Oh, yes. (*Mrs. Frazer does not reply but stares at him as if she were seeing him for the first time.*)

ROYLSTON—(*searching through the things on the table*) God be thanked I haven't a jealous wife; for I must acknowledge that even to the most unprejudiced observer the events of last night would appear dubious. (*irritably*) Where did Benton put—? Oh, here it is. (*finds the fountain pen he has been looking for and puts it in his pocket*) You see Mrs. Frazer missed the last train and when I explained that you were away it was all I could do to persuade her to occupy Guest Chamber No. 1 instead of melting to death in the rain. Nice situation, wasn't it? Nothing if not compromising. Married man, married lady—not to each other—lonely country house—stormy night—wife returns home unexpectedly the next morning and—does not believe the worst. (*with a laugh which has a trace of mockery in it*) My dear Alice, you are really the perfect wife. (*goes over to her and puts his arm around her carelessly and continues in the same bantering tone*) I told you, Mrs. Frazer, that Caesar's wife was above harboring suspicion. I welcome you to the model household, where truth reigns, where conventions are as naught, where we believe in each other implicitly because we have found each other so worthy of belief. And I salute you, My Angel of Trustfulness. (*He bends to kiss his wife. She gently pushes him away.*)

MRS. ROYLSTON—Don't, David, please!

ROYLSTON—(*glancing from one to the other. Mrs. Frazer is looking at him with frank disgust.*) Hm—I was too hasty in my reliance on mutual confidence it seems. You two have had a run-in already, I see. (*to his wife, impatiently*) I am sorry you should have jumped at conclusions before you heard my explanation. Mrs. Frazer is going to do some work for me and—

MRS. ROYLSTON—(*her eyes filling*) Ah.

ROYLSTON—Which will necessitate her being here for some time, and we must clear away all unpleasantness—

MRS. FRAZER—(*interrupting him coldly*) You are mistaken. I have decided I cannot accept the work you offer me.

ROYLSTON—(*perplexed*) Hm,—it's as bad as that, eh?

MRS. ROYLSTON—(*turning to Mrs. Frazer*) But you must!

MRS. FRAZER—(*indignantly*) Must?

MRS. ROYLSTON—What good can your refusal do now?

MRS. FRAZER—(*to Roylston*) Your wife has plainly told me that she is firmly convinced I am your mistress. She has read letters to you from someone and thinks I am the author. You see how plainly impossible it would be for me to work for you or accept your assistance in any way. Besides, there are other reasons. I have made a mistake, a great mistake, and it only remains for me to go. Before I leave I should like to have you try to convince Mrs. Roylston that her suspicions are groundless—as far as I am concerned.

ROYLSTON—(*turning to his wife*) So you read my letters?

MRS. ROYLSTON—Yes; you left them on your table and I—couldn't resist the temptation. (*Roylston turns away from her contemptuously.*) I saw I was losing you, that you were becoming indifferent to me and the children—

ROYLSTON—And you thought opening my letters would cure that?

MRS. ROYLSTON—They were already open.

ROYLSTON—Reading them, then.

MRS. ROYLSTON—I did not stop to think. I love you.

ROYLSTON—(*coldly*) Indeed? You have strange ways of showing it.

MRS. ROYLSTON—I wanted to fight for you. I had to know who my enemy was.

ROYLSTON—Well, who was this so-called enemy of yours?

MRS. ROYLSTON—The letters were signed: Julia Wainright.

MRS. FRAZER—(*eagerly*) You see!

ROYLSTON—What has she to do with Mrs. Frazer? Why, in heaven's name, should you connect the two? Your insults to Mrs. Frazer are unpardonable and nonsensical. You are letting a narrow-minded suspicion blot out all that is best in you. Appearances have been against me before and yet you never took this attitude.

MRS. ROYLSTON—There is such a thing as the last straw.

ROYLSTON—(*sternly*) Alice, what has come over you? You are not yourself. When I tell you we are both blameless do you still persist—

MRS. ROYLSTON—(*frenziedly*) I don't believe you or her or anyone. I can't, I can't! You call her Mrs. Frazer and expect me to believe her innocent—and she wears no wedding ring. (*Mrs. Frazer instinctively hides her hand behind her back.*) Why are you up and out so early? You never get up before ten—Because she is up!

MRS. FRAZER—(*growing crimson*) Oh! (*The doorbell is heard ringing.*)

ROYLSTON—(*bitingly*) You need not tell your woes to the servants, Alice. Please try to control yourself. Here comes Benton. (*A moment later Benton appears in the doorway.*)

BENTON—Dr. Morse is here, ma'am.

MRS. ROYLSTON—(*faintly*) Very well, Benton. Tell him I'll be right out; and call the children in.

BENTON—Yes, ma'am. (*He goes out.*)

ROYLSTON—(*turning to his wife—cuttingly*) Your conduct has been rather a revelation to me.

MRS. ROYLSTON—(*wincing*) Don't, David!

ROYLSTON—You have called me a liar and you have insulted Mrs. Frazer who is my friend. (*Mrs. Frazer makes an angry gesture repudiating this statement.*) You will have no cause for any suspicions in the future for I shall not trouble you with my presence in this house any longer. I will have Benton pack up my things at once. I do not care to live with a wife who is also an evil-minded spy. I could vindicate myself beyond all possibility of doubt, in ten words; but I prefer to have you think whatever your jealous whim dictates. I will explain to Mrs. Frazer and she may tell you if she considers your charges against her worth the trouble of refuting.

MRS. ROYLSTON—(*shrinking from him as if he had struck her*) Don't, don't David! Please don't speak like that—to me. You are killing me. I love you, you must not go away. This is your home. It is I who have no reason here. I will give you (*sobbing and walking toward the door on the left*) your freedom. I want you to be happy, and—I know I'm only in your way—now. Please forgive me if I can't believe. (*stretching out her arms to him supplicatingly*) Please forgive me! (*He turns away from her coldly.*)

MRS. FRAZER—(*indignantly*) For shame, Mr. Roylston!

MRS. ROYLSTON—(*turning to her furiously*) How dare you intercede for me! Don't you know how I hate you? (*She rushes out the door to the left as*

The Curtain Falls)

ACT III

SCENE—*The same. Roylston and Mrs. Frazer are still staring at the door through which Mrs. Roylston has just gone.*

ROYLSTON—(*shrugging his shoulders turns to Mrs. F. with a short laugh*) I have lived with that woman for eleven years, and have never known her until ten minutes ago. (*Benton appears in the doorway to the left. He stands there irresolutely for a second and is turning to go out again when Roylston sees him.*)

ROYLSTON—(*sharply*) Well, Benton? What is it?

BENTON—(*confused*) Nothing of any importance, sir—just something the gardener, Weson, asked me to tell you. (*He hesitates, plainly indicating he does not wish to speak before Mrs. F.*)

ROYLSTON—(*to Mrs. Frazer*) Excuse me. (*goes over to Benton in the doorway*) Well?

BENTON—Weson says he saw a suspicious character hanging around and looking at the house early this morning. Weson shouted at him to find out what he wanted and he ran away.

ROYLSTON—(*with a groan*) Damn Weson! Are you never going to get over your idiotic burglar scares, Benton?

BENTON—(*darkly*) I wasn't thinking of burglars—this time. (*with a meaning glance in Mrs. F.'s direction*) Look out for the badger game, sir.

ROYLSTON—(*irritably*) Go to the devil! (*Benton smiles craftily and goes out. Roylston comes back to the table.*) When I outgrew a governess they gave me Benton. I thought it was a change for the better but it wasn't. I have never been able to outgrow him. He won't let me. (*Mrs. Frazer remains silent. Roylston strides up and down nervously, clasping and unclasping his hands and scowling at his disagreeable thoughts. Suddenly he strikes his fist into the palm of his hand with an impatient exclamation.*) What a blind fool I am! If there was anything in the world I would have trusted Alice not to do, it was to read my letters. What a contemptible thing to do—to read my letters! And what a trustful simpleton I was to leave them around! (*with an ironical smile*) Do you remember what I said last night about not caring to analyze my home relations provided the surface remained smooth? Well, your visit has stirred up the depths with a vengeance—the muddy depths.

MRS. FRAZER—(*sarcastically*) What a crushing blow for you!

ROYLSTON—In all seriousness it really is appalling. I feel as if the world were turned topsy-turvy. When you have taken a thing for granted for years, when a faith in it has been one of the main props of your life, although you might not have realized its importance at the time,—and suddenly you make the discovery that you have trusted in a sham, that your prop is worm-eaten!—It is rather a rough tumble, isn't it?

MRS. FRAZER—(*in the same sarcastic tone*) I have found it so myself.

ROYLSTON—That's so; I was forgetting. We're in the same boat, aren't we? (*with a sigh*) Well, I shall get bravely over it, as you have escaped from yours. A few bruises, I suppose, must be expected after such a hard fall.

MRS. FRAZER—Yes, bruises on the soul.

ROYLSTON—I will have to hunt a new illusion. You remember you said last night that when you came here you feared the crowning disillusionment?

MRS. FRAZER—My fears were well grounded.

ROYLSTON—Hm—you mean you have seen my illusion go up in smoke, too? It is discouraging—as if everything in life were founded upon false appearances. (*He quotes ironically*) "Yea, faileth now dream the dreamer and the lute the lutanist."

MRS. FRAZER—You are deceiving yourself as to the nature of my awakening. I have come to regard the prop, as you call it, which I cast aside with scorn as the sound one. The new one, I find, is worm-eaten.

ROYLSTON—The new one? Meaning that I am?

MRS. FRAZER—Exactly! I asked you to guide my future because I thought you were far-sighted. I have discovered you are only in-sighted—as pitifully in-sighted as I was.

ROYLSTON—(*surprised*) In-sighted?

MRS. FRAZER—Yes, you see nothing beyond yourself. You are so preoccupied with the workings of your own brain that your vision of outside things is clouded. You are only a cruel egotist.

ROYLSTON—Know thyself, sayeth the law.

MRS. FRAZER—You make no allowance for the individual.

ROYLSTON—Oh, come now, Mrs. Frazer; you have read what I have written. You know if there is one thing I harp on ad nauseam—

MRS. FRAZER—It is the duty of the individual to triumph over environment; but in your life you regard yourself as the only individual in the world. You cannot see beyond that. You have reconstructed the world for yourself—well and good. Why try to force your conception on others? Why judge their thoughts by what you would think in their place? When you do so you deprive them of personality. You make them man-ikins and yourself the master of the show; and you care not a whit how you hurt their feelings when they fail to answer your pull of the string.

ROYLSTON—(*with a bitter smile*) You, too? It seems this is my day to be properly humbled in spirit.

MRS. FRAZER—I know you will never pardon my effron-tery in wounding your vanity so. Such colossal conceit!

ROYLSTON—(*flushing*) Mrs. Frazer!

MRS. FRAZER—(*calmly*) Your cruel vanity has torn off the mask. How could *you* help me? You can only help yourself. Perhaps if I were in love with you—but then you know, Mr. Narcissus, I would only be your reflection. However, I do not love you. Last night I thought—you were on such a high pedestal—I thought of the superman, of the creator, the maker of new values. This morning I saw merely an egotist whose hands are bloody with the human sacrifices he has made—to himself!

ROYLSTON—(*jumping from his chair—excitedly*) You are unjust, Mrs. Frazer.

MRS. FRAZER—Now you are begining to be angry.

ROYLSTON—(*indignantly*) Angry? Why should I be? You have a perfect right to your opinion, preposterous as it may be. Go on, let me hear the tale of my iniquities. It is very interesting.

MRS. FRAZER—(*teasingly*) You are losing your temper, you spoiled child.

ROYLSTON—I am not losing my temper. (*pettishly*) I am growing inured to insults this morning.

MRS. FRAZER—Why, so am I! I must beg your forgiveness for one thing I said. It was too cruel of me. (*She pauses, smiling mischievously at him.*)

ROYLSTON—(*sulkily*) To what are you alluding?

MRS. FRAZER—(*mockingly*) I was truthful enough to tell you I did not love you. That was horrible of me. How could you endure hearing a woman say she did not love you? And how bored you must be when you hear them say they do love you! Eternal repetition, you know. The petted favorite of fortune stands between the devil and the deep blue sea.

ROYLSTON—(*angrily*) Mrs. Frazer, these personalities are— (*looking at her and catching the twinkle in her eyes—with an embarrassed laugh*) I'm beaten; I acknowledge defeat. I surrender to the superwoman—only don't hit me when I'm down.

MRS. FRAZER—(*contritely*) I shouldn't have said all this to you, but I had to cure myself of my attack of hero-worship in some way. Besides the wounds I received in this morning's interview with your wife cried aloud for vengeance. I had to vent my spleen on someone.

ROYLSTON—(*bitterly*) I shall never forgive myself for subjecting you to such a breach of hospitality. It was shameful of her.

MRS. FRAZER—(*sternly*) No, it is shameful of you to speak of her in that way. She is not to blame for her suspicions. She loves you: how could she help thinking what she did? She is the most wonderful woman I have ever known—worlds above poor blind selfish creatures like you and me.

ROYLSTON—I am afraid I cannot see it in that light.

MRS. FRAZER—No, because in this case truth offends your pride and you will not see. You never misunderstood her as grossly as you do at the present moment.

ROYLSTON—And *I* think I have only just begun to understand her.

MRS. FRAZER—Take care! You are doing exactly what you rail against in others—judging by appearances. Is the keen analytical eye obstinately closed by wounded vanity?

ROYLSTON—(*impatiently*) No, no—but my letters?

MRS. FRAZER—With such a wife you had no right to receive such letters.

ROYLSTON—(*scornfully*) Right?

MRS. FRAZER—You'll admit that needless cruelty is wrong, I hope?

ROYLSTON—Yes, but I don't see what—

MRS. FRAZER—Do you love this woman of the letters?

ROYLSTON—No, of course not!

MRS. FRAZER—Yet you persuaded her to leave her home—

ROYLSTON—Persuaded? No, certainly not! She came to me for advice. She had been impressed by what I had written about the narrowing influence of the conventional home. She had practically the same environment you described to me as yours before your marriage. She was engaged to be married to some cut-and-dried young simpleton. Her life was unsatisfying, gave her no scope for realizing the best that was in her. I saw she had brains, ability. I advised her to learn some occupation which would make her self-sustaining, and then go out into life and see things for herself.

MRS. FRAZER—She is young?

ROYLSTON—Twenty-one.

MRS. FRAZER—And pretty?

ROYLSTON—Yes.

MRS. FRAZER—You are sure you are not in love with her?

ROYLSTON—(*irritably*) I am sure, yes! (*with a bored smile*) I have been too busy to love anyone.

MRS. FRAZER—But yourself. Then you have not even that justification.

ROYLSTON—(*coldly*) I see no necessity for justifying my actions.

MRS. FRAZER—You cannot deny this girl loves you?

ROYLSTON—(*cynically*) She may think she does.

MRS. FRAZER—And you think she does! It tickles your vanity to think so.

ROYLSTON—You are breaking me on the wheel. (*He laughs helplessly.*)

MRS. FRAZER—You are a poor blind bat, not a butterfly; you can stand it. It may open your eyes. Can't you see that you have forever ruined all chance of her being happy with her cut-and-dried simpleton or any of his kind? And where is she to find the superman? Even if she gained your love, what a disappointment! What an awakening when she really came to know you!

ROYLSTON—(*forcing a laugh and looking down at his feet*) Poor clay feet!

MRS. FRAZER—There is only one salvation for her. You must write to her at once and say— (*She hesitates.*)

ROYLSTON—Say what?

MRS. FRAZER—Reveal your true self.

ROYLSTON—(*smiling confidently*) You guarantee that will cure the infatuation?

MRS. FRAZER—Absolutely!

ROYLSTON—Are you sure she won't read her ideal into my words?

MRS. FRAZER—(*biting her lip*) Perhaps you are right. That won't do. I must go to her and tell her—

ROYLSTON—She would think you were jealous. She would not believe you.

MRS. FRAZER—Tell her flatly you don't love her.

ROYLSTON—How about needless cruelty?

MRS. FRAZER—(*alarmed*) But you see yourself you must end it someway.

ROYLSTON—I have a way (*smiling at her*) tried and proved by experience.

MRS. FRAZER—(*scornfully*) I have no doubt.

ROYLSTON—(*in a bantering tone*) Shall I tell you what it is? Don't try to look so indifferent. You know you're dying with curiosity. (*Mrs. Frazer shakes her head indignantly.*) Well, I write a letter to this effect: "I love you but we must see each other no more."

MRS. FRAZER—(*contemptuously*) Oh!

ROYLSTON—(*continues with a great show of affected pathos*) I cannot make you unhappy. Our love is forbidden by cruel, man-made laws and it is on your frail shoulders their punishment would fall, etc., ad nauseam. So you must forget me— or rather, do not forget. Remember in my heart of hearts, my soul of souls, etc., ad lib, your image will remain, the inspiration of my work; that in spirit all my work will be dedicated to you—and so on ad infinitum.

MRS. FRAZER—That is disgusting drivel.

ROYLSTON—Of course it is! But don't you know, haven't you ever been in love?

MRS. FRAZER—Why?

ROYLSTON—Love is the world upside down. Sense is drivel and drivel is sense.

MRS. FRAZER—You mean to tell me she will be ridiculous enough to believe that?

ROYLSTON—She will revel in it. She will telephone—I cannot be found. She will write—no answer. She may even try to see me—I am invisible. Then she will say: That wonderful man has the strength to sacrifice himself for my sake. Voila! She goes home, marries the cut-and-dried simpleton, adopts a superior air which holds him in awed servitude, pities him—pity is love without jealousy—and whenever his uncouth matter-of-factness grates on her sensitive nerves she reverently takes my image from the inner shrine and indulges in the sweet happiness of melancholy retrospection. The memory of another's sacrifice for love of oneself— That is the most soothing narcotic a woman can possess. I recommend it to you.

MRS. FRAZER—(*dryly*) Thank you.

ROYLSTON—(*enthusiastically*) Just think of the ecstatic joy of a woman grown old and fat when she remembers that in her younger days a discarded lover committed suicide because she refused him. What a recompense for a double chin the memory of such a corpse must be!

MRS. FRAZER—(*controlling an impulse to laugh—coldly*) I was attempting to consider this matter seriously.

ROYLSTON—What! Consider love seriously? Set your mind at rest. I have written the letter and I have ordered Benton to stifle the appeals of the telephone. You see you need not have warned me.

MRS. FRAZER—She had become serious, then?

ROYLSTON—Why do you say that?

MRS. FRAZER—When they become serious you grow afraid of complications. A little bird told me.

ROYLSTON—A little bird?

MRS. FRAZER—A man is never a hero to his—

ROYLSTON—(*groaning*) Valet! That scoundrel Benton!

The model of discretion. Another illusion gone! My house of cards is tumbling about my ears.

MRS. FRAZER—No more than you deserve.

ROYLSTON—I admit it, Mrs. Frazer. (*eagerly*) I may mock but I see it just the same. In the future I will send my tickled vanity a-packing and have done with such foolishness. After all, it was only an amusing flirtation—nothing more.

MRS. FRAZER—Go and tell Mrs. Roylston that.

ROYLSTON—(*his expression growing hard and cold*) Thank you for reminding me. (*He goes to the electric bell-button in the wall near the door on left.*)

MRS. FRAZER—(*anxiously*) What are you going to do?

ROYLSTON—Ring for Benton to pack my things.

MRS. FRAZER—Please don't!

ROYLSTON—Why not?

MRS. FRAZER—(*pleadingly*) Not yet at any rate. Please sit down again. I have something to say to you.

ROYLSTON—(*sitting down*) Whatever you may say, Mrs. Frazer, will not alter my opinion in the least. I have my own ideas of the way Alice has acted and what I must do. With your permission I will go back to New York on the train with you.

MRS. FRAZER—No, no, no! Think of how that would hurt her? Have you no pity? I will not allow it. Furthermore you will never see me again when I leave this house. I have been the cause of too much unhappiness already.

ROYLSTON—Don't accuse yourself. I have only gratitude to you for opening my eyes, and I want to help you in every way as I promised I would.

MRS. FRAZER—(*vehemently*) No!

ROYLSTON—Surely you don't mean you refuse—

MRS. FRAZER—Yes, I refuse your assistance in any way, shape or manner. I am not going to take any position and I will not need your help; so let us drop that part of the matter. And as for opening your eyes you have never been as sightless as you are now, poor blind mole!

ROYLSTON—(*with smiling protest*) Odious comparisons! First I am a bat, then a mole!

MRS. FRAZER—Would you like to see clearly?

ROYLSTON—Granted that I am blind—will sight make me any the less miserable?

MRS. FRAZER—(*enthusiastically*) It will make you happy, truly happy. (*R. smiles skeptically.*) Have I your permission to teach you the lesson I was given this morning.

ROYLSTON—(*frowning*) Lesson?

MRS. FRAZER—Yes, a lesson in life your wife gave me this morning.

ROYLSTON—(*icily*) My wife also gave me a lesson in life, if you will remember. (*dryly*) Her first lesson was not so pleasing that I crave for a second.

MRS. FRAZER—For her sake, for my sake, for your own sake you must.

ROYLSTON—(*indifferently*) Very well. (*He gets up from his chair.*) In the meantime Benton can be packing up my things.

MRS. FRAZER—No, please, not yet. Hear me out first—then pack away if you still care to. (*He hesitates uncertainly.*) Come, I ask it as a favor. (*He sits down in his chair again.*)

ROYLSTON—I warn you, Mrs. Frazer, I am not to be cajoled into altering my plans. You are wasting your time and eloquence.

MRS. FRAZER—We shall see. Remember you are to hear me from begining to end—of the lesson. All ready? When I came down this morning I found the irreproachable Benton in this room.

ROYLSTON—And he showed you the crack in my armor.

MRS. FRAZER—He convinced me, without meaning to do so, that the idol's feet were—well—at least only plated.

ROYLSTON—(*sarcastically*) Of course, he meant well.

MRS. FRAZER—He meant to flatter me. He had his own convictions as to my status in this household, and when I saw him growing confidential I did not attempt to show him his mistake.

ROYLSTON—(*accusingly*) You wanted to listen to his gossip?

MRS. FRAZER—(*with a frank laugh*) I wanted to play detective and find out if my you was the real you. Benton, having approved of your choice of a mistress, flattered me by revealing the fact that you had never cared enough for any of the others to dare to install them in your household.

ROYLSTON—(*raging*) The evil-minded wretch! Others, indeed! I tell you that there never have been any others in the sense he meant. And you allowed him to talk to you like that?

MRS. FRAZER—I was making an ineffectual attempt to put him in his place when we heard Mrs. Roylston coming in with the children. And what do you think I did?—I, the bold emancipated woman? I ran and hid in that room like the guiltiest of cravens. When I regained control of myself I was furious, and to prove I was not a coward I came in to face your wife. I went to the other extreme in my display of daring. She was not certain I had been here all night but I immediately told her the truth of the whole affair.

ROYLSTON—What else could you have done?

MRS. FRAZER—Oh, I could have lied a little for the good of her soul. Just consider how damning the facts are! She returns unexpectedly to find me sneaking out of a darkened room, the picture of guilt. I brazenly acknowledge I have been here all night and tell her an absurd story of missing a train, and so forth. She has read letters and—

ROYLSTON—(impatiently) I know how sadly the circumstantial evidence is against the truth. I was relying on the implicit trust she has always seemed to have for me.

MRS. FRAZER—Trust? After she had read those letters—letters which seemed all the more guilty because you had never mentioned them to her? Trust! You want an angel for a wife, not a human being.

ROYLSTON—She had no business to read those letters. The whole thing rests upon that.

MRS. FRAZER—You had no business to receive the letters. The whole thing rests upon that. But to go on with my lesson: I asserted my innocence. Your wife refused to believe me—naturally enough. She spoke despondently of having expected something of the sort for a long time because you had been growing indifferent to her and the children.

ROYLSTON—(indignantly) That is not so. It's true I haven't had much time. I have been very busy, but—

MRS. FRAZER—(looking at him searchingly) Are you sure what you are saying now is the truth. Come, be frank! Remember your statement to me last night when I asked you if you loved her.

ROYLSTON—(*after a pause—grudgingly*) Well, I confess I may have seemed indifferent; but, good heavens—

MRS. FRAZER—She said she blamed no one but herself for what had happened. How could it be expected that a brilliant genius like you could continue to love a poor ignorant creature like herself?

ROYLSTON—(*a bit shamefaced*) She said that?

MRS. FRAZER—Those are almost her exact words. She blamed herself for marrying you in the first place. Marriages like yours were cursed, she thought.

ROYLSTON—Marriages like ours?

MRS. FRAZER—(*meaningly—looking steadily into his eyes*) She told me of the events which preceded your marriage—of the discovery of your love affair.

ROYLSTON—(*gripping the arms of his chair tensely, and speaking hoarsely*) Good God, she told you that! Poor Alice! (*half to himself*) What could have made her do that?

MRS. FRAZER—She said she thought that perhaps you blamed her for your father's death.

ROYLSTON—What an absurd idea!

MRS. FRAZER—She described your early life together—the days of struggle with poverty before your first play was produced; the days when you remained home in the little flat to write while she worked in an office as stenographer. She used to typewrite what you had written during the day when she came home at night—after she had cooked dinner and washed the dishes.

ROYLSTON—(*his face slowly flushing crimson*) You are right! I see what you are driving at. Whatever I am she has made me. I have been forgetting those early days for the past few years. They do not chime well with the tickled vanity. (*with sudden ingenuousness*) But I did used to dry the dishes, you know.

MRS. FRAZER—(*laughing*) Bravo! Richard is himself again. You only sold a few articles that first year, she said.

ROYLSTON—She flattered me. I never sold one. Every cent came through her.

MRS. FRAZER—She said those days were the happiest of her life. She had often been selfish enough to wish, since you became indifferent, that you had never succeeded and it could always have been as it was in the little flat.

ROYLSTON—Good heavens, she was nothing but a slave in those days.

MRS. FRAZER—She knew how hard it must have been for you, who had been used to having everything, to have her drag you down into privation and—

ROYLSTON—(*deeply moved*) What a horribly mistaken thought! I joyed in losing everything for her. It was like paying off part of my debt.

MRS. FRAZER—(*continuing as if he had not interrupted*) So she resolved that as soon as your first book or play was published or produced, and you did not need her any longer, she would leave you, permit you to regain your freedom.

ROYLSTON—(*stupefied—his voice trembling*) Why that's what she proposed to do—for me—when she was here a little while ago!

MRS. FRAZER—Oh yes, she only desires your happiness and, as she thinks you love me, she is perfectly willing to give you up to me—because she loves you so much.

ROYLSTON—How is it possible to lose oneself like that—I cannot grasp it—there is too much clay in my make-up— For me, too! Good heavens! She intended to leave me when my first play was produced, you say? But she didn't.

MRS. FRAZER—For a very good reason. It was about that time your son was born, wasn't it?

ROYLSTON—(*getting up from his chair and walking nervously about the room—in great agitation*) I see, I see! Poor Alice! What a woman she is! And I—good heavens! You threatened to open my eyes—I've lived with her all these years and forgotten how much I owed to her. She has protected and shielded me from everything—made my opportunity for me, you might say—and I took it all for granted— the finest thing in my life! Took it all for granted without a thought of gratitude, as my due. Lord, what a cad I've been! What a rotten cad! (*He throws himself into the chair and stares moodily before him.*)

MRS. FRAZER—(*with a faint smile*) I'd like to deny your statement but I'm afraid it's only too true.

ROYLSTON—What I cannot get through my head is why she should tell you all this. Alice is proud. To reveal all this to you, a stranger—it must have humbled her spirit to the breaking point.

Mrs. Frazer—I cannot quite understand, myself. She wished to justify you, of course, to prove you were in no way to blame.

Roylston—(*groaning*) Oh!

Mrs. Frazer—You see she persisted in regarding this misfortune as the retribution for her sin in the beginning.

Roylston—(*jumping up—excitedly*) Ah, by heavens, that is going too far! Retribution for *her* sin! What a preposterous idea! As if the blame, the sin if it was one, were not all mine! (*looking at his hands*) Bloody with sacrifices at my own altar—yes, you were right—and she is the woman whom I tortured with my blind egotism not half an hour ago—the woman who pleaded for forgiveness—and I refused and was going to desert her. I am beginning to hate myself for a monster! Those letters! If any woman ever dares to write to me again I'll have her letters burned by the—no, we haven't one—I'll hand them over to the police. (*Mrs. Frazer bursts out laughing.*) And my children— Good God, do you know the horrible thought came to me just now that I do not even know my own children?

Mrs. Frazer—(*protestingly*) Now you are carrying your self-accusation too far.

Roylston—(*vehemently*) I tell you it's the truth. I speak to them. I kiss them sometimes; but I do the same for other people's. For all the loving interest I have taken in them they might just as well be the gardener's—or Benton's.

Mrs. Frazer—You have the whole future before you for retribution.

Roylston—(*catching at the word eagerly*) Yes, retribution, joyful retribution every day, every hour! Pay off a part of this enormous debt of love which has accumulated against me! Why, life is going to mean more, be finer and happier than I ever dreamed!

Mrs. Frazer—Happiness is servitude.

Roylston—(*enthusiastically*) Of course it is! Servitude in love, love in servitude! Logos in Pan, Pan in Logos! That is the great secret—and I never knew! Thank you, thank you! But how did you guess it?

MRS. FRAZER—Mrs. Roylston told me this morning—her lesson in life.

ROYLSTON—That, too! Her love is great enough to solve all enigmas.

MRS. FRAZER—(*laughing*) But your work? The sovereign individual? The superman? The great lonely one?

ROYLSTON—My love will be a superlove worthy of the superman, and— (*hesitating*) Besides this is the exceptional case which proves the contrary rule—what are you laughing at?

MRS. FRAZER—At your determination to be exceptional though the heavens fall.

ROYLSTON—(*laughing himself*) I have to be exceptional to be worthy of such an exceptional wife.

MRS. FRAZER—(*rising from her chair*) And now I must go. My mission is accomplished.

ROYLSTON—Your mission? (*The doorbell is heard ringing.*)

MRS. FRAZER—Remember what you said about fatality? I am convinced I had to accomplish something here. It was not what I thought it was, but no matter. I, too, have learned the secret. It was my mission to open your eyes—and my own.

ROYLSTON—You are going back to your husband?

MRS. FRAZER—Yes, back to the chains which have suddenly become dear to me. Like you I had grown so accustomed to the best thing in life that I scorned it. I, too, have my joyful retribution to make, my debt of love to pay.

ROYLSTON—(*going to her and taking her hand*) And how can I ever thank you for my awakening?

MRS. FRAZER—The fact that you have wakened is thanks enough.

ROYLSTON—And will you not become—my wife's friend?

MRS. FRAZER—With all my heart—if she will allow it. (*Benton appears in the doorway on the left. He is greatly excited.*)

BENTON—Excuse me, sir, but there's a man who insisted on seeing you and— (*George Frazer pushes Benton roughly aside and steps into the room. He is a man of about thirty-five, thick-set, of medium height, black hair grey at the temples, square jaw, irregular features, broad clean-shaven face, and shrewd blue eyes. His face is haggard and shows plainly the traces of deep-rooted grief and anxiety with their consequent sleepless nights. He is dressed in a business suit of dark material.*)

FRAZER—(*gives a groan of suppressed rage as he sees the two standing together*) Ethel!

MRS. FRAZER—George! (*She makes a movement toward him. He throws himself at Roylston, pulling a revolver from his coat pocket. Mrs. Frazer springs between them.*)

MRS. FRAZER—For my sake! George! (*Frazer hurls the revolver on the floor and sinks into the chair by the table, hiding his face in his hands and sobbing heavily. Mrs. Frazer goes to him and puts her arm around his shoulder. He makes a feeble effort to shake her off. Benton creeps stealthily over and picks up the revolver.*)

ROYLSTON—(*severely*) You may go, Benton. (*Benton looks at him irresolutely, then goes out. Frazer finally regains his composure somewhat and turns his grief-stricken face to his wife.*)

FRAZER—Ethel—why?— My God!

MRS. FRAZER—(*distractedly*) Will this misunderstanding never be cleared up!

ROYLSTON—Yes, I will clear it up.

FRAZER—(*furiously*) Shut up, you—. You lie! I know what I know. You have done me harm enough without trying to treat me like a fool. I'd have shot you for the skulking liar you are—but—it wasn't for your sake I didn't—

ROYLSTON—(*with calm dignity*) I choose to ignore your insults for the present, Mr. Frazer. When you are calmer you will hear what I have to say and this ludicrous melodrama will end. (*He turns to go out door in back.*)

MRS. FRAZER—No, please stay; you must. (*R. remains standing by the door.*)

MRS. FRAZER—(*her voice trembling*) George, how did you find out?

FRAZER—I always knew you'd wind up here sooner or later. Before you left, when I was certain you didn't care for me any more, I suspected you were in love with this (*with bitter scorn*) gentleman. His books, his plays all over the place, his photograph on the middle of your dresser. (*Mrs. Frazer flushes. Roylston looks at her in astonishment.*) That was why I had you followed.

MRS. FRAZER—(*with a frown*) I thought you had given up spying on me.

FRAZER—(*pleadingly*) It wasn't spying. You mustn't think that, Ethel. It was for your own sake I did it.

MRS. FRAZER—(*with a hard laugh*) For my sake!

FRAZER—I wanted to protect you. You don't know the world. I knew you'd do something foolish sooner or later with your head full of his crazy ideas. You don't know the game these gentlemen play.

ROYLSTON—(*angrily*) Oh! (*He turns and goes out door in rear.*)

MRS. FRAZER—So I was followed to this house?

FRAZER—Yes.

MRS. FRAZER—When I came—last night?

FRAZER—(*with a groan*) Yes.

MRS. FRAZER—How is it you gave up waiting for me? Why haven't you tried to see me yourself—it's nearly two months.

FRAZER—I could see you didn't want me bothering you— and I've been sick.

MRS. FRAZER—(*alarmed*) Sick?

FRAZER—(*lightly*) Nothing serious—overwork—nervous breakdown, the doctor said. Had to go to bed—he pre-scribed perfect rest. (*ironically*) Perfect rest!

MRS. FRAZER—(*with tender anxiety*) But you're all right now, de— (*She bites back the term of endearment at his won-dering look.*) George?

FRAZER—(*sarcastically*) Fine—as you can see.

MRS. FRAZER—Why couldn't you have sent me word? It would have changed things so.

FRAZER—You mean you wouldn't be here? Well, I couldn't. I didn't want you to come back because you pitied me. (*bitterly*) I didn't think you'd care.

MRS. FRAZER—(*wincing*) Oh. (*after a pause*) Why did you come here this morning?

FRAZER—The detective telephoned me—when he was sure. I wanted to kill this man and you too, at first. I didn't know what I was doing.

MRS. FRAZER—(*sadly*) And now I suppose it's all over— forever—between us. You can't want me any longer—believ-ing what you do.

FRAZER—(*turning away from her to hide his emotion*) Don't say that, Ethel. I can't give you up—this way. Life is too— hard to bear—without you. I can't help loving you—in spite of everything. I shouldn't—I suppose—now. (*Mrs. Frazer is looking at him with eyes full of tenderness.*) If you'd only—love me a little—I could forget this foolishness—not your fault—if we'd had children—you were always alone—my fault. (*A sob shakes his shoulders.*)

MRS. FRAZER—(*softly*) So you still want me—to come back?

FRAZER—Yes—that's why I came—to ask you—if you would.

MRS. FRAZER—(*kneeling down beside him—eagerly*) Then look into my eyes quick—now! (*He looks down at her.*) I swear to you I am innocent—that I love you more now than I ever did, even on our honeymoon; and I am as innocent of wrong now as I was then. Can you believe me?

FRAZER—(*wonderingly*) Then you don't love him?

MRS. FRAZER—No, no, a thousand times no! I love you, and he loves his wife. My presence here is folly, nothing more. Let me explain the whole thing to you.

FRAZER—(*joyfully*) No, no, I believe you without that. (*He takes her into his arms and kisses her. Mrs. Roylston enters from the door on the left. She has a small travelling bag in her hand. Her eyes are red from weeping. She stops in astonishment and her bag drops from her hand when she sees the Frazers.*)

MRS. ROYLSTON—(*timidly*) I beg your pardon. (*Startled, they both jump to their feet and face Mrs. Roylston in confusion.*)

MRS. FRAZER—(*joyfully*) I want you to meet my husband, Mrs. Roylston. George, this is Mrs. Roylston.

MRS. ROYLSTON—(*astonished*) I'm very happy—

FRAZER—A great pleasure, etc.

MRS. FRAZER—Mrs. Roylston is the most wonderful woman in the world. (*Mrs. Roylston smiles feebly.*) If you don't believe me, ask her husband. (*as Frazer stammers and Mrs. Roylston is equally nonplussed*) And now you and I will be going—home! (*She walks over toward the door on the left.*) Good-bye, Mrs. Roylston. I hope when you understand everything you will become my friend. (*She holds out her hand which Mrs. Roylston takes uncertainly as if in a daze.*) Come, George, out into the open air. I have so much to say to you. (*She goes out. Frazer follows her but stops at the door and turns to Mrs. Roylston.*)

FRAZER—Mrs. Roylston, will you tell your husband I wish to take back all I said to him a while ago. He'll understand.

MRS. ROYLSTON—(*dully*) I'll tell him.

FRAZER—Thank you; good-bye. (*He goes out. A moment later the front door is heard closing.*)

MRS. ROYLSTON—(*mechanically*) Good-bye. (*She takes her bag and sets it down beside the table; then sinks wearily into the chair and leans both elbows on the table, holding her face in her hands in an attitude of deep dejection. Roylston enters from the door in the rear. He gives a joyful exclamation on seeing his wife.*)

ROYLSTON—(*coming over quickly, stands beside her*) Alice.

MRS. ROYLSTON—(*startled, turns and looks up at him— dully*) Yes.

ROYLSTON—They have gone—Mr. and Mrs. Frazer—together?

MRS. ROYLSTON—Yes.

ROYLSTON—(*jubilantly*) Good! And without hearing my explanation! That is a proof of love and trust on his part which I would hardly have expected of him. You see, Alice, the most ludicrous part of this whole misunderstanding is the fact that I did not spend last night in this house.

MRS. ROYLSTON—(*slowly—as if she could not believe her ears*) You—were not here?

ROYLSTON—No. After I directed Mrs. Frazer to her room I ran away—spent the night at the roadhouse. I was afraid to stay, I must confess—afraid of myself—afraid of how the situation might be misconstrued. I didn't want to be the cause of any more trouble to Mrs. Frazer, who had suffered enough already.

MRS. ROYLSTON—(*her eyes brimming with happy tears*) Oh, I'm so glad!

ROYLSTON—I want you to prove my statement—to be completely satisfied that I am speaking the truth. My name is on the register at the roadhouse and they all know me and can testify to my story. I wanted to explain before but your doubts hurt my obstinate pride—I had boasted to Mrs. Frazer that you would not judge by appearances, you know. As for Frazer's detective, he must have taken everything for granted—as you and all the rest did. I'll have to write to

Frazer and tell him. In spite of his fine confidence there might be some secret suspicions in the back of his mind.

MRS. ROYLSTON—David—forgive me—

ROYLSTON—(*impetuously*) Forgive you? What nonsense! (*He bends down to kneel beside her and knocks his knee against her bag. He holds it up wonderingly.*) What's this? Your bag all packed! Then you were really going to leave me?

MRS. ROYLSTON—(*tremblingly*) I thought you loved her. I wanted you to be happy.

ROYLSTON—And the children?

MRS. ROYLSTON—I had no right— It was best for them to stay.

ROYLSTON—You were going to leave them, too—and all for my sake! Good heavens! And you ask for forgiveness! (*kneeling down beside her and putting his arms around her*) Ah, my dear, my dear, how deeply you make me feel my unworthiness! I am the one who must plead for pardon, pardon for a lifetime of selfish neglect, of vain posing, of stupid conceit—

MRS. ROYLSTON—(*kissing him*) Ssshhh!

ROYLSTON—(*his voice vibrating with tenderness*) Dear, the future will be all that the past has not been, I swear it. We start on our honeymoon today—a lifelong honeymoon. (*jumping to his feet, with mock severity*) But haven't you read your husband's books, you wonderful, foolish woman? Don't you know it was your duty to claim your right as an individual, to shake off the shackles my insufferable egotism had forced upon you? Don't you understand that you have stifled your own longings, given up your own happiness that I might feel self-satisfied—

MRS. ROYLSTON—(*interrupting him—softly and tenderly*) That was my happiness. (*He bends down and kisses her reverently as*

The Curtain Falls)

THE SNIPER

A Play in One Act

CHARACTERS

ROUGON, *a Belgian peasant*
THE VILLAGE PRIEST
A GERMAN CAPTAIN OF INFANTRY
FOUR PRIVATES OF THE REGIMENT
JEAN, *a peasant boy*

The Sniper

SCENE—*The main room of a ruined cottage on the outskirts of a small Belgian village. The rear wall has two enormous breaches made by the shells of the artillery. The right wall is partly hidden by a mass of wreckage from the roof, which has caved in leaving a jagged hole through which the sky can be seen. The ceiling slants drunkenly downward toward the right, ending abruptly in a ragged edge of splintered boards and beams which forms a fantastic fretwork against the sky. The floor is littered with all kinds of debris.*

In the rear wall near the right corner, a window, its panes of glass all broken, with a torn white curtain. No trace of the doorway to the road remains. The larger breach in the rear wall is used as exit and entrance.

The left wall, with a door in the middle, is uninjured. Over the door a large black crucifix hangs from a nail.

In the center of the room, an overturned table. A solitary chair, the only thing left standing, is beside it. On the right of the table a smashed armchair.

The time is about sundown on a September day. Through the breaches in the wall a dark green vista of rolling fields can be seen. Where they meet the horizon they are already shimmering in the golden dust of the sunset. Muffled and far-off, the booming of distant cannon reverberates slowly over the fields.

The sound of shuffling footsteps is heard from the road before the cottage and a great hulking old man of sixty-five or so appears at the larger breach in the rear wall. He is dressed in the usual peasant fashion and wears wooden sabots on his feet. He is bent under some burden which, as he enters the room, is seen to be the body of a young man dressed in the uniform of a Belgian infantryman. He lays the body down carefully in a cleared space between the table and the left wall, pillowing the soldier's head upon his knapsack. The body lies with its feet toward the rear wall.

He stands looking down at the still form, his attitude one of abject despair. A heavy sob shakes his round shoulders. He murmurs brokenly: "Charles! My little one!"; *then turns abruptly and stumbles to the middle of the room where he mechanically rights the overturned table. He sits down on the chair, and stares at the ruins about him with an expression of dazed bewilderment on his broad face, his round, child-like eyes wandering dully from one object to another. His gaze finally rests on the smashed arm-chair on the other side of the table, and suddenly overcome by a flood of anguished horror, he hides his face in his hands, rocking from side to side on his chair, moaning to himself like a wounded animal.*

The slight black-robed figure of a priest appears on the road outside. He casts a quick glance into the room and, seeing the bowed figure on the chair quickly picks his way to the peasant's side. The priest is old, white-haired, with a kindly, spiritual face.

THE PRIEST—Rougon!

ROUGON—(*not hearing him*) God, oh God!

THE PRIEST—(*laying a thin white hand compassionately on Rougon's broad back*) There, there, my son! It is the will of God.

ROUGON—(*startled by the sound of a voice, jumps up from his chair*) Eh? (*stares at the priest with dazed eyes*)

THE PRIEST—(*with a sad smile*) Oh, come now, it isn't possible that you've forgotten me.

ROUGON—(*snatching off his cap respectfully*) Pardon, Father. I was—I didn't know—you see—all this—

THE PRIEST—(*gently*) I have heard of your loss. I understand.

ROUGON—But take the chair, Father. (*bitterly*) I am lucky to have it left to offer you.

THE PRIEST—(*sitting down*) You must not brood over your misfortunes. Many, a great many, have suffered even more than you. You must learn to bear these burdens as they come, at such a dreadful time as this, and pray to God for strength. We must all bow ourselves before His will.

ROUGON—His will? Ha! No, the good God would not punish me so,—I, who have harmed no one. (*furiously*) It is all these cursed Pruss—

THE PRIEST—Ssshh! (*after a pause*) Such thoughts may rest in the heart, but to let them rise to the lips is hardly wise—now.

ROUGON—What matter if they should hear? I am finished,

me! They can do no more but kill me. (*He sits on the edge of the table. A heavy sob shakes his bowed shoulders.*)

THE PRIEST—(*after a pause during which he gazes sadly at the face of the dead young soldier*) You must not mourn his loss so bitterly. He has given his life for his country. He is at rest with God. You should feel proud of him.

ROUGON—(*dully*) Yes, he is—at rest—in heaven. And, look you, Father, you remember, this was the day—today he was to have been married.

THE PRIEST—(*in accents of deep grief*) True, true, I had forgotten. Poor boy, poor boy—and poor Louise!

ROUGON—And my poor old woman— Ah, good God, what have we done? All this—in one day!

THE PRIEST—Your wife—she doesn't know?

ROUGON—No. This morning, look you, I sent her away. It was Charles who came to me this morning—in his new uniform—he who lies there so still now—he whom they have murdered, those cursed Prussians!

THE PRIEST—Ssshh! Would you bring more misfortune upon yourself?

ROUGON—(*springing to his feet in a frenzy*) Ah, how I would love to slaughter them, to grind my heel in their fat faces, to,—to—

THE PRIEST—Calm yourself, for the love of heaven, my good Rougon! Will it improve matters, think you, to have you, too, shot? Do not forget your poor old wife. You must be careful for her sake, if for nothing else.

ROUGON—(*sullenly slouching back to his seat on the table*) It is hard, name of a dog, it is hard. I feel like a coward, me, to stand by and do nothing.

THE PRIEST—(*in low tones*) Be comforted. The hour of retribution will yet strike. The end is not yet. Your son Charles will be avenged.

ROUGON—(*shaking his head doubtfully*) There are so many.

THE PRIEST—But you were telling me about your wife. You sent her away this morning?

ROUGON—If the good God so pleases she is in Brussels by now. For, look you, Charles came to me this morning. "My father" he said, "I am afraid there will be fighting here today. I have warned the family of Louise and she is to flee with them to Brussels. I have arranged that Mother should go with them; and you, too, my father." "But no," I said, "It is right for your mother. She shall go. As you say, it will be no place for women if there be fighting. But me, no, I shall stay." "Mind you, then, Father, no shooting!" Charles said as he kissed me good-bye and ran to join the regiment on the village place, "or they will shoot you like a dog".

THE PRIEST—You see! Your son gave you the best advice. Remember you are not a soldier.

ROUGON—(*proudly*) If I were not too old I should have been in a uniform this long time gone. Too old! The fools! As if I could not shoot straighter than all these boys!

THE PRIEST—There are other things to consider, my poor Rougon. Someone must gather in the harvest if we are not all to starve.

ROUGON—(*fiercely*) The harvest? What is there left? First it is the French who take away my two fine horses that I have saved up every centime two years to buy—and leave me a scrap of paper; then—

THE PRIEST—The French are our friends; in due time you shall be paid.

ROUGON—Bah, promises!

THE PRIEST—(*earnestly*) At a time like this all must bear their share of sacrifice.

ROUGON—All who wanted war, yes; but we who desired nothing more than to be left in peace to till our fields? Look you, my Father, why should we be robbed and plundered and our homes blown apart by their accursed cannon?

THE PRIEST—(*shaking his head, sadly*) God knows. Our poor country is a lamb among wolves.

ROUGON—(*raising his voice excitedly*) The first shell that burst in our village—do you know where it struck?

THE PRIEST—No.

ROUGON—Out there—on my barn—setting it in flames—killing my two cows one of which I was to have given Charles, with half of my farm, as a wedding present— burning up all my hay I had gathered for the winter. (*stamping his foot in his rage*) Ah, those dirty beasts!

THE PRIEST—Ssshh! They are all around.

ROUGON—And then, look you, the cavalry ride over my

fields trampling my grain beneath their horses, the artillery wheels tear up the earth, the cannon blow my home to pieces—as you see. (*bitterly*) Harvest? There is nothing left to harvest but dirt and stones!

THE PRIEST—(*to change the subject which is rapidly infuriating the old man*) You may well give thanks to the good God that your wife is safe in Brussels.

ROUGON—They started early this morning, as I have said, and the family of Louise has relatives in Brussels. She is safe, God be thanked. (*with a grief-stricken glance at the body of his son*) But when she knows—and Louise who also loved him so— Oh, my God! (*He chokes back a sob.*)

THE PRIEST—God give them strength to bear it.

ROUGON—(*indicating his son*) He wanted me to go with them. He was afraid I would do something rash if I stayed. But I have been calm. But, name of a dog, it has been hard—when I saw them trampling my wheat—those pigs—when I saw the ashes which had been my barn—and this house, as you see, where I had lived so many years—this finger itched to press the trigger and send at least one to hell for payment.

THE PRIEST—My son, my son!

ROUGON—Your pardon, my Father. Had it not been for the promise I had given Charles, I would have taken the old rifle from where I have it hidden in there (*he indicates with a nod of his head the room on the left*) and—

THE PRIEST—(*casting an apprehensive glance toward the street*) Ssshh! Be careful what you say in so loud a tone. Their soldiers are everywhere. But where were you when all this fighting was taking place?

ROUGON—I was hiding in the well. I had placed a board across, on which I could stand and see what took place through the chinks in the stones. I wanted to see—him.

THE PRIEST—See—Charles? How could—

ROUGON—His part of the regiment was behind the wall in the orchard not one hundred meters away. I could watch him clearly.

THE PRIEST—(*to himself, half-aloud*) Poor man!

ROUGON—At first it was all right. Their infantry came up so close to each other that not even a child could have missed them. Bang! and they were toppled over before they had even reached the foot of the hill. I laughed. I thought it was all finished. I could see Charles laughing and talking with his comrades—and then— (*He stops, shaking his head despondently.*)

THE PRIEST—And then?

ROUGON—One of their devilish flying machines which look like the great birds flew overhead, far-up. All shot at it but it was too far away. It flew back to them, and a minute later, look you, I saw white puffs of smoke on all the hills over to the west; then bang! crash! I could not hear; my ears were cracked with the din. There was dust, and falling walls, and my barn blazing. Ah, those accursed cannon! I climbed out of the well and ran to the barn.

THE PRIEST—In the midst of all those bursting shells?

ROUGON—I trembled with rage. I had no fear of their cannon. I remembered only the cow, the pretty little cow, I was to give to Charles. But I could do nothing. Not all the fire-engines in Belgium could have saved it. I ran back to the well. Ssszzz! went the bullets all round. As I was climbing over I was stunned by a terrible crash. The roof of this house tumbled in—as you see.

THE PRIEST—And you remained in the well all during the battle?

ROUGON—Yes—until I saw Charles fall. He was just aiming his rifle over the wall when I saw him throw up his hands, spin around like a top, and fall on his face. I ran down and carried him back on my shoulders to the well—but it was too late. He was dead. (*He stops abruptly, choking back a sob.*)

THE PRIEST—(*after a pause*) Requiescat in pace. His life was ever a happy one. He never knew the cares and worries that come with the years and the ceaseless struggle for bread. He loved and was loved. He died the death of the brave. (*gently*) Is it not better after all—as it is? (*Rougon does not answer.*) Can you not console yourself with that thought?

ROUGON—Perhaps. Who knows? But, look you, it is hard for me—and for Louise—and most of all for his mother whose baby he was.

THE PRIEST—You all loved him, did everything in your power to make him happy. You have nothing with which to reproach yourselves.

ROUGON—But now—what shall I do? Look you, it was for him we worked and saved, his mother and I; that he might never have to know, as we had known, what it is to be poor and hungry. (*despondently*) And now—we are old—what use to work? There is nothing left but death.

THE PRIEST—You have each other.

ROUGON—Yes, we have each other. Were it not for the thought of my poor Margot I had let these butchers kill me before this.

THE PRIEST—(*sternly*) I do not like to hear you talk in that manner. You must realize well, that in its time of stress, your country has need of you; as much need of you as of her soldiers. You must not be rash. You must live and help and bear your part of her burden as best you can. It is your duty.

ROUGON—Yes, yes, I well know it; but—

THE PRIEST—Above all, you have to exercise control over your hasty temper. You must realize that you will best serve your country and revenge your personal wrongs by living and helping, not by willfully seeking death. You must remember you are a civilian and, according to the rules of war, you have no right to fight. Your part lies elsewhere. Let others shoot the guns.

ROUGON—(*disgustedly*) Bah! The children they have as soldiers cannot shoot. With my little rifle in there I could pick off more Prussian swine than a whole regiment of youngsters like my poor Charles. (*scornfully*) Yet they tell me I am too old to enlist! Dolts!

THE PRIEST—(*rising and laying his hand on Rougon's back—with solemn earnestness*) My son, before I leave, I want you to swear to me before the God who watches over us, that you will remember what I have said and not allow your temper to force you to violence.

ROUGON—(*sullenly*) I promise. I swear it.

THE PRIEST—(*patting him on the back*) There, now you are sensible, more like yourself. (*He stands looking down at Charles.*) I would advise you as to the burial of Charles. (*Rougon groans.*) Let it be done as secretly as possible. Let us avoid all provocation, and on their heads be it if misfortune happens. Perhaps tonight would be best.

ROUGON—Ah, no, no, no! Please, my Father, not yet!

Tonight let him remain here in his home, the house he was born in, with me.

THE PRIEST—So be it. Tomorrow night, then. You will let me know what time you wish it to be.

ROUGON—Very well, my Father.

THE PRIEST—And now I must go; but first let us kneel down and humbly offer up a prayer for the repose of his soul. (*They kneel down beside the dead body. The priest commences to intone a prayer in which the words* "Almighty God," "Merciful," "Infinite justice," "Infinite love," "Infinite pity," "Thy son Jesus," "We, Thy children," "Praise Thy infinite goodness," *stand out from the general mumble of sing-song sentences. Perhaps a sense of the crushing irony of this futile prayer penetrates the sorrow-numbed brain of Rougon and proves the last straw which breaks down his self-control; for he interrupts the droning supplications of the priest with a groan of agony, throws himself beside the young soldier's body, and sobs brokenly:* "Charles, Charles, my little one! Oh, why did not God take me instead!")

THE PRIEST—(*after a pause—wiping the tears from his eyes with his large handkerchief*) Come, come, it is hard, I know, but you must bear it like a man. God's will be done! He, too, had a Son who died for others. Pray to Him and He will comfort you in your affliction.

ROUGON—(*placing his hand gently on his son's face*) Cold! Cold! He who was so alive and smiling only this morning. (*A step is heard on the road outside. The two get hastily to their feet as a young man in the grey uniform of a German captain of infantry appears at one of the gaps of the wall.*)

THE CAPTAIN—(*entering and turning to the priest*) Are you the— (*seeing the body on the floor*) I beg your pardon.

THE PRIEST—(*coldly*) What is your wish?

THE CAPTAIN—(*twirling his blond mustache fiercely to hide his embarrassment*) Again, I ask pardon. I meant no disrespect. (*Taking off his helmet impressively—he is a very young captain.*) I honor the brave dead on whichever side they fall.

THE PRIEST—(*indicating Rougon who has slunk off to the other side of the table and is controlling his hatred and rage with very apparent effort*) It is his son.

THE CAPTAIN—Ah! Too bad! The fortunes of war. Today, him; tomorrow, me, perhaps. Are you the curé of the village?

THE PRIEST—I am.

THE CAPTAIN—I have been seeking you ever since we occupied the place.

THE PRIEST—I returned but a short time ago from Brussels where I had been called to make my report to the Bishop. I knew nothing of the fighting here or I should have returned sooner. (*sadly*) There were many, perhaps, who died needing me. But what is it you wish?

THE CAPTAIN—I was sent by the colonel to find you and deliver his orders. There seems to be no one of civil authority left in the village—else I should not intrude upon you.

THE PRIEST—I am listening.

THE CAPTAIN—(*oratorically*) It is the colonel's wish that you warn the inhabitants against committing any violence against our soldiers. Civilians caught with arms will be immediately shot. (*The priest casts a significant glance at Rougon who scowls and mutters to himself.*) Is that clear?

THE PRIEST—Quite.

THE CAPTAIN—On the other hand all we demand of you will be paid for in cash. Let all your parishioners return to their work without fear of molestation. We make no war upon the helpless. (*with complacent pride*) I hope I make my meaning clear. I flatter myself my French is not so bad.

THE PRIEST—(*with cold politeness*) You speak it very well, Monsieur. You may tell your colonel that I will do all in my power to impress his words upon the minds of my people— not that I respect his orders or admit his right to give them to a man of peace, but because I have the welfare of my people at heart.

THE CAPTAIN—Good. I will tell him. And now I will say "au revoir" for I, too, have my duties to perform. We march from here immediately.

THE PRIEST—(*significantly*) Adieu. (*The Captain goes out.*)

ROUGON—(*raging*) Dog of a Prussian!

THE PRIEST—Silence! Are you a fool? (*While he is speaking an awkward peasant boy of about fifteen with a broad face appears at the breech in the rear wall. His clothes are mud-stained and ragged and he is trembling with fear. He breathes in great shud-*

dering gasps. There is a cut on his forehead beneath which the blood has dried in reddish-brown streaks.)

ROUGON—(*hears the noise*) What's that? (*They both turn around and see the boy.*)

THE PRIEST—Why, it's Jean! Whatever are you doing skulking around like that?

JEAN—(*stopping uneasily as if he intended to run away again*) Nothing, nothing.

THE PRIEST—Come over here. (*Jean does not move but stares at him with frightened eyes.*) Don't you hear me speaking to you? What is the matter with you?

JEAN—(*faintly*) I am afraid.

THE PRIEST—Of me? Come, this is ridiculous.

JEAN—(*his lips trembling*) I am afraid—of them. Everything—blows up.

ROUGON—Come to the good father when he speaks to you, stupid dolt! Or I shall find a good strong stick and—

THE PRIEST—Hush, you are only frightening him. Come to me, Jean, like a good boy. (*Jean goes slowly to the priest who puts an arm about his shoulders.*) Why, you're trembling like a leaf! Did the battle frighten you?

JEAN—No, no, no! I don't know.

ROUGON—(*contemptuously*) The battle? He was never near the fighting. It was bad enough for we others without having this half-witted calf around. So we sent him away with the women this morning. (*to Jean*) Answer me, you, how is it you are back here?

JEAN—(*trembling*) I don't know.

ROUGON—(*roughly*) Name of a dog, what do you know? Did we send you away with the women this morning or didn't we?

JEAN—(*uncertainly*) Yes—I went away—this morning.

THE PRIEST—Hush, Rougon, you are only frightening the poor fellow. Jean, listen to me and stop trembling. I shall not let anyone hurt you. I have always been your good friend, have I not?

JEAN—Yes—you are my friend.

THE PRIEST—Of course I am; and while I am around there is nothing you need fear. Come now, tell me like a good lad; you went away with the others this morning, didn't you?

JEAN—Yes, Father.

THE PRIEST—Then how do you happen to be here now? Why did you return to the village? Your clothes are in a shocking state. Where have you been hiding and how did you get that cut on your forehead?

JEAN—(*feeling the cut on his forehead with a dazed air*) It hurts.

THE PRIEST—You will come home with me presently and we will wash that nasty cut and wrap it up in a nice clean bandage. Then you may be sure you will no longer feel any hurt at all. But first tell me—

JEAN—I don't know. I ran and ran—and I came here.

THE PRIEST—But something must have happened to make you run. Come, tell us, what was it?

JEAN—(*vaguely*) We left here and walked a long, long ways. Some rode in wagons but I was walking.

ROUGON—And did you see Mother Rougon there, and Louise?

JEAN—(*in a strange tone—with a shudder*) Yes, I saw them, I saw them. (*Rougon gives a grunt of satisfaction.*)

THE PRIEST—Go on, my son, tell us what happened next.

JEAN—We could hear shots. We hurried faster. The horses galloped. The women commenced to scream and cry. Always the firing was louder. We didn't see any soldiers for a long time. Then we came upon lots of bodies—men from our army and others dressed in grey.

ROUGON—(*in growing alarm*) Name of a dog, why didn't you turn back, eh?

JEAN—(*vaguely*) I don't know. (*He drones on in his expressionless voice.*) The women were praying. They were afraid. They wanted us to hurry up and get to Brussels. We beat the horses. The hills were covered with white spots like,—like daisies; and they floated 'way up in the air. (*He makes a queer awkward gesture upward.*)

ROUGON—Idiot! What is all this foolish talk?

THE PRIEST—(*gently*) It was the smoke from the guns you saw, my child.

JEAN—(*very slowly—trying his best to imitate the exact sound*) Boom! Boom! Boom! I couldn't hear what anyone was saying. (*He pauses.*)

ROUGON—Why do you stop, stupid? Go on, go on, or—
(*He shakes his clenched fist at the boy.*)

THE PRIEST—Silence, Rougon! Give the poor lad a chance.

JEAN—(*in flat, monotonous tones*) Something blew up in a
field by the road and threw dirt and stones on us. The horses
were afraid. They ran faster. Then we came to the top of a
hill. Lots of the soldiers in our army were there hiding in a
long ditch. They shouted for us to run away. Then—then—
then—

THE PRIEST—(*anxiously*) Yes? (*Rougon stands tensely with
averted face as if afraid to listen.*)

JEAN—(*throwing both his arms into the air with a wild gesture*) Then everything around blew up. (*in flat tones*) Something hit me on the head. I laid down for a while. When I
got up I couldn't see any of the rest. There were bodies all
around. I saw Mother Rougon—

THE PRIEST—(*clinging to a last shred of hope*) Alive and
unharmed? (*But Rougon has guessed the worst and stands as if
in a stupor, clenching and unclenching his big red hands, his features working convulsively.*)

JEAN—She was lying on the ground. She had a big hole
here (*pointing to his chest*) and blood all over—bright and red
like—like flowers.

ROUGON—(*dully*) Dead! She, too!

JEAN—And Louise had a hole in her head, here (*pointing
to his forehead*) and—

THE PRIEST—(*distracted with horror*) Enough! Stop! We
have heard all we care to, do you hear?

JEAN—So I ran, and ran, and ran, and ran, and ran. (*His
words die away into a murmur— He stares straight before him
like one in a trance.*)

THE PRIEST—Merciful God, have pity!

ROUGON—(*slowly—as if the meaning of Jean's words were
just commencing to dawn on him*) So—they are gone, too—
the old woman—and Louise— (*licks his lips with his dry
tongue*) Everything is gone.

(*There is a long silence. The priest dabs with his big handkerchief at the tears which are welling into his eyes. Jean wanders over
to the breach in the wall and stands looking down the road. A
loud bugle call is heard. Jean darts back into the room.*)

JEAN—(*waving his arms, cries in terrified tones*) They are coming. They are coming this way! (*He runs to the right corner of the room and crouches there trembling, seeking to hide himself in the fallen ruins.*)

ROUGON—So—*they* are coming? (*He strides resolutely across the room and enters the room on left.*)

THE PRIEST—(*alarmed by the expression on Rougon's face*) Rougon! Rougon! What are you going to do? (*He receives no answer. A moment later Rougon re-enters the room carrying a long-barrelled rifle.*)

THE PRIEST—(*seizing him by the arm*) No, no, I beseech you!

ROUGON—(*roughly throwing the priest aside*) Let me alone! (*He half-kneels beside one of the breeches in the wall—then speaks in a voice of deadly calmness.*) They will not pass here. They are going to turn off at the fork in the road. It is near enough, however. (*The rhythmic tramp of the marching troops can be faintly heard.*)

THE PRIEST—(*in agony*) In the name of God I implore you—

ROUGON—Bah, God! (*He takes careful aim and fires.*) That for Margot! (*loads and fires again*) That for Louise! (*Cries of rage and running footsteps are heard. Rougon is reloading his rifle when the Captain and four German privates rush in. Rougon struggles but is disarmed and forced back to the wall on left. He stands proudly, calmly awaiting his fate. One of the soldiers seizes the priest.*)

THE SOLDIER—(*to the Captain*) Was mit dem Priester?

ROUGON—(*to the Captain*) The good father did nothing. He but did his best to hold my arm and stop me. It is I alone who did the shooting, Dog of a Prussian!

THE CAPTAIN—Is this true, priest?

THE PRIEST—It is as he tells you. I tried to restrain him—not for your sakes, but for his own.

THE CAPTAIN—(*to the soldier*) Las den Priester gehen! (*The soldier releases the priest. The Captain turns to Rougon.*) If you have a prayer to say, be quick! (*The four soldiers line up in front of Rougon and face him across the body of Charles.*)

ROUGON—(*with angry scorn*) I want no prayers!

THE PRIEST—Rougon!

ROUGON—(*furiously*) To hell with your prayers!

THE PRIEST—(*supplicatingly*) Make your peace with God, my son!

ROUGON—(*spitting on the floor, fiercely*) That for your God who allows such things to happen! (*to the Captain*) I am ready, pig!

THE CAPTAIN—(*to the soldiers*) Gewehr! Heraus! (*The soldiers take aim.*)

THE PRIEST—May God have mercy on—

THE CAPTAIN—Feuer! (*A crashing report. Rougon pitches forward on his face, quivers for a moment, is still. The soldiers file out to the road. The Captain turns to the horrified priest.*)

THE CAPTAIN—(*shrugging his shoulders*) It is the law. (*He follows the soldiers.*)

THE PRIEST—(*looking down with infinite compassion at the still bodies of father and son*) Alas, the laws of men! (*The sun has set. The twilight is fading grayly into night. From the heap of wreckage in the right corner comes the sound of stifled weeping.*)

(*The Curtain Falls*)

THE PERSONAL EQUATION

A Play in Four Acts

CHARACTERS

THOMAS PERKINS, *2nd engineer of the* S. S. San Francisco
TOM, *his son*
HENDERSON, *1st engineer of the* S. S. Empress
OLGA TARNOFF ⎫
HARTMANN ⎪ *Members of the International*
ENWRIGHT ⎬ *Workers Union*
WHITELY ⎪
MRS. ALLEN ⎭
O'ROURKE ⎫
COCKY ⎪
HARRIS ⎬ *Stokers of the* San Francisco
SCHMIDT ⎪
HOGAN ⎭
MURPHY, *an oiler*
JACK, *an engineer's apprentice*
A DOCTOR
MISS BROWN

ACT I: Headquarters of the I.W.U. in Hoboken
ACT II: Home of Thomas Perkins
ACT III: SCENE I—Fireman's fo'castle of the *San Francisco*, docked at Liverpool
        SCENE II—Engine room of the *San Francisco*
ACT IV: Private room in hospital in Liverpool

The Personal Equation

ACT I

SCENE—*Main room of the headquarters of the International Workers Union in Hoboken—a large bare room with white-washed walls. In the rear, two windows looking out on a dingy back street. On the wall between the windows, a large framed engraving of a naked woman with a liberty cap on her head, leaning back against the two upright beams of a guillotine. In the left hand corner, a desk with chair. In the middle of left wall, a door opening into hall. In right corner, a small table with type-writer on it. In the middle of left wall, a door opening into hall. In the middle of right wall, another door. In the center of room, a long table with four or five straight-backed chairs placed around it. On the table, newspapers, periodicals, stacks of pamphlets, etc. Flooring of coarse, uncovered boards. Framed cartoons, mostly in color, from* Jugend, Simplissimus, *etc., are hung here and there on the walls.*

It is evening and already dark. Two gas lights of the Welsbach type, fixed on the tarnished chandelier which hangs over the table, throw a cold white light about the room, revealing every detail of its bare ugliness.

Olga stands at one end of the table reading a newspaper. She is very dark; strong, fine features; large spirited black eyes, slender, supple figure. Enwright sits on the chair nearest her. He is thin, round-shouldered, middle-aged, clean-shaven, wears glasses.

ENWRIGHT—(*languidly*) What have our dear friends, the Socialists, to say about us today? Are we luring their honest working man to his ruin; are we planting the insidious seeds of anarchy in the unsuspecting bosoms of their voters, or, or—what?

OLGA—Bah, the same old stuff! What's the use of repeating it? (*her eyes flashing*) Oh, these Socialists! How I loathe their eternal platitudes, their milk-and-water radicalism, their cut-and-dried sermons for humble voters! As if to vote were not also to acquiesce in the present order of things, to become a cog in the machine which grinds the voter himself to bits! Revolution by act of Congress! The dolts! (*as*

Enwright smiles amusedly and glances at his watch) What time is it?

ENWRIGHT—Nearly eight. Are you waiting for Tom, or Hartmann?

OLGA—Both. Tom ought to be here now. Hartmann sent word he wanted to see us here tonight on something important.

ENWRIGHT—Something to do with the talked-of strike of the dock-laborers, seamen and firemen, I expect. I hear there's a contemplated move in that direction.

OLGA—Ah, so that's it. I couldn't imagine what it could be.

ENWRIGHT—(*after a pause*) May I ask an impertinent question, Olga? Do you think Tom's zeal in our activities is inspired by deep inward conviction, or—I'll be plain—do you think it's merely an outcropping of his love for you?

OLGA—(*indignantly*) How can you imagine such a thing? You know Tom. You know how hard he has worked with us.

ENWRIGHT—It's just a feeling I have. Somehow he doesn't seem to fit in. He's a fine intelligent fellow and all that, but he isn't our type, now is he?

OLGA—He was interested in our movement and used to come to our meetings before I ever met him.

ENWRIGHT—Curiosity and a craving for adventure might account for that. He probably wanted to see a real bomb thrown.

OLGA—(*angrily*) Oh! (*then coldly*) You're wrong and you know it.

ENWRIGHT—Hm, am I? Well, I shouldn't have asked you. You love him. What do you know of the real man? Now, don't fly into a rage. Tom is my good friend, and no matter what he's inspired by, a valuable addition to our ranks. I must go and see if those pamphlets have come. (*He goes to door on right. Tom enters just as Enwright is closing door. Enwright shouts:* "Hello, Tom" *and shuts door behind him. Olga runs to Tom and they embrace and kiss each other passionately.*)

(*Tom is a husky six-footer in his early twenties, large intelligent eyes, handsome in a rough, manly, strong-featured way. His manner is one of boyishly naive enthusiasm with a certain note of defiance creeping in as if he were fighting an inward embarrassment and was determined to brave it down.*)

OLGA—I thought you'd never get here and yet you're on time. (*They laugh and come over and sit down—Olga in chair at end of the table, Tom on edge of the table beside her.*)

TOM—Hartmann showed up yet?

OLGA—Not yet.

TOM—Wonder what he wants us for.

OLGA—It's something to do with a coming strike of dock-laborers and firemen, Enwright thinks.

TOM—Anything in the paper about it?

OLGA—Not much; they're trying to hush it up. (*She picks up a paper.*) But there's quite an editorial here about you and me and other dangerous inciters to riot—you know—for our speeches in Union Square last Saturday. Listen to this. He's referring to what I said against war with Mexico. (*reads*) "A crack-brained young female, Olga something-or-other, arose to howl invective against the government which protects her, against all sense of decency and national honor"—and so forth. Here again: "Over-strung lady anarchists of the Olga type are a constant and dangerous menace to society and should be confined in some asylum for the criminal-insane."

TOM—(*fiercely*) Damn him! (*puts his arm protectingly around Olga*)

OLGA—(*resisting this protective attitude*) It seems I'm a dangerous anarchist inciting to murder because I call upon men not to shoot their brother men for a fetish of red, white and blue, a mockery called patriotism. (*She laughs angrily.*)

TOM—The cowardly hound!

OLGA—(*throwing the paper on the floor scornfully*) I won't read what he said about you—something about your looking like a broken-down college boy whom a desire for cheap notoriety had led into the International Workers. (*fiercely*) Liar!

TOM—(*with a smile*) Well, I'm a college boy if that one year I wasted in college makes me one. (*slowly*) I don't care what they say about me; but, damn him, he ought to have the manhood not to sling his muddy ink at a woman.

OLGA—What an old-fashioned idea! Aren't we equals when we fight for liberty—regardless of sex?

TOM—(*a bit sheepishly*) I know it's a mistaken notion—logically. I can feel that way about all the others—the other women who are working with us, I mean—but where you are concerned, I can't. It's different, somehow. (*slowly*) You see—I love you, Olga.

OLGA—(*calmly*) And I love you, Tom; but what difference does that make? Are we not comrades fighting in the ranks—before everything? Don't you put that before our own miserable little egos?

TOM—Before my own little miserable ego, yes; but not before yours. (*as Olga looks at him reproachfully*) I can't help it. Our love comes first. (*moodily*) That's why calumnies against you like the one in that paper drive me wild. I'd like to take that editor and twist his measly neck for him.

OLGA—(*frowning at his attitude of protection*) I'm used to such things, I'm strong enough to bear them. You ought to know that.

TOM—I do, Olga. Good Lord, you're strong enough to bear anything. I'm not, that's the thing. I'm not strong enough to bear the insults against you, and by God, I never will be.

OLGA—(*rather impatiently*) Don't take them so seriously.

TOM—I can't help it—especially the things they say against you—(*he hesitates*) on account of me.

OLGA—On account of you? What do you mean?

TOM—On account of—our relationship.

OLGA—You mean that stupid Philistines sneer at me because I'm living with you and we're not married?

TOM—Yes.

OLGA—(*indifferently*) Very well; let them. They do not enter into my world. I expect their denunciations and I revel in them.

TOM—But don't you see I can't help blaming myself—

OLGA—(*impatiently*) Blame yourself for what? Because when I knew I loved you I gave myself to you freely and openly? It seems to me the responsibility is mine. Don't be foolishly sentimental.

TOM—(*doggedly*) Still, I wish you— (*He hesitates—blurting it out*) Marry me.

OLGA—(*frowning*) We've argued this out before.

TOM—(*lamely*) I thought you might have reconsidered.

OLGA—(*vehemently*) I haven't done so, and I won't do so. I tell you I won't marry you or anyone. (*seeing the hurt look on Tom's face —contritely*) You dear old Tom, you, don't you know I love you with all the love I have in me? Isn't that enough?

TOM—Yes, of course, but—

OLGA—Listen: Am I not all to you that a wife could be?

TOM—Yes.

OLGA—You don't believe in marriage as an institution, do you? You know that the voluntary union of two people is something which concerns them and them alone. You don't believe that the sanction of the law we hate or a religion we despise could make our relationship any holier, do you?

TOM—No.

OLGA—Then why speak of marriage?

TOM—(*doggedly*) It's just this Olga. Though we know it is all wrong, we've got to face the facts as they are. Marriage is a fact. I agree with you it ought to be abolished. But what are we to do? It won't be destroyed in our time in spite of all our efforts and we're living now, not in the future. We've got to make some concessions to society in order to be free to do our work. It's foolish to waste time butting one's head against a stone wall.

OLGA—(*getting up and walking up and down —vehemently*) What are we beside the ideal we fight for? We cannot change conditions in our lives, perhaps, but we can make our lives a living protest against those conditions.

TOM—I don't want you to be a martyr—on my account.

OLGA—It's not on your account. I'm fighting for an ideal. You're only the man I love. Oh, can't you see? Some of us must be pioneers, some of us must prove by our lives that the dream we're striving for can be realized. (*passionately*) We love each other. Our love is a fine love, freed from all the commonplaces of marriage. Why would you change it. There's no feeling of enforced servitude on my part. There can be no complacent sense of ownership on yours. (*with smiling irony*) Perhaps that's what you regret?

TOM—(*indignantly*) Olga!

OLGA—Do you want a signed certificate proving I am yours—like a house and lot?

TOM—(*hurt*) Don't, Olga! (*impatiently*) You don't understand.

OLGA—I understand this: To compromise is to acknowledge defeat. (*more and more determinedly*) No, we'll live as we believe! And let all the self-righteous jackasses go to the devil!

TOM—You'll have to pay; I won't. It's the devilish unfairness which drives me wild. I want you to be happy, that's all.

OLGA—Then let me fight for my own soul with my own life. That's my happiness. And don't adopt that protective masculine attitude. I'm better able to bear my share of the burden than you are. It's in my blood—the exultation of the fight against tyranny. I was born with it. My father was exiled from his country for living and speaking what he thought; and I shall preserve his heritage in this country where I was born. It's harder for you, Tom, with years of conventional prudery behind you.

TOM—(*shaking his head*) You haven't considered the most important reason for my proposal. (*slowly*) Supposing we should have children? Would it be fair to them?

OLGA—(*passionately*) We'll never have children. No, no, anything but that! I would go through anything, kill myself rather than have that happen!

TOM—Olga!

OLGA—No. To me the birth of a child is a horrible tragedy. To bring a helpless little one into a world of drudgery and unhappiness, to force upon it a mouldy crust of life— what heartlessness and needless cruelty! There are much too many of us here already. No; I will wait until life becomes a gift and not a punishment before I bestow it upon a child of mine. I will offer no children to Moloch as sacrifices. (*Tom stares at the floor but does not answer—a pause.*) Make me a better world, O Husband-Man, and I'll be proud and not ashamed to bear children.

TOM—(*frowning*) I was only asking you to consider the possibility—

OLGA—(*fiercely*) There's no possibility! There never will be a possibility I tell you, I'd die first!

TOM—(*hopelessly*) Let's drop the subject, then.

OLGA—(*coming over to kiss him*) I love you, Tom; and there's only one way to be true to you and to myself at the same time, and that's our present comradeship.

Tom—(*giving in—tenderly*) All right, as long as you are happy.

Olga—I am! I am! (*Enwright enters from door on right with a pile of pamphlets in under his arm.*)

Enwright—What are you, pray? (*comes over to them*)

Olga—Happy.

Enwright—Why not—with youth and love and (*with a smile*) inexperience. (*sets pamphlets on table*) Hartmann hasn't come yet? He's late as usual.

Tom—You think he wants to see us about the seamen and firemen's strike?

Enwright—Yes, I imagine so—can't think what else it could be.

Tom—They're talking of nothing else down at the office. (*with sudden recollection—laughing*) Oh, I'd forgotten to tell you the tragic news, Olga. I've lost my job.

Olga—(*smiling*) Really?

Tom—Yes, I'm bounced. No longer is your co-revolutionist assistant cashier of the Ocean Steamship Co. No longer is he a wage-slave.

Olga—When did all this happen?

Tom—This evening. You know those pamphlets Hartmann gave me to distribute among the crew of the *San Francisco* when she arrived from Liverpool?

Enwright—Yes.

Tom—Well, in spite of the fact that my revered old man is, as I've told you, second engineer of the *San Francisco,* I managed to get rid of every single one of them without, as I thought, getting caught at it. I was wrong. Some coward must have reported me, for the manager called me into his office tonight at closing time—and fired me.

Enwright—What did he have to say?

Tom—Gave me a silly sermon for the good of my soul: told me of my evil ways and so forth. Said he hated to discharge the son of one of the company's oldest and most faithful employees—he might just as well have said servants—but my outrageous conduct made it necessary, as I must see for myself. Stirring up mutiny among the crew of the Company's largest and finest ship! Oh, he's a smooth party, that manager.

Talked to me in a regular it-hurts-me-more-than-it-does-you way. Damn his nerve.

ENWRIGHT—Has your father heard the news yet?

TOM—(*frowning*) Haven't seen him except for a moment at the office since the *San Francisco* docked. I promised I'd go up home for dinner tonight but I can't make it now. I suppose I'll have to go up later, and break the bad news to him then.

OLGA—What'll he say?

TOM—(*shrugging his shoulders*) Go off into a nervous spasm of fear the Company will hold it against him for having such a son.

ENWRIGHT—Is he as bad as that?

TOM—Bad? No, nothing as alive as the word bad. Weak is a better term. You'd have to know him to understand what I mean.

OLGA—Tell me about him. I'm interested. We've been together for nearly half a year now and you've hardly ever mentioned him except to say that he was second-engineer on the *San Francisco*.

TOM—There's nothing much about him to tell except that. He's a common type, more's the pity. No backbone, no will power, no individuality, nothing. Just a poor servile creature living in constant fear of losing his job. You know the kind of man I mean. (*They nod.*) He's been a second engineer on the boats of the Ocean Steamship company ever since I can remember. That fact gives you a glimpse into his character. He really knows marine engines from a to z—that's the strange part of it. Thirty years in the same little rut—and contented! Good God, think of it! They've never promoted him because he's never had the courage to demand it. They've taken him at his own valuation.

ENWRIGHT—But surely there must be some positive side to his character.

TOM—Oh, he's got a positive love for his engines, for his ship, and even for the rotten old Ocean Company itself. I remember he actually cried—real tears—when he was transferred from the old ship to the *San Francisco*—said he hated to leave the old engines he was used to. His life is bound up in just that one thing—marine engines. He'll talk to anyone who'll listen for hours on that subject. He knows nothing else. (*with a groan*) I think I was lulled to sleep in my cradle with a triple-expansion, twin-screw lullaby.

OLGA—(*with a smile*) But how do you two ever get along together?

TOM—We don't. He's too afraid of me to have any affection for me. Cringes before me as abjectly as if I were his chief engineer. It's sickening but I guess it's just as well. I've none of that feeling for him we're supposed to have for our parents. How could I? He stands for everything I hate. (*Hartmann enters from the door on left. He is an undersized man in his late forties, dressed in black, white shirt with soft collar, flowing black Windsor tie. His head is massive, too large for his body, with long black hair brushed straight back from his broad forehead. His large dark eyes peer near-sightedly from behind a pair of thick-rimmed spectacles. His voice is low and musical. He continually strokes his mustache and imperial with thin nervous hands.*)

HARTMANN—Ah you are already here. I am late, nicht war? Ach, such a talk we've been having. Phew! I could not make my exit. (*He comes over to the table and sits down, after patting Olga affectionately on the back.*)

ENWRIGHT—Same old subject, I suppose—Colorado?

HARTMANN—Nein, nein, we did not Colorado mention, this evening. It was of something far more important we spoke; but have you not the evening papers read?

TOM—Haven't seen one.

OLGA—What is it, Hartmann?

HARTMANN—(*shaking his head slowly*) It may be nothing or it may be much. I am wrong to have such fear but there is in me a premonition, a dread unspeakable. I seem to see coming a disaster to us and to our hopes. (*as the others show signs of impatience*) War, I am speaking of—war which it is rumored, not without foundation, will soon break out.

TOM—Nothing new in that. They've been writing up war with Mexico for months.

HARTMANN—Nein, I mean not Mexico, or this country—yet. That, in truth, would be horrible enough, but this, that I mean, is more terrible a thousand times. It will all the nations involve (*nodding his head*) over there—in Europe. Too long have the jealous dogs growled over their bones. This time, I fear, they will fight. If they do—(*he makes a hopeless gesture*)—it will be the smash-up, le débâcle. And our cause will most of all suffer. The revolution will be fifty years put back.

OLGA—(*jumping to her feet impulsively*) Then now is the time for us to show what we can do. We're strongly organized over there. The socialists—surely their millions will fight shoulder to shoulder with us on this issue. We'll declare the general strike if they declare war. We'll defy them to make war when production ceases. Let every working man in those nations refuse to work, refuse to bear arms, and there will be no war. (*enthusiastically*) Think of what it would mean—that strike! No electricity, no cars, no trains, no steamers, the factories dark and deserted, no newspapers, no wireless, nothing. The whole world of workers on a holiday. Think of how foolish those kings and emperors, those cabinets and parliaments would look when they found no one to fight for them, when they realized if they wanted war, they would have to fight themselves.

HARTMANN—(*shaking his head—with a sad smile*) The general strike is a solution possible in fifty years, perhaps. Now, no. All their lives the comrades shall proclaim it, fight for it—and gradually the workers will their stupid patriotism unlearn, will feel their power and take what is theirs. But now—how is it possible? They have not yet outgrown their silly awe when a stained rag on the end of a stick is waved over their heads. (*solemnly*) And that is why I am afraid—that they are yet too ignorant, these workers; that at the first blare of a band, the first call to fatherland or motherland or some such sentimental phantom, they will all our teachings forget. Time, time is necessary for our ideas to grow into the hearts of men. Now they are in his brain only. The emotional crisis blots them out. We must the hearts of mankind touch—for it is what is in his heart he fights and dies for, and his brain is as nothing, that foolish animal. Yes, we must reach his heart, nicht war? And that time is not yet.

TOM—(*after a pause—cheerfully*) Well, the war hasn't started yet, and I'll be willing to bet it'll be like this Mexican business of ours. Much talking, much writing, much patriotic gush—and that's all. They go through the same thing in Europe every few years, don't they?

HARTMANN—(*shaking his head—slowly*) But this time—(*throwing off his depression*) Ach well, it is on the lap of the Gods. Yet I would not see millions of madmen butchering each other for (*with an expressive wave of his hand*) wheels in the head. (*a pause*) The soul of man is an uninhabited house haunted by the ghosts of old ideals. And man in those ghosts still believes! He so slowly unlearns, or understands, or loves what is true and beautiful, the stupid animal! (*with a sardonic laugh*) And he dreams he is God's masterpiece, wie, was? Ha-ha. And yet God is his masterpiece—that is truth. (*He chuckles to himself.*)

ENWRIGHT—(*slowly*) Why not encourage war? It's the great purgative. It destroys the unenlightened. Let them fight until nothing but weaklings are left—and we others who refused to fight. Then we'll come into our own. We'll take what we want. Then we can start life anew with a new generation, a new art, a new ideal. Therefore vive la guerre!

HARTMANN—(*amused*) There is much in what you say—if we could those armies persuade to fight until annihilated. Unhappily there remains always so many still in uniform.

OLGA—And the women remain. How would they be remodeled into your new world?

ENWRIGHT—The civilized woman has long been living beyond her mental means. She will be only too glad to find a good excuse to throw aside her pretence of equality with man to return to polygamy. Her pose was interesting to her when it was new. Now it bores her. The constant strain of keeping up mental appearances, of having a soul,—

OLGA—(*with a disdainful toss of her head*) When you once start, Enwright, you're impossible.

ENWRIGHT—(*in same thoughtful tone—as if he had not heard her*) At the end of my supposititious war of manly extermination there will be ten or twenty womanly women for every unmanly man who has refused to die on the field of honor. Yet breeding must go on. The women, above all, will demand it. The new race must be created in order to enjoy the new freedom. What will be the result?

OLGA—(*at first irritably—finally breaking into a laugh*) Hartmann, please tell him to shut up; or, at least, tell us the reason you wanted to see Tom and me, and let us make our escape. Enwright has found a pretty little strange idea. He's going to play with it, cuddle it, turn it over and over to see what's inside—and I refuse to waste an evening listening to him.

ENWRIGHT—I'm serious, Olga. All that might very well happen. (*taking hat from table*) You people want to talk, and so do I, so I better leave in search of an audience.

HARTMANN—Ach no, Enwright, sit down. It is necessary also that you know what is to be done, and to have your opinion of our plan.

ENWRIGHT—That's different; if I can be of any use—

TOM—(*looking at his watch*) Is it going to take long, Hartmann?

HARTMANN—Nein, my boy, a few moments only. You must go? This is very important that you should at once know the facts and to a decision come.

TOM—I promised to run up and see my father tonight. He sails in a day or so and I won't have another chance. (*impatiently*) Damned bore! (*sitting down at table*) Well, let him wait.

HARTMANN—Attention, then. (*All assume attitudes of tense expectation. Tom closes his hand over one of Olga's on the table but she releases it with a frown at his childishness. Hartmann commences slowly.*) You have rumors heard, no?, of a strike, a strike which would be truly international, among the seamen and firemen of all ocean steamships, and of all the dock laborers?

ENWRIGHT—I was saying I thought that was what you had in mind.

HARTMANN—What you do not know is that this strike is hanging fire; it hesitates. There is needed a push to start it on its way. It is for us of the International to strike a blow, to give courage to those wavering ones. This we have decided to do. (*They nod in assent.*) You know the Ocean Steamship Company?

TOM—(*smiling*) I have made its acquaintance.

HARTMANN—Ach, it is there you work, nicht war? For the moment I had forgotten.

TOM—(*with emphasis*) It was there I *worked*.

HARTMANN—(*puzzled*) Was?

TOM—I was fired—for distributing pamphlets.

HARTMANN—So. So much the better. You are free to undertake—(*he raises his brows with a questioning look*) anything?

TOM—(*steadily*) Anything! Anything you think would help.

HARTMANN—I need not to ask you, Olga.

OLGA—(*quietly*) Anything. Go on.

HARTMANN—And now before I go further I must a question ask. (*to Tom*) Did you not tell me once that you had worked as a stoker, fireman, on an ocean steamer.

TOM—Yes, two summers ago. Did it for a stunt more than anything else. (*with an abashed smile*) I had no serious conception of anything in those days. I and a pal of mine made the round trip. (*boyishly*) I tell you, though, it opened my eyes to conditions I had never dreamt of. It made me think—seeing the contrast between us grimy stokers and the first cabin people lolling in their deck-chairs.

OLGA—It was on one of the Ocean Company's boats you made the trip, wasn't it, Tom?

TOM—Yes.

HARTMANN—(*with an air of satisfaction*) Then, you know all the ropes, no? You would make no blunders which would attract attention should you ever again as fireman work?

TOM—I guess not. It was drilled into me hard enough.

HARTMANN—That is good, very good. I told them, the others, that you were the exact one for it.

TOM—I don't see what shipping as stoker—

HARTMANN—It is just that you must do if you would help us.

TOM—(*beginning to understand*) Ah.

OLGA—And I?

HARTMANN—A moment and you will clearly understand. (*slowly*) The unions on both sides of the ocean were all in favor of this strike. It was to be in bitterness waged to the end. There was to be no compromise. But now the unions are afraid, they seek to waste time doing nothing. The Steamship Companies fear this strike. They are endeavoring before its birth to crush it, to buy off the union leaders so no strike will be declared.

ENWRIGHT—Are you sure of this—that the union leaders are dickering with the Companies?

HARTMANN—Very sure. They have a traitor among them who is true to us. He has written us everything from Liverpool, where, it was intended, the strike should break out first.

ENWRIGHT—Do you mean Whitely?

HARTMANN—Yes, Whitely—the one strong soul among them over there. (*He takes a letter from his pocket and hands it to Olga.*) Here is a letter to Whitely, Olga. You must to him present it the moment you reach Liverpool. (*Olga nods.*)

TOM—But—I don't see—

HARTMANN—It is time for us to strike, to prove the International no foolish dream. Let these rumors of a great war of nations but continue, and in a short time, these seamen and firemen and dock laborers will be in the streets like foolish school boys cheering for the flag which their oppression symbolizes. We must strike now, immediately, or not at all. We must from their lethargy awake these workers, these unions. We must put fear into the hearts of capitalism. (*rising to his feet, his voice trembling with his earnestness*) We must at the heart of capital strike. There is necessary in this crisis a blow which, like the spark in a magazine of gunpowder, will the conflagration establish. A blow must be struck so powerful that on it will the eyes and minds of all be focussed. We must the attention of the world call to the International Workers of the Earth and to the issue of this strike.

TOM—(*his eyes growing bright*) But what is my part in this?

HARTMANN—Wait! Have patience! Soon you shall know. Our blow is at the heart of the Ship Trust to be directed, at the Company which controls the whole ship combine.

TOM—You mean the Ocean Company? (*Hartmann nods.*) Good enough!

HARTMANN—(*solemnly*) There is something I must warn you of before you accept definitely this mission. It is very dangerous, very dangerous. The one who undertakes it risks death, imprisonment.

TOM—(*steadily*) I understand. Go on.

HARTMANN—You accept?

TOM—Yes.

OLGA—(*taking his hand with impulsive admiration*) Tom!

ENWRIGHT—Good boy!

HARTMANN—My boy, I am glad. Whatever happens, your soul will rejoice. It will know you are the good fight fighting, the fight of suffering humanity.

TOM—What is it I am to do?

HARTMANN—A steamer, the finest steamer of the Ocean Company, sails the day after tomorrow. (*Tom is struck with some thought and glances quickly at Olga.*) You will ship—is it that you call it?—on her as a fireman. Here are your fireman's papers. (*takes papers from pocket*) They are made out in the name of Tom Donovan. You will know, better than I, where you can find clothes suitable, and how to disguise yourself.

TOM—But where does Olga come in?

HARTMANN—She will as second class passenger on the same ship go. When Liverpool is reached she will the letter to Whitely present, and he will give her dynamite which she will give to you when you come on shore.

TOM—Dynamite?

HARTMANN—Whitely will instruct you how to use it, and when. Some time during the steamship's stop in Liverpool you will dynamite the engines—without loss of life—if possible.

TOM—(*confused by the suddenness of all this*) But what good will that do—to dynamite the engines?

ENWRIGHT—(*breaking in*) Just this. All the men will realize that it was one of their number who did it. There will be no attempt at concealment of that fact. It will give them confidence in their power; and it will hit the Ocean Company a hard blow. The Companies will make no compromise after that. Instead they will probably adopt harsh retaliatory measures. The strike will break out and it will be a fight to the finish.

OLGA—(*eagerly*) And this explosion will point to sabotage as the logical method of waging the war of labor—that force alone can be effective against force. For many years the workers have appealed to the humanity and fairness of capital, and they have always found it unfair and cruel. They have thought

Capitalism impregnable behind its fortress of law, and they have been afraid. A few successful assaults of this kind and their eyes will be opened. They will realize their strength and they will unite and *demand*, not beg.

HARTMANN—The words of Danton— "It is necessary to dare, and again to dare, and still again to dare."

TOM—(*resentfully*) It wasn't the daring I was thinking of, Hartmann. If I'm to risk my life I want to know it's going to do some good. (*still more resentfully*) And I don't see why you have to drag Olga into all this.

OLGA—(*impatiently*) Tom! Please!

TOM—Oh, I know it makes you sore to have me say that. I don't care. I don't think it's right to make a woman run risks—

OLGA—But don't you see? I won't be running risks. They'll never suspect me.

ENWRIGHT—That's the answer, Tom.

TOM—Maybe it's safe enough—still—I feel—

OLGA—Tom! You're not going to back out now?

TOM—(*fiercely*) Olga! (*turning to Hartmann*) You haven't even told me the name of the steamer yet.

HARTMANN—Ach, so it is. (*reaches in pocket and peers at the card he takes out*) Hmmm—yes—here it is—the *San Francisco*. (*In a flash of understanding Enwright and Olga look at each other and then at Tom.*)

OLGA—Good heavens.

ENWRIGHT—The devil!

TOM—(*with a grim smile*) By God, I thought so.

HARTMANN—Thought what? I do not understand— (*looks from one to the other*)

TOM—My father is second engineer of the *San Francisco*.

HARTMANN—(*stunned*) Ach Gott! So? So? I remember— you said your father was engineer on a boat—but there are of boats so many, wie? was? How could I know?

TOM—(*slowly*) It makes no difference. (*with a meaning look at Olga*) I am not going to *back out*.

HARTMANN—What! In spite of this you will—

TOM—I said I would do it, Hartmann, and I'm going to.

HARTMANN—But your father? He will recognize—

TOM—I'll see that he doesn't, never fear; and I'll see that the thing happens when he's off watch and ashore.

HARTMANN—(*unconvinced—wringing his hands*) Ach, the miserable luck of it. It was all so fine, so certain.

TOM—(*picking up his hat*) If you knew what kind of man my father is you wouldn't worry. (*contemptuously*) He isn't much of an obstacle. I'll take care of him. (*moving toward door*) I'm going up to see him now. (*He laughs.*)

HARTMANN—(*jumping to his feet in a flurry of angry fear*) Gott in Himmel, you will not tell him?

OLGA—(*indignantly*) Hartmann!

HARTMANN—(*as he sees the expression on Tom's face—haltingly*) A thousand pardons.

TOM—(*coldly*) You needn't have asked that question, Hartmann. I'll see you here tomorrow morning about nine. Goodnight. I won't be long, Olga. (*He goes out as*

The Curtain Falls)

ACT II

SCENE—*Sitting-room of Thomas Perkins' small home in Jersey City—a small room crowded with cheap furniture. On the right, two windows with drawn shades and stiff white curtains. In the right corner, a sofa. In the middle of rear wall, a door leading into the hall. On the right of door, a bookcase half filled with a few books and stacks of magazines. In the left corner, a stand on which is a potted rubber plant. In the left wall, forward, a door. Ugly straight-backed chairs are pushed back against the walls which are papered in some dreary floral design.*

It is about nine o'clock on the same night. Thomas Perkins and Henderson are discovered at the table playing cards. Perkins is a nervous, self-conscious, awkward little man with a soft timid voice. He is half bald but an unkempt fringe of thin grey hair straggles about his ears. He wears spectacles, carpet slippers, ill-fitting shabby clothes. Henderson is a tall, lean Scotchman with grey hair and bristly mustache. He is dressed in the uniform of a ship's engineer.

They are just finishing a hand at euchre. Henderson is fiercely intent upon the game, a gleam of triumph in his eye. Perkins pays but little attention to his cards but continually glances at the door in rear. His manner is worried, his expression troubled, and evidently his playing is ragged in the extreme for Henderson grunts with contemptuous satisfaction as he rakes in the tricks.

HENDERSON—(*whacking his last card down*) That does for ye, I tak' it, Perkins.

PERKINS—(*with a nervous start*) Eh? Oh yes, yes, of course. (*hopefully*) That makes game, don't it, Henderson?

HENDERSON—(*looking at his counters—grumblingly*) I ha' one more to go. (*Perkins sighs, casts a quick glance at the door, takes up cards and prepares to deal again.*) Shuffle the cards, mon, shuffle the cards! (*A sudden thought strikes him.*) It's no your deal, mon, it's no your deal! Gie them here to me!

PERKINS—(*timidly apologetic*) I was forgetting. (*hands cards to Henderson*)

HENDERSON—(*shuffling the cards with a great clatter—sar-*

328

castically) Forgettin'. Na doot ye'll be likewise forgettin' yon's the seventh game ye've lost and ye arre thrupence hapenny my debtor. (*He licks his thumb and commences to deal.*)

PERKINS—Seven cents, that is. (*commences to fumble in his pockets*)

HENDERSON—(*irritably*) Dinna bother wi' it the noo. Canna ye take a joke? Play your hand! (*Perkins snatches up his hand, and plays. Whenever Henderson looks at his hand, Perkins glances with pitiful hopefulness at the door. Henderson takes a trick, ponders with knit brows, plays a card. Perkins hears the flap of the card. He has been taking advantage of Henderson's preoccupation to glance surreptitiously at his watch. He hurriedly plays the first card his hand touches and starts to pull in the trick. Henderson's big hand grips his wrist.*)

HENDERSON—No, ye don't! (*Perkins stares at him with amazement.*) I little kenned I'd see the day I'd be gamblin' for gold wi' a card sharp.

PERKINS—A card sharp!

HENDERSON—D'ye ken the trumps?

PERKINS—Diamonds.

HENDERSON—An' this card I played? (*holding it up accusingly before Perkins*)

PERKINS—Ten of diamonds.

HENDERSON—(*solemnly, impressing him with the terrible outrage*) An' ye played the jock o' spades on it—*and took the trick!*

PERKINS—I was thinking it was right bower.

HENDERSON—(*picking up Perkins' hand and looking at it*) An' ye had diamonds to follow suit wi' (*shakes his head solemnly*) an' ye dinna do it. Mon alive, whur are your wits? (*throws the cards disgustedly on the table*) We'll play na more the nicht. 'Tis na sport playin' wi' one so ha'-witted.

PERKINS—(*gathering up the cards with a sigh of relief*) I'm sorry. I couldn't keep my mind on the game. I kept wondering if Tom—

HENDERSON—(*with a grunt*) Ay, Tam, Tam—always Tam!

PERKINS—(*looking at his watch*) It's early yet, isn't it? He said he'd come. I do hope— (*with a sigh*) I told Mrs. Allen to keep supper warm for him. (*apprehensively*) She'll be mad.

I do hope he'll come. (*hopefully*) Don't you think he will? (*He plays nervously with the cards on the table.*)

HENDERSON—Ay, ay, he'll come—when he's good an' ready.

PERKINS—(*goes to the window and peers out—returns with a sigh*) Will you have a little something to drink now?

HENDERSON—I'll sup a wee drop o' whiskey. (*Perkins goes slowly out of the door on the left. Henderson fills and lights his pipe. The sound of a woman's shrill, irritated voice comes from left. Henderson smiles grimly and remarks to himself, half-aloud:* "Ay, he's catchin' it the noo." *A moment later Perkins enters hastily from the left carrying a bottle of Scotch, a pitcher of water and two glasses. He places these on the table. The woman's voice still shrills on from the left.*)

PERKINS—(*agitated*) Mrs. Allen is very mad—about the dinner. She says she won't try to keep it any longer. It's burnt, she says. (*worriedly*) And I know Tom will be hungry.

HENDERSON—(*grunting*) Ay, you wi' your Tam an' your Mrs. Allen.

PERKINS—(*fearfully*) Ssshh! Here she comes now. (*The flow of shrill talk grows quickly louder and Mrs. Allen enters from left. She is a thin, angular, middle-aged woman with sharp features. Her voice is unpleasantly high and rasping.*)

MRS. ALLEN—(*taking a hat pin from her mouth and jabbing it into her hat*) And not another minute, not another second will I stay if you was to git down on your knees to me. I ain't one, and I never was one to balk at workin', and no one knows it better'n you, Thomas Perkins. Ain't I come in regular every day you was here for the past five years, and once a week when you was on ship, scrubbin' my hands off, and dustin', and lookin' after things? And I ain't never missed once—and all the time I got a husband and family of my own to tend to besides. And what d'you suppose my man'll think when I come back this late in the night? Liable to accuse me of skylarkin' with you, Thomas Perkins, that's what he is, with his temper, and you a widower.

PERKINS—(*faintly*) No, no, Mrs. Allen, I'm sure he won't.

HENDERSON—(*gruffly*) Tush, tush, woman, is your mon daft?

MRS. ALLEN—(*turning furiously*) Don't you tush me, Mr.

Henderson! And don't you be slingin' slurs at Mister Allen. He's a better man than you are or ever will be for all your bein' a chief engineer. He ain't daft! No, nor he ain't a sot with a bottle of whiskey at his elbow all the day, neither. (*Henderson nearly bursts with rage at this but makes no reply.*)

PERKINS—(*interposing*) It was just this once, Mrs. Allen. I won't ask you to do it again. It was very, very nice of you indeed. You see I thought Tom would be hungry, and—

MRS. ALLEN—(*with a snort*) Tom! You're always thinkin' about him; and much he cares about you, never comin' to see you, and leavin' you here eatin' your heart out with lonesomeness night after night. Why isn't he here for dinner at seven o'clock like he said he would be, and him knowin' you was here all alone?

PERKINS—They kept him at the office, I'm sure; or something came up to prevent him, or— (*pitiably*) It's early yet for a young man like him. Don't you think he'll come, Mrs. Allen?

MRS. ALLEN—Lawd knows! And if I was you I wouldn't bother whether he did or not. A pretty way he's treated you after you've sweated in a dirty engine room—

PERKINS—(*hastily resenting this slur*) The engine room is not dirty, Mrs. Allen. It's as clean as—as—as your kitchen. Isn't it, Henderson? (*Henderson grunts.*)

MRS. ALLEN—(*ignoring this correction*) After you've sweated in a dirty engine room to send him through school—

PERKINS—(*feebly expostulating*) Mrs. Allen!

MRS. ALLEN—Oh he can't pull the wool over my eyes like he does you. That's what you get for eddicating him so much. It's just what Mr. Allen tells me when I spoke about sending our Jim to high school. No, he says, none of those high-fangled schools for a son of mine. I wants 'em to be workers, not loafers, he says; and he was right.

PERKINS—No doubt, no doubt, Mrs. Allen.

MRS. ALLEN—(*proudly*) And that same boy's a good plumber right now, and earns good wages, and has a wife and children, and never drinks 'cept on Saturday nights like his father told him.

PERKINS—Yes, of course, of course, a fine boy.

MRS. ALLEN—And when I think of your Tom it jest makes

my blood boil—the best part of a good dinner burnt up. How long is it since he's been here to so much as eat a bite with you, tell me that!

PERKINS—(*vaguely*) Why—er—not so long ago—

MRS. ALLEN—It's more than three months, that's what it is! And three times during that time I've cooked dinners for him, and he ain't never come till the dinner was spoiled and I'd gone home.

HENDERSON—(*drily*) I dinna blame the lad. (*He puffs furiously on his pipe. Mrs. Allen glares at him.*)

MRS. ALLEN—And are you foolish enough to think, Thomas Perkins, that it's that job you got for him that keeps him from coming up here? Well you may think so, but t'ain't; (*impressively*) Your Tom is skylarkin' around with some girl, that's what he is, and that's the reason he ain't got no time for his father.

PERKINS—(*eagerly*) A girl?

MRS. ALLEN—Yes, young Dugan says he sees him every night pretty near, and always with the same girl.

PERKINS—(*delighted*) Why that explains everything, doesn't it? You couldn't expect him to be coming up here in that case, Mrs. Allen. And he's never let on a word about it, the young rascal. (*with pitiful eagerness for more details*) She must be a nice girl, Mrs. Allen?

MRS. ALLEN—(*grudgingly*) Well, young Dugan says he didn't notice nothin' wrong about her—but he's a man.

PERKINS—She must be a pretty girl, Mrs. Allen?

MRS. ALLEN—Young Dugan says she was pretty enough, but Lawd knows what people think is pretty nowadays.

PERKINS—And does young Dugan know who she is, Mrs. Allen?

MRS. ALLEN—No, he don't know nothin' 'bout her 'cept what I've told you, but he heard Tom call her Olga once.

PERKINS—(*fascinated by the name*) Olga. Olga. A pretty name, isn't it, Mrs. Allen?

MRS. ALLEN—(*with a sniff*) Sounds furrin to me. (*with a sigh*) I'm glad you take it so easy, Thomas Perkins.

PERKINS—(*smiling happily*) Thank you so much for telling me, Mrs. Allen. I'm very glad. A young man like Tom ought to get married.

MRS. ALLEN—(*with a martyred air*) Course it ain't none of my business and I ain't got no right to be talkin' about it; but you've been kind to me, Thomas Perkins, and you've been a friend to me and Mr. Allen when we needed a friend bad, and you've always paid me well, and— (*She is on the verge of tears.*)

PERKINS—(*terrified by this demonstration*) It's nothing, nothing, nothing at all, nothing—

MRS. ALLEN—(*swallowing her tears—indignantly*) And even if you do take it so easy, I say again that you been treated shameful—and I know Mr. Henderson will agree with me. (*Henderson, during the conversation between Perkins and the housekeeper, has been fidgeting in his chair as if on pins and needles. Several times it has seemed as if his irritation would compel him to speech but with mighty—and apparent efforts—he has controlled these impulses.*)

HENDERSON—(*jumping at this unexpected question, turns around and surveys Mrs. Allen icily for a second; then ejaculates forcibly*) I dinna agree wi' one word that ever came from your mouth, Mrs. Allen; and I would considerr it a kindness of ye not to address me. (*Mrs. Allen is dumb with fury. Henderson turns his back to her and puffs on his pipe; then turns with a satisfied air to the bottle at his elbow and starts to pour out a drink.*)

MRS. ALLEN—(*seeing her chance—as Henderson lifts the bottle—in a loud stage whisper*) Keep you eye on that bottle is what I says, Thomas Perkins. He might git vilent. (*Henderson sets down the bottle on the table with a crash—but before his rage can find expression, Mrs. Allen sweeps out the door in rear with a good-night to Perkins.*)

PERKINS—(*coming over to the table with a sigh of relief*) She's gone.

HENDERSON—Mon, mon, what a deeil of a woman! The Lord God pity puir Mr. Allen. (*smiting his clenched fist on the table*) Was I her husband I'd drop poison in her tea, on ma conscience I would. (*testily*) How can ye put up wi' her?

PERKINS—(*sitting down*) It's just her way. She's a very good woman, really—very good-hearted—and works very, very hard. (*Henderson grunts.*) You haven't taken your drink yet, Henderson.

HENDERSON—Ay, I ha' forgotten it. (*takes a sip*) Yon woman's clatter addled my wits. (*Perkins sips his glass of water. The two men are silent for a moment, Henderson engrossed by his Scotch and Perkins staring mournfully before him.*)

PERKINS—(*with a sigh*) The *San Francisco* sails the day after tomorrow.

HENDERSON—Ay, and the *Empress* as well.

PERKINS—I was down on board this morning.

HENDERSON—Canna ye keep off the bloody ship when ye've no call to be there. I never saw a mon sae fond of his job as ye are.

PERKINS—(*simply*) I was lonely.

HENDERSON—(*genuinely sympathetic*) Ye puir unfortunate body! And so ye go doon to your engines for companionship! Mon, but you're the queer person!

PERKINS—(*his eyes lighting up*) I love those engines—all engines.

HENDERSON—An' I hate the bloody things—most o' the time.

PERKINS—No, you don't. You can't mean that.

HENDERSON—Ay, I do. Twenty-five years I ha' been sweatin' in the bowels of a ship till my stomach's turned wi' the lot o' them. (*very seriously*) An' I tell ye now, Perkins, I'm goin' to chuck the sea an' spend the remainderr of my days on shore.

PERKINS—(*horrified*) You're going to work on shore!

HENDERSON—Ay; in the marine engine works at Liverpool.

PERKINS—You don't mean—you won't sail on the *Empress* any more?

HENDERSON—I ha' given in my notice. At the end of this trip, I'm through.

PERKINS—(*stunned by this news, sits blinking his eyes rapidly—clears his throat huskily—in a trembling voice*) I'm sorry— (*quickly*) Of course, I'm glad for your sake, very glad—see you better yourself—you know that. What I meant was— sorry we won't— (*He falters.*) Have many more nights together here—like this.

HENDERSON—(*with feeling*) On that point, Perkins, ye are na more sorry than I am. (*drily but kindly*) 'Tis a wet walk from Liverpool to the States, Perkins. (*a pause*)

PERKINS—(*sadly*) Twenty years, isn't it, Henderson?—We've known each other.

HENDERSON—Ay, in the neighborhood o' that.

PERKINS—You were fourth engineer on the same ship I was second on, the old *Roumania*, when we first met.

HENDERSON—Ay.

PERKINS—(*with a pitiful attempt at a smile*) And now you're a chief engineer and I'm still where I was—second.

HENDERSON—(*forcibly*) An' ye ken more about a ship's engines than I everr had in my head. I canna understand it. (*savagely*) They're a rotten lot—that Ocean Steamship Company—or ye'd ha' received promotion years agone.

PERKINS—(*protestingly*) No, no, they're all right.

HENDERSON—Bosh! If ye'd threatened them to chuck your job—if ye had more push to ye—

PERKINS—Yes, that's it; of course you're right enough, maybe; but you see I never was born that way. (*slowly*) It isn't in me. (*brightening*) But I'm not complaining. I'm contented enough where I am. I don't think after all I'd be happy with the whole responsibility of the engines on my shoulders. I think maybe I wouldn't make a good first—and the Company knows that.

HENDERSON—(*disgustedly*) The deeil damn the Company.

PERKINS—You see—I know—they all know—I've no strength, no force of character.

HENDERSON—(*scornfully—knocking out his pipe*) Na force of characterr? I suppose ye'd na force of characterr the day the boiler burst on the *Roumania* an' ye went below in the scaldin' steam.

PERKINS—(*embarrassed*) It was nothing. Someone had to. I was young then. (*abruptly*) You haven't finished your drink.

HENDERSON—'Tis no use talkin' to you. Ye will na credit aught good o' yourself. I ha' neverr encounterred such a mon. (*He finishes his drink—starts to fill pipe.*)

PERKINS—It's going to be lonely—when you're gone—

HENDERSON—Ye can live on the ship then and be near the dear engines all o' the time.

PERKINS—(*seriously*) Yes, I'm thinking of that.

HENDERSON—(*surprised*) Surely ye canna mean that.

PERKINS—Yes, I do. I have a reason now, after something I heard tonight.

HENDERSON—(*with sly sarcasm*) I dinna dream I'd ever be rivals in a body's affections wi' a quadruple expansion engine.

PERKINS—(*not knowing whether Henderson is really offended or not*) No, no! (*seeing the twinkle in Henderson's eye*) Oh, now you're joking. But I do love those engines. (*enthusiastically*) Seems as if I could never get tired watching them. (*shyly*) I've got to know them so well, and sometimes I think—I know this sounds foolish to you—that they know me. (*Henderson grunts.*) Oh I know it sounds foolish, doesn't it, but I can't help believing it. Sometimes when I touch them I seem to know they feel me. I seem to hear them speaking like a friend to me, times when I'm lonely and, well, sort of sick of things—and they're a comfort. (*eagerly*) And in a storm, I know I can hear them groan with pain, and suffer, and I feel so sorry and try to do all I can to help them. (*nervously*) I know you'll think all this is very silly and—childish, don't you.

HENDERSON—No, I canna say I ha' na felt somewhat o' the same at times, myself.

PERKINS—(*pleased*) Then it's only natural, isn't it? You see I've been with them so much. One gets to be friends with them—and even (*hesitating shyly*) love them, in a manner of speaking— (*sadly*) People never have seemed to understand or like me, somehow—except you.

HENDERSON—The deeil damn them for a pack o' fools.

PERKINS—Oh, it isn't their fault. It's just that I don't know how to act with people. I'm stupid. I can't say the things I want to say. You—you know how I act. Why even Tom, I feel embarrassed even with him, he's been so much away. (*looking anxiously at his watch*) I wonder what can be keeping him.

HENDERSON—(*fiercely*) Ah, Tam, Tam! 'Tis a shame the mannerr you've spoilt that boy. And what thanks does he give ye? Were he mine I'd take a whip to him, big as he is.

PERKINS—(*with real anger*) Henderson! You mustn't talk that way about Tom. I can't permit it, even from you.

HENDERSON—Ah weel, dinna fly off the handle. I'll say naught more.

PERKINS—You don't understand, Henderson. Tom isn't like me. He takes after his mother. (*a pause*) You remember his mother, don't you?

HENDERSON—(*with an expression indicating his disapproval of that lady*) Ay.

PERKINS—She was just like Tom—large and forceful.

HENDERSON—(*grimly*) Ay she was; an' neverr perrmitted ye to call your soul your ain.

PERKINS—Oh not as bad as that, Henderson; but she never could understand why I didn't become president of the Steamship Company. (*quaintly*) I was lonely—after she died. That's why I came to love the engines so. Of course I couldn't have Tom at home alone when he was only a little chap, and I was away most of the time. So he's been away ever since then till he grew up, and I haven't seen much of him. (*sadly*) That's the whole trouble. He doesn't know me.

HENDERSON—'Tis time he did. (*disgustedly*) Larkin' around wi' lasses!

PERKINS—I was very glad to hear that, Henderson. If he would only marry—

HENDERSON—There are many ways wi' lasses besides takin' them for wife.

PERKINS—That couldn't be so in this case. Tom isn't the kind to trifle or do anything wrong.

HENDERSON—An' why are ye so anxious to ha' him married?

PERKINS—Well you know I spoke of closing up this house and living on board—I couldn't stand it here alone when you can't come any more. But if Tom gets married I was thinking— You know I've just paid off the last of the mortgage, and I've always intended to give this house to Tom for a wedding present. That's what I've been saving for. I've been thinking that when Tom and his wife came to live here they might let me stay with them when I was in port, and—it would be like home again. (*shyly*) And maybe there'd be children and I'd be a grandfather, wouldn't I? (*He falls into a smiling reverie.*)

HENDERSON—I had na thought Tam was earrnin' enough to take on a wife.

PERKINS—Oh, Tom has a very good position now.

HENDERSON—He has you to thank for it.

PERKINS—I only got him a start, that was all. Very good of the Company to have done me the favor, don't you think? (*proudly*) Tom's been promoted twice since then. He's well liked in the office and— (*He stops abruptly as if struck by some alarming thought. An expression of dismay comes over his face.*) I do hope nothing will happen, Henderson.

HENDERSON—(*surprised by his change of tone*) Eh?

PERKINS—(*greatly agitated*) I have so set my mind on having him rise in the Company—and what I heard today— Oh, I know it can't be true. There must be some mistake.

HENDERSON—(*impatiently*) Speak your mind! What is it?

PERKINS—It's had me so upset, ever since. Listen. When I was passing by the manager's office this morning Mr. Griffin stopped me and said he wanted to warn me about Tom.

HENDERSON—(*as if this was no more than he expected*) Hmm!

PERKINS—I couldn't say a word I was so frightened. He said he wanted me to say a word to Tom about the company he was keeping. It seems one of Tom's best friends in the office was discharged a short time ago for being an Anarchist or a Socialist or a—I forget the other—it's three letters, I remember.

HENDERSON—The I.W.E.?

PERKINS—Yes, that's it. What does it mean?

HENDERSON—The International Workers of the Earth they call themselves.

PERKINS—What kind of people are they? What is it? A club? A secret society?

HENDERSON—They're a lot of scamps who will na work themselves an' canna endure the thought of anyone else worrkin'. They go around makin' speeches, an' gettin' men discontented wi' their jobs. 'Tis they who help start all the strikes. Ha' ye no heard about the seamen and firemen's strike they say is going to break out in a week or two?

PERKINS—Yes, the Chief spoke about it this morning.

HENDERSON—The same I.W.E. you were speakin' of is back of it all. They'll be askin' for a Turkish bath in the stokehold next. I would be verra sorry to hear Tam had any truck wi' such rogues.

PERKINS—(*hastily*) Oh, I'm sure not. Mr. Griffin didn't say that. He only said Tom's friend was one of their members. (*brightening*) Mr. Griffin said everyone in the office liked Tom, and it would be a pity if— But of course there must be some mistake. Don't you think so?

HENDERSON—I ha' na doot there is. Tam's no a scoundrel. (*A knock at the door. Without waiting for anyone to come Tom pushes open the door and walks into the room.*)

TOM—(*with careless indifference*) Evening, father. Sorry I wasn't here for dinner but I couldn't make it. (*to Henderson, curtly*) Good evening.

HENDERSON—(*coldly*) Good evening to ye.

PERKINS—(*pitiably self-conscious, nervous, and confused*) Oh, it doesn't matter. I tried to have Mrs. Allen keep something warm for you but it was so late for her—poor woman—you know how she is.

TOM—(*irritably*) Is that old pest still coming here?

PERKINS—Oh, she isn't so bad. I'm used to her, you see. (*Tom smiles at him with amused contempt. Perkins cringes before this smile.*)

HENDERSON—(*getting up and picking up his hat*) I'll be gettin' doon to the ship, I'm thinkin'. (*goes to door*)

PERKINS—(*beseechingly*) Oh, don't go yet. It's so early. Surely you can stay a while—

HENDERSON—(*firmly*) I ha' some letters to write before I turn in. (*nodding*)

TOM—(*carelessly*) Good night.

PERKINS—(*going over and shaking Henderson's hand*) But you'll come up again tomorrow night, won't you? the last night, you know.

HENDERSON—Ay.

PERKINS—We'll have another hand at euchre, wouldn't you like to?

HENDERSON—Verra weel. (*with a smile*) But dinna forget ye are already thrupence hapenny my debtor. (*He goes out. Tom sits down in his chair. Perkins comes over and sits down in his old place. Tom looks steadily at his father but remains silent. Perkins squirms. A pause.*)

PERKINS—(*at last—desperately*) Henderson's going to give up his position on the *Empress* and work on shore—marine engine works at Liverpool.

TOM—Ah.

PERKINS—I'll miss him coming up here nights.

TOM—(*with a significant glance at the bottle*) He'll probably miss it too—in a way.

PERKINS—Oh no, Tom, you mustn't think that. He's my best friend in the world. It's going to be lonely without him.

TOM—(*banteringly*) You'll have no one to talk engines with any longer, will you? Except on ship.

PERKINS—(*innocently*) No.

TOM—But you'll still have the engines themselves—that's a comfort.

PERKINS—(*seriously*) Yes, that's a comfort.

TOM—And you'll have the ship—the *San Francisco*.

PERKINS—Yes.

TOM—And the Ocean Steamship Company—L—T—D.

PERKINS—(*feeling the mockery in Tom's voice for the first time—fidgeting miserably*) Now you're trying to have a joke on me, aren't you?

TOM—Not at all. I was only reminding you of the many sources of consolation for the loss of Henderson.

PERKINS—(*desperately*) I wish you could get up oftener. (*as Tom frowns*) Oh I know you're very busy. I mean just once in a while.

TOM—(*with a sigh*) I'll try and do so.

PERKINS—It's been such a long time since you've been here. (*gulping*) It doesn't seem like home anymore, when you're not here.

TOM—Well, you didn't need me as long as Henderson was here. He understands all about engines—and I don't.

PERKINS—(*humbly*) I'll promise not to talk about engines in future.

TOM—(*perfunctorily*) Oh, I like to hear about them well enough, when you're not so technical I can't follow you.

PERKINS—It's the only thing I know about, you see—and like.

TOM—(*who has been relenting, hardens*) Yes, I realize that.

PERKINS—(*feeling he has said something offensive is in a piti-*

able quandary. A pause.) I'm thinking of giving up the house and living on board, after this.

TOM—(*surprised*) Why, I thought you liked the house.

PERKINS—I do, but—it's lonely.

TOM—What do you intend to do? Sell it?

PERKINS—Oh no, no, I couldn't do that.

TOM—Rent it?

PERKINS—No, no—you see—er—you see—I was— (*He stutters with confusion before Tom's steady look.*) I just paid off the last of the mortgage a month ago.

TOM—Ah.

PERKINS—(*with satisfaction*) It's all mine now.

TOM—(*not interested*) That's fine.

PERKINS—I was thinking that you—

TOM—What?

PERKINS—Might want to live here.

TOM—And if I did? Why should you live on board ship in that case?

PERKINS—(*confused*) Well, you see, I—er—

TOM—Do you think I'd live way out here alone?

PERKINS—No, no, not alone.

TOM—Not alone?

PERKINS—You see—I thought—maybe— (*with a feeble attempt at slyness*) Mrs. Allen has been telling me all about it.

TOM—(*frowning*) About what? What bit of gossip has the old witch got hold of now?

PERKINS—About—about—the girl.

TOM—What girl?

PERKINS—She said—name—was Olga.

TOM—(*wonderingly*) The old witch! How did she ever hear of that?

PERKINS—She said young Dugan—

TOM—So he's the one, eh? I remember we've met him a couple of times. (*with a sudden laugh*) So you're willing that Olga and I should come here to live?

PERKINS—(*beaming*) Yes, yes, of course!

TOM—But you'll preserve your sense of propriety by staying on the ship. (*in half-angry amusement*) If that isn't just like you!

PERKINS—I—I—I don't know what you mean.

TOM—(*with real gratitude*) At that, it's darn nice of you, father, and I want you to know I appreciate it, and Olga would, too. I never suspected you of being so broadminded. Thank you just the same; but Olga and I will stay where we are for the present.

PERKINS—You live—at the same place?

TOM—(*perplexed in his turn*) Certainly.

PERKINS—Together? I mean—with her?

TOM—Why yes.

PERKINS—(*eagerly*) Then you're married already! And you never told me! (*joyfully*) I'm so glad to hear it, so glad— (*He stops in confusion at the look on Tom's face.*)

TOM—(*slowly*) Olga and I are not married.

PERKINS—(*bewildered*) Not married?

TOM—No.

PERKINS—And you're living together—as man and wife!

TOM—Yes; as comrades.

PERKINS—But you are going to be married—you're intending—

TOM—No. Look here, what did Mrs. Allen tell you?

PERKINS—That you were keeping company—with a girl—named Olga.

TOM—That all?

PERKINS—Yes.

TOM—And I thought— (*thoughtfully*) Now I see what the use of the house was to be—a wedding present. (*looking at his father keenly*) Now you know the truth of it.

PERKINS—(*all at sea*) You're joking, aren't you, Tom? You wouldn't do that. Live with a girl—and not married. It's—it's wicked.

TOM—That's a matter of opinion.

PERKINS—But I can't see— It's not right, Tom. What if they heard of this at the office?

TOM—Damn the office!

PERKINS—(*shocked*) Don't say that, Tom. (*miserably*) I never thought you'd go around with that kind of girl.

TOM—(*sternly*) She's the girl I love, and I respect her as much as I would my own mother if she were alive. That's enough for you to know, father. We won't talk about it any more—unless you want me to leave.

PERKINS—(*abjectly cringing*) No, no, please don't go. I won't speak of it. Don't go! (*obsessed by the idea*) That's what Mr. Griffin warned me of.

TOM—Eh?

PERKINS—He said you'd be getting into trouble.

TOM—Then you knew——? When did Griffin speak to you?

PERKINS—This morning.

TOM—Ah. What did he say?

PERKINS—He said you were keeping bad company.

TOM—(*enraged*) The imbecile! Who did he mean by bad company?

PERKINS—Some friend of yours in the office who was discharged for being a member of the I.W.—the I.W.—

TOM—The I.W.E.?

PERKINS—Yes, that's it.

TOM—(*grimly*) Did he say that I belonged to the I.W.E. too?

PERKINS—Oh no, nothing as serious, as bad as that.

TOM—Well I do.

PERKINS—You—what?

TOM—I am a member of the I.W.E.

PERKINS—(*trying to force a smile*) You're trying to make fun of me now, I know.

TOM—I mean it. I'm serious.

PERKINS—But aren't they—don't they start strikes—and throw bombs—and blow up places with dynamite?

TOM—They use force when force is used against them, when they have to.

PERKINS—But you wouldn't do anything like that—I mean dynamite.

TOM—Yes, I would. (*looking keenly at his father*) If they asked me to dynamite the engines of the *San Francisco* tomorrow, I'd do it.

PERKINS—Dynamite my engines! (*with surprising firmness and decision*) I'd never permit that.

TOM—(*with a contemptuous smile*) How would you stop it?

PERKINS—I don't know, but I would, somehow. (*seeing Tom's smile*) Or the Chief would.

TOM—Ah, I thought you'd wait for the Chief's orders.

PERKINS—Of course you're joking. Who would ever think of such a thing.

TOM—(*easily*) Yes, I was only joking.

PERKINS—(*excitedly*) Dynamite the engines of a ship! Why it would be a crime. No one but Anarchists or criminals would do such a thing.

TOM—Don't get excited about it. It would be a good lesson to the rotten old Ocean Steamship Company if someone did something of the sort.

PERKINS—(*flushing*) I don't like to hear you speak of the Company so disrespectfully.

TOM—(*throwing his hands in the air*) Disrespectfully! Why, good heavens, that thieving Line is owned by the biggest financial bandits in Wall Street or in the country, and you ought to know it.

PERKINS—(*rising from his chair—tensely*) I know nothing of the kind.

TOM—Then it's time you did. The sooner you do, the sooner you'll get over your servile fidelity to the Line and everyone connected with it. Don't you know that the Ocean Company is the head of the ship combine, and that the ship combine was organized by the greatest gang of crooked capitalists in the world?

PERKINS—(*breathing hard*) I know nothing of the kind.

TOM—Don't you know that the seamen and firemen on their ships, and on your own ship, the *San Francisco*, are shamefully underpaid and overworked? That the Company will not listen to their just demands, but grinds them down and gives them no chance? Oh, but what's the use of talking to you? I tell you right now the Ocean Steamship Company is rotten from top to bottom.

PERKINS—(*bristling with indignant rage*) It's a lie. (*Tom looks at him in amused astonishment.*) It's a lie! (*sputtering*) How dare you say such things? About the Company I have worked for for thirty years and never had a complaint to make.

TOM—And who have promoted men over your head time after time! A lot you have to be grateful to them for! Why you ought to hate them as—as much as I do.

PERKINS—(*commencing to wilt before Tom's contempt*) No,

no, Tom, you're very wrong. It's my own fault I haven't been promoted. I haven't the ability and they know it.

Tom—You haven't got the pull behind you, that's the answer. Ability? You know twice as much about marine engines as the fleet engineer. I've heard him say so myself.

Perkins—(*beaming for a second*) Did he really say that? He must have been only joking. (*then worriedly*) You're wrong to run down the Company, indeed you are. It's all this I.W.—whatever-their-name-is foolishness you've got in your head. (*anxiously*) You mustn't go around with them any more. You mustn't belong to them. Supposing the Company should hear of it!

Tom—They have heard of it.

Perkins—What!

Tom—(*slowly—letting the words sink in*) Yes. They fired me this afternoon for just that.

Perkins—(*staring wildly at Tom—aghast*) They—discharged—you?

Tom—I was fired this afternoon. So you see your warning is too late.

Perkins—You've lost your position! (*He crumples up into his chair.*)

Tom—I meant to tell you before. (*with airy indifference*) It's of so little importance I'd forgotten it.

Perkins—(*half-aloud*) They've discharged you! My son discharged in disgrace! After the thirty years I've worked for them! What will they think of me?

Tom—(*with angry contempt*) What will *they* think of *you*? I knew that was how you'd take it—the damned old Company before everything else in the world! (*disgustedly*) Hell! (*rises to his feet*)

Perkins—(*hastily*) I didn't mean that, Tom, not in that way. You don't understand. I was only thinking they might discharge me too, because—because—

Tom—Because I was your son, eh?

Perkins—No, no, Tom, not that! I mean they might think I was connected with this I.W.—

Tom—(*scornfully*) Don't worry. There's no danger of their getting rid of so faithful a *servant*! They'd have a hard time finding another like you.

PERKINS—(*pitifully*) I know you think it's weak of me—
I can't help it— Don't look at me that way, Tom. I wouldn't
lose my position on the *San Francisco* for anything in the
world. I love the work—and the ship—and the engines—
I'm just beginning to know them.

TOM—Bah!

PERKINS—If you've lost your position, Tom, you must
need money. Let me give you some, won't you?

TOM—No.

PERKINS—Let me help you, won't you? Let me loan you
some. You can pay it back sometime.

TOM—I don't want any more of the *Company's* money.

PERKINS—Listen! If I went to them— I've worked faith-
fully for thirty years. They've never had a complaint to make
of me—if I went and asked them—

TOM—(*frowning*) What?

PERKINS—And you were to promise them to give up this
I.W. foolishness—you're only a boy, you know—and you
promised not to live with that woman any more—I think—
I think—they might—

TOM—(*in hard tones*) Take me back?

PERKINS—Yes, yes, I'm almost sure. I'll see Mr. Griffin the
first thing in the morning and I'll—

TOM—And *you* advise me to do this?

PERKINS—(*faltering*) I think—I think—

TOM—You advise me to cringe like a yellow mongrel and
lick the boot which has kicked me out?

PERKINS—(*half-insane with nervous fear of everything*) I
don't know—I don't know— You must go back to your position, really you must— I've dreamed so much— You'll be
president of the Company some day— I've failed— You
must succeed— Please, Tom, please go back! I know they'll
take you if you'll only—

TOM—(*with cold rage*) By God, I'm through! I've had
enough of all this. I've tried to think of you as my father,
tried to feel like a son toward you, but it's time to give up
the pretence. You're in one world and I'm in another. We'd
better say goodbye now while we still have some kindly feelings for each other. When the best you can advise your son is
to become a cur, it's time to quit. Goodbye!

PERKINS—No, no, no! Please! You mustn't go, Tom, you mustn't leave me this way! I can't say goodbye to you! (*But Tom has gone out shutting the door behind him. Perkins stares at the closed door in dumb anguish for a moment—then stumbles to chair and leans forward on the table, his head hidden in his arms.*)

PERKINS—(*sobbing wildly*) Tom! Tom!

(*The Curtain Falls*)

ACT III
Scene I

Scene—*A section of the firemen's forecastle on the* S.S. San Francisco *at dock in Liverpool—two weeks or so later. Bunks, ranged three deep with a space of two and a half to three feet between them, occupy the rear and left walls. Over the upper tier of bunks in rear, several open portholes. In front of the bunks, low wooden benches. In under the lower tier a glimpse can be had of seachests, suit cases, etc. jammed in indiscriminately. In the middle of right wall, a door. On either side of it, more tiers of bunks. A row of steel stanchions extends down the middle of the room. Everything is steel, painted white, except the board floor.*

It is night. As the curtain rises, the ship's bell is heard ringing four bells.

A number of stokers are seated on the benches or lying in their bunks, the majority smoking clay pipes. Most of them are either stripped to the waist or in their undershirts, for the smoke-laden air in the forecastle on this August night is stiflingly hot. Tom is seated in their midst, smoking a cigarette, staring moodily before him.

O'ROURKE—(*a giant of a red-headed Irishman—knocking out his pipe—savagely to Tom*) Let thim do somethin' and be quick about ut, and not be maikin' bloody fools av the lot av us.

TOM—They will, O'Rourke. Give them a chance.

O'ROURKE—A chance, is ut? Wid us sailin' tomorry and the rist av the ships durin' the week, and a new lot comin' in. (*Tom gets up impatiently and strides up and down the forecastle.*)

HARRIS—(*a tall, wiry, grey-headed man with round shoulders*) I think the whole damned thing's off, s'what I think.

TOM—I tell you it isn't, Harris. I tell you—

COCKY—(*squat, broad-shouldered, pasty-faced—interrupting scornfully*) Tell 'im! That's wot you been tellin' us arll the parst week 'ere. I ain't seen nothink 'appen yet, I 'avent. (*still more scornfully*) International Workers of the bleedin' world! Bloody swankers I calls the lot uv them.

TOM—(*contemptuously*) Shut up, Cocky. The heat's bad enough without having to listen to your drivel.

348

COCKY—(*with injured indignation*) Gawd blimey! Listen to 'im! Carnt a man say wot 'e thinks?

O'ROURKE—(*savagely*) Close yer big mout', ye little scut, or I'll close ut for ye.

COCKY—(*whiningly*) Aw naw!

HARRIS—Just the same, Cocky's right. (*to Tom*) Ain't you been sayin' all week even if the union's gone back on us, this I.W.E. would help us out and start the strike?

TOM—Yes; and I still say it.

HARRIS—Well, it looks 's if the union is afraid to start anything, don't it?

TOM—Yes, damn them. It looks that way.

HARRIS—(*rising to a climax*) Then where's the I.W.E. comin' in, that's what we wants to know?

TOM—There's still time for that.

SCHMIDT—(*a giant of a shock-headed German —spitting disgustedly*) Time? Mit one more night in port only?

TOM—(*with decision*) It'll be done tonight.

HARRIS—It? What's it? That's what we wants to know, Donovan.

TOM—You'll know soon enough. (*evasively*) I'm waiting for someone now.

O'ROURKE—Divil take all this sneakin' business! Who is ut you're waitin' for?

TOM—I don't know exactly or I'd have told you— Whitely, probably.

O'ROURKE—(*encouraged*) Whitely's a man that'd stop at nothin'. I know that, none betther. Betune the two av ye ye should be able to think av somethin'; but for the love av the saints be quick. The rest av us'll folly ye to the divil, if need be. (*a murmur of assent from the others*) Only, be quick wid ut. Wid only wan night more in Liverpool, there's little toime to be speech-maikin', and I'm not for puttin' up wid this dog's life wan day longer. (*chorus of assent*)

TOM—(*resolutely*) Look here, men, I've promised you if the union leaders failed you—

HARRIS—Well, they have, ain't they?

TOM—We're not absolutely sure yet. They've been weakening. Tonight's meeting of the officers of the union will decide whether they intend standing to their guns or not.

HARRIS—'N if they don't?

TOM—(*firmly*) I'll act—we'll act immediately.

O'ROURKE—That's the talkin'.

COCKY—But 'ow are we to know—abaht this 'ere meetin'?

TOM—Whitely's there. He'll be down to tell us what happened. He ought to be here any minute now.

O'ROURKE—(*savagely*) Thin let thim go back on us for the black scuts av traithors they arr, and be damned to thim. We're men enough widout the say-so av the unions to show a thing or two to the ship's officers and teach thim to be swillin' their guts wid wine and champagne at the Company's dinner on shore, and us dyin' wid the heat and thirst in this stinkin' rat's hole. (*a chorus of angry growls*)

HARRIS—The Company thinks they'll be no strike. That's why they're givin' this rotten dinner on shore to the ship's officers.

TOM—Well, we'll show them they haven't got us whipped, and never can have as long as we're men enough to demand our rights. We'll hit them a blow they'll never forget.

HARRIS—How're you goin' to do it, 's what I want to know?

TOM—When the time comes you'll know.

O'ROURKE—No betther toime than this night wid no officers on board the auld hooker but the mate and the second engineer. And meanin' no disrespect to Molly Perkins he's nat the wan to sthop us if we once get starthed.

TOM—(*easily*) We'll get the second engineer out of the way easy enough. He'll be too stunned to do anything.

O'ROURKE—He's a civil-spoken bit av a man, is the second, and I'd not loike to see him hurted.

TOM—I'll warn him in time. He won't bother us.

SCHMIDT—Ha ha! If he gets funny, dot leedle man, I vill— (*makes a gesture with his great hands as if he were breaking a stick across his knee*)

TOM—(*promptly*) No, you won't, Schmidt! Remember that! Every man in this fo'castle has got to promise, no matter what happens, he won't touch the second engineer, or—you can all shift for yourselves as far as I'm concerned, or the I.W.E. either.

THE STOKERS—Aye—a dacint little man— Wouldn't

hurt a fly, he wouldn't— Who'd wanta mash him?—Shut up, Dutch! etc. (*Schmidt is sullenly silent before this criticism.*)

O'ROURKE—(*walking over to Schmidt and laying a hand on his shoulder—fiercely*) Ye'll not lay a hand on him, me bucko!

SCHMIDT—(*defiantly*) Iss it you would stop me, was?

O'ROURKE—The same—Red O'Rourke. Ye've guessed ut, Dutchy.

SCHMIDT—I am not Dutch. I am German.

O'ROURKE—'Tis all the same breed av swine, I'm thinkin'. Kape this in your thick skull: If ye lay a finger on the little second engineer, ye deal wid me.

SCHMIDT—(*jumping to his feet*) I am not fraid of you or no Irish, py damn!

TOM—(*jumping in between the two men*) Here! Here! Stop this nonsense. What chance have you against the Company if you don't fight shoulder to shoulder and stop scrapping among yourselves. Don't you know that's just what the Company would like to see you do, you fools, you! (*Schmidt sulkily sits down again.*)

O'ROURKE—(*walking back to his place*) I'll see ye again, Dutchy.

TOM—(*addressing the crowd—earnestly*) If you men want to win the big fight you'll have to put aside your private scraps. Remember if you don't work together, you're licked before you start. I thought Olga Tarnoff had impressed that on your minds at the meeting on shore the other night.

COCKY—I 'eard 'er but it fair drove me balmy—sick of 'er silly jossin', I wuz—like one of them blushin' Suffrygette meetings, it wuz. Blimey if any female can stand jawin' at me. Let 'er be 'ome a-nursin' of 'er babies, I says. Men is men and—

O'ROURKE—(*stretching out a long arm and placing a big hand over Cocky's mouth*) Will ye be still, ye insect? Or must I choke ye. 'Tis too hot entoirely to listen to your squakin'.

TOM—Never mind the fool, Red. (*O'Rourke releases Cocky who is about to continue his outburst when the sound of maudlin singing is heard. As it grows nearer the words can be distinguished.*)

THE VOICE—"Whiskey is the life of man
                Whiskey! O Johnny!"

O'ROURKE—'Tis Hogan comin' back wid his skin full av ale. I wish I had half av ut. Where'd he get the dough, I wonder.

HOGAN—(*appearing in the doorway—a stout, broad-shouldered man*) "O whiskey killed my poor aunt Ann.
Whiskey for my Johnny!"

(*He stands reeling and blinking in the doorway, holding a newspaper in one hand. The others look at him with broad grins.*)

O'ROURKE—(*genially*) Won't ye come in, ye drunken baboon?

HOGAN—(*singing*) "Beer, beer, glorious beer!
Fill yourselves right up to here."

(*waving his newspaper*) War! War! Bloody war wid the Dutchmen comin'. 'Tis truth I'm tellin' ye. 'Tis here in black and white.

SCHMIDT—(*getting up quickly*) Gif me dot baper. (*snatches it out of Hogan's hand, and, sitting down, commences laboriously to pick out the words*)

HOGAN—(*dazedly*) Aisy, aisy, me son. Ye'll know all about it soon enough. (*He hiccoughs.*) When the British navy gets after ye. The war is not yet, the paper says, but 'tis apt to come any day if things kape on the way they are. (*angrily*) Give me back that paper, ye Dutch swine! (*lays his hand roughly on Schmidt's shoulder*)

SCHMIDT—Oud! (*Jumps to his feet and throws Hogan aside. Hogan goes down in a heap.*)

O'ROURKE—(*fiercely*) Hit a helpless man, wud ye? (*He hits Schmidt. They grapple. Tom and the others rush in and pull them apart.*)

HARRIS—No fightin' in the fo'castle. Out on the for'ard square if you wants to settle it.

THE OTHERS—(*delighted at the prospect of seeing a fight*) Come out and settle it! See who's the better man! Out on the for'ard square! etc.

O'ROURKE—Will ye see who's the betther man, Dutchy, or are ye a coward?

SCHMIDT—(*raging*) Come oud! I show you! I show you! (*All crowd out the doorway except Tom and Hogan.*)

HOGAN—(*weaving drunkenly toward his bunk—sings*) "We are the boys of Wexford." (*speaks*) 'Tis my fight but no matther. I'm too drunk, God help me. (*climbing into his bunk—philosophically*) No matther! O'Rourke will bate him. (*He falls asleep and is soon snoring. Tom walks up and down impatiently. A moment later Olga enters. She is dressed in a dirty sweater and dungaree jumper, patched dungaree trousers, rough shoes, and has a cap pulled down over her eyes, hiding her hair. Her face and hands are grimed with dirt.*)

OLGA—Tom!

TOM—(*in surprise*) Olga! (*takes her in his arms and kisses her—pulls the cap from over her face*)

OLGA—Don't!

TOM—There's no one here.

OLGA—Where are they all?

TOM—(*disgustedly*) Out on the for'ard square fighting as usual. But how do you happen to be here?

OLGA—Whitely sent me to warn you.

TOM—When did you see him?

OLGA—Not half an hour ago. He had just left the meeting of the union officers.

TOM—What happened at the meeting?

OLGA—(*contemptuously*) Just what we expected. They decided not to declare the strike at present. Whitely says they have been bought off by the Companies, every one of them. He himself was offered money by one of the Companies' agents if he would go away for a time and stop his agitating.

TOM—The scoundrels!

OLGA—Whitely was wild with rage. He pleaded with them but they wouldn't listen. Finally he told them what he thought of them and resigned his office. (*with a smile*) They're not liable to forget what he said, I'll bet.

TOM—But didn't they offer some excuse?

OLGA—Traitors are always full of excuses. They crawled behind patriotism, said it wouldn't be right. (*contemptuously*) Right! To call a strike now when beloved Britannia might become involved in a great war.

TOM—What hypocrites!

OLGA—(*indignantly*) Whitely told them that now, above all times, was the moment to strike in all branches of organized labor and thus paralyze the sinews of war. They couldn't see it that way; or rather, with the Companies' money in their pockets, they decided not to see it.

TOM—(*shaking his head*) It looks as if all this war talk would result in something this time.

OLGA—Oh, how can they be such idiots!

TOM—I've been thinking of what Hartmann said—that such a war would put back the cause of true liberty fifty years.

OLGA—There's no doubt of that. (*with deep feeling*) Oh, it can't happen. Men can't be such fools—after all they've been taught, all we've preached to them, all the Socialists have done—

TOM—You forget they've been taught patriotism at home, in government schools along with their first reader. It's in their hearts, as Hartmann said. You can't make them forget it by reasoning.

OLGA—You're right. (*impulsively*) Ah, I'll bring up our child with a soul freed from all adorations of Gods and governments if I have to live alone on a mountain top to do it.

TOM—(*quickly*) Our child?

OLGA—(*avoiding his look—betraying confusion—hurriedly*) Why do you pick me up like that? You know I was only stating a supposition. (*hurriedly*) You haven't asked me how I sneaked on board.

TOM—No need to. The master-at-arms on the gangway is one of us. Even if he'd recognized you he wouldn't have stopped you.

OLGA—But isn't my disguise good?

TOM—(*with a grin*) You look exactly like—like an adorable woman with a dirty face.

OLGA—(*disappointedly*) Oh. (*But this time she allows herself to be kissed.*)

TOM—(*after a pause*) Now that the unions have backed down it's up to us.

OLGA—Yes.

TOM—Did Whitely say anything about the dynamite?

OLGA—That's what he asked me to tell you—that he had gone to Sims' shop to get it and would be down immediately. He wanted you to be prepared.

TOM—(*frowning*) Tonight's the best time, if it must be done. All the officers are on shore at that dinner the Company is giving. The curse of it is that the only engineer left on the boat is the very one—

OLGA—Your father?

TOM—Yes.

OLGA—He hasn't found out that you're on the boat?

TOM—No.

OLGA—You think he'll make trouble?

TOM—Not trouble in the sense you mean. But he's sure to be pottering around in the engine room petting his engines, and—I'll have to explain, threaten, get him out of danger somehow. (*irritably*) I wish it could have been some time when he wasn't on duty. I could use force if it was anyone else.

OLGA—There won't be anyone else in the engine room?

TOM—All the men are with us.

OLGA—(*anxiously*) Do you know anything about dynamite?

TOM—Only what Whitely has told me.

OLGA—(*with growing agitation*) Isn't it liable to go off prematurely sometimes?

TOM—I suppose so; but there isn't much danger of that as long as one is careful, Whitely says.

OLGA—As long as one is careful. You *will* be careful, won't you, dear?

TOM—(*struck by her tone*) Of course I will.

OLGA—(*after a pause—with growing embarrassment*) Whitely said that he—don't you think it might be better— more sure—if Whitely were to do it?

TOM—(*looks keenly at her for a moment—she turns away— slowly*) So you still think I'm a quitter, do you?

OLGA—No, no, it isn't that.

TOM—You must or you wouldn't propose such a thing.

OLGA—(*lamely*) I was only thinking the results would be more certain if a man who knew all about dynamite—

TOM—(*shortly*) I know enough for the purpose.

OLGA—(*impulsively*) I wish you'd let him do it. I don't know why but I've a premonition, a fear—

TOM—(*going to her and putting his hands on her shoulders, and looking into her eyes*) Olga, what's the matter? Tell me.

OLGA—(*avoiding his look*) Nothing at all.

TOM—Yes, there is. Ever since we arrived in Liverpool you've been different, changed from the old Olga. What is it? Tell me.

OLGA—Nothing. It's only your imagination.

TOM—No, it isn't. (*tenderly*) You know I love you.

OLGA—Yes, yes, you must!

TOM—And you love me, don't you?

OLGA—Yes, I do, I do!

TOM—Then tell me.

OLGA—I can't. There's nothing to tell.

TOM—Olga! In New York you would have scorned me if I had shown the slightest sign of shirking; and now you are advising me to—

OLGA—Conditions have changed since then.

TOM—What conditions?

OLGA—Oh, everything is different now.

TOM—How?

OLGA—(*haltingly*) It doesn't seem— I don't think— (*desperately*) I don't think it's going to do any good, this dynamiting. I don't believe it will have the effect Hartmann expected.

TOM—(*quietly*) Why?

OLGA—(*wildly*) Don't ask me so many questions. It's just what I think.

TOM—I should say the present conditions of things demanded drastic action on our part more than ever. We have this coming war to fight against now. The strike must be started.

OLGA—(*trying to collect herself*) Yes, perhaps you're right. Then all the more reason for your letting Whitely do the dynamiting. It can't fail, then.

TOM—You know that's impossible. Whitely is well known. He'll be suspected as it is. He must be able to furnish an iron-clad alibi. You see it's impossible, don't you?

OLGA—(*dully*) Yes.

TOM—And you know you'd despise me for a quitter if I gave up at this point. It's my duty. I've got to do it. (*resolutely*) You needn't worry about my lack of ability. I know exactly what to do. (*to reassure her*) They'll never find out who did it—unless some of the men squeal on me.

OLGA—(*sitting down on one of the benches—sadly*) Ah—unless!

TOM—They're real men, all of them. They won't squeal.

OLGA—I wouldn't trust them.

TOM—Even if it is known that I'm the one, the men only know me as Tom Donovan; and Whitely has arranged a hiding place where even the devil himself couldn't find me.

OLGA—But you'd never be able to come out. They'd always be looking for you.

TOM—(*coming over to her*) What you've been saying doesn't sound like you at all, Olga. There *is* something the matter. Please tell me—like a good comrade.

OLGA—I've overtaxed my strength, I think. I feel—run down. That's all.

TOM—(*tenderly*) Poor little girl.

OLGA—(*wildly—breaking away from him*) Don't pity me. I don't want pity. I want to be someplace all alone—and think.

TOM—When we get back we'll both take a trip into the country. I know a place—a farm in the Jersey hills—nice people—be glad to have us. We'll go there.

OLGA—(*slowly giving way to the dream*) That would be wonderful. I feel as if I could lie for days in the cool grass, looking up at the sky—and dreaming. (*coming back to the present with a start*) But you may never— (*Her eyes widen with horror.*)

TOM—(*putting his arm around her*) Olga, you mustn't have such thoughts.

OLGA—(*half-sobbing, her head on his shoulder*) Tom, please let Whitely do it.

TOM—Olga!

OLGA—If you knew—if I could tell you—why I ask this— (*regaining control of herself, walks up and down fighting down her emotion. Tom looks at her wonderingly. Finally she speaks quite calmly.*) You're right. You're the only one who can do it. I've been making a fool of myself.

TOM—(*cheerfully*) I'm glad you see it that way again. I couldn't quit. I've promised the men—and you would despise me later.

(*Whitely enters quietly and stands for a moment in the doorway looking at them. He is a swarthy, dark-eyed, bull-necked, powerfully-built man of about 35. He wears a black mustache and is dressed in a dirty suit of dungarees.*)

OLGA—(*seeing him*) Here's Whitely now.

TOM—(*shaking hands with him*) I've heard the bad news.

WHITELY—(*his eyes flashing*) The yellow cowards! They sold themselves like the slaves they are—and I told them so. The meeting nearly broke up in a riot. Where are all the men?

TOM—Watching a fight in the for'ard square. O'Rourke and Schmidt are at it. I stopped them once but— (*He shrugs his shoulders.*)

WHITELY—(*grimly*) The war has commenced already, eh?

TOM—It can't last much longer. They'll be back soon.

WHITELY—Before they come back I've more bad news for you.

TOM—What?

WHITELY—There'll be no dynamiting.

OLGA—(*in spite of herself—joyfully*) Ah!

TOM—You mean?

WHITELY—Sims, the man in whose shop the stuff is hidden, has been arrested.

TOM—On suspicion?

WHITELY—I don't know whether it has anything to do with this affair or not. I didn't go around to learn particulars. I was afraid they might nab me. I went home and put on these clothes and slipped down here to tell you.

TOM—Then it's all off—the whole thing?

WHITELY—That part of it, at least.

TOM—And I had promised the men— What can we do?

WHITELY—If there was only some way to prevent the *San Francisco* from sailing tomorrow! If we could only start a little strike of our own on board this ship and keep her here, I know the crowd from the other ships would join in. It only needs a spark and the strike will spread everywhere—unions or no unions. Haven't you some influence with the men?

TOM—I did have.

WHITELY—You *did* have?

TOM—I've been losing it lately. They've been waiting for me to do something, and they're beginning to think it was all talk.

WHITELY—Then now is your time to show them.

TOM—Yes; but how?

WHITELY—How? Can't you think of something, man? You know a ship better than I do.

TOM—I'm trying to think.

WHITELY—If we can throw the *San Francisco* off her schedule—delay the mails. That will hit the Company hard. They stake their reputation on this ship. Think of the encouragement it will give to the men.

TOM—I've a plan, but it means mutiny.

WHITELY—What of it? So much the better. It means a fight and that's what we're looking for. It means the consolidation of the men under the International Workers, and the destruction of their petty unions. If you can only get this thing going here, I'll guarantee to keep it going.

TOM—(*resolutely*) I'll do my best.

WHITELY—(*enthusiastically*) Good!

OLGA—(*apprehensively*) What are you going to do, Tom?

TOM—If I can get them to follow me, I'll prevent the ship from sailing on time all right. When the men come in I leave it to you to tell them the way the union leaders have betrayed them. If that doesn't make them fighting mad, then they've lost their spirit and there's nothing to be done.

WHITELY—I'll rouse them—by telling the truth—just what happened.

TOM—They're coming now. (*noise of voices from without*)

WHITELY—Hadn't Olga better go ashore?

TOM—(*turning to her*) Yes, Olga, I think you—

OLGA—(*vehemently*) Why should I? They've heard me speak. They all know I'm their friend.

TOM—(*protestingly*) But—

OLGA—(*firmly*) I insist upon staying. (*Tom shrugs his shoulders helplessly.*)

WHITELY—Oh, there's no harm, I suppose. (*The crowd of excited stokers pour in the doorway. In their admiring midst is the conqueror O'Rourke, stripped to the waist, his face bloody, one eye closed, his swollen lips parted in a triumphant grin. Schmidt is not among them.*)

COCKY—Gawd blimey, wot a swipe!

HARRIS—That last punch knocked him cold. (*All the stokers lower their voices and cease their admiring oaths when they see Olga and recognize her. She nods calmly from one to the other of them.*)

O'ROURKE—Give me me shirt, ye scuts. Am I fit appearin'

to be in the presence av a lady— (*with a comical glance at Olga's pants*) Aven if she is a man. (*One of the crowd hands him his shirt which he puts on.*)

Tom—Where's Schmidt?

Harris—The other Dutchies are pourin' water on him.

O'Rourke—(*jovially*) Down wid the Dutch and success to the British army—the Irish part av ut I mane.

Tom—Men, Whitely has just come from the meeting of the officers of your union. He wants to tell you what happened there.

Cocky—(*in a loud aside to the man next to him*) Glad it ain't one of them blarsted Suffrygette speeches we've got to 'ear. (*with a withering glance at Olga*) Wearin' of men's clothes naw.

O'Rourke—Spake up, Whitely. We know it's the truth you'll be tellin' us.

Whitely—(*stands on one of the benches. The men crowd around him.*) You all know me. (*chorus of assent*) You know I've always fought my damndest for you whenever I've had the chance. The Companies have had me pinched, and they've tried to buy me off only a few weeks ago; but they've never been able to shut my mouth, and I'm still here fighting them.

O'Rourke—Divil a lie, ye arr. Three cheers for Whitely, boys!

Tom—(*hurriedly interposing*) Not now, not now, O'Rourke! We've got to be quiet if we want to do anything.

Whitely—Donovan's right. We can't let them suspect there's anything up.

O'Rourke—Right ye arr, and I'm an auld fool. (*gleefully*) If there's throuble comin' 'tis Red O'Rourke'll be in the midst av ut. (*All the stokers show pleased expectation.*)

Whitely—I've just come from the meeting and I want to say this about the officers of the union, of which I was one before I resigned tonight— They're traitors to you, every rotten one of them! (*an angry growl from the crowd*) They've decided to let the Companies go on oppressing you without your saying a word. They've decided not to strike! (*a chorus of angry exclamations from the stokers*)

HARRIS—And what reason do they give, s'what I wants to know.

WHITELY—It's not the reason they give that counts. They say it isn't the right time to strike but they're liars and they know it. They know this is the grandest opportunity to get their rights the workers on the ships have ever had. Never before have you had the same chance of waging a successful war against the thieving ship corporations.

COCKY—'Ear! 'Ear!

O'ROURKE—True for ye, thieves they arr, iviry divil's wan av thim.

WHITELY—The officers of your union knew they were lying when they gave that excuse for not striking. It wasn't the real reason. The real reason was that every rotten one of them had some of the Company's dirty money in his pocket. They had sold you to the Companies. The Companies had bought every cowardly one of them—and I told them so! (*He is interrupted by a clamor of rage from all sides.*)

O'ROURKE—The dirthy blackguards!

HARRIS—How do you know all this, Whitely?

WHITELY—How do I know it? Because a week ago, when I was still an officer of your union, one of the agents of the Companies came to me and offered me one hundred pounds—five hundred dollars—if I would betray you. And do you know what I told him? I told him to go to hell! (*expressions of enthusiastic approval from all sides*)

O'ROURKE—That's the talkin'.

WHITELY—But the others didn't tell him that—not them. They took the money and sold themselves, and all of you into the bargain. That's why I resigned tonight as an officer of your union. I wouldn't lower myself by being associated with such a pack of yellow curs.

COCKY—Dahn with the bleedin' swine, says I!

O'ROURKE—Let me catch wan av thim face to face. (*He brandishes his fists.*)

WHITELY—Are you going to stand for this treatment?

ALL—No, no!

WHITELY—Then listen to Tom Donovan. He's one of you, a stoker himself. He represents the International Workers, the only organization true to the interests of the workers. He'll tell you what to do; and if you're real men with guts you'll follow him. (*He gets down amid acclamations. Tom gets up in his place.*)

Tom—(*in determined tones*) *Are* you willing to follow me?

O'Rourke—To the divil and back, me boy.

All—Yes, yes.

Tom—Then we'll start the strike here and teach them a lesson. If we just went ashore on strike they'd get a crew of scabs tomorrow morning and sail on time. We want to make the Company pay for the way they've treated us. We want to keep the *San Francisco* from sailing tomorrow.

O'Rourke—(*in his element now*) We'll sink the auld scow.

Tom—I had a plan by which I alone was going to put the engines on the bum, but, through no fault of mine, the plan fell through. Now I've got to have your help. Will you help me?

All—Yes! Yes!

Tom—Then we'll go to the stokehold and get the men there to join us. We'll pull out the fires. We'll get splice bars and shovels and everything else that's handy. We'll go to the engine room and smash everything we can. We may not be able to do any permanent damage, but, by God, we'll keep the *San Francisco* from sailing tomorrow! (*a chorus of delighted approval*)

Whitely—And I'll go to the other ships and get their men to join you.

Tom—Come on then, those of you who are with me.

O'Rourke—We're all av us wid you! (*They crowd toward the door, waiting for Tom to lead the way. Olga steps to his side.*)

Tom—Where are you going, Olga?

Olga—With you.

Tom—(*sternly*) You can't!

Olga—I must! (*She throws her arms about his neck.*)

Tom—(*kisses her*) It's impossible. Take her ashore, will you, Whitely? (*to the grinning stokers who stand waiting for him*) Come on! (*He goes out. The men crowd after him. Olga covers her face with her hands. A sob shakes her shoulders.*)

One of the Last Stokers—(*as he is going out the door*) It's easy. There's no one on watch but old Molly Perkins.

WHITELY—(*gently—after a pause*) We'd better go, Olga.

(*End of Scene One*)

SCENE II

SCENE—*The engine room of the* San Francisco *facing the engines. Perkins is discovered in his working clothes, his face and hands smeared with grease. He stands back, surveying the engines lovingly, humming a tune with a satisfied air. He comes forward and rubs off a speck of dust with the sleeve of his coat; then stands back and watches the oiler, Murphy, who is busy above.*

PERKINS—That will do, I guess, Murphy.

MURPHY—Yes, sir. (*He comes down and stands beside Perkins.*)

PERKINS—Everything look right to you, Murphy.

MURPHY—Right as rain, sir.

PERKINS—(*rubbing his hands with satisfaction*) That's good, that's very good indeed.

MURPHY—Yes, sir.

PERKINS—(*his admiring eyes taking in every detail of his pets*) Beauties, aren't they.

MURPHY—Fine engines, sir.

PERKINS—And old Henderson of the *Empress* tried to tell me that his were better—just imagine! You've worked on the *Empress*, haven't you, Murphy?

MURPHY—Yes, sir.

PERKINS—Well—er—hm—do you think her engines are as good as these?

MURPHY—(*diplomatically*) Not on your life, sir. A regular, rattlin' bunch o' junk they are, it's the truth.

PERKINS—(*pleased*) Oh come, Murphy, that's exaggeration, now, isn't it? They're very good engines, I'm told; but not as good as these. Haven't we beaten the *Empress* nearly every time? Isn't that proof enough, eh, Murphy?

MURPHY—Proof enough, yes sir.

PERKINS—I wish I could make Henderson see it. He's so pig-headed. (*a slight pause*) You might as well go, Murphy.

MURPHY—(*gladly*) Thank you, sir. (*prepares to go up*)

PERKINS—(*uncertainly*) Er—hm—there isn't any trouble among the men, is there?

MURPHY—(*closing up*) I don't know, sir.

PERKINS—Er—surely—hm—surely you wouldn't think of striking, would you, Murphy—I mean you seem satisfied.

MURPHY—It all depends on what the union says, sir.

PERKINS—Hmm—yes, yes, of course, the union. You—er—you don't belong to the I.W.—?

MURPHY—The I.W., sir? No, sir.

PERKINS—You know something about them, don't you?

MURPHY—Yes, sir.

PERKINS—Well—er—do you think a young man—say 22—would come to any harm belonging to them?

MURPHY—Couldn't say, sir.

PERKINS—(*with a troubled sigh*) I hope not, indeed I hope not. They say there's some of them been making speeches in Liverpool.

MURPHY—(*cautiously*) Don't know, sir.

PERKINS—All right, Murphy, you can go. I'll stay here for awhile.

MURPHY—Good night, sir. (*He climbs up.*)

PERKINS—Good night. (*He walks up and down the engine room with a troubled air. A moment later the clattering sound of running steps is heard on the iron stairs and Jack, an engineer's apprentice, hurries down to where Perkins is standing. He is a shock-headed, freckle-faced youth, wildly excited and breathless.*)

JACK—(*breathlessly*) Mr.—Mr. Perkins! (*He gasps.*)

PERKINS—(*with nervous solicitude*) There, there, get your breath. What under the sun brings you down here?

JACK—They're coming!

PERKINS—Who are coming? What do you mean? Have you had the nightmare?

JACK—N—no. I wasn't asleep. I was listening.

PERKINS—Listening?

JACK—Outside the door of the fo'castle.

PERKINS—What fo'castle?

JACK—The firemen's fo'castle. I heard everything they said, him and her.

PERKINS—Him? What him?

JACK—The one they call Donovan.

PERKINS—Did you say her? Do you mean there was a woman in the fo'castle?

JACK—Yes, sir.

PERKINS—You must have been dreaming.

JACK—No, I wasn't, sir, honest I wasn't. I saw her plain as anything—even if she was dressed up in men's clothes.

PERKINS—Dressed in men's clothes! Are you sure?

JACK—Yes, sir; I am, sir.

PERKINS—Why didn't the man-at-arms stop her from getting on board? (*unable to believe*) You're sure you saw her, Jack?

JACK—Yes, sir; and I know who she is too. I heard her make a speech last Wednesday. She's that I.W. woman who's been talking about striking.

PERKINS—(*frightened*) I.W. woman!

JACK—Her and that Tom Donovan were talking while the men was out fighting on the for'ard square. I heard them talking about dynamite—

PERKINS—(*terrified*) Dynamite!

JACK—The Chief told me to listen whenever I got a chance; and I was outside where no one could see me. They were talking about dynamite.

PERKINS—Good heavens!

JACK—Then another fellow came in and they all talked low, but I heard them say dynamite again.

PERKINS—(*as if the name fascinated him*) Dynamite!

JACK—Then all the stokers came back and the last fellow made a speech to them about the unions and strikes and things and they all got crazy mad.

PERKINS—Strikes! Unions! What are they going to do? (*helplessly*) I wish the chief was here.

JACK—Then this Donovan fellow makes a speech and tells them to smash the engines—

PERKINS—(*indignation showing beneath his terror*) Smash the engines! No, he couldn't have urged them to do that.

JACK—Yes, he did, sir. I heard him plain as can be.

PERKINS—That Donovan fellow must be a rascal.

JACK—Then they all rushed outa the fo'castle to get splice-bars and shovels in the stokehold, like Donovan told 'em, to smash everything with.

PERKINS—Smash the engines! (*He walks up and down.*) No, no that's impossible. They wouldn't do that. (*growing more and more indignant*) Only scoundrels would do such a thing.

JACK—Then I ran down here fast as I could to tell you. (*more and more excited*) They'll be down here in a few minutes, sir. You better look out.

PERKINS—(*in an agony of perplexity*) What shall I do? I do wish the Chief was here.

JACK—Probably they'll bring the dynamite with them.

PERKINS—(*aghast*) Do you think they really mean to blow up the engines?

JACK—They're crazy mad, sir. They'd do anything.

PERKINS—Dynamite these engines! (*resolutely*) No, I'll never permit them to do that. I couldn't. (*miserably*) I wish the chief was here.

JACK—You better give them a wide berth, sir. They're fighting mad. You better go up on deck, sir, before they come.

PERKINS—(*paying no attention*) Blow up those engines! (*his anger rising*) The blackguards!

JACK—(*glancing around apprehensively*) Better hurry, sir, or it'll be too late. They'll be here soon. Come up on deck, sir.

PERKINS—(*goes toward the stairs irresolutely, then stops, then resolutely*) No, I'll stay here. They mustn't harm the engines. I must see to that.

JACK—But how, sir?

PERKINS—(*helplessly*) I don't know, yet. (*bursting into rage*) The scoundrels. The scoundrels! Why can't they go on strike and leave the engines alone? (*suddenly goes to his uniform coat which hangs on one side and takes a revolver from the pocket and holds it in his hand gingerly*) The Chief told me to carry this, in case of trouble. (*holding it out to Jack*) Is it loaded? I can't tell. I've never touched one of the things before.

JACK—(*takes the revolver and breaks it—then hands it back*) Yes, sir, it's all loaded.

PERKINS—I might scare them off with this.

JACK—(*astonished*) You're not going to wait here till they come, sir?

PERKINS—Yes, of course. I can't let them touch the engines, you know, can I? (*furiously*) The scoundrels!

JACK—(*his eyes wide with surprised admiration*) Gee, you've got some nerve, sir.

PERKINS—You better run up and tell the mate to go ashore and get the police—and tell him to send someone to the Chief and ask what I better do.

JACK—(*reluctantly*) They're crazy, sir; and it's a hundred to one against you.

PERKINS—(*sharply*) Hurry now and do what I told you. (*Jack runs up the stairs. Perkins looks wildly around, terrified at finding himself alone—takes up his stand with his back to the engines, his knees trembling, his expression one of hopeless indecision. A moment later a crowd of the stokers enter the engine room. Many of them carry shovels, steel bars, etc.*)

PERKINS—(*weakly—the revolver hidden behind his back*) What do you men want here?

COCKY—Blimey, if it ain't old Molly Perkins.

HARRIS—(*derisively*) What do *you* want down here, 's what we wants to know.

COCKY—Better sling yer 'ook aht of 'ere, Molly.

PERKINS—(*dazed with terror at the threatening attitude of the crowd*) What do you want here?

HARRIS—We wants to repair yer engines for yer, that's what. (*a burst of laughter from the crowd*)

THE MEN—Tell him the air's better on deck.
　　　　　　　Push him outa the road!
　　　　　　　Let's get to work!

COCKY—Yes, the blarsted hofficers'll be 'ere in 'arf a mo.

A VOICE—(*angrily*) Fetch him a crack!

OTHER VOICES—Outa the way, Molly!
　　　　　　　Git up on deck!
　　　　　　　We don't wanta hurt you, Molly!
　　　　　　　Where's Tom Donovan? He said he'd fix
　　　　　　　　him.
　　　　　　　Hell! Let's do something!
　　　　　　　Where's Tom?

THE ANGRY VOICE—Kick the little runt outa the way! (*The crowd move threateningly toward Perkins.*)

PERKINS—(*protesting weakly*) Wait a minute, men. I want to say something to you.

THE ANGRY VOICE—Shut up!

OTHER VOICES—Let him talk if he wants to!
					Hurry up, Molly!
					To hell with him!
					Let's do something!
					No bloody speeches!

HARRIS—If yer got somethin' to say be quick about it; but I tells yer it ain't no use. We got a purpose in comin' here and we ain't goin' to weaken. (*to the crowd*) Are we, boys? (*a negative growl from the crowd*)

COCKY—'Urry, Molly, yer not standin' for Parliament.

PERKINS—Does—does this mean—you're on strike?

COCKY—Righto yer bloody well are, guv'nor.

HARRIS—That's what it means, Molly Perkins.

O'ROURKE—(*coming in from behind and pushing through the crowd*) Lave me pass, ye scuts!

HARRIS—Where's Tom?

O'ROURKE—Pershuadin' some av the white-livered wans in the stokehold to jine the party. I was for mashin' in their faces but he said no. (*He stands in front of Perkins.*) Well if it ain't me auld friend, Molly Perkins. The top av the evenin' to ye, Molly. T'was to see ye were not hurted by these rough bhoys here Tom sent me ahead av him.

PERKINS—(*pleadingly*) You're not going to harm the engines, are you, O'Rourke? (*a roar of angry laughter from the crowd*)

O'ROURKE—(*winking at them*) Indade not; how cud ye think ut? We've been commishuned by the Company to mend them a bit. T'was thought they needed fixin'. (*laughter from crowd*) And now, me little man, ye'd best be goin' up on deck to take a bit av fresh air. We've work to do, and 'tis no fit place for the loikes av you. (*taking a step toward Perkins*) Will ye go up on deck wid your own legs, or shall I carry ye?

PERKINS—(*producing the revolver from behind his back—in a frenzy of fear*) Don't you—don't you touch me! (*The crowd shrink back involuntarily.*)

HARRIS—Look out, Red, it might go off.

O'ROURKE—Put down that pisthol! It makes me nervous. Your hand is tremblin' so ye might pull the thrigger unbeknownst. I'll not touch ye yet awhile. (*Perkins lowers the revolver.*)

COCKY—'Eres a bloody mess!

O'ROURKE—(*scratching his head*) What I'm to do, I dunno. Were it not for what Tom Donovan made us promise I'd not be afraid av that squirt gun av his.

A VOICE—Here's Tom, now. (*They make way for Tom, who hurries through the crowd and confronts his father. He carries an iron bar on his shoulder. Perkins looks at him as if he could not believe his eyes. His arm falls to his side. He seems to crumple up, grow small and pitiful.*)

PERKINS—Tom!

TOM—(*quietly*) You'd better go up on deck.

PERKINS—Tom! Tom! Tom! Oh, who could think— (*He chokes with his emotion. The crowd murmurs:* "Molly knows him!" *etc.*)

TOM—(*with quiet contempt*) You'd better go up on deck where you'll be safe; and give me that revolver. (*He reaches out his hand for it. Perkins seems about to hand it over when one of the stokers reaches out with an iron bar and smashes the face of one of the steam gauges. Perkins starts as if coming out of a dream, stiffens, a look of resolution coming into his face. He backs away from Tom.*)

PERKINS—(*pointing his revolver in the direction of the man who smashed the gauge—in a firm voice*) Here, stop that! I can't permit that!

TOM—(*surprised*) Will you go up on deck, now?

PERKINS—(*firmly*) No, not until you have promised me not to touch the engines. (*breaking down for a second*) Tom, how could you? What have I done to you?

TOM—(*coldly*) We won't discuss personal matters. I'm a stranger to you. I'm Tom Donovan.

PERKINS—(*horrified*) You—Donovan—that scoundrel. Don't talk like that, Tom—to me—please don't talk like that to me! (*The hand holding the revolver drops to his side. He is crushed.*)

TOM—I've urged these men to revenge their wrongs at the Company's hands and we're going to do it.

PERKINS—No, no, I won't permit it! Not the engines! (*a threatening murmur from the crowd*)

HARRIS—You've done your best to help him, Donovan. If he want to act foolish then let him take the consequences, 's what I say.

A VOICE—Smash his damn head in!

TOM—(*whirling around*—*fiercely*) Who said that? (*No one answers*—*threateningly*.) If anyone touches the second engineer—

THE VOICE—(*sneeringly*) Who is he—your old man?

TOM—He *is* my father; and I won't have him touched!

PERKINS—(*wildly*) Tom! Tom! (*murmurs of astonishment from the crowd;* "Molly's his father! His name ain't Donovan. Maybe he's stallin'." *etc.*)

O'ROURKE—Ain't ut the divil's own luck now—wid all the other engineers we cud bate to a jelly!

TOM—(*pleadingly*) Please go up on deck, father.

PERKINS—Will you promise—

TOM—No. For the last time will you go up on deck or must I have you carried there by force?

PERKINS—(*weakening for a second*) Don't, Tom! Don't talk to me like that! (*The crowd push forward, jeering. Perkins flushes with anger*—*points his revolver at the crowd.*) Don't come too near, do you hear me! (*The men stop awed by the resolution in his tones.*)

TOM—(*with angry contempt*) What rot! What will you do if they do come nearer?

PERKINS—(*bravely*) I'll shoot the first man who touches the engines.

TOM—(*looks at his father for a moment with wonder*—*then laughs mockingly*) Oh, you will? (*He steps carelessly toward the engines, gripping the iron bar with both hands.*)

PERKINS—(*frenziedly*) Tom! Don't! (*lowers the revolver*)

TOM—(*pausing for a moment*—*laughs*) I knew you were only bluffing.

PERKINS—(*lifting the revolver again and pointing it in Tom's direction*—*in dead tones as if he didn't know what he was saying*) I'll shoot the first one who touches the engines.

TOM—(*laughing contemptuously*) Well, shoot then! (*With his iron bar he smashes the face of a gauge. There is a tinkle of glass followed by the report of a revolver. The expression on Tom's face turns to one of bewildered amazement. His knees sag and he pitches forward on his face and lies still.*)

PERKINS—(*dully*) Stand back, or I'll shoot! (*The crowd push away from him in horror, saying to each other:* "He's killed him! Dead as hell! His own son!")

A VOICE—(*loud with fear*) Let's get outa this! (*A sort of panic seizes the men. They rush from the engine room fighting with each other to be the first out. O'Rourke alone stands his ground.*)

O'ROURKE—(*looking down at Tom's body in horror*) He's hit in the head! (*to Perkins in hoarse voice*) Ye've murdered him, I'm tellin' you! (*Olga comes running down the ladder.*)

PERKINS—(*The revolver slips from his nerveless grasp and clatters on the floor. He looks down at Tom with eyes full of a dull amazement; then turns to O'Rourke with an air of stupid bewilderment.*) But I pointed it over his head, O'Rourke, I pointed it—over his head!

(*The Curtain Falls*)

ACT IV

SCENE—*A private room in a hospital in Liverpool—three weeks or so later. A dazzlingly-white, sunshiny room with a large, open, white-curtained window in the middle of left wall. Near the window, a rocking chair with cushions and a wicker table. In the rear, a white iron bed placed so that its occupant faces the audience. To the right of bed, a door. On the left of bed, a small stand with glass shelves on which are medicine bottles, glasses, etc. Two straight-backed chairs stand against the right wall.*

Tom is discovered sitting in the rocking chair, gazing out of the window with listless, half-closed eyes. His head is bandaged and his face is pale and thin. He wears a light colored bathrobe over his pajamas, and slippers.

A nurse is just finishing making up the bed. She is a short, stout, fresh-looking woman in her late thirties.

THE NURSE—(*coming over to Tom*) You must go back to bed now, Mr. Donovan. (*Tom looks at her blankly but does not answer or move. The nurse gives an irritated sigh.*) Bed! Bed! (*She points to the bed.*) Can't you understand? (*She puts her hand in under his arm. He gets out of the chair, slowly, mechanically, like a man in a dream. She supports him over to the bed, takes off his bathrobe and slippers, and tucks him in. He lies quietly, staring up at the ceiling. The doctor enters. He is an elderly man with grey mustache and beard.*)

THE DOCTOR—Well? Any change?

THE NURSE—No, Doctor, not a word out of him.

THE DOCTOR—(*looking keenly at Tom*) He seems much better, physically.

THE NURSE—He's getting stronger all the time. He slept well last night and ate a hearty breakfast.

THE DOCTOR—Good! Any temperature?

THE NURSE—No, Doctor. 98.6 the last time I took it.

THE DOCTOR—Perfectly normal, then. He'll be able to leave us soon. That trepanning saved his life. (*shakes his head sadly*) But I'm afraid his reason is gone.

THE NURSE—You don't think he'll ever be right in the head again?

THE DOCTOR—I'm afraid not—like a little child for the rest of his life.

THE NURSE—How awful! It would have been better if— (*She makes a suggestive gesture.*)

THE DOCTOR—(*solemnly*) You cannot set yourself against the laws of God and men without being punished. This is his punishment.

THE NURSE—And theirs?

THE DOCTOR—Theirs?

THE NURSE—All those who cared anything about him— his family.

THE DOCTOR—He doesn't seem to have any relatives alive. It's a pity. He might have been different if he had had the influence of a home. As it is, there's no trace of who he is or where he came from. He's one of those strange human strays one sometimes runs across.

THE NURSE—Didn't some say the engineer who shot him—was his father?

THE DOCTOR—Just a sensational fairy tale. It was absolutely discredited by the Ocean Company and by Mr. Perkins himself. Why, they're no more alike than—than you and I are.

THE NURSE—But the Anarchist woman whom they arrested and let go for lack of evidence—Olga something-or-other— She evidently cares about him. I was talking to her yesterday downstairs. She's been around every day to try and see him.

THE DOCTOR—(*shrugging his shoulders*) She may care—in the way such people do. She was probably his mistress.

THE NURSE—She told me they were engaged to be married.

THE DOCTOR—(*with a yawn*) Perhaps they were; but I thought their tribe went in for free love. (*suddenly*) Now that you remind me of it, she's waiting downstairs—she and that rascal, Whitely. I told her I might let her see him. (*indicating Tom*) She might as well know his state first as last. I think I'll try an experiment. The sight of her might bring him back to himself. One can never tell in such cases. Will you go down and ask them to come up?

THE NURSE—Yes, Doctor. (*goes out*)

THE DOCTOR—(*goes over and stands beside bed. Tom is still motionless, staring at the ceiling. The doctor speaks in sharp tones.*) San Francisco! Engine room! Olga! Strike! (*Tom does not move but turns and stares at the doctor blankly.*)

THE DOCTOR—(*turning away*) He's gone, poor chap! (*He goes to the window and stands looking out.*)

THE NURSE—(*entering*) This way, please. (*Olga enters followed by Whitely. Her face is weary and drawn, with dark circles in under the eyes. The doctor turns around and watches keenly the scene which follows.*)

OLGA—Tom! (*She goes quickly to bed and leans over and kisses him, hiding her face on his shoulder.*) Ah, how good it is to see you looking so well and your old self again— (*Tom pushes her away. He is staring at her blankly. She looks at his expressionless face in horror for a moment.*) Tom! Tom! Speak to me! (*Dead silence. She continues in tones of anguish*) Tom! Don't you know me? I love you, Tom! It's Olga! Olga!

TOM—(*slowly—childishly mimicking her voice*) Olga! Olga! (*He turns his eyes away from her and stares at the ceiling. She shrinks away from the bed, hiding her face in her hands.*)

THE DOCTOR—(*with satisfaction*) Ah, he spoke. (*comes over to bed*)

THE NURSE—First words I've ever heard him say.

THE DOCTOR—(*studying Tom keenly*) He spoke; but it was only the mimicking of a child. There was no recognition, no intelligence behind the words. I'm afraid— (*turns from the bed with a hopeless gesture*)

OLGA—(*taking her hands away from her face—to the doctor*) So—this was what you meant when you said his health would return but he would never be the same again!

THE DOCTOR—Yes.

OLGA—(*in agonized tones*) Ah, why didn't you tell me?

THE DOCTOR—(*coldly*) I hoped you would understand.

OLGA—And will he always be—like this?

THE DOCTOR—(*evidently voicing an opinion he does not feel*) Oh no, not necessarily. With care and the proper surroundings he will learn to speak again.

OLGA—*Learn* to speak again!

THE DOCTOR—He may even recover a part of his reason and memory.

OLGA—You are saying things you don't believe.

THE DOCTOR—(*sharply*) Don't jump at such hasty conclusions, Miss—er—Miss Tarnoff. The best of us are never absolutely sure in cases like this.

OLGA—(*pinning him down*) But *you* don't think he will ever recover.

THE DOCTOR—(*stiffly*) I must decline to answer such questions except to the immediate members of the man's family, if he has any.

OLGA—(*fiercely*) I love him and he—*loved* me!

THE DOCTOR—(*moved in spite of himself*) I understand from Miss Brown that you and he were engaged to be married?

OLGA—(*with a momentary show of hesitation*) Yes.

THE DOCTOR—Ah then, it is just as well to tell you that there is little hope for his reason—*but*—there is always a hope!

OLGA—(*despairingly*) Oh!

THE DOCTOR—(*looking at his watch*) I must be on my rounds. Perhaps if we leave the two of you alone with him—he knew you both well—it might—. We who are strangers to him may constitute an unfavorable influence. You might try to rouse some emotion, some memory. (*to nurse*) Come, Miss Brown. (*They go out. Whitely moves over to window and looks out.*)

OLGA—(*going to the bedside*) Tom! (*His eyes fix on her face but there is no expression in them.*) Tom, don't you remember me? (*She tries to kiss him, but he draws away from her with a frightened whimper—heartbrokenly*) Tom, don't you remember the happy days together—in our flat? And Hartmann? And Enwright? Surely you remember them! And the engine room on the *San Francisco*, and your father, and how you were shot? (*His eyes turn away from her face and he stares at the ceiling.*) Tom! (*her voice breaking*) Say you know me! I love you, Tom. It's Olga who is speaking to you! Olga! Olga!

TOM—(*mimicking her childishly*) Olga! Olga!

OLGA—(*turning from the bed—in a dead voice*) It's no use.

WHITELY—Shall I try?

OLGA—It's no use. Look at his eyes. They look at you and they don't see you. Oh, it's horrible! (*She shudders.*)

WHITELY—(*standing at the foot of the bed—in loud, commanding tones*) Look here, Tom, you haven't forgotten me, have you? (*A look of terror comes over Tom's face. He whimpers softly and draws the clothes up as if he were going to hide his head under them.*)

OLGA—Stop, Whitely. He doesn't recognize you and your loud voice frightens him. See! He is going to hide his head in under the clothes. (*tenderly*) Just like a child, a little child. (*She goes and puts her hand on Tom's forehead. He immediately grows quiet.*)

WHITELY—And to think of his being that way all his life! Good God!

OLGA—Don't! I can't bear to think of it.

WHITELY—Was it true, what you told the doctor—that he and you were engaged?

OLGA—No; we were just comrades.

WHITELY—I see.

OLGA—I had to tell them something which would give me a claim on him in their eyes. (*bitterly*) That I love him doesn't count.

WHITELY—Then when he is able to be taken away, you—?

OLGA—I shall take care of him.

WHITELY—Are you able to?—I mean, financially.

OLGA—I have a little in the bank, the remnant of what my father left me. It will be enough to keep us for a time—till I get work. And I am sure the comrades in New York will do all they can to help, when they know.

WHITELY—But his father?

OLGA—(*fiercely*) His father has no claim on him now.

WHITELY—He may not think so.

OLGA—No, the coward will be only too glad to get rid of such a living reproach. (*scornfully*) The Company has promoted him, made him a chief engineer, presented him with a gold watch for his heroism!

WHITELY—Strange the papers didn't say more about Tom being his son. They must have heard. All the men knew it.

OLGA—His father denied it himself, and, then, I suppose, the Company had it hushed up for the hero's sake.

WHITELY—Yes, that must be it.

OLGA—(*scornfully*) And then the papers gushed on about his sorrow! How he had hired a special room in the hospital for his victim! They would be sentimentalizing about it yet if the war hadn't broken out and given their silly patriotism an opportunity to slop over into pages of words.

WHITELY—It's just as well the *San Francisco* episode is forgotten. What a rotten fizzle it all was!

OLGA—(*slowly*) Yes, a rotten fizzle.

WHITELY—And the attempted strike! What a fiasco!

OLGA—And now all your brave strikers are waving flags and singing "God save the King!"

WHITELY—(*frowning*) This isn't an ordinary war, Olga. You can't condemn it on England's part.

OLGA—(*looking at him searchingly for a moment*) You, too!

WHITELY—(*flushing*) What do you mean?

OLGA—I mean that you are one of those Hartmann spoke of when he said that the ideal of the new freedom had interested their brains, but had not touched their hearts.

WHITELY—You're unjust, Olga. No one has fought for the I.W.E. more than I have or has suffered more for it!

OLGA—(*with a little sad smile—looking over at the bed*) Suffered?

WHITELY—(*shame-facedly*) I had forgotten.

OLGA—Here we are arguing about war and the I.W.E.—as if we were alone. (*She goes over to bed and puts her hand on Tom's forehead.*) Poor Tom! Forgotten already!

WHITELY—I wonder if his father is still on the *San Francisco.* She docks this morning.

OLGA—I suppose so. The papers said he wasn't to receive his new position till some boat they're overhauling gets out of dry dock. (*She comes away from bed.*)

WHITELY—He'll be up here, then.

OLGA—(*fiercely*) I hope he does come. They told him before he left that Tom was sure to get well. They wanted to get rid of him. He'll know now how true his aim was.

WHITELY—You think he'll let you take Tom? He has the right, you know.

OLGA—He must! He must! Do you think I would let him have Tom after he has done his best to murder him? Never!

WHITELY—You might not be able to prevent it.

OLGA—He can't refuse when he knows—when I tell him— (*She stops abruptly with a frightened glance at Whitely.*)

WHITELY—(*curiously*) What?

OLGA—Why it must be so.

WHITELY—This means giving up all your I.W.E. work, doesn't it?

OLGA—I will still do all I can. Even if it did mean giving up everything else in the world I would do it gladly. (*proudly*) For I love him! He went to death or worse for me, not the I.W.E. I see that now. He was only a great big boy and he followed blindly where I led him. (*choking with her emotion*) That is what makes it so hard. I realize it was all through me—this—all my fault. I owe him a lifetime of reparation.

WHITELY—(*looking at Tom compassionately*) It's well he has someone, poor old chap!

OLGA—I had a foreboding of misfortune to him that night in the fo'castle. I had my moment of womanly weakness when, ideals or no ideals, I wanted to save the man I loved. I thought you were going to bring the dynamite, and I implored him to step out, to quit, as he said, and let you destroy the engines.

WHITELY—I wanted him to let me do it.

OLGA—I knew that; and I was afraid the dynamite would explode prematurely, or something of the sort.

WHITELY—(*with a grim smile*) It was perfectly right for me to blow up, eh?

OLGA—I was only thinking of saving him; I didn't care how. But he wouldn't. He thought I would despise him if he failed in his mission.

WHITELY—And you would have—afterwards.

OLGA—You don't understand. I love him.

THE NURSE—(*knocks and enters—looks from one to the other*) He hasn't recognized you?

OLGA—No.

THE NURSE—The engineer, Perkins, is coming up.

OLGA—(*fiercely*) Ah!

WHITELY—Then I'll be going.

OLGA—And I'll stay.

WHITELY—I'll come back for you in, say, a quarter of an hour, Olga?

OLGA—Yes. (*Whitely goes out.*) Has the Doctor told him about Tom?

THE NURSE—Yes. He's all broken up, poor little man, but he insisted on seeing him. (*The nurse indicates Tom.*) He told the doctor that it was true what they were saying—that this really is his son.

OLGA—Ah. (*Perkins enters accompanied by the doctor. Perkins is bowed down by grief. He is sobbing and holds a handkerchief to his eyes.*)

THE DOCTOR—See if he knows you.

PERKINS—(*at foot of bed—faintly*) Tom! (*then louder*) Tom! (*Tom turns his eyes and looks at his father blankly, without recognition. Perkins puts the handkerchief to his eyes and turns away.*)

THE DOCTOR—(*shaking his head*) Not a gleam of recognition. (*turning to Olga*) You were unsuccessful?

OLGA—Yes.

THE DOCTOR—(*to Perkins*) You know Miss—er—Miss Tarnoff, the fiancée of your son?

PERKINS—(*looking at Olga—timidly*) Is this—Olga?

OLGA—(*coldly*) Yes.

PERKINS—And you and Tom—were to be—married?

OLGA—Yes. (*to the doctor*) Would you mind leaving Mr. Perkins and myself alone for a few minutes? I have something to say to him. And we might (*indicating the form in the bed*) try again together.

THE DOCTOR—(*with a shrug of his shoulders at the uselessness of such efforts*) Certainly. (*He and the nurse go out.*)

PERKINS—(*nervously*) Something—to say—to me?

OLGA—(*in hard tones*) So you finally acknowledged he is your son? I should think you would have kept on denying it, as you started out to do.

PERKINS—It was for his sake—I denied it before. I was afraid—when he got well that it would hurt his chances—having people know what he had done.

OLGA—And what you had done. (*a pause*) Well? Are you satisfied?

PERKINS—Satisfied?

OLGA—Satisfied with your work by which you earned promotion?

PERKINS—(*wildly*) Don't, Miss Olga, please! If you knew how I have suffered since they told me. They said before I went away that Tom would be all right—and I believed them, really I did, or I wouldn't have made the trip. And now— (*raises handkerchief to his eyes*)

OLGA—(*cruelly*) Your aim was better than you thought.

PERKINS—Aim? (*brokenly*) I couldn't aim. I never had one of those things in my hand before, really I didn't; and I pointed it over his head. I never meant to fire. I meant to scare them—and then—it went off. (*seeing the incredulous look on Olga's face*) Oh, how can you think such a thing—that I could mean to shoot—Tom? He was the only one in the world I loved, the only one left to me—

OLGA—(*with cruel enjoyment of his anguish*) You have your engines.

PERKINS—Don't! I hate them, now. I have ever since. I will always hate them. It's all changed, now.

OLGA—When it's too late.

PERKINS—I pointed it over his head! I didn't mean to fire it—I swear I didn't. (*sobbing*) Oh why can't someone believe me? Nobody does. They say yes but I feel they don't. Why don't you believe me?

OLGA—It doesn't matter much now whether you meant to fire or not. It's done—and it can't be undone!

PERKINS—But the doctor said, with good care—there was hope.

OLGA—He says that but he knows it isn't so. There is no hope. Tom will be like that, like a child, for the rest of his life.

PERKINS—(*with an apprehensive glance at the bed*) Sshh! He may hear you.

OLGA—(*slowly*) You forget—he can hear nothing now.

PERKINS—No, no, it can't be true! (*going to bed—pitifully*) Tom! Tom! (*But Tom's eyes are now closed.*)

OLGA—(*going over to bed quickly*) Sshh! He is asleep! (*They both lower their voices for the moment and come over by the window.*)

OLGA—The doctor says he is getting stronger every day—physically. He will soon be able to leave.

PERKINS—Yes; he told me, too.

OLGA—(*with a defiant look at Perkins*) I shall take him out in the country some place where no one knows us—

PERKINS—(*angrily*) You—you will take him!

OLGA—Yes.

PERKINS—Take him—away from me!

OLGA—Yes. You must realize that you have forfeited all right by—what you did.

PERKINS—No! No!

OLGA—And you will be on ship. How could you look after him?

PERKINS—I am leaving—the Company.

OLGA—You have not accepted the promotion?

PERKINS—No.

OLGA—What will you do?

PERKINS—I don't know. I hate the engines. I can't work with them any more.

OLGA—(*with a frightened expression*) Then you're going to live on shore?

PERKINS—Yes; in the house I meant for him. I resolved on this during the last trip—when I found I hated the engines. They've promised me a position on shore.

OLGA—And you mean to take him with you?

PERKINS—Yes. I have Mrs. Allen—

OLGA—He hated her.

PERKINS——to keep house for me, and she will help to take care of him.

OLGA—And I?

PERKINS—You? (*with a burst of angry grief*) I wish he had never seen you. You are to blame for everything. It was you who got him in with the dynamite people. It was you who drove him to lead those men on strike. It's all your fault, all your fault!

OLGA—(*defiantly*) I love him.

PERKINS—And don't his own father love him?

OLGA—You shot him!

PERKINS—(*wildly*) I pointed it over his head! It was only to scare them. Oh, why can't anyone believe me? He was all I had to live for. You are young and I am over sixty. He is all I have in the world. I won't let you take him!

OLGA—You must! He loved me, and not you.

PERKINS—(*wildly*) It's a lie, a wicked lie! He did! He did! He was only a boy—and thoughtless—and you led him away from me—

OLGA—(*relentlessly*) If he could choose, he would come with me. You know it.

PERKINS—It's a lie, a lie! You can't have him. They know I'm his father. They won't let you have him.

OLGA—(*realizing the truth of this—pleadingly*) I will forget all—I will forgive all you have done to make my life miserable if you will let me take him.

PERKINS—(*touched in spite of himself*) No, I can't. What would I have left to live for alone—with the memory of him. I couldn't stand it.

OLGA—I implore you, if you love him. You know he loved me. He must have told you.

PERKINS—(*in a whisper*) Yes. He told me—once.

OLGA—You know it would be his wish to be with me if he could speak.

PERKINS—You don't know what you're asking. You would rob me—of everything. I must bring him back to himself so he can forgive me. I must make up to him—for what I have done—as far as possible.

OLGA—I owe him reparation too, for my sin against him. You were right—when you said it was my fault—as well as yours.

PERKINS—Ah, you admit it!

OLGA—He did follow where I led, but, oh, I never thought—I didn't realize the danger to him till it was too late. I didn't realize he was doing it only for me. (*pleadingly*) So you see I have my debt to pay back, my forgiveness to win. Let him come with me!

PERKINS—No! It's impossible. You have no money, have you?

OLGA—I will work!

PERKINS—And no home of your own?

OLGA—I will make one for him!

PERKINS—You see? It's impossible. How would he get proper care? Who would look after him?

OLGA—(*wildly—begging*) Please, Mr. Perkins! You love

him, you say; and you know he loved me. I cannot live without him. Would you kill me, too?

PERKINS—(*affected—raising the handkerchief to his eyes*) It is too much for you to ask, Miss Olga. Haven't you any pity for me? No! He has met harm through being with you.

OLGA—(*furiously*) You dare to say that to me! And *you* shot him! Shot your own son in cold blood! Murderer! Murderer!

PERKINS—(*faintly*) No, no! Not that name! I can't bear it! (*sobbing*) Won't you believe me? I pointed it over his head.

OLGA—And not content with killing him, you will kill his child!

PERKINS—(*stupidly*) His child? What child?

OLGA—The child I will bear which is his, your son's. If you do not let me have Tom, I will kill it, I will never allow it to be born. I will kill my child as you have yours! (*She leans against the table, nearly fainting.*)

PERKINS—(*tremblingly*) Dear God! You are going to have a child?—Tom's child? Did he know this before—

OLGA—No—unless he guessed—that last night on the *San Francisco*—I tried to make him understand—why I had changed so—grown so weak and tender toward him—

PERKINS—(*as if he didn't yet understand*) My Tom's child!

OLGA—(*pleadingly*) Yes! The child of our love. You will not take its father away from me, will you? You cannot be as bad, as hard-hearted as that.

PERKINS—(*after a pause—hesitatingly*) Do you—hate me so very much?

OLGA—I will hate you from the bottom of my soul if you take him away from me. But I will forgive you everything— I will even love you, as his father if you will let me take care of him.

PERKINS—(*slowly*) I have hated you too, God forgive me, because I thought—you were to blame. (*a slight pause*) If I let you have him—will you bring him to my home—and live there—with me?

OLGA—Live—in your home?

PERKINS—No one will ever know you were not married. We will say you were married over here.

OLGA—*Your* home! No, I couldn't, I couldn't.

PERKINS—You have no place to take him, you know—and I have the home I meant for him—for his wedding present. It will be his home and his child's. He has a right to come there—and you—

OLGA—Give me time—to think.

PERKINS—You have no money and you will not be able to work—soon. Who will take care of you and Tom—and the child—then? Please let me do it. It is my right, isn't it? When Tom knows—when he is in his right mind again—he might forgive—

OLGA—(*with deep sorrow*) He will never be himself again!

PERKINS—(*obstinately*) The doctor said there was still a hope—with good care. I will work on shore or on the ship—anything for him—and I won't bother you much if I am on ship. And Mrs. Allen will take care of you when—

OLGA—Oh, this is good of you—but—

PERKINS—Please consent—if you don't hate me—too much. You are his wife, really. I know he loved you, and would have married you—if—if it wasn't for what I did. (*Olga is silent—simply*) It is settled, then. When he's strong enough we'll take him home together.

OLGA—(*holding out her hand to Perkins*) I am very grateful—and I know you love him—and I know you didn't mean—what happened.

PERKINS—(*taking her hand—humbly*) Thank you so for believing that. You're the only one. (*He gulps.*)

OLGA—We'll take good care of him together, you and I, and we'll fight for that one hope the doctor held out. Who knows? It may be a real hope, after all.

PERKINS—And do you think—when he gets back his mind—and knows—he'll forgive me?

OLGA—I'm sure he will forgive—both of us.

PERKINS—I do hope and pray so, I do, indeed. (*as an afterthought*) And when he's all right again, you can be married, can't you? (*Olga doesn't answer—Tom stirs in the bed and opens his eyes.*)

PERKINS—Look! He's awake again. He's looking at us. (*They both go to the side of the bed.*)

OLGA—(*tenderly*) Poor little child! (*Tom reaches up and takes one of her hands.*) See! He's taken my hand. (*Tom holds his other hand out toward his father*.) He wants to take yours. (*Perkins puts his hand in Tom's. He and Olga look at each other in wonder across the bed.*)

PERKINS—(*in stifled tones*) Tom! (*to Olga*) Do you suppose—he understands.

OLGA—Yes, I feel sure he does.

PERKINS—Then—he has forgiven me.

OLGA—He has forgiven *us*. (*Tom lets both of their hands go and turns his eyes again to the ceiling.*)

PERKINS—(*dabbing at his eyes with his handkerchief*) I must go and tell the doctor what we have decided—if you'll excuse me. He wanted to know what arrangements I would make.

OLGA—Yes, you'd better tell him.

PERKINS—I'll be right back, right back. (*He goes to the door. In the doorway he nearly collides with Whitely, who enters as Perkins goes out.*)

WHITELY—(*in a state of great excitement—pointing to the newspaper in his hand*) See what they've done now!

OLGA—Who?

WHITELY—The Germans—dropped bombs on an orphan asylum and killed twenty children! (*then exultantly*) But they've paid for it, the swine! The Russians have beaten them in a big battle in East Prussia.

OLGA—(*amazed*) And *you* are rejoicing over a *Russian* victory!

WHITELY—(*abashed*) Anything to beat *them*.

OLGA—(*scornfully*) You'll enlist next.

WHITELY—(*flushing angrily*) By God, if they keep on doing things like this—(*slapping the newspaper*) I *will* enlist! And so will every other red-blooded man.

OLGA—(*with quiet scorn*) Don't you know these stories are written just to make people like you enlist?

WHITELY—(*insisting*) But this is true—vouched for by a person who was in the town and saw it. (*a faint sound of music*) Ssshh! Listen! (*The strains of a far-off marching tune come through the open window. Whitely's face lights up.*) Troops! Off for the front. (*He hums the tune, beating time with his feet.*)

OLGA—Poor sheep!

WHITELY—You'd understand—if it was your country engaged.

OLGA—Liberty—that is my country.

WHITELY—Can't you see that these swine must be crushed, or—it's a case of eat or be eaten. The country must be defended.

OLGA—Every soldier in each one of the nations at war was called to arms to defend his country.

WHITELY—(*lamely*) Our case is—well, it's right, you can't deny it.

OLGA—And each one thinks that. (*a pause*) So, as far as you are concerned, the social revolution can take care of itself, now when it needs you most!

WHITELY—It's no time for it now. What's the use? Who would listen to you? This is the upheaval of everything.

OLGA—You might be true to our ideals. We have preached against war always.

WHITELY—This is different, Olga. This is a just war, a war forced upon us.

OLGA—And each one of them thinks the same, poor fools!

WHITELY—(*angrily*) How about most of the great Radical leaders? Socialist, Syndicalist, or Anarchist, here and in France and Russia? Haven't they all realized that this was no time to quibble over theories.

OLGA—Theories!

WHITELY—Kropotkin, the great Communist? Hasn't he come out and said it was the duty of every man, no matter what he believes, to crush German militarism? I tell you we've got to back up the government until this war is won; and they're all doing it—Socialists, Syndicalists and all of them.

OLGA—Then they are all blind fools—or traitors.

WHITELY—(*irritably*) I can't talk to you. You won't see. (*after a pause, brutally*) I shouldn't think you'd care much about the social revolution—now!

OLGA—(*slowly*) You mean—after it has ruined my life? (*Whitely nods, a bit ashamed of what he has said. Olga's eyes flash.*) Oh, you fool! You blind fool! What am I? What is my small happiness worth in the light of so great a struggle? We fight, and at times like the present, it seems hopelessly. We fight and we go down before the might of Society; but the

Revolution marches on over our bodies. It moves forward though we may not see it. We are the bridge. Our sacrifice is never in vain. It is enough for us to know we are doing our small part, and that our little lives and little deaths count after all. No, let the others wave flags and cheer and forswear their faith. (*proudly*) I have suffered and will suffer more than any of them; and I am proud that I can still cry from the depths of my soul: It is well done! Long live the Revolution! (*She stands proudly erect, inspired, exalted. Whitely is awed in spite of himself. And then*—)

TOM—(*with a low, chuckling laugh—mimicking Olga*) Long—live—the Revolution. (*His vacant eyes turn from one to the other of them. A stupid smile plays about his loose lips. Whitely turns away with a shudder. Olga stares at the figure in the bed with fascinated horror—then covers her face with her hands as*

The Curtain Falls)

BEFORE BREAKFAST

A Play in One Act

CHARACTER

MRS. ROWLAND

Before Breakfast

SCENE—*A small room serving both as kitchen and dining room in a flat on Christopher Street, New York City. In the rear, to the right, a door leading to the outer hallway. On the left of the doorway, a sink, and a two-burner gas stove. Over the stove, and extending to the left wall, a wooden closet for dishes, etc. On the left, two windows looking out on a fire escape where several potted plants are dying of neglect. Before the windows, a table covered with oilcloth. Two cane-bottomed chairs are placed by the table. Another stands against the wall to the right of door in rear. In the right wall, rear, a doorway leading into a bedroom. Farther forward, different articles of a man's and a woman's clothing are hung on pegs. A clothes line is strung from the left corner, rear, to the right wall, forward.*

It is about eight-thirty in the morning of a fine, sunshiny day in the early fall.

Mrs. Rowland enters from the bedroom, yawning, her hands still busy putting the finishing touches on a slovenly toilet by sticking hairpins into her hair which is bunched up in a drab-colored mass on top of her round head. She is of medium height and inclined to a shapeless stoutness, accentuated by her formless blue dress, shabby and worn. Her face is characterless, with small regular features and eyes of a nondescript blue. There is a pinched expression about her eyes and nose and her weak, spiteful mouth. She is in her early twenties but looks much older.

She comes to the middle of the room and yawns, stretching her arms to their full length. Her drowsy eyes stare about the room with the irritated look of one to whom a long sleep has not been a long rest. She goes wearily to the clothes hanging on the right and takes an apron from a hook. She ties it about her waist, giving vent to an exasperated "damn" when the knot fails to obey her clumsy fingers. Finally gets it tied and goes slowly to the gas stove and lights one burner. She fills the coffee pot at the sink and sets it over the flame. Then slumps down into a chair by the table and puts a hand over her forehead as if she were suffering from headache. Suddenly her face brightens as though she had remembered something, and she casts a quick glance at the dish closet; then looks sharply at the bedroom door and listens intently for a moment or so.

MRS. ROWLAND—(*in a low voice*) Alfred! Alfred! (*There is no answer from the next room and she continues suspiciously in a louder tone*) You needn't pretend you're asleep. (*There is no reply to this from the bedroom, and, reassured, she gets up from her chair and tiptoes cautiously to the dish closet. She slowly opens one door, taking great care to make no noise, and slides out, from their hiding place behind the dishes, a bottle of Gordon gin and a glass. In doing so she disturbs the top dish, which rattles a little. At this sound she starts guiltily and looks with sulky defiance at the doorway to the next room.*)

(*Her voice trembling*) Alfred!

(*After a pause, during which she listens for any sound, she takes the glass and pours out a large drink and gulps it down; then hastily returns the bottle and glass to their hiding place. She closes the closet door with the same care as she had opened it, and, heaving a great sigh of relief, sinks down into her chair again. The large dose of alcohol she has taken has an almost immediate effect. Her features become more animated, she seems to gather energy, and she looks at the bedroom door with a hard, vindictive smile on her lips. Her eyes glance quickly about the room and are fixed on a man's coat and vest which hang from a hook at right. She moves stealthily over to the open doorway and stands there, out of sight of anyone inside, listening for any movement.*)

(*Calling in a half-whisper*) Alfred!

(*Again there is no reply. With a swift movement she takes the coat and vest from the hook and returns with them to her chair. She sits down and takes the various articles out of each pocket but quickly puts them back again. At last, in the inside pocket of the vest, she finds a letter.*)

(*Looking at the handwriting—slowly to herself*) Hmm! I knew it.

(*She opens the letter and reads it. At first her expression is one of hatred and rage, but as she goes on to the end it changes to one of triumphant malignity. She remains in deep thought for a moment, staring before her, the letter in her hands, a cruel smile on her lips. Then she puts the letter back in the pocket of the vest, and still careful not to awaken the sleeper, hangs the clothes up again on the same hook, and goes to the bedroom door and looks in.*)

(*In a loud, shrill voice*) Alfred! (*still louder*) Alfred! (*There is a muffled, yawning groan from the next room.*) Don't you think it's about time you got up? Do you want to stay in bed all day? (*turning around and coming back to her chair*) Not that I've got any doubts about your being lazy enough to stay in bed forever. (*She sits down and looks out of the window, irritably*) Goodness knows what time it is. We haven't even got any way of telling the time since you pawned your watch like a fool. The last valuable thing we had, and you knew it. It's been nothing but pawn, pawn, pawn, with you—anything to put off getting a job, anything to get out of going to work like a man. (*She taps the floor with her foot nervously, biting her lips.*)

(*After a short pause*) Alfred! Get up, do you hear me? I want to make that bed before I go out. I'm sick of having this place in a continual muss on your account. (*with a certain vindictive satisfaction*) Not that we'll be here long unless you manage to get some money some place. Heaven knows I do my part— and more—going out to sew every day while you play the gentleman and loaf around bar rooms with that good-for-nothing lot of artists from the Square.

(*A short pause during which she plays nervously with a cup and saucer on the table.*)

And where are you going to get money, I'd like to know? The rent's due this week and you know what the landlord is. He won't let us stay a minute over our time. You say you *can't* get a job. That's a lie and you know it. You never even look for one. All you do is moon around all day writing silly poetry and stories that no one will buy—and no wonder they won't. I notice I can always get a position, such as it is; and it's only that which keeps us from starving to death.

(*Gets up and goes over to the stove—looks into the coffee pot to see if the water is boiling; then comes back and sits down again.*)

You'll have to get money to-day some place. I can't do it all, and I won't do it all. You've got to come to your senses. You've got to beg, borrow, or steal it somewheres. (*with a contemptuous laugh*) But where, I'd like to know? You're too proud to beg, and you've borrowed the limit, and you haven't the nerve to steal.

(*After a pause—getting up angrily*) Aren't you up yet, for heaven's sake? It's just like you to go to sleep again, or pretend to. (*She goes to the bedroom door and looks in.*) Oh, you are up. Well, it's about time. You needn't look at me like that. Your airs don't fool me a bit any more. I know you too well—better than you think I do—you and your goings-on. (*turning away from the door—meaningly*) I know a lot of things, my dear. Never mind what I know, now. I'll tell you before I go, you needn't worry. (*She comes to the middle of the room and stands there, frowning.*)

(*Irritably*) Hmm! I suppose I might as well get breakfast ready—not that there's anything much to get. (*questioningly*) Unless you have some money? (*She pauses for an answer from the next room which does not come.*) Foolish question! (*She gives a short, hard laugh.*) I ought to know you better than that by this time. When you left here in such a huff last night I knew what would happen. You can't be trusted for a second. A nice condition you came home in! The fight we had was only an excuse for you to make a beast of yourself. What was the use pawning your watch if all you wanted with the money was to waste it in buying drink?

(*Goes over to the dish closet and takes out plates, cups, etc., while she is talking.*)

Hurry up! It don't take long to get breakfast these days, thanks to you. All we got this morning is bread and butter and coffee; and you wouldn't even have that if it wasn't for me sewing my fingers off. (*She slams the loaf of bread on the table with a bang.*)

The bread's stale. I hope you'll like it. *You* don't deserve any better, but I don't see why *I* should suffer.

(*Going over to the stove*) The coffee'll be ready in a minute, and you needn't expect me to wait for you.

(*Suddenly with great anger*) What on earth are you doing all this time? (*She goes over to the door and looks in.*) Well, you're *almost* dressed at any rate. I expected to find you back in bed. That'd be just like you. How awful you look this morning! For heaven's sake, shave! You're disgusting! You look like a tramp. No wonder no one will give you a job. I don't blame them—when you don't even look half-way decent. (*She goes to the stove.*) There's plenty of hot water right here. You've got no excuse. (*gets a bowl and pours some of the water from the coffee pot into it*) Here.

(*He reaches his hand into the room for it. It is a sensitive hand with slender fingers. It trembles and some of the water spills on the floor.*)

(*Tauntingly*) Look at your hand tremble! You'd better give up drinking. You can't stand it. It's just your kind that get the D. T's. *That would be* the last straw! (*looking down at the floor*) Look at the mess you've made of this floor—cigarette butts and ashes all over the place. Why can't you put them on a plate? No, you wouldn't be considerate enough to do that. You never think of me. You don't have to sweep the room and that's all you care about.

(*Takes the broom and commences to sweep viciously, raising a cloud of dust. From the inner room comes the sound of a razor being stropped.*)

(*Sweeping*) Hurry up! It must be nearly time for me to go. If I'm late I'm liable to lose my position, and then I couldn't support you any longer. (*As an afterthought she adds sarcastically*) And then you'd have to go to work or something dreadful like that. (*sweeping under the table*) What I want to know is whether you're going to look for a job to-day or not. You know your family won't help us any more. They've had enough of you, too. (*after a moment's silent sweeping*) I'm about sick of all this life. I've a good notion to go home, if I wasn't too proud to let them know what a failure you've been—you, the millionaire Rowland's only son, the Harvard graduate, the poet, the catch of the town—Huh! (*with bitterness*) There wouldn't be many of them now envy my catch if they knew the truth. What has our marriage been, I'd like to know? Even before your *millionaire* father died owing every one in the world money, you certainly never wasted any of your time on your wife. I suppose you thought I'd ought to be glad you were *honorable* enough to marry me—after getting me into trouble. You were ashamed of me with your fine friends because my father's only a grocer, that's what you were. At least he's honest, which is more than any one could say about yours. (*She is sweeping steadily toward the door. Leans on her broom for a moment.*)

You hoped every one'd think you'd been forced to marry me, and pity you, didn't you? You didn't hesitate much about telling me you loved me, and making me believe your lies, before it happened, did you? You made me think you didn't want your father to buy me off as he tried to do. I know better now. I haven't lived with you all this time for nothing. (*somberly*) It's lucky the poor thing was born dead, after all. What a father you'd have been!

(*Is silent, brooding moodily for a moment—then she continues with a sort of savage joy.*)

But I'm not the only one who's got you to thank for being unhappy. There's one other, at least, and *she* can't hope to marry you now. (*She puts her head into the next room.*) How about Helen? (*She starts back from the doorway, half frightened.*)

Don't look at me that way! Yes, I read her letter. What about it? I got a right to. I'm your wife. And I know all there is to know, so don't lie. You needn't stare at me so. You can't bully me with your superior airs any longer. Only for me you'd be going without breakfast this very morning. (*She sets the broom back in the corner—whiningly*) You never did have any gratitude for what I've done. (*She comes to the stove and puts the coffee into the pot.*) The coffee's ready. I'm not going to wait for you. (*She sits down in her chair again.*)

(*After a pause—puts her hand to her head—fretfully*) My head aches so this morning. It's a shame I've got to go to work in a stuffy room all day in my condition. And I wouldn't if you were half a man. By rights I ought to be lying on my back instead of you. You know how sick I've been this last year; and yet you object when I take a little something to keep up my spirits. You even didn't want me to take that tonic I got at the drug store. (*with a hard laugh*) I know you'd be glad to have me dead and out of your way; then you'd be free to run after all these silly girls that think you're such a wonderful, misunderstood person—this Helen and the others. (*There is a sharp exclamation of pain from the next room.*)

(*With satisfaction*) There! I knew you'd cut yourself. It'll be a lesson to you. You know you oughtn't to be running around nights drinking with your nerves in such an awful shape. (*She goes to the door and looks in.*)

What makes you so pale? What are you staring at yourself in the mirror that way for? For goodness sake, wipe that blood off your face! (*with a shudder*) It's horrible. (*in relieved tones*) There, that's better. I never could stand the sight of blood. (*She shrinks back from the door a little.*) You better give up trying and go to a barber shop. Your hand shakes dreadfully. Why do you stare at me like that? (*She turns away from the door.*) Are you still mad at me about that letter? (*defiantly*) Well, I had a right to read it. I'm your wife. (*She comes to the chair and sits down again. After a pause*)

I knew all the time you were running around with some one. Your lame excuses about spending the time at the library didn't fool me. Who is this Helen, anyway? One of those artists? Or does she write poetry, too? Her letter sounds that way. I'll bet she told you your things were the best ever, and you believed her, like a fool. Is she young and pretty? I was young and pretty, too, when you fooled me with your fine, poetic talk; but life with you would soon wear anyone down. What I've been through!

(*Goes over and takes the coffee off the stove*) Breakfast is ready. (*with a contemptuous glance*) Breakfast! (*pours out a cup of coffee for herself and puts the pot on the table*) Your coffee'll be cold. What are you doing—still shaving, for heaven's sake? You'd better give it up. One of these mornings you'll give yourself a serious cut. (*She cuts off bread and butters it. During the following speeches she eats and sips her coffee.*)

I'll have to run as soon as I've finished eating. One of us has got to work. (*angrily*) Are you going to look for a job today or aren't you? I should think some of your fine friends would help you, if they really think you're so much. But I guess they just like to hear you talk. (*sits in silence for a moment*)

I'm sorry for this Helen, whoever she is. Haven't you got any feelings for other people? What will her family say? I see she mentions them in her letter. What is she going to do— have the child—or go to one of those doctors? That's a nice thing, I must say. Where can she get the money? Is she rich? (*She waits for some answer to this volley of questions.*)

Hmm! You won't tell me anything about her, will you? Much I care. Come to think of it, I'm not so sorry for her after all. She knew what she was doing. She isn't any schoolgirl, like I was, from the looks of her letter. Does she know you're married? Of course, she must. All your friends know about your unhappy marriage. I know they pity you, but they don't know my side of it. They'd talk different if they did.

(*Too busy eating to go on for a second or so.*)

This Helen must be a fine one, if she knew you were married. What does she expect, then? That I'll divorce you and let her marry you? Does she think I'm crazy enough for that—after all you've made me go through? I guess not! And you can't get a divorce from me and you know it. No one can say *I've* ever done anything wrong. (*drinks the last of her cup of coffee*)

She deserves to suffer, that's all I can say. I'll tell you what I think; I think your Helen is no better than a common street-walker, that's what I think. (*There is a stifled groan of pain from the next room.*)

Did you cut yourself again? Serves you right. (*gets up and takes off her apron*) Well, I've got to run along. (*peevishly*) This is a fine life for me to be leading! I won't stand for your loafing any longer. (*Something catches her ear and she pauses and listens intently.*) There! You've overturned the water all over everything. Don't say you haven't. I can hear it dripping on the floor. (*A vague expression of fear comes over her face.*) Alfred! Why don't you answer me?

(*She moves slowly toward the room. There is the noise of a chair being overturned and something crashes heavily to the floor. She stands, trembling with fright.*)

Alfred! Alfred! Answer me! What is it you knocked over? Are you still drunk? (*Unable to stand the tension a second longer she rushes to the door of the bedroom.*)

Alfred!

(*She stands in the doorway looking down at the floor of the inner room, transfixed with horror. Then she shrieks wildly and runs to the other door, unlocks it and frenziedly pulls it open, and runs shrieking madly into the outer hallway.*)

(*The Curtain Falls*)

NOW I ASK YOU

A Play in Three Acts, a Prologue,
and an Epilogue

CHARACTERS

RICHARD ASHLEIGH
MRS. ASHLEIGH, *his wife*
LUCY, *their daughter*
TOM DRAYTON
LEONORA BARNES
GABRIEL ADAMS
DRAYTON'S CHAUFFER
A MAID AT THE ASHLEIGH'S
A MAID AT THE DRAYTON'S

PROLOGUE: The Library of the Drayton's home in the suburbs of New York City.
ACT ONE: The sitting room of the Ashleigh's house near Gramercy Park, New York City.
ACT TWO: Same as Prologue. Three months later.
ACT THREE: Same as Act Two. A month later.
EPILOGUE: Same as Prologue.

Now I Ask You
PROLOGUE

SCENE—*A dark room, the library of a house in a fashionable New York suburb. In the rear, french windows looking out on the lawn and the driveway in front of the house. On the left, a doorway leading to the main hall. On the right, another doorway screened by heavy portieres. Bookcases around the walls. In the center of the room, a table with books, periodicals, and a reading lamp on it.*

The room is in darkness except for the light from the hallway. The portieres on the right are cautiously parted and Lucy enters. She stops and stands motionless for a moment or so in an attitude of strained attention, evidently listening for some sound from the hallway. Hearing nothing, she goes to the table and throws herself into a chair beside it. She rests her head on her outstretched arms and sobs softly. Making an effort to control herself, she dries her eyes hastily with her handkerchief, gets up, and walks nervously from the table to the windows and back again.

She stands by the table for a minute staring straight before her, her expression betraying the somber thoughts which are passing through her brain. Then, with a quick movement of decision, she pulls out a drawer in the table and slowly takes a revolver from it. She looks at it with frightened eyes and puts it down on the table with a convulsive shudder.

There is the sound of a motor from the roadway outside. Lucy gives a nervous start and looks quickly around the room as if searching for a hiding place. She finally hurries back into the room on the right, pulling the portieres together behind her. The noise of the motor grows steadily louder. At last the machine stops in front of the main entrance of the house, and only the soft purr of the engine is heard. The glare from the headlamps pierces the darkness beyond the french windows.

Someone is heard walking along the hallway to the front door. The outer door is heard opening. There is a brief murmur of the voices of chauffer and the maid. Then the door is closed again. Tom's voice is heard calling from the top of the hall stairs: "Is that the car?" *The maid's voice answers:* "Yes, sir.", *and she is heard returning to the rear of the house.*

*Tom and Leonora are heard conversing as they come down the stairs in the hall. Leonora's infectious laughter rings out. Tom appears in evening dress in the doorway, left, and looks toward the door at the right. He calls softly: "*Lucy*"; then takes a step forward into the room. Leonora calls to him from the hall: "*We'll be late.*" Tom makes a movement of impatience and raises his voice:* "Lucy!"

LEONORA—(*from the hallway*) She's probably out in the garden mooning with Gab. Come on!

Tom allows a muttered "damn" *to escape him, and walks back into the hall.*

The outer door is again opened and shut. Lucy comes out from behind the portieres and goes quickly to the table. The sound of the limousine door being slammed is heard. A wild look of determination comes into Lucy's face and she snatches the revolver from the table. The noise of the motor increases in volume. The curtain starts to fall. The car outside starts. Closing her eyes tightly, Lucy lifts the revolver to her temple. The curtain hides her from view. As it touches the stage there is the sound of a shot.

ACT ONE

SCENE—*The living room of the Ashleighs home in the neigh-borhood of Gramercy Park, New York City. It is a large, high-ceilinged room furnished in sober, old-fashioned good taste with here and there a quaint, half-humourously protesting modern touch. Dingy portraits of severely-sedate ancestors are hung on the walls. There are well-filled bookcases, sufficient in size and the number of volumes contained to denote a creditable amount of sound classic culture on the part of the occupants.*

In the center of the rear wall, a doorway leading to the main hall. On the right, two large open double windows looking out on the street. At left, an open doorway hidden by heavy portieres.

The time is the present. It is about eight-thirty of a warm June evening.

Mr. and Mrs. Ashleigh are discovered sitting by the ponderous oak table in the center of the room. Mrs. Ashleigh is a handsome, white-haired woman of fifty, calm, unruffled, with a charmingly-girlish smile and dark eyes dancing with a keen sense of humour. Ashleigh is sixty and rather bald. He is tall and portly, and suggests by his clothes and demeanor the retired banker whose life has been uneventful and prosperous. Inefficiently pompous, he becomes easily aroused to nervous irritability when his own respectable dog-mas are questioned.

ASHLEIGH—(*rustling the evening paper he is pretending to read—irritably*) This has simply got to stop! (*He turns to his wife.*) I won't put up with it any longer.

MRS. ASHLEIGH—(*looking up from the book she is reading—quietly*) Won't put up with what?

ASHLEIGH—With Lucy's continual attacks of insane faddism.

MRS. ASHLEIGH—(*with a smile*) So its Lucy again.

ASHLEIGH—Yes, its Lucy again! (*indignantly*) You simply won't realize how serious the situation is. Why her conduct for the past year since she left college has been—there is no other word for it—absolutely indecent!

MRS. ASHLEIGH—(*calmly*) Don't take it so seriously. Its just her youth—effervescence of an active mind striving to find itself, needing an outlet somewhere.

ASHLEIGH—(*obstinately*) But a healthy outlet—not a lot of half-baked theories.

MRS. ASHLEIGH—(*teasingly*) Lucy's new theories are very interesting. (*Ashleigh looks shocked at this remark. Mrs. Ashleigh laughs at him.*) No, you needn't be alarmed. I'm not catching the fever. Our daughter has hopelessly outdistanced me, and you are far behind. She is tomorrow, I am today, and you, my dear Dick, are yesterday. (*She leans across the table and pats his hand.*) Don't worry about Lucy. I understand her better than you do, and she's just her mother over again. (*a trace of sadness creeping into her tones*) Besides, you won't have her at home to plague you into tempers—after tomorrow.

ASHLEIGH—(*slowly*) Tomorrow. Our little Lucy married tomorrow! It doesn't seem possible. Why it seems only yesterday she was running around in short skirts, singing at the top of her lungs and raising the devil generally. (*with a smile*) She's always had a will of her own, that little lady. (*after a pause—slowly*) Its going to be lonely here at home without her.

MRS. ASHLEIGH—We must try to accept it philosophically. Its simply the law of nature—when the little birds learn to fly, they fly away.

ASHLEIGH—Its a cruel law.

MRS. ASHLEIGH—No, its a just law. Lucy would stagnate here. Our desire to keep her is selfish. She must go out into the sunlight and the shadow and accumulate her little store of memories just as you and I have done, just as her children will do after her. (*Ashleigh sighs.*) And I think we ought to be as cheerful as two about-to-be-bereaved parents can be under the circumstances. Lucy is fortunate in her choice. Tom Drayton is a rare type—the clean, wholesome young American.

ASHLEIGH—Yes, Tom's a fine fellow, right enough; a splendid young chap with plenty of go to him. That's why I can't understand why he doesn't put a stop to all this foolishness of her's. Its ridiculous to see a man of his stamp play the meek little lamb. Why the way she twists him around her finger is—is disgusting.

ASHLEIGH—Perhaps Tom has seen enough of our family life to hope that the meek lamb will succeed where the—(*she smiles over at him*) roaring lion has failed.

ASHLEIGH—Well, even you'll admit I've good cause to roar tonight, when I tell you her latest escapade.

MRS. ASHLEIGH—(*smiling*) What was it this time? Did she buy another Futurist painting and bring it home to show you?

ASHLEIGH—No.

MRS. ASHLEIGH—Has she written another five-act tragedy in free verse?

ASHLEIGH—No.

MRS. ASHLEIGH—Has she bought another Greenwich eucalalie which she can't play?

ASHLEIGH—No!

MRS. ASHLEIGH—Did she bring home a tramp poet to live in our garret?

ASHLEIGH—No!

MRS. ASHLEIGH—Not even a long-haired sculptor smelling of absinthe?

ASHLEIGH—(*exasperated*) No, no, no, I tell you!

MRS. ASHLEIGH—This must have been one of Lucy's idle days. (*her eyes dancing with merriment*) Has she gone in for psycho-analysis again?

ASHLEIGH—No.

MRS. ASHLEIGH—Don't tell me she has disinterred another Yogi mystic in a cerise turban!

ASHLEIGH—(*huffed*) If you'll stop questioning me for a moment, my dear, I might be able to enlighten you. (*Mrs. A. puts her finger on her lips.*) You remember last night when she said she and Tom were going to the theatre?

MRS. ASHLEIGH—I thought she merely said they were going out.

ASHLEIGH—(*crossly*) Well, anyway, I thought she must be going to the theatre. Where else do normal people go when they don't stay at home? (*Receiving no answer, he continues with impressive slowness*) Do—you—know where she—did go?

MRS. ASHLEIGH—No; not to—? Oh, I forgot. I mustn't guess. Well, then, where—did—she—go?

ASHLEIGH—To an Anarchist lecture!

MRS. ASHLEIGH—And dragged Tom along with her?

ASHLEIGH—Yes; the idiot!

MRS. ASHLEIGH—Did Tom tell you?

ASHLEIGH—No. Lucy cooly informed me that *I* ought to go and hear it.

MRS. ASHLEIGH—Well, I can't see the enormity of her going.

ASHLEIGH—I tell you the woman who gave the lecture was an Anarchist. Most of the audience were Anarchists. And do you know what the subject was?

MRS. ASHLEIGH—Yes.

ASHLEIGH—(*astonished*) What? Did Lucy tell—

MRS. ASHLEIGH—No. She's been too busy talking trousseau to me. I meant to say I can guess what the lecture was about.

ASHLEIGH—What?

MRS. ASHLEIGH—Birth control, of course. Everyone is lecturing on that subject now, judging from the papers. Its quite the rage.

ASHLEIGH—And you don't think its infamous?

MRS. ASHLEIGH—On the contrary I'm enough of a radical myself on that question to quite approve of it.

ASHLEIGH—Well, I'll be—

MRS. ASHLEIGH—Damned! There, I said it for you. (*Then as he rises from his chair and gets ready to crush her with the weight of his eloquence, she shakes her finger at him.*) Now Dick! Now Dick! Every time you've read the words "birth control" in the newspapers you've condemned them at length and in detail, and I've listened with wifely patience. (*coming over to him still shaking her finger*) So I know all you're going to say beforehand. So don't say it. (*as he is going to speak*) Don't say it! (*She laughingly puts a finger over his lips.*)

ASHLEIGH—(*mollified—with a sigh*) All right, I won't; but—

MRS. ASHLEIGH—(*kissing him*) That's a dear. (*A ring of the bell is heard.*) There's the bell. I wonder who it can be. (*A moment later the maid appears at the door.*)

THE MAID—Its Miss. Barnes, m'am. She has a picture for Miss. Lucy, she says, m'am.

ASHLEIGH—(*with a groan*) Another painting! Good heavens!

MRS. ASHLEIGH—(*to the maid*) Show her in here, please. (*The maid goes out.*) Now, Dick, you run up and make your peace with Lucy. You know you'll have it on your conscience and be miserable if you don't. (*She kisses him. He goes toward the door on left.*) And don't loose your temper again.

ASHLEIGH—I won't. (*He goes out. Leonora Barnes enters from the doorway in rear. She is a tiny bit of a person, rather pretty, but pale and aenemic looking with great dark circles in under her bright, restless eyes. She is dressed in a pink painter's smock, dark skirt, and wears sandals on her bare feet. Immediately on entering she throws aside her queer hat revealing thick blond hair bobbed in a Dutch clip.*)

LEONORA—(*breezily*) Hello. (*She stands the small canvas she is carrying against the wall near the door.*)

MRS. ASHLEIGH—(*shaking hands with her*) How do you do, Leonora.

LEONORA—(*flitting nervously about the room with quick, bird-like movements*) Oh, I'm fair. Terribly bored with everything, though. (*She squints scornfully at the portraits.*) Now I ask you, aren't those rotten daubs! Never been in this room before. Who are they?

MRS. ASHLEIGH—Only a few ancestors.

LEONORA—Oh. (*Then she says to herself, not realizing she is talking out loud*) Philistines! Chinese ancestor worship!

MRS. ASHLEIGH—(*amused*) Won't you sit down?

LEONORA—(*throwing herself into an easy chair*) Thanks. (*She takes a bag of tobacco and cigarette papers from the pocket of her smock and starts to roll a cigarette—then stops and looks questioningly at Mrs. Ashleigh.*) Oh, I forgot where I was. You don't mind?

MRS. ASHLEIGH—Not at all.

LEONORA—(*finishes rolling her cigarette, takes a long ivory cigarette holder from her pocket, and fixes the cigarette in it*) I didn't think you would, being Lucy's mother, but you never can tell. Most of the older generation do object, you know.

MRS. ASHLEIGH—(*with a smile*) Yes, we're dreadfully behind the times, I'm afraid.

LEONORA—(*flitting to the table to light her cigarette—philosophically*) Its hard to live out of one's period, I dare say.

(*musingly*) I suppose even I'll be respectable when I'm too old to be anything else. (*throwing herself back in the chair*) Where's Lucy?

MRS. ASHLEIGH—She's resting. You know tomorrow—

LEONORA—(*exhaling a cloud of smoke*) Oh yes, the marriage! Don't blame her for resting up. Frightful ordeal—I imagine. Too bad. Lucy has talent and temperament. What does she want to marry for?

MRS. ASHLEIGH—(*gently*) Perhaps because she is in love.

LEONORA—(*airily*) Mid-Victorian sentimentality! Love is no excuse. Marriage is for propagation, and artists shouldn't propagate. Takes up too much of their time.

MRS. ASHLEIGH—But artists fall in love the same as ordinary people—so I've heard.

LEONORA—Oh, love, of course; but free love! I'd argue with you about it only I'm not much on sociology. That's more in Lucy's line. I'm only interested in it superficially. Art takes up all my time. (*her eyes falling on the canvas she brought in*) Oh, I was forgetting. (*She jumps up and goes over to it.*) Here's something of mine I brought for Lucy. (*making a wry face*) You may call it a wedding present, if you like. Lucy admired it when she was up at the studio and I thought she might like to have it.

MRS. ASHLEIGH—That's very sweet of you, my dear. I know Lucy will be delighted. May I see it?

LEONORA—(*bringing over the canvas*) It's good, I think. It expresses something of what I tried to put into it. (*She holds the painting on the table in front of Mrs. Ashleigh. The audience can see Mrs. Ashleigh's face but not the painting.*)

MRS. ASHLEIGH—(*trying to conceal the look of blank amazement on her face*) Er—what wonderful colors.

LEONORA—(*complacently*) Yes, the color is rather fine. Everyone agrees on that. Its much more effective in daylight, though.

MRS. ASHLEIGH—Has it—er—any title?

LEONORA—I call it the Great Blond Beast—you know, Nietzsche. (*raptly*) It is the expression of my passion to create something or someone great and noble—the Superman or the work of great art.

MRS. ASHLEIGH—(*with perfect courtesy*) Hm—yes—I can feel that in it.

LEONORA—(*delighted*) Oh, can you? How wonderful! I knew you couldn't be as Mid-Victorian as your environment. (*She indicates the room with a disdainful gesture.*)

MRS. ASHLEIGH—(*smiling*) I'm afraid I am.

LEONORA—(*enthusiastically*) Nonsense! You're not at all. You're one of us. (*She throws her arms around Mrs. Ashleigh and kisses her.*) You're an old dear. (*suddenly standing off and regarding Mrs. Ashleigh critically*) Why don't you dye your hair red? You'd be splendidly decorative. (*without waiting for an answer*) I'll put this out of the way. (*She stands the canvas against the wall near the window. As she is doing this, Tom Drayton enters. He is a tall, blond, finely-built man of about thirty with large, handsome features.*)

MRS. ASHLEIGH—Hello, Tom.

TOM—Hello, mother. (*He comes over and kisses her.*)

LEONORA—(*waving her hand to him from the window*) Hello-hello! (*as he turns to her with a puzzled expression*) I've met you. You needn't be shocked. You came to my studio with Lucy. Remember?

TOM—Oh, yes, of course; I remember now. How do you do, Miss.—er—

LEONORA—Never mind the Miss. Call me Leo. They all do. (*She comes forward and shakes his hand.*) Are you interested in any form of art? What are you—I mean what do you do?

TOM—I'm afraid I'm merely a—business man.

LEONORA—(*disdainfully*) Hmm! (*suddenly*) You see you attract me physically. (*Tom is stunned. Mrs. Ashleigh smiles at his confusion.*)

TOM—(*at last*) Oh, yes, I see. You're a painter, aren't you?

LEONORA—I don't mean I want you for a model. I mean you have all the outward appearance of my ideal of what the Great Blond Beast should look like. (*scrutinizing him closely*) Ever read Nietzsche? No, business men don't, do they? They go to the Follies. (*measuring him with a searching glance*) Maybe there is something more to you than you realize yourself. (*decisively*) Some day I'm going to find out. (*She carelessly tosses the butt of her cigarette on the rug and stamps on it, much to Mrs. Ashleigh's consternation.*) I'll have to be getting along.

(*puts on her hat*) You two must have no end of details to fuss over and chatter about.

MRS. ASHLEIGH—You're surely coming to the wedding?

LEONORA—No, I think not. Too much stir over nothing. Tell Lucy I'll see her when she gets back. And tell her I think she's a fool to marry. And don't forget the painting. Ta-ta! (*She runs out the doorway in the rear.*)

TOM—(*smiling*) A breezy sprite, isn't she? Where's Lucy?

MRS. ASHLEIGH—Upstairs—resting, I hope. I'll send for her in a moment. But now, sit down (*pointing to the chair opposite her*) for I have something (*she smiles*) *very serious* to say to you!

TOM—You may fire when you are ready.

MRS. ASHLEIGH—I ask permission to play the mother-in-law before the fact, promising in return to forever hold my peace after the ceremony.

TOM—(*affectionately*) Oh come now, you mustn't say that. Your advice will always be invaluable. It would be downright unkind of you to keep any such promise.

MRS. ASHLEIGH—Well, then, in extremis you may call on me. Now for what I was going to say to you. You've known Lucy now for two years and yet I'm afraid you may not know her at all.

TOM—I *think* I understand her.

MRS. ASHLEIGH—Let me ask you a question then. How do you accept her wild ideas about society and the world in general?

TOM—I attribute them to youth and inexperience and an active mind and body. They are part of Lucy—and I love Lucy.

MRS. ASHLEIGH—And their startling manifestations don't annoy you?

TOM—Annoy? Good heavens, no. (*smiling*) But the outbreaks are a trifle disconcerting at times, I must confess.

MRS. ASHLEIGH—That means you don't take them seriously. (*thoughtfully*) That's where you're both right and very wrong. (*Tom looks at her with a puzzled expression.*) Right in believing that beneath the high-strung girl of flighty impulses there exists the woman whose sense of humour will soon awake and make her laugh at all her present extravagant poses. (*warningly*) But you must not expect a drastic change immediately. Lucy has been our spoiled child all her life and is used to having her whims respected.

TOM—Oh, I know that a period of transition— (*boyishly*) Besides, hang it all, her poses are adorable. I don't want her ever to lose them—all of them, at least.

MRS. ASHLEIGH—You may love them for a time, but they're hard to live with—even after one has become inured.

TOM—(*smiling*) Perhaps I've become acclimated already. (*Mrs. A. shakes her head doubtfully.*) But you said a moment ago I was also very wrong in my attitude. How?

MRS. ASHLEIGH—In not *pretending* to take Lucy seriously. That's the most important thing of all.

TOM—But I do pretend.

MRS. ASHLEIGH—Not very successfully. I've been observing you.

TOM—(*protestingly*) But haven't I gone to impossible lectures, impossible exhibitions, listened to impossible poems, met millions of impossible lunatics of every variety? Haven't I done all this gladly, nay, even enthusiastically?

MRS. ASHLEIGH—Yes, you've done all of that, I must acknowledge; but, seriously, Tom, don't you know that your attitude has been that of kindly tolerance—the kindly tolerance of an elder brother toward an irresponsible child?

TOM—But Lucy *is* a child in such things.

MRS. ASHLEIGH—A child feels lack of sympathy with its dreams more keenly than anything else.

TOM—But everyone around her, her father, even you—

MRS. ASHLEIGH—We've all been wrong and its too late for us to change. You're just beginning and you must profit by our mistakes. That's why I wanted this talk with you— because the most vital thing left to me in life is that you and Lucy should be happy together.

TOM—(*gratefully*) I know that, Mrs. Ashleigh, and I'll do whatever you suggest.

MRS. ASHLEIGH—Then try to feel something of the spirit of Lucy's rainbow chasing, and show her you feel it. Its the old, ever young, wild spirit of youth which tramples rudely on the grave-mound of the Past to see more clearly to the future dream. We are all thrilled by it sometime, in someway or another. In most of us it flickers out, more's the pity. In some of us it becomes tempered to a fine, sane, progressive ideal which is of infinite help to the race. I think Lucy will develope into one of those rare ones.

TOM—(*impulsively*) I'm sure of it.

MRS. ASHLEIGH—(*warningly*) *If* she is not goaded into wilder and wilder revolts by the lack of sympathetic understanding in those around her. (*seeing Tom's troubled frown*) Don't be alarmed, though. Lucy looks on you as a promising neophyte. That's one reason why she's marrying you.

TOM—To convert me? All right then, I'm converted. (*with a wild gesture*) Down with everything!

MRS. ASHLEIGH—(*approvingly*) That's the spirit! See that you stay converted. Agree with her. Encourage her. Be earnest with her, and—(*she smiles*) trust to your wife's dormant sense of humour to eventually end your agony. You won't have long to suffer. Lucy has advanced to the ridiculous stage even now. Its only a step to the return to reason. Now I'm through lecturing and you may breathe easier. I'll send for Lucy. Will you ring for the maid? (*Tom goes over and pushes the button.*) Do smoke. You look so unoccupied.

TOM—(*laughing*) Thank you. (*He lights a cigarette.*)

MRS. ASHLEIGH—(*as the maid comes in*) Annie, will you tell Lucy that Mr. Drayton is here?

THE MAID—Yes, m'am. (*She goes out.*)

TOM—(*wandering around the room, stops on seeing the canvas against the wall*) Is this the painting our little Leo was urging you not to forget?

MRS. ASHLEIGH—Yes. Bring it over to the light. You'll enjoy it. Its a wedding present for Lucy. (*Tom brings it to the table and holds it in the light. It is an orgy of colors done in the wildest Synchromist manner. Tom looks at it with an expression of amused contempt. Mrs. Ashleigh watches his face with a smile. Ashleigh enters from the left. He appears wildly excited, and his face is red with indignant rage.*)

ASHLEIGH—What do you suppose—? (*He sees Tom and comes and shakes hands with him warmly.*) Hello, Tom. Its lucky you're here to put a stop to— (*He turns to his wife.*) Mary, what do you suppose—?

MRS. ASHLEIGH—Ssshh! Don't interrupt our mood.

Come and look at this work of art. Its a wedding present for Lucy. (*He comes and stands beside Tom and looks at it blankly.*)

ASHLEIGH—What in the name of— Who made it?

MRS. ASHLEIGH—That little Miss. Barnes; you know; you met her the other day with Lucy.

ASHLEIGH—(*growling*) Oh, that short-haired lunatic! I might have guessed it. (*indignantly*) Does she call that a picture of something? What tommyrot! Its blithering idiocy, eh, Tom?

TOM—I can't even get mad at them any more. I've been to too many exhibitions. I'm hardened.

ASHLEIGH—(*disgustedly*) What's it supposed to be, I'd like to know? (*He peers at it sideways.*) You must have it upside down. (*Mrs. Ashleigh turns it around.*)

MRS. ASHLEIGH—(*oratorically*) Approach it with an open mind and soul freed from all conventional prejudices and categorical judgements, and tell me what emotion it arouses in you, what feeling you get from it.

ASHLEIGH—You're beginning to talk as absurdly as the craziest of them. I'll be going mad myself the next thing.

MRS. ASHLEIGH—(*insisting*) But, Dick, tell me what you think it is, just for curiousity.

ASHLEIGH—Tommyrot! Tommyrot! That's what I know it is.

MRS. ASHLEIGH—And you, Tom?

TOM—I can't make out whether its the Aurora Borealis or an explosion in a powder mill. (*Ashleigh laughs.*)

MRS. ASHLEIGH—(*impressively*) You are both wrong. It is the longing of the soul for the Great Blond Beast.

ASHLEIGH—Great Blond Rot! (*to Tom*) Never mind that thing. Listen to me for a moment. Mary, do you know what Lucy was doing when I went up to her room (*sarcastically*) where *you* thought she was resting.

MRS. ASHLEIGH—Reading, I suppose.

ASHLEIGH—Yes; reading some trashy novel by some damn Russian; and she insisted on reading it out loud to me—a lot of nonsense condemning marriage—on the night before her wedding. (*He appeals to the ceiling.*) Trying to convert me to free love—at my age! Then she said she'd decided not to marry Tom after all and—

TOM—(*appalled*) What!

MRS. ASHLEIGH—Remember what you promised me, Tom. (*He immediately smiles and becomes composed again.*)

ASHLEIGH—Yes, that's what she said. (*Lucy appears in the doorway on left.*) Here she is now. (*with grim satisfaction as he sits down in a chair*) Now *you* can listen to her for a while!

(*Lucy comes slowly into the room. She is slender, dark, beautiful, with large eyes which she attempts to keep always mysterious and brooding, smiling lips which she resolutely compresses to express melancholy determination, a healthy complexion subdued by powder to a proper prison pallor, a vigorous, lithe body which frets restlessly beneath the restriction of studied, artificial movements. In short, Lucy is an intelligent, healthy American girl suffering from an overdose of undigested reading, and has mistaken herself for the heroine of a Russian novel. She is dressed in a dark, somber kimona, and Turkish slippers.*)

LUCY—Good evening, Tom. (*She comes to the center of the room and gives him her hand with a drooping gesture. Tom stares at her in embarrassment. Lucy glides into a chair near her mother, rests her chin on her hand, and gazes into the immensities. There is a long silence.*)

ASHLEIGH—(*drums on the arm of his chair in extreme irritation*) Well? (*then as Lucy gives no sign of having heard him, in a louder tone*) Well?

LUCY—(*coming out of her dream—slowly*) I beg your pardon. I'm afraid I interrupted you. You must keep on talking as if I were not here. I'm so distrait this evening. There is so much turmoil in my soul. (*appealing to them with a sad smile*) Strindberg's daughter of Indra discovered the truth. Life is horrible, is it not?

ASHLEIGH—(*fuming*) Bosh! Bosh! You know very well what we were discussing, Miss., and you're trying to avoid the subject.

MRS. ASHLEIGH—(*interrupting quickly*) We were discussing the meaning of this painting Leonora brought for you.

LUCY—(*abandoning her pose for an unguarded moment— with real, girlish pleasure*) A painting? From Leo? How charming of her! (*She goes quickly to the table and looks at the painting. While she is doing so she remembers herself and resumes her pose.*)

Tom—(*feeling bound to say something*) Beautiful, isn't it?

Ashleigh—(*looking at Tom scornfully*) Beautiful! Why you just said— (*Mrs. Ashleigh makes violent signs to him to be silent. He grunts disgustedly.*)

Lucy—(*holding the painting at arm's length and examining it critically*) Beautiful? Yes, perhaps as a photograph is beautiful. The technique is perfect, but—is that the meaning of Art? (*She lays the canvas down with an expression of mild disdain and resumes her chair.*) I am somewhat disappointed in Leonora. She seems to have little to express after all.

Ashleigh—(*with satisfaction*) Hmm!

Lucy—(*with a glance at her father*) She is too old-fashioned. Her methods are those of yesterday.

Ashleigh—What?

Lucy—(*not noticing his interruption*) I once thought she would soar to the heights but I see now it is hopeless. The wings of her soul are weighed down by the dust of too many dead yesterdays.

Ashleigh—I don't know what you're talking about but I'm glad to learn you've sense enough to know that thing is tommyrot. (*He points scornfully at the canvas.*)

Lucy—(*with real indignation*) I never said such a thing. As usual you misunderstand me. I think its fine and I deeply appreciate her giving it to me.

Ashleigh—(*sarcastically*) Then maybe you can tell us what it represents? (*He winks at Tom who pretends not to see him and wears a face of deadly seriousness.*)

Lucy—(*glances doubtfully at the painting—then lightly*) What would be the use? You would only misinterpret what I said. Besides, Art is not to be limited by definitions.

Mrs. Ashleigh—(*as Ashleigh is about to answer*) It was very thoughtful of her to give Lucy a wedding present. She doesn't look any too prosperous, poor child, and it must have taken up a lot of her time.

Lucy—(*slowly*) Wedding present?

Mrs. Ashleigh—Yes. She said you might regard it as such.

Lucy—(*after a pause—turning to her father accusingly*) Then you haven't told them?

Ashleigh—I haven't had a chance; and, anyway, I refuse to believe that rubbish you were telling me.

MRS. ASHLEIGH—What rubbish?

ASHLEIGH—(*indicating Lucy who is gazing moodily into space*) I will leave it to our lady anarchist to explain.

LUCY—(*slowly—after a pause*) There will be no wedding.

ASHLEIGH—(*looking at the others with an I-told-you-so air of satisfaction*) There! Now you know!

MRS. ASHLEIGH—(*with the utmost calm*) You mean you want it postponed?

LUCY—(*firmly*) I mean there will be no wedding—ever! (*Tom squirms in his chair and seems about to protest but catches Mrs. Ashleigh's meaning glance and stops abruptly. Lucy revels in the impression she knows she has made. Wearing her best Russian heroine pose she comes slowly over to Tom's chair and takes his hand.*) I am sorry, Tom. I would not hurt you for anything in the world, but this—must be! My highest duty is toward myself, and my ego demands freedom, wide horizons to develope in, (*she makes a sweeping gesture*) Castles in the air, not homes for human beings! (*tenderly*) You understand, don't you Tom?

TOM—(*with an effort—matter-of-factedly*) Yes, Lucy, I understand.

ASHLEIGH—What's that?

LUCY—(*a trace of disappointment in her manner in spite of herself*) You mean you will give up the idea of our marriage, tomorrow or at any future time?

TOM—Since it's your wish, yes, Lucy.

LUCY—(*showing her hurt*) Oh. (*She tries to speak calmly.*) I knew you would understand. (*She goes back and sits down. This time her eyes are full of a real emotion as she stares before her.*)

ASHLEIGH—(*to Tom—angrily*) So! Its your turn to play the damn fool, is it? I thought you had some sense. (*He snatches a paper from the table and pretends to read.*)

TOM—I love Lucy. I'll do whatever she thinks necessary to her happiness.

ASHLEIGH—Humph! She doesn't know what she thinks.

LUCY—(*agonizingly*) Oh, I've thought and thought and thought until my brain seemed bursting. I've lain awake in the still, long hours and struggled with myself. I've fought against it. I've tried to force myself to submit—for Tom's sake. But I cannot. I cannot play the hypocrite to the extent of binding myself by a pact which means nothing to me. It would be the meanest form of slavery—to marry when I am convinced marriage is the most despicable of all the laws of society. (*Ashleigh rustles his paper angrily—Lucy continues scornfully*) What is it Nietzsche says of marriage? "Ah, the poverty of soul in the twain! Ah, the filth of soul in the twain! Ah, the pitiable self-complacency in the twain!"

ASHLEIGH—(*enraged*) There! That's the stuff she was reading to me. Look here, young lady! Don't you know that all the invitations are sent out and everything is arranged? Do you want to make all this infernal mess at the last moment? Think what people will say.

LUCY—(*scornfully*) As if I cared for the opinion of the mob—the much-too-many!

ASHLEIGH—They're not mob. They're my friends!

LUCY—Stupid bourgeois!

MRS. ASHLEIGH—(*hastily—forseeing a row*) I can quite sympathize with your objections to marriage as an institution, Lucy,—

ASHLEIGH—(*bursting out*) Mary!

MRS. ASHLEIGH—Even if your father cannot. (*spiritedly*) Its high time women should refuse to be treated like dumb beasts with no souls of their own.

LUCY—(*surprised but triumphant*) Thank you, mother.

MRS. ASHLEIGH—When we have the right to make our own laws we ought to abolish marriage the first thing. (*violently*) Its an outrage against decency, that's what it is. (*catching Lucy's look of amazement*) I see you're surprised, Lucy, but you shouldn't be. I know more of the evils of marriage than you do. You've escaped it so far, but you must remember I've been in the toils for over twenty years.

LUCY—(*a bit shocked in spite of herself*) Why, mother—I never— (*She hesitates, at a loss to account for her mother's outburst.*)

ASHLEIGH—Well, I'll be damned! (*He burries his nose in the paper, choking with suppressed rage.*)

MRS. ASHLEIGH—(*with a great sigh—hopelessly*) But in the present we are hopeless—for we must still fall in love in spite of ourselves. You love Tom, don't you, Lucy?

LUCY—I do.

MRS. ASHLEIGH—And Tom loves you. Then, notwith-standing, the fact that your decision is just, it is bound to make both of you unhappy.

LUCY—(*resolutely*) No, not if Tom agrees to the plan I have in mind.

ALL—(*astonished*) Plan?

LUCY—(*going over to Tom*) You are sure you love me, Tom?

TOM—How can you ask, Lucy!

LUCY—And you will dare anything that we may be to-gether?

TOM—Anything!

LUCY—(*fervidly*) Then why this useless formality of mar-riage? Let us go forth into the world together, not shackled for better or for worse, but as free spirits, comrades who have no other claims upon each other than what our hearts dictate. (*All are overwhelmed. Even Mrs. Ashleigh is evidently taken off her feet for a moment. Lucy looks from one to the other to enjoy the effect she is producing and then continues calmly*) We need not change one of our plans. Let the marriage only be omit-ted and I will go with you.

ASHLEIGH—(*turning to his wife*) The girl's out of her head!

LUCY—I was never saner in my life than at this moment.

ASHLEIGH—(*exasperated beyond endurance*) But don't you see, can't you understand that what you're proposing is noth-ing more or less than—than—than free love!

LUCY—Yes, free! free! *free* love!

ASHLEIGH—Have you no shame?

LUCY—(*grandly*) None where my liberty is concerned.

ASHLEIGH—(*furiously—to Tom*) And you—why don't you say something and put a stop to this disgusting nonsense?

TOM—I must— Give me time. I—I want to think it over.

ASHLEIGH—(*indignantly*) Think it over! (*Lucy turns away from Tom who looks questioningly at Mrs. Ashleigh. She nods at him approvingly.*)

LUCY—(*seeming to be reassured after the moment's suspense— triumphantly*) That means you are *afraid* to go with me in free comradeship, *afraid* of what people will say, *afraid* of your conventional conscience. Well, perhaps you are right from your light, but—

Tom—One moment, Lucy. I didn't say I refused. On the contrary, I see your way is the one way out for both of us. (*He stands up and takes Lucy's hand. She seems bewildered by his acceptance.*)

Ashleigh—(*white with rage*) So you—a gentleman—encourage this infamous proposal?

Mrs. Ashleigh—(*calmly*) Be reasonable, Dick. It seems the only thing they can do.

Ashleigh—(*wildly*) I won't listen to you any longer. This is all a filthy joke or—or—my God, you're all insane! (*He rushes out of the door in rear.*)

Lucy—(*to Tom—evidently trying to dissuade him*) I want you to think deeply over your decision. It probably involves greater sacrifice for you than it does for me. We will have to go far away and start again together, or else, remain—

Tom—(*quickly*) Yes, it will be braver to remain.

Lucy—Then you'll have to face the stupid sneers and snubs of all your associates. It will be hard. You're not accustomed—

Tom—Its all right. I'll manage somehow.

Mrs. Ashleigh—Lucy, how can you ask such a sacrifice of Tom—if you really love him as you say?

Lucy—(*sees a way out and eagerly clutches at this straw. She stands for a moment as if a tremendous mental conflict were taking place within her, then turns to Tom sadly.*) No, Tom, mother is right. I cannot be so selfish. I cannot tear your life to pieces. No, you are free. Time heals everything—you will forget.

Tom—(*putting his arm around her*) No, Lucy, I could never forget. (*firmly*) So tomorrow we'll start life together as you desire it.

Lucy—(*releasing herself—with infinite sadness*) No—for your sake—I cannot.

Mrs. Ashleigh—Why not sacrifice yourself, Lucy? You might marry Tom as you intended to do. (*with a pretence of annoyance*) Where is your sense of humour, you two? Why all this seriousness? Good heavens, the marriage ceremony is merely a formula which you can take with as many grains of salt as you please. You needn't live up to it in any way. Few people do. You can have your own private understanding—and divorce is easy enough.

LUCY—(*feeling bound to protest*) But, mother, that would be hypocritical—ignoble!

MRS. ASHLEIGH—Ignoble, fudge! Hypocritical, rats! Be sensible! What is the use of butting your heads against a stone wall? You have work to do in this world and you can't afford to leave yourselves open to the malicious badgering and interference of all the moral busy-bodies if you expect to accomplish your purpose in life. Now I would have nothing to say against free love if it could be free. I object to it because its less free than marriage.

LUCY—(*tragically*) There must be martyrs for every step of progress.

MRS. ASHLEIGH—Martyrs are people with no imaginations. No; make your marriage a model of all that's best in free love, if you must set an example. True progress lies along those lines.

LUCY—(*vaguely*) But—

MRS. ASHLEIGH—But nothing. You agree with me, don't you, Tom?

TOM—Perfectly. I never intended to regard our marriage in any other way.

MRS. ASHLEIGH—(*hustling Lucy*) Then make out your own wedding contract and sign it yourselves without the sanction of church or state or anything. You're willing that Lucy should draw up the terms of your mutual agreement, aren't you, Tom? She's the chief objector.

TOM—I repeat again for the hundredth time—anything Lucy wishes I will agree to.

LUCY—(*embarrassed*) I believe I've already written down what I thought— I was going to ask Tom—

MRS. ASHLEIGH—Have you it with you? No? Then run and get it. I'll keep Tom company while you're gone. (*Lucy hesitates a moment; then goes out left. After she has gone Tom comes over to Mrs. Ashleigh and takes her hand. They both commence to laugh.*)

MRS. ASHLEIGH—There! I've given you the best example of how to manage Lucy. See that you profit by it.

TOM—I won't forget, I promise you. Do you think I'm learning to be a better actor?

MRS. ASHLEIGH—My dear boy, you were splendid. Poor Lucy! She was frightened to death when you decided to accept her in unshackled free love.

TOM—(*with a laugh*) But where did you learn all this radical rigamarole? You had me fooled at times. I didn't know whether you were serious or not.

MRS. ASHLEIGH—Oh, Lucy has sown me with tracts on the sex problem and I'm commencing to yield a harvest of wild words.

TOM—(*with a comic groan*) I can imagine the terms of this agreement Lucy has written out.

MRS. ASHLEIGH—Pooh! Keep up your courage, agree to anything, be married tomorrow, and live happy ever after. Its simple enough. (*Lucy enters from the left with the paper in her hand. She has regained her composure and wears a serious, purposeful expression. She lays the paper on the table.*)

MRS. ASHLEIGH—(*getting up*) And now I'll leave you to yourselves. Your poor father must have torn out his few remaining hairs by this time. I'll go and reassure him. (*She goes out, rear. Tom sits down at the table.*)

LUCY—(*standing by him—impressively*) I wrote this out last night. It is my idea of what the ideal relationship between a free man and woman should be. Of course, its tentative, and you can suggest any changes you think proper. One thing I must insist on. It is mutually agreed there shall be no children by our union. (*directing a searching look at Tom*) I know you're far too intelligent not to believe in birth control.

TOM—Er—for the very poor I consider it desirable.

LUCY—We of the well-to-do class must devote all our time to caring for the children of the poor instead of pampering our own. To do this effectively and unselfishly we must remain childless. The little proletarians will take the place of our own flesh and blood. (*seeing the badly-concealed look of disapproval on Tom's face*) Don't think I wish to shirk the burden of motherhood. You know how I love children.

TOM—(*hastily*) Of course. I understand, Lucy.

Lucy—And you agree to the provision?

Tom—I do.

Lucy—Then read the whole contract and tell me what you think.

Tom—(*reading*) Our union is to be one of mutual help and individual freedom. Agreed. Under no conditions shall I ever question any act of your's or attempt to restrict the expression of your ego in any way. Agreed. I will love you as long as my heart dictates, and not one second longer. Agreed. I will honor you only in so far as you prove yourself worthy of it in my eyes. Agreed. I will not obey you. (*with a smile*) According to the old formula it isn't necessary for *me* to promise that, Lucy.

Lucy—The slips are identical. I made a carbon copy of mine to save time. Here. (*She takes his slip from him.*) You can scratch out what doesn't apply to you. (*She takes a pencil and scratches out the sentence and hands the slip back to him.*)

Tom—(*reading*) For sociological reasons I shall have no children. That hardly applies to me either. (*He takes the pencil from her and scratches it out.*) In our economic relations we shall be strictly independent of each other. Hmm. Agreed. I may have lovers without causing jealousy or in any way breaking our compact as herein set forth. Lovers? Hmm, that must be your part, too. (*He pauses and sits looking down at the paper with a frown.*)

Lucy—But you agree that I may, don't you? (*as Tom still hesitates—with sudden indignation*) Why, you seem to suspect I desire to have them!

Tom—(*hastily*) Indeed I don't! I was only thinking—

Lucy—Its only a clause to show you I am free.

Tom—I know, Lucy, I know; and I agree. (*He marks off the clause on his sheet and continues his reading.*) Under the above conditions I will live with you in the true comradship of a free man and woman. Agreed, emphatically! (*He looks up at her.*) And now, what?

Lucy—We exchange slips after we've both signed our names to them. (*They write down their names and pass over each other's slips.*)

Tom—And now, what?

LUCY—(*with a smile*) Now you may kiss me. (*He jumps to his feet and takes her in his arms and kisses her.*)

LUCY—And now run along home like a dear. I'm so worn out. I'm going upstairs.

TOM—(*anxiously*) I wouldn't sit up any more tonight reading the books. It—er—it might hurt your eyes. (*He goes toward door in rear.*)

LUCY—(*yawning*) I promise. I'm too sleepy.

TOM—(*turning at the door—uncertainly*) You'll be sure to be at the church, dear?

LUCY—(*resuming her pose as if by magic at the word "church"*) I will be there, but—(*she looks at him questioningly*) its *absolutely meaningless*, remember!

TOM—(*moving back toward her*) Oh, *absolutely!*

LUCY—And a terrible bore, isn't it?

TOM—(*very near her again*) Terrible! (*He catches her in his arms and kisses her.*) Good-night. (*He runs out of the door in rear.*)

LUCY—Good-night. (*looking after him with a smile*) Silly!

(*The Curtain Falls*)

ACT TWO

SCENE—*The library of the Drayton's home in a fashionable New York suburb. The room is light and airy, furnished unpretentiously but in perfect taste. The only jarring note is supplied by two incredible paintings in the Synchromist manner which are hung in conspicuous places, and not to be ignored.*

In the rear, french windows looking out on the driveway which runs from the road to the front of the house, and the stretch of lawn beyond. On the left, a doorway leading into the main hall. On the right, rear, a window opening on the garden. Farther forward, a doorway, screened by heavy portieres, leading into another room. In the center, a table with books, periodicals, and an electric reading lamp on it.

Three months have elapsed since Act One. It is about noon on a warm day in September.

Mrs. Ashleigh and Lucy are discovered. Mrs. Ashleigh is seated by the table reading a magazine. Lucy is standing by the windows looking out over the grounds. She sighs fretfully and comes forward to where her mother is sitting; picks up a magazine, turns over the pages disgustedly, and throws it back on the table with an exclamation of contempt.

LUCY—Pah, what silly, shallow stuff! How can you waste your time reading it, mother?

MRS. ASHLEIGH—(*laying down her magazine resignedly*) I find it pleasant these warm days. Its light and frivolous, to be sure, but it serves to while away the hours.

LUCY—(*scornfully*) While away the hours! That's because your mind is unoccupied. Now, if you had a vital purpose—

MRS. ASHLEIGH—(*hurriedly*) Stop right there, my dear Lucy. I suffered from an overdose of your vital purposes when you were my daughter and I had to submit to keep peace in the family; but now that you are Mrs. Drayton, I rebel!

LUCY—(*laughing, sits down on the arm of her mother's chair and puts her arm around her—girlishly*) But I still am your daughter, mother. (*She kisses her.*) Unless you've disowned me.

MRS. ASHLEIGH—(*fondly*) Indeed I haven't; but I'm

424

determined to shun your stern principles. They're too rigorous for a lazy old lady.

LUCY—You're nothing of the kind. Only if you're going to read why don't you read something worth while? Have you looked over that copy of the new radical monthly, The Crash, I loaned you?

MRS. ASHLEIGH—No. My brain perspired at the sight of it.

LUCY—(*laughing*) Mother, you're incorrigible. You must read it. Theres a wonderful poem by Gabriel—

MRS. ASHLEIGH—Now, Lucy, you know I think Gabriel's poetry is—well—unmentionable.

LUCY—(*loftily*) That's blind prejudice, mother. You don't like Gabriel and you won't see the beauty of his work on that account.

MRS. ASHLEIGH—(*with a sigh*) Have it your own way, my dear. As you say, I don't like him overmuch. I can't for the life of me imagine what you find interesting in him.

LUCY—(*in the same lofty manner*) You don't understand him.

MRS. ASHLEIGH—(*with a trace of irritation*) Perhaps not. Certainly I don't understand why he should be always hanging around here. You never used to see much of him, did you?

LUCY—I used to run into him around the Square quite frequently.

MRS. ASHLEIGH—Where did you first meet him?

LUCY—Leo introduced me to him. He and she have a studio together.

MRS. ASHLEIGH—(*raising her eyebrows a trifle*) And I suppose they—live together?

LUCY—(*assertively*) Yes. They do. In *free* comradship!

MRS. ASHLEIGH—Hmm!

LUCY—Don't be bourgeois, mother.

MRS. ASHLEIGH—Oh, I wasn't belittling their morals. They're free to do as they please, of course. I was only thinking of little Leo. I like her quite well, and I didn't think she had such bad taste in the matter of companions.

LUCY—(*indignantly*) Mother! (*The front door is opened and shut, and Tom appears in the doorway on the left.*)

TOM—Ah, here you are. (*He comes over and kisses Lucy who submits rather constrainedly and walks away from him to the windows where she stands with her back toward him. Tom looks at her with a puzzled expression; then turns quickly to Mrs. Ashleigh.*) This is an unexpected pleasure, mother. (*He bends down and kisses her.*) I didn't think I'd find you out here.

MRS. ASHLEIGH—It was so warm and sunshiny, I just couldn't bear to remain in the city.

TOM—(*with boyish enthusiasm*) Bully out here, isn't it? I don't regret the half-hour train trip. One breath of this air after all those sultry streets puts new life into you. (*turning to Lucy*) Eh, Lucy?

LUCY—(*without enthusiasm*) Yes, its very nice.

TOM—You don't say that as if you meant it. Do you know, Mother, I think Lucy still pines for the stuffy studios of Greenwich Village.

LUCY—(*coldly*) You're mistaken.

MRS. ASHLEIGH—I can hardly believe that of her. Anyway, she can motor in whenever she feels homesick. She has the car. You seem hardly ever to use it.

TOM—No, that's Lucy's plaything. The old train is good enough for a hard-working business slave who can't afford to take chances on blow-outs.

MRS. ASHLEIGH—But you used to be such an enthusiastic motor fiend.

TOM—Married life has had it's sobering effect. I'm less frivolous.

LUCY—(*turning to him abruptly*) I suppose you forgot the tickets I asked you to get for the concert this afternoon?

TOM—(*looking at her for a moment—gently*) Do I usually forget anything you ask me?

LUCY—(*abashed*) No—I—I didn't mean it that way, Tom. I merely wanted to know if you had them.

TOM—I sure have. (*He takes the tickets out of his pocket and holds them up for her to see.*) Just to show you I'm a man of my word.

LUCY—Thank you. What time does it begin?

TOM—Two-thirty, I believe. We'll have to leave a little before two if we want to make it in the car. (*He takes a bundle of papers from his pocket.*) I've got to run over these papers. I'll have time before lunch, I guess. (*He goes out left. Lucy stands staring moodily out of the windows. Her mother looks at her searchingly.*)

MRS. ASHLEIGH—(*after a pause*) Come, Lucy, what's the matter? Its ungrateful of you to be blue on a beautiful day like this.

LUCY—(*with a sigh—fretfully*) I don't like weather which is so glaring and sunshiny. Nature makes too vulgar a display of it's kind intentions. (*with a toss of her head*) Besides, the weather can't heal my mood. (*with exaggerated melancholy*) My blue devils live deep down in my soul.

MRS. ASHLEIGH—Don't you like it out here any more? You seemed so enthusiastic when you first came.

LUCY—Oh, I knew it was what Tom wanted, and, well, I'd never had the experience before so how could I know?

MRS. ASHLEIGH—Experience? Why, you've only been here three weeks.

LUCY—That's long enough—to realize. But, Mother, it doesn't make any difference where I am, the conditions are the same. I feel—cramped in. (*with an affected yawn, throwing herself into a chair*) And I'm mortally bored.

MRS. ASHLEIGH—(*with a sigh*) Ever since you saw that play the other night you've done nothing but talk and act Hedda Gabbler; so I suppose its no use trying to argue with her.

LUCY—(*irritated at having her pose seen through*) I'm not talking Hedda Gabler. I'm simply telling you how I feel. (*somberly*) Though I'll confess there are times when General Gabbler's pistols have their fascination.

MRS. ASHLEIGH—(*with a smile*) Tut-tut, Lucy. You're too morbid today. You'll be longing next for someone to come "with vine leaves in his hair."

LUCY—(*maliciously*) And perhaps he will come.

MRS. ASHLEIGH—Hmm; well, it won't be our friend Gabriel, to be sure. I'm certain he's one of your precise modern poets who drowns his sorrows in unfermented grape juice, and goes in for scientific eating—counts his calories and proteins over one by one, so to speak.

LUCY—(*not deigning to smile at this*) There's much more to Gabriel than you have any idea of.

MRS. ASHLEIGH—(*with a smile*) As Leonora said to Tom once.

LUCY—(*with affected carelessness*) What did she say?

MRS. ASHLEIGH—She began by saying she was attracted to him physically! Imagine! Tom was flabbergasted. He hardly knew her at that time.

LUCY—(*stiffly*) She is *rather* rude.

MRS. ASHLEIGH—It would have been impossible in anyone else, but Leonora has a way with her. Tom didn't mind. Then she went on to make it worse—said he had more to him than he dreamed of and she was determined to find it out some day.

LUCY—(*with a short laugh*) Perhaps she will.

MRS. ASHLEIGH—I think Tom was inclined to regard her as a freak at first but he likes her quite well now. Does she come out here much?

LUCY—Quite often—with Gabriel.

MRS. ASHLEIGH—Leonora is a charming little elf.

LUCY—(*frowning*) She gets on my nerves at times now, and bores me with her chatter.

MRS. ASHLEIGH—(*in surprise*) Why I thought you and she were— Oh, well, this is one of your days, Miss. Hedda Gabbler, to be bored with everything and everybody.

LUCY—(*vexed*) Do stop calling me Hedda Gabbler, Mother. What has that to do with it? Leo wearies me with her silly talk of the Great Blond Beast.

MRS. ASHLEIGH—That's what she said Tom reminded her of.

LUCY—(*with a sneer*) She must be imaginative.

MRS. ASHLEIGH—(*after a pause*) When you came back from your honeymoon you were so full of healthy good spirits; and now you're falling back into the old morbid rut again.

LUCY—I'm not morbid. Is it morbid to look the truth in the face? (*pettishly*) I suppose its all my own fault. I was never intended for a hausfrau. I should never have allowed myself to be bullied into marrying when all my instincts were against it.

MRS. ASHLEIGH—(*astonished*) Bullied into marrying? Why, Lucy!

LUCY—(*peevishly*) Yes, you did. You and father and Tom

were all so set on it. What could I do? If I had only known—
And now— (*dramatically*) Oh, I want air! I want freedom to
love and dream beyond all these deadly commonplaces!

MRS. ASHLEIGH—It seems to me you're perfectly free to
do as you please.

LUCY—(*scornfully*) Do you call this freedom—this bourgeois paradise?

MRS. ASHLEIGH—(*with asperity*) I certainly call it as lovely
a home as anyone could wish for.

LUCY—Home? I don't want a home. I want a space to
grow in.

MRS. ASHLEIGH—(*with a sigh of vexation*) I believe all this
talk of your's comes from your association with Gabriel.

LUCY—(*excitedly*) He's the only real sympathetic human
being who comes into this house. He understands me. He
can talk to me in terms of the things I love. You and Tom—
you take me for granted.

MRS. ASHLEIGH—(*seeing Lucy's excitement, comes over and
puts her arm around her*) I'm sure we try our best to be sympathetic, dear. (*She kisses her.*) But let's not talk any more
about it now. The humidity is too oppressive for argument.
Let's go out in the garden for awhile.

LUCY—(*getting up*) I can only stay a moment, Mother.
I'm expecting Gabriel and Leo any minute. I asked them out
for lunch before I knew about the concert. (*with a defiant
glance at her mother*) Gabriel promised to read some new
poems to me.

MRS. ASHLEIGH—(*eagerly—much to Lucy's surprise*) I'd
like to hear them, if I may. You see I want to know Gabriel
more intimately. I'm afraid, after what you've told me, I must
be wrongly prejudiced against him.

LUCY—I assure you you are, Mother. (*They walk together
to the windows in rear.*)

MRS. ASHLEIGH—How beautiful everything looks! Let's
walk around in back where those lovely, shady maple trees are.
(*They go out and walk off right. A moment later the hall door is
heard being opened and shut and Gabriel and Leonora enter from
the doorway on the left. Gabriel has rather long black hair and
big soulful eyes. His face is thin and intelligent, with irregular
large features. He wears clothes sufficiently unconventional to*

attract attention. His manner is that of a spoiled child who is used to being petted and enjoys every moment of it. Leonora is dressed in her usual bizarre fashion.)

LEONORA—Now I ask you, why didn't you ring, you impossible person?

GABRIEL—(*throwing himself into the easiest chair*) I don't need to. I belong with the Lares and Penates of this house. In fact, I am them. I am more than they are. I am the great god, persona grata.

LEONORA—(*peering around*) There isn't a soul here.

GABRIEL—I quite agree with you. If there is one thing this home could harbor without fear of overcrowding, its a soul.

LEONORA—(*throwing herself into a chair*) I say! Why do you trot out here so much, then?

GABRIEL—(*reproachfully*) And you have the naivete to ask me that? (*He takes a box of cigarettes from his pocket and lights one.*)

LEONORA—Give me one. (*She takes a cigarette.*) And a light. (*She lights her cigarette from his.*) Yes, I do ask you that.

GABRIEL—(*shaking his head*) You who are familiar with the asininity of editors and the emaciated condition of my form and purse. You, whose cooking will eventually make a Carlyle out of me—

LEONORA—I don't pretend to be a cook.

GABRIEL—Because the most unworldly stomach would see through such a pretence. No, my adored Leonora, your cooking is very much akin to your painting—difficult to absorb.

LEONORA—(*with outraged dignity*) You know nothing at all about painting.

GABRIEL—But I have a sensitive appreciation where true Art is concerned, Leo, my own; and as I have told you so many times, your paintings are rubbish.

LEONORA—(*her face flushing with rage*) And your verse is nonsense.

GABRIEL—(*airily*) You're speaking of something you're too small of soul to understand.

LEONORA—(*judicially*) I understand the beauty of *real* poetry. That's why I've always told you your stuff is only sentimental journalism.

GABRIEL—(*outraged*) What! (*sputtering*) Your opinion is

worthless. No, by God, its even flattering, considering the source.

LEONORA—Its worth as much as *your* criticism of *my* Art.

GABRIEL—(*with a sneering laugh*) Your Art? Good heavens, do you call that stuff Art?

LEONORA—(*bursting forth*) Conceited ass!

GABRIEL—Idiot!

LEONORA—Fool!

GABRIEL—Imbecile!

LEONORA—Bourgeois rhymster!

GABRIEL—(*quivering with fury*) Have the last word, you little simpleton! (*He springs to his feet and, picking a book from the table, appears about to hurl it on the floor.*)

LEONORA—Now I ask you, what are you doing with that book? This isn't our place. You can't work out your rage by smashing things here.

GABRIEL—I won't endure this relationship a moment longer!

LEONORA—You've said that before. Ta-ta! Go! You know noone else would put up with you—and you can't take care of yourself.

GABRIEL—(*crashing the book on the floor*) Damn! (*He strides up and down holding his head.*)

LEONORA—(*calmly*) Shall I ring and have the maid pick up that book for you?

GABRIEL—(*picking the book up and putting it back on the table with a great show of dignity*) I don't desire menial service. Its abhorrent to my love of freedom.

LEONORA—So I've observed. Certainly there have never been any menials around the studio since I arrived. (*as she sees Gabriel is about to give vent to his anger again*) Now don't fly off into another tantrum, Gab.

GABRIEL—Don't call me Gab. Its vulgar, and it makes me ridiculous. How often must I tell you?

LEONORA—Very well, then—Gabriel. (*suddenly bursting into peals of laughter*) Now I ask you, wasn't that a lovely brawl?

GABRIEL—(*with a sigh*) Well, its over for today, at any rate. You know what we swore to each other?

LEONORA—Only one row a day.

GABRIEL—(*smiling*) What if the Philistines had heard us! They would perish with the rapture of a revelation—at last, Bohemia!

LEONORA—We must be careful. The dignity of free love is at stake. (*laughing*) If they only knew—

GABRIEL—Ssshh! Someone'll hear you. Do you want to ruin us? Remember the high cost of eating.

LEONORA—Where are they all, I wonder—and more important, where is lunch? I'm as hungry as a tiger. (*turning to him—suddenly*) How is your affair coming on with the Blessed Damozel, Lucy?

GABRIEL—Too well.

LEONORA—I've noticed she's been cool to me lately. You must have been making love to her.

GABRIEL—I haven't; I've simply been reading my poems; but I'm afraid the time has come to be prosy.

LEONORA—Poor Lucy! I like her so much, but she's such a nut.

GABRIEL—She's exceeding fair to look upon, at least, and that's something. If she only knew the wisdom of silence, the charm of vocal inaction in the female—but no, I must listen to all her brainstorms. Its a bit thick, you know. She's just been to see Hedda Gabbler for the Nth time, and she's obsessed by it. So I have to play the drunken gentleman with the vine leaves in his hair, whatever his name is.

LEONORA—If she saw you on some of your nights she wouldn't doubt your ability to fill the bill. I'm afraid she's becoming quite impossible—Ibsen, in this advanced age! Imagine a modern husband living with an old-fashioned Ibsen woman! I begin to pity the Blond Beast.

GABRIEL—There, you're wrong. After all, with all her fits, Lucy is delightful. I see nothing in her husband but an overgrown clod.

LEONORA—Ah, so? You don't know him. There's more than you dream of beneath his boyish exterior.

GABRIEL—How do you know? (*indignantly*) Have you been flirting with him?

LEONORA—(*airily*) Perhaps. Attend to your own love affairs and I'll attend to mine.

GABRIEL—Great Blond Beast! Great Big Imbecile!

LEONORA—It seems you're getting jealous again. Why, Gabriel, how refreshing! Kiss me!

GABRIEL—I won't; don't be an idiot! (*angrily*) I tell you I won't stand—

LEONORA—Don't.

GABRIEL—I won't endure being made a fool of behind my back.

LEONORA—(*calmly*) Don't.

GABRIEL—If I thought for one second—I'd leave you instantly.

LEONORA—Do.

GABRIEL—What? (*They are interrupted by the entrance of the maid. Gabriel strides around the room fuming. Leo turns to the maid.*)

LEONORA—Is Mrs. Drayton around anywhere?

THE MAID—Yes, Miss, in the garden, I think. Shall I tell her you're here?

LEONORA—Yes, do, will you? (*The maid goes out rear.*)

GABRIEL—(*stands in front of Leonora with his arms folded*) Remember. I've warned you.

LEONORA—Pooh! (*She snaps her fingers.*) That for your warning. When I brought Lucy to our studio you didn't hesitate to start right in casting your spells in under my nose.

GABRIEL—But she's necessary to my work.

LEONORA—Stuff! The old excuse! You've said that about every one of them. Its your own love of being adored, that's the real reason. Don't think I'm jealous. Go right ahead and amuse yourself. I don't mind.

GABRIEL—(*incredulously*) You don't?

LEONORA—Not a bit; but you've got to let me have my own little fling.

GABRIEL—Little fling! You mean that lout, Drayton?

LEONORA—Perhaps. He appeals to me terrifically—physically; and I'm sure he has a good mind, too.

GABRIEL—(*with an attempt at superior disdain*) I must say your tastes are very low. (*furiously*) And am I to submit while you make a monkey of me in this fashion?

LEONORA—I've had to. It'll do you good to find out how a monkey feels.

GABRIEL—I tell you I'll leave you flat at the first inkling—

LEONORA—Run along, then. (*He turns away from her and strides toward the windows.*) Farewell, my beloved! Aren't you going to kiss me good'bye?

GABRIEL—(*coming back to her—intensely*) You're an empty-headed nincompoop!

LEONORA—(*gets up and dances around him singing*) Empty-headed nincompoop! But I do not give a hoop! (*Lucy appears at the windows in the rear. Leonora sees her and runs and flings her arms around her as she enters.*) What a dear you look today! (*She kisses her effusively. Gabriel stands biting his lips, trying to subdue his ill temper.*)

LUCY—(*embarrassed by Leonora's reception*) Have you been here long? I went for a stroll in the garden with mother.

LEONORA—Where is she? Never mind, I'll find her. I must see her. She's a dear. Ta-ta! (*She runs out into the garden.*)

GABRIEL—(*is himself again. He comes and takes Lucy's hand and looks into her eyes ardently.*) Leo was right. You are beautiful today—as ever. (*He kisses her hand passionately.*)

LUCY—(*embarrassed; taking her hand away, hurriedly*) Have you brought your poems? (*She comes forward and sits down on the lounge. He pulls up a chair close to her.*)

GABRIEL—Yes; but I won't bore you with them yet awhile.

LUCY—(*reproachfully*) Bore? It isn't kind of you to say that when you know how deeply I admire them.

GABRIEL—Life is the most beautiful poem of all, if we can make it so. Let me simply breathe, live, here in the same room with you for an eternal moment or so. That will be a more wonderful poem than any I could read.

LUCY—(*haltingly*) I'm afraid you'd soon find it—very tiresome.

GABRIEL—It would be heaven! I am weary of reading, writing, thinking. I want to feel, to live a poem. I want to sit and let my soul drink in your beauty, and forget everything else.

LUCY—(*archly*) Ah, sir poet, but you mustn't. If you don't feel in the mood for reading, then you must talk. I am lonely, and you are the only one who can understand my solitude. I cannot talk to the others. They live in another world. You are the only one who loves the things I love.

GABRIEL—(*kissing her hand*) How can I thank you for feeling that? (*She allows him to keep her hand in both of his.*)

LUCY—No, it is I who should thank you.

GABRIEL—Ah no, no, Princess!

LUCY—But yes. You do not mock my dreams, my longings, with the old thread-bare platitudes. (*then wearily with a great sigh*) My life appeared so futilely hopeless; I was so alone, until you came; and I was mortally bored with everything.

GABRIEL—(*hastily*) I know how you feel—crushed in, tied down by the petty round of family life. (*with affected melancholy*) Do you think I haven't mentally rebelled against the same bonds, suffered from the same irritating restraints as you? Ah, you don't know.

LUCY—But you—you're not married. Its hardly the same.

GABRIEL—(*hurriedly*) Of course—in that sense, you're right. Nevertheless— (*He heaves a great, unhappy sigh.*)

LUCY—(*with awakened curiosity*) But I thought your relationship with Leonora was ideally happy.

GABRIEL—(*with a scornful smile*) What is ideal in this miserable existence? I was born to be unhappy, I suppose. All poets are; and I must achieve my punishment with the rest.

LUCY—(*softly*) Then you aren't—happy?

GABRIEL—(*bitterly*) Happiness? What is it? A mirage? A reality? I don't know. (*looking at her meaningly*) I see it before me now, within my reach, and yet so far from me; guarded, withheld by every damnable convention in the world. (*She drops her eyes before his intense gaze. He laughs shortly.*) But I'm talking about myself. What do I matter? "Dear God, what means a poet more or less?" I am used to suffering, but you, you must not! You are too good, too wonderful, too beautiful to know anything but joy. Your life should express itself only in beauty, in growth, like a flowers.

LUCY—(*immensely pleased*) I'm afraid you have much too high an opinion of me. I'm not what you would believe— (*with a sad smile*) Simply a discontented, morbid, spoiled child, perhaps, as my mother thinks.

GABRIEL—(*indignantly*) How can she misunderstand you so? Why shouldn't your fine spiritual inner nature revolt against all this sordidness? (*With a sweeping gesture he indicates the room and the grounds outside*.) All this bourgeois sty! At least, I understand you. (*with tender appeal in his voice*) Do I not?

LUCY—(*slowly*) Yes, you do. You are the only one who does.

GABRIEL—Ah, if you would only let me help you!

LUCY—You have—so much, already.

GABRIEL—If you only felt that someone from without could come into your life and take you away, to the mountain tops, to the castles in the air, to the haunt of brave dreams where life is free, and joyous, and noble! If you only felt the need of such a person— (*He looks at her questioningly*.)

LUCY—(*hesitatingly*) Perhaps—I do.

GABRIEL—(*impulsively*) Then let *me* be the one! Your very presence fills me with strength. For you I could do anything, everything! (*Lucy grows ill at ease at this excited outburst and casts an anxious look toward the door on left. Gabriel continues passionately:*) Can't you read the secret in my heart? Don't you hear the song my soul has been singing ever since I first looked into your eyes? (*He kisses her hand ardently. She is frightened and attempts to withdraw it.*) I love you, Lucy! Don't you know that I love you? (*Tom appears in the doorway at the left. He stands there looking at them, an expression of anger coming over his face. Lucy suddenly catches sight of him and tears her hand from Gabriel's grasp with a little cry. Gabriel turns around and jumps to his feet when he sees Tom.*)

TOM—(*icily*) I beg your pardon! (*Then, overcome by his anger he advances toward Gabriel threateningly. The latter shrinks away from him, and looks around wildly for some place of escape.*)

LUCY—(*stepping in between them*) Tom!

TOM—(*recovering himself with an effort, forces a smile, and holds out his hand to Gabriel*) Hello, Adams. I didn't know you were here.

GABRIEL—(*looks at the outstretched hand uncertainly— finally takes it*) Er—just got here—Leo and I—a moment ago. (*He pulls away his hand hurriedly.*) Er—where is Leo, by the way? (*He looks around as if he had thought she was in the same room.*) She was here a second ago. She's always running away like that. Must be in the garden. I'll go and find her— if you'll excuse me.

TOM—(*ironically*) Oh, certainly. (*Gabriel makes his escape. Tom comes over and stands before Lucy who is sitting down on the lounge again, staring at the floor, her cheek resting on her hand.*) Lucy!

LUCY—(*raising her head slowly*) Yes?

TOM—(*awkwardly*) Isn't this—going a bit too far?

LUCY—(*calmly*) What?

TOM—I mean—you know—in my own house—

LUCY—(*coldly*) I'm glad you recognize the fact that its your house and not mine.

TOM—You know I didn't mean that.

LUCY—But I mean it.

TOM—But—what I meant was—I don't understand—

LUCY—No, that's the tragedy of it—you don't understand.

TOM—(*hurt*) You're not fair, Lucy.

LUCY—Fair? And do you think you're fair after the scene you created a minute ago?

TOM—I don't see that I made any scene. I think I held myself in pretty well, considering the circumstances.

LUCY—(*lifting her eyebrows—haughtily*) Considering the circumstances!

TOM—Yes. (*wrathfully*) Dirty little cad!

LUCY—What circumstances are you referring to?

TOM—Now, Lucy, you must acknowledge its rather hard on me to come down here and find that little puppy licking your hand.

LUCY—Don't be vulgar!

TOM—Well, then, kissing your hand.

LUCY—And what of that? Gabriel is one of my dearest friends, and—

TOM—You can't deny he was making love to you, right here in under my nose, the insolent scribbler!

LUCY—(*stiffly*) I deny your right to talk to me in this manner.

TOM—(*hurriedly*) Oh, I'm not blaming you; I know you don't realize what he really is or you wouldn't stand for him a minute. I know his kind—making love to every woman he sees, getting off a lot of poetic slush which sounds good to them; and the worst part of it is all the romantic fools think its genuine!

Lucy—(*jumping to her feet in angry indignation*) So that's
what you consider me—a romantic fool!

Tom—(*realizing he has put his foot in it*) I didn't say you
were one of them. I only said—

Lucy—I don't care to hear your excuses. Besides, what
does it matter? I tell you quite frankly: Gabriel *was* making
love to me.

Tom—Of course he was. He does to everyone. I've heard
all about him.

Lucy—(*wincing*) Don't try to revenge yourself by repeating all the cheap scandal of your stupid friends. How could
they ever know the real Gabriel?

Tom—But that's just what they do know—the real
Gabriel.

Lucy—(*stiffly*) I prefer to rely on my own judgement, not
on theirs. I believe, not his words, but my own intuition.

Tom—And, thinking he was serious, you permitted it?

Lucy—(*defiantly*) Yes.

Tom—But why? Why? (*fearfully*) Don't you—love me?

Lucy—(*rising to the occasion—moodily*) I don't know.

Tom—You don't know! Surely you don't—you can't—
you don't love him?

Lucy—I don't know.

Tom—(*furiously*) The measly little shrimp! I've a good notion to break him in half.

Lucy—(*scornfully*) Leonora should see you now. She
would think you were the blond beast. (*Tom subsides a bit at
this.*) You've no right to ask me if I love Gabriel or anyone
else. You should rely on my frankness to tell you of my own
free will. I won't be forced.

Tom—(*with a hollow laugh*) No right. No, I'm only your
husband!

Lucy—(*with a lofty disdain*) Husband? You know that
word has no meaning for me.

Tom—Well, it has for me. (*pathetically*) You see *I* love *you*.

Lucy—(*continuing as if she hadn't heard*) You are honor-
ably bound by our agreement—

Tom—(*roughly*) That was all foolishness!

Lucy—(*angrily*) You may think so but I do not. For me
its the only thing which is binding. Our being married in the

regular sense means nothing to me at all. If I find I love Gabriel I'll leave with him that instant.

TOM—(*suffering*) Lucy! Please! (*He tries to take her hand but she holds it away from him.*)

LUCY—No, its no use being sentimental about it. I advise you to reread the agreement you signed as a man of honor, and you'll have a clearer idea of the conditions of our life together. You seem to have forgotten. Until your misconceptions are cleared up I prefer not to discuss the matter with you further. (*She starts to sweep past him out into the garden.*)

TOM—(*bitterly*) I remember I'm allowed the same liberty of action as you are by that agreement. I haven't forgotten that.

LUCY—(*stopping*) Certainly you are. What do you mean?

TOM—(*with a hard laugh*) I mean its about time I made use of some of my—freedom.

LUCY—(*trying to appear indifferent—coldly*) You may do as you please. (*She goes out. Tom throws himself into a chair, lights a cigarette, throws it away, gets up and walks up and down irritably. Mrs. Ashleigh enters from the garden and stands for a moment looking at Tom who does not see her. She comes forward.*)

TOM—(*trying to conceal his irritation*) Ah, Mother, too hot for you outside? (*He arranges an easy chair for her and she sits down.*)

MRS. ASHLEIGH—(*smiling at him—gently*) What's the matter, Tom? Even if I couldn't read you like a book, I've seen Gabriel, and I've seen Lucy, and I know something unpleasant has occurred. What was it?

TOM—(*hesitatingly*) Oh—nothing much—only I came to get something in here, and I found that little insect— (*He stops, frowning.*)

MRS. ASHLEIGH—Yes?

TOM—(*blurting it out*) Holding her hand and kissing it.

MRS. ASHLEIGH—(*with a smile*) Oh, is that all? That's a favorite mannerism of Gabriel's, I believe. Its so romantic, and it gives one such an air. Why, he kissed my hand out in the garden not ten minutes ago.

TOM—(*angrily*) It was the way he did it.

MRS. ASHLEIGH—And what happened afterward?

TOM—Oh—nothing.

MRS. ASHLEIGH—Now, Tom! Surely you can confide in me.

TOM—Oh, well, he ran away as soon as he could; and then Lucy and I had a regular row. (*He throws himself into a chair and frowns fiercely.*)

MRS. ASHLEIGH—(*smiling*) Your first row?

TOM—Yes.

MRS. ASHLEIGH—What? Not one on your honeymoon?

TOM—No.

MRS. ASHLEIGH—The first row is always a blow. I can remember mine—the day after my marriage. So you see you're lucky. The tenth one won't be so bad, and the hundredeth—not to mention the thousandth—poof! Mere puffs of wind ruffling the surface.

TOM—(*indignantly*) Its serious to me.

MRS. ASHLEIGH—Then I'll be serious, too; but you must answer my questions. Did you tell Lucy you objected to this Gabriel?

TOM—Certainly I did! I've stood it long enough. He's around the house more than the cat is. Wherever I go I find him. If I start to sit down in a chair I discover he's in it. I can't see Lucy alone for a minute. I have to sit and listen to his everlasting poems. Its got to stop.

MRS. ASHLEIGH—You're on the wrong tack. I made the same mistake myself this morning—became irritated because Lucy kept quoting his banal epigrams—on this hot day! So I allowed myself a few disparaging remarks about the gentleman. (*shaking her head*) Its foolish. I shouldn't have done it. You shouldn't either. We ought to know better.

TOM—Oh, I know what you preached to me the night before we were married, and I've tried to follow your plan religiously. Lot of good its done!

MRS. ASHLEIGH—You're ungrateful. If it wasn't for my advice I think your first quarrell would have taken place ten minutes after leaving the church instead of four months later.

TOM—Its too humiliating. I can't give in all the time.

MRS. ASHLEIGH—You must—if you want to have your own way.

TOM—There's a limit to everything. Why last evening I went to the bathroom and found him there shaving—with my razor!

MRS. ASHLEIGH—(*laughs—then becomes serious*) It seems we've both made a frightful mess of things today. Lucy will make Gabriel the leading issue after this, out of pure defiance.

TOM—Well, I can't knuckle down now—after our row.

MRS. ASHLEIGH—What did Lucy have to say in answer to your objections?

TOM—Referred me to that silly agreement I was foolish enough to sign.

MRS. ASHLEIGH—(*horrified*) You didn't put it that way to her?

TOM—(*with a great show of manliness*) Yes, I did—only stronger.

MRS. ASHLEIGH—Oh, this is frightful! Why *did* you do it? The agreement of agreements, Lucy's masterpiece of free, unfettered radicalism—and you dared to cast slurs on it! What did you say, in heaven's name?

TOM—I told her if she was going to use her guaranteed-by-agreement liberty in the way she's been doing, it was about time I began to use some of mine along the same lines.

MRS. ASHLEIGH—(*aghast at first*) You did! (*then thoughtfully*) Hmm. (*her face suddenly lighting up*) Why, Tom, its an inspiration! I have underestimated your wiles.

TOM—(*modestly*) I only meant it as a bluff.

MRS. ASHLEIGH—Bluff? Indeed not! Its exactly what you must do.

TOM—What do you mean?

MRS. ASHLEIGH—And now I remember something which ought to be valuable to us. Its right in line with your idea.

TOM—(*puzzled*) My idea? You don't think I've any intention of carrying out that foolish threat of mine?

MRS. ASHLEIGH—But you must! (*as Tom shakes his head decisively*) Of course I mean you must pretend to, you great baby!

TOM—(*commencing to smile*) Oh, I see.

MRS. ASHLEIGH—Did Lucy act taken back when you asserted your right to bestow your affections elsewhere?

TOM—(*grinning*) She didn't look very pleased.

MRS. ASHLEIGH—Then it will be all plain sailing. (*She leans back in her chair with a sigh of relief.*) So that's settled.

TOM—Yes; but what's settled?

Mrs. Ashleigh—Why, that you're to fall in love with Leo.

Tom—(*astonished*) Leo?

Mrs. Ashleigh—Leo—Leonora— The little Nietzsche lady—Gabriel's Leo. You shall be her Great Blond Beast.

Tom—But I don't see—why Leo?

Mrs. Ashleigh—For many reasons. First, you like her, don't you?

Tom—Yes; but I never thought of her in that light.

Mrs. Ashleigh—Of course you didn't, silly boy. I assure you I've no suspicions regarding you whatever. The second reason is—revenge! You'll be getting back at Gabriel. It will hurt his pride dreadfully and I know he'll be infernally jealous.

Tom—I'd like to make him sweat.

Mrs. Ashleigh—And the third reason I'm not going to tell you. You wouldn't believe it, and I've no proof to offer you. Its just what you'd call a hunch of mine, but I know it will turn out to be the best reason of all.

Tom—Well, granting my willingness to carry out my part, how do you know Leo will fall in with this idea?

Mrs. Ashleigh—Why she's just perishing to start a flirtation with you. Are you blind? She'll think its the greatest lark.

Tom—(*uncertainly*) But is all this fair to Lucy?

Mrs. Ashleigh—(*with a sigh*) Its the only way I can see to bring her back to earth and get her to take up the business of married life seriously. She'll never realize the worth of her good fortune until she sees it slipping from her.

Tom—Well—if you think its best—I'll try it.

Mrs. Ashleigh—Do; and I'll let you know from the inside how things are developing. (*She gets up from her chair.*) I need fresh air after all this intrigue. It must be nearly lunch time. I'll go and tell them.

Tom—(*going over with her to the windows*) Here comes my light-of-love now. (*Leonora comes running breathlessly into the room. She stops suddenly on seeing them.*)

Leonora—I'm not interrupting anything, am I? Every where I go I seem to be one too many.

Mrs. Ashleigh—(*putting her arm around her*) Certainly not, dear.

LEONORA—Gab's in the garden doing the book-reading scene from Francesca da Rimini with Lucy, and they treated me as if I were a contagious disease. (*Tom frowns.*) What time is it? How long before lunch?

TOM—Oh, ten minutes or so?

LEONORA—Then I'll have time to take a bath! (*She dances around gleefully, snapping her fingers.*)

MRS. ASHLEIGH—A bath? In ten minutes?

LEONORA—Oh, I just hop in and out. There's never any hot water where we live. (*to Tom*) Is there plenty of hot water here?

TOM—(*with a smile*) I think so.

LEONORA—And towels?

TOM—I hope so.

LEONORA—Now I say, I forgot! I should have asked you, shouldn't I? May I, please, use your honorable bath tub?

TOM—(*making a deep bow*) It is at your disposal.

MRS. ASHLEIGH—(*with a significant glance at Tom*) I'll walk out and tell them how late its getting to be. If Lucy's going to the concert with you she ought to get ready.

TOM—(*after a moment's hesitation—as Mrs. A. is going out*) Perhaps you'd better tell Lucy I'm not sure whether I can go with her or not.

MRS. ASHLEIGH—(*with a comprehending smile*) Very well, I'll tell her. (*She goes into the garden and off right.*)

LEONORA—That's right, you are going to a concert, aren't you? Don't you think they're a bore on a day like this?

TOM—Yes, I emphatically do.

LEONORA—Then don't go.

TOM—But I've practically promised Lucy.

LEONORA—She won't mind. Let her take Gab. He pretends he just dotes on the new music. There'll be a pair of them. One ought to suffer for one's poses, don't you think?

TOM—I sure do. But how will I spend the afternoon?

LEONORA—Come with me.

TOM—Where to?

LEONORA—Oh, I have to drop in at an exhibition for a few minutes but I won't be longer than that. You like paintings, anyway, don't you?

TOM—*Some* paintings.

LEONORA—Now I say, don't be bourgeois! Come down with me and you'll see enough art to talk about with the country folk for years. Don't look so glum. I won't keep you there long. You can take me to the Lafayette afterwards and we'll have an absinthe together. I'll blow you. I've got seventy cents. We can get quite squiffy on that.

TOM—(*after a moment's hesitation*) Its a go. I'm with you.

LEONORA—Ta-ta, then. I'm off for my dip. (*She looks up at him scrutinizingly for a moment.*) Bend down your head. (*He obediently does so. Lucy appears at the windows in the rear and stands looking at them. Leo runs her fingers through his hair, and squints her eye at it.*) I say, you have got nice hair, haven't you? Well, au revoir, Blond Beast. See you later. (*She skips laughingly out of the room. Lucy walks into the room.*)

TOM—(*turning to her—with a forced laugh*) Leo's the devil of a tease, isn't she?

LUCY—(*coldly*) Yes? (*trying to conceal her irritation*) I can remember when you considered her a freak.

TOM—Yes; strange how erroneous one's first impressions sometimes are. Now that I know her better I like her more than any of your friends.

LUCY—So I perceive.

TOM—Eh?

LUCY—Nothing. Mother said you didn't know whether you'd go to the concert or not. Isn't it rather late to back out?

TOM—You can easily find a substitute. Take Gab along. He'll pretend to enjoy that stuff better than I could. (*He takes the tickets out of his pocket and hands them to her.*) Here's the tickets. (*She masters her impulse to fly into a rage, and takes them from him.*)

LUCY—Do you have to go back to the office?

TOM—Oh, no. I'm through with work for the day.

LUCY—Then why do you break this engagement with me?

TOM—You know I don't care about concerts. I'd only be bored to death if I went.

LUCY—(*insistently*) Won't it be just as much of a bore to stay in—(*scornfully*) this place?

TOM—(*warmly*) For you it might. You see our tastes differ. Anyway, I don't intend to remain here. I feel like a little re-laxation.

LUCY—(*scornfully*) The baseball game?

TOM—(*regretfully*) No.

LUCY—Then what, if I'm not too inquisitive?

TOM—(*playing his part—jubilantly*) A regular lark—with Leo. I'm going to take her to an exhibition of paintings some-place, and—

LUCY—(*laughing sarcastically*) That will be interesting—for you.

TOM—Yes, it will. Leo promises to explain them all to me. I've often wanted to get a clear comprehension of what some of those chaps were driving at; and she being one of them herself can put me on to all the inside stuff.

LUCY—You must have changed to take such a sudden interest in Art.

TOM—I have.

LUCY—(*with a sneer*) Strange I haven't noticed it.

TOM—I haven't let you see it. I was sure you'd misunderstand me.

LUCY—(*flushing*) Are you trying to be humourous at my expense?

TOM—Heaven forbid! I mean what I say. Don't think you're the only misunderstood person about this house. I have my own aspirations which you will never understand; only I'm resigned to my fate.

LUCY—(*caustically*) You *are* trying to be funny, aren't you?

TOM—Please forgive me for feeling cheerful. I can't help it. You see Leo has promised to take me to the Lafayette, blow me to absinthe, tea me at her studio, and I feel light-headed at the prospect of such a bust-up. (*Mrs. Ashleigh and Gabriel enter from the rear. Gabriel keeps as far away from Tom as he can.*)

LUCY—Would you like to go with me to the concert, Gabriel?

GABRIEL—(*looking at Tom*) Why—er—you see—I'm not sure—

TOM—(*heartily*) You've got to go. I can't; and Lucy insists on someone being bored with her.

GABRIEL—Oh, in that case, I'd love to, Luc-—Mrs. Drayton.

TOM—Then that's fixed, and Leo and I can have our bust-up.

GABRIEL—(*frowning*) Leo?

TOM—Yes; she and I are going to have a real party together.

GABRIEL—(*looking angrily round the room*) Where is Leo?

TOM—Upstairs, taking a bath.

LUCY—(*indignantly*) Bath!

TOM—Yes, I gave her the freedom of the tub. (*to Gab*) You know there's never any hot water at your place.

THE MAID—(*entering from the right*) Lunch is served.

LUCY—(*petulantly*) We'll be late for the concert if we wait for her. I'd better run up and tell her to hurry.

GABRIEL—(*furiously*) I'll go up and tell her.

TOM—(*stepping before him*) Oh no, we couldn't think of putting you to the trouble. You three go in and start lunch. I'll run up and tell her. (*Lucy and Gabriel both show very apparent disapproval of this proposition. While all are standing in hesitation, Leonora enters hurriedly from the left. She has on Tom's bathrobe which trails in a long train in back of her, her bare feet peeping out from beneath the front of it.*)

LEONORA—(*calmly critical and absolutely unembarrassed*) Now I must say, this is a nice home! Why there isn't any soap up there! I want some soap!

(*The Curtain Falls*)

ACT THREE

SCENE—*Same as Act Two—a month later. It is about seven o'clock in the evening. Tom and Leonora are discovered. Tom is sitting by the table, frowning, his mind evidently troubled about something. He is making a polite but ineffectual attempt to appear interested in Leonora's effervescent chatter. She is never still for a moment but flits from chair to chair, sitting on the arms, perching on the edge of the table, picking up books and throwing them down again, going to look out of the windows, etc.*

LEONORA—(*coming over to Tom and looking at him with a quizzical smile*) Now I ask you, what are you so gloomy about? (*Tom attempts a smile.*) Heavens, what a movie-actor smile! Don't do it again. You needn't be polite with me, you know. I love to talk to myself, and your replies are no good anyway. A second ago you said "no" when any perfect gentleman should have said "yes" and agreed with me.

TOM—(*a bit confused*) I guess I'm a little off color tonight.

LEONORA—(*sitting on the edge of the table*) Indigestion. I ate too much myself. We all do out here. (*Tom looks at her impatiently.*) But its jolly to be a glutton for once in a way after a starve-and-grow-thin studio diet. (*with a chuckle*) How Gab gorges himself! He's losing his spiritual waist line since he began coming out here. Have you noticed?

TOM—(*explosively*) No!

LEONORA—Yes, he's gradually assuming the blubber of prosperity—given up free verse for free food. He hasn't written a poem since my last Welch rabbit.

TOM—(*bitingly*) Thank God the situation has some redeeming features.

LEONORA—Oh, he does real stuff every now and then, when he forgets himself for a moment. (*She goes over to the window and looks out at the garden.*) Where's mother? I haven't seen her since dinner.

TOM—Mother?

LEONORA—Your mother-in-law—Mrs. Ashleigh.

TOM—(*sarcastically*) Oh!

LEONORA—She told me I could call her that. She's a dear. Where is she, I wonder?

447

TOM—(*grumpily*) I don't know.

LEONORA—Probably chaperoning those two. (*Tom winces. She comes back to the table and commences to roll a cigarette.*) How bored they must be with each other! Its too dark for Gab to read his poems, and without the sound of his own voice to spur him on, he's a stick. (*She fixes the cigarette in her holder and lights it.*) I'll bet they're holding hands and saying: "Ain't nature grand!"

TOM—Damn! (*He gets up and strides up and down the room.*)

LEONORA—(*sitting on the edge of the table and smoking— calmly*) You're not jealous of Gab, are you?

TOM—(*trying to appear scornful*) Jealous? Do you think I'm crazy?

LEONORA—I don't know. You would be if you were. I assure you Gab's entirely harmless. He's in love with himself and there's not a rival in sight. (*looking at him keenly*) Do sit down! (*He does so.*) There's something wrong with you. What is it? Tell me. (*doubtfully*) You're not falling in love with me, are you?

TOM—(*decidedly*) I am not.

LEONORA—You needn't be so unflatteringly emphatic about it. But its just as well. You have a certain physical appeal, as I've often said, but I've given up sex for good. I've been through it all, and there's nothing in it for anyone who wants to accomplish something real.

TOM—(*forced to smile*) I'll take your word for it, Miss. Barnes.

LEONORA—The next time you call me that I hope you choke. What's the matter with Leo? Of course, it isn't my real name. I'll bet you can't guess the horrible title my silly parents wished on me.

TOM—What was it?

LEONORA—Pearl! Imagine, Pearl! I simply couldn't put up with Pearl. We once had a colored cook who was called Leonora—she was named after a race horse, she said—and I liked the sound and swiped it. So Leonora I've been ever since. (*She sees that Tom is staring grumpily before him and not paying any attention to her.*) What ho! (*Tom comes to with a start.*) There *is* something wrong. Don't you feel well?

TOM—Oh, its nothing.

LEONORA—Is it business worries, then?

TOM—(*grasping eagerly at this excuse*) Yes—sort of.

LEONORA—(*interestedly*) You haven't been dabbling in Wall street and robbing the till, have you? (*clapping her hands*) I say! That would give me a moment—seeing a movie crook in real life.

TOM—(*dryly*) I'm sorry, but I'll have to disappoint you.

LEONORA—(*putting out her cigarette*) I suppose its the price of paper or some other dull thing that's bothering you. (*She jumps to the floor and stretches, yawning.*) This is a bore! (*Lucy, Mrs. Ashleigh and Gabriel enter from the french windows in the rear.*) Hello, hello, hello! Here you are at last. (*Lucy looks at her coldly, Mrs. Ashleigh smiles, while Gabriel appears furious at finding Leo and Tom together.*)

TOM—(*getting up from his chair, and adopting a pose of smiling joviality*) Hello! We didn't expect you back from your walk so soon. (*Lucy and Gabriel sit down on right. Mrs. Ashleigh takes the chair in the middle. Leo hops to the edge of the table again.*)

MRS. ASHLEIGH—It was becoming chilly outside so we thought we'd better come back. (*There is an uncomfortable silence following this. Each one appears to be trying desperately to find something to say.*)

LEO—(*bursting out impulsively*) I say! This *is* a bore! You're all as glum as a tree full of owls. Let's do something, anything!

TOM—(*forcing a smile*) I'm game. What do you suggest?

LEONORA—Lets all motor down and take in some theatre.

MRS. ASHLEIGH—That's a good idea, Leo. What do you think, Lucy?

LUCY—(*with a wan smile*) I don't care, Mother.

LEONORA—Isn't there some perfectly shocking burlesque we can see? (*clapping her hands*) That *would* be a lark!

GABRIEL—What silly nonsense!

LEO—(*airily*) Speak when you're spoken to, Gab, my dear. (*to Tom*) Isn't there one?

TOM—(*with a smile*) I'm hardly posted on that subject.

LUCY—(*coldly*) Of course, Leo is only joking. She knows Mother wouldn't go.

LEO—I'll bet she would. She's more of a sport than any of

us. Now I ask you, wouldn't you, Mother? (*Lucy shows her indignation at this familiarity and turns to Gabriel who is biting his lips and glowering at Leo.*)

MRS. ASHLEIGH—(*gently*) Its so long since I've been to one, my dear, I'm afraid I'm not young enough to enjoy them any more. (*Lucy looks at her mother in shocked surprise.*) However I suggest that we eliminate all serious plays for tonight. I'd like something cheerful—something with jokes and music—say, a good musical comedy.

GABRIEL—You won't find that, Mrs. Ashleigh, in a country where vulgarity is mistaken for humour.

TOM—(*sarcastically*) They do it differently in Jersey City, eh, Gabriel?

LEONORA—Don't mind Gab. He's only posing. He went with me to see "Oh, You Cutey!" last winter—the press agent gave us passes, you know—and nearly went into hysterics laughing. And then the papers came out next day and called it the most vulgar exhibition that had ever disgraced a New York theatre.

GABRIEL—(*jumping from his chair—furiously*) I was not myself that night—and you know it!

LEONORA—You were squiffy, you mean? All the rest of the audience knew that, too. But that's no excuse. In vino veritas, you know, and all the rest of it.

TOM—(*who has been glancing over the paper*) This looks good—the new show at the Casino. (*getting up*) I'll phone for the tickets and order the car.

GABRIEL—I'm afraid— Thank you just the same, Drayton, but—the fact is I've just remembered an engagement—

LEONORA—Liar!

GABRIEL—(*raging*) Will you hold your tongue, you little— (*He controls himself by a violent effort. Leo laughs and makes a face at him.*)

TOM—(*perfunctorily*) Sorry you can't come. That'll make it four. (*He starts for the door.*)

LUCY—(*languidly*) I don't think I care much for that type of amusement either.

LEONORA—Oh I say, here's our party breaking up already.

TOM—(*frowning*) Then you won't come?

LUCY—(*coldly*) I think not.

MRS. ASHLEIGH—(*coaxingly*) Do come, dear! I'm sure you'll enjoy a little foolishness for a change.

LUCY—(*wearily*) No, I've a headache, Mother. I think I'll stay home.

MRS. ASHLEIGH—Then perhaps we'd all better stay.

LUCY—No. You three go. (*looking at Tom defiantly*) I'm sure Gabriel will keep me company, part of the time at least— (*she turns to Gab, questioningly*) if his engagement—?

GABRIEL—(*looking at Leo with malicious satisfaction*) Oh, that was nothing of any importance. I can phone. I'll be delighted to remain, Mrs. Drayton.

LEONORA—(*breezily*) Then that's settled. (*She flits up to Tom who is standing uncertainly, glaring at Gabriel, and gives him a push.*) Hurry on now, and phone. They may be sold out.

TOM—(*gloomily*) That'll be three. (*He goes out left.*)

LEONORA—I do hope there'll be acrobats in it! I *adore* acrobats! They're so decorative in their tights and spangles. I'd just love to paint them.

GABRIEL—(*sneeringly*) I'm sure the acrobats would recognize you as a fellow-craftsman if they ever saw your work.

LEONORA—I *could* say something of your trapeze stunts in free verse but I won't. You can't pick a fight with me tonight, Gab. I ate too much dinner.

MRS. ASHLEIGH—(*hastily—as Gabriel is framing some biting retort*) When does it start, I wonder? Look in the paper, Leonora, will you? (*Leo picks up the paper and commences glancing through it.*)

LUCY—(*boredly*) You won't miss anything if you're late, Mother. Those productions were concocted with an eye for the comfort of the Tired Business Man.

GABRIEL—Exactly!

LEONORA—Well, we'll have one with us—Tom; so he ought to enjoy it. (*She turns over the paper angrily.*) I never could find anything in the beastly papers. (*Tom enters from the left.*)

TOM—They had nothing left but a stage box. I told them to save that for us.

MRS. ASHLEIGH—A box! Good heavens, look at me. I can't go in a box.

LEONORA—Why? You're all right.

TOM—Why yes, Mother.

MRS. ASHLEIGH—(*giving Tom a significant look in the direction of Lucy and Gabriel*) No, really, I couldn't go looking like this. Besides, I've been thinking while you were gone that perhaps, after all, I better not go.

LEONORA—Oh, do come along.

MRS. ASHLEIGH—I'm sure Mr. Ashleigh will expect me home early after my staying out here for the past two nights. So I really don't think I'd better go. You take Leo, Tom, and send the car back for me.

TOM—(*reluctantly*) All right, Mother, if you think its best. (*Lucy and Gab show very evident disapproval of this plan.*)

GABRIEL—Why not call it all off for tonight?

LEONORA—Well, I guess not! I must have my acrobats tonight or die. (*She looks ruefully at her smock.*) But what am I going to wear, I ask you? If I go this way they'll think I'm one of the performers.

TOM—(*boldly*) Lucy can let you have something, I'm sure.

LUCY—(*starting to her feet—her eyes blazing*) I—I'd be glad to, but you seem to forget Leo is much smaller than me.

LEONORA—(*delighted*) Oh, I can fix that all right. I've worn too many hired costumes to masquerades not to know how to make things look a fit. With a few pins— You can let your maid help me. I'll be ready in no time. I can wear your fur coat till we get in the box and then sit in back. Noone'll know the difference. Lucy, you're a dear!

TOM—(*looking at his watch*) We'll have to hurry. The car'll be here at quarter of.

LEONORA—Don't worry, ole love. I'll be in my soup and fish as soon as you will. Show me what I can wear, Lucy. I promise not to tear it.

LUCY—(*her voice trembling a little*) Very well—if *you* don't mind. (*She walks toward doorway on left, biting her lips.*)

LEONORA—Mind? I think its no end of a lark. You must come up too, Mother, and help tuck me in. Will you?

MRS. ASHLEIGH—(*with an uneasy glance at Lucy—uncertainly*) Of course, my dear. (*They all go out left leaving Gabriel alone.*)

GABRIEL—(*sitting for a moment in silent rage*) Of all the

damned cheek! (*He gets up and strides furiously up and down the room, running his hands through his hair. Suddenly he utters a loud "damn" and picks a book from the table as if he were going to hurl it at someone. He still has the book held high in the air when Lucy returns. He puts it back on the table sheepishly.*)

LUCY—(*her face still flushed with anger—irritably*) What in the world are you doing with that book?

GABRIEL—(*following her and sitting down on a chair close to the lounge on which she throws herself*) Er—to tell you the truth I was about to give way to a stupid fit of rage.

LUCY—(*coldly*) About what?

GABRIEL—Why the way Leo jumped at wearing your gown. It was so nervy of her, so ill-mannered, so—

LUCY—I'm sure she's perfectly welcome to it if she thinks she can make it fit.

GABRIEL—I was never so ashamed of anything in my life.

LUCY—I wouldn't take it so seriously if I were you.

GABRIEL—Leo is too preposterous at times.

LUCY—(*irritably*) Please! Let's drop the subject.

GABRIEL—(*with an ill grace*) I beg your pardon. (*There is an uncomfortable silence. Lucy stares straight in front of her, now and then casting a side glance of irritation at Gabriel who is fidgetting nervously in his chair, and biting his nails fiercely.*)

LUCY—(*endeavoring to make talk*) Do you know anything good for a headache?

GABRIEL—Why—bromo-seltzer, isn't it?

LUCY—It never brought me any relief.

GABRIEL—Its supposed to be good.

LUCY—It isn't. (*The talk abruptly ceases.*)

GABRIEL—(*after an unpleasant pause—desperately*) Is it very bad?

LUCY—What?

GABRIEL—Your toothache.

LUCY—(*icily*) My toothache? I haven't—

GABRIEL—(*hastily*) I mean your headache.

LUCY—Splitting.

GABRIEL—(*perfunctorily*) I'm so sorry. Isn't there anything I can do?

LUCY—No, thank you, I think not. (*Another long silence. Gabriel becomes more nervous than ever. He is evidently re-*

straining an outburst of rage only by a mighty effort. Lucy's lips are compressed and she glares at him angrily.)

GABRIEL—(*in an exasperated tone*) How shall we spend the evening? Can't we—? (*He can find nothing to suggest.*)

LUCY—Yes?

GABRIEL—What do you say to a walk?

LUCY—We've just come from one; and besides, its too chilly.

GABRIEL—(*jumping up from his chair*) There must be something we can do. We can't sit here all night like a couple of— (*he hesitates, then blurts it out*) of mummies. Its ridiculous!

LUCY—(*her eyebrows raised*) If you would rather go home—

GABRIEL—(*quickly takes her hand in both of his, much against her will*) You know I didn't mean that, Lucy. I'm terribly out of key. Don't be cruel to me. I only want— I love you so much I can't bear to have anyone— Forgive me, Lucy! (*He raises her hand and kisses it.*)

LUCY—(*snatching her hand away—pettishly*) Don't be silly!

GABRIEL—(*in accents of wounded pride*) Silly!

LUCY—Someone is liable to come in any moment.

GABRIEL—(*relieved*) Oh! Yes, of course, you're right. I'm too impulsive. I forget—these infernally stupid conditions. (*Lucy tries to wither him with a look but he does not see it. He sits down again and leans his chin on his hands and stares soulfully into space. Lucy taps her foot nervously on the floor. There is a long pause.*)

GABRIEL—(*suddenly*) What are they doing all this time?

LUCY—(*coldly*) They haven't been gone five minutes.

GABRIEL—(*rudely*) It seems five years. (*Lucy stiffens at this remark.*) You wouldn't care to have me read to you, would you? (*He reaches into his pocket with a complacent smile and takes out some manuscript.*) I've a couple of new poems here I'm sure you haven't heard. I think they're some of the best things I've done—and it was your inspiration which gave birth to them all. Shall I read them?

LUCY—(*harshly*) No, please, not now! (*Gabriel is dumbfounded. Lucy attempts a feeble smile.*) I've such a headache I'm afraid I couldn't appreciate them tonight.

GABRIEL—(*crestfallen*—*stuffs the poems back in his pocket—in hurt tones*) I'm afraid my poems are commencing to bore you. (*He waits for Lucy to deny this, but as she does not, he continues huffily*) In fact, I'm quite sure they bore you.

LUCY—(*with weary vexation*) Please don't misunderstand me. I meant nothing of the kind.

GABRIEL—But there was something in your voice which— (*with hurt dignity*) I promise I won't bore you with them in future.

LUCY—(*coldly*) One doesn't feel in the mood for poetry all the time. We can't all be poets.

GABRIEL—(*with a superior air*) Decidedly not.

LUCY—(*meanly*) And some of your poems are—well— rather difficult to understand.

GABRIEL—(*stung*) One must possess a fine soul to really appreciate any true poetry.

LUCY—(*indignantly*) By which you mean I haven't?

GABRIEL—(*fuming*) I don't mean anything. I wasn't thinking of what I was saying. What difference does it make what I meant? My mind is on something else. What time is it, I wonder? They'll be late. What can be keeping them up there so long? (*Lucy makes no reply but sighs wearily. Gabriel walks up and down, frowning, muttering to himself, on the verge of an outburst.*)

LUCY—(*a trace of contempt in her voice*) You're in a fine temper tonight.

GABRIEL—(*roughly*) And why shouldn't I be?

LUCY—Why should you be?

GABRIEL—(*drawing a deep breath*) Because— (*bursting forth*) I tell you I won't endure it any longer! (*He bangs his fist on the table.*)

LUCY—(*contemptuously*) I don't know what you're talking about.

GABRIEL—Oh yes, you do! You aren't blind. You can see what's in front of your eyes, can't you? (*raging*) I'll tell you what I mean. I mean this shameless affair between your husband and Leo which is going on openly right here, right in your own house. And if you don't put a stop to it, I will!

LUCY—(*freezingly*) I refuse to discuss the matter with you.

GABRIEL—(*miserably*) Please don't be angry with me, Lucy. Don't take that attitude. Why shouldn't we discuss it with each other? Noone else cares. (*flying off again*) Its an insult to our intelligence—the way they flaunt it before us. Its—its revolting! We've got to put a stop to it, that's all!

LUCY—Speak for yourself. (*her voice trembling*) For my part, Tom is free to do as he chooses.

GABRIEL—Ha! Just you try and see how far you're free to do as you choose. You'll soon have your eyes opened.

LUCY—You're mistaken. We are both equally free. We signed a mutual agreement to that effect the night before we were married.

GABRIEL—(*scornfully*) Pooh! A lot of attention he'd pay to that if you ever dared go as far as he has.

LUCY—(*growing pale*) I don't understand you.

GABRIEL—You mean you *won't* understand me. It seems you prefer to be blind.

LUCY—(*indignantly*) I see a purely harmless flirtation, if that's what you're driving at.

GABRIEL—(*with a sneer*) Purely harmless? Flirtation? Well, you are a little innocent—if this isn't a pose of your's.

LUCY—It isn't a pose! Its what I believe in spite of all your nasty insinuations. (*her eyes filling*) I know Tom would tell me if— (*She catches herself in time to choke back a sob.*)

GABRIEL—(*vehemently*) Its a shame, a beastly shame, for him to treat you this way. And Leo—she's a little fool. But you must face the truth. Its decidedly serious, this affair of their's, when you come to know the facts.

LUCY—(*stubbornly*) You must be mad. You've no proof of what you're saying.

GABRIEL—(*cunningly*) Haven't I? How do you know? You've heard Leo rave about him as her cursed Great Blond Beast, haven't you? Have you read Nietzsche? Do you think Leo has any moral scruples about anything? Well, I don't. And where have they gone on all these motor trips?

LUCY—They always told us where they went.

GABRIEL—And do you think they told us the truth? Well, I am hardly as naive as that.

LUCY—Do you mean they lied? Why do you say such a thing?
GABRIEL—I know—and that's enough. And how about

all those teas alone together at the studio? Do you think—
Oh, but what's the use? If you won't see—

LUCY—(*hysterically*) Its a lie! I won't listen to you!

GABRIEL—(*becoming more and more excited*) Its the truth!
And you've got to realize it. Things can't go on in this way.
I won't stand for it. Its too humiliating!

LUCY—(*trying to calm herself*) *You* won't stand for it. How
about me?

GABRIEL—Its a thousand times easier for you. If he goes
away you can always get a million more just like him; while
I—I can't live with any woman but Leo. She's the only one
who understands me, who can protect me from the others—
and from myself. I tell you she's necessary to me and I won't
give her up to any Philistine like him.

LUCY—(*scornfully*) So this is your free comradship! Hasn't
she a right to her own soul?

GABRIEL—No! She's a fool!

LUCY—And if she loves someone else?

GABRIEL—She doesn't. She only thinks she does. She's a
fool, I tell you! (*after a pause*) You must break up this shameless intrigue.

LUCY—*I* must?

GABRIEL—Yes, you must. Tell him I won't permit it. Tell
him he mustn't see Leo any more.

LUCY—This is absurd. Can you possibly think I'd degrade
my pride to that extent?

GABRIEL—(*imploringly*) But you must save me! I implore
you, Lucy—for my sake! I'd be lost without her, the fool! I
couldn't even find my toothbrush. I wouldn't even know
when to get up. Besides, its nothing to you but your hurt
pride because he's your husband. You don't really care anything about him.

LUCY—(*her eyes flashing*) How dare you say that!

GABRIEL—(*staring at her in amazement*) But—you love
me, don't you?

LUCY—(*with supreme contempt*) Love *you*? Do you think
I've lost my mind, you stupid little egotist?

GABRIEL—(*stands stunned for a moment*) But—your
actions—the things you've said—the things you've let me
believe—

Lucy—It was *you* who said you loved me.

Gabriel—But I say that to every woman. They know I'm a poet and they expect it.

Lucy—And does your conceit make you think I took you seriously—had fallen in love with you? Oh, this is too disgusting!

Gabriel—Think of the confessions you made about your unhappy home life. You can't deny them. (*Lucy covers her face with her hands.*) What was I to believe, in heaven's name? (*She doesn't answer or look up at him.*) But you'll persuade him not to run away with Leo, won't you? All the more reason to do so if you love him and don't want to loose him. They're liable to fly off tonight, I tell you. You have no idea what a fool Leo is.

Lucy—(*angrily*) Why don't *you* speak to *her*?

Gabriel—She's such a fool! She wouldn't listen to me. You're the only hope I've got.

Lucy—(*furiously*) And you ask me—to do this!

Gabriel—You must! There's no other way.

Lucy—(*choking back her tears of rage*) And you can dare to continue to insult me by suggesting such a thing?

Gabriel—(*horrified*) Then you won't?

Lucy—(*tearfully*) No! No! Let him go if he wants to. After what you've told me I never want to see him again. And Leo has a right to go. She isn't married to you.

Gabriel—(*frenziedly*) Did she tell you that? Its a lie! Its cowardly of her to deny it.

Lucy—(*looking at him in amazement*) You mean to say you are married?

Gabriel—Of course we are! We've been married for two years. (*Lucy suddenly commences to laugh hysterically. Gabriel is irritated.*) What are you laughing at? Its the truth.

Lucy—(*wildly*) Nothing! Nothing! (*She continues to laugh.*)

Gabriel—The only reason we concealed it was because we were taking a studio in Greenwich Village together when we moved to New York and we were afraid they'd consider us provincial down there if they knew. (*angrily*) Why, in God's name, do you laugh like that?

Lucy—(*hysterically—between laughter and tears*) Go! Go

away! I can't bear the sight of you. Please go! I want to be alone. (*She makes a motion as if she were pushing him out of the room.*)

GABRIEL—(*stands looking down at her for a moment—angrily*) Well— Oh, I'll go crazy if you don't stop that racket! I must get out of this rabbit hutch. (*dramatically*) I must go out under the stars—to think! I must have clean air to breathe! (*He rushes out of the french windows in the rear to the garden. Lucy stops laughing and hides her face in her hands and sobs violently. After a moment Mrs. Ashleigh enters from the hallway. She comes quickly over to Lucy with an anxious expression.*)

MRS. ASHLEIGH—(*putting her hand on Lucy's shoulder*) Lucy! Lucy! What's the matter? (*Lucy doesn't answer but sobs more violently than ever. Mrs. Ashleigh sits down beside her on the lounge and puts her arm around her—soothingly*) There, there, dear. Have a good cry and get it over with. (*Lucy gradually grows calmer and finally lifts her tear-stained face to her mother's. Mrs. Ashleigh kisses her and smiles.*) And now tell me the cause of this breakdown.

LUCY—(*rising from the lounge—a bit wildly*) Its nothing, Mother. I'm tired and my nerves are worn out, I suppose. I haven't slept much the past week.

MRS. ASHLEIGH—You poor child!

LUCY—And I've a splitting headache; and, oh, I'm so sick of everything and everybody—I wish I were dead—or away off someplace alone!

MRS. ASHLEIGH—(*rebukingly*) Now, dear, you musn't begin again in that foolish morbid strain.

LUCY—(*wildly*) Leave me alone! I'll be what I want to be in spite of all of you!

MRS. ASHLEIGH—Lucy!

LUCY—Oh, I didn't mean that, Mother. I don't know what I'm saying or doing any more. Just let me alone.

MRS. ASHLEIGH—But what happened? Please tell me. Did Gabriel—

LUCY—(*irritably*) No! No! What has he to do with me?

MRS. ASHLEIGH—It seems to me, my dear, he's had a lot too much to do with you during the last month.

LUCY—Then all I can say is you must all have evil minds if you're so suspicious of everything.

MRS. ASHLEIGH—(*indignantly*) Why, Lucy! Do you realize what you're saying?

LUCY—He's nothing to me, less than nothing. I don't care if he lives or dies. He was amusing, that was all.

MRS. ASHLEIGH—(*insinuatingly*) Even his love-making, Lucy? Was that amusing?

LUCY—He's a poet and he makes love to every woman. He told me so himself. I never took him seriously.

MRS. ASHLEIGH—There's one person who was made very unhappy by it—someone who loves you very much.

LUCY—(*sceptically*) Who? You, Mother?

MRS. ASHLEIGH—Indeed not. I gave you credit for too much good sense. Gabriel didn't bother me in the least.

LUCY—(*a trace of defiance in her tone*) It couldn't have been anyone else.

MRS. ASHLEIGH—(*gently*) I was speaking of—Tom.

LUCY—(*with a bitter laugh*) Tom!

MRS. ASHLEIGH—Why do you adopt that tone? Don't you believe me? Do you imagine its been pleasant for him to see you always with that crack-brained piece of conceit?

LUCY—(*sarcastically*) He's had plenty of consolation.

MRS. ASHLEIGH—(*with a smile*) You mean little Leo? Don't be silly, child.

LUCY—(*indignantly*) Silly! If you knew—

MRS. ASHLEIGH—(*interrupting her—calmly*) I do know all about it, and its your own fault. What could you expect? When you and Gabriel were eternally mooning around together, did you think Leo and Tom would mope in separate corners until you were through amusing yourselves? Remember the contract you drew up yourself—equal liberty of action. You've no reason to complain, my dear. It serves you right.

LUCY—(*tensely*) And you can taunt me with it in this manner?

MRS. ASHLEIGH—Yes, I can. You deserve it.

LUCY—This shameless, disgusting liason!

MRS. ASHLEIGH—(*with smiling reproof*) Those are strong words. I didn't think they were used any more outside of cheap melodrama.

LUCY—There are no words vile enough to describe what I feel.

MRS. ASHLEIGH—(*a trifle impatiently*) Come, Lucy! Don't overact your part of the abused wife. Vile? Shameless, disgusting liason? What extravagant terms to apply to an *amusing* flirtation.

LUCY—(*scornfully*) Flirtation? Then you don't know, after all. (*bitterly*) Or are you just trying to hide it from me? It seems as if there weren't a word of truth left in the world.

MRS. ASHLEIGH—(*hurt*) Lucy! Is that the way you speak to your mother? (*Lucy does not answer and her face remains hard. Mrs. Ashleigh, plainly worried now, speaks with an attempt at calmness.*) Let's get to the bottom of this. I don't understand you. What is it I don't know?

LUCY—(*fiercely*) You don't seem to know—or you couldn't taunt me with it—that Leo is now Tom's mistress!

MRS. ASHLEIGH—(*shocked and stunned, stares at the distracted Lucy in amazement for a moment*) Oh!

LUCY—Now you know! Now tell me its my fault—that it serves me right—that I brought it on myself!

MRS. ASHLEIGH—Lucy! What a wicked lie! I'm ashamed of you!

LUCY—(*with a hard laugh*) Of course, I knew you wouldn't believe it. You think everyone's so nice and proper. People don't do such things in your world. (*She laughs mockingly.*)

MRS. ASHLEIGH—Lucy, has your mind become so distorted that you can believe an infamous falsehood like that?

LUCY—I believe what I've seen, what I've suspected, what I now know to be the truth. Do you think I'm blind, that everyone else is blind? Where did they go on all their motor trips? Do you think I can put any trust in the foolish tales they told us?

MRS. ASHLEIGH—(*severely*) Stop, Lucy! I refuse to listen to you when you accuse Tom of deliberately lieing to you, of deceiving you in the basest manner.

LUCY—(*wildly*) Of course he's a liar! They're all liars. Everyone lies! What about their teas together all alone in the studio? And the times they were supposed to be at exhibitions of paintings, which I know he hates? And the night he said he had to stay in town? Do you—does he think I'm a fool?

MRS. ASHLEIGH—Are you out of your mind? Do you realize what you're saying?

LUCY—(*frantically*) Her Great Blond Beast! Well, she can
have him! (*She shudders.*) You must give him a message from
me. I loathe him too much to speak to him.

MRS. ASHLEIGH—Lucy!

LUCY—Tell him I'll leave this house tomorrow—and I
never want to see him again.

MRS. ASHLEIGH—(*resolving to be diplomatic—suppressing
her grief and anxiety*) I will if you'll stop talking wildly and
listen to me for a moment. (*Lucy looks at her mother with stubborn defiance.*) Come, Lucy, please sit down. You're trembling
all over. I'm afraid you'll be ill. Sit down and rest for a while
and try to calm yourself. (*Lucy reluctantly sits down on the
lounge beside her mother.*) What a state you've worked yourself
into! And all for nothing. There. Sit still and listen to me.

LUCY—(*stubbornly*) I warn you in advance, Mother, that
nothing you can say will make me change the resolve I've
taken.

MRS. ASHLEIGH—(*gently*) You may do whatever you
think is best, dear. You can come home tomorrow and stay
with your father and me for a while if you like. The change
may do you good.

LUCY—(*harshly*) Come home? And be driven insane by
father's eternal nagging and questioning? And even you—
(*she chokes back her tears*) are against me.

MRS. ASHLEIGH—(*tenderly*) You know that isn't so,
dear.

LUCY—I won't go home. I don't need any help or sympathy. I'll go out alone and live my own life as I choose.

MRS. ASHLEIGH—As you like, dear. No one is objecting
to that. And now listen and I'll explain all this misunderstanding away. (*coaxingly*) Will you believe your mother when she
swears to you that this apparent affair between Leo and Tom
was all a secret plot of our's—Tom's and mine—to make you
jealous, to rid you of the nasty influence of that detestable
Gabriel person? (*But Lucy has gone too far to believe anything
but her own suspicions. She stares at her mother with wild-eyed
scorn.*)

LUCY—Stop, Mother! I can't bear it! Do you expect me to

believe that silly cock-and-bull story—that you and Tom suspected me of something terrible and deliberately planned to do your best to make me unhappy and miserable? Do you think I'm a child to be put off with a silly tale like that?

MRS. ASHLEIGH—But, my dear, you haven't heard—

LUCY—(*weeping hysterically and clapping her hands over her ears*) I don't want to hear any more! Let me alone!

MRS. ASHLEIGH—(*seeing the futility of argument*) All right, dear. I won't mention the matter again. (*Lucy gradually grows calmer.*) And now don't you think you'd better go upstairs and go to bed? You'll be sick tomorrow if you don't.

LUCY—(*hoarsely*) Upstairs? With her? I'd die first!

MRS. ASHLEIGH—(*indicating the room on right*) Then go in there and lie down on the couch. The darkness will rest your eyes. (*Tom enters from the hallway. He is in evening clothes but his tie has not yet been tied. Lucy gets up abruptly and, without looking at him, walks into the next room pulling the portieres shut behind her. Tom looks after her gloomily.*)

TOM—(*savagely*) Did you see that? She never even looked at me.

MRS. ASHLEIGH—You mustn't mind her tonight, Tom. She's dreadfully upset.

TOM—It isn't only tonight. Its every night. (*throwing himself into a chair*) And I'm sick of it.

MRS. ASHLEIGH—Ssshh! She might hear you.

TOM—(*grumpily*) I don't care if she does. Its about time she knew the way I feel about some things.

MRS. ASHLEIGH—Why, Tom!

TOM—(*morosely*) I'm tired of being treated like a dog. And that fine plan of your's seems to be messing things up worse than ever. This Leo is getting on my nerves. She's too—too exuberant. I'm not in love with the idea of this theatre party. I've a good notion to chuck it.

MRS. ASHLEIGH—(*thoughtfully*) Perhaps you'd better.

TOM—(*defiantly*) No, I'll be darned if I will. Lucy'd only think I wanted to spy on her and that little doggie of her's.

MRS. ASHLEIGH—(*with a sigh of comic despair*) I see I've two big children who need spanking instead of one.

TOM—Its nothing to laugh at. (*getting up from his chair*) I've half a mind to go in and have it out with her right now.

Mrs. Ashleigh—(*grasping his arm*) No, Tom. Please don't—now.

Tom—(*stubbornly*) Why not?

Mrs. Ashleigh—Because she's in a dreadful state of nerves. She'd only become hysterical if you started to quarrell with her. Wait until you come back. I'll see to it she gets rested up before then, and willing to listen to reason.

Tom—(*with real anxiety*) She isn't really ill, is she?

Mrs. Ashleigh—No— (*in almost a whisper*) Someone's been telling her some nasty tales and—

Tom—About me? (*Mrs. Ashleigh nods and puts her finger to her lips. Tom clenches his fists.*) I'll bet it was that—

Mrs. Ashleigh—(*hurriedly interrupting him*) No, no. I'll explain it all to you later. Not here. I can't now. She might hear me. (*aloud*) Do you want me to tie that tie for you, you big baby, you?

Tom—(*ruefully*) I can tie it all right but I left it for Lucy— she usually—I thought I'd have an excuse—

Mrs. Ashleigh—(*with a smile*) Poor boy. (*Leo comes tripping in from the hallway. She is dressed in a white evening gown of Lucy's which shows every evidence of having been shortened, tightened, and otherwise made over with the aid of pins and basting thread. However Leo has an air which carries it off. She is bubbling over with delight at the strangeness of her make-up.*)

Leonora—Now I ask you, amn't I the ultimate gasp! My dear, if I dare to heave a sigh I'll be in the nude. *That* will give the audience a moment. (*to Tom*) You don't mind, do you?

Tom—(*sullenly*) You can go the limit as far as I'm concerned.

Mrs. Ashleigh—You look quite bewitching in that dress, doesn't she, Tom? (*The portieres on the right are parted a trifle and Lucy's pale face is seen for a moment and hurriedly withdrawn.*) White is your color.

Leonora—(*making a mocking grimace*) Blessed are the pure—whatever it is they inherit. (*seeing Tom's tie*) I thought you were all ready. I say, look at your tie. You can't go with me like that. Here. Let me fix it. Bend down, my Beast—or page me a stepladder. (*She ties the tie for him and slaps his face roguishly.*) There. Now aren't we beautiful?

Tom—(*looking at his watch—sulkily*) You've got three

minutes to put on the rest of your armor if there's anything missing.

LEONORA—I'm all ready, I think, excepting my coat. (*suddenly feeling her face with her hands*) Oh, I've forgotten my beauty spots. I *must* have beauty spots! They'll help cover my nakedness. (*She lifts up her skirts and skips out of the room, shouting back over her shoulder*) I'll be right down.

TOM—(*suddenly beginning to feel in his pockets*) Dammit, here I am starting out without a cent in my pockets—a nice pickle we'd have been in. (*He starts for the doorway, left.*)

MRS. ASHLEIGH—Just a minute. I'm going up to phone to Mr. Ashleigh. (*in a low voice*) And I've a few words to say to you before you go.

TOM—All right, Mother.

MRS. ASHLEIGH—Not here. (*She casts a significant glance at the room on the right.*) We'll turn these lights out so they won't disturb her. I hope she's asleep, poor dear. (*She switches off the lights. The room is in darkness except for the light from the hallway. She and Tom go out, left, and can be heard conversing as they go up the stairs. The portieres on the right are carefully parted and Lucy enters. She stops and stands motionless for a moment or so in an attitude of strained attention, listening for some sound from the hallway. Hearing nothing, she goes to the table and throws herself into a chair beside it. She rests her head on her outstretched arms and sobs softly. Making an effort to control herself, she dries her eyes hastily with her handkerchief, gets up, and walks nervously from the table to the windows in rear and back again.*

(*She stands by the table for a minute staring straight before her, her expression betraying the somber thoughts which are passing through her brain. Then, with a quick movement of decision, she pulls out a drawer in the table and slowly takes a revolver from it. She looks at it with frightened eyes and puts it down on the table with a convulsive shudder.*

(*There is the sound of a motor from the roadway outside. Lucy gives a nervous start and looks quickly around the room as if searching for a hiding place. She finally hurries back into the room on the right, pulling the portieres together behind her. The noise of the motor grows steadily louder. At last the machine stops in front of the main entrance to the house, and only the soft purr of the engine is heard. The glare from the headlamps pierces the darkness beyond the french windows.*

(*Someone is heard walking along the hallway to the front door. The outer door is heard opening. There is the brief murmur of the voices of the chauffer and the maid. Then the door is closed again. Tom's voice is heard calling from the top of the stairs:* "Is that the car?" *The maid's voice answers:* "Yes, sir", *and she is heard returning to the back of the house.*

(*Tom and Leonora are heard conversing as they come down the stairs in the hall. Leonora's infectious laughter rings out. Tom appears in evening dress in the doorway left, and looks toward the door on the right. He calls softly:* "Lucy"; *then takes a step forward into the room. Leonora calls to him from the hall:* "We'll be late." *Tom makes a movement of impatience and raises his voice:* "Lucy!")

LEONORA—(*from the hallway*) She's probably out in the garden mooning with Gab. Come on.

(*Tom allows a muttered* "damn" *to escape him, and walks back into the hall.*

(*The outer door is again opened and shut. Lucy comes out from behind the portieres and goes quickly to the table. The sound of the limousine door being slammed is heard. A wild look of determination comes into Lucy's face and she snatches the revolver from the table. The noise of the motor increases in volume. The curtain starts to fall. The car outside starts. Closing her eyes tightly, Lucy lifts the revolver to her temple. The curtain hides her from view. As it touches the stage there is the sound of a shot.*)

EPILOGUE

After an interval of three minutes during which the theatre remains darkened, the curtain is again raised.

The second that the curtain starts to rise the shot is again heard. As the curtain goes up Lucy is discovered standing in an attitude of abject terror, the revolver still clutched in her trembling hand. Suddenly it drops from her nerveless grasp and she crumples up and falls to the floor. She lies there motionless.

The outside door is opened and shut and Tom comes into the room from the hallway followed by Leonora. He switches on the lights. Both of them utter exclamations of terror as they see the prostrate form of Lucy almost at their feet.

Tom—Good God!

Leonora—Heavens! She must have fainted. (*She sinks to her knees beside Lucy and starts rubbing one of her wrists. Gabriel appears outside the french windows. He takes one look at the scene inside and then hurries into the room.*)

Tom—(*He is looking at the revolver with an expression of dazed stupefaction.*) No. (*He picks the revolver from the floor.*) Look! (*Mrs. Ashleigh enters from the left.*)

Mrs. Ashleigh—(*rushing over to her daughter*) Lucy! (*She leans down and puts her hand over Lucy's heart.*)

Tom—(*dazedly*) She shot herself!

Gabriel—Shot herself! (*He stands petrified.*)

Leonora—(*in matter-of-fact tones*) Well, if she did she must have missed. She has no wound anywhere. (*peremptorily*) You, Gab, don't stand there like an idiot. Get some water. (*Gabriel hurries out.*)

Tom—(*opens up the revolver and stares at it stupidly—a sheepish relieved grin spreads slowly over his face. He chuckles.*) Hmm!

Leonora—(*looking up at him*) Well?

Tom—I forgot—its never been loaded. (*Gabriel comes back with a glass of water. Leo dips her handkerchief in it and dabs it on Lucy's face. Lucy gasps and opens her eyes; then struggles hastily to her feet. She backs away from Tom to the right of room. Gabriel follows her.*)

Gabriel—(*hurriedly—in a low voice*) You weren't going to

467

do—that—on account of what I said this evening—about them, were you? (*Lucy nods slowly. Gabriel goes on earnestly.*) Don't be a fool and take me seriously. Noone ever does, you know. Not a word of truth in what I said. Perfectly harmless. Just my infernal jealous imagination. Believe that! (*He comes back beside Leo.*)

TOM—(*receiving a nudge from Mrs. Ashleigh, goes to Lucy—pleadingly*) Lucy. (*She throws herself into his arms and sobs softly. He pats her shoulder and soothes her.*) There! There! Its all over, little sweetheart.

LEONORA—(*throwing her arms around Gabriel*) Kiss me, Gab. Its being done just now.

GABRIEL—(*very dignified*) You *are* a fool! (*But he kisses her.*)

LUCY—(*suddenly breaking away from Tom—in tones of frightened wonder*) But the shot—the shot!

ALL—(*puzzled*) Shot? What shot? (*The chauffer comes into the room carrying a removable wheel with a flat tire.*)

THE CHAUFFER—Pardon, sir. (*They all turn and look at him.*) It isn't bad, sir. (*He points to the tire.*) See, sir. Fix up as good as new. (*There is a roar of laughter as the realization of what the shot really was comes to them. The chauffer looks from one to the other of them with open mouth, as if he thought they were crazy.*)

LEONORA—(*turning to Lucy and pointing dramatically to the tire*) General Gabbler's pistol! Fancy that, Hedda!

(*The Curtain Falls*)

IN THE ZONE

A Play in One Act

CHARACTERS

SMITTY
DAVIS
SWANSON
SCOTTY
IVAN   *Seamen on the British*
PAUL   *tramp steamer* Glencairn
JACK
DRISCOLL
COCKY

In the Zone

SCENE—*The seamen's forecastle. On the right above the bunks three or four portholes covered with black cloth can be seen. On the floor near the doorway is a pail with a tin dipper. A lantern in the middle of the floor, turned down very low, throws a dim light around the place. Five men, Scotty, Ivan, Swanson, Smitty and Paul, are in their bunks apparently asleep. It is about ten minutes of twelve on a night in the fall of the year 1915.*

Smitty turns slowly in his bunk and, leaning out over the side, looks from one to another of the men as if to assure himself that they are asleep. Then he climbs carefully out of his bunk and stands in the middle of the forecastle fully dressed, but in his stocking feet, glancing around him suspiciously. Reassured, he leans down and cautiously pulls out a suit-case from under the bunks in front of him.

Just at this moment Davis appears in the doorway, carrying a large steaming coffee-pot in his hand. He stops short when he sees Smitty. A puzzled expression comes over his face, followed by one of suspicion, and he retreats farther back in the alleyway, where he can watch Smitty without being seen.

All the latter's movements indicate a fear of discovery. He takes out a small bunch of keys and unlocks the suit-case, making a slight noise as he does so. Scotty wakes up and peers at him over the side of the bunk. Smitty opens the suit-case and takes out a small black tin box, carefully places this under his mattress, shoves the suit-case back under the bunk, climbs into his bunk again and closes his eyes.

Davis enters the forecastle, places the coffee-pot beside the lantern, and goes from one to the other of the sleepers and shakes them vigorously, saying to each in a low voice: Near eight bells, Scotty. Arise and shine, Swanson. Eight bells, Ivan. *Smitty yawns loudly with a great pretense of having been dead asleep. All of the rest of the men tumble out of their bunks, stretching and gaping, and commence to pull on their shoes. They go one by one to the cupboard near the open door, take out their cups and spoons, and sit down together on the benches. The coffee-pot is passed around. They munch their biscuits and sip their coffee in dull silence.*)

DAVIS—(*suddenly jumping to his feet—nervously*) Where's
that air comin' from? (*All are startled and look at him wonderingly.*)

SWANSON—(*a squat, surly-faced Swede—grumpily*) What
air? I don't feel nothing.

DAVIS—(*excitedly*) I kin feel it—a draft. (*He stands on the
bench and looks around—suddenly exploding*) Damn fool
square-head! (*He leans over the upper bunk in which Paul is
sleeping and slams the porthole shut.*) I got a good notion to
report him. Serve him bloody well right! What's the use o'
blindin' the ports when that thick-head goes an' leaves 'em
open?

SWANSON—(*yawning—too sleepy to be aroused by anything—carelessly*) Dey don't see what little light go out yust
one port.

SCOTTY—(*protesting*) Dinna be a loon, Swanson! D'ye no
ken the dangerr o' showin' a licht wi' a pack o' submarrines
lyin' aboot?

IVAN—(*shaking his shaggy ox-like head in an emphatic affirmative*) Dot's right, Scotty. I don' li-ike blow up, no, by
devil!

SMITTY—(*his manner slightly contemptuous*) I don't think
there's much danger of meeting any of their submarines, not
until we get into the War Zone, at any rate.

DAVIS—(*He and Scotty look at Smitty suspiciously—
harshly*) You don't, eh? (*He lowers his voice and speaks slowly.*)
Well, we're in the war zone right this minit if you wants to
know. (*The effect of this speech is instantaneous. All sit bolt upright on their benches and stare at Davis.*)

SMITTY—How do you know, Davis?

DAVIS—(*angrily*) 'Cos Drisc heard the First send the Third
below to wake the skipper when we fetched the zone—bout
five bells, it was. Now whata y' got to say?

SMITTY—(*conciliatingly*) Oh, I wasn't doubting your word,
Davis; but you know they're not pasting up bulletins to let
the crew know when the zone is reached—especially on ammunition ships like this.

IVAN—(*decidedly*) I don't li-ike dees voyage. Next time I
ship on windjammer Boston to River Plate, load with wood
only so it float, by golly!

SWANSON—(*fretfully*) I hope British navy blow 'em to hell, those submarines, py damn!

SCOTTY—(*looking at Smitty, who is staring at the doorway in a dream, his chin on his hands—meaningly*) It is no the submarrines only we've to fear, I'm thinkin'.

DAVIS—(*assenting eagerly*) That's no lie, Scotty.

SWANSON—You mean the mines?

SCOTTY—I wasna thinkin' o' mines eitherr.

DAVIS—There's many a good ship blown up and at the bottom of the sea, what never hit no mine or torpedo.

SCOTTY—Did ye neverr read of the Gerrman spies and the dirrty work they're doin' all the war? (*He and Davis both glance at Smitty, who is deep in thought and is not listening to the conversation.*)

DAVIS—An' the clever way they fool you!

SWANSON—Sure; I read it in paper many time.

DAVIS—Well—(*he is about to speak but hesitates and finishes lamely*) you got to watch out, that's all I says.

IVAN—(*drinking the last of his coffee and slamming his fist on the bench explosively*) I tell you dis rotten coffee give me belly-ache, yes! (*They all look at him in amused disgust.*)

SCOTTY—(*sardonically*) Dinna fret about it, Ivan. If we blow up ye'll no be mindin' the pain in your middle. (*Jack enters. He is a young American with a tough, good-natured face. He wears dungarees and a heavy jersey.*)

JACK—Eight bells, fellers.

IVAN—(*stupidly*) I don' hear bell ring.

JACK—No, and yuh won't hear any ring, yuh boob— (*lowering his voice unconsciously*) now we're in the war zone.

SWANSON—(*anxiously*) Is the boats all ready?

JACK—Sure; we can lower 'em in a second.

DAVIS—A lot o' good the boats'll do, with us loaded deep with all kinds o' dynamite and stuff the like o' that! If a torpedo hits this hooker we'll all be in hell b'fore you could wink your eye.

JACK—They ain't goin' to hit us, see? That's my dope. Whose wheel is it?

IVAN—(*sullenly*) My wheel. (*He lumbers out.*)

JACK—And whose lookout?

SWANSON—Mine, I tink. (*He follows Ivan.*)

JACK—(*scornfully*) A hell of a lot of use keepin' a lookout! We couldn't run away or fight if we wanted to. (*to Scotty and Smitty*) Better look up the bo'sun or the Fourth, you two, and let 'em see you're awake. (*Scotty goes to the doorway and turns to wait for Smitty, who is still in the same position, head on hands, seemingly unconscious of everything. Jack slaps him roughly on the shoulder and he comes to with a start.*) Aft and report, Duke! What's the matter with yuh—in a dope dream? (*Smitty goes out after Scotty without answering. Jack looks after him with a frown.*) He's a queer guy. I can't figger him out.

DAVIS—Nor no one else. (*lowering his voice—meaningly*) An' he's liable to turn out queerer than any of us think if we ain't careful.

JACK—(*suspiciously*) What d'yuh mean? (*They are interrupted by the entrance of Driscoll and Cocky.*)

COCKY—(*protestingly*) Blimey if I don't fink I'll put in this 'ere watch ahtside on deck. (*He and Driscoll go over and get their cups.*) I down't want to be caught in this 'ole if they 'its us. (*He pours out coffee.*)

DRISCOLL—(*pouring his*) Divil a bit ut wud matther where ye arre. Ye'd be blown to smithereens b'fore ye cud say your name. (*He sits down, overturning as he does so the untouched cup of coffee which Smitty had forgotten and left on the bench. They all jump nervously as the tin cup hits the floor with a bang. Driscoll flies into an unreasonable rage.*) Who's the dirty scut left this cup where a man 'ud sit on ut?

DAVIS—It's Smitty's.

DRISCOLL—(*kicking the cup across the forecastle*) Does he think he's too much av a bloody gentleman to put his own away loike the rist av us? If he does I'm the bye'll beat that noshun out av his head.

COCKY—Be the airs 'e puts on you'd think 'e was the Prince of Wales. Wot's 'e doin' on a ship, I arsks yer? 'E ain't now good as a sailor, is 'e?—dawdlin' abaht on deck like a chicken wiv 'is 'ead cut orf!

JACK—(*good-naturedly*) Aw, the Duke's all right. S'posin' he did ferget his cup—what's the diff? (*He picks up the cup and puts it away—with a grin*) This war zone stuff's got yer goat, Drisc—and yours too, Cocky—and I ain't cheerin' much fur it myself, neither.

COCKY—(*with a sigh*) Blimey, it ain't no bleedin' joke, yer first trip, to know as there's a ship full of shells li'ble to go orf in under your bloomin' feet, as you might say, if we gets 'it be a torpedo or mine. (*with sudden savagery*) Calls themselves 'uman bein's, too! Blarsted 'Uns!

DRISCOLL—(*gloomily*) 'Tis me last trip in the bloody zone, God help me. The divil take their twenty-foive percent bonus—and be drowned like a rat in a trap in the bargain, maybe.

DAVIS—Wouldn't be so bad if she wasn't carryin' ammunition. Them's the kind the subs is layin' for.

DRISCOLL—(*irritably*) Fur the love av hivin, don't be talkin' about ut. I'm sick wid thinkin' and jumpin' at iviry bit av a noise. (*There is a pause during which they all stare gloomily at the floor.*)

JACK—Hey, Davis, what was you sayin' about Smitty when they come in?

DAVIS—(*with a great air of mystery*) I'll tell you in a minit. I want to wait an' see if he's comin' back. (*impressively*) You won't be callin' him all right when you hears what I seen with my own eyes. (*He adds with an air of satisfaction*) An' you won't be feelin' no safer, neither. (*They all look at him with puzzled glances full of a vague apprehension.*)

DRISCOLL—God blarst ut! (*He fills his pipe and lights it. The others, with an air of remembering something they had forgotten, do the same. Scotty enters.*)

SCOTTY—(*in awed tones*) Mon, but it's clear outside the nicht! Like day.

DAVIS—(*in low tones*) Where's Smitty, Scotty?

SCOTTY—Out on the hatch starin' at the moon like a mon half-daft.

DAVIS—Kin you see him from the doorway?

SCOTTY—(*goes to doorway and carefully peeks out*) Aye; he's still there.

DAVIS—Keep your eyes on him for a moment. I've got something I wants to tell the boys and I don't want him walkin' in in the middle of it. Give a shout if he starts this way.

SCOTTY—(*with suppressed excitement*) Aye, I'll watch him. And I've somethin' myself to tell aboot his Lordship.

DRISCOLL—(*impatiently*) Out wid ut! You're talkin' more than a pair av auld women wud be standin' in the road, and gittin' no further along.

DAVIS—Listen! You 'member when I went to git the coffee, Jack?

JACK—Sure, I do.

DAVIS—Well, I brings it down here same as usual and got as far as the door there when I sees him.

JACK—Smitty?

DAVIS—Yes, Smitty! He was standin' in the middle of the fo'c's'tle there (*pointing*) lookin' around sneakin'-like at Ivan and Swanson and the rest 's if he wants to make certain they're asleep. (*He pauses significantly, looking from one to the other of his listeners. Scotty is nervously dividing his attention between Smitty on the hatch outside and Davis's story, fairly bursting to break in with his own revelations.*)

JACK—(*impatiently*) What of it?

DAVIS—Listen! He was standin' right there—(*pointing again*) in his stockin' feet—no shoes on, mind, so he wouldn't make no noise!

JACK—(*spitting disgustedly*) Aw!

DAVIS—(*not heeding the interruption*) I seen right away somethin' on the queer was up so I slides back into the alleyway where I kin see him but he can't see me. After he makes sure they're all asleep he goes in under the bunks there—bein' careful not to raise a noise, mind!—an' takes out his bag there. (*By this time everyone, Jack included, is listening breathlessly to his story.*) Then he fishes in his pocket an' takes out a bunch o' keys an' kneels down beside the bag an' opens it.

SCOTTY—(*unable to keep silent longer*) Mon, didn't I see him do that same thing wi' these two eyes. 'Twas just that moment I woke and spied him.

DAVIS—(*surprised, and a bit nettled to have to share his story with anyone*) Oh, you seen him, too, eh? (*to the others*) Then Scotty kin tell you if I'm lyin' or not.

DRISCOLL—An' what did he do whin he'd the bag opened?

DAVIS—He bends down and reaches out his hand sort o'

scared-like, like it was somethin' dang'rous he was after, an' feels round in under his duds—hidden in under his duds an' wrapped up in 'em, it was—an' he brings out a black iron box!

COCKY—(*looking around him with a frightened glance*) Gawd blimey! (*The others likewise betray their uneasiness, shuffling their feet nervously.*)

DAVIS—Ain't that right, Scotty?

SCOTTY—Right as rain, I'm tellin' ye'!

DAVIS—(*to the others with an air of satisfaction*) There you are! (*lowering his voice*) An' then what d'you suppose he did? Sneaks to his bunk an' slips the black box in under his mattress—in under his mattress, mind!—

JACK—And it's there now?

DAVIS—Course it is! (*Jack starts toward Smitty's bunk. Driscoll grabs him by the arm.*)

DRISCOLL—Don't be touchin' ut, Jack!

JACK—You needn't worry. I ain't goin' to touch it. (*He pulls up Smitty's mattress and looks down. The others stare at him, holding their breaths. He turns to them, trying hard to assume a careless tone.*) It's there, aw right.

COCKY—(*miserably upset*) I'm gointer 'op it aht on deck. (*He gets up but Driscoll pulls him down again. Cocky protests*) It fair guvs me the trembles sittin' still in 'ere.

DRISCOLL—(*scornfully*) Are ye frightened, ye toad? 'Tis a hell av a thing fur grown men to be shiverin' loike childer at a bit av a black box. (*scratching his head in uneasy perplexity*) Still, ut's damn queer, the looks av ut.

DAVIS—(*sarcastically*) A bit of a black box, eh? How big d'you think them—(*he hesitates*)—things has to be—big as this fo'c's'tle?

JACK—(*in a voice meant to be reassuring*) Aw, hell! I'll bet it ain't nothin' but some coin he's saved he's got locked up in there.

DAVIS—(*scornfully*) That's likely, ain't it? Then why does he act so s'picious? He's been on ship near two year, ain't he? He knows damn well there ain't no thiefs in this fo'c's'tle, don't he? An' you know 's well 's I do he didn't have no money when he came on board an' he ain't saved none since. Don't you? (*Jack doesn't answer.*) Listen! D'you know what he done after he put that thing in under his mattress?—an' Scotty'll tell you if I ain't speakin' truth. He looks round to see if anyone's woke up—

SCOTTY—I clapped my eyes shut when he turned round.

DAVIS—An' then he crawls into his bunk an' shuts his eyes, *pretendin'* he was asleep, mind!

SCOTTY—Aye, I could see him.

DAVIS—An' when I goes to call him, I don't even shake him. I just says, "Eight bells, Smitty," in a'most a whisper-like, an' up he gets yawnin' an' stretchin' fit to kill hisself 's if he'd been dead asleep.

COCKY—Gawd blimey!

DRISCOLL—(*shaking his head*) Ut looks bad, divil a doubt av ut.

DAVIS—(*excitedly*) An' now I come to think of it, there's the porthole. How'd it come to git open, tell me that? I know'd well Paul never opened it. Ain't he grumblin' about bein' cold all the time?

SCOTTY—The mon that opened it meant no good to this ship, whoever he was.

JACK—(*sourly*) What porthole? What're yuh talkin' about?

DAVIS—(*pointing over Paul's bunk*) There. It was open when I come in. I felt the cold air on my neck an' shut it. It would'a been clear's a lighthouse to any sub that was watchin'—an' we s'posed to have all the ports blinded! Who'd do a dirty trick like that? It wasn't none of us, nor Scotty here, nor Swanson, nor Ivan. Who would it be, then?

COCKY—(*angrily*) Must'a been 'is bloody Lordship.

DAVIS—For all's we know he might'a been signalin' with it. They does it like that by winkin' a light. Ain't you read how they gets caught doin' it in London an' on the coast?

COCKY—(*firmly convinced now*) An' wots 'e doin' aht alone on the 'atch—keepin' 'isself clear of us like 'e was afraid?

DRISCOLL—Kape your eye on him, Scotty.

SCOTTY—There's no a move oot o' him.

JACK—(*in irritated perplexity*) But, hell, ain't he an Englishman? What'd he wanta—

DAVIS—English? How d'we know he's English? Cos he talks it? That ain't no proof. Ain't you read in the papers how all them German spies they been catchin' in England has been livin' there for ten, often as not twenty years, an' talks English as good's anyone? An' look here, ain't you noticed he don't talk natural? He talks it too damn good, that's what I mean. He don't talk exactly like a toff, does he, Cocky?

COCKY—Not like any toff as I ever met up wiv.

DAVIS—No; an' 'e don't talk it like us, that's certain. An' he don't look English. An' what d'we know about him when you come to look at it? Nothin'! He ain't ever said where he comes from or why. All we knows is he ships on here in London 'bout a year b'fore the war starts, as an A. B.—stole his papers most lik'ly—when he don't know how to box the compass, hardly. Ain't that queer in itself? An' was he ever open with us like a good shipmate? No; he's always had that sly air about him 's if he was hidin' somethin'.

DRISCOLL—(slapping his thigh—angrily) Divil take me if I don't think ye have the truth av ut, Davis.

COCKY—(scornfully) Lettin' on be 'is silly airs, and all, 'e's the son of a blarsted earl or somethink!

DAVIS—An' the name he calls hisself—Smith! I'd risk a quid of my next pay day that his real name is Schmidt, if the truth was known.

JACK—(evidently fighting against his own conviction) Aw, say, you guys give me a pain! What'd they want puttin' a spy on this old tub for?

DAVIS—(shaking his head sagely) They're deep ones, an' there's a lot o' things a sailor'll see in the ports he puts in ought to be useful to 'em. An' if he kin signal to 'em an' they blows us up it's one ship less, ain't it? (lowering his voice and indicating Smitty's bunk) Or if he blows us up hisself.

SCOTTY—(in alarmed tones) Hush, mon! Here he comes! (Scotty hurries over to a bench and sits down. A thick silence settles over the forecastle. The men look from one to another with uneasy glances. Smitty enters and sits down beside his bunk. He is seemingly unaware of the dark glances of suspicion directed at him from all sides. He slides his hand back stealthily over his mattress and his fingers move, evidently feeling to make sure the box is still there. The others follow this movement carefully with quick looks out of the corners of their eyes. Their attitudes grow tense as if they were about to spring at him. Satisfied the box is safe, Smitty draws his hand away slowly and utters a sigh of relief.)

SMITTY—(*in a casual tone which to them sounds sinister*) It's a good light night for the subs if there's any about. (*For a moment he sits staring in front of him. Finally he seems to sense the hostile atmosphere of the forecastle and looks from one to the other of the men in surprise. All of them avoid his eyes. He sighs with a puzzled expression and gets up and walks out of the doorway. There is silence for a moment after his departure and then a storm of excited talk breaks loose.*)

DAVIS—Did you see him feelin' if it was there?

COCKY—'E ain't arf a sly one wiv 'is talk of submarines, Gawd blind 'im!

SCOTTY—Did ye see the sneakin' looks he gave us?

DRISCOLL—If ivir I saw black shame on a man's face 'twas on his whin he sat there!

JACK—(*thoroughly convinced at last*) He looked bad to me. He's a crook, aw right.

DAVIS—(*excitedly*) What'll we do? We gotter do somethin' quick or— (*He is interrupted by the sound of something hitting against the port side of the forecastle with a dull, heavy thud. The men start to their feet in wild-eyed terror and turn as if they were going to rush for the deck. They stand that way for a strained moment, scarcely breathing and listening intently.*)

JACK—(*with a sickly smile*) Hell! It's on'y a piece of driftwood or a floatin' log. (*He sits down again.*)

DAVIS—(*sarcastically*) Or a mine that didn't go off—that time—or a piece o' wreckage from some ship they've sent to Davy Jones.

COCKY—(*mopping his brow with a trembling hand*) Blimey! (*He sinks back weakly on a bench.*)

DRISCOLL—(*furiously*) God blarst ut! No man at all cud be puttin' up wid the loike av this—an' I'm not wan to be fearin' anything or any man in the worrld'll stand up to me face to face; but this divil's trickery in the darrk— (*He starts for Smitty's bunk.*) I'll throw ut out wan av the portholes an' be done wid ut. (*He reaches toward the mattress.*)

SCOTTY—(*grabbing his arm—wildly*) Arre ye daft, mon?

DAVIS—Don't monkey with it, Drisc. I knows what to do. Bring the bucket o' water here, Jack, will you? (*Jack gets it and brings it over to Davis.*) An' you, Scotty, see if he's back on the hatch.

SCOTTY—(*cautiously peering out*) Aye, he's sittin' there the noo.

DAVIS—Sing out if he makes a move. Lift up the mattress, Drisc—careful now! (*Driscoll does so with infinite caution.*) Take it out, Jack—careful—don't shake it now, for Christ's sake! Here—put it in the water—easy! There, that's fixed it! (*They all sit down with great sighs of relief.*) The water'll git in and spoil it.

DRISCOLL—(*slapping Davis on the back*) Good wurrk for ye, Davis, ye scut! (*He spits on his hands aggressively.*) An' now what's to be done wid that black-hearted thraitor?

COCKY—(*belligerently*) Guv 'im a shove in the marf and 'eave 'im over the side!

DAVIS—An' serve him right!

JACK—Aw, say, give him a chance. Yuh can't prove nothin' till yuh find out what's in there.

DRISCOLL—(*heatedly*) Is ut more proof ye'd be needin' afther what we've seen an' heard? Then listen to me—an' ut's Driscoll talkin'—if there's divilment in that box an' we see plain 'twas his plan to murrdher his own shipmates that have served him fair— (*He raises his fist.*) I'll choke his rotten heart out wid me own hands, an' over the side wid him, and one man missin' in the mornin'.

DAVIS—An' no one the wiser. He's the balmy kind what commits suicide.

COCKY—They 'angs spies ashore.

JACK—(*resentfully*) If he's done what yuh think I'll croak him myself. Is that good enough for yuh?

DRISCOLL—(*looking down at the box*) How'll we be openin' this, I wonder?

SCOTTY—(*from the doorway—warningly*) He's standin' up.

DAVIS—We'll take his keys away from him when he comes in. Quick, Drisc! You an' Jack get beside the door and grab him. (*They get on either side of the door. Davis snatches a small coil of rope from one of the upper bunks.*) This'll do for me an' Scotty to tie him.

SCOTTY—He's turnin' this way—he's comin'! (*He moves away from the door.*)

DAVIS—Stand by to lend a hand, Cocky.

COCKY—Righto. (*As Smitty enters the forecastle he is seized roughly from both sides, and his arms pinned behind him. At first he struggles fiercely, but seeing the uselessness of this, he finally stands calmly and allows Davis and Scotty to tie up his arms.*)

SMITTY—(*when they have finished—with cold contempt*) If this is your idea of a joke I'll have to confess it's a bit too thick for me to enjoy.

COCKY—(*angrily*) Shut yer marf, 'ear!

DRISCOLL—(*roughly*) Ye'll find ut's no joke, me bucko, b'fore we're done wid you. (*to Scotty*) Kape your eye peeled, Scotty, and sing out if anyone's comin'. (*Scotty resumes his post at the door.*)

SMITTY—(*with the same icy contempt*) If you'd be good enough to explain—

DRISCOLL—(*furiously*) Explain, is ut? 'Tis you'll do the explainin'—an' damn quick, or we'll know the reason why. (*to Jack and Davis*) Bring him here, now. (*They push Smitty over to the bucket.*) Look here, ye murrdherin' swab. D'you see ut? (*Smitty looks down with an expression of amazement which rapidly changes to one of anguish.*)

DAVIS—(*with a sneer*) Look at him! S'prised, ain't you? If you wants to try your dirty spyin' tricks on us you've gotter git up earlier in the mornin'.

COCKY—Thorght yer weren't 'arf a fox, didn't yer?

SMITTY—(*trying to restrain his growing rage*) What—what do you mean? That's only— How dare—what are you doing with my private belongings?

COCKY—(*sarcastically*) Ho yus! Private b'longings!

DRISCOLL—(*shouting*) What is ut, ye swine? Will you tell us to our faces? What's in ut?

SMITTY—(*biting his lips—holding himself in check with a great effort*) Nothing but— That's my business. You'll please attend to your own.

DRISCOLL—Oho, ut is, is ut? (*shaking his fist in Smitty's face*) Talk aisy now if ye know what's best for you. Your business, indade! Then we'll be makin' ut ours, I'm thinkin'. (*to Jack and Davis*) Take his keys away from him an' we'll see if there's one'll open ut, maybe. (*They start in searching Smitty, who tries to resist and kicks out at the bucket. Driscoll leaps forward and helps them push him away.*) Try to kick ut over, would

ye? Did ye see him then? Tryin' to murrdher us all, the scut!
Take that pail out av his way, Cocky. (*Smitty struggles with all
of his strength and keeps them busy for a few seconds. As Cocky
grabs the pail Smitty makes a final effort and, lunging forward,
kicks again at the bucket but only succeeds in hitting Cocky on the
shin. Cocky immediately sets down the pail with a bang and,
clutching his knee in both hands, starts hopping around the forecastle, groaning and swearing.*)

COCKY—Ooow! Gawd strike me pink! Kicked me, 'e did!
Bloody, bleedin', rotten Dutch 'og! (*approaching Smitty, who
has given up the fight and is pushed back against the wall near
the doorway with Jack and Davis holding him on either side—
wrathfully, at the top of his lungs*) Kick me, will yer? I'll show
yer what for, yer bleedin' sneak! (*He draws back his fist. Driscoll
pushes him to one side.*)

DRISCOLL—Shut your mouth! D'you want to wake the
whole ship? (*Cocky grumbles and retires to a bench, nursing his
sore shin.*)

JACK—(*taking a small bunch of keys from Smitty's pocket*)
Here yuh are, Drisc.

DRISCOLL—(*taking them*) We'll soon be knowin'. (*He takes
the pail and sits down, placing it on the floor between his feet.
Smitty again tries to break loose but he is too tired and is easily
held back against the wall.*)

SMITTY—(*breathing heavily and very pale*) Cowards!

JACK—(*with a growl*) Nix on the rough talk, see! That
don't git yuh nothin'.

DRISCOLL—(*looking at the lock on the box in the water and
then scrutinizing the keys in his hand*) This'll be ut, I'm thinkin'.
(*He selects one and gingerly reaches his hand in the water.*)

SMITTY—(*his face grown livid—chokingly*) Don't you open
that box, Driscoll. If you do, so help me God, I'll kill you if
I have to hang for it.

DRISCOLL—(*pausing—his hand in the water*) Whin I open
this box I'll not be the wan to be kilt, me sonny bye! I'm no
dirty spy.

SMITTY—(*his voice trembling with rage. His eyes are fixed on
Driscoll's hand.*) Spy? What are you talking about? I only
put that box there so I could get it quick in case we were
torpedoed. Are you all mad? Do you think I'm— (*chokingly*)

You stupid curs! You cowardly dolts! (*Davis claps his hand over Smitty's mouth.*)

DAVIS—That'll be enough from you! (*Driscoll takes the dripping box from the water and starts to fit in the key. Smitty springs forward furiously, almost escaping from their grasp, and drags them after him half-way across the forecastle.*)

DRISCOLL—Hold him, ye divils! (*He puts the box back in the water and jumps to their aid. Cocky hovers on the outskirts of the battle, mindful of the kick he received.*)

SMITTY—(*raging*) Cowards! Damn you! Rotten curs! (*He is thrown to the floor and held there.*) Cowards! Cowards!

DRISCOLL—I'll shut your dirty mouth for you. (*He goes to his bunk and pulls out a big wad of waste and comes back to Smitty.*)

SMITTY—Cowards! Cowards!

DRISCOLL—(*with no gentle hand slaps the waste over Smitty's mouth*) That'll teach you to be misnamin' a man, ye sneak. Have ye a handkerchief, Jack? (*Jack hands him one and he ties it tightly around Smitty's head over the waste.*) That'll fix your gab. Stand him up, now, and tie his feet, too, so he'll not be movin'. (*They do so and leave him with his back against the wall near Scotty. Then they all sit down beside Driscoll, who again lifts the box out of the water and sets it carefully on his knees. He picks out the key, then hesitates, looking from one to the other uncertainly.*) We'd best be takin' this to the skipper, d'you think, maybe?

JACK—(*irritably*) To hell with the Old Man. This is our game and we c'n play it without no help.

COCKY—Now bleedin' horficers, I says!

DAVIS—They'd only be takin' all the credit and makin' heroes of theyselves.

DRISCOLL—(*boldly*) Here goes, thin! (*He slowly turns the key in the lock. The others instinctively turn away. He carefully pushes the cover back on its hinges and looks at what he sees inside with an expression of puzzled astonishment. The others crowd up close. Even Scotty leaves his post to take a look.*) What is ut, Davis?

DAVIS—(*mystified*) Looks funny, don't it? Somethin' square tied up in a rubber bag. Maybe it's dynamite—or somethin'—you can't never tell.

JACK—Aw, it ain't got no works so it ain't no bomb, I'll bet.

DAVIS—(*dubiously*) They makes them all kinds, they do.

JACK—Open it up, Drisc.

DAVIS—Careful now! (*Driscoll takes a black rubber bag resembling a large tobacco pouch from the box and unties the string which is wound tightly around the top. He opens it and takes out a small packet of letters also tied up with string. He turns these over in his hands and looks at the others questioningly.*)

JACK—(*with a broad grin*) On'y letters! (*slapping Davis on the back*) Yuh're a hell of a Sherlock Holmes, ain't yuh? Letters from his best girl too, I'll bet. Let's turn the Duke loose, what d'yuh say? (*He starts to get up.*)

DAVIS—(*fixing him with a withering look*) Don't be so damn smart, Jack. Letters, you says, 's if there never was no harm in 'em. How d'you s'pose spies gets their orders and sends back what they finds out if it ain't by letters and such things? There's many a letter is worser'n any bomb.

COCKY—Righto! They ain't as innercent as they looks, I'll take me oath, when you read 'em. (*pointing at Smitty*) Not 'is Lordship's letters; not be no means!

JACK—(*sitting down again*) Well, read 'em and find out. (*Driscoll commences untying the packet. There is a muffled groan of rage and protest from Smitty.*)

DAVIS—(*triumphantly*) There! Listen to him! Look at him tryin' to git loose! Ain't that proof enough? He knows well we're findin' him out. Listen to me! Love letters, you says, Jack, 's if they couldn't harm nothin'. Listen! I was readin' in some magazine in New York on'y two weeks back how some German spy in Paris was writin' love letters to some woman spy in Switzerland who sent 'em on to Berlin, Germany. To read 'em you wouldn't s'pect nothin'—just mush and all. (*impressively*) But they had a way o' doin' it—a damn sneakin' way. They had a piece o' plain paper with pieces cut out of it an' when they puts it on top o' the letter they sees on'y the words what tells them what they wants to know. An' the Frenchies gets beat in a fight all on account o' that letter.

COCKY—(*awed*) Gawd blimey! They ain't 'arf smart bleeders!

DAVIS—(*seeing his audience is again all with him*) An' even if these letters of his do sound all right they may have what they calls a code. You can't never tell. (*to Driscoll, who has finished untying the packet*) Read one of 'em, Drisc. My eyes is weak.

DRISCOLL—(*takes the first one out of its envelope and bends down to the lantern with it. He turns up the wick to give him a better light.*) I'm no hand to be readin' but I'll try ut. (*Again there is a muffled groan from Smitty as he strains at his bonds.*)

DAVIS—(*gloatingly*) Listen to him! He knows. Go ahead, Drisc!

DRISCOLL—(*his brow furrowed with concentration*) Ut begins: Dearest Man— (*His eyes travel down the page.*) An' thin there's a lot av blarney tellin' him how much she misses him now she's gone away to singin' school—an' how she hopes he'll settle down to rale worrk an' not be skylarkin' around now that she's away loike he used to before she met up wid him—and ut ends: "I love you betther than anythin' in the worrld. You know that, don't you, dear? But b'fore I can agree to live out my life wid you, you must prove to me that the black shadow—I won't menshun uts hateful name but you know what I mean—which might wreck both our lives, does not exist for you. You can do that, can't you, dear? Don't you see you must for my sake?" (*He pauses for a moment—then adds gruffly*) Uts signed: "Edith." (*At the sound of the name Smitty, who has stood tensely with his eyes shut as if he were undergoing torture during the reading, makes a muffled sound like a sob and half turns his face to the wall.*)

JACK—(*sympathetically*) Hell! What's the use of readin' that stuff even if—

DAVIS—(*interrupting him sharply*) Wait! Where's that letter from, Drisc?

DRISCOLL—There's no address on the top av ut.

DAVIS—(*meaningly*) What'd I tell you? Look at the postmark, Drisc,—on the envelope.

DRISCOLL—The name that's written is Sidney Davidson, wan hundred an'—

DAVIS—Never mind that. O' course it's a false name. Look at the postmark.

DRISCOLL—There's a furrin stamp on ut by the looks av

ut. The mark's blurred so it's hard to read. (*He spells it out laboriously.*) B-e-r—the nixt is an l, I think—i—an' an n.

DAVIS—(*excitedly*) Berlin! What did I tell you? I knew them letters was from Germany.

COCKY—(*shaking his fist in Smitty's direction*) Rotten 'ound! (*The others look at Smitty as if this last fact had utterly condemned him in their eyes.*)

DAVIS—Give me the letter, Drisc. Maybe I kin make somethin' out of it.` (*Driscoll hands the letter to him.*) You go through the others, Drisc, and sing out if you sees anythin' queer. (*He bends over the first letter as if he were determined to figure out its secret meaning. Jack, Cocky and Scotty look over his shoulder with eager curiosity. Driscoll takes out some of the other letters, running his eyes quickly down the pages. He looks curiously over at Smitty from time to time, and sighs frequently with a puzzled frown.*)

DAVIS—(*disappointedly*) I gotter give it up. It's too deep for me, but we'll turn 'em over to the perlice when we docks at Liverpool to look through. This one I got was written a year before the war started, anyway. Find anythin' in yours, Drisc?

DRISCOLL—They're all the same as the first—lovin' blarney, an' how her singin' is doin', and the great things the Dutch teacher says about her voice, an' how glad she is that her Sidney bye is worrkin' harrd an' makin' a man av himself for her sake.

(*Smitty turns his face completely to the wall.*)

DAVIS—(*disgustedly*) If we on'y had the code!

DRISCOLL—(*taking up the bottom letter*) Hullo! Here's wan addressed to this ship—s. s. Glencairn, ut says—whin we was in Cape Town sivin months ago— (*looking at the postmark*) Ut's from London.

DAVIS—(*eagerly*) Read it! (*There is another choking groan from Smitty.*)

DRISCOLL—(*reads slowly—his voice becomes lower and lower as he goes on*) Ut begins wid simply the name Sidney Davidson—no dearest or sweetheart to this wan. "Ut is only from your chance meetin' wid Harry—whin you were drunk—that I happen to know where to reach you. So you have run away to sea loike the coward you are because you knew I had found out the truth—the truth you have covered over with your mean little lies all the time I was away in Berlin and blindly trusted you. Very well, you have chosen. You have shown that your drunkenness means more to you than any love or faith av mine. I am sorry—for I loved you, Sidney Davidson—but this is the end. I lave you—the mem'ries; an' if ut is any satisfaction to you I lave you the real-i-zation that you have wrecked my loife as you have wrecked your own. My one remainin' hope is that nivir in God's worrld will I ivir see your face again. Good-by. Edith." (*As he finishes there is a deep silence, broken only by Smitty's muffled sobbing. The men cannot look at each other. Driscoll holds the rubber bag limply in his hand and some small white object falls out of it and drops noiselessly on the floor. Mechanically Driscoll leans over and picks it up, and looks at it wonderingly.*)

DAVIS—(*in a dull voice*) What's that?

DRISCOLL—(*slowly*) A bit av a dried-up flower. (*He drops it into the bag and gathers up the letters and puts them back. He replaces the bag in the box, and locks it and puts it back under Smitty's mattress. The others follow him with their eyes. He steps softly over to Smitty and cuts the ropes about his arms and ankles with his sheath knife, and unties the handkerchief over the gag. Smitty does not turn around but covers his face with his hands and leans his head against the wall. His shoulders continue to heave spasmodically but he makes no further sound.*)

DRISCOLL—(*stalks back to the others—there is a moment of silence, in which each man is in agony with the hopelessness of finding a word he can say—then Driscoll explodes*) God stiffen us, are we never goin' to turn in fur a wink av sleep? (*They all start as if awakening from a bad dream and gratefully crawl into their bunks, shoes and all, turning their faces to the wall, and pulling their blankets up over their shoulders. Scotty tiptoes past Smitty out into the darkness. Driscoll turns down the light and crawls into his bunk as*

The Curtain Falls)

ILE

A Play in One Act

CHARACTERS

BEN, *the cabin boy*
THE STEWARD
CAPTAIN KEENEY
SLOCUM, *second mate*
MRS. KEENEY
JOE, *a harpooner*
Members of the crew of the
steam whaler Atlantic Queen

Ile

SCENE—*Captain Keeney's cabin on board the steam whaling ship* Atlantic Queen—*a small, square compartment about eight feet high with a skylight in the center looking out on the poop deck. On the left (the stern of the ship) a long bench with rough cushions is built in against the wall. In front of the bench, a table. Over the bench, several curtained portholes.*

In the rear, left, a door leading to the Captain's sleeping quarters. To the right of the door a small organ, looking as if it were brand new, is placed against the wall.

On the right, to the rear, a marble-topped sideboard. On the sideboard, a woman's sewing basket. Farther forward, a doorway leading to the companion way, and past the officer's quarters to the main deck.

In the center of the room, a stove. From the middle of the ceiling a hanging lamp is suspended. The walls of the cabin are painted white.

There is no rolling of the ship, and the light which comes through the skylight is sickly and faint, indicating one of those gray days of calm when ocean and sky are alike dead. The silence is unbroken except for the measured tread of some one walking up and down on the poop deck overhead.

It is nearing two bells—one o'clock—in the afternoon of a day in the year 1895.

At the rise of the curtain there is a moment of intense silence. Then the Steward enters and commences to clear the table of the few dishes which still remain on it after the Captain's dinner. He is an old, grizzled man dressed in dungaree pants, a sweater, and a woolen cap with ear flaps. His manner is sullen and angry. He stops stacking up the plates and casts a quick glance upward at the skylight; then tiptoes over to the closed door in rear and listens with his ear pressed to the crack. What he hears makes his face darken and he mutters a furious curse. There is a noise from the doorway on the right and he darts back to the table.

Ben enters. He is an over-grown, gawky boy with a long, pinched face. He is dressed in sweater, fur cap, etc. His teeth are chattering with the cold and he hurries to the stove, where he stands for a moment shivering, blowing on his hands, slapping them against his sides, on the verge of crying.

491

THE STEWARD—(*in relieved tones—seeing who it is*) Oh, 'tis you, is it? What're ye shiverin' 'bout? Stay by the stove where ye belong and ye'll find no need of chatterin'.

BEN—It's c-c-cold. (*trying to control his chattering teeth— derisively*) Who d'ye think it were—the Old Man?

THE STEWARD—(*makes a threatening move—Ben shrinks away.*) None o' your lip, young un, or I'll learn ye. (*more kindly*) Where was it ye've been all o' the time—the fo'c's'tle?

BEN—Yes.

THE STEWARD—Let the Old Man see ye up for'ard mon-keyshinin' with the hands and ye'll get a hidin' ye'll not forget in a hurry.

BEN—Aw, he don't see nothin'. (*A trace of awe in his tones—he glances upward.*) He just walks up and down like he didn't notice nobody—and stares at the ice to the no'the'ard.

THE STEWARD—(*the same tone of awe creeping into his voice*) He's always starin' at the ice. (*in a sudden rage, shaking his fist at the skylight*) Ice, ice, ice! Damn him and damn the ice! Holdin' us in for nigh on a year—nothin' to see but ice—stuck in it like a fly in molasses!

BEN—(*apprehensively*) Ssshh! He'll hear ye.

THE STEWARD—(*raging*) Aye, damn him, and damn the Arctic seas, and damn this stinkin' whalin' ship of his, and damn me for a fool to ever ship on it! (*subsiding as if realizing the uselessness of this outburst—shaking his head—slowly, with deep conviction*) He's a hard man—as hard a man as ever sailed the seas.

BEN—(*solemnly*) Aye.

THE STEWARD—The two years we all signed up for are done this day. Blessed Christ! Two years o' this dog's life, and no luck in the fishin', and the hands half starved with the food runnin' low, rotten as it is; and not a sign of him turnin' back for home! (*bitterly*) Home! I begin to doubt if ever I'll set foot on land again. (*excitedly*) What is it he thinks he's goin' to do? Keep us all up here after our time is worked out till the last man of us is starved to death or frozen? We've grub enough hardly to last out the voyage back if we started now. What are the men goin' to do 'bout it? Did ye hear any talk in the fo'c's'tle?

BEN—(*going over to him—in a half whisper*) They said if he don't put back south for home to-day they're goin' to mutiny.

THE STEWARD—(*with grim satisfaction*) Mutiny? Aye, 'tis the only thing they can do; and serve him right after the manner he's treated them—'s if they wern't no better nor dogs.

BEN—The ice is all broke up to s'uth'ard. They's clear water 's far 's you can see. He ain't got no excuse for not turnin' back for home, the men says.

THE STEWARD—(*bitterly*) He won't look nowheres but no'the'ard where they's only the ice to see. He don't want to see no clear water. All he thinks on is gittin' the ile—'s if it was our fault he ain't had good luck with the whales. (*shaking his head*) I think the man's mighty nigh losin' his senses.

BEN—(*awed*) D'you really think he's crazy?

THE STEWARD—Aye, it's the punishment o' God on him. Did ye ever hear of a man who wasn't crazy do the things he does? (*pointing to the door in rear*) Who but a man that's mad would take his woman—and as sweet a woman as ever was—on a stinkin' whalin' ship to the Arctic seas to be locked in by the rotten ice for nigh on a year, and maybe lose her senses forever—for it's sure she'll never be the same again.

BEN—(*sadly*) She useter be awful nice to me before—(*his eyes grow wide and frightened*) she got—like she is.

THE STEWARD—Aye, she was good to all of us. 'Twould have been hell on board without her; for he's a hard man—a hard, hard man—a driver if there ever was one. (*with a grim laugh*) I hope he's satisfied now—drivin' her on till she's near lost her mind. And who could blame her? 'Tis a God's wonder we're not a ship full of crazed people—with the damned ice all the time, and the quiet so thick you're afraid to hear your own voice.

BEN—(*with a frightened glance toward the door on right*) She don't never speak to me no more—jest looks at me 's if she didn't know me.

THE STEWARD—She don't know no one—but him. She talks to him—when she does talk—right enough.

BEN—She does nothin' all day long now but sit and sew—and then she cries to herself without makin' no noise. I've seen her.

THE STEWARD—Aye, I could hear her through the door a while back.

BEN—(*tiptoes over to the door and listens*) She's cryin' now.

THE STEWARD—(*furiously—shaking his fist*) God send his soul to hell for the devil he is! (*There is the noise of some one coming slowly down the companionway stairs. The Steward hurries to his stacked up dishes. He is so nervous from fright that he knocks off the top one, which falls and breaks on the floor. He stands aghast, trembling with dread. Ben is violently rubbing off the organ with a piece of cloth which he has snatched from his pocket. Captain Keeney appears in the doorway on right and comes into the cabin, removing his fur cap as he does so. He is a man of about forty, around five-ten in height but looking much shorter on account of the enormous proportions of his shoulders and chest. His face is massive and deeply lined, with gray-blue eyes of a bleak hardness, and a tightly clenched, thin-lipped mouth. His thick hair is long and gray. He is dressed in a heavy blue jacket and blue pants stuffed into his seaboots.*

(*He is followed into the cabin by the Second Mate, a rangy six-footer with a lean weather-beaten face. The Mate is dressed about the same as the Captain. He is a man of thirty or so.*)

KEENEY—(*comes toward the Steward—with a stern look on his face. The Steward is visibly frightened and the stack of dishes rattles in his trembling hands. Keeney draws back his fist and the Steward shrinks away. The fist is gradually lowered and Keeney speaks slowly.*) 'Twould be like hitting a worm. It is nigh on two bells, Mr. Steward, and this truck not cleared yet.

THE STEWARD—(*stammering*) Y-y-yes, sir.

KEENEY—Instead of doin' your rightful work ye've been below here gossipin' old woman's talk with that boy. (*to Ben, fiercely*) Get out o' this, you! Clean up the chart room. (*Ben darts past the Mate to the open doorway.*) Pick up that dish, Mr. Steward!

THE STEWARD—(*doing so with difficulty*) Yes, sir.

KEENEY—The next dish you break, Mr. Steward, you take a bath in the Bering Sea at the end of a rope.

THE STEWARD—(*tremblingly*) Yes, sir. (*He hurries out. The Second Mate walks slowly over to the Captain.*)

MATE—I warn't 'specially anxious the man at the wheel

should catch what I wanted to say to you, sir. That's why I asked you to come below.

KEENEY—(*impatiently*) Speak your say, Mr. Slocum.

MATE—(*unconsciously lowering his voice*) I'm afeard there'll be trouble with the hands by the look o' things. They'll likely turn ugly, every blessed one o' them, if you don't put back. The two years they signed up for is up to-day.

KEENEY—And d'you think you're tellin' me somethin' new, Mr. Slocum? I've felt it in the air this long time past. D'you think I've not seen their ugly looks and the grudgin' way they worked? (*The door in rear is opened and Mrs. Keeney stands in the doorway. She is a slight, sweet-faced little woman primly dressed in black. Her eyes are red from weeping and her face drawn and pale. She takes in the cabin with a frightened glance and stands as if fixed to the spot by some nameless dread, clasping and unclasping her hands nervously. The two men turn and look at her.*)

KEENEY—(*with rough tenderness*) Well, Annie?

MRS. KEENEY—(*as if awakening from a dream*) David, I— (*She is silent. The Mate starts for the doorway.*)

KEENEY—(*turning to him—sharply*) Wait!

MATE—Yes, sir.

KEENEY—D'you want anything, Annie?

MRS. KEENEY—(*after a pause, during which she seems to be endeavoring to collect her thoughts*) I thought maybe—I'd go up on deck, David, to get a breath of fresh air. (*She stands humbly awaiting his permission. He and the Mate exchange a significant glance.*)

KEENEY—It's too cold, Annie. You'd best stay below to-day. There's nothing to look at on deck—but ice.

MRS. KEENEY—(*monotonously*) I know—ice, ice, ice! But there's nothing to see down here but these walls. (*She makes a gesture of loathing.*)

KEENEY—You can play the organ, Annie.

MRS. KEENEY—(*dully*) I hate the organ. It puts me in mind of home.

KEENEY—(*a touch of resentment in his voice*) I got it jest for you.

MRS. KEENEY—(*dully*) I know. (*She turns away from them and walks slowly to the bench on left. She lifts up one of the cur-*

tains and looks through a porthole; then utters an exclamation of joy.) Ah, water! Clear water! As far as I can see! How good it looks after all these months of ice! (*She turns round to them, her face transfigured with joy.*) Ah, now I must go upon deck and look at it, David.

KEENEY—(*frowning*) Best not to-day, Annie. Best wait for a day when the sun shines.

MRS. KEENEY—(*desperately*) But the sun never shines in this terrible place.

KEENEY—(*a tone of command in his voice*) Best not to-day, Annie.

MRS. KEENEY—(*crumbling before this command—abjectly*) Very well, David. (*She stands there staring straight before her as if in a daze. The two men look at her uneasily.*)

KEENEY—(*sharply*) Annie!

MRS. KEENEY—(*dully*) Yes, David.

KEENEY—Me and Mr. Slocum has business to talk about—ship's business.

MRS. KEENEY—Very well, David. (*She goes slowly out, rear, and leaves the door three-quarters shut behind her.*)

KEENEY—Best not have her on deck if they's goin' to be any trouble.

MATE—Yes, sir.

KEENEY—And trouble they's goin' to be. I feel it in my bones. (*takes a revolver from the pocket of his coat and examines it*) Got your'n?

MATE—Yes, sir.

KEENEY—Not that we'll have to use 'em—not if I know their breed of dog—jest to frighten 'em up a bit. (*grimly*) I ain't never been forced to use one yit; and trouble I've had by land and by sea 's long as I kin remember, and will have till my dyin' day, I reckon.

MATE—(*hesitatingly*) Then you ain't goin'—to turn back?

KEENEY—Turn back! Mr. Slocum, did you ever hear 'o me pointin' s'uth for home with only a measly four hundred barrel of ile in the hold?

MATE—(*hastily*) No, sir—but the grub's gittin' low.

KEENEY—They's enough to last a long time yit, if they're careful with it; and they's plenty o' water.

MATE—They say it's not fit to eat—what's left; and the

two years they signed on fur is up to-day. They might make trouble for you in the courts when we git home.

KEENEY—To hell with 'em! Let them make what law trouble they kin. I don't give a damn 'bout the money. I've got to git the ile! (*glancing sharply at the Mate*) You ain't turnin' no damned sea lawyer, be you, Mr. Slocum?

MATE—(*flushing*) Not by a hell of a sight, sir.

KEENEY—What do the fools want to go home fur now? Their share o' the four hundred barrel wouldn't keep 'em in chewin' terbacco.

MATE—(*slowly*) They wants to git back to their folks an' things, I s'pose.

KEENEY—(*looking at him searchingly*) 'N you want to turn back, too. (*The Mate looks down confusedly before his sharp gaze.*) Don't lie, Mr. Slocum. It's writ down plain in your eyes. (*with grim sarcasm*) I hope, Mr. Slocum, you ain't agoin' to jine the men agin me.

MATE—(*indignantly*) That ain't fair, sir, to say sich things.

KEENEY—(*with satisfaction*) I warn't much afeard o' that, Tom. You been with me nigh on ten year and I've learned ye whalin'. No man kin say I ain't a good master, if I be a hard one.

MATE—I warn't thinkin' of myself, sir—'bout turnin' home, I mean. (*desperately*) But Mrs. Keeney, sir—seems like she ain't jest satisfied up here, ailin' like—what with the cold an' bad luck an' the ice an' all.

KEENEY—(*his face clouding—rebukingly but not severely*) That's my business, Mr. Slocum. I'll thank you to steer a clear course o' that. (*a pause*) The ice'll break up soon to no'th'ard. I could see it startin' to-day. And when it goes and we git some sun Annie'll perk up. (*another pause—then he bursts forth*) It ain't the damned money what's keepin' me up in the Northern seas, Tom. But I can't go back to Homeport with a measly four hundred barrel of ile. I'd die fust. I ain't never come back home in all my days without a full ship. Ain't that truth?

MATE—Yes, sir; but this voyage you been ice-bound, an'—

KEENEY—(*scornfully*) And d'you s'pose any of 'em would believe that—any o' them skippers I've beaten voyage after voyage? Can't you hear 'em laughin' and sneerin'—Tibbots 'n' Harris 'n' Simms and the rest—and all o' Homeport makin' fun o' me? "Dave Keeney what boasts he's the best whalin' skipper out o' Homeport comin' back with a measly four hundred barrel of ile?" (*The thought of this drives him into a frenzy, and he smashes his fist down on the marble top of the sideboard.*) Hell! I got to git the ile, I tell you. How could I figger on this ice? It's never been so bad before in the thirty year I been acomin' here. And now it's breakin' up. In a couple o' days it'll be all gone. And they's whale here, plenty of 'em. I know they is and I ain't never gone wrong yit. I got to git the ile! I got to git it in spite of all hell, and by God, I ain't agoin' home till I do git it! (*There is the sound of subdued sobbing from the door in rear. The two men stand silent for a moment, listening. Then Keeney goes over to the door and looks in. He hesitates for a moment as if he were going to enter—then closes the door softly. Joe, the harpooner, an enormous six-footer with a battered, ugly face, enters from right and stands waiting for the Captain to notice him.*)

KEENEY—(*turning and seeing him*) Don't be standin' there like a gawk, Harpooner. Speak up!

JOE—(*confusedly*) We want—the men, sir—they wants to send a depitation aft to have a word with you.

KEENEY—(*furiously*) Tell 'em to go to— (*checks himself and continues grimly*) Tell 'em to come. I'll see 'em.

JOE—Aye, aye, sir. (*He goes out.*)

KEENEY—(*with a grim smile*) Here it comes, the trouble you spoke of, Mr. Slocum, and we'll make short shift of it. It's better to crush such things at the start than let them make headway.

MATE—(*worriedly*) Shall I wake up the First and Fourth, sir? We might need their help.

KEENEY—No, let them sleep. I'm well able to handle this alone, Mr. Slocum. (*There is the shuffling of footsteps from outside and five of the crew crowd into the cabin, led by Joe. All are dressed alike—sweaters, seaboots, etc. They glance uneasily at the Captain, twirling their fur caps in their hands.*)

KEENEY—(*after a pause*) Well? Who's to speak fur ye?

JOE—(*stepping forward with an air of bravado*) I be.

KEENEY—(*eyeing him up and down coldly*) So you be. Then speak your say and be quick about it.

JOE—(*trying not to wilt before the Captain's glance and avoiding his eyes*) The time we signed up for is done to-day.

KEENEY—(*icily*) You're tellin' me nothin' I don't know.

JOE—You ain't pintin' fur home yit, far 's we kin see.

KEENEY—No, and I ain't agoin' to till this ship is full of ile.

JOE—You can't go no further no'the with the ice afore ye.

KEENEY—The ice is breaking up.

JOE—(*after a slight pause during which the others mumble angrily to one another*) The grub we're gittin' now is rotten.

KEENEY—It's good enough fur ye. Better men than ye are have eaten worse. (*There is a chorus of angry exclamations from the crowd.*)

JOE—(*encouraged by this support*) We ain't agoin' to work no more less you puts back for home.

KEENEY—(*fiercely*) You ain't, ain't you?

JOE—No; and the law courts'll say we was right.

KEENEY—To hell with your law courts! We're at sea now and I'm the law on this ship. (*edging up toward the harpooner*) And every mother's son of you what don't obey orders goes in irons. (*There are more angry exclamations from the crew. Mrs. Keeney appears in the doorway in rear and looks on with startled eyes. None of the men notice her.*)

JOE—(*with bravado*) Then we're agoin' to mutiny and take the old hooker home ourselves. Ain't we, boys? (*As he turns his head to look at the others, Keeney's fist shoots out to the side of his jaw. Joe goes down in a heap and lies there. Mrs. Keeney gives a shriek and hides her face in her hands. The men pull out their sheath knives and start a rush, but stop when they find themselves confronted by the revolvers of Keeney and the Mate.*)

KEENEY—(*his eyes and voice snapping*) Hold still! (*The men stand huddled together in a sullen silence. Keeney's voice is full of mockery.*) You've found out it ain't safe to mutiny on this ship, ain't you? And now git for'ard where ye belong, and— (*He gives Joe's body a contemptuous kick.*) Drag him with you. And remember the first man of ye I see shirkin' I'll shoot dead as sure as there's a sea under us, and you can tell the rest the same. Git for'ard now! Quick! (*The men leave in cowed silence, carrying Joe with them. Keeney turns to the Mate with a short laugh and puts his revolver back in his pocket.*) Best get up on deck, Mr. Slocum, and see to it they don't try none of their skulkin' tricks. We'll have to keep an eye peeled from now on. I know 'em.

MATE—Yes, sir. (*He goes out, right. Keeney hears his wife's hysterical weeping and turns around in surprise—then walks slowly to her side.*)

KEENEY—(*putting an arm around her shoulder—with gruff tenderness*) There, there, Annie. Don't be afeard. It's all past and gone.

MRS. KEENEY—(*shrinking away from him*) Oh, I can't bear it! I can't bear it any longer!

KEENEY—(*gently*) Can't bear what, Annie?

MRS. KEENEY—(*hysterically*) All this horrible brutality, and these brutes of men, and this terrible ship, and this prison cell of a room, and the ice all around, and the silence. (*After this outburst she calms down and wipes her eyes with her handkerchief.*)

KEENEY—(*after a pause during which he looks down at her with a puzzled frown*) Remember, I warn't hankerin' to have you come on this voyage, Annie.

MRS. KEENEY—I wanted to be with you, David, don't you see? I didn't want to wait back there in the house all alone as I've been doing these last six years since we were married—waiting, and watching, and fearing—with nothing to keep my mind occupied—not able to go back teaching school on account of being Dave Keeney's wife. I used to dream of sailing on the great, wide, glorious ocean. I wanted to be by your side in the danger and vigorous life of it all. I wanted to see you the hero they make you out to be in Homeport. And instead— (*Her voice grows tremulous.*) All I find is ice and cold—and brutality! (*Her voice breaks.*)

KEENEY—I warned you what it'd be, Annie. "Whalin' ain't no ladies' tea party," I says to you, and "you better stay to home where you've got all your woman's comforts." (*shaking his head*) But you was so set on it.

MRS. KEENEY—(*wearily*) Oh, I know it isn't your fault, David. You see, I didn't believe you. I guess I was dreaming about the old Vikings in the story books and I thought you were one of them.

KEENEY—(*protestingly*) I done my best to make it as cozy

and comfortable as could be. (*Mrs. Keeney looks around her in wild scorn.*) I even sent to the city for that organ for ye, thinkin' it might be soothin' to ye to be playin' it times when they was calms and things was dull like.

MRS. KEENEY—(*wearily*) Yes, you were very kind, David. I know that. (*She goes to left and lifts the curtains from the porthole and looks out—then suddenly bursts forth*) I won't stand it—I can't stand it—pent up by these walls like a prisoner. (*She runs over to him and throws her arms around him, weeping. He puts his arm protectingly over her shoulders.*) Take me away from here, David! If I don't get away from here, out of this terrible ship, I'll go mad! Take me home, David! I can't think any more. I feel as if the cold and the silence were crushing down on my brain. I'm afraid. Take me home!

KEENEY—(*holds her at arm's length and looks at her face anxiously*) Best go to bed, Annie. You ain't yourself. You got fever. Your eyes look so strange like. I ain't never seen you look this way before.

MRS. KEENEY—(*laughing hysterically*) It's the ice and the cold and the silence—they'd make any one look strange.

KEENEY—(*soothingly*) In a month or two, with good luck, three at the most, I'll have her filled with ile and then we'll give her everything she'll stand and pint for home.

MRS. KEENEY—But we can't wait for that—I can't wait. I want to get home. And the men won't wait. They want to get home. It's cruel, it's brutal for you to keep them. You must sail back. You've got no excuse. There's clear water to the south now. If you've a heart at all you've got to turn back.

KEENEY—(*harshly*) I can't, Annie.

MRS. KEENEY—Why can't you?

KEENEY—A woman couldn't rightly understand my reason.

MRS. KEENEY—(*wildly*) Because it's a stupid, stubborn reason. Oh, I heard you talking with the second mate. You're afraid the other captains will sneer at you because you didn't come back with a full ship. You want to live up to your silly reputation even if you do have to beat and starve men and drive me mad to do it.

KEENEY—(*his jaw set stubbornly*) It ain't that, Annie. Them skippers would never dare sneer to my face. It ain't so much what any one'd say—but— (*He hesitates, struggling to express his meaning.*) You see—I've always done it—since my first voyage as skipper. I always come back—with a full ship—and—it don't seem right not to—somehow. I been always first whalin' skipper out o' Homeport, and— Don't you see my meanin', Annie? (*He glances at her. She is not looking at him but staring dully in front of her, not hearing a word he is saying.*) Annie! (*She comes to herself with a start.*) Best turn in, Annie, there's a good woman. You ain't well.

MRS. KEENEY—(*resisting his attempts to guide her to the door in rear*) David! Won't you please turn back?

KEENEY—(*gently*) I can't, Annie—not yet awhile. You don't see my meanin'. I got to git the ile.

MRS. KEENEY—It'd be different if you needed the money, but you don't. You've got more than plenty.

KEENEY—(*impatiently*) It ain't the money I'm thinkin' of. D'you think I'm as mean as that?

MRS. KEENEY—(*dully*) No—I don't know—I can't understand— (*intensely*) Oh, I want to be home in the old house once more and see my own kitchen again, and hear a woman's voice talking to me and be able to talk to her. Two years! It seems so long ago—as if I'd been dead and could never go back.

KEENEY—(*worried by her strange tone and the far-away look in her eyes*) Best go to bed, Annie. You ain't well.

MRS. KEENEY—(*not appearing to hear him*) I used to be lonely when you were away. I used to think Homeport was a stupid, monotonous place. Then I used to go down on the beach, especially when it was windy and the breakers were rolling in, and I'd dream of the fine free life you must be leading. (*She gives a laugh which is half a sob.*) I used to love the sea then. (*She pauses; then continues with slow intensity.*) But now—I don't ever want to see the sea again.

KEENEY—(*thinking to humor her*) 'Tis no fit place for a woman, that's sure. I was a fool to bring ye.

MRS. KEENEY—(*after a pause—passing her hand over her eyes with a gesture of pathetic weariness*) How long would it take us to reach home—if we started now?

KEENEY—(*frowning*) 'Bout two months, I reckon, Annie, with fair luck.

MRS. KEENEY—(*counts on her fingers—then murmurs with a rapt smile*) That would be August, the latter part of August, wouldn't it? It was on the twenty-fifth of August we were married, David, wasn't it?

KEENEY—(*trying to conceal the fact that her memories have moved him—gruffly*) Don't *you* remember?

MRS. KEENEY—(*vaguely—again passes her hand over her eyes*) My memory is leaving me—up here in the ice. It was so long ago. (*A pause—then she smiles dreamily.*) It's June now. The lilacs will be all in bloom in the front yard—and the climbing roses on the trellis to the side of the house—they're budding. (*She suddenly covers her face with her hands and commences to sob.*)

KEENEY—(*disturbed*) Go in and rest, Annie. You're all wore out cryin' over what can't be helped.

MRS. KEENEY—(*suddenly throwing her arms around his neck and clinging to him*) You love me, don't you, David?

KEENEY—(*in amazed embarrassment at this outburst*) Love you? Why d'you ask me such a question, Annie?

MRS. KEENEY—(*shaking him—fiercely*) But you do, don't you, David? Tell me!

KEENEY—I'm your husband, Annie, and you're my wife. Could there be aught but love between us after all these years?

MRS. KEENEY—(*shaking him again—still more fiercely*) Then you do love me. Say it!

KEENEY—(*simply*) I do, Annie.

MRS. KEENEY—(*gives a sigh of relief—her hands drop to her sides. Keeney regards her anxiously. She passes her hand across her eyes and murmurs half to herself*) I sometimes think if we could only have had a child. (*Keeney turns away from her, deeply moved. She grabs his arm and turns him around to face her—intensely*) And I've always been a good wife to you, haven't I, David?

KEENEY—(*his voice betraying his emotion*) No man has ever had a better, Annie.

MRS. KEENEY—And I've never asked for much from you, have I, David? Have I?

KEENEY—You know you could have all I got the power to give ye, Annie.

MRS. KEENEY—(*wildly*) Then do this this once for my sake, for God's sake—take me home! It's killing me, this life—the brutality and cold and horror of it. I'm going mad. I can feel the threat in the air. I can hear the silence threatening me—day after gray day and every day the same. I can't bear it. (*sobbing*) I'll go mad, I know I will. Take me home, David, if you love me as you say. I'm afraid. For the love of God, take me home! (*She throws her arms around him, weeping against his shoulder. His face betrays the tremendous struggle going on within him. He holds her out at arm's length, his expression softening. For a moment his shoulders sag, he becomes old, his iron spirit weakens as he looks at her tear-stained face.*)

KEENEY—(*dragging out the words with an effort*) I'll do it, Annie—for your sake—if you say it's needful for ye.

MRS. KEENEY—(*with wild joy—kissing him*) God bless you for that, David! (*He turns away from her silently and walks toward the companionway. Just at that moment there is a clatter of footsteps on the stairs and the Second Mate enters the cabin.*)

MATE—(*excitedly*) The ice is breakin' up to no'the'ard, sir. There's a clear passage through the floe, and clear water beyond, the lookout says. (*Keeney straightens himself like a man coming out of a trance. Mrs. Keeney looks at the Mate with terrified eyes.*)

KEENEY—(*dazedly—trying to collect his thoughts*) A clear passage? To no'the'ard?

MATE—Yes, sir.

KEENEY—(*his voice suddenly grim with determination*) Then get her ready and we'll drive her through.

MATE—Aye, aye, sir.

MRS. KEENEY—(*appealingly*) David!

KEENEY—(*not heeding her*) Will the men turn to willin' or must we drag 'em out?

MATE—They'll turn to willin' enough. You put the fear o' God into 'em, sir. They're meek as lambs.

KEENEY—Then drive 'em—both watches. (*with grim determination*) They's whale t'other side o' this floe and we're going to git 'em.

MATE—Aye, aye, sir. (*He goes out hurriedly. A moment later there is the sound of scuffling feet from the deck outside and the Mate's voice shouting orders.*)

KEENEY—(*speaking aloud to himself—derisively*) And I was agoin' home like a yaller dog!

MRS. KEENEY—(*imploringly*) David!

KEENEY—(*sternly*) Woman, you ain't adoin' right when you meddle in men's business and weaken 'em. You can't know my feelin's. I got to prove a man to be a good husband for ye to take pride in. I got to git the ile, I tell ye.

MRS. KEENEY—(*supplicatingly*) David! Aren't you going home?

KEENEY—(*ignoring this question—commandingly*) You ain't well. Go and lay down a mite. (*He starts for the door.*) I got to git on deck. (*He goes out. She cries after him in anguish*) David! (*A pause. She passes her hand across her eyes—then commences to laugh hysterically and goes to the organ. She sits down and starts to play wildly an old hymn. Keeney reënters from the doorway to the deck and stands looking at her angrily. He comes over and grabs her roughly by the shoulder.*)

KEENEY—Woman, what foolish mockin' is this? (*She laughs wildly and he starts back from her in alarm.*) Annie! What is it? (*She doesn't answer him. Keeney's voice trembles.*) Don't you know me, Annie? (*He puts both hands on her shoulders and turns her around so that he can look into her eyes. She stares up at him with a stupid expression, a vague smile on her lips. He stumbles away from her, and she commences softly to play the organ again.*)

KEENEY—(*swallowing hard—in a hoarse whisper, as if he had difficulty in speaking*) You said—you was a-goin' mad—God! (*A long wail is heard from the deck above. Ah bl-o-o-o-ow! A moment later the Mate's face appears through the skylight. He cannot see Mrs. Keeney.*)

MATE—(*in great excitement*) Whales, sir—a whole school of 'em—off the star'b'd quarter 'bout five mile away—big ones!

KEENEY—(*galvanized into action*) Are you lowerin' the boats?

MATE—Yes, sir.

KEENEY—(*with grim decision*) I'm a-comin' with ye.

MATE—Aye, aye, sir. (*jubilantly*) You'll git the ile now right enough, sir. (*His head is withdrawn and he can be heard shouting orders.*)

KEENEY—(*turning to his wife*) Annie! Did you hear him? I'll git the ile. (*She doesn't answer or seem to know he is there. He gives a hard laugh, which is almost a groan.*) I know you're foolin' me, Annie. You ain't out of your mind—(*anxiously*) be you? I'll git the ile now right enough—jest a little while longer, Annie—then we'll turn hom'ard. I can't turn back now, you see that, don't ye? I've got to git the ile. (*in sudden terror*) Answer me! You ain't mad, be you? (*She keeps on playing the organ, but makes no reply. The Mate's face appears again through the skylight.*)

MATE—All ready, sir. (*Keeney turns his back on his wife and strides to the doorway, where he stands for a moment and looks back at her in anguish, fighting to control his feelings.*)

MATE—Comin', sir?

KEENEY—(*his face suddenly grown hard with determination*) Aye. (*He turns abruptly and goes out. Mrs. Keeney does not appear to notice his departure. Her whole attention seems centered in the organ. She sits with half-closed eyes, her body swaying a little from side to side to the rhythm of the hymn. Her fingers move faster and faster and she is playing wildly and discordantly as*

The Curtain Falls)

THE LONG VOYAGE HOME

A Play in One Act

CHARACTERS

FAT JOE, *proprietor of a dive*

NICK, *a crimp*

MAG, *a barmaid*

OLSON

DRISCOLL

COCKY *Seamen of the British tramp steamer, Glencairn*

IVAN

KATE

FREDA

TWO ROUGHS

The Long Voyage Home

SCENE—*The bar of a low dive on the London water front—a squalid, dingy room dimly lighted by kerosene lamps placed in brackets on the walls. On the left, the bar. In front of it, a door leading to a side room. On the right, tables with chairs around them. In the rear, a door leading to the street.*

A slovenly barmaid with a stupid face sodden with drink is mopping off the bar. Her arm moves back and forth mechanically and her eyes are half shut as if she were dozing on her feet. At the far end of the bar stands Fat Joe, the proprietor, a gross bulk of a man with an enormous stomach. His face is red and bloated, his little piggish eyes being almost concealed by rolls of fat. The thick fingers of his big hands are loaded with cheap rings and a gold watch chain of cable-like proportions stretches across his checked waistcoat.

At one of the tables, front, a round-shouldered young fellow is sitting, smoking a cigarette. His face is pasty, his mouth weak, his eyes shifting and cruel. He is dressed in a shabby suit, which must have once been cheaply flashy, and wears a muffler and cap.

It is about nine o'clock in the evening.

JOE—(*yawning*) Blimey if bizness ain't 'arf slow to-night. I donnow wot's 'appened. The place is like a bleedin' tomb. Where's all the sailor men, I'd like to know? (*raising his voice*) Ho, you Nick! (*Nick turns around listlessly.*) Wot's the name o' that wessel put in at the dock below jest arter noon?

NICK—(*laconically*) Glencairn—from Bewnezerry. (Buenos Aires)

JOE—Ain't the crew been paid orf yet?

NICK—Paid orf this afternoon, they tole me. I 'opped on board of 'er an' seen 'em. 'Anded 'em some o' yer cards, I did. They promised faithful they'd 'appen in to-night—them as whose time was done.

JOE—Any two-year men to be paid orf?

NICK—Four—three Britishers an' a square-'ead.

JOE—(*indignantly*) An' yer popped orf an' left 'em? An' me a-payin' yer to 'elp an' bring 'em in 'ere!

NICK—(*grumblingly*) Much you pays me! An' I ain't

509

slingin' me 'ook abaht the 'ole bleedin' town fur now man. See?

JOE—I ain't speakin' on'y fur meself. Down't I always give yer yer share, fair an' square, as man to man?

NICK—(*with a sneer*) Yus—b'cause you 'as to.

JOE—'As to? Listen to 'im! There's many'd be 'appy to 'ave your berth, me man!

NICK—Yus? Wot wiv the peelers li'ble to put me away in the bloody jail fur crimpin', an' all?

JOE—(*indignantly*) We down't do no crimpin'.

NICK—(*sarcastically*) Ho, now! Not arf!

JOE—(*a bit embarrassed*) Well, on'y a bit now an' agen when there ain't no reg'lar trade. (*To hide his confusion he turns to the barmaid angrily. She is still mopping off the bar, her chin on her breast, half-asleep.*) 'Ere, me gel, we've 'ad enough o' that. You been a-moppin', an' a-moppin', an' a-moppin' the blarsted bar fur a 'ole 'our. 'Op it aht o' this! You'd fair guv a bloke the shakes a-watchin' yer.

MAG—(*beginning to sniffle*) Ow, you do frighten me when you 'oller at me, Joe. I ain't a bad gel, I ain't. Gawd knows I tries to do me best fur you. (*She bursts into a tempest of sobs.*)

JOE—(*roughly*) Stop yer grizzlin'! An' 'op it aht of 'ere!

NICK—(*chuckling*) She's drunk, Joe. Been 'ittin' the gin, eh, Mag?

MAG—(*ceases crying at once and turns on him furiously*) You little crab, you! Orter wear a muzzle, you ort! A-openin' of your ugly mouth to a 'onest woman what ain't never done you no 'arm. (*commencing to sob again*) H'abusin' me like a dawg cos I'm sick an' orf me oats, an' all.

JOE—Orf yer go, me gel! Go hupstairs and 'ave a sleep. I'll wake yer if I wants yer. An' wake the two gels when yer goes hup. It's 'arpas' nine an' time as some one was a-comin' in, tell 'em. D'yer 'ear me?

MAG—(*stumbling around the bar to the door on left—sobbing*) Yus, yus, I 'ears you. Gawd knows wot's goin' to 'appen to me, I'm that sick. Much you cares if I dies, down't you? (*She goes out.*)

JOE—(*still brooding over Nick's lack of diligence—after a pause*) Four two-year men paid orf wiv their bloody pockets full o' sovereigns—an' yer lorst 'em. (*He shakes his head sorrowfully.*)

NICK—(*impatiently*) Stow it! They promised faithful they'd come, I tells yer. They'll be walkin' in in 'arf a mo'. There's lots o' time yet. (*in a low voice*) 'Ave yer got the drops? We might wanter use 'em.

JOE—(*taking a small bottle from behind the bar*) Yus; 'ere it is.

NICK—(*with satisfaction*) Righto! (*His shifty eyes peer about the room searchingly. Then he beckons to Joe, who comes over to the table and sits down.*) Reason I arst yer about the drops was 'cause I seen the capt'n of the Amindra this arternoon.

JOE—The Amindra? Wot ship is that?

NICK—Bloody windjammer—skys'l yarder—full rigged—painted white—been layin' at the dock above 'ere fur a month. You knows 'er.

JOE—Ho, yus. I knows now.

NICK—The capt'n says as 'e wants a man special bad—ter-night. They sails at daybreak ter-morrer.

JOE—There's plenty o' 'ands lyin' abaht waitin' fur ships, I should fink.

NICK—Not fur this ship, ole buck. The capt'n an' mate are bloody slave-drivers, an' they're bound down round the 'Orn. They 'arf starved the 'ands on the larst trip 'ere, an' no one'll dare ship on 'er. (*after a pause*) I promised the capt'n faithful I'd get 'im one, and ter-night.

JOE—(*doubtfully*) An' 'ow are yer goin' to git 'im?

NICK—(*with a wink*) I was thinkin' as one of 'em from the Glencairn'd do—them as was paid orf an' is comin' 'ere.

JOE—(*with a grin*) It'd be a good 'aul, that's the troof. (*frowning*) If they comes 'ere.

NICK—They'll come, an' they'll all be rotten drunk, wait an' see. (*There is the noise of loud, boisterous singing from the street.*) Sounds like 'em, now. (*He opens the street door and looks out.*) Gawd blimey if it ain't the four of 'em! (*turning to Joe in triumph*) Naw, what d'yer say? They're lookin' for the place. I'll go aht an' tell 'em. (*He goes out. Joe gets into position behind the bar, assuming his most oily smile. A moment later the door is opened, admitting Driscoll, Cocky, Ivan and Olson. Driscoll is a tall, powerful Irishman; Cocky, a wizened runt of a man with a straggling gray mustache; Ivan, a hulking oaf of a peasant; Olson, a stocky, middle-aged Swede with round, child-ish blue eyes. The first three are all very drunk, especially Ivan, who is managing his legs with difficulty. Olson is perfectly sober. All are dressed in their ill-fitting shore clothes and look very uncomfortable. Driscoll has unbuttoned his stiff collar and its ends stick out sideways. He has lost his tie. Nick slinks into the room after them and sits down at a table in rear. The seamen come to the table, front.)*

JOE—(*with affected heartiness*) Ship ahoy, mates! 'Appy to see yer 'ome safe an' sound.

DRISCOLL—(*turns round, swaying a bit, and peers at him across the bar*) So ut's you, is ut? (*He looks about the place with an air of recognition.*) 'An the same damn rat's-hole, sure enough. I remimber foive or six years back 'twas here I was sthripped av me last shillin' whin I was aslape. (*with sudden fury*) God stiffen ye, come none av your dog's thricks on me this trip or I'll— (*He shakes his fist at Joe.*)

JOE—(*hastily interrupting*) Yer must be mistaiken. This is a 'onest place, this is.

COCKY—(*derisively*) Ho, yus! An' you're a bleedin' angel, I s'pose?

IVAN—(*vaguely taking off his derby hat and putting it on again—plaintively*) I don' li-ike dis place.

DRISCOLL—(*going over to the bar—as genial as he was furious a moment before*) Well, no matther, 'tis all past an' gone an' forgot. I'm not the man to be holdin' harrd feelin's on me first night ashore, an' me dhrunk as a lord. (*He holds out his hand, which Joe takes very gingerly.*) We'll all be havin' a dhrink, I'm thinkin'. Whiskey for the three av us—*Irish* whiskey!

COCKY—(*mockingly*) An' a glarse o' ginger beer fur our blarsted love-child 'ere. (*He jerks his thumb at Olson.*)

OLSON—(*with a good-natured grin*) I bane a good boy dis night, for one time.

DRISCOLL—(*bellowing, and pointing to Nick as Joe brings the drinks to the table*) An' see what that crimpin' son av a crimp'll be wantin'—an' have your own pleasure. (*He pulls a sovereign out of his pocket and slams it on the bar.*)

NICK—Guv me a pint o' beer, Joe. (*Joe draws the beer and takes it down to the far end of the bar. Nick comes over to get it and Joe gives him a significant wink and nods toward the door on the left. Nick signals back that he understands.*)

COCKY—(*drink in hand—impatiently*) I'm that bloody dry! (*lifting his glass to Driscoll*) Cheero, ole dear, cheero!

DRISCOLL—(*pocketing his change without looking at it*) A toast for ye: Hell roast that divil av a bo'sun! (*He drinks.*)

COCKY—Righto! Gawd strike 'im blind! (*He drains his glass.*)

IVAN—(*half-asleep*) Dot's gude. (*He tosses down his drink in one gulp. Olson sips his ginger ale. Nick takes a swallow of his beer and then comes round the bar and goes out the door on left.*)

COCKY—(*producing a sovereign*) Ho there, you Fatty! Guv us another!

JOE—The saime, mates?

COCKY—Yus.

DRISCOLL—No, ye scut! I'll be havin' a pint av beer. I'm dhry as a loime kiln.

IVAN—(*suddenly getting to his feet in a befuddled manner and nearly upsetting the table*) I don' li-ike dis place! I wan' see girls—plenty girls. (*pathetically*) I don't li-ike dis place. I wan' dance with girl.

DRISCOLL—(*pushing him back on his chair with a thud*) Shut up, ye Rooshan baboon! A foine Romeo you'd make in your condishun. (*Ivan blubbers some incoherent protest—then suddenly falls asleep.*)

JOE—(*bringing the drinks—looks at Olson*) An' you, matey?

OLSON—(*shaking his head*) Noting dis time, thank you.

COCKY—(*mockingly*) A-saivin' of 'is money, 'e is! Goin' back to 'ome an' mother. Goin' to buy a bloomin' farm an' punch the blarsted dirt, that's wot 'e is! (*spitting disgustedly*) There's a funny bird of a sailor man for yer, Gawd blimey!

OLSON—(*wearing the same good-natured grin*) Yust what I like, Cocky. I wus on farm long time when I wus kid.

DRISCOLL—Lave him alone, ye bloody insect! 'Tis a foine sight to see a man wid some sense in his head instead av a damn fool the loike av us. I only wisht I'd a mother alive to call me own. I'd not be dhrunk in this divil's hole this minute, maybe.

COCKY—(*commencing to weep dolorously*) Ow, down't talk, Drisc! I can't bear to 'ear you. I ain't never 'ad no mother, I ain't—

DRISCOLL—Shut up, ye ape, an' don't be makin' that squealin'. If ye cud see your ugly face, wid the big red nose av ye all screwed up in a knot, ye'd never shed a tear the rist av your loife. (*roaring into song*) We ar-re the byes av We-e-ex-ford who fought wid hearrt an' hand! (*speaking*) To hell wid Ulster! (*He drinks and the others follow his example.*) An' I'll strip to any man in the city av London won't dhrink to that toast. (*He glares truculently at Joe, who immediately downs his beer. Nick enters again from the door on the left and comes up to Joe and whispers in his ear. The latter nods with satisfaction.*)

DRISCOLL—(*glowering at them*) What divil's thrick are ye up to now, the two av ye? (*He flourishes a brawny fist.*) Play fair wid us or ye deal wid me!

JOE—(*hastily*) No trick, shipmate! May Gawd kill me if that ain't troof!

NICK—(*indicating Ivan, who is snoring*) On'y your mate there was arskin' fur gels an' I thorght as 'ow yer'd like 'em to come dawhn and 'ave a wet wiv yer.

JOE—(*with a smirking wink*) Pretty, 'olesome gels they be, ain't they, Nick?

NICK—Yus.

COCKY—Aar! I knows the gels you 'as, not 'arf! They'd fair blind yer, they're that 'omely. None of yer bloomin' gels fur me, ole Fatty. Me an' Drisc knows a place, down't we, Drisc?

DRISCOLL—Divil a lie, we do. An' we'll be afther goin' there in a minute. There's music there an' a bit av a dance to liven a man.

JOE—Nick, 'ere, can play yer a tune, can't yer, Nick?

NICK—Yus.

JOE—An' yer can 'ave a dance in the side room 'ere.

DRISCOLL—Hurroo! Now you're talkin'. (*The two women, Freda and Kate, enter from the left. Freda is a little, sallow-faced blonde. Kate is stout and dark.*)

COCKY—(*in a loud aside to Driscoll*) Gawd blimey, look at 'em! Ain't they 'orrible? (*The women come forward to the table, wearing their best set smiles.*)

FREDA—(*in a raspy voice*) 'Ullo, mates.

KATE—'Ad a good voyage?

DRISCOLL—Rotten; but no matther. Welcome, as the

sayin' is, an' sit down, an' what'll ye be takin' for your thirst? (*to Kate*) You'll be sittin' by me, darlin'—what's your name?

KATE—(*with a stupid grin*) Kate. (*She stands by his chair.*)

DRISCOLL—(*putting his arm around her*) A good Irish name, but you're English by the trim av ye, an' be damned to you. But no matther. Ut's fat ye are, Katy dear, an' I never cud endure skinny wimin. (*Freda favors him with a viperish glance and sits down by Olson.*) What'll ye have?

OLSON—No, Drisc. Dis one bane on me. (*He takes out a roll of notes from his inside pocket and lays one on the table. Joe, Nick, and the women look at the money with greedy eyes. Ivan gives a particularly violent snore.*)

FREDA—Waike up your fren'. Gawd, 'ow I 'ates to 'ear snorin'.

DRISCOLL—(*springing to action, smashes Ivan's derby over his ears*) D'you hear the lady talkin' to ye, ye Rooshan swab? (*The only reply to this is a snore. Driscoll pulls the battered remains of the derby off Ivan's head and smashes it back again.*) Arise an' shine, ye dhrunken swine! (*Another snore. The women giggle. Driscoll throws the beer left in his glass into Ivan's face. The Russian comes to in a flash, spluttering. There is a roar of laughter.*)

IVAN—(*indignantly*) I tell you—dot's someting I don' li-ike!

COCKY—Down't waste good beer, Drisc.

IVAN—(*grumblingly*) I tell you—dot is not ri-ight.

DRISCOLL—Ut's your own doin', Ivan. Ye was moanin' for girrls an' whin they come you sit gruntin' loike a pig in a sty. Have ye no manners? (*Ivan seems to see the women for the first time and grins foolishly.*)

KATE—(*laughing at him*) Cheero, ole chum, 'ows Russha?

IVAN—(*greatly pleased—putting his hand in his pocket*) I buy a drink.

OLSON—No; dis one bane on me. (*to Joe*) Hey, you faller!

JOE—Wot'll it be, Kate?

KATE—Gin.

FREDA—Brandy.

DRISCOLL—An' Irish whiskey for the rist av us—wid the excipshun av our timperance friend, God pity him!

FREDA—(*to Olson*) You ain't drinkin'?

OLSON—(*half-ashamed*) No.

FREDA—(*with a seductive smile*) I down't blame yer. You got sense, you 'ave. I on'y tike a nip o' brandy now an' agen fur my 'ealth. (*Joe brings the drinks and Olson's change. Cocky gets unsteadily to his feet and raises his glass in the air.*)

COCKY—'Ere's a toff toast for yer: The ladies, Gawd— (*he hesitates—then adds in a grudging tone*)—bless 'em.

KATE—(*with a silly giggle.*) Oo-er! That wasn't what you was goin' to say, you bad Cocky, you! (*They all drink.*)

DRISCOLL—(*to Nick*) Where's the tune ye was promisin' to give us?

NICK—Come ahn in the side 'ere an' you'll 'ear it.

DRISCOLL—(*getting up*) Come on, all av ye. We'll have a tune an' a dance if I'm not too dhrunk to dance, God help me. (*Cocky and Ivan stagger to their feet. Ivan can hardly stand. He is leering at Kate and snickering to himself in a maudlin fashion. The three, led by Nick, go out the door on the left. Kate follows them. Olson and Freda remain seated.*)

COCKY—(*calling over his shoulder*) Come on an' dance, Ollie.

OLSON—Yes, I come. (*He starts to get up. From the side room comes the sound of an accordion and a boisterous whoop from Driscoll, followed by a heavy stamping of feet.*)

FREDA—Ow, down't go in there. Stay 'ere an' 'ave a talk wiv me. They're all drunk an' you ain't drinkin'. (*with a smile up into his face*) I'll think yer don't like me if yer goes in there.

OLSON—(*confused*) You wus wrong, Miss Freda. I don't— I mean I do like you.

FREDA—(*smiling—puts her hand over his on the table*) An' I likes you. Yer a genelman. You don't get drunk an' hinsult poor gels wot 'as a 'ard an' uneppy life.

OLSON—(*pleased but still more confused—wriggling his feet*) I bane drunk many time, Miss Freda.

FREDA—Then why ain't yer drinkin' now? (*She exchanges a quick, questioning glance with Joe, who nods back at her— then she continues persuasively*) Tell me somethin' abaht yeself.

OLSON—(*with a grin*) There ain't noting to say, Miss Freda. I bane poor devil sailor man, dat's all.

FREDA—Where was you born—Norway? (*Olson shakes his head.*) Denmark?

OLSON—No. You guess once more.

FREDA—Then it must be Sweden.

OLSON—Yes. I wus born in Stockholm.

FREDA—(*pretending great delight*) Ow, ain't that funny! I was born there, too—in Stockholm.

OLSON—(*astonished*) You wus born in Sweden?

FREDA—Yes; you wouldn't think it, but it's Gawd's troof. (*She claps her hands delightedly.*)

OLSON—(*beaming all over*) You speak Swedish?

FREDA—(*trying to smile sadly*) Now. Y'see my ole man an' woman come 'ere to England when I was on'y a baby an' they was speakin' English b'fore I was old enough to learn. Sow I never knew Swedish. (*sadly*) Wisht I 'ad! (*with a smile*) We'd 'ave a bloomin' lark of it if I 'ad, wouldn't we?

OLSON—It sound nice to hear the old talk yust once in a time.

FREDA—Righto! No place like yer 'ome, I says. Are yer goin' up to—to Stockholm b'fore yer ships away agen?

OLSON—Yes. I go home from here to Stockholm. (*proudly*) As passenger!

FREDA—An' you'll git another ship up there arter you've 'ad a vacation?

OLSON—No. I don't never ship on sea no more. I got all sea I want for my life—too much hard work for little money. Yust work, work, work on ship. I don't want more.

FREDA—Ow, I see. That's why you give up drinkin'.

OLSON—Yes. (*with a grin*) If I drink I yust get drunk and spend all money.

FREDA—But if you ain't gointer be a sailor no more, what'll yer do? You been a sailor all yer life, ain't yer?

OLSON—No. I work on farm till I am eighteen. I like it, too—it's nice—work on farm.

FREDA—But ain't Stockholm a city same's London? Ain't no farms there, is there?

OLSON—We live—my brother and mother live—my father iss dead—on farm yust a little way from Stockholm. I have plenty money, now. I go back with two years' pay and buy more land yet; work on farm. (*grinning*) No more sea, no more bum grub, no more storms—yust nice work.

FREDA—Ow, ain't that luv'ly! I s'pose you'll be gittin' married, too?

OLSON—(*very much confused*) I don't know. I like to, if I find nice girl, maybe.

FREDA—Ain't yer got some gel back in Stockholm? I bet yer 'as.

OLSON—No. I got nice girl once before I go on sea. But I go on ship, and I don't come back, and she marry other faller. (*He grins sheepishly.*)

FREDA—Well, it's nice for yer to be goin' 'ome, anyway.

OLSON—Yes. I tank so. (*There is a crash from the room on left and the music abruptly stops. A moment later Cocky and Driscoll appear, supporting the inert form of Ivan between them. He is in the last stage of intoxication, unable to move a muscle. Nick follows them and sits down at the table in rear.*)

DRISCOLL—(*as they zigzag up to the bar*) Ut's dead he is, I'm thinkin', for he's as limp as a blarsted corpse.

COCKY—(*puffing*) Gawd, 'e ain't 'arf 'eavy!

DRISCOLL—(*slapping Ivan's face with his free hand*) Wake up, ye divil, ye. Ut's no use. Gabriel's trumpet itself cudn't rouse him. (*to Joe*) Give us a dhrink for I'm perishing wid the thirst. 'Tis harrd worrk, this.

JOE—Whiskey?

DRISCOLL—*Irish* whiskey, ye swab. (*He puts down a coin on the bar. Joe serves Cocky and Driscoll. They drink and then swerve over to Olson's table.*)

OLSON—Sit down and rest for time, Drisc.

DRISCOLL—No, Ollie, we'll be takin' this lad home to his bed. Ut's late for wan so young to be out in the night. An' I'd not trust him in this hole as dhrunk as he is, an' him wid a full pay day on him. (*shaking his fist at Joe*) Oho, I know your games, me sonny bye!

JOE—(*with an air of grievance*) There yer goes again—hin-sultin' a 'onest man!

COCKY—Ho, listen to 'im! Guv 'im a shove in the marf, Drisc.

OLSON—(*anxious to avoid a fight—getting up*) I help you take Ivan to boarding house.

FREDA—(*protestingly*) Ow, you ain't gointer leave me, are yer? An' we 'avin' sech a nice talk, an' all.

DRISCOLL—(*with a wink*) Ye hear what the lady says,

Ollie. Ye'd best stay here, me timperance lady's man. An' we need no help. 'Tis only a bit av a way and we're two strong men if we are dhrunk. Ut's no hard shift to take the remains home. But ye can open the door for us, Ollie. (*Olson goes to the door and opens it.*) Come on, Cocky, an' don't be fallin' aslape yourself. (*They lurch toward the door. As they go out Driscoll shouts back over his shoulder*) We'll be comin' back in a short time, surely. So wait here for us, Ollie.

OLSON—All right. I wait here, Drisc. (*He stands in the doorway uncertainly. Joe makes violent signs to Freda to bring him back. She goes over and puts her arm around Olson's shoulder. Joe motions to Nick to come to the bar. They whisper together excitedly.*)

FREDA—(*coaxingly*) You ain't gointer leave me, are yer, dearie? (*then irritably*) Fur Gawd's sake, shet that door! I'm fair freezin' to death wiv the fog. (*Olson comes to himself with a start and shuts the door.*)

OLSON—(*humbly*) Excuse me, Miss Freda.

FREDA—(*leading him back to the table—coughing*) Buy me a drink o' brandy, will yer? I'm sow cold.

OLSON—All you want, Miss Freda, all you want. (*to Joe, who is still whispering instructions to Nick*) Hey, Yoe! Brandy for Miss Freda. (*He lays a coin on the table.*)

JOE—Righto! (*He pours out her drink and brings it to the table.*) 'Avin' somethink yeself, shipmate?

OLSON—No. I don't tank so. (*He points to his glass with a grin.*) Dis iss only belly-wash, no? (*He laughs.*)

JOE—(*hopefully*) 'Ave a man's drink.

OLSON—I would like to—but no. If I drink one I want drink one tousand. (*He laughs again.*)

FREDA—(*responding to a vicious nudge from Joe's elbow*) Ow, tike somethin'. I ain't gointer drink all be meself.

OLSON—Den give me a little yinger beer—small one. (*Joe goes back of the bar, making a sign to Nick to go to their table. Nick does so and stands so that the sailor cannot see what Joe is doing.*)

NICK—(*to make talk*) Where's yer mates popped orf ter? (*Joe pours the contents of the little bottle into Olson's glass of ginger beer.*)

OLSON—Dey take Ivan, dat drunk faller, to bed. They come back. (*Joe brings Olson's drink to the table and sets it before him.*)

JOE—(*to Nick—angrily*) 'Op it, will yer? There ain't no time to be dawdlin'. See? 'Urry!

NICK—Down't worry, ole bird, I'm orf. (*He hurries out the door. Joe returns to his place behind the bar.*)

OLSON—(*after a pause—worriedly*) I tank I should go after dem. Cocky iss very drunk, too, and Drisc—

FREDA—Aar! The big Irish is all right. Don't yer 'ear 'im say as 'ow they'd surely come back 'ere, an' fur you to wait fur 'em?

OLSON—Yes; but if dey don't come soon I tank I go see if dey are in boarding house all right.

FREDA—Where is the boardin' 'ouse?

OLSON—Yust little way back from street here.

FREDA—You stayin' there, too?

OLSON—Yes—until steamer sail for Stockholm—in two day.

FREDA—(*She is alternately looking at Joe and feverishly trying to keep Olson talking so he will forget about going away after the others.*) Yer mother won't be arf glad to see yer agen, will she? (*Olson smiles.*) Does she know yer comin'?

OLSON—No. I tought I would yust give her surprise. I write to her from Bonos Eres but I don't tell her I come home.

FREDA—Must be old, ain't she, yer ole lady?

OLSON—She iss eighty-two. (*He smiles reminiscently.*) You know, Miss Freda, I don't see my mother or my brother in—let me tank—(*he counts laboriously on his fingers*) must be more than ten year. I write once in while and she write many time; and my brother he write me, too. My mother say in all letter I should come home right away. My brother he write same ting, too. He want me to help him on farm. I write back always I come soon; and I mean all time to go back home at end of voyage. But I come ashore, I take one drink, I take many drinks, I get drunk, I spend all money, I have to ship away for other voyage. So dis time I say to myself: Don't drink one drink, Ollie, or, sure, you don't get home. And I want go home dis time. I feel homesick for farm and to see my people again. (*He smiles.*) Yust like little boy, I feel home-sick. Dat's why I don't drink noting to-night but dis—belly-wash! (*He roars with childish laughter, then suddenly becomes serious.*) You know, Miss Freda, my mother get very old, and I want see her. She might die and I would never—

FREDA—(*moved a lot in spite of herself*) Ow, don't talk like that! I jest 'ates to 'ear any one speakin' abaht dyin'. (*The door to the street is opened and Nick enters, followed by two rough-looking, shabbily-dressed men, wearing mufflers, with caps pulled down over their eyes. They sit at the table nearest to the door. Joe brings them three beers, and there is a whispered consultation, with many glances in the direction of Olson.*)

OLSON—(*starting to get up—worriedly*) I tank I go round to boarding house. I tank someting go wrong with Drisc and Cocky.

FREDA—Ow, down't go. They kin take care of theyselves. They ain't babies. Wait 'arf a mo'. You ain't 'ad yer drink yet.

JOE—(*coming hastily over to the table, indicates the men in the rear with a jerk of his thumb*) One of them blokes wants yer to 'ave a wet wiv 'im.

FREDA—Righto! (*to Olson*) Let's drink this. (*She raises her glass. He does the same.*) 'Ere's a toast fur yer: Success to yer bloomin' farm an' may yer live long an' 'appy on it. Skoal! (*She tosses down her brandy. He swallows half his glass of ginger beer and makes a wry face.*)

OLSON—Skoal! (*He puts down his glass.*)

FREDA—(*with feigned indignation*) Down't yer like my toast?

OLSON—(*grinning*) Yes. It iss very kind, Miss Freda.

FREDA—Then drink it all like I done.

OLSON—Well— (*He gulps down the rest.*) Dere! (*He laughs.*)

FREDA—Done like a sport!

ONE OF THE ROUGHS—(*with a laugh*) Amindra, ahoy!

NICK—(*warningly*) Sssshh!

OLSON—(*turns around in his chair*) Amindra? Iss she in port? I sail on her once long time ago—three mast, full rig, skys'l yarder? Iss dat ship you mean?

THE ROUGH—(*grinning*) Yus; right you are.

OLSON—(*angrily*) I know dat damn ship—worst ship dat

sail to sea. Rotten grub and dey make you work all time—
and the Captain and Mate wus Bluenose devils. No sailor
who know anyting ever ship on her. Where iss she bound
from here?

THE ROUGH—Round Cape 'Orn—sails at daybreak.

OLSON—Py yingo, I pity poor fallers make dat trip round
Cape Stiff dis time year. I bet you some of dem never see
port once again. (*He passes his hand over his eyes in a dazed
way. His voice grows weaker.*) I'y golly, I feel dizzy. All the
room go round and round like I wus drunk. (*He gets weakly
to his feet.*) Good night, Miss Freda. I bane feeling sick. Tell
Drisc—I go home. (*He takes a step forward and suddenly collapses over a chair, rolls to the floor, and lies there unconscious.*)

JOE—(*from behind the bar*) Quick, nawh! (*Nick darts forward with Joe following. Freda is already beside the unconscious
man and has taken the roll of money from his inside pocket. She
strips off a note furtively and shoves it into her bosom, trying to
conceal her action, but Joe sees her. She hands the roll to Joe, who
pockets it. Nick goes through all the other pockets and lays a handful of change on the table.*)

JOE—(*impatiently*) 'Urry, 'urry, can't yer? The other
blokes'll be 'ere in 'arf a mo'. (*The two roughs come forward.*)
'Ere, you two, tike 'im in under the arms like 'e was drunk.
(*They do so.*) Tike 'im to the Amindra—yer knows that,
don't yer?—two docks above. Nick'll show yer. An' you,
Nick, down't yer leave the bleedin' ship till the capt'n guvs yer
this bloke's advance—full month's pay—five quid, d'yer 'ear?

NICK—I knows me bizness, ole bird. (*They support Olson
to the door.*)

THE ROUGH—(*as they are going out*) This silly bloke'll 'ave
the s'prise of 'is life when 'e wakes up on board of 'er. (*They
laugh. The door closes behind them. Freda moves quickly for the
door on the left but Joe gets in her way and stops her.*)

JOE—(*threateningly*) Guv us what yer took!

FREDA—Took? I guv yer all 'e 'ad.

JOE—Yer a liar! I seen yer a-playin' yer sneakin' tricks, but
yer can't fool Joe. I'm too old a 'and. (*furiously*) Guv it to me,
yer bloody cow! (*He grabs her by the arm.*)

FREDA—Lemme alone! I ain't got no—

JOE—(*hits her viciously on the side of the jaw. She crumples up *on the floor.*) That'll learn yer! (*He stoops down and fumbles in her bosom and pulls out the banknote, which he stuffs into his pocket with a grunt of satisfaction. Kate opens the door on the left and looks in—then rushes to Freda and lifts her head up in her arms.*)

KATE—(*gently*) Pore dearie! (*looking at Joe angrily*) Been 'ittin' 'er agen, 'ave yer, yer cowardly swine!

JOE—Yus; an' I'll 'it you, too, if yer don't keep yer marf shut. Tike 'er aht of 'ere! (*Kate carries Freda into the next room. Joe goes behind the bar. A moment later the outer door is opened and Driscoll and Cocky come in.*)

DRISCOLL—Come on, Ollie. (*He suddenly sees that Olson is not there, and turns to Joe.*) Where is ut he's gone to?

JOE—(*with a meaning wink*) 'E an' Freda went aht t'gether 'bout five minutes past. 'E's fair gone on 'er, 'e is.

DRISCOLL—(*with a grin*) Oho, so that's ut, is ut? Who'd think Ollie'd be sich a divil wid the wimin? 'Tis lucky he's sober or she'd have him stripped to his last ha'penny. (*turning to Cocky, who is blinking sleepily*) What'll ye have, ye little scut? (*to Joe*) Give me whiskey, *Irish* whiskey!

(*The Curtain Falls*)

THE MOON OF THE
CARIBBEES

A Play in One Act

CHARACTERS

YANK
DRISCOLL
OLSON
DAVIS   *Seamen of the British tramp*
COCKY   *steamer, Glencairn*
SMITTY
PAUL

LAMPS, *the lamptrimmer*
CHIPS, *the carpenter*
OLD TOM, *the donkeyman*

BIG FRANK
DICK   *Firemen on the Glencairn*
MAX
PADDY

BELLA
SUSIE   *West Indian Negresses*
VIOLET
PEARL

THE FIRST MATE

Two other seamen—SCOTTY and IVAN—and several other members of the stokehole-engine-room crew

The Moon of the Caribbees

SCENE—*A forward section of the main deck of the British tramp Steamer* Glencairn, *at anchor off an island in the West Indies. The full moon, half-way up the sky, throws a clear light on the deck. The sea is calm and the ship motionless.*

On the left two of the derrick booms of the foremast jut out at an angle of forty-five degrees, black against the sky. In the rear the dark outline of the port bulwark is sharply defined against a distant strip of coral beach, white in the moonlight, fringed with coco palms whose tops rise clear of the horizon. On the right is the forecastle with an open doorway in the center leading to the sea-men's and firemen's compartments. On either side of the doorway are two closed doors opening on the quarters of the Bo'sun, the ship's carpenter, the messroom steward, and the donkeyman— what might be called the petty officers of the ship. Near each bul-wark there is also a short stairway, like a section of fire escape, leading up to the forecastle head (the top of the forecastle)—the edge of which can be seen on the right.

In the center of the deck, and occupying most of the space, is the large, raised square of the number one hatch, covered with canvas, battened down for the night.

A melancholy negro chant, faint and far-off, drifts, crooning, over the water.

Most of the seamen and firemen are reclining or sitting on the hatch. Paul is leaning against the port bulwark, the upper part of his stocky figure outlined against the sky. Smitty and Cocky are sitting on the edge of the forecastle head with their legs dangling over. Nearly all are smoking pipes or cigarettes. The majority are dressed in patched suits of dungaree. Quite a few are in their bare feet and some of them, especially the firemen, have nothing on but a pair of pants and an undershirt. A good many wear caps.

There is the low murmur of different conversations going on in the separate groups as the curtain rises. This is followed by a sud-den silence in which the singing from the land can be plainly heard.

DRISCOLL—(*a powerfully built Irishman who is sitting on the edge of the hatch, front—irritably*) Will ye listen to them naygurs? I wonder now, do they call that keenin' a song?

SMITTY—(*a young Englishman with a blond mustache. He is sitting on the forecastle head looking out over the water with his chin supported on his hands.*) It doesn't make a chap feel very cheerful, does it? (*He sighs.*)

COCKY—(*a wizened runt of a man with a straggling gray mustache—slapping Smitty on the back*) Cheero, ole dear! Down't be ser dawn in the marf, Duke. She loves yer.

SMITTY—(*gloomily*) Shut up, Cocky! (*He turns away from Cocky and falls to dreaming again, staring toward the spot on shore where the singing seems to come from.*)

BIG FRANK—(*a huge fireman sprawled out on the right of the hatch—waving a hand toward the land*) They bury somebody—py chiminy Christmas, I tink so from way it sound.

YANK—(*a rather good-looking rough who is sitting beside Driscoll*) What d'yuh mean, bury? They don't plant 'em down here, Dutchy. They eat 'em to save fun'ral expenses. I guess this guy went down the wrong way an' they got indigestion.

COCKY—Indigestion! Ho yus, not 'arf! Down't yer know as them blokes 'as two stomacks like a bleedin' camel?

DAVIS—(*a short, dark man seated on the right of hatch*) An' you seen the two, I s'pect, ain't you?

COCKY—(*scornfully*) Down't be showin' yer igerance be tryin' to make a mock o' me what has seen more o' the world than yeself ever will.

MAX—(*a Swedish fireman—from the rear of hatch*) Spin dat yarn, Cocky.

COCKY—It's Gawd's troof, what I tole yer. I 'eard it from a bloke what was captured pris'ner by 'em in the Solomon Islands. Shipped wiv 'im one voyage. 'Twas a rare treat to 'ear 'im tell what 'appened to 'im among 'em. (*musingly*) 'E was a funny bird, 'e was—'ailed from Mile End, 'e did.

DRISCOLL—(*with a snort*) Another lyin' Cockney, the loike av yourself!

LAMPS—(*a fat Swede who is sitting on a camp stool in front of his door talking with Chips*) Where you meet up with him, Cocky?

CHIPS—(*a lanky Scotchman—derisively*) In New Guinea, I'll lay my oath!

COCKY—(*defiantly*) Yus! It *was* in New Guinea, time I was shipwrecked there. (*There is a perfect storm of groans and laughter at this speech.*)

YANK—(*getting up*) Yuh know what we said yuh'd get if yuh sprung any of that lyin' New Guinea dope on us again, don't yuh? Close that trap if yuh don't want a duckin' over the side.

COCKY—Ow, I was on'y tryin' to edicate yer a bit. (*He sinks into dignified silence.*)

YANK—(*nodding toward the shore*) Don't yuh know this is the West Indies, yuh crazy mut? There ain't no cannibals here. They're only common niggers.

DRISCOLL—(*irritably*) Whativir they are, the divil take their cryin'. It's enough to give a man the jigs listenin' to 'em.

YANK—(*with a grin*) What's the matter, Drisc? Yuh're as sore as a boil about somethin'.

DRISCOLL—I'm dyin' wid impatience to have a dhrink; an' that blarsted bumboat naygur woman took her oath she'd bring back rum enough for the lot av us whin she came back on board to-night.

BIG FRANK—(*overhearing this—in a loud eager voice*) You say the bumboat voman vill bring booze?

DRISCOLL—(*sarcastically*) That's right—tell the Old Man about ut, an' the Mate, too. (*All of the crew have edged nearer to Driscoll and are listening to the conversation with an air of suppressed excitement. Driscoll lowers his voice impressively and addresses them all.*) She said she cud snake ut on board in the bottoms av thim baskets av fruit they're goin' to bring wid 'em to sell to us for'ard.

THE DONKEYMAN—(*an old gray-headed man with a kindly, wrinkled face. He is sitting on a camp stool in front of his door, right front.*) She'll be bringin' some black women with her this time—or times has changed since I put in here last.

DRISCOLL—She said she wud—two or three—more, maybe, I dunno. (*This announcement is received with great enthusiasm by all hands.*)

COCKY—Wot a bloody lark!

OLSON—Py yingo, we have one hell of a time!

DRISCOLL—(*warningly*) Remimber ye must be quiet about ut, ye scuts—wid the dhrink, I mane—ivin if the bo'sun is ashore. The Old Man ordered her to bring no booze on board or he wudn't buy a thing av her for the ship.

PADDY—(*a squat, ugly Liverpool Irishman*) To the divil wid him!

BIG FRANK—(*turning on him*) Shud up, you tamn fool, Paddy! You vant make trouble? (*to Driscoll*) You und me, ve keep dem quiet, Drisc.

DRISCOLL—Right ye are, Dutchy. I'll split the skull av the first wan av ye starts to foight. (*Three bells are heard striking.*)

DAVIS—Three bells. When's she comin', Drisc?

DRISCOLL—She'll be here any minute now, surely. (*to Paul, who has returned to his position by the bulwark after hearing Driscoll's news*) D'you see 'em comin', Paul?

PAUL—I don't see anyting like bumboat. (*They all set themselves to wait, lighting pipes, cigarettes, and making themselves comfortable. There is a silence broken only by the mournful singing of the negroes on shore.*)

SMITTY—(*slowly—with a trace of melancholy*) I wish they'd stop that song. It makes you think of—well—things you ought to forget. Rummy go, what?

COCKY—(*slapping him on the back*) Cheero, ole love! We'll be 'avin our rum in arf a mo', Duke. (*He comes down to the deck, leaving Smitty alone on the forecastle head.*)

BIG FRANK—Sing someting, Drisc. Den ve don't hear dot yelling.

DAVIS—Give us a chanty, Drisc.

PADDY—Wan all av us knows.

MAX—We all sing in on chorus.

OLSON—"Rio Grande," Drisc.

BIG FRANK—No, ve don't know dot. Sing "Viskey Johnny."

CHIPS—"Flyin' Cloud."

COCKY—Now! Guv us "Maid o' Amsterdam."

LAMPS—"Santa Anna" iss good one.

DRISCOLL—Shut your mouths, all av you. (*scornfully*) A chanty is ut ye want? I'll bet me whole pay day there's not wan in the crowd 'ceptin' Yank here, an' Ollie, an' meself, an'

Lamps an' Cocky, maybe, wud be sailors enough to know the main from the mizzen on a windjammer. Ye've heard the names av chanties but divil a note av the tune or a loine av the words do ye know. There's hardly a rale deep-water sailor lift on the seas, more's the pity.

YANK—Give us "Blow The Man Down." We all know some of that. (*A chorus of assenting voices:* Yes!—Righto!— Let 'er drive! Start 'er, Drisc! *etc.*)

DRISCOLL—Come in then, all av ye. (*He sings*) As I was a-roamin' down Paradise Street—

ALL—Wa-a-ay, blow the man down!

DRISCOLL—As I was a-roamin' down Paradise Street—

ALL—Give us some time to blow the man down!

CHORUS

Blow the man down, boys, oh, blow the man down!
    Wa-a-ay, blow the man down!
  As I was a-roamin' down Paradise Street—
    Give us some time to blow the man down!

DRISCOLL—A pretty young maiden I chanced for to meet.

ALL—Wa-a-ay, blow the man down!

DRISCOLL—A pretty young maiden I chanced for to meet.

ALL—Give us some time to blow the man down!

CHORUS

Blow the man down, boys, oh, blow the man down!
    Wa-a-ay, blow the man down!
  A pretty young maiden I chanced for to meet.
    Give us some time to blow the man down!

PAUL—(*just as Driscoll is clearing his throat preparatory to starting the next verse*) Hay, Drisc! Here she come, I tink. Some bumboat comin' dis way. (*They all rush to the side and look toward the land.*)

YANK—There's five or six of them in it—and they paddle like skirts.

DRISCOLL—(*wildly elated*) Hurroo, ye scuts! 'Tis thim right enough. (*He does a few jig steps on the deck.*)

OLSON—(*after a pause during which all are watching the approaching boat*) Py yingo, I see six in boat, yes, sir.

DAVIS—I kin make out the baskets. See 'em there amidships?

BIG FRANK—Vot kind booze dey bring—viskey?

DRISCOLL—Rum, foine West Indy rum wid a kick in ut loike a mule's hoind leg.

LAMPS—Maybe she don't bring any; maybe skipper scare her.

DRISCOLL—Don't be throwin' cold water, Lamps. I'll skin her black hoide off av her if she goes back on her worrd.

YANK—Here they come. Listen to 'em gigglin'. (*calling*) Oh, you kiddo! (*The sound of women's voices can be heard talking and laughing.*)

DRISCOLL—(*calling*) Is ut you, Mrs. Old Black Joe?

A WOMAN'S VOICE—Ullo, Mike! (*There is loud feminine laughter at this retort.*)

DRISCOLL—Shake a leg an' come abord thin.

THE WOMAN'S VOICE—We're a-comin'.

DRISCOLL—Come on, Yank. You an' me'd best be goin' to give 'em a hand wid their truck. 'Twill put 'em in good spirits.

COCKY—(*as they start off left*) Ho, you ain't 'arf a fox, Drisc. Down't drink it all afore we sees it.

DRISCOLL—(*over his shoulder*) You'll be havin' yours, me sonny bye, don't fret. (*He and Yank go off left.*)

COCKY—(*licking his lips*) Gawd blimey, I can do wiv a wet.

DAVIS—Me, too!

CHIPS—I'll bet there ain't none of us'll let any go to waste.

BIG FRANK—I could trink a whole barrel mineself, py chimminy Christmas!

COCKY—I 'opes all the gels ain't as bloomin' ugly as 'er. Looked like a bloody organ-grinder's monkey, she did. Gawd, I couldn't put up wiv the likes of 'er!

PADDY—Ye'll be lucky if any of thim looks at ye, ye squint-eyed runt.

COCKY—(*angrily*) Ho, yus? You ain't no bleedin' beauty prize yeself, me man. A 'airy ape, I calls yer.

PADDY—(*walking toward him—truculently*) Whot's thot? Say ut again if ye dare.

COCKY—(*his hand on his sheath knife—snarling*) 'Airy ape! That's wot I says! (*Paddy tries to reach him but the others keep them apart.*)

BIG FRANK—(*pushing Paddy back*) Vot's the matter mit you, Paddy. Don't you hear vat Driscoll say—no fighting?

PADDY—(*grumblingly*) I don't take no back talk from that deck-scrubbin' shrimp.

COCKY—Blarsted coal-puncher! (*Driscoll appears wearing a broad grin of satisfaction. The fight is immediately forgotten by the crowd who gather around him with exclamations of eager curiosity.* How is it, Drisc? Any luck? Vot she bring, Drisc? Where's the gels? *etc.*)

DRISCOLL—(*with an apprehensive glance back at the bridge*) Not so loud, for the love av hivin! (*The clamor dies down.*) Yis, she has ut wid her. She'll be here in a minute wid a pint bottle or two for each wan av ye—three shillin's a bottle. So don't be impashunt.

COCKY—(*indignantly*) Three bob! The bloody cow!

SMITTY—(*with an ironic smile*) Grand larceny, by God! (*They all turn and look up at him, surprised to hear him speak.*)

OLSON—Py yingo, we don't pay so much.

BIG FRANK—Tamn black tief!

PADDY—We'll take ut away from her and give her nothin'.

THE CROWD—(*growling*) Dirty thief! Dot's right! Give her nothin'! Not a bloomin' 'apenny! etc.

DRISCOLL—(*grinning*) Ye can take ut or lave ut, me sonny byes. (*He casts a glance in the direction of the bridge and then reaches inside his shirt and pulls out a pint bottle.*) 'Tis foine rum, the rale stuff. (*He drinks.*) I slipped this wan out av wan av the baskets whin they wasn't lookin'. (*He hands the bottle to Olson who is nearest him.*) Here ye are, Ollie. Take a small sup an' pass ut to the nixt. 'Tisn't much but 'twill serve to take the black taste out av your mouths if ye go aisy wid ut. An' there's buckets more av ut comin'. (*The bottle passes from hand to hand, each man taking a sip and smacking his lips with a deep "Aaah" of satisfaction.*)

DAVIS—Where's she now, Drisc?

DRISCOLL—Up havin' a worrd wid the skipper, makin' arrangements about the money, I s'pose.

DAVIS—An' where's the other gels?

DRISCOLL—Wid her. There's foive av thim she took aboard—two swate little slips av things, near as white as you an' me are, for that gray-whiskered auld fool, an' the mates—

an' the engineers too, maybe. The rist av thim'll be comin' for'ard whin she comes.

COCKY—'E ain't 'arf a funny ole bird, the skipper. Gawd blimey! 'Member when we sailed from 'ome 'ow 'e stands on the bridge lookin' like a bloody ole sky pilot? An' 'is missus dawn on the bloomin' dock 'owlin' fit to kill 'erself? An' 'is kids 'owlin' an' wavin' their 'andkerchiefs? (*with great moral indignation*) An' 'ere 'e is makin' up to a bleedin' nigger! There's a captain for yer! Gawd blimey! Bloody crab, I calls 'im!

DRISCOLL—Shut up, ye insect! Sure, it's not you should be talkin', an' you wid a woman an' childer weepin' for ye in iviry divil's port in the wide worrld, if we can believe your own tale av ut.

COCKY—(*still indignant*) I ain't no bloomin' captain, I ain't. I ain't got no missus—reg'lar married, I means. I ain't—

BIG FRANK—(*putting a huge paw over Cocky's mouth*) You ain't going talk so much, you hear? (*Cocky wriggles away from him.*) Say, Drisc, how ve pay dis voman for booze? Ve ain't got no cash.

DRISCOLL—It's aisy enough. Each girl'll have a slip av paper wid her an' whin you buy anythin' you write ut down and the price beside ut and sign your name. If ye can't write have some one who can do ut for ye. An' rimimber this: Whin ye buy a bottle av dhrink or (*with a wink*) somethin' else forbid, ye must write down tobaccy or fruit or somethin' the loike av that. Whin she laves the skipper'll pay what's owin' on the paper an' take ut out av your pay. Is ut clear to ye now?

ALL—Yes—Clear as day—Aw right, Drisc—Righto—Sure. etc.

DRISCOLL—An' don't forgit what I said about bein' quiet wid the dhrink, or the Mate'll be down on our necks an' spile the fun. (*a chorus of assent*)

DAVIS—(*looking aft*) Ain't this them comin'? (*They all look in that direction. The silly laughter of a woman is heard.*)

DRISCOLL—Look at Yank, wud ye, wid his arrm around the middle av wan av thim. That lad's not wastin' any toime. (*The four women enter from the left, giggling and whispering to each other. The first three carry baskets on their heads. The youngest and best-looking comes last. Yank has his arm about her waist and is carrying her basket in his other hand. All four are distinct negro types. They wear light-colored, loose-fitting clothes and have bright bandana handkerchiefs on their heads. They put down their baskets on the hatch and sit down beside them. The men crowd around, grinning.*)

BELLA—(*she is the oldest, stoutest, and homeliest of the four— grinning back at them*) Ullo, boys.

THE OTHER GIRLS—'Ullo, boys.

THE MEN—Hello, yourself—Evenin'—Hello—How are you? etc.

BELLA—(*genially*) Hope you had a nice voyage. My name's Bella, this here's Susie, yander's Violet, and her there (*pointing to the girl with Yank*) is Pearl. Now we all knows each other.

PADDY—(*roughly*) Never mind the girls. Where's the dhrink?

BELLA—(*tartly*) You're a hawg, ain't you? Don't talk so loud or you don't git any—you nor no man. Think I wants the ole captain to put me off the ship, do you?

YANK—Yes, nix on hollerin', you! D'yuh wanta queer all of us?

BELLA—(*casting a quick glance over her shoulder*) Here! Some of you big strapping boys sit back of us on the hatch there so's them officers can't see what we're doin'. (*Driscoll and several of the others sit and stand in back of the girls on the hatch. Bella turns to Driscoll.*) Did you tell 'em they gotter sign for what they gits—and *how* to sign?

DRISCOLL—I did—what's your name again—oh, yis— Bella, darlin'.

BELLA—Then it's all right; but you boys has gotter go inside the fo'castle when you gits your bottle. No drinkin' out here on deck. I ain't takin' no chances. (*An impatient murmur of assent goes up from the crowd.*) Ain't that right, Mike?

DRISCOLL—Right as rain, darlin'. (*Big Frank leans over and says something to him in a low voice. Driscoll laughs and slaps his thigh.*) Listen, Bella, I've somethin' to ask ye for my little friend here who's bashful. Ut has to do wid the ladies so I'd best be whisperin' ut to ye meself to kape them from blushin'. (*He leans over and asks her a question.*)

BELLA—(*firmly*) Four shillin's.

DRISCOLL—(*laughing*) D'you hear that, all av ye? Four shillin's ut is.

PADDY—(*angrily*) To hell wid this talkin'. I want a dhrink.

BELLA—Is everything all right, Mike?

DRISCOLL—(*after a look back at the bridge*) Sure. Let her droive!

BELLA—All right, girls. (*The girls reach down in their baskets in under the fruit which is on top and each pulls out a pint bottle. Four of the men crowd up and take the bottles.*) Fetch a light, Lamps, that's a good boy. (*Lamps goes to his room and returns with a candle. This is passed from one girl to another as the men sign the sheets of paper for their bottles.*) Don't you boys forget to mark down cigarettes or tobacco or fruit, remember! Three shillin's is the price. Take it into the fo'castle. For Gawd's sake, don't stand out here drinkin' in the moonlight. (*The four go into the forecastle. Four more take their places. Paddy plants himself in front of Pearl who is sitting by Yank with his arm still around her.*)

PADDY—(*gruffly*) Gimme thot! (*She holds out a bottle which he snatches from her hand. He turns to go away.*)

YANK—(*sharply*) Here, you! Where d'yuh get that stuff? You ain't signed for that yet.

PADDY—(*sullenly*) I can't write me name.

YANK—Then I'll write it for yuh. (*He takes the paper from Pearl and writes.*) There ain't goin' to be no welchin' on little Bright Eyes here—not when I'm around, see? Ain't I right, kiddo?

PEARL—(*with a grin*) Yes, suh.

BELLA—(*seeing all four are served*) Take it into the fo'castle, boys. (*Paddy defiantly raises his bottle and gulps down a drink in the full moonlight. Bella sees him.*) Look at 'im! Look at the dirty swine! (*Paddy slouches into the forecastle.*) Wants to git me in trouble. That settles it! We all got to git inside, boys, where we won't git caught. Come on, girls. (*The girls pick up their baskets and follow Bella. Yank and Pearl are the last to reach the doorway. She lingers behind him, her eyes fixed on Smitty, who is still sitting on the forecastle head, his chin on his hands, staring off into vacancy.*)

PEARL—(*waving a hand to attract his attention*) Come ahn in, pretty boy. Ah likes you.

SMITTY—(*coldly*) Yes; I want to buy a bottle, please. (*He goes down the steps and follows her into the forecastle. No one remains on deck but the Donkeyman, who sits smoking his pipe in front of his door. There is the subdued babble of voices from the crowd inside but the mournful cadence of the song from the shore can again be faintly heard. Smitty reappears and closes the door to the forecastle after him. He shudders and shakes his shoulders as if flinging off something which disgusted him. Then he lifts the bottle which is in his hand to his lips and gulps down a long drink. The Donkeyman watches him impassively. Smitty sits down on the hatch facing him. Now that the closed door has shut off nearly all the noise the singing from shore comes clearly over the moonlit water.*)

SMITTY—(*listening to it for a moment*) Damn that song of theirs. (*He takes another big drink.*) What do you say, Donk?

THE DONKEYMAN—(*quietly*) Seems nice an' sleepy-like.

SMITTY—(*with a hard laugh*) Sleepy! If I listened to it long—sober—I'd never go to sleep.

THE DONKEYMAN—'Tain't sich bad music, is it? Sounds kinder pretty to me—low an' mournful—same as listenin' to the organ outside o' church of a Sunday.

SMITTY—(*with a touch of impatience*) I didn't mean it was bad music. It isn't. It's the beastly memories the damn thing brings up—for some reason. (*He takes another pull at the bottle.*)

THE DONKEYMAN—Ever hear it before?

SMITTY—No; never in my life. It's just a something about the rotten thing which makes me think of—well—oh, the devil! (*He forces a laugh.*)

THE DONKEYMAN—(*spitting placidly*) Queer things, mem'ries. I ain't ever been bothered much by 'em.

SMITTY—(*looking at him fixedly for a moment—with quiet scorn*) No, you wouldn't be.

THE DONKEYMAN—Not that I ain't had my share o' things goin' wrong; but I puts 'em out o' me mind, like, an' fergets 'em.

SMITTY—But suppose you couldn't put them out of your

mind? Suppose they haunted you when you were awake and when you were asleep—what then?

THE DONKEYMAN—(*quietly*) I'd git drunk, same's you're doin'.

SMITTY—(*with a harsh laugh*) Good advice. (*He takes another drink. He is beginning to show the effects of the liquor. His face is flushed and he talks rather wildly.*) We're poor little lambs who have lost our way, eh, Donk? Damned from here to eternity, what? God have mercy on such as we! True, isn't it, Donk?

THE DONKEYMAN—Maybe; I dunno. (*after a slight pause*) Whatever set you goin' to sea? You ain't made for it.

SMITTY—(*laughing wildly*) My old friend in the bottle here, Donk.

THE DONKEYMAN—I done my share o' drinkin' in my time. (*regretfully*) Them was good times, those days. Can't hold up under drink no more. Doctor told me I'd got to stop or die. (*He spits contentedly.*) So I stops.

SMITTY—(*with a foolish smile*) Then I'll drink one for you. Here's your health, old top! (*He drinks.*)

THE DONKEYMAN—(*after a pause*) S'pose there's a gel mixed up in it someplace, ain't there?

SMITTY—(*stiffly*) What makes you think so?

THE DONKEYMAN—Always is when a man lets music bother 'im. (*after a few puffs at his pipe*) An' she said she threw you over 'cause you was drunk; an' you said you was drunk 'cause she threw you over. (*He spits leisurely.*) Queer thing, love, ain't it?

SMITTY—(*rising to his feet with drunken dignity*) I'll trouble you not to pry into my affairs, Donkeyman.

THE DONKEYMAN—(*unmoved*) That's everybody's affair, what I said. I been through it many's the time. (*genially*) I always hit 'em a whack on the ear an' went out and got drunker'n ever. When I come home again they always had somethin' special nice cooked fur me to eat. (*puffing at his pipe*) That's the on'y way to fix 'em when they gits on their high horse. I don't s'pose you ever tried that?

SMITTY—(*pompously*) Gentlemen don't hit women.

THE DONKEYMAN—(*placidly*) No; that's why they has mem'ries when they hears music. (*Smitty does not deign to reply to this but sinks into a scornful silence. Davis and the girl Violet come out of the forecastle and close the door behind them. He is staggering a bit and she is laughing shrilly.)*

DAVIS—(*turning to the left*) This way, Rose, or Pansy, or Jessamine, or black Tulip, or Violet, or whatever the hell flower your name is. No one'll see us back here. (*They go off left.*)

THE DONKEYMAN—There's love at first sight for you—an' plenty more o' the same in the fo'c's'tle. No mem'ries jined with that.

SMITTY—(*really repelled*) Shut up, Donk. You're disgusting. (*He takes a long drink.*)

THE DONKEYMAN—(*philosophically*) All depends on how you was brung up, I s'pose. (*Pearl comes out of the forecastle. There is a roar of voices from inside. She shuts the door behind her, sees Smitty on the hatch, and comes over and sits beside him and puts her arm over his shoulder.*)

THE DONKEYMAN—(*chuckling*) There's love for you, Duke.

PEARL—(*patting Smitty's face with her hand*) 'Ullo, pretty boy. (*Smitty pushes her hand away coldly.*) What you doin' out here all alone by yourself?

SMITTY—(*with a twisted grin*) Thinking and,—(*he indicates the bottle in his hand*)—drinking to stop thinking. (*He drinks and laughs maudlinly. The bottle is three-quarters empty.*)

PEARL—You oughtn't drink so much, pretty boy. Don' you know dat? You have big, big headache come mawnin'.

SMITTY—(*dryly*) Indeed?

PEARL—Tha's true. Ah knows what Ah say. (*cooingly*) Why you run 'way from me, pretty boy? Ah likes you. Ah don' like them other fellahs. They act too rough. You ain't rough. You're a genelman. Ah knows. Ah can tell a genelman fahs Ah can see 'im.

SMITTY—Thank you for the compliment; but you're wrong, you see. I'm merely—a ranker. (*He adds bitterly*) And a rotter.

PEARL—(*patting his arm*) No, you ain't. Ah knows better. You're a genelman. (*insinuatingly*) Ah wouldn't have nothin' to do with them other men, but (*she smiles at him enticingly*) you is diff'rent. (*He pushes her away from him disgustedly. She pouts*) Don' you like me, pretty boy?

SMITTY—(*a bit ashamed*) I beg your pardon. I didn't mean to be rude, you know, really. (*His politeness is drunkenly exaggerated.*) I'm a bit off color.

PEARL—(*brightening up*) Den you do like me—little ways?

SMITTY—(*carelessly*) Yes, yes, why shouldn't I? (*He suddenly laughs wildly and puts his arm around her waist and presses her to him.*) Why not? (*He pulls his arm back quickly with a shudder of disgust, and takes a drink. Pearl looks at him curiously, puzzled by his strange actions. The door from the forecastle is kicked open and Yank comes out. The uproar of shouting, laughing and singing voices has increased in violence. Yank staggers over toward Smitty and Pearl.*)

YANK—(*blinking at them*) What the hell—oh, it's you, Smitty the Duke. I was goin' to turn one loose on the jaw of any guy'd cop my dame, but seein' it's you— (*sentimentally*) Pals is pals and any pal of mine c'n have anythin' I got, see? (*holding out his hand*) Shake, Duke. (*Smitty takes his hand and he pumps it up and down.*) You'n me's frens. Ain't I right?

SMITTY—Right it is, Yank. But you're wrong about this girl. She isn't with me. She was just going back to the fo'c's'tle to you. (*Pearl looks at him with hatred gathering in her eyes.*)

YANK—Tha' right?

SMITTY—On my word!

YANK—(*grabbing her arm*) Come on then, you, Pearl! Le's have a drink with the bunch. (*He pulls her to the entrance where she shakes off his hand long enough to turn on Smitty furiously.*)

PEARL—You swine! You can go to hell! (*She goes in the forecastle, slamming the door.*)

THE DONKEYMAN—(*spitting calmly*) There's love for you. They're all the same—white, brown, yeller 'n' black. A whack on the ear's the only thing'll learn 'em. (*Smitty makes no reply but laughs harshly and takes another drink; then sits staring before him, the almost empty bottle tightly clutched in one hand. There is an increase in volume of the muffled clamor from the forecastle and a moment later the door is thrown open and the whole mob, led by Driscoll, pours out on deck. All of them are very drunk and several of them carry bottles in their hands. Bella is the only one of the women who is absolutely sober. She tries in vain to keep the men quiet. Pearl drinks from Yank's bottle every moment or so, laughing shrilly, and leaning against Yank, whose arm is about her waist. Paul comes out last carrying an accordion. He staggers over and stands on top of the hatch, his instrument under his arm.)*

DRISCOLL—Play us a dance, ye square-head swab!—a rale, Godforsaken son av a turkey trot wid guts to ut.

YANK—Straight from the old Barbary Coast in Frisco!

PAUL—I don' know. I try. (*He commences tuning up.*)

YANK—Ataboy! Let 'er rip! (*Davis and Violet come back and join the crowd. The Donkeyman looks on them all with a detached, indulgent air. Smitty stares before him and does not seem to know there is any one on deck but himself.*)

BIG FRANK—Dance? I don't dance. I trink! (*He suits the action to the word and roars with meaningless laughter.*)

DRISCOLL—Git out av the way thin, ye big hulk, an' give us some room. (*Big Frank sits down on the hatch, right. All of the others who are not going to dance either follow his example or lean against the port bulwark.*)

BELLA—(*on the verge of tears at her inability to keep them in the forecastle or make them be quiet now they are out*) For Gawd's sake, boys, don't shout so loud! Want to git me in trouble?

DRISCOLL—(*grabbing her*) Dance wid me, me cannibal quane. (*Some one drops a bottle on deck and it smashes.*)

BELLA—(*hysterically*) There they goes! There they goes! Captain'll hear that! Oh, my Lawd!

DRISCOLL—Be damned to him! Here's the music! Off ye go! (*Paul starts playing "You Great Big Beautiful Doll" with a note left out every now and then. The four couples commence dancing—a jerk-shouldered version of the old Turkey Trot as it was done in the sailor-town dives, made more grotesque by the fact that all the couples are drunk and keep lurching into each other every moment. Two of the men start dancing together, intentionally bumping into the others. Yank and Pearl come around in front of Smitty and, as they pass him, Pearl slaps him across the side of the face with all her might, and laughs viciously. He jumps to his feet with his fists clenched but sees who hit him and sits down again smiling bitterly. Yank laughs boisterously.*)

YANK—Wow! Some wallop! One on you, Duke.

DRISCOLL—(*hurling his cap at Paul*) Faster, ye toad! (*Paul makes frantic efforts to speed up and the music suffers in the process.*)

BELLA—(*puffing*) Let me go. I'm wore out with you steppin' on my toes, you clumsy Mick. (*She struggles but Driscoll holds her tight.*)

DRISCOLL—God blarst you for havin' such big feet, thin. Aisy, aisy, Mrs. Old Black Joe! 'Tis dancin'll take the blubber off ye. (*He whirls her around the deck by main force. Cocky, with Susie, is dancing near the hatch, right, when Paddy, who is sitting on the edge with Big Frank, sticks his foot out and the wavering couple stumble over it and fall flat on the deck. A roar of laughter goes up. Cocky rises to his feet, his face livid with rage, and springs at Paddy, who promptly knocks him down. Driscoll hits Paddy and Big Frank hits Driscoll. In a flash a wholesale fight has broken out and the deck is a surging crowd of drink-maddened men hitting out at each other indiscriminately, although the general idea seems to be a battle between seamen and firemen. The women shriek and take refuge on top of the hatch, where they huddle in a frightened group. Finally there is the flash of a knife held high in the moonlight and a loud yell of pain.*)

DAVIS—(*somewhere in the crowd*) Here's the Mate comin'! Let's git out o' this! (*There is a general rush for the forecastle. In a moment there is no one left on deck but the little group of women on the hatch; Smitty, still dazedly rubbing his cheek; the Donkeyman quietly smoking on his stool; and Yank and Driscoll, their faces battered up considerably, their undershirts in shreds, bending over the still form of Paddy, which lies stretched out on the deck between them. In the silence the mournful chant from the shore creeps slowly out to the ship.*)

DRISCOLL—(*quickly—in a low voice*) Who knoifed him?

YANK—(*stupidly*) I didn't see it. How do I know? Cocky, I'll bet. (*The First Mate enters from the left. He is a tall, strongly-built man dressed in a plain blue uniform.*)

THE MATE—(*angrily*) What's all this noise about? (*He sees the man lying on the deck.*) Hello! What's this? (*He bends down on one knee beside Paddy.*)

DRISCOLL—(*stammering*) All av us—was in a bit av a harmless foight, sir,—an'—I dunno— (*The Mate rolls Paddy over and sees a knife wound on his shoulder.*)

THE MATE—Knifed, by God. (*He takes an electric flash from his pocket and examines the cut.*) Lucky it's only a flesh wound. He must have hit his head on deck when he fell. That's what knocked him out. This is only a scratch. Take him aft and I'll bandage him up.

DRISCOLL—Yis, sor. (*They take Paddy by the shoulders and feet and carry him off left. The Mate looks up and sees the women on the hatch for the first time.*)

THE MATE—(*surprised*) Hello! (*He walks over to them.*) Go to the cabin and get your money and clear off. If I had my way, you'd never— (*His foot hits a bottle. He stoops down and picks it up and smells of it.*) Rum, by God! So that's the trouble! I thought their breaths smelled damn queer. (*to the women, harshly*) You needn't go to the skipper for any money. You won't get any. That'll teach you to smuggle rum on a ship and start a riot.

BELLA—But, Mister—

THE MATE—(*sternly*) You know the agreement—rum—no money.

BELLA—(*indignantly*) Honest to Gawd, Mister, I never brung no—

THE MATE—(*fiercely*) You're a liar! And none of your lip or I'll make a complaint ashore to-morrow and have you locked up.

BELLA—(*subdued*) Please, Mister—

THE MATE—Clear out of this, now! Not another word out of you! Tumble over the side damn quick! The two others are waiting for you. Hop, now! (*They walk quickly—almost run—off to the left. The Mate follows them, nodding to the Donkeyman, and ignoring the oblivious Smitty.*)

(*There is absolute silence on the ship for a few moments. The melancholy song of the negroes drifts crooning over the water. Smitty listens to it intently for a time; then sighs heavily, a sigh that is half a sob.*)

SMITTY—God! (*He drinks the last drop in the bottle and throws it behind him on the hatch.*)

THE DONKEYMAN—(*spitting tranquilly*) More mem'ries? (*Smitty does not answer him. The ship's bell tolls four bells. The Donkeyman knocks out his pipe.*) I think I'll turn in. (*He opens the door to his cabin, but turns to look at Smitty—kindly*) You can't hear it in the fo'c's'tle—the music, I mean—an' there'll likely be more drink in there, too. Good night. (*He goes in and shuts the door.*)

SMITTY—Good night, Donk. (*He gets wearily to his feet and walks with bowed shoulders, staggering a bit, to the forecastle entrance and goes in. There is silence for a second or so, broken only by the haunted, saddened voice of that brooding music, faint and far-off, like the mood of the moonlight made audible.*)

(*The Curtain Falls*)

THE ROPE

A Play in One Act

CHARACTERS

ABRAHAM BENTLEY

ANNIE, *his daughter*

PAT SWEENEY, *her husband*

MARY, *their child*

LUKE BENTLEY, *Abe's son by a second marriage*

The Rope

SCENE—*The interior of an old barn situated on top of a high headland of the seacoast. In the rear, to the left, a stall in which lumber is stacked up. To the right of it, an open double doorway looking out over the ocean. Outside the doorway, the faint trace of what was once a road leading to the barn. Beyond the road, the edge of a cliff which rises sheer from the sea below. On the right of the doorway, three stalls with mangers and hay-ricks. The first of these is used as a woodbin and is half full of piled-up cordwood. Near this bin, a chopping block with an ax driven into the top of it.*

The left section of the barn contains the hay loft, which extends at a height of about twelve feet from the floor as far to the right as the middle of the doorway. The loft is bare except for a few scattered mounds of dank-looking hay. From the edge of the loft, halfway from the door, a rope about five feet long with an open running noose at the end is hanging. A rusty plow and various other farming implements, all giving evidence of long disuse, are lying on the floor near the left wall. Farther forward an old cane-bottomed chair is set back against the wall.

In front of the stalls on the right stands a long, roughly constructed carpenter's table, evidently home-made. Saws, a lathe, a hammer, chisel, a keg containing nails and other tools of the carpentry trade are on the table. Two benches are placed, one in front, one to the left of it.

The right side of the barn is a bare wall.

It is between six and half-past in the evening of a day in early spring. At the rising of the curtain some trailing clouds near the horizon, seen through the open doorway, are faintly tinged with gold by the first glow of the sunset. As the action progresses this reflected light gradually becomes brighter, and then slowly fades into a smoky crimson. The sea is a dark slate color. From the rocks below the headland sounds the muffled monotone of breaking waves.

As the curtain rises Mary is discovered squatting cross-legged on the floor, her back propped against the right side of the doorway, her face in profile. She is a skinny, over-grown girl of ten with thin, carroty hair worn in a pig-tail. She wears a shabby gingham dress. Her face is stupidly expressionless. Her hands flutter about aimlessly in relaxed, flabby gestures.

She is staring fixedly at a rag doll which she has propped up against the doorway opposite her. She hums shrilly to herself.

At a sudden noise from outside she jumps to her feet, peeks out, and quickly snatches up the doll, which she hugs fiercely to her breast. Then, after a second's fearful hesitation, she runs to the carpenter's table and crawls under it.

As she does so Abraham Bentley appears in the doorway and stands, blinking into the shadowy barn. He is a tall, lean stoop-shouldered old man of sixty-five. His thin legs, twisted by rheumatism, totter feebly under him as he shuffles slowly along by the aid of a thick cane. His face is gaunt, chalky-white, furrowed with wrinkles, surmounted by a shiny bald scalp fringed with scanty wisps of white hair. His eyes peer weakly from beneath bushy, black brows. His mouth is a sunken line drawn in under his large, beak-like nose. A two weeks' growth of stubby patches of beard covers his jaws and chin. He has on a threadbare brown overcoat but wears no hat.

BENTLEY—(*comes slowly into the barn, peering around him suspiciously. As he reaches the table and leans one hand on it for support, Mary darts from underneath and dashes out through the doorway. Bentley is startled; then shakes his cane after her.*) Out o' my sight, you Papist brat! Spawn o' Satan! Spyin' on me! They set her to it. Spyin' to watch me! (*He limps to the door and looks out cautiously. Satisfied, he turns back into the barn.*) Spyin' to see—what they'll never know. (*He stands staring up at the rope and taps it testingly several times with his stick, talking to himself as he does so.*) It's tied strong—strong as death— (*He cackles with satisfaction.*) They'll see, then! They'll see! (*He laboriously creeps over to the bench and sits down wearily. He looks toward the sea and his voice quavers in a doleful chant.*) "Woe unto us! for the day goeth away, for the shadows of the evening are stretched out." (*He mumbles to himself for a moment—then speaks clearly.*) Spyin' on me! Spawn o' the Pit! (*He renews his chant.*) "They hunt our steps that we cannot go in our streets; our end is near, our days are fulfilled; for our end is come."

(*As he finishes Annie enters. She is a thin, slovenly, worn-out looking woman of about forty with a drawn, pasty face. Her ha-bitual expression is one of a dulled irritation. She talks in a high-pitched, sing-song whine. She wears a faded gingham dress and a torn sunbonnet.)*

ANNIE—(*comes over to her father but warily keeps out of range of his stick. He doesn't answer or appear to see her.*) Paw! Paw! You ain't fergittin' what the doctor told you when he was here last, be you? He said you was to keep still and not go a-walkin' round. Come on back to the house, Paw. It's gittin' near supper time and you got to take your medicine b'fore it, like he says.

BENTLEY—(*his eyes fixed in front of him*) "The punishment of thine iniquity is accomplished, O daughter of Zion: he will visit thine iniquity, O daughter of Edom; he will discover thy sins."

ANNIE—(*waiting resignedly until he has finished—wearily*) You better take watch on your health, Paw, and not be sneakin' up to this barn no more. Lord sakes, soon 's ever my back is turned you goes sneakin' off agen. It's enough to drive a body outa their right mind.

BENTLEY—"Behold, everyone that useth proverbs shall use this proverb against thee, saying, As is the mother, so is her daughter!" (*He cackles to himself.*) So is her daughter!

ANNIE—(*her face flushing with anger*) And if I am, I'm glad I take after her and not you, y'old wizard! (*scornfully*) A fine one you be to be shoutin' Scripture in a body's ears all the live-long day—you that druv Maw to her death with your naggin', and pinchin', and miser stinginess. If you've a mind to pray, it's down in the medder you ought to go, and kneel down by her grave, and ask God to forgive you for the mean-ness you done to her all her life.

BENTLEY—(*mumbling*) "As is the mother, so is her daughter."

ANNIE—(*enraged by the repetition of this quotation*) You quotin' Scripture! Why, Maw wasn't cold in the earth b'fore you was down in the port courtin' agen—courtin' that harlot that was the talk o' the whole town. And then you disgraces yourself and me by marryin' her—*her*—and bringin' her back home with you; and me still goin' every day to put flowers on Maw's grave that you'd fergotten. (*She glares at him vin-*

dictively, pausing for breath.) And between you you'd have
druv me into the grave like you done Maw if I hadn't married
Pat Sweeney so's I could git away and live in peace. Then you
took on so high and mighty 'cause he was a Cath'lic—*you*
gittin' religion all of a moment just for spite on me 'cause I'd
left—and b'cause she egged you on against me; *you* sayin' it
was a sin to marry a Papist, after not bein' at Sunday meetin'
yourself for more'n twenty years!

BENTLEY—(*loudly*) "He will visit thine iniquity—"

ANNIE—(*interrupting*) And the carryin's-on you had the
six years at home after I'd left you—the shame of the whole
county! Your wife, indeed, with a child she *claimed* was
yourn, and her goin' with this farmer and that, and even men
off the ships in the port, and you blind to it! And then when
she got sick of you and ran away—only to meet her end at
the hands of God a year after—she leaves you alone with
that—*your* son, Luke, *she* called him—and him only five years
old!

BENTLEY—(*babbling*) Luke? Luke?

ANNIE—(*tauntingly*) Yes, Luke! "As is the mother, so is
her son"—that's what you ought to preach 'stead of puttin'
curses on me. You was glad enough to git me back home
agen, and Pat with me, to tend the place, and help bring up
that brat of hers. (*jealously*) You was fond enough of him all
them years—and how did he pay you back? Stole your
money and ran off and left you just when he was sixteen and
old enough to help. Told you to your face he'd stolen and
was leavin'. He only laughed when you was took crazy and
cursed him; and he only laughed harder when you hung up
that silly rope there (*she points*) and told him to hang himself
on it when he ever came home agen.

BENTLEY—(*mumbling*) You'll see, then. You'll see!

ANNIE—(*wearily—her face becoming dull and emotionless
again*) I s'pose I'm a bigger fool than you be to argy with a
half-witted body. But I tell you agen that Luke of yours ain't
comin' back; and if he does he ain't the kind to hang himself,
more's the pity. He's like her. He'd hang *you* more likely if he
s'pected you had any money. So you might 's well take down
that ugly rope you've had tied there since he run off. He's
probably dead anyway by this.

BENTLEY—(*frightened*) No! No!

ANNIE—Them as bad as him comes to a sudden end. (*irritably*) Land sakes, Paw, here I am argyin' with your lunatic notions and the supper not ready. Come on and git your medicine. You can see no one ain't touched your old rope. Come on! You can sit 'n' read your Bible. (*He makes no movement. She comes closer to him and peers into his face—uncertainly*) Don't you hear me? I do hope you ain't off in one of your fits when you don't know nobody. D'you know who's talkin'? This is Annie—your Annie, Paw.

BENTLEY—(*bursting into senile rage*) None o' mine! Spawn o' the Pit! (*With a quick movement he hits her viciously over the arm with his stick. She gives a cry of pain and backs away from him, holding her arm.*)

ANNIE—(*weeping angrily*) That's what I git for tryin' to be kind to you, you ugly old devil! (*The sound of a man's footsteps is heard from outside, and Sweeney enters. He is a stocky, muscular, sandy-haired Irishman dressed in patched corduroy trousers shoved down into high laced boots, and a blue flannel shirt. The bony face of his bullet head has a pressed-in appearance except for his heavy jaw, which sticks out pugnaciously. There is an expression of mean cunning and cupidity about his mouth and his small, round, blue eyes. He has evidently been drinking and his face is flushed and set in an angry scowl.*)

SWEENEY—Have ye no supper at all made, ye lazy slut? (*seeing that she has been crying*) What're you blubberin' about?

ANNIE—It's all his fault. I was tryin' to git him home but he's that set I couldn't budge him; and he hit me on the arm with his cane when I went near him.

SWEENEY—He did, did he? I'll soon learn him better. (*He advances toward Bentley threateningly.*)

ANNIE—(*grasping his arm*) Don't touch him, Pat. He's in one of his fits and you might kill him.

SWEENEY—An' good riddance!

BENTLEY—(*hissing*) Papist! (*chants*) "Pour out thy fury upon the heathen that knows thee not, and upon the families that call not on thy name: for they have eaten up Jacob, and devoured him, and consumed him, and made his habitation desolate."

SWEENEY—(*instinctively crosses himself—then scornfully*) Spit curses on me till ye choke. It's not likely the Lord God'll be listenin' to a wicked auld sinner the like of you. (*to Annie*) What's got into him to be roamin' up here? When I left for the town he looked too weak to lift a foot.

ANNIE—Oh, it's the same crazy notion he's had ever since Luke left. He wanted to make sure the rope was still here.

BENTLEY—(*pointing to the rope with his stick*) He-he! Luke'll come back. Then you'll see. You'll see!

SWEENEY—(*nervously*) Stop that mad cacklin' for the love of heaven! (*with a forced laugh*) It's great laughter I should be havin' at you, mad as you are, for thinkin' that thief of a son of yours would come back to hang himself on account of your curses. It's five years he's been gone, and not a sight of him; an' you cursin' an' callin' down the wrath o' God on him by day an' by night. That shows you what God thinks of your curses—an' Him deaf to you!

ANNIE—It's no use talkin' to him, Pat.

SWEENEY—I've small doubt but that Luke is hung long since—by the police. He's come to no good end, that lad. (*his eyes on the rope*) I'll be pullin' that thing down, so I will; an' the auld loon'll stay in the house, where he belongs, then, maybe. (*He reaches up for the rope as if to try and yank it down. Bentley waves his stick frantically in the air, and groans with rage.*)

ANNIE—(*frightened*) Leave it alone, Pat. Look at him. He's liable to hurt himself. Leave his rope be. It don't do no harm.

SWEENEY—(*reluctantly moves away*) It looks ugly hangin' there open like a mouth. (*The old man sinks back into a relieved immobility. Sweeney speaks to his wife in a low tone.*) Where's the child? Get her to take him out o' this. I want a word with you he'll not be hearin'. (*She goes to the door and calls out:* Ma-ry! Ma-ry! *A faint, answering cry is heard and a moment later Mary rushes breathlessly into the barn. Sweeney grabs her roughly by the arm. She shrinks away, looking at him with terrified eyes.*) You're to take your grandfather back to the house—an' see to it he stays there.

ANNIE—And give him his medicine.

SWEENEY—(*As the child continues to stare at him silently with eyes stupid from fear, he shakes her impatiently.*) D'you hear me, now? (*to his wife*) It's soft-minded she is, like I've always told you, an' stupid; and you're not too firm in the head yourself at times, God help you! An' look at him! It's the curse is in the wits of your family, not mine.

ANNIE—You've been drinkin' in town or you wouldn't talk that way.

MARY—(*whining*) Maw! I'm skeered!

SWEENEY—(*lets go of her arm and approaches Bentley*) Get up out o' this, ye auld loon, an' go with Mary. She'll take you to the house. (*Bentley tries to hit him with the cane.*) Oho, ye would, would ye? (*He wrests the cane from the old man's hands.*) Bad cess to ye, you're the treach'rous one! Get up, now! (*He jerks the old man to his feet.*) Here, Mary, take his hand. Quick now! (*She does so tremblingly.*) Lead him to the house.

ANNIE—Go on, Paw. I'll come and git your supper in a minute.

BENTLEY—(*stands stubbornly and begins to intone*) "O Lord, thou hast seen my wrong; judge thou my cause. Thou hast seen all their vengeance and all their imaginations against me—"

SWEENEY—(*pushing him toward the door. Bentley tries to resist. Mary pulls at his hand in a sudden fit of impish glee, and laughs shrilly.*) Get on now an' stop your cursin'.

BENTLEY—"Render unto them a recompense, O Lord, according to the work of their hands."

SWEENEY—Shut your loud quackin'! Here's your cane. (*He gives it to the old man as they come to the doorway and quickly steps back out of reach.*) An' mind you don't touch the child with it or I'll beat you to a jelly, old as ye are.

BENTLEY—(*resisting Mary's efforts to pull him out, stands shaking his stick at Sweeney and his wife*) "Give them sorrow of heart, thy curse unto them. Persecute and destroy them in anger from under the heavens of the Lord."

MARY—(*tugging at his hand and bursting again into shrill laughter*) Come on, gran'paw. (*He allows himself to be led off, right.*)

SWEENEY—(*making the sign of the cross furtively—with a sigh of relief*) He's gone, thank God! What a snake's tongue he has in him! (*He sits down on the bench to the left of table.*)

Come here, Annie, till I speak to you. (*She sits down on the bench in front of table. Sweeney winks mysteriously.*) Well, I saw him, sure enough.

ANNIE—(*stupidly*) Who?

SWEENEY—(*sharply*) Who? Who but Dick Waller, the lawyer, that I went to see. (*lowering his voice*) An' I found out what we was wishin' to know. (*with a laugh*) Ye said I'd been drinkin'—which is true; but 'twas all in the plan I'd made. I've a head for strong drink, as ye know, but he hasn't. (*He winks cunningly.*) An' the whisky loosened his tongue till he'd told all he knew.

ANNIE—He told you—about Paw's will?

SWEENEY—He did. (*disappointedly*) But for all the good it does us we might as well be no wiser than we was before. (*He broods for a moment in silence—then hits the table furiously with his fist.*) God's curse on the auld miser!

ANNIE—What did he tell you?

SWEENEY—Not much at the first. He's a cute one, an' he'd be askin' a fee to tell you your own name, if he could get it. His practice is all dribbled away from him lately on account of the drink. So I let on I was only payin' a friendly call, havin' known him for years. Then I asked him out to have a drop o' drink, knowin' his weakness; an' we had rashers of them, an' I payin' for it. Then I come out with it straight and asked him about the will—because the auld man was crazy an' on his last legs, I told him, an' he was the lawyer made out the will when Luke was gone. So he winked at me an' grinned—he was drunk by this—an' said: "It's no use, Pat. He left the farm to the boy." "To hell with the farm," I spoke back. "It's mortgaged to the teeth; but how about the money?" "The money?" an' he looks at me in surprise, "What money?" "The cash he has," I says. "You're crazy," he says. "There wasn't any cash—only the farm." "D'you mean to say he made no mention of money in his will?" I asked. You could have knocked me down with a feather. "He did not—on my oath," he says. (*Sweeney leans over to his wife—indignantly*) Now what d'you make o' that? The auld divil!

ANNIE—Maybe Waller was lyin'.

SWEENEY—He was not. I could tell by his face. He was surprised to hear me talkin' of money.

ANNIE—But the thousand dollars Paw got for the mortgage just before that woman ran away—

SWEENEY—An' that I've been slavin' me hands off to pay the in'trist on!

ANNIE—What could he have done with that? He ain't spent it. It was in twenty dollar gold pieces he got it, I remember Mr. Keller of the bank tellin' me once.

SWEENEY—Divil a penny he's spent. Ye know as well as I do if it wasn't for my hammerin', an' sawin', an' nailin', he'd be in the poor house this minute—or the mad house, more likely.

ANNIE—D'you suppose that harlot ran off with it?

SWEENEY—I do not; I know better—an' so do you. D'you not remember the letter she wrote tellin' him he could support Luke on the money he'd got on the mortgage she'd signed with him; for he'd made the farm over to her when he married her. An' where d'you suppose Luke got the hundred dollars he stole? The auld loon must have had cash with him then, an' it's only five years back.

ANNIE—He's got it hid some place in the house most likely.

SWEENEY—Maybe you're right. I'll dig in the cellar this night when he's sleepin'. He used to be down there a lot recitin' Scripture in his fits.

ANNIE—What else did Waller say?

SWEENEY—Nothin' much; except that we should put notices in the papers for Luke, an' if he didn't come back by sivin years from when he'd left—two years from now, that'd be—the courts would say he was dead an' give us the farm. Divil a lot of use it is to us now with no money to fix it up; an' himself ruinin' it years ago by sellin' everythin' to buy that slut new clothes.

ANNIE—Don't folks break wills like his'n in the courts?

SWEENEY—Waller said 'twas no use. The auld divil was plain in his full senses when he made it; an' the courts cost money.

ANNIE—(resignedly) There ain't nothin' we can do then.

SWEENEY—No—except wait an' pray that young thief is dead an' won't come back; an' try an' find where it is the auld man has the gold hid, if he has it yet. I'd take him by the neck an' choke him till he told it, if he wasn't your father. (*He takes a full quart flask of whisky from the pocket of his coat and has a big drink.*) Aahh! If we'd on'y the thousand we'd stock the farm good an' I'd give up this dog's game (*he indicates the carpentry outfit scornfully*) an' we'd both work hard with a man or two to help, an' in a few years we'd be rich; for 'twas always a payin' place in the auld days.

ANNIE—Yes, yes, it was always a good farm then.

SWEENEY—He'll not last long in his senses, the doctor told me. His next attack will be very soon an' after it he'll be a real lunatic with no legal claims to anythin'. If we on'y had the money— 'Twould be the divil an' all if the auld fool should forget where he put it, an' him takin' leave of his senses altogether. (*He takes another nip at the bottle and puts it back in his pocket—with a sigh*) Ah, well, I'll save what I can an' at the end of two years, with good luck in the trade, maybe we'll have enough. (*They are both startled by the heavy footfalls of someone approaching outside. A shrill burst of Mary's laughter can be heard and the deep voice of a man talking to her.*)

SWEENEY—(*uneasily*) It's Mary; but who could that be with her? It's not himself. (*As he finishes speaking Luke appears in the doorway, holding the dancing Mary by the hand. He is a tall, strapping young fellow about twenty-one with a coarse-featured, rather handsome face bronzed by the sun. What his face lacks in intelligence is partly forgiven for his good-natured, half-foolish grin, his hearty laugh, his curly dark hair, a certain devil-may-care recklessness and irresponsible youth in voice and gesture. But his mouth is weak and characterless; his brown eyes are large but shifty and acquisitive. He wears a dark blue jersey, patched blue pants, rough sailor shoes, and a gray cap. He advances into the stable with a mocking smile on his lips until he stands directly under the rope. The man and woman stare at him in petrified amazement.*)

ANNIE—Luke!

SWEENEY—(*crossing himself*) Glory be to God—it's him!

MARY—(*hopping up and down wildly*) It's Uncle Luke, Uncle Luke, Uncle Luke! (*She runs to her mother, who pushes her away angrily.*)

LUKE—(*regarding them both with an amused grin*) Sure, it's

Luke—back after five years of bummin' round the rotten old earth in ships and things. Paid off a week ago—had a bust-up—and then took a notion to come out here—bummed my way—and here I am. And you're both of you tickled to death to see me, ain't yuh?—like hell! (*He laughs and walks over to Annie.*) Don't yuh even want to shake flippers with your dear, long-lost brother, Annie? I remember you and me used to git on so fine together—like hell!

ANNIE—(*giving him a venomous look of hatred*) Keep your hands to yourself.

LUKE—(*grinning*) You ain't changed, that's sure—on'y yuh're homlier'n ever. (*He turns to the scowling Sweeney.*) How about you, brother Pat?

SWEENEY—I'd not lower myself to take the hand of a—

LUKE—(*with a threat in his voice*) Easy goes with that talk! I'm not so soft to lick as I was when I was a kid; and don't forget it.

ANNIE—(*to Mary, who is playing catch with a silver dollar which she has had clutched in her hand—sharply*) Mary! What have you got there? Where did you get it? Bring it here to me this minute! (*Mary presses the dollar to her breast and remains standing by the doorway in stubborn silence.*)

LUKE—Aw, let her alone! What's bitin' yuh? That's on'y a silver dollar I give her when I met her in front of the house. She told me you was up here; and I give her that as a present to buy candy with. I got it in Frisco—cart-wheels, they call 'em. There ain't none of them in these parts I ever seen, so I brung it along on the voyage.

ANNIE—(*angrily*) I don't know or care where you got it—but I know you ain't come by it honest. Mary! Give that back to him this instant! (*As the child hesitates, she stamps her foot furiously.*) D'you hear me? (*Mary starts to cry softly, but comes to Luke and hands him the dollar.*)

LUKE—(*taking it—with a look of disgust at his half-sister*) I was right when I said you ain't changed, Annie. You're as stinkin' mean as ever. (*to Mary, consolingly*) Quit bawlin', kid. You 'n' me'll go out on the edge of the cliff here and chuck some stones in the ocean same's we useter, remember? (*Mary's tears immediately cease. She looks up at him with shining eyes, and claps her hands.*)

MARY—(*pointing to the dollar he has in his hand*) Throw that! It's flat 'n' it'll skip.

LUKE—(*with a grin*) That's the talk, kid. That's all it's good for—to throw away; not buryin' it like your miser folks'd tell you. Here! You take it and chuck it away. It's yourn. (*He gives her the dollar and she hops to the doorway. He turns to Pat with a grin.*) I'm learnin' your kid to be a sport, Tight-Wad. I hope you ain't got no objections.

MARY—(*impatiently*) Come on, Uncle Luke. Watch me throw it.

LUKE—Aw right. (*to Pat*) I'll step outside a second and give you two a chanct to git all the dirty things yuh're thinkin' about me off your chest. (*threateningly*) And then I'm goin' ter come and talk turkey to you, see? I didn't come back here for fun, and the sooner you gets that in your beans, the better.

MARY—Come on and watch me!

LUKE—Aw right, I'm comin'. (*He walks out and stands, leaning his back against the doorway, left. Mary is about six feet beyond him on the other side of the road. She is leaning down, peering over the edge of the cliff and laughing excitedly.*)

MARY—Can I throw it now? Can I?

LUKE—Don't git too near the edge, kid. The water's deep down there, and you'd be a drowned rat if you slipped. (*She shrinks back a step.*) You chuck it when I say three. Ready now. (*She draws back her arm.*) One! Two! Three! (*She throws the dollar away and bends down to see it hit the water.*)

MARY—(*clapping her hands and laughing*) I seen it! I seen it! I seen it splash! It's deep down now, ain't it?

LUKE—Yuh betcher it is! Now watch how far I kin chuck rocks. (*He picks up a couple and goes to where she is standing. During the following conversation between Sweeney and his wife he continues to play this way with Mary. Their voices can be heard but the words are indistinguishable.*)

SWEENEY—(*glancing apprehensively toward the door—with a great sigh*) Speak of the divil an' here he is! (*furiously*) Flingin' away dollars, the dirty thief, an' us without—

ANNIE—(*interrupting him*) Did you hear what he said? A thief like him ain't come back for no good. (*lowering her voice*) D'you s'pose he knows about the farm bein' left to him?

SWEENEY—(*uneasily*) How could he? An' yet—I dunno—(*with sudden decision*) You'd best lave him to me to watch out for. It's small sense you have to hide your hate from him. You're as looney as the rist of your breed. An' he needs to be blarneyed round to fool him an' find out what he's wantin'. I'll pritind to make friends with him, God roast his soul! An' do you run to the house an' break the news to the auld man; for if he seen him suddin its likely the little wits he has left would leave him; an' the thief could take the farm from us to-morrow if himself turned a lunatic.

ANNIE—(*getting up*) I'll tell him a little at a time till he knows.

SWEENEY—Be careful, now, or we'll lose the farm this night. (*She starts towards the doorway. Sweeney speaks suddenly in a strange, awed voice.*) Did you see Luke when he first came in to us? He stood there with the noose of the rope almost touchin' his head. I was almost wishin'— (*He hesitates.*)

ANNIE—(*viciously*) I was wishin' it was round his neck chokin' him, that's what I was—hangin' him just as Paw says.

SWEENEY—Ssshh! He might hear ye. Go along, now. He's comin' back.

MARY—(*pulling at Luke's arm as he comes back to the doorway*) Lemme throw 'nother! Lemme throw 'nother!

LUKE—(*enters just as Annie is going out and stops her*) Goin' to the house? Do we get any supper? I'm hungry.

ANNIE—(*glaring at him but restraining her rage*) Yes.

LUKE—(*jovially*) Good work! And tell the old man I'm here and I'll see him in a while. He'll be glad to see me, too—like hell! (*He comes forward. Annie goes off, right.*)

MARY—(*in an angry whine, tugging at his hand*) Lemme throw 'nother. Lemme—

LUKE—(*shaking her away*) There's lots of rocks, kid. Throw them. Dollars ain't so plentiful.

MARY—(*screaming*) No! No! I don' wanter throw rocks. Lemme throw 'nother o' them.

SWEENEY—(*severely*) Let your uncle in peace, ye brat! (*She commences to cry.*) Run help your mother now or I'll give ye a good hidin'. (*Mary runs out of the door, whimpering. Pat turns to Luke and holds out his hand.*)

Luke—(*looking at it in amazement*) Ahoy, there! What's this?

Sweeney—(*with an ingratiating smile*) Let's let by-gones be by-gones. I'm harborin' no grudge agen you these past years. Ye was only a lad when ye ran away an' not to be blamed for it. I'd have taken your hand a while back, an' glad to, but for her bein' with us. She has the divil's own tongue, as ye know, an' she can't forget the rowin' you an' her used to be havin'.

Luke—(*still looking at Sweeney's hand*) So that's how the wind blows! (*with a grin*) Well, I'll take a chanct. (*They shake hands and sit down by the table, Sweeney on the front bench and Luke on the left one.*)

Sweeney—(*pulls the bottle from his coat pocket—with a wink*) Will ye have a taste? It's real stuff.

Luke—Yuh betcher I will! (*He takes a big gulp and hands the bottle back.*)

Sweeney—(*after taking a drink himself, puts bottle on table*) I wasn't wishin' herself to see it or I'd have asked ye sooner. (*There is a pause, during which each measures the other with his eyes.*)

Luke—Say, how's the old man now?

Sweeney—(*cautiously*) Oh, the same as ivir—older an' uglier, maybe.

Luke—I thought he might be in the bug-house by this time.

Sweeney—(*hastily*) Indeed not; he's foxy to pritind he's looney but he's his wits with him all the time.

Luke—(*insinuatingly*) Is he as stingy with his coin as he used to be?

Sweeney—If he owned the ocean he wouldn't give a fish a drink; but I doubt if he's any money left at all. Your mother got rid of it all, I'm thinkin'. (*Luke smiles a superior, knowing smile.*) He has on'y the farm, an' that mortgaged. I've been payin' the in'trist an' supportin' himself an' his doctor's bills by the carpentryin' these five years past.

Luke—(*with a grin*) Huh! Yuh're slow. Yuh oughter get wise to yourself.

Sweeney—(*inquisitively*) What d'ye mean by that?

Luke—(*aggravatingly*) Aw, nothin'. (*He turns around and*

his eyes fix themselves on the rope.) What the hell— (*He is suddenly convulsed with laughter and slaps his thigh.*) Hahaha! If that don't beat the Dutch! The old nut!

SWEENEY—What?

LUKE—That rope. Say, has he had that hangin' there ever since I skipped?

SWEENEY—(*smiling*) Sure; an' he thinks you'll be comin' home to hang yourself.

LUKE—Hahaha! Not this chicken! And you say he ain't crazy! Gee, that's too good to keep. I got to have a drink on that. (*Sweeney pushes the bottle toward him. He raises it toward the rope.*) Here's how, old chum! (*He drinks. Sweeney does likewise.*) Say, I'd a'most forgotten about that. Remember how hot he was that day when he hung that rope up and cussed me for pinchin' the hundred? He was standin' there shakin' his stick at me, and I was laughin' 'cause he looked so funny with the spit dribblin' outa his mouth like he was a mad dog. And when I turned round and beat it he shouted after me: "Remember, when you come home again there's a rope waitin' for yuh to hang yourself on, yuh bastard!" (*He spits contemptuously.*) What a swell chanct. (*His manner changes and he frowns.*) The old slave driver! That's a hell of a fine old man for a guy to have!

SWEENEY—(*pushing the bottle toward him*) Take a sup an' forget it. 'Twas a long time past.

LUKE—But the rope's there yet, ain't it? And he keeps it there. (*He takes a large swallow. Sweeney also drinks.*) But I'll git back at him aw right, yuh wait 'n' see. I'll git every cent he's got this time.

SWEENEY—(*slyly*) If he has a cent. I'm not wishful to discourage ye, but— (*He shakes his head doubtfully, at the same time fixing Luke with a keen glance out of the corner of his eye.*)

LUKE—(*with a cunning wink*) Aw, he's got it aw right. You watch me! (*He is beginning to show the effects of the drink he has had. He pulls out tobacco and a paper and rolls a cigarette and lights it. As he puffs he continues boastfully.*) You country jays oughter wake up and see what's goin' on. Look at me. I was green as grass when I left here, but bummin' round the world, and bein' in cities, and meetin' all kinds, and keepin' your two eyes open—that's what'll learn yuh a cute trick or two.

SWEENEY—No doubt but you're right. Us country folks is stupid in most ways. We've no chance to learn the things a travelin' lad like you'd be knowin'.

LUKE—(*complacently*) Well, you watch me and I'll learn yuh. (*He snickers.*) So yuh think the old man's flat broke, do yuh?

SWEENEY—I do so.

LUKE—Then yuh're simple; that's what—simple! You're lettin' him kid yuh.

SWEENEY—If he has any, it's well hid, I know that. He's a sly old bird.

LUKE—And I'm a slyer bird. D'yuh hear that? I c'n beat his game any time. You watch me! (*He reaches out his hand for the bottle. They both drink again. Sweeney begins to show signs of getting drunk. He hiccoughs every now and then and his voice grows uncertain and husky.*)

SWEENEY—It'd be a crafty one who'd find where he'd hidden it, sure enough.

LUKE—You watch me! I'll find it. I betcher anything yuh like I find it. You watch me! Just wait till he's asleep and I'll show yuh—ternight. (*There is a noise of shuffling footsteps outside and Annie's whining voice raised in angry protest.*)

SWEENEY—Ssshh! It's himself comin' now. (*Luke rises to his feet and stands, waiting in a defensive attitude, a surly expression on his face. A moment later Bentley appears in the doorway, followed by Annie. He leans against the wall, in an extraordinary state of excitement, shaking all over, gasping for breath, his eyes devouring Luke from head to foot.*)

ANNIE—I couldn't do nothin' with him. When I told him *he'd* come back there was no holdin' him. He was a'most frothin' at the mouth till I let him out. (*whiningly*) You got to see after him, Pat, if you want any supper. I can't—

SWEENEY—Shut your mouth! We'll look after him.

ANNIE—See that you do. I'm goin' back. (*She goes off, right. Luke and his father stand looking at each other. The surly expression disappears from Luke's face, which gradually expands in a broad grin.*)

LUKE—(*jovially*) Hello, old sport! I s'pose yuh're tickled

to pieces to see me—like hell! (*The old man stutters and stammers incoherently as if the very intensity of his desire for speech had paralyzed all power of articulation. Luke turns to Pat.*) I see he ain't lost the old stick. Many a crack on the nut I used to get with that.

BENTLEY—(*suddenly finding his voice—and chants*) "Bring forth the best robe, and put it on him; and put a ring on his hand, and shoes on his feet: And bring hither the fatted calf, and kill it; and let us eat, and be merry: For this my son was dead, and is alive again; he was lost, and is found." (*He ends up with a convulsive sob.*)

LUKE—(*disapprovingly*) Yuh're still spoutin' the rotten old Word o' God same's ever, eh? Say, give us a rest on that stuff, will yuh? Come on and shake hands like a good sport. (*He holds out his hand. The old man totters over to him, stretching out a trembling hand. Luke seizes it and pumps it up and down.*) That's the boy!

SWEENEY—(*genuinely amazed*) Look at that, would ye—the two faced auld liar. (*Bentley passes his trembling hand all over Luke, feeling of his arms, his chest, his back. An expression of overwhelming joy suffuses his worn features.*)

LUKE—(*grinning at Sweeney*) Say, watch this. (*with tolerant good-humor*) On the level I b'lieve the old boy's glad to see me at that. He looks like he was tryin' to grin; and I never seen him grin in my life, I c'n remember. (*as Bentley attempts to feel of his face*) Hey, cut it out! (*He pushes his hand away, but not roughly.*) I'm all here, yuh needn't worry. Yuh needn't be scared I'm a ghost. Come on and sit down before yuh fall down. Yuh ain't got your sea-legs workin' right. (*He guides the old man to the bench at left of table.*) Squat here for a spell and git your wind. (*Bentley sinks down on the bench. Luke reaches for the bottle.*) Have a drink to my makin' port. It'll buck yuh up.

SWEENEY—(*alarmed*) Be careful, Luke. It might likely end him.

LUKE—(*holds the bottle up to the old man's mouth, supporting his head with the other hand. Bentley gulps, the whisky drips over his chin, and he goes into a fit of convulsive coughing. Luke laughs.*) Hahaha! Went down the wrong way, did it? I'll show yuh the way to do it. (*He drinks.*) There yuh are—smooth as silk. (*He hands the bottle to Sweeney, who drinks and puts it back on the table.*)

SWEENEY—He must be glad to see ye or he'd not drink. 'Tis dead against it he's been these five years past. (*shaking his head*) An' him cursin' you day an' night! I can't put head or tail to it. Look out he ain't meanin' some bad to ye underneath. He's crafty at pritindin'.

LUKE—(*as the old man makes signs to him with his hand*) What's he after now? He's lettin' on he's lost his voice again. What d'yuh want? (*Bentley points with his stick to the rope. His lips move convulsively as he makes a tremendous effort to utter words.*)

BENTLEY—(*mumbling incoherently*) Luke—Luke—rope—Luke—hang.

SWEENEY—(*appalled*) There ye are! What did I tell you? It's to see you hang yourself he's wishin', the auld fiend!

BENTLEY—(*nodding*) Yes—Luke—hang.

LUKE—(*taking it as a joke—with a loud guffaw*) Hahaha! If that don't beat the Dutch! The old nanny-goat! Aw right, old sport. Anything to oblige. Hahaha! (*He takes the chair from left and places it under the rope. The old man watches him with eager eyes and seems to be trying to smile. Luke stands on the chair.*)

SWEENEY—Have a care, now! I'd not be foolin' with it in your place.

LUKE—All out for the big hangin' of Luke Bentley by hisself. (*He puts the noose about his neck with an air of drunken bravado and grins at his father. The latter makes violent motions for him to go on.*) Look at him, Pat. By God, he's in a hurry. Hahaha! Well, old sport, here goes nothin'. (*He makes a movement as if he were going to jump and kick the chair from under him.*)

SWEENEY—(*half starts to his feet—horrified*) Luke! Are ye gone mad?

LUKE—(*stands staring at his father, who is still making gestures for him to jump. A scowl slowly replaces his good-natured grin.*) D'yuh really mean it—that yuh want to see me hangin' myself? (*Bentley nods vigorously in the affirmative. Luke glares at him for a moment in silence.*) Well, I'll be damned! (*to Pat*) An' I thought he was only kiddin'. (*He removes the rope *gingerly from his neck. The old man stamps his foot and gesticulates wildly, groaning with disappointment. Luke jumps to the floor and looks at his father for a second. Then his face grows white with a vicious fury.*) I'll fix your hash, you stinkin' old murderer. (*He grabs the chair by its back and swings it over his head as if he were going to crush Bentley's skull with it. The old man cowers on the bench in abject terror.*)

SWEENEY—(*jumping to his feet with a cry of alarm*) Luke! For the love of God! (*Luke hesitates; then hurls the chair in back of him under the loft, and stands menacingly in front of his father, his hands on his hips.*)

LUKE—(*grabbing Bentley's shoulder and shaking him— hoarsely*) Yuh wanted to see me hangin' there in real earnest, didn't yuh? You'd hang me yourself if yuh could, wouldn't yuh? And you my own father! Yuh damned son of a gun! Yuh would, would yuh? I'd smash your brains out for a nickel! (*He shakes the old man more and more furiously.*)

SWEENEY—Luke! Look out! You'll be killin' him next.

LUKE—(*giving his father one more shake, which sends him sprawling on the floor*) Git outa here! Git outa this b'fore I kill yuh dead! (*Sweeney rushes over and picks the terrified old man up.*) Take him outa here, Pat! (*His voice rises to a threatening roar.*) Take him outa here or I'll break every bone in his body! (*He raises his clenched fists over his head in a frenzy of rage.*)

SWEENEY—Ssshh! Don't be roarin'! I've got him. (*He steers the whimpering, hysterical Bentley to the doorway.*) Come out o' this, now. Get down to the house! Hurry now! Ye've made enough trouble for one night. (*They disappear off right. Luke flings himself on a bench, breathing heavily. He picks up the bottle and takes a long swallow. Sweeney re-enters from rear. He comes over and sits down in his old place.*) Thank God he's off down to the house, scurryin' like a frightened hare as if he'd never a kink in his legs in his life. He was moanin' out loud so you could hear him a long ways. (*with a sigh*) It's a murd'rous auld loon he is, sure enough.

LUKE—(*thickly*) The damned son of a gun!

SWEENEY—I thought you'd be killin' him that time with the chair.

LUKE—(*violently*) Serve him damn right if I done it.

SWEENEY—An' you laughin' at him a moment sooner! I thought 'twas jokin' ye was.

LUKE—(*sullenly*) So I was kiddin'; but I thought he was tryin' to kid me, too. And then I seen by the way he acted he really meant it. (*banging the table with his fist*) Ain't that a hell of a fine old man for yuh!

SWEENEY—He's a mean auld swine.

LUKE—He meant it aw right, too. Yuh shoulda seen him lookin' at me. (*with sudden lugubriousness*) Ain't he a hell of a nice old man for a guy to have? Ain't he?

SWEENEY—(*soothingly*) Hush! It's all over now. Don't be thinkin' about it.

LUKE—(*on the verge of drunken tears*) How kin I help thinkin'—and him my own father? After me bummin' and starvin' round the rotten earth, and workin' myself to death on ships and things—and when I come home he tries to make me bump off—wants to see me a corpse—my own father, too! Ain't he a hell of an old man to have? The rotten son of a gun!

SWEENEY—It's past an' done. Forget it. (*He slaps Luke on the shoulder and pushes the bottle toward him.*) Let's take a drop more. We'll be goin' to supper soon.

LUKE—(*takes a big drink—huskily*) Thanks. (*He wipes his mouth on his sleeve with a snuffle.*) But I'll tell yuh something you can put in your pipe and smoke. It ain't past and done, and it ain't goin' to be! (*more and more aggressively*) And I ain't goin' to ferget it, either! Yuh kin betcher life on that, pal. And *he* ain't goin' to ferget it—not if he lives a million—not by a damned sight! (*with sudden fury*) I'll fix his hash! I'll git even with him, the old skunk! You watch me! And this very night, too!

SWEENEY—How d'you mean?

LUKE—You just watch me, I tell yuh! (*banging the table*) I said I'd git even and I will git even—this same night, with no long waits, either! (*frowning*) Say, you don't stand up for him, do yuh?

SWEENEY—(*spitting—vehemently*) That's child's talk. There's not a day passed I've not wished him in his grave.

LUKE—(*excitedly*) Then we'll both git even on him—you 'n' me. We're pals, ain't we?

SWEENEY—Sure.

LUKE—And yuh kin have half what we gits. That's the kinda feller I am! That's fair enough, ain't it?

SWEENEY—Surely.

LUKE—I don't want no truck with this rotten farm. You kin have my share of that. I ain't made to be no damned dirt puncher—not me! And I ain't goin' to loaf round here more'n I got to, and when I goes this time I ain't never comin' back. Not me! Not to punch dirt and milk cows. You kin have the rotten farm for all of me. What I wants is cash—regular coin yuh kin spend—not dirt. I want to show the gang a real time, and then ship away to sea agen or go bummin' agen. I want coin yuh kin throw away—same's your kid chucked that dollar of mine overboard, remember? A real dollar, too! She's a sport, aw right!

SWEENEY—(*anxious to bring him back to the subject*) But where d'you think to find his money?

LUKE—(*confidently*) Don't yuh fret. I'll show yuh. You watch me! I know his hidin' places. I useter spy on him when I was a kid— Maw used to make me—and I seen him many a time at his sneakin'. (*indignantly*) He used to hide stuff from the old lady. What d'yuh know about him—the mean skunk!

SWEENEY—That was a long time back. You don't know—

LUKE—(*assertively*) But I do know, see! He's got two places. One was where I swiped the hundred.

SWEENEY—It'll not be there, then.

LUKE—No; but there's the other place; and he never knew I was wise to that. I'd have left him clean on'y I was a kid and scared to pinch more. So you watch me! We'll git even on him, you 'n' me, and go halfs, and yuh kin start the rotten farm goin' agen and I'll beat it where there's some life.

SWEENEY—But if there's no money in that place, what'll you be doin' to find out where it is, then?

LUKE—Then you 'n' me 'ull make him tell!

SWEENEY—Oho, don't think it! 'Tis not him'd be tellin'.

LUKE—Aw, say, you're simple! You watch me! I know a trick or two about makin' people tell what they don't wanter. (*He picks up the chisel from the table.*) Yuh see this? Well, if he don't answer up nice and easy we'll show him! (*A ferocious*

grin settles over his face.) We'll git even on him, you 'n' me—
and he'll tell where it's hid. We'll just shove this into the stove
till it's red hot and take off his shoes and socks and warm the
bottoms of his feet for him. (*savagely*) He'll tell then—anything we wants him to tell.

SWEENEY—But Annie?

LUKE—We'll shove a rag in her mouth so's she can't yell.
That's easy.

SWEENEY—(*his head lolling drunkenly—with a cruel leer*)
'Twill serve him right to heat up his hoofs for him, the
limpin', auld miser!—if ye don't hurt him too much.

LUKE—(*with a savage scowl*) We won't hurt him—more'n
enough. (*suddenly raging*) I'll pay him back aw right! He
won't want no more people to hang themselves when I git
through with him. I'll fix his hash! (*He sways to his feet, the
chisel in his hand.*) Come on! Let's git to work. Sooner we
starts the sooner we're rich. (*Sweeney rises. He is steadier on
his feet than Luke. At this moment Mary appears in the doorway.*)

MARY—Maw says supper's ready. I had mine. (*She comes
into the room and jumps up, trying to grab hold of the rope.*) Lift
me, Uncle Luke. I wanter swing.

LUKE—(*severely*) Don't yuh dare touch that rope, d'yuh
hear?

MARY—(*whining*) I wanter swing.

LUKE—(*with a shiver*) It's bad, kid. Yuh leave it alone, take
it from me.

SWEENEY—She'll get a good whalin' if I catch her jumpin'
at it.

LUKE—Come on, pal. T'hell with supper. We got work to
do first. (*They go to the doorway.*)

SWEENEY—(*turning back to the sulking Mary*) And you stay
here, d'you hear, ye brat, till we call ye—or I'll skin ye alive.

LUKE—And termorrer mornin', kid, I'll give yuh a whole
handful of them shiny, bright things yuh chucked in the
ocean—and yuh kin be a real sport.

MARY—(*eagerly*) Gimme 'em now! Gimme 'em now,
Uncle Luke. (*as he shakes his head—whiningly*) Gimme one!
Gimme one!

LUKE—Can't be done, kid. Termorrer. Me 'n' your old man

is goin' to git even now—goin' to make him pay for—

SWEENEY—(*interrupting—harshly*) Hist with your noise!
D'you think she's no ears? Don't be talkin' so much. Come
on, now.

LUKE—(*permitting himself to be pulled out the doorway*) Aw
right! I'm with yuh. We'll git even—you 'n' me. The damned
son of a gun! (*They lurch off to the right.*)

(*Mary skips to the doorway and peeps after them for a moment.
Then she comes back to the center of the floor and looks around her
with an air of decision. She sees the chair in under the loft and
runs over to it, pulling it back and setting it on its legs directly
underneath the noose of the rope. She climbs and stands on the top
of the chair and grasps the noose with both her upstretched hands.
Then with a shriek of delight she kicks the chair from under her
and launches herself for a swing. The rope seems to part where it
is fixed to the beam. A dirty gray bag tied to the end of the rope
falls to the floor with a muffled, metallic thud. Mary sprawls forward on her hands and knees, whimpering. Straggly wisps from
the pile of rank hay fall silently to the floor in a mist of dust. Mary,
discovering she is unhurt, glances quickly around and sees the bag.
She pushes herself along the floor and, untying the string at the
top, puts in her hand. She gives an exclamation of joy at what she
feels and, turning the bag upside down, pours its contents in her
lap. Giggling to herself, she gets to her feet and goes to the doorway, where she dumps what she has in her lap in a heap on the
floor just inside the barn. They lie there in a little glittering pile,
shimmering in the faint sunset glow—fifty twenty-dollar gold
pieces. Mary claps her hands and sings to herself: "Skip—skip—
skip." Then she quickly picks up four or five of them and runs out
to the edge of the cliff. She throws them one after another into the
ocean as fast as she can and bends over to see them hit the water.
Against the background of horizon clouds still tinted with blurred
crimson she hops up and down in a sort of grotesque dance, clapping her hands and laughing shrilly. After the last one is thrown
she rushes back into the barn to get more.*)

MARY—(*picking up a handful—giggling ecstastically*) Skip!
Skip! Skip! (*She turns and runs out to throw them as*

The Curtain Falls)

BEYOND THE HORIZON

A Play in Three Acts

To Agnes

CHARACTERS

James Mayo, *a farmer*
Kate Mayo, *his wife*
Captain Dick Scott, *of the bark* Sunda, *her brother*
Andrew Mayo ⎫
Robert Mayo ⎭ *sons of James Mayo*
Ruth Atkins
Mrs. Atkins, *her widowed mother*
Mary
Ben, *a farm hand*
Doctor Fawcett

Beyond the Horizon

ACT ONE
SCENE ONE

A section of country highway. The road runs diagonally from the left, forward, to the right, rear, and can be seen in the distance winding toward the horizon like a pale ribbon between the low, rolling hills with their freshly plowed fields clearly divided from each other, checkerboard fashion, by the lines of stone walls and rough snake fences.

The forward triangle cut off by the road is a section of a field from the dark earth of which myriad bright-green blades of fall-sown rye are sprouting. A straggling line of piled rocks, too low to be called a wall, separates this field from the road.

To the rear of the road is a ditch with a sloping, grassy bank on the far side. From the center of this an old, gnarled apple tree, just budding into leaf, strains its twisted branches heavenwards, black against the pallor of distance. A snake-fence sidles from left to right along the top of the bank, passing beneath the apple tree.

The hushed twilight of a day in May is just beginning. The horizon hills are still rimmed by a faint line of flame, and the sky above them glows with the crimson flush of the sunset. This fades gradually as the action of the scene progresses.

At the rise of the curtain, Robert Mayo is discovered sitting on the fence. He is a tall, slender young man of twenty-three. There is a touch of the poet about him expressed in his high forehead and wide, dark eyes. His features are delicate and refined, leaning to weakness in the mouth and chin. He is dressed in gray corduroy trousers pushed into high laced boots, and a blue flannel shirt with a bright colored tie. He is reading a book by the fading sunset light. He shuts this, keeping a finger in to mark the place, and turns his head toward the horizon, gazing out over the fields and hills. His lips move as if he were reciting something to himself.

His brother Andrew comes along the road from the right, returning from his work in the fields. He is twenty-seven years old, an opposite type to Robert—husky, sun-bronzed, handsome in a large-featured, manly fashion—a son of the soil, intelligent in a shrewd way, but with nothing of the intellectual about him. He wears overalls, leather boots, a gray flannel shirt open at the neck, and a soft, mud-stained hat pushed back on his head. He stops to talk to Robert, leaning on the hoe he carries.

ANDREW—(*seeing Robert has not noticed his presence—in a loud shout*) Hey there! (*Robert turns with a start. Seeing who it is, he smiles.*) Gosh, you do take the prize for daydreaming! And I see you've toted one of the old books along with you. (*He crosses the ditch and sits on the fence near his brother.*) What is it this time—poetry, I'll bet. (*He reaches for the book.*) Let me see.

ROBERT—(*handing it to him rather reluctantly*) Look out you don't get it full of dirt.

ANDREW—(*glancing at his hands*) That isn't dirt—it's good clean earth. (*He turns over the pages. His eyes read something and he gives an exclamation of disgust.*) Hump! (*With a provoking grin at his brother he reads aloud in a doleful, sing-song voice*) "I have loved wind and light and the bright sea. But holy and most sacred night, not as I love and have loved thee." (*He hands the book back.*) Here! Take it and bury it. I suppose it's that year in college gave you a liking for that kind of stuff. I'm darn glad I stopped at High School, or maybe I'd been crazy too. (*He grins and slaps Robert on the back affectionately.*) Imagine me reading poetry and plowing at the same time! The team'd run away, I'll bet.

ROBERT—(*laughing*) Or picture me plowing.

ANDREW—You should have gone back to college last fall, like I know you wanted to. You're fitted for that sort of thing—just as I ain't.

ROBERT—You know why I didn't go back, Andy. Pa didn't like the idea, even if he didn't say so; and I know he wanted the money to use improving the farm. And besides, I'm not keen on being a student, just because you see me reading books all the time. What I want to do now is keep on moving so that I won't take root in any one place.

ANDREW—Well, the trip you're leaving on tomorrow will keep you moving all right. (*At this mention of the trip they both fall silent. There is a pause. Finally Andrew goes on, awkwardly, attempting to speak casually.*) Uncle says you'll be gone three years.

ROBERT—About that, he figures.

ANDREW—(*moodily*) That's a long time.

ROBERT—Not so long when you come to consider it. You know the *Sunda* sails around the Horn for Yokohama first, and that's a long voyage on a sailing ship; and if we go to any of the other places Uncle Dick mentions—India, or Australia, or South Africa, or South America—they'll be long voyages, too.

ANDREW—You can have all those foreign parts for all of me. (*after a pause*) Ma's going to miss you a lot, Rob.

ROBERT—Yes—and I'll miss her.

ANDREW—And Pa ain't feeling none too happy to have you go—though he's been trying not to show it.

ROBERT—I can see how he feels.

ANDREW—And you can bet that I'm not giving any cheers about it. (*He puts one hand on the fence near Robert.*)

ROBERT—(*putting one hand on top of Andrew's with a gesture almost of shyness*) I know that, too, Andy.

ANDREW—I'll miss you as much as anybody, I guess. You see, you and I ain't like most brothers—always fighting and separated a lot of the time, while we've always been together—just the two of us. It's different with us. That's why it hits so hard, I guess.

ROBERT—(*with feeling*) It's just as hard for me, Andy —believe that! I hate to leave you and the old folks— but—I feel I've got to. There's something calling me— (*He points to the horizon.*) Oh, I can't just explain it to you, Andy.

ANDREW—No need to, Rob. (*angry at himself*) Hell! You want to go—that's all there is to it; and I wouldn't have you miss this chance for the world.

ROBERT—It's fine of you to feel that way, Andy.

ANDREW—Huh! I'd be a nice son-of-a-gun if I didn't, wouldn't I? When I know how you need this sea trip to make a new man of you—in the body, I mean—and give you your full health back.

ROBERT—(*a trifle impatiently*) All of you seem to keep harping on my health. You were so used to seeing me lying around the house in the old days that you never will get over the notion that I'm a chronic invalid. You don't realize how

I've bucked up in the past few years. If I had no other excuse for going on Uncle Dick's ship but just my health, I'd stay right here and start in plowing.

ANDREW—Can't be done. Farming ain't your nature. There's all the difference shown in just the way us two feel about the farm. You—well, you like the home part of it, I expect; but as a place to work and grow things, you hate it. Ain't that right?

ROBERT—Yes, I suppose it is. For you it's different. You're a Mayo through and through. You're wedded to the soil. You're as much a product of it as an ear of corn is, or a tree. Father is the same. This farm is his life-work, and he's happy in knowing that another Mayo, inspired by the same love, will take up the work where he leaves off. I can understand your attitude, and Pa's; and I think it's wonderful and sincere. But I—well, I'm not made that way.

ANDREW—No, you ain't; but when it comes to understanding, I guess I realize that you've got your own angle of looking at things.

ROBERT—(*musingly*) I wonder if you do, really.

ANDREW—(*confidently*) Sure I do. You've seen a bit of the world, enough to make the farm seem small, and you've got the itch to see it all.

ROBERT—It's more than that, Andy.

ANDREW—Oh, of course. I know you're going to learn navigation, and all about a ship, so's you can be an officer. That's natural, too. There's fair pay in it, I expect, when you consider that you've always got a home and grub thrown in; and if you're set on traveling, you can go anywhere you're a mind to without paying fare.

ROBERT—(*with a smile that is half sad*) It's more than that, Andy.

ANDREW—Sure it is. There's always a chance of a good thing coming your way in some of those foreign ports or other. I've heard there are great opportunities for a young fellow with his eyes open in some of those new countries that are just being opened up. (*jovially*) I'll bet that's what you've been turning over in your mind under all your quietness! (*He slaps his brother on the back with a laugh.*) Well, if you get to be a millionaire all of a sudden, call 'round once in a while and I'll pass the plate to you. We could use a lot of money right here on the farm without hurting it any.

ROBERT—(*forced to laugh*) I've never considered that practical side of it for a minute, Andy.

ANDREW—Well, you ought to.

ROBERT—No, I oughtn't. (*pointing to the horizon —dreamily*) Supposing I was to tell you that it's just Beauty that's calling me, the beauty of the far off and unknown, the mystery and spell of the East which lures me in the books I've read, the need of the freedom of great wide spaces, the joy of wandering on and on—in quest of the secret which is hidden over there, beyond the horizon? Suppose I told you that was the one and only reason for my going?

ANDREW—I should say you were nutty.

ROBERT—(*frowning*) Don't, Andy. I'm serious.

ANDREW—Then you might as well stay here, because we've got all you're looking for right on this farm. There's wide space enough, Lord knows; and you can have all the sea you want by walking a mile down to the beach; and there's plenty of horizon to look at, and beauty enough for anyone, except in the winter. (*He grins.*) As for the mystery and spell, I haven't met 'em yet, but they're probably lying around somewheres. I'll have you understand this is a first class farm with all the fixings. (*He laughs.*)

ROBERT—(*joining in the laughter in spite of himself*) It's no use talking to you, you chump!

ANDREW—You'd better not say anything to Uncle Dick about spells and things when you're on the ship. He'll likely chuck you overboard for a Jonah. (*He jumps down from fence.*) I'd better run along. I've got to wash up some as long as Ruth's Ma is coming over for supper.

ROBERT—(*pointedly—almost bitterly*) And Ruth.

ANDREW—(*confused—looking everywhere except at Robert —trying to appear unconcerned*) Yes, Ruth'll be staying too. Well, I better hustle, I guess, and— (*He steps over the ditch to the road while he is talking.*)

ROBERT—(*who appears to be fighting some strong inward emotion—impulsively*) Wait a minute, Andy! (*He jumps down from the fence.*) There is something I want to— (*He stops abruptly, biting his lips, his face coloring.*)

ANDREW—(*facing him; half-defiantly*) Yes?

ROBERT—(*confusedly*) No— never mind—it doesn't matter, it was nothing.

ANDREW—(*after a pause, during which he stares fixedly at Robert's averted face*) Maybe I can guess—what you were going to say—but I guess you're right not to talk about it. (*He pulls Robert's hand from his side and grips it tensely; the two brothers stand looking into each other's eyes for a minute.*) We can't help those things, Rob. (*He turns away, suddenly releasing Robert's hand.*) You'll be coming along shortly, won't you?

ROBERT—(*dully*) Yes.

ANDREW—See you later, then. (*He walks off down the road to the left. Robert stares after him for a moment; then climbs to the fence rail again, and looks out over the hills, an expression of deep grief on his face. After a moment or so, Ruth enters hurriedly from the left. She is a healthy, blonde, out-of-door girl of twenty, with a graceful, slender figure. Her face, though inclined to roundness, is undeniably pretty, its large eyes of a deep blue set off strikingly by the sun-bronzed complexion. Her small, regular features are marked by a certain strength—an underlying, stubborn fixity of purpose hidden in the frankly-appealing charm of her fresh youthfulness. She wears a simple white dress but no hat.*)

RUTH—(*seeing him*) Hello, Rob!

ROBERT—(*startled*) Hello, Ruth!

RUTH—(*jumps the ditch and perches on the fence beside him*) I was looking for you.

ROBERT—(*pointedly*) Andy just left here.

RUTH—I know. I met him on the road a second ago. He told me you were here. (*tenderly playful*) I wasn't looking for Andy, Smarty, if that's what you mean. I was looking for you.

ROBERT—Because I'm going away tomorrow?

RUTH—Because your mother was anxious to have you come home and asked me to look for you. I just wheeled Ma over to your house.

ROBERT—(*perfunctorily*) How is your mother?

RUTH—(*a shadow coming over her face*) She's about the same. She never seems to get any better or any worse. Oh,

Rob, I do wish she'd try to make the best of things that can't be helped.

ROBERT—Has she been nagging at you again?

RUTH—(*nods her head, and then breaks forth rebelliously*) She never stops nagging. No matter what I do for her she finds fault. If only Pa was still living— (*She stops as if ashamed of her outburst.*) I suppose I shouldn't complain this way. (*She sighs.*) Poor Ma, Lord knows it's hard enough for her. I suppose it's natural to be cross when you're not able ever to walk a step. Oh, I'd like to be going away some place—like you!

ROBERT—It's hard to stay—and equally hard to go, sometimes.

RUTH—There! If I'm not the stupid body! I swore I wasn't going to speak about your trip—until after you'd gone; and there I go, first thing!

ROBERT—Why didn't you want to speak of it?

RUTH—Because I didn't want to spoil this last night you're here. Oh, Rob, I'm going to—we're all going to miss you so awfully. Your mother is going around looking as if she'd burst out crying any minute. You ought to know how I feel. Andy and you and I—why it seems as if we'd always been together.

ROBERT—(*with a wry attempt at a smile*) You and Andy will still have each other. It'll be harder for me without anyone.

RUTH—But you'll have new sights and new people to take your mind off; while we'll be here with the old, familiar place to remind us every minute of the day. It's a shame you're going—just at this time, in spring, when everything is getting so nice. (*with a sigh*) I oughtn't to talk that way when I know going's the best thing for you. You're bound to find all sorts of opportunities to get on, your father says.

ROBERT—(*heatedly*) I don't give a damn about that! I wouldn't take a voyage across the road for the best opportunity in the world of the kind Pa thinks of. (*He smiles at his own irritation.*) Excuse me, Ruth, for getting worked up over it; but Andy gave me an overdose of the practical considerations.

RUTH—(*slowly, puzzled*) Well, then, if it isn't— (*with sudden intensity*) Oh, Rob, why *do* you want to go?

ROBERT—(*turning to her quickly, in surprise—slowly*) Why do you ask that, Ruth?

RUTH—(*dropping her eyes before his searching glance*) Because— (*lamely*) It seems such a shame.

ROBERT—(*insistently*) Why?

RUTH—Oh, because—everything.

ROBERT—I could hardly back out now, even if I wanted to. And I'll be forgotten before you know it.

RUTH—(*indignantly*) You won't! I'll never forget— (*She stops and turns away to hide her confusion.*)

ROBERT—(*softly*) Will you promise me that?

RUTH—(*evasively*) Of course. It's mean of you to think that any of us would forget so easily.

ROBERT—(*disappointedly*) Oh!

RUTH—(*with an attempt at lightness*) But you haven't told me your reason for leaving yet?

ROBERT—(*moodily*) I doubt if you'll understand. It's difficult to explain, even to myself. Either you feel it, or you don't. I can remember being conscious of it first when I was only a kid—you haven't forgotten what a sickly specimen I was then, in those days, have you?

RUTH—(*with a shudder*) Let's not think about them.

ROBERT—You'll have to, to understand. Well, in those days, when Ma was fixing meals, she used to get me out of the way by pushing my chair to the west window and telling me to look out and be quiet. That wasn't hard. I guess I was always quiet.

RUTH—(*compassionately*) Yes, you always were—and you suffering so much, too!

ROBERT—(*musingly*) So I used to stare out over the fields to the hills, out there—(*he points to the horizon*) and somehow after a time I'd forget any pain I was in, and start dreaming. I knew the sea was over beyond those hills,—the folks had told me—and I used to wonder what the sea was like, and try to form a picture of it in my mind. (*with a smile*) There was all the mystery in the world to me then about that—far-off sea—and there still is! It called to me then just as it does now. (*after a slight pause*) And other times my eyes would follow this road, winding off into the distance, toward the hills, as if it, too, was searching for the sea. And I'd promise myself that when I grew up and was strong, I'd follow that road, and it and I would find the sea together. (*with a smile*) You see, my making this trip is only keeping that promise of long ago.

RUTH—(*charmed by his low, musical voice telling the dreams of his childhood*) Yes, I see.

ROBERT—Those were the only happy moments of my life then, dreaming there at the window. I liked to be all alone—those times. I got to know all the different kinds of sunsets by heart. And all those sunsets took place over there—(*he points*) beyond the horizon. So gradually I came to believe that all the wonders of the world happened on the other side of those hills. There was the home of the good fairies who performed beautiful miracles. I believed in fairies then. (*with a smile*) Perhaps I still do believe in them. Anyway, in those days they were real enough, and sometimes I could actually hear them calling to me to come out and play with them, dance with them down the road in the dusk in a game of hide-and-seek to find out where the sun was hiding himself. They sang their little songs to me, songs that told of all the wonderful things they had in their home on the other side of the hills; and they promised to show me all of them, if I'd only come, come! But I couldn't come then, and I used to cry sometimes and Ma would think I was in pain. (*He breaks off suddenly with a laugh.*) That's why I'm going now, I suppose. For I can still hear them calling. But the horizon is as far away and as luring as ever. (*He turns to her—softly*) Do you understand now, Ruth?

RUTH—(*spellbound, in a whisper*) Yes.

ROBERT—You feel it then?

RUTH—Yes, yes, I do! (*Unconsciously she snuggles close against his side. His arm steals about her as if he were not aware of the action.*) Oh, Rob, how could I help feeling it? You tell things so beautifully!

ROBERT—(*suddenly realizing that his arm is around her, and that her head is resting on his shoulder, gently takes his arm away.*

Ruth, brought back to herself, is overcome with confusion.) So now you know why I'm going. It's for that reason—that and one other.

RUTH—You've another? Then you must tell me that, too.

ROBERT—(*looking at her searchingly. She drops her eyes before his gaze.*) I wonder if I ought to! You'll promise not to be angry—whatever it is?

RUTH—(*softly, her face still averted*) Yes, I promise.

ROBERT—(*simply*) I love you. That's the other reason.

RUTH—(*hiding her face in her hands*) Oh, Rob!

ROBERT—I wasn't going to tell you, but I feel I have to. It can't matter now that I'm going so far away, and for so long—perhaps forever. I've loved you all these years, but the realization never came 'til I agreed to go away with Uncle Dick. Then I thought of leaving you, and the pain of that thought revealed to me in a flash—that I loved you, had loved you as long as I could remember. (*He gently pulls one of Ruth's hands away from her face.*) You mustn't mind my telling you this, Ruth. I realize how impossible it all is—and I understand; for the revelation of my own love seemed to open my eyes to the love of others. I saw Andy's love for you— and I knew that you must love him.

RUTH—(*breaking out stormily*) I don't! I don't love Andy! I don't! (*Robert stares at her in stupid astonishment. Ruth weeps hysterically.*) Whatever—put such a fool notion into— into your head? (*She suddenly throws her arms about his neck and hides her head on his shoulder.*) Oh, Rob! Don't go away! Please! You mustn't, now! You can't! I won't let you! It'd break my—my heart!

ROBERT—(*the expression of stupid bewilderment giving way to one of overwhelming joy. He presses her close to him—slowly and tenderly*) Do you mean that—that you love me?

RUTH—(*sobbing*) Yes, yes—of course I do—what d'you s'pose? (*She lifts up her head and looks into his eyes with a tremulous smile.*) You stupid thing! (*He kisses her.*) I've loved you right along.

ROBERT—(*mystified*) But you and Andy were always together!

RUTH—Because you never seemed to want to go any place with me. You were always reading an old book, and not paying any attention to me. I was too proud to let you see I cared because I thought the year you had away to college had made you stuck-up, and you thought yourself too educated to waste any time on me.

ROBERT—(*kissing her*) And I was thinking— (*with a laugh*) What fools we've both been!

RUTH—(*overcome by a sudden fear*) You won't go away on the trip, will you, Rob? You'll tell them you can't go on account of me, won't you? You can't go now! You can't!

ROBERT—(*bewildered*) Perhaps—you can come too.

RUTH—Oh, Rob, don't be so foolish. You know I can't. Who'd take care of ma? Don't you see I couldn't go—on her account? (*She clings to him imploringly.*) Please don't go—not now. Tell them you've decided not to. They won't mind. I know your mother and father'll be glad. They'll all be. They don't want you to go so far away from them. Please, Rob! We'll be so happy here together where it's natural and we know things. Please tell me you won't go!

ROBERT—(*face to face with a definite, final decision, betrays the conflict going on within him*) But—Ruth—I—Uncle Dick—

RUTH—He won't mind when he knows it's for your happiness to stay. How could he? (*As Robert remains silent she bursts into sobs again.*) Oh, Rob! And you said—you loved me!

ROBERT—(*conquered by this appeal—an irrevocable decision in his voice*) I won't go, Ruth. I promise you. There! Don't cry! (*He presses her to him, stroking her hair tenderly. After a pause he speaks with happy hopefulness.*) Perhaps after all Andy was right—righter than he knew—when he said I could find all the things I was seeking for here, at home on the farm. I think love must have been the secret—the secret that called to me from over the world's rim—the secret beyond every horizon; and when I did not come, it came to me. (*He clasps Ruth to him fiercely.*) Oh, Ruth, our love is sweeter than any distant dream! (*He kisses her passionately and steps to the ground, lifting Ruth in his arms and carrying her to the road where he puts her down.*)

RUTH—(*with a happy laugh*) My, but you're strong!

ROBERT—Come! We'll go and tell them at once.

RUTH—(*dismayed*) Oh, no, don't, Rob, not 'til after I've

gone. There'd be bound to be such a scene with them all together.

ROBERT—(*kissing her—gayly*) As you like—little Miss Common Sense!

RUTH—Let's go, then. (*She takes his hand, and they start to go off left. Robert suddenly stops and turns as though for a last look at the hills and the dying sunset flush.*)

ROBERT—(*looking upward and pointing*) See! The first star. (*He bends down and kisses her tenderly.*) Our star!

RUTH—(*in a soft murmur*) Yes. Our very own star. (*They stand for a moment looking up at it, their arms around each other. Then Ruth takes his hand again and starts to lead him away.*) Come, Rob, let's go. (*His eyes are fixed again on the horizon as he half turns to follow her. Ruth urges*) We'll be late for supper, Rob.

ROBERT—(*shakes his head impatiently, as though he were throwing off some disturbing thought—with a laugh*) All right. We'll run then. Come on! (*They run off laughing as*

The Curtain Falls)

SCENE TWO

The sitting room of the Mayo farm house about nine o'clock the same night. On the left, two windows looking out on the fields. Against the wall between the windows, an old-fashioned walnut desk. In the left corner, rear, a sideboard with a mirror. In the rear wall to the right of the sideboard, a window looking out on the road. Next to the window a door leading out into the yard. Farther right, a black horse-hair sofa, and another door opening on a bedroom. In the corner, a straight-backed chair. In the right wall, near the middle, an open doorway leading to the kitchen. Farther forward a double-heater stove with coal scuttle, etc. In the center of the newly carpeted floor, an oak dining-room table with a red cover. In the center of the table, a large oil reading lamp. Four chairs, three rockers with crocheted tidies on their backs, and one straight-backed, are placed about the table. The walls are papered a dark red with a scrolly-figured pattern.

Everything in the room is clean, well-kept, and in its exact place, yet there is no suggestion of primness about the whole. Rather the atmosphere is one of the orderly comfort of a simple, hard-earned prosperity, enjoyed and maintained by the family as a unit.

James Mayo, his wife, her brother, Captain Dick Scott, and Andrew are discovered. Mayo is his son Andrew over again in body and face—an Andrew sixty-five years old with a short, square, white beard. Mrs. Mayo is a slight, round-faced, rather prim-looking woman of fifty-five who had once been a school teacher. The labors of a farmer's wife have bent but not broken her, and she retains a certain refinement of movement and expression foreign to the Mayo part of the family. Whatever of resemblance Robert has to his parents may be traced to her. Her brother, the Captain, is short and stocky, with a weather-beaten, jovial face and a white mustache—a typical old salt, loud of voice and given to gesture. He is fifty-eight years old.

James Mayo sits in front of the table. He wears spectacles, and a farm journal which he has been reading lies in his lap. The Captain leans forward from a chair in the rear, his hands on the table in front of him. Andrew is tilted back on the straight-backed chair to the left, his chin sunk forward on his chest, staring at the carpet, preoccupied and frowning.

As the Curtain rises the Captain is just finishing the relation of some sea episode. The others are pretending an interest which is belied by the absent-minded expressions on their faces.

THE CAPTAIN—(*chuckling*) And that mission woman, she hails me on the dock as I was acomin' ashore, and she says—with her silly face all screwed up serious as judgment—"Captain," she says, "would you be so kind as to tell me where the sea-gulls sleeps at nights?" Blow me if them warn't her exact words! (*He slaps the table with the palm of his hands and laughs loudly. The others force smiles.*) Ain't that just like a fool woman's question? And I looks at her serious as I could, "Ma'm," says I, "I couldn't rightly answer that question. I ain't never seed a sea-gull in his bunk yet. The next time I hears one snorin'," I says, "I'll make a note of where he's turned in, and write you a letter 'bout it." And then she calls me a fool real spiteful and tacks away from me quick. (*He laughs again uproariously.*) So I got rid of her that way.

(*The others smile but immediately relapse into expressions of gloom again.*)

MRS. MAYO—(*absent-mindedly—feeling that she has to say something*) But when it comes to that, where *do* sea-gulls sleep, Dick?

SCOTT—(*slapping the table*) Ho! Ho! Listen to her, James. 'Nother one! Well, if that don't beat all hell—'scuse me for cussin', Kate.

MAYO—(*with a twinkle in his eyes*) They unhitch their wings, Katey, and spreads 'em out on a wave for a bed.

SCOTT—And then they tells the fish to whistle to 'em when it's time to turn out. Ho! Ho!

MRS. MAYO—(*with a forced smile*) You men folks are too smart to live, aren't you? (*She resumes her knitting. Mayo pretends to read his paper; Andrew stares at the floor.*)

SCOTT—(*looks from one to the other of them with a puzzled air. Finally he is unable to bear the thick silence a minute longer, and blurts out*) You folks look as if you was settin' up with a corpse. (*with exaggerated concern*) God A'mighty, there ain't anyone dead, be there?

MAYO—(*sharply*) Don't play the dunce, Dick! You know as well as we do there ain't no great cause to be feelin' chipper.

SCOTT—(*argumentatively*) And there ain't no cause to be wearin' mourning, either, I can make out.

MRS. MAYO—(*indignantly*) How can you talk that way, Dick Scott, when you're taking our Robbie away from us, in the middle of the night, you might say, just to get on that old boat of yours on time! I think you might wait until morning when he's had his breakfast.

SCOTT—(*appealing to the others hopelessly*) Ain't that a woman's way o' seein' things for you? God A'mighty, Kate, I can't give orders to the tide that it's got to be high just when it suits me to have it. I ain't gettin' no fun out o' missin' sleep and leavin' here at six bells myself. (*protestingly*) And the *Sunda* ain't an old ship—leastways, not very old—and she's good's she ever was.

MRS. MAYO—(*her lips trembling*) I wish Robbie weren't going.

MAYO—(*looking at her over his glasses—consolingly*) There, Katey!

MRS. MAYO—(*rebelliously*) Well, I *do* wish he wasn't!

SCOTT—You shouldn't be taking it so hard, 's far as I kin see. This vige'll make a man of him. I'll see to it he learns how to navigate, 'n' study for a mate's c'tificate right off—and it'll give him a trade for the rest of his life, if he wants to travel.

MRS. MAYO—But I don't want him to travel all his life. You've got to see he comes home when this trip is over. Then he'll be all well, and he'll want to—to marry—(*Andrew sits forward in his chair with an abrupt movement*)—and settle down right here. (*She stares down at the knitting in her lap—after a pause*) I never realized how hard it was going to be for me to have Robbie go—or I wouldn't have considered it a minute.

SCOTT—It ain't no good goin' on that way, Kate, now it's all settled.

MRS. MAYO—(*on the verge of tears*) It's all right for *you* to talk. You've never had any children. You don't know what it means to be parted from them—and Robbie my youngest, too. (*Andrew frowns and fidgets in his chair.*)

ANDREW—(*suddenly turning to them*) There's one thing none of you seem to take into consideration—that Rob wants to go. He's dead set on it. He's been dreaming over this trip ever since it was first talked about. It wouldn't be fair to him not to have him go. (*A sudden uneasiness seems to strike him.*) At least, not if he still feels the same way about it he did when he was talking to me this evening.

MAYO—(*with an air of decision*) Andy's right, Katey. That ends all argyment, you can see that. (*looking at his big silver watch*) Wonder what's happened to Robert? He's been gone long enough to wheel the widder to home, certain. He can't be out dreamin' at the stars his last night.

MRS. MAYO—(*a bit reproachfully*) Why didn't you wheel Mrs. Atkins back tonight, Andy? You usually do when she and Ruth come over.

ANDREW—(*avoiding her eyes*) I thought maybe Robert wanted to tonight. He offered to go right away when they were leaving.

MRS. MAYO—He only wanted to be polite.

ANDREW—(*gets to his feet*) Well, he'll be right back, I

guess. (*He turns to his father.*) Guess I'll go take a look at the black cow, Pa—see if she's ailing any.

MAYO—Yes—better had, son. (*Andrew goes into the kitchen on the right.*)

SCOTT—(*as he goes out—in a low tone*) There's the boy that would make a good, strong sea-farin' man—if he'd a mind to.

MAYO—(*sharply*) Don't you put no such fool notions in Andy's head, Dick—or you 'n' me's goin' to fall out. (*Then he smiles.*) You couldn't tempt him, no ways. Andy's a Mayo bred in the bone, and he's a born farmer, and a damn good one, too. He'll live and die right here on this farm, like I expect to. (*with proud confidence*) And he'll make this one of the slickest, best-payin' farms in the state, too, afore he gits through!

SCOTT—Seems to me it's a pretty slick place right now.

MAYO—(*shaking his head*) It's too small. We need more land to make it amount to much, and we ain't got the capital to buy it. (*Andrew enters from the kitchen. His hat is on, and he carries a lighted lantern in his hand. He goes to the door in the rear leading out.*)

ANDREW—(*opens the door and pauses*) Anything else you can think of to be done, Pa?

MAYO—No, nothin' I know of. (*Andrew goes out, shutting the door.*)

MRS. MAYO—(*after a pause*) What's come over Andy to-night, I wonder? He acts so strange.

MAYO—He does seem sort o' glum and out of sorts. It's 'count o' Robert leavin', I s'pose. (*to Scott*) Dick, you wouldn't believe how them boys o' mine sticks together. They ain't like most brothers. They've been thick as thieves all their lives, with nary a quarrel I kin remember.

SCOTT—No need to tell me that. I can see how they take to each other.

MRS. MAYO—(*pursuing her train of thought*) Did you notice, James, how queer everyone was at supper? Robert seemed stirred up about something; and Ruth was so flustered and giggly; and Andy sat there dumb, looking as if he'd lost his best friend; and all of them only nibbled at their food.

MAYO—Guess they was all thinkin' about tomorrow, same as us.

MRS. MAYO—(*shaking her head*) No. I'm afraid somethin's happened—somethin' else.

MAYO—You mean—'bout Ruth?

MRS. MAYO—Yes.

MAYO—(*after a pause—frowning*) I hope her and Andy ain't had a serious fallin'-out. I always sorter hoped they'd hitch up together sooner or later. What d'you say, Dick? Don't you think them two'd pair up well?

SCOTT—(*nodding his head approvingly*) A sweet, wholesome couple they'd make.

MAYO—It'd be a good thing for Andy in more ways than one. I ain't what you'd call calculatin' generally, and I b'lieve in lettin' young folks run their affairs to suit themselves; but there's advantages for both o' them in this match you can't overlook in reason. The Atkins farm is right next to ourn. Jined together they'd make a jim-dandy of a place, with plenty o' room to work in. And bein' a widder with only a daughter, and laid up all the time to boot, Mrs. Atkins can't do nothin' with the place as it ought to be done. She needs a man, a first-class farmer, to take hold o' things; and Andy's just the one.

MRS. MAYO—(*abruptly*) I don't think Ruth loves Andy.

MAYO—You don't? Well, maybe a woman's eyes is sharper in such things, but—they're always together. And if she don't love him now, she'll likely come around to it in time. (*as Mrs. Mayo shakes her head*) You seem mighty fixed in your opinion, Katey. How d'you know?

MRS. MAYO—It's just—what I feel.

MAYO—(*a light breaking over him*) You don't mean to say— (*Mrs. Mayo nods. Mayo chuckles scornfully.*) Shucks! I'm losin' my respect for your eyesight, Katey. Why, Robert ain't got no time for Ruth, 'cept as a friend!

MRS. MAYO—(*warningly*) Sss-h-h! (*The door from the yard opens, and Robert enters. He is smiling happily, and humming a song to himself, but as he comes into the room an undercurrent of nervous uneasiness manifests itself in his bearing.*)

MAYO—So here you be at last! (*Robert comes forward and sits on Andy's chair. Mayo smiles slyly at his wife.*) What have you been doin' all this time—countin' the stars to see if they all come out right and proper?

ROBERT—There's only one I'll ever look for any more, Pa.

MAYO—(*reproachfully*) You might've even not wasted time lookin' for that one—your last night.

MRS. MAYO—(*as if she were speaking to a child*) You ought to have worn your coat a sharp night like this, Robbie.

SCOTT—(*disgustedly*) God A'mighty, Kate, you treat Robert as if he was one year old!

MRS. MAYO—(*notices Robert's nervous uneasiness*) You look all worked up over something, Robbie. What is it?

ROBERT—(*swallowing hard, looks quickly from one to the other of them—then begins determinedly*) Yes, there *is* something—something I must tell you—all of you. (*As he begins to talk Andrew enters quietly from the rear, closing the door behind him, and setting the lighted lantern on the floor. He remains standing by the door, his arms folded, listening to Robert with a repressed expression of pain on his face. Robert is so much taken up with what he is going to say that he does not notice Andrew's presence.*) Something I discovered only this evening—very beautiful and wonderful—something I did not take into consideration previously because I hadn't dared to hope that such happiness could ever come to me. (*appealingly*) You must all remember that fact, won't you?

MAYO—(*frowning*) Let's get to the point, son.

ROBERT—(*with a trace of defiance*) Well, the point is this, Pa: I'm not going—I mean—I can't go tomorrow with Uncle Dick—or at any future time, either.

MRS. MAYO—(*with a sharp sigh of joyful relief*) Oh, Robbie, I'm so glad!

MAYO—(*astounded*) You ain't serious, be you, Robert? (*severely*) Seems to me it's a pretty late hour in the day for you to be upsettin' all your plans so sudden!

ROBERT—I asked you to remember that until this evening I didn't know myself. I had never dared to dream—

MAYO—(*irritably*) What is this foolishness you're talkin' of?

ROBERT—(*flushing*) Ruth told me this evening that—she loved me. It was after I'd confessed I loved her. I told her I hadn't been conscious of my love until after the trip had been arranged, and I realized it would mean—leaving her. That was the truth. I *didn't* know until then. (*as if justifying himself to the others*) I hadn't intended telling her anything but—suddenly—I felt I must. I didn't think it would matter, because I was going away. And I thought she loved—someone else. (*slowly—his eyes shining*) And then she cried and said it was I she'd loved all the time, but I hadn't seen it.

MRS. MAYO—(*rushes over and throws her arms about him*) I knew it! I was just telling your father when you came in—and, Oh, Robbie, I'm so happy you're not going!

ROBERT—(*kissing her*) I knew you'd be glad, Ma.

MAYO—(*bewilderedly*) Well, I'll be damned! You do beat all for gettin' folks' minds all tangled up, Robert. And Ruth too! Whatever got into her of a sudden? Why, I was thinkin'—

MRS. MAYO—(*hurriedly—in a tone of warning*) Never mind what you were thinking, James. It wouldn't be any use telling us that now. (*meaningly*) And what you were hoping for turns out just the same almost, doesn't it?

MAYO—(*thoughtfully—beginning to see this side of the argument*) Yes; I suppose you're right, Katey. (*scratching his head in puzzlement*) But how it ever come about! It do beat anything ever I heard. (*Finally he gets up with a sheepish grin and walks over to Robert.*) We're glad you ain't goin', your Ma and I, for we'd have missed you terrible, that's certain and sure; and we're glad you've found happiness. Ruth's a fine girl and'll make a good wife to you.

ROBERT—(*much moved*) Thank you, Pa. (*He grips his father's hand in his.*)

ANDREW—(*his face tense and drawn comes forward and holds out his hand, forcing a smile*) I guess it's my turn to offer congratulations, isn't it?

ROBERT—(*with a startled cry when his brother appears before him so suddenly*) Andy! (*confused*) Why—I—I didn't see you. Were you here when—

ANDREW—I heard everything you said; and here's wishing you every happiness, you and Ruth. You both deserve the best there is.

ROBERT—(*taking his hand*) Thanks, Andy, it's fine of you to— (*His voice dies away as he sees the pain in Andrew's eyes.*)

ANDREW—(*giving his brother's hand a final grip*) Good luck to you both! (*He turns away and goes back to the rear where he bends over the lantern, fumbling with it to hide his emotion from the others.*)

MRS. MAYO—(*to the Captain, who has been too flabbergasted by Robert's decision to say a word*) What's the matter, Dick? Aren't you going to congratulate Robbie?

SCOTT—(*embarrassed*) Of course I be! (*He gets to his feet and shakes Robert's hand, muttering a vague*) Luck to you, boy. (*He stands beside Robert as if he wanted to say something more but doesn't know how to go about it.*)

ROBERT—Thanks, Uncle Dick.

SCOTT—So you're not acomin' on the *Sunda* with me? (*His voice indicates disbelief.*)

ROBERT—I can't, Uncle—not now. I wouldn't miss it for anything else in the world under any other circumstances. (*He sighs unconsciously.*) But you see I've found—a bigger dream. (*then with joyous high spirits*) I want you all to understand one thing—I'm not going to be a loafer on your hands any longer. This means the beginning of a new life for me in every way. I'm going to settle right down and take a real interest in the farm, and do my share. I'll prove to you, Pa, that I'm as good a Mayo as you are—or Andy, when I want to be.

MAYO—(*kindly but skeptically*) That's the right spirit, Robert. Ain't none of us doubts your willin'ness, but you ain't never learned—

ROBERT—Then I'm going to start learning right away, and you'll teach me, won't you?

MAYO—(*mollifyingly*) Of course I will, boy, and be glad to, only you'd best go easy at first.

SCOTT—(*who has listened to this conversation in mingled consternation and amazement*) You don't mean to tell me you're goin' to let him stay, do you, James?

MAYO—Why, things bein' as they be, Robert's free to do as he's a mind to.

MRS. MAYO—*Let him!* The very idea!

SCOTT—(*more and more ruffled*) Then all I got to say is, you're a soft, weak-willed critter to be permittin' a boy—and women, too—to be layin' your course for you wherever they damn pleases.

MAYO—(*slyly amused*) It's just the same with me as 'twas with you, Dick. You can't order the tides on the seas to suit you, and I ain't pretendin' I can reg'late love for young folks.

SCOTT—(*scornfully*) Love! They ain't old enough to know love when they sight it! Love! I'm ashamed of you, Robert, to go lettin' a little huggin' and kissin' in the dark spile your chances to make a man out o' yourself. It ain't common sense—no siree, it ain't—not by a hell of a sight! (*He pounds the table with his fists in exasperation.*)

MRS. MAYO—(*laughing provokingly at her brother*) A fine one you are to be talking about love, Dick—an old cranky bachelor like you. Goodness sakes!

SCOTT—(*exasperated by their joking*) I've never been a damn fool like most, if that's what you're steerin' at.

MRS. MAYO—(*tauntingly*) Sour grapes, aren't they, Dick? (*She laughs. Robert and his father chuckle. Scott sputters with annoyance.*) Good gracious, Dick, you do act silly, flying into a temper over nothing.

SCOTT—(*indignantly*) Nothin'! You talk as if I wasn't concerned nohow in this here business. Seems to me I've got a right to have my say. Ain't I made all arrangements with the owners and stocked up with some special grub all on Robert's account?

ROBERT—You've been fine, Uncle Dick; and I appreciate it. Truly.

MAYO—'Course; we all does, Dick.

SCOTT—(*unplacated*) I've been countin' sure on havin' Robert for company on this vige—to sorta talk to and show things to, and teach, kinda, and I got my mind so set on havin' him I'm goin' to be double lonesome this vige. (*He pounds on the table, attempting to cover up this confession of weakness.*) Darn all this silly lovin' business, anyway. (*irritably*) But all this talk ain't tellin' me what I'm to do with that sta'b'd cabin I fixed up. It's all painted white, an' a bran new mattress on the bunk, 'n' new sheets 'n' blankets 'n' things. And Chips built in a book-case so's Robert could take his books along—with a slidin' bar fixed across't it, mind, so's they couldn't fall out no matter how she rolled. (*with excited consternation*) What d'you suppose my officers is goin' to think when there's no one comes aboard to occupy that sta'b'd cabin? And the men what did the work on it—what'll *they* think? (*He shakes his finger indignantly.*) They're liable as not to suspicion it was a *woman* I'd planned to ship along, and that she gave me the go-by at the last moment! (*He wipes his perspiring brow in anguish at this thought.*) Gawd A'mighty! They're only lookin' to have the laugh on me for something like that. They're liable to b'lieve anything, those fellers is!

MAYO—(*with a wink*) Then there's nothing to it but for you to get right out and hunt up a wife somewheres for that spick 'n' span cabin. She'll have to be a pretty one, too, to match it. (*He looks at his watch with exaggerated concern.*) You ain't got much time to find her, Dick.

SCOTT—(*as the others smile—sulkily*) You kin go to thunder, Jim Mayo!

ANDREW—(*comes forward from where he has been standing by the door, rear, brooding. His face is set in a look of grim determination.*) You needn't worry about that spare cabin, Uncle Dick, if you've a mind to take me in Robert's place.

ROBERT—(*turning to him quickly*) Andy! (*He sees at once the fixed resolve in his brother's eyes, and realizes immediately the reason for it—in consternation*) Andy, you mustn't!

ANDREW—You've made your decision, Rob, and now I've made mine. You're out of this, remember.

ROBERT—(*hurt by his brother's tone*) But Andy—

ANDREW—Don't interfere, Rob—that's all I ask. (*turning to his uncle*) You haven't answered my question, Uncle Dick.

SCOTT—(*clearing his throat, with an uneasy side glance at James Mayo who is staring at his elder son as if he thought he had suddenly gone mad*) O' course, I'd be glad to have you, Andy.

ANDREW—It's settled then. I can pack the little I want to take in a few minutes.

MRS. MAYO—Don't be a fool, Dick. Andy's only joking you.

SCOTT—(*disgruntedly*) It's hard to tell who's jokin' and who's not in this house.

ANDREW—(*firmly*) I'm not joking, Uncle Dick. (*as Scott looks at him uncertainly*) You needn't be afraid I'll go back on my word.

ROBERT—(*hurt by the insinuation he feels in Andrew's tone*) Andy! That isn't fair!

MAYO—(*frowning*) Seems to me this ain't no subject to joke over—not for Andy.

ANDREW—(*facing his father*) I agree with you, Pa, and I tell you again, once and for all, that I've made up my mind to go.

MAYO—(*dumbfounded—unable to doubt the determination in Andrew's voice—helplessly*) But why, son? Why?

ANDREW—(*evasively*) I've always wanted to go.

ROBERT—Andy!

ANDREW—(*half angrily*) You shut up, Rob! (*turning to his father again*) I didn't ever mention it because as long as Rob was going I knew it was no use; but now Rob's staying on here, there isn't any reason for me not to go.

MAYO—(*breathing hard*) No reason? Can you stand there and say that to me, Andrew?

MRS. MAYO—(*hastily—seeing the gathering storm*) He doesn't mean a word of it, James.

MAYO—(*making a gesture to her to keep silence*) Let me talk, Katey. (*in a more kindly tone*) What's come over you so sudden, Andy? You know's well as I do that it wouldn't be fair o' you to run off at a moment's notice right now when we're up to our necks in hard work.

ANDREW—(*avoiding his eyes*) Rob'll hold his end up as soon as he learns.

MAYO—Robert was never cut out for a farmer, and you was.

ANDREW—You can easily get a man to do my work.

MAYO—(*restraining his anger with an effort*) It sounds strange to hear you, Andy, that I always thought had good sense, talkin' crazy like that. (*scornfully*) Get a man to take your place! You ain't been workin' here for no hire, Andy, that you kin give me your notice to quit like you've done. The farm is your'n as well as mine. You've always worked on it with that understanding; and what you're sayin' you intend doin' is just skulkin' out o' your rightful responsibility.

ANDREW—(*looking at the floor—simply*) I'm sorry, Pa. (*after a slight pause*) It's no use talking any more about it.

MRS. MAYO—(*in relief*) There! I knew Andy'd come to his senses!

ANDREW—Don't get the wrong idea, Ma. I'm not backing out.

MAYO—You mean you're goin' in spite of—everythin'?

ANDREW—Yes. I'm going. I've got to. (*He looks at his father defiantly.*) I feel I oughn't to miss this chance to go out into the world and see things, and—I want to go.

MAYO—(*with bitter scorn*) So—you want to go out into the world and see thin's! (*his voice raised and quivering with anger*) I never thought I'd live to see the day when a son o' mine 'd look me in the face and tell a bare-faced lie! (*bursting out*) You're a liar, Andy Mayo, and a mean one to boot!

MRS. MAYO—James!

ROBERT—Pa!

SCOTT—Steady there, Jim!

MAYO—(*waving their protests aside*) He is and he knows it.

ANDREW—(*his face flushed*) I won't argue with you, Pa. You can think as badly of me as you like.

MAYO—(*shaking his finger at Andy, in a cold rage*) You know I'm speakin' truth—that's why you're afraid to argy! You lie when you say you want to go 'way—and see thin's! You ain't got no likin' in the world to go. I've watched you grow up, and I know your ways, and they're my ways. You're runnin' against your own nature, and you're goin' to be a'mighty sorry for it if you do. 'S if I didn't know your real reason for runnin' away! And runnin' away's the only words to fit it. You're runnin' away 'cause you're put out and riled 'cause your own brother's got Ruth 'stead o' you, and—

ANDREW—(*his face crimson—tensely*) Stop, Pa! I won't stand hearing that—not even from you!

MRS. MAYO—(*rushing to Andy and putting her arms about him protectingly*) Don't mind him, Andy dear. He don't mean a word he's saying! (*Robert stands rigidly, his hands clenched, his face contracted by pain. Scott sits dumbfounded and open-mouthed. Andrew soothes his mother who is on the verge of tears.*)

MAYO—(*in angry triumph*) It's the truth, Andy Mayo! And you ought to be bowed in shame to think of it!

ROBERT—(*protestingly*) Pa!

MRS. MAYO—(*coming from Andrew to his father; puts her hands on his shoulders as though to try and push him back in the chair from which he has risen*) Won't you be still, James? Please won't you?

MAYO—(*looking at Andrew over his wife's shoulder—stubbornly*) The truth—God's truth!

MRS. MAYO—Sh-h-h! (*She tries to put a finger across his lips, but he twists his head away.*)

ANDREW—(*who has regained control over himself*) You're wrong, Pa, it isn't truth. (*with defiant assertiveness*) I don't love Ruth. I never loved her, and the thought of such a thing never entered my head.

MAYO—(*with an angry snort of disbelief*) Hump! You're pilin' lie on lie!

ANDREW—(*losing his temper—bitterly*) I suppose it'd be hard for you to explain anyone's wanting to leave this blessed farm except for some outside reason like that. But I'm sick and tired of it—whether you want to believe me or not—and that's why I'm glad to get a chance to move on.

ROBERT—Andy! Don't! You're only making it worse.

ANDREW—(*sulkily*) I don't care. I've done my share of work here. I've earned my right to quit when I want to. (*suddenly overcome with anger and grief; with rising intensity*) I'm sick and tired of the whole damn business. I hate the farm and every inch of ground in it. I'm sick of digging in the dirt and sweating in the sun like a slave without getting a word of thanks for it. (*tears of rage starting to his eyes—hoarsely*) I'm through, through for good and all; and if Uncle Dick won't take me on his ship, I'll find another. I'll get away somewhere, somehow.

MRS. MAYO—(*in a frightened voice*) Don't you answer him, James. He doesn't know what he's saying. Don't say a word to him 'til he's in his right senses again. Please James, don't—

MAYO—(*pushes her away from him; his face is drawn and pale with the violence of his passion. He glares at Andrew as if he hated him.*) You dare to—you dare to speak like that to me? You talk like that 'bout this farm—the Mayo farm—where you was born—you—you— (*He clenches his fist above his head and advances threateningly on Andrew.*) You damned whelp!

MRS. MAYO—(*with a shriek*) James! (*She covers her face with her hands and sinks weakly into Mayo's chair. Andrew remains standing motionless, his face pale and set.*)

SCOTT—(*starting to his feet and stretching his arms across the table toward Mayo*) Easy there, Jim!

ROBERT—(*throwing himself between father and brother*) Stop! Are you mad?

MAYO—(*grabs Robert's arm and pushes him aside—then stands for a moment gasping for breath before Andrew. He points to the door with a shaking finger.*) Yes—go!—go!—You're no son o' mine—no son o' mine! You can go to hell if you want to! Don't let me find you here—in the mornin'—or—or—I'll *throw* you out!

ROBERT—Pa! For God's sake! (*Mrs. Mayo bursts into noisy sobbing.*)

MAYO—(*He gulps convulsively and glares at Andrew.*) You go—tomorrow mornin'—and by God—don't come back—don't dare come back—by God, not while I'm livin'—or I'll—I'll— (*He shakes over his muttered threat and strides toward the door rear, right.*)

MRS. MAYO—(*rising and throwing her arms around him—hysterically*) James! James! Where are you going?

MAYO—(*incoherently*) I'm goin'—to bed, Katey. It's late, Katey—it's late. (*He goes out.*)

MRS. MAYO—(*following him, pleading hysterically*) James! Take back what you've said to Andy. James! (*She follows him out. Robert and the Captain stare after them with horrified eyes. Andrew stands rigidly looking straight in front of him, his fists clenched at his sides.*)

SCOTT—(*the first to find his voice—with an explosive sigh*) Well, if he ain't the devil himself when he's roused! You oughtn't to have talked to him that way, Andy 'bout the damn farm, knowin' how touchy he is about it. (*with another sigh*) Well, you won't mind what he's said in anger. He'll be sorry for it when he's calmed down a bit.

ANDREW—(*in a dead voice*) You don't know him. (*defiantly*) What's said is said and can't be unsaid; and I've chosen.

ROBERT—(*with violent protest*) Andy! You can't go! This is all so stupid—and terrible!

ANDREW—(*coldly*) I'll talk to you in a minute, Rob. (*Crushed by his brother's attitude Robert sinks down into a chair, holding his head in his hands.*)

SCOTT—(*comes and slaps Andrew on the back*) I'm damned glad you're shippin' on, Andy. I like your spirit, and the way you spoke up to him. (*lowering his voice to a cautious whisper*) The sea's the place for a young feller like you that isn't half dead 'n' alive. (*He gives Andy a final approving slap.*) You 'n' me 'll get along like twins, see if we don't. I'm goin' aloft to turn in. Don't forget to pack your dunnage. And git some sleep, if you kin. We'll want to sneak out extra early b'fore they're up. It'll do away with more argyments. Robert can drive us down to the town, and bring back the team. (*He goes to the door in the rear, left.*) Well, good night.

ANDREW—Good night. (*Scott goes out. The two brothers remain silent for a moment. Then Andrew comes over to his brother and puts a hand on his back. He speaks in a low voice, full of feeling.*) Buck up, Rob. It ain't any use crying over spilt milk; and it'll all turn out for the best—let's hope. It couldn't be helped—what's happened.

ROBERT—(*wildly*) But it's a lie, Andy, a lie!

ANDREW—Of course it's a lie. You know it and I know it,—but that's all ought to know it.

ROBERT—Pa'll never forgive you. Oh, the whole affair is so senseless—and tragic. Why did you think you must go away?

ANDREW—You know better than to ask that. You know why. (*fiercely*) I can wish you and Ruth all the good luck in the world, and I do, and I mean it; but you can't expect me to stay around here and watch you two together, day after day—and me alone. I couldn't stand it—not after all the plans I'd made to happen on this place thinking—(*his voice breaks*) thinking she cared for me.

ROBERT—(*putting a hand on his brother's arm*) God! It's horrible! I feel so guilty—to think that I should be the cause of your suffering, after we've been such pals all our lives. If I could have foreseen what'd happen, I swear to you I'd have never said a word to Ruth. I swear I wouldn't have, Andy!

ANDREW—I know you wouldn't; and that would've been worse, for Ruth would've suffered then. (*He pats his brother's shoulder.*) It's best as it is. It had to be, and I've got to stand the gaff, that's all. Pa'll see how I felt—after a time. (*as Robert shakes his head*) —and if he don't—well, it can't be helped.

ROBERT—But think of Ma! God, Andy, you can't go! You can't!

ANDREW—(*fiercely*) I've got to go—to get away! I've got to, I tell you. I'd go crazy here, bein' reminded every second of the day what a fool I'd made of myself. I've got to get away and try and forget, if I can. And I'd hate the farm if I stayed, hate it for bringin' things back. I couldn't take interest in the work any more, work with no purpose in sight. Can't you see what a hell it'd be? You love her too, Rob. Put yourself in my place, and remember I haven't stopped loving her, and couldn't if I was to stay. Would that be fair to you or to her? Put yourself in my place. (*He shakes his brother fiercely by the shoulder.*) What'd you do then? Tell me the truth! You love her. What'd you do?

ROBERT—(*chokingly*) I'd—I'd go, Andy! (*He buries his face in his hands with a shuddering sob.*) God!

ANDREW—(*seeming to relax suddenly all over his body—in a low, steady voice*) Then you know why I got to go; and there's nothing more to be said.

ROBERT—(*in a frenzy of rebellion*) Why did this have to happen to us? It's damnable! (*He looks about him wildly, as if his vengeance were seeking the responsible fate.*)

ANDREW—(*soothingly—again putting his hands on his brother's shoulder*) It's no use fussing any more, Rob. It's done. (*forcing a smile*) I guess Ruth's got a right to have who she likes. She made a good choice—and God bless her for it!

ROBERT—Andy! Oh, I wish I could tell you half I feel of how fine you are!

ANDREW—(*interrupting him quickly*) Shut up! Let's go to bed. I've got to be up long before sun-up. You, too, if you're going to drive us down.

ROBERT—Yes. Yes.

ANDREW—(*turning down the lamp*) And I've got to pack yet. (*He yawns with utter weariness.*) I'm as tired as if I'd been plowing twenty-four hours at a stretch. (*dully*) I feel—dead. (*Robert covers his face again with his hands. Andrew shakes his head as if to get rid of his thoughts, and continues with a poor attempt at cheery briskness.*) I'm going to douse the light. Come on. (*He slaps his brother on the back. Robert does not move. Andrew bends over and blows out the lamp. His voice comes from the darkness.*) Don't sit there mourning, Rob. It'll all come out in the wash. Come on and get some sleep. Everything'll turn out all right in the end. (*Robert can be heard stumbling to his feet, and the dark figures of the two brothers can be seen groping their way toward the doorway in the rear as*

The Curtain Falls)

ACT TWO
Scene One

Same as Act One, Scene Two. Sitting room of the farm house about half past twelve in the afternoon of a hot, sun-baked day in mid-summer, three years later. All the windows are open, but no breeze stirs the soiled white curtains. A patched screen door is in the rear. Through it the yard can be seen, its small stretch of lawn divided by the dirt path leading to the door from the gate in the white picket fence which borders the road.

The room has changed, not so much in its outward appearance as in its general atmosphere. Little significant details give evidence of carelessness, of inefficiency, of an industry gone to seed. The chairs appear shabby from lack of paint; the table cover is spotted and askew; holes show in the curtains; a child's doll, with one arm gone, lies under the table; a hoe stands in a corner; a man's coat is flung on the couch in the rear; the desk is cluttered up with odds and ends; a number of books are piled carelessly on the sideboard. The noon enervation of the sultry, scorching day seems to have penetrated indoors, causing even inanimate objects to wear an aspect of despondent exhaustion.

A place is set at the end of the table, left, for someone's dinner. Through the open door to the kitchen comes the clatter of dishes being washed, interrupted at intervals by a woman's irritated voice and the peevish whining of a child.

At the rise of the curtain Mrs. Mayo and Mrs. Atkins are discovered sitting facing each other, Mrs. Mayo to the rear, Mrs. Atkins to the right of the table. Mrs. Mayo's face has lost all character, disintegrated, become a weak mask wearing a helpless, doleful expression of being constantly on the verge of comfortless tears. She speaks in an uncertain voice, without assertiveness, as if all power of willing had deserted her. Mrs. Atkins is in her wheel chair. She is a thin, pale-faced, unintelligent looking woman of about forty-eight, with hard, bright eyes. A victim of partial paralysis for many years, condemned to be pushed from day to day of her life in a wheel chair, she has developed the selfish, irritable nature of the chronic invalid. Both women are dressed in black. Mrs. Atkins knits nervously as she talks. A ball of unused yarn, with needles stuck through it, lies on the table before Mrs. Mayo.

MRS. ATKINS—(*with a disapproving glance at the place set on the table*) Robert's late for his dinner again, as usual. I don't see why Ruth puts up with it, and I've told her so. Many's the time I've said to her "It's about time you put a stop to his nonsense. Does he suppose you're runnin' a hotel—with no one to help with things?" But she don't pay no attention. She's as bad as he is, a'most—thinks she knows better than an old, sick body like me.

MRS. MAYO—(*dully*) Robbie's always late for things. He can't help it, Sarah.

MRS. ATKINS—(*with a snort*) Can't help it! How you do go on, Kate, findin' excuses for him! Anybody can help anything they've a mind to—as long as they've got health, and ain't rendered helpless like me—(*she adds as a pious afterthought*)—through the will of God.

MRS. MAYO—Robbie can't.

MRS. ATKINS—Can't! It do make me mad, Kate Mayo, to see folks that God gave all the use of their limbs to potterin' round and wastin' time doin' everything the wrong way— and me powerless to help and at their mercy, you might say. And it ain't that I haven't pointed the right way to 'em. I've talked to Robert thousands of times and told him how things ought to be done. You know that, Kate Mayo. But d'you s'pose he takes any notice of what I say? Or Ruth, either— my own daughter? No, they think I'm a crazy, cranky old woman, half dead a'ready, and the sooner I'm in the grave and out o' their way the better it'd suit them.

MRS. MAYO—You mustn't talk that way, Sarah. They're not as wicked as that. And you've got years and years before you.

MRS. ATKINS—You're like the rest, Kate. You don't know how near the end I am. Well, at least I can go to my eternal rest with a clear conscience. I've done all a body could do to avert ruin from this house. On their heads be it!

MRS. MAYO—(*with hopeless indifference*) Things might be worse. Robert never had any experience in farming. You can't expect him to learn in a day.

MRS. ATKINS—(*snappily*) He's had three years to learn, and he's gettin' worse 'stead of better. Not on'y your place but mine too is driftin' to rack and ruin, and I can't do nothin' to prevent.

MRS. MAYO—(*with a spark of assertiveness*) You can't say but Robbie works hard, Sarah.

MRS. ATKINS—What good's workin' hard if it don't accomplish anythin', I'd like to know?

MRS. MAYO—Robbie's had bad luck against him.

MRS. ATKINS—Say what you've a mind to, Kate, the proof of the puddin's in the eatin'; and you can't deny that things have been goin' from bad to worse ever since your husband died two years back.

MRS. MAYO—(*wiping tears from her eyes with her handkerchief*) It was God's will that he should be taken.

MRS. ATKINS—(*triumphantly*) It was God's punishment on James Mayo for the blasphemin' and denyin' of God he done all his sinful life! (*Mrs. Mayo begins to weep softly.*) There, Kate, I shouldn't be remindin' you, I know. He's at peace, poor man, and forgiven, let's pray.

MRS. MAYO—(*wiping her eyes—simply*) James was a good man.

MRS. ATKINS—(*ignoring this remark*) What I was sayin' was that since Robert's been in charge things've been goin' down hill steady. You don't know *how* bad they are. Robert don't let on to you what's happenin'; and you'd never see it yourself if 'twas under your nose. But, thank the Lord, Ruth still comes to me once in a while for advice when she's worried near out of her senses by his goin's-on. Do you know what she told me last night? But I forgot, she said not to tell you—still I think you've got a right to know, and it's my duty not to let such things go on behind your back.

MRS. MAYO—(*wearily*) You can tell me if you want to.

MRS. ATKINS—(*bending over toward her—in a low voice*) Ruth was almost crazy about it. Robert told her he'd have to mortgage the farm—said he didn't know how he'd pull through 'til harvest without it, and he can't get money any other way. (*She straightens up—indignantly*) Now what do you think of your Robert?

MRS. MAYO—(*resignedly*) If it has to be—

MRS. ATKINS—You don't mean to say you're goin' to sign away your farm, Kate Mayo—after me warnin' you?

MRS. MAYO—I'll do what Robbie says is needful.

MRS. ATKINS—(*holding up her hands*) Well, of all the foolishness!—well, it's your farm, not mine, and I've nothin' more to say.

MRS. MAYO—Maybe Robbie'll manage till Andy gets back and sees to things. It can't be long now.

MRS. ATKINS—(*with keen interest*) Ruth says Andy ought to turn up any day. When does Robert figger he'll get here?

MRS. MAYO—He says he can't calculate exactly on account o' the *Sunda* being a sail boat. Last letter he got was from England, the day they were sailing for home. That was over a month ago, and Robbie thinks they're overdue now.

MRS. ATKINS—We can give praise to God then that he'll be back in the nick o' time. He ought to be tired of travelin' and anxious to get home and settle down to work again.

MRS. MAYO—Andy *has* been working. He's head officer on Dick's boat, he wrote Robbie. You know that.

MRS. ATKINS—That foolin' on ships is all right for a spell, but he must be right sick of it by this.

MRS. MAYO—(*musingly*) I wonder if he's changed much. He used to be so fine-looking and strong. (*with a sigh*) Three years! It seems more like three hundred. (*her eyes filling—piteously*) Oh, if James could only have lived 'til he came back—and forgiven him!

MRS. ATKINS—He never would have—not James Mayo! Didn't he keep his heart hardened against him till the last in spite of all you and Robert did to soften him?

MRS. MAYO—(*with a feeble flash of anger*) Don't you dare say that! (*brokenly*) Oh, I know deep down in his heart he forgave Andy, though he was too stubborn ever to own up to it. It was that brought on his death—breaking his heart just on account of his stubborn pride. (*She wipes her eyes with her handkerchief and sobs.*)

MRS. ATKINS—(*piously*) It was the will of God. (*The whining crying of the child sounds from the kitchen. Mrs. Atkins frowns irritably.*) Drat that young one! Seems as if she cries all the time on purpose to set a body's nerves on edge.

MRS. MAYO—(*wiping her eyes*) It's the heat upsets her. Mary doesn't feel any too well these days, poor little child!

MRS. ATKINS—She gets it right from her Pa—bein' sickly all the time. You can't deny Robert was always ailin' as a child. (*She sighs heavily.*) It was a crazy mistake for them two to get married. I argyed against it at the time, but Ruth was so spelled with Robert's wild poetry notions she wouldn't listen to sense. Andy was the one would have been the match for her.

MRS. MAYO—I've often thought since it might have been better the other way. But Ruth and Robbie seem happy enough together.

MRS. ATKINS—At any rate it was God's work—and His will be done. (*The two women sit in silence for a moment. Ruth enters from the kitchen, carrying in her arms her two year old daughter, Mary, a pretty but sickly and ænemic looking child with a tear-stained face. Ruth has aged appreciably. Her face has lost its youth and freshness. There is a trace in her expression of something hard and spiteful. She sits in the rocker in front of the table and sighs wearily. She wears a gingham dress with a soiled apron tied around her waist.*)

RUTH—Land sakes, if this isn't a scorcher! That kitchen's like a furnace. Phew! (*She pushes the damp hair back from her forehead.*)

MRS. MAYO—Why didn't you call me to help with the dishes?

RUTH—(*shortly*) No. The heat in there'd kill you.

MARY—(*sees the doll under the table and struggles on her mother's lap*) Dolly, Mama! Dolly!

RUTH—(*pulling her back*) It's time for your nap. You can't play with Dolly now.

MARY—(*commencing to cry whiningly*) Dolly!

MRS. ATKINS—(*irritably*) Can't you keep that child still? Her racket's enough to split a body's ears. Put her down and let her play with the doll if it'll quiet her.

RUTH—(*lifting Mary to the floor*) There! I hope you'll be satisfied and keep still. (*Mary sits down on the floor before the table and plays with the doll in silence. Ruth glances at the place set on the table.*) It's a wonder Rob wouldn't try to get to meals on time once in a while.

MRS. MAYO—(*dully*) Something must have gone wrong again.

RUTH—(*wearily*) I s'pose so. Something's always going wrong these days, it looks like.

MRS. ATKINS—(*snappily*) It wouldn't if you possessed a bit of spunk. The idea of you permittin' him to come in to meals at all hours—and you doin' the work! I never heard of such a thin'. You're too easy goin', that's the trouble.

RUTH—Do stop your nagging at me, Ma! I'm sick of hearing you. I'll do as I please about it; and thank you for not interfering. (*She wipes her moist forehead—wearily*) Phew! It's too hot to argue. Let's talk of something pleasant. (*curiously*) Didn't I hear you speaking about Andy a while ago?

MRS. MAYO—We were wondering when he'd get home.

RUTH—(*brightening*) Rob says any day now he's liable to drop in and surprise us—him and the Captain. It'll certainly look natural to see him around the farm again.

MRS. ATKINS—Let's hope the farm'll look more natural, too, when he's had a hand at it. The way thin's are now!

RUTH—(*irritably*) Will you stop harping on that, Ma? We all know things aren't as they might be. What's the good of your complaining all the time?

MRS. ATKINS—There, Kate Mayo! Ain't that just what I told you? I can't say a word of advice to my own daughter even, she's that stubborn and self-willed.

RUTH—(*putting her hands over her ears—in exasperation*) For goodness sakes, Ma!

MRS. MAYO—(*dully*) Never mind. Andy'll fix everything when he comes.

RUTH—(*hopefully*) Oh, yes, I know he will. He always did know just the right thing ought to be done. (*with weary vexation*) It's a shame for him to come home and have to start in with things in such a topsy-turvy.

MRS. MAYO—Andy'll manage.

RUTH—(*sighing*) I s'pose it isn't Rob's fault things go wrong with him.

MRS. ATKINS—(*scornfully*) Hump! (*She fans herself nervously.*) Land o' Goshen, but it's bakin' in here! Let's go out in under the trees in back where there's a breath of fresh air.

Come, Kate. (*Mrs. Mayo gets up obediently and starts to wheel the invalid's chair toward the screen door.*) You better come too, Ruth. It'll do you good. Learn him a lesson and let him get his own dinner. Don't be such a fool.

RUTH—(*going and holding the screen door open for them—listlessly*) He wouldn't mind. He doesn't eat much. But I can't go anyway. I've got to put baby to bed.

MRS. ATKINS—Let's go, Kate. I'm boilin' in here. (*Mrs. Mayo wheels her out and off left. Ruth comes back and sits down in her chair.*)

RUTH—(*mechanically*) Come and let me take off your shoes and stockings, Mary, that's a good girl. You've got to take your nap now. (*The child continues to play as if she hadn't heard, absorbed in her doll. An eager expression comes over Ruth's tired face. She glances toward the door furtively—then gets up and goes to the desk. Her movements indicate a guilty fear of discovery. She takes a letter from a pigeon-hole and retreats swiftly to her chair with it. She opens the envelope and reads the letter with great interest, a flush of excitement coming to her cheeks. Robert walks up the path and opens the screen door quietly and comes into the room. He, too, has aged. His shoulders are stooped as if under too great a burden. His eyes are dull and lifeless, his face burned by the sun and unshaven for days. Streaks of sweat have smudged the layer of dust on his cheeks. His lips drawn down at the corners, give him a hopeless, resigned expression. The three years have accentuated the weakness of his mouth and chin. He is dressed in overalls, laced boots, and a flannel shirt open at the neck.*)

ROBERT—(*throwing his hat over on the sofa—with a great sigh of exhaustion*) Phew! The sun's hot today! (*Ruth is startled. At first she makes an instinctive motion as if to hide the letter in her bosom. She immediately thinks better of this and sits with the letter in her hands looking at him with defiant eyes. He bends down and kisses her.*)

RUTH—(*feeling of her cheek—irritably*) Why don't you shave? You look awful.

ROBERT—(*indifferently*) I forgot—and it's too much trouble this weather.

MARY—(*throwing aside her doll, runs to him with a happy cry*) Dada! Dada!

ROBERT—(*swinging her up above his head—lovingly*) And how's this little girl of mine this hot day, eh?

MARY—(*screeching happily*) Dada! Dada!

RUTH—(*in annoyance*) Don't do that to her! You know it's time for her nap and you'll get her all waked up; then I'll be the one that'll have to sit beside her till she falls asleep.

ROBERT—(*sitting down in the chair on the left of table and cuddling Mary on his lap*) You needn't bother. I'll put her to bed.

RUTH—(*shortly*) You've got to get back to your work, I s'pose.

ROBERT—(*with a sigh*) Yes, I was forgetting. (*He glances at the open letter on Ruth's lap.*) Reading Andy's letter again? I should think you'd know it by heart by this time.

RUTH—(*coloring as if she'd been accused of something—defiantly*) I've got a right to read it, haven't I? He says it's meant for all of us.

ROBERT—(*with a trace of irritation*) Right? Don't be so silly. There's no question of right. I was only saying that you must know all that's in it after so many readings.

RUTH—Well, I don't. (*She puts the letter on the table and gets wearily to her feet.*) I s'pose you'll be wanting your dinner now.

ROBERT—(*listlessly*) I don't care. I'm not hungry.

RUTH—And here I been keeping it hot for you!

ROBERT—(*irritably*) Oh, all right then. Bring it in and I'll try to eat.

RUTH—I've got to get her to bed first. (*She goes to lift Mary off his lap.*) Come, dear. It's after time and you can hardly keep your eyes open now.

MARY—(*crying*) No, no! (*appealing to her father*) Dada! No!

RUTH—(*accusingly to Robert*) There! Now see what you've done! I told you not to—

ROBERT—(*shortly*) Let her alone, then. She's all right where she is. She'll fall asleep on my lap in a minute if you'll stop bothering her.

RUTH—(*hotly*) She'll not do any such thing! She's got to learn to mind me! (*shaking her finger at Mary*) You naughty child! Will you come with Mama when she tells you for your own good?

MARY—(*clinging to her father*) No, Dada!

RUTH—(*losing her temper*) A good spanking's what you need, my young lady—and you'll get one from me if you don't mind better, d'you hear? (*Mary starts to whimper frightenedly.*)

ROBERT—(*with sudden anger*) Leave her alone! How often have I told you not to threaten her with whipping? I won't have it. (*soothing the wailing Mary*) There! There, little girl! Baby mustn't cry. Dada won't like you if you do. Dada'll hold you and you must promise to go to sleep like a good little girl. Will you when Dada asks you?

MARY—(*cuddling up to him*) Yes, Dada.

RUTH—(*looking at them, her pale face set and drawn*) A fine one you are to be telling folks how to do things! (*She bites her lips. Husband and wife look into each other's eyes with something akin to hatred in their expressions; then Ruth turns away with a shrug of affected indifference.*) All right, take care of her then, if you think it's so easy. (*She walks away into the kitchen.*)

ROBERT—(*smoothing Mary's hair—tenderly*) We'll show Mama you're a good little girl, won't we?

MARY—(*crooning drowsily*) Dada, Dada.

ROBERT—Let's see: Does your mother take off your shoes and stockings before your nap?

MARY—(*nodding with half-shut eyes*) Yes, Dada.

ROBERT—(*taking off her shoes and stockings*) We'll show Mama we know how to do those things, won't we? There's one old shoe off—and there's the other old shoe—and here's one old stocking—and there's the other old stocking. There we are, all nice and cool and comfy. (*He bends down and kisses her.*) And now will you promise to go right to sleep if Dada takes you to bed? (*Mary nods sleepily.*) That's the good little girl. (*He gathers her up in his arms carefully and carries her into the bedroom. His voice can be heard faintly as he lulls the child to sleep. Ruth comes out of the kitchen and gets the plate from the table. She hears the voice from the room and tiptoes to the door to look in. Then she starts for the kitchen but stands for a moment thinking, a look of ill-concealed jealousy on her face. At a noise from inside she hurriedly disappears into the kitchen. A moment later Robert re-enters. He comes forward and picks up the shoes and stockings which he shoves carelessly under the table. Then, seeing no one about, he goes to the sideboard and selects a book. Coming back to his chair, he sits down and immediately becomes absorbed in reading. Ruth returns from the kitchen bringing his plate heaped with food, and a cup of tea. She sets those before him and sits down in her former place. Robert continues to read, oblivious to the food on the table.)*

RUTH—*(after watching him irritably for a moment)* For heaven's sakes, put down that old book! Don't you see your dinner's getting cold?

ROBERT—*(closing his book)* Excuse me, Ruth. I didn't notice. *(He picks up his knife and fork and begins to eat gingerly, without appetite.)*

RUTH—I should think you might have some feeling for me, Rob, and not always be late for meals. If you think it's fun sweltering in that oven of a kitchen to keep things warm for you, you're mistaken.

ROBERT—I'm sorry, Ruth, really I am. Something crops up every day to delay me. I mean to be here on time.

RUTH—*(with a sigh)* Mean-tos don't count.

ROBERT—*(with a conciliating smile)* Then punish me, Ruth. Let the food get cold and don't bother about me.

RUTH—I'd have to wait just the same to wash up after you.

ROBERT—But I can wash up.

RUTH—A nice mess there'd be then!

ROBERT—*(with an attempt at lightness)* The food is lucky to be able to get cold this weather. *(As Ruth doesn't answer or smile he opens his book and resumes his reading, forcing himself to take a mouthful of food every now and then. Ruth stares at him in annoyance.)*

RUTH—And besides, you've got your own work that's got to be done.

ROBERT—*(absent-mindedly, without taking his eyes from the book)* Yes, of course.

RUTH—*(spitefully)* Work you'll never get done by reading books all the time.

ROBERT—*(shutting the book with a snap)* Why do you persist in nagging at me for getting pleasure out of reading? Is it because— *(He checks himself abruptly.)*

RUTH—(*coloring*) Because I'm too stupid to understand them, I s'pose you were going to say.

ROBERT—(*shame-facedly*) No—no. (*in exasperation*) Why do you goad me into saying things I don't mean? Haven't I got my share of troubles trying to work this cursed farm without your adding to them? You know how hard I've tried to keep things going in spite of bad luck—

RUTH—(*scornfully*) Bad luck!

ROBERT—And my own very apparent unfitness for the job, I was going to add; but you can't deny there's been bad luck to it, too. Why don't you take things into consideration? Why can't we pull together? We used to. I know it's hard on you also. Then why can't we help each other instead of hindering?

RUTH—(*sullenly*) I do the best I know how.

ROBERT—(*gets up and puts his hand on her shoulder*) I know you do. But let's both of us try to do better. We can both improve. Say a word of encouragement once in a while when things go wrong, even if it is my fault. You know the odds I've been up against since Pa died. I'm not a farmer. I've never claimed to be one. But there's nothing else I can do under the circumstances, and I've got to pull things through somehow. With your help, I can do it. With you against me— (*He shrugs his shoulders. There is a pause. Then he bends down and kisses her hair—with an attempt at cheerfulness*) So you promise that; and I'll promise to be here when the clock strikes—and anything else you tell me to. Is it a bargain?

RUTH—(*dully*) I s'pose so. (*They are interrupted by the sound of a loud knock at the kitchen door.*) There's someone at the kitchen door. (*She hurries out. A moment later she reappears.*) It's Ben.

ROBERT—(*frowning*) What's the trouble now, I wonder? (*in a loud voice*) Come on in here, Ben. (*Ben slouches in from the kitchen. He is a hulking, awkward young fellow with a heavy, stupid face and shifty, cunning eyes. He is dressed in overalls, boots, etc., and wears a broad-brimmed hat of coarse straw pushed back on his head.*) Well, Ben, what's the matter?

BEN—(*drawlingly*) The mowin' machine's bust.

ROBERT—Why, that can't be. The man fixed it only last week.

BEN—It's bust just the same.

ROBERT—And can't you fix it?

BEN—No. Don't know what's the matter with the goll-darned thing. 'Twon't work, anyhow.

ROBERT—(*getting up and going for his hat*) Wait a minute and I'll go look it over. There can't be much the matter with it.

BEN—(*impudently*) Don't make no diff'rence t' me whether there be or not. I'm quittin'.

ROBERT—(*anxiously*) You don't mean you're throwing up your job here?

BEN—That's what! My month's up today and I want what's owin' t' me.

ROBERT—But why are you quitting now, Ben, when you know I've so much work on hand? I'll have a hard time getting another man at such short notice.

BEN—That's for you to figger. I'm quittin'.

ROBERT—But what's your reason? You haven't any complaint to make about the way you've been treated, have you?

BEN—No. 'Tain't that. (*shaking his finger*) Look-a-here. I'm sick o' being made fun at, that's what; an' I got a job up to Timms' place; an' I'm quittin' here.

ROBERT—Being made fun of? I don't understand you. Who's making fun of you?

BEN—They all do. When I drive down with the milk in the mornin' they all laughs and jokes at me—that boy up to Harris' and the new feller up to Slocum's, and Bill Evans down to Meade's, and all the rest on 'em.

ROBERT—That's a queer reason for leaving me flat. Won't they laugh at you just the same when you're working for Timms?

BEN—They wouldn't dare to. Timms is the best farm here-abouts. They was laughin' at me for workin' for *you*, that's what! "How're things up to the Mayo place?" they hollers every mornin'. "What's Robert doin' now—pasturin' the cattle in the cornlot? Is he seasonin' his hay with rain this year, same as last?" they shouts. "Or is he inventin' some 'lectrical milkin' engine to fool them dry cows o' his into givin' hard cider?" (*very much ruffled*) That's like they talks; and I ain't goin' to put up with it no longer. Everyone's always knowed me as a first-class hand hereabouts, and I ain't wantin' 'em to get no different notion. So I'm quittin' you. And I wants what's comin' to me.

ROBERT—(*coldly*) Oh, if that's the case, you can go to the devil. You'll get your money tomorrow when I get back from town—not before!

BEN—(*turning to doorway to kitchen*) That suits me. (*As he goes out he speaks back over his shoulder.*) And see that I do get it, or there'll be trouble. (*He disappears and the slamming of the kitchen door is heard.*)

ROBERT—(*as Ruth comes from where she has been standing by the doorway and sits down dejectedly in her old place*) The stupid damn fool! And now what about the haying? That's an example of what I'm up against. No one can say I'm responsible for that.

RUTH—He wouldn't dare act that way with anyone else! (*spitefully, with a glance at Andrew's letter on the table*) It's lucky Andy's coming back.

ROBERT—(*without resentment*) Yes, Andy'll see the right thing to do in a jiffy. (*with an affectionate smile*) I wonder if the old chump's changed much? He doesn't seem to from his letters, does he? (*shaking his head*) But just the same I doubt if he'll want to settle down to a hum-drum farm life, after all he's been through.

RUTH—(*resentfully*) Andy's not like you. He likes the farm.

ROBERT—(*immersed in his own thoughts—enthusiastically*) Gad, the things he's seen and experienced! Think of the places he's been! All the wonderful far places I used to dream about! God, how I envy him! What a trip! (*He springs to his feet and instinctively goes to the window and stares out at the horizon.*)

RUTH—(*bitterly*) I s'pose you're sorry now you didn't go?

ROBERT—(*too occupied with his own thoughts to hear her—vindictively*) Oh, those cursed hills out there that I used to think promised me so much! How I've grown to hate the sight of them! They're like the walls of a narrow prison yard shutting me in from all the freedom and wonder of life! (*He turns back to the room with a gesture of loathing.*) Sometimes I think if it wasn't for you, Ruth, and—(*his voice softening*) —little Mary, I'd chuck everything up and walk down the road with just one desire in my heart—to put the whole rim of the world between me and those hills, and be able to breathe freely once more! (*He sinks down into his chair and smiles with bitter self-scorn.*) There I go dreaming again—my old fool dreams.

RUTH—(*in a low, repressed voice—her eyes smoldering*) You're not the only one!

ROBERT—(*buried in his own thoughts—bitterly*) And Andy, who's had the chance—what has he got out of it? His letters read like the diary of a—of a farmer! "We're in Singapore now. It's a dirty hole of a place and hotter than hell. Two of the crew are down with fever and we're short-handed on the work. I'll be damn glad when we sail again, although tacking back and forth in these blistering seas is a rotten job too!" (*scornfully*) That's about the way he summed up his impressions of the East.

RUTH—(*her repressed voice trembling*) You needn't make fun of Andy.

ROBERT—When I think—but what's the use? You know I wasn't making fun of Andy personally, but his attitude toward things is—

RUTH—(*her eyes flashing—bursting into uncontrollable rage*) You was too making fun of him! And I ain't going to stand for it! You ought to be ashamed of yourself! (*Robert stares at her in amazement. She continues furiously*) A fine one to talk about anyone else—after the way you've ruined everything with your lazy loafing!—and the stupid way you do things!

ROBERT—(*angrily*) Stop that kind of talk, do you hear?

RUTH—You findin' fault—with your own brother who's ten times the man you ever was or ever will be! You're jealous, that's what! Jealous because he's made a man of himself, while you're nothing but a—but a— (*She stutters incoherently, overcome by rage.*)

ROBERT—Ruth! Ruth! You'll be sorry for talking like that.

RUTH—I won't! I won't never be sorry! I'm only saying what I've been thinking for years.

ROBERT—(*aghast*) Ruth! You can't mean that!

RUTH—What do you think—living with a man like you—having to suffer all the time because you've never been man enough to work and do things like other people. But no! You

never own up to that. You think you're so much better than
other folks, with your college education, where you never
learned a thing, and always reading your stupid books instead
of working. I s'pose you think I ought to be *proud* to be your
wife—a poor, ignorant thing like me! (*fiercely*) But I'm not.
I hate it! I hate the sight of you. Oh, if I'd only known! If I
hadn't been such a fool to listen to your cheap, silly, poetry
talk that you learned out of books! If I could have seen how
you were in your true self—like you are now—I'd have killed
myself before I'd have married you! I was sorry for it before
we'd been together a month. I knew what you were really
like—when it was too late.

ROBERT—(*his voice raised loudly*) And now—I'm finding
out what you're really like—what a—a creature I've been
living with. (*with a harsh laugh*) God! It wasn't that I haven't
guessed how mean and small you are—but I've kept on
telling myself that I must be wrong—like a fool!—like a
damned fool!

RUTH—You were saying you'd go out on the road if it
wasn't for me. Well, you can go, and the sooner the better! I
don't care! I'll be glad to get rid of you! The farm'll be better
off too. There's been a curse on it ever since you took hold.
So go! Go and be a tramp like you've always wanted. It's all
you're good for. I can get along without you, don't you
worry. (*exulting fiercely*) Andy's coming back, don't forget
that! He'll attend to things like they should be. He'll show
what a man can do! I don't need you. Andy's coming!

ROBERT—(*They are both standing. Robert grabs her by the
shoulders and glares into her eyes.*) What do you mean? (*He
shakes her violently.*) What are you thinking of? What's in your
evil mind, you—you— (*His voice is a harsh shout.*)

RUTH—(*in a defiant scream*) Yes I do mean it! I'd say it if
you was to kill me! I do love Andy. I do! I do! I always loved
him. (*exultantly*) And he loves me! He loves me! I know he
does. He always did! And you know he did, too! So go! Go
if you want to!

ROBERT—(*throwing her away from him. She staggers back
against the table—thickly*) You—you slut! (*He stands glaring
at her as she leans back, supporting herself by the table, gasping
for breath. A loud frightened whimper sounds from the awakened

*child in the bedroom. It continues. The man and woman stand
looking at one another in horror, the extent of their terrible quarrel suddenly brought home to them. A pause. The noise of a horse
and carriage comes from the road before the house. The two, suddenly struck by the same premonition, listen to it breathlessly, as to
a sound heard in a dream. It stops. They hear Andy's voice from
the road shouting a long hail*—"Ahoy there!")

RUTH—(*with a strangled cry of joy*) Andy! Andy! (*She rushes
and grabs the knob of the screen door, about to fling it open.*)

ROBERT—(*in a voice of command that forces obedience*) Stop!
(*He goes to the door and gently pushes the trembling Ruth away
from it. The child's crying rises to a louder pitch.*) I'll meet Andy.
You better go in to Mary, Ruth. (*She looks at him defiantly for
a moment, but there is something in his eyes that makes her turn
and walk slowly into the bedroom.*)

ANDY'S VOICE—(*in a louder shout*) Ahoy there, Rob!

ROBERT—(*in an answering shout of forced cheeriness*) Hello,
Andy! (*He opens the door and walks out as*

The Curtain Falls)

SCENE TWO

*The top of a hill on the farm. It is about eleven o'clock the next
morning. The day is hot and cloudless. In the distance the sea can
be seen.*

*The top of the hill slopes downward slightly toward the left. A
big boulder stands in the center toward the rear. Further right, a
large oak tree. The faint trace of a path leading upward to it from
the left foreground can be detected through the bleached, sun-
scorched grass.*

*Robert is discovered sitting on the boulder, his chin resting on
his hands, staring out toward the horizon seaward. His face is pale
and haggard, his expression one of utter despondency. Mary is
sitting on the grass near him in the shade, playing with her doll,
singing happily to herself. Presently she casts a curious glance at
her father, and, propping her doll up against the tree, comes over
and clambers to his side.*

MARY—(*pulling at his hand—solicitously*) Dada sick?

ROBERT—(*looking at her with a forced smile*) No, dear. Why?

MARY—Play wif Mary.

ROBERT—(*gently*) No, dear, not today. Dada doesn't feel like playing today.

MARY—(*protestingly*) Yes, Dada!

ROBERT—No, dear. Dada does feel sick—a little. He's got a bad headache.

MARY—Mary see. (*He bends his head. She pats his hair.*) Bad head.

ROBERT—(*kissing her—with a smile*) There! It's better now, dear, thank you. (*She cuddles up close against him. There is a pause during which each of them looks out seaward. Finally Robert turns to her tenderly.*) Would you like Dada to go away?—far, far away?

MARY—(*tearfully*) No! No! No, Dada, no!

ROBERT—Don't you like Uncle Andy—the man that came yesterday—not the old man with the white mustache—the other?

MARY—Mary loves Dada.

ROBERT—(*with fierce determination*) He won't go away, baby. He was only joking. He couldn't leave his little Mary. (*He presses the child in his arms.*)

MARY—(*with an exclamation of pain*) Oh! Hurt!

ROBERT—I'm sorry, little girl. (*He lifts her down to the grass.*) Go play with Dolly, that's a good girl; and be careful to keep in the shade. (*She reluctantly leaves him and takes up her doll again. A moment later she points down the hill to the left.*)

MARY—Mans, Dada.

ROBERT—(*looking that way*) It's your Uncle Andy. (*A moment later Andrew comes up from the left, whistling cheerfully. He has changed but little in appearance, except for the fact that his face has been deeply bronzed by his years in the tropics; but there is a decided change in his manner. The old easy-going good-nature seems to have been partly lost in a breezy, business-like briskness of voice and gesture. There is an authoritative note in his speech as though he were accustomed to give orders and have them obeyed as a matter of course. He is dressed in the simple blue uniform and cap of a merchant ship's officer.*)

ANDREW—Here you are, eh?

ROBERT—Hello, Andy.

ANDREW—(*going over to Mary*) And who's this young lady I find you all alone with, eh? Who's this pretty young lady? (*He tickles the laughing, squirming Mary, then lifts her up at arm's length over his head.*) Upsy—daisy! (*He sets her down on the ground again.*) And there you are! (*He walks over and sits down on the boulder beside Robert who moves to one side to make room for him.*) Ruth told me I'd probably find you up top-side here; but I'd have guessed it, anyway. (*He digs his brother in the ribs affectionately.*) Still up to your old tricks, you old beggar! I can remember how you used to come up here to mope and dream in the old days.

ROBERT—(*with a smile*) I come up here now because it's the coolest place on the farm. I've given up dreaming.

ANDREW—(*grinning*) I don't believe it. You can't have changed that much. (*after a pause—with boyish enthusiasm*) Say, it sure brings back old times to be up here with you having a chin all by our lonesomes again. I feel great being back home.

ROBERT—It's great for us to have you back.

ANDREW—(*after a pause—meaningly*) I've been looking over the old place with Ruth. Things don't seem to be—

ROBERT—(*his face flushing—interrupts his brother shortly*) Never mind the damn farm! Let's talk about something interesting. This is the first chance I've had to have a word with you alone. Tell me about your trip.

ANDREW—Why, I thought I told you everything in my letters.

ROBERT—(*smiling*) Your letters were—sketchy, to say the least.

ANDREW—Oh, I know I'm no author. You needn't be afraid of hurting my feelings. I'd rather go through a typhoon again than write a letter.

ROBERT—(*with eager interest*) Then you were through a typhoon?

ANDREW—Yes—in the China sea. Had to run before it under bare poles for two days. I thought we were bound down for Davy Jones, sure. Never dreamed waves could get so big or the wind blow so hard. If it hadn't been for Uncle Dick being such a good skipper we'd have gone to the sharks, all of us. As it was we came out minus a main top-mast and had to beat back to Hong-Kong for repairs. But I must have written you all this.

ROBERT—You never mentioned it.

ANDREW—Well, there was so much dirty work getting things ship-shape again I must have forgotten about it.

ROBERT—(*looking at Andrew—marveling*) Forget a typhoon? (*with a trace of scorn*) You're a strange combination, Andy. And is what you've told me all you remember about it?

ANDREW—Oh, I could give you your bellyful of details if I wanted to turn loose on you. It was all-wool-and-a-yard-wide-Hell, I'll tell you. You ought to have been there. I remember thinking about you at the worst of it, and saying to myself: "This'd cure Rob of them ideas of his about the beautiful sea, if he could see it." And it would have too, you bet! (*He nods emphatically.*)

ROBERT—(*dryly*) The sea doesn't seem to have impressed you very favorably.

ANDREW—I should say it didn't! I'll never set foot on a ship again if I can help it—except to carry me some place I can't get to by train.

ROBERT—But you studied to become an officer!

ANDREW—Had to do something or I'd gone mad. The days were like years. (*He laughs.*) And as for the East you used to rave about—well, you ought to see it, and *smell* it! One walk down one of their filthy narrow streets with the tropic sun beating on it would sicken you for life with the "wonder and mystery" you used to dream of.

ROBERT—(*shrinking from his brother with a glance of aversion*) So all you found in the East was a stench?

ANDREW—*A* stench! Ten thousand of them!

ROBERT—But you did like some of the places, judging from your letters—Sydney, Buenos Aires—

ANDREW—Yes, Sydney's a good town. (*enthusiastically*) But Buenos Aires—there's the place for you. Argentine's a country where a fellow has a chance to make good. You're right I like it. And I'll tell you, Rob, that's right where I'm going just as soon as I've seen you folks a while and can get a ship. I can get a berth as second officer, and I'll jump the ship when I get there. I'll need every cent of the wages Uncle's paid me to get a start at something in B. A.

ROBERT—(*staring at his brother—slowly*) So you're not going to stay on the farm?

ANDREW—Why sure not! Did you think I was? There wouldn't be any sense. One of us is enough to run this little place.

ROBERT—I suppose it does seem small to you now.

ANDREW—(*not noticing the sarcasm in Robert's tone*) You've no idea, Rob, what a splendid place Argentine is. I had a letter from a marine insurance chap that I'd made friends with in Hong-Kong to his brother, who's in the grain business in Buenos Aires. He took quite a fancy to me, and what's more important, he offered me a job if I'd come back there. I'd have taken it on the spot, only I couldn't leave Uncle Dick in the lurch, and I'd promised you folks to come home. But I'm going back there, you bet, and then you watch me get on! (*He slaps Robert on the back.*) But don't you think it's a big chance, Rob?

ROBERT—It's fine—for you, Andy.

ANDREW—We call this a farm—but you ought to hear about the farms down there—ten square miles where we've got an acre. It's a new country where big things are opening up—and I want to get in on something big before I die. I'm no fool when it comes to farming, and I know something about grain. I've been reading up a lot on it, too, lately. (*He notices Robert's absent-minded expression and laughs.*) Wake up, you old poetry book worm, you! I know my talking about business makes you want to choke me, doesn't it?

ROBERT—(*with an embarrassed smile*) No, Andy, I—I just happened to think of something else. (*frowning*) There've been lots of times lately that I've wished I had some of your faculty for business.

ANDREW—(*soberly*) There's something I want to talk about, Rob,—the farm. You don't mind, do you?

ROBERT—No.

ANDREW—I walked over it this morning with Ruth—and she told me about things— (*evasively*) I could see the place had run down; but you mustn't blame yourself. When luck's against anyone—

ROBERT—Don't, Andy! It *is* my fault. You know it as well as I do. The best I've ever done was to make ends meet.

ANDREW—(*after a pause*) I've got over a thousand saved, and you can have that.

ROBERT—(*firmly*) No. You need that for your start in Buenos Aires.

ANDREW—I don't. I can—

ROBERT—(*determinedly*) No, Andy! Once and for all, no! I won't hear of it!

ANDREW—(*protestingly*) You obstinate old son of a gun!

ROBERT—Oh, everything'll be on a sound footing after harvest. Don't worry about it.

ANDREW—(*doubtfully*) Maybe. (*after a pause*) It's too bad Pa couldn't have lived to see things through. (*with feeling*) It cut me up a lot—hearing he was dead. He never—softened up, did he—about me, I mean?

ROBERT—He never understood, that's a kinder way of putting it. He does now.

ANDREW—(*after a pause*) You've forgotten all about what—caused me to go, haven't you, Rob? (*Robert nods but keeps his face averted.*) I was a slushier damn fool in those days than you were. But it was an act of Providence I did go. It opened my eyes to how I'd been fooling myself. Why, I'd forgotten all about—that—before I'd been at sea six months.

ROBERT—(*turns and looks into Andrew's eyes searchingly*) You're speaking of—Ruth?

ANDREW—(*confused*) Yes. I didn't want you to get false notions in your head, or I wouldn't say anything. (*looking Robert squarely in the eyes*) I'm telling you the truth when I say I'd forgotten long ago. It don't sound well for me, getting over things so easy, but I guess it never really amounted to more than a kid idea I was letting rule me. I'm certain now I never was in love—I was getting fun out of thinking I was— and being a hero to myself. (*He heaves a great sigh of relief.*) There! Gosh, I'm glad that's off my chest. I've been feeling sort of awkward ever since I've been home, thinking of what you two might think. (*a trace of appeal in his voice*) You've got it all straight now, haven't you, Rob?

ROBERT—(*in a low voice*) Yes, Andy.

ANDREW—And I'll tell Ruth, too, if I can get up the

nerve. She must feel kind of funny having me round—after what used to be—and not knowing how I feel about it.

ROBERT—(*slowly*) Perhaps—for her sake—you'd better not tell her.

ANDREW—For her sake? Oh, you mean she wouldn't want to be reminded of my foolishness? Still, I think it'd be worse if—

ROBERT—(*breaking out—in an agonized voice*) Do as you please, Andy; but for God's sake, let's not talk about it! (*There is a pause. Andrew stares at Robert in hurt stupefaction. Robert continues after a moment in a voice which he vainly attempts to keep calm.*) Excuse me, Andy. This rotten headache has my nerves shot to pieces.

ANDREW—(*mumbling*) It's all right, Rob—long as you're not sore at me.

ROBERT—Where did Uncle Dick disappear to this morning?

ANDREW—He went down to the port to see to things on the *Sunda*. He said he didn't know exactly when he'd be back. I'll have to go down and tend to the ship when he comes. That's why I dressed up in these togs.

MARY—(*pointing down the hill to the left*) See! Mama! Mama! (*She struggles to her feet. Ruth appears at left. She is dressed in white, shows she has been fixing up. She looks pretty, flushed and full of life.*)

MARY—(*running to her mother*) Mama!

RUTH—(*kissing her*) Hello, dear! (*She walks toward the rock and addresses Robert coldly.*) Jake wants to see you about something. He finished working where he was. He's waiting for you at the road.

ROBERT—(*getting up—wearily*) I'll go down right away. (*As he looks at Ruth, noting her changed appearance, his face darkens with pain.*)

RUTH—And take Mary with you, please. (*to Mary*) Go with Dada, that's a good girl. Grandma has your dinner most ready for you.

ROBERT—(*shortly*) Come, Mary!

MARY—(*taking his hand and dancing happily beside him*) Dada! Dada! (*They go down the hill to the left.*)

RUTH—(*Looks after them for a moment, frowning—then turns to Andy with a smile.*) I'm going to sit down. Come on, Andy.

It'll be like old times. (*She jumps lightly to the top of the rock and sits down.*) It's so fine and cool up here after the house.

ANDREW—(*half-sitting on the side of the boulder*) Yes. It's great.

RUTH—I've taken a holiday in honor of your arrival. (*laughing excitedly*) I feel so free I'd like to have wings and fly over the sea. You're a man. You can't know how awful and stupid it is—cooking and washing dishes all the time.

ANDREW—(*making a wry face*) I can guess.

RUTH—Besides, your mother just insisted on getting your first dinner to home, she's that happy at having you back. You'd think I was planning to poison you the flurried way she shooed me out of the kitchen.

ANDREW—That's just like Ma, bless her!

RUTH—She's missed you terrible. We all have. And you can't deny the farm has, after what I showed you and told you when we was looking over the place this morning.

ANDREW—(*with a frown*) Things are run down, that's a fact! It's too darn hard on poor old Rob.

RUTH—(*scornfully*) It's his own fault. He never takes any interest in things.

ANDREW—(*reprovingly*) You can't blame him. He wasn't born for it; but I know he's done his best for your sake and the old folks and the little girl.

RUTH—(*indifferently*) Yes, I suppose he has. (*gayly*) But thank the Lord, all those days are over now. The "hard luck" Rob's always blaming won't last long when you take hold, Andy. All the farm's ever needed was someone with the knack of looking ahead and preparing for what's going to happen.

ANDREW—Yes, Rob hasn't got that. He's frank to own up to that himself. I'm going to try and hire a good man for him—an experienced farmer—to work the place on a salary and percentage. That'll take it off of Rob's hands, and he needn't be worrying himself to death any more. He looks all worn out, Ruth. He ought to be careful.

RUTH—(*absent-mindedly*) Yes. I s'pose. (*Her mind is filled with premonitions by the first part of his statement.*) Why do you want to hire a man to oversee things? Seems as if now that you're back it wouldn't be needful.

ANDREW—Oh, of course I'll attend to everything while I'm here. I mean after I'm gone.

RUTH—(*as if she couldn't believe her ears*) Gone!

ANDREW—Yes. When I leave for the Argentine again.

RUTH—(*aghast*) You're going away to sea!

ANDREW—Not to sea, no; I'm through with the sea for good as a job. I'm going down to Buenos Aires to get in the grain business.

RUTH—But—that's far off—isn't it?

ANDREW—(*easily*) Six thousand miles more or less. It's quite a trip. (*with enthusiasm*) I've got a peach of a chance down there, Ruth. Ask Rob if I haven't. I've just been telling him all about it.

RUTH—(*a flush of anger coming over her face*) And didn't he try to stop you from going?

ANDREW—(*in surprise*) No, of course not. Why?

RUTH—(*slowly and vindictively*) That's just like him—not to.

ANDREW—(*resentfully*) Rob's too good a chum to try and stop me when he knows I'm set on a thing. And he could see just as soon's I told him what a good chance it was.

RUTH—(*dazedly*) And you're bound on going?

ANDREW—Sure thing. Oh, I don't mean right off. I'll have to wait for a ship sailing there for quite a while, likely. Anyway, I want to stay to home and visit with you folks a spell before I go.

RUTH—(*dumbly*) I s'pose. (*with sudden anguish*) Oh, Andy, you can't go! You can't. Why we've all thought—we've all been hoping and praying you was coming home to stay, to settle down on the farm and see to things. You mustn't go! Think of how your Ma'll take on if you go—and how the farm'll be ruined if you leave it to Rob to look after. You can see that.

ANDREW—(*frowning*) Rob hasn't done so bad. When I get a man to direct things the farm'll be safe enough.

RUTH—(*insistently*) But your Ma—think of her.

ANDREW—She's used to me being away. She won't object when she knows it's best for her and all of us for me to go. You ask Rob. In a couple of years down there I'll make my pile, see if I don't; and then I'll come back and settle down and turn this farm into the crackiest place in the whole state. In the meantime, I can help you both from down there. (*earnestly*) I tell you, Ruth, I'm going to make good right from the minute I land, if working hard and a determination to get on can do it; and I *know* they can! (*excitedly—in a rather boastful tone*) I tell you, I feel ripe for bigger things than settling down here. The trip did that for me, anyway. It showed me the world is a larger proposition than ever I thought it was in the old days. I couldn't be content any more stuck here like a fly in molasses. It all seems trifling, somehow. You ought to be able to understand what I feel.

RUTH—(*dully*) Yes—I s'pose I ought. (*after a pause—a sudden suspicion forming in her mind*) What did Rob tell you—about me?

ANDREW—Tell? About you? Why, nothing.

RUTH—(*staring at him intensely*) Are you telling me the truth, Andy Mayo? Didn't he say—I— (*She stops confusedly.*)

ANDREW—(*surprised*) No, he didn't mention you, I can remember. Why? What made you think he did?

RUTH—(*wringing her hands*) Oh, I wish I could tell if you're lying or not!

ANDREW—(*indignantly*) What're you talking about? I didn't used to lie to you, did I? And what in the name of God is there to lie for?

RUTH—(*still unconvinced*) Are you sure—will you swear—it isn't the reason— (*She lowers her eyes and half turns away from him.*) The same reason that made you go last time that's driving you away again? 'Cause if it is—I was going to say—you mustn't go—on that account. (*Her voice sinks to a tremulous, tender whisper as she finishes.*)

ANDREW—(*confused—forces a laugh*) Oh, is *that* what you're driving at? Well, you needn't worry about that no more— (*soberly*) I don't blame you, Ruth, feeling embarrassed having me around again, after the way I played the dumb fool about going away last time.

RUTH—(*her hope crushed—with a gasp of pain*) Oh, Andy!

ANDREW—(*misunderstanding*) I know I oughtn't to talk about such foolishness to you. Still I figure it's better to get it out of my system so's we three can be together same's years ago, and not be worried thinking one of us might have the wrong notion.

RUTH—Andy! Please! Don't!

ANDREW—Let me finish now that I've started. It'll help clear things up. I don't want you to think once a fool always a fool, and be upset all the time I'm here on my fool account. I want you to believe I put all that silly nonsense back of me a long time ago—and now—it seems—well—as if you'd always been my sister, that's what, Ruth.

RUTH—(*at the end of her endurance—laughing hysterically*) For God's sake, Andy—won't you please stop talking! (*She again hides her face in her hands, her bowed shoulders trembling.*)

ANDREW—(*ruefully*) Seem's if I put my foot in it whenever I open my mouth today. Rob shut me up with almost the same words when I tried speaking to him about it.

RUTH—(*fiercely*) You told him—what you've told me?

ANDREW—(*astounded*) Why sure! Why not?

RUTH—(*shuddering*) Oh, my God!

ANDREW—(*alarmed*) Why? Shouldn't I have?

RUTH—(*hysterically*) Oh, I don't care what you do! I don't care! Leave me alone! (*Andrew gets up and walks down the hill to the left, embarrassed, hurt, and greatly puzzled by her behavior.*)

ANDREW—(*after a pause—pointing down the hill*) Hello! Here they come back—and the Captain's with them. How'd he come to get back so soon, I wonder? That means I've got to hustle down to the port and get on board. Rob's got the baby with him. (*He comes back to the boulder. Ruth keeps her face averted from him.*) Gosh, I never saw a father so tied up in a kid as Rob is! He just watches every move she makes. And I don't blame him. You both got a right to feel proud of her. She's surely a little winner. (*He glances at Ruth to see if this very obvious attempt to get back in her good graces is having any effect.*) I can see the likeness to Rob standing out all over her, can't you? But there's no denying she's your young one, either. There's something about her eyes—

RUTH—(*piteously*) Oh, Andy, I've a headache! I don't want to talk! Leave me alone, won't you please?

ANDREW—(*stands staring at her for a moment—then walks*

away saying in a hurt tone) Everybody hereabouts seems to be on edge today. I begin to feel as if I'm not wanted around. (*He stands near the path, left, kicking at the grass with the toe of his shoe. A moment later Captain Dick Scott enters, followed by Robert carrying Mary. The Captain seems scarcely to have changed at all from the jovial, booming person he was three years before. He wears a uniform similar to Andrew's. He is puffing and breathless from his climb and mops wildly at his perspiring countenance. Robert casts a quick glance at Andrew, noticing the latter's discomfited look, and then turns his eyes on Ruth who, at their approach, has moved so her back is toward them, her chin resting on her hands as she stares out seaward.*)

MARY—Mama! Mama! (*Robert puts her down and she runs to her mother. Ruth turns and grabs her up in her arms with a sudden fierce tenderness, quickly turning away again from the others. During the following scene she keeps Mary in her arms.*)

SCOTT—(*wheezily*) Phew! I got great news for you, Andy. Let me get my wind first. Phew! God A'mighty, mountin' this damned hill is worser'n goin' aloft to the skys'l yard in a blow. I got to lay to a while. (*He sits down on the grass, mopping his face.*)

ANDREW—I didn't look for you this soon, Uncle.

SCOTT—I didn't figger it, neither; but I run across a bit o' news down to the Seamen's Home made me 'bout ship and set all sail back here to find you.

ANDREW—(*eagerly*) What is it, Uncle?

SCOTT—Passin' by the Home I thought I'd drop in an' let 'em know I'd be lackin' a mate next trip count o' your leavin'. Their man in charge o' the shippin' asked after you 'special curious. "Do you think he'd consider a berth as Second on a steamer, Captain?" he asks. I was goin' to say no when I thinks o' you wantin' to get back down south to the Plate agen; so I asks him: "What is she and where's she bound?" "She's the *El Paso*, a brand new tramp," he says, "and she's bound for Buenos Aires."

ANDREW—(*his eyes lighting up—excitedly*) Gosh, that is luck! When does she sail?

SCOTT—Tomorrow mornin'. I didn't know if you'd want to ship away agen so quick an' I told him so. "Tell him I'll hold the berth open for him until late this afternoon," he says. So there you be, an' you can make your own choice.

ANDREW—I'd like to take it. There may not be another ship for Buenos Aires with a vacancy in months. (*his eyes roving from Robert to Ruth and back again—uncertainly*) Still—damn it all—tomorrow morning *is* soon. I wish she wasn't leaving for a week or so. That'd give me a chance—it seems hard to go right away again when I've just got home. And yet it's a chance in a thousand— (*appealing to Robert*) What do you think, Rob? What would you do?

ROBERT—(*forcing a smile*) He who hesitates, you know. (*frowning*) It's a piece of good luck thrown in your way—and—I think you owe it to yourself to jump at it. But don't ask me to decide for you.

RUTH—(*turning to look at Andrew—in a tone of fierce resentment*) Yes, go, Andy! (*She turns quickly away again. There is a moment of embarrassed silence.*)

ANDREW—(*thoughtfully*) Yes, I guess I will. It'll be the best thing for all of us in the end, don't you think so, Rob? (*Robert nods but remains silent.*)

SCOTT—(*getting to his feet*) Then, that's settled.

ANDREW—(*Now that he has definitely made a decision his voice rings with hopeful strength and energy.*) Yes, I'll take the berth. The sooner I go the sooner I'll be back, that's a certainty; and I won't come back with empty hands next time. You bet I won't!

SCOTT—You ain't got so much time, Andy. To make sure you'd best leave here soon's you kin. I got to get right back aboard. You'd best come with me.

ANDREW—I'll go to the house and repack my bag right away.

ROBERT—(*quietly*) You'll both be here for dinner, won't you?

ANDREW—(*worriedly*) I don't know. Will there be time? What time is it now, I wonder?

ROBERT—(*reproachfully*) Ma's been getting dinner especially for you, Andy.

ANDREW—(*flushing—shamefacedly*) Hell! And I was forgetting! Of course I'll stay for dinner if I missed every damned ship in the world. (*He turns to the Captain—*

briskly) Come on, Uncle. Walk down with me to the house and you can tell me more about this berth on the way. I've got to pack before dinner. (*He and the Captain start down to the left. Andrew calls back over his shoulder*) You're coming soon, aren't you, Rob?

ROBERT—Yes. I'll be right down. (*Andrew and the Captain leave. Ruth puts Mary on the ground and hides her face in her hands. Her shoulders shake as if she were sobbing. Robert stares at her with a grim, somber expression. Mary walks backward toward Robert, her wondering eyes fixed on her mother.*)

MARY—(*her voice vaguely frightened, taking her father's hand*) Dada, Mama's cryin', Dada.

ROBERT—(*bending down and stroking her hair—in a voice he endeavors to keep from being harsh*) No, she isn't, little girl. The sun hurts her eyes, that's all. Aren't you beginning to feel hungry, Mary?

MARY—(*decidedly*) Yes, Dada.

ROBERT—(*meaningly*) It must be your dinner time now.

RUTH—(*in a muffled voice*) I'm coming, Mary. (*She wipes her eyes quickly and, without looking at Robert, comes and takes Mary's hand—in a dead voice*) Come on and I'll get your dinner for you. (*She walks out left, her eyes fixed on the ground, the skipping Mary tugging at her hand. Robert waits a moment for them to get ahead and then slowly follows as*

The Curtain Falls)

ACT THREE

Scene One

Same as Act Two, Scene One—The sitting room of the farm house about six o'clock in the morning of a day toward the end of October five years later. It is not yet dawn, but as the action progresses the darkness outside the windows gradually fades to gray.

The room, seen by the light of the shadeless oil lamp with a smoky chimney which stands on the table, presents an appearance of decay, of dissolution. The curtains at the windows are torn and dirty and one of them is missing. The closed desk is gray with accumulated dust as if it had not been used in years. Blotches of dampness disfigure the wall paper. Threadbare trails, leading to the kitchen and outer doors, show in the faded carpet. The top of the coverless table is stained with the imprints of hot dishes and spilt food. The rung of one rocker has been clumsily mended with a piece of plain board. A brown coating of rust covers the unblacked stove. A pile of wood is stacked up carelessly against the wall by the stove.

The whole atmosphere of the room, contrasted with that of former years, is one of an habitual poverty too hopelessly resigned to be any longer ashamed or even conscious of itself.

At the rise of the curtain Ruth is discovered sitting by the stove, with hands outstretched to the warmth as if the air in the room were damp and cold. A heavy shawl is wrapped about her shoulders, half-concealing her dress of deep mourning. She has aged horribly. Her pale, deeply lined face has the stony lack of expression of one to whom nothing more can ever happen, whose capacity for emotion has been exhausted. When she speaks her voice is without timbre, low and monotonous. The negligent disorder of her dress, the slovenly arrangement of her hair, now streaked with gray, her muddied shoes run down at the heel, give full evidence of the apathy in which she lives.

Her mother is asleep in her wheel chair beside the stove toward the rear, wrapped up in a blanket.

There is a sound from the open bedroom door in the rear as if someone were getting out of bed. Ruth turns in that direction with a look of dull annoyance. A moment later Robert appears in the doorway, leaning weakly against it for support. His hair is long and unkempt, his face and body emaciated. There are bright patches of crimson over his cheek bones and his eyes are burning with fever. He is dressed in corduroy pants, a flannel shirt, and wears worn carpet slippers on his bare feet.

RUTH—(*dully*) S-s-s-h-! Ma's asleep.

ROBERT—(*speaking with an effort*) I won't wake her. (*He walks weakly to a rocker by the side of the table and sinks down in it exhausted.*)

RUTH—(*staring at the stove*) You better come near the fire where it's warm.

ROBERT—No. I'm burning up now.

RUTH—That's the fever. You know the doctor told you not to get up and move round.

ROBERT—(*irritably*) That old fossil! He doesn't know anything. Go to bed and stay there—that's his only prescription.

RUTH—(*indifferently*) How are you feeling now?

ROBERT—(*buoyantly*) Better! Much better than I've felt in ages. Really I'm fine now—only very weak. It's the turning point, I guess. From now on I'll pick up so quick I'll surprise you—and no thanks to that old fool of a country quack, either.

RUTH—He's always tended to us.

ROBERT—Always helped us to die, you mean! He "tended" to Pa and Ma and—(*his voice breaks*)—and to—Mary.

RUTH—(*dully*) He did the best he knew, I s'pose. (*after a pause*) Well, Andy's bringing a specialist with him when he comes. That ought to suit you.

ROBERT—(*bitterly*) Is that why you're waiting up all night?

RUTH—Yes.

ROBERT—For Andy?

RUTH—(*without a trace of feeling*) Somebody had got to. It's only right for someone to meet him after he's been gone five years.

ROBERT—(*with bitter mockery*) Five years! It's a long time.

RUTH—Yes.

ROBERT—(*meaningly*) To *wait*!

RUTH—(*indifferently*) It's past now.

ROBERT—Yes, it's past. (*after a pause*) Have you got his

two telegrams with you? (*Ruth nods.*) Let me see them, will you? My head was so full of fever when they came I couldn't make head or tail to them. (*hastily*) But I'm feeling fine now. Let me read them again. (*Ruth takes them from the bosom of her dress and hands them to him.*)

RUTH—Here. The first one's on top.

ROBERT—(*opening it*) New York. "Just landed from steamer. Have important business to wind up here. Will be home as soon as deal is completed." (*He smiles bitterly.*) Business first was always Andy's motto. (*He reads*) "Hope you are all well. Andy." (*He repeats ironically*) "Hope you are all well!"

RUTH—(*dully*) He couldn't know you'd been took sick till I answered that and told him.

ROBERT—(*contritely*) Of course he couldn't. I'm a fool. I'm touchy about nothing lately. Just what did you say in your reply?

RUTH—(*inconsequentially*) I had to send it collect.

ROBERT—(*irritably*) What did you say was the matter with me?

RUTH—I wrote you had lung trouble.

ROBERT—(*flying into a petty temper*) You *are* a fool! How often have I explained to you that it's *pleurisy* is the matter with me. You can't seem to get it in your head that the pleura is outside the lungs, not in them!

RUTH—(*callously*) I only wrote what Doctor Smith told me.

ROBERT—(*angrily*) He's a damned ignoramus!

RUTH—(*dully*) Makes no difference. I had to tell Andy something, didn't I?

ROBERT—(*after a pause, opening the other telegram*) He sent this last evening. Let's see. (*He reads*) "Leave for home on midnight train. Just received your wire. Am bringing specialist to see Rob. Will motor to farm from Port." (*He calculates.*) What time is it now?

RUTH—Round six, must be.

ROBERT—He ought to be here soon. I'm glad he's bringing a doctor who knows something. A specialist will tell you in a second that there's nothing the matter with my lungs.

RUTH—(*stolidly*) You've been coughing an awful lot lately.

ROBERT—(*irritably*) What nonsense! For God's sake, haven't you ever had a bad cold yourself? (*Ruth stares at the stove in silence. Robert fidgets in his chair. There is a pause. Finally Robert's eyes are fixed on the sleeping Mrs. Atkins.*) Your mother is lucky to be able to sleep so soundly.

RUTH—Ma's tired. She's been sitting up with me most of the night.

ROBERT—(*mockingly*) Is she waiting for Andy, too? (*There is a pause. Robert sighs.*) I couldn't get to sleep to save my soul. I counted ten million sheep if I counted one. No use! I gave up trying finally and just laid there in the dark thinking. (*He pauses, then continues in a tone of tender sympathy.*) I was thinking about you, Ruth—of how hard these last years must have been for you. (*appealingly*) I'm sorry, Ruth.

RUTH—(*in a dead voice*) I don't know. They're past now. They were hard on all of us.

ROBERT—Yes; on all of us but Andy. (*with a flash of sick jealousy*) Andy's made a big success of himself—the kind he wanted. (*mockingly*) And now he's coming home to let us admire his greatness. (*frowning—irritably*) What am I talking about? My brain must be sick, too. (*after a pause*) Yes, these years have been terrible for both of us. (*His voice is lowered to a trembling whisper.*) Especially the last eight months since Mary—died. (*He forces back a sob with a convulsive shudder—then breaks out in a passionate agony*) Our last hope of happiness! I could curse God from the bottom of my soul—if there was a God! (*He is racked by a violent fit of coughing and hurriedly puts his handkerchief to his lips.*)

RUTH—(*without looking at him*) Mary's better off—being dead.

ROBERT—(*gloomily*) We'd all be better off for that matter. (*with a sudden exasperation*) You tell that mother of yours she's got to stop saying that Mary's death was due to a weak constitution inherited from me. (*on the verge of tears of weakness*) It's got to stop, I tell you!

RUTH—(*sharply*) S-h-h! You'll wake her; and then she'll nag at me—not you.

ROBERT—(*coughs and lies back in his chair weakly—a pause*) It's all because your mother's down on me for not begging Andy for help.

RUTH—(*resentfully*) You might have. He's got plenty.

ROBERT—How can *you* of all people think of taking money from *him*?

RUTH—(*dully*) I don't see the harm. He's your own brother.

ROBERT—(*shrugging his shoulders*) What's the use of talking to you? Well, *I* couldn't. (*proudly*) And I've managed to keep things going, thank God. You can't deny that without help I've succeeded in— (*He breaks off with a bitter laugh.*) My God, what am I boasting of? Debts to this one and that, taxes, interest unpaid! I'm a fool! (*He lies back in his chair closing his eyes for a moment, then speaks in a low voice.*) I'll be frank, Ruth. I've been an utter failure, and I've dragged you with me. I couldn't blame you in all justice—for hating me.

RUTH—(*without feeling*) I don't hate you. It's been my fault too, I s'pose.

ROBERT—No. You couldn't help loving—Andy.

RUTH—(*dully*) I don't love anyone.

ROBERT—(*waving her remark aside*) You needn't deny it. It doesn't matter. (*after a pause—with a tender smile*) Do you know Ruth, what I've been dreaming back there in the dark? (*with a short laugh*) I was planning our future when I get well. (*He looks at her with appealing eyes as if afraid she will sneer at him. Her expression does not change. She stares at the stove. His voice takes on a note of eagerness.*) After all, why shouldn't we have a future? We're young yet. If we can only shake off the curse of this farm! It's the farm that's ruined our lives, damn it! And now that Andy's coming back—I'm going to sink my foolish pride, Ruth! I'll borrow the money from him to give us a good start in the city. We'll go where people live instead of stagnating, and start all over again. (*confidently*) I won't be the failure there that I've been here, Ruth. You won't need to be ashamed of me there. I'll prove to you the reading I've done can be put to some use. (*vaguely*) I'll write, or something of that sort. I've always wanted to write. (*pleadingly*) You'll want to do that, won't you, Ruth?

RUTH—(*dully*) There's Ma.

ROBERT—She can come with us.

RUTH—She wouldn't.

ROBERT—(*angrily*) So that's your answer! (*He trembles*

with violent passion. His voice is so strange that Ruth turns to look at him in alarm.) You're lying, Ruth! Your mother's just an excuse. You want to stay here. You think that because Andy's coming back that— (*He chokes and has an attack of coughing.*)

RUTH—(*getting up—in a frightened voice*) What's the matter? (*She goes to him.*) I'll go with you, Rob. Stop that coughing for goodness' sake! It's awful bad for you. (*She soothes him in dull tones.*) I'll go with you to the city—soon's you're well again. Honest I will, Rob, I promise! (*Rob lies back and closes his eyes. She stands looking down at him anxiously.*) Do you feel better now?

ROBERT—Yes. (*Ruth goes back to her chair. After a pause he opens his eyes and sits up in his chair. His face is flushed and happy.*) Then you *will* go, Ruth?

RUTH—Yes.

ROBERT—(*excitedly*) We'll make a new start, Ruth—just you and I. Life owes us some happiness after what we've been through. (*vehemently*) It must! Otherwise our suffering would be meaningless—and that is unthinkable.

RUTH—(*worried by his excitement*) Yes, yes, of course, Rob, but you mustn't—

ROBERT—Oh, don't be afraid. I feel completely well, really I do—now that I can hope again. Oh if you knew how glorious it feels to have something to look forward to! Can't you feel the thrill of it, too—the vision of a new life opening up after all the horrible years?

RUTH—Yes, yes, but do be—

ROBERT—Nonsense! I won't be careful. I'm getting back all my strength. (*He gets lightly to his feet.*) See! I feel light as a feather. (*He walks to her chair and bends down to kiss her— smilingly*) One kiss—the first in years, isn't it?—to greet the dawn of a new life together.

RUTH—(*submitting to his kiss—worriedly*) Sit down, Rob, for goodness' sake!

ROBERT—(*with tender obstinacy—stroking her hair*) I won't sit down. You're silly to worry. (*He rests one hand on the back of her chair.*) Listen. All our suffering has been a test through which we had to pass to prove ourselves worthy of a finer realization. (*exultingly*) And we did pass through it! It hasn't broken us! And now the dream is to come true! Don't you see?

RUTH—(*looking at him with frightened eyes as if she thought he had gone mad*) Yes, Rob, I see; but won't you go back to bed now and rest?

ROBERT—No. I'm going to see the sun rise. It's an augury of good fortune. (*He goes quickly to the window in the rear left, and pushing the curtains aside, stands looking out. Ruth springs to her feet and comes quickly to the table, left, where she remains watching Robert in a tense, expectant attitude. As he peers out his body seems gradually to sag, to grow limp and tired. His voice is mournful as he speaks.*) No sun yet. It isn't time. All I can see is the black rim of the damned hills outlined against a creeping grayness. (*He turns around; letting the curtains fall back, stretching a hand out to the wall to support himself. His false strength of a moment has evaporated leaving his face drawn and hollow-eyed. He makes a pitiful attempt to smile.*) That's not a very happy augury, is it? But the sun'll come—soon. (*He sways weakly.*)

RUTH—(*hurrying to his side and supporting him*) Please go to bed, won't you, Rob? You don't want to be all wore out when the specialist comes, do you?

ROBERT—(*quickly*) No. That's right. He mustn't think I'm sicker than I am. And I feel as if I could sleep now—(*cheerfully*)—a good, sound, restful sleep.

RUTH—(*helping him to the bedroom door*) That's what you need most. (*They go inside. A moment later she reappears calling back*) I'll shut this door so's you'll be quiet. (*She closes the door and goes quickly to her mother and shakes her by the shoulder.*) Ma! Ma! Wake up!

MRS. ATKINS—(*coming out of her sleep with a start*) Glory be! What's the matter with you?

RUTH—It was Rob. He's just been talking to me out here. I put him back to bed. (*Now that she is sure her mother is awake her fear passes and she relapses into dull indifference. She sits down in her chair and stares at the stove—dully*) He acted—funny; and his eyes looked so—so wild like.

MRS. ATKINS—(*with asperity*) And is that all you woke me out of a sound sleep for, and scared me near out of my wits?

RUTH—I was afraid. He talked so crazy. I couldn't quiet

him. I didn't want to be alone with him that way. Lord knows what he might do.

MRS. ATKINS—(*scornfully*) Humph! A help I'd be to you and me not able to move a step! Why didn't you run and get Jake?

RUTH—(*dully*) Jake isn't here. He quit last night. He hasn't been paid in three months.

MRS. ATKINS—(*indignantly*) I can't blame him. What decent person'd want to work on a place like this? (*with sudden exasperation*) Oh, I wish you'd never married that man!

RUTH—(*wearily*) You oughtn't to talk about him now when he's sick in his bed.

MRS. ATKINS—(*working herself into a fit of rage*) You know very well, Ruth Mayo, if it wasn't for me helpin' you on the sly out of my savin's, you'd both been in the poor house— and all 'count of his pigheaded pride in not lettin' Andy know the state thin's were in. A nice thin' for me to have to support him out of what I'd saved for my last days—and me an invalid with no one to look to!

RUTH—Andy'll pay you back, Ma. I can tell him so's Rob'll never know.

MRS. ATKINS—(*with a snort*) What'd Rob think you and him was livin' on, I'd like to know?

RUTH—(*dully*) He didn't think about it, I s'pose. (*after a slight pause*) He said he'd made up his mind to ask Andy for help when he comes. (*as a clock in the kitchen strikes six*) Six o'clock. Andy ought to get here directly.

MRS. ATKINS—D'you think this special doctor'll do Rob any good?

RUTH—(*hopelessly*) I don't know. (*The two women remain silent for a time staring dejectedly at the stove.*)

MRS. ATKINS—(*shivering irritably*) For goodness' sake put some wood on that fire. I'm most freezin'!

RUTH—(*pointing to the door in the rear*) Don't talk so loud. Let him sleep if he can. (*She gets wearily from the chair and puts a few pieces of wood in the stove.*) This is the last of the wood. I don't know who'll cut more now that Jake's left. (*She sighs and walks to the window in the rear, left, pulls the curtains aside, and looks out.*) It's getting gray out. (*She comes back to the stove.*) Looks like it'd be a nice day. (*She stretches out her hands to warm them.*) Must've been a heavy frost last night. We're paying for the spell of warm weather we've been having. (*The throbbing whine of a motor sounds from the distance outside.*)

MRS. ATKINS—(*sharply*) S-h-h! Listen! Ain't that an auto I hear?

RUTH—(*without interest*) Yes. It's Andy, I s'pose.

MRS. ATKINS—(*with nervous irritation*) Don't sit there like a silly goose. Look at the state of this room! What'll this strange doctor think of us? Look at that lamp chimney all smoke! Gracious sakes, Ruth—

RUTH—(*indifferently*) I've got a lamp all cleaned up in the kitchen.

MRS. ATKINS—(*peremptorily*) Wheel me in there this minute. I don't want him to see me looking a sight. I'll lay down in the room the other side. You don't need me now and I'm dead for sleep. (*Ruth wheels her mother off right. The noise of the motor grows louder and finally ceases as the car stops on the road before the farmhouse. Ruth returns from the kitchen with a lighted lamp in her hand which she sets on the table beside the other. The sound of footsteps on the path is heard—then a sharp rap on the door. Ruth goes and opens it. Andrew enters, followed by Doctor Fawcett carrying a small black bag. Andrew has changed greatly. His face seems to have grown highstrung, hardened by the look of decisiveness which comes from being constantly under a strain where judgments on the spur of the moment are compelled to be accurate. His eyes are keener and more alert. There is even a suggestion of ruthless cunning about them. At present, however, his expression is one of tense anxiety. Doctor Fawcett is a short, dark, middle-aged man with a Vandyke beard. He wears glasses.*)

RUTH—Hello, Andy! I've been waiting—

ANDREW—(*kissing her hastily*) I got here as soon as I could. (*He throws off his cap and heavy overcoat on the table, introducing Ruth and the doctor as he does so. He is dressed in an expensive business suit and appears stouter.*) My sister-in-law, Mrs. Mayo—Doctor Fawcett. (*They bow to each other silently. Andrew casts a quick glance about the room.*) Where's Rob?

RUTH—(*pointing*) In there.

ANDREW—I'll take your coat and hat, Doctor. (*as he helps the doctor with his things*) Is he very bad, Ruth?

RUTH—(*dully*) He's been getting weaker.

ANDREW—Damn! This way, Doctor. Bring the lamp, Ruth. (*He goes into the bedroom, followed by the doctor and Ruth carrying the clean lamp. Ruth reappears almost immediately closing the door behind her, and goes slowly to the outside door, which she opens, and stands in the doorway looking out. The sound of Andrew's and Robert's voices comes from the bedroom. A moment later Andrew re-enters, closing the door softly. He comes forward and sinks down in the rocker on the right of table, leaning his head on his hand. His face is drawn in a shocked expression of great grief. He sighs heavily, staring mournfully in front of him. Ruth turns and stands watching him. Then she shuts the door and returns to her chair by the stove, turning it so she can face him.*)

ANDREW—(*glancing up quickly—in a harsh voice*) How long has this been going on?

RUTH—You mean—how long has he been sick?

ANDREW—(*shortly*) Of course! What else?

RUTH—It was last summer he had a bad spell first, but he's been ailin' ever since Mary died—eight months ago.

ANDREW—(*harshly*) Why didn't you let me know—cable me? Do you want him to die, all of you? I'm damned if it doesn't look that way! (*his voice breaking*) Poor old chap! To be sick in this out-of-the-way hole without anyone to attend to him but a country quack! It's a damned shame!

RUTH—(*dully*) I wanted to send you word once, but he only got mad when I told him. He was too proud to ask anything, he said.

ANDREW—Proud? To ask *me*? (*He jumps to his feet and paces nervously back and forth.*) I can't understand the way you've acted. Didn't you see how sick he was getting? Couldn't you realize—why, I nearly dropped in my tracks when I saw him! He looks—(*he shudders*)—terrible! (*with fierce scorn*) I suppose you're so used to the idea of his being delicate that you took his sickness as a matter of course. God, if I'd only known!

RUTH—(*without emotion*) A letter takes so long to get where you were—and we couldn't afford to telegraph. We owed everyone already, and I couldn't ask Ma. She'd been giving me money out of her savings till she hadn't much left. Don't say anything to Rob about it. I never told him. He'd only be mad at me if he knew. But I had to, because—God knows how we'd have got on if I hadn't.

ANDREW—You mean to say— (*His eyes seem to take in the poverty-stricken appearance of the room for the first time.*) You sent that telegram to me collect. Was it because— (*Ruth nods silently. Andrew pounds on the table with his fist.*) Good God! And all this time I've been—why I've had everything! (*He sits down in his chair and pulls it close to Ruth's—impulsively*) But—I can't get it through my head. Why? Why? What has happened? How did it ever come about? Tell me!

RUTH—(*dully*) There's nothing much to tell. Things kept getting worse, that's all—and Rob didn't seem to care. He never took any interest since way back when your Ma died. After that he got men to take charge, and they nearly all cheated him—he couldn't tell—and left one after another. Then after Mary died he didn't pay no heed to anything any more—just stayed indoors and took to reading books again. So I had to ask Ma if she wouldn't help us some.

ANDREW—(*surprised and horrified*) Why, damn it, this is frightful! Rob must be mad not to have let me know. Too proud to ask help of *me*! What's the matter with him in God's name? (*a sudden, horrible suspicion entering his mind*) Ruth! Tell me the truth. His mind hasn't gone back on him, has it?

RUTH—(*dully*) I don't know. Mary's dying broke him up terrible—but he's used to her being gone by this, I s'pose.

ANDREW—(*looking at her queerly*) Do you mean to say *you're* used to it?

RUTH—(*in a dead tone*) There's a time comes—when you don't mind any more—anything.

ANDREW—(*looks at her fixedly for a moment—with great pity*) I'm sorry, Ruth—if I seemed to blame you. I didn't realize— The sight of Rob lying in bed there, so gone to pieces—it made me furious at everyone. Forgive me, Ruth.

RUTH—There's nothing to forgive. It doesn't matter.

ANDREW—(*springing to his feet again and pacing up and down*) Thank God I came back before it was too late. This doctor will know exactly what to do. That's the first thing to think of. When Rob's on his feet again we can get the farm working on a sound basis once more. I'll see to that—before I leave.

RUTH—You're going away again?

ANDREW—I've got to.

RUTH—You wrote Rob you was coming back to stay this time.

ANDREW—I expected to—until I got to New York. Then I learned certain facts that make it necessary. (*with a short laugh*) To be candid, Ruth, I'm not the rich man you've probably been led to believe by my letters—not now. I was when I wrote them. I made money hand over fist as long as I stuck to legitimate trading; but I wasn't content with that. I wanted it to come easier, so like all the rest of the idiots, I tried speculation. Oh, I won all right! Several times I've been almost a millionaire—on paper—and then come down to earth again with a bump. Finally the strain was too much. I got disgusted with myself and made up my mind to get out and come home and forget it and really live again. (*He gives a harsh laugh.*) And now comes the funny part. The day before the steamer sailed I saw what I thought was a chance to become a millionaire again. (*He snaps his fingers.*) That easy! I plunged. Then, before things broke, I left—I was so confident I couldn't be wrong. But when I landed in New York—I wired you I had business to wind up, didn't I? Well, it was the business that wound me up! (*He smiles grimly, pacing up and down, his hands in his pockets.*)

RUTH—(*dully*) You found—you'd lost everything?

ANDREW—(*sitting down again*) Practically. (*He takes a cigar from his pocket, bites the end off, and lights it.*) Oh, I don't mean I'm dead broke. I've saved ten thousand from the wreckage, maybe twenty. But that's a poor showing for five years' hard work. That's why I'll have to go back. (*confidently*) I can make it up in a year or so down there—and I don't need but a shoestring to start with. (*A weary expression comes over his face and he sighs heavily.*) I wish I didn't have to. I'm sick of it all.

RUTH—It's too bad—things seem to go wrong so.

ANDREW—(*shaking off his depression—briskly*) They might be much worse. There's enough left to fix the farm O. K.

before I go. I won't leave 'til Rob's on his feet again. In the meantime I'll make things fly around here. (*with satisfaction*) I need a rest, and the kind of rest I need is hard work in the open—just like I used to do in the old days. (*stopping abruptly and lowering his voice cautiously*) Not a word to Rob about my losing money! Remember that, Ruth! You can see why. If he's grown so touchy he'd never accept a cent if he thought I was hard up; see?

RUTH—Yes, Andy. (*After a pause, during which Andrew puffs at his cigar abstractedly, his mind evidently busy with plans for the future, the bedroom door is opened and Doctor Fawcett enters, carrying a bag. He closes the door quietly behind him and comes forward, a grave expression on his face. Andrew springs out of his chair.*)

ANDREW—Ah, Doctor! (*He pushes a chair between his own and Ruth's.*) Won't you have a chair?

FAWCETT—(*glancing at his watch*) I must catch the nine o'clock back to the city. It's imperative. I have only a moment. (*sitting down and clearing his throat—in a perfunctory, impersonal voice*) The case of your brother, Mr. Mayo, is— (*He stops and glances at Ruth and says meaningly to Andrew*) Perhaps it would be better if you and I—

RUTH—(*with dogged resentment*) I know what you mean, Doctor. (*dully*) Don't be afraid I can't stand it. I'm used to bearing trouble by this; and I can guess what you've found out. (*She hesitates for a moment—then continues in a monotonous voice*) Rob's going to die.

ANDREW—(*angrily*) Ruth!

FAWCETT—(*raising his hand as if to command silence*) I am afraid my diagnosis of your brother's condition forces me to the same conclusion as Mrs. Mayo's.

ANDREW—(*groaning*) But, Doctor, surely—

FAWCETT—(*calmly*) Your brother hasn't long to live—perhaps a few days, perhaps only a few hours. It's a marvel that he's alive at this moment. My examination revealed that both of his lungs are terribly affected.

ANDREW—(*brokenly*) Good God! (*Ruth keeps her eyes fixed on her lap in a trance-like stare.*)

FAWCETT—I am sorry I have to tell you this. If there was anything that could be done—

ANDREW—There isn't anything?

FAWCETT—(*shaking his head*) It's too late. Six months ago there might have—

ANDREW—(*in anguish*) But if we were to take him to the mountains—or to Arizona—or—

FAWCETT—That might have prolonged his life six months ago. (*Andrew groans.*) But now— (*He shrugs his shoulders significantly.*)

ANDREW—(*appalled by a sudden thought*) Good heavens, you haven't told him this, have you, Doctor?

FAWCETT—No. I lied to him. I said a change of climate— (*He looks at his watch again nervously.*) I must leave you. (*He gets up.*)

ANDREW—(*getting to his feet—insistently*) But there must still be some chance—

FAWCETT—(*as if he were reassuring a child*) There is always that last chance—the miracle. (*He puts on his hat and coat—bowing to Ruth.*) Good-by, Mrs. Mayo.

RUTH—(*without raising her eyes—dully*) Good-by.

ANDREW—(*mechanically*) I'll walk to the car with you, Doctor. (*They go out of the door. Ruth sits motionlessly. The motor is heard starting and the noise gradually recedes into the distance. Andrew re-enters and sits down in his chair, holding his head in his hands.*) Ruth! (*She lifts her eyes to his.*) Hadn't we better go in and see him? God! I'm afraid to! I know he'll read it in my face. (*The bedroom door is noiselessly opened and Robert appears in the doorway. His cheeks are flushed with fever, and his eyes appear unusually large and brilliant. Andrew continues with a groan*) It can't be, Ruth. It can't be as hopeless as he said. There's always a fighting chance. We'll take Rob to Arizona. He's *got* to get well. There *must* be a chance!

ROBERT—(*in a gentle tone*) Why must there, Andy? (*Ruth turns and stares at him with terrified eyes.*)

ANDREW—(*whirling around*) Rob! (*scoldingly*) What are you doing out of bed? (*He gets up and goes to him.*) Get right back now and obey the Doc, or you're going to get a licking from me!

ROBERT—(*ignoring these remarks*) Help me over to the chair, please, Andy.

ANDREW—Like hell I will! You're going right back to bed,

that's where you're going, and stay there! (*He takes hold of Robert's arm.*)

ROBERT—(*mockingly*) Stay there 'til I die, eh, Andy? (*coldly*) Don't behave like a child. I'm sick of lying down. I'll be more rested sitting up. (*as Andrew hesitates—violently*) I swear I'll get out of bed every time you put me there. You'll have to sit on my chest, and that wouldn't help my health any. Come on, Andy. Don't play the fool. I want to talk to you, and I'm going to. (*with a grim smile*) A dying man has some rights, hasn't he?

ANDREW—(*with a shudder*) Don't talk that way, for God's sake! I'll only let you sit down if you'll promise that. Remember. (*He helps Robert to the chair between his own and Ruth's.*) Easy now! There you are! Wait, and I'll get a pillow for you. (*He goes into the bedroom. Robert looks at Ruth who shrinks away from him in terror. Robert smiles bitterly. Andrew comes back with the pillow which he places behind Robert's back.*) How's that?

ROBERT—(*with an affectionate smile*) Fine! Thank you! (*as Andrew sits down*) Listen, Andy. You've asked me not to talk—and I won't after I've made my position clear. (*slowly*) In the first place I know I'm dying. (*Ruth bows her head and covers her face with her hands. She remains like this all during the scene between the two brothers.*)

ANDREW—Rob! That isn't so!

ROBERT—(*wearily*) It *is* so! Don't lie to me. After Ruth put me to bed before you came, I saw it clearly for the first time. (*bitterly*) I'd been making plans for our future—Ruth's and mine—so it came hard at first—the realization. Then when the doctor examined me, I knew—although he tried to lie about it. And then to make sure I listened at the door to what he told you. So don't mock me with fairy tales about Arizona, or any such rot as that. Because I'm dying is no reason you should treat me as an imbecile or a coward. Now that I'm sure what's happening I can say Kismet to it with all my heart. It was only the silly uncertainty that hurt. (*There is a pause. Andrew looks around in impotent anguish, not knowing what to say. Robert regards him with an affectionate smile.*)

ANDREW—(*finally blurts out*) It isn't foolish. You *have* got a chance. If you heard all the Doctor said that ought to prove it to you.

ROBERT—Oh, you mean when he spoke of the miracle? (*dryly*) I don't believe in miracles—in my case. Besides, I know more than any doctor on earth *could* know—because I *feel* what's coming. (*dismissing the subject*) But we've agreed not to talk of it. Tell me about yourself, Andy. That's what I'm interested in. Your letters were too brief and far apart to be illuminating.

ANDREW—I meant to write oftener.

ROBERT—(*with a faint trace of irony*) I judge from them you've accomplished all you set out to do five years ago?

ANDREW—That isn't much to boast of.

ROBERT—(*surprised*) Have you really, honestly reached that conclusion?

ANDREW—Well, it doesn't seem to amount to much now.

ROBERT—But you're rich, aren't you?

ANDREW—(*with a quick glance at Ruth*) Yes, I s'pose so.

ROBERT—I'm glad. You can do to the farm all I've undone. But what did you do down there? Tell me. You went in the grain business with that friend of yours?

ANDREW—Yes. After two years I had a share in it. I sold out last year. (*He is answering Robert's questions with great reluctance.*)

ROBERT—And then?

ANDREW—I went in on my own.

ROBERT—Still in grain?

ANDREW—Yes.

ROBERT—What's the matter? You look as if I were accusing you of something.

ANDREW—I'm proud enough of the first four years. It's after that I'm not boasting of. I took to speculating.

ROBERT—In wheat?

ANDREW—Yes.

ROBERT—And you made money—gambling?

ANDREW—Yes.

ROBERT—(*thoughtfully*) I've been wondering what the great change was in you. (*after a pause*) You—a farmer—to gamble in a wheat pit with scraps of paper. There's a spiritual significance in that picture, Andy. (*He smiles bitterly.*) I'm a failure, and Ruth's another—but we can both justly lay some of the blame for our stumbling on God. But you're the deepest-dyed failure of the three, Andy. You've spent eight years running away from yourself. Do you see what I mean? You used to be a creator when you loved the farm. You and life were in harmonious partnership. And now— (*He stops as if seeking vainly for words.*) My brain is muddled. But part of what I mean is that your gambling with the thing you used to love to create proves how far astray— So you'll be punished. You'll have to suffer to win back— (*His voice grows weaker and he sighs wearily.*) It's no use. I can't say it. (*He lies back and closes his eyes, breathing pantingly.*)

ANDREW—(*slowly*) I think I know what you're driving at, Rob—and it's true, I guess. (*Robert smiles gratefully and stretches out his hand, which Andrew takes in his.*)

ROBERT—I want you to promise me to do one thing, Andy, after—

ANDREW—I'll promise anything, as God is my Judge!

ROBERT—Remember, Andy, Ruth has suffered double her share. (*his voice faltering with weakness*) Only through contact with suffering, Andy, will you—awaken. Listen. You must marry Ruth—afterwards.

RUTH—(*with a cry*) Rob! (*Robert lies back, his eyes closed, gasping heavily for breath.*)

ANDREW—(*making signs to her to humor him—gently*) You're tired out, Rob. You better lie down and rest a while, don't you think? We can talk later on.

ROBERT—(*with a mocking smile*) Later on! You always were an optimist, Andy! (*He sighs with exhaustion.*) Yes, I'll go and rest a while. (*as Andrew comes to help him*) It must be near sunrise, isn't it?

ANDREW—It's after six.

ROBERT—(*as Andrew helps him into the bedroom*) Shut the door, Andy. I want to be alone. (*Andrew reappears and shuts the door softly. He comes and sits down on his chair again, supporting his head on his hands. His face is drawn with the intensity of his dry-eyed anguish.*)

RUTH—(*glancing at him—fearfully*) He's out of his mind now, isn't he?

ANDREW—He may be a little delirious. The fever would

do that. (*with impotent rage*) God, what a shame! And there's
nothing we can do but sit and—wait! (*He springs from his
chair and walks to the stove.*)

RUTH—(*dully*) He was talking—wild—like he used to—
only this time it sounded—unnatural, don't you think?

ANDREW—I don't know. The things he said to me had
truth in them—even if he did talk them way up in the air,
like he always sees things. Still— (*He glances down at Ruth
keenly.*) Why do you suppose he wanted us to promise we'd—
(*confusedly*) You know what he said.

RUTH—(*dully*) His mind was wandering, I s'pose.

ANDREW—(*with conviction*) No—there was something
back of it.

RUTH—He wanted to make sure I'd be all right—after
he'd gone, I expect.

ANDREW—No, it wasn't that. He knows very well I'd naturally look after you without—anything like that.

RUTH—He might be thinking of—something happened
five years back, the time you came home from the trip.

ANDREW—What happened? What do you mean?

RUTH—(*dully*) We had a fight.

ANDREW—A fight? What has that to do with me?

RUTH—It was about you—in a way.

ANDREW—(*amazed*) About *me*?

RUTH—Yes, mostly. You see I'd found out I'd made a mistake
about Rob soon after we were married—when it was too late.

ANDREW—Mistake? (*slowly*) You mean—you found out
you didn't love Rob?

RUTH—Yes.

ANDREW—Good God!

RUTH—And then I thought that when Mary came it'd be
different, and I'd love him; but it didn't happen that way.
And I couldn't bear with his blundering and book-reading—
and I grew to hate him, almost.

ANDREW—Ruth!

RUTH—I couldn't help it. No woman could. It had to be
because I loved someone else, I'd found out. (*She sighs wearily.*) It can't do no harm to tell you now—when it's all past
and gone—and dead. *You* were the one I really loved—only
I didn't come to the knowledge of it 'til too late.

ANDREW—(*stunned*) Ruth! Do you know what you're saying?

RUTH—It was true—then. (*with sudden fierceness*) How could I help it? No woman could.

ANDREW—Then—you loved me—that time I came home?

RUTH—(*doggedly*) I'd known your real reason for leaving home the first time—everybody knew it—and for three years I'd been thinking—

ANDREW—That I loved you?

RUTH—Yes. Then that day on the hill you laughed about what a fool you'd been for loving me once—and I knew it was all over.

ANDREW—Good God, but I never thought— (*He stops, shuddering at his remembrance.*) And did Rob—

RUTH—That was what I'd started to tell. We'd had a fight just before you came and I got crazy mad—and I told him all I've told you.

ANDREW—(*gaping at her speechlessly for a moment*) You told Rob—you loved me?

RUTH—Yes.

ANDREW—(*shrinking away from her in horror*) You—you—you mad fool, you! How could you do such a thing?

RUTH—I couldn't help it. I'd got to the end of bearing things—without talking.

ANDREW—Then Rob must have known every moment I stayed here! And yet he never said or showed— God, how he must have suffered! Didn't you know how much he loved you?

RUTH—(*dully*) Yes. I knew he liked me.

ANDREW—Liked you! What kind of a woman are you? Couldn't you have kept silent? Did you have to torture him? No wonder he's dying! And you've lived together for five years with this between you?

RUTH—We've lived in the same house.

ANDREW—Does he still think—

RUTH—I don't know. We've never spoke a word about it since that day. Maybe, from the way he went on, he s'poses I care for you yet.

ANDREW—But you don't. It's outrageous. It's stupid! You don't love me!

RUTH—(*slowly*) I wouldn't know how to feel love, even if I tried, any more.

ANDREW—(*brutally*) And I don't love you, that's sure! (*He sinks into his chair, his head between his hands.*) It's damnable such a thing should be between Rob and me. Why, I love Rob better'n anybody in the world and always did. There isn't a thing on God's green earth I wouldn't have done to keep trouble away from him. And I have to be the very one—it's damnable! How am I going to face him again? What can I say to him now? (*He groans with anguished rage. After a pause*) He asked me to promise—what am I going to do?

RUTH—You can promise—so's it'll ease his mind—and not mean anything.

ANDREW—What? Lie to him now—when he's dying? (*determinedly*) No! It's *you* who'll have to do the lying, since it must be done. You've got a chance now to undo some of all the suffering you've brought on Rob. Go in to him! Tell him you never loved me—it was all a mistake. Tell him you only said so because you were mad and didn't know what you were saying! Tell him something, anything, that'll bring him peace!

RUTH—(*dully*) He wouldn't believe me.

ANDREW—(*furiously*) You've got to make him believe you, do you hear? You've got to—now—hurry—you never know when it may be too late. (*as she hesitates—imploringly*) For God's sake, Ruth! Don't you see you owe it to him? You'll never forgive yourself if you don't.

RUTH—(*dully*) I'll go. (*She gets wearily to her feet and walks slowly toward the bedroom.*) But it won't do any good. (*Andrew's eyes are fixed on her anxiously. She opens the door and steps inside the room. She remains standing there for a minute. Then she calls in a frightened voice*) Rob! Where are you? (*Then she hurries back, trembling with fright.*) Andy! Andy! He's gone!

ANDREW—(*misunderstanding her—his face pale with dread*) He's not—

RUTH—(*interrupting him—hysterically*) He's gone! The bed's empty. The window's wide open. He must have crawled out into the yard!

ANDREW—(*springing to his feet. He rushes into the bedroom*

and returns immediately with an expression of alarmed amazement on his face.) Come! He can't have gone far! (*Grabbing his hat he takes Ruth's arm and shoves her toward the door.*) Come on! (*opening the door*) Let's hope to God— (*The door closes behind them, cutting off his words as*

The Curtain Falls)

SCENE TWO

Same as Act One, Scene One—A section of country highway. The sky to the east is already alight with bright color and a thin, quivering line of flame is spreading slowly along the horizon rim of the dark hills. The roadside, however, is still steeped in the grayness of the dawn, shadowy and vague. The field in the foreground has a wild uncultivated appearance as if it had been allowed to remain fallow the preceding summer. Parts of the snake-fence in the rear have been broken down. The apple tree is leafless and seems dead.

Robert staggers weakly in from the left. He stumbles into the ditch and lies there for a moment; then crawls with a great effort to the top of the bank where he can see the sun rise, and collapses weakly. Ruth and Andrew come hurriedly along the road from the left.

ANDREW—(*stopping and looking about him*) There he is! I knew it! I knew we'd find him here.

ROBERT—(*trying to raise himself to a sitting position as they hasten to his side—with a wan smile*) I thought I'd given you the slip.

ANDREW—(*with kindly bullying*) Well you didn't, you old scoundrel, and we're going to take you right back where you belong—in bed. (*He makes a motion to lift Robert.*)

ROBERT—Don't, Andy. Don't, I tell you!

ANDREW—You're in pain?

ROBERT—(*simply*) No. I'm dying. (*He falls back weakly. Ruth sinks down beside him with a sob and pillows his head on her lap. Andrew stands looking down at him helplessly. Robert moves his head restlessly on Ruth's lap.*) I couldn't stand it back there in the room. It seemed as if all my life—I'd been cooped in a room. So I thought I'd try to end as I might have—if I'd had the courage—alone—in a ditch by the open road—watching the sun rise.

ANDREW—Rob! Don't talk. You're wasting your strength. Rest a while and then we'll carry you—

ROBERT—Still hoping, Andy? Don't. I know. (*There is a pause during which he breathes heavily, straining his eyes toward the horizon.*) The sun comes so slowly. (*with an ironical smile*) The doctor told me to go to the far-off places—and I'd be cured. He was right. That was always the cure for me. It's too late—for this life—but— (*He has a fit of coughing which racks his body.*)

ANDREW—(*with a hoarse sob*) Rob! (*He clenches his fists in an impotent rage against Fate.*) God! God! (*Ruth sobs brokenly and wipes Robert's lips with her handkerchief.*)

ROBERT—(*in a voice which is suddenly ringing with the happiness of hope*) You mustn't feel sorry for me. Don't you see I'm happy at last—free—free!—freed from the farm—free to wander on and on—eternally! (*He raises himself on his elbow, his face radiant, and points to the horizon.*) Look! Isn't it beautiful beyond the hills? I can hear the old voices calling me to come— (*exultantly*) And this time I'm going! It isn't the end. It's a free beginning—the start of my voyage! I've won to my trip—the right of release—beyond the horizon! Oh, you ought to be glad—glad—for my sake! (*He collapses weakly.*) Andy! (*Andrew bends down to him.*) Remember Ruth—

ANDREW—I'll take care of her, I swear to you, Rob!

ROBERT—Ruth has suffered—remember, Andy—only through sacrifice—the secret beyond there— (*He suddenly raises himself with his last remaining strength and points to the horizon where the edge of the sun's disc is rising from the rim of the hills.*) The sun! (*He remains with his eyes fixed on it for a moment. A rattling noise throbs from his throat. He mumbles*) Remember! (*and falls back and is still. Ruth gives a cry of horror and springs to her feet, shuddering, her hands over her eyes. Andrew bends on one knee beside the body, placing a hand over Robert's heart, then he kisses his brother reverentially on the forehead and stands up.*)

ANDREW—(*facing Ruth, the body between them—in a dead voice*) He's dead. (*with a sudden burst of fury*) God damn you, you never told him!

RUTH—(*piteously*) He was so happy without my lying to him.

ANDREW—(*pointing to the body—trembling with the violence of his rage*) This is your doing, you damn woman, you coward, you murderess!

RUTH—(*sobbing*) Don't, Andy! I couldn't help it—and he knew how I'd suffered, too. He told you—to remember.

ANDREW—(*stares at her for a moment, his rage ebbing away, an expression of deep pity gradually coming over his face. Then he glances down at his brother and speaks brokenly in a compassionate voice*) Forgive me, Ruth—for his sake—and I'll remember— (*Ruth lets her hands fall from her face and looks at him uncomprehendingly. He lifts his eyes to hers and forces out falteringly*) I— you—we've both made a mess of things! We must try to help each other—and—in time—we'll come to know what's right— (*desperately*) And perhaps we— (*But Ruth, if she is aware of his words, gives no sign. She remains silent, gazing at him dully with the sad humility of exhaustion, her mind already sinking back into that spent calm beyond the further troubling of any hope.*)

(*The Curtain Falls*)

SHELL SHOCK

A Play in One Act

CHARACTERS

JACK ARNOLD, *Major of Infantry, U.S.A.*
HERBERT ROYLSTON, *Lieutenant of Infantry, U.S.A.*
ROBERT WAYNE, *Medical Corps, U.S.A.*
WAITER

Shell Shock

SCENE—*A corner in the grill of the New York club of a large Eastern University. Six tables with chairs placed about them are set at regular intervals in two rows of three from left to right. On the left, three windows looking out on a side street. In the rear, four windows opening on an avenue. On the right, forward, the main entrance to the grill.*

It is the middle of the afternoon of a hot day in September, 1918. Through the open windows, the white curtains of which hang motionless, unstirred by the faintest breeze, a sultry vapor of dust-clogged sunlight can be seen steaming over the hot asphalt. Here, in the grill, it is cool. The drowsy humming of an electric fan on the left wall lulls to inertness. A bored, middle-aged waiter stands leaning wearily against the wall between the tables in the rear, gaping and staring listlessly out at the avenue. Every now and then he casts an indifferent glance at the only other occupant of the room, a young man of about thirty dressed in the uniform of an officer in the Medical Corps who is sitting at the middle table, front, sipping a glass of iced coffee and reading a newspaper. The officer is under medium height, slight and wiry, with a thin, pale face, light brown hair and mustache, and grey eyes peering keenly through tortoise-rimmed spectacles.

As the curtain rises there is a sound of footsteps from the entrance. The waiter half-straightens into an attitude of respectful attention. A moment later Herbert Roylston enters. He is a brawny young fellow of twenty-seven or so, clad in the uniform of a first lieutenant of infantry. Blond and clean-shaven, his rather heavy, good-natured face noticeably bears the marks of a recent convalescence from serious illness. Lines of suffering about the lips contrast with his ever-ready, jovial grin; and his blue eyes of a healthy child seem shadowed by the remembrance of pain, witnessed and not by them to be forgotten.

Roylston stands at the entrance and glances about the grill. The waiter starts forward with an inquiring "Yes, sir?". The medical officer is engrossed in some bit of news and does not look up. Roylston walks forward to his table and glances at the other curiously. Then the paper is put down and the eyes of the two men meet. A look of perplexed recognition comes over both their faces.

ROYLSTON—(*with a boyish grin*) I know you. Wait a minute! (*The other smiles.*) Ah! Now I've got it— Wayne, isn't it— Bobby Wayne? You used to room with Jack Arnold at college.

WAYNE—That's right; and this is—Roylston, isn't it? I met you here with Jack?

ROYLSTON—That's who. (*The two men shake hands heartily, evidently greatly pleased at this chance meeting.*)

WAYNE—I'm very glad to see you again. Sit down. Won't you have something to drink? (*He beckons to the waiter.*)

ROYLSTON—Sure thing. That's what I came in for—that, and to try and find someone to talk to, and write a couple of letters. (*to the waiter*) Iced coffee, please. (*The waiter goes out.*) Its a sure enough broiler in the streets. Whew! (*He mops his face with his handkerchief—then continues apologetically*) I guess I'm still a bit weak. You know I had rather a close shave, thanks to the Bosche.

WAYNE—(*nodding*) I can see by your face that you've been through the mill. What was it—scrapnel?

ROYLSTON—(*with a grin*) A touch of that in both legs; and afterward machine gun here and here. (*He touches the upper part of his chest.*) They nearly had me. (*showing emotion*) If it hadn't been for Jack—

WAYNE—(*interestedly*) Eh? You don't mean Jack Arnold?

ROYLSTON—I sure do! He came out into No Mans Land and got me.

WAYNE—(*quickly*) When was this—after Chateau Thierry?

ROYLSTON—Yes.

WAYNE—(*astonished*) Then you were the one he brought back—that exploit—

ROYLSTON—I don't know about *the* one. I was *a* one, at any rate. (*with enthusiasm*) Jack's got a whole caboodle of such stunts to his credit. I wouldn't dare say that I—

WAYNE—(*puzzled*) But I heard—they didn't give the name—but I understood it was the body of a *dead* officer he risked his life to get.

ROYLSTON—(*laughing*) I guess they did think I was a gone goose at the time; but I managed to pull through. You can't put a squirrel in the ground. (*The waiter comes back bringing the iced coffee which he sets on the table. Roylston takes a sip and sighs contentedly.*)

WAYNE—(*when the waiter has resumed his post by the rear windows*) Tell me about it, will you, Roylston? The reports have been so meager, and I'm so damn interested in all Jack does. You see Jack and I have palled together ever since we were knee-high.

ROYLSTON—Yes. He's told me.

WAYNE—But he's such a rotten correspondent that, even when I was in France, I had to depend on the war correspondents and the official reports for any news about him. So it'd be a favor if you'd—

ROYLSTON—(*embarrassed*) There isn't much to tell. We got caught in a bit of barrage half-way to the third Bosche trench—we'd captured the first two and should have stopped, but you get drunk with the joy of chasing them back and you don't stop to think.

WAYNE—I can understand that!

ROYLSTON—Well, that was where I got mine—in both legs. I went down and couldn't get up. The boys had to go back to the trench we'd just captured. They didn't have time to do any picking up. I must have seemed dead anyway. I remember the Bosche counter-attacked and caught hell. Then the lights went out completely as far as I was concerned.

WAYNE—(*eagerly*) But you've heard how Jack's company got cut off in that second trench, haven't you? How the Hun barrage cut all communication between them and the rest of the army? (*enthusiastically*) Jack's company held out for three days and nights against all kinds of terrific shelling and counter attacks, without support or relief, until the rest of the division advanced again and caught up with them. Nearly every member of the company was either killed or wounded—but they stuck it out! It was a wonderful example of what our boys can do in a pinch!

ROYLSTON—It sure was great stuff! I heard about that part of it afterward in hospital; but at the time it all happened I wasn't especially interested in what was going on around me.

WAYNE—Then— When was it Jack came out to get you?

ROYLSTON—Just after the division pushed up and they were relieved.

WAYNE—(*astonished*) That third night?

ROYLSTON—It was at night, I know.

WAYNE—(*looking at him with wondering admiration*) Then—you were lying in No Mans Land three days and nights—badly wounded?

ROYLSTON—(*embarrassed*) I must have been, I guess. I didn't notice time much. I was sort of out of my head with thirst and pain, or in a numb trance most of the time. You know how one gets. (*Wayne nods.*) I'd see dark and light but—I didn't think of anything at all—not even of death. (*He pauses and then continues shamefacedly.*) Finally I came to in the dark. I heard someone screaming—damn horribly! I listened and discovered that *I* was doing it—screaming at the top of my lungs! Honestly, I was ashamed to death of myself. I managed to get to my feet. I had a mad hunch to get back to our lines. Then a Bosche machine gun commenced to rattle, and I felt a terrific thud in the chest—and the ground came up and hit me. The Bosche artillery loosened up and a shower of star shells made it light as day. I saw a man come running through that hell straight for me. The air was fairly sizzling with bullets but he kept right on, and then when he came close I saw it was Jack. He shouted: Roylston, and hauled me up on his shoulder. The pain of it knocked me into a faint. When I came to I was in hospital. (*with a shy grin of relief*) So that's all I know about it.

WAYNE—You certainly had a frightful time of it, old man.

ROYLSTON—No worse than the rest of the boys. We all have to take our medicine sooner or later. But its lucky for me Jack saw me stand up that time.

WAYNE—You think he saw you?

ROYLSTON—(*making a wry face*) I hope so. I'd hate to think he heard me balling out there. I guess they all thought me dead or they'd have been out looking for me before that. (*He drinks the rest of his coffee.*) Well, I've got to toddle upstairs and write—

WAYNE—Wait a minute, will you, Roylston? There's something I want to talk over with you. It's about Jack—and perhaps you can help me.

ROYLSTON—Certainly. (*as the other hesitates*) Something about Jack, you say?

WAYNE—Yes. But first let me explain how I happen to be here at home. I'm not on leave, and I wasn't sent back from

France on account of ill health, as you might think. At the base hospital over there I was assigned to treating victims of shell-shock. I'd made quite a study of the disease since it first became known and as a consequence was more successful than most at treating it. So a few months ago when the sick commenced to be sent home in appreciable numbers, I was ordered back here to help on shock patients.

ROYLSTON—I see.

WAYNE—(*with a keen glance at the other—lowering his voice*) And, this is strictly confidential, of course, it appears from a letter I recently received, as if Jack Arnold is likely to become one of my patients.

ROYLSTON—(*amazed*) What! Not shell shock?

WAYNE—Yes.

ROYLSTON—Good God! But there must be some mistake. Why Jack has the nerves of an ox!

WAYNE—*Did have*. Don't forget he's been in there three years now without a let-up—when you come to count the two he was with the Canadians before he was transferred to ours. That's a long stretch.

ROYLSTON—But the last I remember of him he was A1.

WAYNE—It hits you all of a sudden usually; besides, it's by no means certain in Jacks case. The letter I spoke of was from a Doctor Thompson over there, one of the heads. He wrote that Jack had been sent to the base hospital with a leg wound, nothing serious in itself. But, knowing I was a friend of Jack's, Thompson wrote to tell me Jack had been invalided home, and for me to study him carefully when he arrived. His trouble seemed to be plain nervous break-down, Thompson said, but still there was something queer about the case he couldn't get hold of and he hadn't the time to devote to individuals. So he left it up to me.

ROYLSTON—Didn't he give you some hint as to just what he meant was the trouble with Jack?

WAYNE—Only a postscript evidently scribbled in a hurry. He wrote: "Watch Arnold—cigarettes!"—with the word cigarettes deeply underlined.

ROYLSTON—(*wonderingly*) Cigarettes?

WAYNE—Sounds ridiculous, doesn't it? Especially as Jack never smokes.

ROYLSTON—(*quickly*) Oh, he did over there—a great deal. As I remember him he had one stuck in his mouth all the time.

WAYNE—(*astonished*) What? Why, when I knew him he wouldn't touch one on a bet. (*The two men look at each other for a moment deeply puzzled.*) There's something queer about it, evidently—from that postscript.

ROYLSTON—(*after a moment*) Oh, I guess it's just that your Thompson is one of those anti-cigarette fiends.

WAYNE—(*frowning*) Quite the contrary. He smokes incessantly himself. There must be something in it. Thompson is one of our keenest diagnosticians.

WAYNE—(*confidently*) No matter how sharp he is I'll bet he's all wrong about Jack. Why—hell—Jack's made of iron. I've seen him in the trenches and I know. If he'd been shot or gassed or—but shell shock— Bosh! Jack'd laugh at that. (*eagerly*) But when do you expect him to get here?

WAYNE—Any day now.

ROYLSTON—Gad, I sure hope he arrives before I leave. I want to see him above all other people in the world—to thank him, if I can, for my presence in our midst. (*impulsively*) If you only knew how I feel about Jack! (*inconsequentially*) You remember his senior year at college when he was All-American half—and his touchdown that won the Harvard game? (*Wayne nods.*) I was just a Freshman then and you can imagine what a hero he was to me. (*Wayne smiles.*) And then to go over there and find myself directly under his command—to become his friend! It meant a devil of a lot, I tell you!

WAYNE—It must have.

ROYLSTON—And then to cap the climax he saved my life when not one man in a million would have tried it—and no blame to them, either! It was rank suicide. The chances were a thousand to one against his coming out of it alive. (*with a grin*) When I get started on that subject I never stop, so I guess I better beat it to my letter writing. Be sure and let me know when Jack arrives, I sure want to see him.

WAYNE—(*as they both stand and shake hands*) I'll be sure to.

ROYLSTON—Thanks. Well, so long for the present.

WAYNE—So long. (*He sits down again. Roylston goes out.*

Wayne drums on the table with his fingers and stares before him, deep in his thoughts. After a moment steps are heard from the entrance, right, and Jack Arnold comes into the grill. He is a tall, broad-shouldered, and sinewy-built man of about thirty with black hair and mustache. The sun tan on his strong-featured, handsome face has been faded to a sickly yellow by illness. Lines of nervous tension are deep about his mouth and nose, and his cheeks are hollow, the skin drawn taut over the cheek bones. His dark eyes have a strained expression of uncertain expectancy as if he were constantly holding himself in check while he waited for a mine to explode. His hands tremble a little. He has a queer mannerism of continually raising the fore and middle fingers of his right hand to his lips as though he were smoking an invisible cigarette. He wears the uniform of a major of infantry.)

ARNOLD—(*immediately recognizes Wayne and calls out casually*) Hello, Bobby. (*He strides toward the table.*)

WAYNE—(*jumps to his feet, nearly upsetting the table*) Jack! (*his face glowing with pleasure as he pumps his friend's hand up and down*) By all that's wonderful! When did you get in?

ARNOLD—This morning.

WAYNE—(*pushing him into a chair*) Sit down, you old scoundrel! I've been expecting to hear of your arrival every day. (*slapping him on the back affectionately*) It's certainly a sight for sore eyes to see you alive and kicking again!

ARNOLD—Yes, I'm glad to be back for a bit. I was rather done up in a nervous way.

WAYNE—So Doctor Thompson wrote me.

ARNOLD—(*betraying uneasiness*) Oh, he wrote you, did he?

WAYNE—Yes; said you were coming back.

ARNOLD—(*irritably*) He's a fossilized old woman, your Thompson—fusses like a wet hen about imaginary symptoms.

WAYNE—Yet he's one of the best in his line.

ARNOLD—(*dryly*) Perhaps; but you'll not convince me of it. (*He makes the peculiar motion of fingers to his lips.*) He got on my nerves frightfully with his incessant examinations—pure rot, if you want my opinion.

WAYNE—(*with a keen professional glance at his friend's face—from this time he studies Arnold as a patient*) But, honestly, you do look as if you'd been knocked out for a time.

ARNOLD—(*annoyed*) No; fit as a fiddle. (*vaguely*) It's only the silence. (*He again makes the motion to his lips.*)

WAYNE—(*mystified*) Silence?

ARNOLD—(*not appearing to notice this question—with sudden eagerness*) Have you a cigarette, Bobby?

WAYNE—(*takes out his case and offers it to Arnold*) You're smoking now?

ARNOLD—Naturally. (*He lights the cigarette and, drawing in a deep inhale, exhales it with a sigh of relief.*)

WAYNE—How, naturally? You didn't use to, you know— nary a puff.

ARNOLD—Had to over there. (*with sudden remembrance*) I was forgetting—it's such a damn long while since I've seen you, Bobby.

WAYNE—Three years.

ARNOLD—(*vaguely*) A lot of things can happen in that time, what? (*With a detached air, as if he were unconscious of what he is doing, he puts out the cigarette from which he has hardly taken more than a few puffs, and carefully puts the butt into a pocket of his uniform.*)

WAYNE—(*watching him curiously*) What—? (*He suddenly thinks better of his question and stops.*)

ARNOLD—(*sharply*) Eh?

WAYNE—Oh, nothing. (*as Jack stares at him*) How's the wound in your leg?

ARNOLD—All O.K. Only a scratch. (*He again puts his fingers to his lips nervously—then his eyes fall on the cigarette case on the table.*) I'll graft another of your fags, Bobby, if I may.

WAYNE—Help yourself.

ARNOLD—(*lighting up*) I went straight to your house from the dock. Saw your mother. She told me I'd probably find you here. (*with a display of affection*) It's good to see you again, Bobby, damn good! Like a tonic, by Jove! I feel bucked up already.

WAYNE—(*with a smile*) I'm glad of that, Jack.

ARNOLD—(*reminiscently*) What times we used to have together, eh?

WAYNE—Bully!

ARNOLD—Those week-ends in the city when you came on

from Baltimore—when you were a grinding medical stude
and I was a—(*scornfully*) scribbler!

WAYNE—Have you managed to get any writing done over
there?

ARNOLD—(*with a frown*) No. What's the use? It's not a
thing one can write about, is it? (*There is a pause. Arnold mechanically puts out his cigarette and is just placing it in his pocket
when he looks up and catches his friend's eye probing into his
strange action. He immediately becomes conscious of what he is
doing and shame-facedly hurls his cigarette on the floor and stamps
on it.*) Damn it all! (*irritably*) What are you staring at, Bobby?

WAYNE—(*flushing*) Nothing—er—

ARNOLD—You must think me a thundering ass when you
catch me in a childish act like that—just like a kid on the
streets "sniping butts". I can't seem to break myself of the
devilish habit—must have contracted it in the front line
trenches—saving up butts for an emergency when I'd be
without a smoke. And now I do it mechanically—(*hesitates—
then moodily in a low voice*) whenever the silence comes over me.

WAYNE—(*seeing his friend's embarrassment—soothingly*) It's
natural enough.

ARNOLD—(*as if he were talking to himself*) There's something back of it I can't get at—something that drives me to
do it. (*He shakes his head as if banishing some painful thought,
and producing an unopened box of cigarettes from each of his pockets, turns to Wayne with a forced laugh.*) Here I've got a full
box in each pocket and yet I'll bet I've been grafting yours as
though there wasn't one for sale in the whole world. It's a
disgusting obsession. I've got to break myself of it or people
will think I've a screw loose somewhere. It's up to you,
Bobby, to call me down every time you catch me. That'll do
the trick. (*Forgetful of the full boxes on the table he calls to the
waiter roughly*) Hey, waiter!

THE WAITER—(*starting out of his doze*) Yes, sir?

ARNOLD—A box of cigarettes.

THE WAITER—What kind would you like, sir?

ARNOLD—(*vaguely*) Any kind.

WAYNE—But you've all those unopened on the table, Jack.

ARNOLD—(*flushing—awkwardly*) Yes—so I have—I was

forgetting. (*to the waiter*) Never mind about them now. (*There is a pause during which Arnold presses his hands to his forehead as if he were trying to focus his thoughts. Finally he mutters in a low voice*) It's the silence. That does it.

WAYNE—(*staring at him keenly*) That's the third time you've mentioned the silence, Jack. What do you mean, exactly? What silence?

ARNOLD—(*after a pause*) Just that—*the* silence. It hits you when you're sent back home after you've been in the lines for a long time—say a year or more without a holiday. (*He laughs mockingly.*) A holiday! A rest period! Rest! Good God! (*He turns to Wayne excitedly.*) Understand that I'm only speaking from my own experience and my feelings may have no general significance. But I believe they have. I've seen them verified in the faces of those men who come back to the trenches after a leave at home—their expression of genuine happiness at being back— Why, man, they look relieved, freed from slavery! (*He pauses for a moment, reflecting—then continues intensely.*) You've been hearing the rumble and crash of the big guns, the rat-a-pet rivetting of the machine-guns, the crack of rifles, the whine of bullets, the roar of bursting shells. Everything whirls in a constant feverish movement around you; the earth trembles and quakes beneath your feet; even the darkness is only an intermittent phenomena snatching greedily at the earth between the wane of one star shell and the bursting brilliance of the next; even the night is goaded into insomnia by the everlasting fireworks. Nothing is fixed or certain. The next moment of your life never attains to the stability of even a probable occurrence. It hits you with the speed of a bullet, passes through you, is gone. (*He pauses.*) And then you come out into the old peaceful world you once knew—for a rest—and it seems as if you were burried in the tomb of a pyramid erected before the stars were born. Time has died of old age; and the silence, like the old Chinese water torture, drips leadenly drop by drop—on your brain—and then you think—you have to think—about the things you ought to forget—

WAYNE—(*in a brisk voice—trying to rouse his friend*) You'll get used to the quiet after a bit. You're letting your imagination run away with you. (*Arnold looks at him with a curious, haggard smile.*) Do you know—it's a curious coincidence—I was just talking about you with a friend of yours before you came in. Speak of the devil, you know. Guess who it was?

ARNOLD—(*indifferently*) I don't know. Who?

WAYNE—Roylston. It's funny you didn't run into him.

ARNOLD—(*showing no interest—as if he hadn't heard the name*) I saw someone in uniform going up the stairs—didn't get a look at his face. Who did you say it was?

WAYNE—(*laying emphasis on the name*) Roylston—Herb Roylston—the man you dragged out of No Mans Land after Chateau Thierry when you won your load of medals, you chump!

ARNOLD—(*stunned*) You don't mean—Herb?

WAYNE—That's exactly who I do mean.

ARNOLD—(*pale and excited*) Here—in this club—Herb? But that's impossible. Herb was dead, I tell you.

WAYNE—You may think so; but you'll be doubly glad to hear he's very much alive, and he wants to see you and thank you for—

ARNOLD—(*covering his face with his hands*) Oh God!

WAYNE—(*alarmed*) Jack! What's the trouble?

ARNOLD—(*controlling himself with an effort*) Nothing—only it brings it all back. (*His fingers flutter to his mouth. He murmurs hoarsely*) Got a cigarette, Bobby?

WAYNE—There—on the table.

ARNOLD—Thanks. (*He does not touch his own boxes but picks a cigarette from his friend's case and lights it. He takes a deep inhale and commences to talk volubly in a forced tone as if he were trying to cover up his apparent indifference in the matter of Roylston.*) I'm damn glad to hear about Herb. So he's alive—really alive! It seems incredible. He was swimming in his own blood. I carried him over my shoulder. I was soaked with it. Ugh! (*He shudders at the recollection but talks rapidly again, trying to drown his memories.*) I'll be damn glad to see him again—damn glad. Herb's a corking chap—one of the best. He and I were great chums over there. (*He puts his cigarette out and sticks it hastily in his pocket. Wayne sees this and seems about to speak but thinks better of it. Arnold goes on in an agitated tone.*) Yes, Herb's one fine chap. That was an awful mess—the worst ever—that Chateau Thierry affair. I'll have to tell you about it. We ran out of cigarettes you know—not a damn one in the whole company—not a smoke of any description. It was hell. Speaking of smokes—you've another fag, haven't you, Bobby?

WAYNE—(*quietly*) On the table, Jack.

ARNOLD—Thanks. (*He again takes one from Wayne's case and puffs nervously.*) You can't realize what a smoke comes to mean to you in a first line trench. You'd have to have been there, Bobby. You wondered at my smoking now when I never had in the old days. I didn't at first—then I had to—had to, I tell you! You know—the stench and the lice and the rest of it. A smoke takes your mind off them, somehow.

WAYNE—(*soothingly*) I know it's a good thing.

ARNOLD—(*complainingly*) And that time in that Chateau Thierry trench there was nothing. The Bosche barrage cut us off completely from the rest of the army—not a smoke in the whole company! No chance of getting one! We only had emergency field rations and when they gave out some of the boys—toward the end—those who were still unwounded—were wild with hunger and thirst. I can remember Billy Sterett—a corporal—he went west with a bullet through his heart later on, poor fellow—singing some idiotic nonsense about beef steak pie over and over again—till it drove you nearly mad to listen to him. He must have been clean out of his head. But I didn't feel hunger or thirst at all. All I wanted was a smoke—and not a one! (*He puffs furiously at his cigarette.*)

WAYNE—I've read about your famous three days, Jack. It was a glorious thing but I can well imagine how terrible it was also.

ARNOLD—(*excitedly*) Terrible? No word for it! Man alive, you couldn't know! We'd crouch down in the mud with the trench rats squeaking and scampering with fright over our feet—nipping at your legs—while we waited for the next counter attack, wondering if the Bosche would get through the next time, gritting our teeth to stick it out. Their artillery played hell with us. The world seemed flying to bits. The concussions of the bursting shells—all about us—would jar your heart right back against your spine. It rained shell splinters. Men kept falling, writhing and groaning in the muck—one's friends!—and nothing to do. A little Italian private—Tony—he used to sing for us in camp—don't know his second name—used to be a bootblack here at home—was standing near me. A shell fragment came down on his skull—his brains spattered all over—(*shuddering*)—over my face. And all that time not a cigarette—not a damned smoke of any kind—to take your mind off—all that!

WAYNE—(*worried by Arnold's rapidly increasing excitement*) You ought to try and forget those unavoidable horrors, Jack. War has to be what it is—until we make an end to it forever.

ARNOLD—(*waving this remark aside*) You've got to know about it, all you others—then you'll send us the things we need, smokes and the rest. (*He throws his cigarette away and lights another.*) And at nights it was frightful, expecting a surprise attack every minute—watching—straining your eyes! We had to pile the dead up against the rear wall of the trench; and when you'd stumble in the dark you'd put your hand out and touch a—a face, or a leg—or—something sticky with blood. Not a wink of sleep! You couldn't! Even when the guns let up for a moment there were the screams of the wounded out in No Mans Land. They'd keep the dead awake—lying out there dying by bits. And you couldn't go out to get them in that fire. It was suicide. I told the men that. They wanted to go out and get their friends, and I couldn't give permission. We needed every man. It was suicide. I told them so. They wept and cursed. It was my duty. They would have been killed—uselessly.

WAYNE—But you went out yourself—for Roylston.

ARNOLD—(*vaguely—shaking his head*) No; Roylston was dead. I saw him fall flat on his face. Then after that for three days I didn't see or hear him—so he must have been dead. (*He hurries on volubly as if this thought of Roylston disturbed him.*) I thought I'd go mad. No place for the wounded to be cared for—groans and shrieks on all sides! And not a thing to smoke! You had to think—think about it! And the stench of the bodies rotting in the sun between the Bosche trench and ours! God! And not a single cigarette, do you understand? Not one! You'd feel sick clear down to the soles of your feet. You finally came to believe you were putrefying yourself—alive!—and the living men around you—they too—rotten!

WAYNE—(*revolted*) For heavens sake, Jack, cut it out!

ARNOLD—A cigarette would have been heaven—to fill your lungs with clean smoke—to cleanse the stench out of your nostrils! But no! Not the tiniest butt! Not a damn thing! Its unbelievable! (*growing more and more excited*) And when the relief came—our boys—and I was weeping with the joy of it—and I prayed to them—yes, actually prayed—Give me a cigarette, for God's sake! Not a one, Bobby, do you hear? Not a blessed one of them had any. There'd been a delay, a mistake, something. None had come up with the supplies. I was wild. I cursed them. I suddenly remembered Roylston. He'd given me one just before we charged. He had a whole case full I remembered, and I knew the spot where he went down—the exact spot. After that—I forget. It's all a blank. I must have gone over the top and brought him back. (*His voice sinks to a dull whisper. He notices the half-smoked cigarette in his hand and throws it away with a gesture of loathing.*)

WAYNE—(*gazing at him with horrified eyes*) Then that was why—you saved Roylston—for a cigarette—God! (*As Arnold hides his face in his hands with a half-sob Wayne hastens to add compassionately*) No, it couldn't have been that. Your mind is sick, old pal, do you know it? Very sick. Come with me, Jack. Let's get out of here. (*He gets to his feet putting his hand on his friend's shoulder.*)

ARNOLD—(*getting to his feet—in agonized tones*) What have I been saying? I've never talked about it before—but that's the thought that's been eating into my brain, Bobby— what you just said. That's why I'm going mad—thinking about it—day and night! (*with frenzied protest*) It couldn't have been that! I must have gone out for him—for Herb! I must have suddenly realized that he was out there—still alive—suffering! (*breaking down*) But how could I have known that? I thought he was dead. How? I can't remember.

WAYNE—(*quickly*) You saw him when he stood up, of course—when he tried to get back to our lines.

ARNOLD—(*hopelessly—with a groan*) No—no—I saw noone—nothing.

WAYNE—(*forcibly*) Then you heard him screaming out there—screaming with pain in his delirium. Think!

ARNOLD—(*his eyes widening*) Screaming? Yes—there was screaming—driving you mad— (*His face contracts convulsively. He beats his head with his hands, his eyes shut in his effort to visualize the scene.*) Yes—and then—God!—one voice—when all the others were silent for a second—like this— (*He throws his head back and screams as if in horrible pain.*)

WAYNE—(*as the waiter shrinks back against a window terrified*) Jack! Stop!

ARNOLD—(*in a frenzy of joy*) I remember it all now. It was his voice—Herb's—screaming—just at the moment we were relieved! Then I knew he was out there alive. I couldn't bear it! That's why I went over—to save him—Herb!—not the damned cigarettes! (*His face lights up and he grabs Wayne's hand and pumps it up and down.*) That's why I've been sick—queer—crazy—off my nut, Bobby! They've all been telling what a hero I was—and I thought I'd done it all for—I couldn't remember why I'd gone for him—except the cigarettes—and they gave me medals for bravery—and all the time I've been going mad—slowly—inside—thinking I was a damned cur! But now I know, Bobby. I remember every bit that happened. I heard him scream—and I did go over to save Herb, Bobby! Thank God! (*He sinks down into a chair, weak but radiant.*)

WAYNE—(*calmly*) Why sure you did. It's only a touch of shock got the other fool notion into your head. (*with a grin*) And now I can dismiss your case. You're cured already. I'm some doctor, eh? (*While he is speaking Roylston appears in the doorway. When he sees Jack he gives a shout of delight and rushes over throwing his arms around Arnold in a bear hug.*)

ROYLSTON—(*shaking him affectionately*) Hello, Jack! (*He holds him at arm's length—with embarrassment*) Here you are at last—I've wanted to see you—to try and tell—to try and thank—damn it! (*He fumbles in his pocket and pulls out his cigarette case which he offers to Jack.*) Its hard to speak about such things—but you know— Have a cigarette.

ARNOLD—Not on your life! Never another! A pipe for

mine for the rest of my life! (*He beckons wildly to the waiter.*) Hey, waiter! Bring on a gallon of wine! Camouflage it in a teapot, if you have to, and pour it through a strainer. Here's where we celebrate! (*The astonished waiter stands gaping at him in petrified wonder as Jack grabs Herb's hand and shakes it up and down.*) How are you, Herb, you old son of a gun?

(*The Curtain Falls*)

THE DREAMY KID

A Play in One Act

CHARACTERS

Mammy Saunders
Abe, *her grandson, "The Dreamy Kid"*
Ceely Ann
Irene

The Dreamy Kid

SCENE—*Mammy Saunders' bedroom in a house just off of Carmine Street, New York City. The left of the room, forward, is taken up by a heavy, old-fashioned wooden bedstead with a feather mattress. A gaudy red-and-yellow quilt covers the other bedclothes. In back of the bed, a chest of drawers placed against the left wall. On top of the chest, a small lamp. A rocking-chair stands beside the head of the bed on the right. In the rear wall, toward the right, a low window with ragged white curtains. In the right corner, a washstand with bowl and pitcher. Bottles of medicine, a spoon, a glass, etc., are also on the stand. Farther forward, a door opening on the hall and stairway.*

It is soon after nightfall of a day in early winter. The room is in shadowy half darkness, the only light being a pale glow that seeps through the window from the arc lamp on the nearby corner, and by which the objects in the room can be dimly discerned. The vague outlines of Mammy Saunders' figure lying in the bed can be seen, and her black face stands out in sharp contrast from the pillows that support her head.

MAMMY SAUNDERS—*(weakly)* Ceely Ann! *(with faint querulousness)* Light de lamp, will you? Hits mighty dark in yere. *(after a slight pause)* Ain't you dar, Ceely Ann? *(Receiving no reply she sighs deeply and her limbs move uneasily under the bedclothes. The door is opened and shut and the stooping form of another colored woman appears in the semi-darkness. She goes to the foot of the bed sobbing softly, and stands there evidently making an effort to control her emotion.)*

MAMMY SAUNDERS—Dat you, Ceely Ann?

CEELY—*(huskily)* Hit ain't no yuther, Mammy.

MAMMY—Light de lamp, den. I can't see no whars.

CEELY—Des one second till I finds a match. *(She wipes her eyes with her handkerchief—then goes to the chest of drawers and feels around on the top of it—pretending to grumble)* Hit beat all how dem pesky little sticks done hide umse'fs. Shoo! Yere dey is. *(She fumbles with the lamp.)*

MAMMY—*(suspiciously)* You ain't been cryin', is you?

CEELY—*(with feigned astonishment)* Cryin'? I clar' ter goodness you does git de mos' fool notions lyin' dar.

675

MAMMY—(*in a tone of relief*) I mos' thought I yeard you.

CEELY—(*lighting the lamp*) 'Deed you ain't. (*The two women are revealed by the light. Mammy Saunders is an old, white-haired negress about ninety with a weazened face furrowed by wrinkles and withered by old age and sickness. Ceely is a stout woman of fifty or so with grey hair and a round fat face. She wears a loose-fitting gingham dress and a shawl thrown over her head.*)

CEELY—(*with attempted cheeriness*) Bless yo' soul, I ain't got nothin' to cry 'bout. Yere. Lemme fix you so you'll rest mo' easy. (*She lifts the old woman gently and fixes the pillows.*) Dere. Now ain't you feelin' better?

MAMMY—(*dully*) My strenk don' all went. I can't lift a hand.

CEELY—(*hurriedly*) Dat'll all come back ter you de doctor tole me des now when I goes down to de door with him. (*glibly*) He say you is de mos' strongest 'oman fo' yo' years ever he sees in de worl'; and he tell me you gwine ter be up and walkin' agin fo' de week's out. (*As she finds the old woman's eyes fixed on her she turns away confusedly and abruptly changes the subject.*) Hit ain't too wo'm in dis room, dat's a' fac'.

MAMMY—(*shaking her head—in a half whisper*) No, Ceely Ann. Hit ain't no use'n you tellin' me nothin' but de trufe. I feels mighty poo'ly. En I knows hit's on'y wid de blessin' er God I kin las' de night out.

CEELY—(*distractedly*) Ain't no sich a thing! Hush yo' noise Mammy!

MAMMY—(*as if she hadn't heard—in a crooning sing-song*) I'se gwine soon fum dis wicked yearth—and may de Lawd have mercy on dis po' ole sinner. (*after a pause—anxiously*) All I'se prayin' fer is dat God don' take me befo' I sees Dreamy agin. Whar's Dreamy, Ceely Ann? Why ain't he come yere? Ain't you done sent him word I'se sick like I tole you?

CEELY—I tole dem boys ter tell him speshul, and dey swar dey would soon's dey find him. I s'pose dey ain't kotch him yit. Don' you pester yo'se'f worryin'. Dreamy 'ull come fo' ve'y long.

MAMMY—(*after a pause—weakly*) Dere's a feelin' in my

haid like I was a-floatin' yander whar I can't see nothin', or 'member nothin', or know de sight er any pusson I knows; en I wants ter see Dreamy agin befo'—

CEELY—(*quickly*) Don' waste yo strenk talkin'. You git a wink er sleep en I wake you when he comes, you heah me?

MAMMY—(*faintly*) I does feel mighty drowsy. (*She closes her eyes. Ceely goes over to the window and pulling the curtains aside stands looking down into the street as if she were watching for someone coming. A moment later there is a noise of footfalls from the stairs in the hall, followed by a sharp rap on the door.*)

CEELY—(*turning quickly from the window*) Ssshh! Ssshh! (*She hurries to the door, glancing anxiously toward Mammy. The old woman appears to have fallen asleep. Ceely cautiously opens the door a bare inch or so and peeks out. When she sees who it is she immediately tries to slam it shut again but a vigorous shove from the outside forces her back and Irene pushes her way defiantly into the room. She is a young, good-looking negress, highly rouged and powdered, dressed in gaudy, cheap finery.*)

IRENE—(*in a harsh voice—evidently worked up to a great state of nervous excitement*) No you don't, Ceely Ann! I said I was comin' here and it'll take mo'n you to stop me!

CEELY—(*almost speechless with horrified indignation—breathing heavily*) Yo' bad 'oman! Git back ter yo' bad-house whar yo' b'longs!

IRENE—(*raising her clenched hand—furiously*) Stop dat talkin' to me, nigger, or I'll split yo' fool head! (*As Ceely shrinks away Irene lowers her hand and glances quickly around the room.*) Whar's Dreamy?

CEELY—(*scornfully*) Yo' axe me dat! Whar's Dreamy? Axe yo'se'f. Yo's de one ought ter know whar he is.

IRENE—Den he ain't come here?

CEELY—I ain't tellin' de likes er you wedder he is or not.

IRENE—(*pleadingly*) Tell me, Ceely Ann, ain't he been here? He'd be sure to come here 'count of Mammy dyin', dey said.

CEELY—(*pointing to Mammy—apprehensively*) Ssshh! (*then lowering her voice to a whisper—suspiciously*) Dey said? Who said?

IRENE—(*equally suspicious*) None o' your business who

said. (*then pleading again*) Ceely Ann, I jest got ter see him dis minute, dis secon'! He's in bad, Dreamy is, and I knows somep'n I gotter tell him, somep'n I jest heard—

CEELY—(*uncomprehendingly*) In bad? What you jest heah?

IRENE—I ain't tellin' no one but him. (*desperately*) For Gawd's sake, tell me whar he is, Ceely!

CEELY—I don' know no mo'n you.

IRENE—(*fiercely*) You's lyin', Ceely! You's lyin' ter me jest 'cause I'se bad.

CEELY—De good Lawd bar witness I'se tellin' you de trufe!

IRENE—(*hopelessly*) Den I gotter go find him, high and low, somewheres. (*proudly*) You ain't got de right not ter trust me, Ceely, where de Dreamy's mixed in it. I'd go ter hell for Dreamy!

CEELY—(*indignantly*) Hush yo' wicked cussin'! (*then anxiously*) Is Dreamy in trouble?

IRENE—(*with a scornful laugh*) Trouble? Good Lawd, it's worser'n dat! (*then in surprise*) Ain't you heerd what de Dreamy done last night, Ceely?

CEELY—(*apprehensively*) What de Dreamy do? Tell me, gal. Somep'n bad?

IRENE—(*with the same scornful laugh*) Bad? Worser'n bad, what he done!

CEELY—(*lamenting querulously*) Oh good Lawd, I knowed it! I knowed with all his carryin's-on wid dat passel er tough young niggers—him so uppity 'cause he's de boss er de gang—sleepin' all de day 'stead er workin' an' Lawd knows what he does in de nights—fightin' wid white folks, an' totin' a pistol in his pocket—(*with a glance of angry resentment at Irene*)—an' as fo' de udder company he's been keepin'—

IRENE—(*fiercely*) Shut your mouth, Ceely! Dat ain't your business.

CEELY—Oh, I knowed Dreamy'd be gittin' in trouble fo' long! De lowflung young trash! An' here's his ole Mammy don' know no dif'frunt but he's de mos' innercent young lamb in de worl'. (*in a strained whisper*) What he do? Is he been stealin' somep'n?

IRENE—(*angrily*) You go ter hell, Ceely Ann! You ain't no

fren' of de Dreamy's, you talk dat way, and I ain't got no time ter waste argyin' wid your fool notions. (*She goes to the door.*) Dreamy'll go ter his death sho's yo' born, if I don't find him an' tell him quick!

CEELY—(*terrified*) Oh Lawd!

IRENE—(*anxiously*) He'll sho'ly try ter come here and see his ole Mammy befo' she dies, don't you think, Ceely?

CEELY—Fo' Gawd I hopes so! She's been a-prayin' all de day—

IRENE—(*opening the door*) You hopes so, you fool nigger! I tells you it's good-bye to de Dreamy, he come here! I knows! I gotter find an' stop him. If he come here, Ceely, you tell him git out quick and hide, he don't wanter git pinched. You hear? You tell him dat, Ceely, for Gawd's sake! I'se got ter go—find him—high an' low— (*She goes out leaving Ceely staring at her in speechless indignation.*)

CEELY—(*drawing a deep breath*) Yo' street gal! I don' b'lieve one word you says—stuffin' me wid yo' bad lies so's you kin keep de Dreamy frum leavin' you! (*Mammy Saunders awakes and groans faintly. Ceely hurries over to her bedside.*) Is de pain hurtin' agin, Mammy?

MAMMY—(*vaguely*) Dat you, Dreamy?

CEELY—No, Mammy, dis is Ceely. Dreamy's comin' soon. Is you restin' easy?

MAMMY—(*as if she hadn't heard*) Dat you, Dreamy?

CEELY—(*sitting down in the rocker by the bed and taking one of the old woman's hands in her's*) No. Dreamy's comin'.

MAMMY—(*after a pause—suddenly*) Does you 'member yo' dead Mammy, chile?

CEELY—(*mystified*) My dead Mammy?

MAMMY—Didn' I heah yo' talkin' jest now, Dreamy?

CEELY—(*very worried*) I clar ter goodness, she don' know me ary bit. Dis is Ceely Ann talkin' ter yo', Mammy.

MAMMY—Who was yo' talkin' wid, Dreamy?

CEELY—(*shaking her head—in a trembling voice*) Hit can't be long befo' de en'. (*in a louder tone*) Hit was me talkin' wid a pusson fum ovah de way. She say tell you Dreamy comin' heah ter see yo' right away. You heah dat, Mammy? (*The old woman sighs but does not answer. There is a pause.*)

MAMMY—(*suddenly*) Does yo' 'member yo' dead Mammy,

chile? (*then with a burst of religious exaltation*) De Lawd have mercy!

CEELY—(*like an echo*) Bless de Lawd! (*then in a frightened half-whisper to herself*) Po' thing! Her min's done leavin' her jest like de doctor said. (*She looks down at the old woman helplessly. The door on the right is opened stealthily and the Dreamy Kid slinks in on tiptoe.*)

CEELY—(*hearing a board creak, turns quickly toward the door and gives a frightened start*) Dreamy!

DREAMY—(*puts his fingers to his lips—commandingly*) Ssshh! (*He bends down to a crouching position and holding the door about an inch open, peers out into the hallway in an attitude of tense waiting, one hand evidently clutching some weapon in the side pocket of his coat. After a moment he is satisfied of not being followed, and, after closing the door carefully and locking it, he stands up and walks to the center of the room casting a look of awed curiosity at the figure in the bed. He is a well-built, good looking young negro, light in color. His eyes are shifty and hard, their expression one of tough, scornful defiance. His mouth is cruel and perpetually drawn back at the corner into a snarl. He is dressed in well-fitting clothes of a flashy pattern. A light cap is pulled down on the side of his head.*)

CEELY—(*coming from the bed to meet him*) Bless de Lawd, here you is at las'!

DREAMY—(*with a warning gesture*) Nix on de loud talk! Talk low, can't yuh! (*He glances back at the door furtively—then continues with a sneer*) Yuh're a fine nut, Ceely Ann! What for you sendin' out all ober de town for me like you was crazy! D'yuh want ter git me in de cooler? Don' you know dey're after me for what I done last night?

CEELY—(*fearfully*) I heerd somep'n—but—what you done, Dreamy?

DREAMY—(*with an attempt at a careless bravado*) I croaked a guy, dat's what! A white man.

CEELY—(*in a frightened whisper*) What you mean—croaked?

DREAMY—(*boastfully*) I shot him dead, dat's what! (*as Ceely shrinks away from him in horror—resentfully*) Aw say, don' gimme none o'dem looks o'yourn. 'T'warn't my doin' nohow. He was de one lookin' for trouble. I wasn't seekin' for no mess wid him dat I would help. But he tole folks he was gwine ter git me for a fac', and dat fo'ced my hand. I had ter git him ter pertect my own life. (*with cruel satisfaction*) And I got him right, you b'lieve me!

CEELY—(*putting her hands over her face with a low moan of terror*) May de good Lawd pardon yo' wickedness! Oh Lawd! What yo' po' ole Mammy gwine say if she hear tell—an' she never knowin' how bad you's got.

DREAMY—(*fiercely*) Hell! You ain't tole her, is you?

CEELY—Think I want ter kill her on the instant? An' I didn' know myse'f—what you done—till you tells me. (*frightenedly*) Oh, Dreamy, what you gwine do now? How you gwine git away? (*almost wailing*) Good Lawd, de perlice gon' kotch you suah!

DREAMY—(*savagely*) Shut yo' loud mouth, damn yo'! (*He stands tensely listening for some sound from the hall. After a moment he points to the bed.*) Is Mammy sleepin'?

CEELY—(*tiptoes to the bed*) Seems like she is. (*She comes back to him.*) Dat's de way wid her—sleep fo' a few minutes, den she wake, den sleep agin.

DREAMY—(*scornfully*) Aw, dere ain't nothin' wrong wid her 'ceptin' she's ole. What yuh wanter send de word tellin' me she's croakin', and git me comin' here at de risk o' my life, and den find her sleepin'. (*clenching his fist threateningly*) I gotter mind ter smash yo' face for playin' de damn fool and makin' me de goat. (*He turns toward the door.*) Ain't no us'en me stayin' here when dey'll likely come lookin' for me. I'm gwine out where I gotta chance ter make my git-away. De boys is all fixin' it up for me. (*his hand on the doorknob*) When Mammy wakes, you tell her I couldn't wait, you hear?

CEELY—(*hurrying to him and grabbing his arm—pleadingly*) Don' yo' go now, Dreamy—not jest yit. Fo' de good Lawd's sake, don' yo' go befo' you speaks wid her! If yo' knew how she's been a-callin' an' a-prayin' for yo' all de day—

DREAMY—(*scornfully but a bit uncertainly*) Aw, she don' need none o' me. What good kin I do watchin' her do a kip? It'd be dif'frunt if she was croakin' on de level.

CEELY—(*in an anguished whisper*) She's gwine wake up in a secon' an' den she call: "Dreamy. Whar's Dreamy?"—an' what I gwine tell her den? An' yo' Mammy is dyin', Dreamy, sho's fate! Her min' been wanderin' an' she don' even recernize me no mo', an' de doctor say when dat come it ain't but a sho't time befo' de en'. Yo' gotter stay wid yo' Mammy long 'nuff ter speak wid her, Dreamy. Yo' jest gotter stay wid her in her las' secon's on dis yearth when she's callin' ter yo'. (*with conviction as he hesitates*) Listen heah, yo' Dreamy! Yo' don' never git no bit er luck in dis worril ary agin, yo' leaves her now. De perlice gon' kotch yo' suah.

DREAMY—(*with superstitious fear*) Ssshh! Can dat bull, Ceely! (*then boastfully*) I wasn't pinin' to beat it up here, git me? De boys was all persuadin' me not ter take de chance. It's takin' my life in my hands, dat's what. But when I heerd it was ole Mammy croakin' and axin' ter see me, I says ter myse'f: "Dreamy, you gotter make good wid ole Mammy no matter what come—or you don' never git a bit of luck in yo' life no more." And I was game and come, wasn't I? Nary body in dis worril kin say de Dreamy ain't game ter de core, n'matter what. (*With sudden decision walks to the foot of the bed and stands looking down at Mammy. A note of fear creeps into his voice.*) Gawd, she's quiet 'nuff. Maybe she done passed away in her sleep like de ole ones does. You go see, Ceely; an' if she's on'y sleepin', you wake her up. I wanter speak wid her quick—an' den I'll make a break outa here. You make it fast, Ceely Ann, I tells yo'.

CEELY—(*bends down beside the bed*) Mammy! Mammy! Here's de Dreamy.

MAMMY—(*opens her eyes—drowsily and vaguely, in a weak voice*) Dreamy?

DREAMY—(*shuffling his feet and moving around the bed*) Here I is, Mammy.

MAMMY—(*fastening her eyes on him with fascinated joy*) Dreamy! Hits yo'! (*then uncertainly*) I ain't dreamin' nor seein' ha'nts, is I?

DREAMY—(*coming forward and taking her hand*) 'Deed I ain't no ghost. Here I is, sho' 'nuff.

MAMMY—(*clutching his hand tight and pulling it down on her breast—in an ecstasy of happiness*) Didn' I know you'd come! Didn' I say: "Dreamy ain't gwine let his ole Mammy die all lone by he'se'f an' him not dere wid her." I knows yo'd come. (*She starts to laugh joyously, but coughs and sinks back weakly.*)

DREAMY—(*shudders in spite of himself as he realizes for the first time how far gone the old woman is—forcing a tone of joking reassurance*) What's dat foolishness I hears you talkin', Mammy? Wha' d'yuh mean pullin' dat bull 'bout croakin' on me? Shoo! Tryin' ter kid me, ain't yo'? Shoo! You live ter plant de flowers on my grave, see if you don'.

MAMMY—(*sadly and very weakly*) I knows! I knows! Hit ain't long now. (*bursting into a sudden weak hysteria*) Yo' stay heah, Dreamy! Yo' stay heah by me, yo' stay heah—till de good Lawd take me home. Yo' promise me dat! Yo' do dat fo' po' ole Mammy, won't yo'?

DREAMY—(*uneasily*) 'Deed I will, Mammy, 'deed I will.

MAMMY—(*closing her eyes with a sigh of relief—calmly*) Bless de Lawd for dat. Den I ain't skeered no mo'. (*She settles herself comfortably in the bed as if preparing for sleep.*)

CEELY—(*in a low voice*) I gotter go home fo' a minute, Dreamy. I ain't been dere all de day and Lawd knows what happen. I'll be back yere befo' ve'y long.

DREAMY—(*his eyes fixed on Mammy*) Aw right, beat it if yuh wanter. (*turning to her—in a fierce whisper*) On'y don' be long. I can't stay here an' take dis risk, you hear?

CEELY—(*frightenedly*) I knows, chile. I come back, I swar! (*She goes out quietly. Dreamy goes quickly to the window and cautiously searches the street below with his eyes.*)

MAMMY—(*uneasily*) Dreamy. (*He hurries back and takes her hand again.*) I got de mos' 'culiar feelin' in my head. Seems like de years done all roll away an' I'm back down home in de ole place whar yo' was bo'n. (*after a short pause*) Does yo' 'member yo' own mammy, chile?

DREAMY—No.

MAMMY—Yo' was too young, I s'pec'. Yo' was on'y a baby w'en she tuck 'n' die. My Sal was a mighty fine 'oman, if I does say hit my se'f.

DREAMY—(*fidgeting nervously*) Don' you talk, Mammy. Better you'd close yo' eyes an' rest.

MAMMY—(*with a trembling smile—weakly*) Shoo! W'at is I done come ter wid my own gran' chile bossin' me 'bout. I wants ter talk. You knows you ain't give me much chance ter talk wid yo' dese las' years.

DREAMY—(*sullenly*) I ain't had de time, Mammy; but you knows I was always game ter give you anything I got. (*a note of appeal in his voice*) You knows dat, don' you, Mammy?

MAMMY—Sho'ly I does. Yo' been a good boy, Dreamy; an' if dere's one thing more'n nother makes me feel like I mighter done good in de sight er de Lawd, hits dat I raised yo' fum a baby.

DREAMY—(*clearing his throat gruffly*) Don' you talk so much, Mammy.

MAMMY—(*querulously*) I gotter talk, chile. Come times— w'en I git thinkin' yere in de bed—w'at's gwine ter come ter me a'mos' b'fore I knows hit—like de thief in de night—en den I gits skeered. But w'en I talks wid yo' I ain't skeered a bit.

DREAMY—(*defiantly*) You ain't got nothin' to be skeered of—not when de Dreamy's here.

MAMMY—(*after a slight pause, faintly*) Dere's a singin' in my ears all de time. (*seized by a sudden religious ecstasy*) Maybe hits de singin' hymns o' de blessed angels I done heah fum above. (*wildly*) Bless Gawd! Bless Gawd! Pity dis po' ole sinner!

DREAMY—(*with an uneasy glance at the door*) Ssshh, Mammy! Don' shout so loud.

MAMMY—De pictures keep a whizzin' fo' my eyes like de thread in a sewing machine. Seems s'if all my life done fly back ter me all ter once. (*with a flickering smile —weakly*) Does you know how yo' come by dat nickname dey alls call yo'— de Dreamy? Is I ever tole yo' dat?

DREAMY—(*evidently lying*) No, Mammy.

MAMMY—Hit was one mawnin' b'fo' we come No'th. Me an' yo' mammy—yo' was des a baby in arms den—

DREAMY—(*hears a noise from the hall*) Ssshh, Mammy! For God's sake, don't speak for a minute. I hears somep'n. (*He stares at the door, his face hardening savagely, and listens intently.*)

MAMMY—(*in a frightened tone*) W'at's de matter, chile?

DREAMY—Ssshh! Somebody comin'. (*A noise of footsteps comes from the hall stairway. Dreamy springs to his feet.*) Leggo my hand, Mammy—jest for a secon'. I come right back to you. (*He pulls his hand from the old woman's grip. She falls back on the pillows moaning. Dreamy pulls a large automatic revolver from his coat pocket and tiptoes quickly to the door. As he does so there is a sharp rap. He stands listening at the crack for a moment, then noiselessly turns the key, unlocking the door. Then he crouches low down by the wall so that the door, when opened, will hide him from the sight of anyone entering. There is another and louder rap on the door.*)

MAMMY—(*groaning*) W'at's dat, Dreamy? Whar is yo'?

DREAMY—Ssshh! (*Then muffling his voice he calls*) Come in. (*He raises the revolver in his hand. The door is pushed open and Irene enters, her eyes peering wildly about the room. Her bosom is heaving as if she had been running and she is trembling all over with terrified excitement.*)

IRENE—(*not seeing him calls out questioningly*) Dreamy?

DREAMY—(*lowering his revolver and rising to his feet roughly*) Close dat door!

IRENE—(*whirling about with a startled cry*) Dreamy!

DREAMY—(*shutting the door and locking it—aggressively*) Shut yo' big mouth, gal, or I'll bang it shut for you! You wanter let de whole block know where I is?

IRENE—(*hysterical with joy—trying to put her arms around him*) Bless God, I foun' you at last!

DREAMY—(*pushing her away roughly*) Leggo o' me! Why you come here follerin' me? Ain't yo' got 'nuff sense in yo' fool head ter know de bulls is liable ter shadow you when dey knows you's my gal? Is you pinin' ter git me kotched an' sent to de chair?

IRENE—(*terrified*) No, no!

DREAMY—(*savagely*) I gotter mind ter hand you one you won't ferget! (*He draws back his fist.*)

IRENE—(*shrinking away*) Don' you hit me, Dreamy! Don' you beat me up now! Jest lemme 'xplain, dat's all.

MAMMY—(*in a frightened whimper*) Dreamy! Come yere to me. Whar is yo'? I'se skeered!

DREAMY—(*in a fierce whisper to Irene*) Can dat bull or I'll fix you. (*He hurries to the old woman and pats her hand.*) Here I is, Mammy.

MAMMY—Who dat yo's a-talkin' wid?

DREAMY—On'y a fren' o' Ceely Ann's, Mammy, askin' where she is. I gotter talk wid her some mo' yit. You sleep, Mammy? (*He goes to Irene.*)

MAMMY—(*feebly*) Don' yo' leave me, Dreamy.

DREAMY—I'se right here wid you. (*fiercely to Irene*) You git the hell outa here, you Reeny, you heah—quick! Dis ain't no place for de likes o' you wid ole Mammy dyin'.

IRENE—(*with a horrified glance at the bed*) Is she dyin'—honest?

DREAMY—Ssshh! She's croakin', I tells yo'—an' I gotter stay wid her fo' a while—an' I ain't got no time ter be pesterin' wid you. Beat it, now! Beat it outa here befo' I knocks yo' cold, git me?

IRENE—Jest wait a secon' for de love o' Gawd. I got somep'n ter tell you—

DREAMY—I don' wanter hear yo' fool talk. (*He gives her a push toward the door.*) Git outa dis, you hear me?

IRENE—I'll go. I'm going soon—soon's ever I've had my say. Lissen Dreamy! It's about de coppers I come ter tell you.

DREAMY—(*quickly*) Why don' you say dat befo'? What you know, gal?

IRENE—Just befo' I come here to find you de first time, de Madam sends me out to Murphy's ter git her a bottle o' gin. I goes in de side door but I ain't rung de bell yet. I hear yo' name spoken an' I stops ter lissen. Dey was three or four men in de back room. Dey don't hear me open de outside door, an' dey can't see me, course. It was Big Sullivan from de Central Office talkin'. He was talkin' 'bout de killin' you done last night and he tells dem odders he's heerd 'bout de ole woman gittin' so sick, and dat if dey don't fin' you none of de udder places dey's lookin', dey's goin' wait for you here. Dey s'pecs you come here say good-bye to Mammy befo' you make yo' get-away.

DREAMY—It's aw right den. Dey ain't come yit. Twister Smith done tole me de coast was clear befo' I come here.

IRENE—Dat was den. It ain't now.

DREAMY—(*excitedly*) What you mean, gal?

IRENE—I was comin' in by de front way when I sees some pusson hidin' in de doorway 'cross de street. I gits a good peek at him and when I does—it's a copper, Dreamy, suah's yo' born, in his plain clo'se, and he's a watchin' de door o' dis house like a cat.

DREAMY—(*goes to the window and stealthily crouching by the dark side peeks out. One glance is enough. He comes quickly back to Irene.*) You got de right dope, gal. It's dat Mickey. I knows him even in de dark. Dey're waitin'—so dey ain't wise I'm here yit, dat's suah.

IRENE—But dey'll git wise befo' long.

DREAMY—He don't pipe you comin' in here?

IRENE—I skulked roun' and sneaked in by de back way froo de yard. Dey ain't none o' dem dar yit. (*raising her voice—excitedly*) But dere will be soon. Dey're boun' to git wise to dat back door. You ain't got no time to lose, Dreamy. Come on wid me now. Git back where yo' safe. It's de cooler for you certain if you stays here. Dey'll git you like a rat in de trap. (*as Dreamy hesitates*) For de love of Gawd, Dreamy, wake up to youse'f!

DREAMY—(*uncertainly*) I can't beat it—wid Mammy here alone. My luck done turn bad all my life, if I does.

IRENE—(*fiercely*) What good's you gittin' pinched and sent to de chair gwine do her? Is you crazy mad? Come away wid me, I tells you!

DREAMY—(*half-persuaded—hesitatingly*) I gotter speak wid her. You wait a secon'.

IRENE—(*wringing her hands*) Dis ain't no time now for fussin' wid her.

DREAMY—(*gruffly*) Shut up! (*He makes a motion for her to remain where she is and goes over to the bed—in a low voice*) Mammy.

MAMMY—(*hazily*) Dat you, Dreamy? (*She tries to reach out her hand and touch him.*)

DREAMY—I'm gwine leave you—jest for a moment, Mammy. I'll send de word for Ceely Ann—

MAMMY—(*wide awake in an instant—with intense alarm*) Don' yo' do dat! Don' yo' move one step out er yere or yo'll be sorry, Dreamy.

DREAMY—(*apprehensively*) I gotter go, I tells you. I'll come back.

MAMMY—(*with wild grief*) O good Lawd! W'en I's drawin' de las' bre'fs in dis po' ole body— (*frenziedly*) De Lawd have mercy! Good Lawd have mercy!

DREAMY—(*fearfully*) Stop dat racket, Mammy! You bring all o' dem down on my head! (*He rushes over and crouches by the window again to peer out—in relieved tones*) He ain't heerd nothin'. He's dar yit.

IRENE—(*imploringly*) Come on, Dreamy! (*Mammy groans with pain.*)

DREAMY—(*hurrying to the bed*) What's de matter, Mammy?

IRENE—(*stamping her foot*) Dreamy! Fo' Gawd's sake!

MAMMY—Lawd have mercy! (*She groans.*) Gimme yo' han', chile. Yo' ain't gwine leave me now, Dreamy? Yo' ain't, is yo'? Yo' ole Mammy won't bodder yo' long. Yo' know w'at yo' promise me, Dreamy! Yo' promise yo' sacred word yo' stay wid me till de en'. (*with an air of somber prophecy—slowly*) If yo' leave me now, yo' ain't gwine git no bit er luck s'long's yo' live, I tells yo' dat!

DREAMY—(*frightened—pleadingly*) Don' you say dat, Mammy!

IRENE—Come on, Dreamy!

DREAMY—(*slowly*) I can't. (*in awed tones*) Don' you hear de curse she puts on me if I does?

MAMMY—(*her voice trembling with weak tears*) Don' go, chile!

DREAMY—(*hastily*) I won't leave dis room, I swar ter you! (*Relieved by the finality in his tones, the old woman sighs and closes her eyes. Dreamy frees his hand from her's and goes to Irene. He speaks with a strange calm.*) De game's up, gal. You better beat it while de goin's good.

IRENE—(*aghast*) You gwine stay?

DREAMY—I gotter, gal. I ain't gwine agin her dyin' curse. No, suh!

IRENE—(*pitifully*) But dey'll git you suah!

DREAMY—(*slapping the gun in his pocket significantly*) Dey'll have some gittin'. I git some o' dem fust. (*with gloomy determination*) Dey don' git dis chicken alive! Lawd Jesus, no suh. Not de Dreamy!

IRENE—(*helplessly*) Oh Lawdy, Lawdy! (*She goes to the*

window—with a short cry) He's talkin' wid someone. Dere's two o' dem. (*Dreamy hurries to her side.*)

DREAMY—I knows him—de udder. It's Big Sullivan. (*pulling her away roughly*) Come out o' dat! Dey'll see you. (*He pushes her toward the door.*) Dey won't wait down dere much longer. Dey'll be comin' up here soon. (*prayerfully, with a glance at the bed*) I hopes she's croaked by den', fo' Christ I does!

IRENE—(*as if she couldn't believe it*) Den you ain't gwine save youse'f while dere's time? (*pleadingly*) Oh Dreamy, you can make it yet!

DREAMY—De game's up, I tole you. (*with gloomy fatalism*) I s'pect it hatter be. Yes, suh. Dey'd git me in de long run anyway—and wid her curse de luck'd be agin me. (*with sudden anger*) Git outa here, you Reeny! You ain't aimin' ter get shot up too, is you? Ain't no sense in dat.

IRENE—(*fiercely*) I'se stayin' too, here wid you!

DREAMY—No you isn't! None o' dat bull! You ain't got no mix in dis jamb.

IRENE—Yes, I is! Ain't you my man?

DREAMY—Don' make no dif. I don' wanter git you in Dutch more'n you is. It's bad 'nuff fo' me. (*He pushes her toward the door.*) Blow while you kin, I tells you!

IRENE—(*resisting him*) No, Dreamy! What I care if dey kills me? I'se gwine stick wid you.

DREAMY—(*gives her another push*) No, you isn't, gal. (*unlocking the door—relentlessly*) Out wid you!

IRENE—(*hysterically*) You can't gimme no bum's rush. I'm gwine stay.

DREAMY—(*gloomily*) On'y one thing fo' me ter do den. (*He hits her on the side of the face with all his might knocking her back against the wall where she sways as if about to fall. Then he opens the door and grabs her two arms from behind.*) Out wid you, gal!

IRENE—(*moaning*) Dreamy! Dreamy! Lemme stay wid you! (*He pushes her into the hallway and holds her there at arm's length.*) Fo' Gawd's sake, Dreamy!

MAMMY—(*whimperingly*) Dreamy! I'se skeered!

IRENE—(*from the hall*) I'se gwine stay right here at de door. You might s'well lemme in.

DREAMY—(*frowning*) Don' do dat, Reeny. (*then with a sudden idea*) You run roun' and tell de gang what's up. Maybe dey git me outa dis, you hear?

IRENE—(*with eager hope*) You think dey kin?

DREAMY—Never kin tell. You hurry—through de back yard, 'member—an' don' git pinched, now.

IRENE—(*eagerly*) I'm gwine! I'll bring dem back!

DREAMY—(*stands listening to her retreating footsteps—then shuts and locks the door—gloomily to himself*) Ain't no good. Dey dassent do nothin'—but I hatter git her outa dis somehow.

MAMMY—(*groaning*) Dreamy!

DREAMY—Here I is. Jest a secon'. (*He goes to the window.*)

MAMMY—(*weakly*) I feels—like—de en's comin'. Oh Lawd, Lawd!

DREAMY—(*absent-mindedly*) Yes, Mammy. (*aloud to himself*) Dey're sneakin' cross de street. Dere's anudder of 'em. Dat's tree. (*He glances around the room quickly—then hurries over and takes hold of the chest of drawers. As he does so the old woman commences to croon shrilly to herself.*)

DREAMY—Stop dat noise, Mammy! Stop dat noise!

MAMMY—(*wanderingly*) Dat's how come yo' got dat—dat nickname—Dreamy.

DREAMY—Yes, Mammy. (*He puts the lamp on the floor to the rear of the door, turning it down low. Then he carries the chest of drawers over and places it against the door as a barricade.*)

MAMMY—(*rambling as he does this—very feebly*) Does yo' know—I gives you dat name—w'en yo's des a baby—lyin' in my arms—

DREAMY—Yes, Mammy.

MAMMY—Down by de crik—under de ole willow—whar I uster take yo'—wid yo' big eyes a-chasin'—de sun flitterin' froo de grass—an' out on de water—

DREAMY—(*takes the revolver from his pocket and puts it on top of the chest of drawers*) Dey don' git de Dreamy alive—not for de chair! Lawd Jesus, no suh!

MAMMY—An' yo' was always—a-lookin'—an' a-thinkin' ter yo'se'f—an' yo' big eyes jest a-dreamin' an' a-dreamin' —an' dat's w'en I gives yo' dat nickname—Dreamy— Dreamy—

DREAMY—Yes, Mammy. (*He listens at the crack of the door—in a tense whisper*) I don' hear dem—but dey're comin' sneakin' up de stairs, I knows it.

MAMMY—(*faintly*) Whar is yo', Dreamy? I can't—ha'dly—breathe—no mo'. Oh Lawd have mercy!

DREAMY—(*goes over to the bed*) Here I is, Mammy.

MAMMY—(*speaking with difficulty*) Yo'—kneel down—chile—say a pray'r—Oh Lawd!

DREAMY—Jest a secon', Mammy. (*He goes over and gets his revolver and comes back.*)

MAMMY—Gimme—yo' hand—chile. (*Dreamy gives her his left hand. The revolver is in his right. He stares nervously at the door.*) An' yo' kneel down—pray fo' me. (*Dreamy gets on one knee beside the bed. There is a sound from the hallway as if some-one had made a misstep on the stairs—then silence. Dreamy starts and half aims his gun in the direction of the door. Mammy groans weakly.*) I'm dyin', chile. Hit's de en'. You pray for me—out loud—so's I can heah. Oh Lawd! (*She gasps to catch her breath.*)

DREAMY—(*abstractedly, not having heard a word she has said*) Yes, Mammy. (*aloud to himself with an air of grim deter-mination as if he were making a pledge*) Dey don't git de Dreamy! Not while he's 'live! Lawd Jesus, no suh!

MAMMY—(*falteringly*) Dat's right—yo' pray—Lawd Jesus—Lawd Jesus— (*There is another slight sound of movement from the hallway.*)

(*The Curtain Falls*)

WHERE THE CROSS IS MADE

IS MADE

A Play in One Act

CHARACTERS

CAPTAIN ISAIAH BARTLETT
NAT BARTLETT, *his son*
SUE BARTLETT, *his daughter*
DOCTOR HIGGINS
SILAS HORNE, *mate*
CATES, *bo'sun*   } *of the schooner* Mary Allen
JIMMY KANAKA, *harpooner*

Where the Cross Is Made

SCENE—*Captain Bartlett's "cabin"—a room erected as a lookout post at the top of his house situated on a high point of land on the California coast. The inside of the compartment is fitted up like the captain's cabin of a deep-sea sailing vessel. On the left, forward, a porthole. Farther back, the stairs of the companionway. Still farther, two more portholes. In the rear, left, a marble-topped sideboard with a ship's lantern on it. In the rear, center, a door opening on stairs which lead to the lower house. A cot with a blanket is placed against the wall to the right of the door. In the right wall, five portholes. Directly under them, a wooden bench. In front of the bench, a long table with two straight-backed chairs, one in front, the other to the left of it. A cheap, dark-colored rug is on the floor. In the ceiling, midway from front to rear, a skylight extending from opposite the door to above the left edge of the table. In the right extremity of the skylight is placed a floating ship's compass. The light from the binnacle sheds over this from above and seeps down into the room, casting a vague globular shadow of the compass on the floor.*

The time is an early hour of a clear windy night in the fall of the year 1900. Moonlight, winnowed by the wind which moans in the stubborn angles of the old house, creeps wearily in through the portholes and rests like tired dust in circular patches upon the floor and table. An insistent monotone of thundering surf, muffled and far-off, is borne upward from the beach below.

After the curtain rises the door in the rear is opened slowly and the head and shoulders of Nat Bartlett appear over the sill. He casts a quick glance about the room, and seeing no one there, ascends the remaining steps and enters. He makes a sign to some one in the darkness beneath: "All right, Doctor." *Doctor Higgins follows him into the room and, closing the door, stands looking with great curiosity around him. He is a slight, medium-sized professional-looking man of about thirty-five. Nat Bartlett is very tall, gaunt, and loose-framed. His right arm has been amputated at the shoulder and the sleeve on that side of the heavy mackinaw he wears hangs flabbily or flaps against his body as he moves. He appears much older than his thirty years. His shoulders have a weary stoop as if worn down by the burden of his massive head*

*with its heavy shock of tangled black hair. His face is long, bony,
and sallow, with deep-set black eyes, a large aquiline nose, a wide
thin-lipped mouth shadowed by an unkempt bristle of mustache.
His voice is low and deep with a penetrating, hollow, metallic
quality. In addition to the mackinaw, he wears corduroy trousers
stuffed down into high laced boots.*

NAT—Can you see, Doctor?

HIGGINS—(*in the too-casual tones which betray an inward
uneasiness*) Yes—perfectly—don't trouble. The moonlight is
so bright—

NAT—Luckily. (*walking slowly toward the table*) He doesn't
want any light—lately—only the one from the binnacle
there.

HIGGINS—He? Ah—you mean your father?

NAT—(*impatiently*) Who else?

HIGGINS—(*a bit startled—gazing around him in embarrassment*) I suppose this is all meant to be like a ship's cabin?

NAT—Yes—as I warned you.

HIGGINS—(*in surprise*) Warned me? Why, warned? I think
it's very natural—and interesting—this whim of his.

NAT—(*meaningly*) Interesting, it may be.

HIGGINS—And he lives up here, you said—never comes
down?

NAT—Never—for the past three years. My sister brings his
food up to him. (*He sits down in the chair to the left of the
table.*) There's a lantern on the sideboard there, Doctor. Bring
it over and sit down. We'll make a light. I'll ask your pardon
for bringing you to this room on the roof—but—no one'll
hear us here; and by seeing for yourself the mad way he
lives— Understand that I want you to get all the facts—just
that, facts!—and for that light is necessary. Without that—
they become dreams up here—dreams, Doctor.

HIGGINS—(*with a relieved smile carries over the lantern*) It
is a trifle spooky.

NAT—(*not seeming to notice this remark*) He won't take any
note of this light. His eyes are too busy—out there. (*He flings
his left arm in a wide gesture seaward.*) And if he does notice—
well, let him come down. You're bound to see him sooner or
later. (*He scratches a match and lights the lantern.*)

HIGGINS—Where is—he?

NAT—(*pointing upward*) Up on the poop. Sit down, man! He'll not come—yet awhile.

HIGGINS—(*sitting gingerly on the chair in front of table*) Then he has the roof too rigged up like a ship?

NAT—I told you he had. Like a deck, yes. A wheel, compass, binnacle light, the companionway there (*he points*), a bridge to pace up and down on—*and keep watch*. If the wind wasn't so high you'd hear him now—back and forth—all the live-long night. (*with a sudden harshness*) Didn't I tell you he's mad?

HIGGINS—(*with a professional air*) That was nothing new. I've heard that about him from all sides since I first came to the asylum yonder. You say he only walks at night—up there?

NAT—Only at night, yes. (*grimly*) The things he wants to see can't be made out in daylight—dreams and such.

HIGGINS—But just what is he trying to see? Does any one know? Does he tell?

NAT—(*impatiently*) Why, every one knows what Father looks for, man! The ship, of course.

HIGGINS—What ship?

NAT—His ship—the Mary Allen—named for my dead mother.

HIGGINS—But—I don't understand— Is the ship long overdue—or what?

NAT—Lost in a hurricane off the Celebes with all on board—three years ago!

HIGGINS—(*wonderingly*) Ah. (*after a pause*) But your father still clings to a doubt—

NAT—There is no doubt for him or any one else to cling to. She was sighted bottom up, a complete wreck, by the whaler John Slocum. That was two weeks after the storm. They sent a boat out to read her name.

HIGGINS—And hasn't your father ever heard—

NAT—He was the first to hear, naturally. Oh, he *knows* right enough, if that's what you're driving at. (*He bends toward the doctor—intensely*) He *knows*, Doctor, he *knows*— but he won't *believe*. He can't—and keep living.

HIGGINS—(*impatiently*) Come, Mr. Bartlett, let's get

down to brass tacks. You didn't drag me up here to make things more obscure, did you? Let's have the facts you spoke of. I'll need them to give sympathetic treatment to his case when we get him to the asylum.

NAT—(*anxiously—lowering his voice*) And you'll come to take him away to-night—for sure?

HIGGINS—Twenty minutes after I leave here I'll be back in the car. That's positive.

NAT—And you know your way through the house?

HIGGINS—Certainly, I remember—but I don't see—

NAT—The outside door will be left open for you. You must come right up. My sister and I will be here—with him. And you understand— Neither of us knows anything about this. The authorities have been complained to—not by us, mind—but by some one. He must never know—

HIGGINS—Yes, yes—but still I don't— Is he liable to prove violent?

NAT—No—no. He's quiet always—too quiet; but he might do something—anything—if he knows—

HIGGINS—Rely on me not to tell him, then; but I'll bring along two attendants in case— (*He breaks off and continues in matter-of-fact tones*) And now for the facts in this case, if you don't mind, Mr. Bartlett.

NAT—(*shaking his head—moodily*) There are cases where facts— Well, here goes—the brass tacks. My father was a whaling captain as his father before him. The last trip he made was seven years ago. He expected to be gone two years. It was four before we saw him again. His ship had been wrecked in the Indian Ocean. He and six others managed to reach a small island on the fringe of the Archipelago—an island barren as hell, Doctor—after seven days in an open boat. The rest of the whaling crew never were heard from again—gone to the sharks. Of the six who reached the island with my father only three were alive when a fleet of Malay canoes picked them up, mad from thirst and starvation, the four of them. These four men finally reached Frisco. (*with great emphasis*) They were my father; Silas Horne, the mate; Cates, the bo'sun, and Jimmy Kanaka, a Hawaiian harpooner. Those four! (*with a forced laugh*) There are facts for you. It was all in the papers at the time—my father's story.

HIGGINS—But what of the other three who were on the island?

NAT—(*harshly*) Died of exposure, perhaps. Mad and jumped into the sea, perhaps. That was the told story. Another was whispered—killed and eaten, perhaps! But gone—vanished—that, undeniably. That was the fact. For the rest—who knows? And what does it matter?

HIGGINS—(*with a shudder*) I should think it would matter—a lot.

NAT—(*fiercely*) We're dealing with facts, Doctor! (*with a laugh*) And here are some more for you. My father brought the three down to this house with him—Horne and Cates and Jimmy Kanaka. We hardly recognized my father. He had been through hell and looked it. His hair was white. But you'll see for yourself—soon. And the others—they were all a bit queer, too—mad, if you will. (*He laughs again.*) So much for the facts, Doctor. They leave off there and the dreams begin.

HIGGINS—(*doubtfully*) It would seem—the facts are enough.

NAT—Wait. (*He resumes deliberately.*) One day my father sent for me and in the presence of the others told me the dream. I was to be heir to the secret. Their second day on the island, he said, they discovered in a sheltered inlet the rotten, water-logged hulk of a Malay prau—a proper war prau such as the pirates used to use. She had been there rotting—God knows how long. The crew had vanished—God knows where, for there was no sign on the island that man had ever touched there. The Kanakas went over the prau—they're devils for staying under water, you know—and they found—in two chests— (*He leans back in his chair and smiles ironically.*) —Guess what, Doctor?

HIGGINS—(*with an answering smile*) Treasure, of course.

NAT—(*leaning forward and pointing his finger accusingly at the other*) You see! The root of belief is in you, too! (*Then he leans back with a hollow chuckle.*) Why, yes. Treasure, to be sure. What else? They landed it and—you can guess the rest, too—diamonds, emeralds, gold ornaments—innumerable, of course. Why limit the stuff of dreams? Ha-ha! (*He laughs sardonically as if mocking himself.*)

HIGGINS—(*deeply interested*) And then?

NAT—They began to go mad—hunger, thirst, and the rest—and they began to forget. Oh, they forgot a lot, and lucky for them they did, probably. But my father realizing, as he told me, what was happening to them, insisted that while they still knew what they were doing they should—guess again now, Doctor. Ha-ha!

HIGGINS—Bury the treasure?

NAT—(*ironically*) Simple, isn't it? Ha-ha. And then they made a map—the same old dream, you see—with a charred stick, and my father had care of it. They were picked up soon after, mad as hatters, as I have told you, by some Malays. (*He drops his mocking and adopts a calm, deliberate tone again.*) But the map isn't a dream, Doctor. We're coming back to facts again. (*He reaches into the pocket of his mackinaw and pulls out a crumpled paper.*) Here. (*He spreads it out on the table.*)

HIGGINS—(*craning his neck eagerly*) Dammit! This is interesting. The treasure, I suppose, is where—

NAT—Where the cross is made.

HIGGINS—And here are the signatures, I see. And that sign?

NAT—Jimmy Kanaka's. He couldn't write.

HIGGINS—And below? That's yours, isn't it?

NAT—As heir to the secret, yes. We all signed it here the morning the Mary Allen, the schooner my father had mortgaged this house to fit out, set sail to bring back the treasure. Ha-ha.

HIGGINS—The ship he's still looking for—that was lost three years ago?

NAT—The Mary Allen, yes. The other three men sailed away on her. Only father and the mate knew the approximate location of the island—and I—as heir. It's— (*He hesitates, frowning.*) No matter. I'll keep the mad secret. My father wanted to go with them—but my mother was dying. I dared not go either.

HIGGINS—Then you wanted to go? You believed in the treasure then?

NAT—Of course. Ha-ha. How could I help it? I believed until my mother's death. Then *he* became mad, entirely mad. He built this cabin—to wait in—and he suspected my growing doubt as time went on. So, as final proof, he gave me a thing he had kept hidden from them all—a sample of the richest of the treasure. Ha-ha. Behold! (*He takes from his pocket a heavy bracelet thickly studded with stones and throws it on the table near the lantern.*)

HIGGINS—(*picking it up with eager curiosity—as if in spite of himself*) Real jewels?

NAT—Ha-ha! You want to believe, too. No—paste and brass—Malay ornaments.

HIGGINS—You had it looked over?

NAT—Like a fool, yes. (*He puts it back in his pocket and shakes his head as if throwing off a burden.*) Now you know why he's mad—waiting for that ship—and why in the end I had to ask you to take him away where he'll be safe. The mortgage—the price of that ship—is to be foreclosed. We have to move, my sister and I. We can't take him with us. She is to be married soon. Perhaps away from the sight of the sea he may—

HIGGINS—(*perfunctorily*) Let's hope for the best. And I fully appreciate your position. (*He gets up, smiling.*) And thank you for the interesting story. I'll know how to humor him when he raves about treasure.

NAT—(*somberly*) He is quiet always—too quiet. He only walks to and fro—watching—

HIGGINS—Well, I must go. You think it's best to take him to-night?

NAT—(*persuasively*) Yes, Doctor. The neighbors—they're far away but—for my sister's sake—you understand.

HIGGINS—I see. It must be hard on her—this sort of thing— Well.— (*He goes to the door, which Nat opens for him.*) I'll return presently. (*He starts to descend.*)

NAT—(*urgently*) Don't fail us, Doctor. And come right up. He'll be here. (*He closes the door and tiptoes carefully to the companionway. He ascends it a few steps and remains for a moment listening for some sound from above. Then he goes over to the table, turning the lantern very low, and sits down, resting his elbows, his chin on his hands, staring somberly before him. The door in the rear is slowly opened. It creaks slightly and Nat jumps to his feet—in a thick voice of terror*) Who's there? (*The door swings wide open, revealing Sue Bartlett. She ascends into the room and shuts the door behind her. She is a tall, slender woman of twenty-five, with a pale, sad face framed in a mass of dark red hair. This hair furnishes the only touch of color about her. Her full lips are pale; the blue of her wistful wide eyes is fading into a twilight gray. Her voice is low and melancholy. She wears a dark wrapper and slippers.*)

SUE—(*stands and looks at her brother accusingly*) It's only I. What are you afraid of?

NAT—(*averts his eyes and sinks back on his chair again*) Nothing. I didn't know—I thought you were in your room.

SUE—(*comes to the table*) I was reading. Then I heard some one come down the stairs and go out. Who was it? (*with sudden terror*) It wasn't—Father?

NAT—No. He's up there—watching—as he always is.

SUE—(*sitting down—insistently*) Who was it?

NAT—(*evasively*) A man—I know.

SUE—What man? What is he? You're holding something back. Tell me.

NAT—(*raising his eyes defiantly*) A doctor.

SUE—(*alarmed*) Oh! (*with quick intuition*) You brought him up here—so that I wouldn't know!

NAT—(*doggedly*) No. I took him up here to see how things were—to ask him about Father.

SUE—(*as if afraid of the answer she will get*) Is he one of them—from the asylum? Oh, Nat, you haven't—

NAT—(*interrupting her—hoarsely*) No, no! Be still.

SUE—That would be—the last horror.

NAT—(*defiantly*) Why? You always say that. What could be more horrible than things as they are? I believe—it would be better for him—away—where he couldn't see the sea. He'll forget his mad idea of waiting for a lost ship and a treasure that never was. (*as if trying to convince himself—vehemently*) I believe this!

SUE—(*reproachfully*) You don't, Nat. You know he'd die if he hadn't the sea to live with.

NAT—(*bitterly*) And you know old Smith will foreclose the mortgage. Is that nothing? We cannot pay. He came yesterday and talked with me. He knows the place is his—to all purposes. He talked as if we were merely his tenants, curse him! And he swore he'd foreclose immediately unless—

SUE—(*eagerly*) What?

NAT—(*in a hard voice*) Unless we have—Father—taken away.

SUE—(*in anguish*) Oh! But why, why? What is Father to him?

NAT—The value of the property—our home which is his, Smith's. The neighbors are afraid. They pass by on the road at nights coming back to their farms from the town. They see *him* up there walking back and forth—waving his arms against the sky. They're afraid. They talk of a complaint. They say for his own good he must be taken away. They even whisper the house is haunted. Old Smith is afraid of his property. He thinks that *he* may set fire to the house—do anything—

SUE—(*despairingly*) But you told him how foolish that was, didn't you? That Father is quiet, always quiet.

NAT—What's the use of telling—when they believe—when they're afraid? (*Sue hides her face in her hands—a pause—Nat whispers hoarsely*) I've been afraid myself—at times.

SUE—Oh, Nat! Of what?

NAT—(*violently*) Oh, him and the sea he calls to! Of the damned sea he forced me on as a boy—the sea that robbed me of my arm and made me the broken thing I am!

SUE—(*pleadingly*) You can't blame Father—for your misfortune.

NAT—He took me from school and forced me on his ship, didn't he? What would I have been now but an ignorant sailor like him if he had had his way? No. It's the sea I should not blame, that foiled him by taking my arm and then throwing me ashore—another one of *his* wrecks!

SUE—(*with a sob*) You're bitter, Nat—and hard. It was so long ago. Why can't you forget?

NAT—(*bitterly*) Forget! You can talk! When Tom comes home from this voyage you'll be married and out of this with life before you—a captain's wife as our mother was. I wish you joy.

SUE—(*supplicatingly*) And you'll come with us, Nat—and father, too—and then—

NAT—Would you saddle your young husband with a madman and a cripple? (*fiercely*) No, no, not I! (*vindictively*) And not him, either! (*with sudden meaning—deliberately*) I've got to stay here. My book is three-fourths done—my book that will set me free! But I know, I feel, as sure as I stand here living before you, that I must finish it here. It could not live for me outside of this house where it was born. (*staring at her fixedly*) So I will stay—in spite of hell! (*Sue sobs hopelessly. After a pause he continues.*) Old Smith told me I could live here indefinitely without paying—as caretaker—if—

SUE—(*fearfully—like a whispered echo*) If?

NAT—(*staring at her—in a hard voice*) If I have *him* sent—where he'll no longer harm himself—nor others.

SUE—(*with horrified dread*) No—no, Nat! For our dead mother's sake.

NAT—(*struggling*) Did I say I had? Why do you look at me—like that?

SUE—Nat! Nat! For our mother's sake!

NAT—(*in terror*) Stop! Stop! She's dead—and at peace. Would you bring her tired soul back to him again to be bruised and wounded?

SUE—Nat!

NAT—(*clutching at his throat as though to strangle something within him—hoarsely*) Sue! Have mercy! (*His sister stares at him with dread foreboding. Nat calms himself with an effort and continues deliberately.*) Smith said he would give two thousand cash if I would sell the place to him—and he would let me stay, rent free, as caretaker.

SUE—(*scornfully*) Two thousand! Why, over and above the mortgage its worth—

NAT—It's not what it's worth. It's what one can get, cash—for my book—for freedom!

SUE—So that's why he wants Father sent away, the wretch! He must know the will Father made—

NAT—Gives the place to me. Yes, he knows. I told him.

SUE—(*dully*) Ah, how vile men are!

NAT—(*persuasively*) If it were to be done—if it were, I say—there'd be half for you for your wedding portion. That's fair.

SUE—(*horrified*) Blood money! Do you think I could touch it?

NAT—(*persuasively*) It would be only fair. I'd give it you.

SUE—My God, Nat, are you trying to bribe me?

NAT—No. It's yours in all fairness. (*with a twisted smile*) You forget I'm heir to the treasure, too, and can afford to be generous. Ha-ha.

SUE—(*alarmed*) Nat! You're so strange. You're sick, Nat. You couldn't talk this way if you were yourself. Oh, we must go away from here—you and father and I! Let Smith foreclose. There'll be something over the mortgage; and we'll move to some little house—by the sea so that father—

NAT—(*fiercely*) Can keep up his mad game with me—whispering dreams in my ear—pointing out to sea—mocking me with stuff like this! (*He takes the bracelet from his pocket. The sight of it infuriates him and he hurls it into a corner, exclaiming in a terrible voice*) No! No! It's too late for dreams now. It's too late! I've put them behind me to-night—forever!

SUE—(*looks at him and suddenly understands that what she dreads has come to pass—letting her head fall on her outstretched arms with a long moan*) Then—you've done it! You've sold him! Oh, Nat, you're cursed!

NAT—(*with a terrified glance at the roof above*) Ssshh! What are you saying? He'll be better off—away from the sea.

SUE—(*dully*) You've sold him.

NAT—(*wildly*) No! No! (*He takes the map from his pocket.*) Listen, Sue! For God's sake, listen to me! See! The map of the island. (*He spreads it out on the table.*) And the treasure—where the cross is made. (*He gulps and his words pour out incoherently.*) I've carried it about for years. Is that nothing? You don't know what it means. It stands between me and my book. It's stood between me and life—driving me mad! *He* taught me to wait and hope with him—wait and hope—day after day. He made me doubt my brain and give the lie to my eyes—when hope was dead—when I knew it was all a dream—I couldn't kill it! (*his eyes starting from his head*) God forgive me, I still believe! And that's mad—mad, do you hear?

SUE—(*looking at him with horror*) And that is why—you hate him!

NAT—No, I don't— (*then in a sudden frenzy*) Yes! I do hate him! He's stolen my brain! I've got to free myself, can't you see, from him—and his madness.

SUE—(*terrified—appealingly*) Nat! Don't! You talk as if—

NAT—(*with a wild laugh*) As if I were mad? You're right—but I'll be mad no more! See! (*He opens the lantern and sets fire to the map in his hand. When he shuts the lantern again it flickers and goes out. They watch the paper burn with fascinated eyes as he talks.*) See how I free myself and become sane. And now for facts, as the doctor said. I lied to you about him. He was a doctor from the asylum. See how it burns! It must all be destroyed—this poisonous madness. Yes, I lied to you—see—it's gone—the last speck—and the only other map is the one Silas Horne took to the bottom of the sea with him. (*He lets the ash fall to the floor and crushes it with his foot.*) Gone! I'm free of it—at last! (*His face is very pale, but he goes on calmly.*) Yes, I sold him, if you will—to save my soul. They're coming from the asylum to get him— (*There is a loud, muffled cry from above, which sounds like "Sail-ho," and a stamping of feet. The slide to the companionway above is slid back with a bang. A gust of air tears down into the room. Nat and Sue have jumped to their feet and stand petrified. Captain Bartlett tramps down the stairs.*)

NAT—(*with a shudder*) God! Did he hear?

SUE—Ssshh! (*Captain Bartlett comes into the room. He bears a striking resemblance to his son, but his face is more stern and formidable, his form more robust, erect and muscular. His mass of hair is pure white, his bristly mustache the same, contrasting with the weather-beaten leather color of his furrowed face. Bushy gray brows overhang the obsessed glare of his fierce dark eyes. He wears a heavy, double-breasted blue coat, pants of the same material, and rubber boots turned down from the knee.*)

BARTLETT—(*in a state of mad exultation strides toward his son and points an accusing finger at him. Nat shrinks backward a step.*) Bin thinkin' me mad, did ye? Thinkin' it for the past three years, ye bin—ever since them fools on the Slocum tattled their damn lie o' the Mary Allen bein' a wreck.

NAT—(*swallowing hard—chokingly*) No—Father—I—

BARTLETT—Don't lie, ye whelp! You that I'd made my heir—aimin' to git me out o' the way! Aimin' to put me behind the bars o' the jail for mad folk!

SUE—Father—no!

BARTLETT—(*waving his hand for her to be silent*) Not you, girl, not you. You're your mother.

NAT—(*very pale*) Father—do you think—I—

BARTLETT—(*fiercely*) A lie in your eyes! I bin a-readin' 'em. My curse on you!

SUE—Father! Don't!

BARTLETT—Leave me be, girl. He believed, didn't he? And ain't he turned traitor—mockin' at me and sayin' it's all a lie—mockin' at himself, too, for bein' a fool to believe in dreams, as he calls 'em.

NAT—(*placatingly*) You're wrong, Father. I do believe.

BARTLETT—(*triumphantly*) Aye, now ye do! Who wouldn't credit their own eyes?

NAT—(*mystified*) Eyes?

BARTLETT—Have ye not seen her, then? Did ye not hear me hail?

NAT—(*confusedly*) Hail? I heard a shout. But—hail what? —seen what?

BARTLETT—(*grimly*) Aye, now's your punishment, Judas. (*explosively*) The Mary Allen, ye blind fool, come back from the Southern Seas—come back as I swore she must!

SUE—(*trying to soothe him*) Father! Be quiet. It's nothing.

BARTLETT—(*not heeding her—his eyes fixed hypnotically on his son's*) Turned the pint a half-hour back—the Mary Allen— loaded with gold as I swore she would be—carryin' her lowers—not a reef in 'em—makin' port, boy, as I swore she must—too late for traitors, boy, too late!—droppin' her anchor just when I hailed her.

NAT—(*a haunted, fascinated look in his eyes, which are fixed immovably on his father's*) The Mary Allen! But how do you know?

BARTLETT—Not know my own ship! 'Tis you 're mad!

NAT—But at night—some other schooner—

BARTLETT—No other, I say! The Mary Allen—clear in the moonlight. And heed this: D'you call to mind the signal I gave to Silas Horne if he made this port o' a night?

NAT—(*slowly*) A red and a green light at the mainmasthead.

BARTLETT—(*triumphantly*) Then look out if ye dare! (*He goes to the porthole, left forward.*) Ye can see it plain from here.

(*commandingly*) Will ye believe your eyes? Look—and then call me mad! (*Nat peers through the porthole and starts back, a dumbfounded expression on his face.*)

NAT—(*slowly*) A red and a green at the mainmast-head. Yes—clear as day.

SUE—(*with a worried look at him*) Let me see. (*She goes to the porthole.*)

BARTLETT—(*to his son with fierce satisfaction*) Aye, ye see now clear enough—too late for you. (*Nat stares at him spellbound.*) And from above I saw Horne and Cates and Jimmy Kanaka plain on the deck in the moonlight lookin' up at me. Come! (*He strides to the companionway, followed by Nat. The two of them ascend. Sue turns from the porthole, an expression of frightened bewilderment on her face. She shakes her head sadly. A loud* "Mary Allen, ahoy!" *comes from above in Bartlett's voice, followed like an echo by the same hail from Nat. Sue covers her face with her hands, shuddering. Nat comes down the companionway, his eyes wild and exulting.*)

SUE—(*brokenly*) He's bad to-night, Nat. You're right to humor him. It's the best thing.

NAT—(*savagely*) Humor him? What in hell do you mean?

SUE—(*pointing to the porthole*) There's nothing there, Nat. There's not a ship in harbor.

NAT—You're a fool—or blind! The Mary Allen's there in plain sight of any one, with the red and the green signal lights. Those fools lied about her being wrecked. And I've been a fool, too.

SUE—But, Nat, there's nothing. (*She goes over to the porthole again.*) Not a ship. See.

NAT—I saw, I tell you! From above it's all plain. (*He turns from her and goes back to his seat by the table. Sue follows him, pleading frightenedly*)

SUE—Nat! You mustn't let this— You're all excited and trembling, Nat. (*She puts a soothing hand on his forehead.*)

NAT—(*pushing her away from him roughly*) You blind fool! (*Bartlett comes down the steps of the companionway. His face is transfigured with the ecstasy of a dream come true.*)

BARTLETT—They've lowered a boat—the three—Horne and Cates and Jimmy Kanaka. They're a-rowin' ashore. I heard the oars in the locks. Listen! (*a pause*)

NAT—(*excitedly*) I hear!

SUE—(*who has taken the chair by her brother—in a warning whisper*) It's the wind and sea you hear, Nat. Please!

BARTLETT—(*suddenly*) Hark! They've landed. They're back on earth again as I swore they'd come back. They'll be a-comin' up the path now. (*He stands in an attitude of rigid attention. Nat strains forward in his chair. The sound of the wind and sea suddenly ceases and there is a heavy silence. A dense green glow floods slowly in rhythmic waves like a liquid into the room — as of great depths of the sea faintly penetrated by light.*)

NAT—(*catching at his sister's hand—chokingly*) See how the light changes! Green and gold! (*He shivers.*) Deep under the sea! I've been drowned for years! (*hysterically*) Save me! Save me!

SUE—(*patting his hand comfortingly*) Only the moonlight, Nat. It hasn't changed. Be quiet, dear, it's nothing. (*The green light grows deeper and deeper.*)

BARTLETT—(*in a crooning, monotonous tone*) They move slowly—slowly. They're heavy, I know, heavy—the two chests. Hark! They're below at the door. You hear?

NAT—(*starting to his feet*) I hear! I left the door open.

BARTLETT—For them?

NAT—For them.

SUE—(*shuddering*) Ssshh! (*The sound of a door being heavily slammed is heard from way down in the house.*)

NAT—(*to his sister—excitedly*) There! You hear?

SUE—A shutter in the wind.

NAT—There is no wind.

BARTLETT—Up they come! Up, bullies! They're heavy—heavy! (*The paddling of bare feet sounds from the floor below—then comes up the stairs.*)

NAT—You hear them now?

SUE—Only the rats running about. It's nothing, Nat.

BARTLETT—(*rushing to the door and throwing it open*) Come in, lads, come in!—and welcome home! (*The forms of Silas Horne, Cates, and Jimmy Kanaka rise noiselessly into the room from the stairs. The last two carry heavy inlaid chests. Horne is a parrot-nosed, angular old man dressed in gray cotton trousers and a singlet torn open across his hairy chest. Jimmy is a tall, sinewy, bronzed young Kanaka. He wears only a breech cloth. Cates is squat and stout and is dressed in dungaree pants and a shredded white sailor's blouse, stained with iron rust. All are in their bare feet. Water drips from their soaked and rotten clothes. Their hair is matted, intertwined with slimy strands of seaweed. Their eyes, as they glide silently into the room, stare frightfully wide at nothing. Their flesh in the green light has the suggestion of decomposition. Their bodies sway limply, nervelessly, rhythmically as if to the pulse of long swells of the deep sea.)*

NAT—(*making a step toward them*) See! (*frenziedly*) Welcome home, boys!

SUE—(*grabbing his arm*) Sit down, Nat. It's nothing. There's no one there. Father—sit down!

BARTLETT—(*grinning at the three and putting his finger to his lips*) Not here, boys, not here—not before him. (*He points to his son.*) He has no right, now. Come. The treasure is ours only. We'll go away with it together. Come. (*He goes to the companionway. The three follow. At the foot of it Horne puts a swaying hand on his shoulder and with the other holds out a piece of paper to him. Bartlett takes it and chuckles exultantly.*) That's right—for him—that's right! (*He ascends. The figures sway up after him.*)

NAT—(*frenziedly*) Wait! (*He struggles toward the companionway.*)

SUE—(*trying to hold him back*) Nat—don't! Father—come back!

NAT—Father! (*He flings her away from him and rushes up the companionway. He pounds against the slide, which seems to have been shut down on him.*)

SUE—(*hysterically—runs wildly to the door in rear*) Help! Help! (*As she gets to the door Doctor Higgins appears, hurrying up the stairs.*)

HIGGINS—(*excitedly*) Just a moment, Miss. What's the matter?

SUE—(*with a gasp*) My father—up there!

HIGGINS—I can't see—where's my flash? Ah. (*He flashes it on her terror-stricken face, then quickly around the room. The green glow disappears. The wind and sea are heard again. Clear moonlight floods through the portholes. Higgins springs to the companionway. Nat is still pounding.*) Here, Bartlett. Let me try.

NAT—(*coming down—looking dully at the doctor*) They've locked it. I can't get up.

HIGGINS—(*looks up—in an astonished voice*) What's the matter, Bartlett? It's all open. (*He starts to ascend.*)

NAT—(*in a voice of warning*) Look out, man! Look out for them!

HIGGINS—(*calls down from above*) Them? Who? There's no one here. (*suddenly—in alarm*) Come up! Lend a hand here! He's fainted! (*Nat goes up slowly. Sue goes over and lights the lantern, then hurries back to the foot of the companionway with it. There is a scuffling noise from above. They reappear, carrying Captain Bartlett's body.*)

HIGGINS—Easy now! (*They lay him on the couch in rear. Sue sets the lantern down by the couch. Higgins bends and listens for a heart-beat. Then he rises, shaking his head.*) I'm sorry—

SUE—(*dully*) Dead?

HIGGINS—(*nodding*) Heart failure, I should judge. (*with an attempt at consolation*) Perhaps it's better so, if—

NAT—(*as if in a trance*) There was something Horne handed him. Did you see?

SUE—(*wringing her hands*) Oh, Nat, be still! He's dead. (*to Higgins with pitiful appeal*) Please go—go—

HIGGINS—There's nothing I can do?

SUE—Go—please— (*Higgins bows stiffly and goes out. Nat moves slowly to his father's body, as if attracted by some irresistible fascination.*)

NAT—Didn't you see? Horne handed him something.

SUE—(*sobbing*) Nat! Nat! Come away! Don't touch him, Nat! Come away. (*But her brother does not heed her. His gaze is fixed on his father's right hand, which hangs downward over the side of the couch. He pounces on it and forcing the clenched fingers open with a great effort, secures a crumpled ball of paper.*)

NAT—(*flourishing it above his head with a shout of triumph*) See! (*He bends down and spreads it out in the light of the lantern.*) The map of the island! Look! It isn't lost for me after all! There's still a chance—*my* chance! (*with mad, solemn decision*) When the house is sold I'll go—and I'll find it! Look! It's written here in his hand writing: "The treasure is buried where the cross is made."

SUE—(*covering her face with her hands—brokenly*) Oh, God! Come away, Nat! Come away!

(*The Curtain Falls*)

THE STRAW

A Play in Three Acts

CHARACTERS

BILL CARMODY

MARY
NORA
TOM } *his children*
BILLY

DOCTOR GAYNOR

FRED NICHOLLS

EILEEN CARMODY, *Bill's eldest child*

STEPHEN MURRAY

MISS HOWARD, *a nurse in training*

MISS GILPIN, *superintendent of the Infirmary*

DOCTOR STANTON, *of the Hill Farm Sanatorium*

DOCTOR SIMMS, *his assistant*

MR. SLOAN

PETERS, *a patient*

MRS. TURNER, *matron of the Sanatorium*

MISS BAILEY
MRS. ABNER } *patients*
FLYNN

OTHER PATIENTS OF THE SANATORIUM

MRS. BRENNAN

SCENES

ACT I

ACT II

ACT III

The Straw

ACT ONE

SCENE ONE

The kitchen of the Carmody home on the outskirts of a manu-facturing town in Connecticut. On the left, forward, the sink. Farther back, two windows looking out on the yard. In the left corner, rear, the icebox. Immediately to the right of it, in the rear wall, a window opening on the side porch. To the right of this, a dish closet, and a door leading into the hall where the main front entrance to the house and the stairs to the floor above are situated. On the right, to the rear, a door opening on the dining room. Farther forward, the kitchen range with scuttle, wood box, etc. In the center of the room, a table with a red and white cover. Four cane-bottomed chairs are pushed under the table. In front of the stove, two battered, wicker rocking chairs. The floor is partly cov-ered by linoleum strips. The walls are papered a light cheerful color. Several old framed picture-supplement prints hang from nails. Everything has a clean, neatly-kept appearance. The supper dishes are piled in the sink ready for washing. A dish pan of water simmers on the stove.

It is about eight o'clock in the evening of a bitter cold day in late February.

As the curtain rises, Bill Carmody is discovered sitting in a rocker by the stove, reading a newspaper and smoking a blackened clay pipe. He is a man of fifty, heavy-set and round-shouldered, with long muscular arms and swollen-veined, hairy hands. His face is bony and ponderous; his nose, short and squat; his mouth large, thick-lipped and harsh; his complexion mottled—red, pur-ple-streaked, and freckled; his hair, short and stubby with a bald spot on the crown. The expression of his small, blue eyes is one of selfish cunning. His voice is loud and hoarse. He wears a flannel shirt, open at the neck, criss-crossed by red suspenders; black, baggy trousers gray with dust; muddy brogans.

His youngest daughter, Mary, is sitting on a chair by the table, front, turning over the pages of a picture book. She is a delicate, dark-haired, blue-eyed, quiet little girl about eight years old.

CARMODY—(*after watching the child's preoccupation for a*

moment, in a tone of half-exasperated amusement) Well, but you're the quiet one, surely! It's the dead spit and image of your sister, Eileen, you are, with your nose always in a book; and you're like your mother, too, God rest her soul. (*He crosses himself with pious unction and Mary also does so.*) It's Nora and Tom has the high spirits in them like their father; and Billy, too,—if he is a lazy shiftless divil—has the fightin' Carmody blood like me. You're a Cullen like your mother's people. They always was dreamin' their lives out. (*He lights his pipe and shakes his head with ponderous gravity.*) It's out rompin' and playin' you ought to be at your age, not carin' a fig for books. (*with a glance at the clock*) Is that auld fool of a doctor stayin' the night? Run out in the hall, Mary, and see if you hear him.

MARY—(*goes out into the hall, rear, and comes back*) He's upstairs. I heard him talking to Eileen.

CARMODY—Close the door, ye little divil! There's a freezin' draught comin' in. (*She does so and comes back to her chair. Carmody continues with a sneer.*) I've no use for their drugs at all. They only keep you sick to pay more visits. I'd not have sent for this bucko if Eileen didn't scare me by faintin'.

MARY—(*anxiously*) Is Eileen very sick, Papa?

CARMODY—(*spitting—roughly*) If she is, it's her own fault entirely—weakenin' her health by readin' here in the house. (*irritably*) Put down that book on the table and leave it be. I'll have no more readin' or I'll take the strap to you!

MARY—(*laying the book on the table*) It's only pictures.

CARMODY—No back talk! Pictures or not, it's all the same mopin' and lazin' in it. (*after a pause—morosely*) Who's to do the work and look after Nora and Tom and yourself, if Eileen is bad took and has to stay in her bed? All that I've saved from slavin' and sweatin' in the sun with a gang of lazy Dagoes'll be up the spout in no time. (*bitterly*) What a fool a man is to be raisin' a raft of children and him not a millionaire! (*with lugubrious self-pity*) Mary, dear, it's a black curse God put on me when he took your mother just when I needed her most. (*Mary commences to sob. Carmody starts and looks at her angrily.*) What are you snifflin' at?

MARY—(*tearfully*) I was thinking—of Mama.

CARMODY—(*scornfully*) It's late you are with your tears,

and her cold in her grave for a year. Stop it, I'm tellin' you! (*Mary gulps back her sobs.*)

(*There is a noise of childish laughter and screams from the street in front. The outside door is opened and slammed, footsteps pound along the hall. The door in the rear is shoved open, and Nora and Tom rush in breathlessly. Nora is a bright, vivacious, red-haired girl of eleven—pretty after an elfish, mischievous fashion—light-hearted and robust.*)

(*Tom resembles Nora in disposition and appearance. A healthy, good-humored youngster with a shock of sandy hair. He is a year younger than Nora. They are followed into the room, a moment later, by their brother, Billy, who is evidently loftily disgusted with their antics. Billy is a fourteen-year-old replica of his father, whom he imitates even to the hoarse, domineering tone of voice.*)

CARMODY—(*grumpily*) Ah, here you are, the lot of you. Shut that door after you! What's the use in me spendin' money for coal if all you do is to let the cold night in the room itself?

NORA—(*hopping over to him—teasingly*) Me and Tom had a race, Papa. I beat him. (*She sticks her tongue out at her younger brother.*) Slow poke!

TOM—You didn't beat me, neither!

NORA—I did, too!

TOM—You tripped me comin' up the steps. Brick-top! Cheater!

NORA—(*flaring up*) You're a liar! I beat you fair. Didn't I, Papa?

CARMODY—(*with a grin*) You did, darlin'. (*Tom slinks back to the chair in the rear of the table, sulking. Carmody pats Nora's red hair with delighted pride.*) Sure it's you can beat the divil himself!

NORA—(*sticks out her tongue again at Tom*) See? Liar! (*She goes and perches on the table near Mary who is staring sadly in front of her.*)

CARMODY—(*to Billy—irritably*) Did you get the plug I told you?

BILLY—Sure. (*He takes a plug of tobacco from his pocket and hands it to his father. Nora slides down off her perch and disappears, unnoticed, under the table.*)

CARMODY—It's a great wonder you didn't forget it—and me without a chew. (*He bites off a piece and tucks it into his cheek.*)

TOM—(*suddenly clutching at his leg with a yell*) Ouch! Darn you! (*He kicks frantically at something under the table, but Nora scrambles out at the other end, grinning.*)

CARMODY—(*angrily*) Shut your big mouth!

TOM—(*indignantly*) She pinched me—hard as she could, too—and look at her laughin'!

NORA—(*hopping on the table again*) Cry-baby!

TOM—I'll tell Eileen, wait 'n' see!

NORA—Tattle-tale! Eileen's sick.

TOM—That's why you dast do it. You dasn't if she was up.

CARMODY—(*exasperated*) Go up to bed, the two of you, and no more talk, and you go with them, Mary.

NORA—(*giving a quick tug at Mary's hair*) Come on, Mary.

MARY—Ow! (*She begins to cry.*)

CARMODY—(*raising his voice furiously*) Hush your noise! It's nothin' but blubberin' you do be doin' all the time. (*He stands up threateningly.*) I'll have a moment's peace, I will! Go on, now! (*They scurry out of the rear door.*)

NORA—(*sticks her head back in the door*) Can I say goodnight to Eileen, papa?

CARMODY—No. The doctor's with her yet. (*Then he adds hastily*) Yes, go in to her, Nora. It'll drive himself out of the house maybe, bad cess to him, and him stayin' half the night. (*Nora waits to hear no more but darts back, shutting the door behind her. Billy takes the chair in front of the table. Carmody sits down again with a groan.*) The rheumatics are in my leg again. (*shakes his head*) If Eileen's in bed long those brats'll have the house down. Ara, well, it's God's will, I suppose, but where the money'll come from, I dunno. (*with a disparaging glance at his son*) They'll not be raisin' your wages soon, I'll be bound.

BILLY—(*surlily*) Naw.

CARMODY—(*still scanning him with contempt*) A divil of a lot of good it was for me to go against Eileen's wish and let you leave off your schoolin' this year thinkin' the money you'd earn would help with the house.

BILLY—Aw, goin' to school didn't do me no good. The teachers was all down on me. I couldn't learn nothin' there.

CARMODY—(*disgustedly*) Nor any other place, I'm thinkin', you're that thick. (*There is a noise from the stairs in the hall.*) Wisht! It's the doctor comin' down from Eileen. (*The door in the rear is opened and Doctor Gaynor enters. He is a stout, bald, middle-aged man, forceful of speech, who in the case of patients of the Carmodys' class dictates rather than advises. Carmody adopts a whining tone.*) Aw, Doctor, and how's Eileen now?

GAYNOR—(*does not answer this but comes forward into the room holding out two slips of paper—dictatorially*) Here are two prescriptions that'll have to be filled immediately.

CARMODY—(*frowning*) You take them, Billy, and run round to the drug store. (*Gaynor hands them to Billy.*)

BILLY—Give me the money, then.

CARMODY—(*reaches down into his pants pocket with a sigh*) How much will they come to, Doctor?

GAYNOR—About a dollar, I guess.

CARMODY—(*protestingly*) A dollar! Sure it's expensive medicines you're givin' her for a bit of a cold. (*He meets the doctor's cold glance of contempt and he wilts—grumblingly, as he peels a dollar bill off a small roll and gives it to Billy*) Bring back the change—if there is any. And none of your tricks!

BILLY—Aw, what do you think I am? (*He takes the money and goes out.*)

CARMODY—(*grudgingly*) Take a chair, Doctor, and tell me what's wrong with Eileen.

GAYNOR—(*seating himself by the table—gravely*) Your daughter is very seriously ill.

CARMODY—(*irritably*) Aw, Doctor, didn't I know you'd be sayin' that, anyway!

GAYNOR—(*ignoring this remark—coldly*) She has tuberculosis of the lungs.

CARMODY—(*with puzzled awe*) Too-ber-c'losis?

GAYNOR—Consumption, if that makes it plainer to you.

CARMODY—(*with dazed terror—after a pause*) Consumption? Eileen? (*with sudden anger*) What lie is it you're tellin' me?

GAYNOR—(*icily*) Look here, Carmody!

CARMODY—(*bewilderedly*) Don't be angry, now. Sure I'm out of my wits entirely. Ah, Doctor, sure you must be mistaken!

GAYNOR—There's no chance for a mistake, I'm sorry to say. Her right lung is badly affected.

CARMODY—(*desperately*) It's a cold only, maybe.

GAYNOR—(*curtly*) Don't talk nonsense. (*Carmody groans. Gaynor continues authoritatively.*) She'll have to go to a sanatorium at once. She ought to have been sent to one months ago. (*Casts a look of indignant scorn at Carmody who is sitting staring at the floor with an expression of angry stupor on his face.*) It's a wonder to me you didn't see the condition she was in and force her to take care of herself.

CARMODY—(*with vague fury*) God blast it!

GAYNOR—She kept on doing her work, I suppose—taking care of her brothers and sisters, washing, cooking, sweeping, looking after your comfort—worn out—when she should have been in bed—and— (*He gets to his feet with a harsh laugh.*) But what's the use of talking? The damage is done. We've got to set to work to repair it at once. I'll write tonight to Dr. Stanton of the Hill Farm Sanatorium and find out if he has a vacancy.

CARMODY—(*his face growing red with rage*) Is it sendin' Eileen away to a hospital you'd be? (*exploding*) Then you'll not! You'll get that notion out of your head damn quick. It's all nonsense you're stuffin' me with, and lies, makin' things out to be the worst in the world. She'll not move a step out of here, and I say so, and I'm her father!

GAYNOR—(*who has been staring at him with contempt—coldly angry*) You refuse to let her go to a sanatorium?

CARMODY—I do.

GAYNOR—(*threateningly*) Then I'll have to report her case to the Society for the Prevention of Tuberculosis of this county and tell them of your refusal to help her.

CARMODY—(*wavering a bit*) Report all you like, and be damned to you!

GAYNOR—(*ignoring the interruption—impressively*) A majority of the most influential men of this city are back of the Society. (*grimly*) We'll find a way to move you, Carmody, if you try to be stubborn.

CARMODY—(*thoroughly frightened but still protesting*) Ara, Doctor, you don't see the way of it at all. If Eileen goes to the hospital, who's to be takin' care of the others, and mindin' the house when I'm off to work?

GAYNOR—You can easily hire some woman.

CARMODY—(*at once furious again*) Hire? D'you think I'm a millionaire itself?

GAYNOR—(*contemptuously*) That's where the shoe pinches, eh? (*in a rage*) I'm not going to waste any more words on you, Carmody, but I'm damn well going to see this thing through! You might as well give in first as last.

CARMODY—(*wailing*) But where's the money comin' from?

GAYNOR—The weekly fee at the Hill Farm is only seven dollars. You can easily afford that—the price of a few rounds of drinks.

CARMODY—Seven dollars! And I'll have to pay a woman to come in—and the four of the children eatin' their heads off! Glory be to God, I'll not have a penny saved for me old age—and then it's the poor house!

GAYNOR—Well, perhaps I can get the Society to pay half for your daughter—if you're really as hard up as you pretend.

CARMODY—(*brightening*) Ah, Doctor, thank you.

GAYNOR—(*abruptly*) Then it's all settled?

CARMODY—(*grudgingly—trying to make the best of it*) I'll do my best for Eileen, if it's needful—and you'll not be tellin' them people about it at all, Doctor?

GAYNOR—Not unless you force me to.

CARMODY—And they'll pay the half, surely?

GAYNOR—I'll see what I can do.

CARMODY—God bless you, Doctor! (*grumblingly*) It's the whole of it they ought to be payin', I'm thinkin', and them with sloos of money. 'Tis them builds the hospitals and why should they be wantin' the poor like me to support them?

GAYNOR—(*disgustedly*) Bah! (*abruptly*) I'll telephone to Doctor Stanton tomorrow morning. Then I'll know something definite when I come to see your daughter in the afternoon.

CARMODY—(*darkly*) You'll be comin' again tomorrow? (*half to himself*) Leave it to the likes of you to be drainin' a man dry. (*Gaynor has gone out to the hall in rear and does not hear this last remark. There is a loud knock from the outside door. The doctor comes back into the room carrying his hat and overcoat.*)

GAYNOR—There's someone knocking.

CARMODY—Who'll it be? Ah, it's Fred Nicholls, maybe. (*in a low voice to Gaynor who has started to put on his overcoat*) Eileen's young man, Doctor, that she's engaged to marry, as you might say.

GAYNOR—(*thoughtfully*) Hmm—yes—she spoke of him. (*As another knock sounds Carmody hurries to the rear. Gaynor, after a moment's indecision, takes off his overcoat again and sits down. A moment later Carmody reënters followed by Fred Nicholls, who has left his overcoat and hat in the hallway. Nicholls is a young fellow of twenty-three, stockily built, fair-haired, handsome in a commonplace, conventional mold. His manner is obviously an attempt at suave gentility; he has an easy, taking smile and a ready laugh, but there is a petty, calculating expression in his small, observing, blue eyes. His well-fitting, readymade clothes are carefully pressed. His whole get-up suggests an attitude of man-about-small-town complacency.*)

CARMODY—(*as they enter*) I had a mind to phone to your house but I wasn't wishful to disturb you, knowin' you'd be comin' to call tonight.

NICHOLLS—(*with disappointed concern*) It's nothing serious, I hope.

CARMODY—(*grumblingly*) Ah, who knows? Here's the doctor. You've not met him?

NICHOLLS—(*politely, looking at Gaynor who inclines his head stiffly*) I haven't had the pleasure. Of course I've heard—

CARMODY—It's Doctor Gaynor. This is Fred Nicholls, Doctor. (*The two men shake hands with conventional pleased-to-meet yous.*) Sit down, Fred, that's a good lad, and be talkin' to the Doctor a moment while I go upstairs and see how is Eileen.

NICHOLLS—Certainly, Mr. Carmody—and tell her how sorry I am to learn she's under the weather.

CARMODY—I will so. (*He goes out.*)

GAYNOR—(*after a pause in which he is studying Nicholls*) Do you happen to be any relative to Albert Nicholls over at the Downs Manufacturing Company?

NICHOLLS—(*smiling*) He's sort of a near relative—my father.

GAYNOR—Ah, yes?

NICHOLLS—(*with satisfaction*) I work for the Downs Company myself—bookkeeper.

GAYNOR—Miss Carmody had a position there also, didn't she, before her mother died?

NICHOLLS—Yes. She had a job as stenographer for a time. When she graduated from the business college—I was already working at the Downs—and through my father's influence—you understand. (*Gaynor nods curtly.*) She was getting on finely, too, and liked the work. It's too bad—her mother's death, I mean—forcing her to give it up and come home to take care of those kids.

GAYNOR—It's a damn shame. That's the main cause of her breakdown.

NICHOLLS—(*frowning*) I've noticed she's been looking badly lately. Well, it's all her father's fault—and her own, too, because whenever I raised a kick about his making a slave of her, she always defended him. (*with a quick glance at the doctor—in a confidential tone*) Between us, Carmody's as selfish as they make 'em, if you want my opinion.

GAYNOR—(*with a growl*) He's a hog on two legs.

NICHOLLS—(*with a gratified smile*) You bet! (*with a patronizing air*) I hope to get Eileen away from all this as soon as—things pick up a little. (*making haste to explain his connection with the dubious household*) Eileen and I have gone around together for years—went to Grammar and High School together—in different classes, of course. She's really a corker—very different from the rest of the family you've seen—like her mother. My folks like her awfully well. Of course, they'd never stand for him.

GAYNOR—You'll excuse my curiosity, but you and Miss Carmody are engaged, aren't you? Carmody said you were.

NICHOLLS—(*embarrassed*) Why, yes, in a way—but nothing definite—no official announcement or anything of that kind. (*with a sentimental smile*) It's always been sort of understood between us. (*He laughs awkwardly.*)

GAYNOR—(*gravely*) Then I can be frank with you. I'd like

to be because I may need your help. Besides, you're bound to know anyway. She'd tell you.

NICHOLLS—(*a look of apprehension coming over his face*) Is it—about her sickness?

GAYNOR—Yes.

NICHOLLS—Then—it's serious?

GAYNOR—It's pulmonary tuberculosis—consumption.

NICHOLLS—(*stunned*) Consumption? Good heavens! (*after a dazed pause—lamely*) Are you sure, Doctor?

GAYNOR—Positive. (*Nicholls stares at him with vaguely frightened eyes.*) It's had a good start—thanks to her father's blind selfishness—but let's hope that can be overcome. The important thing is to ship her off to a sanatorium immediately. That's where you can be of help. It's up to you to help me convince Carmody that it's imperative she be sent away at once—for the safety of those around her as well as her own.

NICHOLLS—(*confusedly*) I'll do my best, Doctor. (*as if he couldn't yet believe his ears—shuddering*) Good heavens! She never said a word about—being so ill. She's had a cold. But Doctor,—do you think this sanatorium will—?

GAYNOR—(*with hearty hopefulness*) She has every chance. The Hill Farm has a really surprising record of arrested cases. Of course, she'll never be able to live as carelessly as before, even after the most favorable results. (*apologetically*) I'm telling you all this as being the one most intimately concerned. You're the one who'll have to assume responsibility when she returns to everyday life.

NICHOLLS—(*answering as if he were merely talking to screen the thoughts in his mind*) Yes—certainly—. Where is this sanatorium, Doctor?

GAYNOR—Half an hour by train to the town. The sanatorium is two miles out on the hills. You'll be able to see her whenever you've a day off.

NICHOLLS—(*A look of horrified realization has been creeping into his eyes.*) You said—Eileen ought to be sent away—for the sake of those around her—?

GAYNOR—T. B. is extremely contagious, you must know that. Yet I'll bet she's been fondling and kissing those brothers and sisters of hers regardless. (*Nicholls fidgets uneasily on his chair.*)

NICHOLLS—(*his eyes shiftily avoiding the doctor's face*) Then the kids might have gotten it—by kissing Eileen?

GAYNOR—It stands to reason that's a common means of communication.

NICHOLLS—(*very much shaken*) Yes. I suppose it must be. But that's terrible, isn't it? (*with sudden volubility, evidently extremely anxious to wind up this conversation and conceal his thoughts from Gaynor*) I'll promise you, Doctor, I'll tell Carmody straight what's what. He'll pay attention to me or I'll know the reason why.

GAYNOR—(*getting to his feet and picking up his overcoat*) Good boy! Tell him I'll be back tomorrow with definite information about the sanatorium.

NICHOLLS—(*helping him on with his overcoat, anxious to have him go*) All right, Doctor.

GAYNOR—(*puts on his hat*) And do your best to cheer the patient up. Give her confidence in her ability to get well. That's half the battle.

NICHOLLS—(*hastily*) I'll do all I can.

GAYNOR—(*turns to the door and shakes Nicholls' hand sympathetically*) And don't take it to heart too much yourself. In six months she'll come back to you her old self again.

NICHOLLS—(*nervously*) It's hard on a fellow—so suddenly —but I'll remember—and— (*abruptly*) Good-night, Doctor.

GAYNOR—Good-night. (*He goes out. The outer door is heard shutting behind him. Nicholls closes the door, rear, and comes back and sits in the chair in front of table. He rests his chin on his hands and stares before him, a look of desperate, frightened calculation coming into his eyes. Carmody is heard clumping heavily down the stairs. A moment later he enters. His expression is glum and irritated.*)

CARMODY—(*coming forward to his chair by the stove*) Has he gone away?

NICHOLLS—(*turning on him with a look of repulsion*) Yes. He said to tell you he'd be back tomorrow with definite information—about the sanatorium business.

CARMODY—(*darkly*) Oho, he did, did he? Maybe I'll surprise him. I'm thinkin' it's lyin' he is about Eileen's sickness, and her lookin' as fresh as a daisy with the high color in her cheeks when I saw her now.

NICHOLLS—(*impatiently*) Gaynor knows his business. (*after a moment's hesitation*) He told me all about Eileen's sickness.

CARMODY—(*resentfully*) Small thanks to him to be tellin' our secrets to the town.

NICHOLLS—(*exasperated*) He only told me because you'd said I and Eileen were engaged. You're the one who was telling—secrets.

CARMODY—(*irritated*) Ara, don't be talkin'! That's no secret at all with the whole town watchin' Eileen and you spoonin' together from the time you was kids.

NICHOLLS—(*vindictively*) Well, the whole town is liable to find out— (*He checks himself.*)

CARMODY—(*too absorbed in his own troubles to notice this threat*) So he told you he'd send Eileen away to the hospital? I've half a mind not to let him—and let him try to make me! (*with a frown*) But Eileen herself says she's wantin' to go, now. (*angrily*) It's all that divil's notion he put in her head that the children'd be catchin' her sickness that makes her willin' to go.

NICHOLLS—(*with a superior air*) From what he told me, I should say it's the only thing for Eileen to do if she wants to get well quickly. (*spitefully*) And I'd certainly not go against Gaynor, if I was you.

CARMODY—(*worriedly*) But what can he do—him and his Sasiety? I'm her father.

NICHOLLS—(*seeing Carmody's uneasiness with revengeful satisfaction*) You'll make a mistake if you think he's bluffing. It'd probably get in all the papers about you refusing. Everyone would be down on you. (*as a last jab—spitefully*) You might even lose your job over it, people would be so sore.

CARMODY—(*jumping to his feet*) Ah, divil take him! Let him send her where he wants, then.

NICHOLLS—(*as an afterthought*) And, honestly, Mr. Carmody, I don't see how you can object for a second. (*Seeing Carmody's shaken condition, he finishes boldly.*) You've some feeling for your own daughter, haven't you?

CARMODY—(*apprehensively*) Whisht! She might hear you. Let her do what she's wishful.

NICHOLLS—(*complacently—feeling his duty in the matter well done*) That's the right spirit. And you and I'll do all we can to help her. (*He gets to his feet.*) Well, I guess I'll have to go. Tell Eileen—

CARMODY—You're not goin'? Sure, Eileen is puttin' on her clothes to come down and have a look at you.

NICHOLLS—(*suddenly panic-stricken by the prospect of facing her*) No—no—I can't stay—I only came for a moment— I've got an appointment—honestly. Besides, it isn't right for her to be up. You should have told her. (*The door in the rear is opened and Eileen enters. She is just over eighteen. Her wavy mass of dark hair is parted in the middle and combed low on her forehead, covering her ears, to a knot at the back of her head. The oval of her face is spoiled by a long, rather heavy, Irish jaw contrasting with the delicacy of her other features. Her eyes are large and blue, confident in their compelling candor and sweetness; her lips, full and red, half-open, over strong even teeth, droop at the corners into an expression of wistful sadness; her clear complexion is unnaturally striking in its contrasting colors, rose and white; her figure is slight and undeveloped. She wears a plain black dress with a bit of white at the neck and wrists. She stands looking appealingly at Nicholls who avoids her glance. Her eyes have a startled, stunned expression as if the doctor's verdict were still in her ears.*)

EILEEN—(*faintly—forcing a smile*) Good-evening, Fred. (*Her eyes search his face anxiously.*)

NICHOLLS—(*confusedly*) Hello, Eileen. I'm so sorry to—. (*Clumsily trying to cover up his confusion, he goes over and leads her to a chair.*) You sit down. You've got to take care of yourself. You never ought to have gotten up tonight.

EILEEN—(*sits down*) I wanted to talk to you. (*She raises her face with a pitiful smile. Nicholls hurriedly moves back to his own chair.*)

NICHOLLS—(*almost brusquely*) I could have talked to you from the hall. You're silly to take chances just now. (*Eileen's eyes show her hurt at his tone.*)

CARMODY—(*seeing his chance—hastily*) You'll be stayin' a while now, Fred? I'll take a walk down the road. I'm needin' a drink to clear my wits. (*He goes to the door in rear.*)

EILEEN—(*reproachfully*) You won't be long, Father? And please don't—you know.

CARMODY—(*exasperated*) Sure who wouldn't get drunk with all the sorrows of the world piled on him? (*He stamps out. A moment later the outside door bangs behind him. Eileen sighs. Nicholls walks up and down with his eyes on the floor.*)

NICHOLLS—(*furious at Carmody for having left him in this situation*) Honestly, Eileen, your father is the limit. I don't see how you stand for him. He's the most selfish—

EILEEN—(*gently*) Sssh! You mustn't, Fred. He just doesn't understand. (*Nicholls snorts disdainfully.*) Don't! Let's not talk about him now. We won't have many more evenings together for a long, long time. Did Father or the doctor tell you—(*She falters.*)

NICHOLLS—(*not looking at her—glumly*) Everything there was to tell, I guess.

EILEEN—(*hastening to comfort him*) You mustn't worry, Fred. Please don't! It'd make it so much worse for me if I thought you did. I'll be all right. I'll do exactly what they tell me, and in a few months I'll be back so fat and healthy you won't know me.

NICHOLLS—(*lamely*) Oh, there's no doubt of that. No one's worrying about your not getting well quick.

EILEEN—It won't be long. We can write often, and it isn't far away. You can come out and see me every Sunday—if you want to.

NICHOLLS—(*hastily*) Of course I will!

EILEEN—(*looking at his face searchingly*) Why do you act so funny? Why don't you sit down—here, by me? Don't you want to?

NICHOLLS—(*drawing up a chair by hers—flushing guiltily*) I—I'm all bawled up, Eileen. I don't know what I'm doing.

EILEEN—(*putting her hand on his knee*) Poor Fred! I'm so sorry I have to go. I didn't want to at first. I knew how hard it would be on Father and the kids—especially little Mary. (*Her voice trembles a bit.*) And then the doctor said if I stayed I'd be putting them all in danger. He even ordered me not to kiss them any more. (*She bites her lips to restrain a sob—then coughs, a soft, husky cough. Nicholls shrinks away from her to the edge of his chair, his eyes shifting nervously with fright. Eileen continues gently.*) So I've got to go and get well, don't you see?

NICHOLLS—(*wetting his dry lips*) Yes—it's better.

EILEEN—(*sadly*) I'll miss the kids so much. Taking care of them has meant so much to me since Mother died. (*With a half-sob she suddenly throws her arms about his neck and hides her face on his shoulder. He shudders and fights against an impulse to push her away.*) But I'll miss you most of all, Fred. (*She lifts her lips towards his, expecting a kiss. He seems about to kiss her—then averts his face with a shrinking movement, pretending he hasn't seen. Eileen's eyes grow wide with horror. She throws herself back into her own chair, staring accusingly at Nicholls. She speaks chokingly.*) Fred! Why—why didn't you kiss—what is it? Are you—afraid? (*with a moaning sound*) Oooh!

NICHOLLS—(*goaded by this accusation into a display of manhood, seizes her fiercely by the arms*) No! What—what d'you mean? (*He tries to kiss her but she hides her face.*)

EILEEN—(*in a muffled voice of hysterical self-accusation, pushing his head away*) No, no, you mustn't! The doctor told you not to, didn't he? Please don't, Fred! It would be awful if anything happened to you—through me. (*Nicholls gives up his attempts, recalled to caution by her words. She raises her face and tries to force a smile through her tears.*) But you can kiss me on the forehead, Fred. That can't do any harm. (*His face crimson, he does so. She laughs hysterically.*) It seems so silly—being kissed that way—by you. (*She gulps back a sob and continues to attempt to joke.*) I'll have to get used to it, won't I?

(*The Curtain Falls*)

SCENE TWO

The reception room of the Infirmary, a large, high-ceilinged room painted white, with oiled, hardwood floor. In the left wall, forward, a row of four windows. Farther back, the main entrance from the driveway, and another window. In the rear wall left, a glass partition looking out on the sleeping porch. A row of white beds, with the faces of patients barely peeping out from under piles of heavy bedclothes, can be seen. To the right of this partition, a bookcase, and a door leading to the hall past the patients' rooms. Farther right, another door opening on the examining room. In the right wall, rear, a door to the office. Farther forward, a row of windows. In front of the windows, a long dining table with chairs. On the left of the table, toward the center of the room, a chimney with two open fireplaces, facing left and right. Several wicker armchairs are placed around the fireplace on the left in which a cheerful wood fire is crackling. To the left of center, a round reading and writing table with a green-shaded electric lamp. Other electric lights are in brackets around the walls. Easy chairs stand near the table which is stacked with magazines. Rocking chairs are placed here and there about the room, near the windows, etc. A Victrola stands near the left wall, forward.

It is nearing eight o'clock of a cold evening about a week later.

At the rise of the curtain Stephen Murray is discovered sitting in a chair in front of the fireplace, left. Murray is thirty years old — a tall, slender, rather unusual looking fellow with a pale face, sunken under high cheek bones, lined about the eyes and mouth, jaded and worn for one still so young. His intelligent, large hazel eyes have a tired, dispirited expression in repose, but can quicken instantly with a concealment mechanism of mocking, careless humor whenever his inner privacy is threatened. His large mouth aids this process of protection by a quick change from its set apathy to a cheerful grin of cynical good nature. He gives off the impression of being somehow dissatisfied with himself but not yet embittered enough by it to take it out on others. His manner, as revealed by his speech — nervous, inquisitive, alert — seems more an acquired quality than any part of his real nature. He stoops a trifle, giving him a slightly round-shouldered appearance. He is dressed in a shabby dark suit, baggy at the knees. He is staring into the fire, dreaming, an open book lying unheeded on the arm of his chair. The Victrola is whining out the last strains of Dvorak's Humoresque. In the doorway to the office, Miss Gilpin stands talking to Miss Howard. The former is a slight, middle-aged woman with black hair, and a strong, intelligent face, its expression of resolute efficiency softened and made kindly by her warm, sympathetic gray eyes. Miss Howard is tall, slender and blond — decidedly pretty and provokingly conscious of it, yet with a certain air of seriousness underlying her apparent frivolity. She is twenty years old. The elder woman is dressed in the all white of a full-fledged nurse. Miss Howard wears the gray-blue uniform of one still in training. The record peters out. Murray sighs with relief but makes no move to get up and stop the grinding needle. Miss Howard hurries across to the machine. Miss Gilpin goes back into the office.

MISS HOWARD—(*takes off the record, glancing at Murray with amused vexation*) It's a wonder you wouldn't stop this machine grinding itself to bits, Mr. Murray.

MURRAY—(*with a smile*) I was hoping the darn thing would bust. (*Miss Howard sniffs. Murray grins at her teasingly.*) It keeps you from talking to me. That's the real music.

MISS HOWARD—(*comes over to his chair laughing*) I think you're a natural born kidder. All newspaper reporters are like that, I've heard.

MURRAY—You wrong me terribly. (*then frowning*) And it isn't charitable to remind me of my job.

MISS HOWARD—(*surprised*) I think it's great to be able to write. You ought to be proud of it.

MURRAY—(*glumly*) I'm not. You can't call it writing—not what I did—small town stuff. (*changing the subject*) Do you know when I'm to be moved to the shacks?

MISS HOWARD—In a few days, I guess. (*Murray grunts and moves nervously on his chair.*) What's the matter? Don't you like us here at the Infirmary?

MURRAY—(*smiling*) Oh—you—yes! (*then seriously*) I don't care for the atmosphere, though. (*He waves his hand toward the partition looking out on the porch.*) All those people in bed out there on the porch seem so sick. It's depressing.

MISS HOWARD—All the patients have to come here first until Doctor Stanton finds out whether they're well enough to be sent out to the shacks and cottages. And remember you're a patient.

MURRAY—I know it. But I don't feel as if I were—really sick like them.

MISS HOWARD—(*wisely*) None of them do, either.

MURRAY—(*after a moment's reflection—cynically*) Yes, I suppose it's that pipe dream keeps us all going, eh?

MISS HOWARD—Well, you ought to be thankful. (*lowering*

her voice) Shall I tell you a secret? I've seen your chart and *you've* no cause to worry. Doctor Stanton joked about it. He said you were too uninteresting—there was so little the matter with you.

MURRAY—(*pleased but pretending indifference*) Humph! He's original in that opinion.

MISS HOWARD—I know it's hard your being the only one up the week you've been here; but there's another patient due today. Maybe she'll be well enough to be around with you. (*with a quick glance at her wrist watch*) She can't be coming unless she got in on the last train.

MURRAY—(*interestedly*) It's a she, eh?

MISS HOWARD—Yes.

MURRAY—(*grinning provokingly*) Young?

MISS HOWARD—Eighteen, I believe. (*seeing his grin—with feigned pique*) I suppose you'll be asking if she's pretty next! Her name is Carmody, that's the only other thing I know. So there!

MISS GILPIN—(*appearing in the office doorway*) Miss Howard.

MISS HOWARD—Yes, Miss Gilpin. (*in an aside to Murray as she leaves him*) It's time for those horrid diets. (*She hurries back into the office. Murray stares into the fire. Miss Howard reappears from the office and goes out by the door to the hall, rear. Carriage wheels are heard from the driveway in front of the house on the left. They stop. After a pause there is a sharp rap on the door and a bell rings insistently. Men's muffled voices are heard in argument. Murray turns curiously in his chair. Miss Gilpin comes from the office and walks quickly to the door, unlocking and opening it. Eileen enters, followed by Nicholls, who is carrying her suitcase, and by her father.*)

EILEEN—I'm Miss Carmody. I believe Doctor Gaynor wrote—

MISS GILPIN—(*taking her hand—with kind affability*) We've been expecting you all day. How do you do? I'm Miss Gilpin. You came on the last train, didn't you?

EILEEN—(*heartened by the other woman's kindness*) Yes. This is my father, Miss Gilpin—and Mr. Nicholls. (*Miss Gilpin shakes hands cordially with the two men who are staring about the room in embarrassment. Carmody has very evidently been drinking. His voice is thick and his face puffed and stupid. Nicholls' manner is that of one who is accomplishing a necessary but disagreeable duty with the best grace possible, but is frightfully eager to get it over and done with. Carmody's condition embarrasses him acutely and when he glances at him it is with hatred and angry disgust.*)

MISS GILPIN—(*indicating the chairs in front of the windows on the left, forward*) Won't you gentlemen sit down? (*Carmody grunts sullenly and plumps himself into the one nearest the door. Nicholls hesitates, glancing down at the suit-case he carries. Miss Gilpin turns to Eileen.*) And now we'll get you settled immediately. Your room is all ready for you. If you'll follow me— (*She turns toward the door in rear, center.*)

EILEEN—Let me take the suit-case now, Fred.

MISS GILPIN—(*as he is about to hand it to her—decisively*) No, my dear, you mustn't. Put the case right down there, Mr. Nicholls. I'll have it taken to Miss Carmody's room in a moment. (*She shakes her finger at Eileen with kindly admonition.*) That's the first rule you'll have to learn. Never exert yourself or tax your strength. You'll find laziness is a virtue instead of a vice with us.

EILEEN—(*confused*) I— I didn't know—

MISS GILPIN—(*smiling*) Of course you didn't. And now if you'll come with me I'll show you your room. We'll have a little chat there and I can explain all the other important rules in a second. The gentlemen can make themselves comfortable in the meantime. We won't be gone more than a moment.

NICHOLLS—(*feeling called upon to say something*) Yes— we'll wait—certainly, we're all right. (*Carmody remains silent, glowering at the fire. Nicholls sits down beside him. Miss Gilpin and Eileen go out. Murray switches his chair so he can observe the two men out of the corner of his eye while pretending to be absorbed in his book.*)

CARMODY—(*looking about shiftily and reaching for the inside pocket of his overcoat*) I'll be havin' a nip now we're alone, and that cacklin' hen gone. (*He pulls out a pint flask, half full.*)

NICHOLLS—(*excitedly*) Put that bottle away! (*in a whisper*) Don't you see that fellow in the chair there?

CARMODY—(*taking a big drink*) Ah, I'm not mindin' a man at all. Sure I'll bet it's himself would be likin' a taste of the same. (*He appears about to get up and invite Murray to join him but Nicholls grabs his arm.*)

NICHOLLS—(*with a frightened look at Murray who appears buried in his book*) Stop it, you— Don't you know he's probably a patient and they don't allow them—

CARMODY—(*scornfully*) It's queer they'd be allowin' the sick ones to read books when I'll bet it's the same lazy readin' in the house brought the half of them down with the consumption itself. (*raising his voice*) I'm thinkin' this whole she-bang is a big, thievin' fake—and I've always thought so.

NICHOLLS—(*furiously*) Put that bottle away, damn it! And don't shout. You're not in a barrel-house.

CARMODY—(*with provoking calm*) I'll put it back when I'm ready, not before, and no lip from you!

NICHOLLS—(*with fierce disgust*) You're drunk now.

CARMODY—(*raging*) Drunk, am I? Is it the like of a young jackass like you that's still wet behind the ears to be tellin' me I'm drunk?

NICHOLLS—(*half-rising from his chair—pleadingly*) For heaven's sake, Mr. Carmody, remember where we are and don't raise any rumpus. What'll Eileen say?

CARMODY—(*puts the bottle away hastily, mumbling to himself—then glowers about the room scornfully with blinking eyes*) It's a grand hotel this is, I'm thinkin', for the rich to be takin' their ease, and not a hospital for the poor, but the poor has to pay for it.

NICHOLLS—(*fearful of another outbreak*) Sshh!

CARMODY—Don't be shshin' at me! I'd make Eileen come back out of this tonight if that divil of a doctor didn't have me by the throat.

NICHOLLS—(*glancing at him nervously*) I wonder how soon she'll be back? We'll have to hurry to make that last train.

CARMODY—(*angrily*) Is it anxious to get out of her sight you are, and you engaged to marry her? (*Nicholls flushes guiltily. Murray pricks up his ears and stares over at Nicholls. The latter meets his glance, scowls, and hurriedly averts his eyes. Carmody goes on accusingly.*) Sure, it's no heart at all you have—and her your sweetheart for years—and her sick with the consumption—and you wild to run away and leave her alone.

NICHOLLS—(*springing to his feet—furiously*) That's a—! (*He controls himself with an effort. His voice trembles.*) You're not responsible for the idiotic things you're saying or I'd— (*He turns away, seeking some escape from the old man's tongue.*) I'll see if the man is still there with the rig. (*He goes to the door on left and goes out.*)

CARMODY—(*following him with his eyes*) Go to hell, for all I'm preventin'. You've got no guts of a man in you. (*He addresses Murray with the good nature inspired by the flight of Nicholls.*) Is it true you're one of the consumptives, young fellow?

MURRAY—(*delighted by this speech—with a grin*) Yes, I'm one of them.

CARMODY—My name's Carmody. What's yours, then?

MURRAY—Murray.

CARMODY—(*slapping his thigh*) Irish as Paddy's pig! (*Murray nods. Carmody brightens and grows confidential.*) I'm glad to be knowin' you're one of us. You can keep an eye on Eileen.

MURRAY—I'll be glad to do all I can.

CARMODY—Thanks to you—though it's a grand life she'll be havin' here from the fine look of the place. (*with whining self-pity*) It's me it's hard on, God help me, with four small children and me widowed, and havin' to hire a woman to come in and look after them and the house now that Eileen's sick; and payin' for her curin' in this place, and me with only a bit of money in the bank for my old age. That's hard, now, on a man, and who'll say it isn't?

MURRAY—(*made uncomfortable by this confidence*) Hard luck always comes in bunches. (*to head off Carmody who is about to give vent to more woe—quickly, with a glance toward the door from the hall*) If I'm not mistaken, here comes your daughter now.

CARMODY—(*as Eileen comes into the room*) I'll make you acquainted. Eileen! (*She comes over to them, embarrassed to find her father in his condition so chummy with a stranger. Murray rises to his feet.*) This is Mr. Murray, Eileen. He's Irish and he'll put you on to the ropes of the place. He's got the consumption, too, God pity him.

EILEEN—(*distressed*) Oh, Father, how can you— (*with a*

look at Murray which pleads for her father) I'm glad to meet you, Mr. Murray.

MURRAY—(*with a straight glance at her which is so frankly admiring that she flushes and drops her eyes*) I'm glad to meet you. (*The front door is opened and Nicholls re-appears, shivering with the cold. He stares over at the others with ill-concealed irritation.*)

CARMODY—(*noticing him—with malicious satisfaction*) Oho, here you are again. (*Nicholls scowls and turns away. Carmody addresses his daughter with a sly wink at Murray.*) I thought Fred was slidin' down hill to the train, and him so desperate hurried to get away from here. Look at the knees on him clappin' together with the great fear he'll be catchin' a sickness in this place! (*Nicholls, his guilty conscience stabbed to the quick, turns pale with impotent rage.*)

EILEEN—(*remonstrating pitifully*) Father! Please! (*She hurries over to Nicholls.*) Oh, please don't mind him, Fred! You know what he is when he's drinking.

NICHOLLS—(*thickly*) That's all right—for you to say. But I won't forget—I'm sick and tired standing for—I'm not used to—such people.

EILEEN—(*shrinking from him*) Fred!

NICHOLLS—(*with a furious glance at Murray*) Before that cheap slob, too.

EILEEN—(*faintly*) He seems—very nice.

NICHOLLS—You've got your eyes set on him already, have you?

EILEEN—Fred!

NICHOLLS—Well, go ahead if you want to. I don't care. I'll— (*Startled by the look of anguish which comes over her face, he hastily swallows his words. He takes out watch—fiercely*) We'll miss that train, damn it!

EILEEN—(*in a stricken tone*) Oh, Fred! (*Then forcing back her tears she calls to Carmody in a strained voice*) Father! You'll have to go now.

CARMODY—(*shaking hands with Murray*) Keep your eye on her. I'll be out soon to see her and you and me'll have another chin.

MURRAY—Glad to. Good-by for the present. (*He walks to*

windows on the far right, turning his back considerately on their leave-taking.)

EILEEN—(comes to Carmody and hangs on his arm as they proceed to the door) Be sure and kiss them all for me—and bring them out to see me as soon as you can, Father, please! And don't forget to tell Mrs. Brennan all the directions I gave you coming out on the train. I told her but she mightn't remember—about Mary's bath—and to give Tom his—

CARMODY—(impatiently) Hasn't she brought up brats of her own, and doesn't she know the way of it?

EILEEN—(helplessly) Never mind telling her, then. I'll write to her.

CARMODY—You'd better not. She'll not wish you mixin' in with her work and tellin' her how to do it.

EILEEN—(aghast) Her work! (She seems at the end of her tether—wrung too dry for any further emotion. She kisses her father at the door with indifference and speaks calmly.) Good-by, Father.

CARMODY—(in a whining tone of injury) A cold kiss! Is your heart a stone? (Drunken tears well from his eyes and he blubbers) And your own father going back to a lone house with a stranger in it!

EILEEN—(wearily in a dead voice) You'll miss your train, Father.

CARMODY—(raging in a second) I'm off, then! Come on, Fred. It's no welcome we have with her here in this place—and a great curse on this day I brought her to it! (He stamps out.)

EILEEN—(in the same dead tone) Good-by, Fred.

NICHOLLS—(repenting his words of a moment ago—confusedly) I'm sorry, Eileen—for what I said. I didn't mean—you know what your father is—excuse me, won't you?

EILEEN—(without feeling) Yes.

NICHOLLS—And I'll be out soon—in a week if I can make it. Well then,—good-by for the present. (He bends down as if to kiss her but she shrinks back out of his reach.)

EILEEN—(a faint trace of mockery in her weary voice) No, Fred. Remember you mustn't now.

NICHOLLS—(*in an instant huff*) Oh, if that's the way you feel about— (*He strides out and slams the door viciously behind him. Eileen walks slowly back toward the fireplace, her face fixed in the dead calm of despair. As she sinks into one of the armchairs, the strain becomes too much. She breaks down, hiding her face in her hands, her frail shoulders heaving with the violence of her sobs. At this sound, Murray turns from the windows and comes over near her chair.*)

MURRAY—(*after watching her for a moment—in an embarrassed tone of sympathy*) Come on, Miss Carmody, that'll never do. I know it's hard at first—but— It isn't so bad up here—really—once you get used to it! (*The shame she feels at giving way in the presence of a stranger only adds to her loss of control and she sobs heartbrokenly. Murray walks up and down nervously, visibly nonplussed and upset. Finally he hits upon something.*) One of the nurses will be in any minute. You don't want them to see you like this.

EILEEN—(*chokes back her sobs and finally raises her face and attempts a smile*) I'm sorry—to make such a sight of myself.

MURRAY—(*jocularly*) Well, they say a cry does you a lot of good.

EILEEN—(*forcing a smile*) I do feel—better.

MURRAY—(*staring at her with a quizzical smile—cynically*) You shouldn't take those lovers' squabbles so seriously. Tomorrow he'll be sorry. He'll write begging forgiveness. Result—all serene again.

EILEEN—(*a shadow of pain on her face—with dignity*) Don't—please.

MURRAY—(*angry at himself—hanging his head contritely*) Pardon me. I'm rude sometimes—before I know it. (*He shakes off his confusion with a renewed attempt at a joking tone.*) You can blame your father for any breaks I make. He told me to see that you behaved.

EILEEN—(*with a genuine smile*) Oh, Father! (*flushing*) You mustn't mind anything he said tonight.

MURRAY—(*thoughtlessly*) Yes, he was well lit up. I envied him. (*Eileen looks very shame-faced. Murray sees it and exclaims in exasperation at himself*) Darn! There I go again putting my foot in it! (*with an irrepressible grin*) I ought to have my tongue operated on—that's what's the matter with me. (*He laughs and throws himself in a chair.*)

EILEEN—(*forced in spite of herself to smile with him*) You're candid, at any rate, Mr. Murray.

MURRAY—I said I envied him his jag and that's the truth. The same candor compels me to confess that I was pickled to the gills myself when I arrived here. Fact! I made love to all the nurses and generally disgraced myself—and had a wonderful time.

EILEEN—I suppose it does make you forget your troubles.

MURRAY—(*waving this aside*) I didn't want to forget—not for a second. I wasn't drowning my sorrow. I was hilariously celebrating.

EILEEN—(*astonished—by this time quite interested in this queer fellow to the momentary forgetfulness of her own grief*) Celebrating—coming here? But—aren't you sick?

MURRAY—Yes, of course. (*confidentially*) But it's only a matter of time when I'll be all right again. I hope it won't be too soon.

EILEEN—(*with wide eyes*) I wonder if you really mean—

MURRAY—I sure do—every word of it!

EILEEN—(*puzzled*) I can't understand how anyone could— (*with a worried glance over her shoulder*) I think I'd better look for Miss Gilpin, hadn't I? She may wonder— (*She half rises from her chair.*)

MURRAY—(*quickly*) No. Please don't go yet. (*She glances at him irresolutely, then resumes her chair.*) I'll see to it that you don't fracture any rules. (*hitching his chair nearer hers, —impulsively*) In all charity to me you've got to stick awhile. I haven't had a chance to really talk to a soul for a week. You found what I said a while ago hard to believe, didn't you?

EILEEN—(*with a smile*) You said you hoped you wouldn't get well too soon!

MURRAY—And I meant it! This place is honestly like heaven to me—a lonely heaven till your arrival. (*Eileen looks embarrassed.*) And why wouldn't it be? Just let me tell you what I was getting away from— (*with a sudden laugh full of a weary bitterness*) Do you know what it means to work from seven at night till three in the morning on a morning newspaper in a town of twenty thousand people—for *ten years*? No. You don't. You can't. But what it did to me—it made me happy—yes, happy!—to get out here!

EILEEN—(*looking at him curiously*) But I always thought being a reporter was so interesting.

MURRAY—(*with a cynical laugh*) On a small town rag? A month of it, perhaps, when you're new to the game. But ten years! With only a raise of a couple of dollars every blue moon or so, and a weekly spree on Saturday night to vary the monotony. (*He laughs again.*) Interesting, eh? Getting the dope on the Social of the Queen Esther Circle in the basement of the Methodist Episcopal Church, unable to sleep through a meeting of the Common Council on account of the noisy oratory caused by John Smith's application for a permit to build a house; making a note that a tug boat towed two barges loaded with coal up the river, that Mrs. Perkins spent a week-end with relatives in Hickville, that John Jones— Oh help! Why go on? I'm a broken man. God, how I used to pray that our Congressman would commit suicide, or the Mayor murder his wife—just to be able to write a real story!

EILEEN—(*with a smile*) Is it as bad as that? But weren't there other things that were interesting?

MURRAY—(*decidedly*) Nope. Never anything new—and I knew everyone and everything in town by heart years ago. (*with sudden bitterness*) Oh, it was my own fault. Why didn't I get out of it? Well, I was always going to—tomorrow— and tomorrow never came. I got in a rut—and stayed put. People seem to get that way, somehow—in that town. It took T. B. to blast me loose.

EILEEN—(*wonderingly*) But—your family—

MURRAY—I haven't much of a family left. My mother died when I was a kid. My father—he was a lawyer—died when I was nineteen, just about to go to college. He left nothing, so I went to work instead. I've two sisters, respectably married and living in another part of the state. We don't get along—but they're paying for me here, so I suppose I've no kick. (*cynically*) A family wouldn't have changed things. From what I've seen that blood-thicker-than-water dope is all wrong. It's thinner than table-d'hôte soup. You may have seen a bit of that truth in your own case already.

EILEEN—(*shocked*) How can you say that? You don't know—

MURRAY—Don't I, though? Wait till you've been here three months or four. You'll see then!

EILEEN—(*angrily, her lips trembling*) You must be crazy to say such things! (*fighting back her tears*) Oh, I think it's hateful—when you see how badly I feel!

MURRAY—(*in acute confusion—stammering*) Look here, Miss Carmody, I didn't mean to— Listen—don't feel mad at me, please. I was only talking. I'm like that. You mustn't take it seriously.

EILEEN—(*still resentful*) I don't see how you can talk—when you've just said you had no family of your own, really.

MURRAY—(*eager to return to her good graces*) Of course I don't know. I was just talking regardless for the fun of it.

EILEEN—(*after a pause*) Hasn't either of your sisters any children?

MURRAY—One of them has—two squally little brats.

EILEEN—(*disapprovingly*) You don't like babies?

MURRAY—(*bluntly*) No. (*then with a grin at her shocked face*) I don't get them. They're something I can't seem to get acquainted with.

EILEEN—(*with a smile, indulgently*) You're a funny person. (*then with a superior motherly air*) No wonder you couldn't understand how badly I feel. (*with a tender smile*) I've four of them—my brothers and sisters—though they're not what you'd call babies, except to me. I've been a mother to them now for a whole year—ever since our mother died. (*sadly*) And I don't know how they'll ever get along while I'm away.

MURRAY—(*cynically*) Oh, they'll—(*he checks what he was going to say and adds lamely*)—get along somehow.

EILEEN—(*with the same superior tone*) It's easy for you to say that. You don't know how children grow to depend on you for everything. You're not a woman.

MURRAY—(*with a grin*) Are you? (*then with a chuckle*) You're as old as the pyramids, aren't you? I feel like a little boy. Won't you adopt me, too?

EILEEN—(*flushing, with a shy smile*) Someone ought to. (*quickly changing the subject*) Do you know, I can't get over what you said about hating your work so. I should think it would be wonderful—to be able to write things.

MURRAY—My job had nothing to do with writing. To write—really write—yes, that's something worth trying for. That's what I've always meant to have a stab at. I've run across ideas enough for stories—that sounded good to me, anyway. (*with a forced laugh*) But—like everything else—I never got down to it. I started one or two—but—either I thought I didn't have the time or— (*He shrugs his shoulders.*)

EILEEN—Well, you've plenty of time now, haven't you?

MURRAY—(*instantly struck by this suggestion*) You mean— I could write up here? (*She nods. His face lights up with enthusiasm.*) Say! That is an idea! Thank you! I'd never have had sense enough to have thought of that myself. (*Eileen flushes with pleasure.*) Sure there's time—nothing but time up here—

EILEEN—Then you seriously think you'll try it?

MURRAY—(*determinedly*) Yes. Why not? I've got to try and do something real sometime, haven't I? I've no excuse not to, now. My mind isn't sick.

EILEEN—(*excitedly*) That'll be wonderful!

MURRAY—(*confidently*) Listen. I've had ideas for a series of short stories for the last couple of years—small town experiences, some of them actual. I know that life too darn well. I ought to be able to write about it. And if I can sell one—to the *Post*, say—I'm sure they'd take the others, too. And then—I should worry! It'd be easy sailing. But you must promise to help—play critic for me—read them and tell me where they're rotten.

EILEEN—(*pleased but protesting*) Oh, no, I'd never dare. I don't know anything—

MURRAY—Yes, you do. And you started me off on this thing, so you've got to back me up now. (*suddenly*) Say, I wonder if they'd let me have a typewriter up here?

EILEEN—It'd be fine if they would. I'd like to have one, too—to practice.

MURRAY—I don't see why they wouldn't allow it. You're not sick enough to be kept in bed, I'm sure of that.

EILEEN—I— I don't know—

MURRAY—Here! None of that! You just think you're not and you won't be. Say, I'm keen on that typewriter idea.

EILEEN—(*eagerly*) And I could type your stories after you've written them! I *could* help that way.

MURRAY—(*smiling*) But I'm quite able— (*Then seeing how interested she is he adds hurriedly*) That'd be great! I've always been a bum at a machine. And I'd be willing to pay whatever— (*Miss Gilpin enters from the rear and walks toward them.*)

EILEEN—(*quickly*) Oh, no! I'd be glad to get the practice. I wouldn't accept— (*She coughs slightly.*)

MURRAY—(*with a laugh*) Maybe, after you've read my stuff, you won't type it at any price.

MISS GILPIN—Miss Carmody, may I speak to you for a moment, please. (*She takes Eileen aside and talks to her in low tones of admonition. Eileen's face falls. She nods a horrified acquiescence. Miss Gilpin leaves her and goes into the office, rear.*)

MURRAY—(*as Eileen comes back, noticing her perturbation— kindly*) Well? Now, what's the trouble?

EILEEN—(*her lips trembling*) She told me I mustn't forget to shield my mouth with my handkerchief when I cough.

MURRAY—(*consolingly*) Yes, that's one of the rules, you know.

EILEEN—(*falteringly*) She said they'd give me—a—cup to carry around— (*She stops, shuddering.*)

MURRAY—(*easily*) It's not as bad as it sounds. They're only little paste-board things you carry in your pocket.

EILEEN—(*as if speaking to herself*) It's so horrible. (*She holds out her hand to Murray.*) I'm to go to my room now. Good-night, Mr. Murray.

MURRAY—(*holding her hand for a moment—earnestly*) Don't mind your first impressions here. You'll look on everything as a matter of course in a few days. I felt your way at first. (*He drops her hand and shakes his finger at her.*) Mind your guardian, now! (*She forces a trembling smile.*) See you at breakfast. Good-night. (*Eileen goes out to the hall in rear. Miss Howard comes in from the door just after her, carrying a glass of milk.*)

MISS HOWARD—Almost bedtime, Mr. Murray. Here's your diet. (*He takes the glass. She smiles at him provokingly.*) Well, is it love at first sight?

MURRAY—(*with a grin*) Sure thing! You can consider yourself heartlessly jilted. (*He turns and raises his glass toward the door through which Eileen has just gone, as if toasting her.*)

"A glass of milk, and thou
Coughing beside me in the wilderness—
Ah—wilderness were Paradise enow!"

(*He takes a sip of milk.*)

MISS HOWARD—(*peevishly*) That's old stuff, Mr. Murray. A patient at Saranac wrote that parody.

MURRAY—(*maliciously*) Aha, you've discovered it's a parody, have you, you sly minx! (*Miss Howard turns from him huffily and walks back towards the office, her chin in the air.*)

(*The Curtain Falls*)

ACT TWO

Scene One

The assembly room of the main building of the sanatorium—early in the morning of a fine day in June, four months later. The room is large, light and airy, painted a fresh white. On the left forward, an armchair. Farther back, a door opening on the main hall. To the rear of this door a pianola on a raised platform. In back of the pianola, a door leading into the office. In the rear wall, a long series of French windows looking out on the lawn, with wooded hills in the far background. Shrubs in flower grow immediately outside the windows. Inside, there is a row of potted plants. In the right wall, rear, four windows. Farther forward, a long, well-filled bookcase, and a doorway leading into the dining room. Following the walls, but about five feet out from them a stiff line of chairs placed closely against each other forms a sort of right-angled auditorium of which the large, square table that stands at center, forward, would seem to be the stage.

From the dining room comes the clatter of dishes, the confused murmur of many voices, male and female—all the mingled sounds of a crowd of people at a meal.

After the curtain rises, Doctor Stanton enters from the hall, followed by a visitor, Mr. Sloan, and the assistant physician, Doctor Simms. Doctor Stanton is a handsome man of forty-five or so with a grave, care-lined, studious face lightened by a kindly, humorous smile. His gray eyes, saddened by the suffering they have witnessed, have the sympathetic quality of real understanding. The look they give is full of companionship, the courage-renewing, human companionship of a hope which is shared. He speaks with a slight Southern accent, soft and slurring. Doctor Simms is a tall, angular young man with a long, sallow face and a sheepish, self-conscious grin. Mr. Sloan is fifty, short and stout, well dressed—one of the successful business men whose endowments have made the Hill Farm a possibility.

STANTON—(*as they enter*) This is the general assembly room, Mr. Sloan—where the patients of both sexes are allowed to congregate together after meals, for diets, and in the evening.

SLOAN—(*looking around him*) Couldn't be more pleasant, I must say. (*He walks where he can take a peep into the dining room.*) Ah, they're all at breakfast, I see.

STANTON—(*smiling*) Yes, and with no lack of appetite, let me tell you. (*with a laugh of proud satisfaction*) They'd sure eat us out of house and home at one sitting, if we'd give them the opportunity.

SLOAN—(*with a smile*) That's fine. (*with a nod toward the dining room*) The ones in there are the sure cures, aren't they?

STANTON—(*a shadow coming over his face*) Strictly speaking, there are no sure cures in this disease, Mr. Sloan. When we permit a patient to return to take up his or her activities in the world, the patient is what we call an arrested case. The disease is overcome, quiescent; the wound is healed over. It's then up to the patient to so take care of himself that this condition remains permanent. It isn't hard for them to do this, usually. Just ordinary, bull-headed common sense— added to what they've learned here—is enough. And the pre- cautions we teach them to take don't diminish their social usefulness in the slightest, either, as I can prove by our statis- tics of former patients. (*with a smile*) It's rather early in the morning for statistics, though.

MR. SLOAN—(*with a wave of the hand*) Oh, you needn't. Your reputation in that respect, Doctor— (*Stanton inclines his head in acknowledgment. Sloan jerks his thumb toward the dining room.*) But the ones in there *are* getting well, aren't they?

STANTON—To all appearances, yes. You don't dare swear to it, though. Sometimes, just when a case looks most favor- able, there's a sudden, unforeseen breakdown and they have to be sent back to bed, or, if it's very serious, back to the Infirmary again. These are the exceptions, however, not the rule. You can bank on most of those eaters being out in the world and usefully employed within six months.

SLOAN—You couldn't say more than that. (*abruptly*) But— the unfortunate ones—do you have many deaths?

STANTON—(*with a frown*) No. We're under a very hard, almost cruel imperative which prevents that. If, at the end of six months, a case shows no response to treatment, continues to go down hill—if, in a word, it seems hopeless—we send them away, to one of the State Farms if they have no private means. (*apologetically*) You see, this sanatorium is over-crowded and has a long waiting list most of the time of others who demand their chance for life. We have to make places for them. We have no time to waste on incurables. There are other places for them—and sometimes, too, a change is bene-ficial and they pick up in new surroundings. You never can tell. But we're bound by the rule. It may seem cruel—but it's as near justice to all concerned as we can come.

SLOAN—(*soberly*) I see. (*His eyes fall on the pianola—in sur-prise*) Ah—a piano.

STANTON—(*replying to the other's thought*) Yes, the patients play and sing. (*with a smile*) If you'd call the noise they make by those terms. They'd dance, too, if we permitted it. There's only one song taboo—Home, Sweet Home—for obvious reasons.

SLOAN—I see. (*with a final look around*) Did I understand you to say this is the only place where the sexes are permitted to mingle?

STANTON—Yes, sir.

SLOAN—(*with a smile*) Not much chance for a love affair, then.

STANTON—(*seriously*) We do our best to prevent them. We even have a strict rule which allows us to step in and put a stop to any intimacy which grows beyond the casual. People up here, Mr. Sloan, are expected to put aside all ideas except the one—getting well.

SLOAN—(*somewhat embarrassed*) A damn good rule, too, under the circumstances.

STANTON—(*with a laugh*) Yes, we're strictly anti-Cupid, sir, from top to bottom. (*turning to the door to the hall*) And now, if you don't mind, Mr. Sloan, I'm going to turn you foot-loose to wander about the grounds on an unconducted tour. Today is my busy morning—Saturday. We weigh each patient immediately after breakfast.

SLOAN—Every week?

STANTON—Every Saturday. You see we depend on fluctua-tions in weight to tell us a lot about the patient's condition. If they gain, or stay at normal, all's usually well. If they lose week after week, we keep careful watch. It's a sign that something's wrong.

SLOAN—(*with a smile*) Well, you just shoo me off wherever you please and go on with the good work. I'll be glad of a ramble in the open.

STANTON—After the weighing is over, sir, I'll be free to— (*His words are lost as the three go out. A moment later, Eileen enters from the dining room. She has grown stouter, her face has more of a healthy, out-of-door color, but there is still about her the suggestion of being worn down by a burden too oppressive for her strength. She is dressed in shirtwaist and dark skirt. She goes to the armchair, left forward, and sinks down on it. She is evidently in a state of nervous depression; she twists her fingers together in her lap; her eyes stare sadly before her; she clenches her upper lip with her teeth to prevent its trembling. She has hardly regained control over herself when Stephen Murray comes in hurriedly from the dining room and, seeing her at his first glance, walks quickly over to her chair. He is the picture of health, his figure has filled out solidly, his tanned face beams with suppressed exultation.*)

MURRAY—(*excitedly*) Eileen! I saw you leave your table. I've something to tell you. I didn't get a chance last night after the mail came. Just listen, Eileen—it's too good to be true—but on that mail—guess what?

EILEEN—(*forgetting her depression—with an excited smile*) I know! You've sold your story!

MURRAY—(*triumphantly*) Go to the head of the class. What d'you know about that for luck! My first, too—and only the third magazine I sent it to! (*He cuts a joyful caper.*)

EILEEN—(*happily*) Isn't that wonderful, Stephen! But I knew all the time you would. The story's so good.

MURRAY—Well, you might have known but I didn't think there was a chance in the world. And as for being good— (*with superior air*)—wait till I turn loose with the real big ones, the kind I'm going to write. Then I'll make them sit up and take notice. They can't stop me now. And I haven't told you the best part. The editor wrote saying how much he liked the yarn and asked me for more of the same kind.

EILEEN—And you've the three others about the same person—just as good, too! (*She claps her hands delightedly.*)

MURRAY—And I can send them out right away. They're all typed, thanks to you. That's what's brought me luck, I know. I never had a bit by myself. (*Then, after a quick glance around to make sure they are alone, he bends down and kisses her.*) There! A token of gratitude—even if it is against the rules.

EILEEN—(*flushing—with timid happiness*) Stephen! You mustn't! They'll see.

MURRAY—(*boldly*) Let them!

EILEEN—But you know—they've warned us against being so much together, already.

MURRAY—Let them! We'll be out of this prison soon. (*Eileen shakes her head sadly but he does not notice.*) Oh, I wish you could leave when I do. We'd have some celebration together.

EILEEN—(*her lips trembling*) I was thinking last night—that you'd be going away. You look so well. Do you think—they'll let you go—soon?

MURRAY—You bet I do. I caught Stanton in the hall last night and asked him if I could go.

EILEEN—(*anxiously*) What did he say?

MURRAY—He only smiled and said: "We'll see if you gain weight tomorrow." As if that mattered now! Why, I'm way above normal as it is! But you know Stanton—always putting you off.

EILEEN—(*slowly*) Then—if you gain today—

MURRAY—He'll let me go. I'm going to insist on it.

EILEEN—Then—you'll leave—?

MURRAY—The minute I can get packed.

EILEEN—(*trying to force a smile*) Oh, I'm so glad—for your sake; but—I'm selfish—it'll be so lonely here without you.

MURRAY—(*consolingly*) You'll be going away yourself before long. (*Eileen shakes her head. He goes on without noticing, wrapped in his own success.*) Oh, Eileen, you can't imagine all it opens up for me—selling that story. I can go straight to New York, and live, and meet real people who are doing things. I can take my time, and try and do the work I hope to. (*feelingly*) You don't know how grateful I am to you, Eileen—how you've helped me. Oh, I don't mean just the typing, I mean your encouragement, your faith! The stories would never have been written if it hadn't been for you.

EILEEN—(*choking back a sob*) I didn't do—anything.

MURRAY—(*staring down at her—with rough kindliness*) Here, here, that'll never do! You're not weeping about it, are you, silly? (*He pats her on the shoulder.*) What's the matter, Eileen? You didn't eat a thing this morning. I was watching you. (*with kindly severity*) That's no way to gain weight you know. You'll have to feed up. Do you hear what your guardian commands, eh?

EILEEN—(*with dull hopelessness*) I know I'll lose again. I've been losing steadily the past three weeks.

MURRAY—Here! Don't you dare talk that way! Why, you've been picking up wonderfully—until just lately. Even the old Doc has told you how much he admired your pluck, and how much better you were getting. You're not going to quit now, are you?

EILEEN—(*despairingly*) Oh, I don't care! I don't care—now.

MURRAY—Now? What do you mean by that? What's happened to make things any different?

EILEEN—(*evasively*) Oh—nothing. Don't ask me, Stephen.

MURRAY—(*with sudden anger*) I don't have to ask you. I can guess. Another letter from home—or from that ass, eh?

EILEEN—(*shaking her head*) No, it isn't that. (*She looks at him as if imploring him to comprehend.*)

MURRAY—(*furiously*) Of course, you'd deny it. You always do. But don't you suppose I've got eyes? It's been the same damn thing all the time you've been here. After every nagging letter—thank God they don't write often any more!—you've been all in; and after their Sunday visits—you can thank God they've been few, too—you're utterly knocked out. It's a shame!

EILEEN—Stephen!

MURRAY—(*relentlessly*) They've done nothing but worry and torment you and do their best to keep you from getting well.

EILEEN—(*faintly*) You're not fair, Stephen.

MURRAY—Rot! When it isn't your father grumbling about expense, it's the kids, or that stupid housekeeper, or that slick Aleck, Nicholls, with his cowardly lies. Which is it this time?

EILEEN—(*pitifully*) None of them.

MURRAY—(*explosively*) But him, especially—the dirty cad! Oh, I've got a rich notion to pay a call on that gentleman when I leave and tell him what I think of him.

EILEEN—(*quickly*) No—you mustn't ever! He's not to blame. If you knew— (*She stops, lowering her eyes in confusion.*)

MURRAY—(*roughly*) Knew what? You make me sick, Eileen—always finding excuses for him. I never could understand what a girl like you could see— But what's the use? I've said all this before. You're wasting yourself on a— (*rudely*) Love must be blind. And yet you say you don't love him, really?

EILEEN—(*shaking her head—helplessly*) But I do—like Fred. We've been good friends so many years. I don't want to hurt him—his pride—

MURRAY—That's the same as answering no to my question. Then, if you don't love him, why don't you write and tell him to go to—break it off? (*Eileen bows her head but doesn't reply. Irritated, Murray continues brutally.*) Are you afraid it would break his heart? Don't be a fool! The only way you could do that would be to deprive him of his meals.

EILEEN—(*springing to her feet—distractedly*) Please stop, Stephen! You're cruel! And you've been so kind—the only real friend I've had up here. Don't spoil it all now.

MURRAY—(*remorsefully*) I'm sorry, Eileen. I won't say another word. (*irritably*) Still someone ought to say or do something to put a stop to—

EILEEN—(*with a broken laugh*) Never mind. Everything will stop—soon, now!

MURRAY—(*suspiciously*) What do you mean?

EILEEN—(*with an attempt at a careless tone*) Nothing. If you can't see— (*She turns to him with sudden intensity.*) Oh, Stephen, if you only knew how wrong you are about everything you've said. It's all true; but it isn't that—any of it—any more—that's— Oh, I can't tell you!

MURRAY—(*with great interest*) Please do, Eileen!

EILEEN—(*with a helpless laugh*) No.

MURRAY—Please tell me what it is! Let me help you.

EILEEN—No. It wouldn't be any use, Stephen.

MURRAY—(*offended*) Why do you say that? Haven't I helped before?

EILEEN—Yes—but this—

MURRAY—Come now! 'Fess up! What is "this"?

EILEEN—No. I couldn't speak of it here, anyway. They'll all be coming out soon.

MURRAY—(*insistently*) Then when? Where?

EILEEN—Oh, I don't know—perhaps never, nowhere. I don't know— Sometime before you leave, maybe.

MURRAY—But I may go tomorrow morning—if I gain weight and Stanton lets me.

EILEEN—(*sadly*) Yes, I was forgetting—you were going right away. (*dully*) Then nowhere I suppose—never. (*glancing toward the dining room*) They're all getting up. Let's not talk about it any more—now.

MURRAY—(*stubbornly*) But you'll tell me later, Eileen? You must.

EILEEN—(*vaguely*) Perhaps. It depends— (*The patients, about forty in number, straggle in from the dining room by twos and threes, chatting in low tones. The men and women with few exceptions separate into two groups, the women congregating in the left right angle of chairs, the men sitting or standing in the right right angle. In appearance, most of the patients are tanned, healthy, and cheerful looking. The great majority are under middle age. Their clothes are of the cheap, readymade variety. They are all distinctly of the wage-earning class. They might well be a crowd of cosmopolitan factory workers gathered together after a summer vacation. A hollow-chestedness and a tendency to round shoulders may be detected as a common characteristic. A general air of tension, marked by frequent bursts of laughter in too high a key, seems to pervade the throng. Murray and Eileen, as if to avoid contact with the others, come over to the right in front of the dining-room door.*)

MURRAY—(*in a low voice*) Listen to them laugh. Did you ever notice—perhaps it's my imagination—how forced they act on Saturday mornings before they're weighed?

EILEEN—(*dully*) No.

MURRAY—Can't you tell me that secret now? No one'll hear.

EILEEN—(*vehemently*) No, no, how could I? Don't speak

of it! (*A sudden silence falls on all the groups at once. Their eyes, by a common impulse turn quickly toward the door to the hall.*)

A WOMAN—(*nervously—as if this moment's silent pause oppressed her*) Play something, Peters. They ain't coming yet. (*Peters, a stupid-looking young fellow with a sly, twisted smirk which gives him the appearance of perpetually winking his eye, detaches himself from a group on the right. All join in with urging exclamations:* Go on, Peters! Go to it! Pedal up, Pete! Give us a rag! That's the boy, Peters! *etc.*)

PETERS—Sure, if I got time. (*He goes to the pianola and puts in a roll. The mingled conversation and laughter bursts forth again as he sits on the bench and starts pedaling.*)

MURRAY—(*disgustedly*) It's sure good to think I won't have to listen to that old tin-pan being banged much longer! (*The music interrupts him—a quick rag. The patients brighten, hum, whistle, sway their heads or tap their feet in time to the tune. Doctor Stanton and Doctor Simms appear in the doorway from the hall. All eyes are turned on them.*)

STANTON—(*raising his voice*) —They all seem to be here, Doctor. We might as well start. (*Mrs. Turner, the matron, comes in behind them—a stout, motherly, capable-looking woman with gray hair. She hears Stanton's remark.*)

MRS. TURNER—And take temperatures after, Doctor?

STANTON—Yes, Mrs. Turner. I think that's better today.

MRS. TURNER—All right, Doctor. (*Stanton and the assistant go out. Mrs. Turner advances a step or so into the room and looks from one group of patients to the other, inclining her head and smiling benevolently. All force smiles and nod in recognition of her greeting. Peters, at the pianola, lets the music slow down, glancing questioningly at the matron to see if she is going to order it stopped. Then, encouraged by her smile, his feet pedal harder than ever.*)

MURRAY—Look at old Mrs. Grundy's eyes pinned on us! She'll accuse us of being too familiar again, the old wench!

EILEEN—Ssshh. You're wrong. She's looking at me, not at us.

MURRAY—At you? Why?

EILEEN—I ran a temperature yesterday. It must have been over a hundred last night.

MURRAY—(*with consoling scepticism*) You're always suffering for trouble, Eileen. How do you know you ran a temp? You didn't see the stick, I suppose?

EILEEN—No—but—I could tell. I felt feverish and chilly. It must have been way up.

MURRAY—Bosh! If it was you'd have been sent to bed.

EILEEN—That's why she's looking at me. (*piteously*) Oh, I do hope I won't be sent back to bed! I don't know what I'd do. If I could only gain this morning. If my temp has only gone down! (*hopelessly*) But I feel— I didn't sleep a wink— thinking—

MURRAY—(*roughly*) You'll persuade yourself you've got leprosy in a second. Don't be a nut! It's all imagination, I tell you. You'll gain. Wait and see if you don't. (*Eileen shakes her head. A metallic rumble and jangle comes from the hallway. Everyone turns in that direction with nervous expectancy.*)

MRS. TURNER—(*admonishingly*) Mr. Peters!

PETERS—Yes, ma'am. (*He stops playing and rejoins the group of men on the right. In the midst of a silence broken only by hushed murmurs of conversation, Doctor Stanton appears in the hall doorway. He turns to help his assistant wheel in a Fairbanks scale on castors. They place the scale against the wall immediately to the rear of the doorway. Doctor Simms adjusts it to a perfect balance.*)

DOCTOR STANTON—(*takes a pencil from his pocket and opens the record book he has in his hand*) All ready, Doctor?

DOCTOR SIMMS—Just a second, sir.

MURRAY—(*with a nervous smile*) Well, we're all set. Here's hoping!

EILEEN—You'll gain, I'm sure you will. You look so well.

MURRAY—Oh—I—I wasn't thinking of myself, I'm a sure thing. I was betting on you. I've simply got to gain to-day, when so much depends on it.

EILEEN—Yes, I hope you— (*She falters brokenly and turns away from him.*)

DOCTOR SIMMS—(*straightening up*) All ready, Doctor.

STANTON—(*nods and glances at his book—without raising his voice—distinctly*) Mrs. Abner. (*A middle-aged woman comes and gets on the scales. Simms adjusts it to her weight of the previous week which Stanton reads to him from the book in a low voice, and weighs her.*)

MURRAY—(*with a relieved sigh*) They're off. (*noticing Eileen's downcast head and air of dejection*) Here! Buck up, Eileen! Old Lady Grundy's watching you—and it's your turn in a second. (*Eileen raises her head and forces a frightened smile. Mrs. Abner gets down off the scales with a pleased grin. She has evidently gained. She rejoins the group of women, chattering volubly in low tones. Her exultant* "gained half a pound" *can be heard. The other women smile their perfunctory congratulations, their eyes absent-minded, intent on their own worries. Stanton writes down the weight in the book.*)

STANTON—Miss Bailey. (*A young girl goes to the scales.*)

MURRAY—Bailey looks badly, doesn't she?

EILEEN—(*her lips trembling*) She's been losing, too.

MURRAY—Well, *you're* going to gain today. Remember, now!

EILEEN—(*with a feeble smile*) I'll try to obey your orders. (*Miss Bailey gets down off the scales. Her eyes are full of despondency although she tries to make a brave face of it, forcing a laugh as she joins the women. They stare at her with pitying looks and murmur consoling phrases.*)

EILEEN—She's lost again. Oh, I wish I didn't have to get weighed—

STANTON—Miss Carmody. (*Eileen starts nervously.*)

MURRAY—(*as she leaves him*) Remember now! Break the scales! (*She walks quickly to the scales, trying to assume an air of defiant indifference. The balance stays down as she steps up. Eileen's face shows her despair at this. Simms weighs her and gives the poundage in a low voice to Stanton. Eileen steps down mechanically, then hesitates as if not knowing where to turn, her anguished eyes flitting from one group to another.*)

MURRAY—(*savagely*) Damn! (*Doctor Stanton writes the figures in his book, glances sharply at Eileen, and then nods significantly to Mrs. Turner who is standing beside him.*)

STANTON—(*calling the next*) Miss Doeffler. (*Another woman comes to be weighed.*)

MRS. TURNER—Miss Carmody! Will you come here a moment, please?

EILEEN—(*her face growing very pale*) Yes, Mrs. Turner. (*The heads of the different groups bend together. Their eyes follow Eileen as they whisper. Mrs. Turner leads her down front, left. Behind them the weighing of the women continues briskly. The great majority have gained. Those who have not have either remained stationary or lost a negligible fraction of a pound. So, as the weighing proceeds, the general air of smiling satisfaction rises among the groups of women. Some of them, their ordeal over, go out through the hall doorway by twos and threes with suppressed laughter and chatter. As they pass behind Eileen they glance at her with pitying curiosity. Doctor Stanton's voice is heard at regular intervals calling the names in alphabetical order:* Mrs. Elbing, Miss Finch, Miss Grimes, Miss Haines, Miss Hayes, Miss Jutner, Miss Linowski, Mrs. Marini, Mrs. McCoy, Miss McElroy, Miss Nelson, Mrs. Nott, Mrs. O'Brien, Mrs. Olson, Miss Paul, Miss Petrovski, Mrs. Quinn, Miss Robersi, Mrs. Stattler, Miss Unger.)

MRS. TURNER—(*putting her hand on Eileen's shoulder— kindly*) You're not looking so well, lately, my dear, do you know it?

EILEEN—(*bravely*) I feel—fine. (*Her eyes, as if looking for encouragement, seek Murray who is staring at her worriedly.*)

MRS. TURNER—(*gently*) You lost weight again, you know.

EILEEN—I know—but—

MRS. TURNER—This is the fourth week.

EILEEN—I— I know it is—

MRS. TURNER—I've been keeping my eye on you. You seem—worried. Are you upset about—something we don't know?

EILEEN—(*quickly*) No, no! I haven't slept much lately. That must be it.

MRS. TURNER—Are you worrying about your condition? Is that what keeps you awake?

EILEEN—No.

MRS. TURNER—You're sure it's not that?

EILEEN—Yes, I'm sure it's not, Mrs. Turner.

MRS. TURNER—I was going to tell you if you were: Don't do it! You can't expect it to be all smooth sailing. Even the most favorable cases have to expect these little setbacks. A few days' rest in bed will start you on the right trail again.

EILEEN—(*in anguish, although she has realized this was coming*) Bed? Go back to bed? Oh, Mrs. Turner!

MRS. TURNER—(*gently*) Yes, my dear, Doctor Stanton thinks it best. So when you go back to your cottage—

EILEEN—Oh, please—not today—not right away!

MRS. TURNER—You had a temperature and a high pulse yesterday, didn't you realize it? And this morning you look quite feverish. (*She tries to put her hand on Eileen's forehead but the latter steps away defensively.*)

EILEEN—It's only—not sleeping last night. Oh, I'm sure it'll go away.

MRS. TURNER—(*consolingly*) When you lie still and have perfect rest, of course it will.

EILEEN—(*with a longing look over at Murray*) But not to-day—please, Mrs. Turner.

MRS. TURNER—(*looking at her keenly*) There is something upsetting you. You've something on your mind that you can't tell me, is that it? (*Eileen maintains a stubborn silence.*) But think—*can't* you tell me? (*with a kindly smile*) I'm used to other people's troubles. I've been playing mother-confessor to the patients for years now, and I think I've usually been able to help them. Can't you confide in me, child? (*Eileen drops her eyes but remains silent. Mrs. Turner glances meaningly over at Murray who is watching them whenever he thinks the matron is not aware of it—a note of sharp rebuke in her voice*) I think I can guess your secret. You've let other notions become more important to you than the idea of getting well. And you've no excuse for it. After I had to warn you a month ago, I expected *that* silliness to stop instantly.

EILEEN—(*her face flushed—protesting*) Nothing like that has anything to do with it.

MRS. TURNER—(*sceptically*) What is it that has, then?

EILEEN—(*lying determinedly*) It's my family. They keep writing—and worrying me—and— That's what it is, Mrs. Turner.

MRS. TURNER—(*not exactly knowing whether to believe this or not—probing the girl with her eyes*) Your father?

EILEEN—Yes, all of them. (*suddenly seeing a way to discredit all of the matron's suspicions—excitedly*) And principally the young man I'm engaged to—the one who came to visit me several times—

MRS. TURNER—(*surprised*) So—you're engaged? (*Eileen*

nods. Mrs. Turner immediately dismisses her suspicions.) Oh, pardon me. I didn't know that, you see, or I wouldn't— (*She pats Eileen on the shoulder comfortingly.*) Never mind. You'll tell me all about it, won't you?

EILEEN—(*desperately*) Yes. (*She seems about to go on but the matron interrupts her.*)

MRS. TURNER—Oh, not here, my dear. Not now. Come to my room—let me see—I'll be busy all morning—sometime this afternoon. Will you do that?

EILEEN—Yes. (*joyfully*) Then I needn't go to bed right away?

MRS. TURNER—No—on one condition. You mustn't take any exercise. Stay in your recliner all day and rest and remain in bed tomorrow morning.

EILEEN—I promise, Mrs. Turner.

MRS. TURNER—(*smiling in dismissal*) Very well, then. I'll see you this afternoon.

EILEEN—Yes, Mrs. Turner. (*The matron goes to the rear where Miss Bailey is sitting with Mrs. Abner. She beckons to Miss Bailey who gets up with a scared look, and they go to the far left corner of the room. Eileen stands for a moment hesitating—then starts to go to Murray, but just at this moment Peters comes forward and speaks to Murray.*)

PETERS—(*with his sly twisted grin*) Say, Carmody musta lost fierce. Did yuh see the Old Woman handin' her an earful? Sent her back to bed, I betcha. What d'yuh think?

MURRAY—(*impatiently, showing his dislike*) How the hell do I know?

PETERS—(*sneeringly*) Huh, you don't know nothin' 'bout her, I s'pose? Where d'yuh get that stuff?

MURRAY—(*with cold rage before which the other slinks away*) If it wasn't for other people losing weight you couldn't get any joy out of life, could you? (*roughly*) Get away from me! (*He makes a threatening gesture.*)

PETERS—(*beating a snarling retreat*) Wait'n' see if yuh don't lose too, yuh stuck-up boob! (*Seeing that Murray is alone again, Eileen starts toward him but this time she is intercepted by Mrs. Abner who stops on her way out. The weighing of the women is now finished, and that of the men, which proceeds much quicker, begins.*)

DOCTOR STANTON—Anderson! (*Anderson comes to the scales. The men all move down to the left to wait their turn, with the exception of Murray, who remains by the dining room door, fidgeting impatiently, anxious for a word with Eileen.*)

MRS. ABNER—(*taking Eileen's arm*) Coming over to the cottage, dearie?

EILEEN—Not just this minute, Mrs. Abner. I have to wait—

MRS. ABNER—For the Old Woman? You lost today, didn't you? Is she sendin' you to bed, the old devil?

EILEEN—Yes, I'm afraid I'll have to—

MRS. ABNER—She's a mean one, ain't she? I gained this week—half a pound. Lord, I'm gettin' fat! All my clothes are gittin' too small for me. Don't know what I'll do. Did you lose much, dearie?

EILEEN—Three pounds.

MRS. ABNER—Ain't that awful! (*hastening to make up for this thoughtless remark*) All the same, what's three pounds! You can git them back in a week after you're resting more. You've been runnin' a temp, too, ain't you? (*Eileen nods.*) Don't worry about it, dearie. It'll go down. Worryin's the worst. Me, I don't never worry none. (*She chuckles with satisfaction—then soberly*) I just been talkin' with Bailey. She's got to go to bed, too, I guess. She lost two pounds. She ain't runnin' no temp though.

STANTON—Barnes! (*Another man comes to the scales.*)

MRS. ABNER—(*in a mysterious whisper*) Look at Mr. Murray, dearie. Ain't he nervous today? I don't know as I blame him, either. I heard the doctor said he'd let him go home if he gained today. Is it true, d'you know?

EILEEN—(*dully*) I don't know.

MRS. ABNER—Gosh, I wish it was me! My old man's missin' me like the dickens, he writes. (*She starts to go.*) You'll be over to the cottage in a while, won't you? Me'n' you'll have a game of casino, eh?

EILEEN—(*happy at this deliverance*) Yes, I'll be glad to.

STANTON—Cordero! (*Mrs. Abner goes out. Eileen again starts toward Murray but this time Flynn, a young fellow with a brick-colored, homely, good-natured face, and a shaven-necked haircut, slouches back to Murray. Eileen is brought to a halt in front of the table where she stands, her face working with nervous strain, clasping and unclasping her trembling hands.*)

FLYNN—(*curiously*) Say, Steve, what's this bull about the Doc lettin' yuh beat it if yuh gain today? Is it straight goods?

MURRAY—He said he might, that's all. (*impatiently*) How the devil did that story get traveling around?

FLYNN—(*with a grin*) Wha' d'yuh expect with this gang of skirts chewin' the fat? Well, here's hopin' yuh come home a winner, Steve.

MURRAY—(*gratefully*) Thanks. (*with confidence*) Oh, I'll gain all right; but whether he'll let me go or not— (*He shrugs his shoulders.*)

FLYNN—Make 'em behave. I wisht Stanton'd ask waivers on me. (*with a laugh*) I oughter gain a ton today. I ate enough spuds for breakfast to plant a farm.

STANTON—Flynn!

FLYNN—Me to the plate! (*He strides to the scales.*)

MURRAY—Good luck! (*He starts to join Eileen but Miss Bailey, who has finished her talk with Mrs. Turner, who goes out to the hall, approaches Eileen at just this moment. Murray stops in his tracks, fuming. He and Eileen exchange a glance of helpless annoyance.*)

MISS BAILEY—(*her thin face full of the satisfaction of misery finding company—plucks at Eileen's sleeve*) Say, Carmody, she sent you back to bed, too, didn't she?

EILEEN—(*absent-mindedly*) I suppose—

MISS BAILEY—You suppose? Of course she did. I got to go, too. (*pulling Eileen's sleeve*) Come on. Let's get out of here. I hate this place, don't you?

STANTON—(*calling the next*) Hopper!

FLYNN—(*shouts to Murray as he is going out to the hall*) I hit 'er for a two-bagger, Steve. Come on now, Bo, and bring me home! 'Atta boy! (*Grinning gleefully, he slouches out. Doctor Stanton and all the patients laugh.*)

MISS BAILEY—(*with irritating persistence*) Come on, Carmody. You've got to go to bed, too.

EILEEN—(*at the end of her patience—releasing her arm from the other's grasp*) Let me alone, will you? I don't have to go to bed now—not till tomorrow morning.

MISS BAILEY—(*in a whining rage*) Why not? You've been

running a temp, too, and I haven't! You must have a pull, that's what! It isn't fair. I'll bet you lost more than I did, too! What right have you got— Well, I'm not going to bed if you don't. Wait 'n' see!

EILEEN—(*turning away revolted*) Go away! Leave me alone, please.

STANTON—Lowenstein!

MISS BAILEY—(*turns to the hall door, whining*) All right for you! I'm going to find out. It isn't square. I'll write home. (*She disappears in the hallway. Murray strides over to Eileen whose strength seems to have left her and who is leaning weakly against the table.*)

MURRAY—Thank God—at last! Isn't it hell—all these fools! I couldn't get to you. What did Old Lady Grundy have to say to you? I saw her giving me a hard look. Was it about us—the old stuff? (*Eileen nods with downcast eyes.*) What did she say? Never mind now. You can tell me in a minute. It's my turn next. (*His eyes glance toward the scales.*)

EILEEN—(*intensely*) Oh, Stephen, I wish you weren't going away!

MURRAY—(*excitedly*). Maybe I'm not. It's like gambling— if I win—

STANTON—Murray!

MURRAY—Wait here, Eileen. (*He goes to the scales. Eileen keeps her back turned. Her body stiffens rigidly in the intensity of her conflicting emotions. She stares straight ahead, her eyes full of anguish. Murray steps on the scales nervously. The balance rod hits the top smartly. He has gained. His face lights up and he heaves a great sigh of relief. Eileen seems to sense this outcome and her head sinks, her body sags weakly and seems to shrink to a smaller size. Murray gets off the scales, his face beaming with a triumphant smile. Doctor Stanton smiles and murmurs something to him in a low voice. Murray nods brightly; then turns back to Eileen.*)

STANTON—Nathan! (*Another patient advances to the scales.*)

MURRAY—(*trying to appear casual*) Well—three rousing cheers! Stanton told me to come to his office at eleven. That means a final exam—and release!

EILEEN—(*dully*) So you gained?

MURRAY—Three pounds.

EILEEN—Funny—I lost three. (*with a pitiful effort at a smile*) I hope you gained the ones I lost. (*Her lips tremble.*) So you're surely going away.

MURRAY—(*his joy fleeing as he is confronted with her sorrow—slowly*) It looks that way, Eileen.

EILEEN—(*in a trembling whisper broken by rising sobs*) Oh— I'm so glad—you gained—the ones I lost, Stephen— So glad! (*She breaks down, covering her face with her hands, stifling her sobs.*)

MURRAY—(*alarmed*) Eileen! What's the matter? (*desperately*) Stop it! Stanton'll see you!

(*The Curtain Falls*)

SCENE TWO

Midnight of the same day. A crossroads near the sanatorium. The main road comes down forward from the right. A smaller road, leading down from the left, joins it toward left, center.

Dense woods rise sheer from the grass and bramble-grown ditches at the road's sides. At the junction of the two roads there is a signpost, its arms pointing toward the right and the left, rear. A pile of round stones is at the road corner, left forward. A full moon, riding high overhead, throws the roads into white shadowless relief and masses the woods into walls of compact blackness. The trees lean heavily together, their branches motionless, unstirred by any trace of wind.

As the curtain rises, Eileen is discovered standing in the middle of the road, front center. Her face shows white and clear in the bright moonlight as she stares with anxious expectancy up the road to the left. Her body is fixed in an attitude of rigid immobility as if she were afraid a slightest movement would break the spell of silence and awaken the unknown. She has shrunk instinctively as far away as she can from the mysterious darkness which rises at the road's sides like an imprisoning wall. A sound of hurried footfalls, muffled by the dust, comes from the road she is watching. She gives a startled gasp. Her eyes strain to identify the oncomer. Uncertain, trembling, with fright, she hesitates a second; then darts to the side of the road and crouches down in the shadow.

Stephen Murray comes down the road from the left. He stops by the sign post and peers about him. He wears a cap, the peak of which casts his face into shadow. Finally he calls in a low voice:

MURRAY—Eileen!

EILEEN—(*coming out quickly from her hiding place—with a glad little cry*) Stephen! At last! (*She runs to him as if she were going to fling her arms about him but stops abashed. He reaches out and takes her hands.*)

MURRAY—It can't be twelve yet. (*He leads her to the pile of stones to the left.*) I haven't heard the village clock.

EILEEN—I must have come early. It seemed as if I'd been waiting for ages.

MURRAY—How your hands tremble! Were you frightened?

EILEEN—(*forcing a smile*) A little. The woods are so black and queer looking. I'm all right now.

MURRAY—Sit down. You must rest. (*in a tone of annoyed reproof*) I am going to read you a lecture, young lady. You shouldn't ever have done this—running a temp and— Good heavens, don't you want to get well?

EILEEN—(*dully*) I don't know—

MURRAY—(*irritably*) You make me ill when you talk that way, Eileen. It doesn't sound like you at all. What's come over you lately? I was—knocked out—when I read the note you slipped me after supper. I didn't get a chance to read it until late, I was so busy packing, and by that time you'd gone to your cottage. If I could have reached you any way I'd have refused to come here, I tell you straight. But I couldn't—and I knew you'd be here waiting—and—still, I feel guilty. Damn it, this isn't the thing for you! You ought to be in bed asleep.

EILEEN—(*humbly*) Please, Stephen, don't scold me.

MURRAY—How the devil did you ever get the idea— meeting me here at this ungodly hour?

EILEEN—You'd told me about your sneaking out to go to the village, and I thought there'd be no harm this one night—the last night.

MURRAY—But I'm well. I've been well. It's different. You— Honest, Eileen, you shouldn't lose sleep and tax your strength.

EILEEN—Don't scold me, please. I'll make up for it. I'll rest all the time—after you're gone. I just had to see you some way. (*A clock in the distant village begins striking.*) Ssshh! Listen.

MURRAY—That's twelve now. You see I was early. (*In a pause of silence they wait motionlessly until the last mournful note dies in the hushed woods.*)

EILEEN—(*in a stifled voice*) It isn't tomorrow now, is it? It's today—the day you're going.

MURRAY—(*something in her voice making him avert his face and kick at the heap of stones on which she is sitting—brusquely*) Well, I hope you took precautions so you wouldn't be caught sneaking out.

EILEEN—I did just what you'd told me you did—stuffed the pillows under the clothes so the watchman would think I was there.

MURRAY—None of the patients on your porch saw you leave, did they?

EILEEN—No. They were all asleep.

MURRAY—That's all right, then. I wouldn't trust any of that bunch of women. They'd be only too tickled to squeal on you. (*There is an uncomfortable pause. Murray seems waiting for her to speak. He looks about him at the trees, up into the moonlit sky, breathing in the fresh night air with a healthy delight. Eileen remains with downcast head, staring at the road.*) It's beautiful tonight, isn't it? Worth losing sleep for.

EILEEN—(*dully*) Yes. (*Another pause—finally she murmurs faintly*) Are you leaving early?

MURRAY—The ten-forty. Leave the San at ten, I guess.

EILEEN—You're going home?

MURRAY—Home? No. But I'm going to see my sisters—just to say hello. I've got to, I suppose.

EILEEN—I'm sure—I've often felt—you're unjust to your sisters. (*with conviction*) I'm sure they must both love you.

MURRAY—(*frowning*) Maybe, in their own way. But what's love without a glimmer of understanding—a nuisance! They've never seen the real me and never wanted to.

EILEEN—(*as if to herself*) What is—the real you? (*Murray kicks at the stones impatiently without answering. Eileen hastens to change the subject.*) And then you'll go to New York?

MURRAY—(*interested at once*) Yes. You bet.

EILEEN—And write more?

MURRAY—Not in New York, no. I'm going there to take a vacation and really enjoy myself for a while. I've enough money for that as it is and if the other stories you typed sell— I'll be as rich as Rockefeller. I might even travel— No, I've got to make good with my best stuff first. I know what I'll do. When I've had enough of New York, I'll rent a place in the country—some old farmhouse—and live alone there and work. (*lost in his own plans—with pleasure*) That's the right idea, isn't it?

EILEEN—(*trying to appear enthused*) It ought to be fine for your work. (*after a pause*) They're fine, those stories you wrote here. They're—so much like you. I'd know it was you wrote them even if—I didn't know.

MURRAY—(*pleased*) Wait till you read the others I'm going to do! (*after a slight pause—with a good-natured grin*) Here I am talking about myself again! But you don't know how good it is to have your dreams coming true. It'd make an egotist out of anyone.

EILEEN—(*sadly*) No. I don't know. But I love to hear you talk of yours.

MURRAY—(*with an embarrassed laugh*) Thanks. Well, I've certainly told you all of them. You're the only one— (*He stops and abruptly changes the subject.*) You said in your note that you had something important to tell me. (*He sits down beside her, crossing his legs.*) Is it about your interview with Old Mrs. Grundy this afternoon?

EILEEN—No, that didn't amount to anything. She seemed mad because I told her so little. I think she guessed I only told her what I did so she'd let me stay, maybe—your last day,—and to keep her from thinking what she did—about us.

MURRAY—(*quickly, as if he wishes to avoid this subject*) What is it you wanted to tell me, then?

EILEEN—(*sadly*) It doesn't seem so important now, some-how. I suppose it was silly of me to drag you out here, just for that. It can't mean anything to you—much.

MURRAY—(*encouragingly*) How do you know it can't?

EILEEN—(*slowly*) I only thought—you might like to know.

MURRAY—(*interestedly*) Know what? What is it? If I can help—

EILEEN—No. (*after a moment's hesitation*) I wrote to him this afternoon.

MURRAY—Him?

EILEEN—The letter you've been advising me to write.

MURRAY—(*as if the knowledge of this alarmed him—haltingly*) You mean—Fred Nicholls?

EILEEN—Yes.

MURRAY—(*after a pause—uncomfortably*) You mean—you broke it all off?

EILEEN—Yes—for good. (*She looks up at his averted face. He remains silent. She continues apprehensively.*) You don't say anything. I thought—you'd be glad. You've always told me it was the honorable thing to do.

MURRAY—(*gruffly*) I know. I say more than my prayers, damn it! (*with sudden eagerness*) Have you mailed the letter yet?

EILEEN—Yes. Why?

MURRAY—(*shortly*) Humph. Oh—nothing.

EILEEN—(*with pained disappointment*) Oh, Stephen, you don't think I did wrong, do you—now—after all you've said?

MURRAY—(*hurriedly*) Wrong? No, not if you were convinced it was the right thing to do yourself—if you know you don't love him. But I'd hate to think you did it just on my say-so. I shouldn't— I didn't mean to interfere. I don't know enough about your relations for my opinion to count.

EILEEN—(*hurt*) You know all there is to know.

MURRAY—I know you've been frank. But him—I don't know him. He may be quite different from my idea. That's what I'm getting at. I don't want to be unfair to him.

EILEEN—(*bitterly scornful*) You needn't worry. You weren't unfair. And you needn't be afraid you were responsible for my writing. I'd been going to for a long time before you ever spoke.

MURRAY—(*with a relieved sigh*) I'm glad of that—honestly, Eileen. I felt guilty. I shouldn't have knocked him behind his back without knowing him at all.

EILEEN—You said you could read him like a book from his letters I showed you.

MURRAY—(*apologetically*) I know. I'm a fool.

EILEEN—(*angrily*) What makes you so considerate of Fred Nicholls all of a sudden? What you thought about him was right.

MURRAY—(*vaguely*) I don't know. One makes mistakes.

EILEEN—(*assertively*) Well, I know! You needn't waste pity on him. He'll be only too glad to get my letter. He's been anxious to be free of me ever since I was sent here, only he thought it wouldn't be decent to break it off himself while I was sick. He was afraid of what people would say about him when they found it out. So he's just gradually stopped writing and coming for visits, and waited for me to realize. And if I didn't, I know he'd have broken it off himself the first day I got home. I've kept persuading myself that, in spite of the way he's acted, he did love me as much as he could love anyone, and that it would hurt him if I— But now I know that he never loved me, that he couldn't love anyone but himself. Oh, I don't hate him for it. He can't help being what he is. And all people seem to be—like that, mostly. I'm only going to remember that he and I grew up together, and that he was kind to me then when he thought he liked me—and forget all the rest. (*with agitated impatience*) Oh, Stephen, you know all this I've said about him. Why don't you admit it? You've read his letters.

MURRAY—(*haltingly*) Yes, I'll admit that was my opinion—only I wanted to be sure you'd found out for yourself.

EILEEN—(*defiantly*) Well, I have! You see that now, don't you?

MURRAY—Yes; and I'm glad you're free of him, for your own sake. I knew he wasn't the person. (*with an attempt at a joking tone*) You must get one of the right sort—next time.

EILEEN—(*springing to her feet with a cry of pain*) Stephen! (*He avoids her eyes which search his face pleadingly.*)

MURRAY—(*mumbling*) He wasn't good enough—to lace your shoes—nor anyone else, either.

EILEEN—(*with a nervous laugh*) Don't be silly. (*after a pause during which she waits hungrily for some words from him—with a sigh of despair—faintly*) Well, I've told you—all there is. I might as well go back.

MURRAY—(*not looking at her—indistinctly*) Yes. You

mustn't lose too much sleep. I'll come to your cottage in the morning to say good-by. They'll permit that, I guess.

EILEEN—(*stands looking at him imploringly, her face convulsed with anguish, but he keeps his eyes fixed on the rocks at his feet. Finally she seems to give up and takes a few uncertain steps up the road toward the right—in an exhausted whisper*) Good night, Stephen.

MURRAY—(*his voice choked and husky*) Good night, Eileen.

EILEEN—(*walks weakly up the road but, as she passes the sign-post, she suddenly stops and turns to look again at Murray who has not moved or lifted his eyes. A great shuddering sob shatters her pent-up emotions. She runs back to Murray, her arms outstretched, with a choking cry.*) Stephen!

MURRAY—(*startled, whirls to face her and finds her arms thrown around his neck—in a terrified tone*) Eileen!

EILEEN—(*brokenly*) I love you, Stephen—you! That's what I wanted to tell! (*She gazes up into his eyes, her face transfigured by the joy and pain of this abject confession.*)

MURRAY—(*wincing as if this were the thing he had feared to hear*) Eileen!

EILEEN—(*pulling down his head with fierce strength and kissing him passionately on the lips*) I love you! I will say it! There! (*with sudden horror*) Oh, I know I shouldn't kiss you! I mustn't! You're all well—and I—

MURRAY—(*protesting frenziedly*) Eileen! Damn it! Don't say that! What do you think I am! (*He kisses her fiercely two or three times until she forces a hand over her mouth.*)

EILEEN—(*with a hysterically happy laugh*) No! Just hold me in your arms—just a little while—before—

MURRAY—(*his voice trembling*) Eileen! Don't talk that way! You're—it's killing me. I can't stand it!

EILEEN—(*with soothing tenderness*) Listen, dear—listen—and you won't say a word—I've so much to say—till I get through—please, will you promise?

MURRAY—(*between clinched teeth*) Yes—anything, Eileen!

EILEEN—Then I want to say—I know your secret. You don't love me— Isn't that it? (*Murray groans.*) Ssshh! It's all right, dear. You can't help what you don't feel. I've guessed you didn't—right along. And I've loved you—such a long time now—always, it seems. And you've sort of guessed—

that I did—didn't you? No, don't speak! I am sure you've guessed—only you didn't want to know—that—did you?—when you didn't love me. That's why you were lying—but I saw, I knew! Oh, I'm not blaming you, darling. How could I—never! You mustn't look so—so frightened. I know how you felt, dear. I've—I've watched you. It was just a flirtation for you at first. Wasn't it? Oh, I know. It was just fun, and—Please don't look at me so. I'm not hurting you, am I? I wouldn't for worlds, dear—you know—hurt you! And then afterwards—you found we could be such good friends—helping each other—and you wanted it to stay just like that always, didn't you?—I know—and then I had to spoil it all—and fall in love with you—didn't I? Oh, it was stupid—I shouldn't—I couldn't help it, you were so kind and—and different—and I wanted to share in your work and—and everything. I knew you wouldn't want to know I loved you—when you didn't—and I tried hard to be fair and hide my love so you wouldn't see—and I did, didn't I, dear? You never knew till just lately—maybe not till just today—did you?—when I knew you were going away so soon—and couldn't help showing it. You never knew before, did you? Did you?

MURRAY—(*miserably*) No. Oh, Eileen—Eileen, I'm so sorry!

EILEEN—(*in heart-broken protest*) Sorry? Oh no, Stephen, you mustn't be! It's been beautiful—all of it—for me! That's what makes your going—so hard. I had to see you tonight—I'd have gone—crazy—if I didn't know you knew, if I hadn't made you guess. And I thought—if you knew about my writing to Fred—that—maybe—it'd make some difference. (*Murray groans—and she laughs hysterically.*) I must have been crazy—to think that—mustn't I? As if that could—when you don't love me. Sshh! Please! Let me finish. You mustn't feel sad—or anything. It's made me happier than I've ever been—loving you—even when I did know—you didn't. Only now—you'll forgive me telling you all this, won't you, dear? Now, it's so terrible to think I won't see you any more. I'll feel so—without anybody.

MURRAY—(*brokenly*) But I'll—come back. And you'll be out soon—and then—

EILEEN—(*brokenly*) Sshh! Let me finish. You don't know how alone I am now. Father—he'll marry that house-keeper—and the children—they've forgotten me. None of them need me any more. They've found out how to get on without me—and I'm a drag—dead to them—no place for me home any more—and they'll be afraid to have me back—afraid of catching—I know she won't want me back. And Fred—he's gone—he never mattered, anyway. Forgive me, dear—worrying you—only I want you to know how much you've meant to me—so you won't forget—ever—after you've gone.

MURRAY—(*in grief-stricken tones*) Forget? Eileen! I'll do anything in God's world—

EILEEN—I know—you like me a lot even if you can't love me—don't you? (*His arms tighten about her as he bends down and forces a kiss on her lips again.*) Oh, Stephen! That was for good-by. You mustn't come tomorrow morning. I couldn't bear having you—with people watching. But you'll write after—often—won't you? (*heartbrokenly*) Oh, please do that, Stephen!

MURRAY—I will! I swear! And when you get out I'll—we'll—I'll find something— (*He kisses her again.*)

EILEEN—(*breaking away from him with a quick movement and stepping back a few feet*) Good-by, darling. Remember me—and perhaps—you'll find out after a time—I'll pray God to make it so! Oh, what am I saying? Only—I'll hope—I'll hope—till I die!

MURRAY—(*in anguish*) Eileen!

EILEEN—(*her breath coming in tremulous heaves of her bosom*) Remember, Stephen—if ever you want—I'll do any-thing—anything you want—no matter what—I don't care—there's just you and—don't hate me, dear. I love you—love you—remember! (*She suddenly turns and runs away up the road.*)

MURRAY—Eileen! (*He starts to run after her but stops by the signpost and stamps on the ground furiously, his fists clenched in impotent rage at himself and at Fate.*) Christ!

(*The Curtain Falls*)

ACT THREE

SCENE—*Four months later. An isolation room at the Infirmary with a sleeping porch at the right of it. Late afternoon of a Sunday toward the end of October. The room, extending two-thirds of the distance from left to right, is, for reasons of space economy, scantily furnished with the bare necessities—a bureau with mirror in the left corner, rear—two straight-backed chairs— a table with a glass top in the center. The floor is varnished hardwood. The walls and furniture are painted white. On the left, forward, a door to the hallway. On the right, rear, a double glass door opening on the porch. Farther front two windows. The porch, a screened-in continuation of the room, contains only a single iron bed painted white, and a small table placed beside the bed.*

The woods, the leaves of the trees rich in their autumn coloring, rise close about this side of the Infirmary. Their branches almost touch the porch on the right. In the rear of the porch they have been cleared away from the building for a narrow space, and through this opening the distant hills can be seen with the tree tops glowing in the sunlight.

As the curtain rises, Eileen is discovered lying in the bed on the porch, propped up into a half-sitting position by pillows under her back and head. She seems to have grown much thinner. Her face is pale and drawn with deep hollows under her cheek-bones. Her eyes are dull and lusterless. She gazes straight before her into the wood with the unseeing stare of apathetic indifference. The door from the hall in the room behind her is opened and Miss Howard enters followed by Bill Carmody, Mrs. Brennan, and Mary. Carmody's manner is unwontedly sober and subdued. This air of respectable sobriety is further enhanced by a black suit, glaringly new and stiffly pressed, a new black derby hat, and shoes polished like a mirror. His expression is full of a bitter, if suppressed, resentment. His gentility is evidently forced upon him in spite of himself and correspondingly irksome. Mrs. Brennan is a tall, stout woman of fifty, lusty and loud-voiced, with a broad, snub-nosed, florid face, a large mouth, the upper lip darkened by a suggestion of mustache, and little round blue eyes, hard and restless with a continual fuming irritation. She is got up regardless in her ridiculous Sunday-best. Mary appears tall and skinny-legged in a starched, outgrown frock. The sweetness of her face has disappeared, giving way to a

773

hangdog sullenness, a stubborn silence, with sulky, furtive glances of rebellion directed at her stepmother.

MISS HOWARD—(*pointing to the porch*) She's out there on the porch.

MRS. BRENNAN—(*with dignity*) Thank you, ma'am.

MISS HOWARD—(*with a searching glance at the visitors as if to appraise their intentions*) Eileen's been very sick lately, you know, so be careful not to worry her about anything. Do your best to cheer her up.

CARMODY—(*mournfully*) We'll try to put life in her spirits, God help her. (*with an uncertain look at Mrs. Brennan*) Won't we, Maggie?

MRS. BRENNAN—(*turning sharply on Mary who has gone over to examine the things on the bureau*) Come away from that, Mary. Curiosity killed a cat. Don't be touchin' her things. Remember what I told you. Or is it admirin' your mug in the mirror you are? (*turning to Miss Howard as Mary moves away from the bureau, hanging her head—shortly*) Don't you worry, ma'am. We won't trouble Eileen at all.

MISS HOWARD—Another thing. You mustn't say anything to her of what Miss Gilpin just told you about her being sent away to the State Farm in a few days. Eileen isn't to know till the very last minute. It would only disturb her.

CARMODY—(*hastily*) We'll not say a word of it.

MISS HOWARD—(*turning to the hall door*) Thank you. (*She goes out, shutting the door.*)

MRS. BRENNAN—(*angrily*) She has a lot of impudent gab, that one, with her don't do this and don't do that! (*gazing about the room critically*) Two sticks of chairs and a table! They don't give much for the money.

CARMODY—Catch them! It's a good thing she's clearin' out of this and her worse off after them curin' her eight months than she was when she came. She'll maybe get well in the new place.

MRS. BRENNAN—(*indifferently*) It's God's will, what'll happen. (*irritably*) And I'm thinkin' it's His punishment she's under now for having no heart in her and never writin' home a word to you or the children in two months or more. If the doctor hadn't wrote us himself to come see her, we'd have been no wiser.

CARMODY—Whisht. Don't be blamin' a sick girl.

MARY—(*who has drifted to one of the windows at right—curiously*) There's somebody in bed out there. Is it Eileen?

MRS. BRENNAN—Don't be goin' out there till I tell you, you imp! (*coming closer to him and lowering her voice*) Are you going to tell her about it?

CARMODY—(*pretending ignorance*) About what?

MRS. BRENNAN—About what, indeed! About our marryin' two weeks back, of course. What else?

CARMODY—(*uncertainly*) Yes—I disremembered she didn't know. I'll have to tell her, surely.

MRS. BRENNAN—(*flaring up*) You speak like you wouldn't. Are you afraid of a slip of a girl? Well, then, I'm not! I'll tell her to her face soon enough.

CARMODY—(*angry in his turn—assertively*) You'll not, now! Keep your mouth out of this and your rough tongue! I tell you I'll tell her.

MRS. BRENNAN—(*satisfied*) Let's be going out to her, then. (*They move toward the door to the porch.*) And keep your eye on your watch. We mustn't miss the train. Come with us, Mary, and remember to keep your mouth shut. (*They go out on the porch and stand just outside the door waiting for Eileen to notice them; but the girl in bed continues to stare into the woods, oblivious to their presence.*)

MRS. BRENNAN—(*nudging Carmody with her elbow—in a harsh whisper*) Glory be, it's bad she's lookin'. The look on her face'd frighten you. Speak to her, you! (*Eileen stirs uneasily as if this whisper had disturbed her unconsciously.*)

CARMODY—(*wetting his lips and clearing his throat huskily*) Eileen.

EILEEN—(*startled, turns and stares at them with frightened eyes. After a pause she ventures uncertainly as if she were not sure but what these figures might be creatures of her dream.*) Father. (*Her eyes shift to Mrs. Brennan's face and she shudders.*) Mrs. Brennan.

MRS. BRENNAN—(*quickly—in a voice meant to be kindly*) Here we are, all of us, come to see you. How is it you're feelin' now, Eileen? (*While she is talking she advances to the bedside, followed by Carmody, and takes one of the sick girl's hands in hers. Eileen withdraws it as if stung and holds it out to her father. Mrs. Brennan's face flushes angrily and she draws back from the bedside.*)

CARMODY—(*moved—with rough tenderness patting her hand*) Ah, Eileen, sure it's a sight for sore eyes to see you again! (*He bends down as if to kiss her, but, struck by a sudden fear, hesitates, straightens himself, and shamed by the understanding in Eileen's eyes, grows red and stammers confusedly*) How are you now? Sure it's the picture of health you're lookin'. (*Eileen sighs and turns her eyes away from his with a resigned sadness.*)

MRS. BRENNAN—What are you standin' there for like a stick, Mary? Haven't you a word to say to your sister?

EILEEN—(*twisting her head around and seeing Mary for the first time—with a glad cry*) Mary! I—why I didn't see you before! Come here. (*Mary approaches gingerly with apprehensive side glances at Mrs. Brennan who watches her grimly. Eileen's arms reach out for her hungrily. She grasps her about the waist and seems trying to press the unwilling child to her breast.*)

MARY—(*fidgeting nervously—suddenly in a frightened whine*) Let me go! (*Eileen releases her, looks at her face dazedly for a second, then falls back limply with a little moan and shuts her eyes. Mary, who has stepped back a pace, remains fixed there as if fascinated with fright by her sister's face. She stammers*) Eileen—you look so—so funny.

EILEEN—(*without opening her eyes—in a dead voice*) You, too! I never thought you— Go away, please.

MRS. BRENNAN—(*with satisfaction*) Come here to me, Mary, and don't be botherin' your sister. (*Mary avoids her stepmother but retreats to the far end of the porch where she stands shrunk back against the wall, her eyes fixed on Eileen with the same fascinated horror.*)

CARMODY—(*after an uncomfortable pause, forcing himself to speak*) Is the pain bad, Eileen?

EILEEN—(*dully—without opening her eyes*) There's no pain. (*There is another pause—then she murmurs indifferently*) There are chairs in the room you can bring out if you want to sit down.

MRS. BRENNAN—(*sharply*) We've not time to be sittin'. We've the train back to catch.

EILEEN—(*in the same lifeless voice*) It's a disagreeable trip. I'm sorry you had to come.

CARMODY—(*fighting against an oppression he cannot understand, bursts into a flood of words*) Don't be talking of the trip. Sure we're glad to take it to get a sight of you. It's three months since I've had a look at you and I was anxious. Why haven't you written a line to us? You could do that without trouble, surely. Don't you ever think of us at all any more? (*He waits for an answer but Eileen remains silent with her eyes closed. Carmody starts to walk up and down talking with an air of desperation.*) You're not asking a bit of news from home. I'm thinkin' the people out here have taken all the thought of us out of your head. We're all well, thank God. I've another good job on the streets from Murphy and one that'll last a long time, praise be! I'm needin' it surely, with all the expenses—but no matter. Billy had a raise from his old skinflint of a boss a month back. He's gettin' seven a week now and proud as a turkey. He was comin' out with us today but he'd a date with his girl. Sure, he's got a girl now, the young bucko! What d'you think of him? It's old Malloy's girl he's after—the pop-eyed one with glasses, you remember—as ugly as a blind sheep, only he don't think so. He said to give you his love. (*Eileen stirs and sighs wearily, a frown appearing for an instant on her forehead.*) And Tom and Nora was comin' out too, but Father Fitz had some doin's or other up to the school, and he told them to be there, so they wouldn't come with us, but they sent their love to you too. They're growin' so big you'd not know them. Tom's no good at the school. He's like Billy was. I've had to take the strap to him often. He's always playin' hooky and roamin' the streets. And Nora— (*with pride*) There's the divil for you! Up to everything she is and no holdin' her high spirits. As pretty as a picture, and the smartest girl in her school, Father Fitz says. Am I lyin', Maggie?

MRS. BRENNAN—(*grudgingly*) She's smart enough—and too free with her smartness.

CARMODY—(*pleased*) Ah, don't be talkin'! She'll know more than the lot of us before she's grown even. (*He pauses in his walk and stares down at Eileen, frowning.*) Are you sick, Eileen, that you're keepin' your eyes shut without a word out of you?

EILEEN—(*wearily*) No. I'm tired, that's all.

CARMODY—(*resuming his walk*) And who else is there, let me think? Oh, Mary—she's the same as ever, you can see for yourself.

EILEEN—(*bitterly*) The same? Oh, no!

CARMODY—She's grown, you mean? I suppose. You'd notice, not seeing her so long? (*He can think of nothing else to say but walks up and down with a restless, uneasy expression.*)

MRS. BRENNAN—(*sharply*) What time is it gettin'?

CARMODY—(*fumbles for his watch*) Half past four, a bit after.

MRS. BRENNAN—We'll have to leave soon. It's a long jaunt down the hill in that buggy. (*She catches his eye and makes violent signs to him to tell Eileen what he has come to tell.*)

CARMODY—(*after an uncertain pause—clenching his fists and clearing his throat*) Eileen.

EILEEN—Yes.

CARMODY—(*irritably*) Can't you open your eyes on me? It's like talkin' to myself I am.

EILEEN—(*looking at him—dully*) What is it?

CARMODY—(*stammering—avoiding her glance*) It's this, Eileen—me and Maggie—Mrs. Brennan, that is—we—

EILEEN—(*without surprise*) You're going to marry her?

CARMODY—(*with an effort*) Not goin' to. It's done.

EILEEN—(*without a trace of feeling*) Oh, so you've been married already? (*Without further comment, she closes her eyes.*)

CARMODY—Two weeks back we were, by Father Fitz. (*He stands staring down at his daughter, irritated, perplexed and confounded by her silence, looking as if he longed to shake her.*)

MRS. BRENNAN—(*angry at the lack of enthusiasm shown by Eileen*) Let us get out of this, Bill. It's little she's caring about you, and little thanks she has for all you've done for her and the money you've spent.

CARMODY—(*with a note of pleading*) Is that a proper way to be treatin' your father, Eileen, after what I've told you? Is it nothin' to you you've a good, kind woman now for mother?

EILEEN—(*fiercely, her eyes flashing open on him*) No, No! Never!

MRS. BRENNAN—(*plucking at Carmody's elbow. He stands looking at Eileen helplessly, his mouth open, a guilty flush spreading over his face.*) Come out of here, you big fool, you! Is it to listen to insults to your livin' wife you're waiting?

CARMODY—(*turning on her threateningly*) Will you shut your gab?

EILEEN—(*with a moan*) Oh, go away. Father! Please! Take her away!

MRS. BRENNAN—(*pulling at his arm*) Take me away this second or I'll never speak again to you till the day I die!

CARMODY—(*pushes her violently away from him—raging, his fist uplifted*) Shut your gab, I'm saying!

MRS. BRENNAN—The devil mend you and yours then! I'm leavin' you. (*She starts for the door.*)

CARMODY—(*hastily*) Wait a bit, Maggie. I'm coming. (*She goes into the room, slamming the door, but once inside she stands still, trying to listen. Carmody glares down at his daughter's pale twitching face with closed eyes. Finally he croaks in a whining tone of fear*) Is your last word a cruel one to me this day, Eileen? (*She remains silent. His face darkens. He turns and strides out of the door. Mary darts after him with a frightened cry of* "Papa." *Eileen covers her face with her hands and a shudder of relief runs over her body.*)

MRS. BRENNAN—(*as Carmody enters the room—in a mollified tone*) So you've come, have you? Let's go, then! (*Carmody stands looking at her in silence, his expression full of gloomy rage. She bursts out impatiently*) Are you comin' or are you goin' back to her? (*She grabs Mary's arm and pushes her toward the door to the hall.*) Are you comin' or not, I'm asking?

CARMODY—(*somberly—as if to himself*) There's something wrong in the whole of this—that I can't make out. (*With sudden fury he brandishes his fists as though defying someone and growls threateningly*) And I'll get drunk this night—dead, rotten drunk! (*He seems to detect disapproval in Mrs. Brennan's face for he shakes his fist at her and repeats like a solemn oath*) I'll get drunk if my soul roasts for it—and no one in the whole world is strong enough to stop me! (*Mrs. Brennan turns from him with a disgusted shrug of her shoulders and hustles Mary out of the door. Carmody, after a second's pause, follows them. Eileen lies still, looking out into the woods with empty, desolate eyes. Miss Howard comes into the room from the hall and goes to the porch, carrying a glass of milk in her hand.*)

MISS HOWARD—Here's your diet, Eileen. I forgot it until just now. Did you have a nice visit with your folks?

EILEEN—(*forcing a smile*) Yes.

MISS HOWARD—I hope they didn't worry you over home affairs?

EILEEN—No. (*She sips her milk and sets it back on the table with a shudder of disgust.*)

MISS HOWARD—(*with a smile*) What a face! You'd think you were taking poison.

EILEEN—(*with deep passion*) I wish it was poison!

MISS HOWARD—(*jokingly*) Oh, come now! That isn't a nice way to feel on the Sabbath. (*with a meaning smile*) I've some news that'll cheer you up, I bet. (*archly*) Guess who's here on a visit?

EILEEN—(*startled—in a frightened whisper*) Who?

MISS HOWARD—Mr. Murray. (*Eileen closes her eyes wincingly for a moment and a shadow of pain comes over her face.*) He came just about the time your folks did. I saw him for a moment, not to speak to. (*beaming—with a certain curiosity*) What do you think of that for news?

EILEEN—(*trying to conceal her agitation and assume a casual tone*) He must have come to be examined.

MISS HOWARD—(*with a meaning laugh*) Oh, I'd hardly say that was his main reason. (*in business-like tones*) Well, I've got to get back on the job. (*She turns to the door calling back jokingly*) He'll be in to see you of course, so look your prettiest. (*She goes out and shuts the door to the porch. Eileen gives a frightened gasp and struggles up in bed as if she wanted to call the nurse to return. Then she lies back in a state of great nervous excitement, twisting her head with eager, fearful glances toward the door, listening, clasping and unclasping her thin fingers on the white spread. As Miss Howard walks across the room to the hall door, it is opened and Stephen Murray enters. A great change is visible in his face. It is much thinner and the former healthy tan has faded to a sallow pallor. Puffy shadows of sleeplessness and dissipation are marked under his heavy-lidded eyes. He is dressed in a well-fitting, expensive, dark suit, a white shirt with a soft collar and bright-colored tie.*)

MISS HOWARD—(*with pleased surprise, holding out her hand*) Hello, Mr. Murray.

MURRAY—(*shaking her hand—with a forced pleasantness*) How are you, Miss Howard?

MISS HOWARD—Fine as ever. It certainly looks natural to see you around here again—not that I hope you're here to stay, though. (*with a smile*) I suppose you're on your way to Eileen now. Well, I won't keep you. I've oodles of work to do. (*She opens the hall door. He starts for the porch.*) Oh, I was forgetting— Congratulations! I've read those stories—all of us have. They're great. We're all so proud of you. You're one of our graduates, you know.

MURRAY—(*indifferently*) Oh,—that stuff.

MISS HOWARD—(*gayly*) Don't be so modest. Well, see you later, I hope.

MURRAY—Yes. Doctor Stanton invited me to stay for supper and I may—

MISS HOWARD—Fine! Be sure to! (*She goes out. Murray walks to porch door and steps out. He finds Eileen's eyes waiting for him. As their eyes meet she gasps involuntarily and he stops short in his tracks. For a moment they remain looking at each other in silence.*)

EILEEN—(*dropping her eyes—faintly*) Stephen.

MURRAY—(*much moved, strides to her bedside and takes her hands awkwardly*) Eileen. (*then after a second's pause in which he searches her face and is shocked by the change illness has made—anxiously*) How are you feeling, Eileen? (*He grows confused by her gaze and his eyes shift from hers, which search his face with wild yearning.*)

EILEEN—(*forcing a smile*) Oh, I'm all right. (*eagerly*) But you, Stephen? How are you? (*excitedly*) Oh, it's good to see you again! (*Her eyes continue fixed on his face pleadingly, questioningly.*)

MURRAY—(*haltingly*) And it's sure great to see you again, Eileen. (*He releases her hand and turns away.*) And I'm fine and dandy. I look a little done up, I guess, but that's only the result of too much New York.

(*Eileen, sensing from his manner that whatever she has hoped for from his visit is not to be, sinks back on the pillows, shutting her eyes hopelessly, and cannot control a sigh of pain.*)

MURRAY—(*turning to her anxiously*) What's the matter, Eileen? You're not in pain, are you?

EILEEN—(*wearily*) No.

MURRAY—You haven't been feeling badly lately, have you? Your letters suddenly stopped—not a line for the past three weeks—and I—

EILEEN—(*bitterly*) I got tired of writing and never getting any answer, Stephen.

MURRAY—(*shame-faced*) Come, Eileen, it wasn't as bad as that. You'd think I never—and I did write, didn't I?

EILEEN—Right after you left here, you did, Stephen. Lately—

MURRAY—I'm sorry, Eileen. It wasn't that I didn't mean to—but—in New York it's so hard. You start to do one thing and something else interrupts you. You never seem to get any one thing done when it ought to be. You can understand that, can't you, Eileen?

EILEEN—(*sadly*) Yes. I understand everything now.

MURRAY—(*offended*) What do you mean by everything? You said that so strangely. You mean you don't believe— (*But she remains silent with her eyes shut. He frowns and takes to pacing up and down beside the bed.*) Why have they got you stuck out here on this isolation porch, Eileen?

EILEEN—(*dully*) There was no room on the main porch, I suppose.

MURRAY—You never mentioned in any of your letters—

EILEEN—It's not very cheerful to get letters full of sickness. I wouldn't like to, I know.

MURRAY—(*hurt*) That isn't fair, Eileen. You know I— How long have you been back in the Infirmary?

EILEEN—About a month.

MURRAY—(*shocked*) A month! But you were up and about—on exercise, weren't you—before that?

EILEEN—No. I had to stay in bed while I was at the cottage.

MURRAY—You mean—ever since that time they sent you back—the day before I left?

EILEEN—Yes.

MURRAY—But I thought from the cheery tone of your letters that you were—

EILEEN—(*uneasily*) Getting better? I am, Stephen. I'm strong enough to be up now but Doctor Stanton wants me to take a good long rest this time so that when I get up again I'll be sure— (*She breaks off impatiently.*) But don't let's talk about it. I'm all right. (*Murray glances down at her face worriedly. She changes the subject.*) You've been over to see Doctor Stanton, haven't you?

MURRAY—Yes.

EILEEN—Did he examine you?

MURRAY—Yes. (*carelessly*) Oh, he found me O.K.

EILEEN—I'm glad, Stephen. (*after a pause*) Tell about yourself—what you've been doing. You've written a lot lately, haven't you?

MURRAY—(*frowning*) No. I haven't been able to get down to it—somehow. There's so little time to yourself once you get to know people in New York. The sale of the stories you typed put me on easy street as far as money goes, so I've felt no need— (*He laughs weakly.*) I guess I'm one of those who have to get down to hard pan before they get the kick to drive them to hard work.

EILEEN—(*surprised*) Was it hard work writing them up here? You used to seem so happy just in doing them.

MURRAY—I was—happier than I've been before or afterward. (*cynically*) But—I don't know—it was a new game to me then and I was chuck full of illusions about the glory of it. (*He laughs half-heartedly.*) Now I'm hardly a bit more enthusiastic over it than I used to be over newspaper work. It's like everything else, I guess. When you've got it, you find you don't want it.

EILEEN—(*looking at him wonderingly—disturbed*) But isn't just the writing itself worth while?

MURRAY—(*as if suddenly ashamed of himself—quickly*) Yes. Of course it is. I'm talking like a fool. I'm sore at everything because I'm dissatisfied with my own cussedness and laziness—and I want to pass the buck. (*with a smile of cheerful confidence*) It's only a fit. I'll come out of it all right and get down to brass tacks again.

EILEEN—(*with an encouraging smile*) That's the way you ought to feel. It'd be wrong—I've read the two stories that have come out so far over and over. They're fine, I think. Every line in them sounds like you, and at the same time sounds natural and like people and things you see every day. Everybody thinks they're fine, Stephen.

MURRAY—(*pleased but pretending cynicism*) Then they must be rotten. (*then with self-assurance*) Well, I've plenty more of those stories in my head. (*spiritedly*) And I'll make them so much better than what I've done so far, you won't recognize them. (*smiling*) Darn it, do you know just talking about it makes me feel as if I could sit right down now and start in on one. Is it the fact I've worked here before—or is it seeing you, Eileen? (*gratefully*) I really believe it's you. I haven't forgotten how you helped me before.

EILEEN—(*in a tone of pain*) Don't, Stephen. I didn't do anything.

MURRAY—(*eagerly*) Yes, you did. You made it possible. And since I've left the San, I've looked forward to your letters to boost up my spirits. When I felt down in the mouth over my own idiocy, I used to reread them, and they always were good medicine. I can't tell you how grateful I've felt, honestly!

EILEEN—(*faintly*) You're kind to say so, Stephen—but it was nothing, really.

MURRAY—And I can't tell you how I've missed those letters for the past three weeks. They left a big hole in things. I was worried about you—not having heard a word. (*with a smile*) So I came to look you up.

EILEEN—(*faintly, forcing an answering smile*) Well, you see now I'm all right.

MURRAY—(*concealing his doubt*) Yes, of course you are. Only I'd a darn sight rather see you up and about. We could take a walk, then—through the woods. (*A wince of pain shadows Eileen's face. She closes her eyes. Murray continues softly, after a pause.*) You haven't forgotten that last night—out there—Eileen?

EILEEN—(*her lips trembling—trying to force a laugh*) Please don't remind me of that, Stephen. I was so silly and so sick, too. My temp was so high it must have made me—completely crazy—or I'd never dreamed of doing such a stupid thing. My head must have been full of wheels because I don't remember anything I did or said, hardly.

MURRAY—(*his pride taken down a peg by this—in a hurt tone*) Oh! Well—I haven't forgotten and I never will, Eileen. (*Then his face clears up as if a weight had been taken off his conscience.*) Well—I rather thought you wouldn't take it seriously—afterward. You were all up in the air that night. And you never mentioned it in your letters—

EILEEN—(*pleadingly*) Don't talk about it! Forget it ever happened. It makes me feel—(*with a half-hysterical laugh*)—like a fool!

MURRAY—(*worried*) All right, Eileen. I won't. Don't get worked up over nothing. That isn't resting, you know. (*looking down at her closed eyes—solicitously*) Perhaps all my talking has tired you out? Do you feel done up? Why don't you try and take a nap now?

EILEEN—(*dully*) Yes, I'd like to sleep.

MURRAY—(*clasps her hands gently*) I'll leave you then. I'll drop back to say good-by and stay awhile before I go. I won't leave until the last train. (*as she doesn't answer*) Do you hear, Eileen?

EILEEN—(*weakly*) Yes. You'll come back—to say good-by.

MURRAY—Yes. I'll be back sure. (*He presses her hand and after a kindly glance of sympathy down at her face, tiptoes to the door and goes into the room, shutting the door behind him. When she hears the door shut Eileen struggles up in bed and stretches her arms after him with an agonized sob "Stephen!" She hides her face in her hands and sobs brokenly. Murray walks across to the hall door and is about to go out when the door is opened and Miss Gilpin enters.*)

MISS GILPIN—(*hurriedly*) How do you do, Mr. Murray. Doctor Stanton just told me you were here.

MURRAY—(*as they shake hands—smiling*) How are you, Miss Gilpin?

MISS GILPIN—He said he'd examined you, and that you were O.K. I'm glad. (*glancing at him keenly*) You've been talking to Eileen?

MURRAY—Just left her this second. She wanted to sleep for a while.

MISS GILPIN—(*wonderingly*) Sleep? (*then hurriedly*) It's too bad. I wish I'd known you were here sooner. I wanted very much to talk to you before you saw Eileen. (*with a worried smile*) I still think I ought to have a talk with you.

MURRAY—Certainly, Miss Gilpin.

MISS GILPIN—(*takes a chair and places it near the hall door*) Sit down. She can't hear us here. Goodness knows this is hardly the place for confidences, but there are visitors all over and it'll have to do. Did you close the door tightly? She mustn't hear me above all. (*She goes to the porch door and peeks out for a moment; then comes back to him with flashing eyes.*) She's crying! What have you been saying to her? Oh, it's too late, I know! What has happened out there? Tell me!

MURRAY—(*stammering*) Nothing. She's crying? Why Miss Gilpin—you know I wouldn't hurt her for worlds.

MISS GILPIN—(*more calmly*) Intentionally, I know you wouldn't. But something has happened. (*then briskly*) Since you don't seem inclined to confide in me, I'll have to in you. You noticed how badly she looks, didn't you?

MURRAY—Yes, I did.

MISS GILPIN—(*gravely*) She's been going down hill steadily—(*meaningly*)—ever since you left. She's in a very serious state, let me impress you with that. Doctor Stanton has given up hope of her improving here, and her father is unwilling to pay for her elsewhere now he knows there's a cheaper place—the State Farm. So she's to be sent there in a day or so.

MURRAY—(*springing to his feet—horrified*) To the State Farm!

MISS GILPIN—Her time here is long past. You know the rule—and she isn't getting better.

MURRAY—(*appalled*) That means—!

MISS GILPIN—(*forcibly*) Death! That's what it means for her!

MURRAY—(*stunned*) Good God, I never dreamed—

MISS GILPIN—In her case, it's certain. She'll die. And it wouldn't do any good to keep her here, either. She'd die here. She'll die anywhere because lately she's given up hope, she hasn't wanted to live any more. She's let herself go—and now it's too late.

MURRAY—Too late? You mean there's no chance—now? (*Miss Gilpin nods. Murray is overwhelmed—after a pause— stammering*) Isn't there—anything—we can do?

MISS GILPIN—(*sadly*) I don't know. I should have talked to you before. You see, she's seen you now. She knows. (*As he looks mystified she continues slowly.*) I suppose you know that Eileen loves you, don't you?

MURRAY—(*as if defending himself against an accusation— with confused alarm*) No—Miss Gilpin. She may have felt something like that—once—but that was long ago before I left the San. She's forgotten all about it since, I know she has. (*Miss Gilpin smiles bitterly.*) Why—just now—she said that part of it had all been so silly she felt she'd acted like a fool and didn't ever want to be reminded of it.

MISS GILPIN—She saw that you didn't love her—any more than you did in the days before you left. Oh, I used to watch you then. I sensed what was going on between you. I would have stopped it then out of pity for her, if I could have, if I didn't know that any interference would only make matters worse. (*She sighs—then after a pause*) You'll have to forgive me for speaking to you so boldly on a delicate subject. But, don't you see, it's for her sake. I love Eileen. We all do. (*averting her eyes from his—in a low voice*) I know how Eileen feels, Mr. Murray. Once—a long time ago—I suffered as she is suffering—from the same mistake. But I had resources to fall back upon that Eileen hasn't got—a family who loved me and understood—friends—so I pulled through. But it spoiled my life for a long time. (*looking at him again and forc- ing a smile*) So I feel that perhaps I have a right to speak for Eileen who has no one else.

MURRAY—(*huskily—much moved*) Say anything you like, Miss Gilpin.

MISS GILPIN—(*after a pause—sadly*) You don't love her— do you?

MURRAY—No—I—I don't believe I've ever thought much of loving anyone—that way.

MISS GILPIN—(*sadly*) Oh, it's too late, I'm afraid. If we had only had this talk before you had seen her! I meant to

talk to you frankly and if I found out you didn't love Eileen—
there was always the forlorn hope that you might—I was
going to tell you not to see her, for her sake—not to let her
face the truth. For I'm sure she continued to hope in spite of
everything, and always would—to the end—if she didn't see
you. I was going to implore you to stay away, to write her
letters that would encourage her hope, and in that way she'd
never learn the truth. I thought of writing you all this—
but—it's so delicate a matter—I didn't have the courage.
(*with intense grief*) And now Doctor Stanton's decision to
send her away makes everything doubly hard. When she
knows *that*—she'll throw everything that holds her to life—
out of the window! And think of it—her dying there
alone!

MURRAY—(*very pale*) Don't! That shan't happen. I have
money enough—I'll make more—to send her any place you
think—

MISS GILPIN—That's something—but it doesn't touch
the source of her unhappiness. If there were only some way
to make her happy in the little time that's left to her! She has
suffered so much through you. Oh, Mr. Murray, can't you
tell her you love her?

MURRAY—(*after a pause—slowly*) But she'll never believe
me, I'm afraid, now.

MISS GILPIN—(*eagerly*) But you must make her believe!
And you must ask her to marry you. If you're engaged it will
give you the right in her eyes to take her away. You can take
her to some private San. There's a small place but a very good
one at White Lake. It's not too expensive, and it's a beautiful
spot, out of the world, and you can live and work nearby.
And she'll be happy to the very last. Don't you think that's
something you can give in return for her love for you?

MURRAY—(*slowly—deeply moved*) Yes. (*then determinedly*)
But I won't go into this thing by halves. It isn't fair to her.
I'm going to marry her—yes, I mean it. I owe her that if it
will make her happy.

MISS GILPIN—(*with a sad smile*) She'll never consent—for
your sake—until she's well again. And stop and think, Mr.
Murray. Even if she did consent to marry you right now the
shock—it'd be suicide for her. I'd have to warn her against it

myself. I've talked with Dr. Stanton. God knows I'd be the first one to hold out hope if there was any. There isn't. It's merely a case of prolonging the short time left to her and making it happy. You must bear that in mind—as a fact!

MURRAY—(*dully*) All right. I'll remember. But it's hell to realize— (*He turns suddenly toward the porch door.*) I'll go out to her now while I feel—that—yes, I know I can make her believe me now.

MISS GILPIN—You'll tell me—later on?

MURRAY—Yes. (*He opens the door to the porch and goes out. Miss Gilpin stands for a moment looking after him worriedly. Then she sighs helplessly and goes out to the hall. Murray steps noiselessly out on the porch. Eileen is lying motionless with her eyes closed. Murray stands looking at her, his face showing the emotional stress he is under, a great pitying tenderness in his eyes. Then he seems to come to a revealing decision on what is best to do for he tiptoes to the bedside and bending down with a quick movement, takes her in his arms, and kisses her.*) Eileen!

EILEEN—(*startled at first, resists automatically for a moment*) Stephen! (*Then she succumbs and lies back in his arms with a happy sigh, putting both hands to the sides of his face and staring up at him adoringly.*) Stephen, dear!

MURRAY—(*quickly questioning her before she can question him*) You were fibbing—about that night—weren't you? You do love me, don't you, Eileen?

EILEEN—(*breathlessly*) Yes—I—but you, Stephen—you don't love me. (*She makes a movement as if to escape from his embrace.*)

MURRAY—(*genuinely moved—with tender reassurance*) Why do you suppose I came away up here if not to tell you I did? But they warned me—Miss Gilpin—that you were still weak and that I mustn't excite you in any way. And I—I didn't want—but I had to come back and tell you.

EILEEN—(*convinced—with a happy laugh*) And is that why you acted so strange—and cold? Aren't they silly to tell you that! As if being happy could hurt me! Why, it's just that, just you I've needed!

MURRAY—(*his voice trembling*) And you'll marry me, Eileen?

EILEEN—(*a shadow of doubt crossing her face momentarily*) Are you sure—you want me, Stephen?

MURRAY—(*a lump in his throat—huskily*) Yes. I do want you, Eileen.

EILEEN—(*happily*) Then I will—after I'm well again, of course. (*She kisses him.*)

MURRAY—(*chokingly*) That won't be long now, Eileen.

EILEEN—(*joyously*) No—not long—now that I'm happy for once in my life. I'll surprise you, Stephen, the way I'll pick up and grow fat and healthy. You won't know me in a month. How can you ever love such a skinny homely thing as I am now! (*with a laugh*) I couldn't if I was a man—love such a fright.

MURRAY—Ssshh!

EILEEN—(*confidently*) But you'll see now. I'll make myself get well. We won't have to wait long, dear. And can't you move up to the town near here where you can see me every day, and you can work and I can help you with your stories just as I used to—and I'll soon be strong enough to do your typing again. (*She laughs.*) Listen to me—talking about helping you—as if they weren't all your own work, those blessed stories!—as if I had anything to do with it!

MURRAY—(*hoarsely*) You had! You did! They're yours. (*trying to calm himself*) But you mustn't stay here, Eileen. You'll let me take you away, won't you?—to a better place— not far away—White Lake, it's called. There's a small private sanatorium there. Doctor Stanton says it's one of the best. And I'll live nearby—it's a beautiful spot—and see you every day.

EILEEN—(*in the seventh heaven*) And did you plan out all this for me beforehand, Stephen? (*He nods with averted eyes. She kisses his hair.*) You wonderful, kind dear! And it's a small place—this White Lake? Then we won't have so many people around to disturb us, will we? We'll be all to ourselves. And you ought to work so well up there. I know New York wasn't good for you—alone—without me. And I'll get well and strong so quick! And you say it's a beautiful place? (*intensely*) Oh, Stephen, any place in the world would be beautiful to me—if you were with me! (*His face is hidden in the pillow beside her. She is suddenly startled by a muffled sob—anxiously*) Why—Stephen—you're—you're crying! (*The tears start to her own eyes.*)

MURRAY—(*raising his face which is this time alight with a passionate awakening—a revelation*) Oh, I do love you, Eileen! I do! I love you, love you!

EILEEN—(*thrilled by the depths of his present sincerity—but with a teasing laugh*) Why, you say that as if you'd just made the discovery, Stephen!

MURRAY—Oh, what does it matter, Eileen! Oh, what a blind selfish ass I've been! You are my life—everything! I love you, Eileen! I do! I do! And we'll be married— (*Suddenly his face grows frozen with horror as he remembers the doom. For the first time Death confronts him face to face as a menacing reality.*)

EILEEN—(*terrified by the look in his eyes*) What is it, Stephen? What—?

MURRAY—(*with a groan—protesting half-aloud in a strangled voice*) No! No! It can't be—! My God! (*He clutches her hands and hides his face in them.*)

EILEEN—(*with a cry*) Stephen! What is the matter? (*Her face suddenly betrays an awareness, an intuitive sense of the truth.*) Oh—Stephen— (*then with a childish whimper of terror*) Oh, Stephen, I'm going to die! I'm going to die!

MURRAY—(*lifting his tortured face—wildly*) No!

EILEEN—(*her voice sinking to a dead whisper*) I'm going to die.

MURRAY—(*seizing her in his arms in a passionate frenzy and pressing his lips to hers*) No, Eileen, no, my love, no! What are you saying? What could have made you think it? You—die? Why, of course, we're all going to die—but—Good God! What damned nonsense! You're getting well—every day. Everyone—Miss Gilpin—Stanton—everyone told me that. I swear before God, Eileen, they did! You're still weak, that's all. They said—it won't be long. You mustn't think that—not now.

EILEEN—(*miserably—unconvinced*) But why did you look at me—that way—with that awful look in your eyes—? (*While she is speaking Miss Gilpin enters the room from the hallway. She appears worried, agitated. She hurries toward the porch but stops inside the doorway, arrested by Murray's voice.*)

MURRAY—(*takes Eileen by the shoulders and forces her to look into his eyes*) I wasn't thinking about you then— No,

Eileen—not you. I didn't mean you—but me—yes, me! I couldn't tell you before. They'd warned me—not to excite you—and I knew that would—if you loved me.

EILEEN—(*staring at him with frightened amazement*) You mean you— you're sick again?

MURRAY—(*desperately striving to convince her*) Yes. I saw Stanton. I lied to you before—about that. It's come back on me, Eileen—you see how I look—I've let myself go. I don't know how to live without you, don't you see? And you'll—marry me now—without waiting—and help me to get well—you and I together—and not mind their lies—what they say to prevent you? You'll do that, Eileen?

EILEEN—I'll do anything for you— And I'd be so happy— (*She breaks down.*) But, Stephen, I'm so afraid. I'm all mixed up. Oh, Stephen, I don't know what to believe!

MISS GILPIN—(*who has been listening thunderstruck to Murray's wild pleading, at last summons up the determination to interfere—steps out on the porch—in a tone of severe remonstrance*) Mr. Murray!

MURRAY—(*starts to his feet with wild, bewildered eyes—confusedly*) Oh—you— (*Miss Gilpin cannot restrain an exclamation of dismay as she sees his face wrung by despair. Eileen turns her head away with a little cry as if she would hide her face in the bedclothes. A sudden fierce resolution lights up Murray's countenance—hoarsely*) You're just in time, Miss Gilpin! Eileen! Listen! You'll believe Miss Gilpin, won't you? She knows all about it. (*Eileen turns her eyes questioningly on the bewildered nurse.*)

MISS GILPIN—What—?

MURRAY—(*determinedly*) Doctor Stanton—he must have told you about me. Eileen doesn't believe me—when I tell her I got T. B. again. She thinks—I don't know what. I know you're not supposed to, but—can't you tell her—?

MISS GILPIN—(*stunned by being thus defiantly confronted—stammeringly*) Mr. Murray! I—I—how can you ask—

MURRAY—(*quickly*) She loves me—and I—I—love her! (*He holds her eyes and speaks with a passion of sincerity that compels belief.*) I love her, do you hear?

MISS GILPIN—(*falteringly*) You—love—Eileen?

MURRAY—Yes! I do! (*entreatingly*) So—tell her—won't you?

MISS GILPIN—(*swallowing hard, her eyes full of pity and sorrow fixed on Eileen*) Yes—Eileen— (*She turns away slowly toward the door.*)

EILEEN—(*with a little cry of alarmed concern, stretches out her hands to Murray protectingly*) Poor Stephen—dear! (*He grasps her hands and kisses them.*)

MISS GILPIN—(*in a low voice*) Mr. Murray. May I speak to you?

MURRAY—(*with a look of questioning defiance at her*) Certainly.

MISS GILPIN—(*turns to Eileen with a forced smile*) I won't steal him away for more than a moment, Eileen. (*Eileen smiles happily.*)

MURRAY—(*follows Miss Gilpin into the room. She leads him to the far end of the room near the door to the hall, after shutting the porch door carefully behind him. He looks at her defiantly.*) Well?

MISS GILPIN—(*in low agitated tones*) What has happened? I feel as if I may have done a great wrong to myself—to you—to her—by that lie. And yet—something forced me.

MURRAY—(*moved*) It has saved her—us. Oh, how can I explain what happened? I suddenly saw—how beautiful and sweet and good she is—how I couldn't bear the thought of life without her— That's all. (*determinedly*) She must marry me at once and I'll take her away—the far West—any place Stanton thinks can help. And she can take care of me— as she thinks—and I know she'll grow well as I seem to grow well. Oh Miss Gilpin, don't you see? No half and half measures can help us—help her. (*fiercely as if defying her*) But we'll win together. We can! We must! There are things doctors can't value—can't know the strength of! (*exultantly*) You'll see! I'll make Eileen get well, I tell you! Happiness will cure! Love is stronger than— (*He suddenly breaks down before the pitying negation she cannot keep from her eyes. He sinks on a chair, shoulders bowed, face hidden in his hands, with a groan of despair.*) Oh, why did you give me a hopeless hope?

MISS GILPIN—(*putting her hand on his shoulder—with tender compassion—sadly*) Isn't all life just that—when you think of it? (*her face lighting up with a consoling revelation*) But there must be something back of it—some promise of fulfillment,—somehow—somewhere—in the spirit of hope itself.

MURRAY—(*dully*) What do words mean to me now? (*then suddenly starting to his feet and flinging off her hand with disdainful strength—violently and almost insultingly*) What damned rot! I tell you we'll win! We must! All the verdicts of all the doctors—what do they matter? This is—beyond you! And we'll win in spite of you! (*scornfully*) How dare you use the word hopeless—as if it were the last! Come now, confess, damn it! There's always hope, isn't there? What do you *know*? Can you say you *know* anything?

MISS GILPIN—(*taken aback by his violence for a moment, finally bursts into a laugh of helplessness which is close to tears*) I? I know nothing—absolutely nothing! God bless you both! (*She raises her handkerchief to her eyes and hurries out to the hallway without turning her head. Murray stands looking after her for a moment; then strides out to the porch.*)

EILEEN—(*turning and greeting him with a shy smile of happiness as he comes and kneels by her bedside*) Stephen! (*He kisses her. She strokes his hair and continues in a tone of motherly, self-forgetting solicitude.*) I'll have to look out for you, Stephen, won't I? From now on? And see that you rest so many hours a day—and drink your milk when I drink mine—and go to bed at nine sharp when I do—and obey everything I tell you—and—

(*The Curtain Falls*)

CHRIS CHRISTOPHERSEN

A Play in Three Acts

CHARACTERS

JOHNNY "THE PRIEST"

JACK BURNS

ADAMS

TWO LONGSHOREMEN

LARRY, *bartender*

A POSTMAN

CHRIS CHRISTOPHERSEN

MICKEY

DEVLIN

MARTHY OWEN

ANNA CHRISTOPHERSEN, *Chris' daughter*

CAPTAIN JESSUP, *of the British tramp steamer* Londonderry

MR. HALL, *First Mate*

THE STEWARD

PAUL ANDERSEN, *Second Mate*

EDWARDS, *seaman*

JONESY, *seaman*

GLASS, *messroom steward*

(Note—The characters are named in the order in which they appear.)

The action of the play takes place in the year 1910.

Chris Christophersen

ACT ONE
SCENE I

SCENE—*Johnny "the Priest's" bar near South Street, New York City. On the left, forward, a large window looking out on the street. Beyond it, the main entrance, a double swinging door. Farther back, another window. The bar runs from left to right nearly the whole length of the rear wall. In back of the bar, a small show case displaying a few bottles of case goods, for which there is evidently little call. The remainder of the rear space in front of the large mirrors is occupied by half-barrels of cheap whiskey of the nickel-a-shot variety, from which the liquor is drawn by means of brass spigots. On the right is an open doorway leading to the back room. Down front, at center and right of center, are two round, wooden tables with five chairs grouped about each.*

It is late afternoon of a day in the fall of the year 1910.

As the curtain rises, Johnny, Adams, and Jack Burns are discovered. Johnny "the Priest" deserves his nickname. With his pale, thin, clean-shaven face, his mild blue eyes, white hair, and decorous mouth set in a fixed smile of kindly tolerance, a cassock would seem more suited to him than the white apron he wears. Neither his voice nor his general manner dispel this illusion which has made him a personage of the waterfront. They are soft and bland. But beneath all this mildness one senses the man behind the mask—cynical, callous, hard as nails. He is lounging at ease behind the bar, a pair of spectacles on his nose, reading an evening newspaper.

Adams and Jack Burns are seated at the table, right front. The former is a man of fifty or so with grizzled hair, his face bloated and unshaven, his eyes puffed and bleary. His grey suit is baggy and wrinkled as if he had slept in it for nights; his stiff collar, the tie of which is awry, and the cuffs of his shirt are crumpled and grimy; his mouth hangs open; his eyes are half shut; his head, resting on one hand, bobs up and down in a drunken half-slumber. Jack Burns, bull-necked and squat, with a battered, pushed-in countenance, sits smoking a cigarette, looking at his companion with an amused leer of contempt. Burns is middle-aged, dressed in a patched working suit.

BURNS—(*catching Johnny's eye over the newspaper, nodding toward Adams*) Dead to the world! (*He takes hold of Adams by the shoulder and shakes him.*) Hey, you! Wake up! Wha's matter with yuh?

JOHNNY—(*frowning*) Leave him alone, Jack. He's been talking me deaf, dumb and blind all day. I'm sick o' listening to him. Let him sleep it off.

BURNS—You? Huh! How about me? I'm goin' to make him buy 'nother drink, that's what—to pay me for listenin' to his bull, see? (*He pushes Adams' elbow off the table. The latter jerks forward in his chair, his eyes blinking open in a sodden surprise.*) Say you, Adams! Rise 'n' shine! Where's that ball you was goin' to blow me to, huh? Yuh was beefin' about bein' a gentleman a second ago. Well, if y'are one, buy a drink.

ADAMS—(*in a whine*) No—not another—not for you, Jack Burns. I've got the money too, but you needn't think I'm a sucker.

BURNS—(*disgustedly*) Aw, yuh're full of prunes!

ADAMS—(*maudlinly*) I'm a sport, Jack Burns, and a gentleman—and that's more than you can say—or anyone who hangs out in this low, waterfront, barrel-house—where I only come when I'm on a drunk—and then only to see my old friend Johnny there—for old friendship's sake, understan'—

JOHNNY—(*irritably*) I told you you'd get him started again, Jack.

BURNS—(*with a wink at Johnny*) I'll stop him. I'll trow a scare into him, huh? (*He turns on Adams with a threatening fist.*) Close your trap, Old Prunejuice, or I'll hand yuh a punch in the puss that'll knock you dead, get me? I ain't kiddin', neither. (*Adams shrinks back on his chair in frightened silence. Burns continues grumblingly.*) Beefin' about losin' your job! Huh! Yuh're lucky not to have one. How'd yuh like to have mine? I gotter go down the bay on the mail boats tonight and work mail. That's a job for yuh—break yuh in half in a minit. You and your job! Go ter hell! I ain't had no sleep, see? I gotter git some sleep. So keep your mouth shut. Yuh're full of prunes, anyway. (*He leans his head on outstretched arms.*) Don't fergit now if yuh don't wanta git lammed for a goal. (*He closes his eyes. Adams sits staring at him with sodden stupidity. Two longshoremen enter from the street, wearing their working aprons, the button of the union pinned conspicuously on their caps pulled sideways on their heads at an aggressive angle.*)

FIRST LONGSHOREMAN—(*as they range themselves at the bar*) Gimme a shock—Number Two. (*He tosses a coin on the bar.*)

SECOND LONGSHOREMAN—Same here. (*Johnny sets two glasses of barrel whiskey before them.*)

FIRST LONGSHOREMAN—Here's luck! (*The other nods. They gulp down their whiskey.*)

SECOND LONGSHOREMAN—(*putting money on the bar*) Give us another.

FIRST LONGSHOREMAN—Gimme a scoop this time—lager and porter. I'm dry.

SECOND LONGSHOREMAN—Same here. (*Johnny draws the lager and porter and sets the big, foaming schooners before them. They drink down half the contents of their glasses and start to talk together hurriedly in low tones. The door on the left is swung open and Larry enters. He is a boyish, red-cheeked, rather good-looking young fellow of twenty or so.*)

LARRY—(*nodding to Johnny—cheerily*) Hello, boss.

JOHNNY—Hello, Larry. (*with a glance at his watch*) Just on time. (*Larry goes to the right behind the bar, takes off his coat, and puts on an apron.*)

FIRST LONGSHOREMAN—(*abruptly*) Let's drink up and get back to it. (*They finish their drinks and go out left. The postman enters as they leave. He exchanges nods with Johnny and throws a letter on the bar.*)

THE POSTMAN—Addressed care of you, Johnny. Know him?

JOHNNY—(*picks up the letter, adjusting his spectacles. Larry comes over and peers over his shoulders. Johnny reads slowly*) Christopher Christophersen.

THE POSTMAN—(*helpfully*) Squarehead name.

LARRY—Old Chris—that's who.

JOHNNY—Oh sure. That's who. I was forgetting Chris carried a hell of a name like that. Letters come here for him sometimes before. I remember now. Long time ago, though.

THE POSTMAN—It'll get him all right then?

JOHNNY—Sure thing. He comes here whenever he's in port.

THE POSTMAN—(*turning to go*) Sailor, eh?

JOHNNY—(*with a grin*) Captain of a coal barge. (*as if he were reciting a piece*) Captain, mate, cook and crew!

THE POSTMAN—(*laughing*) Some job! Well, s'long.

JOHNNY—S'long. I'll see he gets it. (*The postman goes out. Johnny scrutinizes the letter.*) Furrin' stamp, it looks like. You got good eyes, Larry. Where's it from?

LARRY—(*after a glance*) British—same's them I get from the old country. It's marked Leeds. That'll be in England, I'm thinkin'. Who the divil'd be writing to the Swede from England? Looks like a woman's writing, too, the old divil!

JOHNNY—He's got a daughter somewhere the other side, I think he told me once. (*He puts the letter on the cash register.*) Come to think of it, I ain't seen old Chris in a dog's age. Where was he bound last trip, d'you know, Larry?

LARRY—Boston, he said. Up the Sound. He'd ought to be back by this. (*after a pause—thoughtfully*) That's a hell of a job now, when you come to think of it—getting towed on a rope from place to place on a rotten, dirty old tub.

JOHNNY—Captain, mate, cook and crew! Seems to suit Chris all right. He's been at it a long time. Used to be a regular, deep-sea sailor years ago when he first got to comin' here—bo'sun on sailing ships. A good one on a windjammer, too, I guess. All them squareheads is good sailors. He cut it out all of a sudden when he got back here after some long voyage or other. Never said why. Got sick of it, I guess— work too hard. He ain't so young no more. He had a tough time gettin' this job. Bummed around here broke for months before he landed it. He was stubborn. Them Swedes are when they git a notion. He wouldn't hear of going back to sailing—not if he starved to death. Funny! I used to stake him when he was broke. He always paid me back. Good old boy, Chris! Good spender, too—when he's got it. Just like all sailors, though. Throws it away on a drunk.

LARRY—Aye. He's been drunk every time I've seen him. A divil to sing that song of his, too!

JOHNNY—(*laughing*) Oh—my Yosephine?

LARRY—He'd drive you mad with that silly tune.

JOHNNY—(*good-naturedly*) Oh well—that's Chris. He means well.

ADAMS—(*suddenly coming to life—with loud assertiveness*) Chris is a gentleman same's you and me, Johnny. That's all that counts. I don't care what a man is or does as long as he's a gentleman. I don't care if old Chris is only a poor devil working on a stinking old coal barge, he's a gentleman just the same. And I know it. He and I have had many a drink in your place, Johnny the Priest, sitting right here at this very table treating each other as man to man. Chris is a gentleman and a sport, and anyone that says different is a liar! Where's Chris, Johnny? I want to buy him a drink right this minute.

LARRY—(*with amused exasperation*) Cuckoo! He's at it again, divil take him! Let you keep your loud mouth shut, I'm tellin' you, or the toe of my boot'll be boosting you out to get the air.

JOHNNY—No more drinks for him, Larry, till he's slept this one off.

ADAMS—That isn't fair, Johnny. I need a drink—

JOHNNY—(*decisively*) I said no. That goes. You've got a skin full now. And you've talked too much, too. (*He comes from behind the bar and takes Adams by the shoulder.*) Come on. Go upstairs and do a flop. Take the end room. Come on. You'll feel better after.

ADAMS—(*resisting*) No. I don't want to go to bed.

JOHNNY—(*losing patience, jerks him to his feet*) Get in the back room then and sleep at a table. Or do you want me to give you the bounce outside?

ADAMS—(*whining*) No. Leggo, Johnny. I'll go—back room. (*He staggers to the door on right and goes out.*)

LARRY—(*as Johnny comes behind the bar to get his overcoat*) He's a pest, that one, with his loud gab.

JOHNNY—Smart fellow, too—when he's sober. I've known him for twenty or thirty years. Used to be clerk at a ship chandlers. Left that and became a travelling salesman. Good one, too, they say. Never stays long on one job, though. Booze got a strangle hold on him. He's been fired again now. Good schoolin'—every chance, too. He's one of the kind ought to leave red eye alone. Always ends up his drunk here. Knows no one'll know him here 'cept me and he ain't shamed to go the limit. (*philosophically*) Well, he's a good spender as long as he's got it. Don't be too rough with him. (*His overcoat on, he comes around the end of the bar.*) Guess I'll be gettin' home. See you tomorrow.

LARRY—Good-night to ye, boss. (*As Johnny goes toward the street door, it is pushed open and Christopher Christophersen enters. He is a short, squat, broad-shouldered man of about fifty with a round, weather-beaten red face from which his light blue eyes peer short-sightedly, twinkling with a simple good humor. His large mouth, overhung by a thick, drooping yellow mustache, is childishly self-willed and weak, and of an obstinate kindliness. His heavy jaw is set at an angle denoting an invincible stubbornness. A thick neck is jammed like a post into the heavy trunk of his body. His arms with their big, hairy freckled hands, and his stumpy legs terminating in large flat feet, are awkwardly short and muscular. He walks with a clumsy, rolling gait. His voice, when not raised in a hollow boom, is toned down to a sly, confidential half-whisper with something vaguely plaintive in its quality. He is dressed in a wrinkled, ill-fitting dark suit of shore clothes, and wears a faded cap of grey cloth over his mop of grizzled blond hair. Just now his face beams with a too-blissful happiness, and he has evidently been drinking. He reaches his hand out to Johnny.*)

CHRIS—Hello, Yohnny! Have a drink on me. Come on, Larry. Give us drink. Have one yourself. (*putting his hand in his pocket*) Ay gat money—plenty money.

JOHNNY—(*shakes Chris by the hand*) Speak of the divil! We was just talkin' about you.

LARRY—(*coming to the end of the bar*) Hello, Chris. Put it there. (*They shake hands.*)

CHRIS—(*beaming*) Give us a drink.

JOHNNY—(*with a grin*) You got a half snoot-full now. Where'd you get it?

CHRIS—(*grinning*) Oder fallar on oder barge—Irish fallar—he gat bottle vhiskey and ve drank it, yust us two. Dot vhiskey gat kick, py yingo! Ay just come ashore. Don't gat drink no oder place. Come straight here. Give us drink, Larry. Ay vas little drunk, no much. Yust feel good. (*He laughs and commences to sing in a nasal, high-pitched quaver*) "My Yosephine, come board de ship. Long time Ay vait for you. De moon, she shi-i-i-ine. She looka yust like you. Tchee-tchee. Tchee-tchee. Tchee-tchee. Tchee-tchee." (*To the accom-*

paniment of this last he waves his hand as if he were conducting an orchestra.)

JOHNNY—(*with a laugh*) Same old Yosie, eh, Chris?

LARRY—(*with a grin*) I'll be hearin' that all night now, I s'pose.

CHRIS—You don't know good song when you hear him. Give us drink. (*He throws change on the bar.*)

LARRY—(*with a professional air*) What's your pleasure, gentlemen?

JOHNNY—Small beer, Larry.

CHRIS—Vhiskey—Number two.

LARRY—(*as he gets their drinks*) I'll take a cigar on you.

CHRIS—(*lifting his glass*) Skoal! (*He drinks.*)

JOHNNY—Drink hearty.

CHRIS—(*immediately*) Have oder drink.

JOHNNY—No. Some other time. Got to go home now. So you just landed? Where are you in from this time?

CHRIS—Boston. Ve make slow voyage—anchor all time—dirty vedder—yust fog, fog, fog all bloody time!

JOHNNY—Oh, I was forgettin'. Letter just come for you here a minute ago—from the other side. Give him that letter, Larry. (*Larry hands it to Chris who peers at it blinkingly.*)

LARRY—It's from Leeds, England—and a lady's writin'.

CHRIS—(*quickly*) Oh, dan it come from my daughter, Anna. She live in Leeds. (*He turns the letter over in his hands uncertainly.*) Ay don't gat letter from Anna—must be year. Ay forgat answer her last letter and she gat mad, Ay tank.

JOHNNY—(*turning away*) Well, s'long, Chris. See you later.

CHRIS—Good'bye, Yohnny. (*Johnny goes out.*)

LARRY—(*jokingly*) That's a fine fairy tale to be tellin'—your daughter! Sure I'll bet it's some English bum ye've left back there on the street with a child on her lap!

CHRIS—(*soberly*) No. Dis come from Anna. (*then with a grin*) Oh, Ay gat nice gel too—kind of gel you mean, Larry. She live with me on barge. Make all voyage—everytang. Nice, fat gel. You come on board barge sometime, Larry. Ay introduce you. Ay bet you tank she's svell gel for ole fallar like me.

LARRY—(*sardonically*) Aye. I got a picture of her. Thim kind that lives with the men on coal barges must be beauts.

CHRIS—(*as if he hadn't heard this last—engrossed by the letter in his hand—uncertainly*) Py golly, Ay tank Ay'm too drunk for read dis letter from Anna. She give me hell, Ay bet.

LARRY—A good strong lemon and seltzer'll fix you up. (*He makes it and hands it to Chris.*) Drink up, now—all of it.

CHRIS—(*after he has done so*) Ay tank Ay sat down for a minute. (*He goes to a table, front center, and sits down. After staring at the letter for a moment, he slowly opens it and, squinting his eyes, commences to read laboriously, his lips moving as he spells out the words. As he reads his face lights up with an expression of mingled joy and bewilderment.*)

LARRY—(*who has been watching him curiously*) Good news?

CHRIS—(*pauses for a moment after finishing the letter as if to let the news sink in—then suddenly pounds his fist on the table with happy excitement*) Py yimminy, Ay tank so! Yust tank, Anna say she's comin' here—to dis country—comin' here to gat yob and live with me! She gat sick of living with dem cousins and vorking in England, she say. It's short letter don't tal me much more'n dat. (*beaming*) Py golly, dat's good news all at one time for ole fallar! (*then rather shame-facedly*) You know, Larry, Ay don't see my Anna since she vas little girl five year ole.

LARRY—How old'll she be now?

CHRIS—She must be—lat me see—fifteen year ago Ay vent home Sweden for last time—she must be twenty year ole, py Yo!

LARRY—(*surprised*) You've not seen her in fifteen years?

CHRIS—(*suddenly growing somber—in a low voice*) No. Ven she vas little girl Ay vas bo'sun on windjammer. Ay never gat home only few time dem year. Ay'm fool sailor fallar. Ven mo'der die, Ay tank it's better dem cousins in England—her mo'der's people—take Anna. And Ay stay in dis country—get yob on barge. Ay tank it's better Anna never know she gat fa'der like me. Ay vas no good for her mo'der—damn fool drunk sailor fallar—and Ay tank Ay vas no good for have little gel grow up with. So Ay stay here on barge. Ay write her letter once in vhile, dat's all. (*with a sigh of relief*) But she's grown voman now. Ay can't do her harm no more, py golly.

LARRY—It's too bad her mother's dead, now.

CHRIS—(*in melancholy tones*) She die ven Ay vas on voyage—twelve year ago.

LARRY—And has your daughter no brothers at all?

CHRIS—Ay once gat two sons—dey was eighteen and sixteen—good, big boys—sailing on fishing boat. Dey get drowned in storm year before deir mo'der die. Ay vas avay on voyage dat time, too.

LARRY—(*wiping off the bar to hide his embarrassment at Chris' sorrow—after a pause*) You're a family of sailors, God help you, like some in Ireland. This girl, now, 'll be marryin' a sailor herself, likely. It's in the blood.

CHRIS—(*suddenly springing to his feet and smashing his fist on the table in a rage*) No, py God! She don't do dat! Not if Ay gat kill her first!

LARRY—(*amazed*) Oho, what's up with you? Ain't you a sailor yourself, now and always been?

CHRIS—(*slowly*) Dat's yust why Ay say it. (*forcing a smile*) Sailor vas all right fallar, but not for marry gel. No. Ay know dat. Anna's mo'der, she know it, too. (*with an expression of intense hatred*) Dat damn, dirty sea, she spoil all tangs. She's dirty ole davil, Ay tal you! Ay know her many year. (*spitting with disgust*) Yes. Ay know all her dirty tricks.

LARRY—(*as Chris remains sunk in gloomy reflection*) When is your daughter comin'? Soon?

CHRIS—(*roused*) Py yimminy, Ay forgat. (*reads through the letter hurriedly*) She say she come on *Caronia*—dat's Cunard Line—leave Liverpool on fourteenth. (*anxiously*) Vat day vas today, Larry?

LARRY—Eighteenth. That's a six-day boat, likely. She'll be gettin' in day after tomorrow, then.

CHRIS—(*astounded*) So quick! (*He gets to his feet excitedly.*) Py golly, dat ain't long for vait. (*alarmed by a sudden thought*) Py yingo, Ay gat get my voman, Marthy, ashore off barge b'fore Anna come! Anna raise hell if she find dat out. Marthy raise hell, too, for go, py golly!

LARRY—(*with a chuckle*) Serve ye right, ye old divil—havin' a woman at your age!

CHRIS—(*scratching his head in a quandary*) You tal me lie for tal Marthy, Larry, so's she gat off barge quick.

LARRY—Tell her the truth, man—that your daughter's comin', and to get the hell out of it.

CHRIS—No. She's good voman. Ay don't like make her feel bad.

LARRY—You're an old mush! Keep your girl away from the barge, then. She'll likely want to stop ashore anyway, and her lookin' for a job. (*curiously*) What does she work at, your Anna?

CHRIS—She vas nurse gel, but she say in letter she learn new business. Typewriter. (*proudly*) She's smart gel—go to school all time till tree year ago. Yust like her mo'der, she know everytang. Look at fine writing she make! (*He holds up the letter—then shakes his head resolutely.*) But Ay don't vant for her gat yob. Ay don't see her since she's little gel. Ay vant for her stay with me for vhile.

LARRY—(*scornfully*) On a dirty coal barge! She'll not like that, I'm thinkin'.

CHRIS—Ay never write in letter Ay vork on barge. Ay'm goin' tal her it's new yob Ay gat 'cause Ay'm sick on land. (*He chuckles at his cunning.*) Dat'a good lie, Larry. Dan she stay with me sure. (*seriously*) It's nice on barge—everytang nice and clean—nice stove and bed. Anna like it ven she see. And voyage ve make—yust nice and quiet—no rough vedder—plenty fresh air, good grub, make her strong and healthy. Ay gat 'nuff money on pay day so Anna don't have gat yob. (*having convinced himself—confidently*) Anna like it pooty good, Ay bet.

LARRY—I'd not bet on it. She'll be wantin' to work for herself and go about and see things, you'll find out.

CHRIS—(*a shadow coming over his face*) Ay don't tank— (*with a sigh*) Vell, anyhow, so long's dat ole davil, sea, don't gat her, make her life sorry, like her mo'der, Ay don't vorry. And Anna don't know sea, don't know ships or sailor fallars. She live inland in Leeds most all her life. Ay tank God for dat.

LARRY—But if ye keep her on the barge, ye old fool, won't that be sea for her?

CHRIS—(*contemptuously*) No. Barge vas nutting. It ain't sea or it ain't land eider. Barge ain't ship no more dan coal vagon is ship. Dat's vhy Ay like dat yob. Ay svore ven Anna's mo'der die Ay never go to sea again. If barge is ship Ay never go on her, py golly! And Anna's with me on barge. Ay look after her. (*vindictively*) Old davil sea don't gat her ven Ay'm looking, no!

LARRY—(*shaking his head*) You're a crazy old nut.

CHRIS—(*worriedly—after a pause*) Ay must gat dat Marthy voman off barge so Anna don't see her. (*Larry snickers. Chris grins sheepishly.*) Oh vell, Ay gat plenty time for dat— two day. (*He sighs with ponderous relief.*) Phooh! Ay don't tank so much in long time. Gimme whiskey, Larry. Ay bet dis is last night Ay'm able gat drunk, now Anna come.

LARRY—(*handing him the drink*) Its better off you'll be— and richer.

CHRIS—Skoal! (*He drinks and tosses money on the bar.*) Give me oder one. Ay'm going celabrate, py golly! (*musingly*) Yust tank, Ay don't see Anna since she vas little gel so high. Ay vonder vat she look like now she's big gel. Py golly, Ay'm glad Ay don't turn up toes and die b'fore Ay see her again. (*hugging himself with childish glee*) Py golly, it make me happy, dat letter. Have drink on me, Larry. You celabrate with me.

LARRY—(*with virtuous severity*) I never touch it. Wake up Jack Burns there. He'll be only too glad to drink with you.

CHRIS—Hey, Yack! Yack! Ahoy, Yack!

BURNS—(*raises his face off his arms, blinking sleepily*) What the—

CHRIS—(*beaming*) Have drink, Yack. Ay celabrate.

BURNS—(*shaking himself to alertness and rising to his feet*) Sure. (*then grinning as he joins Chris*) Hello, Captain. How's things?

CHRIS—(*shaking his head*) Pooty good, Yack.

BURNS—Gimme Number Two, Larry. (*Larry serves them. The door from the street is pushed open and Mickey and Devlin enter and take up a position at the end of the bar. Both show signs of having been drinking. Mickey is about forty-five, short and round-shouldered, monkey-like in the disproportionate length of arms and legs. His pock-marked face, weather-tanned, has a broken nose twisted askew which gives him a grotesque expression when he grins. His eyes are a wishy-washy blue, his hair a muddy red, his voice hoarse and raspy. He is dressed in a blue coat, flannel shirt, and dungaree pants. Devlin is a lanky, loose-jointed man of about thirty-five with a lean, boney face, a hooked nose, beady dark eyes, and a bristly, black mustache shadowing a wide, thin-lipped mouth. His speech is sharp and explosive. He is dressed much the same as his companion.*)

MICKEY—(*as Larry comes down to them*) Whiskey—and a scoop of ale.

DEVLIN—The same. (*Larry serves them.*)

CHRIS—(*picking up his drink—to Burns*) Skoal!

BURNS—Good luck, Chris. (*They drink.*)

CHRIS—(*with a childish chuckle*) Ay celabrate, py yimminy. Dis vas last night—dan Ay go on vater vagon long time. Have oder drink, Yack.

BURNS—Sure.

CHRIS—(*begins to sing*) "My Yosephine, come board the ship. Long time Ay vait for you. De moon, she shi-i-i-ine. She looka yust like you. Tchee-tchee. Tchee-tchee. Tchee-tchee. Tchee-tchee." (*He laughs and speaks*) Good song, eh, Yack? Ay learn him from Italian fallar on oder barge one time.

BURNS—(*with a grin*) Great stuff. Yuh got Caruso skinned a block. (*calling*) Hey, Larry, give us some service.

MICKEY—(*who has listened to Chris as if the voice were familiar*) D'yo mind that singin', Dev? I'll take my oath I've heard that voice somewheres before.

DEVLIN—(*glancing down the bar to where Chris stands with back turned to them*) The old squarehead, you mean?

MICKEY—Yes. I've been mates with him on some hooker long ago or I'm a liar. You'd not forget a screechin' like his, ever. (*to Larry*) What's his name—the Dutchy there?

LARRY—Old Chris, you mean. That's his name. He used to be a sailor once—a bo'sun on windjammers.

MICKEY—(*slapping his thigh*) Bo'sun? Chris? Now I know him and his singin'. 'Twas on the old *Neptune*—full-rigged ship, Dev. Let me get a look at his mug to make sure. (*He goes down the bar, peers at Chris' face for a second, then slaps him heartily on the back and holds out his hand.*) Put it there, matey. I knew I'd seen the cut of your jib before. (*as Chris looks at him in bewilderment*) D'ye not remember Mickey on the old *Neptune* when you was bo'sun?

CHRIS—(*suddenly beaming and pumping his hand up and*

down) Py golly, yes! You vas Mickey? Ay remember your face. Old *Neptune*—dat vas long time back.

MICKEY—A damn long time—but I knew your singin', Dutchy. Who'd forget it?

CHRIS—Have drink, you Mickey. Bring fallar with you. Ve sit at table. Ve all have drink, py yimminy!

MICKEY—That's a bloody good plan. Come on, Dev. We'll sit down a bit. (*to Larry*) Bring us all a drink—whiskey—the best. (*then as Devlin comes up*) This is ole Chris, Dev, as good a bo'sun as ever was. (*They shake hands and sit down at table, center. Burns remains standing at the bar.*)

CHRIS—(*his head nodding—dreamily*) Ole *Neptune*. She vas mighty smart ship, dat one. Ay vas bo'sun board of her tree year. Ain't no more fine ships like her on sea no more, py golly. (*He spits disgustedly.*) All is steamers now—damn tea-kettles. Dey ain't ships. (*He pats Mickey on the back affectionately.*) It's yust good for see ole shipmate once again. Ay vas celabrating tonight. (*Larry brings their drinks and Mickey pays.*) Bring oder drink, Larry. Den ve don't loose time.

DEVLIN—Hold up. The next is mine.

MICKEY—Down with this one. Here's luck, Chris. (*They drink. Larry takes glasses to refill them.*) We're on the bust ourselves after a vige down to the Plate and back. We was paid off this morning—a stinkin', starvation, lime-juice tramp!

DEVLIN—(*with an emphatic grunt of assent*) Aye!

MICKEY—What are you doin' now, Chris? Workin' ashore? Ye have sense, then. The sea ain't what it used to be.

DEVLIN—Rotten!

CHRIS—(*with a grin*) Ay don't vork ashore and Ay don't work on sea, neider. Ay'm captain on coal barge. Ha-ha.

MICKEY—You're jokin'. (*Larry brings drinks again. Devlin pays.*)

DEVLIN—Here's a go! (*They drink.*)

CHRIS—Bring oder drink, Larry.

LARRY—You'll be fallin' on your nose, I'm thinkin'. Well, it'll be your big head. (*He goes to get the drinks.*)

MICKEY—(*who has been frowning at Chris*) You're jokin', Chris—about the coal barge. (*with drunken insistence*) Tell me it's a lie, I'm sayin'.

CHRIS—No. It ain't a lie.

MICKEY—Is it truth, then? (*Chris nods. Mickey spits.*) Divil take you! Who'd think it—a fine, smart sailor man the like of you doin' the like of that! On a rotten coal barge! Hell's fire!

DEVLIN—(*drunkenly quarrelsome*) A damn rotten job, I say, for a sailor!

CHRIS—(*gloomily*) Ay know all dat. (*then grinning*) You don't know dat yob, you fallars. Nice, easy yob, Ay tal you. Ay gat cabin, nice and clean, no bugs. Gat own grub for cook mysalf—good grub. No one on board ship to tal me vat Ay do. Gat nice gel, too. (*He winks at their scowling, hostile faces.*) She make all voyage with me. Ay tal you Ay vas captain, mate, cook and crew on board my boat, py golly! (*He tries to force a jovial laugh.*)

MICKEY—(*disgustedly*) An old woman's job—for a smart sailor like you—gettin' towed on a rope from one dock to another.

DEVLIN—(*smashing his fist on the table*) A stinking, coal-punchers berth!

CHRIS—(*raising his voice defiantly*) It's nice, Ay say!

MICKEY—(*with drunken superiority*) For a smart bo'sun of the old *Neptune*! You'd ought to be shamed to own it!

DEVLIN—(*morosely*) He never was a bo'sun. Not him! No bo'sun'd punch stinking coal.

MICKEY—(*emphatically*) He was so! Don't I know him? As smart a bo'sun as ever signed on a windbag.

DEVLIN—(*heatedly*) Not him! You're a liar, Mickey!

MICKEY—(*belligerently—starting to get up*) What's that?

LARRY—(*interrupting*) No scrappin' now, d'ye hear? Here's your drinks. (*He brings them. Devlin subsides into sullen silence. Mickey glares at Chris rebukingly. Chris pays for the drinks, shame-faced, avoiding Mickey's eyes.*)

CHRIS—(*taking up his drink—placatingly*) Skoal, you fallars.

MICKEY—(*reprovingly*) I don't know as I'd ought to drink with you—and you what you are!

DEVLIN—(*gruffly*) I won't drink with him—a coal-puncher! (*He pours his drink on the floor. Chris flushes guiltily and swallows his drink, sputtering.*)

MICKEY—I oughtn't but—(*he takes his glass*) it's a shame to waste it. (*He drinks and fixes Chris with a sorrowful eye.*) Old Chris—as smart a bo'sun as ever—on a coal scow!

DEVLIN—(*scornfully*) Calls himself a man, too!

CHRIS—(*crushed—at the point of drunken tears*) Ay tal you, you fallars, you make big mistake. You don't know—

MICKEY—Mistake, is it? God stiffen you! (*suddenly leaning over and grasping Chris by the arm—fiercely*) Will you ship away with us, Chris, when our money's gone? Will you make a man of yourself again, or stay a rat?

DEVLIN—And a barge rat at that!

CHRIS—(*His eyes stare at Mickey in amazement.*) Ship away—on sea? (*He seems to begin to comprehend this proposition, and, as Mickey goes on, his face grows white with rage.*)

MICKEY—(*intense emotion trembling in his voice*) Will you do that, Chris, for old friendship's sake—ship away to sea again?

DEVLIN—(*maudlinly*) Ship away, old Chris, ship away!

MICKEY—We'll find a clean, smart ship for the three of us—when our money's spent.

DEVLIN—When our money's spent, we'll do that!

MICKEY—No lime-juice tramp this time! I've my bellyfull of steam. To hell with it!

DEVLIN—To hell with steam!

MICKEY—(*almost chanting the words*) We'll find a tall, smart daisy of a full-rigged ship with skys'ls—a beautiful, swift hooker that'll take us flyin' south through the Trades.

DEVLIN—(*sings*) Oh, away Rio!

MICKEY—A sweet, slim clipper like the old ones, Chris. If there's one left on the seas, we'll find her!

DEVLIN—Aye, we'll find her!

MICKEY—(*this time imploringly*) Will you ship with us, Chris, for the love of God? Or has this dirty scow of yours destroyed you entirely? (*Chris glares at him with hatred, his lips moving as if his seething rage were vainly seeking for words strong enough.*)

DEVLIN—(*with a groan*) No use, Mickey. He's damned and done for. Hell's full of his like.

MICKEY—(*shaking Chris' arm—violently*) Answer me, Dutchy!

CHRIS—(*shaking off his hand furiously—sputtering*) You damn Irish fallar—you vas damn fool, you! (*He shakes his fist in Mickey's astounded face and lurches to his feet.*) You shut dat big mouth, py yingo! You try for gat me back on sea ven Ay'm drunk? Dat's oder one sea's dirty tricks. She try gat me back many time, dirty ole davil! (*He shakes his fist at the door as if visualizing the sea outside.*) She's try all tricks on me for gat me back but Ay tal her go to hell all time last twelve year. Ay tal her go to hell now once again. She kill my fa'der, my tree bro'der, dan my mo'der's all lone, she die too. Dan Ay gat married and Ay don't see my vife only five time in twenty year. Ven my boys vas born, Ay vas away on voyage. Ven my gel, Anna, is born, Ay vas on odder voyage, too. Dan dat first voyage on ole *Neptune*, my two boys gat drowned by home on fishing boat. Ay don't never see them again. Second voyage on ole *Neptune*, my vife die in England, and Ay don't never see her again, neider. All years Ay vas at sea Ay gat drunk on pay day, spend all money, ship avay again, never gat home. Dat's vat dirty tricks of dat ole davil, sea, do to me. Dan, ven my voman die, Ay hate dat ole davil so much Ay say: "You tank you gat me next. Ay fool you yust dis one time, py yingo." Dan Ay gat yob on barge here. Ay know Ay can't vork on land. Ay'm too ole dog for learn new tricks. But vork on barge ain't on land, ain't on sea, neider. Barge ain't sea boat, Ay tal you! It ain't nutting. Dat's only vay Ay gat for beat ole davil sea. And you vant for me ship avay on sea with you fallars—yust now ven Anna come to me? Ay tal you, dat ole davil sea don't gat me no more! (*He strikes table with his clenched fist.*) No, py God! No more!

LARRY—(*irritably*) Easy, there! Don't break the table, ye old loon!

CHRIS—(*brought up abruptly, sputters and then grins*) Poof! Ay'm old fool for gat mad at you drunk fallars. Ay forgat Ay celabrate. My Anna's coming home. Give us oder drink, Larry.

MICKEY—(*with a characteristic drunken reversal of opinion—getting up and slapping Chris on the back*) You're right, old Chris, right as rain!

DEVLIN—(*half-asleep*) Right as rain.

MICKEY—(*feelingly—on the verge of tears*) Sure, why

shouldn't an old man that the sea's taken all from be shut of it and have his peace? It's a dog's life, anyway.

DEVLIN—A dog's life.

CHRIS—(*again beaming with bliss—drunkenly*) Have odder drink, you fallars. Ay sing song. (*He starts to sing his Josephine song beginning in the middle:*) "De moon, she shi-i-i-ine. She looka yust like you. Tchee-tchee. Tchee-tchee. Tchee-tchee."

as

(*The Curtain Falls*)

SCENE II

SCENE—*The interior of the cabin on the barge,* Simeon Winthrop (*at dock in New York harbor*)—*a narrow, low-ceilinged compartment the walls of which are painted a light brown with white trimmings. On the left, forward, a small cooking range with wood and coal box beside it. On nails in the wall over the stove hang a few cooking utensils, pots and a frying pan. In the rear of stove, a door leading to Chris' sleeping quarters. In the far left corner, a locker for dishes, painted white, on the door of which a mirror hangs on a nail. In the rear wall, two small, square windows and a door opening out on the deck toward the stern. In the right wall, two more windows looking out on the port deck. White curtains, clean and stiff, are at all the windows. A table with two cane-bottomed chairs stands in the center of the cabin. A dilapidated wicker rocker, painted brown, is placed before the stove.*

It is around the noon hour of a sunny day two days later. From the harbor and docks outside, muffled by the closed door and windows, comes the sound of steamers' whistles and the puffing snort of donkey engines of some ship unloading nearby.

As the curtain rises, Marthy Owen and Chris are discovered. Marthy is not beautiful. She might be forty or fifty. Her jowly, mottled face with its thick red nose is streaked with interlacing, purple veins. Her big mouth is thick-lipped and droops laxly. Some of her teeth are missing. Her thick grey hair is piled anyhow in a greasy mop on top of her round head. Her figure is flabby and fat; her breath comes in wheezy gasps; she speaks in a loud mannish voice, punctuated by explosions of hoarse laughter. But there still twinkles in her blood-shot blue eyes a youthful lust for life which hard usage has failed to entirely stifle, a sense of humor mocking but good tempered. She wears a man's cap, a double-breasted man's jacket, and a grimy calico skirt. Her bare feet are incased in a man's brogans several sizes too large for her, which gives her a shuffling, wobbly gait. She is relaxed comfortably in the rocker in front of the stove, her eyes drowsily following a wheezing whisp of steam ascending upwards from the spout of the kettle on the stove. Chris wanders nervously about the room, casting quick, uneasy side glances at her face. He carefully turns his back to her to take a secret peep at his dollar watch, and sighs helplessly. His attitude betrays an overwhelming anxiety which has him on tenterhooks. He pretends to be busily engaged in setting things shipshape but this occupation is confined to picking up some object, staring at it stupidly for a second, then aimlessly putting it down again. He attempts to whistle a few bars of "Josephine" with careless bravado but the whistle peeters out futilely. Then he clears his throat huskily and sings in a voice incredibly doleful: "My Yosephine, come board de ship. Long time Ay vait for you—" *But this reminds him of impending disaster and he abruptly stops. He is dressed in his very best, a blue suit somewhat frayed by time, black shoes glistening with polish, and an immaculate, white cotton shirt with a soft collar and blue tie.*

CHRIS—(*clearing his throat and approaching Marthy's chair with the courage of desperation—stammeringly*) Ay vas expecting company come aboard barge dis morning, Marthy, and—

MARTHY—(*startled from her doze—explosively*) Wha's that? (*then stretching herself with a sleepy grin*) Gawd, I musta been dozin' off. What did yuh say, Dutchy?

CHRIS—(*whose courage has fled at the force of her first exclamation—feebly*) Ay vas sayin'— Don't kettle bile yet?

MARTHY—It will in a secon'. Yuh want some tea, don't yuh?

CHRIS—(*peevishly*) No. No, Ay don't vant nutting.

MARTHY—Why didn't yuh say so before? Here I been waitin'. (*She gets up, stretching.*) I'm dopey with sleep. Guess I'll beat it ashore and git a scoop of ale to open me lamps. Come on and blow me, Chris. (*She grins at him quizzically.*)

CHRIS—(*with haste—uneasily*) No. Ay can't. Ay gat stay aboard.

MARTHY—Wha' for? (*making as if to sit down again—provokingly*) Then I won't go on me lonesome.

CHRIS—(*eagerly*) Yes. You go. Ay give you money for treat on me. (*He takes half a dollar from his pocket and hands it to her.*)

MARTHY—(*takes it—peers at him for a moment keenly, grinning*) Wha's up, Dutchy, yuh're gittin' so gen'rous?

CHRIS—(*takes her arm persuasively—forcing a smile*) You go gat drink, Marthy, dat's good gel.

MARTHY—(*shaking his hand off*) Leggo me. Wha's the rush? (*She pretends to fly into a rage, her twinkling eyes enjoying Chris' misery.*) Wha' yuh tryin' to do, huh? Git rid o' me, huh? Gimme the bum's rush ashore, huh? Lemme tell yuh somethin', Dutchy. There ain't a squarehead workin' on a boat man enough to git away with that. Don't start nothin' yuh can't finish.

CHRIS—(*miserably*) Ay don't start nutting, Marthy. Ay vant treat you, dat's all.

MARTHY—(*glares at him for a second—then cannot control a burst of laughter*) Ho-ho! Yuh're a scream, Squarehead—an honest-ter-Gawd knockout! Ho-ho! (*She wheezes, panting for breath.*)

CHRIS—(*with childish pique*) Ay don't see nutting for laugh at.

MARTHY—(*pointing to the mirror*) Take a look in that and yuh'll see. Ho-ho! (*recovering from her mirth—chucklingly*) Think I was really sore at yuh, Dutchy? It's a shame ter kid yuh. (*She slaps him on the back.*) Say, wha's been the matter with yuh since yestiday mornin'? Yuh been goin' round s'if yuh was nutty, washin' and scrubbin' this dump till yuh near had me nuts, too. Think I ain't noticed, huh? Why don't yuh speak up—git it off yer chest? (*scornfully*) A squarehead tryin' to kid Marthy Owen at this late day! After me campin' with barge men the last twenty years! I'm wise to the game up, down and sideways. I'm hep to all the dirty tricks yuh could play on me b'fore yuh start 'em.

CHRIS—Dis vasn't no dirty trick, Ay svear!

MARTHY—(*warningly*) It'd better not be. (*then kindly*) Say, lissen: I was wise to yer game yestiday mornin' at the start. I been trou the mill b'fore, and I know the signs in a man when I see 'em. I ain't been born and dragged up on the waterfront for nothin'. (*She claps the bewildered Chris on the back.*) And I packed all me duds noon yestiday. I'm quittin' yuh, get me? Think I'd give yuh the satisfaction of tellin' me ter beat it? Not much. Not this chicken! I'm tellin' yuh I'm sick o' stickin' with yuh, and I'm leavin' yuh flat, see? There's plenty o' guys on other barges waitin' for me. Always was, I always found. (*She slaps Chris on the back again.*) So cheer up, Dutchy! When I go ter git this drink yuh'll be rid o' me for good— and me o' you—good riddance for both of us. Ho-ho.

CHRIS—(*soberly*) Ay don't tank dat. You vas good gel, Marthy.

MARTHY—(*grinning*) Good girl? Aw, can the bull! Well, yuh treated me square, yuhself. So it's fifty-fifty. Nobody's sore at nobody. We're still good frens, huh?

CHRIS—(*beaming now that he sees his troubles disappearing*) Yes, py yingo!

MARTHY—That's the talk! In all my time I tried never to split with a guy with no hard feelin's; and that way I got lots o' frens stead o' soreheads. But why didn't yuh tell me straight yuh was trou. Why'd yuh try to hide it? Scared I'd kick up a row? That ain't my way. No one man's worth gittin' sore about. There's too many others.

CHRIS—No. Ay vasn't scared. Ay yust don't vant for hurt you.

MARTHY—(*angrily*) Hurt me? You? (*Then she laughs.*) Ho-ho! What a chanct! At my age! (*then regarding him with kindly scorn*) Say, yuh're a simple kind o' guy, ain't yuh?

CHRIS—(*grinning*) Ay tank, maybe.

MARTHY—What I can't figger, 's this: Wha's come over yuh all of a sudden? Yuh never went cheatin' with other women like most guys. Yuh're no lady killer, Dutchy. Was it some dame yuh met ashore night b'fore last yuh liked better'n me? Or are yuh just tired o' the same old thing?

CHRIS—(*hastily*) No, don't tank dat, py yimminy! (*hesitatingly*) You know, Ay tal you Ay gat daughter in England? (*Marthy nods. Chris scratches his head in embarrassment.*) Vell,

Ay gat letter from her oder night. She's—Anna's comin' to dis country.

MARTHY—(*looks at him keenly for a moment to make out whether he's lying or not—then satisfied*) She's comin'? When?

CHRIS—Dis morning. Steamer vas due for dock dis morning.

MARTHY—This mornin'? (*then suspiciously*) Why ain't you down ter meet her, then?

CHRIS—Ay gat no good clothes for dat. She go from boat to Yohnny the Priest to look for me, and Ay've tole Yohnny tal her, pay for carriage bring her to dis dock. She find barge all right.

MARTHY—Thank she'd mind yer clothes? Yuh're a simple nut, Dutchy. How old's she?

CHRIS—Twenty, Ay tank.

MARTHY—(*disapprovingly*) Yuh think? (*then laughing*) Ho-ho! Yuh're a funny stiff! Say, she's only a kid. Yuh ain't goin' to have her livin' on the barge, are yuh?

CHRIS—Yes. Ay try for keep her with me.

MARTHY—(*severely*) It's no dump for a kid, lemme tell yuh.

CHRIS—Ay tank—it's nice.

MARTHY—Nice? Ho-ho! Fur Gawd's sake! (*She suddenly assumes a bustling air.*) If the boat was docked this mornin' she'd ought to be here now—if she ain't got lost by your fool directions. I'll blow outa this quick. If she ever lamped me here yuh'd have to do some explainin', huh? (*irritably*) Why didn't yuh tell me this b'fore, yuh thickhead? Think I'd get sore when it's your kid comin'? Not much! That ain't Marthy's way. (*scornfully*) Think I'd break my heart to lose yuh? Commit suicide, huh? Ho-ho! Gawd! The world's full o' men, if that's all I'd worry about! (*sharply*) Heft me bag out o' there. I got a head on me this mornin'. (*Chris goes in room on left and returns with her bag, an aged rattan suitcase bound up with rope.*) Now I'll be beatin' it. I ain't lookin' for no hair-pullin' with no angry daughters when I ain't in shape. Gimme a dollar, huh? I'll drink her health for yuh. What's her name—Anna? I'll say: "Here's luck to Anna."

CHRIS—(*eagerly*) Sure tang. You have good celabrate for

me. (*He takes out a bill.*) Ay ain't gat one. You take dis two. (*with a grin*) Dat's better.

MARTHY—(*takes it—with a smile*) Yuh're a good guy, old Chris. I on'y hope my next's as good. (*abruptly, taking her bag under her arm*) Well, I'll be makin' a move. So long, Chris. (*They shake hands. She goes to the door.*) I'll see yuh sometime someplace if yuh're still of the boats and we'll have a drink together—to show we're frens, see?

CHRIS—Yes, py golly! Ve do dat for sure.

MARTHY—(*holding the door open*) And take a fool's advice and keep your Anna offen the barge. It's a bum game. So long. (*She starts to go out.*)

CHRIS—Good'bye.

MARTHY—(*suddenly retreating into the cabin—in a harsh whisper*) There's some dame just comin' aboard. Must be her, huh? She's comin' astern. Don't look so scared, yuh fool! I'll fix it. Leave it ter me. (*She digs him in the ribs.*) I'm tryin' ter sell yer somethin', get me? (*Chris stands waiting with a look of dazed apprehension. Anna appears on the deck before the doorway, carrying a suitcase. She can just make out Marthy's figure inside the doorway.*)

ANNA—(*addressing her*) Is there a Mr. Christophersen here?

MARTHY—In here, ma'am. (*then turning to Chris—in a loud tone*) I can't sell yuh nothin' for the cabin today, huh? Well, I'll try yuh again next time yuh're in port. Good day. (*She goes out, casting a critical look at Anna as she passes her just outside the door.*)

CHRIS—(*faintly—in answer to Marthy*) Good day. (*then raising his voice*) Anna?

ANNA—(*putting her head inside the cabin—uncertainly, as if the word were a strange one to her*) Father?

CHRIS—(*his eyes fixed hungrily on her face—in a whisper*) Anna! (*He is terribly nonplused at seeing her so pretty, so full grown, so well dressed, so modern, so different from what his idea of her had been. He shrinks back against the wall with an air of servile deference, murmuring*) Von't you come in cabin?

ANNA—(*her eyes still blinded by the sunshine outside*) Where are you, Father? The sun's in my eyes still. It's so dark in here at first. (*She comes into the cabin and stands before him, hesitating, confused, looking at him as at a stranger. She is a tall, blond, fully developed girl of twenty, built on a statuesque, beautifully moulded plan—a subject for a sculptor with the surprising size of her figure so merged into harmonious lines of graceful youth and strength as to pass unnoticed. There is something, too, of the statue in the perfect modelling of her face. But her expression is alert, mobile, intelligent. Only her wide blue eyes betray anything of the dreamer. They shine with an eager, wistful light. Her smile reveals her father's good nature, but in her it is more detached, induced by a feeling of confident self-sufficiency. She has her father's firm jaw also, but toned down from obstinacy to strength in repose. She speaks slowly with an English accent, her voice low but distinct and clear toned. She is dressed simply in a blue, tailormade suit.)*

CHRIS—*(looking about him with pitiful nervousness as if to avoid the appraising glance with which she takes in his face, his clothes, the surrounding room—his voice seeming to plead for her forbearance)* Anna!

ANNA—*(reminded of her duty, comes and kisses him self-consciously—then with a trace of genuine feeling awakening in her voice)* It's so good to see you, Father—at last—after all these years.

CHRIS—*(grasps her arms and looks into her face—then, overcome by a wave of fierce tenderness)* My little Anna, my darling girl . . . *kära flicka* . . .

ANNA—*(shrinks away from him, half-frightened)* I've forgotten it, Father—the old language. I have not spoken it since Mother died.

CHRIS—*(lets go of her arms and looks away)* Don't dem cousins speak Swedish?

ANNA—No. They forced me always to talk English to make me learn. I had to know it well to get on over there.

CHRIS—*(with a sigh)* Yes. Ay tank it's better, too. *(suddenly reminded of the situation—with a bustling air)* Py yimminy, Ay'm losing mind. Give me dat bag. *(He takes her bag and goes into room on the left saying as he does so)* Sat down, Anna, in dat rocker. Dat's best chair. You gat varm near stove. Ay put your bag in here. *(Anna sits down, staring about her with amused curiousity. Chris reappears.)* You like some tea? Ay make some right avay—good tea. *(He winks at her, begin-*

ning to recover his joviality now that the first strain of meeting is over.) You see! Ay'm first-rate cook for ole fallar. (*He goes to the locker to get tea.*)

ANNA—(*perfunctorily*) Yes, I would like a cup of tea.

CHRIS—(*coming back to the stove and making the tea*) You gat in dis morning all right?

ANNA—Yes. (*then frowning*) Why did you allow me to go to that awful dive to look for you? (*Chris hangs his head, shame-facedly. Anna continues with a trace of irritation.*) Didn't you receive my letter saying I was coming on the *Caronia*? I expected you'd be at the wharf when the ship docked. I looked all over for you for half an hour. I thought I must have missed you. I remembered we might not recognize each other.

CHRIS—(*with a sudden grunt of pain*) Eeh! Dat's so. Ay forgat dat.

ANNA—But why didn't you meet me? Didn't you want me to come to America? Is that why?

CHRIS—(*forcibly*) No, no, Anna! Ay vant you come. Ay vant it like hell, py golly!

ANNA—(*shocked for a second—then with an amused laugh*) Father!

CHRIS—(*with an embarrassed grin*) Eeh! Ay svear too much. All ole sailor fallar like me svear all time. Don't mean nutting. (*then seriously*) Ay ain't gat good clothes for meet you at steamer, dat's vhy Ay don't come. Only gat vork clothes. Ay never need clothes for dress up, ole fallar like me. (*He gets cups from the locker. Anna's amused eyes soften with a growing affection as she watches his clumsy bustling. He pours out the tea.*) Here. You take cup of tea and gat varm inside. It's chilly out in air.

ANNA—(*looking around her with an expression of amused wonderment*) You don't live here on this boat all the time, do you?

CHRIS—Yes. It's nice here.

ANNA—What a funny place for anyone to live in!

CHRIS—(*anxiously*) It's nice place—nice and clean—yust like home. Don't you like it, too?

ANNA—But it's so small. There's no room to turn about in.

CHRIS—Oh, Ay know it ain't big like house on shore, but

it's pooty good for ole fallar like me. (*persuasively*) Ay tank you like him very much, too, ven you gat used to place.

ANNA—And do you do all your cooking and washing yourself—right in this same tiny little room?

CHRIS—(*uneasily*) Yes. It's more easy for me dat vay. (*He gives her hand a kindly pat. She smiles up at him.*) Here. You drink tea—dan talk.

ANNA—(*after a hesitating sip, makes a wry face*) Ugh! Do you call that tea, Father? (*with a smile*) I see I'll have to teach you how to make tea sometime.

CHRIS—(*beaming at once*) Yes. You yust show me. Ay like learn from you.

ANNA—Sometime. (*after a pause*) You never said in your letters that you worked on a boat. I thought—

CHRIS—(*lying glibly*) Oh, Ay vork on land long time—as yanitor in house. Yust short time ago Ay gat dis yob 'cause Ay vas sick, need open air.

ANNA—(*with a laugh*) You'd never think so. You look healthy enough now. (*interestedly*) But what do you do on this boat? What does it do?

CHRIS—Oh, yust vork about. She's towed one port for load coal; dan towed oder port for unload. Ay yust keep watch on tow line, anchor her in harbor, sometimes raise small sail, tend to tangs on deck, steer sometime—yust easy vork for ole fallar.

ANNA—(*thoughtfully*) I remember that you wrote once, a long time ago, that you'd never go back to sea again.

CHRIS—(*his face darkening*) Yes. Ay svear dat ven your mo'der die.

ANNA—That was long ago. (*after a pause*) I can hardly remember her any more. (*leaning forward in her chair*) Tell me about Mother, Father. My cousins never seemed to care to speak much about her. I imagine she didn't get on well with them—that one year in Leeds before she died. But she was an educated woman—a clergyman's daughter—wasn't she?

CHRIS—(*gloomily—with evident reluctance*) Yes. Her mo'der die ven she vas kit. Her fa'der die yust couple months before she marry me. (*slowly*) It's better for him dat vay, so he never know she marry crazy, sailor fallar like Ay vas. He vas proud, hard man. Oh, your mo'der vas smart voman. She go to school all time till she marry me. She learn everytang. (*with a sad smile*) Only foolish tang she ever do is marry me. Ay vas vild, young sailor fallar dem day—good sailor, too—but good sailor don't make good husband, no!

ANNA—(*looking at him curiously, not knowing what to make of this confession*) But she—loved you, didn't she?—always?

CHRIS—(*flushing guiltily and trying to force a laugh*) Yes—Ay guess, Anna—but she vas fool for do it. Ay vasn't good enough, no. (*then with great feeling*) And Ay love her, Anna—alvays—and now, too!

ANNA—(*much moved, is silent for a while—then after a pause*) You were away at sea most of the time when I was little, weren't you? I don't remember you at all. And my cousins never mentioned you. I don't think they approve of—sailors. (*she laughs*) Why, if it hadn't been for your letters, I'd never have known I had a father.

CHRIS—(*sadly*) Yes. Ay vas on deep-sea voyage all time dem year.

ANNA—And my two brothers—I don't remember them at all, either.

CHRIS—Dey vas drowned ven you vas so little—fine, big boys.

ANNA—(*coming out of her reverie—with a sigh*) Well, you're back as a sailor again in spite of all your promises.

CHRIS—(*scornfully*) Dis ain't sailor yob. Any ole land-lubber do dis, py golly!

ANNA—But it's on the sea; and you wrote how you'd grown to hate the sea, I remember. Didn't you?

CHRIS—(*intensely*) An Ay do hate dat ole davil, py yimminy! (*argumentatively*) Dis ain't on sea, dis barge. She don't make no voyage at sea out sight of land. She yust gat towed on harbor, on canal, on river, on Sound—no deep sea—no rough vedder. She ain't ship. She's yust ole tub—like piece of land with house on it dat float but can't go no place by itself. Yob on her ain't sea yob.

ANNA—(*perplexed by his vehemence in proving this point of distinction*) Well—it doesn't matter, does it, as long as it's good for your health?

CHRIS—No, Ay don't gat yob on sea, Anna, if Ay die first!

Ay svear dat once. Ay keep my vord, py yingo! (*looking at her anxiously*) You don't like sea eider, Anna, Ay bet?

ANNA—I? I didn't like it coming over. I was sick most of the trip. The steerage was so dirty, and I didn't have money enough after I'd bought clothes to come second class. (*shaking her head*) No. I've lived inland so long. I like that best.

CHRIS—(*joyously*) Ay'm glad for hear you say dat, py golly! Dat ole davil sea, she ain't good for nobody. She kill your two bro'der, she kill your mo'der, too; she kill me too, if Ay stay on her.

ANNA—(*slowly—not understanding*) She killed Mother? But Mother died in Leeds.

CHRIS—(*shaking his head—darkly*) She kill her yust the same—by me. Ay vas avay on voyage. Ay don't come home.

ANNA—(*with a shudder*) Don't. Let's talk of something else.

CHRIS—(*after a pause—inquisitively*) You like sailor fallars, Anna?

ANNA—I've never known one. Why?

CHRIS—Dey vas bad fallars for young gel, Ay tank. (*Anna smiles.*) Never save money, gat drunk in port. Ay vas sailor myself. Ay know dat gang.

ANNA—(*laughing*) Oh, Father! And are the officers as bad as the men?

CHRIS—(*forcibly*) No good, eider. Yust slave drivers. Dey're vorser'n before the mast, py golly. (*suspiciously*) Vhy you ask about officer? You know one, yes?

ANNA—(*with a laugh*) No. Why? Does it worry you?

CHRIS—(*pleased*) Vorry? Not for you, Anna. Ay can tal you gat sense.

ANNA—(*more and more amused*) Thank you, Father.

CHRIS—(*sitting down beside her*) And now you tal me about yourself. You say in letter you learn oder yob—typewriter?

ANNA—Yes, indeed. I'm a full-fledged typist now, Father. (*Chris looks vague at this but nods his head.*) I only took a situation as a nurse temporarily. (*with a smile*) You didn't think I'd picked that out for a life work, did you?

CHRIS—You don't like take care of kits?

ANNA—Oh, I liked the children well enough, and the people themselves were kind to me. I was really more of a governess than anything else—a privileged character. I was allowed the use of their library and read a lot. (*impatiently*) Oh, it was nice and homelike—and stuffy!—and it bored me to death! I'd never have remained with them as long as I did—a year—if I hadn't an end in view. I wanted the money, I hoarded it like a miser, so that when I left them I could afford a course in stenography. That meant independence—a step along the right path. Besides, our cousins are not rich and they had made sacrifices to keep me in school until I was seventeen. I owed it to them to take myself off their hands.

CHRIS—You liked dem cousins?

ANNA—Indeed I did. They were always kind. I was like a daughter to them. (*with the same irrepressible impatience*) But they were so religious and strict, Father—prayers morning and evening—and so old-fashioned in their ideas—and so humble—and stuffy! I had to get out of their house finally—to breathe freely. And as a typist I made enough to live on my own and be myself.

CHRIS—(*vaguely mystified and impressed by all this*) And you vorked on dis new yob over dere?

ANNA—For over a year past—in a barrister's office—a first-class position.

CHRIS—Den why you leave dat yob? You vant travel, eh? (*hopefully*) You vant see your ole fa'der, maybe?

ANNA—Yes, that was part of the reason, I fancy. I was becoming fed up after the novelty wore off. But the thing which made me decide was that my employer—the barrister—a man of forty with a wife and children, fancy!—suddenly took it into his head to make love to me!

CHRIS—(*angrily*) Dirty svine!

ANNA—(*laughing*) Father! How funny you are! (*then making a gesture to silence him*) At first I pretended not to notice, but he wouldn't let me alone. I asked him to stop his silliness—he *was* ugly and silly—but that only made him worse. There was only one thing to do—leave. Then it came to me that I might as well make an entire new start if I wanted to get on in the world. I dreamed of the big opportunities for a woman over here in America—and here I am.

CHRIS—(*patting her hand approvingly*) Ay tank God for dat!

ANNA—(*her eyes sparkling*) And I'm not going to stop as a typist, either. My big hope is to work and save until I have enough to take a course in college. (*She laughs with a trace of self-mockery.*) You'd think to hear me I had some big life ambition. I haven't. I don't even know what course I want to take, or what I eventually want to become. It's all—in the air. (*intensely*) I only know I want to get away from being just a woman, to lead a man's life; to know as much as I can, and see and live as much as I can—to always have something new to work for. I won't grow stale—and married. I won't!

CHRIS—(*who has been staring at her face with awed admiration as if he were becoming aware of her beauty for the first time—enthusiastically*) You know you vas awful pooty gel, Anna? Ay don't blame dat fallar fall in love with you, py yimminy! Ay fall in love with you too, Ay vas him.

ANNA—(*embarrassed for a second—then with a smile*) That's just the way he used to talk, Father.

CHRIS—(*hurt—humbly*) Ain't no harm for your fa'der tal you dat, Anna.

ANNA—No, of course not. Only—it's so funny to see you and not remember anything. You're like a—a stranger at first.

CHRIS—(*sadly*) Ay s'pose. Dat's all my fault, too. Ay never come home only five time ven you vas kit in Sveden. You don't remember dat?

ANNA—No. (*thoughtfully*) But why did you never come home in those days? Why have you never come to Leeds?

CHRIS—(*slowly*) Ay tank, after your mo'der die, it's better for you you don't ever see me. And dem cousins don't vant it. Dey always hate me. (*He goes to a window in the rear and stands for a moment looking out at the harbor—then he turns to Anna—sadly*) Ay don't know, Anna, vhy Ay never come home Sveden in ole year. Ay alvays vant for come home end of every voyage. Ay vant see your mo'der, your bro'der, you ven you vas born—but—Ay don't come. Ay sign on oder ships—go South America, go Australia, go China, go every port all over vorld many time—but Ay never gat board ship sail for Sveden. Ven Ay gat money for pay passage home as passenger, den—(*he bows his head guiltily*) Ay forgat and Ay spend all money. Ven Ay tank again, it's too late. (*He sighs.*) Ay don't know vhy but dat's vay with most sailor fallar, Anna. Dat ole davil sea make dem crazy fools with her dirty tricks. It's so!

ANNA—(*who has watched him keenly while he has been speaking*—*musingly, with a trace of scorn in her voice*) Then you blame it all—on the sea. (*Then as if ashamed of her thoughts, she hastily summons a smile.*) Do you know you speak frightful English, Father? It's strange you don't know it better after so many years over here.

CHRIS—(*This strikes him funny and he slaps his thigh.*) Ho-ho! Ay'm stupid ole fallar, Ay guess. You teach me speak good, eh?

ANNA—(*laughing*) I'll try. You need it. When I begin a lesson I'll stop you every word you speak wrongly.

CHRIS—(*delighted*) Ho-ho! You stop me every vord Ay say, Ay tank. (*He starts to his feet as if suddenly reminded of something.*) Py golly, Ay forgat you ain't had nutting for eat yet. You must be hungry like shark, yes?

ANNA—I am—a little.

CHRIS—(*bustling to the stove*) Ay gat nice fresh eggs, bacon, bread and butter yust for you.

ANNA—(*rising to her feet*) I'll get an apron out of my bag, and you must let me get the lunch, Father.

CHRIS—(*shaking his head decidedly*) No, Ay don't stand for dat. (*He takes her gently by the shoulders and forces her to sit down again.*) Ay'm boss on dis boat. Ay do all vork. You sat down, Anna, dat's good gel.

ANNA—(*smilingly*) But I refuse to let you make the tea again, Father.

CHRIS—(*chuckling*) You vas English gel, Ay tank—so fussy with tea. Vell, you make tea. Dat's all. (*He gets down the frying pan, unconsciously singing his Josephine song. Anna listens, controlling her mirth with an effort until he comes to the "Tchee-tchee. Tchee-tchee," doing his pantomime conducting with the frying pan. Then she bursts into laughter.*)

ANNA—What a silly song! Where in heaven's name did you learn it?

CHRIS—(*with a grin*) Italian fallar on oder barge. Ay learn from him. (*He opens the locker door. A loud hail is heard from the dock above:* "Ahoy, on board the barge!" *Chris makes a quick movement toward the door.*) Ay tank dat's me dey call, Anna. Dey vant move barge fadder down dock for load, Ay guess. Ay come back in second. (*A louder hail, this time in angry impatient tones is heard. Chris opens the door and bawls out cheerfully*) Aye-aye. Ay'm comin'. (*He goes out, slamming the door, and can be heard stamping about at the stern, slacking the lines, yelling replies to the orders from the dock. Anna rises, gets an apron from her bag in the next room, and takes up the luncheon preparations where he left off. She puts bacon in the pan, sets the table, etc. She is standing at the stove with her back to the door when Chris reenters, his face red with exertion but grinning cheerfully. As he looks at Anna in her apron his face beams with a great happiness.*)

CHRIS—(*pretending to feel aggrieved*) Dat ain't fair, py yingo. You sat down.

ANNA—No, indeed. You sit down. You're the one who's tired now—after that work.

CHRIS—Ho-ho. Dat ain't vork for tough ole bird like me.

ANNA—Well, sit down. I've everything started and you're only in the way.

CHRIS—(*sits down and follows her every movement with a gloating happiness—with a great sigh*) Dis vas yust like home, see you cook in my ole cabin. Make me feel good, py golly, Anna, for see you!

ANNA—You've only one frying pan. I'll have to cook the eggs and potatoes together.

CHRIS—(*grinning*) Dat's vay Ay do—mix 'em all up in hash. Dat's easiest tang.

ANNA—What an uncomfortable way to live! And in there, where you sleep, there's hardly room for my bag. I don't see how you manage.

CHRIS—(*fidgeting uneasily*) Oh, Ay don't need large place. Dis is nice, Anna.

ANNA—(*authoritatively*) I don't think much of this kind of life at your age, Father. It's too hard. I could hear that man cursing at you from the dock just now.

CHRIS—(*with a grin*) Oh, dey all do dat.

ANNA—It's a shame. He shouldn't be allowed to speak that way to an old man. (*decidedly*) There'll be no excuse for your keeping this position, once I'm at work. I know it can't be good for you living this way at your time of life. And you hate the sea so much too. I know you'd be better off someplace where you wouldn't have the sea around you all the time to remind you of the past and make you sad. Don't you think so yourself?

CHRIS—(*vaguely alarmed*) Maybe, Anna.

ANNA—You've worked hard all your life, and you've recently been sick, you say. It's time you had a good rest. Let me do the working from now on. (*with a laugh*) I'm strong, sober and industrious; and two can live as cheaply as one if they make up their minds to it. We'll rent a little house together someplace.

CHRIS—(*trying to laugh it off*) Ay gat little house right here.

ANNA—(*disdainfully*) This wretched cabin—on a sooty, old barge!

CHRIS—(*squirming—with an attempt at carelessness*) Vell, ve don't talk no more about dat now, eh? Dere's plenty of time for tank of dat.

ANNA—(*throwing him a quick glance over her shoulder as she cooks*) Time? I'm not going to waste a moment. I can't afford to. I've very little money left. I read the employment advertisements in the New York papers on the boat coming over. I'm going to the city right after lunch. I shall simply have to find work at the first possible moment, Father.

CHRIS—(*stunned*) You go ashore—right after eat?

ANNA—Yes. Among other things, I've got to look for a room. Why, I've no place to sleep yet.

CHRIS—(*swallowing hard—in a choked tone*) But—you stay here, Anna.

ANNA—(*turning to him in surprise—sharply*) Stay here? On board this barge? You're joking, aren't you, Father?

CHRIS—No. You stay here.

ANNA—But how silly! How could I even if I cared to? Where could I sleep?

CHRIS—(*eagerly*) In oder room. Ay fix it all up for you— nice, clean blanket. Ay scrub all place yesterday for you.

ANNA—But that's your room. Where would you sleep?

CHRIS—Ay gat mattress, blanket for put on deck in here.

ANNA—No.

CHRIS—(*excitedly*) Yust suits ole fallar like me, sleep dat vay, Ay tal you, Anna!

ANNA—(*turns to the stove again, shaking her head*) No. Even if I'd consent to putting you out, I don't want to stay. These docks must be terribly awkward to get to and get from, aren't they?

CHRIS—(*not answering—sadly*) You don't like it here with me on barge—not even little bit, Anna?

ANNA—(*with a laugh*) Like it? It's funny and queer enough. I like it that way—but hardly as a place to live. Do you?

CHRIS—(*dully*) Yes, Ay do. It's nice for me. (*Anna turns and stares at him wonderingly. He hesitates—then continues more and more pleadingly.*) You don't know how nice it's on barge, Anna. You vait! You see! Here in dock, it's nutting. It's dirty ven ve load coal, Ay know. But you vait! Dat ain't for long. Dan tug come and ve gat towed out on voyage. No docks, no more dirt, no noise no more. Yust vater all around, and sun, and fresh air for make you strong, healthy gel. Ve go up Sound, up to Boston, around Cape Cod, Ay tank. You see many new tangs you don't see before. You like it on barge on vater, Ay'm sure you do, Anna. You gat moonlight at night, maybe; see steamer pass; see schooner make sail; see everytang dat's pooty. You need take rest like dat. You vork too much for young gel already. You don't vant for gat yob right avay soon's you land dis country.

ANNA—(*who has listened to him with growing amazement—hastily*) But I do! That's exactly what I want to do. I want to start in earning money the first minute I can. I've got to.

CHRIS—No. Ay gat money 'nuff for us two live on here.

ANNA—(*as if she still couldn't believe her ears*) Do you really mean to tell me that you expected me to live on this barge with you and go on trips with you?

CHRIS—(*earnestly*) Yes. Ay tank dat, Anna.

ANNA—(*half-exasperated*) But, Father, how silly! How could you ever dream—

CHRIS—(*imploringly—in excited tones*) No, Anna! Don't make fun for it! Ay tank maybe you vant stay with me. Ay don't see you for long time, you don't forget dat. Ay vant have you with me now. (*his voice trembles*) Ay'm gatting ole. Ay gat no one in vorld but you, Anna; and Ay'm so happy ven Ay know you come dis country. Now Ay see you yust one second—and you say you run avay again!

ANNA—(*deeply touched*) I *do* want to be with you, Father. That's why I'm anxious to get to work so that we can have a home together.

CHRIS—(*eagerly*) Ve do dat sometime. But please, Anna, don't go for gat yob right avay! (*as he sees signs of relenting in her face*) You vork too much. You take vacation, yes?

ANNA—(*her excited eyes plainly showing that the strangeness of his proposal appeals to her—hesitatingly*) Don't tempt me. I can't afford a vacation, Father. The trip over was my vacation.

CHRIS—(*pushing his argument*) In steerage! Dat's hell of fun for young gel! (*insistently*) For live on here don't cost nutting. You gat yob ashore whenever you vant—smart, pooty gel like you. It's cinch. But you vait. You take one voyage with me on barge, and you see. You like it.

ANNA—(*evidently considering it seriously—excitedly*) Fancy! It would be funny—and jolly. (*She laughs.*) A trip on a coal barge—seeing America! I'd almost like to, Father. It'd be such a queer thing to do, wouldn't it? But—I oughtn't—

CHRIS—(*hastily*) You come. Dat's good gel, py golly!

ANNA—Wait. How long will it take to Boston and back?

CHRIS—(*evasively*) Not very long. All depend on vedder.

ANNA—But how long?

CHRIS—Tree veek or so, about. Ay can't tell 'xactly. But only short time.

ANNA—And we'll leave here soon?

CHRIS—Yes, in couple day.

ANNA—And you'll promise this one trip will be your last, and you'll start living with me on land the minute I get a position?

CHRIS—At end of trip, if you still vant dat, Ay promise. Ve'll see den.

ANNA—(*bends down and kisses him—with a smile*) Then I'll go. (*with an excited laugh*) It'll be such a lark! Now, are you satisfied?

CHRIS—(*beaming*) Yes, Ay'm happy so, py golly, Anna!

ANNA—(*turning to the stove*) Then that's settled. Now we'll have lunch.

CHRIS—Ay tank Ay'm hungry for eat cow, py yimminy!

ANNA—(*turning on him and shaking a fork at him admonishingly*) Good gracious! Is that English you're speaking? Repeat after me or you get no lunch. I think. Say it!

CHRIS—(*chuckles—then carefully*) I think.

ANNA—*I'm* hungry enough.

CHRIS—*I'm* hungry enough.

ANNA—To eat a cow.

CHRIS—To eat a cow.

ANNA—(*pronouncing it herself with an effort*) By jimminy.

CHRIS—By yimminy.

ANNA—No! By jimminy.

CHRIS—By jim— No, Ay can't say dat.

ANNA—Yes, you can. It's easy. Listen! By yimminy.

CHRIS—(*delighted*) What's dat? Say it again.

ANNA—What's the matter? I said it right. By— (*She screws up her mouth.*)

CHRIS—(*prompting gleefully*) Yimminy!

ANNA—Yimminy. No. That's wrong. You're awful, Father. You've got me all mixed up.

CHRIS—(*jumping to his feet with a roar of laughter*) Ho-ho! (*He puts an arm around her waist—teasingly*) You vas Squarehead Svede just like me, py golly! (*She laughs in confusion, putting her hands over her ears as Chris bursts into the first lines of his Josephine song:*) "My Yosephine, come board de ship. Long time Ay vait for you—"

(*The Curtain Falls*)

ACT TWO
Scene I

SCENE—*Ten days later. The stern of the deeply laden barge,* Simeon Winthrop. *It is about midnight. Dense, impenetrable fog shrouds the barge on all sides, and she floats motionless on the dead calm of a silent sea. The bow of the barge is off right, the starboard bulwark facing front. Between the stern and the extreme left of stage, a blank wall of fog. The deck is about four feet above the water (the stage). In the stern, a lantern set up on an immense coil of thick hawser sheds a dull, filtering light on objects near it— the two heavy steel bits for making fast the tow lines, the wheel, its spokes glistening with drops of moisture. In the center, slightly right, of the visible stretch of deck, is the cabin, its two misty starboard windows glowing wanly from the light of the lamp inside, like two rheumy, old eyes peering into the fog. The chimney from the cabin stove rises a few feet above the roof.*

As the curtain rises, Anna is discovered standing near the coil of rope on which the lantern is placed. She has on a black, oilskin coat, dripping with moisture, but wears no hat. No trace of fear is revealed in her expression which is rather one of awed wonder. From inside the cabin comes the muffled sound of hammering. A moment later the door is flung open and Chris appears. He carries in one hand a box foghorn, worked by a lever on the side, and in the other another lantern which he sets on the cabin roof above the doorway. He is dressed in yellow oilskins—coat, pants, and sou'wester—and wears high sea-boots.

CHRIS—(*the glare from the cabin still in his eyes, peers blinkingly astern*) Anna! (*Receiving no reply, he calls again, this time with very apparent apprehension*) Anna!

ANNA—(*with a start—making a gesture with her hand as if to impose silence—in a strange, hushed voice*) Yes, Father. I'm here.

CHRIS—(*walks over to her, carrying the horn—solicitously*) You better go in cabin vere it's light. It ain't good for you to stay out here in fog.

ANNA—No. I'd rather stay on deck. I love the fog. It's so—(*she hesitates, groping for a word*) strange—and still. I feel as if I were—out of the world altogether.

CHRIS—(*spitting disgustedly*) Damn fog! (*Then he pats her on the shoulder comfortingly.*) It all come out all right, don't worry. In morning fog lift, Ay tank, and ve gat picked up. Tug boat come looking for us sure. (*His tone of reassurance does not ring true. He is plainly worried, casting quick glances from side to side into the fog bank.*) Dey ain't nutting you gat be scared for, Anna.

ANNA—(*with a trace of scorn*) Do I seem afraid? I'm not—not the least bit.

CHRIS—(*letting it out before he thinks*) Vell, if you ain't, Ay am, py yingo!

ANNA—You're afraid. Why? What of?

CHRIS—(*trying to cover up*) Oh, nutting. Ay only make yoke.

ANNA—No, you weren't. What is it? Tell me. (*as he hesitates*) Whatever it is, I want to know it. I won't be treated like a silly girl, Father. (*as he still hesitates*) Isn't the barge safe? Is anything wrong with it?

CHRIS—(*hastily*) No, she's all right. It's only fog vorry me.

ANNA—(*looking around her with confidence*) I'm sure it won't hurt us. (*in an awed tone*) It's so still—and beautiful.

CHRIS—(*moodily*) You don't talk like that, if you know her like me. Damn fog! It's vorst one her dirty tricks, py golly!

ANNA—Her?

CHRIS—Damn ole davil, sea.

ANNA—(*with a sigh of weary impatience*) Oh.

CHRIS—(*confessing his apprehension*) Ve must drift long vay since dat tow line bust. Tide going out, too. Ve drift right out to sea, dat's vorst; and Ay tank ve gat right in south steamer track from Boston, maybe. (*shaking his head*) Steamer don't see us, eider, in dis fog till she's right on board. Dat's tang vorry me. Ve don't vant gat run down.

ANNA—(*slowly*) It's strange to think of other ships being on this sea. It's so still. You wouldn't think there was another ship in the world.

CHRIS—(*displeased—staring at her for a moment—gruffly*) It's too much still, dat's yust trouble. (*He bends down over the horn.*) Maybe, Ay fixed dis horn so she vork now. Py golly, Ay hope so! (*He seizes the level and pumps it back and forth furiously. The horn gives a wheezing grunt, a last gasp, and then refuses to give forth a sound.*)

ANNA—(*frowning*) Don't.

CHRIS—(*glancing up at her*) Don't? Vat you mean?

ANNA—(*a bit confused*) Nothing—only—it makes a horrible noise, doesn't it? And it's so peaceful all around.

CHRIS—(*giving the lever a last, desperate jerk, straightens up panting*) Don't talk dat vay, Anna. Dat's foolish business. You don't tank or you don't say it. How's a steamer going look out for us, steer clear, if ve don't make noise? She can't see us in fog. (*kicking the useless horn irritably*) Py damn! It's queer, Ay tal you. Ain't it yust luck dis horn gat bust yust ven ve need him most? Ay try hard for fix him, too. Ain't no use. He's alvays been good, loud horn oder time. It's funny, yes. (*shaking his fist out at the sea—angrily*) Dat's oder one your dirty tricks, ole davil! (*then grumblingly*) Your first voyage on barge, Anna, all dis gat happen. No, it's Yonah voyage from time ve sail.

ANNA—(*with a smile at his childishness*) And am I the Jonah? Don't be superstitious, Father. The trip has been wonderful. Everything's been so jolly—and different—since we left New York. And now—drifting all alone in the fog—I wouldn't miss it for the world. I never knew living on ships was so—different from land. And the sea—I hadn't the slightest idea of what it could mean, before. Why, I'd love to work on it, I know I would, if I were a man. I don't wonder you've always been a sailor.

CHRIS—(*vehemently*) Dat's fool talk, Anna. You only see nice part so far. Dat ain't sea, Ay tal you. (*then returning to a grumbling tone*) But it's funny, dis voyage. Sometang wrong somevere. Vyh dey put dis barge last one on tow? Oder time she's alvays first or second one. If she's first or second dis time, nutting don't happen. Ven tow rope break dat vay, dan tug know right quick, come right back and pick us up. But she's last barge dis time, and tug don't know right avay ven she steam slow in fog. Ven she do know ve're adrift, it's too late. She can't stop, anyhow, drop oder barges in fog, look for us. She gat keep dem oder barges safe.

ANNA—Where were we when the tow rope broke, do you think, Father?

CHRIS—Ve vas somevere near end Cape Cod, Ay guess. Dan rope bust and ve drift out on tide—straight for deep sea, too!

ANNA—(*thrilled*) Then we're out on the deep sea now?

CHRIS—Py golly, Ay'm afraid, yes.

ANNA—(*drawing a deep breath and staring into the fog*) But it's so still! There don't seem to be any waves.

CHRIS—It's calm dat vay sometime in heavy fog. It's luck for us, py yingo! Dis barge is load so deep, she ship big vave, she go to bottom like stone, Ay bet.

ANNA—(*not frightened—railingly*) Then we *are* having *some* good luck, in spite of my being a Jonah.

CHRIS—(*shaking his head*) Yust look at oder tangs happen. It's funny. Yust look at dat fallar on barge tree. He's drunk ven ve sail, and he heave me rotten ole tow line ain't no good. Ay know dat tow line break, Anna, if big svell come; and it happen yust like dat. Ay tal him at time, dan he curse, call me Squarehead fool, tal me go to hell, vouldn't heave me oder rope. Dan he keep drunk all voyage on bottles, Ay bet, and dis evening he's asleep ven fog come down, and ven line snap he asleep, he's too drunk, he don't know notting happen— don't give damn, eider, dat fallar don't, ve gat drowned, gat wrecked, py yimminy! (*with a sudden burst of fury*) Py golly, Ay bet you dat fallar's sorry ven Ay next meet him ashore! Py golly, Ay bet Ay grab hold his ears, knock his head on ground till he gat sense in it. Yes, Ay svear Ay beat hell of him, py yingo!

ANNA—(*astonished*) Father!

CHRIS—Oh, Ay'm nice, quiet ole fallar till Ay gat mad. Dan Ay'm not so, no!

ANNA—(*pointedly changing the subject*) Whereabouts do you think we are now, Father—near what land, I mean?

CHRIS—Ay can't tal. Maybe ve're yet near end Cape. Dere's two big lights end of Cape. Maybe ve see dem, but fog's so damn tick, Ay don't know. (*He peers about him and then shakes his head hopelessly.*) Ve ought for hear fog horn anyvay, ve gat near shore. Maybe tide turn and ve drift back ashore on Cape some place. Dat's all right calm night like dis. Py golly, Ay hope so!

ANNA—(*staring seaward*) I don't. I'd like everything to stay just as it is—just drift on and on like this.

CHRIS—(*angrily*) Till steamer run us down and ve gat drowned, eh?

ANNA—(*recklessly*) Oh, I don't care what happens! (*then looking at her father with a sudden curiosity*) But you—an old sailor—why are you so—so afraid?

CHRIS—(*sullenly*) Ay'm not scared for myself, Anna. Ay've seen many storm, many fog vorse dan dis, but Ay'm still alive. Ay'm scared for you, yes, py yimminy!

ANNA—(*easily*) You needn't be. I'm not.

CHRIS—All ole sailor gat alvays scared of sea a little ven dey gat sense. Only young fallar dat don't know don't gat scared, and dey gat drowned very quick if dey don't learn better. Dat ole davil, she don't like for fallar gat fresh with her. She kill dem fallar.

ANNA—(*with a little laugh*) So you think I don't know enough to be afraid?

CHRIS—(*nodding his head solemnly*) You don't know dat ole davil, Anna. (*abruptly*) Ve keep quiet one minute, Anna. Ay vant listen. (*He stands turning his head, vainly endeavoring to catch some sound.*) Ay'm going up in bow, take look, and listen for horn.

ANNA—All right. I'll stay here.

CHRIS—You better go in cabin, read book. Dan you don't tank so much.

ANNA—(*impatiently*) Why don't you want me to think? Are you afraid I'll get frightened? I promise you—

CHRIS—(*interrupting*) No, not dat. (*doggedly*) Only it ain't good—tank so much out here in fog. (*She turns away without answering. He stares at her for a moment with troubled eyes.*) You ain't gat no hat on head, eider. You catch cold, Anna.

ANNA—I don't want a hat. The fog makes my head feel so nice and cool. (*as he still stands staring at her—with sudden irritation*) I'm all right, Father. Attend to whatever you have to, and don't bother about me.

CHRIS—(*goes to the cabin and takes the lantern off the roof. Then he turns again to Anna—uneasily*) You act funny tonight, Anna. You ain't sick?

ANNA—(*shortly*) No. How silly! I'm feeling better than I ever did.

CHRIS—(*gloomily—as if struck by some change in her voice*) You vas queer gel, Anna. Ay tank maybe Ay'm damn fool for bring you on dis voyage. (*with a sigh*) Vell, you gat yob on shore— Ay gat yob, too—yust soon ve gat back to New York. Dat's best tang for you—yob in country, py yingo!

ANNA—(*with a shudder of disgust*) Please don't talk about—that—not until we do get back, Father. All those things, all my plans seem so far away now—and dead! I don't care to think of them. They're only the outside of me. They don't matter one way or the other. It's too—big—out here—to even consider them. I feel—something way down inside me—something I've never felt before—tonight. (*She laughs helplessly.*) But I'm talking silly, aren't I, Father?

CHRIS—(*stares at her moodily for a moment—then sadly*) Ay'm going up bow. Ay be back in minute. (*He goes along the deck on the port side and disappears forward. Anna sighs with relief when he is gone, and sits down on the coil of rope beside the lantern, her eyes fixed with a dreamy gaze out into the fog. After a pause Chris returns carrying the lantern, dragging along the deck behind him the line of the broken hawser.*)

CHRIS—(*stops and holds the lantern so the light shines full on the frayed rope—in querulous tones of vexation*) Look at dis, Anna. Yust look once! All rotten, py golly! It's ole rope must be made fast on Noah's Ark one time, Ay bet! (*indignantly*) Dats nice trick for dat fallar heave me tow line like dis! Drunk fool! Ay beat his head for him, py yimminy!

ANNA—(*impatiently*) It's too late to get mad about it now.

CHRIS—Dey ought put him in yail ten year for dis.

ANNA—(*irritably*) Oh! (*Then seeing the hurt expression on her father's face, she forces a smile.*) Drop the old rope, Father. It's no use crying over spilt milk. (*patting the coil of hawser invitingly*) Come. Sit down by me. There's nothing else you can do, is there?

CHRIS—(*dully*) No. Ain't nutting Ay can do more.

ANNA—You must be tired, too. Sit down.

CHRIS—(*sinks down beside her with a sigh. There is a pause during which he stares at the lantern despondently—worriedly*) It's gatting pooty late in night, Anna. You better turn in in cabin, get some sleep.

ANNA—Sleep? You don't think I could sleep tonight, do you?

CHRIS—Ay know you must be vorried, but ve come out all right, you see.

ANNA—Worried? It isn't that. How often must I tell you— (*She bites her lips and turns away from him.*)

CHRIS—(*after a pause*) You gat rest anyvay, you lay down. Must be near eight bells now, Ay guess.

ANNA—(*interestedly*) Eight bells? What time is that?

CHRIS—Twelve o'clock.

ANNA—It's queer I know so little about sea language. Coming from a family of sailors, I ought to.

CHRIS—No. It's better you don't. It don't do nobody no good, know dem tangs.

ANNA—(*as if she hadn't heard*) Funny my cousins never talked about the sea. I don't think I ever heard them mention it.

CHRIS—(*with a grunt of satisfaction*) Dey're farm people. Deir fa'der and mo'der lived on farm in Sveden before dey go to England.

ANNA—Yes, now I remember, they were always talking about farms. It was stupid listening to them.

CHRIS—You don't like live on farm, Anna? It must be nice, Ay tank.

ANNA—No, I would not. (*with a laugh*) And you wouldn't, either. You'd die if they put you on a farm—and you know it. You belong out here. (*She makes a sweeping gesture seaward.*) It's so much finer. But not on a coal barge. You belong on a ship—a real ship—sailing on every ocean— going all over the world.

CHRIS—(*moodily*) Ay've done dat many year, Anna, ven Ay vas damn fool. Ay gat better sense, now Ay'm ole fallar.

ANNA—(*disappointed*) Oh. (*After a pause she speaks dreamily*) Were the men in our family always sailors—as far back as you know about?

CHRIS—(*shortly*) Yes. Damn fools.

ANNA—(*with keen interest*) Tell me about them.

CHRIS—(*disgustedly*) Ain't anytang for tal much. It's all same fool tang every one. All men in our village on coast, dey go to sea. Ain't nutting else for dem to do. Dat ole davil sea, she kill dem all sooner, later. My fa'der die on board ship in Indian Ocean. He's buried at sea. Ay don't never know him only little bit. He only gat home in village once in long, long time. Dan my tree bro'der, older'n me, dey go on ships, too.

Dan Ay ship to sea, too. Dan my mo'der—Ay ain't gat no sister—she's left all lone. She die pooty quick after dat—all lone. Ve vas all avay on voyage ven she die. (*He pauses sadly.*)

ANNA—(*absorbed*) And the others—your brothers—and my mother's people?

CHRIS—Your mo'der's uncle, he's vashed overboard in Western Ocean. One my uncles, he die ashore in hospital, Singapore. He gat fever ven his ship's dere. Two my bro'der, dey gat lost on fishing boat same like your bro'der vas drowned. My oder bro'der, he save money, give up sea, den he die home in bed. He's only one dat ole davil don't kill. (*defiantly*) But me, Ay bet you Ay die ashore in bed, too! Ay bet you dat, Anna! Ay'm not fool like Ay vas no more.

ANNA—Were all these men just sailors?

CHRIS—Able body seamen, most of dem. (*with a certain pride*) Dey vas all smart seamen, too—A one.

ANNA—(*with a trace of disappointment*) None of them ever rose to be officers?

CHRIS—No. Ay don't tank so. (*then shyly*) Ay vas bo'sun.

ANNA—Bo'sun?

CHRIS—Dat's kind of officer. He's next to mates on ship.

ANNA—(*with a glad smile*) I didn't know that. Why didn't you tell me before? Tell me about it now. What does he do?

CHRIS—(*after a second's satisfaction, plunged into gloom again by his fear of her enthusiasm*) Hard vork all time. Bum grub and small pay. It's rotten, Ay tal you, for go to sea.

ANNA—(*hurt*) Oh!

CHRIS—(*determined to disgust her with sea life—volubly*) Dey're all fool fallar, dem fallar in our family. Dey all vork rotten yob on sea like dog for nutting. Ay know! Dey ain't kind fallar make officer. Dey're damn fool stupid fallar don't know nutting but yust sailor vork, don't vant for know, don't care nutting but yust gat big pay day in pocket, gat drunk, gat robbed, ship avay again on oder voyage. Dey don't come home. Dey don't do anytang like good man do. And dat ole davil, sea, sooner later, she swallow dem up!

ANNA—(*after a pause—thoughtfully*) And did all the women of the family marry sailors?

CHRIS—(*eagerly, seeing a chance to drive home his point*) Yes; only your grandmo'der she's only one gat sense, she don't.

And it's bad on dem vomen like hell vorst of all. Dey don't see deir men only once in long vile. Dey sit and vait all lone. Maybe, every day, deir men gat wrecked, gat sick, gat drowned—dey don't know. And ven deir boys grow up, go on sea, dey sit and vait some more. (*vehemently*) Any gel marry sailor, she's crazy fool! Ay know it! Your mo'der, she tal you same tang if she's alive. She know it! (*with great sorrow*) Dat kill her, too. It's my fault for going on sea after Ay marry her. Ay vas stupid fallar dem day. Ay don't gat sense till too late, and Ay'm sorry all year after for dat. (*He shakes his fist seaward.*) And Ay hate dat ole davil, sea, for make me crazy like dat! (*He relapses into an attitude of somber brooding—after a pause*) Ay tank dat ole davil, she hate vomen, yes? She take all men avay and kill dem so's dey never go back home to vomen.

ANNA—(*very thoughtfully—saddened by his words*) It is a strange life—people who go to sea and the ones they leave behind. But I don't feel that the sea hates me—not tonight. (*Chris grunts disapprovingly but makes no reply. After a pause Anna continues dreamily.*) It's funny, Father. I do feel strange tonight. I feel—so old!

CHRIS—(*mystified*) Ole?

ANNA—Yes—as if I'd lived a long, long time—out here in the fog; as if I'd come back home after a long visit away someplace. It all seems so—familiar—as if I'd been here before many times—on boats—in this same fog. And yet of course I know that's silly.

CHRIS—(*gruffly*) Anybody feel funny dat vay in fog.

ANNA—(*persistently*) But why don't I feel afraid? I ought to, oughtn't I, a girl who's always lived inland? And you've told me what danger we're in. But I don't feel afraid the least bit. I don't feel anything—but—(*she gropes helplessly for words*) restful—as if I'd found something I'd always been seeking—as if this were the place for me to be—and I feel happy! (*exultantly*) Yes—happier than I've ever been anywhere before! (*As Chris makes no comment but a heavy sigh, she continues wonderingly.*) It's queer for me to feel that way, don't you think?

CHRIS—(*a grim foreboding in his voice*) Ay tank Ay'm damn fool for bring you on voyage, Anna.

ANNA—But why—if I'm happy here with you? Don't you want me to be?

CHRIS—(*gloomingly*) It ain't right kind, dat happiness, no!

ANNA—(*impressed by his tone—in a low voice*) How do you know? You talk—queer—tonight, yourself, Father. You act as if you thought—as if you were afraid something was going to happen to us.

CHRIS—Only God know dat, Anna.

ANNA—(*slowly*) Then it will be God's will—what does happen.

CHRIS—(*starts to his feet—with fierce protest*) No! Dat ole davil, sea, she ain't God! (*In the abrupt silence which follows these words a steamer's whistle sounds—faint, far-off, mournful, muffled by the fog. Anna straightens herself; a tense quiver runs over her body; a glow of excitement comes into her eyes. Chris, his hand instantly raised to his ear, strains his whole body in the direction of the sound in a desperate effort to solve its significance. As the sound flows into silence, his face lights up with tremendous relief. He stutters frantically with a joy bordering on hysteria*) Tug boat! Tug boat vistle! Ay know him, py golly! She come look for us, Anna! Pick us up! All's vell! Ve fetch Boston in morning. You take train back to New York. Gat yob. No more voyage for you, py yimminy! It ain't good for you on sea, no! (*He shuffles his feet in a kind of grotesque dance and sings with wild joy:*) "My Yosephine, come board de ship. Long time Ay vait for you. Tchee-tchee. Tchee-tchee."

ANNA—(*who, at the first mention of the tug boat, has bent forward in a dejected, listless attitude, puts her hands over her ears—in sharp annoyance*) Please stop that, Father! (*He stops, open-mouthed. She adds vehemently*) I hate that silly song! (*then apathetically*) It is the tug boat looking for us, you think?

CHRIS—Ay'm sure. Must be tug boat. She's closer dan she sound, too. Vind blow sound avay from us.

ANNA—(*half to herself—bitterly*) So it's all going to end—like that!

CHRIS—Ssshh! Time ve hear oder vistle. (*They listen. After a moment the same whistle is heard, perceptibly louder and clearer. As the sound dies away, Chris' expression falls into gloom again.*)

ANNA—(*watching his face—eagerly*) Well? Is it—?

CHRIS—(*shaking his head*) No. Ay make mistake. Ain't tug

boat. (*with terrified bewilderment*) Ay vas sure—but no—ain't tug boat—no—py damn—Ay know dat now. (*He stands as if facing this new situation had benumbed his body.*)

ANNA—(*her voice thrilling once more with life and energy—springing to her feet*) Then what can it be, do you think?

CHRIS—(*his voice trembling*) Steamer vistle—big steamer. (*appalled, as if he hadn't thought of this before*) Ve're in her course! She's coming dis vay! Ve're in track! (*overcome with terror*) She don't know ve're here. Ve gat make noise, py God! (*He pounces down on the foghorn, pumping the lever back and forth frenziedly, forgetting in his terror that this is useless.*)

ANNA—(*in a calm tone of command*) Stop that, Father! (*He stops and stares up at her stupidly.*) You know the horn is broken. Don't get so excited. (*She lays her hand on his shoulder reassuringly.*)

CHRIS—(*brought back to himself, gets to his feet—dully*) Ay vas sure it's tug boat. (*hanging his head sheepishly with a shamed side glance at his daughter*) You tank Ay'm big coward, Anna, for gat scared dat vay?

ANNA—(*quickly*) No. You were excited, that's all. (*Chris lifts his head with a relieved expression and is about to speak when Anna lifts her hand warningly.*) Ssshh! (*The whistle sounds again with a loud full note.*)

CHRIS—(*shocked this time into an instant, calculated activity*) She's bearing down fast, py golly! She pass close by. (*He grabs up his lantern and strides with quick heavy steps astern. He points to one of the steel bits to which a small rope is made fast.*) Look, Anna! (*commandingly, as she remains motionless, staring spellbound out into the fog*) You look here quick, Anna! Ve ain't gat time for dream now, py golly! Dat steamer run us down, maybe, py yimminy!

ANNA—(*aroused—running to his side—excitedly*) What is it, Father?

CHRIS—(*taking hold of rope*) You see dis rope?

ANNA—Yes, Father.

CHRIS—It's painter—painter of small boat. Ay launch her early in night ven you vas in cabin. Ay don't tal you for fear Ay make you scared. (*holding his lantern over the stern on the far [port] side*) See. She's all right. Ay fix her so's ve gat avay if anytang happen to barge. Ay put in tinned meat, cracker, plenty vater. She's all right. (*He strides back to the bit.*) Look, Anna! Ay make half turn on painter. She's easy for cast off dat vay, see? (*He illustrates.*)

ANNA—Yes, Father, I see.

CHRIS—If anytang happen you cast dis off. You tumble over side ven Ay yell to you. You gat in boat damn quick, you hear? You push off, you find oars in her, you row avay like hell, you hear?

ANNA—(*protestingly—her voice frightened for the first time*) But you? I won't go till you—

CHRIS—(*fiercely*) Don't vait for me, you hear! (*The whistle of the steamer sounds again seemingly very much nearer this time.*)

ANNA—(*with a startled gasp*) Oh!

CHRIS—She's pooty close, by golly! She steam full speed ahead, Ay tank—take chance. Dey don't care for poor davil like us. (*grasping her arm as he turns away*) You stay here, Anna. Don't move one step now! (*He strides toward the cabin.*)

ANNA—(*a bit hysterically*) Where are you going?

CHRIS—In cabin. Gat life preserver. You vait. (*He disappears in the cabin but returns almost immediately with two life preservers.*) Here! You gat dis on you. (*He adjusts it on her with quick, capable fingers.*) Dere! You're all right. You halp me, now. (*She helps him get his on. Her hands tremble as she fumbles awkwardly with the straps. He pats her on the back reassuringly.*) Don't gat scared, Anna. Keep your head now! Maybe dat steamer don't—but if she do, you yump quick, Anna, gat in boat. Ain't no time for stop, tank. (*The steamer's whistle sounds again, close on the port side.*)

ANNA—(*with a gasp*) But you? I won't get in the boat without you.

CHRIS—(*roughly*) Shut up! No time for talk more. You do vat Ay tal you, Anna. (*then more kindly*) Ay'm all right. Ay gat stay on ship till Ay know she's lost for sure. Dan Ay yump over side. You pick me up in boat. (*He puts the end of the painter in her hand.*) Remember! Ven Ay yell, you cast off and yump in boat. Ay gat go now. Ay vave light, maybe dey see it. (*He hurries to the cabin.*)

ANNA—(*fearfully—in a trembling whisper*) Father!

CHRIS—(*clambers to the roof of the cabin and peers out to*

port) Ay can't see no lights. (*He swings the lantern in a circle over his head. The steamer's whistle again sounds, this time seeming to boom out of the fog right over the barge. Chris waves the lantern frenziedly and curses*) Py God! Dem damn fools! (*Then he sets the lantern down and, forming a megaphone with his two hands, shouts stridently:*) Ahoy! Ahoy dere! Ahoy on board steamer! (*As through a sudden break in the fog a loud noise of throbbing engines and swishing waves sweeps over the barge. Chris' face is turned toward the bow. He gives a loud yell of angry dismay*) Dere she come! She hit us on port bow sure! Cast off, Anna! (*Lantern in hand, he jumps to the deck and leaps madly astern to where the white-faced Anna stands with the painter she has freed from the bit in her hands. He snatches it from her.*) Good gel! (*He grabs her in one arm around the waist, letting the lantern go, and slings her over the port side like a bag of meal.*) Over with you! (*A thin wail sounds from the fog overhead:* "Barge dead ahead!" *Chris stands with one foot on the port bulwark, ready to jump, his eyes turned toward the bow. A prolonged, ear-racking blast of the steamer's whistle seems to shatter the fog to fragments as*

The Curtain Falls)

SCENE II

SCENE—*The main cabin on board the British tramp steamer* Londonderry—*a quadrangular room with a row of portholes on the right looking out toward the bow of the ship. Beneath the portholes, a long bench with cushions. In front of the bench, a large table with a lighted, green-shaded reading lamp in the center. In the rear wall, several portholes looking out to port. In the left wall, two doors opening on the officers' quarters and, past them, to the bridge deck beyond. Against the wall between the doors, a lounge. Several chairs are placed near the table. A large, dark-colored rug covers most of the floor.*

The time is in the half hour immediately following the running down of the barge by the Londonderry.

As the curtain rises, Captain Jessup enters from the doorway in rear. He is a slim, well-knit man of sixty or so with iron-grey hair, beard and mustache. His voice is high-pitched and shrill, with a querulous, irritated quality which is belied by his good-humored smile, and the kindly expression of his keen blue eyes. His immaculate, well-fitting uniform gives him the general, dapper aspect of a naval officer. He speaks back to some one who is following him — irritably) A loaded barge—we were right aboard of her in the fog before you could say Jack Robinson.

MR. HALL—(*follows his chief into the cabin, his eyes still blinking with sleep, buttoning up his coat as if he were just finishing dressing. He is a tall, spare man of middle age, with a long, gaunt clean-shaven face. His thin-lipped, wide mouth seems perpetually in a grim determination not to smile and to utter as few words as possible. His uniform is old and shiney. He mutters drowsily in answer to the captain)* They'd just given me a call for the watch, sir. I was turning out—half-asleep—when the smash came.

CAPTAIN JESSUP—This damn fog! Bad as the Channel! No horn, no lights, no warning of any sort—and there she was dead ahead! Just time to throw the wheel hard a-port and—bang!—we were into her. We'd slowed down a minute before, though. Lucky!

HALL—(*with awakening concern*) A hard hit, sir?

CAPTAIN JESSUP—No. Not to appearances, at least. Andersen is forward having a look. Glancing blow on the starb'rd quarter. Enough to finish the scow, though. She heeled over and went down like a rock, I believe. Loaded deep. A stroke of fortune we didn't hit her full on or—(*he shrugs his shoulders*) we'd have been damned unlucky, too.

HALL—I thought I heard Andersen getting a boat lowered.

CAPTAIN JESSUP—(*disgusted*) Yes—had to do it. One of the men reported having seen a small boat almost alongside right after we hit. Two men in it. They hailed us, too. Oh yes, plenty of hails when it was too late! Not a second before. Couldn't leave the beggars adrift, though. So—stopped.

HALL—Will we have to put back to Boston, sir?

CAPTAIN JESSUP—Dammit, no! The damage won't be serious enough to warrant that. Can't be. You'll see. Nothing so bad that we can't patch up at sea and keep our course. Temporary repairs'll do. By Jove, they'll have to! Now we're at sea, we'll keep at sea, Hall.

HALL—Yes, sir.

CAPTAIN JESSUP—Hmmph! You'd better get forward. Have a look at things and see what you think. And set her going on her course as soon as those beggars are aboard.

MR. HALL—Yes, sir. (*He turns to go.*)

CAPTAIN JESSUP—Oh, and tell the steward I want him, will you?

HALL—Yes, sir. (*He goes out. The captain paces back and forth nervously. A moment later the steward appears in the doorway, rear. He is a thin, undersized young fellow whose weak, characterless face wears a look of ingratiating servility. A suggestion of feeble blond mustache fringes his upper lip. He coughs respectfully to attract the captain's attention.*)

CAPTAIN JESSUP—Oh, Steward. Have they picked up those barge beggars yet?

THE STEWARD—They're bringing them alongside now, sir, I think. I heard their voices. Sounded quite close up, sir.

CAPTAIN JESSUP—(*grimly—as if speaking aloud to himself*) Drunk, I suppose—and forgot to blow any horn. A nice go! Well, we'll make the beggars sweat for their passage down to give them a lesson.

THE STEWARD—(*concealing a smile—volunteers the information apologetically*) One of them—seems to be a woman, sir.

CAPTAIN JESSUP—Eh? What's that? A woman?

THE STEWARD—Yes, sir.

CAPTAIN JESSUP—What would a woman be doing on that tub? You must be mistaken.

THE STEWARD—(*noncommittally—fearing he has put his foot in it*) Perhaps I'm wrong, sir.

CAPTAIN JESSUP—(*irritably*) What made you think— How do you know, eh?

THE STEWARD—One of the voices sounded like a woman's, sir.

CAPTAIN JESSUP—Oh, that—voices in fog—may sound like anything. (*But he shakes his head, muttering with half-*

amused vexation) A woman—hmmph! Some drunken slut, too, I'll wager—a barge woman! Eh, well— (*He notices the steward still waiting and is brought back to himself.*) Oh yes, what I wanted you for. The beggars may have taken a wetting over board. They'll need coffee—something hot. Turn out the cook—or—see to it, eh?

THE STEWARD—Yes, sir.

CAPTAIN JESSUP—And tell them to bring the barge— hmmph—persons in to me here. I'll want to have a look at them at once.

THE STEWARD—Yes, sir. (*He goes out. The captain resumes his pacing. Paul Andersen appears in the doorway, left rear. He is a tall, broad-shouldered, blond young fellow of about twenty-five with a strong-featured, handsome face marred by a self-indulgent mouth continually relaxed in a smile of lazy good humor. His blue eyes, large and intelligent, have a dreamy, absent-minded expression. His low deep voice drawls a little as he speaks. He is dressed in the simple blue uniform of a second mate.*)

ANDERSEN—I've had a look up for'ard, sir.

CAPTAIN JESSUP—Eh, well? How does it look?

ANDERSEN—No harm done, sir, to speak of. No leak any-where that I could find. A few of the plates to starb'rd are bent in a bit. That seems to be all, sir.

CAPTAIN JESSUP—(*rubbing his hands together with a grunt of satisfaction*) Hmmph! That's good, Andersen. That's excellent, eh? I was afraid we might have to put back to Boston for repairs. No end of a nasty business, that! No end of ex-planation to make on all sides. Not our fault, though. They couldn't say that. No horn, no lights, nothing!

ANDERSEN—(*amused at the captain's warmth—with his lazy smile*) Yes, sir. They could hardly blame us.

CAPTAIN JESSUP—(*abruptly*) She's on her course again. Those barge beggars must be on board, eh?

ANDERSEN—Yes, sir. The steward said you wanted to see them. They're waiting on deck.

CAPTAIN JESSUP—Tell them to come in. (*as Andersen turns to the door*) Oh—the steward was saying he thought one of them was a woman?

ANDERSEN—Yes, sir.

CAPTAIN JESSUP—(*disgustedly*) I was hoping he was mistaken. You've seen—the lady?

ANDERSEN—Yes, sir. I talked with her for a second.

CAPTAIN JESSUP—Some drunken wench, I suppose?

ANDERSEN—(*smiling*) No, sir—not exactly.

CAPTAIN JESSUP—Eh? A barge woman!

ANDERSEN—(*with a laugh*) Oh, I know the kind they usually are. But she isn't that. She's the daughter of the old Swede on the barge. It seems she was keeping him company on this one trip for the fun of the thing.

CAPTAIN JESSUP—Fun! A likely story! Even so—what kind of girl—daughter of a barge hand!

ANDERSEN—I don't know. I only spoke with her a second. But you'll be surprised, sir, when you see her. She seems very well educated. Spoke correct English without any accent. (*He smiles.*) And as far as looks go—she's a corker.

CAPTAIN JESSUP—(*with a twinkle in his eye*) Aha! That's a reason for standing up for her, what? Well, let me have a look at beauty in distress. Tell them to come in.

ANDERSEN—Yes, sir. (*He goes out and can be heard calling*) This way, please. (*A moment later Anna enters, followed by her father and Andersen. Once inside, after a quick glance at the captain, Anna stands hesitatingly. She does not seem embarrassed but looks about the room with eager curiosity. Chris pulls off his sou'wester as he enters, and stands awkwardly, turning it over in his hands. His eyes avoid the captain. He is full of an old sailor's uneasiness at being called before the Old Man. Andersen remains by the door, observing every move of Anna's with a greedy admiration.*)

CAPTAIN JESSUP—(*The stern frown he has prepared for their reception disappears as his eyes meet Anna's. He is plainly astounded by her appearance and becomes embarrassed in his turn. Finally he points to a chair by the table.*) Hmmph! Won't you—er—sit down, Miss—?

ANNA—(*with smiling assurance*) Thank you, Captain. (*She sits down.*)

CAPTAIN JESSUP—(*more than ever taken aback by the unexpected refinement of her tone*) Sorry this—unfortunate accident—couldn't be avoided, you know. Fog so cursed thick, couldn't see your hand before you. No horn, you know.

(*Angry at himself for this blundering explanation, he turns furiously on Chris.*) You, bargee! Why didn't you keep your horn going, eh, you idiot? Were you drunk—or asleep—or what?

CHRIS—(*humbly*) Horn vas broke, sir. Ay try for fix him but Ay can't gat him vork. He vas alvays good, loud horn before dis time.

CAPTAIN JESSUP—Bah! Excuses! Damn carelessness, that's what! Too lazy to fix it, I'll wager.

ANNA—(*indignantly*) My father is telling the truth, Captain. He did his best to repair the horn; and he waved a lantern from the roof of the cabin and shouted to you. But you were coming so fast through the fog— (*The captain starts at this and glances uneasily at Andersen, who puts his hand to his face to hide a smile.*)

CAPTAIN JESSUP—(*clearing his throat—testily*) Not fast, young lady. Nothing of the sort. We were feeling our way carefully. Never expected— (*He turns to Chris.*) How did your tub get out here, eh? Where's the rest of the tow?

CHRIS—Tow rope part and ve gat adrift in fog about four bells in evening, sir. Ve vas last barge on tow of four, so tug can't stop look for us, Ay guess. (*eagerly explaining*) Crazy, drunk fallar on oder barge heave me rotten tow line, sir. Ay tal him it's rotten and he say—

CAPTAIN JESSUP—(*sharply*) Never mind that. It's none of my business how you came to get adrift (*He sits down at the table and takes a notebook and pencil from his pocket.*) What was the name of your tub?

CHRIS—*Simeon Winthrop*—load with coal, New York for Boston, sir.

CAPTAIN JESSUP—(*writing*) Coal—New York for Boston. (*He makes a few other notes then replaces book and pencil in his pocket, and looks up, taking Chris' measure with a keen eye.*) You're an old deep-sea sailor, aren't you? You've not worked on barges all your life by the cut of you.

CHRIS—Ay vas sailor on deep-sea many year, sir. (*with pride*) Ay don't never vork on steam. Ay vas bo'sun on vind-yammer.

CAPTAIN JESSUP—(*with appreciation*) Good. We can use you. I suppose you're willing to work your passage down, eh?

CHRIS—(*pleadingly*) If you could put us ashore end of Cape, sir—

CAPTAIN JESSUP—(*impatiently*) We left Cape Cod astern long ago. Do you think we'll turn back for you, eh? No, this'll teach you to be careless next time. You'll work your way down, my man, and no shirking about it either. And then we'll turn you over to your consul.

CHRIS—(*pointing to his daughter*) Ay vasn't thinking for mysalf, sir. Ay ain't scared for vork, sir. But Anna—

CAPTAIN JESSUP—(*starts as if he had forgotten all about her—staring at her in perplexity*) Hmmph! The devil!

ANNA—(*eagerly*) Oh, you mustn't turn back for me, Captain. Just put me anywhere. I can sleep on deck if need be.

CHRIS—(*angrily*) Anna!

ANNA—(*her face flushed with excitement*) And, after all, there's nothing to keep me in America. I'd only arrived from England a short time ago—to see my father. I was taking this one trip on his barge—as a vacation—for a lark—and—

CAPTAIN JESSUP—(*surprised*) From England?

ANNA—Yes. Although I was born in Sweden I was brought up by relatives in Leeds. Afterward, I worked as a typist there.

CAPTAIN JESSUP—(*his face clearing now that he knows her exact status*) Ah—a typist indeed. (*then he smiles*) But, with all due respect to your calling, I don't see how we can make use of it on this ship.

ANNA—But I can work at anything. I can cook, and wash dishes, and sweep—

CAPTAIN JESSUP—I'm afraid those positions are already filled. No, Miss—er—

ANNA—Christophersen.

CAPTAIN JESSUP—Miss Christophersen. I think you'll have to be content to remain a passenger. Your father can do enough work for the two passages. As to finding fit quarters for you, I don't know how we'll manage.

ANDERSEN—(*eagerly*) She can have my cabin, sir. I'll have the steward get my things out at once, and I'll bunk in with the Fourth. He won't mind, under the circumstances.

CAPTAIN JESSUP—(*snapping him up*) Then that's settled.

ANNA—(*quickly*) Oh, no. I'm very grateful but I couldn't think of putting out Mr.—

CAPTAIN JESSUP—Mr. Andersen doesn't mind, I'm sure. And you've no choice, you know.

ANDERSEN—(*smiling and looking Anna boldly in the eyes*) Not a bit of it! It's a pleasure, Miss Christophersen.

ANNA—(*flushing and dropping her eyes*) Then—thank you. You're very kind.

ANDERSEN—(*a touch of triumph in his drawling tones*) Not at all. (*His glance turns to Chris, who has been watching this handsome second mate with a dislike which has turned to immediate jealous hatred as he notices the impression made upon Anna. Andersen senses this feeling on the father's part and frowns. He speaks to Chris in a tone of command.*) You'll find a bunk up in the fo'c's'tle.

CHRIS—(*sullenly*) Yes, sir. (*But he stubbornly holds his ground, his eyes fixed on Anna.*)

CAPTAIN JESSUP—(*carelessly*) We'll leave Mr. Hall to decide about him.

ANDERSEN—(*turning to the door*) I'd better go look up the steward and have him get my things out of that cabin. (*with a look at Anna which again causes her to drop her eyes*) Miss Christophersen must be tired.

ANNA—Oh, no. Don't trouble. I'm not tired—not a bit.

CAPTAIN JESSUP—Yes. Better see to it, Andersen.

ANDERSEN—Yes, sir. (*He goes out, smiling back at Anna over his shoulder.*)

CAPTAIN JESSUP—(*after a slight pause*) You're dry, eh? I mean, you didn't get a wetting over the side?

ANNA—No, Captain. We were safe in the small rowboat.

CAPTAIN JESSUP—(*with a grunt*) Lucky! (*Mr. Hall enters from the doorway, left rear. The captain turns to him.*) Eh, Hall? Well? No damage, eh? Nothing to get excited about, what?

HALL—Starb'rd plates bent in a little. That's all, sir.

CAPTAIN JESSUP—(*rubbing his hands together gleefully*) Good! We're fortunate, eh?

HALL—Yes, sir. (*He turns to go out again.*)

CAPTAIN JESSUP—One minute, Hall. (*He waves his hand to indicate Chris.*) This man—Christophersen—bo'sun on windbags for years, he says—put him to work tomorrow.

HALL—(*measuring Chris with a calculating eye*) Glad to get him, sir. I'll put him on as a day man.

CAPTAIN JESSUP—Better take him up for'ard, eh? See that he gets a bunk in the fo'c's'tle.

HALL—Yes, sir. (*He beckons to Chris.*) Come on.

CHRIS—(*looks from him to the captain to Anna with a dazed, stupid expression on his face—stammeringly*) Ay tank— (*He mumbles in a silly bewilderment.*)

HALL—(*gruffly*) Never mind what you think. Come on.

CHRIS—(*abjectly*) Yes, sir. (*He turns to follow Hall, casting a pleading glance at Anna.*)

ANNA—(*quickly*) You'll come back to say good night after you're settled, won't you, Father? (*Chris does not answer but looks at the captain. The latter frowns impatiently. Hall's lips part in a sardonic grin.*) You'll permit that, won't you, Captain?

CAPTAIN JESSUP—(*flustered*) Yes—under the circumstances. Tonight, yes—let him come. (*then irritably*) But kindly don't make any such requests in future. You'll see him on deck, after working hours, quite enough. (*frowning authoritatively*) There's such a thing as discipline on a ship, young lady.

ANNA—(*smiling at him gratefully*) Thank you so much, Captain. You're so kind. (*The captain clears his throat importantly but he feels that the wind has been taken from his sails. Anna turns to her father.*) So be sure and come back, Father.

CHRIS—(*dully*) Yes, Anna. Ay come back.

HALL—(*impatiently*) Come along now. (*Chris slowly follows him out.*)

CAPTAIN JESSUP—(*fidgeting with embarrassment now that he is alone with Anna*) Er—you must pardon me for insisting—that matter—Miss Christophersen. Captain's cabin, you know. Members of the crew—no business here. Bad for discipline. Create ill feeling. Make it harder for him up for'ard with the others, too. They wouldn't like it. Well—you understand—they're like children. Very like.

ANNA—Yes, I think I understand, Captain. I won't ask it again, now that you've told me. (*after a pause—with excited curiosity*) What is the name of your ship, Captain, and where is she going?

CAPTAIN JESSUP—She's the *Londonderry*. Boston for Buenos Aires.

ANNA—(*musingly*) Buenos Aires. That's a long way off, isn't it?

CAPTAIN JESSUP—Six thousand miles, more or less.

ANNA—(*her eyes glowing*) Six thousand miles at sea—without a stop?

CAPTAIN JESSUP—Yes. You're in for nearly a month of nothing but water.

ANNA—(*with excited pleasure*) What a wonderful trip! (*smiling at the captain*) Oh, Captain, I'm so glad—it happened! (*She laughs.*) Does that sound silly of me?

CAPTAIN JESSUP—(*smiling*) Well, after a coal barge, I suppose the *Londonderry*'s not so bad. (*As he is speaking Andersen comes in, left rear. He carries a cup of steaming coffee in his hand which he brings to Anna.*)

ANDERSEN—Here's something to warm you up. The steward was busy changing me so I thought I might as well bring it.

ANNA—(*flushing with pleasure*) Thank you.

ANDERSEN—(*smiling down at her upturned face*) Look out. It's hot.

CAPTAIN JESSUP—I'll take a turn on the bridge, I think—smoke a cigar. Don't feel sleepy. That business still has me jumpy. Narrow escape, by Gad! I'll have a look up for'ard, too, I believe—not that I doubt your word. (*He walks to the doorway, left rear, making a motion to Andersen to follow him. He speaks in a low tone.*) I leave it to you, Andersen, to see the steward has her fixed up all right.

ANDERSEN—(*with his lazy smile*) I'll see that she's comfortable, sir.

CAPTAIN JESSUP—(*struck by something in the other's manner*) No monkey business, now, Andersen.

ANDERSEN—(*with a laugh*) Of course not, sir.

CAPTAIN JESSUP—(*with half-amused severity*) Mind! (*He goes out. Andersen comes over and sits down in a chair beside Anna.*)

ANDERSEN—You're forgetting your coffee. Better drink it while it's hot. (*He laughs.*) Pardon me, did I call it coffee? Well, anyway, it tastes good when you're cold.

ANNA—(*avoiding the direct gaze of his eyes and sipping her coffee—shyly*) It *is* good.

ANDERSEN—(*watching her with an admiring smile*) You're certainly a cool customer, for a girl, if you'll excuse my saying so. Aren't you frightened—or nervous—or disturbed the least bit?

ANNA—(*smiling at him confidently*) No. Why should I be?

ANDERSEN—But weren't you scared when you heard us in the fog getting nearer and nearer—when you saw us looming up on top of you?

ANNA—I did feel—queer—for a moment, but I knew it would come out all right.

ANDERSEN—(*puzzled*) You knew? How?

ANNA—(*vaguely*) I can't explain it. I simply felt sure. It didn't seem as if I'd been made to be drowned tonight, that's all.

ANDERSEN—You were close to it, though. It was only the merest luck.

ANNA—(*indifferently*) Yes, I suppose we were in great danger.

ANDERSEN—(*with a low chuckle*) Danger? You *suppose*?

ANNA—(*wrinkling her brows in the effort to express what she feels*) But, at the same time, I *felt* there was no danger. I knew it couldn't be the end of everything—so soon. Somehow—I can't explain what I mean—something—perhaps it was the sea—I don't know what—told me that it was a new beginning of my life, not an end.

ANDERSEN—(*curiously*) And you still think that?

ANNA—(*nodding her head emphatically*) Oh, yes. Now more than ever.

ANDERSEN—(*with a laugh*) Then you must be glad you were shipwrecked?

ANNA—(*smiling*) Indeed I am. Otherwise this—(*she makes a gesture to indicate the ship*) could never have happened.

ANDERSEN—And you've no regrets?

ANNA—Regrets?

ANDERSEN—For what you've left behind?

ANNA—Oh, I've left nothing behind. I've only been in America less than a fortnight. All of that time I spent on Father's horrid old barge, and now the barge is sunk.

And as for England, I left nothing behind there worth regretting.

ANDERSEN—(*slyly*) Not even a sweetheart or two?

ANNA—(*laughing candidly*) Not even half of one.

ANDERSEN—(*jokingly*) Sure?

ANNA—Positive!

ANDERSEN—(*in the same joking tone*) A beautiful girl like you! I can't believe it. I think you're fibbing.

ANNA—(*flushing*) Now you're chaffing, aren't you? No, seriously, I'm glad it happened the way it did, shipwreck and everything. (*with earnest enthusiasm*) Why, I feel free for the first time in my life! It's like playing truant from my stupid old work. It's not very interesting, you know, doing the same thing over again day after day, cooped up in an office.

ANDERSEN—(*sympathetically*) I know what that means. I tried it once.

ANNA—(*smiling*) And the best part of it is that this vacation—this wonderful trip—is forced on me. I have no choice in the matter. So I can't feel guilty about not working and earning money, can I? (*She laughs.*)

ANDERSEN—(*smiling*) Nope. Your guilty conscience went down with the barge.

ANNA—(*growing serious again*) And it *is* a beginning of new things for me, in a way I've just begun to know the sea—and love it! It seemed to come over me suddenly—while we were drifting in that fog with that queer silence all about. I'd always lived inland in Leeds ever since the time I was a little girl. The sea was only a name to me. And on the steamer coming over, in the steerage—that was nothing. It was only on the barge when the fog swept over us that I began to feel—it. (*She glances at his intent face, flushes, and laughs awkwardly.*) You must think I'm dreadfully silly—talking this way—don't you?

ANDERSEN—(*earnestly*) Not a bit of it! It's darned interesting. And I think I know how you felt.

ANNA—You mean you've felt—the same way?

ANDERSEN—(*with an encouraging smile*) Tell me more about it, and I'll see.

ANNA—It's so hard to put into words. (*intensely*) As if you'd come home after being away a long, long time; as if everything suddenly had changed, and nothing could ever be the same again; as if everything you'd lived through before was small—and wrong—and could never mean anything to you again.

ANDERSEN—(*nodding slowly—his eyes wide and dreamy*) That's it. You've got it. That's the feeling exactly.

ANNA—Oh, I'm so glad that someone else has had the same experience, that it's not just a silly notion of mine.

ANDERSEN—(*absent-mindedly patting her hand which is on the table beside him. She draws it away quickly, her face crimson, but one glance at his face convinces her of the innocence of this action. He speaks thoughtfully.*) Foolish? Not a bit of it. It's a big, big thing—and a true thing. But why is it, I wonder? Where does it come from—for instance in your case?

ANNA—(*self-possessed again*) Perhaps it's in my blood. My father was a sailor most of his life. All the men, my father has told me, on both sides of the family have been sailors as far back as he knows about. Many of them were drowned, or died on ships and were buried at sea. (*awed by a sudden idea*) Perhaps it is they—calling! (*then shaking her head with a forced laugh*) But I don't believe in ghosts, do you?

ANDERSEN—Sometimes when I'm on the bridge in a thick fog, I do.

ANNA—(*with a nervous laugh*) Yes, that would be the time for them, wouldn't it? But when the ghosts interrupted me I was going to tell you that all the women of the family, with one exception, had married sailors. So you see—if there's anything in heredity—I must have a lot of sea concealed about me someplace.

ANDERSEN—(*thoughtfully*) Heredity might account for me, too. I've often wondered if it could be that: for my case is similar to yours—I mean, I was born and bred inland— (*with a smile*) and yet here I am.

ANNA—But your family have been sailors?

ANDERSEN—(*with a laugh*) Not my father! Far be it! Nor any of my brothers. Not on your life! They're all wedded to the soil. They have the greatest scorn for anyone who works on a ship.

ANNA—Then, if they're that kind, why did you say—

ANDERSEN—Oh, I had two uncles, my father's brothers,

who went to sea. One of them died when he was captain of a steamer like this—a Swedish steamer.

ANNA—(*smiling*) I thought from your name you might be Swedish too.

ANDERSEN—(*with a laugh*) Oh, but I'm not. I'm an American, born and brought up in Minnesota. My father is a Swede but an American citizen. He came over when he was a young man.

ANNA—And what does he do?

ANDERSEN—Farming, on a small scale. He owns a small farm and works like a slave on it—my brothers, too. It's all right for them. They like it. I tried it for a while—but it wasn't for me.

ANNA—What does your father think of your going to sea?

ANDERSEN—He makes the best of it. He knows I wasn't made for farming. He discovered that quite early—after I left high school. High school was my privilege as the youngest child. My three brothers were put to work on the farm after grammar school—and wanted to be. Well—I couldn't go the farm. I saw a chance to work my way through the university, and the farm and I parted company. Two years at college were enough. It hardly came up to my dreams. Then I bummed my way around the country for a while—as a hobo. Off and on I worked, manual labor of different kinds, but I found that slavery worse than the farm. So I drifted East and got a position with an insurance company—office work—a year of it—enough to disgust me with all indoor work for all time. I resigned on a sudden hunch and shipped away as a seaman on a tramp steamer—Australia, South Africa, the Far East—all over. Then—and then only—I began to feel the sense of finding home, you speak of. And here I am still—quite contented and unrepentant.

ANNA—(*staring at him with a fascinated astonishment*) It's wonderful—to have lived all of that!

ANDERSEN—(*with a laugh*) Well, at any rate, I'm like you. I'm glad it all happened. It brought me—home.

ANNA—But you look so young! And this must have happened long ago.

ANDERSEN—Why? I haven't been at sea long—only a little over three years.

ANNA—(*with admiration*) And you're a second officer already!

ANDERSEN—(*laughing*) Does that sound so hard? It isn't. It was an easy examination, and I got this berth without much trouble.

ANNA—Then it shouldn't be long before you're a captain—at that rate.

ANDERSEN—(*grinning*) Not on your life! Never!

ANNA—(*surprised*) But why not?

ANDERSEN—Don't want to be.

ANNA—You mean to say— You're not serious, I know.

ANDERSEN—Yes I am—dead serious. Why should I want such a job? The skipper has the whole responsibility of the ship on his shoulders. (*smiling*) I'm not looking for material responsibilities. I'm doing my best to avoid them.

ANNA—But—you must have changed, then. Didn't you start as a common sailor?

ANDERSEN—Yes.

ANNA—And didn't you work up to the responsible position you hold now?

ANDERSEN—(*laughing*) Responsible? A second mate? Well, perhaps, in a sense; but for me at least this job is a cinch—the easiest berth on the ship. I'm merely the captain's shadow. I toil and spin very little. The first mate has a dog's life of it—toil and trouble unending. So I don't care to be first mate any more than I do to be captain. (*with a trace of self-contempt in his mocking tones*) I'm free from the sin of ambition, you see. I'm quite content to remain where I am and let others do the aspiring. (*He laughs again rather bitterly.*) It was only my laziness which made me work up so far.

ANNA—Laziness?

ANDERSEN—(*amused by her bewilderment*) Exactly. The crew have to work and sweat for their pay. That was never my idea of living. I hated it, but I knew I couldn't quit—that once on the sea, I'd never be happy again away from it. I calculated carefully. I grew wise to the berth of second mate—a jewel of a position—sweatless and without a care. I resolved I'd be a second mate. So I worked like the devil for a time to fit myself to be free of hard work for all time. (*He laughs.*) So you see that my laziness was the spur that goaded me on.

ANNA—(*looking at him queerly*) You're funny. I don't know now whether you aren't making fun of me.

ANDERSEN—I'm not. Honor bright!

ANNA—(*frowning*) You don't look that kind.

ANDERSEN—(*taken aback*) What kind? (*He tries to laugh it off carelessly.*) Oh, you mean—lazy? A waster?

ANNA—There's more to it than you've told, I know.

ANDERSEN—No. Honestly.

ANNA—But there must be something back of it. Else— what are you doing it all for?

ANDERSEN—(*shrugging his shoulders*) What is anyone doing anything for? If one could answer that question— (*He gets to his feet and paces back and forth. Her gaze follows him wonderingly, full of a pity mingled with contempt. Finally he stops abruptly by her chair, throwing his head back defiantly, his face stubborn, his eyes staring beyond her.*) To live! That's the answer to your question. That's why I'm doing it all. (*disdainfully*) Working, slaving, sweating to get something which only disgusts you when you've got it! That's ambition for you! But is it living? Not to me! Freedom—that's life! No ties, no responsibilities—no guilty feelings. Like the sea—always moving, never staying, never held by anything, never giving a damn—but absorbing, taking it all in, grabbing every opportunity to see it all—making the world part of you and not being a grain of sand buried and lost and held fast by other grains! Not American, Swede—but citizen of the sea which belongs to no one. Not love in the sense of a wife—marriage—an anchor—but love that is free—women of all kinds and races—Woman!

ANNA—(*who has been listening to him with fascinated eyes, gives a startled gasp at this last*) Oh! (*disapprovingly*) That's stupid. It spoils all the rest.

ANDERSEN—(*his outburst broken off short, stares down at her for a moment uncomprehendingly—then with a mocking laugh*) That last doesn't please you, eh? I suppose you're all for marriage—and stability. Naturally. (*with a quizzical smile*) But what do you think of my ambitionless ambition—as a whole?

ANNA—(*her eyes glowing*) I think it's wonderful! It's fine! It's what I feel, too.

ANDERSEN—(*astonished—half-scornfully*) What *you* feel?

ANNA—(*intensely*) What the sea has made me feel. What I felt on the barge in the fog—waiting, knowing that something was going to happen—and not caring what it was if only it led to—something different—something new.

ANDERSEN—(*looking at her with puzzled admiration*) Yes. That's it. It's strange that you— (*quickly resuming his tone of mocking raillery*) Then you confess you're a waster, too!

ANNA—Oh, no. For I don't see why you shouldn't keep on working up, become a captain, own your own ship even, and still—

ANDERSEN—(*waving this idea aside*) Responsibilities! A captain belongs to his ship first, last, and always. So does a first mate. But a second mate belongs to himself.

ANNA—But if they love their ship?

ANDERSEN—Then they don't love themselves enough. The sea doesn't love ships. She plays with them, destroys them, endures them because she expresses herself through them— but they belong to her, not she to them. (*While he is speaking the steward enters from the door, left forward.*)

THE STEWARD—Your cabin is all ready for the young lady, sir.

ANDERSEN—All right, Steward. Thank you. (*The steward goes out. Andersen turns to Anna with a smile.*) You must be worn out—by my foolish talk as much as anything.

ANNA—(*protesting excitedly*) No. It's been wonderful. I've never heard anyone talk of those things before.

ANDERSEN—(*dismissing this with a laugh*) And I swear I've never said those things to anyone before. One doesn't tell one's secrets to all comers. But I had to make some defence against your waster charge. And, from what you've told me of your own symptoms, I knew you'd contracted the same disease—seasickness, eh? (*He laughs mockingly—then as she doesn't reply but looks hurt by his remarks*) Shall I show you where your quarters are?

ANNA—(*getting up—matter-of-factly*) Yes, please. (*She follows him to the doorway, left forward.*)

ANDERSEN—(*pointing*) The open door on your left where

the light is. That's it. (*She nods. He smiles down into her eyes.*) I won't keep you up any longer. I've got to go on watch again at four myself. I'll need a wink of sleep—if I can sleep, *now*. It's been great sport, our talk. We'll have plenty of time for more of the same—if you like.

ANNA—Yes.

ANDERSEN—You might convert me, you know.

ANNA—(*with a confused laugh*) I'm afraid you're past reforming.

ANDERSEN—Not—by you. (*coming nearer to her*) Well—good night.

ANNA—(*faintly*) Good night. (*Suddenly he takes her in his arms and kisses her. She struggles fiercely and pushes him away. They stand looking at each other. She wipes her lips unconsciously with an expression of aversion, her eyes flaming at him with defiant rage and hurt. Something in her glance convinces him of his mistake. He turns away, his face growing red in his awkward shame.*)

ANDERSEN—(*pleading for forbearance—in a husky voice*) You were—so beautiful—then.

ANNA—(*her voice quivering*) You've spoiled it all. You've proved you are—what you said you were.

ANDERSEN—(*with a sad laugh*) A cad? Yes, I guess so. (*then suddenly turning to her with impassioned entreaty*) No! Don't believe that! It wasn't I then—who did that. I knew all the time I was wrong—about you. I felt it deep down. But a mocking devil whispered that you were too good to be true. So I wanted to be convinced— But it wasn't I—not the real myself! I swear to you it was not! Don't think of me—as that. It means so much now—your opinion—after the talk we've had—somehow. So don't—please— I'm a rotten damn fool, I know—but not— Say you don't believe it, won't you?

ANNA—(*deeply moved by his sincerity*) I don't want—to believe it.

ANDERSEN—And you'll forgive me—and forget—that?

ANNA—If you'll promise to remember—I will. (*Chris appears in the doorway, left rear. The two in the doorway, front, do not notice his coming. His eyes harden with rage and hatred as they fasten themselves on Andersen. He half crouches, his thick fingers twitching, as if he would like to spring at the second mate.*)

ANDERSEN—(*very humbly*) And will you shake hands—as a token—for good night—with the real me? (*He advances his hand slowly as if fearing a refusal.*)

ANNA—(*with impulsive tenderness, seeing him so abject*) Of course! (*She grasps his hand.*) Good night.

ANDERSEN—(*looks in her eyes for a moment*) Good night. (*He releases her hand and turns away. As he does so he sees Chris. He starts in surprise—then speaks in his mate's voice of authority.*) Hello! Haven't they found you a bunk up for'ard yet?

CHRIS—(*sullenly*) Yes, Ay gat bunk—sir. (*He plainly has to force out the "sir."*) Ay come for say good night to Anna.

ANDERSEN—(*repeats the name to himself half-aloud*) Anna!

ANNA—The captain gave him permission, Mr. Andersen.

ANDERSEN—(*absent-mindedly*) Oh, that's all right. (*He goes out, left rear. Chris walks forward to his daughter.*)

CHRIS—(*stares at her for a moment—then somberly*) Anna! Don't go for do dat, Anna. (*his voice breaking into a pitiful pleading*) Don't go for do dat, Anna, Ay tal you!

ANNA—(*with astonished bewilderment*) What, Father? Do what?

CHRIS—(*bursting into a rage*) Ay know! Ay see! Dat rotten fallar, he make fool of you, Anna. You look out! Ay know his kind fallar. Ay've seen many like him my time. He look pooty, he's yentleman, but he's no good sailor fallar yust same as in fo'c's'tle. You look out! He talk pooty talk, dan he gat you for marry him—

ANNA—(*staring at him as if he were mad*) Father!

CHRIS—(*not heeding*) He gat you for marry him, and dan you might yust s'well be dead. He go avay on ship, he leave you for vait alone, he gat new gel every port. Dan you gat kits, he don't care, he don't come home, he don't know his kits even, he don't vant be bothered with kits. Oh, Ay know it's so! Your mo'der, she tal you same tang, if she's alive. She know it kill her, Ay bet you! It make you ole soon, it kill you too, Anna! (*raising his hand as if he were taking an oath*) Ay svear, Anna, Ay vould like better you vas never been born dan you marry man dat go to sea! And Ay von't let you, no, Ay von't—no matter vat Ay gat do for stop you, py God!

ANNA—(*indignantly*) Are you insane? What crazy talk,

Father! What—as if I were dreaming of marrying anyone! How ridiculous you are!

CHRIS—(*not convinced*) Dat ole davil, sea, she's gat us on voyage. You gat look out for her tricks now, Ay tal you!

ANNA—(*with impatient scorn*) Are you cursing the sea again? (*defiantly*) Well, I love the sea! (*The situation suddenly strikes her as absurd, and she bends down and kisses her father laughingly.*) Go to bed, you silly old goose! You're still nervous and upset or you wouldn't talk such nonsense. Get a good rest now. Good night. (*She goes out, left forward, shutting the door behind her.*)

CHRIS—(*dully*) Good night, Anna. (*He stands still for a moment, brooding somberly. Then he shakes his fist at the sea outside with a hopeless rage.*) Damn ole davil! (*He turns, his shoulders bowed wearily, and plods toward the doorway, left rear as*

The Curtain Falls)

ACT THREE

Scene I

Scene—*About a month later—The seamen's section of the forecastle on the* Londonderry, *at anchor in the roadstead, Buenos Aires. The forecastle is a small, low, triangular-shaped compartment with tiers of bunks, three deep, built in along the sides. It narrows to an apex at the far end (toward the bow of the ship). The left wall, with its rows of bunks, runs straight back, following the line of the alleyway outside which separates the seamen's from the firemen's quarters. The bunks on the right follow the line of the ship's hull curving in at the bow. Several portholes are seen over the upper tier on this side. Low, wooden benches border the edge of the constricted floor space. Blankets lie in heaps as they were tossed aside in most of the bunks. On the left, forward, a doorway opening on the alleyway leading to the main deck. To the rear of the door top, a lighted lamp stands in a bracket fastened to the wall.*

It is about nine o'clock at night.

As the curtain rises, Chris, Jonesy, and Edwards are discovered. Chris is lying on his side in a lower bunk on the right, his head propped on his hand. He stares moodily before him, evidently deep in somber thought. Jonesy is seated on a bench on the left near the doorway, as close to the light as he can get. He is a stout, heavy-faced, good-natured-looking young fellow. His sleeves are rolled up to the elbows; he has a battered suitcase on his knees serving as desk; he is writing a letter, his brow furrowed by the effort at concentration, his thick, red fingers clenched about the pencil as if it were a chisel. He makes the letters with difficulty, with painstaking slowness, sticking out his tongue as he completes each sentence. Edwards, a tall, lanky, dark-complected boy of eighteen, sits by his side, bent forward, smoking a pipe, watching his mate's efforts impatiently with a scornful amusement. All are dressed in dungarees, flannel shirts, etc.

EDWARDS—(*impatiently*) Aw, chuck the bloody letter, Jonesy. Finish it some other time. It's hot 's hell in here. Let's get out on deck. The moon's up. All the rest is out there.

JONESY—(*without looking up*) Must be all dead. I don't 'ear no talkin'.

EDWARDS—That's count o' the bo'sun. He's bad tonight, they says—fever and stuff—and the skipper sends orders to douse the noise. They're takin' the bos to the hospital first thing in the mornin', I heard. The rheumatics has him done for.

JONESY—(*unfeelingly*) Serve 'im bloody right—the slave-drivin' image!

EDWARDS—He'll not be with us next trip, that's safe. We'll be signin' on another bo'sun. (*nudging Jonesy with his elbow— with a grin*) Maybe skipper'll give ole Chris the job. He useter to bo'sun, he says. (*Jonesy looks up with a chuckle.*)

CHRIS—(*surlily*) Ay don't take yob on dis scow dey give me hundred dollar a day.

EDWARDS—(*imitating Chris' accent*) Dat's fallar, py golly! (*He and Jonesy roar with laughter. Chris grunts angrily.*)

JONESY—(*bending to his writing again*) Hush your jaw, Eds. Don't you see I'm tryin' to think? I can't when you're blatherin'. (*He finishes a sentence and looks up.*) I got to finish the damn thing now I'm started—or I never will.

EDWARDS—(*disgustedly*) What's the good of it? What's there to write about? Nothin' never happens on this old hooker.

JONESY—That's what bloody well makes it 'ard on a bloke. I got to make it up out o' me own 'ead.

EDWARDS—Then chuck it!

JONESY—No. I ain't written the old woman a line in a year a'most. She'll think I'm gone to Davy Jones. No, blarst it, I'm at it, and I'll finish, and then the rotten thing'll be off my mind. (*with exasperation*) But what in 'ell can yer write your mother about? Yer can't tell 'er what 'appened in port, can yer? You can't say: "Dear Ma, when I was in Boston I was as drunk as drunk and spent all my money." Ho! That'd set 'er cursin' and blindin' 'er old 'ead off! And, same's you said, nothin' never 'appens on this tub to write about. (*He grips his pencil again savagely.*) But I'm goin' to finish the blarsted thing, Gawd blind it!

EDWARDS—You're off your chump! (*He turns and regards*

Chris curiously for a moment.) What's up with you, old Chris? Feelin' off your oats?

CHRIS—(*glumly*) No. Ay'm all right.

EDWARDS—You'd never think it, lookin' at you. You're a funny bloke. Ain't you glad the voyage is over? I'd be dancin' out on deck if I was in your boots. You'll go ashore tomorrer in Bonos Ares and be your own boss again. And the skipper'll give you a month's pay, I'll bet. He's a soft old bird like that. You'll be able to have a bloody good drunk 'fore the consul ships you back to the States.

CHRIS—(*angrily*) Ay don't vant for go on drunk any more, Ay tal you!

EDWARDS—(*with a chuckle*) Oh, I was forgettin' your girl was on board. She'd give you hell if you did, eh?

CHRIS—(*irritably*) Dat ain't none of your business.

JONESY—(*looking up—with a grin*) 'Is gel? She won't be 'is gel long, you can take my word for it.

CHRIS—(*glancing at him with dark suspicion*) Vat you mean, Yonesy?

JONESY—(*derisively*) Don't arsk me. Arsk the second mate.

CHRIS—(*furiously—half scrambling out of his bunk*) You mind your own damn business, you fallar!

JONESY—(*grinning*) You ain't gettin' mad at me, are yer? No 'arm meant, ole Chris, s'elp me! I was on'y sayin' what all of us 'as seen with our two eyes. 'E's dead gone on 'er, the second, it's plain 's the nose on yer face. (*placatingly, as Chris continues to glare at him*) I didn't mean nothin' bad, ole Chris, s'elp me. 'Is missis, reg'lar married is what I meant.

CHRIS—(*furiously*) Shut up, you damn liar, you! (*He springs out of his bunk threateningly.*)

JONESY—(*as Edwards roars with laughter—provokingly*) You do take it to 'eart, don't yer? What's the trouble? Don't yer like Andersen?

EDWARDS—(*with sudden scorn*) Aw, he's a crazy Dutchy. A second mate ain't good enough for his girl, I s'pose. Wants a skipper—or the King of England. And him takin' his watch on deck with the rest of us!

CHRIS—(*his anger passing away*) Ay'm big fool for gat angry. You is yust young boys. You don't know. Ay don't vant

King of England for Anna, Ay don't vant no man. Ay vant her for mysalf. She's all Ay gat in vorld. (*He sits down on a bench dejectedly. The two boys are a bit shame-faced and remain silent, Jonesy pretending to write again.*)

EDWARDS—(*getting to his feet*) Well, I wisht I was in your boots just the same—gettin' paid off tomorrer. How'd you like to be me, eh?—signed on for a year more on this lousy lime-juicer. (*He grunts—then stretches lazily.*) You won't chuck the writin' and come out on deck, Jonesy?

JONESY—No. I'll be finished in 'arf a mo.

EDWARDS—I'll sling my hook, then. It'd choke you in here. (*He saunters out. There is a pause. Jonesy scowls and sweats over his letter.*)

CHRIS—(*kindly*) You write your mo'der, Yonesy?

JONESY—Yes.

CHRIS—(*approvingly*) Dat's good boy. Don't let dat fallar Ed stop you from write. Your mo'der, she vorry like thunder, she tank maybe you're drowned, you don't write.

JONESY—(*looking up—with cynical amusement*) Worry? Not 'er! She ain't got time. There's 'leven of us boys and gels she's got. If she was to start worryin' over each of us, she'd go balmy quick. Ho, no! She ain't worrin'. But I might 's well let 'er know I'm live and kickin'. (*He starts in writing.*) She ain't a bad one, the ole woman—'less she's got a cargo of gin aboard. (*As he finishes speaking, Glass the messroom steward, comes into the forecastle. He is a slight, dark young fellow of twenty-five or so. His thin face with its long pointed nose; its large mouth twisted to one side, the upper lip shadowed by a wisp of mustache; its sharp, mocking, pale blue eyes; has the expression of half-cruel, malicious humor which characterizes the practical joker. He wears a short, white jacket, white duck pants, and sneakers— all passably clean.*)

GLASS—(*breezily*) What ho, Jonesy, me lad. (*His eyes fix themselves immediately on Chris with the eager satisfaction of one who has found his victim. He grins.*) And hello, if here ain't old Chris, old scuttle!

CHRIS—(*with a grunt of dislike*) Vell, vat about ole Chris? You try make fun, you fallar?

GLASS—(*with feigned indignation*) Can't I say a civil word to you without you gettin' on your ear? Do you think I'm always jokin'? I never seed the like of the mob on this kettle. They don't believe a word a man says. (*He catches Jonesy's eye and winks at him slyly. Jonesy, anticipating fun from this signal, puts his suitcase and letter on the bench beside him and leans back against the bunks with an expectant smirk.*)

CHRIS—(*a bit mollified*) You don't act like crazy fool, ve believe you.

GLASS—(*sitting down opposite Chris*) Well, I'm not acting like a fool now, am I? If you think I am, say so, and I'll get out of this. There ain't no use tryin' to tell things to a man that won't believe you.

CHRIS—(*suspiciously*) You vant tal *me* sometang?

GLASS—That's what I came here for. You don't s'pose, when it's cool and moonlight on deck so clear you'd read a book by it, that I'd be comin' to this sweet room for pleasure do you? No, I was lookin' you up to have a talk with you as man to man. You can believe or not. Just the same, I'm dead serious, old Chris.

CHRIS—(*looking at him doubtfully*) Vat you gat for tal me, Glass?

GLASS—A lot o' things you've a right to know.

CHRIS—(*his curiosity aroused*) Vat tangs?

GLASS—(*staring upward—carelessly*) About two people— on this boat.

CHRIS—(*frowning*) Vat two people?

GLASS—One is an officer.

CHRIS—(*savagely*) Hmmph!

GLASS—The other's a passenger.

CHRIS—(*springing to his feet and shaking his fist in Glass' face*) Shut up, you! Don't make no lying yoke with me, you fool fallar! Ay break your face, you do!

GLASS—(*rising with an air of hurt dignity*) Did you ever see the beat of him, Jonesy? (*turning to Chris with well-feigned anger*) All right, you goat-nose Swede, if that's the way you feel about it! No one's forcin' you to lissen, is there? That's the thanks I get for tryin' to do a good turn for you. Well, you can go to hell now, for all of me. Keep on bein' as blind as a bat and have the whole world laughin' at you—till it's too late. All I was goin' to do was to tell you somethin' that'd maybe open your eyes, and put some sense in your thick, square head—and make you show if you was a sheep or had the guts of a man. (*He takes a few steps toward the door.*) You're scared to learn the truth, that's what. You're a sheep.

CHRIS—(*stares at his back for a moment undecidedly, then sits down again—with angry contempt*) Ay'm not scared any man on dis ship, py golly! Ay break you in half with little finger, you skinny grasshopper!

GLASS—(*pretending to ignore this—with a wink at Jonesy— pleasantly*) Writin' a letter to your girl, Jonesy?

JONESY—(*grinning back at him*) No—the ole woman.

CHRIS—(*in a loud tone of scorn which nevertheless reveals a troubled curiosity*) Fallars on dis ship make anyone sick! Yust talk, talk—tangs dey don't know nutting about—yust like pack of ole vomen round stove!

GLASS—(*keeping his back turned but raising his voice—with elaborate sarcasm*) Of course, *I* couldn't know nothin' 'bout *them*. *I'm* on'y up on the bridge deck, where *they* are, most of the time. So you couldn't expect *me* to know nothin', or *see* nothin', or *hear* nothin', could you, Jonesy?

JONESY—Ho! You sees a lot ole Chris don't see, I'll lay my oath!

CHRIS—(*This shaft has bitten deep but he growls*) He don't see nutting, dat fallar. He make up lies. (*As Glass makes no reply, he is forced to address him directly—scornfully*) Vat you *tank* you see, Glass?

GLASS—(*turning to him—stiffly*) Nothin'—as if I'd tell you any more, old Dutchy.

CHRIS—(*after a pause—insinuatingly*) Ay tank you make fun. Dat make me angry. You alvays make fun, you know dat, Glass. If Ay tank you talk straight and don't lie—

GLASS—And be insulted again for my pains, eh? Not much!

CHRIS—Ay'm not angry no more. (*questioningly*) Ay'm sure you don't make fun dis time, Glass?

GLASS—(*very earnestly*) I won't deny I like my joke—in most things. But when it comes to talkin' as man to man with a man—about serious things, mind!—you'll find I'm the last one in the world to laugh. (*He turns to Jonesy with a wink.*) You can ask Jonesy. He's known me a while and he'll tell you. Ain't that right, Jonesy?

JONESY—(*concealing his grin—heartily*) Right as rain!

CHRIS—(*persuasively*) Sat down, dan. You tal me—(*with an attempt to belittle the matter*)—all dem big tangs, eh?

GLASS—(*pretending reluctance*) You'll promise you'll not get on your high horse at anythin'—the truth, man!—I tells you?

CHRIS—Yes. Ay'm cool as cucumber now. (*forcing a grin*) You ain't gat nothin' for tal, Ay bet you.

GLASS—Oho, ain't I! (*He sits down and leans over to Chris confidentially.*) I won't beat about the bush. I'll come straight to the point to prove I'm not foolin'. I'll tell you straight out, if I was you, I'd not trust any girl of mine with that second mate.

CHRIS—(*his face darkening—tries to force a careless laugh*) Is dat all you gat tal? You don't know. Anna's strong gel. She know how for take care of herself, py yingo!

GLASS—(*with provoking scorn*) You like the second, I'll bet, in spite of all your talk.

CHRIS—(*violently*) Like? Ay hate dat fallar! He's no good for no one.

GLASS—(*eagerly, seeing that he now has his victim where he wants him*) No good? You ain't tellin' no lie, old Chris! He ain't no good, that's a fact. You must've heard something about him, ain't you?

CHRIS—No, Ay hear tangs about him, but Ay don't care for dat. Ay can tal dem kind fallar ven Ay see him, vithout Ay hear nutting.

GLASS—(*thoughtfully*) Man, I could tell you a few things that'd make you prick up your ears.

CHRIS—(*scowling*) Vat tangs you mean?

GLASS—I'm not findin' fault with his doin's on my own account, mind! The second's a good sport from his toes up—a man as ain't afraid to go on a bloody drunk when he's a mind to, and don't care who knows it. And the girls—they all go crazy after him, man! He's left them broken-hearted after him in every port we've touched since he's been aboard—and he goes laughin' on to the next one. What's a girl more or less to him? He's that big and handsome, there's not one of the lot wouldn't leave home and mother if he crooked his little finger.

CHRIS—(*savagely*) It's so, Ay guess. (*suspiciously*) But how you come for know all dem tangs, Glass?

GLASS—(*in scornful amazement*) Know them? Do you think I'm tellin' you a secret? Every blarsted man on board the *Londonderry* could tell you the same thing. Couldn't they, Jonesy?

JONESY—(*concealing a snicker*) Aye.

GLASS—He's not the one to hide what he's doin', the second. He's proud of it, s'help me! Why, last time we was here in Buenos Aires I went to the Casino to see the wrestling match—and there was Andersen in a box, as drunk as a lord, with a big, blond girl—a beauty, man!—sittin' on his lap. They was kissin' each other, not givin' a damn for no one, and the whole crowd in the place watchin' 'em and laughin'.

CHRIS—(*clenching his fists and growling*) Dirty svine!

GLASS—(*with a grin over his shoulder at Jonesy*) Oh, he ain't so bad—as a man with men. He spends his pay day like a sport and a sailor. No savin' money, no stinginess about him. He worked up from the fo'c's'tle, he did. He wasn't no lady-boy apprentice, ever. So he's a good sport and a real seaman of the old school—like you, old Chris.

CHRIS—(*with hatred*) Dat's vorst tang he can be, Ay tank. Dat's damn fool business. Dat's dat ole davil sea's dirty tricks. (*He shakes his fist—then with bewilderment*) You're crazy fallar, Glass. One minute you say he's no good, next minute say he is good. Vat you talkin' about, eh?

GLASS—Lissen! I say he's a sport after my own heart, and I like him well enough myself even if he is a Yank—*but*—I ain't got no young daughter that's a nice girl, don't forget!

CHRIS—(*glumly*) Anna look out for hersalf, Ay tal you!

GLASS—(*indignantly*) That's a sweet way for you to talk! Are you her father, or ain't you? Ain't you bound to look after her when her mother's dead? It's your fault, her gettin' aboard, ain't it? Look out for herself? There's lots he's left behind that thought— Well, if you don't care that much, I s'pose there's no good talkin'. But remember that I did my best to give you a hand.

CHRIS—(*trying to reassure himself*) Oh, you Glass, you make all tangs bigger. It's all right. Ve're in port now, ve go ashore in morning, she don't see him again. (*spitting disgustedly*) She don't care for fool fallar dat go on sea, anyvay. She's gat too much sense for dat.

GLASS—(*mockingly*) She don't, eh? Lissen to him, Jonesy! Just lissen to him!

JONESY—'E's a silly bird.

CHRIS—(*vehemently*) Ay tal you it's so. She make fun, dat's all.

GLASS—Fun! Lissen to him! If you'd seen what I seed last night—

CHRIS—Vat? (*threateningly*) Don't you go for lie now, you hear?

GLASS—Did I say it was anythin' wrong? Don't I know your Anna ain't that kind? Can't I tell by the looks of her? It ain't nothin' not right I'm speakin' of; but Ed was tellin' me you don't even want her to marry him.

CHRIS—(*savagely*) No! Anna marry dat drunk, no good, sailor fallar? Ay svear Ay kill him first!

GLASS—(*with an air of decision—calmly*) Then you lose, Chris, old love.

CHRIS—(*perplexed*) Eh?

GLASS—You lose, I said.

CHRIS—Ay lose? Vat Ay lose?

GLASS—Her! (*with a grin*) You better get out your old pistol and shoot him. You ain't got so much time, either. They'll both be ashore tomorrow.

CHRIS—(*menacingly*) Yes—but Ay—Ay vill be ashore, too.

GLASS—Oh, they'll give you the slip—after you're good and drunk.

CHRIS—(*angrily*) Ay don't gat drunk no more, Ay tal you!

GLASS—Many a man's sworn the same and woke up in jail next mornin' with a drunk and disorderly against him. (*tormentingly*) They'll be man and wife when they come to bail you out. (*Jonesy laughs.*)

CHRIS—(*starting to his feet—furiously*) Shut up, you big fool! All you talk is crazy tangs. Anna don't care nutting, vouldn't marry dat fallar, he gat million dollar. You make joke, ain't it so?

GLASS—(*carelessly*) If it's a joke, it's one on you. You wouldn't call it a joke if you seen 'em last night.

CHRIS—(*in rage and misery*) You don't see dem. You're liar, dat's vat!

GLASS—I was going up the starb'rd ladder to the bridge deck when I seen 'em—'bout six bells, it was. I stopped when I heard the voices and bent down in the shadow, listenin'. Says I to myself: Here's where I can do a good turn for old Chris, likely. They'll maybe be sayin' somethin' as he had ought to know about. They didn't heed me comin'. They was too busy with themselves. And it was that still and calm, if you remember, I could hear every word. Andersen was tellin' your girl how much he loved and all that stuff. It took him a long time to get to the point but in the end he says: "Will you marry me?" And she waits a bit and then answers: "Yes," says she.

CHRIS—(*raging, grabs Glass by the shoulders and shakes him furiously*) Anna don't say dat! Dat's lie, Ay tal you!

GLASS—(*writhing in his grip*) On my oath! Believe it or not. (*whining with pain*) Leggo me, Dutchy, blarst you! (*Chris seems to come to himself. He takes his hands away and drops down on a bench, staring before him with beaten, wounded eyes, his spirit broken, his shoulders sagging wearily. Glass moves his sore shoulders and glares at him resentfully.*) That's what I get for tryin' to beat some brains into your square head, is it? (*viciously*) Well, I hope the second does make a bleedin' fool of you, that's what!

CHRIS—(*gets up distractedly as if he couldn't bear to listen to the other's voice a second longer*) Shut up! Shut up! Ay gat go out on deck vere I don't hear you. (*He goes out.*)

GLASS—(*shouting after him*) Take a jump over the side and drown ye'self for all I cares! (*He turns to Jonesy grumblingly.*) He near broke my shoulders, the fathead Swede! Arms on him like a hairy gorilla, he has.

JONESY—(*chuckling*) You didn't 'arf 'ave 'im on a string. 'E swallowed it all, 'ook, line and sinker. And did yer look at 'im? 'E's mad as a bloody 'ornet at the second. (*He laughs gleefully.*) Blimey, but 'e'll kick up a bloody row with 'im, wait 'n' see!

GLASS—(*grinning*) And the second won't dare beat him, 'count of the girl.

JONESY—(*still more tickled*) Ho-ho! You're a foxey joker,

Glass. If you'd seed the serious face on you when you was tellin' it. I was almost taken in by it myself. Was any of it truth?

GLASS—(*with a chuckle*) Sure—a good bit of it—on'y not the way I told it, exactly. You know right enough what I said about the second is Gospel. He does spend his money like a sport, and he does go on sprees, and he does fool with the girls. (*He grins.*) But what I told of the blond girl sittin' on his lap in the Casino and kissin' him—I made that up out of my head.

JONESY—Ho-ho! Blimey!

GLASS—Still, why ain't it true? He's the kind to do it. It might have happened just 's well 's not.

JONESY—And that about him askin' Chris' gel to marry 'im?

GLASS—(*candidly*) That's Gawd's truth, Jonesy! And I was there listenin' to hear what I could hear, like I says. (*He grins.*) But the end of it wasn't hardly what I told him.

JONESY—(*excitedly*) It wasn't? What'd they do, then?

GLASS—She didn't say yes, Chris' girl didn't. She said no. (*As Jonesy stares at him with astonished doubt, he continues impressively*) She doesn't speak for a long time, keepin' him waitin' while she's lookin' out over the water—then "no," she says—and you could tell she meant it, too—very low but clear so's I heard it plain as you hear me now.

JONESY—(*the humor of the situation suddenly striking him*) And you told ole Chris—Gawd's truth!—but you've made a bloody mess of it! The second'll bash 'is 'ead in! Blimey! Ho-ho!

GLASS—Serve him right! Someone had ought to bust his face in. Silly fathead! Him talkin' 'bout not lettin' his girl marry a sailor, or anyone'd go to sea, not even a bloody officer! He's a fine one to talk—deck hand on a rotten coal barge! Who does he think he is, I wonder—a squarehead furriner! He'd ought to be glad the second'd look at his girl, and mean decent. And her! She seems nice enough; but puttin' on airs, talkin' like a bloody lady! If it wasn't for her looks she'd be scrubbin' floors. She'd ought to get down on her knees to nab a man like the second, with officer's pay.

JONESY—Maybe she's 'eard of 'is foolin' with other gels.

Maybe she's got another bloke in the States. (*philosophically*) Gels is funny blokes. (*good-naturedly*) And ole Chris is all right—a good mate in the fo'c's'tle and a smart sailor—bo'sun, 'e was once—on'y 'e's a bit off 'is 'ead. (*laughing*) Ho-ho! There'll be some bloody fun on this bloody hooker in the mornin' if ole Chris gets started! You'd better lie low till 'e gets ashore, Glass. If 'e finds out you was lyin' to 'im, it won't be 'ealthy for you to meet 'im.

GLASS—(*with a smile*) I'll get the fourth engineer to sneak me in his cabin if there's any trouble. (*yawning*) Well, it'll give the Swede somethin' to think about for one night, anyway. He won't sleep much, I'll bet. I wonder why he's so down on sailors.

JONESY—'E don't seem to be with us 'ere. It's on'y with 'is gel, 'e means.

GLASS—He's off his chump, like you says, must be. (*stretching*) I'm for out on deck. Goin' to finish your letter?

JONESY—(*taking suitcase, paper and pencil again—obstinately*) Yes, blarst it!

GLASS—I'll pop off. (*He saunters out. Jonesy, scowling fiercely, bends to his labors. A moment later Chris reenters and sits down again. Jonesy looks up, then goes on writing. Chris broods somberly.*)

CHRIS—(*after a pause—with a grim determination—aloud to himself*) Only one tang left for do, py yingo! (*Jonesy looks up. Chris takes his sheath knife from his belt and holds it in his hands, regarding it with a morbid fascination.*) Only one vay for save Anna from dat ole davil. Eh—oh—it's so!

JONESY—(*jeeringly*) What ole devil? The second?

CHRIS—Eh, him? He don't count, dat fool fallar. He don't count for himself. But he's sailor—yust like Ay vas once—he's no good—he belong to sea—he's one of her dirty tricks.

JONESY—(*with a guffaw*) 'Er? Your gel?

CHRIS—No—ole davil, sea.

JONESY—The sea? What in 'ell are yer talkin' 'bout? (*contemptuously*) Blimey! You're a balmy ole bird!

CHRIS—(*not heeding this—in the same strange, determined way as if he were giving speech to something he had worked out carefully in his own mind*) Ay gat do it. Ay beat dat ole davil yet, py yimminy! She don't gat Anna like her mo'der, no, Ay svear! And Anna forgat in time. Forgat him, forgat me. She hate sea like hell after—dis—happen. (*He nods his head.*) It's only tang, yes. Ay can't help it.

JONESY—(*irritably*) Hush your bleedin' gab! 'Ow the 'ell can I write when you're ravin' like a lunatic?

CHRIS—(*fingering the edge of the knife—dully*) You ain't gat stone for sharpen knife, Yonesy?

JONESY—No. Shut yer marf! Chips 'as got one.

CHRIS—Ay got gat him. It's dull—dis knife. (*He goes out slowly.*)

JONESY—(*stares after him for a second, seized with a vague foreboding. Then he shakes this off irritably.*) Ho, t'ell with 'im! (*He starts writing again as*

The Curtain Falls)

SCENE II

SCENE—*A section of the midship of the* Londonderry, *looking astern. In the foreground, a short stretch of the main deck about ten feet deep from front to rear. On both sides of this, fencing it in, are the steel bulwarks of the ship, about three and a half feet high. In the rear, the bridge deck rises eight feet above the main. It is reached by two steel ladders, placed port and starboard. On the bridge deck, allowing a free deck space of about six feet on each side, stands the cabin with its row of brass-rimmed portholes. It sets back a little from the front edge of the bridge deck, allowing a narrow space in front of it, shut in by a steel rail, along which one can walk in passing from port to starboard. Over the cabin, extending the full width of the ship, is the bridge itself, a glimpse of which can be seen with its canvas awning, its wheel house and chart room in the center, its deck, rail high, fenced in by taut, canvas strips.*

All of this superstructure of the ship is painted white. The rest—bulwarks, main deck, everything below the bridge deck is painted black.

Bright, intense moonlight falls full on the ship. The shadows stretch astern. Every object stands plainly revealed. The vessel rides, motionless, on the calm waters of the roadstand. Silence and moon-light brood as one spirit over the ship. It is evidently late, for there is no sound of any human activity. The row of portholes toward the center of the cabin are alight, however, showing there is still someone awake. Their bright, yellow light sheds forth in golden strips, then filters into the lucent moon-grey and is lost. Over the bulwarks a vista of still-flowing river, spattered with silver rain, can be seen, a black line of low-lying land marking the horizon. The sky is wan and withdrawn, faintly glimmering with stars.

As the curtain rises, there is silence for a moment. Then a slight noise, like the shuffling of a foot, is heard from the left where the bulwark curves upward to the bridge deck. There is a black patch of shadow there between the ladder and the bulwark. The figure of Chris can be dimly made out, crouching on his haunches, his body pressed into the angle to avoid discovery from above. His head is tilted back; his eyes stare up at the bridge deck; he listens intently for some sound of movement from that direction.

His watch is rewarded. A door on the left of the cabin is opened and Andersen comes out. For a moment he stands in the block of thin yellow light from the open door; then he closes it behind him. Chris starts and half straightens his bent body. Andersen goes to the rail on the left of the bridge deck and stands there for a second. He sighs heavily, his eyes staring out over the water. Then he shakes his head doggedly as if to get rid of his thoughts, and clears his throat impatiently. Chris stiffens into an attitude of threatening vigilance. He has recognized the voice. Andersen takes out his watch and peers at it in the moonlight. Then, putting it back, he walks slowly around the corner of the cabin to the strip of railed-in deck in front of the portholes. He walks across toward the right. As he does so, Chris slinks quickly from his hiding place and bounds up the ladder, his bare feet making no noise on the steel rungs. Gaining the deck above, he crouches against the left wall of the cabin in the shadow falling from the bridge overhead. Andersen stops as he nears the end of the cabin on the right and, leaning against the rail, his face turned toward the right, he remains as if waiting for someone. Chris moves forward silently out of the shadow and peers around the corner of the cabin. He has a knife clutched in his right hand. He sees that the second mate's back is toward him, and, bending low so as to be beneath the sweep of the lighted portholes, he advances noiselessly three slow, careful steps. Then he gathers himself together and seems to be about to make a rushing spring at Andersen when the silence is shattered by the ship's bell which tolls with a mellow booming six times. Panic-stricken by this unforeseen interruption, Chris turns tail and darts back around the corner to his hiding place in the shadow of the bridge. Andersen stands motionless until the sound of the bell dies away. Then a door is opened on the right of the cabin and Anna comes out. Andersen hears this and strides forward eagerly around the corner of the cabin to meet her. He takes her hand without speaking. She withdraws it quickly.

ANDERSEN—(*in a low voice*) Out there in front of the cabin. The moonlight's beautiful there. (*He motions her to precede him.*)

ANNA—(*walking before the portholes and looking out over the sea—raptly*) It's beautiful everywhere tonight. What a night! It's like living in a dream. (*She has stopped at the center of the strip of deck.*)

ANDERSEN—Let's go further on. The skipper's still up, you know, going over his papers, and if he heard us talking he'd probably come out and join in. We don't want any number three—tonight.

ANNA—(*walking along almost to the end of the cabin on left—uncertainly*) It might be better—if—

ANDERSEN—(*fiercely*) No, no, Anna! Not our last night together!

ANNA—(*sadly*) This *is* the end, isn't it? Tomorrow I'll have to say good'bye to this dear old ship.

ANDERSEN—(*in a tone of pain*) Don't, Anna. Don't speak of it.

ANNA—(*as if she had not heard him*) And then I suppose it'll be steerage passage back to the States for me and Father—and then a beginning of the old, dull life all over again. (*She sighs. Chris slinks out of the shadow of the bridge and cautiously peers around the corner. They are side by side, their faces turned toward the bow, and they cannot see him. Chris discovers that his daughter is now between him and Andersen. He draws his head back quickly, his face working with baffled fury. He cannot escape toward the forecastle now; he is afraid to move; he is forced to remain an eavesdropper. Besides, he is consumed by curiosity. He leans against the side of the cabin, his head cocked to one side, trying to hear every word that passes between them.*)

ANDERSEN—(*eagerly*) You don't have to go back to the old life, Anna. (*pleadingly*) If you'd only—

ANNA—(*shrinking away from him—in a frightened tone*) Please! You promised you'd not speak of that again—or I'd not have come tonight. (*He groans helplessly. There is an uncomfortable pause—then she goes on sadly.*) When I was inside waiting for six bells to strike, I got to thinking of things. I tried to argue sensibly with myself and make myself become at least as hopeful about the future as I used to be in England. I tried to feel assured that I'd be contented again with my old plans and dreams. (*She gives an unhappy laugh.*) But they seemed too dreadful—and stupid—and such a waste of life.

ANDERSEN—Then why go back to them, Anna?

ANNA—(*ignoring this question*) This trip has been too splendid. It's spoiled me for commonplace things, I'm afraid. The sea has made me discover so many feelings I never knew I had before. (*She laughs unhappily.*) Perhaps it's only my natural laziness sprouting out, but the way I feel now I'd be happy—oh, so happy!—just forever sailing here and there, watching the sun rise and sink into the sea again day after day—and never do anything but love the sea.

ANDERSEN—(*impatiently*) You could do all that if you'd only—

ANNA—(*putting her hands over her ears—frightenedly*) Ssshh! Please!

ANDERSEN—(*with a helpless groan*) Oh—the devil take promises!

ANNA—(*after a pause—rebelliously*) I don't want to go back to any life I've ever lived before—but what else can I do?

ANDERSEN—Are you asking me? (*with a bitter smile*) I made a suggestion last night.

ANNA—Don't. We're talking of things that are—possible. And you're not trying to help me.

ANDERSEN—I tried to help us both, but—

ANNA—(*shortly*) Please!

ANDERSEN—(*offended—sarcastically*) Well then, when your

father becomes captain, mate and crew of another barge, you might sign on as general housekeeper.

ANNA—(*hurt—coldly*) It's serious with me. (*After a pause she continues slowly.*) No, I'm afraid Father and I will have to separate. (*Chris gives a start as he hears this. His face winces as if he had been struck.*) I don't think I have a good effect on him, or he on me. In the first days, after I grew to know him on the barge, I was happy because I thought I had found a real father I could love and respect. He was so kind and gentle—and different—and he worked so hard and uncomplainingly, and he seemed so happy to have me with him. I thought I had at last found something real to work for—to give him a home, a real home, in his old age. (*She sighs. Chris makes a movement as if he wanted to hide himself in the shadow again.*) But since the fog—since we've been on the steamer—he's changed, and he seems a stranger to me now more than ever. We've hardly spoken to each other in the last two weeks. He glares at me as if he hated me. And when he does speak he says such strange things—over and over—that silly idea I've told you of about the sea—the old devil, he calls her—that will swallow me up. (*with a shudder of fear*) It's silly—but I'm growing afraid of him—and of what he says. It sinks in. It gets on my nerves until I'm in terror of the sea myself. (*She points out and smiles raptly.*) Imagine being afraid of anything so lovely!

ANDERSEN—(*frowning*) He hates to see me with you. That's it.

ANNA—No, I really believe this enforced trip to sea again has affected his mind. He's so queer.

ANDERSEN—(*contemptuously*) Queer? We're all queer. Your father's brand of queerness is common enough, only he's got enough of the old sea superstitions in his blood to make him believe in his ghosts. But I tell you what: It's fear, that's what's the matter with him. He's afraid. He swallowed the anchor, as the sailors say. (*Chris half opens his mouth as if he were going to shout an indignant denial of this charge.*)

ANNA—(*curiously*) What a funny expression. What does it mean?

ANDERSEN—To swallow the anchor? It means just this: To

loose your grip, to whine and blame something outside of yourself for your misfortunes, to quit and refuse to fight back any more, to be afraid to take any more chances because you're sure you're no longer strong enough to make things come out right, to shrink from any more effort and be content to anchor fast in the thing you are!

ANNA—(*looking at him with wonder*) It's strange to hear you talk that way—with your ideas of things.

ANDERSEN—(*bitterly*) Oh, you're not the only one who has changed since you came on board—though you probably haven't been interested enough to see it. But we'll let that pass. I was telling you that your father had swallowed the anchor. The sea was his life, wasn't it? And now he blames it for all that happened to him, and hates and fears it accordingly. It's life he's really afraid of, if he only knew it—his own life.

ANNA—(*kindly*) I suppose that is it. Poor Father!

ANDERSEN—He has an excuse—if there ever is any. He's an old man. Oh, I'm not blaming him. I've hardly the right to. We've all of us done the same thing at times—swallowed the anchor!

ANNA—(*astonished*) Why do you talk so bitterly?

ANDERSEN—(*with a laugh*) Why not? Who has a better right? For I know the game. I swallowed the anchor the day I became second mate.

ANNA—(*rising to his defense*) That's not true. You wanted to live differently—to see the world.

ANDERSEN—That was my sugar-coated illusion. But the truth is that I wanted to enjoy everything and go scot free of payment. I want to sponge, to let someone else pay. It's a good enough idea, if you're small enough for it, though I don't doubt that you'd be forced to pay tenfold in the end—when you were old. Yes, I was small enough for it—then. I'm not now. I can see—bigger things. (*She turns away her head to hide the fact that she is moved by his talk. He goes on bitterly again.*) And you—oh, yes, you've swallowed the anchor, too! You're afraid to go on, afraid to be yourself. You whine: "what else can I do?" You're stuck fast. You'll go back to the old things.

ANNA—(*her face flushing—turning on him indignantly*) What are you saying? Please don't meddle— (*But she drops her eyes before his—in a trembling voice*) You're insulting.

ANDERSEN—You know it's true, Anna. (*She turns away. There is a pause. He goes on bitterly.*) And I? I had just heaved my anchor up on deck again, and got my ship refitted for sea. It wasn't such an easy job as you might think. And now there's no port to sail to! So it's overboard—down my throat—it'll have to go again, once and for all time.

ANNA—(*instinctively putting her hand on his arm—pleadingly*) Don't. It hurts me to hear you talk that way.

ANDERSEN—(*taking her hand in both of his*) Then why won't you—why won't you marry me, Anna? (*Chris stands up straight at this, an expression of amazed joy coming over his face as he knows that Glass' story must have been a lie. Anna opens her lips to voice a frightened protest but Andersen interrupts her fiercely.*) Oh, I know I promised not to speak of it again—after last night. But how can I help it? What else in God's world can I talk about? What else matters? What is my life now but you?

ANNA—(*struggling to free her hands—weakly*) Don't. I'm going—in.

ANDERSEN—Not till we've thrashed this thing out, you're not! No, not if I have to tie you here. (*Chris raises the knife in his hand and seems about to spring around the corner of the cabin.*)

ANNA—(*pleading—weakly*) But it's no good—it will only hurt us, Paul—it's better—as it is.

ANDERSEN—(*insistently*) Hurt *us*? But that means—it hurts you too, Anna. And if you don't care—why should it hurt you? (*intensely*) Then you do care, Anna! You do care!

ANNA—(*struggling—feebly*) No. I didn't mean—

ANDERSEN—(*triumphantly*) You do love me, Anna! You do! I told you last night I knew you must—must!

ANNA—(*trying to force her hand away from his*) No, Paul! No!

ANDERSEN—(*his voice thrilling with joy*) You're lying, Anna. You know you are. You can't blot it out of your eyes. It's there—giving you the lie— (*He tries to press her to him. Chris again takes a step forward, crouching, his face convulsed with rage; but there is some fear which stays him, holds him motionless in his position of eavesdropper.*)

ANNA—(*desperately*) No! (*half-hysterically*) I—I don't—(*then breaking down*) Yes—I don't know— Oh, what am I lying for this last night— Yes, I do—I think I do—I do love you, Paul. (*Chris shrinks back, seeming to crumple up as if he had been struck a mortal blow.*)

ANDERSEN—(*drawing her to him fiercely*) Anna! (*He bends to kiss her.*)

ANNA—(*with real entreaty*) Don't kiss me! Please, Paul! I ask you—please!

ANDERSEN—(*releasing her—tenderly*) But why?—dear.

ANNA—It will only make it harder for us. I've said I loved you—and I do—but—I can't do what you wish—I can't marry you—never!

ANDERSEN—(*with fierce grief*) But why not, Anna—if you love me?

ANNA—I should never have told you that. Why did you force me? But it can't be—I can't—I won't—I'm—I'm afraid.

ANDERSEN—Afraid? Of what, Anna?

ANNA—Of everything. Of myself—of you.

ANDERSEN—Of me, Anna? Of me? For God's sake, why?

ANNA—(*wildly*) Don't ask me! It's enough to know it's impossible for us. (*brokenly*) It'll be all right, Paul, in the end. After a time—when we haven't seen each other—we'll forget.

ANDERSEN—(*wounded*) Forget? You can say that—but I—

ANNA—You've loved other women before me. You've forgotten them.

ANDERSEN—(*frowning*) Has someone been carrying silly tales to you? Your father, eh. Oh, Anna, be sensible! Those things are nothing. They have nothing to do with the me who loves you. They are dead things, just as the old me is dead. I've played the damn fool, I know, but can't you see the change my love for you has made in me? Can't you believe in the sincerity of that change, its lasting quality? Why, I never knew the real myself till I knew you, Anna! Before that I just drifted with the tide, and let things happen. It was all a game to play. How could I know you—your love—

would come to me? I was a fool. I never dreamed anything so splendid could enter into a life like mine. But now—it *has* come! Oh, Anna, I've never known real love till I knew you! I swear it! Can't you believe me?

ANNA—(*faintly*) Yes, I believe you feel that way—now. But—you'd never leave the sea—

ANDERSEN—(*wildly*) Yes, I will. I'll work on land. I'll do anything you wish, Anna.

ANNA—(*sadly*) No. Don't you see I couldn't ask that? Your life is here. You'd soon grow tired on land—and then you'd leave me—and blame me—and hate me!

ANDERSEN—Anna!

ANNA—You would—in time. And I—I don't want to settle down, either—not the way most people do. I've known the sea now, too. (*sorrowfully*) I think Father is right, after all. The sea does put a curse on the men who go down to it—and their women—the women most of all.

ANDERSEN—(*roughly*) Your father is a superstitious old ass! He blames the sea for his own weakness.

ANNA—(*shaking her head*) No. He knows it better than you. He has seen for many years what it has done. The women wait, he says—and it's true. They wait. And the men sail over the world—and there are the other women in every port—fresh faces—and the men forget their home. And when they do return for a short while between voyages they and their wives are strangers—and if children are born, the father and child are strangers—as I and my father were—and are. When my mother died—he was at sea. (*breaking down*) No, no, I'm afraid, Paul. I couldn't live that way—waiting for you—not knowing what you were doing, thinking you might be drowned, fearing that even if you were alive, you had forgotten me for the other woman. No, no, it's best to end it now—in the beginning. I can't let my life be tortured like that! I can't!

ANDERSEN—But your father is speaking of the old sailing-ship days. What he says might have been true then. It isn't any longer.

ANNA—But you've told me yourself this ship has no regular route—that it goes any place in the world where there are cargoes, and takes them any place. If I were in the States now—married to you—when would you be home to me? You don't know. It might be a year—two years.

ANDERSEN—(*taking her by the shoulders and shaking her gently—compellingly*) Listen, Anna. I've found a way to beat your father's bogie stories. You won't have to settle down in a landman's way—to a house and lot. I wouldn't want you to. I wouldn't love you if you did. I love the you who is different from the rest of the pack—the girl with the sea in her eyes, and the love of it in her blood—the girl who loves and feels the things I love and feel! (*then buoyantly as if the vision of it were clear before his eyes*) We'll not leave the sea, you and I. We'll keep it in spite of everything. And we'll go to all the ports of the world and see them all—together! And the sea shall be our mother, and the mother of our children. And you won't have to wait for me as your mother waited for him—watching and hoping and despairing. No, you will be with me, beside me, a part of me—always!

ANNA—(*who has been leaning toward him, drinking in his words with shining eyes*) Oh, if that could only be! (*then with a despairing laugh*) But it's only a dream you're dreaming, Paul. How is it possible?

ANDERSEN—It is—when I'm a captain, Anna. A captain can have his wife to live on board with him if he gets the right ship and insists upon it. (*resolutely*) And I'll win to a master's certificate just as soon as it's humanly possible.

ANNA—(*staring at him*) You? A captain? But you don't want that, Paul, you know you don't. You remember what you told me that very first night—the responsibilities you hated so.

ANDERSEN—(*with a gentle smile*) And that is the biggest thing you've been afraid of—that I might be at heart a waster, after all—isn't it? (*She nods. He pats her shoulder reassuringly.*) Well, you needn't be any more. Didn't I say I had changed? (*with joyous strength*) No, I want responsibilities now—loads of them—to prove to you I can be strong. (*with virile confidence*) And I'll win, Anna! I know I can!

ANNA—Oh, Paul, I know you can, too—if you want to enough.

PAUL—I'll show you! But you won't mind waiting a little at first—till I win to my own ship? I'll make it easy, Anna!

I'll get a berth on some passenger steamer with a regular route out of New York, and you can live there and I'll be with you a lot of the time. And we'll save the money, and every now and then you can take a trip on the ship as a passenger. That won't be so hard for you, will it, Anna?

ANNA—No, dear.

ANDERSEN—And it won't be for long. I'll work my damndest, I promise you.

ANNA—(*suddenly looking at him with a provoking smile*) You seem to be taking a lot for granted. I haven't said I'd marry you yet.

ANDERSEN—(*smiling down at her*) Oh, yes, you did! I heard you! You said you'd marry me tomorrow—in Buenos Aires.

ANNA—Oh, no!

ANDERSEN—Oh, yes!

ANNA—(*with a happy laugh*) Well—let me see—perhaps I did. (*He puts his arms around her. She lifts her lips to his and they kiss and remain clasped in each other's arms. Chris, since he had overheard the declaration of love made by his daughter, has stood motionlessly, the hand with the knife hanging limply by his side, his eyes staring dully out to sea, his whole body seeming to sag and shrink beneath the burden of loss he feels. Now that they are no longer speaking, the silence arouses him. He sticks his head cautiously around the corner of the cabin. He sees them clearly in the moonlight.*)

ANNA—(*her voice thrilling with love*) I was so sad, Paul—I wanted to be dead—and now I'm so, so happy!

ANDERSEN—Dear! (*He kisses her again. The knife drops from Chris' hand with a clatter. At the same moment he stumbles blindly around the cabin toward them. The two break from their embrace and, seeing Chris, stand for a second paralyzed with astonishment.*)

CHRIS—(*with a hoarse cry like a sob*) Anna!

ANNA—(*instinctively stepping forward to protect Andersen— frightenedly*) Father!

ANDERSEN—(*savagely*) Damn! (*His fists clench but he does not move, his eyes watching for some indication of Chris' purpose.*)

CHRIS—(*stopping short in a dazed manner—incoherently*) Ay vas coming for'ard from poop. (*He pauses stupidly.*) It ain't no good—for fight—her. (*He nods out at the moonlit water with a slow motion of his head.*) It's so! (*His chin sinks on his chest. His shoulders heave as if he were stifling a sob.*)

ANNA—(*going and putting her arm about him—compassionately*) Father! What is it? (*then, after a pause, as he makes no reply*) I'm going to marry Mr. Andersen tomorrow, Father.

CHRIS—(*nodding*) Ay know. Ay hear all you say from first.

ANDERSEN—(*indignantly*) You were listening—hiding around the corner of the cabin there?

CHRIS—Yes—sir.

ANDERSEN—(*angrily*) Well, I'll be damned!

ANNA—(*pleading for her father*) Paul!

CHRIS—(*defiantly*) Ay gat right for listen, Ay tank. Anna vas only body Ay gat in vorld. Ay don't know you. (*after a pause during which he struggles to collect his thoughts, to reconcile them*) Yes, Ay hear all you say, sir—all Anna say. Ay don't vant for Anna love fallar go to sea, sir—no, py yingo, Ay don't!

ANDERSEN—(*roughly*) Nonsense, man! If you heard all I said—

CHRIS—(*interrupting him*) Ay know. You say Anna live on board with you—some time—ven you're captain. She don't vait—like her mo'der. Dat's fine tang, too. And you're smart sailor for make captain, Ay know. Ay vatch you on voyage. (*His voice commences to tremble slightly.*) And Anna say she love you. Ay hear. And, maybe—dat's good tang too—for young gel like her. Ay'm too ole fallar for keep young gel. Ay'm ole fool, too, Ay tank. So—Anna—you marry him. It's all right—yes—Ay tank it must be—it's all right.

ANNA—(*joyfully—throwing her arms around his neck and kissing him*) Father! (*Andersen comes forward and takes Chris' limp hand and clasps it silently.*)

CHRIS—(*to Andersen—with slow resentment*) You say wrong tang, sir, Ay hear. Ay don't svallow anchor, no, py yingo! Ay ain't scared. Ay'm ole fallar, but Ay bet you Ay fight dat ole davil, sea, till last end come, py yimminy! (*He shakes his fist defiantly at the horizon. The captain's voice is heard from inside calling: "Andersen."*)

ANDERSEN—(*raising his hand for the others to be silent*) Ssshh!

ANNA—(*confusedly—in a flurried whisper*) He might come out, Paul. Let's hide from him. Good night, Father. (*She kisses him and darts on tip-toe around the cabin to the right. Andersen follows on her heels, bending low to be out of range of the light from the portholes.*)

CHRIS—(*remains standing in a daze, blinking in the moon-light. Then he turns to go to the ladder to the main deck, left. His foot kicks the knife which he picks up. He holds it in his hand for a second, standing at the top of the ladder, staring at it dully. He mutters*) Ay'm ole damn fool fallar. (*He flings the knife over the side disgustedly.*) You take him. He's your dirty trick, ole davil! (*The door on the left of cabin is opened and Captain Jessup comes out.*)

CAPTAIN JESSUP—(*sees the figure standing there*) Andersen? (*then startled*) Eh? Who's that?

CHRIS—(*dully*) It's Chris, sir.

CAPTAIN JESSUP—(*angrily*) Eh? Chris? Oh. What the devil are you doing here, eh?

CHRIS—Ay vas speaking with Anna, sir.

CAPTAIN JESSUP—Oh. (*then in a more friendly tone*) Your daughter's gone in?

CHRIS—Yes, sir.

CAPTAIN JESSUP—Better get forward where you belong, then. (*then as Chris turns to go—as if he suddenly remembered something*) Oh—one moment, Christophersen. Now that you're here, I've something to ask you. The bo'sun is done up with rheumatism, you know that, eh? Pretty serious. Goes ashore to the hospital in the morning. Not a chance of his being fit again in time to go on with us. Hmmph. Mr. Hall reports very favorably on you, Christophersen. He suggests that you—you've had enough of barges, I'll wager—well?—eh?—do you want the berth?

CHRIS—(*in a stupefied voice*) You vant me—for my ole job—bo'sun, sir?

CAPTAIN JESSUP—(*testily*) Eh? Have you lost your wits? Didn't I make it plain to you? Do you want the job—yes or no?

CHRIS—(*looks all around him wildly as if he wanted to run and hide—then in a panic-stricken voice*) Yes, sir. Ay take yob.

CAPTAIN JESSUP—(*with a grunt of satisfaction*) Good

enough. (*He goes to the door—then turns with a smile.*) Good night, bo'sun.

CHRIS—(*automatically*) Good night, sir. (*The captain goes in, shutting the door behind him. Chris stands looking out over the water. As he does so a change gradually comes over his face. It softens, and a grin of admiration and affection which he vainly tries to subdue, forces itself on his face. He shakes his fist again at the far horizon, and growls in a sheepish voice*) Dat's your best dirty trick, ole davil! Eh, vell, you gat me beat for sure dis time. Ay'm ole fool for fight with you. No man dat live going beat you, py yingo! (*He nods appreciatively and turns to the ladder, unconsciously beginning to sing carelessly in a low voice as he clambers slowly down:*) "My Yosephine, come board de ship. Long time Ay vait for you. De moon, she shi-i-i-ine. She looka yust like you. Tchee-tchee. Tchee-tchee. Tchee-tchee. Tchee-tchee." (*He saunters slowly front toward the forecastle along the main deck grumbling cheerfully as he does so:*) It's hard yob, bo'sun on dis rusty tea-kettle—yust vork, vork, vork all time. Ay better turn in for sleep, yes.

as

(*The Curtain Falls*)

GOLD

A Play in Four Acts

CHARACTERS

CAPTAIN ISAIAH BARTLETT, *of the whaling ship* Triton

SILAS HORNE, *boatswain of the* Triton

BEN CATES

JIMMY KANAKA, *an Islander* } *of the* Triton*'s crew*

BUTLER, *cook of the* Triton

ABEL, *the ship's boy*

SARAH ALLEN BARTLETT, *the captain's wife*

SUE, *their daughter*

NAT, *their son*

DANIEL DREW, *officer of a freight steamer*

DOCTOR BERRY

Gold

ACT ONE

SCENE—*A small, barren coral island on the southern fringe of the Malay Archipelago. The coral sand, blazing white under the full glare of the sun, lifts in the right foreground to a long hummock a few feet above sea-level. A stunted coco palm rises from the center of this elevation, its bunch of scraggly leaves drooping motionlessly, casting a small circular patch of shadow directly beneath on the ground about the trunk. About a hundred yards in the distance the lagoon is seen, its vivid blue contrasting with the white coral beach which borders its circular outline. The far horizon to seaward is marked by a broad band of purplish haze which separates the bright blue of the water from the metallic gray-blue of the sky. The island bakes. The intensity of the sun's rays is flung back skyward in a quivering mist of heat-waves which distorts the outlines of things, giving the visible world an intangible eerie quality, as if it were floating submerged in some colorless molten fluid.*

As the curtain rises, Abel is discovered lying asleep, curled up in the patch of shade beneath the coco palm. He is a runty, undersized boy of fifteen, with a shrivelled old face, tanned to parchment by the sun. He has on a suit of dirty dungarees, man's size, much too large for him, which hang in loose folds from his puny frame. A thatch of brown hair straggles in limp wisps from under the peaked canvas cap he wears. He looks terribly exhausted. His dreams are evidently fraught with terror, for he twitches convulsively and moans with fright. Butler enters hurriedly, panting, from the right, rear. He is a tall man of over middle age, dressed in the faded remainder of what was once a brown suit. The coat, the buttons of which have been torn off, hangs open, revealing his nakedness beneath. A cloth cap covers his bald head, with its halo of dirty thin gray hair. His body is emaciated. His face, with its round, blue eyes, is weathered and cracked by the sun's rays. The wreck of a pair of heavy shoes flop about his bare feet. He looks back cautiously, as if he were afraid of being followed; then satisfied that he is not, he approaches the sleeping boy, and bending down, puts his hand on Abel's forehead. Abel groans and opens his eyes. He stares about furtively, as if seeking someone whose presence he dreads to find.

ABEL—(*in a husky voice*) Where's Capt'n and the rest, Butts?

BUTLER—(*in a hoarse, cracked whisper*) On the beach— down there. (*He makes an exhausted gesture, right, and then sinks with a groan at the foot of the tree, leaning back against the trunk, trying vainly to hunch his long legs up so as to be completely in the shade.*)

ABEL—(*with avid eyes*) They ain't found no water yet?

BUTLER—(*shaking his head, his eyes closing wearily*) No. How would they—when there ain't any—not on this devil's island—dry as a bone, my sonny—sand and sun—that's all.

ABEL—(*with a sudden, shrill agony—his lips twitching*) I need a drink of water—something awful! (*with tremulous pleading*) Say, ain't you got 'nother drink left?—honest, ain't you?

BUTLER—(*looking around him cautiously*) Not so loud! (*fixing his eyes sternly on the boy*) This is a dead secret, mind! You'll swear you won't blab—not to him?

ABEL—Sure, Butts, sure! Gawd strike me dead!

BUTLER—(*takes a pint bottle from the hip-pocket of his pants. It is about half full of water.*) He—and the rest—they'd kill me like a dog—and you too, sonny—remember that!

ABEL—Sure! I ain't goin' to tell 'em, Butts. (*stretching out his hands frenziedly*) Aw, give it to me, Butts! Give me a drink, for Christ's sake!

BUTLER—No, you don't! Only a few drops. It's got to last 'til a ship comes past that'll pick us up. That's the only hope. (*holding the bottle at arm's length from the boy*) Hands down, now—or you don't get a drop! (*The boy lets his hands drop to his sides. Butler puts the bottle carefully to his lips, and allows the boy two gulps—then snatches it away.*) That's all now. More later. (*He takes one gulp himself, and making a tremendous effort of will, jerks the bottle from his lips, and corking it quickly, thrusts it back in his pocket and heaves a shuddering sigh.*)

ABEL—Aw, more! Just another swaller—

BUTLER—(*determinedly*) No!

ABEL—(*crying weakly*) Yuh dirty mutt!

BUTLER—(*quietly*) Don't get riled. It only makes you hotter—and thirstier. (*The boy sinks back exhausted and closes his eyes. Butler begins to talk in a more assured voice, as if the sip of water had renewed his courage*.) That'll save us yet, that bit of water. A lucky notion of mine to think of it—at the last moment. They were just lowering the boats. I could hear you calling to me to hurry and come. But I thought of filling this bottle. It'd been lying there in the galley for two years almost. I'd had it on my hip, full of whisky, that night in Oakland when I was shanghied. So I filled it out of a bucket before I ran to the boat. Lucky I did, son—for you and me—not for them—damn 'em! (*as if in self-justification*) Why should I tell 'em, eh? Did I ever get anything better than a kick or a curse from one of them? (*vindictively*) Would they give it to me if they had it? They'd see me in hell first! And besides, it's too late for them. They're mad as hatters right now, the four of them. They ain't had a drop since three nights back, when the water in the cask gave out and we rowed up against this island in the dark. (*Suddenly he laughs queerly*.) Didn't you hear them shouting and yelling like lunatics just before I came?

ABEL—I thought I heard something—on'y maybe I was dreamin'.

BUTLER—It's them that are doing the dreaming. I was with them. (*with rising anger*) He kicked me awake—and every time I tried to get away he beat me back. He's strong yet—(*with threatening vindictiveness*)—but he can't last long, damn him! (*controlling himself, goes on with his story excitedly*) We went looking for water. Then Jimmy Kanaka saw a boat sunk half under down inside the reef—a Malay canoe, only bigger. They thought there might be something to drink on her. All of a sudden they gave an awful yell. They was all standing about a box they'd forced open, yelling and cursing and out of their heads completely. When I looked I seen the box was full of all sorts of metal junk—bracelets and bands and necklaces that I guess the Malays wear. Nothing but brass and copper, and bum imitations of diamonds and things— not worth a damn! I picked up some of the stuff to make sure. Then I told him straight. "This ain't gold. It's brass and copper—not worth a damn." God, he got wild! I had to run, or he'd knifed me. (*with sudden violence*) It serves 'em right, all that's happened and going to happen. Me shanghied when I was drunk—taken away from a good job and forced to cook the swill on a rotten whaler! Oh, I'll pay him back for it! His damn ship is wrecked and lost to him—that's the first of it. I'll see him rot and die—and the three with him! But you and me'll be saved! D'you know why I've let you go halves on this water? It's because they kicked and beat you, too. And now we'll get even! (*He sinks back, exhausted by this outburst. They are both silent, leaning with closed eyes against the bole of the tree. A murmur of men's voices comes from the right, rear, and gradually gets nearer.*)

ABEL—(*opening his eyes with a start*) Butts! I hear 'em comin'!

BUTLER—(*listening, wide-eyed, for a moment*) Yes, it's them. (*He gets up weakly. Abel staggers to his feet. They both move to the left. Butler shades his eyes with his hands and looks toward the beach.*) Look! They're dragging along that box of junk with 'em, the damn fools! (*warningly*) They're crazy as hell. Don't give 'em no chance to pick on you, d'you hear? (*There is a scuffling of heavy footsteps in the sand, and Captain Bartlett appears, followed by Horne, who in turn is followed by Cates and Jimmy Kanaka. Bartlett is a tall, huge-framed figure of a man, dressed in a blue double-breasted coat, pants of the same material, and rubber sea-boots turned down from the knees. In spite of the ravages of hunger and thirst there is still a suggestion of immense strength in his heavy-muscled body. His head is massive, thickly covered with tangled, iron-gray hair. His face is large, bony, and leather-tanned, with a long aquiline nose and a gash of a mouth shadowed by a bristling gray mustache. His broad jaw sticks out at an angle of implacable stubbornness. Bushy gray brows over-hang the obsessed glare of his somber dark eyes. Silas Horne is a thin, parrot-nosed, angular old man, his lean face marked by a life-time of crass lusts and mean cruelty. He is dressed in gray cotton trousers, and a singlet torn open across his hairy chest. The exposed skin of his arms and shoulders and chest has been blistered and seared by the sun. A cap is on his head. Cates is squat and broad chested, with thick, stumpy legs and arms. His square, stu-pid face, with its greedy pig's eyes, is terribly pock-marked. He is gross and bestial, an unintelligent brute. He is dressed in dunga-ree pants and a dirty white sailor's blouse, and wears a brown cap. Jimmy Kanaka is a tall, sinewy, bronzed young Islander. He wears only a loin cloth and a leather belt with a sheath-knife. The last two are staggering beneath the weight of a heavy inlaid chest.*

The eyes of the three white men are wild. They pant exhaustedly, their legs trembling with weakness beneath them. Their lips are puffed and cracked, their voices muffled by their swollen tongues. But there is a mad air of happiness, of excitement, about their scorched faces.)

BARTLETT—(*in a crooning, monotonous voice*) It's heavy, I know, heavy—that chest. Up, bullies! Up with her! (*He flings himself in the shade, resting his back against the tree, and points to the sand at his feet.*) Put 'er there, bullies—there where I kin see!

HORNE—(*echoing his words mechanically*) Put 'er there!

CATES—(*in thick, stupid tones*) Aye-aye, sir! Down she goes, Jimmy. (*They set the chest down.*)

BARTLETT—Sit down, lads, sit down. Ye've earned your spell of rest. (*The three men throw themselves on the sand in attitudes of spent weariness. Bartlett's eyes are fixed gloatingly on the chest. There is a silence suddenly broken by Cates, who leaps to a kneeling position with a choked cry.*)

CATES—(*his eyes staring at the Captain with fierce insistence*) I want a drink—water! (*The others are startled into a rigid, dazed attention. Horne's lips move painfully in a soundless repetition of the word. There is a pause. Then Bartlett strikes the sides of his head with his fist, as if to drive this obsession from his brain. Butler and Abel stand looking at them with frightened eyes.*)

BARTLETT—(*having regained control over himself, in a determined voice, deep-toned and menacing*) If ye speak that word again, Ben Cates—if ye say it once again—ye'll be food for the sharks! Ye hear?

CATES—(*terrified*) Yes, sir. (*He collapses limply on the sand again. Horne and the Kanaka relax hopelessly.*)

BARTLETT—(*with heavy scorn*) Are ye a child to take on like a sick woman—cryin' for what ye know we've not got? Can't ye stand up under a little thirst like a man? (*resolutely*) There'll be water enough—if ye'll wait and keep a stiff upper lip on ye. We'll all be picked up today. I'll stake my word on it. This state o' things can't last. (*His eyes fall on the chest.*) Ye ought to be singin' 'stead o' cryin'—after the find we've made. What's the lack of water amount to—when ye've gold before you? (*with mad exultation*) Gold! Enough of it is your share alone to buy ye rum, and wine, and women, too, for the rest o' your life!

CATES—(*straightening up to a sitting posture—his small eyes staring at the box fascinatedly—in a stupid mumble*) Aye—aye—rum and wine!

BARTLETT—(*half closing his eyes as if the better to enjoy his vision*) Aye, rum and wine and women for you and Horne and Jimmy. No more hard work on the dirty sea for ye, bullies, but a full pay-day in your pockets to spend each day o' the year. (*The three strain their ears, listening eagerly. Even Butler and Abel advance a step or two toward him, as if they, too, were half hypnotized.*) And Cates grumbling because he's thirsty! I'd be the proper one to complain—if complainin' there was to do! Ain't I lost my ship and the work o' two years with her? And what have ye lost, all three, but a few rags o' clothes? (*with savage emphasis*) I tell ye, I be glad the Triton went down! (*He taps the box with his fingers.*) They's more in this than ever was earned by all the whalin' ships afloat. They's gold—heavy and solid—and diamonds and emeralds and rubies!—red and green, they be.

CATES—(*licking his lips*) Aye, I seen 'em there—and emeralds be green, I know, and sell for a ton of gold!

BARTLETT—(*as if he hadn't heard and was dreaming out loud to himself*) Rum and wine for you three, and rest for me. Aye, I'll rest to home 'til the day I die. Aye, woman, I be comin' home now. Aye, Nat and Sue, your father be comin' home for the rest o' his life! I'll give up whalin' like ye've always been askin' me, Sarah. Aye, I'll go to meetin' with ye on a Sunday like ye've always prayed I would. We'll make the damn neighbors open their eyes, curse 'em! Carriages and silks for ye—they'll be nothin' too good—and for Sue and the boy. I've been dreamin' o' this for years. I never give a damn 'bout the oil—that's just trade—but I always hoped on some voyage I'd pick up ambergris—a whole lot of it—and that's worth gold!

HORNE—(*his head bobbing up from his chest drowsily*) Aye, ambergris! It's costly truck.

BUTLER—(*in a whisper to the boy—cautiously*) There! Wasn't I right? Mad as hatters, all of 'em!

BARTLETT—(*his voice more and more that of a somnambulist*)

It's time I settled down to home with ye, Sarah. They's plenty o' big trees on my place, bullies, and shade and green grass, and a cool wind off the sea. (*He shakes off the growing drowsiness and glares about him in a rage.*) Hell's fire! What crazy truck be I thinkin' of? (*But he and the others sink back immediately into stupor. After a pause he begins to relate a tale in a droning voice.*) Years ago, when I was whalin' out o' New Bedford, a man come to me—Spanish-looking, he was—and wanted to charter my ship and me go shares. He showed me a map o' some island off the coast of South America some-where. They was a cross marked on it where treasure had been buried by the old pirates. But I was a fool. I didn't be-lieve him. He got old Scott's schooner—finally. She sailed and never was heard o' since. But I've never forgot him and his map. And often I've thought if I'd 'a' went that vige— (*He straightens up and shouts with aggressive violence*) But here she be! Run right into it—without no map nor nothin'. Gold and diamonds and all—there they be in front o' our eyes! (*to the now alert Jimmy*) Open 'er up, Jimmy!

JIMMY—(*getting up—in his soft voice*) Aye, Captain. (*He reaches down to lift the lid.*)

BARTLETT—(*A sudden change of feeling comes over him, and he knocks Jimmy's arm aside savagely.*) Hands off, ye dog! I'm takin' care o' this chest, and no man's hand's goin' to touch it but mine!

JIMMY—(*stepping back docilely—in the same unmoved, soft tone*) Aye, Captain. (*He squats down to the left of the chest.*)

BARTLETT—(*seeming suddenly to notice the cook for the first time*) So there you be, eh? (*his voice growing thick with rage*) I ain't forgot what ye said down by the shore there! Lucky for ye I didn't catch ye then! "Brass and copper—junk," ye said—"not gold! Not worth a damn," ye said! Ye blasted son o' a liar! (*looking at Abel*) Ye've been tellin' that boy your lies too, I kin tell by the look o' him. (*sternly*) Come here, boy!

ABEL—(*advances with faltering steps*) Y-yes, s-sir?

BARTLETT—Open up that chest! Open it up, ye brat! (*With a desperate movement of fear Abel reaches down and flings open the lid of the chest. As he does so, Bartlett's huge hand fastens on the collar of his coat, and holds him with face bent over the box.*

Horne, Cates, and Jimmy Kanaka pull themselves close, their necks craning for a look inside.)

BARTLETT—(*shaking the terror-stricken boy*) What d'ye see there, ye little swab? What d'ye see there?

ABEL—Aw—leggo—I'm chokin'!

BARTLETT—(*grimly*) Ye'll choke in earnest if ye don't answer me. What d'ye see? Is it gold? Answer me—is it gold?

ABEL—(*stutteringly*) Yes—sure—gold—I see it!

BARTLETT—(*thrusts him away. The boy staggers and falls to the sand. Bartlett turns to Butler triumphantly.*) Ye see, ye liar? Gold! Gold! Even a child can tell it at a look. (*with a somber menace in his tone*) But ye—don't believe—do ye?

BUTLER—(*frightenedly*) Maybe I was wrong, sir. I—didn't—look very careful.

BARTLETT—Come here! (*He stands up, his back against the tree.*) Come here!

BUTLER—Yes, sir. (*But he looks about him shiftily, as if to run away.*)

BARTLETT—Jimmy! (*The Kanaka leaps to his feet.*) Knife him, Jimmy, if he tries to run.

JIMMY—(*His hand goes to his knife, his dark eyes lighting up with savagery—in his soft voice*) Aye, Captain!

BARTLETT—(*to the trembling cook*) Come here!

BUTLER—(*goes to him with the courage of desperation*) Yes, sir.

BARTLETT—(*pointing to the contents of the chest*) Is it gold—or no?

BUTLER—If I can feel of one—

BARTLETT—Pick one up.

BUTLER—(*picks up a heavy anklet encrusted with colored glass, looks at it for a minute—then feigning great assurance*) I was wrong, Captain. It's gold all right enough—worth all kinds of money, I bet.

BARTLETT—(*with mad triumph*) Ha! Ye've come to your senses, have ye? Too late, ye swab! No share for ye! And here's to teach ye for lyin' to me before! (*His fist jerks out from his side, and Butler is knocked sprawling on the sand, where he lies groaning for a moment, the anklet still clutched in his hand. The boy gives a gasp of fright and scampers off, left.*)

BARTLETT—That'll learn ye! (*He sits down beside the chest. The others crouch close. Bartlett shoves in both of his hands—in a tone of mad gloating*) Gold! Better'n whaling, ain't she, boys? Better'n ambergris, even if I ever had luck to find any! (*Butler staggers to his feet. He examines the anklet with contemptuous scorn and even bites it to make sure. Then he edges stealthily toward the left. A sudden transformation comes over his face and he glowers at the Captain with hatred, his features distorted with fury.*)

JIMMY KANAKA—(*pointing to Butler*) He got him, Captain!

BARTLETT—(*glancing at the cook with contemptuous scorn*) Sneakin' away with that piece o' the gold, be ye? Ye thievin' swine! Ye know right enough it's gold now, don't ye? Well, ye kin keep it—for your share for speakin' the truth that once.

HORNE—(*his cupidity protesting*) Don't give it to him, sir! It's so much the less for us that worked for it when he did nothin'!

BUTLER—(*overcome by hysterical rage—stammering*) Who asked you for it—eh? Who—wants the dam thing? Not me! No! (*holding the anklet out contemptuously*) Gold? Ha-ha! Gold? Brass, that's what—and pieces of glass! Junk! Not worth a dam. Here! Take it! (*He flings it on the sand before them. Bartlett snatches it up protectingly.*)

BARTLETT—(*in a frenzy*) Jimmy! (*But Butler runs off left with a terrified cry. Jimmy springs to his feet and stands with his hand on his knife, waiting for a further order.*)

JIMMY—(*eagerly*) I go catch—go stick him, Captain?

BARTLETT—(*pausing—with a frown*) No. They's time enough for that—if need be. Sit down. (*Jimmy sits down again with a childish air of sulking. Bartlett stares at the treasure, continuing to frown, as if Butler's action had made him uneasy, bewildered and confused him. He mutters half to himself*) Queer! Queer! He threw it back as if 'twas a chunk of mud! He knew—and yet he said he didn't want it. Junk, he called it—and he knows it's gold! He said 'twas gold himself a second back. He's queer. Why would he say junk when he knows it's gold? D'ye think—he don't believe?

HORNE—He was mad because you knocked him down.

BARTLETT—(*shaking his head grimly*) It ain't the first time I've knocked him down; but he never spoke up to me—like that—before. No, it's somethin' else is wrong with him— somethin'.

HORNE—No share for him, you told him, sir. That's what's wrong with him.

BARTLETT—(*again shaking his head*) No. His eyes— It's somethin' he's got in his head—somethin' he's hidin'! His share—maybe he thinks he'll get his share anyway, in spite o' us! Maybe he thinks his share wouldn't be all he wants! Maybe he thinks we'll die o' hunger and thirst before we get picked up—and he'll live—and then—he'll come in for the whole chestful! (*suddenly springing to his feet in a rage*) Hell's fire! That's it, bullies! That's his sneakin' plan! To watch us die—and steal it from us!

CATES—(*rising to his knees and shaking his hand threateningly above his head*) Tell Jimmy to knife him, sir! Tell Jimmy—I ain't got a knife, or I'd do it myself. (*He totters weakly to his feet.*)

JIMMY—(*eagerly*) You speak, I stick him, Captain. I stick boy, too.

CATES—(*weakening*) I'm weak, but I kin do for him yet. I'm weak— (*His knees sag under him. He pleads piteously*) If I'd only a drink to put some strength in me! If I'd only a sup o' water, I'd do for him! (*turning, as if to stagger down toward the beach*) There must be water. Let's look again. I'll go look— (*But the effort he makes is too much for his strength and he falls to the sand, panting with open mouth.*)

BARTLETT—(*summoning his will—sternly*) Put a clapper on that jaw of yours, Cates, or I'll do it for ye!

CATES—(*blubbering*) If we don't find water—he'll watch us die.

JIMMY—(*insinuatingly*) Better me knife cook fella—kill boy, too!

BARTLETT—Will killin' 'em give us drink, ye fools? (*After a pause, he shakes his head as if to drive off some thought, and mutters*) No more o' that! (*suddenly, in a tone of sharp command*) No more o' that, I say! We're keepin' no right watch for ships. Go aloft on that tree, Jimmy—and damn quick! (*Kanaka climbs quickly up the bole of the coco palm to the top and looks out on all sides of him. The others rise painfully to their feet and gaze up at him with awakened hope.*)

JIMMY—(*suddenly, in a glad voice*) I see um—see sail, Captain.

CATES—(*waving his arms frenziedly*) Sail—ho!

JIMMY—Look plenty like trade schooner, Captain. She no change course she fetch plenty close by here. She make full sail, she got plenty fella wind out there, she come quick.

HORNE—(*clapping Cates on the back*) Headin' straight for us, Cates, d'you hear?

BARTLETT—Come down. (*The Islander slides down. Bartlett exclaims exultantly*) Didn't I tell ye? In the nick o' time. When she makes in close we'll go down to the reef and yell and wave at her. They'll see! The luck's with us today! (*His eyes fall on the treasure and he starts.*) But now—what's to do with this chest—the gold?

HORNE—(*quickly*) You ain't going to tell them on the schooner about it?

CATES—They'd claim to share with us.

BARTLETT—(*scornfully*) D'ye think I'm cracked? No, we'll bury it here.

CATES—(*regretfully*) Leave it behind for anyone to find?

BARTLETT—We'll bury it deep, where hell itself won't find it—and we'll make a map o' this island. (*He takes a piece of paper and a stub of pencil from his pocket—pointing to the foot of the tree*) Dig a hole here—you, Horne and Jimmy—and dig it deep. (*The two bend down and commence to hollow out the sand with their hands. Bartlett draws on the paper.*) There's the lagoon—and the reef— (*to Cates, who is peering over his shoulder*) And here where the tree is, d'ye see, Cates, I'll make a cross where the gold is hid. (*exultantly*) Oh, all hell'd not stop me from findin' this place again! Let us once get home and I'll fit out a small schooner the four of us can sail, and we'll come back here to dig it up. It won't be long, I swear to ye!

HORNE—(*straightening up*) This deep enough, sir?

JIMMY—(*who has straightened up and is looking off left—suddenly points excitedly*) He look, Captain! Cook fella, he look here! Boy he look, too! They look plenty too much, Captain! (*All four stand staring off at Butler and the boy, whose presence on the island they have forgotten in their mad excitement.*)

CATES—(*in stupid dismay*) They'll know where it's hid, sir!

HORNE—They'll tell 'em on the schooner!

CATES—(*wildly*) We've got to do for 'em, Captain! Gimme your knife, Jimmy—your knife— (*He stumbles toward the Islander, who pushes him aside brusquely, looking questioningly toward the Captain.*)

BARTLETT—(*who has been standing motionless, as if stunned by this forgotten complication—slowly*) There they be watchin' us, the sneakin' dogs! I was forgettin' they was here. (*striking his knee with clenched fist*) We've got to do somethin' damn quick! That schooner'll be up soon where they kin sight her—and they'll wave and yell then—and she'll see 'em!

HORNE—And good-by to the gold for us!

JIMMY—(*eagerly*) You say fella word, Captain, me kill um quick. They no make plenty cry for schooner! They keep dam still plenty too much!

BARTLETT—(*looking at the Islander with mad cunning but replying only to Horne*) Aye, it's good-by to the gold, Horne. That scum of a cook—he's made a mock o' us—sayin' it wasn't gold when he knew it was—he'll tell 'em—he'll get joy o' tellin' 'em!

HORNE—And that scrub of a boy—he's no better. He'll be in with him neck and crop.

CATES—(*hoarsely*) Knife 'em—and be done with it—I say!

BARTLETT—Or, if they don't tell the schooner's skipper it'll only be because they're plannin' to come back themselves—before we kin—and dig it up. That cook—there's somethin' queer in his mind—somethin' he was hidin'—pretendin' not to believe. What d'ye think, Horne?

HORNE—I think—time's gettin' short—and talkin' won't do no good. (*insinuatingly*) They'd do for us soon enough if *they* was able.

BARTLETT—Aye, murder was plain in his eyes when he looked at me.

HORNE—(*lowering his voice to a whisper*) Tell Jimmy—Captain Bartlett—is what I say!

BARTLETT—It's agin the law, Silas Horne!

HORNE—The law don't reach to this island.

BARTLETT—(*monotonously*) It's agin the law a captain's

sworn to keep wherever he sails. They ain't refused duty—nor mutinied.

HORNE—Who'll know they ain't? They're trying to steal what's yours—that's worse'n mutiny. (*as a final persuasion*) And Jimmy's a heathen and under no laws. And he's stronger'n you are. You couldn't stop 'im.

BARTLETT—Aye—I couldn't prevent—

JIMMY—(*eagerly*) I fix um, Captain, they no tell! (*Bartlett doesn't answer, but stares at the treasure. Horne makes violent motions to Jimmy to go. The Islander stares at his master's face. Then, seeming to read the direct command there, he grunts with satisfaction, and pulling his knife from its sheath, he goes stealthily off left. Cates raises himself on his haunches to watch the Islander's movements. Horne and Bartlett sit still in a strained immobility, their eyes on the chest.*)

CATES—(*in an excited whisper*) I see 'em! They're sittin' with their backs this way! (*a slight pause*) There's Jimmy. He's crawlin' on his hands behind 'em. They don't notice—he's right behind—almost atop o' them. (*A pause. Cates gives a fiendish grunt.*) Ugh! (*Butler's muffled cry comes from the left.*) Right in the middle of the back! The cook's done! The boy's runnin'! (*There is a succession of quick screams from the boy, the padding of feet running toward them, the fall of a body, and the boy's dying groan.*)

HORNE—(*with satisfaction*) It's done, sir!

BARTLETT—(*slowly*) I spoke no word, remember that, Silas Horne!

HORNE—(*cunningly*) Nor me neither, sir. Jimmy took it on himself. If blame there is—it's on him.

BARTLETT—(*gloomily*) I spoke no word! (*Jimmy returns noiselessly from the left.*)

JIMMY—(*grinning with savage pride*) I fix um fella plenty, Captain. They no tell. They no open mouth plenty too much!

CATES—(*maudlinly*) You're a man, Jimmy—a man with guts to him—even if you're a— (*He babbles incoherently.*)

JIMMY—(*as the Captain does not look at him*) I go climb fella tree, Captain? I make look for schooner?

BARTLETT—(*rousing himself with an effort*) Aye. (*The Islander climbs the tree.*)

HORNE—(*getting to his feet—eagerly*) Where away, Jimmy?

JIMMY—She come, Captain, she come plenty quick.

HORNE—(*looking in the direction Jimmy indicates*) I kin see her tops'ls from here, sir. Look!

BARTLETT—(*getting to his feet—stares out to sea*) Aye! There she be—and makin' towards us fast. (*In a flash his somber preoccupation is gone, and he is commander once more. He puts the anklet in his hand into his coat pocket—harshly*) Come down out o' that! They's work to do. (*Jimmy clambers down.*) Did ye leave—them—lyin' in plain sight on the open sand?

JIMMY—Yes. I no touch um, Captain.

BARTLETT—Then ye'll touch 'em now. Go, bury 'em, cover 'em up with sand. And mind ye make a good job o' it that none'll see. Jump now!

JIMMY—(*obediently*) I go, Captain. (*He hurries off left.*)

BARTLETT—Down to the reef with ye, Horne! (*giving the prostrate Cates a kick*) Up out o' that, Cates! Go with Horne, and when ye see the schooner hull up, wave to 'em, and yell like mad, d'ye hear?

HORNE—Aye, aye, sir!

BARTLETT—I'll stay here and bury the gold. It's best to be quick about it! They may turn a spyglass on us when they raise the island from deck! Off with ye! (*He gives Cates another kick.*)

CATES—(*groaning*) I'm sick! (*incoherently*) Can't—report for duty—this watch. (*with a shout*) Water!

BARTLETT—(*contemptuously*) Ye dog! Give him a hand, Horne.

HORNE—(*putting a hand under his shoulder*) Up, man! We're to signal the schooner. There'll be water on board o' her—barrels of it!

CATES—(*aroused, scrambles to his feet, violently shaking off Horne's hand*) Water aboard o' her! (*His staring eyes catch the schooner's sails on the horizon. He breaks into a staggering run and disappears down toward the beach, right rear, waving his arms wildly and shouting*) Ahoy! Ahoy! Water! (*Horne walks out quickly after him.*)

BARTLETT—(*after a quick glance around, sinks on his knees beside the chest and shoves both hands into it. From the chest comes a metallic clink as he fingers the pieces in his hands gloatingly.*) Ye're safe now! (*in a dreaming tone, his eyes fixed before him in an ecstatic vision*) No more whalin' on the dirty seas! Rest to home! Gold! I've been dreamin' o' it all my life! (*shaking himself—savagely*) Ye fool! Losin' your senses, be ye? Time ye was picked up! Lucky! (*He shoves down the lid and places the chest in the hole. He pushes the sand in on top of it, whispering hoarsely*) Lay safe, d'ye hear. For I'll be back for ye! Aye—in spite of hell I'll dig ye up again! (*The voices of Horne and Jimmy can be heard from the distance shouting as*

The Curtain Falls)

ACT TWO

SCENE—*Interior of an old boat-shed on the wharf of the Bart-lett place on the California coast. In the rear, a double doorway looking out over the end of the wharf to the bay with the open sea beyond. On the left, two windows, and another door, opening on the dock. Near this door, a cot with blankets and a pillow without a slip. In the center, front, a table with a bottle and glasses on it, and three cane-bottomed chairs. On the right, a fishing dory. Here and there about the shed all sorts of odds and ends pertaining to a ship—old anchors, ropes, tackle, paint-pots, old spars, etc.*

It is late afternoon of a day six months later. Sunlight filters feebly through the stained, cobwebby window panes.

As the curtain rises, Bartlett and Silas Horne are discovered. Horne is in working clothes of paint-stained dungaree. If his sufferings on the island have left any marks on his dry wizened face, they are undiscoverable. In Bartlett, however, the evidence is marked. His hair has turned white. There are deep hollows under his cheek-bones. His jaw and tight-lipped mouth express defiant determination, as if he were fighting back some weakness inside himself, a weakness found in his eyes, which have something in them of fear, of a wishing to avoid other eyes. He is dressed much the same as when on the island. He sits by the table, center, his abstracted gaze bent on the floor before him.

HORNE—(*who is evidently waiting for the Captain to say something—after a pause, glancing at him uneasily*) I'd best be gettin' back aboard the schooner, sir. (*Receiving no answer he starts for the door on the left.*)

BARTLETT—(*rousing himself with an effort*) Wait. (*after a pause*) The full tide's at dawn tomorrow. They know we'll be sailin' then, don't they—Cates and Jimmy?

HORNE—Yes, sir. Oh, they'll be glad o' the word—and me, too, sir. (*with a greedy grin*) It's all we've been talkin' of since ye brought us down here—diggin' up the gold!

BARTLETT—(*passionately*) Aye, the gold! We'll have it before long, now, I reckon. That schooner—the way we've fitted her up—she'd take a man safe to the Pole and back! We'll drop anchor here with the chest on board in six months, unless— (*hesitates*)

HORNE—(*uneasily*) What, sir?

BARTLETT—(*brusquely*) The weather, ye fool!

HORNE—We'll trust to luck for that. (*glancing at the Captain curiously*) And speakin' o' luck, sir—the schooner ain't been christened yet.

BARTLETT—(*betraying a sudden, fierce determination*) She will be!

HORNE—There'd be no luck for a ship sailin' out without a name.

BARTLETT—She'll have a name, I tell ye! She'll be named the Sarah Allen, and Sarah'll christen her herself.

HORNE—It oughter been done, by rights, when we launched her a month back.

BARTLETT—(*sternly*) I know that as well as ye. (*after a pause*) She wasn't willin' to do it then. Women has queer notions—when they're sick, like. (*defiantly—as if he were addressing someone outside of the room*) But Sarah'll be willin' now!

HORNE—Yes, sir. (*He again turns to go, as if he were anxious to get away.*)

BARTLETT—Wait! There's somethin' else I want to ask ye. Nat, he's been hangin' round the schooner all his spare time o' late. (*with rising anger*) I hope ye've remembered what I ordered ye, all three. Not a word o' it to him!

HORNE—(*retreating a step—hastily*) No fear o' that, sir!

BARTLETT—It ain't that I'm afeerd to tell him o' the gold, Silas Horne. (*slowly*) It's them—other things—I'd keep him clear of.

HORNE—(*immediately guessing what he means—reassuringly*) We was all out o' our heads when them things happened, sir.

BARTLETT—Mad? Aye! But I ain't forgot—them two. (*He represses a shudder—then goes on slowly.*) Do they ever come back to you—when you're asleep, I mean?

HORNE—(*pretending mystification*) Who's that, sir?

BARTLETT—(*with somber emphasis*) That cook and that boy. They come to me. I'm gettin' to be afeered o' goin' to sleep— not 'feered o' them, I don't mean. (*with sudden defiant bravado*) Not all the ghosts out o' hell kin keep me from a thing I've set my mind on. (*collecting himself*) But I've waked up talkin' out loud—and I'm afeerd there might be someone hear me.

HORNE—(*uneasily—with an attempt to be reassuring*) You ain't all cured o' that sun and thirst on the island yet, sir.

BARTLETT—(*evidently reassured—with an attempt at conviviality*) Sit down a bit, Horne, and take a grog. (*Horne does so. Bartlett pours out a half-tumbler full of rum for himself and shoves the bottle over to Horne.*)

HORNE—Luck to our vige, sir.

BARTLETT—Aye, luck! (*They drink. Bartlett leans over and taps Horne on the arm.*) Aye, it takes time to get cured o' thirst and sun! (*somberly—after a pause*) I spoke no word, Silas Horne, d'ye remember?

HORNE—Nor me. Jimmy did it alone. (*craftily*) We'd all three swear Bible oaths to that in any court. And even if ye'd given the word, there ain't no good thinkin' more o' it, sir. Didn't they deserve all they got? Wasn't they plottin' on the sly to steal the gold?

BARTLETT—(*his eyes gleaming*) Aye!

HORNE—And when you said he'd get no share of it, didn't he lie to your face that it wasn't gold?

BARTLETT—(*with sudden rage*) Aye, brass and junk, he said, the lyin' scum! That's what he keeps sayin' when I see him in sleep! He didn't believe—an' then he owned up himself 'twas gold! He knew! He lied a-purpose! (*rising to his feet—with confident defiance*) They deserved no better nor they got. Let 'em rot! (*pours out another drink for himself and Horne*)

HORNE—Luck, sir! (*They drink. There is a knock at the door on the left followed by Mrs. Bartlett's voice calling feebly,* "Isaiah! Isaiah!" *Bartlett starts but makes no answer. Horne turns to him questioningly.*) It's Mrs. Bartlett, sir. Shall I open the door?

BARTLETT—No. I ain't aimin' to see her—yet awhile. (*then with sudden reasonless rage*) Let her in, damn ye! (*Horne goes and unhooks the door. Mrs. Bartlett enters. She is a slight, slender little woman of fifty. Sickness, or the inroads of a premature old age, have bowed her shoulders, whitened her hair, and forced her to walk feebly with the aid of a cane. A resolute spirit still flashes from her eyes, however, and there is a look of fixed determination on her face. She stands gazing at her husband. There is something accusing in her stare.*)

BARTLETT—(*avoiding her eyes—brusquely*) Well? What is it ye want o' me, Sarah?

MRS. B.—I want to speak with you alone, Isaiah.

HORNE—I'll be gettin' back aboard, sir. (*starts to go*)

BARTLETT—(*in a tone almost of fear*) Wait. I'm goin' with ye. (*turning to his wife—with a certain rough tenderness*) Ye oughtn't to walk down the hill here, Sarah. The doctor told ye to rest in the house and save your strength.

MRS. B.—I want to speak to you alone, Isaiah.

BARTLETT—(*very uneasily*) I've got to work on the schooner, Sarah.

MRS. B.—She'll be sailin' soon?

BARTLETT—(*suddenly turning on her defiantly*) Tomorrow at dawn!

MRS. B.—(*with her eyes fixed accusingly on his*) And you be goin' with her?

BARTLETT—(*in the same defiant tone*) Yes, I be! Who else'd captain her?

MRS. B.—On a craft without a name.

BARTLETT—She'll have that name!

MRS. B.—No.

BARTLETT—She'll have that name, I tell ye!

MRS. B.—No.

BARTLETT—(*thoroughly aroused, his will tries to break hers, but finds her unbending. He mutters menacingly*) Ye'll see! We'll talk o' that later, you and me. (*Without a further glance at his wife he strides past her and disappears through the doorway, followed by Horne. Mrs. Bartlett sinks down in the chair by the table. She appears suddenly weak and crushed. Then from outside comes a girl's laughing voice. Mrs. Bartlett does not seem to hear, nor to notice Sue and Drew when they enter. Sue is a slender, pretty girl of about twenty, with large blue eyes, reddish-brown hair, and a healthy, sun-tanned, out-of-door complexion. In spite of the slightness of her figure there is a suggestion of great vitality and nervous strength about her. Drew is a well-set-up, tall young fellow of thirty. Not in any way handsome, his boyish face, tanned to a deep brown, possesses an engaging character of healthy, cheerful force-*

fulness that has its compelling charm. There would be no chance of mistaking him for anything but the ship's officer he is. It is written on his face, his walk, his voice, his whole bearing.)

SUE—(*as they enter*) He'll either be here or on the schooner, Danny. (*Then she sees her mother, with startled amazement*) Ma! Good heavens, what are you doing here? Don't you know you shouldn't—

MRS. B.—(*with a start—turning to her daughter with a forced smile*) There, Sue, now! Don't go scoldin' me. (*then seeing Drew—in a tone of forced gayety*) And if there ain't Danny Drew—back home to port at last! You can kiss an old woman, Danny—without makin' her jealous, I reckon.

DREW—(*kissing her—with a smile*) It certainly seems good to see you again—and be back again myself.

MRS. B.—We read in the paper where your ship'd reached San Francisco. Sue's been on pins and needles ever since.

SUE—(*protestingly*) Ma!

DREW—(*with a grin*) It's a long time to be away from Sue—four months. You remember, Ma, I left just after the big excitement here—when Captain Bartlett turned up after we'd all heard the Triton was wrecked and given him up for lost.

MRS. B.—(*her face clouding—in a tone of deep sorrow*) Yes. (*Drew is surprised and glances at Sue questioningly. She sighs. Mrs. Bartlett gets to her feet with difficulty, assisted by Drew.*)

SUE—We'll help you back to the house.

MRS. B.—Shucks! I'm sick o' the house. I need sun and fresh air, and today's so nice I couldn't stay indoors. I'm goin' to set out on the wharf and watch your Pa workin' on the schooner. Ain't much time left to see her, Sue. They're sailin' tomorrow at dawn, your Pa says.

SUE—Tomorrow? Then—you're going to christen her?

MRS. B.—(*with grim determination*) No, I ain't, Sue! (*Catching Drew's glance fixed on her with puzzled curiosity, she immediately attempts to resume her joking tone.*) Shucks! Here's Danny wonderin' what silliness we're talkin' of. It's just this, Danny. Captain Bartlett, he's got a crazy notion in his head that just because his ship was wrecked last vige he'll give up whalin' for life. He's fitted out this little schooner for tradin' in the Islands. More money in that, he says. But I don't agree with no such lunatic notions, and I'm not goin' to set my approval on his craziness by christenin' his ship with my name, like he wants me to. He'd ought to stick to whalin', like he's done all his life. Don't you think so, Danny?

DREW—(embarrassed) Why, sure—he's rated one of the smartest whaling skippers here on the coast—and I should think—

MRS. B.—Just what I tell him—only he's that stubborn. I'd best get out quick while it's still sunny and warm. It's damp in here for an old body. (Drew helps her to the door on the left, opens it, and the two go out, followed by Sue, who carries a chair. After a pause, Sue and Drew return. Sue carefully shuts the door after them. Her face is troubled.)

DREW—(looks at her for a minute, then comes and puts his arm around her and kisses her) What's the trouble, Sue?

SUE—(trying to force a smile) Nothing, Danny.

DREW—Oh, yes there is! No use putting me off that way. Why, I've felt it hanging about in the air ever since I looked at your Ma.

SUE—Yes, she's failed terribly since you saw her last.

DREW—Oh, I don't mean just sickness—only—did you notice how she had to—force herself—to joke about things? She used to be so cheerful natural. (scratching his head in honest puzzlement) But—that ain't what I mean, either. What is it, Sue? Maybe I can help somehow. You look worried, too. Pshaw! You can tell me, can't you?

SUE—Why, yes, Danny—of course—only I'm just as puzzled as you over what it comes from. It's something between Pa and Ma—something only the two of them know. It all seemed to start one morning after you'd left—about a week after he'd come home with those three awful men. During that first week he acted all right—just like he used to—only he'd get talking kind of wild now and then about being glad the Triton was lost, and promising we'd all be millionaires once he started making trips on the schooner. Ma didn't seem to mind his going in for trading then. Then, the night of the day he bought the schooner, something must have happened between them. Neither of them came down to breakfast. I went up to Ma, and found her so sick we sent for the doctor. He said she'd suffered a great shock of some kind, although she wouldn't tell him a word. I found Pa down in this shed. He'd moved that cot down here, and said he'd have to sleep here after that because he wanted to be near the schooner. It's been that way ever since. He's slept down here and never come up to the house except at mealtimes. He's never been alone with Ma one second since then, I don't believe. And she—she's been trying to corner him, to get him alone. I've noticed it, although she does her best to hide it from Nat and me. And she's been failing, growing weaker and sicker looking every day. (*breaking down*) Oh, Danny, these last months have been terrible!

DREW—(*soothing her*) There! It'll all come out right.

SUE—I'm sure that's why she's crept down here today. She's bound she'll see him alone.

DREW—(*frowning*) Seems to me it must be all your Pa's fault, Sue—whatever it is. Have you tried to talk to him?

SUE—Yes—a good many times; but all he's ever said was: "There's things you wouldn't take interest in, Sue. You'll know when it's time to know"—and then he'd break off by asking me what I'd like most to have in the world if he had piles of money. And then, one time, he seemed to be terribly afraid of something, and he said to me: "You hustle up and marry Danny, Sue. You marry him and get out of this."

DREW—(*with an affectionate grin*) I surely wish you'd take his advice, Sue! (*He kisses her.*)

SUE—(*with intense longing*) Oh, I wish I could, Danny.

DREW—I've quite considerable saved now, Sue, and it won't be so long before I get my own ship, I'm hoping, now that I've got my master's certificate. I was hoping at the end of this voyage—

SUE—So was I, Danny—but it can't be this time. With Ma so weak, and no one to take care of her but me—(*shaking her head—in a tone of decision*) I couldn't leave home now, Danny. It wouldn't be right. I couldn't feel really happy—until this thing—whatever it is—is settled between Pa and Ma and they're just as they used to be again. (*pleadingly*) You understand, don't you, Danny?

DREW—(*soberly*) Why—surely I do, Sue. (*He pats her hand.*) Only, it's hard waiting. (*He sighs.*)

Sue—I know. It's just as hard for me.

Drew—I thought maybe I could help; but this isn't anything anyone outside your family could mix in. (*Sue shakes her head. He goes on gloomily after a pause.*) What's the matter with Nat? Seems as if he ought to be able to step in and talk turkey to your Pa.

Sue—(*slowly*) You'll find Nat changed, too, Danny—changed terribly. He's caught the disease—whatever it is. You know how interested in his work he's been ever since they put him in the designing department down in the shipyard?

Drew—Yes.

Sue—(*with emphasis*) Well, all that's changed. He hates it now, or at least he says he does. And when he comes home, he spends all his time prowling around the dock here, talking with those three awful men. And what do you think he told me only the other day? That he was bound he'd throw up his job and make this voyage on the schooner. He even asked me to ask Pa to let him go.

Drew—Your Pa don't want him to, eh?

Sue—Why, of course not! Leave a fine position he worked so hard to get just for this crazy notion! The terrible part is, he's got Ma worried to death—as if she wasn't upset enough already. She's so afraid he'll go—that Pa'll let him at the last moment.

Drew—Maybe I can help after all. I can talk to Nat.

Sue—(*shaking her head*) He's not the same Nat, Danny.

Drew—(*trying to be consoling*) Pshaw, Sue! I think you just get to imagining things. (*As he finishes speaking, the door in the rear opens and Nat appears. He is a tall, loose-framed boy of eighteen, who bears a striking resemblance to his father. His face, like his father's, is large and bony, with deepset black eyes, an aquiline nose, and a wide, thin-lipped mouth. There is no suggestion in Nat, however, of the older man's physical health and great strength. He appears an indoor product, undeveloped in muscle, with a sallow complexion and stooped shoulders. His thick hair is a deep black. His voice recalls his father's, hollow and penetrating. He is dressed in a gray flannel shirt and corduroy trousers. Drew*

calls out to him heartily) Hello, Nat! Speak of the Devil! Sue
and I were just talking about you. (*He goes toward Nat, his
hand outstretched.*)

NAT—(*comes toward them, meets Drew, and shakes his hand
with evident pleasure*) Hello, Danny! You're a sight for sore
eyes! (*His manner undergoes a sudden change. He casts a quick,
suspicious glance from Drew to his sister.*) You were talking about
me? What about?

SUE—(*quickly—with a warning glance at Drew*) About
your work down at the shipyard.

NAT—(*disgustedly*) Oh, that. (*in a tone of reasonless irritation*) For God's sake, Sue, let me alone about my work. Don't
I have to live with the damn thing all day, without your shov-
ing it in my face the minute I get home? I want to forget it—
get away!

DREW—Go to sea, eh?

NAT—(*suspiciously*) Maybe. Why? What do you mean?
(*turning to his sister—angrily*) What have you been telling
Danny?

SUE—I was talking about the schooner—telling him she
sails tomorrow.

NAT—(*dumfounded*) Tomorrow? (*overcome by sudden, nervous excitement*) It can't be. How do you know? Who told
you?

SUE—Ma. Pa told her.

NAT—Then she's been talking to him—telling him not to
take me, I'll bet. (*angrily*) Oh, I wish Ma'd mind her own
business!

SUE—Nat!

NAT—Well, Sue, how would you like it? I'm not a little
boy any more. I know what I want to do. I want to go with
them. I want to go more than I've ever wanted anything else
in my life before. He—he doesn't want me. He's afraid I—
But I think I can force him to— (*He glances at Drew's amazed
face and stops abruptly—sullenly*) Where is Pa?

SUE—He's aboard the schooner.

NAT—(*disappointedly*) Then it's no good trying to see him
now.

DREW—Sound's funny to hear you talking about going to
sea. Why, you always used—

NAT—This is different.

DREW—You want to see the Islands, I suppose?

NAT—(*suspiciously*) Maybe. Why not?

DREW—What group is your Pa heading for first?

NAT—(*more suspiciously*) You'll have to ask him. Why do you want to know? (*abruptly*) You better be getting up to the house, Sue—if we're to have any supper. Danny must be hungry. (*He turns his back on them. They exchange meaning glances.*)

SUE—(*with a sigh*) It must be getting late. Come on, Danny. You can see Pa later on. (*They go toward the door in the rear.*) Aren't you coming, Nat?

NAT—No. I'll wait. (*impatiently*) Go ahead. I'll be up before long.

DREW—See you later, then, Nat.

NAT—Yes. (*They go out, rear. Nat paces up and down in a great state of excitement. The door on the left is opened and Bartlett enters. Father and son stand looking at one another for a second. Nat takes a step backward as if in fear, then straightens up defiantly.*)

BARTLETT—(*slowly*) Is this the way ye mind my orders, boy? I've told ye time an' again not to be sneakin' and spyin' around this wharf.

NAT—I'm not sneaking and spying. I wanted to talk to you, Pa.

BARTLETT—(*sits down by the table*) Well, here I be.

NAT—Sue said the schooner sails tomorrow.

BARTLETT—Aye!

NAT—(*resolutely*) I want to go with you, Pa.

BARTLETT—(*briefly—as if dismissing the matter*) Ye can't. I've told ye that before. Let this be the last time ye ask it.

NAT—But why? Why can't I go?

BARTLETT—Ye've your own work to do—good work. Attend to that and leave me to mine.

NAT—But you always wanted me to go on voyages to learn whaling with you.

BARTLETT—This be different.

NAT—(*with excited indignation*) Yes, this is different! Don't I know it? Do you think you can hide that from me? It is different, and that's why I want to go.

BARTLETT—Ye can't, I say.

NAT—(*pleadingly*) But why not, Pa? I can do a man's work on a ship, or anywhere else.

BARTLETT—(*roughly*) Your place is here, with Sue and your Ma, and here you'll stay.

NAT—(*angrily*) That isn't any reason. But I know your real one. You're afraid—

BARTLETT—(*with a touch of uneasiness—forcing a scornful laugh*) Afeerd! Afeerd o' what? Did ye ever know me to be afeerd?

NAT—Afraid of what I might find out if I went with you.

BARTLETT—(*with the same forced, uneasy scorn*) And what d'ye think ye'd find out, Nat?

NAT—First of all that it's not a trading venture you're going on. Oh, I'm not a fool! That story is all right to fool the neighbors and girls like Sue. But I know better.

BARTLETT—What d'ye know?

NAT—You're going for something else.

BARTLETT—What would that be?

NAT—I don't know—exactly. Something—on that island.

BARTLETT—(*He gets to his feet with a forced burst of laughter.*) Ye fool of a boy! Ye got that notion out o' some fool book ye've been reading, didn't ye? And I thought ye'd growed to be a man! (*more and more wild in his forced scorn*) Ye'll be tellin' me next it's buried treasure I be sailin' after— pirates' gold buried on that island—all in a chest—and a map to guide me with a cross marked on it where the gold is hid! And then they be ghosts guardin' it, ben't they—spirits o' murdered men? They always be, in the books. (*He laughs scornfully.*)

NAT—(*gazing at him with fascinated eyes*) No, not that last. That's silly—but I did think you might have found—

BARTLETT—(*laughing again*) Treasure? Gold? (*with forced sternness*) Nat, I be ashamed of ye. Ye've had schoolin', and ye've been doin' a man's work in the world, and doin' it well, and I'd hoped ye'd take my place here to home when I be away, and look after your Ma and Sue. But ye've owned up to bein' little better nor a boy in short britches, dreamin' o' pirates' gold that never was 'cept in books.

NAT—But you—you're to blame. When you first came

home you did nothing but talk mysteriously of how rich we'd all be when the schooner got back.

BARTLETT—(*roughly*) But what's that to do with silly dreams? It's in the line o' trade I meant.

NAT—But why be so mysterious about trade? There's something you're hiding. You can't say no because I feel it.

BARTLETT—(*insinuatingly—with a crafty glance at his son*) Supposin' in one of them Eastern trading ports I'd run across a bit o' business with a chance for a fortune in it for a man that wasn't afeerd of the law, and could keep his mouth shut?

NAT—(*disappointed*) You mean illegal trading?

BARTLETT—I mean what I mean, Nat—and I'd be a fool to tell an overgrown boy, or two women—or any man in the world, for the matter o' that—what I do mean.

NAT—(*turning toward the door in the rear—disgustedly*) If it's only that, I don't want to hear it. (*He walks toward the door—stops and turns again to his father.*) No, I don't believe it. That's not like you. You're not telling the truth, Pa.

BARTLETT—(*rising to his feet—with a savage sternness in which there is a wild note of entreaty*) I've listened to your fool's talk enough. Get up to the house where ye belong! I'll stand no more o' your meddling in business o' mine. I've been patient with ye, but there's an end to that! Take heed o' what I'm sayin', if ye know what's good for ye! (*with a sort of somber pride*) I'll stand alone in this business and finish it out alone if I go to hell for it. Ye hear me?

NAT—(*alarmed by this outburst—submissively*) Yes, Pa.

BARTLETT—Then see that ye heed. (*after a pause—as Nat lingers*) They'll be waitin' for ye at the house.

NAT—All right. I'll go. (*He turns to the doorway on the left, but before he gets to it, the door is pushed open and Mrs. Bartlett enters. Nat stops, startled.*) Ma!

MRS. BARTLETT—(*with a forced smile*) Run along, Nat. It's all right. I want to speak with your Pa.

BARTLETT—(*uneasily*) Ye'd best go up with Nat, Sarah. I've work to do.

MRS. BARTLETT—(*fixing her eyes on her husband*) I want to talk with you alone, Isaiah.

BARTLETT—(*grimly—as if he were accepting a challenge*) As ye like, then.

MRS. BARTLETT—(*dismissing Nat with a feeble attempt at a smile*) Tell Sue I'll be comin' up directly, Nat.

NAT—(*hesitates for a moment, looking from one to the other uneasily*) All right, Ma. (*He goes out.*)

BARTLETT—(*waits for Nat to get out of hearing*) Won't ye set, Sarah? (*She comes forward and sits by the table. He sits by the other side.*)

MRS. BARTLETT—(*shuddering as she sees the bottle on the table*) Will drinkin' this poison make you forget, Isaiah?

BARTLETT—(*gruffly*) I've naught to forget—leastways naught that's in your mind. But they's things about the stubborn will o' woman I'd like to forget. (*They look at each other across the table. There is a pause. Finally he cannot stand her accusing glance. He looks away, gets to his feet, walks about, then sits down again, his face set determinedly—with a grim smile*) Well, here we be, Sarah—alone together for the first time since—

MRS. BARTLETT—(*quickly*) Since that night, Isaiah.

BARTLETT—(*as if he hadn't heard*) Since I come back to you, almost. Did ye ever stop to think o' how strange it be we'd ever come to this? I never dreamed a day 'd come when ye'd force me to sleep away from ye, alone in a shed like a mangy dog!

MRS. BARTLETT—(*gently*) I didn't drive you away, Isaiah. You came o' your own will.

BARTLETT—Because o' your naggin' tongue, woman—and the wrong ye thought o' me.

MRS. BARTLETT—(*shaking her head, slowly*) It wasn't me you ran from, Isaiah. You ran away from your own self—the conscience God put in you that you think you can fool with lies.

BARTLETT—(*starting to his feet—angrily*) Lies?

MRS. BARTLETT—It's the truth, Isaiah, only you be too weak to face it.

BARTLETT—(*with defiant bravado*) Ye'll find I be strong enough to face anything, true or lie! (*then protestingly*) What call have ye to think evil o' me, Sarah? It's mad o' ye to hold me to account for things I said in my sleep—for the damned nightmares that set me talkin' wild when I'd just come home and my head was still cracked with the thirst and the sun I'd borne on that island. Is that right, woman, to be blamin' me for mad dreams?

MRS. BARTLETT—You confessed the rest of what you said was true—of the gold you'd found and buried there.

BARTLETT—(*with a sudden fierce exultation*) Aye—that be true as Bible, Sarah. When I've sailed back in the schooner, ye'll see for yourself. There be a big chest o' it, yellow and heavy, and fixed up with diamonds, emeralds and sech, that be worth more, even, nor the gold. We'll be rich, Sarah—rich like I've always dreamed we'd be! There'll be silks and carriages for ye—all the woman's truck in the world ye've a mind to want—and all that Nat and Sue'll want, too.

MRS. BARTLETT—(*with a shudder*) Are you tryin' to bribe me, Isaiah—with a treasure that's cursed by God?

BARTLETT—(*as if he hadn't heard*) D'ye remember long ago, how I'd talk to ye o' findin' ambergris, a pile o' it on one vige that'd make us rich? Ye used to take interest then, and all the vige with me ye'd be hopin' I'd find it, too.

MRS. BARTLETT—That was my sin o' greed that I'm bein' punished for now.

BARTLETT—(*again as if he hadn't heard*) And now when the gold's come to us at last—bigger nor I ever dreamed on—ye drive me away from ye and say it's cursed.

MRS. BARTLETT—(*inexorably*) Cursed with the blood o' the man and boy ye murdered!

BARTLETT—(*in a mad rage*) Ye lie, woman! I spoke no word!

MRS. BARTLETT—That's what you kept repeatin' in your sleep, night after night that first week you was home, till I knew the truth, and could bear no more. "I spoke no word!" you kept sayin', as if 'twas your own soul had you at the bar of judgment. And "That cook, he didn't believe 'twas gold," you'd say, and curse him.

BARTLETT—(*wildly*) He was lyin', the thief! Lyin' so's he and the boy could steal th' gold. I made him own up he was lyin'. What if it's all true, what ye heard? Hadn't we the right to do away with two thieves? And we was all mad with thirst and sun. Can ye hold madmen to account for the things they do?

MRS. BARTLETT—You wasn't so crazed but you remember.

BARTLETT—I remember I spoke no word, Sarah—as God's my judge!

MRS. BARTLETT—But you could have prevented it with a word, couldn't you, Isaiah? That heathen savage lives in the fear of you. He'd not have done it if—

BARTLETT—(*gloomily*) That's woman's talk. There be three o' us can swear in any court I spoke no word.

MRS. BARTLETT—What are courts? Can you swear it to yourself? You can't, and it's that's drivin' you mad, Isaiah. Oh, I'd never have believed it of you for all you said in sleep, if it wasn't for the way you looked and acted out of sleep. I watched you that first week, Isaiah, till the fear of it had me down sick. I had to watch you, you was so strange and fearful to me. At first I kept sayin', 'twas only you wasn't rid o' the thirst and the sun yet. But then, all to once, God gave me sight, and I saw 'twas guilt written on your face, on the queer stricken way you acted, and guilt in your eyes. (*She stares into them.*) I see it now, as I always see it when you look at me. (*She covers her face with her hands with a sob.*)

BARTLETT—(*his face haggard and drawn—hopelessly, as if he were too beaten to oppose her further—in a hoarse whisper*) What would ye have me do, Sarah?

MRS. BARTLETT—(*taking her hands from her face—her eyes lighting up with religious fervor*) Confess your sin, Isaiah! Confess to God and men, and make your peace and take your punishment. Forget that gold that's cursed and the voyage you be settin' out on, and make your peace. (*passionately*) I ask you to do this for my sake and the children's, and your own most of all! I'll get down on my knees, Isaiah, and pray you to do it, as I've prayed to God to send you His grace! Confess and wash your soul of the stain o' blood that's on it. I ask you that, Isaiah—and God asks you—to make your peace with Him.

BARTLETT—(*his face tortured by the inward struggle—as if the word strangled him*) Confess and let someone steal the gold! (*This thought destroys her influence over him in a second. His obsession regains possession of him instantly, filling him with rebellious strength. He laughs harshly.*) Ye'd make an old woman o' me, would ye, Sarah?—an old, Sunday go-to-meetin' woman snivelin' and prayin' to God for pardon? Pardon for what? Because two sneakin' thieves are dead and done for? I spoke no word, I tell ye—but if I had, I'd not repent it. What I've done I've done, and I've never asked pardon o' God or men for ought I've done, and never will. Confess, and give up the gold I've dreamed of all my life that I've found at last! By thunder, ye must think I'm crazed!

MRS. BARTLETT—(*seeming to shrivel up on her chair as she sees she has lost—weakly*) You be lost, Isaiah—and no one can stop you.

BARTLETT—(*triumphantly*) Aye, none'll stop me. I'll go my course alone. I'm glad ye see that, Sarah.

MRS. BARTLETT—(*feebly trying to get to her feet*) I'll go to home.

BARTLETT—Ye'll stay, Sarah. Ye've had your say, and I've listened to ye; now I'll have mine and ye listen to me. (*Mrs. Bartlett sinks back in her chair exhaustedly. Bartlett continues slowly.*) The schooner sails at dawn on the full tide. I ask ye again and for the last time, will ye christen her with your name afore she sails?

MRS. BARTLETT—(*firmly*) No.

BARTLETT—(*menacingly*) Take heed, Sarah, o' what ye're sayin'! I'm your husband ye've sworn to obey. By right I kin order ye, not ask.

MRS. BARTLETT—I've never refused in anything that's right—but this be wicked wrong.

BARTLETT—It's only your stubborn woman's spite makes ye refuse. Ye've christened every ship I've ever been skipper on, and it's brought me luck o' a kind, though not the luck I wanted. And ye'll christen this one with your own name to bring me the luck I've always been seekin'.

MRS. BARTLETT—(*resolutely*) I won't, Isaiah.

BARTLETT—Ye will, Sarah, for I'll make ye. Ye force me to it.

MRS. BARTLETT—(*again trying to get up*) Is this the way you talk to me who've been a good wife to you for more than thirty years?

BARTLETT—(*commandingly*) Wait! (*threateningly*) If ye don't christen her afore she sails, I'll take Nat on the vige along with me. (*Mrs. Bartlett sinks back in her chair, stunned.*)

He wants to go, ye know it. He's asked me a hundred times. He s'spects—'bout the gold—but he don't know for sartin. But I'll tell him the truth o' it, and he'll come with me, unless—

MRS. BARTLETT—(*looking at him with terror-stricken eyes—imploringly*) You won't do that, Isaiah? You won't take Nat away from me and drag him into sin? I know he'll go if you give him the word, in spite of what I say. (*pitifully*) You be only frightenin' me! You can't be so wicked cruel as that.

BARTLETT—I'll do it, I take my oath—unless—

MRS. BARTLETT—(*with hysterical anger*) Then I'll tell him myself—of the murders you did, and—

BARTLETT—(*grimly*) And I'll say 'twas done in fair fight to keep them from stealin' the gold! I'll tell him yours is a woman's notion, and he'll believe me, not you. He's his father's son, and he's set to go. Ye know it, Sarah. (*She falls back in the chair hopelessly staring at him with horrified eyes. He turns away and adds after a pause*) So ye'll christen the Sarah Allen in the mornin' afore she sails, won't ye, Sarah?

MRS. BARTLETT—(*in a terrified tone*) Yes—if it's needful to save Nat—and God'll forgive me when He sees my reason. But you— Oh, Isaiah! (*She shudders and then breaks down, sobbing.*)

BARTLETT—(*after a pause, turns to her humbly as if asking forgiveness*) Ye mustn't think hard o' me that I want your name. It's because it's a good woman's name, and I know it'll bring luck to our vige. I'd find it hard to sail without it— the way things be.

MRS. BARTLETT—(*getting to her feet—in a state of feverish fear of him*) I'm goin' to home.

BARTLETT—(*going to her*) I'll help ye to the top o' the hill, Sarah.

MRS. BARTLETT—(*shrinking from him in terror*) No. Don't you touch me! Don't you touch me! (*She hobbles quickly out of the door in the rear, looking back frightenedly over her shoulder to see if he is following as*

The Curtain Falls)

ACT THREE

SCENE—*Dawn of the following morning—exterior of the Bartlett home, showing the main entrance, facing left, toward the harbor. On either side of the door, two large windows, their heavy green shutters tightly closed. In front of the door, a small porch, the roof supported by four white columns. A flight of three steps goes up to this porch from the ground. Two paths lead to the steps through the straggly patches of grass, one around the corner of the house to the rear, the other straight to the left to the edge of the cliff where there is a small projecting iron platform, fenced in by a rail. The top of a steel ladder can be seen. This ladder leads up the side of the cliff from the shore below to the platform. The edge of the cliff extends from the left corner front, half-diagonally back to the right, rear-center.*

In the gray half-light of the dawn, Horne, Cates, and Jimmy Kanaka are discovered. Horne is standing on the steel platform looking down at the shore below. Cates is sprawled on the ground nearby. Jimmy squats on his haunches, his eyes staring out to sea as if he were trying to pierce the distance to the warm islands of his birth. Cates wears dungarees, Jimmy dungaree pants and a black jersey, Horne the same as in Act Two.

CATES—(*with sluggish indifference*) Ain't she finished with it yet?

HORNE—(*irritably*) No, damn her! I kin see 'em all together on the wharf at the bow o' the schooner.

CATES—(*after a pause*) Funny, ain't it—his orderin' us to come up here and wait till it's all done.

HORNE—There's nothin' funny to me that he does no more. He's still out o' his head, d'ye know that, Cates?

CATES—(*stupidly*) I ain't noticed nothin' diff'rent 'bout him.

HORNE—(*scornfully*) He axed me if I ever seen them two in my sleep—that cook and the boy o' the Triton. Said he did often.

CATES—(*immediately protesting uneasily as if he had been accused*) They was with us in the boat b'fore we fetched the island, that's all 'bout 'em I remember. I was crazy, after.

HORNE—(*looking at him with contempt*) I'll not call ye a

925

liar, Cates, but—a hell o' a man ye be! You wasn't so out o' your head that ye forgot the gold, was ye?

CATES—(*his eyes glistening*) Any man'd remember that, even if he was crazy.

HORNE—(*with a greedy grin*) Aye. That's the one thing I see in my sleep. (*There is the faint sound of cries from the beach below. Horne starts and turns to look down again.*) They must 'a' finished it. (*Cates and Jimmy come to the edge to look down.*)

JIMMY—(*suddenly—with an eager childish curiosity*) That falla wife Captain she make strong falla spell on ship, we sail fast, plenty good wind?

HORNE—(*contemptuously*) Aye, that's as near as ye'll come to it. She's makin' a spell. Ye stay here, Jimmy, and tell us when the Old Man is comin'. (*Jimmy remains looking down. Horne motions Cates to follow him, front—then in a low voice, disgustedly*) Did ye hear that damn fool nigger?

CATES—(*grumblingly*) Why the hell is the Old Man givin' him a full share? One piece o' it'd be enough for a nigger like him.

HORNE—(*craftily*) There's a way to get rid o' him—if it comes to that. He knifed them two, ye remember.

CATES—Aye.

HORNE—The two o' us can take oath to that.

CATES—Aye.

HORNE—(*after a calculating look into his companion's greedy eyes—meaningly*) We're two sane men, Cates—and the other two to share is a lunatic and a nigger. The skipper's showed me where there's a copy o' his map o' the island locked up in the cabin—in case anything happens to him I'm to bring back the gold to his woman, he says. (*He laughs harshly.*) Catch me! The fool! I'll be open with ye, Cates. If I could navigate and find the island myself I wouldn't wait for a cracked man to take me there. No, be damned if I would! Me and you'd chance it alone some way or other.

CATES—(*greedily*) The two o' us—share and share alike! (*then shaking his head warningly*) But he's a hard man to git the best on.

HORNE—(*grimly*) And I be a hard man, too.

JIMMY—(*turning to them*) Captain, he come. (*Cates and Horne separate hastily. Bartlett climbs into sight up the ladder to the platform. He is breathing heavily but his expression is one of triumphant exultation.*)

BARTLETT—(*motions with his arms*) Down with ye and git aboard. The schooner's got a name now—a name that'll bring us luck. We'll sail on this tide.

HORNE—Aye—aye, sir.

BARTLETT—I got to wait here till they climb up the path. I'll be aboard afore long. See that ye have her ready to cast off by then.

HORNE—Aye—aye, sir. (*He and Cates disappear down the ladder. Jimmy lingers, looking sidewise at his Captain.*)

BARTLETT—(*noticing him—gruffly*) What are ye waitin' for?

JIMMY—(*volubly*) That old falla wife belong you, Captain, she make strong falla spell for wind blow plenty? She catch strong devil charm for schooner, Captain?

BARTLETT—(*scowling*) What's that, ye brown devil? (*then suddenly laughing harshly*) Yes—a strong spell to bring us luck. (*roughly*) Git aboard, ye dog! Don't let her find ye here with me. (*Jimmy disappears hurriedly down the ladder. Bartlett remains at the edge looking down after him. There is a sound of voices from the right and presently Mrs. Bartlett, Sue, Drew and Nat enter, coming around the house from the rear. Nat and Drew walk at either side of Mrs. Bartlett, who is in a state of complete collapse, so that they are practically carrying her. Sue follows, her handkerchief to her eyes. Nat keeps his eyes on the ground, his expression fixed and gloomy. Drew casts a glance of angry indignation at the Captain, who, after one indifferent look at them, has turned back to watch the operations on the schooner below.*)

BARTLETT—(*as they reach the steps of the house—intent on the work below—makes a megaphone of his hands and shouts in stentorian tones*) Look lively there, Horne!

SUE—(*protestingly*) Pa!

BARTLETT—(*wheels about. When he meets his daughter's eyes he controls his angry impatience and speaks gently.*) What d'ye want, Sue?

SUE—(*pointing to her mother who is being assisted through the door—her voice trembling*) You mustn't shout. She's very sick.

BARTLETT—(*dully, as if he didn't understand*) Sick?

SUE—(*turning to the door*) Wait. I'll be right back. (*She enters the house. As soon as she is gone all of Bartlett's excitement returns. He paces up and down with nervous impatience. Nat comes out of the house.*)

NAT—(*in a tone of anxiety*) Ma seems bad. I'm going for the doctor.

BARTLETT—(*as if he hadn't heard—draws Nat's attention to the schooner*) Smart lines on that schooner, boy. She'll sail hell bent in a breeze. I knowed what I was about when I bought her.

NAT—(*staring down fascinatedly*) How long will the voyage take?

BARTLETT—(*preoccupied*) How long?

NAT—(*insinuatingly*) To get to the island.

BARTLETT—Three months at most—with fair luck. (*exultantly*) And I'll have luck now!

NAT—Then in six months you may be back—with *it*?

BARTLETT—Aye, with— (*stopping abruptly, turns and stares into his son's eyes—angrily*) With what? What boy's foolishness be ye talkin'?

NAT—(*pleading fiercely*) I want to go, Pa! There's no good in my staying here any more. I can't think of anything but—

BARTLETT—(*sternly, to conceal his uneasiness*) Keep clear o' this, boy, I've warned ye!

SUE—(*appearing in doorway—indignantly*) Nat! Haven't you gone for the doctor yet?

NAT—(*shamefacedly*) I forgot.

SUE—Forgot!

NAT—(*starting off*) I'm going, Sue. (*then over his shoulder*) You won't sail before I come back, Pa. (*Bartlett does not answer. Nat stands miserably hesitating.*)

SUE—Nat! For heaven's sake! (*Nat hurries off around the corner of the house, rear. Sue comes to her father who is watching her with a queer, humble, hunted expression.*)

BARTLETT—Well, Sue?

SUE—(*her voice trembling*) Oh, Pa, how could you drag Ma out of bed to christen your old boat—when you knew how sick she's been!

BARTLETT—(*avoiding her eyes*) It's only weakness. She'll get well o' it soon.

SUE—Pa! How can you say things like that—as if you didn't care! (*accusingly*) The way you've acted ever since you've been home almost, anyone would think—you *hated* her!

BARTLETT—(*wincing*) No!

SUE—Oh, Pa, what is it that has come between you? Can't you tell me? Can't I help to set things right again?

BARTLETT—(*mumblingly*) Nothin'—nothin' ye kin help—nor me.

SUE—But things can't go on like this. Don't you see it's killing Ma?

BARTLETT—She'll forget her stubborn notions, now I be sailin' away.

SUE—But you're not—not going for a while now, are you?

BARTLETT—Ain't I been sayin' I'd sail at dawn today?

SUE—(*looking at him for a moment with shocked amazement*) But—you can't mean—right now!

BARTLETT—(*keeping his face averted*) Aye—or we'll miss this tide.

SUE—(*putting her hands on his shoulders and trying to look into his face*) Pa! You can't mean that! (*His face is set with his obsessed determination. She lets her hands fall with a shudder.*) You can't be as cruel as that! Why, I thought, of course, you'd put off— (*wildly*) You have, haven't you, Pa? You did tell those men you couldn't sail when you saw how sick Ma was, didn't you—when she fainted down on the wharf?

BARTLETT—(*implacably*) I said I was sailin' by this tide!

SUE—Pa! (*then pleadingly*) When the doctor comes and you hear what he says—

BARTLETT—(*roughly*) I ain't stoppin' on his word nor any man's. (*intensely*) That schooner's been fit to sail these two weeks past. I been waitin' on her stubborn will (*he gestures toward the house*), eatin' my heart out day and night. Then I swore I'd sail today. I tell ye, Sue, I got a feelin' in my bones if I don't put out now I never will. Aye, I feel it deep down inside me. (*in a tone of superstitious awe*) And when she christened the schooner—jest to the minute, mind ye!—a fair breeze sprung up and come down out o' the land to blow her out to sea—like a sign o' good luck.

SUE—(*aroused to angry indignation*) Oh, I can't believe you're the same man who used to be my father!

BARTLETT—Sue!

SUE—To talk cold-bloodedly of sailing away on a long voyage when Ma's inside—dying for all you seem to know or care! You're not the father I love! You've changed into someone else—hateful and cruel—and I hate him, I hate him! (*She breaks down, sobbing hysterically.*)

BARTLETT—(*who has listened to her with a face suddenly stricken by fear and torturing remorse*) Sue! Ye don't know what ye be sayin', do ye?

SUE—I do! And I hate those three awful men who make you act this way. I hate the schooner! I wish she and they were at the bottom of the sea!

BARTLETT—(*frenziedly—putting his hand over her mouth to stop her words*) Stop, girl! Don't ye dare—

SUE—(*shrinking away from him—frightenedly*) Pa!

BARTLETT—(*bewilderedly, pleading for forgiveness*) Don't heed that, Sue—I didn't mean—ye git me so riled—I'd not hurt ye for all the gold in the world. But don't ye talk wrong o' things ye can't know on.

SUE—Oh, Pa, what kind of things must they be—when you're ashamed to tell them!

BARTLETT—Ye'll know all they be to know—and your Ma and Nat, too—when I come back from this vige. Oh, ye'll be glad enough then—when ye see with your own eyes! Ye'll bless me then 'stead o' turning agin me! (*hesitating for a second—then somberly*) On'y now—till it's all over and done—ye'd best keep clear o' it.

SUE—(*passionately*) I don't want to know anything about it. What I do know is that you can't sail now. Haven't you any heart at all? Can't you see how bad Ma is?

BARTLETT—It's the sight o' me sickens her.

SUE—No. She called your name just a while ago—the only word she's spoken since she christened the ship.

BARTLETT—(*desperately*) I got to git away from her, I tell ye, Sue! She's been houndin' me ever since I got back—houndin' me with her stubborn tongue till she's druv me mad, a'most! Ye've been on'y givin' thought to her, not me. It's for her sake as much as my own I'm goin'—for her and you and Nat. (*with a sudden return of his old resolution*) I've made up my mind, I tell ye, and in the end ye'll know I be right. (*A hail in Horne's voice comes thinly up from the shore below. Bartlett starts, his eyes gleaming.*) Ye hear? It's Horne hailin' me to come. They be ready to cast off. I'll git aboard. (*He starts for the ladder.*)

SUE—Pa! After all I've said—without one word of good-by to Ma! (*hysterically*) Oh, what can I do, what can I say to stop you! She hasn't spoken but that one call for you. She hardly seems to breathe. If it weren't for her eyes I'd believe she was dead—but her eyes look for you. She'll die if you go, Pa!

BARTLETT—No!

SUE—You might just as well kill her now in cold blood as murder her that way!

BARTLETT—(*shaken—raising his hands as if to put them over his ears to shut out her words—hoarsely*) No! Ye lie!

DREW—(*appearing in the doorway, his face working with grief and anger—harshly*) Captain Bartlett! (*then lowering his voice as he sees Sue*) Mrs. Bartlett is asking to see you, Captain, before you go.

SUE—There! Didn't I tell you, Pa!

BARTLETT—(*struggling with himself—dully*) She's wantin' to hound me again, that be all.

SUE—(*seeing him weakening—grasps his hand persuasively*) Pa! Come with me. She won't hound you. How silly you are! Come! (*Hesitatingly, head bowed, he follows her toward the door.*)

BARTLETT—(*As he comes to Drew he stops and looks into the young man's angry, accusing face. He mutters half mockingly*) So ye, too, be agin me, Danny?

DREW—(*unable to restrain his indignation*) What man that's a real man wouldn't be against you, sir?

SUE—(*frightenedly*) Danny! Pa!

BARTLETT—(*in a sudden rage draws back his fist threateningly. Drew stares into his eyes unflinchingly—Bartlett controls himself with an effort and lets his arm fall to his side—scornfully*) Big words from a boy, Danny. I'll forget them this time—on account o' Sue. (*He turns to her.*) I'm goin' in to her to please ye, Sue—but if ye think any words that she kin say'll change my mind, ye make a mistake—for I be sailin' out as I planned

I would in spite o' all hell! (*He walks resolutely into the house. Sue follows him after exchanging a hopeless glance with Danny.*)

DREW—(*to himself—with a shudder*) He's mad, damn him! (*He paces up and down. Horne appears on the ladder from below, followed by Cates.*)

HORNE—(*coming forward and addressing Drew*) Is the skipper about?

DREW—(*curtly*) He's in the house. You can't speak to him now.

HORNE—She's ready to cast off. I hailed him from below but I s'pect he didn't hear. (*as Drew makes no comment—impatiently*) If he don't shake a leg, we'll miss the tide. There's a bit o' fair breeze, too.

DREW—(*glancing at him resentfully*) Don't count on his sailing today. It's just as likely he'll change his mind.

HORNE—(*angrily*) Change his mind again? After us waitin' and wastin' time for weeks! (*to Cates in a loud tone so Drew can hear*) What did I tell ye, Cates? He's crazy as hell.

DREW—(*sharply*) What's that?

HORNE—I was tellin' Cates the skipper's not right in his head. (*angrily*) What man in his senses'd do the way he does?

DREW—(*letting his resentment escape him*) That's no lie, damn it!

HORNE—(*surprised*) Aye, ye've seen it, too, have ye? (*after a pause*) Now I axe ye, as a sailor, how'd ye like to be puttin' out on a vige with a cracked man for skipper? (*Sue comes out of the door, stops with a shudder of disgust as she sees the two sailors, and stands listening. They do not notice her presence.*)

DREW—It seems to me a crazy voyage all round. (*with sudden interest as if a new idea had come to him*) But you know all about it, don't you—what the Captain plans to do on this voyage—and all that?

HORNE—(*dryly*) Aye, as well as himself—but I'm tellin' no man.

DREW—And I'm not asking. What I want to find out is: Do you know enough about this business to make this one voyage alone and attend to everything—in case the Captain can't go?

HORNE—(*exchanging a quick glance with Cates—trying to*

hide his eagerness) Aye, I could do as well as any man alive. He could trust me for it—and I'd make more money for him than he's likely to make with his head out o' gear. (*then scowling*) On'y trouble is, who'd captain her if he ain't goin'?

DREW—(*disappointedly*) Then you don't know navigation enough for that?

HORNE—I've never riz above bo'sun. (*then after a pause in which he appears to be calculating something—curiously*) Why d'ye ask me them questions? (*insinuatingly—almost in a whisper*) It can't be done 'less we got an officer like you aboard.

DREW—(*angrily*) Eh? What're you driving at?

SUE—(*who has been listening with aroused interest*) Danny! (*She comes down to him. Horne and Cates bob their heads respectfully and move back near the platform. Horne watches Sue and Drew out of the corner of his eye.*) Danny, I've been listening to what you were saying, but I don't understand. What are you thinking of?

DREW—(*excitedly*) I was thinking— Listen, Sue! Seems to me your Pa's out of his right mind. Something's got to be done to keep him home in spite of himself. Even leaving your Ma out of it, he's not in any fit state to take a ship to sea; and I was thinking if we could fix it some way so that fellow Horne could take her out on this voyage—

SUE—But, Danny, Pa'd never give in to that.

DREW—I wasn't thinking he would. We—you'd have to give the word—and keep him in the house somehow—and then when he did come out it'd be too late. The schooner'd be gone.

SUE—(*disturbed, but showing that this plan has caught her mind*) But—he'd never forgive—

DREW—When he's back in his right mind again, he would. (*earnestly*) You can't let him sail, and wreck his ship and himself in the bargain, likely. Then, there's your Ma—

SUE—No, no, we can't let him. (*with a glance at Horne and Cates*) But I don't trust those men.

DREW—No more do I; but it would be better to chance them than— (*suddenly interrupting himself—with a shrug of his shoulders*) But I was forgetting. None of them can navigate.

SUE—But didn't I hear him say—if they had an officer on board—like you—

DREW—Yes, but where'll you find one at a second's notice?

SUE—(*meaningly*) And you told me, didn't you, that you'd just got your master's papers.

DREW—(*looking at her with stunned astonishment*) Sue! D'you mean—

SUE—(*a light coming over her face*) Oh, Danny, we could trust you! He'd trust you! And after he'd calmed down I know he wouldn't mind so much. Oh, Danny, it'll break my heart to have you go, to send you away just after you've come back. But I don't see any other way. I wouldn't ask—if it wasn't for Ma being this way—and him— Oh, Danny, can't you see your way to do it—for my sake?

DREW—(*bewilderedly*) Why, Sue, I—I never thought— (*then as he sees the look of disappointment which comes over her face at his hesitancy—resolutely*) Why sure, Sue, I'll do it—if you want me to. I'll do it if it can be done. But we've got to hustle. You've got to keep him in the house some way if he aims to come out. And I'll talk to them. (*Sue goes to the doorway. Drew goes over to Horne and Cates.*)

SUE—(*after listening*) He's still in with Ma. It's all right.

DREW—(*to Horne*) How would you like me for skipper on this one voyage? Listen here. Miss Sue's decided her father isn't in a fit state to captain this trip.

HORNE—That's no lie.

CATES—(*to Horne protestingly*) But if we git ketched the Old Man'll take it out o' our hides, not his'n.

HORNE—(*savagely—with a meaning look at Cates*) Shut up, ye fool!

DREW—(*impatiently*) I'll shoulder all that risk, man!

SUE—(*earnestly*) No harm will come to any of you, I promise you.

HORNE—(*in the tone of one clinching a bargain*) Then we'll chance it. (*warningly*) But it's got to be done smart, sir.

DREW—I've got to get my dunnage. I'll be right back and we'll tumble aboard. (*He goes into the house. Sue follows him in.*)

CATES—(*with stupid anger*) This is a hell o' a mess we're gettin' in, if ye axe me.

HORNE—And I tell ye it's a great stroke o' luck.

CATES—He'll be aboard to spy on us.

HORNE—Leave me to fool him. And when the time comes to git rid o' him, I'll find a means some way or other.

CATES—(*stupidly*) S'long as he don't git no share o' the gold—

HORNE—(*contemptuously*) Share, ye dumbhead! I'd see him in hell first—and send him there myself. (*Drew comes out of the house carrying his bag which he hands to Cates. Sue follows him.*)

DREW—Look lively now!

HORNE—Aye—aye, sir. (*He and Cates clamber hurriedly down the ladder.*)

SUE—(*throwing her arms around his neck and kissing him*) Good-by, Danny. It's so fine of you to do this for us! I'll never forget—

DREW—(*tenderly*) Ssssh! It's nothing, Sue.

SUE—(*tearfully*) Oh, Danny, I hope I'm doing right! I'll miss you so dreadfully! But you'll come back just as soon as you can—

DREW—Of course!

SUE—Danny! Danny! I love you so!

DREW—And I guess you know I love you, don't you? (*kisses her*) And we'll be married when I come back this time sure?

SUE—Yes—yes—Danny—sure!

DREW—I've got to run. Good-by, Sue.

SUE—Good-by, dear. (*They kiss for the last time and he disappears down the ladder. She stands at the top, sobbing, following him with her eyes. Nat comes around the house from the rear and goes to the front door.*)

NAT—(*seeing his sister*) Sue! He hasn't gone yet, has he? (*She doesn't hear him. He hesitates in the doorway for a moment, listening for the sound of his father's voice from inside. Then, very careful to make no noise, he tiptoes carefully into the house. Sue waves her hand to Drew who has evidently now got aboard the ship. Then she covers her face with her hands, sobbing. Nat comes out of the house again and goes to his sister. As she sees him approaching, she dries her eyes hastily, trying to smile.*)

SUE—Did you get the doctor, Nat?

NAT—Yes, he's coming right away, he promised. (*looking at her face*) What—have you been crying?

SUE—No. (*She walks away from the edge of the cliff, drawing him with her.*)

NAT—Yes, you have. Look at your eyes.

SUE—Oh, Nat, everything's so awful! (*She breaks down again.*)

NAT—(*trying to comfort her in an absent-minded way*) There, don't get worked up. Ma'll be all right as soon as the doctor comes. (*then curiously*) Pa's inside with her. They were arguing—have they made it up, d'you think?

SUE—Oh, Nat, I don't know.

NAT—The strain's been too much for him—waiting and hiding his secret from all of us. What do you suppose it is, Sue?

SUE—(*wildly*) I don't know and I don't care!

NAT—Well, there's something— (*starts for the platform. Sue does her best to interpose to hold him back.*) Are they all ready on the schooner? He'll have to hurry if she's going to sail on this tide. (*with sudden passion*) Oh, I've got to go! I can't stay here! (*pleadingly*) Don't you think, Sue, if you were to ask him for me he'd— You're the only one he seems to act sane with or care about any more.

SUE—No! I won't! I can't!

NAT—(*angrily*) Haven't you any sense? Wouldn't it be better for everyone if I went in his place?

SUE—No. You know that's a lie. Ma would lose her mind if you went.

NAT—And I'll lose mine if I stay! (*half aware of Sue's intention to keep him from looking down at the schooner—irritably*) What are you holding my arm for, Sue? I want to see what they're doing. (*He pushes her aside and goes to the platform—excitedly*) Hello, they've got the fores'l and mains'l set. They're setting the stays'l. (*in amazement*) Why—they're casting off! She's moving away from the wharf! (*more and more excitedly*) I see four of them on board! Who—who is that, Sue?

SUE—It's Danny.

NAT—(*furiously*) Danny! What right has he—when I can't! Sue, call Pa! They're sailing, I tell you, you little fool!

SUE—(*trying to calm him—her voice trembling*) Nat! Don't be such a donkey! Danny's only going a little way—just trying the boat to see how she sails while they're waiting for Pa.

NAT—(*uncertainly*) Oh. (*then bitterly*) I was never allowed to do even that—his own son! Look, Sue, that must be Danny at the stern waving.

SUE—(*brokenly*) Yes. (*She waves her handkerchief over her head—then breaks down, sobbing again. There is the noise of Bartlett's voice from inside and a moment later he appears in the doorway. He seems terribly shattered, at the end of his tether. He hesitates uncertainly, looking about him wildly as if he didn't know what to do or where to go.*)

SUE—(*after one look at his face, runs to him and flings her arms about his neck*) Pa! (*She weeps on his shoulder.*)

BARTLETT—Sue, ye did wrong beggin' me to see her. I knowed it'd do no good. Ye promised she'd not hound me— "Confess," she says—when they be naught to tell that couldn't be swore to in any court. "Don't go on this vige," she says, "there be the curse o' God on it." (*with a note of baffled anguish*) She kin say that after givin' the ship her own name! (*with wild, haggard defiance*) But curse or no curse, I be goin'! (*He moves toward the platform, Sue clinging to his arm.*)

SUE—(*frightenedly*) Pa! Go back in the house, won't you?

BARTLETT—I be sorry to go agin your will, Sue, but it's got to be. Ye'll know the reason some day—and be glad o' it. And now good-by to ye. (*With a sudden strange tenderness he bends and kisses his daughter. Then as she seems about to protest further, his expression becomes stern and inflexible.*) No more o' talk, Sue! I be bound out. (*He takes her hand off his arm and strides to the platform. One look down at the harbor and he stands transfixed—in a hoarse whisper*) What damned trick be this? (*He points to the schooner and turns to Nat bewilderedly.*) Ain't that my schooner, boy—the Sarah Allen—reachin' toward the p'int?

NAT—(*surprised*) Yes, certainly. Didn't you know? Danny's trying her to see how she sails while they're waiting for you.

BARTLETT—(*with a tremendous sigh of relief*) Aye. (*then angrily*) He takes a lot o' rope to himself without askin' leave o' me. Don't he know they's no time to waste on boy's foolin'? (*then with admiration*) She sails smart, don't she, boy? I knowed she'd show a pair o' heels.

NAT—(*with enthusiasm*) Yes, she's a daisy! Say, Danny's taking her pretty far out, isn't he?

BARTLETT—(*anxiously*) He'd ought to come about now if he's to tack back inside the p'int. (*furiously*) Come about, damn ye! The swab! That's what comes o' steamer trainin'. I'd sooner trust Sue to sail her nor him. (*waves his arm and shouts*) Come about!

NAT—(*bitterly*) He seems to be heading straight for the open sea. He's taking quite a sail, it seems to me.

BARTLETT—(*as if he couldn't believe his eyes*) He's passed the p'int—and now—headin' her out to sea—so'east by east. By God, that be the course I charted for her! (*Sue bursts out sobbing. He wheels on her, his mouth fallen open, his face full of a stupid despair.*) They be somethin' wrong here. What be it, Sue? What be it, Nat? (*His voice has begun to quiver with passion.*) That schooner—she's sailin' without me— (*He suddenly springs at Nat and grabs him by the throat—with hoarse fury, shaking him*) What be it, ye whelp? It's your doin'—because I wouldn't let ye go. Answer me!

SUE—(*rushing to them with a scream*) Pa! (*She tugs frantically at his hands. Bartlett lets them fall to his side, stepping back from Nat who sinks weakly to the ground, gasping for breath. Bartlett stands looking at him wildly.*)

SUE—Nat didn't know, Pa. It's all my fault. I had to do it. There was no other way—

BARTLETT—(*raging*) What d'ye mean, girl? What is it ye've done? Tell me, I say! Tell me or I'll—

SUE—(*unflinchingly*) You had to be stopped from going some way. So I asked Danny if he wouldn't make the trip in your place. He's just got his captain's papers—and oh, Pa, you can trust him, you know that! That man Horne said he knows about everything you wanted done, and he promised to tell Danny, and Danny'll come back—

BARTLETT—(*chokingly*) So—that be it— (*shaking his clenched fist at the sky as if visualizing the fate he feels in all of this*) Curse ye! Curse ye! (*He subsides weakly, his strength spent, his hand falls limply at his side.*)

MRS. BARTLETT—(*appears in the doorway. Her face is pale with anguish. She gives a cry of joy when she sees her son.*) Nat! (*then with a start of horror as her eyes fall on her husband*) Isaiah! (*He doesn't seem to hear.*) Then—you ain't sailed yet?

SUE—(*going to her—gently*) No, Ma, he isn't going to sail. He's going to stay home with you. But the schooner's gone. See. (*She points and her mother's eyes turn seaward.*)

BARTLETT—(*aloud to himself—in a tone of groping superstitious awe and bewildered fear*) They be somethin' queer—somethin' wrong—they be a curse in this somewhere—

MRS. BARTLETT—(*turning accusing eyes on him—with a sort of fanatical triumph*) I'm glad to hear you confess that, Isaiah. Yes, there be a curse—God's curse on the wicked sinfulness o' men—and I thank God He's saved you from the evil of that voyage, and I'll pray Him to visit His punishment and His curse on them three men on that craft you forced me to give my name— (*She has raised her hand as if calling down retribution on the schooner she can dimly see.*)

SUE—(*terrified*) Ma!

BARTLETT—(*starting toward his wife with an insane yell of fury*) Stop it, I tell ye! (*He towers over her with upraised fist as if to crush her.*)

SUE—Pa!

NAT—(*starting to his feet from where he has been sitting on the ground—hoarsely*) Pa! For God's sake!

MRS. BARTLETT—(*gives a weak, frightened gasp*) Would you murder me too, Isaiah? (*She closes her eyes and collapses in Sue's arms.*)

SUE—(*tremblingly*) Nat! Help me! Quick! We must carry her to bed. (*They take their mother in their arms, carrying her inside the house.*)

BARTLETT—(*while they are doing this, rushes in his mad frenzy to the platform over the edge of the cliff. He puts his hands to his mouth, megaphone-fashion, and yells with despairing rage*) Ahoy! Ahoy! Sarah Allen! Put back! Put back! (*as*

The Curtain Falls)

ACT FOUR

SCENE—*About nine o'clock of a moonlight night one year later—Captain Bartlett's "cabin," a room erected on the top of his house as a lookout post. The interior is fitted up like the cabin of a sailing vessel. On the left, forward, a porthole. Farther back, the stairs of the companionway. Still farther, two more portholes. In the rear, left, a marble-topped sideboard. In the rear, center, a door opening on stairs which lead to the lower house. A cot with a blanket is placed against the wall to the right of door. In the right wall, five portholes. Directly under them, a wooden bench. In front of the bench, a long table with two chairs placed, one in front, one to the left of it. A cheap, dark-colored rug is on the floor. In the ceiling, midway from front to rear, a skylight extending from opposite the door to above the left edge of the table. In the right extremity of the skylight is placed a floating ship's compass. The light from the binnacle sheds down over this and seeps into the room, casting a vague globular shadow of the compass on the floor. Moonlight creeps in through the portholes on the right. A lighted lantern is on the table.*

As the curtain rises, Sue and Doctor Berry are discovered sitting by the table. The doctor is a man of sixty or so, hale and hearty-looking, his white hair and mustache setting off his ruddy complexion. His blue eyes have a gentle expression, his smile is kindly and sympathetic. His whole manner toward Sue is that of the old family doctor and friend, not the least of whose duties is to play father-confessor to his patients. She is dressed in deep mourning. She looks much older. But there is an excited elation in her face at present, her eyes are alight with some unexpected joy.

SUE—(*excitedly*) And here is Danny's letter, Doctor—to prove it's all true. (*She takes a letter from the bosom of her dress and holds it out to him.*)

DOCTOR—(*takes it with a smile, patting her hand*) I can't say how glad I am, Susan. Coming after we'd all given him up for lost—it's like a miracle.

SUE—(*smiling happily*) Read what he says.

DOCTOR—(*hesitating—playfully*) I don't know that it's right for me—love letters at my age!

SUE—I want you to read it. (*He reaches in his pocket for his spectacles. Sue continues gratefully.*) As if I could have any secrets from you after all you've done for us since Ma died. You've been the only friend— (*She stops, her lips trembling.*)

DOCTOR—Tut-tut. (*He adjusts his spectacles and peers at her over them.*) Who wouldn't be of all the service he could to a brave girl like you? This past year—with your mother's death—and then the news of the schooner being reported lost—not many could have stood it—living in this house with him the way he is—even if he was their father.

SUE—(*glancing up at the skylight—apprehensively*) Ssshh! He might hear you.

DOCTOR—(*listening intently*) Not him. There he goes pacing up and down, looking out to sea for that ship that will never come back! (*shaking himself*) Brrr! This house of mad dreams!

SUE—Don't you think Pa'll come to realize the schooner is lost as time goes by and she doesn't come back?

DOCTOR—No, your father won't let himself look the facts in the face. If he did, probably the shock of it would kill him. That darn dream of his has become his life. No, Susan, as time goes on he'll believe in it harder and harder. After observing him for the past year—and I speak for his own sake, too, as his good friend for twenty years or more—my final advice is the same: Send him to an asylum.

SUE—(*with a shudder*) No, Doctor.

DOCTOR—(*shaking his head*) You'll have to come to it in time. He's getting worse. No one can tell—he might get violent—

SUE—How can you say that? You know how gentle and sane he is with me.

DOCTOR—You're his one connecting link with things as they are—but that can't last. Eh, well, my dear, one thing you've got to realize: Your father and Nat must be separated somehow. Nat's going to pieces. I'll bet he doesn't believe that schooner is lost any more than your father does.

SUE—You mean he still hopes it may not be true. That's only natural. He's in San Francisco now tracing down the report again. He saw in the papers where the British freighter that found the derelict was there and he went to talk with the people on board. I'm hoping he'll come back fully convinced, with the whole thing out of his mind.

DOCTOR—(*shaking his head—gravely*) I've watched him and talked with him. You've got to persuade Nat to go away, Susan.

SUE—(*helplessly*) I don't know— (*then brightening*) Just now it's enough to know Danny's alive and coming back. Read his letter, Doctor.

DOCTOR—Yes, yes, let's see. (*He takes the letter from the envelope.*)

SUE—Poor Danny! He's been through terrible things.

DOCTOR—Hmm! Rangoon.

SUE—Yes, he's still in the hospital there. You'll see.

DOCTOR—(*reads the letter—grunts with astonishment— angrily*) By Gad! The damn scoundrels!

SUE—(*shuddering*) Yes, wasn't it hideous—those awful men stabbing him and leaving him for dead in that out of the way native settlement! And then he was laid up for four months there waiting for a vessel to touch and take him back to civilization. And then, think of it, getting the fever on top of all that and nearly dying in the hospital in Rangoon!

DOCTOR—A terrible time of it! He's lucky to be alive. Hmm. I see he foresaw the wreck of the schooner. (*folding the letter and putting it back*) He doesn't seem to have found out what the purpose of that mad trip was. Horne hid it from him to the last, he says. Well, it's queer—damn queer. But I'm glad to know those wretches have gone to their final accounting.

SUE—(*with a shudder*) I was always afraid of them. They looked like—murderers. (*At a noise from below they both start. Steps can be heard climbing the stairs. Sue jumps to her feet frightenedly.*) Why—do you hear—who can that be? (*There is a soft rap on the door. The doctor jumps to his feet. Sue turns to him with a half-hysterical laugh.*) Shall I open? I don't know why— but I'm afraid.

DOCTOR—Tut-tut! I'll see who it is. (*He opens the door and Nat is discovered on the stairs outside.*) Why hello, boy. You gave us a scare. Susan thought it was a ghost knocking.

NAT—(*comes into the room. He has aged, grown thin, his face gaunt and drawn from continual mental strain, his eyes moody and preoccupied. He glances up at the skylight apprehensively, then turns to Sue.*) I didn't find you downstairs so I— (*then to the doctor*) Yes, you do grow to look for ghosts in this house, don't you? (*again glancing upward*) He's up there as usual, I suppose—looking for a ship that'll never, never come now!

DOCTOR—(*with a grunt of approval*) I'm glad to hear you acknowledge that.

SUE—(*who is just recovering from her fright*) But, Nat, I didn't expect you— Did you find out—?

NAT—Yes, I talked with several of the men who were on board at the time. They said they steamed in so close to the schooner it was easy to read the name with the naked eye. All agreed—Sarah Allen, Harborport. They even remembered how her taffrail was painted. There's no chance for mistake. The Sarah Allen is gone. (*with great emphasis*) And I'm glad—damn glad! I feel free again, and I can go back to work—but not here. I've got to go away—start new altogether.

SUE—(*happily, coming and putting her arms around him*) It's so good to hear you talk like your old self again.

DOCTOR—(*earnestly*) Yes, Nat, by Gad, that's sound sense. Get out of this.

NAT—(*giving him a queer look*) I suppose you thought I was doomed, eh?—like him. (*He makes a motion upward—then with an uncertain laugh*) A doctor's always looking for trouble where there isn't any. (*in a tone of finality*) Well, it's all over, anyway.

SUE—(*snatching the letter from the table*) Oh, I was forgetting, Nat. Read this. I got it yesterday.

NAT—(*turns it over in his hands suspiciously*) Who from?

SUE—Open it and see.

NAT—(*does so and turns over the pages to read the signature—he gives a start—hoarsely*) Danny! It can't be! But it's his writing sure enough! (*He exclaims with a sudden wild exultation*) Then they must have been lying to me!

SUE—No, the Sarah Allen was wrecked all right, but that was afterwards. Read it. You'll see. (*Nat sinks back on a chair, evidently depressed by this information. He starts to read the letter with unconcealed indifference, then becomes engrossed, excited, the paper trembling in his hands. The doctor shakes his head at Sue indicating his disapproval of her giving him the letter. Nat finishes and springs to his feet—angrily)*

NAT—The stupid fool! He let Horne pull the wool over his eyes in fine shape.

SUE—(*indignantly*) Nat!

NAT—(*unheedingly*) Oh, if I could only have gone in his place! I knew the kind Horne was. He couldn't have played that trick on me. I'd have forced the secret out of him if I had to— (*He raises his clenched fist in a gesture of threat like his father's—then lets it fall and sits down again—disgustedly*) But what's the use? And what's the use of this? (*tosses the letter contemptuously on the table*) He might just as well not have written.

SUE—(*snatching up the letter—deeply hurt*) Aren't you even glad to hear Danny's alive?

NAT—(*turning to her at once—with remorseful confusion*) Yes—yes—of course, Sue—I don't have to say that, do I? What I mean is, he never found out from Horne—and we're no wiser.

DOCTOR—(*briskly—with a significant glance at Sue*) Well, Susan—Nat—I've got to run along— (*meaningly*) I'll be over again tomorrow, Susan.

SUE—Yes, do come. (*goes with him to the door*) Can you see your way?

DOCTOR—Yes. Good night.

SUE—Good night. (*She closes the door and comes back to Nat. The doctor's footsteps die out.*)

NAT—(*savagely*) That damned old fool! What is he doing, sneaking around here all the time? I've grown to hate the sight of him.

SUE—Nat! You can't mean that. Think of how kind he's been.

NAT—Yes—kindness with a purpose.

SUE—Don't be silly. What purpose could he have except wanting to help us?

NAT—To find out things, of course, you simpleton. To pump Pa when he's not responsible for what he's saying.

SUE—(*indignantly*) Nat!

NAT—Much good it's done him! I know Pa. Sane or not,

he won't tell *that* to anyone—not even you or me, Sue. (*with sudden fury*) I'm going away—but before I go I'm going to make him tell me! He's been so afraid I'd find out, so scared to speak to me even—locking himself up here. But I'll make him tell—yes, I will!

SUE—Careful, Nat. He'll hear you if you shout like that.

NAT—But we have a right to know—his own children. What if he dies without ever speaking?

SUE—(*uneasily*) Be sensible, Nat. There's nothing to tell except in your imagination. (*taking his arm—persuasively*) Come on downstairs. I'll get you something to eat. You must be starved, aren't you?

NAT—No—I don't know—I suppose I ought to be. (*He gets to his feet and glances around with a shudder.*) What a place for him to build to wait in—like the cabin of a ship sunk deep under the sea—like the Sarah Allen's cabin as it is now, probably. (*with a shiver*) There's a chill comes over you. No wonder he's mad. (*He listens.*) Hear him. A year ago today she sailed. I wonder if he knows that. Back and forth, always staring out to sea for the Sarah Allen. Ha-ha! God! It would be funny if it didn't make your flesh creep. (*brusquely*) Come on. Let's leave him and go down where there's light and warmth. (*They go down the stairs, closing the door behind them. There is a pause. Then the door of the companionway above is heard being opened and shut. A gust of wind sweeps down into the room. Bartlett stamps down the stairs. The madness which has taken almost complete possession of him in the past year is clearly stamped on his face, particularly in his eyes which seem to stare through and beyond objects with a hunted, haunted expression. His movements suggest an automaton obeying invisible wires. They are quick, jerky, spasmodic. He appears to be laboring under a state of extraordinary excitement. He stands for a second at the foot of the stairs, peering about him suspiciously. Then he goes to the table and sits down on the edge of a chair, his chin supported on his hands.*)

BARTLETT—(*takes a folded piece of paper from his pocket and spreads it out on the table in the light of the lantern—pointing with his finger—mumblingly*) Where the cross be—ye'll not forget that, Silas Horne. Ye had a copy o' this—no chance for a mistake, bullies—the gold's there, restin' safe—back to

me and we'll share it fair and square. A year ago today—ye
remember the orders I wrote ye, Horne. (*threateningly*) Ye'll
not be gone more nor a year or I'll—and if ye make port to
home here at night, hang a red and a green light at the
mainm'st head so I'll see ye comin'. A red and a green—
(*He springs up suddenly and goes to a porthole to look out at the
sea—disappointedly*) No lights be there—but they'll come.
The year be up today and ye've got to come or I'll— (*He
sinks back on the chair, his head in his hands. Suddenly he starts
and stares straight in front of him as if he saw something in the
air—with angry defiance*) Aye, there ye be again—the two o'
ye! Makin' a mock o' me! Brass and junk, ye say, not worth a
damn! Ye don't believe, do ye? I'll show ye! (*He springs to his
feet and makes a motion as if grabbing someone by the throat and
shaking them—savagely*) Ye lie! Is it gold or no? Answer me!
(*with a mocking laugh*) Aye, ye own up to it now, right
enough. Too late, ye swabs! No share for ye! (*He sinks back
on the chair again—after a pause, dully*) Jimmy's gone. Let
them rot. But I spoke no word, Silas Horne, remember! (*then
in a tone of fear*) Be ye dyin', Sarah? No, ye must live—live
to see your ship come home with the gold—and I'll buy ye
all in the world ye set your heart on. No, not ambergris,
Sarah—gold and diamonds and sech! We're rich at last! (*then
with great anguish*) What woman's stubborn talk be this?
Confess, ye say? But I spoke no word, I swear to ye! Why
will ye hound me and think evil o' what I done? Men's business, I tell ye. They would have killed us and stolen the gold,
can't ye see? (*wildly*) Enough o' talk, Sarah! I'll sail out in
spite o' ye! (*He gets to his feet and paces up and down the room.
The door in the rear is opened and Nat reënters. He glances at his
father, then looks down the stairs behind him cautiously to see if
he is followed. He comes in and closes the door behind him carefully.*)

NAT—(*in a low voice*) Pa! (*then as his father does not appear
to notice his presence—louder*) Pa!

BARTLETT—(*stops short and stares at his son as if he were
gradually awakening from a dream—slowly*) Be that ye, Nat?

NAT—(*coming forward*) Yes. I want to talk with you.

BARTLETT—(*struggling to bring his thoughts under control*)

Talk? Ye want to talk—to me? Men's business—no room for a boy in it—keep clear o' this.

NAT—(*defiantly*) That's what you've always said. But I won't be put off any longer. I won't, do you hear?

BARTLETT—(*angrily*) I've ordered ye not to set foot in this cabin o' mine. Git below where ye belong. Where's Sue? I told her to keep ye away.

NAT—She can't prevent me this time. I've made up my mind. Listen, Pa. I'm going away tomorrow.

BARTLETT—(*uncertainly*) Goin' away?

NAT—Yes, and I'm never coming back. I'm going to start a new life. That's why I want a final talk with you—before I go.

BARTLETT—(*dully*) I've naught to say to ye.

NAT—You will have. Listen. I've absolute proof the Sarah Allen is lost.

BARTLETT—(*fiercely*) Ye lie!

NAT—(*curiously*) Why do you say that? You know it's true. It's just that you *won't believe.*

BARTLETT—(*wanderingly—the word heading his mind into another channel*) Believe? Aye, he wouldn't believe. Brass and junk, he said, not worth a damn—but in the end I made him own up 'twas gold.

NAT—(*repeating the word fascinatedly*) Gold?

BARTLETT—A year ago today she sailed. Ye lie! Ye don't believe either, do ye?—like him. But I'll show ye! I'll make ye own up as I made him! (*with mad exultation*) She's comin' home tonight as I ordered Horne she must! I kin feel her makin' for home, I tell ye! A red an' a green at the mainm'st head if ye make port o' night, I ordered Horne. Ye'll see! (*He goes to look out of a porthole. Nat, as if under a spell, goes to another.*)

NAT—(*turning away disappointedly—making an effort to throw off his thoughts—without conviction*) Nonsense. There's nothing there—no lights—and I don't believe there ever will be.

BARTLETT—(*his wild eyes fixed on his son's with an intense effort of will as if he were trying to break down his resistance*) Ye'll see, I tell ye—a red and a green! It ain't time yet, boy, but when it be they'll be plain in the night afore your eyes. (*He goes and sits down by the table. Nat follows him and sits down in the other chair. He sees the map and stares at it fascinatedly.*)

NAT—What is this—the map of the island? (*He reaches out his hand for it.*)

BARTLETT—(*snatching it up—with a momentary return to reason—frightenedly*) Not for ye, boy. Keep clear o' this for your own good. (*then with a crazed triumph*) Aye! Ye'd believe this soon enough, wouldn't ye?

NAT—(*intensely*) I've always believed there was something—and a moment ago you mentioned gold. (*triumphant in his turn*) So you needn't try to hide the secret any longer. I know now. It's gold—gold you found on that island—gold you fitted out the Sarah Allen to sail back for—gold you buried where I saw that cross marked on the map! (*passionately*) Why have you been afraid to confide in me, your own son? Did you think I wouldn't believe—?

BARTLETT—(*with a mad chuckle*) Aye, ye believe now, right enough.

NAT—I always believed, I tell you. (*pleadingly*) And now that I know so much why can't you tell me the rest? I must know! I have a right to be heir to the secret. Why don't you confess—

BARTLETT—(*interrupting—his brain catching at the word*) Confess? Confess, did ye say, Sarah? To Nat, did ye mean? Aye, Sarah, I'll tell him all and leave it to him to say if I did wrong. (*his gleaming eyes fixed on his son's*) I'll tell ye, boy, from start to finish o' it. I been eatin' my heart to tell someone—someone who'd believe—someone that'd say I did no wrong. Listen, boy, ye know o' our four days in an open boat after the Triton went down. I told ye o' that when I come home. But what I didn't tell ye was they was six o' us in that boat, not four.

NAT—Six? There were you and Horne and Cates and Jimmy—

BARTLETT—The cook o' the Triton and the ship's boy. We'd been on the island two days—an island barren as hell, mind—without food or drink. We was roasted by the sun and nigh mad with thirst. Then, on the second day, I seed a Malay canoe—a proper war canoe such as the pirates use—

sunk down inside the reef. I sent Jimmy down to go over her thinkin' they might be some cask o' water in her the sea'd not got to. (*with impressive emphasis*) He found no water, boy, but he did find—d'ye know what, boy?

NAT—(*exultantly*) The gold, of course!

BARTLETT—(*laughing harshly*) Ha-ha! Ye do believe right enough, don't ye! Aye, the gold—in a chest. We hauled her up ashore and forced the lid open. (*gloatingly*) And there it was afore our eyes in the sun—gold bracelets and rings and ornaments o' all sorts fixed up fancy with diamonds and emeralds and rubies and sech—red and green—shinin' in the sun! (*He stops impressively.*)

NAT—(*fascinatedly*) Diamonds and— But how did they get there?

BARTLETT—Looted treasure o' some Chinese junk, likely. What matter how it come about? There it was afore our eyes. And then, mind ye, that thief o' a cook came runnin' up from where he'd been shirkin' to look at what we'd found. "No share for ye, ye swab," I yelled at him; and then he says: "It ain't gold—brass and junk," he says and run off for fear o' me. Aye, he run off to the boy and told him to jine with his sneakin' plan to steal the gold from us!

NAT—(*savagely*) But why didn't you stop him? Why didn't you—?

BARTLETT—I be comin' to that boy, and ye'll see if I did wrong. We carried the chest to the shade o' a palm and there was that thief o' a cook an' the boy waitin'. I collared 'em both and made 'em look at the gold. "Look and tell me if it's gold or no," I says. (*triumphantly*) They was afeerd to lie. Even that thief o' a cook owned up 'twas gold. Then when I turned 'em loose, because he knowed he'd git no share, he shouted again: "Brass and junk. Not worth a damn."

NAT—(*furiously*) But why did you allow— Why didn't you—

BARTLETT—(*with mad satisfaction*) Aye, ye be seein' the way o' it, boy. It was just then we sighted the schooner that picked us up after. We made a map and was buryin' the gold when we noticed them two thieves sneakin' about to see where we'd hide it. I saw 'em plain, the scum! That thief o' a cook was thinkin' he'd tell the folks on the schooner and go shares with them—and leave us on the island to rot; or he was thinkin' he and the boy'd be able to come back and dig it up afore I could. We had to do somethin' quick to spile their plan afore the schooner come. (*in a tone of savage satisfaction*) And so—though I spoke no word to him—Jimmy knifed 'em both and covered 'em up with sand. But I spoke no word, d'ye hear? Their deaths be on Jimmy's head alone.

NAT—(*passionately*) And what if you had? They deserved what they got.

BARTLETT—Then ye think I did no wrong?

NAT—No! Any man—I'd have done the same myself.

BARTLETT—(*gripping his son's hand tensely*) Ye be true son o' mine, Nat. I ought to told ye before. (*exultantly*) Ye hear, Sarah? Nat says I done no wrong.

NAT—The map! Can I see it?

BARTLETT—Aye. (*He hands it to Nat who spreads it out on the table and pores over it.*)

NAT—(*excitedly*) Why, with this I—we—can go back—even if the Sarah Allen is lost.

BARTLETT—She ain't lost, boy—not her. Don't heed them lies ye been hearin'. She's due now. I'll go up and look. (*He goes up the companionway stairs. Nat does not seem to notice his going, absorbed in the map. Then there is a loud muffled hail in Bartlett's voice.*) Sarah Allen, ahoy! (*Nat starts, transfixed— then rushes to one of the portholes to look. He turns back, passing his hand over his eyes, frowning bewilderedly. The door above is flung open and slammed shut and Bartlett stamps down the stairs.*)

BARTLETT—(*fixing Nat hypnotically with his eyes—triumphantly*) What did I tell ye? D'ye believe now she'll come back? D'ye credit your own eyes?

NAT—(*vaguely*) Eyes? I looked. I didn't see—

BARTLETT—Ye lie! The Sarah Allen, ye blind fool, come back from the Southern Seas as I swore she must! Loaded with gold as I swore she would be!—makin' port!—droppin' her anchor just when I hailed her.

NAT—(*feebly, his will crumbling*) But—how do you know?—some other schooner—

BARTLETT—Not know my own ship—and the signal I'd ordered Horne to make!

NAT—(*mechanically*) I know—a red and a green at the mainm'st head.

BARTLETT—Then look out if ye dare! (*He goes to a porthole*.) Ye kin see it plain from here. (*commandingly*) Will ye believe your eyes? Look! (*Nat comes to him slowly—looks through the porthole—and starts back, a possessed expression coming over his face*.)

NAT—(*slowly*) A red and a green—clear as day!

BARTLETT—(*His face is now transfigured by the ecstasy of a dream come true*.) They've lowered a boat—the three— Horne an' Cates and Jimmy Kanaka. They're rowin' ashore. Listen. I hear the oars in the locks. Listen!

NAT—(*staring into his father's eyes—after a pause during which he appears to be straining his hearing to the breaking point—excitedly*) I hear!

BARTLETT—Listen! They've landed. They'll be comin' up the path now. (*in a crooning, monotonous tone*) They move slowly—slowly. It be heavy, I know—that chest. (*after a pause*) Hark! They're below at the door in front.

NAT—I hear!

BARTLETT—Ye'll see it now in a moment, boy—the gold. Up with it, bullies! Up ye come! Up, bullies! It's heavy, heavy!

NAT—(*madly*) I hear them! They're on the floor below! They're coming! I'll open the door. (*He springs to the door and flings it open, shouting*) Welcome home, boys! (*Sue is discovered outside just climbing up the stairs from below. She steps inside, then stops, looking with amazement and horror from father to brother. Nat pushes her roughly aside to look behind her down the stairs*.)

SUE—Nat!

NAT—(*turning to his father*) I'll go down to the wharf. They must be there or— (*The rest of his words are lost as he hurries down the stairs. Bartlett steps back, shrinking away from his daughter, and sinks on a chair by the table with a groan, his hands over his eyes*.)

SUE—(*comes to him and shakes him by the shoulder— alarmed*) Pa! What has happened? What is the matter with Nat? What have you told him? (*with bitter despair*) Oh, can't you see you're driving him mad, too?

BARTLETT—(*letting his hands fall and staring at her hag-gardly—falteringly, as if reason were slowly filtering back into his brain*) Sue—ye said—drivin' him mad, *too!* Then ye think I be—? (*He staggers to his feet. Sue breaks down, sobbing. Bartlett falters on.*) But I seen her—the Sarah Allen—the signal lights—

SUE—Oh, Pa, there's nothing there! You know it! She was lost months ago.

BARTLETT—Lost? (*He stumbles over to a porthole and looks out. His body sags as if he were going to fall. He turns away and cries hopelessly in a tone of heart-rending grief*) Lost! Aye, they be no Sarah Allen there—no lights—nothin'!

SUE—(*pleading fiercely*) Pa, you've got to save Nat! He won't heed anyone else. Can't you tell him the truth—the whole truth whatever it is—now when I'm here and you're yourself again—and set him free from this crazy dream!

BARTLETT—(*with wild grief*) Confess, ye mean? Sue, ye be houndin' me like your Ma did to her dyin' hour! Confess—that I spoke the word to Jimmy—in my mind! Confess—brass and junk—not worth a damn! (*in frenzied protest*) No! Ye lie!

SUE—Oh, Pa, I don't know what you mean. Tell Nat the truth! Save him!

BARTLETT—The truth? It's a lie! (*as Sue tries to bar his way to the companionway—sternly*) Out o' my way, girl! (*He pulls himself feebly up the stairs. The door is heard slamming above. Sue sits down in a chair in a hopeless, exhausted attitude. After a pause Nat reënters. He is panting heavily from his exertions. His pale face is set in an expression of despair.*)

NAT—(*looking about the room wildly*) Where is he? Sue! (*He comes forward and falls on his knees besides her chair, hiding his face in her lap like a frightened child. He sobs hoarsely*) Sue! What does it all mean? I looked. There was nothing there— no schooner—nothing.

SUE—(*soothing him as if he were a little boy*) Of course there wasn't. Did you expect there would be, you foolish boy? Come, you know better than that. Why, Nat, you told the doctor and I that you were absolutely convinced the Sarah Allen was lost.

NAT—(*dully*) Yes, I know—but I don't believe—like him—

SUE—Sshhhh! You know the state Pa is in. He doesn't realize what he's saying half the time. You ought to have better sense than to pay any attention—

NAT—(*excitedly*) But he told me all he's been hiding from us—all about the gold!

SUE—(*looking at him with alarm—mystified*) Gold? (*then forcing a smile*) Don't be silly, Nat. It doesn't exist except in his poor, deranged mind.

NAT—(*fiercely*) That's a lie, Sue! I saw the map, I tell you—the map of the island with a cross marked on it where they buried the gold.

SUE—He showed a map to you—a real map? (*gently*) Are you sure you're not just imagining that, too?

NAT—I had it in my hands, you fool, you! There—on the table. (*He springs to his feet, sees the map on the table, and snatches it up with an exclamation of joy—showing it to Sue*) See! Now will you believe me! (*She examines the map perplexedly. Nat paces up and down—excitedly*) I tell you it's all true. You can't deny it now. It's lucky for us I forced him to confess. He might have died keeping the secret and then we'd have lost—I'll tell you what I'm going to do now, Sue. I'm going to raise the money somewhere, somehow, and fit out another schooner and this time I'll sail on her myself. No trusting to Danny or anyone else! Yes, Sue, we'll come into our own yet, even if the Sarah Allen is lost— (*He stops— then in accents of bewildered fear*) But—she can't be lost—I saw the lights, Sue—as plain as I see you now— (*He goes to one of the portholes again.*)

SUE—(*who has been watching him worriedly, puts the map back on the table, gets up and, assuming a brisk, matter-of-fact tone, she goes over and takes him by the arm*) Come downstairs, Nat. Don't think any more about it tonight. It's late and you're worn out. You need rest and a good sleep.

NAT—(*following her toward the door—confusedly*) But Sue— I saw them— (*From above in the night comes the muffled hail in Bartlett's voice, "Sarah Allen, ahoy!" Nat stops, tortured, his hands instinctively raised up to cover his ears. Sue gives a startled cry. The door above is slammed and Bartlett comes down the stairs, his face revealing that the delusion has again full possession of his mind.*)

BARTLETT—(*pointing his finger at his son and fixing him with his eyes—in ringing, triumphant tones*) The Sarah Allen, boy—in the harbor below! Come back from the Southern Seas as I swore she must! Loaded with gold as I swore she would be! (*Nat again seems to crumble—to give way to the stronger will. He takes a step toward his father, his eyes lighting up. Sue looks at his face—then rushes to her father.*)

SUE—(*putting her hands to her father's head and forcing him to look down into her face—intensely*) Pa! Stop, do you hear me! It's all mad! You're driving Nat mad, too! (*As she sees her father hesitate, the wild light dying out of his eyes, she summons all her power to a fierce pleading.*) For my sake, Pa! For Ma's sake! Think of how she would feel if she were alive and saw you acting this way with Nat! Tell him! Tell him now—before me—tell him it's all a lie!

BARTLETT—(*trying in an agony of conflict to get hold of his reason—incoherently*) Yes, Sue—I hear ye—confess—aye, Sarah, your dyin' words—keep Nat clear o' this—but—red and green—I seen 'em plain— (*then suddenly after a tremendous struggle, lifting his tortured face to Nat's—in tones of despair*) Nothin' there, boy! Don't ye believe! No red and green! She'll never come! Derelict and lost, boy, the Sarah Allen. (*after another struggle with himself*) And I lied to ye, boy. I gave the word—in my mind—to kill them two. I murdered 'em in cold blood.

SUE—(*shrinking from him in horror*) Pa! You don't know what you're saying.

BARTLETT—The truth, girl. Ye said—confess—

NAT—(*bewilderedly*) But—it was right. They were trying to steal—

BARTLETT—(*overcome by the old obsession for a moment—savagely*) Aye, that's it! The thievin' scum! They was tryin'— (*He stops short, throwing his head back, his whole body tense and quivering with the effort he makes to force this sustaining lie out of his brain—then, broken but self-conquering, he looks again at Nat—gently*) No, Nat. That be the lie I been tellin' myself ever since. That cook—he said 'twas brass— But I'd been lookin' for ambergris—gold—the whole o' my life—and when we found that chest—I *had* to believe, I tell ye! I'd been dreamin' o' it all my days! But he said brass and junk, and told the boy—and I give the word to murder 'em both and cover 'em up with sand.

NAT—(*very pale—despairingly*) But he lied, didn't he? It is gold—real gold—isn't it?

BARTLETT—(*slowly takes the studded anklet from his pocket and holds it out to Nat. The latter brings it to the light of the lantern. Bartlett sits on a chair, covering his face with his hands—in a tone of terrible suffering.*) Ye'll tell me, boy—if it's gold or no. I've had it by me all this time—but I've been afeerd to show—

NAT—(*in a tone of wild scorn*) Why, it's brass, of course! The cheapest kind of junk—not worth a damn! (*He flings it savagely into a corner of the room. Bartlett groans and seems to shrink up and turn into a figure of pitiable feebleness.*)

SUE—(*pityingly*) Don't, Nat. (*She puts her arms around her father's shoulders protectingly.*)

NAT—(*in a stifled voice*) What a damned fool I've been! (*He flings himself down on the cot, his shoulders heaving.*)

BARTLETT—(*uncovers his gray face on which there is now settling an expression of strange peace—stroking his daughter's hand*) Sue—don't think hard o' me. (*He takes the map.*) An end to this! (*He slowly tears it into small pieces, seeming to grow weaker and weaker as he does so. Finally as he lets the fragments filter through his fingers, his whole frame suddenly relaxes. He sighs, his eyes shut, and sags back in his chair, his head bent forward limply on his chest.*)

SUE—(*alarmed*) Pa! (*She sinks to her knees beside him and looks up into his face.*) Pa! Speak to me! It's Sue! (*then turning toward her brother—terrifiedly*) Nat! Run—get the doctor—(*Nat starts to a sitting position. Sue tries with trembling hands to feel of her father's pulse, his heart—then begins to sob hysterically.*) Oh, Nat—he's dead, I think—he's dead!

(*The Curtain Falls*)

"ANNA CHRISTIE"

A Play in Four Acts

CHARACTERS

"Johnny-the-Priest"

Two Longshoremen

A Postman

Larry, *bartender*

Chris. Christopherson, *captain of the barge Simeon Winthrop*

Marthy Owen

Anna Christopherson, *Chris's daughter*

Three men of a steamer's crew

Mat Burke, *a stoker*

Johnson, *deckhand on the barge*

SCENES

Act I
"Johnny-the-Priest's" saloon near the waterfront, New York City.

Act II
The barge, *Simeon Winthrop*, at anchor in the harbor of Provincetown, Mass. Ten days later.

Act III
Cabin of the barge, at dock in Boston. A week later.

Act IV
The same. Two days later.

Time of the Play—About 1910.

"Anna Christie"

ACT I

SCENE—"*Johnny-the-Priest's*" *saloon near South Street, New York City. The stage is divided into two sections, showing a small back room on the right. On the left, forward, of the barroom, a large window looking out on the street. Beyond it, the main entrance—a double swinging door. Farther back, another window. The bar runs from left to right nearly the whole length of the rear wall. In back of the bar, a small showcase displaying a few bottles of case goods, for which there is evidently little call. The remainder of the rear space in front of the large mirrors is occupied by half-barrels of cheap whiskey of the "nickel-a-shot" variety, from which the liquor is drawn by means of spigots. On the right is an open doorway leading to the back room. In the back room are four round wooden tables with five chairs grouped about each. In the rear, a family entrance opening on a side street.*

It is late afternoon of a day in fall.

As the curtain rises, Johnny is discovered. "Johnny-the-Priest" deserves his nickname. With his pale, thin, clean-shaven face, mild blue eyes and white hair, a cassock would seem more suited to him than the apron he wears. Neither his voice nor his general manner dispel this illusion which has made him a personage of the water front. They are soft and bland. But beneath all his mildness one senses the man behind the mask—cynical, callous, hard as nails. He is lounging at ease behind the bar, a pair of spectacles on his nose, reading an evening paper.

Two longshoremen enter from the street, wearing their working aprons, the button of the union pinned conspicuously on the caps pulled sideways on their heads at an aggressive angle.

FIRST LONGSHOREMAN—(*as they range themselves at the bar*) Gimme a shock. Number Two. (*He tosses a coin on the bar.*)

SECOND LONGSHOREMAN—Same here. (*Johnny sets two glasses of barrel whiskey before them.*)

FIRST LONGSHOREMAN—Here's luck! (*The other nods. They gulp down their whiskey.*)

SECOND LONGSHOREMAN—(*putting money on the bar*) Give us another.

FIRST LONGSHOREMAN—Gimme a scoop this time—lager and porter. I'm dry.

SECOND LONGSHOREMAN—Same here. (*Johnny draws the lager and porter and sets the big, foaming schooners before them. They drink down half the contents and start to talk together hurriedly in low tones. The door on the left is swung open and Larry enters. He is a boyish, red-cheeked, rather good-looking young fellow of twenty or so.*)

LARRY—(*nodding to Johnny—cheerily*) Hello, boss.

JOHNNY—Hello, Larry. (*with a glance at his watch*) Just on time. (*Larry goes to the right behind the bar, takes off his coat, and puts on an apron.*)

FIRST LONGSHOREMAN—(*abruptly*) Let's drink up and get back to it. (*They finish their drinks and go out left. The postman enters as they leave. He exchanges nods with Johnny and throws a letter on the bar.*)

THE POSTMAN—Addressed care of you, Johnny. Know him?

JOHNNY—(*picks up the letter, adjusting his spectacles. Larry comes and peers over his shoulders. Johnny reads very slowly*) Christopher Christopherson.

THE POSTMAN—(*helpfully*) Square-head name.

LARRY—Old Chris—that's who.

JOHNNY—Oh, sure. I was forgetting Chris carried a hell of a name like that. Letters come here for him sometimes before, I remember now. Long time ago, though.

THE POSTMAN—It'll get him all right then?

JOHNNY—Sure thing. He comes here whenever he's in port.

THE POSTMAN—(*turning to go*) Sailor, eh?

JOHNNY—(*with a grin*) Captain of a coal barge.

THE POSTMAN—(*laughing*) Some job! Well, s'long.

JOHNNY—S'long. I'll see he gets it. (*The postman goes out. Johnny scrutinizes the letter.*) You got good eyes, Larry. Where's it from?

LARRY—(*after a glance*) St. Paul. That'll be in Minnesota, I'm thinkin'. Looks like a woman's writing, too, the old divil!

JOHNNY—He's got a daughter somewheres out West, I

think he told me once. (*He puts the letter on the cash register.*) Come to think of it, I ain't seen old Chris in a dog's age. (*Putting his overcoat on, he comes around the end of the bar.*) Guess I'll be gettin' home. See you to-morrow.

LARRY—Good-night to ye, boss. (*As Johnny goes toward the street door, it is pushed open and Christopher Christopherson enters. He is a short, squat, broad-shouldered man of about fifty, with a round, weather-beaten, red face from which his light blue eyes peer short-sightedly, twinkling with a simple good humor. His large mouth, overhung by a thick, drooping, yellow mustache, is childishly self-willed and weak, of an obstinate kindliness. A thick neck is jammed like a post into the heavy trunk of his body. His arms with their big, hairy, freckled hands, and his stumpy legs terminating in large flat feet, are awkwardly short and muscular. He walks with a clumsy, rolling gait. His voice, when not raised in a hollow boom, is toned down to a sly, confidential half-whisper with something vaguely plaintive in its quality. He is dressed in a wrinkled, ill-fitting dark suit of shore clothes, and wears a faded cap of gray cloth over his mop of grizzled, blond hair. Just now his face beams with a too-blissful happiness, and he has evidently been drinking. He reaches his hand out to Johnny.*)

CHRIS—Hello, Yohnny! Have drink on me. Come on, Larry. Give us drink. Have one yourself. (*putting his hand in his pocket*) Ay gat money—plenty money.

JOHNNY—(*shakes Chris by the hand*) Speak of the devil. We was just talkin' about you.

LARRY—(*coming to the end of the bar*) Hello, Chris. Put it there. (*They shake hands.*)

CHRIS—(*beaming*) Give us drink.

JOHNNY—(*with a grin*) You got a half-snootful now. Where'd you get it?

CHRIS—(*grinning*) Oder fallar on oder barge—Irish fallar—he gat bottle vhiskey and we drank it, yust us two. Dot vhiskey gat kick, by yingo! Ay yust come ashore. Give us drink, Larry. Ay vas little drunk, not much. Yust feel good. (*He laughs and commences to sing in a nasal, high-pitched quaver.*)

"My Yosephine, come board de ship. Long time Ay vait for you.

De moon, she shi-i-i-ine. She looka yust like you.

Tchee-tchee, tchee-tchee, tchee-tchee, tchee-tchee."

(*To the accompaniment of this last he waves his hand as if he were conducting an orchestra.*)

JOHNNY—(*with a laugh*) Same old Yosie, eh, Chris?

CHRIS—You don't know good song when you hear him. Italian fallar on oder barge, he learn me dat. Give us drink. (*He throws change on the bar.*)

LARRY—(*with a professional air*) What's your pleasure, gentlemen?

JOHNNY—Small beer, Larry.

CHRIS—Vhiskey—Number Two.

LARRY—(*as he gets their drinks*) I'll take a cigar on you.

CHRIS—(*lifting his glass*) Skoal! (*He drinks.*)

JOHNNY—Drink hearty.

CHRIS—(*immediately*) Have oder drink.

JOHNNY—No. Some other time. Got to go home now. So you've just landed? Where are you in from this time?

CHRIS—Norfolk. Ve make slow voyage—dirty vedder— yust fog, fog, fog, all bloody time! (*There is an insistent ring from the doorbell at the family entrance in the back room. Chris gives a start—hurriedly*) Ay go open, Larry. Ay forgat. It vas Marthy. She come with me. (*He goes into the back room.*)

LARRY—(*with a chuckle*) He's still got that same cow livin' with him, the old fool!

JOHNNY—(*with a grin*) A sport, Chris is. Well, I'll beat it home. S'long. (*He goes to the street door.*)

LARRY—So long, boss.

JOHNNY—Oh—don't forget to give him his letter.

LARRY—I won't. (*Johnny goes out. In the meantime, Chris has opened the family entrance door, admitting Marthy. She might be forty or fifty. Her jowly, mottled face, with its thick red nose, is streaked with interlacing purple veins. Her thick, gray hair is piled anyhow in a greasy mop on top of her round head. Her figure is flabby and fat; her breath comes in wheezy gasps; she speaks in a loud, mannish voice, punctuated by explosions of hoarse laughter. But there still twinkles in her blood-shot blue eyes a youthful lust for life which hard usage has failed to stifle, a sense of humor mocking, but good-tempered. She wears a man's cap, double-breasted man's jacket, and a grimy, calico skirt. Her bare*

*feet are encased in a man's brogans several sizes too large for her,
which gives her a shuffling, wobbly gait.*)

MARTHY—(*grumblingly*) What yuh tryin' to do, Dutchy—
keep me standin' out there all day? (*She comes forward and sits
at the table in the right corner, front.*)

CHRIS—(*mollifyingly*) Ay'm sorry, Marthy. Ay talk to
Yohnny. Ay forgat. What you goin' take for drink?

MARTHY—(*appeased*) Gimme a scoop of lager an' ale.

CHRIS—Ay go bring him back. (*He returns to the bar.*)
Lager and ale for Marthy, Larry. Vhiskey for me. (*He throws
change on the bar.*)

LARRY—Right you are. (*Then remembering, he takes the
letter from in back of the bar.*) Here's a letter for you—from
St. Paul, Minnesota—and a lady's writin'. (*He grins.*)

CHRIS—(*quickly—taking it*) Oh, den it come from my
daughter, Anna. She live dere. (*He turns the letter over in his
hands uncertainly.*) Ay don't gat letter from Anna—must be a
year.

LARRY—(*jokingly*) That's a fine fairy tale to be tellin'—
your daughter! Sure I'll bet it's some bum.

CHRIS—(*soberly*) No. Dis come from Anna. (*engrossed by
the letter in his hand—uncertainly*) By golly, Ay tank Ay'm
too drunk for read dis letter from Anna. Ay tank Ay sat down
for a minute. You bring drinks in back room, Larry. (*He goes
into the room on right.*)

MARTHY—(*angrily*) Where's my larger an' ale, yuh big
stiff?

CHRIS—(*preoccupied*) Larry bring him. (*He sits down opposite her. Larry brings in the drinks and sets them on the table.
He and Marthy exchange nods of recognition. Larry stands
looking at Chris curiously. Marthy takes a long draught of her
schooner and heaves a huge sigh of satisfaction, wiping her mouth
with the back of her hand. Chris stares at the letter for a
moment—slowly opens it, and, squinting his eyes, commences to
read laboriously, his lips moving as he spells out the words. As he
reads his face lights up with an expression of mingled joy and bewilderment.*)

LARRY—Good news?

MARTHY—(*her curiosity also aroused*) What's that yuh
got—a letter, fur Gawd's sake?

CHRIS—(*pauses for a moment, after finishing the letter, as if to let the news sink in—then suddenly pounds his fist on the table with happy excitement*) Py yiminy! Yust tank, Anna say she's comin' here right avay! She gat sick on yob in St. Paul, she say. It's short letter, don't tal me much more'n dat. (*beaming*) Py golly, dat's good news all at one time for ole fallar! (*then turning to Marthy, rather shamefacedly*) You know, Marthy, Ay've tole you Ay don't see my Anna since she vas little gel in Sveden five year ole.

MARTHY—How old'll she be now?

CHRIS—She must be—lat me see—she must be twenty year ole, py Yo!

LARRY—(*surprised*) You've not seen her in fifteen years?

CHRIS—(*suddenly growing somber—in a low tone*) No. Ven she vas little gel, Ay vas bo'sun on vindjammer. Ay never gat home only few time dem year. Ay'm fool sailor fallar. My voman—Anna's mother—she gat tired vait all time Sveden for me ven Ay don't never come. She come dis country, bring Anna, dey go out Minnesota, live with her cousins on farm. Den ven her mo'der die ven Ay vas on voyage, Ay tank it's better dem cousins keep Anna. Ay tank it's better Anna live on farm, den she don't know dat ole davil, sea, she don't know fader like me.

LARRY—(*with a wink at Marthy*) This girl, now, 'll be marryin' a sailor herself, likely. It's in the blood.

CHRIS—(*suddenly springing to his feet and smashing his fist on the table in a rage*) No, py God! She don't do dat!

MARTHY—(*grasping her schooner hastily—angrily*) Hey, look out, yuh nut! Wanta spill my suds for me?

LARRY—(*amazed*) Oho, what's up with you? Ain't you a sailor yourself now, and always been?

CHRIS—(*slowly*) Dat's yust vhy Ay say it. (*forcing a smile*) Sailor vas all right fallar, but not for marry gel. No. Ay know dat. Anna's mo'der, she know it, too.

LARRY—(*as Chris remains sunk in gloomy reflection*) When is your daughter comin'? Soon?

CHRIS—(*roused*) Py yiminy, Ay forgat. (*reads through the letter hurriedly*) She say she come right avay, dat's all.

LARRY—She'll maybe be comin' here to look for you, I s'pose. (*He returns to the bar, whistling. Left alone with Marthy,*

*who stares at him with a twinkle of malicious humor in her eyes,
Chris suddenly becomes desperately ill-at-ease. He fidgets, then gets
up hurriedly.)*

CHRIS—Ay gat speak with Larry. Ay be right back. (*mollifyingly*) Ay bring you oder drink.

MARTHY—(*emptying her glass*) Sure. That's me. (*As he retreats with the glass she guffaws after him derisively.*)

CHRIS—(*to Larry in an alarmed whisper*) Py yingo, Ay gat gat Marthy shore off barge before Anna come! Anna raise hell if she find dat out. Marthy raise hell, too, for go, py golly!

LARRY—(*with a chuckle*) Serve ye right, ye old divil—havin' a woman at your age!

CHRIS—(*scratching his head in a quandary*) You tal me lie for tal Marthy, Larry, so's she gat off barge quick.

LARRY—She knows your daughter's comin'. Tell her to get the hell out of it.

CHRIS—No. Ay don't like make her feel bad.

LARRY—You're an old mush! Keep your girl away from the barge, then. She'll likely want to stay ashore anyway. (*curiously*) What does she work at, your Anna?

CHRIS—She stay on dem cousins' farm 'till two year ago. Dan she gat yob nurse gel in St. Paul. (*then shaking his head resolutely*) But Ay don't vant for her gat yob now. Ay vant for her stay with me.

LARRY—(*scornfully*) On a coal barge! She'll not like that, I'm thinkin'.

MARTHY—(*shouts from next room*) Don't I get that bucket o' suds, Dutchy?

CHRIS—(*startled—in apprehensive confusion*) Yes, Ay come, Marthy.

LARRY—(*drawing the lager and ale, hands it to Chris—laughing*) Now you're in for it! You'd better tell her straight to get out!

CHRIS—(*shaking in his boots*) Py golly. (*He takes her drink in to Marthy and sits down at the table. She sips it in silence. Larry moves quietly close to the partition to listen, grinning with expectation. Chris seems on the verge of speaking, hesitates, gulps down his whiskey desperately as if seeking for courage. He attempts to whistle a few bars of "Yosephine" with careless bravado, but the whistle peters out futilely. Marthy stares at him keenly, taking in his embarrassment with a malicious twinkle of amusement in her eye. Chris clears his throat.*) Marthy—

MARTHY—(*aggressively*) Wha's that? (*then, pretending to fly into a rage, her eyes enjoying Chris' misery*) I'm wise to what's in back of your nut, Dutchy. Yuh want to git rid o' me, huh?—now she's comin'. Gimme the bum's rush ashore, huh? Lemme tell yuh, Dutchy, there ain't a square-head workin' on a boat man enough to git away with that. Don't start nothin' yuh can't finish!

CHRIS—(*miserably*) Ay don't start nutting, Marthy.

MARTHY—(*glares at him for a second—then cannot control a burst of laughter*) Ho-ho! Yuh're a scream, Square-head—an honest-ter-Gawd knockout! Ho-ho! (*She wheezes, panting for breath.*)

CHRIS—(*with childish pique*) Ay don't see nutting for laugh at.

MARTHY—Take a slant in the mirror and yuh'll see. Ho-ho! (*recovering from her mirth—chuckling, scornfully*) A square-head tryin' to kid Marthy Owen at this late day!—after me campin' with barge men the last twenty years. I'm wise to the game, up, down, and sideways. I ain't been born and dragged up on the water front for nothin'. Think I'd make trouble, huh? Not me! I'll pack up me duds an' beat it. I'm quittin' yuh, get me? I'm tellin' yuh I'm sick of stickin' with yuh, and I'm leavin' yuh flat, see? There's plenty of other guys on other barges waitin' for me. Always was, I always found. (*She claps the astonished Chris on the back.*) So cheer up, Dutchy! I'll be offen the barge before she comes. You'll be rid o' me for good—and me o' you—good riddance for both of us. Ho-ho!

CHRIS—(*seriously*) Ay don' tank dat. You vas good gel, Marthy.

MARTHY—(*grinning*) Good girl? Aw, can the bull! Well, yuh treated me square, yuhself. So it's fifty-fifty. Nobody's sore at nobody. We're still good frien's, huh? (*Larry returns to bar.*)

CHRIS—(*beaming now that he sees his troubles disappearing*) Yes, py golly.

MARTHY—That's the talkin'! In all my time I tried never to split with a guy with no hard feelin's. But what was yuh so scared about—that I'd kick up a row? That ain't Marthy's way. (*scornfully*) Think I'd break my heart to loose yuh? Commit suicide, huh? Ho-ho! Gawd! The world's full o' men if that's all I'd worry about! (*then with a grin, after emptying her glass*) Blow me to another scoop, huh? I'll drink your kid's health for yuh.

CHRIS—(*eagerly*) Sure tang. Ay go gat him. (*He takes the two glasses into the bar.*) Oder drink. Same for both.

LARRY—(*getting the drinks and putting them on the bar*) She's not such a bad lot, that one.

CHRIS—(*jovially*) She's good gel, Ay tal you! Py golly, Ay calabrate now! Give me vhiskey here at bar, too. (*He puts down money. Larry serves him.*) You have drink, Larry.

LARRY—(*virtuously*) You know I never touch it.

CHRIS—You don't know what you miss. Skoal! (*He drinks—then begins to sing loudly*)

"My Yosephine, come board de ship—"
(*He picks up the drinks for Marthy and himself and walks unsteadily into the back room, singing.*)

"De moon, she shi-i-i-ine. She looks yust like you.

Tche-tchee, tchee-tchee, tchee-tchee, tchee-tchee."

MARTHY—(*grinning, hands to ears*) Gawd!

CHRIS—(*sitting down*) Ay'm good singer, yes? Ve drink, eh? Skoal! Ay calabrate! (*He drinks.*) Ay calabrate 'cause Anna's coming home. You know, Marthy, Ay never write for her to come, 'cause Ay tank Ay'm no good for her. But all time Ay hope like hell some day she vant for see me and den she come. And dat's vay it happen now, py yiminy! (*his face beaming*) What you tank she look like, Marthy? Ay bet you she's fine, good, strong gel, pooty like hell! Living on farm made her like dat. And Ay bet you some day she marry good, steady land fallar here in East, have home all her own, have kits—and dan Ay'm ole grandfader, py golly! And Ay go visit dem every time Ay gat in port near! (*bursting with joy*) By yiminy crickens, Ay calabrate dat! (*shouts*) Bring oder drink, Larry! (*He smashes his fist on the table with a bang.*)

LARRY—(*coming in from bar—irritably*) Easy there! Don't be breakin' the table, you old goat!

CHRIS—(*by way of reply, grins foolishly and begins to sing*) "My Yosephine comes board de ship—"

MARTHY—(*touching Chris' arm persuasively*) You're soused to the ears, Dutchy. Go out and put a feed into you. It'll sober you up. (*then as Chris shakes his head obstinately*) Listen, yuh old nut! Yuh don't know what time your kid's liable to show up. Yuh want to be sober when she comes, don't yuh?

CHRIS—(*aroused—gets unsteadily to his feet*) Py golly, yes.

LARRY—That's good sense for you. A good beef stew'll fix you. Go round the corner.

CHRIS—All right. Ay be back soon, Marthy. (*Chris goes through the bar and out the street door.*)

LARRY—He'll come round all right with some grub in him.

MARTHY—Sure. (*Larry goes back to the bar and resumes his newspaper. Marthy sips what is left of her schooner reflectively. There is the ring of the family entrance bell. Larry comes to the door and opens it a trifle—then, with a puzzled expression, pulls it wide. Anna Christopherson enters. She is a tall, blond, fully-developed girl of twenty, handsome after a large, Viking-daughter fashion but now run down in health and plainly showing all the outward evidences of belonging to the world's oldest profession. Her youthful face is already hard and cynical beneath its layer of make-up. Her clothes are the tawdry finery of peasant stock turned prostitute. She comes and sinks wearily in a chair by the table, left front.*)

ANNA—Gimme a whiskey—ginger ale on the side. (*then, as Larry turns to go, forcing a winning smile at him*) And don't be stingy, baby.

LARRY—(*sarcastically*) Shall I serve it in a pail?

ANNA—(*with a hard laugh*) That suits me down to the ground. (*Larry goes into the bar. The two women size each other up with frank stares. Larry comes back with the drink which he sets before Anna and returns to the bar again. Anna downs her drink at a gulp. Then, after a moment, as the alcohol begins to rouse her, she turns to Marthy with a friendly smile.*) Gee, I needed that bad, all right, all right!

MARTHY—(*nodding her head sympathetically*) Sure—yuh look all in. Been on a bat?

ANNA—No—travelling—day and a half on the train. Had

to sit up all night in the dirty coach, too. Gawd, I thought I'd never get here!

MARTHY—(*with a start—looking at her intently*) Where'd yuh come from, huh?

ANNA—St. Paul—out in Minnesota.

MARTHY—(*staring at her in amazement—slowly*) So— yuh're— (*She suddenly bursts out into hoarse, ironical laughter.*) Gawd!

ANNA—All the way from Minnesota, sure. (*flaring up*) What you laughing at? Me?

MARTHY—(*hastily*) No, honest, kid. I was thinkin' of somethin' else.

ANNA—(*mollified—with a smile*) Well, I wouldn't blame you, at that. Guess I do look rotten—yust out of the hospital two weeks. I'm going to have another 'ski. What d'you say? Have something on me?

MARTHY—Sure I will. T'anks. (*She calls.*) Hey, Larry! Little service! (*He comes in.*)

ANNA—Same for me.

MARTHY—Same here. (*Larry takes their glasses and goes out.*)

ANNA—Why don't you come sit over here, be sociable. I'm a dead stranger in this burg—and I ain't spoke a word with no one since day before yesterday.

MARTHY—Sure thing. (*She shuffles over to Anna's table and sits down opposite her. Larry brings the drinks and Anna pays him.*)

ANNA—Skoal! Here's how! (*She drinks.*)

MARTHY—Here's luck! (*She takes a gulp from her schooner.*)

ANNA—(*taking a package of Sweet Caporal cigarettes from her bag*) Let you smoke in here, won't they?

MARTHY—(*doubtfully*) Sure. (*then with evident anxiety*) On'y trow it away if yuh hear someone comin'.

ANNA—(*lighting one and taking a deep inhale*) Gee, they're fussy in this dump, ain't they? (*She puffs, staring at the table top. Marthy looks her over with a new penetrating interest, taking in every detail of her face. Anna suddenly becomes conscious of this appraising stare—resentfully*) Ain't nothing wrong with me, is there? You're looking hard enough.

MARTHY—(*irritated by the other's tone—scornfully*) Ain't

got to look much. I got your number the minute you stepped in the door.

ANNA—(*her eyes narrowing*) Ain't you smart! Well, I got yours, too, without no trouble. You're me forty years from now. That's you! (*She gives a hard little laugh.*)

MARTHY—(*angrily*) Is that so? Well, I'll tell you straight, kiddo, that Marthy Owen never— (*She catches herself up short—with a grin*) What are you and me scrappin' over? Let's cut it out, huh? Me, I don't want no hard feelin's with no one. (*extending her hand*) Shake and forget it, huh?

ANNA—(*shakes her hand gladly*) Only too glad to. I ain't looking for trouble. Let's have 'nother. What d'you say?

MARTHY—(*shaking her head*) Not for mine. I'm full up. And you— Had anythin' to eat lately?

ANNA—Not since this morning on the train.

MARTHY—Then yuh better go easy on it, hadn't yuh?

ANNA—(*after a moment's hesitation*) Guess you're right. I got to meet someone, too. But my nerves is on edge after that rotten trip.

MARTHY—Yuh said yuh was just outa the hospital?

ANNA—Two weeks ago. (*leaning over to Marthy confidentially*) The joint I was in out in St. Paul got raided. That was the start. The judge give all us girls thirty days. The others didn't seem to mind being in the cooler much. Some of 'em was used to it. But me, I couldn't stand it. It got my goat right—couldn't eat or sleep or nothing. I never could stand being caged up nowheres. I got good and sick and they had to send me to the hospital. It was nice there. I was sorry to leave it, honest!

MARTHY—(*after a slight pause*) Did yuh say yuh got to meet someone here?

ANNA—Yes. Oh, not what you mean. It's my Old Man I got to meet. Honest! It's funny, too. I ain't seen him since I was a kid—don't even know what he looks like—yust had a letter every now and then. This was always the only address he give me to write him back. He's yanitor of some building here now—used to be a sailor.

MARTHY—(*astonished*) Janitor!

ANNA—Sure. And I was thinking maybe, seeing he ain't never done a thing for me in my life, he might be willing to stake me to a room and eats till I get rested up. (*wearily*) Gee, I sure need that rest! I'm knocked out. (*then resignedly*) But I ain't expecting much from him. Give you a kick when you're down, that's what all men do. (*with sudden passion*) Men, I hate 'em—all of 'em! And I don't expect he'll turn out no better than the rest. (*then with sudden interest*) Say, do you hang out around this dump much?

MARTHY—Oh, off and on.

ANNA—Then maybe you know him—my Old Man—or at least seen him?

MARTHY—It ain't old Chris, is it?

ANNA—Old Chris?

MARTHY—Chris Christopherson, his full name is.

ANNA—(*excitedly*) Yes, that's him! Anna Christopherson—that's my real name—only out there I called myself Anna Christie. So you know him, eh?

MARTHY—(*evasively*) Seen him about for years.

ANNA—Say, what's he like, tell me, honest?

MARTHY—Oh, he's short and—

ANNA—(*impatiently*) I don't care what he looks like. What kind is he?

MARTHY—(*earnestly*) Well, yuh can bet your life, kid, he's as good an old guy as ever walked on two feet. That goes!

ANNA—(*pleased*) I'm glad to hear it. Then you think's he'll stake me to that rest cure I'm after?

MARTHY—(*emphatically*) Surest thing you know. (*disgustedly*) But where'd yuh get the idea he was a janitor?

ANNA—He wrote me he was himself.

MARTHY—Well, he was lyin'. He ain't. He's captain of a barge—five men under him.

ANNA—(*disgusted in her turn*) A barge? What kind of a barge?

MARTHY—Coal, mostly.

ANNA—A coal barge! (*with a harsh laugh*) If that ain't a swell job to find your long lost Old Man working at! Gee, I knew something'd be bound to turn out wrong—always does with me. That puts my idea of his giving me a rest on the bum.

MARTHY—What d'yuh mean?

ANNA—I s'pose he lives on the boat, don't he?

MARTHY—Sure. What about it? Can't you live on it, too?

ANNA—(*scornfully*) Me? On a dirty coal barge! What d'you think I am?

MARTHY—(*resentfully*) What d'yuh know about barges, huh? Bet yuh ain't never seen one. That's what comes of his bringing yuh up inland—away from the old devil sea— where yuh'd be safe— Gawd! (*The irony of it strikes her sense of humor and she laughs hoarsely.*)

ANNA—(*angrily*) His bringing me up! Is that what he tells people! I like his nerve! He let them cousins of my Old Woman's keep me on their farm and work me to death like a dog.

MARTHY—Well, he's got queer notions on some things. I've heard him say a farm was the best place for a kid.

ANNA—Sure. That's what he'd always answer back—and a lot of crazy stuff about staying away from the sea—stuff I couldn't make head or tail to. I thought he must be nutty.

MARTHY—He is on that one point. (*casually*) So yuh didn't fall for life on the farm, huh?

ANNA—I should say not! The old man of the family, his wife, and four sons—I had to slave for all of 'em. I was only a poor relation, and they treated me worse than they dare treat a hired girl. (*after a moment's hesitation —somberly*) It was one of the sons—the youngest—started me—when I was sixteen. After that, I hated 'em so I'd killed 'em all if I'd stayed. So I run away—to St. Paul.

MARTHY— (*who has been listening sympathetically*) I've heard Old Chris talkin' about your bein' a nurse girl out there. Was that all a bluff yuh put up when yuh wrote him?

ANNA—Not on your life, it wasn't. It was true for two years. I didn't go wrong all at one jump. Being a nurse girl was yust what finished me. Taking care of other people's kids, always listening to their bawling and crying, caged in, when you're only a kid yourself and want to go out and see things. At last I got the chance—to get into that house. And you bet your life I took it! (*defiantly*) And I ain't sorry neither. (*after a pause —with bitter hatred*) It was all men's fault—the whole business. It was men on the farm ordering and beating me— and giving me the wrong start. Then when I was a nurse, it was men again hanging around, bothering me, trying to see what they could get. (*She gives a hard laugh.*) And now it's men all the time. Gawd, I hate 'em all, every mother's son of 'em! Don't you?

MARTHY—Oh, I dunno. There's good ones and bad ones, kid. You've just had a run of bad luck with 'em, that's all. Your Old Man, now—old Chris—he's a good one.

ANNA—(*sceptically*) He'll have to show me.

MARTHY—Yuh kept right on writing him yuh was a nurse girl still, even after yuh was in the house, didn't yuh?

ANNA—Sure. (*cynically*) Not that I think he'd care a darn.

MARTHY—Yuh're all wrong about him, kid. (*earnestly*) I know Old Chris well for a long time. He's talked to me 'bout you lots o' times. He thinks the world o' you, honest he does.

ANNA—Aw, quit the kiddin'!

MARTHY—Honest! Only, he's a simple old guy, see? He's got nutty notions. But he means well, honest. Listen to me, kid— (*She is interrupted by the opening and shutting of the street door in the bar and by hearing Chris's voice.*) Ssshh!

ANNA—What's up?

CHRIS—(*who has entered the bar. He seems considerably sobered up.*) Py golly, Larry, dat grub taste good. Marthy in back?

LARRY—Sure—and another tramp with her. (*Chris starts for the entrance to the back room.*)

MARTHY—(*to Anna in a hurried, nervous whisper*) That's him now. He's comin' in here. Brace up!

ANNA—Who? (*Chris opens the door.*)

MARTHY—(*as if she were greeting him for the first time*) Why hello, Old Chris. (*Then before he can speak, she shuffles hurriedly past him into the bar, beckoning him to follow her.*) Come here. I wanta tell yuh somethin'. (*He goes out to her. She speaks hurriedly in a low voice.*) Listen! I'm goin' to beat it down to the barge—pack up me duds and blow. That's her in there— your Anna—just come—waitin' for yuh. Treat her right, see? She's been sick. Well, s'long! (*She goes into the back room—to Anna*) S'long, kid. I gotta beat it now. See yuh later.

ANNA—(*nervously*) So long. (*Martha goes quickly out of the family entrance.*)

LARRY—(*looking at the stupefied Chris curiously*) Well, what's up now?

CHRIS—(*vaguely*) Nutting—nutting. (*He stands before the*

door to the back room in an agony of embarrassed emotion —then he forces himself to a bold decision, pushes open the door and walks in. He stands there, casts a shy glance at Anna, whose brilliant clothes, and, to him, high-toned appearance, awe him terribly. He looks about him with pitiful nervousness as if to avoid the appraising look with which she takes in his face, his clothes, etc —his voice seeming to plead for her forebearance.) Anna!

ANNA—*(acutely embarrassed in her turn)* Hello—father. She told me it was you. I yust got here a little while ago.

CHRIS—*(goes slowly over to her chair)* It's good—for see you—after all dem years, Anna. *(He bends down over her. After an embarrassed struggle they manage to kiss each other.)*

ANNA—*(a trace of genuine feeling in her voice)* It's good to see you, too.

CHRIS—*(grasps her arms and looks into her face —then overcome by a wave of fierce tenderness)* Anna lilla! Anna lilla! *(takes her in his arms)*

ANNA—*(shrinks away from him, half-frightened)* What's that—Swedish? I don't know it. *(then as if seeking relief from the tension in a voluble chatter)* Gee, I had an awful trip coming here. I'm all in. I had to sit up in the dirty coach all night—couldn't get no sleep, hardly—and then I had a hard job finding this place. I never been in New York before, you know, and—

CHRIS—*(who has been staring down at her face admiringly, not hearing what she says —impulsively)* You know you vas awful pooty gel, Anna? Ay bet all men see you fall in love with you, py yiminy!

ANNA—*(repelled —harshly)* Cut it! You talk same as they all do.

CHRIS—*(hurt —humbly)* Ain't no harm for your fader talk dat vay, Anna.

ANNA—*(forcing a short laugh)* No—course not. Only— it's funny to see you and not remember nothing. You're like—a stranger.

CHRIS—*(sadly)* Ay s'pose. Ay never come home only few times ven you vas kit in Sveden. You don't remember dat?

ANNA—No. *(resentfully)* But why didn't you never come home them days? Why didn't you never come out West to see me?

CHRIS—(*slowly*) Ay tank, after your mo'der die, ven Ay vas avay on voyage, it's better for you you don't never see me! (*He sinks down in the chair opposite her dejectedly—then turns to her—sadly*) Ay don't know, Anna, vhy Ay never come home Sveden in ole year. Ay vant come home end of every voyage. Ay vant see your mo'der, your two bro'der before dey vas drowned, you ven you vas born—but—Ay—don't go. Ay sign on oder ships—go South America, go Australia, go China, go every port all over world many times—but Ay never go aboard ship sail for Sveden. Ven Ay gat money for pay passage home as passenger den—(*he bows his head guiltily*) Ay forgat and Ay spend all money. Ven Ay tank again, it's too late. (*He sighs.*) Ay don't know vhy but dat's vay with most sailor fallar, Anna. Dat ole davil sea make dem crazy fools with her dirty tricks. It's so.

ANNA—(*who has watched him keenly while he has been speaking—with a trace of scorn in her voice*) Then you think the sea's to blame for everything, eh? Well, you're still workin' on it, ain't you, spite of all you used to write me about hating it. That dame was here told me you was captain of a coal barge—and you wrote me you was yanitor of a building!

CHRIS—(*embarrassed but lying glibly*) Oh, Ay work on land long time as yanitor. Yust short time ago Ay got dis yob cause Ay vas sick, need open air.

ANNA—(*sceptically*) Sick? You? You'd never think it.

CHRIS—And, Anna, dis ain't real sailor yob. Dis ain't real boat on sea. She's yust ole tub—like piece of land with house on it dat float. Yob on her ain't sea yob. No. Ay don't gat yob on sea, Anna, if Ay die first. Ay swear dat, ven your mo'der die. Ay keep my word, py yingo!

ANNA—(*perplexed*) Well, I can't see no difference. (*dismissing the subject*) Speaking of being sick, I been there myself—yust out of the hospital two weeks ago.

CHRIS—(*immediately all concern*) You, Anna? Py golly! (*anxiously*) You feel better now, dough, don't you? You look little tired, dat's all!

ANNA—(*wearily*) I am. Tired to death. I need a long rest and I don't see much chance of getting it.

CHRIS—What you mean, Anna?

ANNA—Well, when I made up my mind to come to see

you, I thought you was a yanitor—that you'd have a place where, maybe, if you didn't mind having me, I could visit a while and rest up—till I felt able to get back on the job again.

CHRIS—(*eagerly*) But Ay gat place, Anna—nice place. You rest all you want, py yiminy! You don't never have to vork as nurse gel no more. You stay with me, py golly!

ANNA—(*surprised and pleased by his eagerness—with a smile*) Then you're really glad to see me—honest?

CHRIS—(*pressing one of her hands in both of his*) Anna, Ay like see you like hell, Ay tal you! And don't you talk no more about gatting yob. You stay with me. Ay don't see you for long time, you don't forgat dat. (*His voice trembles.*) Ay'm gatting ole. Ay gat no one in vorld but you.

ANNA—(*touched—embarrassed by this unfamiliar emotion*) Thanks. It sounds good to hear someone—talk to me that way. Say, though—if you're so lonely—it's funny—why ain't you ever married again?

CHRIS—(*shaking his head emphatically—after a pause*) Ay love your mo'der too much for ever do dat, Anna.

ANNA—(*impressed—slowly*) I don't remember nothing about her. What was she like? Tell me.

CHRIS—Ay tal you all about everytang—and you tal me all tangs happen to you. But not here now. Dis ain't good place for young gel, anyway. Only no good sailor fallar come here for gat drunk. (*He gets to his feet quickly and picks up her bag.*) You come with me, Anna. You need lie down, gat rest.

ANNA—(*half rises to her feet, then sits down again*) Where're you going?

CHRIS—Come. Ve gat on board.

ANNA—(*disappointedly*) On board your barge, you mean? (*dryly*) Nix for mine! (*then seeing his crestfallen look—forcing a smile*) Do you think that's a good place for a young girl like me—a coal barge?

CHRIS—(*dully*) Yes, Ay tank. (*He hesitates—then continues more and more pleadingly.*) You don't know how nice it's on barge, Anna. Tug come and ve gat towed out on voyage— yust water all round, and sun, and fresh air, and good grub for make you strong, healthy gel. You see many tangs you don't see before. You gat moonlight at night, maybe; see steamer pass; see schooner make sail—see everytang dat's pooty. You need take rest like dat. You work too hard for young gel already. You need vacation, yes!

ANNA—(*who has listened to him with a growing interest— with an uncertain laugh*) It sounds good to hear you tell it. I'd sure like a trip on the water, all right. It's the barge idea has me stopped. Well, I'll go down with you and have a look —and maybe I'll take a chance. Gee, I'd do anything once.

CHRIS—(*picks up her bag again*) Ve go, eh?

ANNA—What's the rush? Wait a second. (*Forgetting the situation for a moment, she relapses into the familiar form and flashes one of her winning trade smiles at him.*) Gee, I'm thirsty.

CHRIS—(*sets down her bag immediately—hastily*) Ay'm sorry, Anna. What you tank you like for drink, eh?

ANNA—(*promptly*) I'll take a— (*then suddenly reminded— confusedly*) I don't know. What'a they got here?

CHRIS—(*with a grin*) Ay don't tank dey got much fancy drink for young gel in dis place, Anna. Yinger ale—sas'prilla, maybe.

ANNA—(*forcing a laugh herself*) Make it sas, then.

CHRIS—(*coming up to her—with a wink*) Ay tal you, Anna, ve calabrate, yes—dis one time because ve meet after many year. (*in a half whisper, embarrassedly*) Dey gat good port wine, Anna. It's good for you, Ay tank—little bit—for give you appetite. It ain't strong, neider. One glass don't go to your head, Ay promise.

ANNA—(*with a half hysterical laugh*) All right. I'll take port.

CHRIS—Ay go gat him. (*He goes out to the bar. As soon as the door closes, Anna starts to her feet.*)

ANNA—(*picking up her bag—half-aloud—stammeringly*) Gawd, I can't stand this! I better beat it. (*Then she lets her bag drop, stumbles over to her chair again, and covering her face with her hands, begins to sob.*)

LARRY—(*putting down his paper as Chris comes up—with a grin*) Well, who's the blond?

CHRIS—(*proudly*) Dat vas Anna, Larry.

LARRY—(*in amazement*) Your daughter, Anna? (*Chris nods. Larry lets a long, low whistle escape him and turns away embarrassedly.*)

CHRIS—Don't you tank she vas pooty gel, Larry?

LARRY—(*rising to the occasion*) Sure! A peach!

CHRIS—You bet you! Give me drink for take back—one port vine for Anna—she calabrate dis one time with me—and small beer for me.

LARRY—(*as he gets the drinks*) Small beer for you, eh? She's reformin' you already.

CHRIS—(*pleased*) You bet! (*He takes the drinks. As she hears him coming, Anna hastily dries her eyes, tries to smile. Chris comes in and sets the drinks down on the table—stares at her for a second anxiously—patting her hand*) You look tired, Anna. Vell, Ay make you take good long rest now. (*picking up his beer*) Come, you drink vine. It put new life in you. (*She lifts her glass—he grins.*) Skoal, Anna! You know dat Svedish word?

ANNA—Skoal! (*downing her port at a gulp like a drink of whiskey—her lips trembling*) Skoal? Guess I know that word, all right, all right!

(*The Curtain Falls*)

ACT II

SCENE—*Ten days later. The stern of the deeply-laden barge, "Simeon Winthrop," at anchor in the outer harbor of Provincetown, Mass. It is ten o'clock at night. Dense fog shrouds the barge on all sides, and she floats motionless on a calm. A lantern set up on an immense coil of thick hawser sheds a dull, filtering light on objects near it—the heavy steel bits for making fast the tow lines, etc. In the rear is the cabin, its misty windows glowing wanly with the light of a lamp inside. The chimney of the cabin stove rises a few feet above the roof. The doleful tolling of bells, on Long Point, on ships at anchor, breaks the silence at regular intervals.*

As the curtain rises, Anna is discovered standing near the coil of rope on which the lantern is placed. She looks healthy, transformed, the natural color has come back to her face. She has on a black, oilskin coat, but wears no hat. She is staring out into the fog astern with an expression of awed wonder. The cabin door is pushed open and Chris appears. He is dressed in yellow oilskins— coat, pants, sou'wester—and wears high sea-boots.

CHRIS—(*the glare from the cabin still in his eyes, peers blinkingly astern*) Anna! (*Receiving no reply, he calls again, this time with apparent apprehension*) Anna!

ANNA—(*with a start—making a gesture with her hand as if to impose silence—in a hushed whisper*) Yes, here I am. What d'you want?

CHRIS—(*walks over to her—solicitously*) Don't you come turn in, Anna? It's late—after four bells. It ain't good for you stay out here in fog, Ay tank.

ANNA—Why not? (*with a trace of strange exultation*) I love this fog! Honest! It's so—(*she hesitates, groping for a word*)—funny and still. I feel as if I was—out of things altogether.

CHRIS—(*spitting disgustedly*) Fog's vorst one of her dirty tricks, py yingo!

ANNA—(*with a short laugh*) Beefing about the sea again? I'm getting so's I love it, the little I've seen.

CHRIS—(*glancing at her moodily*) Dat's foolish talk, Anna. You see her more, you don't talk dat vay. (*Then seeing her irritation, he hastily adopts a more cheerful tone.*) But Ay'm glad

979

you like it on barge. Ay'm glad it makes you feel good again. (*with a placating grin*) You like live like dis alone with ole fa'der, eh?

ANNA—Sure I do. Everything's been so different from anything I ever come across before. And now—this fog— Gee, I wouldn't have missed it for nothing. I never thought living on ships was so different from land. Gee, I'd yust love to work on it, honest I would, if I was a man. I don't wonder you always been a sailor.

CHRIS—(*vehemently*) Ay ain't sailor, Anna. And dis ain't real sea. You only see nice part. (*Then as she doesn't answer, he continues hopefully.*) Vell, fog lift in morning, Ay tank.

ANNA—(*the exultation again in her voice*) I love it! I don't give a rap if it never lifts! (*Chris fidgets from one foot to the other worriedly. Anna continues slowly, after a pause.*) It makes me feel clean—out here—'s if I'd taken a bath.

CHRIS—(*after a pause*) You better go in cabin—read book. Dat put you to sleep.

ANNA—I don't want to sleep. I want to stay out here— and think about things.

CHRIS—(*walks away from her toward the cabin—then comes back*) You act funny to-night, Anna.

ANNA—(*her voice rising angrily*) Say, what're you trying to do—make things rotten? You been kind as kind can be to me and I certainly appreciate it—only don't spoil it all now. (*Then, seeing the hurt expression on her father's face, she forces a smile.*) Let's talk of something else. Come. Sit down here. (*She points to the coil of rope.*)

CHRIS—(*sits down beside her with a sigh*) It's gatting pooty late in night, Anna. Must be near five bells.

ANNA—(*interestedly*) Five bells? What time is that?

CHRIS—Half past ten.

ANNA—Funny I don't know nothing about sea talk—but those cousins was always talking crops and that stuff. Gee, wasn't I sick of it—and of them!

CHRIS—You don't like live on farm, Anna?

ANNA—I've told you a hundred times I hated it. (*decidedly*) I'd rather have one drop of ocean than all the farms in the world! Honest! And you wouldn't like a farm, neither. Here's where you belong. (*She makes a sweeping gesture seaward.*) But not on a coal barge. You belong on a real ship, sailing all over the world.

CHRIS—(*moodily*) Ay've done dat many year, Anna, when Ay vas damn fool.

ANNA—(*disgustedly*) Oh, rats! (*After a pause she speaks musingly.*) Was the men in our family always sailors—as far back as you know about?

CHRIS—(*shortly*) Yes. Damn fools! All men in our village on coast, Sveden, go to sea. Ain't nutting else for dem to do. My fa'der die on board ship in Indian Ocean. He's buried at sea. Ay don't never know him only little bit. Den my tree bro'der, older'n me, dey go on ships. Den Ay go, too. Den my mo'der she's left all 'lone. She die pooty quick after dat—all 'lone. Ve vas all avay on voyage when she die. (*He pauses sadly.*) Two my bro'der dey gat lost on fishing boat same like your bro'ders vas drowned. My oder bro'der, he save money, give up sea, den he die home in bed. He's only one dat ole davil don't kill. (*defiantly*) But me, Ay bet you Ay die ashore in bed, too!

ANNA—Were all of 'em yust plain sailors?

CHRIS—Able body seaman, most of dem. (*with a certain pride*) Dey vas all smart seaman, too—A one. (*then after hesitating a moment—shyly*) Ay vas bo'sun.

ANNA—Bo'sun?

CHRIS—Dat's kind of officer.

ANNA—Gee, that was fine. What does he do?

CHRIS—(*after a second's hesitation, plunged into gloom again by his fear of her enthusiasm*) Hard vork all time. It's rotten, Ay tal you, for go to sea. (*determined to disgust her with sea life—volubly*) Dey're all fool fallar, dem fallar in our family. Dey all vork rotten yob on sea for nutting, don't care nutting but yust gat big pay day in pocket, gat drunk, gat robbed, ship avay again on oder voyage. Dey don't come home. Dey don't do anytang like good man do. And dat ole davil, sea, sooner, later she svallow dem up.

ANNA—(*with an excited laugh*) Good sports, I'd call 'em. (*then hastily*) But say—listen—did all the women of the family marry sailors?

CHRIS—(*eagerly—seeing a chance to drive home his point*) Yes—and it's bad on dem like hell vorst of all. Dey don't see deir men only once in long while. Dey set and vait all 'lone. And vhen deir boys grows up, go to sea, dey sit and vait some more. (*vehemently*) Any gel marry sailor, she's crazy fool! Your mo'der she tal you same tang if she vas alive. (*He relapses into an attitude of somber brooding.*)

ANNA—(*after a pause—dreamily*) Funny! I do feel sort of—nutty, to-night. I feel old.

CHRIS—(*mystified*) Ole?

ANNA—Sure—like I'd been living a long, long time—out here in the fog. (*frowning perplexedly*) I don't know how to tell you yust what I mean. It's like I'd come home after a long visit away some place. It all seems like I'd been here before lots of times—on boats—in this same fog. (*with a short laugh*) You must think I'm off my base.

CHRIS—(*gruffly*) Anybody feel funny dat vay in fog.

ANNA—(*persistently*) But why d'you s'pose I feel so—so—like I'd found something I'd missed and been looking for—'s if this was the right place for me to fit in? And I seem to have forgot—everything that's happened—like it didn't matter no more. And I feel clean, somehow—like you feel yust after you've took a bath. And I feel happy for once—yes, honest!—happier than I ever been anywhere before! (*As Chris makes no comment but a heavy sigh, she continues wonderingly.*) It's nutty for me to feel that way, don't you think?

CHRIS—(*a grim foreboding in his voice*) Ay tank Ay'm damn fool for bring you on voyage, Anna.

ANNA—(*impressed by his tone*) You talk—nutty to-night yourself. You act 's if you was scared something was going to happen.

CHRIS—Only God know dat, Anna.

ANNA—(*half-mockingly*) Then it'll be Gawd's will, like the preachers say—what does happen.

CHRIS—(*starts to his feet with fierce protest*) No! Dat ole davil, sea, she ain't God! (*In the pause of silence that comes after his defiance a hail in a man's husky, exhausted voice comes faintly out of the fog to port.* "Ahoy!" *Chris gives a startled exclamation.*)

ANNA—(*jumping to her feet*) What's that?

CHRIS—(*who has regained his composure—sheepishly*) Py golly, dat scare me for minute. It's only some fallar hail, Anna—loose his course in fog. Must be fisherman's power boat. His engine break down, Ay guess. (*The "ahoy" comes again through the wall of fog, sounding much nearer this time. Chris goes over to the port bulwark.*) Sound from dis side. She come in from open sea. (*He holds his hands to his mouth, megaphone-fashion, and shouts back*) Ahoy, dere! Vhat's trouble?

THE VOICE—(*this time sounding nearer but up forward toward the bow*) Heave a rope when we come alongside. (*then irritably*) Where are ye, ye scut?

CHRIS—Ay hear dem rowing. Dey come up by bow, Ay tank. (*then shouting out again*) Dis vay!

THE VOICE—Right ye are! (*There is a muffled sound of oars in oar-locks.*)

ANNA—(*half to herself—resentfully*) Why don't that guy stay where he belongs?

CHRIS—(*hurriedly*) Ay go up bow. All hands asleep 'cepting fallar on vatch. Ay gat heave line to dat fallar. (*He picks up a coil of rope and hurries off toward the bow. Anna walks back toward the extreme stern as if she wanted to remain as much isolated as possible. She turns her back on the proceedings and stares out into the fog. The voice is heard again shouting "Ahoy" and Chris answering "Dis vay." Then there is a pause—the murmur of excited voices—then the scuffling of feet. Chris appears from around the cabin to port. He is supporting the limp form of a man dressed in dungarees, holding one of the man's arms around his neck. The deckhand, Johnson, a young, blond Swede, follows him, helping along another exhausted man similar fashion. Anna turns to look at them. Chris stops for a second—volubly*) Anna! You come help, vill you? You find vhiskey in cabin. Dese fallars need drink for fix dem. Dey vas near dead.

ANNA—(*hurrying to him*) Sure—but who are they? What's the trouble?

CHRIS—Sailor fallars. Deir steamer gat wrecked. Dey been five days in open boat—four fallars—only one left able stand up. Come, Anna. (*She precedes him into the cabin, holding the door open while he and Johnson carry in their burdens. The door is shut, then opened again as Johnson comes out. Chris's voice shouts after him*) Go gat oder faller, Yohnson.

JOHNSON—Yes, sir. (*He goes. The door is closed again. Mat Burke stumbles in around the port side of the cabin. He moves slowly, feeling his way uncertainly, keeping hold of the port bulwark with his right hand to steady himself. He is stripped to the waist, has on nothing but a pair of dirty dungaree pants. He is a powerful, broad-chested six-footer, his face handsome in a hard, rough, bold, defiant way. He is about thirty, in the full power of his heavy-muscled, immense strength. His dark eyes are bloodshot and wild from sleeplessness. The muscles of his arms and shoulders are lumped in knots and bunches, the veins of his forearms stand out like blue cords. He finds his way to the coil of hawser and sits down on it facing the cabin, his back bowed, head in his hands, in an attitude of spent weariness.)*

BURKE—*(talking aloud to himself)* Row, ye divil! Row! *(then lifting his head and looking about him)* What's this tub? Well, we're safe anyway—with the help of God. *(He makes the sign of the cross mechanically. Johnson comes along the deck to port, supporting the fourth man, who is babbling to himself incoherently. Burke glances at him disdainfully.)* Is it losing the small wits ye iver had, ye are? Deck-scrubbing scut! *(They pass him and go into the cabin, leaving the door open. Burke sags forward wearily.)* I'm bate out—bate out entirely.

ANNA—*(comes out of the cabin with a tumbler quarter-full of whiskey in her hand. She gives a start when she sees Burke so near her, the light from the open door falling full on him. Then, overcoming what is evidently a feeling of repulsion, she comes up beside him.)* Here you are. Here's a drink for you. You need it, I guess.

BURKE—*(lifting his head slowly—confusedly)* Is it dreaming I am?

ANNA—*(half smiling)* Drink it and you'll find it ain't no dream.

BURKE—To hell with the drink—but I'll take it just the same. *(He tosses it down.)* Aah! I'm needin' that—and 'tis fine stuff. *(looking up at her with frank, grinning admiration)* But 'twasn't the booze I meant when I said, was I dreaming. I thought you was some mermaid out of the sea come to torment me. *(He reaches out to feel of her arm.)* Aye, rale flesh and blood, divil a less.

ANNA—*(coldly—stepping back from him)* Cut that.

BURKE—But tell me, isn't this a barge I'm on—or isn't it?

ANNA—Sure.

BURKE—And what is a fine handsome woman the like of you doing on this scow?

ANNA—(*coldly*) Never you mind. (*then half-amused in spite of herself*) Say, you're a great one, honest—starting right in kidding after what you been through.

BURKE—(*delighted—proudly*) Ah, it was nothing—aisy for a rale man with guts to him, the like of me. (*He laughs.*) All in the day's work, darlin'. (*then, more seriously but still in a boastful tone, confidentially*) But I won't be denying 'twas a damn narrow squeak. We'd all ought to be with Davy Jones at the bottom of the sea, be rights. And only for me, I'm telling you, and the great strength and guts is in me, we'd be being scoffed by the fishes this minute!

ANNA—(*contemptuously*) Gee, you hate yourself, don't you? (*then turning away from him indifferently*) Well, you'd better come in and lie down. You must want to sleep.

BURKE—(*stung—rising unsteadily to his feet with chest out and head thrown back—resentfully*) Lie down and sleep, is it? Divil a wink I'm after having for two days and nights and divil a bit I'm needing now. Let you not be thinking I'm the like of them three weak scuts come in the boat with me. I could lick the three of them sitting down with one hand tied behind me. They may be bate out, but I'm not—and I've been rowing the boat with them lying in the bottom not able to raise a hand for the last two days we was in it. (*furiously, as he sees this is making no impression on her*) And I can lick all hands on this tub, wan be wan, tired as I am!

ANNA—(*sarcastically*) Gee, ain't you a hard guy! (*then, with a trace of sympathy, as she notices him swaying from weakness*) But never mind that fight talk. I'll take your word for all you've said. Go on and sit down out here, anyway, if I can't get you to come inside. (*He sits down weakly.*) You're all in, you might as well own up to it.

BURKE—(*fiercely*) The hell I am!

ANNA—(*coldly*) Well, be stubborn then for all I care. And I must say I don't care for your language. The men I know don't pull that rough stuff when ladies are around.

BURKE—(*getting unsteadily to his feet again—in a rage*) Ladies! Ho-ho! Divil mend you! Let you not be making game of me. What would ladies be doing on this bloody hulk? (*As Anna attempts to go to the cabin, he lurches into her path.*) Aisy, now! You're not the old Square-head's woman, I suppose you'll be telling me next—living in his cabin with him, no less! (*Seeing the cold, hostile expression on Anna's face, he suddenly changes his tone to one of boisterous joviality.*) But I do be thinking, iver since the first look my eyes took at you, that it's a fool you are to be wasting yourself—a fine, handsome girl—on a stumpy runt of a man like that old Swede. There's too many strapping great lads on the sea would give their heart's blood for one kiss of you!

ANNA—(*scornfully*) Lads like you, eh?

BURKE—(*grinning*) Ye take the words out o' my mouth. I'm the proper lad for you, if it's meself do be saying it. (*With a quick movement he puts his arms about her waist.*) Whisht, now, me daisy! Himself's in the cabin. It's wan of your kisses I'm needing to take the tiredness from me bones. Wan kiss, now! (*He presses her to him and attempts to kiss her.*)

ANNA—(*struggling fiercely*) Leggo of me, you big mut! (*She pushes him away with all her might. Burke, weak and tottering, is caught off his guard. He is thrown down backward and, in falling, hits his head a hard thump against the bulwark. He lies there still, knocked out for the moment. Anna stands for a second, looking down at him frightenedly. Then she kneels down beside him and raises his head to her knee, staring into his face anxiously for some sign of life.*)

BURKE—(*stirring a bit—mutteringly*) God stiffen it! (*He opens his eyes and blinks up at her with vague wonder.*)

ANNA—(*letting his head sink back on the deck, rising to her feet with a sigh of relief*) You're coming to all right, eh? Gee, I was scared for a moment I'd killed you.

BURKE—(*with difficulty rising to a sitting position—scornfully*) Killed, is it? It'd take more than a bit of a blow to crack my thick skull. (*then looking at her with the most intense admiration*) But, glory be, it's a power of strength is in them two fine arms of yours. There's not a man in the world can say the same as you, that he seen Mat Burke lying at his feet and him dead to the world.

ANNA—(*rather remorsefully*) Forget it. I'm sorry it happened, see? (*Burke rises and sits on bench. Then severely*) Only you had no right to be getting fresh with me. Listen, now, and don't go getting any more wrong notions. I'm on this barge because I'm making a trip with my father. The captain's my father. Now you know.

BURKE—The old square—the old Swede, I mean?

ANNA—Yes.

BURKE—(*rising—peering at her face*) Sure I might have known it, if I wasn't a bloody fool from birth. Where else'd you get that fine yellow hair is like a golden crown on your head.

ANNA—(*with an amused laugh*) Say, nothing stops you, does it? (*then attempting a severe tone again*) But don't you think you ought to be apologizing for what you said and done yust a minute ago, instead of trying to kid me with that mush?

BURKE—(*indignantly*) Mush! (*then bending forward toward her with very intense earnestness*) Indade and I will ask your pardon a thousand times—and on my knees, if ye like. I didn't mean a word of what I said or did. (*resentful again for a second*) But divil a woman in all the ports of the world has iver made a great fool of me that way before!

ANNA—(*with amused sarcasm*) I see. You mean you're a lady-killer and they all fall for you.

BURKE—(*offended—passionately*) Leave off your fooling! 'Tis that is after getting my back up at you. (*earnestly*) 'Tis no lie I'm telling you about the women. (*ruefully*) Though it's a great jackass I am to be mistaking you, even in anger, for the like of them cows on the waterfront is the only women I've met up with since I was growed to a man. (*As Anna shrinks away from him at this, he hurries on pleadingly.*) I'm a hard, rough man and I'm not fit, I'm thinking, to be kissing the shoe-soles of a fine, dacent girl the like of yourself. 'Tis only the ignorance of your kind made me see you wrong. So you'll forgive me, for the love of God, and let us be friends from this out. (*passionately*) I'm thinking I'd rather be friends with you than have my wish for anything else in the world. (*He holds out his hand to her shyly.*)

ANNA—(*looking queerly at him, perplexed and worried, but moved and pleased in spite of herself—takes his hand uncertainly*) Sure.

BURKE—(*with boyish delight*) God bless you! (*In his excitement he squeezes her hand tight.*)

ANNA—Ouch!

BURKE—(*hastily dropping her hand—ruefully*) Your pardon, Miss. 'Tis a clumsy ape I am. (*then simply—glancing down his arm proudly*) It's great power I have in my hand and arm, and I do be forgetting it at times.

ANNA—(*nursing her crushed hand and glancing at his arm, not without a trace of his own admiration*) Gee, you're some strong, all right.

BURKE—(*delighted*) It's no lie, and why shouldn't I be, with me shoveling a million tons of coal in the stokeholes of ships since I was a lad only. (*He pats the coil of hawser invitingly.*) Let you sit down, now, Miss, and I'll be telling you a bit of myself, and you'll be telling me a bit of yourself, and in an hour we'll be as old friends as if we was born in the same house. (*He pulls at her sleeve shyly.*) Sit down now, if you plaze.

ANNA—(*with a half laugh*) Well— (*She sits down.*) But we won't talk about me, see? You tell me about yourself and about the wreck.

BURKE—(*flattered*) I'll tell you, surely. But can I be asking you one question, Miss, has my head in a puzzle?

ANNA—(*guardedly*) Well—I dunno—what is it?

BURKE—What is it you do when you're not taking a trip with the Old Man? For I'm thinking a fine girl the like of you ain't living always on this tub.

ANNA—(*uneasily*) No—of course I ain't. (*She searches his face suspiciously, afraid there may be some hidden insinuation in his words. Seeing his simple frankness, she goes on confidently.*) Well, I'll tell you. I'm a governess, see? I take care of kids for people and learn them things.

BURKE—(*impressed*) A governess, is it? You must be smart, surely.

ANNA—But let's not talk about me. Tell me about the wreck, like you promised me you would.

BURKE—(*importantly*) 'Twas this way, Miss. Two weeks out we ran into the divil's own storm, and she sprang wan hell of a leak up for'ard. The skipper was hoping to make Boston before another blow would finish her, but ten days back we met up with another storm the like of the first, only worse. Four days we was in it with green seas raking over her from bow to stern. That was a terrible time, God help us. (*proudly*) And if 'twasn't for me and my great strength, I'm telling you—and it's God's truth—there'd been mutiny itself in the stokehole. 'Twas me held them to it, with a kick to wan and a clout to another, and they not caring a damn for the engineers any more, but fearing a clout of my right arm more than they'd fear the sea itself. (*He glances at her anxiously, eager for her approval.*)

ANNA—(*concealing a smile—amused by this boyish boasting of his*) You did some hard work, didn't you?

BURKE—(*promptly*) I did that! I'm a divil for sticking it out when them that's weak give up. But much good it did anyone! 'Twas a mad, fightin' scramble in the last seconds with each man for himself. I disremember how it come about, but there was the four of us in wan boat and when we was raised high on a great wave I took a look about and divil a sight there was of ship or men on top of the sea.

ANNA—(*in a subdued voice*) Then all the others was drowned?

BURKE—They was, surely.

ANNA—(*with a shudder*) What a terrible end!

BURKE—(*turns to her*) A terrible end for the like of them swabs does live on land, maybe. But for the like of us does be roaming the seas, a good end, I'm telling you—quick and clane.

ANNA—(*struck by the word*) Yes, clean. That's yust the word for—all of it—the way it makes me feel.

BURKE—The sea, you mean? (*interestedly*) I'm thinking you have a bit of it in your blood, too. Your Old Man wasn't only a barge rat—begging your pardon—all his life, by the cut of him.

ANNA—No, he was bo'sun on sailing ships for years. And all the men on both sides of the family have gone to sea as far back as he remembers, he says. All the women have married sailors, too.

BURKE—(*with intense satisfaction*) Did they, now? They had spirit in them. It's only on the sea you'd find rale men with guts is fit to wed with fine, high-tempered girls (*then he adds half-boldly*) the like of yourself.

ANNA—(*with a laugh*) There you go kiddin' again. (*then*

seeing his hurt expression—quickly) But you was going to tell me about yourself. You're Irish, of course I can tell that.

BURKE—(*stoutly*) Yes, thank God, though I've not seen a sight of it in fifteen years or more.

ANNA—(*thoughtfully*) Sailors never do go home hardly, do they? That's what my father was saying.

BURKE—He wasn't telling no lie. (*with sudden melancholy*) It's a hard and lonesome life, the sea is. The only women you'd meet in the ports of the world who'd be willing to speak you a kind word isn't woman at all. You know the kind I mane, and they're a poor, wicked lot, God forgive them. They're looking to steal the money from you only.

ANNA—(*her face averted—rising to her feet—agitatedly*) I think—I guess I'd better see what's doing inside.

BURKE—(*afraid he has offended her—beseechingly*) Don't go, I'm saying! Is it I've given you offence with my talk of the like of them? Don't heed it at all! I'm clumsy in my wits when it comes to talking proper with a girl the like of you. And why wouldn't I be? Since the day I left home for to go to sea punching coal, this is the first time I've had a word with a rale, dacent woman. So don't turn your back on me now, and we beginning to be friends.

ANNA—(*turning to him again—forcing a smile*) I'm not sore at you, honest.

BURKE—(*gratefully*) God bless you!

ANNA—(*changing the subject abruptly*) But if you honestly think the sea's such a rotten life, why don't you get out of it?

BURKE—(*surprised*) Work on land, is it? (*She nods. He spits scornfully.*) Digging spuds in the muck from dawn to dark, I suppose? (*vehemently*) I wasn't made for it, Miss.

ANNA—(*with a laugh*) I thought you'd say that.

BURKE—(*argumentatively*) But there's good jobs and bad jobs at sea, like there'd be on land. I'm thinking if it's in the stokehole of a proper liner I was, I'd be able to have a little house and be home to it wan week out of four. And I'm thinking that maybe then I'd have the luck to find a fine dacent girl—the like of yourself, now—would be willing to wed with me.

ANNA—(*turning away from him with a short laugh—uneasily*) Why sure. Why not?

BURKE—(*edging up close to her—exultantly*) Then you think a girl the like of yourself might maybe not mind the past at all but only be seeing the good herself put in me?

ANNA—(*in the same tone*) Why, sure.

BURKE—(*passionately*) She'd not be sorry for it, I'd take my oath! 'Tis no more drinking and roving about I'd be doing then, but giving my pay day into her hand and staying at home with her as meek as a lamb each night of the week I'd be in port.

ANNA—(*moved in spite of herself and troubled by this half-concealed proposal—with a forced laugh*) All you got to do is find the girl.

BURKE—I have found her!

ANNA—(*half-frightenedly—trying to laugh it off*) You have? When? I thought you was saying—

BURKE—(*boldly and forcefully*) This night. (*hanging his head—humbly*) If she'll be having me. (*then raising his eyes to hers—simply*) 'Tis you I mean.

ANNA—(*is held by his eyes for a moment—then shrinks back from him with a strange, broken laugh*) Say—are you—going crazy? Are you trying to kid me? Proposing—to me!—for Gawd's sake!—on such short acquaintance? (*Chris comes out of the cabin and stands staring blinkingly astern. When he makes out Anna in such intimate proximity to this strange sailor, an angry expression comes over his face.*)

BURKE—(*following her—with fierce, pleading insistence*) I'm telling you there's the will of God in it that brought me safe through the storm and fog to the wan spot in the world where you was! Think of that now, and isn't it queer—

CHRIS—Anna! (*He comes toward them, raging, his fists clenched.*) Anna, you gat in cabin, you hear!

ANNA—(*all her emotions immediately transformed into resentment at his bullying tone*) Who d'you think you're talking to—a slave?

CHRIS—(*hurt—his voice breaking—pleadingly*) You need gat rest, Anna. You gat sleep. (*She does not move. He turns on Burke furiously.*) What you doing here, you sailor fallar? You ain't sick like oders. You gat in fo'c's'tle. Dey give you bunk. (*threateningly*) You hurry, Ay tal you!

ANNA—(*impulsively*) But he is sick. Look at him. He can hardly stand up.

BURKE—(*straightening and throwing out his chest—with a bold laugh*) Is it giving me orders ye are, me bucko? Let you look out, then! With wan hand, weak as I am, I can break ye in two and fling the pieces over the side—and your crew after you. (*stopping abruptly*) I was forgetting. You're her Old Man and I'd not raise a fist to you for the world. (*His knees sag, he wavers and seems about to fall. Anna utters an exclamation of alarm and hurries to his side.*)

ANNA—(*taking one of his arms over her shoulder*) Come on in the cabin. You can have my bed if there ain't no other place.

BURKE—(*with jubilant happiness—as they proceed toward the cabin*) Glory be to God, is it holding my arm about your neck you are! Anna! Anna! Sure it's a sweet name is suited to you.

ANNA—(*guiding him carefully*) Sssh! Sssh!

BURKE—Whisht, is it? Indade, and I'll not. I'll be roaring it out like a fog horn over the sea! You're the girl of the world and we'll be marrying soon and I don't care who knows it!

ANNA—(*as she guides him through the cabin door*) Ssshh! Never mind that talk. You go to sleep. (*They go out of sight in the cabin. Chris, who has been listening to Burke's last words with open-mouthed amazement stands looking after them helplessly.*)

CHRIS—(*turns suddenly and shakes his fist out at the sea— with bitter hatred*) Dat's your dirty trick, damn ole davil, you! (*then in a frenzy of rage*) But, py God, you don't do dat! Not while Ay'm living! No, py God, you don't!

(*The Curtain Falls*)

ACT III

SCENE—*The interior of the cabin on the barge, "Simeon Winthrop" (at dock in Boston)—a narrow, low-ceilinged compartment the walls of which are painted a light brown with white trimmings. In the rear on the left, a door leading to the sleeping quarters. In the far left corner, a large locker-closet, painted white, on the door of which a mirror hangs on a nail. In the rear wall, two small square windows and a door opening out on the deck toward the stern. In the right wall, two more windows looking out on the port deck. White curtains, clean and stiff, are at the windows. A table with two cane-bottomed chairs stands in the center of the cabin. A dilapidated, wicker rocker, painted brown, is also by the table.*

It is afternoon of a sunny day about a week later. From the harbor and docks outside, muffled by the closed door and windows, comes the sound of steamers' whistles and the puffing snort of the donkey engines of some ship unloading nearby.

As the curtain rises, Chris and Anna are discovered. Anna is seated in the rocking-chair by the table, with a newspaper in her hands. She is not reading but staring straight in front of her. She looks unhappy, troubled, frowningly concentrated on her thoughts. Chris wanders about the room, casting quick, uneasy side glances at her face, then stopping to peer absentmindedly out of the window. His attitude betrays an overwhelming, gloomy anxiety which has him on tenter hooks. He pretends to be engaged in setting things ship-shape, but this occupation is confined to picking up some object, staring at it stupidly for a second, then aimlessly putting it down again. He clears his throat and starts to sing to himself in a low, doleful voice: "My Yosephine, come aboard de ship. Long time Ay vait for you."

ANNA—(*turning on him, sarcastically*) I'm glad someone's feeling good. (*wearily*) Gee, I sure wish we was out of this dump and back in New York.

CHRIS—(*with a sigh*) Ay'm glad ven ve sail again, too. (*Then, as she makes no comment, he goes on with a ponderous attempt at sarcasm.*) Ay don't see vhy you don't like Boston, dough. You have good time here, Ay tank. You go ashore all time, every day and night veek ve've been here. You go to

993

movies, see show, gat all kinds fun— (*his eyes hard with hatred*) All with that damn Irish fallar!

ANNA—(*with weary scorn*) Oh, for heaven's sake, are you off on that again? Where's the harm in his taking me around? D'you want me to sit all day and night in this cabin with you—and knit? Ain't I got a right to have as good a time as I can?

CHRIS—It ain't right kind of fun—not with that fallar, no.

ANNA—I been back on board every night by eleven, ain't I? (*then struck by some thought—looks at him with keen suspicion—with rising anger*) Say, look here, what d'you mean by what you yust said?

CHRIS—(*hastily*) Nutting but what Ay say, Anna.

ANNA—You said "ain't right" and you said it funny. Say, listen here, you ain't trying to insinuate that there's something wrong between us, are you?

CHRIS—(*horrified*) No, Anna! No, Ay svear to God, Ay never tank dat!

ANNA—(*mollified by his very evident sincerity—sitting down again*) Well, don't you never think it neither if you want me ever to speak to you again. (*angrily again*) If I ever dreamt you thought that, I'd get the hell out of this barge so quick you couldn't see me for dust.

CHRIS—(*soothingly*) Ay wouldn't never dream— (*then, after a second's pause, reprovingly*) You vas gatting learn to svear. Dat ain't nice for young gel, you tank?

ANNA—(*with a faint trace of a smile*) Excuse me. You ain't used to such language, I know. (*mockingly*) That's what your taking me to sea has done for me.

CHRIS—(*indignantly*) No, it ain't me. It's dat damn sailor fallar learn you bad tangs.

ANNA—He ain't a sailor. He's a stoker.

CHRIS—(*forcibly*) Dat vas million times vorse, Ay tal you! Dem fallars dat vork below shoveling coal vas de dirtiest, rough gang of no-good fallars in vorld!

ANNA—I'd hate to hear you say that to Mat.

CHRIS—Oh, Ay tal him same tang. You don't gat it in head Ay'm scared of him yust 'cause he vas stronger'n Ay vas. (*menacingly*) You don't gat for fight with fists with dem fallars. Dere's oder vay for fix him.

ANNA—(*glancing at him with sudden alarm*) What d'you mean?

CHRIS—(*sullenly*) Nutting.

ANNA—You'd better not. I wouldn't start no trouble with him if I was you. He might forget some time that you was old and my father—and then you'd be out of luck.

CHRIS—(*with smouldering hatred*) Vell, yust let him! Ay'm ole bird maybe, but Ay bet Ay show him trick or two.

ANNA—(*suddenly changing her tone—persuasively*) Aw come on, be good. What's eating you, anyway? Don't you want no one to be nice to me except yourself?

CHRIS—(*placated—coming to her—eagerly*) Yes, Ay do, Anna—only not fallar on sea. But Ay like for you marry steady fallar got good yob on land. You have little home in country all your own—

ANNA—(*rising to her feet—brusquely*) Oh, cut it out! (*scornfully*) Little home in the country! I wish you could have seen the little home in the country where you had me in jail till I was sixteen! (*with rising irritation*) Some day you're going to get me so mad with that talk, I'm going to turn loose on you and tell you—a lot of things that'll open your eyes.

CHRIS—(*alarmed*) Ay don't vant—

ANNA—I know you don't; but you keep on talking yust the same.

CHRIS—Ay don't talk no more den, Anna.

ANNA—Then promise me you'll cut out saying nasty things about Mat Burke every chance you get.

CHRIS—(*evasive and suspicious*) Vhy? You like dat fallar—very much, Anna?

ANNA—Yes, I certainly do! He's a regular man, no matter what faults he's got. One of his fingers is worth all the hundreds of men I met out there—inland.

CHRIS—(*his face darkening*) Maybe you tank you love him, den?

ANNA—(*defiantly*) What of it if I do?

CHRIS—(*scowling and forcing out the words*) Maybe—you tank you—marry him?

ANNA—(*shaking her head*) No! (*Chris' face lights up with relief. Anna continues slowly, a trace of sadness in her voice.*) If I'd met him four years ago—or even two years ago—I'd have jumped at the chance, I tell you that straight. And I would now—only he's such a simple guy—a big kid—and I ain't got the heart to fool him. (*She breaks off suddenly.*) But don't never say again he ain't good enough for me. It's me ain't good enough for him.

CHRIS—(*snorts scornfully*) Py yiminy, you go crazy, Ay tank!

ANNA—(*with a mournful laugh*) Well, I been thinking I was myself the last few days. (*She goes and takes a shawl from a hook near the door and throws it over her shoulders.*) Guess I'll take a walk down to the end of the dock for a minute and see what's doing. I love to watch the ships passing. Mat'll be along before long, I guess. Tell him where I am, will you?

CHRIS—(*despondently*) All right, Ay tal him. (*Anna goes out the doorway on rear. Chris follows her out and stands on the deck outside for a moment looking after her. Then he comes back inside and shuts the door. He stands looking out of the window—mutters—"Dirty ole davil, you." Then he goes to the table, sets the cloth straight mechanically, picks up the newspaper Anna has let fall to the floor and sits down in the rocking-chair. He stares at the paper for a while, then puts it on table, holds his head in his hands and sighs drearily. The noise of a man's heavy footsteps comes from the deck outside and there is a loud knock on the door. Chris starts, makes a move as if to get up and go to the door, then thinks better of it and sits still. The knock is repeated—then as no answer comes, the door is flung open and Mat Burke appears. Chris scowls at the intruder and his hand instinctively goes back to the sheath knife on his hip. Burke is dressed up—wears a cheap blue suit, a striped cotton shirt with a black tie, and black shoes newly shined. His face is beaming with good humor.*)

BURKE—(*as he sees Chris—in a jovial tone of mockery*) Well, God bless who's here! (*He bends down and squeezes his huge form through the narrow doorway.*) And how is the world treating you this afternoon, Anna's father?

CHRIS—(*sullenly*) Pooty goot—if it ain't for some fallars.

BURKE—(*with a grin*) Meaning me, do you? (*He laughs.*) Well, if you ain't the funny old crank of a man! (*then soberly*) Where's herself? (*Chris sits dumb, scowling, his eyes averted. Burke is irritated by this silence.*) Where's Anna, I'm after asking you?

CHRIS—(*hesitating—then grouchily*) She go down end of dock.

BURKE—I'll be going down to her, then. But first I'm thinking I'll take this chance when we're alone to have a word with you. (*He sits down opposite Chris at the table and leans over toward him.*) And that word is soon said. I'm marrying your Anna before this day is out, and you might as well make up your mind to it whether you like it or no.

CHRIS—(*glaring at him with hatred and forcing a scornful laugh*) Ho-ho! Dat's easy for say!

BURKE—You mean I won't? (*scornfully*) Is it the like of yourself will stop me, are you thinking?

CHRIS—Yes, Ay stop it, if it come to vorst.

BURKE—(*with scornful pity*) God help you!

CHRIS—But ain't no need for me do dat. Anna—

BURKE—(*smiling confidently*) Is it Anna you think will prevent me?

CHRIS—Yes.

BURKE—And I'm telling you she'll not. She knows I'm loving her, and she loves me the same, and I know it.

CHRIS—Ho-ho! She only have fun. She make big fool of you, dat's all!

BURKE—(*unshaken—pleasantly*) That's a lie in your throat, divil mend you!

CHRIS—No, it ain't lie. She tal me yust before she go out she never marry fallar like you.

BURKE—I'll not believe it. 'Tis a great old liar you are, and a divil to be making a power of trouble if you had your way. But 'tis not trouble I'm looking for, and me sitting down here. (*earnestly*) Let us be talking it out now as man to man. You're her father, and wouldn't it be a shame for us to be at each other's throats like a pair of dogs, and I married with Anna. So out with the truth, man alive. What is it you're holding against me at all?

CHRIS—(*a bit placated, in spite of himself, by Burke's evident sincerity—but puzzled and suspicious*) Vell—Ay don't vant for Anna gat married. Listen, you fallar. Ay'm a ole man. Ay don't see Anna for fifteen year. She vas all Ay gat in vorld. And now ven she come on first trip—you tank Ay vant her leave me 'lone again?

BURKE—(*heartily*) Let you not be thinking I have no heart at all for the way you'd be feeling.

CHRIS—(*astonished and encouraged—trying to plead persuasively*) Den you do right tang, eh? You ship avay again, leave Anna alone. (*cajolingly*) Big fallar like you dat's on sea, he don't need vife. He gat new gel in every port, you know dat.

BURKE—(*angry for a second*) God stiffen you! (*then controlling himself—calmly*) I'll not be giving you the lie on that. But divil take you, there's a time comes to every man, on sea or land, that isn't a born fool, when he's sick of the lot of them cows, and wearing his heart out to meet up with a fine dacent girl, and have a home to call his own and be rearing up children in it. 'Tis small use you're asking me to leave Anna. She's the wan woman of the world for me, and I can't live without her now, I'm thinking.

CHRIS—You forgat all about her in one veek out of port, Ay bet you!

BURKE—You don't know the like I am. Death itself wouldn't make me forget her. So let you not be making talk to me about leaving her. I'll not, and be damned to you! It won't be so bad for you as you'd make out at all. She'll be living here in the States, and her married to me. And you'd be seeing her often so—a sight more often than ever you saw her the fifteen years she was growing up in the West. It's quare you'd be the one to be making great trouble about her leaving you when you never laid eyes on her once in all them years.

CHRIS—(*guiltily*) Ay taught it vas better Anna stay avay, grow up inland where she don't ever know ole davil, sea.

BURKE—(*scornfully*) Is it blaming the sea for your troubles ye are again, God help you? Well, Anna knows it now. 'Twas in her blood, anyway.

CHRIS—And Ay don't vant she ever know no-good fallar on sea—

BURKE—She knows one now.

CHRIS—(*banging the table with his fist—furiously*) Dat's yust it! Dat's yust what you are—no-good, sailor fallar! You tank Ay lat her life be made sorry by you like her mo'der's vas by me! No, Ay svear! She don't marry you if Ay gat kill you first!

BURKE—(*looks at him a moment, in astonishment—then laughing uproariously*) Ho-ho! Glory be to God, it's bold talk you have for a stumpy runt of a man!

CHRIS—(*threateningly*) Vell—you see!

BURKE—(*with grinning defiance*) I'll see, surely! I'll see myself and Anna married this day, I'm telling you! (*then with contemptuous exasperation*) It's quare fool's blather you have about the sea done this and the sea done that. You'd ought to be shamed to be saying the like, and you an old sailor yourself. I'm after hearing a lot of it from you and a lot more that Anna's told me you do be saying to her, and I'm thinking it's a poor weak thing you are, and not a man at all!

CHRIS—(*darkly*) You see if Ay'm man—maybe quicker'n you tank.

BURKE—(*contemptuously*) Yerra, don't be boasting. I'm thinking 'tis out of your wits you've got with fright of the sea. You'd be wishing Anna married to a farmer, she told me. That'd be a swate match, surely! Would you have a fine girl the like of Anna lying down at nights with a muddy scut stinking of pigs and dung? Or would you have her tied for life to the like of them skinny, shrivelled swabs does be working in cities?

CHRIS—Dat's lie, you fool!

BURKE—'Tis not. 'Tis your own mad notions I'm after telling. But you know the truth in your heart, if great fear of the sea has made you a liar and coward itself. (*pounding the table*) The sea's the only life for a man with guts in him isn't afraid of his own shadow! 'Tis only on the sea he's free, and him roving the face of the world, seeing all things, and not giving a damn for saving up money, or stealing from his friends, or any of the black tricks that a landlubber'd waste his life on. 'Twas yourself knew it once, and you a bo'sun for years.

CHRIS—(*sputtering with rage*) You vas crazy fool, Ay tal you!

BURKE—You've swallowed the anchor. The sea give you a clout once knocked you down, and you're not man enough to get up for another, but lie there for the rest of your life howling bloody murder. (*proudly*) Isn't it myself the sea has nearly drowned, and me battered and bate till I was that close

to hell I could hear the flames roaring, and never a groan out
of me till the sea gave up and it seeing the great strength and
guts of a man was in me?

CHRIS—(*scornfully*) Yes, you vas hell of fallar, hear you
tal it!

BURKE—(*angrily*) You'll be calling me a liar once too
often, me old bucko! Wasn't the whole story of it and my
picture itself in the newspapers of Boston a week back? (*looking Chris up and down belittlingly*) Sure I'd like to see you in
the best of your youth do the like of what I done in the storm
and after. 'Tis a mad lunatic, screeching with fear, you'd be
this minute!

CHRIS—Ho-ho! You vas young fool! In ole years when Ay
was on windyammer, Ay vas through hundred storms vorse'n
dat! Ships vas ships den—and men dat sail on dem vas real
men. And now what you gat on steamers? You gat fallars on
deck don't know ship from mudscow. (*with a meaning glance
at Burke*) And below deck you gat fallars yust know how for
shovel coal—might yust as vell vork on coal vagon ashore!

BURKE—(*stung—angrily*) Is it casting insults at the men
in the stokehole ye are, ye old ape? God stiffen you! Wan of
them is worth any ten stock-fish-swilling Square-heads ever
shipped on a windbag!

CHRIS—(*his face working with rage, his hand going back to
the sheath-knife on his hip*) Irish svine, you!

BURKE—(*tauntingly*) Don't ye like the Irish, ye old baboon? 'Tis that you're needing in your family, I'm telling
you—an Irishman and a man of the stokehole—to put guts
in it so that you'll not be having grandchildren would be fearful cowards and jackasses the like of yourself!

CHRIS—(*half rising from his chair—in a voice choked with
rage*) You look out!

BURKE—(*watching him intently—a mocking smile on his
lips*) And it's that you'll be having, no matter what you'll do
to prevent; for Anna and me'll be married this day, and no
old fool the like of you will stop us when I've made up my
mind.

CHRIS—(*with a hoarse cry*) You don't! (*He throws himself at
Burke, knife in hand, knocking his chair over backwards. Burke
springs to his feet quickly in time to meet the attack. He laughs*

with the pure love of battle. The old Swede is like a child in his hands. Burke does not strike or mistreat him in any way, but simply twists his right hand behind his back and forces the knife from his fingers. He throws the knife into a far corner of the room—tauntingly)

BURKE—Old men is getting childish shouldn't play with knives. *(holding the struggling Chris at arm's length—with a sudden rush of anger, drawing back his fist)* I've half a mind to hit you a great clout will put sense in your square head. Kape off me now, I'm warning you! *(He gives Chris a push with the flat of his hand which sends the old Swede staggering back against the cabin wall, where he remains standing, panting heavily, his eyes fixed on Burke with hatred, as if he were only collecting his strength to rush at him again.)*

BURKE—*(warningly)* Now don't be coming at me again, I'm saying, or I'll flatten you on the floor with a blow, if 'tis Anna's father you are itself! I've no patience left for you. *(then with an amused laugh)* Well, 'tis a bold old man you are just the same, and I'd never think it was in you to come tackling me alone. *(A shadow crosses the cabin windows. Both men start. Anna appears in the doorway.)*

ANNA—*(with pleased surprise as she sees Burke)* Hello, Mat. Are you here already? I was down— *(She stops, looking from one to the other, sensing immediately that something has happened.)* What's up? *(then noticing the overturned chair—in alarm)* How'd that chair get knocked over? *(turning on Burke reproachfully)* You ain't been fighting with him, Mat—after you promised?

BURKE—*(his old self again)* I've not laid a hand on him, Anna. *(He goes and picks up the chair, then turning on the still questioning Anna—with a reassuring smile)* Let you not be worried at all. 'Twas only a bit of an argument we was having to pass the time till you'd come.

ANNA—It must have been some argument when you got to throwing chairs. *(She turns on Chris.)* Why don't you say something? What was it about?

CHRIS—*(relaxing at last—avoiding her eyes—sheepishly)* Ve vas talking about ships and fallars on sea.

ANNA—*(with a relieved smile)* Oh—the old stuff, eh?

BURKE—*(suddenly seeming to come to a bold decision—with*

a defiant grin at Chris) He's not after telling you the whole of it. We was arguing about you mostly.

ANNA—(*with a frown*) About me?

BURKE—And we'll be finishing it out right here and now in your presence if you're willing. (*He sits down at the left of table.*)

ANNA—(*uncertainly—looking from him to her father*) Sure. Tell me what it's all about.

CHRIS—(*advancing toward the table—protesting to Burke*) No! You don't do dat, you! You tal him you don't vant for hear him talk, Anna.

ANNA—But I do. I want this cleared up.

CHRIS—(*miserably afraid now*) Vell, not now, anyvay. You vas going ashore, yes? You ain't got time—

ANNA—(*firmly*) Yes, right here and now. (*She turns to Burke.*) You tell me, Mat, since he don't want to.

BURKE—(*draws a deep breath—then plunges in boldly*) The whole of it's in a few words only. So's he'd make no mistake, and him hating the sight of me, I told him in his teeth I loved you. (*passionately*) And that's God truth, Anna, and well you know it!

CHRIS—(*scornfully—forcing a laugh*) Ho-ho! He tal same tang to gel every port he go!

ANNA—(*shrinking from her father with repulsion—resentfully*) Shut up, can't you? (*then to Burke—feelingly*) I know it's true, Mat. I don't mind what he says.

BURKE—(*humbly grateful*) God bless you!

ANNA—And then what?

BURKE—And then— (*hesitatingly*) And then I said—(*he looks at her pleadingly*) I said I was sure—I told him I thought you have a bit of love for me, too. (*passionately*) Say you do, Anna! Let you not destroy me entirely, for the love of God! (*He grasps both her hands in his two.*)

ANNA—(*deeply moved and troubled—forcing a trembling laugh*) So you told him that, Mat? No wonder he was mad. (*forcing out the words*) Well, maybe it's true, Mat. Maybe I do. I been thinking and thinking—I didn't want to, Mat, I'll own up to that—I tried to cut it out—but—(*she laughs helplessly*) I guess I can't help it anyhow. So I guess I do, Mat.

(*then with a sudden joyous defiance*) Sure I do! What's the use of kidding myself different? Sure I love you, Mat!

CHRIS—(*with a cry of pain*) Anna! (*He sits crushed.*)

BURKE—(*with a great depth of sincerity in his humble gratitude*) God be praised!

ANNA—(*assertively*) And I ain't never loved a man in my life before, you can always believe that—no matter what happens.

BURKE—(*goes over to her and puts his arms around her*) Sure I do be believing ivery word you iver said or iver will say. And 'tis you and me will be having a grand, beautiful life together to the end of our days! (*He tries to kiss her. At first she turns away her head—then, overcome by a fierce impulse of passionate love, she takes his head in both her hands and holds his face close to hers, staring into his eyes. Then she kisses him full on the lips.*)

ANNA—(*pushing him away from her—forcing a broken laugh*) Good-by. (*She walks to the doorway in rear—stands with her back toward them, looking out. Her shoulders quiver once or twice as if she were fighting back her sobs.*)

BURKE—(*too in the seventh heaven of bliss to get any correct interpretation of her word—with a laugh*) Good-by, is it? The divil you say! I'll be coming back at you in a second for more of the same! (*to Chris, who has quickened to instant attention at his daughter's good-by, and has looked back at her with a stirring of foolish hope in his eyes*) Now, me old bucko, what'll you be saying? You heard the words from her own lips. Confess I've bate you. Own up like a man when you're bate fair and square. And here's my hand to you— (*holds out his hand*) And let you take it and we'll shake and forget what's over and done, and be friends from this out.

CHRIS—(*with implacable hatred*) Ay don't shake hands with you fallar—not vhile Ay live!

BURKE—(*offended*) The back of my hand to you then, if that suits you better. (*growling*) 'Tis a rotten bad loser you are, divil mend you!

CHRIS—Ay don't lose— (*trying to be scornful and self-convincing*) Anna say she like you little bit but you don't hear her say she marry you, Ay bet. (*At the sound of her name Anna has turned round to them. Her face is composed and calm again, but it is the dead calm of despair.*)

BURKE—(*scornfully*) No, and I wasn't hearing her say the sun is shining either.

CHRIS—(*doggedly*) Dat's all right. She don't say it, yust same.

ANNA—(*quietly—coming forward to them*) No, I didn't say it, Mat.

CHRIS—(*eagerly*) Dere! You hear!

BURKE—(*misunderstanding her—with a grin*) You're waiting till you do be asked, you mane? Well, I'm asking you now. And we'll be married this day, with the help of God!

ANNA—(*gently*) You heard what I said, Mat—after I kissed you?

BURKE—(*alarmed by something in her manner*) No—I disremember.

ANNA—I said good-by. (*her voice trembling*) That kiss was for good-by, Mat.

BURKE—(*terrified*) What d'you mane?

ANNA—I can't marry you, Mat—and we've said good-by. That's all.

CHRIS—(*unable to hold back his exultation*) Ay know it! Ay know dat vas so!

BURKE—(*jumping to his feet—unable to believe his ears*) Anna! Is it making game of me you'd be? 'Tis a quare time to joke with me, and don't be doing it, for the love of God.

ANNA—(*looking him in the eyes—steadily*) D'you think I'd kid you now? No, I'm not joking, Mat. I mean what I said.

BURKE—Ye don't! Ye can't! 'Tis mad you are, I'm telling you!

ANNA—(*fixedly*) No I'm not.

BURKE—(*desperately*) But what's come over you so sudden? You was saying you loved me—

ANNA—I'll say that as often as you want me to. It's true.

BURKE—(*bewilderedly*) Then why—what, in the divil's name— Oh, God help me, I can't make head or tail to it at all!

ANNA—Because it's the best way out I can figure, Mat. (*her voice catching*) I been thinking it over and thinking it over day and night all week. Don't think it ain't hard on me, too, Mat.

BURKE—For the love of God, tell me then, what is it that's preventing you wedding me when the two of us has love? (*suddenly getting an idea and pointing at Chris—exasperatedly*) Is it giving heed to the like of that old fool ye are, and him hating me and filling your ears full of bloody lies against me?

CHRIS—(*getting to his feet—raging triumphantly before Anna has a chance to get in a word*) Yes, Anna believe me, not you! She know her old fa'der don't lie like you.

ANNA—(*turning on her father angrily*) You sit down, d'you hear? Where do you come in butting in and making things worse? You're like a devil, you are! (*harshly*) Good Lord, and I was beginning to like you, beginning to forget all I've got held up against you!

CHRIS—(*crushed—feebly*) You ain't got nutting for hold against me, Anna.

ANNA—Ain't I yust! Well, lemme tell you— (*She glances at Burke and stops abruptly.*) Say, Mat, I'm s'prised at you. You didn't think anything he'd said—

BURKE—(*glumly*) Sure, what else would it be?

ANNA—Think I've ever paid any attention to all his crazy bull? Gee, you must take me for a five-year-old kid.

BURKE—(*puzzled and beginning to be irritated at her too*) I don't know how to take you, with your saying this one minute and that the next.

ANNA—Well, he has nothing to do with it.

BURKE—Then what is it has? Tell me, and don't keep me waiting and sweating blood.

ANNA—(*resolutely*) I can't tell you—and I won't. I got a good reason—and that's all you need to know. I can't marry you, that's all there is to it. (*distractedly*) So, for Gawd's sake, let's talk of something else.

BURKE—I'll not! (*then fearfully*) Is it married to someone else you are—in the West maybe?

ANNA—(*vehemently*) I should say not.

BURKE—(*regaining his courage*) To the divil with all other reasons then. They don't matter with me at all. (*He gets to his feet confidently, assuming a masterful tone.*) I'm thinking you're the like of them women can't make up their mind till they're drove to it. Well, then, I'll make up your mind for you bloody quick. (*He takes her by the arms, grinning to soften his serious bullying.*) We've had enough of talk! Let you be going into your room now and be dressing in your best and we'll be going ashore.

CHRIS—(*aroused—angrily*) No, py God, she don't do that! (*takes hold of her arm*)

ANNA—(*who has listened to Burke in astonishment. She draws away from him, instinctively repelled by his tone, but not exactly sure if he is serious or not—a trace of resentment in her voice*) Say, where do you get that stuff?

BURKE—(*imperiously*) Never mind, now! Let you go get dressed, I'm saying. (*then turning to Chris*) We'll be seeing who'll win in the end—me or you.

CHRIS—(*to Anna—also in an authoritative tone*) You stay right here, Anna, you hear! (*Anna stands looking from one to the other of them as if she thought they had both gone crazy. Then the expression of her face freezes into the hardened sneer of her experience.*)

BURKE—(*violently*) She'll not! She'll do what I say! You've had your hold on her long enough. It's my turn now.

ANNA—(*with a hard laugh*) Your turn? Say, what am I, anyway?

BURKE—'Tis not what you are, 'tis what you're going to be this day—and that's wedded to me before night comes. Hurry up now with your dressing.

CHRIS—(*commandingly*) You don't do one tang he say, Anna! (*Anna laughs mockingly.*)

BURKE—She will, so!

CHRIS—Ay tal you she don't! Ay'm her fa'der.

BURKE—She will in spite of you. She's taking my orders from this out, not yours.

ANNA—(*laughing again*) Orders is good!

BURKE—(*turning to her impatiently*) Hurry up now, and shake a leg. We've no time to be wasting. (*irritated as she doesn't move*) Do you hear what I'm telling you?

CHRIS—You stay dere, Anna!

ANNA—(*at the end of her patience—blazing out at them pas-*

sionately) You can go to hell, both of you! (*There is something in her tone that makes them forget their quarrel and turn to her in a stunned amazement. Anna laughs wildly.*) You're just like all the rest of them—you two! Gawd, you'd think I was a piece of furniture! I'll show you! Sit down now! (*as they hesitate—furiously*) Sit down and let me talk for a minute. You're all wrong, see? Listen to me! I'm going to tell you something—and then I'm going to beat it. (*to Burke—with a harsh laugh*) I'm going to tell you a funny story, so pay attention. (*pointing to Chris*) I've been meaning to turn it loose on him every time he'd get my goat with his bull about keeping me safe inland. I wasn't going to tell you, but you've forced me into it. What's the dif? It's all wrong anyway, and you might as well get cured that way as any other. (*with hard mocking*) Only don't forget what you said a minute ago about it not mattering to you what other reason I got so long as I wasn't married to no one else.

BURKE—(*manfully*) That's my word, and I'll stick to it!

ANNA—(*laughing bitterly*) What a chance! You make me laugh, honest! Want to bet you will? Wait 'n see! (*She stands at the table rear, looking from one to the other of the two men with her hard, mocking smile. Then she begins, fighting to control her emotion and speak calmly.*) First thing is, I want to tell you two guys something. You was going on 's if one of you had got to own me. But nobody owns me, see?—'cepting myself. I'll do what I please and no man, I don't give a hoot who he is, can tell me what to do! I ain't asking either of you for a living. I can make it myself—one way or other. I'm my own boss. So put that in your pipe and smoke it! You and your orders!

BURKE—(*protestingly*) I wasn't meaning it that way at all and well you know it. You've no call to be raising this rumpus with me. (*pointing to Chris*) 'Tis him you've a right—

ANNA—I'm coming to him. But you—you did mean it that way, too. You sounded—just like all the rest. (*hysterically*) But, damn it, shut up! Let me talk for a change!

BURKE—'Tis quare, rough talk, that—for a dacent girl the like of you!

ANNA—(*with a hard laugh*) Decent? Who told you I was? (*Chris is sitting with bowed shoulders, his head in his hands.*

She leans over in exasperation and shakes him violently by the shoulder.) Don't go to sleep, Old Man! Listen here, I'm talking to you now!

CHRIS—(*straightening up and looking about as if he were seeking a way to escape—with frightened foreboding in his voice*) Ay don't vant for hear it. You vas going out of head, Ay tank, Anna.

ANNA—(*violently*) Well, living with you is enough to drive anyone off their nut. Your bunk about the farm being so fine! Didn't I write you year after year how rotten it was and what a dirty slave them cousins made of me? What'd you care? Nothing! Not even enough to come out and see me! That crazy bull about wanting to keep me away from the sea don't go down with me! You yust didn't want to be bothered with me! You're like all the rest of 'em!

CHRIS—(*feebly*) Anna! It ain't so—

ANNA—(*not heeding his interruption—revengefully*) But one thing I never wrote you. It was one of them cousins that you think is such nice people—the youngest son—Paul—that started me wrong. (*loudly*) It wasn't none of my fault. I hated him worse'n hell and he knew it. But he was big and strong—(*pointing to Burke*)—like you!

BURKE—(*half springing to his feet—his fists clenched*) God blarst it! (*He sinks slowly back in his chair again, the knuckles showing white on his clenched hands, his face tense with the effort to suppress his grief and rage.*)

CHRIS—(*in a cry of horrified pain*) Anna!

ANNA—(*to him—seeming not to have heard their interruptions*) That was why I run away from the farm. That was what made me get a yob as nurse girl in St. Paul. (*with a hard, mocking laugh*) And you think that was a nice yob for a girl, too, don't you? (*sarcastically*) With all them nice inland fellers yust looking for a chance to marry me, I s'pose. Marry me? What a chance! They wasn't looking for marrying. (*as Burke lets a groan of fury escape him—desperately*) I'm owning up to everything fair and square. I was caged in, I tell you—yust like in yail—taking care of other people's kids—listening to 'em bawling and crying day and night—when I wanted to be out—and I was lonesome—lonesome as hell! (*with a sudden weariness in her voice*) So I give up finally. What was the use?

(*She stops and looks at the two men. Both are motionless and silent. Chris seems in a stupor of despair, his house of cards fallen about him. Burke's face is livid with the rage that is eating him up, but he is too stunned and bewildered yet to find a vent for it. The condemnation she feels in their silence goads Anna into a harsh, strident defiance.*) You don't say nothing—either of you—but I know what you're thinking. You're like all the rest! (*to Chris—furiously*) And who's to blame for it, me or you? If you'd even acted like a man—if you'd even been a regular father and had me with you—maybe things would be different!

CHRIS—(*in agony*) Don't talk dat vay, Anna! Ay go crazy! Ay von't listen! (*puts his hands over his ears*)

ANNA—(*infuriated by his action—stridently*) You will too listen! (*She leans over and pulls his hands from his ears—with hysterical rage*) You—keeping me safe inland—I wasn't no nurse girl the last two years—I lied when I wrote you—I was in a house, that's what!—yes, that kind of a house—the kind sailors like you and Mat goes to in port—and your nice inland men, too—and all men, God damn 'em! I hate 'em! Hate 'em! (*She breaks into hysterical sobbing, throwing herself into the chair and hiding her face in her hands on the table. The two men have sprung to their feet.*)

CHRIS—(*whimpering like a child*) Anna! Anna! It's lie! It's lie! (*He stands wringing his hands together and begins to weep.*)

BURKE—(*his whole great body tense like a spring—dully and gropingly*) So that's what's in it!

ANNA—(*raising her head at the sound of his voice—with extreme mocking bitterness*) I s'pose you remember your promise, Mat? No other reason was to count with you so long as I wasn't married already. So I s'pose you want me to get dressed and go ashore, don't you? (*She laughs.*) Yes, you do!

BURKE—(*on the verge of his outbreak—stammeringly*) God stiffen you!

ANNA—(*trying to keep up her hard, bitter tone, but gradually letting a note of pitiful pleading creep in*) I s'pose if I tried to tell you I wasn't—that—no more you'd believe me, wouldn't you? Yes, you would! And if I told you that yust getting out in this barge, and being on the sea had changed me and made me feel different about things, 's if all I'd been through wasn't

me and didn't count and was yust like it never happened—
you'd laugh, wouldn't you? And you'd die laughing sure if I
said that meeting you that funny way that night in the fog,
and afterwards seeing that you was straight goods stuck on
me, had got me to thinking for the first time, and I sized you
up as a different kind of man—a sea man as different from
the ones on land as water is from mud—and that was why I
got stuck on you, too. I wanted to marry you and fool you,
but I couldn't. Don't you see how I'd changed? I couldn't
marry you with you believing a lie—and I was shamed to tell
you the truth—till the both of you forced my hand, and I
seen you was the same as all the rest. And now, give me a
bawling out and beat it, like I can tell you're going to. (*She
stops, looking at Burke. He is silent, his face averted, his features
beginning to work with fury. She pleads passionately.*) Will you
believe it if I tell you that loving you has made me—clean?
It's the straight goods, honest! (*then as he doesn't reply—bitterly*) Like hell you will! You're like all the rest!

BURKE—(*blazing out—turning on her in a perfect frenzy of
rage—his voice trembling with passion*) The rest, is it? God's
curse on you! Clane, is it? You slut, you, I'll be killing you
now! (*He picks up the chair on which he has been sitting and,
swinging it high over his shoulder, springs toward her. Chris rushes
forward with a cry of alarm, trying to ward off the blow from his
daughter. Anna looks up into Burke's eyes with the fearlessness of
despair. Burke checks himself, the chair held in the air.*)

CHRIS—(*wildly*) Stop, you crazy fool! You vant for murder
her!

ANNA—(*pushing her father away brusquely, her eyes still
holding Burke's*) Keep out of this, you! (*to Burke—dully*) Well,
ain't you got the nerve to do it? Go ahead! I'll be thankful to
you, honest. I'm sick of the whole game.

BURKE—(*throwing the chair away into a corner of the room—
helplessly*) I can't do it, God help me, and your two eyes looking at me. (*furiously*) Though I do be thinking I'd have a
good right to smash your skull like a rotten egg. Was there
iver a woman in the world had the rottenness in her that you
have, and was there iver a man the like of me was made the
fool of the world, and me thinking thoughts about you, and
having great love for you, and dreaming dreams of the fine

life we'd have when we'd be wedded! (*his voice high pitched in a lamentation that is like a keen*) Yerra, God help me! I'm destroyed entirely and my heart is broken in bits! I'm asking God Himself, was it for this He'd have me roaming the earth since I was a lad only, to come to black shame in the end, where I'd be giving a power of love to a woman is the same as others you'd meet in any hooker-shanty in port, with red gowns on them and paint on their grinning mugs, would be sleeping with any man for a dollar or two!

ANNA—(*in a scream*) Don't, Mat! For Gawd's sake! (*then raging and pounding on the table with her hands*) Get out of here! Leave me alone! Get out of here!

BURKE—(*his anger rushing back on him*) I'll be going, surely! And I'll be drinking sloos of whiskey will wash that black kiss of yours off my lips; and I'll be getting dead rotten drunk so I'll not remember if 'twas iver born you was at all; and I'll be shipping away on some boat will take me to the other end of the world where I'll never see your face again! (*He turns toward the door.*)

CHRIS—(*who has been standing in a stupor—suddenly grasping Burke by the arm—stupidly*) No, you don't go. Ay tank maybe it's better Anna marry you now.

BURKE—(*shaking Chris off—furiously*) Lave go of me, ye old ape! Marry her, is it? I'd see her roasting in hell first! I'm shipping away out of this, I'm telling you! (*pointing to Anna—passionately*) And my curse on you and the curse of Almighty God and all the Saints! You've destroyed me this day and may you lie awake in the long nights, tormented with thoughts of Mat Burke and the great wrong you've done him!

ANNA—(*in anguish*) Mat! (*But he turns without another word and strides out of the doorway. Anna looks after him wildly, starts to run after him, then hides her face in her outstretched arms, sobbing. Chris stands in a stupor, staring at the floor.*)

CHRIS—(*after a pause, dully*) Ay tank Ay go ashore, too.

ANNA—(*looking up, wildly*) Not after him! Let him go! Don't you dare—

CHRIS—(*somberly*) Ay go for gat drink.

ANNA—(*with a harsh laugh*) So I'm driving you to drink, too, eh? I s'pose you want to get drunk so's you can forget—like him?

CHRIS—(*bursting out angrily*) Yes, Ay vant! You tank Ay like hear dem tangs. (*breaking down—weeping*) Ay tank you vasn't dat kind of gel, Anna.

ANNA—(*mockingly*) And I s'pose you want me to beat it, don't you? You don't want me here disgracing you, I s'pose?

CHRIS—No, you stay here! (*goes over and pats her on the shoulder, the tears running down his face*) Ain't your fault, Anna, Ay know dat. (*She looks up at him, softened. He bursts into rage.*) It's dat ole davil, sea, do this to me! (*He shakes his fist at the door.*) It's her dirty tricks! It vas all right on barge with yust you and me. Den she bring dat Irish fallar in fog, she make you like him, she make you fight with me all time! If dat Irish fallar don't never come, you don't never tal me dem tangs, Ay don't never know, and everytang's all right. (*He shakes his fist again.*) Dirty ole davil!

ANNA—(*with spent weariness*) Oh, what's the use? Go on ashore and get drunk.

CHRIS—(*goes into room on left and gets his cap. He goes to the door, silent and stupid—then turns.*) You vait here, Anna?

ANNA—(*dully*) Maybe—and maybe not. Maybe I'll get drunk, too. Maybe I'll— But what the hell do you care what I do? Go on and beat it. (*Chris turns stupidly and goes out. Anna sits at the table, staring straight in front of her.*)

(*The Curtain Falls*)

ACT IV

SCENE—*Same as Act Three, about nine o'clock of a foggy night two days later. The whistles of steamers in the harbor can be heard. The cabin is lighted by a small lamp on the table. A suit case stands in the middle of the floor. Anna is sitting in the rocking-chair. She wears a hat, is all dressed up as in Act One. Her face is pale, looks terribly tired and worn, as if the two days just past had been ones of suffering and sleepless nights. She stares before her despondently, her chin in her hands. There is a timid knock on the door in rear. Anna jumps to her feet with a startled exclamation and looks toward the door with an expression of mingled hope and fear.*

ANNA—(*faintly*) Come in. (*then summoning her courage— more resolutely*) Come in. (*The door is opened and Chris appears in the doorway. He is in a very bleary, bedraggled condition, suffering from the after effects of his drunk. A tin pail full of foaming beer is in his hand. He comes forward, his eyes avoiding Anna's. He mutters stupidly*) It's foggy.

ANNA—(*looking him over with contempt*) So you come back at last, did you? You're a fine looking sight! (*then jeeringly*) I thought you'd beaten it for good on account of the disgrace I'd brought on you.

CHRIS—(*wincing—faintly*) Don't say dat, Anna, please! (*He sits in a chair by the table, setting down the can of beer, holding his head in his hands.*)

ANNA—(*looks at him with a certain sympathy*) What's the trouble? Feeling sick?

CHRIS—(*dully*) Inside my head feel sick.

ANNA—Well, what d'you expect after being soused for two days? (*resentfully*) It serves you right. A fine thing—you leaving me alone on this barge all that time!

CHRIS—(*humbly*) Ay'm sorry, Anna.

ANNA—(*scornfully*) Sorry!

CHRIS—But Ay'm not sick inside head vay you mean. Ay'm sick from tank too much about you, about me.

ANNA—And how about me? D'you suppose I ain't been thinking, too?

1013

CHRIS—Ay'm sorry, Anna. (*He sees her bag and gives a start.*) You pack your bag, Anna? You vas going—?

ANNA—(*forcibly*) Yes, I was going right back to what you think.

CHRIS—Anna!

ANNA—I went ashore to get a train for New York. I'd been waiting and waiting 'till I was sick of it. Then I changed my mind and decided not to go to-day. But I'm going first thing to-morrow, so it'll all be the same in the end.

CHRIS—(*raising his head—pleadingly*) No, you never do dat, Anna!

ANNA—(*with a sneer*) Why not, I'd like to know?

CHRIS—You don't never gat to do—dat vay—no more, Ay tal you. Ay fix dat up all right.

ANNA—(*suspiciously*) Fix what up?

CHRIS—(*not seeming to have heard her question—sadly*) You vas vaiting, you say? You vasn't vaiting for me, Ay bet.

ANNA—(*callously*) You'd win.

CHRIS—For dat Irish fallar?

ANNA—(*defiantly*) Yes—if you want to know! (*then with a forlorn laugh*) If he did come back it'd only be 'cause he wanted to beat me up or kill me, I suppose. But even if he did, I'd rather have him come than not show up at all. I wouldn't care what he did.

CHRIS—Ay guess it's true you vas in love with him all right.

ANNA—You guess!

CHRIS—(*turning to her earnestly*) And Ay'm sorry for you like hell he don't come, Anna!

ANNA—(*softened*) Seems to me you've changed your tune a lot.

CHRIS—Ay've been tanking, and Ay guess it vas all my fault—all bad tangs dat happen to you. (*pleadingly*) You try for not hate me, Anna. Ay'm crazy ole fool, dat's all.

ANNA—Who said I hated you?

CHRIS—Ay'm sorry for everytang Ay do wrong for you, Anna. Ay vant for you be happy all rest of your life for make up! It make you happy marry dat Irish fallar, Ay vant it, too.

ANNA—(*dully*) Well, there ain't no chance. But I'm glad you think different about it, anyway.

CHRIS—(*supplicatingly*) And you tank—maybe—you forgive me sometime?

ANNA—(*with a wan smile*) I'll forgive you right now.

CHRIS—(*seizing her hand and kissing it—brokenly*) Anna lilla! Anna lilla!

ANNA—(*touched but a bit embarrassed.*) Don't bawl about it. There ain't nothing to forgive, anyway. It ain't your fault, and it ain't mine, and it ain't his neither. We're all poor nuts, and things happen, and we yust get mixed in wrong, that's all.

CHRIS—(*eagerly*) You say right tang, Anna, py golly! It ain't nobody's fault! (*shaking his fist*) It's dat ole davil, sea!

ANNA—(*with an exasperated laugh*) Gee, won't you ever can that stuff? (*Chris relapses into injured silence. After a pause Anna continues curiously.*) You said a minute ago you'd fixed something up—about me. What was it?

CHRIS—(*after a hesitating pause*) Ay'm shipping avay on sea again, Anna.

ANNA—(*astounded*) You're—what?

CHRIS—Ay sign on steamer sail to-morrow. Ay gat my ole yob—bo'sun. (*Anna stares at him. As he goes on, a bitter smile comes over her face.*) Ay tank dat's best tang for you. Ay only bring you bad luck, Ay tank. Ay make your mo'der's life sorry. Ay don't vant make yours dat way, but Ay do yust same. Dat ole davil, sea, she make me Yonah man ain't no good for nobody. And Ay tank now it ain't no use fight with sea. No man dat live going to beat her, py yingo!

ANNA—(*with a laugh of helpless bitterness*) So that's how you've fixed me, is it?

CHRIS—Yes, Ay tank if dat ole davil gat me back she leave you alone den.

ANNA—(*bitterly*) But, for Gawd's sake, don't you see, you're doing the same thing you've always done? Don't you see—? (*But she sees the look of obsessed stubbornness on her father's face and gives it up helplessly.*) But what's the use of talking. You ain't right, that's what. I'll never blame you for nothing no more. But how you could figure out that was fixing me—!

CHRIS—Dat ain't all. Ay gat dem fallars in steamship office to pay you all money coming to me every month vhile Ay'm avay.

ANNA—(*with a hard laugh*) Thanks. But I guess I won't be hard up for no small change.

CHRIS—(*hurt—humbly*) It ain't much, Ay know, but it's plenty for keep you so you never gat go back—

ANNA—(*shortly*) Shut up, will you? We'll talk about it later, see?

CHRIS—(*after a pause—ingratiatingly*) You like Ay go ashore look for dat Irish fallar, Anna?

ANNA—(*angrily*) Not much! Think I want to drag him back?

CHRIS—(*after a pause—uncomfortably*) Py golly, dat booze don't go vell. Give me fever, Ay tank. Ay feel hot like hell. (*He takes off his coat and lets it drop on the floor. There is a loud thud.*)

ANNA—(*with a start*) What you got in your pocket, for Pete's sake—a ton of lead? (*She reaches down, takes the coat and pulls out a revolver—looks from it to him in amazement.*) A gun? What were you doing with this?

CHRIS—(*sheepishly*) Ay forgat. Ain't nutting. Ain't loaded, anyway.

ANNA—(*breaking it open to make sure—then closing it again—looking at him suspiciously*) That ain't telling me why you got it?

CHRIS—(*sheepishly*) Ay'm ole fool. Ay gat it vhen Ay go ashore first. Ay tank den it's all fault of dat Irish fallar.

ANNA—(*with a shudder*) Say, you're crazier than I thought. I never dreamt you'd go that far.

CHRIS—(*quickly*) Ay don't. Ay gat better sense right avay. Ay don't never buy bullets even. It ain't his fault, Ay know.

ANNA—(*still suspicious of him*) Well, I'll take care of this for a while, loaded or not. (*She puts it in the drawer of table and closes the drawer.*)

CHRIS—(*placatingly*) Throw it overboard if you vant. Ay don't care. (*then after a pause*) Py golly, Ay tank Ay go lie down. Ay feel sick. (*Anna takes a magazine from the table. Chris hesitates by her chair.*) Ve talk again before Ay go, yes?

ANNA—(*dully*) Where's this ship going to?

CHRIS—Cape Town. Dat's in South Africa. She's British steamer called Londonderry. (*He stands hesitatingly—finally blurts out*) Anna—you forgive me sure?

ANNA—(*wearily*) Sure I do. You ain't to blame. You're yust—what you are—like me.

CHRIS—(*pleadingly*) Den—you lat me kiss you again once?

ANNA—(*raising her face—forcing a wan smile*) Sure. No hard feelings.

CHRIS—(*kisses her—brokenly*) Anna lilla! Ay— (*He fights for words to express himself, but finds none—miserably—with a sob*) Ay can't say it. Good-night, Anna.

ANNA—Good-night. (*He picks up the can of beer and goes slowly into the room on left, his shoulders bowed, his head sunk forward dejectedly. He closes the door after him. Anna turns over the pages of the magazine, trying desperately to banish her thoughts by looking at the pictures. This fails to distract her, and flinging the magazine back on the table, she springs to her feet and walks about the cabin distractedly, clenching and unclenching her hands. She speaks aloud to herself in a tense, trembling voice.*) Gawd, I can't stand this much longer! What am I waiting for anyway?—like a damn fool! (*She laughs helplessly, then checks herself abruptly, as she hears the sound of heavy footsteps on the deck outside. She appears to recognize these and her face lights up with joy. She gasps*) Mat! (*A strange terror seems suddenly to seize her. She rushes to the table, takes the revolver out of drawer and crouches down in the corner, left, behind the cupboard. A moment later the door is flung open and Mat Burke appears in the doorway. He is in bad shape—his clothes torn and dirty, covered with sawdust as if he had been grovelling or sleeping on barroom floors. There is a red bruise on his forehead over one of his eyes, another over one cheekbone, his knuckles are skinned and raw—plain evidence of the fighting he has been through on his "bat." His eyes are bloodshot and heavy-lidded, his face has a bloated look. But beyond these appearances—the results of heavy drinking—there is an expression in his eyes of wild mental turmoil, of impotent animal rage baffled by its own abject misery.*)

BURKE—(*peers blinkingly about the cabin—hoarsely*) Let you not be hiding from me, whoever's here—though 'tis well you know I'd have a right to come back and murder you. (*He stops to listen. Hearing no sound, he closes the door behind him and comes forward to the table. He throws himself into the rocking-chair—despondently*) There's no one here, I'm thinking, and 'tis a great fool I am to be coming. (*with a sort of dumb, uncomprehending anguish*) Yerra, Mat Burke, 'tis a great jackass you've become and what's got into you at all, at all? She's gone out of this long ago, I'm telling you, and you'll never see her face again. (*Anna stands up, hesitating, struggling between joy and fear. Burke's eyes fall on Anna's bag. He leans over to examine it.*) What's this? (*joyfully*) It's hers. She's not gone! But where is she? Ashore? (*darkly*) What would she be doing ashore on this rotten night? (*his face suddenly convulsed with grief and rage*) 'Tis that, is it? Oh, God's curse on her! (*raging*) I'll wait 'till she comes and choke her dirty life out. (*Anna starts, her face grows hard. She steps into the room, the revolver in her right hand by her side.*)

ANNA—(*in a cold, hard tone*) What are you doing here?

BURKE—(*wheeling about with a terrified gasp*) Glory be to God! (*They remain motionless and silent for a moment, holding each other's eyes.*)

ANNA—(*in the same hard voice*) Well, can't you talk?

BURKE—(*trying to fall into an easy, careless tone*) You've a year's growth scared out of me, coming at me so sudden and me thinking I was alone.

ANNA—You've got your nerve butting in here without knocking or nothing. What d'you want?

BURKE—(*airily*) Oh, nothing much. I was wanting to have a last word with you, that's all. (*He moves a step toward her.*)

ANNA—(*sharply—raising the revolver in her hand*) Careful now! Don't try getting too close. I heard what you said you'd do to me.

BURKE—(*noticing the revolver for the first time*) Is it murdering me you'd be now, God forgive you? (*then with a contemptuous laugh*) Or is it thinking I'd be frightened by that old tin whistle? (*He walks straight for her.*)

ANNA—(*wildly*) Look out, I tell you!

BURKE—(*who has come so close that the revolver is almost touching his chest*) Let you shoot, then! (*then with sudden wild grief*) Let you shoot, I'm saying, and be done with it! Let you end me with a shot and I'll be thanking you, for it's a rotten dog's life I've lived the past two days since I've known what you are, 'til I'm after wishing I was never born at all!

ANNA—(*overcome—letting the revolver drop to the floor, as if her fingers had no strength to hold it—hysterically*) What d'you want coming here? Why don't you beat it? Go on! (*She passes him and sinks down in the rocking-chair.*)

BURKE—(*following her—mournfully*) 'Tis right you'd be asking why did I come. (*then angrily*) 'Tis because 'tis a great weak fool of the world I am, and me tormented with the wickedness you'd told of yourself, and drinking oceans of booze that'd make me forget. Forget? Divil a word I'd forget, and your face grinning always in front of my eyes, awake or asleep, 'til I do be thinking a madhouse is the proper place for me.

ANNA—(*glancing at his hands and face—scornfully*) You look like you ought to be put away some place. Wonder you wasn't pulled in. You been scrapping, too, ain't you?

BURKE—I have—with every scut would take off his coat to me! (*fiercely*) And each time I'd be hitting one a clout in the mug, it wasn't his face I'd be seeing at all, but yours, and me wanting to drive you a blow would knock you out of this world where I wouldn't be seeing or thinking more of you.

ANNA—(*her lips trembling pitifully*) Thanks!

BURKE—(*walking up and down—distractedly*) That's right, make game of me! Oh, I'm a great coward surely, to be coming back to speak with you at all. You've a right to laugh at me.

ANNA—I ain't laughing at you, Mat.

BURKE—(*unheeding*) You to be what you are, and me to be Mat Burke, and me to be drove back to look at you again! 'Tis black shame is on me!

ANNA—(*resentfully*) Then get out. No one's holding you!

BURKE—(*bewilderedly*) And me to listen to that talk from a woman like you and be frightened to close her mouth with a slap! Oh, God help me, I'm a yellow coward for all men to spit at! (*then furiously*) But I'll not be getting out of this 'till I've had me word. (*raising his fist threateningly*) And let you look out how you'd drive me! (*letting his fist fall helplessly*) Don't be angry now! I'm raving like a real lunatic, I'm thinking, and the sorrow you put on me has my brains drownded in grief. (*suddenly bending down to her and grasping her arm intensely*) Tell me it's a lie, I'm saying! That's what I'm after coming to hear you say.

ANNA—(*dully*) A lie? What?

BURKE—(*with passionate entreaty*) All the badness you told me two days back. Sure it must be a lie! You was only making game of me, wasn't you? Tell me 'twas a lie, Anna, and I'll be saying prayers of thanks on my two knees to the Almighty God!

ANNA—(*terribly shaken—faintly*) I can't, Mat. (*as he turns away—imploringly*) Oh, Mat, won't you see that no matter what I was I ain't that any more? Why, listen! I packed up my bag this afternoon and went ashore. I'd been waiting here all alone for two days, thinking maybe you'd come back—thinking maybe you'd think over all I'd said—and maybe—oh, I don't know what I was hoping! But I was afraid to even go out of the cabin for a second, honest—afraid you might come and not find me here. Then I gave up hope when you didn't show up and I went to the railroad station. I was going to New York. I was going back—

BURKE—(*hoarsely*) God's curse on you!

ANNA—Listen, Mat! You hadn't come, and I'd gave up hope. But—in the station—I couldn't go. I'd bought my ticket and everything. (*She takes the ticket from her dress and tries to hold it before his eyes.*) But I got to thinking about you—and I couldn't take the train—I couldn't! So I come back here—to wait some more. Oh, Mat, don't you see I've changed? Can't you forgive what's dead and gone—and forget it?

BURKE—(*turning on her—overcome by rage again*) Forget, is it? I'll not forget 'til my dying day, I'm telling you, and me tormented with thoughts. (*in a frenzy*) Oh, I'm wishing I had wan of them fornest me this minute and I'd beat him with my fists 'till he'd be a bloody corpse! I'm wishing the whole lot of them will roast in hell 'til the Judgment Day—and yourself along with them, for you're as bad as they are.

ANNA—(*shuddering*) Mat! (*then after a pause—in a voice of dead, stony calm*) Well, you've had your say. Now you better beat it.

BURKE—(*starts slowly for the door—hesitates—then after a pause*) And what'll you be doing?

ANNA—What difference does it make to you?

BURKE—I'm asking you!

ANNA—(*in the same tone*) My bag's packed and I got my ticket. I'll go to New York to-morrow.

BURKE—(*helplessly*) You mean—you'll be doing the same again?

ANNA—(*stonily*) Yes.

BURKE—(*in anguish*) You'll not! Don't torment me with that talk! 'Tis a she-divil you are sent to drive me mad entirely!

ANNA—(*her voice breaking*) Oh, for Gawd's sake, Mat, leave me alone! Go away! Don't you see I'm licked? Why d'you want to keep on kicking me?

BURKE—(*indignantly*) And don't you deserve the worst I'd say, God forgive you?

ANNA—All right. Maybe I do. But don't rub it in. Why ain't you done what you said you was going to? Why ain't you got that ship was going to take you to the other side of the earth where you'd never see me again?

BURKE—I have.

ANNA—(*startled*) What—then you're going—honest?

BURKE—I signed on to-day at noon, drunk as I was—and she's sailing to-morrow.

ANNA—And where's she going to?

BURKE—Cape Town.

ANNA—(*the memory of having heard that name a little while before coming to her—with a start, confusedly*) Cape Town? Where's that. Far away?

BURKE—'Tis at the end of Africa. That's far for you.

ANNA—(*forcing a laugh*) You're keeping your word all right, ain't you? (*after a slight pause—curiously*) What's the boat's name?

BURKE—The Londonderry.

ANNA—(*It suddenly comes to her that this is the same ship her father is sailing on.*) The Londonderry! It's the same— Oh, this is too much! (*with wild, ironical laughter*) Ha-ha-ha!

BURKE—What's up with you now?

ANNA—Ha-ha-ha! It's funny, funny! I'll die laughing!

BURKE—(*irritated*) Laughing at what?

ANNA—It's a secret. You'll know soon enough. It's funny. (*controlling herself—after a pause—cynically*) What kind of a place is this Cape Town? Plenty of dames there, I suppose?

BURKE—To hell with them! That I may never see another woman to my dying hour!

ANNA—That's what you say now, but I'll bet by the time you get there you'll have forgot all about me and start in talking the same old bull you talked to me to the first one you meet.

BURKE—(*offended*) I'll not, then! God mend you, is it making me out to be the like of yourself you are, and you taking up with this one and that all the years of your life?

ANNA—(*angrily assertive*) Yes, that's yust what I do mean! You been doing the same thing all your life, picking up a new girl in every port. How're you any better than I was?

BURKE—(*thoroughly exasperated*) Is it no shame you have at all? I'm a fool to be wasting talk on you and you hardened in badness. I'll go out of this and lave you alone forever. (*He starts for the door—then stops to turn on her furiously.*) And I suppose 'tis the same lies you told them all before that you told to me?

ANNA—(*indignantly*) That's a lie! I never did!

BURKE—(*miserably*) You'd be saying that, anyway.

ANNA—(*forcibly, with growing intensity*) Are you trying to accuse me—of being in love—really in love—with them?

BURKE—I'm thinking you were, surely.

ANNA—(*furiously, as if this were the last insult—advancing on him threateningly*) You mutt, you! I've stood enough from you. Don't you dare. (*with scornful bitterness*) Love 'em! Oh, my Gawd! You damn thick-head! Love 'em? (*savagely*) I hated 'em, I tell you! Hated 'em, hated 'em, hated 'em! And may Gawd strike me dead this minute and my mother, too, if she was alive, if I ain't telling you the honest truth!

BURKE—(*immensely pleased by her vehemence—a light beginning to break over his face—but still uncertain, torn between doubt and the desire to believe—helplessly*) If I could only be believing you now!

ANNA—(*distractedly*) Oh, what's the use? What's the use of me talking? What's the use of anything? (*pleadingly*) Oh, Mat, you mustn't think that for a second! You mustn't! Think all the other bad about me you want to, and I won't kick, 'cause you've a right to. But don't think that! (*on the point of tears*) I couldn't bear it! It'd be yust too much to know you was going away where I'd never see you again—thinking that about me!

BURKE—(*after an inward struggle—tensely—forcing out the words with difficulty*) If I was believing—that you'd never had love for any other man in the world but me—I could be forgetting the rest, maybe.

ANNA—(*with a cry of joy*) Mat!

BURKE—(*slowly*) If 'tis truth you're after telling, I'd have a right, maybe, to believe you'd changed—and that I'd changed you myself 'til the thing you'd been all your life wouldn't be you any more at all.

ANNA—(*hanging on his words—breathlessly*) Oh, Mat! That's what I been trying to tell you all along!

BURKE—(*simply*) For I've a power of strength in me to lead men the way I want, and women, too, maybe, and I'm thinking I'd change you to a new woman entirely, so I'd never know, or you either, what kind of woman you'd been in the past at all.

ANNA—Yes, you could, Mat! I know you could!

BURKE—And I'm thinking 'twasn't your fault, maybe, but having that old ape for a father that left you to grow up alone, made you what you was. And if I could be believing 'tis only me you—

ANNA—(*distractedly*) You got to believe it, Mat! What can I do? I'll do anything, anything you want to prove I'm not lying!

BURKE—(*suddenly seems to have a solution. He feels in the pocket of his coat and grasps something—solemnly*) Would you be willing to swear an oath, now—a terrible, fearful oath would send your soul to the divils in hell if you was lying?

ANNA—(*eagerly*) Sure, I'll swear, Mat—on anything!

BURKE—(*takes a small, cheap old crucifix from his pocket and holds it up for her to see*) Will you swear on this?

ANNA—(*reaching out for it*) Yes. Sure I will. Give it to me.

BURKE—(*holding it away*) 'Tis a cross was given me by my mother, God rest her soul. (*He makes the sign of the cross mechanically.*) I was a lad only, and she told me to keep it by me if I'd be waking or sleeping and never lose it, and it'd bring me luck. She died soon after. But I'm after keeping it with me from that day to this, and I'm telling you there's great power in it, and 'tis great bad luck it's saved me from and me roaming the seas, and I having it tied round my neck when my last ship sunk, and it bringing me safe to land when the others went to their death. (*very earnestly*) And I'm warning you now, if you'd swear an oath on this, 'tis my old woman herself will be looking down from Hivin above, and praying Almighty God and the Saints to put a great curse on you if she'd hear you swearing a lie!

ANNA—(*awed by his manner—superstitiously*) I wouldn't have the nerve—honest—if it was a lie. But it's the truth and I ain't scared to swear. Give it to me.

BURKE—(*handing it to her—almost frightenedly, as if he feared for her safety*) Be careful what you'd swear, I'm saying.

ANNA—(*holding the cross gingerly*) Well—what do you want me to swear? You say it.

BURKE—Swear I'm the only man in the world ivir you felt love for.

ANNA—(*looking into his eyes steadily*) I swear it.

BURKE—And that you'll be forgetting from this day all the badness you've done and never do the like of it again.

ANNA—(*forcibly*) I swear it! I swear it by God!

BURKE—And may the blackest curse of God strike you if you're lying. Say it now!

ANNA—And may the blackest curse of God strike me if I'm lying!

BURKE—(*with a stupendous sigh*) Oh, glory be to God, I'm after believing you now! (*He takes the cross from her hand, his face beaming with joy, and puts it back in his pocket. He puts his arm about her waist and is about to kiss her when he stops, appalled by some terrible doubt.*)

ANNA—(*alarmed*) What's the matter with you?

BURKE—(*with sudden fierce questioning*) Is it Catholic ye are?

ANNA—(*confused*) No. Why?

BURKE—(*filled with a sort of bewildered foreboding*) Oh, God, help me! (*with a dark glance of suspicion at her*) There's some divil's trickery in it, to be swearing an oath on a Catholic cross and you wan of the others.

ANNA—(*distractedly*) Oh, Mat, don't you believe me?

BURKE—(*miserably*) If it isn't a Catholic you are—

ANNA—I ain't nothing. What's the difference? Didn't you hear me swear?

BURKE—(*passionately*) Oh, I'd a right to stay away from you—but I couldn't! I was loving you in spite of it all and wanting to be with you, God forgive me, no matter what you are. I'd go mad if I'd not have you! I'd be killing the world— (*He seizes her in his arms and kisses her fiercely.*)

ANNA—(*with a gasp of joy*) Mat!

BURKE—(*suddenly holding her away from him and staring into her eyes as if to probe into her soul—slowly*) If your oath is no proper oath at all, I'll have to be taking your naked word for it and have you anyway, I'm thinking— I'm needing you that bad!

ANNA—(*hurt—reproachfully*) Mat! I swore, didn't I?

BURKE—(*defiantly, as if challenging fate*) Oath or no oath, 'tis no matter. We'll be wedded in the morning, with the help of God. (*still more defiantly*) We'll be happy now, the two of us, in spite of the divil! (*He crushes her to him and kisses her again. The door on the left is pushed open and Chris appears in the doorway. He stands blinking at them. At first the old expression of hatred of Burke comes into his eyes instinctively. Then a look of resignation and relief takes its place. His face lights up with a sudden happy thought. He turns back into the bedroom—reappears immediately with the tin can of beer in his hand—grinning.*)

CHRIS—Ve have drink on this, py golly! (*They break away from each other with startled exclamations.*)

BURKE—(*explosively*) God stiffen it! (*He takes a step toward Chris threateningly.*)

ANNA—(*happily—to her father*) That's the way to talk! (*with a laugh*) And say, it's about time for you and Mat to kiss and make up. You're going to be shipmates on the Londonderry, did you know it?

BURKE—(*astounded*) Shipmates— Has himself—

CHRIS—(*equally astounded*) Ay vas bo'sun on her.

BURKE—The divil! (*then angrily*) You'd be going back to sea and leaving her alone, would you?

ANNA—(*quickly*) It's all right, Mat. That's where he belongs, and I want him to go. You got to go, too; we'll need the money. (*with a laugh, as she gets the glasses*) And as for me being alone, that runs in the family, and I'll get used to it. (*pouring out their glasses*) I'll get a little house somewhere and I'll make a regular place for you two to come back to,—wait and see. And now you drink up and be friends.

BURKE—(*happily—but still a bit resentful against the old man*) Sure! (*clinking his glass against Chris'*) Here's luck to you! (*He drinks.*)

CHRIS—(*subdued—his face melancholy*) Skoal. (*He drinks.*)

BURKE—(*to Anna, with a wink*) You'll not be lonesome long. I'll see to that, with the help of God. 'Tis himself here will be having a grandchild to ride on his foot, I'm telling you!

ANNA—(*turning away in embarrassment*) Quit the kidding, now. (*She picks up her bag and goes into the room on left. As soon as she is gone Burke relapses into an attitude of gloomy thought. Chris stares at his beer absent-mindedly. Finally Burke turns on him.*)

BURKE—Is it any religion at all you have, you and your Anna?

CHRIS—(*surprised*) Vhy yes. Ve vas Lutheran in ole country.

BURKE—(*horrified*) Luthers, is it? (*then with a grim resignation, slowly, aloud to himself*) Well, I'm damned then surely. Yerra, what's the difference? 'Tis the will of God, anyway.

CHRIS—(*moodily preoccupied with his own thoughts—speaks with somber premonition as Anna re-enters from the left*) It's funny. It's queer, yes—you and me shipping on same boat dat vay. It ain't right. Ay don't know—it's dat funny vay ole davil sea do her vorst dirty tricks, yes. It's so. (*He gets up and goes back and, opening the door, stares out into the darkness.*)

BURKE—(*nodding his head in gloomy acquiescence—with a great sigh*) I'm fearing maybe you have the right of it for once, divil take you.

ANNA—(*forcing a laugh*) Gee, Mat, you ain't agreeing with him, are you? (*She comes forward and puts her arm about his shoulder—with a determined gaiety*) Aw say, what's the matter? Cut out the gloom. We're all fixed now, ain't we, me and you? (*pours out more beer into his glass and fills one for herself— slaps him on the back*) Come on! Here's to the sea, no matter what! Be a game sport and drink to that! Come on! (*She gulps down her glass. Burke banishes his superstitious premonitions with a defiant jerk of his head, grins up at her, and drinks to her toast.*)

CHRIS—(*looking out into the night—lost in his somber preoccupation—shakes his head and mutters*) Fog, fog, fog, all bloody time. You can't see vhere you vas going, no. Only dat ole davil, sea—she knows! (*The two stare at him. From the harbor comes the muffled, mournful wail of steamers' whistles.*)

(*The Curtain Falls*)

THE EMPEROR JONES

CHARACTERS

BRUTUS JONES, *Emperor*

HENRY SMITHERS, *a Cockney trader*

AN OLD NATIVE WOMAN

LEM, *a Native Chief*

SOLDIERS, *Adherents of Lem*

The Little Formless Fears; Jeff; The Negro Convicts; The Prison Guard; The Planters; The Auctioneer; The Slaves; The Congo Witch-Doctor; The Crocodile God

The action of the play takes place on an island in the West Indies as yet not self-determined by White Marines. The form of native government is, for the time being, an Empire.

SCENES

SCENE I: In the palace of the Emperor Jones. Afternoon.

SCENE II: The edge of the Great Forest. Dusk.

SCENE III: In the Forest. Night.

SCENE IV: In the Forest. Night.

SCENE V: In the Forest. Night.

SCENE VI: In the Forest. Night.

SCENE VII: In the Forest. Night.

SCENE VIII: Same as Scene Two—the edge of the Great Forest. Dawn.

The Emperor Jones

SCENE ONE

The audience chamber in the palace of the Emperor—a spacious, high-ceilinged room with bare, white-washed walls. The floor is of white tiles. In the rear, to the left of center, a wide archway giving out on a portico with white pillars. The palace is evidently situated on high ground for beyond the portico nothing can be seen but a vista of distant hills, their summits crowned with thick groves of palm trees. In the right wall, center, a smaller arched doorway leading to the living quarters of the palace. The room is bare of furniture with the exception of one huge chair made of uncut wood which stands at center, its back to rear. This is very apparently the Emperor's throne. It is painted a dazzling, eye-smiting scarlet. There is a brilliant orange cushion on the seat and another smaller one is placed on the floor to serve as a footstool. Strips of matting, dyed scarlet, lead from the foot of the throne to the two entrances.

It is late afternoon but the sunlight still blazes yellowly beyond the portico and there is an oppressive burden of exhausting heat in the air.

As the curtain rises, a native negro woman sneaks in cautiously from the entrance on the right. She is very old, dressed in cheap calico, bare-footed, a red bandana handkerchief covering all but a few stray wisps of white hair. A bundle bound in colored cloth is carried over her shoulder on the end of a stick. She hesitates beside the doorway, peering back as if in extreme dread of being discovered. Then she begins to glide noiselessly, a step at a time, toward the doorway in the rear. At this moment, Smithers appears beneath the portico.

Smithers is a tall, stoop-shouldered man about forty. His bald head, perched on a long neck with an enormous Adam's apple, looks like an egg. The tropics have tanned his naturally pasty face with its small, sharp features to a sickly yellow, and native rum has painted his pointed nose to a startling red. His little, washy-blue eyes are red-rimmed and dart about him like a ferret's. His expression is one of unscrupulous meanness, cowardly and dangerous. He is dressed in a worn riding suit of dirty white drill, puttees, spurs, and wears a white cork helmet. A cartridge belt

*with an automatic revolver is around his waist. He carries a rid-
ing whip in his hand. He sees the woman and stops to watch her
suspiciously. Then, making up his mind, he steps quickly on tiptoe
into the room. The woman, looking back over her shoulder continually, does not see him until it is too late. When she does Smithers
springs forward and grabs her firmly by the shoulder. She struggles
to get away, fiercely but silently.*

SMITHERS—(*tightening his grasp—roughly*) Easy! None o'
that, me birdie. You can't wriggle out, now I got me 'ooks
on yer.

WOMAN—(*seeing the uselessness of struggling, gives way to
frantic terror, and sinks to the ground, embracing his knees supplicatingly*) No tell him! No tell him, Mister!

SMITHERS—(*with great curiosity*) Tell 'im? (*then scornfully*)
Oh, you mean 'is bloomin' Majesty. What's the gaime, any-
'ow? What are you sneakin' away for? Been stealin' a bit,
I s'pose. (*He taps her bundle with his riding whip significantly.*)

WOMAN—(*shaking her head vehemently*) No, me no steal.

SMITHERS—Bloody liar! But tell me what's up. There's
somethin' funny goin' on. I smelled it in the air first thing I
got up this mornin'. You blacks are up to some devilment.
This palace of 'is is like a bleedin' tomb. Where's all the
'ands? (*The woman keeps sullenly silent. Smithers raises his whip
threateningly.*) Ow, yer won't, won't yer? I'll show yer what's
what.

WOMAN—(*coweringly*) I tell, Mister. You no hit. They
go—all go. (*She makes a sweeping gesture toward the hills in the
distance.*)

SMITHERS—Run away—to the 'ills?

WOMAN—Yes, Mister. Him Emperor—Great Father. (*She
touches her forehead to the floor with a quick mechanical jerk.*)
Him sleep after eat. Then they go—all go. Me old woman.
Me left only. Now me go too.

SMITHERS—(*his astonishment giving way to an immense,
mean satisfaction*) Ow! So that's the ticket! Well, I know
bloody well wot's in the air—when they runs orf to the 'ills.
The tom-tom 'll be thumping out there bloomin' soon. (*with
extreme vindictiveness*) And I'm bloody glad of it, for one!

Serve 'im right! Puttin' on airs, the stinkin' nigger! 'Is Majesty! Gawd blimey! I only 'opes I'm there when they takes 'im out to shoot 'im. (*suddenly*) 'E's still 'ere all right, ain't 'e?

WOMAN—Him sleep.

SMITHERS—'E's bound to find out soon as 'e wakes up. 'E's cunnin' enough to know when 'is time's come. (*He goes to the doorway on right and whistles shrilly with his fingers in his mouth. The old woman springs to her feet and runs out of the doorway, rear. Smithers goes after her, reaching for his revolver.*) Stop or I'll shoot! (*then stopping—indifferently*) Pop orf then, if yer like, yer black cow. (*He stands in the doorway, looking after her.*)

(*Jones enters from the right. He is a tall, powerfully-built, full-blooded negro of middle age. His features are typically negroid, yet there is something decidedly distinctive about his face—an underlying strength of will, a hardy, self-reliant confidence in himself that inspires respect. His eyes are alive with a keen, cunning intelligence. In manner he is shrewd, suspicious, evasive. He wears a light blue uniform coat, sprayed with brass buttons, heavy gold chevrons on his shoulders, gold braid on the collar, cuffs, etc. His pants are bright red with a light blue stripe down the side. Patent leather laced boots with brass spurs, and a belt with a long-barreled, pearl-handled revolver in a holster complete his make up. Yet there is something not altogether ridiculous about his grandeur. He has a way of carrying it off.*)

JONES—(*not seeing anyone—greatly irritated and blinking sleepily—shouts*) Who dare whistle dat way in my palace? Who dare wake up de Emperor? I'll git de hide frayled off some o' you niggers sho'!

SMITHERS—(*showing himself—in a manner half-afraid and half-defiant*) It was me whistled to yer. (*as Jones frowns angrily*) I got news for yer.

JONES—(*putting on his suavest manner, which fails to cover up his contempt for the white man*) Oh, it's you, Mister Smithers. (*He sits down on his throne with easy dignity.*) What news you got to tell me?

SMITHERS—(*coming close to enjoy his discomfiture*) Don't yer notice nothin' funny today?

JONES—(*coldly*) Funny? No. I ain't perceived nothin' of de kind!

SMITHERS—Then yer ain't so foxy as I thought yer was. Where's all your court? (*sarcastically*) the Generals and the Cabinet Ministers and all?

JONES—(*imperturbably*) Where dey mostly runs to minute I closes my eyes—drinkin' rum and talkin' big down in de town. (*sarcastically*) How come you don't know dat? Ain't you sousin' with 'em most every day?

SMITHERS—(*stung but pretending indifference—with a wink*) That's part of the day's work. I got ter—ain't I—in my business?

JONES—(*contemptuously*) Yo' business!

SMITHERS—(*imprudently enraged*) Gawd blimey, you was glad enough for me ter take yer in on it when you landed here first. You didn' 'ave no 'igh and mighty airs in them days!

JONES—(*his hand going to his revolver like a flash—menacingly*) Talk polite, white man! Talk polite, you heah me! I'm boss heah now, is you fergettin'? (*The Cockney seems about to challenge this last statement with the facts but something in the other's eyes holds and cows him.*)

SMITHERS—(*in a cowardly whine*) No 'arm meant, old top.

JONES—(*condescendingly*) I accepts yo' apology. (*lets his hand fall from his revolver*) No use'n you rakin' up ole times. What I was den is one thing. What I is now 's another. You didn't let me in on yo' crooked work out o' no kind feelin's dat time. I done de dirty work fo' you—and most o' de brain work, too, fo' dat matter—and I was wu'th money to you, dat's de reason.

SMITHERS—Well, blimey, I give yer a start, didn't I?—when no one else would. I wasn't afraid to 'ire you like the rest was—'count of the story about your breakin' jail back in the States.

JONES—No, you didn't have no s'cuse to look down on me fo' dat. You been in jail you'self more'n once.

SMITHERS—(*furiously*) It's a lie! (*then trying to pass it off by an attempt at scorn*) Garn! Who told yer that fairy tale?

JONES—Dey's some tings I ain't got to be tole. I kin see 'em in folk's eyes. (*then after a pause—meditatively*) Yes, you sho' give me a start. And it didn't take long from dat time to git dese fool, woods' niggers right where I wanted dem. (*with pride*) From stowaway to Emperor in two years! Dat's goin' some!

SMITHERS—(*with curiosity*) And I bet you got yer pile o' money 'id safe some place.

JONES—(*with satisfaction*) I sho' has! And it's in a foreign bank where no pusson don't ever git it out but me no matter what come. You didn't s'pose I was holdin' down dis Emperor job for de glory in it, did you? Sho'! De fuss and glory part of it, dat's only to turn de heads o' de low-flung, bush niggers dat's here. Dey wants de big circus show for deir money. I gives it to 'em an' I gits de money. (*with a grin*) De long green, dat's me every time! (*then rebukingly*) But you ain't got no kick agin me, Smithers. I'se paid you back all you done for me many times. Ain't I pertected you and winked at all de crooked tradin' you been doin' right out in de broad day? Sho' I has—and me makin' laws to stop it at de same time! (*He chuckles.*)

SMITHERS—(*grinning*) But, meanin' no 'arm, you been grabbin' right and left yourself, ain't yer? Look at the taxes you've put on 'em! Blimey! You've squeezed 'em dry!

JONES—(*chuckling*) No, dey ain't *all* dry yet. I'se still heah, ain't I?

SMITHERS—(*smiling at his secret thought*) They're dry right now, you'll find out. (*changing the subject abruptly*) And as for me breakin' laws, you've broke 'em all yerself just as fast as yer made 'em.

JONES—Ain't I de Emperor? De laws don't go for him. (*judicially*) You heah what I tells you, Smithers. Dere's little stealin' like you does, and dere's big stealin' like I does. For de little stealin' dey gits you in jail soon or late. For de big stealin' dey makes you Emperor and puts you in de Hall o' Fame when you croaks. (*reminiscently*) If dey's one thing I learns in ten years on de Pullman ca's listenin' to de white quality talk, it's dat same fact. And when I gits a chance to use it I winds up Emperor in two years.

SMITHERS—(*unable to repress the genuine admiration of the small fry for the large*) Yes, yer turned the bleedin' trick, all right. Blimey, I never seen a bloke 'as 'ad the bloomin' luck you 'as.

JONES—(*severely*) Luck? What you mean—luck?

SMITHERS—I suppose you'll say as that swank about the silver bullet ain't luck—and that was what first got the fool blacks on yer side the time of the revolution, wasn't it?

JONES—(*with a laugh*) Oh, dat silver bullet! Sho' was luck! But I makes dat luck, you heah? I loads de dice! Yessuh! When dat murderin' nigger ole Lem hired to kill me takes aim ten feet away and his gun misses fire and I shoots him dead, what you heah me say?

SMITHERS—You said yer'd got a charm so's no lead bullet'd kill yer. You was so strong only a silver bullet could kill yer, you told 'em. Blimey, wasn't that swank for yer—and plain, fat-'eaded luck?

JONES—(*proudly*) I got brains and I uses 'em quick. Dat ain't luck.

SMITHERS—Yer know they wasn't 'ardly liable to get no silver bullets. And it was luck 'e didn't 'it you that time.

JONES—(*laughing*) And dere all dem fool bush niggers was kneelin' down and bumpin' deir heads on de ground like I was a miracle out o' de Bible. Oh Lawd, from dat time on I has dem all eatin' out of my hand. I cracks de whip and dey jumps through.

SMITHERS—(*with a sniff*) Yankee bluff done it.

JONES—Ain't a man's talkin' big what makes him big— long as he makes folks believe it? Sho', I talks large when I ain't got nothin' to back it up, but I ain't talkin' wild just de same. I knows I kin fool 'em—I *knows* it—and dat's backin' enough fo' my game. And ain't I got to learn deir lingo and teach some of dem English befo' I kin talk to 'em? Ain't dat wuk? You ain't never learned ary word er it, Smithers, in de ten years you been heah, dough you knows it's money in you' pocket tradin' wid 'em if you does. But you'se too shiftless to take de trouble.

SMITHERS—(*flushing*) Never mind about me. What's this I've 'eard about yer really 'avin' a silver bullet moulded for yourself?

JONES—It's playin' out my bluff. I has de silver bullet moulded and I tells 'em when de time comes I kills myself wid it. I tells 'em dat's 'cause I'm de on'y man in de world big enuff to git me. No use'n deir tryin'. And dey falls down and bumps deir heads. (*He laughs.*) I does dat so's I kin take a walk in peace widout no jealous nigger gunnin' at me from behind de trees.

SMITHERS—(*astonished*) Then you 'ad it made—'onest?

JONES—Sho' did. Heah she be. (*He takes out his revolver, breaks it, and takes the silver bullet out of one chamber.*) Five lead an' dis silver baby at de last. Don't she shine pretty? (*He holds it in his hand, looking at it admiringly, as if strangely fascinated.*)

SMITHERS—Let me see. (*reaches out his hand for it*)

JONES—(*harshly*) Keep yo' hands whar dey b'long, white man. (*He replaces it in the chamber and puts the revolver back on his hip.*)

SMITHERS—(*snarling*) Gawd blimey! Think I'm a bleedin' thief, you would.

JONES—No, 'tain't dat. I knows you'se scared to steal from me. On'y I ain't 'lowin' nary body to touch dis baby. She's my rabbit's foot.

SMITHERS—(*sneering*) A bloomin' charm, wot? (*venomously*) Well, you'll need all the bloody charms you 'as before long, s' 'elp me!

JONES—(*judicially*) Oh, I'se good for six months yit 'fore dey gits sick o' my game. Den, when I sees trouble comin', I makes my getaway.

SMITHERS—Ho! You got it all planned, ain't yer?

JONES—I ain't no fool. I knows dis Emperor's time is sho't. Dat why I make hay when de sun shine. Was you thinkin' I'se aimin' to hold down dis job for life? No, suh! What good is gittin' money if you stays back in dis raggedy country? I wants action when I spends. And when I sees dese niggers gittin' up deir nerve to tu'n me out, and I'se got all de money in sight, I resigns on de spot and beats it quick.

SMITHERS—Where to?

JONES—None o' yo' business.

SMITHERS—Not back to the bloody States, I'll lay my oath.

JONES—(*suspiciously*) Why don't I? (*then with an easy laugh*) You mean 'count of dat story 'bout me breakin' from jail back dere? Dat's all talk.

SMITHERS—(*skeptically*) Ho, yes!

JONES—(*sharply*) You ain't 'sinuatin' I'se a liar, is you?

SMITHERS—(*hastily*) No, Gawd strike me! I was only thinkin' o' the bloody lies you told the blacks 'ere about killin' white men in the States.

JONES—(*angered*) How come dey're lies?

SMITHERS—You'd 'ave been in jail if you 'ad, wouldn't yer then? (*with venom*) And from what I've 'eard, it ain't 'ealthy for a black to kill a white man in the States. They burns 'em in oil, don't they?

JONES—(*with cool deadliness*) You mean lynchin' 'd scare me? Well, I tells you, Smithers, maybe I does kill one white man back dere. Maybe I does. And maybe I kills another right heah 'fore long if he don't look out.

SMITHERS—(*trying to force a laugh*) I was on'y spoofin' yer. Can't yer take a joke? And you was just sayin' you'd never been in jail.

JONES—(*in the same tone—slightly boastful*) Maybe I goes to jail dere for gettin' in an argument wid razors ovah a crap game. Maybe I gits twenty years when dat colored man die. Maybe I gits in 'nother argument wid de prison guard was overseer ovah us when we're wukin' de road. Maybe he hits me wid a whip and I splits his head wid a shovel and runs away and files de chain off my leg and gits away safe. Maybe I does all dat an' maybe I don't. It's a story I tells you so's you knows I'se de kind of man dat if you evah repeats one word of it, I ends yo' stealin' on dis yearth mighty damn quick!

SMITHERS—(*terrified*) Think I'd peach on yer? Not me! Ain't I always been yer friend?

JONES—(*suddenly relaxing*) Sho' you has—and you better be.

SMITHERS—(*recovering his composure—and with it his malice*) And just to show yer I'm yer friend, I'll tell yer that bit o' news I was goin' to.

JONES—Go ahead! Shoot de piece. Must be bad news from de happy way you look.

SMITHERS—(*warningly*) Maybe it's gettin' time for you to resign—with that bloomin' silver bullet, wot? (*He finishes with a mocking grin.*)

JONES—(*puzzled*) What's dat you say? Talk plain.

SMITHERS—Ain't noticed any of the guards or servants about the place today, I 'aven't.

JONES—(*carelessly*) Dey're all out in de garden sleepin' under de trees. When I sleeps, dey sneaks a sleep, too, and I pretends I never suspicions it. All I got to do is to ring de bell and dey come flyin', makin' a bluff dey was wukin' all de time.

SMITHERS—(*in the same mocking tone*) Ring the bell now an' you'll bloody well see what I means.

JONES—(*startled to alertness, but preserving the same careless tone*) Sho' I rings. (*He reaches below the throne and pulls out a big, common dinner bell which is painted the same vivid scarlet as the throne. He rings this vigorously—then stops to listen. Then he goes to both doors, rings again, and looks out.*)

SMITHERS—(*watching him with malicious satisfaction, after a pause—mockingly*) The bloody ship is sinkin' an' the bleedin' rats 'as slung their 'ooks.

JONES—(*in a sudden fit of anger flings the bell clattering into a corner*) Low-flung, woods' niggers! (*Then catching Smithers' eye on him, he controls himself and suddenly bursts into a low chuckling laugh.*) Reckon I overplays my hand dis once! A man can't take de pot on a bob-tailed flush all de time. Was I sayin' I'd sit in six months mo'? Well, I'se changed my mind den. I cashes in and resigns de job of Emperor right dis minute.

SMITHERS—(*with real admiration*) Blimey, but you're a cool bird, and no mistake.

JONES—No use'n fussin'. When I knows de game's up I kisses it good-by widout no long waits. Dey've all run off to de hills, ain't dey?

SMITHERS—Yes—every bleedin' man jack of 'em.

JONES—Den de revolution is at de post. And de Emperor better git his feet smokin' up de trail. (*He starts for the door in rear.*)

SMITHERS—Goin' out to look for your 'orse? Yer won't find any. They steals the 'orses first thing. Mine was gone when I went for 'im this mornin'. That's wot first give me a suspicion of wot was up.

JONES—(*alarmed for a second, scratches his head, then philosophically*) Well, den I hoofs it. Feet, do yo' duty! (*He pulls out a gold watch and looks at it.*) Three-thuty. Sundown's at six-thuty or dereabouts. (*puts his watch back —with cool confidence*) I got plenty o' time to make it easy.

SMITHERS—Don't be so bloomin' sure of it. They'll be after you 'ot and 'eavy. Ole Lem is at the bottom o' this business an' 'e 'ates you like 'ell. 'E'd rather do for you than eat 'is dinner, 'e would!

JONES—(*scornfully*) Dat fool no-count nigger! Does you think I'se scared o' him? I stands him on his thick head more'n once befo' dis, and I does it again if he comes in my way— (*fiercely*) And dis time I leave him a dead nigger fo' sho'!

SMITHERS—You'll 'ave to cut through the big forest—an' these blacks 'ere can sniff and follow a trail in the dark like 'ounds. You'd 'ave to 'ustle to get through that forest in twelve hours even if you knew all the bloomin' trails like a native.

JONES—(*with indignant scorn*) Look-a-heah, white man! Does you think I'se a natural bo'n fool? Give me credit fo' havin' some sense, fo' Lawd's sake! Don't you s'pose I'se looked ahead and made sho' of all de chances? I'se gone out in dat big forest, pretendin' to hunt, so many times dat I knows it high an' low like a book. I could go through on dem trails wid my eyes shut. (*with great contempt*) Think dese ign'rent bush niggers dat ain't got brains enuff to know deir own names even can catch Brutus Jones? Huh, I s'pects not! Not on yo' life! Why, man, de white men went after me wid bloodhounds where I come from an' I jes' laughs at 'em. It's a shame to fool dese black trash around heah, dey're so easy. You watch me, man. I'll make dem look sick, I will. I'll be 'cross de plain to de edge of de forest by time dark comes. Once in de woods in de night, dey got a swell chance o' findin' dis baby! Dawn tomorrow I'll be out at de oder side and on de coast whar dat French gunboat is stayin'. She picks me up, takes me to Martinique when she go dar, and dere I is safe wid a mighty big bankroll in my jeans. It's easy as rollin' off a log.

SMITHERS—(*maliciously*) But s'posin' somethin' 'appens wrong 'an they do nab yer?

JONES—(*decisively*) Dey don't—dat's de answer.

SMITHERS—But, just for argyment's sake—what'd you do?

JONES—(*frowning*) I'se got five lead bullets in dis gun good enuff fo' common bush niggers—and after dat I got de silver bullet left to cheat 'em out o' gittin' me.

SMITHERS—(*jeeringly*) Ho, I was fergettin' that silver bullet. You'll bump yourself orf in style, won't yer? Blimey!

JONES—(*gloomily*) You kin bet yo' whole roll on one thing, white man. Dis baby plays out his string to de end and when he quits, he quits wid a bang de way he ought. Silver bullet ain't none too good for him when he go, dat's a fac'! (*then shaking off his nervousness—with a confident laugh*) Sho'! What is I talkin' about? Ain't come to dat yit and I never will—not wid trash niggers like dese yere. (*boastfully*) Silver bullet bring me luck anyway. I kin outguess, outrun, outfight, an' outplay de whole lot o' dem all ovah de board any time o' de day er night! You watch me! (*From the distant hills comes the faint, steady thump of a tom-tom, low and vibrating. It starts at a rate exactly corresponding to normal pulse beat—72 to the minute—and continues at a gradually accelerating rate from this point uninterruptedly to the very end of the play. Jones starts at the sound. A strange look of apprehension creeps into his face for a moment as he listens. Then he asks, with an attempt to regain his most casual manner*) What's dat drum beatin' fo'?

SMITHERS—(*with a mean grin*) For you. That means the bleedin' ceremony 'as started. I've 'eard it before and I knows.

JONES—Cer'mony? What cer'mony?

SMITHERS—The blacks is 'oldin' a bloody meetin', 'avin' a war dance, gettin' their courage worked up b'fore they starts after you.

JONES—Let dem! Dey'll sho' need it!

SMITHERS—And they're there 'oldin' their 'eathen religious service—makin' no end of devil spells and charms to 'elp 'em against your silver bullet. (*He guffaws loudly.*) Blimey, but they're balmy as 'ell!

JONES—(*a tiny bit awed and shaken in spite of himself*) Huh! Takes more'n dat to scare dis chicken!

SMITHERS—(*scenting the other's feeling—maliciously*) Ternight when it's pitch black in the forest, they'll 'ave their pet devils and ghosts 'oundin' after you. You'll find yer bloody 'air 'll be standin' on end before termorrow mornin'. (*seri-ously*) It's a bleedin' queer place, that stinkin' forest, even in daylight. Yer don't know what might 'appen in there, it's that rotten still. Always sends the cold shivers down my back min-ute I gets in it.

JONES—(*with a contemptuous sniff*) I ain't no chicken-liver like you is. Trees an' me, we'se friends, and dar's a full moon comin' bring me light. And let dem po' niggers make all de fool spells dey'se a min' to. Does yo' s'pect I'se silly enuff to b'lieve in ghosts an' ha'nts an' all dat ole woman's talk? G'long, white man! You ain't talkin' to me. (*with a chuckle*) Doesn't you know dey's got to do wid a man was member in good standin' o' de Baptist Church? Sho' I was dat when I was porter on de Pullmans, befo' I gits into my little trouble. Let dem try deir heathen tricks. De Baptist Church done per-tect me and land dem all in hell. (*then with more confident satisfaction*) And I'se got little silver bullet o' my own, don't forgit!

SMITHERS—Ho! You 'aven't give much 'eed to your Bap-tist Church since you been down 'ere. I've 'eard myself you 'ad turned yer coat an' was takin' up with their blarsted witch-doctors, or whatever the 'ell yer calls the swine.

JONES—(*vehemently*) I pretends to! Sho' I pretends! Dat's part o' my game from de fust. If I finds out dem niggers believes dat black is white, den I yells it out louder 'n deir loudest. It don't git me nothin' to do missionary work for de Baptist Church. I'se after de coin, an' I lays my Jesus on de shelf for de time bein'. (*stops abruptly to look at his watch—alertly*) But I ain't got de time to waste on no more fool talk wid you. I'se gwine away from heah dis secon'. (*He reaches in under the throne and pulls out an expensive Panama hat with a bright multi-colored band and sets it jauntily on his head.*) So long, white man! (*with a grin*) See you in jail sometime, maybe!

SMITHERS—Not me, you won't. Well, I wouldn't be in yer bloody boots for no bloomin' money, but 'ere's wishin' yer luck just the same.

JONES—(*contemptuously*) You're de frightenedest man evah I see! I tells you I'se safe's 'f I was in New York City. It takes dem niggers from now to dark to git up de nerve to start somethin'. By dat time, I'se got a head start dey never kotch up wid.

SMITHERS—(*maliciously*) Give my regards to any ghosts yer meets up with.

JONES—(*grinning*) If dat ghost got money, I'll tell him never ha'nt you less'n he wants to lose it.

SMITHERS—(*flattered*) Garn! (*then curiously*) Ain't yer takin' no luggage with yer?

JONES—I travels light when I wants to move fast. And I got tinned grub buried on de edge o' de forest. (*boastfully*) Now say dat I don't look ahead an' use my brains! (*with a wide, liberal gesture*) I will all dat's left in de palace to you— and you better grab all you kin sneak away wid befo' dey gits here.

SMITHERS—(*gratefully*) Righto—and thanks ter yer. (*as Jones walks toward the door in rear—cautioningly*) Say! Look 'ere, you ain't goin' out that way, are yer?

JONES—Does you think I'd slink out de back door like a common nigger? I'se Emperor yit, ain't I? And de Emperor Jones leaves de way he comes, and dat black trash don't dare stop him—not yit, leastways. (*He stops for a moment in the doorway, listening to the far-off but insistent beat of the tom-tom.*) Listen to dat roll-call, will you? Must be mighty big drum carry dat far. (*then with a laugh*) Well, if dey ain't no whole brass band to see me off, I sho' got de drum part of it. So long, white man. (*He puts his hands in his pockets and with studied carelessness, whistling a tune, he saunters out of the doorway and off to the left.*)

SMITHERS—(*looks after him with a puzzled admiration*) 'E's got 'is bloomin' nerve with 'im, s'elp me! (*then angrily*) Ho— the bleedin' nigger—puttin' on 'is bloody airs! I 'opes they nabs 'im an' gives 'im what's what!

(*Curtain*)

SCENE TWO

The end of the plain where the Great Forest begins. The fore-ground is sandy, level ground dotted by a few stones and clumps of stunted bushes cowering close against the earth to escape the buf-feting of the trade wind. In the rear the forest is a wall of darkness dividing the world. Only when the eye becomes accustomed to the gloom can the outlines of separate trunks of the nearest trees be made out, enormous pillars of deeper blackness. A somber monotone of wind lost in the leaves moans in the air. Yet this sound serves but to intensify the impression of the forest's relentless immobility, to form a background throwing into relief its brooding, implacable silence.

Jones enters from the left, walking rapidly. He stops as he nears the edge of the forest, looks around him quickly, peering into the dark as if searching for some familiar landmark. Then, apparently satisfied that he is where he ought to be, he throws himself on the ground, dog-tired.

Well, heah I is. In de nick o' time, too! Little mo' an' it'd be blacker'n de ace of spades heahabouts. (*He pulls a bandana handkerchief from his hip pocket and mops off his perspiring face.*) Sho'! Gimme air! I'se tuckered out sho' 'nuff. Dat soft Em-peror job ain't no trainin' fo' a long hike ovah dat plain in de brilin' sun. (*then with a chuckle*) Cheer up, nigger, de worst is yet to come. (*He lifts his head and stares at the forest. His chuckle peters out abruptly. In a tone of awe*) My goodness, look at dem woods, will you? Dat no-count Smithers said dey'd be black an' he sho' called de turn. (*Turning away from them quickly and looking down at his feet, he snatches at a chance to change the subject—solicitously*) Feet, you is holdin' up yo' end fine an' I sutinly hopes you ain't blisterin' none. It's time you git a rest. (*He takes off his shoes, his eyes studiously avoiding the forest. He feels of the soles of his feet gingerly.*) You is still in de pink—on'y a little mite feverish. Cool yo'selfs. Remember you done got a long journey yit befo' you. (*He sits in a weary attitude, listening to the rhythmic beating of the tom-tom. He grumbles in a loud tone to cover up a growing uneasiness*) Bush niggers! Wonder dey wouldn't git sick o' beatin' dat drum. Sound louder, seem like. I wonder if dey's startin' after me?

(*He scrambles to his feet, looking back across the plain.*) Couldn't see dem now, nohow, if dey was hundred feet away. (*then shaking himself like a wet dog to get rid of these depressing thoughts*) Sho', dey's miles an' miles behind. What you gittin' fidgety about? (*But he sits down and begins to lace up his shoes in great haste, all the time muttering reassuringly.*) You know what? Yo' belly is empty, dat's what's de matter wid you. Come time to eat! Wid nothin' but wind on yo' stumach, o' course you feels jiggedy. Well, we eats right heah an' now soon's I gits dese pesky shoes laced up. (*He finishes lacing up his shoes.*) Dere! Now le's see! (*gets on his hands and knees and searches the ground around him with his eyes*) White stone, white stone, where is you? (*He sees the first white stone and crawls to it—with satisfaction*) Heah you is! I knowed dis was de right place. Box of grub, come to me. (*He turns over the stone and feels in under it—in a tone of dismay*) Ain't heah! Gorry, is I in de right place or isn't I? Dere's 'nother stone. Guess dat's it. (*He scrambles to the next stone and turns it over.*) Ain't heah, neither! Grub, whar is you? Ain't heah. Gorry, has I got to go hungry into dem woods—all de night? (*While he is talking he scrambles from one stone to another, turning them over in frantic haste. Finally, he jumps to his feet excitedly.*) Is I lost de place? Must have! But how dat happen when I was followin' de trail across de plain in broad daylight? (*almost plaintively*) I'se hungry, I is! I gotta git my feed. Whar's my strength gonna come from if I doesn't? Gorry, I gotta find dat grub high an' low somehow! Why it come dark so quick like dat? Can't see nothin'. (*He scratches a match on his trousers and peers about him. The rate of the beat of the far-off tom-tom increases perceptibly as he does so. He mutters in a bewildered voice*) How come all dese white stones come heah when I only remembers one? (*Suddenly, with a frightened gasp, he flings the match on the ground and stamps on it.*) Nigger, is you gone crazy mad? Is you lightin' matches to show dem whar you is? Fo' Lawd's sake, use yo' haid. Gorry, I'se got to be careful! (*He stares at the plain behind him apprehensively, his hand on his revolver.*) But how come all dese white stones? And whar's dat tin box o' grub I hid all wrapped up in oilcloth?

(*While his back is turned, the Little Formless Fears creep out from the deeper blackness of the forest. They are black, shapeless, only their glittering little eyes can be seen. If they have any describable form at all it is that of a grubworm about the size of a creeping child. They move noiselessly, but with deliberate, painful effort, striving to raise themselves on end, failing and sinking prone again. Jones turns about to face the forest. He stares up at the tops of the trees, seeking vainly to discover his whereabouts by their conformation.*)

Can't tell nothin' from dem trees! Gorry, nothin' 'round heah looks like I evah seed it befo'. I'se done lost de place sho' 'nuff! (*with mournful foreboding*) It's mighty queer! It's mighty queer! (*with sudden forced defiance—in an angry tone*) Woods, is you tryin' to put somethin' ovah on me?

(*From the formless creatures on the ground in front of him comes a tiny gale of low mocking laughter like a rustling of leaves. They squirm upward toward him in twisted attitudes. Jones looks down, leaps backward with a yell of terror, yanking out his revolver as he does so—in a quavering voice*) What's dat? Who's dar? What is you? Git away from me befo' I shoots you up! You don't?—

(*He fires. There is a flash, a loud report, then silence broken only by the far-off, quickened throb of the tom-tom. The formless creatures have scurried back into the forest. Jones remains fixed in his position, listening intently. The sound of the shot, the reassuring feel of the revolver in his hand, have somewhat restored his shaken nerve. He addresses himself with renewed confidence.*)

Dey're gone. Dat shot fix 'em. Dey was only little animals—little wild pigs, I reckon. Dey've maybe rooted out yo' grub an' eat it. Sho', you fool nigger, what you think dey is— ha'nts? (*excitedly*) Gorry, you give de game away when you fire dat shot. Dem niggers heah dat fo' su'tin! Time you beat it in de woods widout no long waits. (*He starts for the forest— hesitates before the plunge—then urging himself in with manful resolution*) Git in, nigger! What you skeered at? Ain't nothin' dere but de trees! Git in! (*He plunges boldly into the forest.*)

SCENE THREE

In the forest. The moon has just risen. Its beams, drifting through the canopy of leaves, make a barely perceptible, suffused, eerie glow. A dense low wall of underbrush and creepers is in the nearer foreground, fencing in a small triangular clearing. Beyond this is the massed blackness of the forest like an encompassing barrier. A path is dimly discerned leading down to the clearing from left, rear, and winding away from it again toward the right. As the scene opens nothing can be distinctly made out. Except for the beating of the tom-tom, which is a trifle louder and quicker than at the close of the previous scene, there is silence, broken every few seconds by a queer, clicking sound. Then gradually the figure of the negro, Jeff, can be discerned crouching on his haunches at the rear of the triangle. He is middle-aged, thin, brown in color, is dressed in a Pullman porter's uniform and cap. He is throwing a pair of dice on the ground before him, picking them up, shaking them, casting them out with the regular, rigid, mechanical movements of an automaton. The heavy, plodding footsteps of someone approaching along the trail from the left are heard and Jones' voice, pitched on a slightly higher key and strained in a cheery effort to overcome its own tremors.

De moon's rizen. Does you heah dat, nigger? You gits more light from dis out. No mo' buttin' yo' fool head agin' de trunks an' scratchin' de hide off yo' legs in de bushes. Now you sees whar yo'se gwine. So cheer up! From now on you has a snap. (*He steps just to the rear of the triangular clearing and mops off his face on his sleeve. He has lost his Panama hat. His face is scratched, his brilliant uniform shows several large rents.*) What time's it gittin' to be, I wonder? I dassent light no match to find out. Phoo'. It's wa'm an' dat's a fac'! (*wearily*) How long I been makin' tracks in dese woods? Must be hours an' hours. Seems like fo'evah! Yit can't be, when de moon's jes' riz. Dis am a long night fo' yo', yo' Majesty! (*with a mournful chuckle*) Majesty! Der ain't much majesty 'bout dis baby now. (*with attempted cheerfulness*) Never min'. It's all part o' de game. Dis night come to an end like everything else. And when you gits dar safe and has dat bankroll in yo' hands you laughs at all dis. (*He starts to whistle but checks him-*

self abruptly.) What yo' whistlin' for, you po' dope! Want all de worl' to heah you? (*He stops talking to listen.*) Heah dat ole drum! Sho' gits nearer from de sound. Dey's packin' it along wid 'em. Time fo' me to move. (*He takes a step forward, then stops—worriedly*) What's dat odder queer clickety sound I heah? Dere it is! Sound close! Sound like—sound like— Fo' God sake, sound like some nigger was shootin' crap! (*frightenedly*) I better beat it quick when I gits dem notions. (*He walks quickly into the clear space—then stands transfixed as he sees Jeff—in a terrified gasp*) Who dar? Who dat? Is dat you, Jeff? (*starting toward the other, forgetful for a moment of his surroundings and really believing it is a living man that he sees— in a tone of happy relief*) Jeff! I'se sho' mighty glad to see you! Dey tol' me you done died from dat razor cut I gives you. (*stopping suddenly, bewilderedly*) But how you come to be heah, nigger? (*He stares fascinatedly at the other who continues his mechanical play with the dice. Jones' eyes begin to roll wildly. He stutters*) Ain't you gwine—look up—can't you speak to me? Is you—is you—a ha'nt? (*He jerks out his revolver in a frenzy of terrified rage.*) Nigger, I kills you dead once. Has I got to kill you ag'in? You take it den. (*He fires. When the smoke clears away Jeff has disappeared. Jones stands trembling— then with a certain reassurance*) He's gone, anyway. Ha'nt or not ha'nt, dat shot fix him. (*The beat of the far-off tom-tom is perceptibly louder and more rapid. Jones becomes conscious of it— with a start, looking back over his shoulder*) Dey's gittin' near! Dey's comin' fast! And heah I is shootin' shots to let 'em know jes' whar I is! Oh, Gorry, I'se got to run. (*Forgetting the path he plunges wildly into the underbrush in the rear and disappears in the shadow.*)

SCENE FOUR

In the forest. A wide dirt road runs diagonally from right, front, to left, rear. Rising sheer on both sides the forest walls it in. The moon is now up. Under its light the road glimmers ghastly and unreal. It is as if the forest had stood aside momentarily to let the road pass through and accomplish its veiled purpose. This done, the forest will fold in upon itself again and the road will be no more. Jones stumbles in from the forest on the right. His uniform is ragged and torn. He looks about him with numbed surprise when he sees the road, his eyes blinking in the bright moonlight. He flops down exhaustedly and pants heavily for a while. Then with sudden anger

I'm meltin' wid heat! Runnin' an' runnin' an' runnin'! Damn dis heah coat! Like a straitjacket! (*He tears off his coat and flings it away from him, revealing himself stripped to the waist.*) Dere! Dat's better! Now I kin breathe! (*looking down at his feet, the spurs catch his eye*) And to hell wid dese high-fangled spurs. Dey're what's been a-trippin' me up an' breakin' my neck. (*He unstraps them and flings them away disgustedly.*) Dere! I gits rid o' dem frippety Emperor trappin's an' I travels lighter. Lawd! I'se tired! (*after a pause, listening to the insistent beat of the tom-tom in the distance*) I must 'a' put some distance between myself an' dem—runnin' like dat—and yit—dat damn drum sounds jes' de same—nearer, even. Well, I guess I a'most holds my lead anyhow. Dey won't never catch up. (*with a sigh*) If on'y my fool legs stands up. Oh, I'se sorry I evah went in for dis. Dat Emperor job is sho' hard to shake. (*He looks around him suspiciously.*) How'd dis road evah git heah? Good level road, too. I never remembers seein' it befo'. (*shaking his head apprehensively*) Dese woods is sho' full o' de queerest things at night. (*with a sudden terror*) Lawd God, don't let me see no more o' dem ha'nts! Dey gits my goat! (*then trying to talk himself into confidence*) Ha'nts! You fool nigger, dey ain't no such things! Don't de Baptist parson tell you dat many time? Is you civilized, or is you like dese ign'rent black niggers heah? Sho'! Dat was all in yo' own head. Wasn't nothin' dere. Wasn't no Jeff! Know what? You jus' get seein' dem things 'cause yo' belly's empty and you's sick wid hunger inside. Hunger 'fects yo' head and yo' eyes. Any fool know dat. (*then pleading fervently*) But bless God, I don't come across no more o' dem, whatever dey is! (*then cautiously*) Rest! Don't talk! Rest! You needs it. Den you gits on yo' way again. (*looking at the moon*) Night's half gone a'most. You hits de coast in de mawning! Den you's all safe.

(*From the right forward a small gang of negroes enter. They are dressed in striped convict suits, their heads are shaven, one leg drags limpingly, shackled to a heavy ball and chain. Some carry picks, the others shovels. They are followed by a white man dressed in the uniform of a prison guard. A Winchester rifle is slung across his shoulders and he carries a heavy whip. At a signal from the guard they stop on the road opposite where Jones is sitting. Jones, who has been staring up at the sky, unmindful of their noiseless approach, suddenly looks down and sees them. His eyes pop out, he tries to get to his feet and fly, but sinks back, too numbed by fright to move. His voice catches in a choking prayer.*)

Lawd Jesus!

(*The prison guard cracks his whip—noiselessly—and at that signal all the convicts start to work on the road. They swing their picks, they shovel, but not a sound comes from their labor. Their movements, like those of Jeff in the preceding scene, are those of automatons,—rigid, slow, and mechanical. The prison guard points sternly at Jones with his whip, motions him to take his place among the other shovelers. Jones gets to his feet in a hypnotized stupor. He mumbles subserviently*)

Yes, suh! Yes, suh! I'se comin'.

(*As he shuffles, dragging one foot, over to his place, he curses under his breath with rage and hatred.*)

God damn yo' soul, I gits even wid you yit, sometime.

(*As if there were a shovel in his hands he goes through weary, mechanical gestures of digging up dirt, and throwing it to the roadside. Suddenly the guard approaches him angrily, threateningly. He raises his whip and lashes Jones viciously across the shoulders with it. Jones winces with pain and cowers abjectly. The guard turns his back on him and walks away contemptuously. Instantly Jones straightens up. With arms upraised as if his shovel were a club in his hands he springs murderously at the unsuspecting guard. In the act of crashing down his shovel on the white man's*) *skull, Jones suddenly becomes aware that his hands are empty. He cries despairingly)*

Whar's my shovel? Gimme my shovel 'til I splits his damn head! (*appealing to his fellow convicts*) Gimme a shovel, one o' you, fo' God's sake!

(*They stand fixed in motionless attitudes, their eyes on the ground. The guard seems to wait expectantly, his back turned to the attacker. Jones bellows with baffled, terrified rage, tugging frantically at his revolver.*)

I kills you, you white debil, if it's de last thing I evah does! Ghost or debil, I kill you agin!

(*He frees the revolver and fires point blank at the guard's back. Instantly the walls of the forest close in from both sides, the road and the figures of the convict gang are blotted out in an enshrouding darkness. The only sounds are a crashing in the underbrush as Jones leaps away in mad flight and the throbbing of the tom-tom, still far distant, but increased in volume of sound and rapidity of beat.*)

SCENE FIVE

A large circular clearing, enclosed by the serried ranks of gigantic trunks of tall trees whose tops are lost to view. In the center is a big dead stump worn by time into a curious resemblance to an auction block. The moon floods the clearing with a clear light. Jones forces his way in through the forest on the left. He looks wildly about the clearing with hunted, fearful glances. His pants are in tatters, his shoes cut and misshapen, flapping about his feet. He slinks cautiously to the stump in the center and sits down in a tense position, ready for instant flight. Then he holds his head in his hands and rocks back and forth, moaning to himself miserably.

Oh Lawd, Lawd! Oh Lawd, Lawd! (*Suddenly he throws himself on his knees and raises his clasped hands to the sky—in a voice of agonized pleading*) Lawd Jesus, heah my prayer! I'se a po' sinner, a po' sinner! I knows I done wrong, I knows it! When I cotches Jeff cheatin' wid loaded dice my anger overcomes me and I kills him dead! Lawd, I done wrong! When dat guard hits me wid de whip, my anger overcomes me, and I kills him dead. Lawd, I done wrong! And down heah whar dese fool bush niggers raises me up to the seat o' de mighty, I steals all I could grab. Lawd, I done wrong! I knows it! I'se sorry! Forgive me, Lawd! Forgive dis po' sinner! (*then beseeching terrifiedly*) And keep dem away, Lawd! Keep dem away from me! And stop dat drum soundin' in my ears! Dat begin to sound ha'nted, too. (*He gets to his feet, evidently slightly reassured by his prayer—with attempted confidence*) De Lawd'll preserve me from dem ha'nts after dis. (*sits down on the stump again*) I ain't skeered o' real men. Let dem come. But dem odders— (*He shudders—then looks down at his feet, working his toes inside the shoes—with a groan*) Oh, my po' feet! Dem shoes ain't no use no more 'ceptin' to hurt. I'se better off widout dem. (*He unlaces them and pulls them off—holds the wrecks of the shoes in his hands and regards them mournfully.*) You was real, A-one patin' leather, too. Look at you now. Emperor, you'se gittin' mighty low!

(*He sighs dejectedly and remains with bowed shoulders, staring down at the shoes in his hands as if reluctant to throw them away. While his attention is thus occupied, a crowd of figures silently enter the clearing from all sides. All are dressed in Southern costumes of the period of the fifties of the last century. There are middle-aged men who are evidently well-to-do planters. There is one spruce, authoritative individual—the auctioneer. There is a crowd of curious spectators, chiefly young belles and dandies who have come to the slave-market for diversion. All exchange courtly greetings in dumb show and chat silently together. There is something stiff, rigid, unreal, marionettish about their movements. They group themselves about the stump. Finally a batch of slaves is led in from the left by an attendant—three men of different ages, two women, one with a baby in her arms, nursing. They are placed to the left of the stump, beside Jones.*

(The white planters look them over appraisingly as if they were cattle, and exchange judgments on each. The dandies point with their fingers and make witty remarks. The belles titter bewitchingly. All this in silence save for the ominous throb of the tom-tom. The auctioneer holds up his hand, taking his place at the stump. The groups strain forward attentively. He touches Jones on the shoulder peremptorily, motioning for him to stand on the stump— the auction block.

(Jones looks up, sees the figures on all sides, looks wildly for some opening to escape, sees none, screams and leaps madly to the top of the stump to get as far away from them as possible. He stands there, cowering, paralyzed with horror. The auctioneer begins his silent spiel. He points to Jones, appeals to the planters to see for themselves. Here is a good field hand, sound in wind and limb as they can see. Very strong still in spite of his being middle-aged. Look at that back. Look at those shoulders. Look at the muscles in his arms and his sturdy legs. Capable of any amount of hard labor. Moreover, of a good disposition, intelligent and tractable. Will any gentleman start the bidding? The planters raise their fingers, make their bids. They are apparently all eager to possess Jones. The bidding is lively, the crowd interested. While this has been going on, Jones has been seized by the courage of desperation. He dares to look down and around him. Over his face abject terror gives way to mystification, to gradual realization—stutteringly)

What you all doin', white folks? What's all dis? What you all lookin' at me fo'? What you doin' wid me, anyhow? *(suddenly convulsed with raging hatred and fear)* Is dis a auction? Is you sellin' me like dey uster befo' de war? *(jerking out his revolver just as the auctioneer knocks him down to one of the planters—glaring from him to the purchaser*) And *you* sells me? And *you* buys me? I shows you I'se a free nigger, damn yo' souls! (*He fires at the auctioneer and at the planter with such rapidity that the two shots are almost simultaneous. As if this were a signal the walls of the forest fold in. Only blackness remains and silence broken by Jones as he rushes off, crying with fear—and by the quickened, ever louder beat of the tom-tom.*)

SCENE SIX

A cleared space in the forest. The limbs of the trees meet over it forming a low ceiling about five feet from the ground. The interlocked ropes of creepers reaching upward to entwine the tree trunks give an arched appearance to the sides. The space thus enclosed is like the dark, noisome hold of some ancient vessel. The moonlight is almost completely shut out and only a vague wan light filters through. There is the noise of someone approaching from the left, stumbling and crawling through the undergrowth. Jones' voice is heard between chattering moans.

Oh, Lawd, what I gwine do now? Ain't got no bullet left on'y de silver one. If mo' o' dem ha'nts come after me, how I gwine skeer dem away? Oh, Lawd, on'y de silver one left— an' I gotta save dat fo' luck. If I shoots dat one I'm a goner sho'! Lawd, it's black heah! Whar's de moon? Oh, Lawd, don't dis night evah come to an end? (*By the sounds, he is feeling his way cautiously forward.*) Dere! Dis feels like a clear space. I gotta lie down an' rest. I don't care if dem niggers does cotch me. I gotta rest.

(*He is well forward now where his figure can be dimly made out. His pants have been so torn away that what is left of them is no better than a breech cloth. He flings himself full length, face downward on the ground, panting with exhaustion. Gradually it seems to grow lighter in the enclosed space and two rows of seated figures can be seen behind Jones. They are sitting in crumpled, despairing attitudes, hunched, facing one another with their backs touching the forest walls as if they were shackled to them. All are negroes, naked save for loin cloths. At first they are silent and motionless. Then they begin to sway slowly forward toward each other and back again in unison, as if they were laxly letting themselves follow the long roll of a ship at sea. At the same time, a low, melancholy murmur rises among them, increasing gradually by rhythmic degrees which seem to be directed and controlled by the throb of the tom-tom in the distance, to a long, tremulous wail of despair that reaches a certain pitch, unbearably acute, then falls by slow gradations of tone into silence and is taken up again. Jones starts, looks up, sees the figures, and throws himself down again to shut out the sight. A shudder of terror shakes his whole body as the wail rises up about him again. But the next time, his voice, as if under some uncanny compulsion, starts with the others. As their chorus lifts he rises to a sitting posture similar to the others, swaying back and forth. His voice reaches the highest pitch of sorrow, of desolation. The light fades out, the other voices cease, and only darkness is left. Jones can be heard scrambling to his feet and running off, his voice sinking down the scale and receding as he moves farther and farther away in the forest. The tom-tom beats louder, quicker, with a more insistent, triumphant pulsation.)*

SCENE SEVEN

The foot of a gigantic tree by the edge of a great river. A rough structure of boulders, like an altar, is by the tree. The raised river bank is in the nearer background. Beyond this the surface of the river spreads out, brilliant and unruffled in the moonlight, blotted out and merged into a veil of bluish mist in the distance. Jones' voice is heard from the left rising and falling in the long, despairing wail of the chained slaves, to the rhythmic beat of the tomtom. As his voice sinks into silence, he enters the open space. The expression of his face is fixed and stony, his eyes have an obsessed glare, he moves with a strange deliberation like a sleep-walker or one in a trance. He looks around at the tree, the rough stone altar, the moonlit surface of the river beyond, and passes his hand over his head with a vague gesture of puzzled bewilderment. Then, as if in obedience to some obscure impulse, he sinks into a kneeling, devotional posture before the altar. Then he seems to come to himself partly, to have an uncertain realization of what he is doing, for he straightens up and stares about him horrifiedly—in an incoherent mumble

What—what is I doin'? What is—dis place? Seems like I know dat tree—an' dem stones—an' de river. I remember—seems like I been heah befo'. (*tremblingly*) Oh, Gorry, I'se skeered in dis place! I'se skeered. Oh, Lawd, pertect dis sinner!

(*Crawling away from the altar, he cowers close to the ground, his face hidden, his shoulders heaving with sobs of hysterical fright. From behind the trunk of the tree, as if he had sprung out of it, the figure of the Congo witch-doctor appears. He is wizened and old, naked except for the fur of some small animal tied about his waist, its bushy tail hanging down in front. His body is stained all over a bright red. Antelope horns are on each side of his head, branching upward. In one hand he carries a bone rattle, in the other a charm stick with a bunch of white cockatoo feathers tied to the end. A great number of glass beads and bone ornaments are about his neck, ears, wrists, and ankles. He struts noiselessly with a queer prancing step to a position in the clear ground between Jones and the altar. Then with a preliminary, summoning stamp of his foot on the earth, he begins to dance and to chant. As if in*

1057

response to his summons the beating of the tom-tom grows to a fierce, exultant boom whose throbs seem to fill the air with vibrating rhythm. Jones looks up, starts to spring to his feet, reaches a half-kneeling, half-squatting position and remains rigidly fixed there, paralyzed with awed fascination by this new apparition. The witch-doctor sways, stamping with his foot, his bone rattle clicking the time. His voice rises and falls in a weird, monotonous croon, without articulate word divisions. Gradually his dance becomes clearly one of a narrative in pantomime, his croon is an incantation, a charm to allay the fierceness of some implacable deity demanding sacrifice. He flees, he is pursued by devils, he hides, he flees again. Ever wilder and wilder becomes his flight, nearer and nearer draws the pursuing evil, more and more the spirit of terror gains possession of him. His croon, rising to intensity, is punctuated by shrill cries. Jones has become completely hypnotized. His voice joins in the incantation, in the cries, he beats time with his hands and sways his body to and fro from the waist. The whole spirit and meaning of the dance has entered into him, has become his spirit. Finally the theme of the pantomime halts on a howl of despair, and is taken up again in a note of savage hope. There is a salvation. The forces of evil demand sacrifice. They must be appeased. The witch-doctor points with his wand to the sacred tree, to the river beyond, to the altar, and finally to Jones with a ferocious command. Jones seems to sense the meaning of this. It is he who must offer himself for sacrifice. He beats his forehead abjectly to the ground, moaning hysterically)

Mercy, Oh Lawd! Mercy! Mercy on dis po' sinner.

(The witch-doctor springs to the river bank. He stretches out his arms and calls to some God within its depths. Then he starts backward slowly, his arms remaining out. A huge head of a crocodile appears over the bank and its eyes, glittering greenly, fasten upon Jones. He stares into them fascinatedly. The witch-doctor prances up to him, touches him with his wand, motions with hideous command toward the waiting monster. Jones squirms on his belly nearer and nearer, moaning continually)

Mercy, Lawd! Mercy!

(The crocodile heaves more of his enormous hulk onto the land. Jones squirms toward him. The witch-doctor's voice shrills out in furious exultation, the tom-tom beats madly. Jones cries out in a fierce, exhausted spasm of anguished pleading)

Lawd, save me! Lawd Jesus, heah my prayer!

(*Immediately, in answer to his prayer, comes the thought of the one bullet left him. He snatches at his hip, shouting defiantly*)

De silver bullet! You don't git me yit!

(*He fires at the green eyes in front of him. The head of the crocodile sinks back behind the river bank, the witch-doctor springs behind the sacred tree and disappears. Jones lies with his face to the ground, his arms outstretched, whimpering with fear as the throb of the tom-tom fills the silence about him with a somber pulsation, a baffled but revengeful power.*)

SCENE EIGHT

Dawn. Same as Scene Two, the dividing line of forest and plain. The nearest tree trunks are dimly revealed but the forest behind them is still a mass of glooming shadow. The tom-tom seems on the very spot, so loud and continuously vibrating are its beats. Lem enters from the left, followed by a small squad of his soldiers, and by the Cockney trader, Smithers. Lem is a heavy-set, ape-faced old savage of the extreme African type, dressed only in a loin cloth. A revolver and cartridge belt are about his waist. His soldiers are in different degrees of rag-concealed nakedness. All wear broad palm-leaf hats. Each one carries a rifle. Smithers is the same as in Scene One. One of the soldiers, evidently a tracker, is peering about keenly on the ground. He points to the spot where Jones entered the forest. Lem and Smithers come to look.

SMITHERS—(*after a glance, turns away in disgust*) That's where 'e went in right enough. Much good it'll do yer. 'E's miles orf by this an' safe to the Coast, damn 's 'ide! I tole yer yer'd lose 'im, didn't I?—wastin' the 'ole bloomin' night beatin' yer bloody drum and castin' yer silly spells! Gawd blimey, wot a pack!

LEM—(*gutturally*) We cotch him. (*He makes a motion to his soldiers who squat down on their haunches in a semi-circle.*)

SMITHERS—(*exasperatedly*) Well, ain't yer goin' in an' 'unt 'im in the woods? What the 'ell's the good of waitin'?

LEM—(*imperturbably—squatting down himself*) We cotch him.

SMITHERS—(*turning away from him contemptuously*) Aw! Garn! 'E's a better man than the lot o' you put together. I 'ates the sight o' 'im but I'll say that for 'im. (*A sound comes from the forest. The soldiers jump to their feet, cocking their rifles alertly. Lem remains sitting with an imperturbable expression, but listening intently. He makes a quick signal with his hand. His followers creep quickly into the forest, scattering so that each enters at a different spot.*)

SMITHERS—You ain't thinkin' that would be 'im, I 'ope?

LEM—(*calmly*) We cotch him.

SMITHERS—Blarsted fat 'eads! (*then after a second's thought—wonderingly*) Still an' all, it might 'appen. If 'e lost 'is bloody way in these stinkin' woods 'e'd likely turn in a circle without 'is knowin' it.

LEM—(*peremptorily*) Sssh! (*The reports of several rifles sound from the forest, followed a second later by savage, exultant yells. The beating of the tom-tom abruptly ceases. Lem looks up at the white man with a grin of satisfaction.*) We cotch him. Him dead.

SMITHERS—(*with a snarl*) 'Ow d'yer know it's 'im an' 'ow d'yer know 'e's dead?

LEM—My mens dey got um silver bullets. Lead bullet no kill him. He got um strong charm. I cook um money, make um silver bullet, make um strong charm, too.

SMITHERS—(*astonished*) So that's wot you was up to all night, wot? You was scared to put after 'im till you'd moulded silver bullets, eh?

LEM—(*simply stating a fact*) Yes. Him got strong charm. Lead no good.

SMITHERS—(*slapping his thigh and guffawing*) Haw-haw! If yer don't beat all 'ell! (*then recovering himself—scornfully*) I'll bet yer it ain't 'im they shot at all, yer bleedin' looney!

LEM—(*calmly*) Dey come bring him now. (*The soldiers come out of the forest, carrying Jones' limp body. He is dead. They carry him to Lem, who examines his body with great satisfaction.*)

SMITHERS—*leans over his shoulder—in a tone of frightened awe*) Well, they did for yer right enough, Jonesey, me lad! Dead as a 'erring! (*mockingly*) Where's yer 'igh an' mighty airs now, yer bloomin' Majesty? (*then with a grin*) Silver bullets! Gawd blimey, but yer died in the 'eighth o' style, any'ow!

(*Curtain*)

Chronology

1888   Born October 16 at the Barrett House, West 43rd Street and Broadway, New York City, third son of Mary Ellen "Ella" Quinlan (O'Neill) and James O'Neill, and christened November 1 as Eugene Gladstone O'Neill. (Father, born 1846 in Kilkenny, Ireland, came to America with his family in 1855, experienced extreme childhood poverty, and began acting by 1866. After succeeding in Shakespearean roles, he first starred in the Charles Fechter adaptation of Alexandre Dumas' *The Count of Monte Cristo* in 1883 and purchased the lucrative rights to the Fechter dramatization in 1885. Mother, daughter of Irish immigrants, was born 1857 in New Haven, Connecticut, and soon moved with her family to Cleveland, Ohio, where her father became a successful storeowner. She attended St. Mary's Academy, convent school in Notre Dame, Indiana, studied piano, and married James O'Neill in 1877. Their first son, James "Jamie" O'Neill, Jr., was born in 1878, their second, Edmund Burke O'Neill, in 1883. Edmund died in 1885 of measles contracted from Jamie.) Mother is given morphine for pain during and after O'Neill's birth and becomes addicted.

1889–94   Travels with parents (brother is at boarding school) across United States for up to nine months a year as father tours in *Monte Cristo*. Family spends summers at "Monte Cristo" cottage at 325 Pequot Avenue, New London, Connecticut. Becomes close to his Cornish nurse, Sarah Jane Bucknell Sandy, who tells him ghost and murder stories. Father attempts to play new roles during 1890 season, but is rejected by public and soon returns to the financially successful *Monte Cristo* (will perform role about 4,000 times through 1912).

1895–99   October 1895, enrolls at St. Aloysius, boarding school taught by Sisters of Charity on campus of Academy of Mount St. Vincent, Riverdale, New York. Serves as altar boy at Sunday Mass. Reads Kipling (especially enjoys *Captains Courageous* and *The Jungle Book*), the elder Dumas, Victor Hugo, and Shakespeare. Becomes strong swimmer during summers in New London.

1900   Makes First Communion on May 25. Autumn, enters
            De La Salle Institute in New York City, taught by Chris-
            tian Brothers; lives in family's hotel apartment on West
            68th Street near Central Park West.

1901   Becomes boarding student at De La Salle Institute in fall,
            living at school on West 58th Street near Sixth Avenue.
            Does well in history, English, and religion and poorly in
            mathematics.

1902   Fall, enters Betts Academy, non-sectarian boarding school
            in Stamford, Connecticut. Takes long walks in surround-
            ing countryside, enjoys rowing, but does not participate
            in team sports.

1903–05   Summer 1903, learns that mother is morphine addict when
            she attempts to throw herself into Thames River outside
            cottage while undergoing withdrawal. Renounces reli-
            gious faith and refuses to attend Mass with father. Re-
            turns to Betts and explores theaters, restaurants, saloons,
            and brothels of New York City with brother Jamie (now
            acting with father's company). Begins drinking. Patron-
            izes Unique Book Shop in New York, owned by anarchist
            journalist Benjamin Tucker, and reads radical political
            tracts, including those of Emma Goldman, as well as
            works by Shaw, Ibsen, Nietzsche, Baudelaire, Wilde,
            Swinburne, Ernest Dowson, and Edward FitzGerald.
            Corresponds with New London friend Marion Welch
            about school life and his enjoyment of musicals (*The Rog-
            ers Brothers in Ireland*, *Pearl and Pumpkin*) and popular
            novels (including works by Thomas Dixon, Henry Har-
            land, George Barr McCutcheon, and Harold McGrath).

1906   Passes entrance examinations for Princeton University
            in spring and enters college in fall. Frequents bars and
            brothels of Trenton and explores Hell's Kitchen and Green-
            wich Village sections of New York City. Reads *Thus Spake
            Zarathustra* by Nietzsche, *The Ego and His Own* by Max
            Stirner, Tolstoy, Dostoyevsky, and Maxim Gorky.

1907   Sees Alla Nazimova in Ibsen's *Hedda Gabler* ten times.
            Suspended at end of second semester for "poor scholastic
            standing" after failing to take any final examinations.

Takes secretarial job father finds him with mail-order firm, the New York–Chicago Supply Company, for $25 a week. Lives in parents' apartment in Hotel Lucerne on Amsterdam Avenue and 79th Street. Explores saloons and brothels of Tenderloin district. Becomes friends with Greenwich Village restaurant owner Polly Holladay and her brother Louis, painters Edward Keefe and George Bellows, and theater publicist James Findlater Byth. Reads Schopenhauer.

1908   Leaves job and begins receiving $7 a week allowance from parents. Stays with friends as relationship with father becomes increasingly strained.

1909   Spends January with Keefe and Bellows on farm owned by father in Zion, New Jersey, writing sonnets while they paint (later describes poems as "bad imitations of Dante Gabriel Rossetti"). Returns to New York and becomes romantically involved with twenty-year-old Kathleen Jenkins, daughter of prosperous middle-class family. Agrees when father, who disapproves of her Episcopalian background, proposes that he accompany mining engineer Fred C. Stevens on gold prospecting trip to Honduras. Marries Kathleen Jenkins in Hoboken, New Jersey, October 2; ceremony is kept secret from both families. Reads Jack London and Joseph Conrad before leaving for San Francisco in early October. Sails with Stevens and his wife, Ann, to Amapala, Honduras, travels on muleback to Tegucigalpa, and begins prospecting along Rio Seale without success in mid-November. Dislikes Honduran food and is plagued by insect bites.

1910   Contracts malaria and spends three weeks ill with fever in Tegucigalpa before returning to New York in March. Takes job as assistant stage manager with father's company, now touring with play *The White Sister*. Son Eugene Gladstone O'Neill, Jr., born May 4; O'Neill does not see him or Kathleen. Sails from Boston on Norwegian steel barque *Charles Racine* June 4, and arrives in Buenos Aires August 4. Works at Singer sewing machine factory, Swift meat packing plant, and on docks loading ships. Lives in cheap hotels and onboard moored *Charles Racine*, and frequents brothels and rough waterfront bars.

1911   Leaves Buenos Aires March 21 as ordinary seaman on Brit-
        ish freighter *Ikala*, arriving in New York April 15. Calls
        once on Kathleen and sees his son, but does not return
        and never sees her again. Moves to waterfront saloon and
        flophouse run by James "Jimmy the Priest" Condon at 252
        Fulton Street, where he stays for $3 a month. Sails for
        Southampton, England, July 22 as ordinary seaman on
        liner *New York* and returns August 26 as able-bodied sea-
        man on liner *Philadelphia*. Visits New London, but re-
        turns by mid-September to Jimmy the Priest's saloon.
        December, Kathleen requests divorce without asking for
        alimony or child support. O'Neill arranges to substantiate
        adultery charges by being discovered in hotel room with
        prostitute. Sees all of the plays performed by Abbey Play-
        ers from Dublin during six-week New York engagement,
        including T. C. Murray's *Birthright* and J. M. Synge's
        Riders to the Sea and *The Playboy of the Western World*.

1912   Attempts suicide with overdose of sleeping drug Veronal
        at Jimmy the Priest's in early January, but is saved by
        roommate James Byth (Byth will commit suicide at flop-
        house in 1913). Joins family on western vaudeville circuit,
        where father is touring in abridged version of *Monte
        Cristo*, and plays roles of courier and jailer of the Château
        d'If. Returns to New York in March and goes to New
        London in April. Divorce from Kathleen becomes final in
        July. Joins staff of *New London Telegraph* in August, covers
        local events and writes poetry for the paper, and becomes
        friends with editor Frederick Latimer. Falls in love with
        Maibelle Scott, eighteen-year-old neighbor; both families
        disapprove of romance. Develops persistent cough in
        October, and is diagnosed as having tuberculosis in No-
        vember. Resigns newspaper job and enters Fairfield
        County State Sanatorium in Shelton, Connecticut, De-
        cember 9, but leaves after two days. December 24, enters
        Gaylord Farm, private sanatorium in Wallingford, Con-
        necticut.

1913   Has brief romance with fellow patient Catherine MacKay.
        Reads plays of Synge, Eugène Brieux, Gerhart Haupt-
        mann, and August Strindberg. June 3, leaves Gaylord
        Farm with tuberculosis arrested and returns to New Lon-
        don. Writes vaudeville sketch, *A Wife for a Life*, and four
        one-act plays, *The Web*, *Thirst*, *Recklessness*, and *Warnings*.

Moves in autumn into boarding house run by Rippin family near Monte Cristo cottage. Resumes romance with Maibelle Scott. Writes film scenarios to make money, but none are accepted.

1914   Mother overcomes morphine addiction during stay at convent. Romance with Maibelle Scott ends and O'Neill begins to see Beatrice Ashe, eighteen-year-old daughter of New London trolley-car superintendent. Completes two full-length plays, *Bread and Butter* and *Servitude*, and four one-act plays, *Fog*, *Bound East for Cardiff* (then titled *Children of the Sea*), *Abortion*, and *The Movie Man*. First book, *Thirst and Other One Act Plays*, containing *Thirst*, *The Web*, *Warnings*, *Fog*, and *Recklessness*, published by Gorham Press of Boston in August (father pays printing costs). Fall, enrolls as special student in English 47 play-writing workshop at Harvard University, taught by Professor George Pierce Baker. Lives in boarding house at 1105 Massachusetts Avenue. Learns from Baker practice of writing detailed scenario of play before working on the dialogue (will follow this procedure for remainder of career). Writes one-act play "The Dear Doctor" (later destroyed) and full-length play "Belshazzar" (later destroyed), a collaboration with classmate Colin Ford. Studies French and German on his own.

1915   Completes one-act play *The Sniper* and full-length play *The Personal Equation* for course. Spends summer in New London. Father becomes increasingly concerned about financial situation after his producers declare bankruptcy, and O'Neill is unable to study further with Baker. Goes to New York in fall and lives at the Garden Hotel, Madison Avenue and 27th Street. Drinks heavily in hotel saloon and at The Golden Swan (known to patrons as the "Hell Hole") at Sixth Avenue and 4th Street. Becomes friendly at the Hell Hole with the "Hudson Dusters," Irish-American street gang, and Terry Carlin, an anarchistic, alcoholic drifter deeply influenced by Nietzsche. Writes poetry intermittently.

1916   Sees production of Hauptmann's *The Weavers* six times. Watches six-day bicycle races at Madison Square Garden (event becomes a favorite New York pastime of O'Neill's). Goes with Carlin to Provincetown, Massachusetts, in

June. Meets summer colony of writers, including George Cram Cook, his wife, Susan Glaspell, radical journalist John Reed, Louise Bryant, Hutchins and Neith Boyce Hapgood, and Wilbur Daniel Steele, who had started amateur theater in Provincetown wharf shed the previous year. Led by Cook, group stages series of original one-act plays, including *Bound East for Cardiff* on July 28 and *Thirst* in August; O'Neill appears in both plays. Completes one-act plays *Before Breakfast* and "The G.A.N." (later destroyed), three-act *Now I Ask You*, and short story "Tomorrow." Forms friendship with medical student Saxe Commins. Begins affair with Louise Bryant. September, joins others in organizing The Provincetown Players: The Playwrights' Theatre, dedicated to the production of new American plays. Group moves to New York in fall and opens 140-seat theater, The Provincetown Playhouse, at 139 Macdougal Street in Greenwich Village. Provincetown Players stage *Bound East for Cardiff*, November 3, and *Before Breakfast*, December 1. Affair with Louise Bryant continues after she marries John Reed in November.

1917   Provincetown Players stage *Fog*, January 5, and *The Sniper*, February 16. Goes to Provincetown in March. Writes four one-act plays, *In the Zone*, *Ile*, *The Long Voyage Home*, and *The Moon of the Caribbees*, and short story "The Hairy Ape" (later destroyed). "Tomorrow" published in *Seven Arts* magazine, June, earning O'Neill $50. Louise Bryant and John Reed leave for Russia. O'Neill returns to New York in fall and becomes friends with journalist Dorothy Day. October, *The Long Voyage Home* appears in *The Smart Set*. The Washington Square Players stage *In the Zone*, October 31, and Provincetown Players stage *The Long Voyage Home*, November 2, and *Ile*, November 30. Introduced to Agnes Boulton, twenty-four-year-old writer of magazine stories and novelettes, at the Hell Hole in late autumn.

1918   Shaken by death of Louis Holladay from heroin overdose, January. Goes to Provincetown with Agnes Boulton in late winter. Ends affair with Louise Bryant after her return from Russia. Marries Agnes, April 12. Earns money from vaudeville production of *In the Zone*. Completes *Beyond the Horizon* and "Till We Meet" (later destroyed) and four one-act plays, *The Rope* (staged by Provincetown Players

April 26), *Shell Shock*, *Where the Cross Is Made*, and *The Dreamy Kid*. Broadway producer J. D. Williams options *Beyond the Horizon* for $500. Reads *Dubliners* and *A Portrait of the Artist as a Young Man* by James Joyce. Moves in autumn to house owned by Agnes in West Point Pleasant, New Jersey. Provincetown Players stage *Where the Cross Is Made*, November 22, and *The Moon of the Caribbees*, December 20, at their new location, 133 Macdougal Street.

1919 Engages Richard Madden of the American Play Company as literary agent and Harry Weinberger as his attorney; both become trusted friends. *The Moon of the Caribbees and Six Other Plays of the Sea*, published by Boni & Liveright, Inc., receives good reviews (Boni & Liveright will continue to publish his plays, generally coinciding with their first production). Begins long friendship with drama critic George Jean Nathan. Grows closer to father and spends time playing cards with him. Returns to Provincetown in late May and moves to Peaked Hill Bar on eastern side of Cape Cod, living in former Coast Guard station bought for him by father as wedding present (purchase includes furnishings of previous occupant, Mabel Dodge). Becomes enthusiastic kayaker. Completes *The Straw*, *Chris Christophersen*, and three one-act plays, "Exorcism," "Honor Among the Bradleys," and "The Trumpet" (all later destroyed). Broadway producer George C. Tyler options *Chris Christophersen*. Rents cottage in Provincetown at end of summer. Second son, Shane Rudraighe O'Neill, born October 30. Provincetown Players stage *The Dreamy Kid*, October 31, with all-black cast (one of the first productions by a white theater company to cast black actors in black roles).

1920 Goes to New York in early January for rehearsals of *Beyond the Horizon*, which begins series of matinees on February 3. Play is critically praised and runs for 144 evening performances, earning O'Neill $5,264. Father is deeply gratified by play's success, but soon has stroke and is discovered to have intestinal cancer. Production of *Chris Christophersen* is not brought to New York after performances in Atlantic City and Philadelphia. Provincetown Players stage "Exorcism" (O'Neill later recalls and destroys all copies of play, which depicts young man's suicide attempt). Returns to Provincetown in early March and completes *Gold*, longer version of *Where the Cross Is Made*. *Beyond the Horizon* receives Pulitzer Prize for drama in June. Goes to New London in late July and is at father's bedside when he slips into coma. Father dies of cancer, August 10. Jamie stops drinking and stays with mother, who proves capable of managing father's complex estate. Returns to Peaked Hill Bar, completes *"Anna Christie"* (revised version of *Chris Christophersen*), and writes *The Emperor Jones* and *Diff'rent*. *The Emperor Jones*, staged by Provincetown Players, November 1, is widely acclaimed and later moves to Broadway under commercial management, running for 204 performances. *Diff'rent*, produced by Provincetown Players, opens December 27 and runs for 100 performances in Village and on Broadway.

1921   Becomes friends with theatrical critic Kenneth Macgowan and stage designer Robert Edmond Jones. Writes draft of *The First Man* in March. Joins successful protest against New York Drama League's decision not to invite black actor Charles Gilpin, lead player in *The Emperor Jones*, to its annual awards dinner. Has teeth worked on by Saxe Commins, now practicing dentistry in Rochester, New York (O'Neill will continue to have serious dental problems for remainder of his life). *Gold* opens on Broadway June 1 and closes after 13 performances. Finishes draft of *The Fountain* in late August. Agrees to pay child support when Kathleen Jenkins, now married to George Pitt-Smith, contacts him through her lawyer. Goes to New York for rehearsals in October. Meets Eugene, Jr., who had been given name of Richard Pitt-Smith, now attending military school; O'Neill and son both enjoy visit. *"Anna Christie"* opens on Broadway November 2 and runs for 177 performances. *The Straw* opens November 10 at Greenwich Village Theatre and closes after 20 performances. Impressed by German film *The Cabinet of Dr. Caligari*. Returns to Provincetown. Writes *The Hairy Ape* in December.

1922   January, attends rehearsals in New York. Mother dies in Los Angeles after series of strokes, February 28. *The First Man* opens March 4 and closes after 27 performances. March 9, Provincetown Players staging of *The Hairy Ape* opens on same evening that mother's body arrives in New

York, accompanied by Jamie, who has suffered severe alcoholic relapse. O'Neill does not attend opening and remains at his hotel, sending family friend to meet train. *The Hairy Ape* moves to Broadway in April and runs for 120 performances. Returns to Provincetown and completes *The Fountain*. *"Anna Christie"* wins Pulitzer Prize. Visited by Eugene, Jr., and by Jamie, who is drinking heavily. Begins *Welded* in September. Buys Brook Farm, thirty-acre estate with fifteen-room house in Ridgefield, Connecticut, for $32,500, and moves there in autumn. Earns $44,000 during year.

1923   Awarded gold medal by National Institute of Arts and Letters. Successful production of *"Anna Christie"* in London helps establish European reputation. Finishes *Welded* in spring. Lives at Peaked Hill Bar for summer and begins *Marco Millions*. Jamie is committed to sanatorium in June after suffering acute alcoholic breakdown. O'Neill joins Kenneth Macgowan and Robert Edmond Jones in assuming control of Provincetown Players, who have become inactive due to financial difficulties and artistic differences (later adopt name of The Experimental Theatre, Inc., for their productions). Begins *All God's Chillun Got Wings* in September and finishes it after returning to Brook Farm in fall. Visited by Hart Crane and Malcolm Cowley in early November. Jamie dies in Paterson, New Jersey, sanatorium, November 8. O'Neill, recovering from severe drinking episode, does not attend service or burial.

1924   Begins *Desire Under the Elms* in January. Saddened by death in Greece of George Cram Cook. Rehearsals for *All God's Chillun Got Wings* begin in February amid newspaper controversy over play's depiction of interracial marriage, centering on scene in which white actress Mary Blair kisses black actor Paul Robeson's hand. O'Neill, Blair, and Robeson receive hate mail and death threats from Ku Klux Klan and others. *Welded*, produced by O'Neill, Macgowan, Jones, and Edgar Selwyn, opens March 17 and runs for 24 performances. *The Ancient Mariner*, O'Neill's dramatic arrangement of Coleridge's poem, opens April 6 at Provincetown Playhouse and closes after 33 performances. *All God's Chillun Got Wings* opens at Provincetown Playhouse May 15 and runs for 100 performances; first scene is read aloud by director James Light after city refuses to issue permits needed by child actors appearing in production. Finishes *Desire Under the Elms* in June. Resumes work on *Marco Millions* at Peaked Hill Bar in July. Revises and corrects previously published plays for *The Complete Works of Eugene O'Neill*, two-volume limited edition published by Boni & Liveright. Goes to New York in October for rehearsals. *Desire Under the Elms* opens November 11 at Greenwich Village Theatre. O'Neill is dissatisfied with stage set (which is based on his own sketches) but pleased by Walter Huston's performance (tells interviewer for 1948 profile that Huston, Charles Gilpin in *The Emperor Jones*, and Louis Wolheim in *The Hairy Ape* were the only actors in his plays who "lived up to the conceptions I had as I wrote"). Sails to Bermuda November 29 and rents cottage in Paget Parish on south shore.

1925   January, condenses *Marco Millions* from original eight-act length and begins *The Great God Brown*. *Desire Under the Elms* moves to Broadway and is threatened with prosecution for indecency by Manhattan district attorney Joab Banton until panel of citizens serving as "play-jury" clears it; production runs for 208 performances. (Play is later banned in Boston and England.) Finishes *The Great God Brown* in late March. Reads Nietzsche (*The Birth of Tragedy*, *Joyful Wisdom*) and Freud (*Beyond the Pleasure Principle*, *Group Psychology and the Analysis of the Ego*). Begins extended period of heavy drinking in April. Daughter Oona born, May 14. Goes to Nantucket in late July and writes scenarios for *Lazarus Laughed* and *Strange Interlude*. Returns to Ridgefield in October and works on *Lazarus Laughed* for remainder of year. *The Fountain*, produced by Macgowan, Jones, and O'Neill, opens at the Greenwich Village Theatre on December 10 and runs for 24 performances. Continues to drink heavily; Macgowan arranges for him to see psychoanalyst Dr. G. V. Hamilton.

1926   Participates in Hamilton's survey of marital sexual behavior and psychological attitudes (published in 1929 as *A Research in Marriage*) and undergoes six weeks of psychoanalytic treatment with him. Stops drinking (except for intense, short episodes, will abstain for remainder of life). *The Great God Brown*, produced by Macgowan, Jones, and O'Neill, opens on January 23 and runs for 278 performances. Returns to Bermuda in late February and moves to Bellevue, rented estate in Paget Parish. Works on *Lazarus Laughed* and finishes first draft in May. Reads Joyce's *Ulysses*. Buys Spithead, 200-year-old house on Little Turtle Bay, for $17,500. Begins writing *Strange Interlude* in late May. Receives D. Litt. degree from Yale University, June 23, and sees George Pierce Baker, now teaching at Yale. Visits New London before spending summer in Belgrade Lakes, Maine, where he works steadily on *Strange Interlude*. Visited by Eugene, Jr., and Barbara Boulton, Agnes's eleven-year-old daughter by earlier marriage (Barbara lives with her grandparents). Meets again actress Carlotta Monterey (born Hazel Neilson Tharsing, 1888), who had played Mildred in *The Hairy Ape* on Broadway. Interviewed by journalist Elizabeth Shepley Sergeant for profile in *The New Republic*, beginning friendship. Goes to New York in October, sees Carlotta Monterey frequently, and writes film scenarios for *The Hairy Ape* and *Desire Under the Elms* (neither of his scenarios are ever produced). Returns to Bermuda in November and moves into guest cottage at Spithead while main house is renovated. Revises *Marco Millions* for publication by Boni & Liveright in hopes of encouraging its production (appears April 1927).

1927   Finishes first draft of *Strange Interlude* in February. Visited in March by Lawrence Langner, a director of the Theatre Guild, New York producers' organization, who reads first six acts of *Strange Interlude*. April, Theatre Guild board accepts *Marco Millions* for production and options *Strange Interlude*. Revises *Lazarus Laughed* (published in November by Boni & Liveright) and *Strange Interlude* during summer before going to New York at end of August. Suffers from depression and extreme nervousness; consults doctors and is diagnosed as having prostate condition and thyroid deficiency (weighs 137 pounds at height of five feet eleven inches). Eugene, Jr., enters Yale. O'Neill goes to Bermuda in late October before returning to New York in November for rehearsals. Writes increasingly angry letters to Agnes as affair with Carlotta Monterey intensifies.

1928   *Marco Millions* opens January 9 and runs for 92 performances. *Strange Interlude* opens January 30 and runs for 426 performances (published version sells over 100,000 copies by 1931, and O'Neill eventually earns $275,000 from play). Leaves with Carlotta Monterey for Europe on February 10. Goes to London and Paris before renting villa at Guéthary in southern France, March. Keeps whereabouts secret from Agnes and most friends. Begins writing *Dynamo*, first in planned trilogy "Myths for the God-forsaken," to be completed by *Days Without End* (originally titled *Without Endings of Days*) and "It Cannot Be Mad." *Lazarus Laughed* staged by Pasadena Community Playhouse, April 9, and runs for 28 performances. Receives Pulitzer Prize for *Strange Interlude*. Becomes enraged by Agnes's demands in divorce settlement negotiations and by newspaper interview she gives, discussing separation. Finishes draft of *Dynamo* in August and sends it to Saxe Commins, who is living in Paris, to be typed. Leaves with Carlotta Monterey for China, October 5. Becomes ill with influenza during brief stay in Saigon. Arrives in Shanghai, November 9. Drinks heavily and is briefly separated from Carlotta before being hospitalized. Leaves for Manila under assumed name to avoid newspaper reporters, December 12. Resumes drinking onboard ship bound for Singapore.

1929   Carlotta leaves him in Colombo, Ceylon, January 1, but they are reunited in Port Said, Egypt, January 15. Rents villa in late January at Cap d'Ail, on French Riviera near Monte Carlo. Works on scenario for "It Cannot Be Mad." Theatre Guild production of *Dynamo* opens February 11 and receives harsh reviews; runs for 50 performances, mostly to Guild subscribers. O'Neill regrets having had play produced in his absence and makes extensive changes in text while reviewing proofs of published version. Sets trilogy aside in May and begins writing scenarios for *Mourning Becomes Electra*. Sued for $1,250,000 by Gladys Lewis, who claims that *Strange Interlude* was plagiarized from her privately published novel *The Temple of Pallas-Athenæ*, written under name of Georges Lewys. Moves in early June to Château Le Plessis in St. Antoine-du-Rocher, near Tours. Agnes is granted divorce on grounds of desertion in Reno, Nevada, July 2; settlement gives her life interest in Spithead and $6,000–$10,000 per year alimony, depending on O'Neill's income. Marries Carlotta in Paris, July 22. Finishes scenarios for *Mourning Becomes Electra* in early August. Visited by Eugene, Jr. Fall, buys

Bugatti sports car, which he enjoys driving at high speed, and Silverdene Emblem ("Blemie"), prize Dalmatian (dog becomes O'Neill's favorite of several he has owned).

1930   Completes first draft of *Mourning Becomes Electra* in late February. Visits Paris and tours France before beginning second draft at end of March. Film version of *"Anna Christie,"* directed by Clarence Brown and starring Greta Garbo in her first talking role, is popular success (earlier silent version, released in 1923, had starred Blanche Sweet). May, sees *All God's Chillun Got Wings* and *Desire Under the Elms* performed in Russian by Kamerny, experimental Soviet theater company that uses music, dance, and stylized decor in its stagings. Meets its founder, Aleksandr Tairov, and writes letter praising productions. Finishes third draft of *Mourning Becomes Electra* in September and fourth draft in October. Travels in Spain and Morocco. Returns in November and begins fifth draft.

1931   Completes fifth draft in February. Writes sixth draft at Las Palmas in the Canary Islands in March before mailing typescript to Theatre Guild from Paris, April 7. Federal district judge John W. Woolsey rules for defendants in plagiarism case and awards O'Neill $7,500 costs (is unable to collect from bankrupt plaintiff). Resolution of suit allows sale of film rights to *Strange Interlude*, from which O'Neill receives $37,500 (released in 1932, film stars Norma Shearer, Clark Gable, Frank Morgan, and Robert Young, and is directed by Robert Z. Leonard). Returns to United States with Carlotta to prepare for production of *Mourning Becomes Electra*, May 17. Artist Ralph Barton, Carlotta's third husband, commits suicide May 19, leaving note declaring love for her; O'Neills are upset by resulting publicity. Rents house in Northport, Long Island, in June. Takes pride in Eugene, Jr., who recently has won Yale prize for his scholarship in classics. Visited for two weeks in August by Shane, who is entering Lawrenceville School in New Jersey. Works on proofs for published version of *Mourning Becomes Electra* with Saxe Commins, now editor at Horace Liveright, Inc. (formerly Boni & Liveright). Takes duplex apartment at 1095 Park Avenue when rehearsals begin in early September. *Mourning Becomes Electra* opens October 26 to wide critical acclaim and runs for 150 performances. O'Neill is "overjoyed" the following day, but soon writes in work diary: "Reaction—sunk—worn out—depressed—sad that the Mannons exist no more—for me!" November, goes with Carlotta to Sea Island, Georgia, where they decide to build house. Returns to New York in December and meets Mexican artist and writer Miguel Covarrubias.

1932   January, meets Nellie Tharsing, Carlotta's mother, and Cynthia Chapman, Carlotta's fourteen-year-old daughter by her second husband. Sees Oona and Shane. Begins work in February on scenario for *Days Without End*. Sees George Jean Nathan, actress Lillian Gish, Saxe and Dorothy Commins, and James Speyer, wealthy banker and former lover of Carlotta's, who had established trust fund that pays her $14,000 a year. (O'Neill is unaware of Speyer's affair with Carlotta and believes aunt in California is source of her annuity.) Meets German playwright Gerhart Hauptmann. Goes with Carlotta to Sea Island in May, staying in cottage while house is finished. Begins writing *Days Without End*, but work is difficult and he makes little progress. Twenty-room house, costing $100,000 (including land), is finished in late June; O'Neills name it Casa Genotta (name derived from "Eugene" and "Carlotta"). Enjoys swimming and surf fishing. Becomes associate editor of new literary journal *The American Spectator*, edited by George Jean Nathan, and contributes "Memoranda on Masks," "Second Thoughts," and "A Dramatist's Notebook," essays on use of masks in contemporary theater (series appears November 1932–January 1933). Writes in "Memoranda on Masks": "One's outer life passes in a solitude haunted by the masks of others; one's inner life passes in a solitude hounded by the masks of oneself." Resumes work on *Days Without End*, but sets it aside on morning of September 1 to begin *Ah, Wilderness!* (writes in work diary: "Awoke with idea for this 'Nostalgic Comedy' & worked out tentative outline—seems fully formed & ready to write"). Completes first draft by end of September. Returns to *Days Without End* and with difficulty finishes third draft by end of year.

1933   Works on "The Life of Bessie Bowen" (formerly "It Cannot Be Mad") in January, then returns to *Days Without End* in early February and finishes fifth draft by end of March. Sale of film rights to *The Emperor Jones* for $30,000 lessens worries over continuing expenses, which include financial support for Terry Carlin and other friends. (Film, released later in year, is directed by Dudley Murphy and stars Paul Robeson and Dudley Digges.) Saxe Commins secures royalties owed O'Neill by Liveright, Inc., before firm declares bankruptcy in May. O'Neill signs with Bennett Cerf, co-founder of Random House, on condition that Cerf hire Commins as editor (Commins later becomes editor-in-chief of Random House). Contract provides for 20 percent royalty rate and $10,000 advance. Revises *Ah, Wilderness!* in June before beginning sixth draft of *Days Without End*. August, vacations at Big Wolf Lake in Adirondack Mountains. Attends rehearsals of *Ah, Wilderness!* and becomes friends with Russel Crouse, publicist for the Theatre Guild. Play opens in New York, October 2, and runs for 289 performances. Returns to Sea Island in mid-October and revises *Days Without End*. Enjoys player piano "Rosie" given him by Carlotta. Receives $37,500 for screen rights to *Ah, Wilderness!* (film, directed by Clarence Brown and starring Lionel Barrymore, Wallace Beery, and Mickey Rooney, is released in 1935; a musical version, *Summer Holiday*, is released in 1948). Goes to New York in late November for rehearsals.

1934   Theatre Guild production of *Days Without End* opens in New York January 8 and runs for 57 performances; O'Neill is angered by "very prejudiced" reviews. (Play is well received in Ireland when Abbey Theatre stages it later in the year.) Returns to Sea Island at end of January and suffers from severe nervousness and digestive troubles. Told by doctor during visit to New York in March that he must rest for six months to avoid nervous breakdown. Begins taking insulin to gain weight and buys kayak. Has several ship models made for his use in planning "The Calms of Capricorn," play set aboard clipper ship rounding Cape Horn. Goes to Big Wolf Lake in early August and stays until end of September. October, meets Irish playwright Sean O'Casey in New York. Works on notes and outlines for several plays at Sea Island during fall. Visited in December by Shane, now student at Florida Military Academy after doing poorly at Lawrenceville.

1935   January, begins planning cycle of seven plays, incorporating "The Life of Bessie Bowen" and "The Calms of

Capricorn," examining American life since the early nineteenth century through several generations of the Harford family (will eventually adopt title "A Tale of Possessors Self-Dispossessed" for cycle). Writes scenarios for first two plays, *A Touch of the Poet* (originally titled *The Hair of the Dog*) and *More Stately Mansions*, February–April. Visited by Sherwood Anderson and by Eugene, Jr., now graduate student in classics. Works on notes and outlines for scenario through summer and fall despite episodes of nervousness and depression and series of minor ailments. Begins writing draft of *A Touch of the Poet* in November. Visited by Somerset Maugham in December.

1936   Hospitalized with gastritis during visit to New York in February. Suffers from depression, extreme nervousness, and continuing stomach pains after returning to Sea Island. Leaves draft of *A Touch of the Poet* unfinished to work on other plays in cycle. Expands plan to include nine plays, beginning in late eighteenth century. Blames poor health on hot Sea Island climate. Goes to New York in October for medical treatment and is told to rest. November, moves with Carlotta to Seattle at invitation of friend Sophus Keith Winther, professor at University of Washington and author of study of O'Neill's work, who finds house they rent at 4701 West Ruffner Street, overlooking Puget Sound. Awarded Nobel Prize for Literature, November 12. Writes acceptance letter acknowledging influence of Strindberg. Moves with Carlotta to San Francisco in December. Enters Merritt Hospital in Oakland, suffering from abdominal pain and prostate trouble, on December 26, and has appendix removed December 29.

1937   Nearly dies from infection in mid-January, then begins slow recovery. Sells Casa Genotta for $75,000. Leaves hospital in early March but continues to suffer from prostate and stomach ailments. April, moves from San Francisco hotel to house at 2909 Avalon Avenue in Berkeley. Buys 160 acres of land for new home in Las Trampas Hills near Danville, California. Rents house in nearby Lafayette while Danville house is being built, June. Resumes work despite poor health. Writes draft of new first play in cycle that is longer than nine-act *Strange Interlude*, but is uncertain about cutting it. Develops painful neuritis in arm,

November. Moves to Tao House, new Danville home, at end of year.

1938   Neuritis prevents work until late March. Begins draft of *More Stately Mansions*, April. Visited by Shane, now attending ranch school in Colorado. Finishes draft in September and begins rewriting. Disturbed when he learns that Shane is returning to Lawrenceville School, but feels powerless to intervene in his education.

1939   Completes and revises second draft of *More Stately Mansions* in January. Begins rewriting *A Touch of the Poet*, now third play in cycle. Suffers from neuritis, melancholia, low blood pressure, and anxiety over eye operation Carlotta must undergo (surgery is successful). Finishes third draft of *A Touch of the Poet* in mid-May. Decides June 5 to set cycle aside and work on plays outside it. Reviews notes on June 6 and chooses two autobiographical ideas to develop. Finishes outline of first, *The Iceman Cometh*, in late June and of the second, *The Long Day's Journey* (later retitled *Long Day's Journey into Night*), in early July. Visited by Eugene, Jr., now teaching classics at Yale, in July and by Oona in August ("really a charming girl, both in looks and manner—And she has intelligence, too"). Follows outbreak of World War II; writes in diary, "Spengler was right." Finishes first draft of *The Iceman Cometh* in mid-October. Tremor in hands, present intermittently since childhood, becomes more pronounced. Completes third draft of *The Iceman Cometh* in mid-December and considers play to be essentially finished.

1940   Exhaustion prevents steady work on cycle. February, meets director John Ford and screenwriter Dudley Nichols to discuss their plans for filming S. S. *Glencairn* plays (*Bound East for Cardiff*, *The Moon of the Caribbees*, *In the Zone*, and *The Long Voyage Home*) under title *The Long Voyage Home* (O'Neill will see film, which stars John Wayne, Thomas Mitchell, and Barry Fitzgerald, in July and praise it as the best screen adaptation of his work). Begins draft of *Long Day's Journey into Night* in late March, but writes slowly due to continued poor health. Injures back at end of April. Develops "war obsession" after German invasion of France and the Low Countries, May 10, closely following news and doing no writing. Re-

sumes work on *Long Day's Journey into Night* June 26 and
finishes first draft in late September. Writes second draft
before returning to cycle in late October. Decides to di-
vide first two plays into four, creating eleven-play cycle.
November, plans "By Way of Obit.", series of one-act
monologue plays. Dalmatian "Blemie" dies December 17.
O'Neill and Carlotta are deeply grieved; O'Neill writes
"The Last Will and Testament of Silverdene Emblem
O'Neill" as tribute.

1941   Ill with prostate and digestive disorders and bronchitis.
        Begins notes in February for non-cycle play "The Thir-
        teenth Apostle." Works on *Long Day's Journey into Night*
        in March (writes that play "does most with the least—a
        quiet play!—and a great one, I believe"). Writes draft of
        Hughie, one-act play in "By Way of Obit." series, April.
        Has increasing difficulty controlling pencil as hand tremor
        worsens. Tremor diagnosed as Parkinson's disease; re-
        ceives vitamin shots that prove ineffective and doubts that
        he will be able to complete cycle. Visited by Oona in July.
        Eugene, Jr., is deeply moved by reading *Long Day's Jour-
        ney into Night* and *The Iceman Cometh* during visit in Sep-
        tember, which pleases O'Neill. Makes notes at end of
        October for *A Moon for the Misbegotten*. Works on draft
        for remainder of year. Preoccupation with war grows after
        Japanese attack on Pearl Harbor, December 7. Shane joins
        merchant marine.

1942   Finishes first draft of *A Moon for the Misbegotten* in Janu-
        ary. Able to work only sporadically on *A Touch of the Poet*,
        "The Thirteenth Apostle," and *Hughie* as tremor, prostate,
        and other health problems worsen. Carlotta develops se-
        rious back problem. O'Neill is intensely angered by news
        in April that Oona has been chosen "Debutante No. 1" at
        the Stork Club in New York, considering distinction friv-
        olous and inappropriate during wartime. Eugene, Jr.,
        leaves Yale faculty to do war work (rejected for intelli-
        gence and military service, will work in cable factory and
        begin drinking heavily). Sends manuscripts, typescripts,
        and other materials to Princeton and Yale libraries for
        safekeeping. Finishes revising *Hughie* in June. Suffers
        from effects of drugs taken to control Parkinson's (writes
        in diary in late July: "Tough game—take sedatives and
        feel a dull dope—don't take, and feel as if maggots were

crawling all over inside your skin"). Finishes revision of *A Touch of the Poet* in mid-November. Refuses to see Oona when she comes to California to pursue a screen career and writes letter threatening permanent break in relations. Works on "The Last Conquest" (formerly "The Thirteenth Apostle"). Departure of servants for war work, gasoline rationing, and O'Neills' inability to drive leaves them increasingly isolated at Tao House.

1943   Begins second draft of *A Moon for the Misbegotten* in January and finishes in May, working three hours a day despite worsening tremor. Destroys notes for seven plays he no longer expects to write. Tries to begin play "Blind Alley Guy" in June but is forced to stop, no longer capable of controlling pencil and unable to compose on typewriter or dictate. Oona attempts reconciliation with O'Neill after her marriage to Charlie Chaplin on June 16, but he does not respond (will not reply to several other letters from her and never sees any of the five children she will have in his lifetime). Financial worries reduced by sale of film rights to *The Hairy Ape* for $30,000 (film, directed by Alfred Santell and starring William Bendix and Susan Heyward, is released in 1944). Shane suffers nervous collapse after extensive service in North Atlantic and is hospitalized.

1944   Sells Tao House in February and moves to Huntington Hotel in San Francisco. Burns manuscripts of two unfinished cycle plays. Carlotta dangerously ill from kidney infection. Saddened by death of friend and attorney Harry Weinberger. Hires Jane Caldwell, daughter of Carlotta's school friend Myrtle Caldwell, as typist. Revises *A Moon for the Misbegotten* and *A Touch of the Poet*. Meets with Lawrence Langner during summer to discuss production of completed plays, recommending that *The Iceman Cometh* be staged after anticipated mood of post-war optimism recedes. Tremor causes occasional shaking of entire body.

1945   O'Neill's minor flirtation with Jane Caldwell leads to exchange of bitter accusations between him and Carlotta. Moves with Carlotta to New York in October, taking suite at Hotel Barclay. Goes to jazz clubs and sporting events with George Jean Nathan and new attorney, Winfield Aronberg. Sees Eugene, Jr., now pursuing erratic teaching and radio broadcasting career in New York, and Shane, who is drinking heavily, drifting between jobs, and has twice attempted suicide. Grandson Eugene O'Neill III born to Shane and his wife, Catherine Givens, November 19 (O'Neill never sees child, who dies in crib February 10, 1946). Deposits sealed copy of *Long Day's Journey into Night* in Random House safe, November 29, with instructions that it not be published until twenty-five years after his death and never be staged (Carlotta, his literary executor, has play published and produced in 1956; it wins Pulitzer Prize).

1946   Sees Shane and Catherine before they go to Spithead to recover from death of their son. Continuing tension with Carlotta eased when they move in spring into six-room penthouse apartment at 35 East 84th Street. Sees Dudley Nichols about his screen adaptation of *Mourning Becomes Electra* (film, directed by Nichols and starring Rosalind Russell, Michael Redgrave, and Katina Paxinou, is released following year). Works on design and casting of Theatre Guild production of *The Iceman Cometh* and with Saxe Commins on published version. Attends afternoon rehearsals, beginning in early September. Play opens to mixed reviews October 9 and runs for 136 performances.

1947   Attends rehearsals for Theatre Guild staging of *A Moon for the Misbegotten*. Becomes dissatisfied with production, which the Guild decides to try out on tour. Play opens in Columbus, Ohio, February 20 and is performed in Pittsburgh, Detroit, and St. Louis, where it closes March 29. O'Neill does not press for another production and asks Guild to postpone planned staging of *A Touch of the Poet*. Settles remaining alimony claims with Agnes for $17,000. Relationship with Carlotta becomes increasingly strained during fall.

1948   Carlotta leaves after quarrel, January 18. O'Neill drinks, stumbles, and breaks left arm, January 27. Considers leaving Carlotta while in hospital (tells friends that he has learned of her true relationship with James Speyer), but they are reconciled in March. Moves with Carlotta to Boston in April, where they buy shorefront cottage on Point O'Rocks Lane in nearby Marblehead Neck. Purchase and renovation ultimately cost about $85,000 (half coming from Carlotta's savings). Shane is arrested for possession of three vials of heroin, August 10. O'Neill refuses to send $500 bail and breaks off relations (Shane spends four months in federal hospital in Lexington, Kentucky, but is not cured of his addiction). Tremor worsens in legs, making walking difficult, but lessens in hands; O'Neill expresses hope that he may begin writing again. Moves into cottage in fall.

1949   Worsening tremor in hands makes resumption of writing impossible, though O'Neill's desk remains arranged for work. Listens to large collection of jazz and blues records and occasionally visits Boston.

1950   Eugene, Jr., after years of heavy drinking and failed attempt at television career, commits suicide in Woodstock, New York, September 25.

1951   Leaves house, thinly dressed and without cane, after quarrel with Carlotta on night of February 5. Trips over rock beneath snow in garden and breaks right leg at knee. Lies outside for nearly an hour before family doctor arrives and takes him to Salem Hospital (O'Neill later tells friends that Carlotta had tauntingly refused to assist him). Carlotta, severely disoriented, is hospitalized as psychiatric patient February 6, suffering effects of bromide poisoning caused by over-medication (remains in hospital until March 29). O'Neill is visited by New York friends, including Commins, Aronberg, and Langner, who try to arrange permanent separation from Carlotta. Signs petition alleging that Carlotta is insane and incapable, March 23, and enters Doctors' Hospital in New York, March 31. Weighs less than 100 pounds and occasionally hallucinates (is diagnosed as having bromide poisoning less severe than Carlotta's). Develops pneumonia in early April, but responds to penicillin treatment. Declines offer from Saxe and Dorothy Commins to live with them in Princeton. Withdraws petition, April 23. Rejoins Carlotta in Boston on May 17, moving into Suite 401 of Shelton Hotel at 91 Bay State Road (will not leave suite, except for medical reasons, for remainder of his life). Marblehead Neck cottage is sold; O'Neill donates large archive of literary material to Yale, including typescript of *More Stately Mansions*. Visited by Russel Crouse, his only friend still on good terms with Carlotta. Reads mysteries, listens to baseball games on the radio, and takes increasing amounts of sedatives.

1952   Makes Carlotta sole literary executor of his published and unpublished writings. Destroys drafts and scenarios of unfinished cycle plays. *A Moon for the Misbegotten*, published by Random House, receives mixed reviews and sells poorly.

1953   Health deteriorates until he is confined to bed in September. Dies of pneumonia at the Shelton at 4:37 P.M., November 27. Post-mortem examination reveals rare degenerative disease of the cerebellum, possibly inherited and superficially resembling Parkinson's, as primary cause of tremor. Buried at Forest Hills Cemetery in Boston, December 2.

Note on the Texts

This volume includes the first twenty-nine plays of Eugene O'Neill's that are known to be extant, beginning with *A Wife for a Life*, copyrighted August 15, 1913, and ending with *The Emperor Jones*, completed in October 1920. In this seven-year period O'Neill began to write plays while living in New London, attended George Pierce Baker's playwriting class (English 47) at Harvard, joined The Provincetown Players on Cape Cod and went with them to New York, and saw the first Broadway production of one of his plays. O'Neill regarded many of the plays included in this volume, either at the time he wrote them or later, as apprentice pieces. Ten of the plays in this volume were never published by O'Neill, although he registered nine of them with the Copyright Office at the Library of Congress. (After they were copyrighted, he continued to work on some of them, but he later destroyed his typescripts containing the revisions.) He did publish five of his earliest plays (in *Thirst and Other One Act Plays*, 1914, an edition paid for by his father) but these plays were never published again during his lifetime.

When O'Neill joined The Provincetown Players in 1916 he began attending rehearsals of his plays whenever possible, a practice that he would continue for most of his career, preferring to make any revisions considered necessary himself. The printed form became for him at least as important as the staged production, because he had more control over the text. He often made revisions in preparing his plays for publication, including some of those made during productions. A few plays were published before he could incorporate his revisions into them; in these instances he inserted the revisions in the next edition. This volume prints the texts of the plays that incorporate O'Neill's final revisions. For the plays he did not publish, the text is either that of the first printing made from the typescript or, in three instances, that of the typescripts on file in the Library of Congress. The arrangement here follows, as nearly as can be determined, the order O'Neill wrote the plays rather than the order of their first publication.

O'Neill later described his earliest surviving play, *A Wife for a Life* (copyrighted August 15, 1913), as "a vaudeville skit" rather than a play, although the typescript subtitle is "A play in one act." He did not include the play in *Thirst*, his first book of one-act plays. This volume prints the text of the play from the first printing of *Lost Plays of Eugene O'Neill* (introduction by Lawrence Gellert, New York: New Fathoms Press, 1950), an unauthorized edition, printed from the typescripts on file at the Library of Congress, of five plays whose copyrights O'Neill had failed to renew. (The play also appeared in *Ten "Lost" Plays of Eugene O'Neill*, published by Random House in 1964, but that edition was based on the earlier editions *Thirst* and *Lost Plays*.)

The next five plays, beginning with *The Web* (which O'Neill wrote shortly after *A Wife for a Life* and later described as "the first *play* I ever wrote"), are printed in the order of their composition. The revised manuscript of *Thirst* is dated fall 1913; *Recklessness*, November 25, 1913; *Warnings*, dated 1913, is thought to have been written in December; and O'Neill placed *Fog* in 1914. Final arrangements for their publication by The Gorham Press in Boston were made in March 1914, with James O'Neill, O'Neill's father, paying the costs. *Thirst and Other One Act Plays* was published in an edition of 1,000 copies in August 1914. Though two of the plays in the book were staged at least once by The Provincetown Players, *Thirst* on the wharf in Provincetown in August 1916, and *Fog* in New York City on January 5, 1917, O'Neill never republished any of them (although he did renew the copyright in 1942). The texts of the five plays in The Gorham Press edition (1914) are printed here.

O'Neill completed at least five more plays before he left New London for Harvard University in the fall of 1914: *Bread and Butter*, *Bound East for Cardiff*, *Abortion*, *The Movie Man*, and *Servitude*. *Bread and Butter* was copyrighted May 2, 1914. He continued to work on the play after that date; in a letter of May 5, 1914, he wrote to a friend that he was "pruning the first act" of this four-act drama. Later in the summer he sent a revised version to his father's friend, producer George C. Tyler, but nothing came of this submission and O'Neill destroyed his own copy. This volume prints the text of the typescript copy deposited for copyright in the Library of Congress.

Bound East for Cardiff, copyrighted under the title *Children of the Sea* on May 14, 1914, was the first play of O'Neill's to be produced and the earliest play included in his collected works. O'Neill carefully revised the typescript of *Children of the Sea*: he changed the title, cut and revised some of the speeches and stage directions, and rewrote the dialect spelling. He also changed the order of the names in the list of characters, giving more prominence to the larger roles, and made the "First Officer" into "The Second Mate." (The typescript of *Children of the Sea* was published in transcript form in *"Children of the Sea" and Three Other Unpublished Plays by Eugene O'Neill*, edited by Jennifer McCabe Atkinson, Washington, D.C.: NCR Microcard Editions, 1972.) The play was produced at The Wharf Theatre in Provincetown on July 28, 1916; a second production was staged by The Provincetown Players in New York City, November 3, 1916. It was first published in pamphlet form with two other plays in *The Provincetown Plays, First Series*, edited by Frank Shay, November 1916. O'Neill made less extensive revisions in the play when he prepared it for inclusion in *The Moon of the Caribbees and Six Other Plays of the Sea*, the first book of his published by the firm of Boni & Liveright, which appeared in May 1919. The tramp steamer was given the name *Glencairn*, and "The Norwegian" was identified as "Paul." Driscoll was changed from a "red haired giant" to a "brawny Irishman," and "blond" was no longer used to describe the Norwegian Paul. He changed or added a few descriptive sentences and changed the spelling of "Oleson" to "Olson." O'Neill made his last revisions when he prepared the play for inclusion in *The Complete Works of Eugene O'Neill* (a limited, autographed, two-volume edition published by Boni & Liveright, dated 1924 but not distributed until early 1925). O'Neill went over the proofs for this edition with particular care, revising many of the plays, some more extensively than others. Only a few revisions were made in *Bound East for Cardiff*: two of the captain's speeches were changed and one sentence deleted; some dialect was corrected. None of the plays from *The Moon of the Caribbees and Six Other Plays of the Sea* were included in the four-volume uniform trade edition made from the type used for *The Complete Works* that Boni & Liveright published in 1925. Later editions of the seven sea plays were set from the 1919 edition (the type set for *The Complete Works* possibly having been dispersed by then) and therefore did not incorporate the revisions O'Neill made for *The Complete Works* edition. The text of *Bound East for Cardiff* printed in this volume is from *The Complete Works of Eugene O'Neill* (1924).

The next three plays in this volume were not published by O'Neill, nor were they produced. *Abortion* was copyrighted on May 19, 1914, *The Movie Man* on July 1, 1914, and *Servitude* on September 23, 1914. O'Neill believed that all three had been destroyed, but the typescripts remained in the Copyright Office at the Library of Congress and were printed in *Lost Plays of Eugene O'Neill* (1950). The texts printed here of the three plays are from that edition.

The Sniper and *The Personal Equation* are the only two plays known to survive from those O'Neill wrote while attending George Pierce Baker's English 47 playwrighting course at Harvard in 1914–15. O'Neill never published them. *The Sniper* was copyrighted March 13, 1915, and was staged once by The Provincetown Players in New York City on February 16, 1917. The play was first printed, from the text of the copyrighted typescript in the Library of Congress, in *Lost Plays of Eugene O'Neill* (1950); the text of that edition is printed here. *The Personal Equation*, written at Harvard during the spring 1915 semester, was never copyrighted by O'Neill, published by him, or produced on the stage. A typescript of the play was deposited in the Houghton Library at Harvard University. The play is published for the first time in *The Unknown O'Neill*, edited by Travis Bogard (New Haven: Yale University Press, 1988). The text of that edition is printed in this volume.

Before Breakfast was written in the summer of 1916, while O'Neill was living in Provincetown. The one-act play was staged in New York by The Provincetown Players, December 1, 1916, and published in *Provincetown Plays, Third Series*, edited by Frank Shay, December 1916. A second edition appeared in *A Treasury of Plays for Women*, edited by Frank Shay (Boston: Little, Brown, and Company, 1922), but O'Neill was not involved in this edition. He made his last revisions in the play, deleting words in both dialogue and stage directions, when he prepared the proofs for *The Complete Works of Eugene O'Neill* (Boni & Liveright, 1924). The text of *Before Breakfast* in *The Complete Works* is printed in this volume.

Now I Ask You was written while O'Neill was in Provincetown in the summer and fall of 1916, but not copyrighted until May 23, 1917, and was never staged or published in his lifetime. The text printed here is from the typescript on file in the Library of Congress Copyright Office.

O'Neill wrote four plays in rapid succession in Provincetown during the spring of 1917. All of them were produced, and all appeared in book form for the first time in *The Moon of the Caribbees and Six Other Plays of the Sea*, published by Boni & Liveright in May 1919. *In the Zone* was presented by the Washington Square Players on October 31, 1917; *Ile*, staged by The Provincetown Players, November 30, 1917, was printed in *The Smart Set*, a journal edited by H. L. Mencken and George Jean Nathan, in May 1918; *The Long Voyage Home*, staged by The Provincetown Players, November 2, 1917, was printed in *The Smart Set*, October 1917; and *The Moon of the Caribbees*, presented by The Provincetown Players, December 20, 1918, was printed in *The Smart Set*, August 1918. Following its editorial policy, the language of the seamen was toned down in the plays printed in *The Smart Set*. O'Neill restored his original language in *The Moon of the Caribbees and Six Other Plays of the Sea*. O'Neill read proofs of the plays once more in 1924 for the two-volume Boni & Liveright edition, *The Complete Works of Eugene O'Neill*. At this time he made a few small revisions in the stage directions for Smitty, the central character of *In the Zone*. A few dialect spellings in the play were inadvertently normalized in the new typesetting, but O'Neill's own revisions outweigh this defect. Later editions of the play were printed from the 1919 edition, not *The Complete Works*; although new editorial elements were introduced, O'Neill's last revisions were not included. The text of *In the Zone* printed in this volume is from *The Complete Works* (1924). O'Neill did not revise *Ile* or *The Long Voyage Home* for the 1924 edition. He may have been responsible for the deletion of two clauses in the stage directions setting the scene in

The Moon of the Caribbees in the 1924 edition, but in this case the loss of original dialect readings through inadvertent normalization seems to outweigh the possibly authorial deletions in the stage directions. He made no other revisions in later editions. The texts of *Ile*, *The Long Voyage Home*, and *The Moon of the Caribbees* printed here are therefore from the first book publication, *The Moon of the Caribbees and Six Other Plays of the Sea* (1919).

O'Neill finished writing *The Rope* in Provincetown in March 1918; the play, produced by The Provincetown Players, opened on April 26, 1918. It was first published in *The Moon of the Caribbees and Six Other Plays of the Sea* (1919). O'Neill worked on the play again in October 1924 when he read proofs for *The Complete Works* edition, making several revisions: he added repetitions in speeches by Mary, corrected Luke's age to twenty-one, and altered a few other words. Because later editions of the play were set from the 1919 edition, these last revisions were not included in them. This volume prints the text of *The Rope* in *The Complete Works of Eugene O'Neill* (1924).

O'Neill obtained two copyrights for *Beyond the Horizon*: the first on June 7, 1918, and the second on August 5, 1918. The play was produced by John D. Williams; it opened (after a tryout the day before in Yonkers, New York) at the Morosco Theatre for a series of special matinee performances on February 3, 1920. O'Neill made cuts in the play during rehearsals and helped with the direction. This was both his first long play to be produced and his first experience with the commercial theater. A few days before the play opened he wrote his wife, Agnes: "I have learned a lot. I'm a better playwright already, I feel it." The first edition, *Beyond the Horizon*, published by Boni & Liveright on March 10, 1920, appeared too close to production to incorporate revisions made during rehearsals; they were included in the second edition, *The Complete Works of Eugene O'Neill* (1924). O'Neill made no other revisions in later editions; the text of *Beyond the Horizon* in *The Complete Works* is printed here.

Shell Shock, written in Provincetown and copyrighted August 5, 1918, was never produced or published in O'Neill's lifetime. The text here is from the typescript deposited for copyright in the Library of Congress.

The Dreamy Kid was written in Provincetown in the summer of 1918, but The Provincetown Players decided not to use it in their opening program that year; the play was staged the following year on October 31, 1919, and first published in *Theatre Arts Magazine* in January 1920. Its first book publication was in *Contemporary One-Act Plays of 1921 (American)*, selected and edited by Frank Shay (Cincinnati, Ohio: Stewart Kidd Company, 1922), but O'Neill had nothing to do with this edition. He reviewed it again when he prepared *The Complete Works* edition in 1924, but made no revisions in the play. This volume prints the text of the play's first appearance in *Theatre Arts Magazine*.

O'Neill apparently decided to write *Where the Cross Is Made* after The Provincetown Players expressed doubts about *The Dreamy Kid*. The manuscript is dated "1918, fall." The Provincetown Players gave its first performance on November 22, 1918. The one-act play was made from the last act of another play, *Gold*, which he did not complete until 1920. As O'Neill explained in a letter to George Jean Nathan, "I merely took the last act situation and jammed it into the one-act form because I wanted to be represented on the Provincetown Players' opening bill." *Where the Cross Is Made* was first published in *The Moon of the Caribbees and Six Other Plays of the Sea* (1919) and was never revised by O'Neill. The text from that edition is printed in this volume.

O'Neill began *The Straw* in the fall of 1918 and finished it in May 1919. Boni & Liveright published it on April 7, 1921, in *The Emperor Jones, Diff'rent, The Straw*; it was produced by George C. Tyler and opened, after a tryout in New London on November 4, at The Greenwich Village Theatre on November 10, 1921. O'Neill attended rehearsals and made cuts and revisions in the play at that time, but he was not able to incorporate them into print until he prepared the play for inclusion in *The Complete Works of Eugene O'Neill* (1924). O'Neill made no further revisions; the text of the second edition of *The Straw* from *The Complete Works* edition is printed here.

Chris Christophersen was copyrighted June 5, 1919; it was

produced by George C. Tyler and opened with the title *Chris* in Atlantic City, New Jersey, on March 8, 1920, but it never opened in New York. O'Neill then rewrote the play and re-titled it *"Anna Christie."* The earlier version, taken from the typescript deposited for copyright in the Library of Congress, was published as *Chris Christophersen* by Random House in 1982, edited by Leslie Eric Comens. The text of that edition is printed here.

Gold, the long version of *Where the Cross Is Made*, was com-pleted in the spring of 1920. O'Neill attended only three re-hearsals before the play opened on June 1, 1921, and he felt too discouraged by what he saw to do further work on the play. The first edition, *Gold*, was published by Boni & Live-right, September 10, 1921. O'Neill extensively revised the play in 1924, when he was preparing it for inclusion in *The Com-plete Works* edition; the text of this second edition is printed here.

O'Neill completed *"Anna Christie"* (the play made from *Chris Christophersen*) in the summer of 1920, and it was copy-righted November 29, 1920, as *The Ole Davil*. O'Neill made some revisions while attending rehearsals. The play, produced by Arthur Hopkins, opened in New York City on November 2, 1921. The first edition was published by Boni & Liveright, July 24, 1922, in *The Hairy Ape, Anna Christie, The First Man*. O'Neill made no revisions in the play in later editions; the text of the first edition (1922) is printed here.

O'Neill began writing *The Emperor Jones* late in September 1920 and finished it in early October. It was immediately put into production by The Provincetown Players and opened in New York on November 1, 1920. The first publication was in the January 1921 number of *Theatre Arts Magazine*. O'Neill made a few revisions and cuts in the play when he prepared it for book publication by Boni & Liveright in *The Emperor Jones, Diff'rent, The Straw*, on April 7, 1921. He gave permis-sion for a third edition, *The Emperor Jones* (Cincinnati: Stew-art Kidd Company, 1921), but took no part in its preparation. O'Neill made his last revisions in the play when he prepared it for *The Complete Works of Eugene O'Neill*, including cutting two of Smithers' speeches, one from the end of Scene One and the second from the end of the play. (The deleted words are given in the notes to this volume.) The text printed here is from *The Complete Works* (1924).

This volume presents the texts of the editions and typescripts chosen for inclusion here. It does not attempt to reproduce features of the physical layout or design of these documents, such as the typography of speech headings and stage directions. The texts are reproduced without change, except for the correction of errors in the lists of characters and typographical errors. Spelling, punctuation, and capitalization are often expressive features, and they are not altered, even when inconsistent or irregular. O'Neill's own usage in spelling is retained: for example, "burries" for "buries"; "balling" for "bawling"; "dam" for "damn"; "mantle" for "mantel"; "lieing" for "lying"; "kitchinette" for "kitchenette"; "shrugg" for "shrug"; "loose" for "lose"; "beseaching" for "beseeching"; "liason" for "liaison"; "noone" for "no one"; "comradship" for "comradeship"; "begining" for "beginning"; "Gabbler" for "Gabler"; "breech" for "breach"; "Miss." for "Miss"; "curiousity" for "curiosity"; "chauffer" for "chauffeur." His handling of apostrophes is also retained: for example, "its" for "it's", or "it's" for "its"; "her's," "your's," "our's," and "their's"; "thats" for "that's"; "Mauds" for "Maud's," and "Ashleigh's" for "Ashleighs'"; and "o'ny" for "on'y," etc.

The following is a list of typographical errors corrected, cited by page and line number: 15.36–37, *murmus*; 21.6, peoples; 23.16, starvin.'; 23.40, *is if*; 24.36, dont; 51.25, *errie*; 56.38, musn't; 58.30, in; 65.26, *wonder*; 66.4, *lipe*; 69.19, women; 87.13, mechanist?; 88.28, *officer's*; 89.16, Damnation?; 92.34, bulkhead; 94.23, *stupified*; 98.25, Your're; 108.2, *stubborness*; 108.28, *then*; 115.19, *grooped*; 115.28, *the*; 121.27, lot things; 129.33, hasnt; 130.16, every I; 131.33, But let; 136.17, temperment; 136.34, CARTER; 137.7, ladies; 139.16, amm; 140.12, Might; 140.20, WE'll; 144.36, isn'T; 147.30, acquinance; 152.39, woman's; 166.13, *place*; 170.31, condider; 178.35, is; 179.1, *concieve*; 181.40, od; 189.13, e'; 193.35, do feel; 195.28, gittin; 205.9, *aggresively*; 212.37, time; 213.26, Love; 214.21, exhorbitant; 231.1, Senior; 232.4, fights; 237.35, light; 239.13, A lady; 247.23, born; 250.19, county; 272.11, Dr. Morse is here, ma'am.; 278.17, wont't; 286.24, things; 300.12, by; 300.12, cannon?; 302.40, village.; 307.26, *siezes*; 318.31, it?; 319.10, hate."; 321.27, pretense; 323.1, is where; 323.27, not,; 332.38, telling,; 334.39, *dryly*; 335.31, them; 336.34, T'is; 337.35, again, 338.11, Oh.; 339.36, Verra'; 343.21, —You; 349.28, nothing'; 352.39, Wexford"; 355.6, means; 356.40, they're; 357.13, *breaaking*; 363.18, *his eyes*; 367.17, s'what; 368.23, *pleading*; 371.2, son!; 373.28, *shoulder*; 375.23, memory; 376.37, The; 379.13, Tom; 381.23, you.; 403.4, high-celinged; 403.30, fadism; 408.19, *he*; 409.34, *scrutenizing*; 410.1, You too; 411.27, then enything; 413.16–17, catagorical; 413.37, marriage.; 416.24, mean will; 419.12, *disuade*; 429.31, hii him; 430.21, assinity; 431.28, abhorent; 435.27, witheld; 437.23, refering; 440.10, mine.—; 443.32, just just; 447.11, *quizical*; 447.22, spirituel; 454.11, mumies; 457.15, conradship; 461.32, *severly*; 464.39, *rouguishly*; 467.26, *preremptorily*; 472.17, sumbarrines; 472.31, 'Cose; 473.37, goin; 478.33, isself; 487.25, making; 492.35, he'; 535.39, blushin; 542.38, *deck.) dressed . . . uniform.)*; 550.30, there.; 555.31, everything; 566.4, trying; 623.38, *left. Ruth*; 658.20, her; 659.4, paled; 661.19, transfered; 665.18, do [ ]; 666.29, occurence; 666.34, brain.—; 668.16, army.—; 668.39, jarr; 670.22, *hafl*; 676.37, aint; 681.14, don'; 681.19, her sleep; 681.33, doin'; 683.29, *agin*; 683.31, you'; 727.23–24, suddenly but; 734.7, you're; 736.24, thinkin,'; 736.28, me?; 762.4, Is is; 769.1, *apolegetically*; 774.35, God; 777.39, talkin; 779.40, *for she*; 798.26, *Tommy*; 803.9, gentleman; 807.2, Ann's; 816.18, *see*; 872.27, Ay-Ay; 886.8, damdest; 889.11, *appreciately*; 969.7, *burst*; 979.30, Funny; 1000.26–27, babboon; 1003.18, Good-bye; 1005.5–6, *exasperately*; 1061.25, Jonsey.

Notes

In the notes below, the reference numbers denote page and line of the present volume (the line count includes act and scene headings). No note is made for material included in a standard desk-reference book. Quotations from Shakespeare have been keyed to *The Riverside Shakespeare*, ed. G. Blakemore Evans (Boston: Houghton Mifflin, 1974). For more detailed notes, references to other studies, and further biographical background, see: *The Unknown O'Neill*, edited by Travis Bogard (New Haven: Yale University Press, 1988); *Selected Letters of Eugene O'Neill*, edited by Travis Bogard and Jackson R. Bryer (New Haven: Yale University Press, 1988); *"Love and Admiration and Respect": The O'Neill-Commins Correspondence*, edited by Dorothy Commins (Durham: Duke University Press, 1986); *"As Ever, Gene": The Letters of Eugene O'Neill to George Jean Nathan*, edited by Nancy L. Roberts and Arthur W. Roberts (Rutherford, New Jersey: Farleigh Dickinson University Press, 1987); *"The Theatre We Worked For": The Letters of Eugene O'Neill to Kenneth Macgowan*, edited by Jackson R. Bryer, introductions by Travis Bogard (New Haven: Yale University Press, 1982); *Eugene O'Neill Work Diary 1924–1943*, preliminary edition, edited by Donald Gallup (2 vols.; New Haven: Yale University Library, 1981); Jennifer McCabe Atkinson, *Eugene O'Neill: A Descriptive Bibliography* (Pittsburgh: University of Pittsburgh Press, 1974); Travis Bogard, *Contour in Time: The Plays of Eugene O'Neill*, revised edition (New York: Oxford University Press, 1987); Arthur and Barbara Gelb, *O'Neill*, enlarged edition (New York: Harper & Row, 1973); Jordan Y. Miller, *Playwright's Progress: O'Neill and the Critics* (Chicago: Scott, Foresman and Company, 1965); Margaret Loftus Ranald, *The Eugene O'Neill Companion* (Westport, Connecticut: Greenwood Press, 1984); Louis Sheaffer, *O'Neill: Son and Playwright* (Boston: Little, Brown and Company, 1968) and *O'Neill: Son and Artist* (Boston: Little, Brown and Company, 1973).

The cast lists of the first productions below are supplied from the opening-night playbills and do not always correspond exactly with the character lists in the texts of the plays.

Contrary to current practice, O'Neill described stage settings from the point of view of the audience rather than the actors.

A WIFE FOR A LIFE

11.10–11   Greater . . . friend.]   Cf. John 15:13.

THE WEB

19.16   the Island]   Blackwells (later Welfare, now Roosevelt) Island in the East River, then the site of a prison.

21.8   hand . . . call]   To warn or challenge.

22.33   the "con"]   Consumption; tuberculosis.

THIRST

First produced by The Provincetown Players, September 1, 1916, at The Wharf Theatre, Provincetown, Massachusetts.

Direction: George Cram Cook   *A Gentleman:* George Cram Cook
Design: William Zorach   *A Dancer:* Louise Bryant
                                    A West Indian Sailor: Eugene G.
                                       O'Neill

FOG

First produced by The Provincetown Players, January 5, 1917, at The Playwrights' Theatre, New York City. The director is not known, but in the early years of the Players, O'Neill frequently directed his own plays.

Design: Margaret Swain and   *A Man of Business:* Hutchinson
   B. J. Nordfeldt   Collins
                                    A Peasant Woman: Margaret
A Poet: John Held   Swain
                                    The Third Officer: Karl Karstens

100.38   Hecuba . . . her.]   Cf. *Hamlet*, II, ii, 559–60.

BREAD AND BUTTER

141.4   Carter . . . Nick]   Nick Carter, the detective hero of a series of pulp novels.

151.26–27   Have . . . cup.]   Edward FitzGerald, *The Rubáiyát of Omar Khayyám* (1879 edition), stanza 93.

157.12   R.E.s]   See "Oh, stop that noise, Mr. Ree Morse!" (page 151.28). In a letter to John Weaver, January 13, 1921, O'Neill speaks of recovering from a hangover with "the Brooklyn Boys sounding the full brass band of Remorse after me."

BOUND EAST FOR CARDIFF

First produced by The Provincetown Players, July 28, 1916, at The Wharf Theatre, Provincetown, Massachusetts.

Direction: Eugene G. O'Neill and E. J. Ballantine

Yank: George Cram Cook
Driscoll: Frederic Burt
Cocky: E. J. Ballantine

Davis: Harry Kemp
The Captain: David Carb
The Second Mate: Eugene G. O'Neill
John Reed and Wilbur Daniel Steele were also in the cast.

SERVITUDE

273.23   badger game]   Blackmailing scheme in which a woman entices a man into a compromising situation so that they can be "discovered" by her male partner.

274.26–27   "Yea, . . . lutanist."]   Francis Thompson, "The Hound of Heaven" (1890), a poem O'Neill frequently recited from memory.

283.33–34   Richard . . . again.]   A line taken from Colley Cibber's adaptation (1700) of Shakespeare's *Richard III* and used in performances of the play by John Philip Kemble (1757–1823).

THE SNIPER

First produced by The Provincetown Players, February 16, 1917, at The Playwrights' Theatre in New York City.

Direction: Nina Moise

Rougon: George Cram Cook
The Village Priest: Donald Corley
A German Captain: Theron M. Bamberger

Privates: Morton Stafford and Robert Montcarr
Jean: Ida Rauh

THE PERSONAL EQUATION

311.16   Jugend, Simplissimus]   Radical German periodicals.

319.22   Colorado]   Scene of violent labor conflict in 1913–14, culminating in a massacre of striking mine workers and their families by the National Guard at Ludlow on April 20, 1914. More than forty people, including thirteen children, were killed when the Guard set fire to the strikers' tent city and machine-gunned the fleeing survivors.

BEFORE BREAKFAST

First produced by The Provincetown Players, December 1, 1916, at The Playwrights' Theatre, New York City.

Direction: Advice by James   *Mrs. Rowland:* Mary Pyne
   O'Neill and re-direction by   *Alfred:* Eugene G. O'Neill
   Eugene G. O'Neill

NOW I ASK YOU

417.5–7   "Ah, . . . twain!"]   Friedrich Nietzsche, *Thus Spake Zarathustra*, "About Marriage and Children," translation by Thomas Common.

425.25   the Square]   Washington Square, in Greenwich Village, New York City.

IN THE ZONE

First produced by The Washington Square Players, October 31, 1917, at The Comedy Theatre, New York City.

Design: Rollo Peters   *Scotty:* Eugene Lincoln
                                    Ivan: Edward Balzerit
Smitty: Frederick Roland   *Yank:* Jay Strong
Davis: Robert Strange   *Driscoll:* Arthur Hohl
Olsen: Abram Gillette   *Cocky:* Rienzi de Cordova

When the play was published Olsen was changed to Swanson, Yank to Jack.

479.11–12   box the compass]   Name the thirty-two points of the compass.

ILE

First produced by The Provincetown Players, November 30, 1917, at The Playwrights' Theatre, New York City.

Direction: Nina Moise   *Captain Keeney:* Hutchinson
Design: Louis B. Ell   Collins
                                    Slocum: Ira Remsen
Ben: Harold Conley   *Mrs. Keeney:* Clara Savage
The Steward: Robert Edwards   *Joe:* Louis B. Ell

THE LONG VOYAGE HOME

First produced by The Provincetown Players, November 2, 1917, at The Playwrights' Theatre, New York City.

Fat Joe: George Cram Cook
Nick: Harold Conley
Olson: Ira Remson
Driscoll: Hutchinson Collins

Cocky: O. K. Liveright
Ivan: Donald Dean Young
Kate: Alice MacDougal
Freda: Ida Rauh

THE MOON OF THE CARIBBEES

First produced by The Provincetown Players, December 20, 1918, at The Playwrights' Theatre, New York City.

Direction: Thomas Mitchell

Yank: Harry Winston
Driscoll: Hutchinson Collins
Olson: William Forster
  Batterham
Davis: W. Clay Hill
Cocky: O. K. Liveright
Smitty: Charles Ellis
Paul: Percy Winner

Lamps: Phil Lyons
Chips: Fred Booth
Old Tom: William Stuart
Big Frank: Howard Scott
Max: Jimmy Spike
Paddy: Charles Garland Kemper
Bella: Jean Robb
Susie: Bernice Abbott
Pearl: Ruth Collins Allen
The First Mate: Louis B. Ell

526.23   crew] In *The Moon of the Caribbees and Six Other Plays of the Sea*, which included *Moon of the Caribbees*, *Bound East for Cardiff*, *The Long Voyage Home*, *In the Zone*, *Ile*, *Where the Cross Is Made*, and *The Rope*, this note followed: "With the exception of 'In the Zone,' the action of all the plays in this volume takes place in years preceding the outbreak of the World War."

538.7−8   We're . . . way,] Rudyard Kipling, "Gentleman-Rankers" (1898).

THE ROPE

First produced by The Provincetown Players, April 26, 1918, at The Playwrights' Theatre, New York City.

Direction: Nina Moise

Abraham Bentley: O. K.
  Liveright

Annie: Dorothy Upjohn
Pat Sweeney: H. B. Tisdale
Mary: Edna Smith
Luke Bentley: Charles Ellis

548.32−34   "Woe . . . out."] Jeremiah 6:4.

548.36−38   "They . . . come."] Lamentations 4:18.

549.12−15   "The punishment . . . sins."] Lamentations 4:22.

549.21–23   "Behold, . . . daughter!"]   Ezekiel 16:44.

551.35–39   "Pour . . . desolate."]   Jeremiah 10:25.

553.18–21   "O Lord . . . me—"]   Lamentations 3:59–60.

553.25–26   "Render . . . hands."]   Lamentations 3:64.

553.32–34   "Give . . . Lord."]   Lamentations 3:65–66.

563.6–10   "Bring . . . found."]   Luke 15:22–24.

BEYOND THE HORIZON

First produced by John D. Williams, February 3, 1920, at the Morosco
Theatre, New York City.

Design: Homer Saint-Gaudens

James Mayo: Erville Alderson
Kate Mayo: Mary Jeffery
Captain Dick Scott: Max Mitzel
Andrew Mayo: Edward Arnold

Robert Mayo: Richard Bennett
Ruth Atkins: Helen MacKellar
Mrs. Atkins: Louise Closser Hale
Mary: Elfin Finn
Ben: George Hadden
Doctor Fawcett: George Riddell

574.17–19   "I . . . thee."]   Arthur Symons (1865–1945), "To Night."

THE DREAMY KID

First produced by The Provincetown Players, October 31, 1919, at The Playwrights' Theatre, New York City.

Direction: Ida Rauh
Design: Glenn Coleman

Mammy Saunders: Ruth
   Anderson

Abe: Harold Simmelkjaer
Ceely Ann: Leathe Colvert
Irene: Margaret Rhodes

WHERE THE CROSS IS MADE

First produced by The Provincetown Players, November 22, 1918, at The
Playwrights' Theatre, New York City.

Direction: Ida Rauh

Captain Isaiah Bartlett:
   Hutchinson Collins
Nat Bartlett: James Light

Sue Bartlett: Ida Rauh
Doctor Higgins: O. K. Liveright
Silas Horne: Louis B. Ell
Cates: Foster Damon
Jimmy Kanaka: F. Ward Roege

701.36–37   *elbows . . . hands*]   Never corrected by O'Neill.

THE STRAW

First produced by George C. Tyler; after a November 4 tryout in New London, Connecticut, it opened November 10, 1921, at The Greenwich Village Theatre, New York City.

Direction: John Westley
Design: Gates & Morange

Bill Carmody: Harry Harwood
Nora: Viola Cecil Ormonde
Tom: Richard Ross
Billy: Norris Millington
Doctor Gaynor: George Woodward
Fred Nicholls: Robert Strange

Eileen Carmody: Margalo Gillmore
Stephen Murray: Otto Kruger
Miss Howard: Dorothea Fisher
Miss Gilpin: Katherine Grey
Doctor Stanton: George Farren
Mrs. Turner: Grace Henderson
Miss Bailey: Alice Haynes
Mrs. Abner: Nora O'Brien
Mrs. Brennan: Jennie Lamont

746.4–6   "A glass . . . enow!"]   Cf. Edward FitzGerald, *The Rubáiyát of Omar Khayyám* (1879 edition), stanza 12.

CHRIS CHRISTOPHERSEN

Titled *Chris,* the play was first produced by George C. Tyler, March 8, 1920, at the Apollo Theatre, Atlantic City, New Jersey, and played for one more week, beginning March 15, at the Broad Street Theatre in Philadelphia.

Direction: Frederick Stanhope

Johnny "the Priest": James C. Mack
Jack Burns: Claude Gourand
Adams: Max L. Schrade
Longshoreman: Frank Devlin
Larry: William E. Hallman
A Postman: Harry MacFayden
Chris Christophersen: Emmett Corrigan
Mickey: Dan Moyles

Devlin: George A. Lawrence
Marthy Owen: Mary Hampton
Anna Christophersen: Lynn Fontanne
Captain Jessup: Roy Cochrane
The Steward: George Spelvin
Paul Andersen: Arthur Ashley
Edwards: William Smith
Jonesy: John Rogers
Glass: Gerald Rogers

795.1   CHRISTOPHERSEN]   O'Neill later learned that the Swedish spelling is "Christopherson," and he changed it in *"Anna Christie."*

802.38–40   "My . . . Tchee-tchee."]   According to a letter from O'Neill to his wife, Agnes, written in December 1919, this song was composed by "Lefty," a bartender at the "Hell Hole" (the Golden Swan saloon) in Greenwich Village: "He swears—(and I believe him)—that Josephine is his own stuff, a song he made up when he was singing in a tough Wop cabaret—'my own bull-s—t,' he exclaims proudly. That it is to be heard on Broadway is a great event in his life. He offers, as soon as rehearsals start, to go up for a couple of hours every morning to instruct Corrigan how to sing it—without desiring pay for his services! All he wants is two seats to take his girl to surprise her with his song—on Broadway!" The tune is as follows:

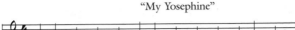

"My Yosephine"

My   Yo- se- phine, come   board de ship. Long   time Ay vait for

you.   De   moon, she shine. She   look-a   yust like   you.—

809.23   the Plate]   The Rio de la Plata, estuary between Argentina and Uruguay.

GOLD

First produced by John D. Williams, June 1, 1921, at Frazee Theatre, New York City.

Direction: Homer
   Saint-Gaudens
Scenery: Joseph Physioc
Decorations: Mrs. Sidney B.
   Harris

Captain Isaiah Bartlett: Willard
   Mack
Silas Horne: J. Fred Holloway
Ben Cates: Charles D. Brown

Jimmy Kanaka: T. Tamamoto
Butler: George Marion
Abel: Ashley Buck
Sarah Allen Bartlett: Katherine
   Grey
Sue: Geraldine O'Brien
Nat: E. J. Ballantine
Daniel Drew: Charles Francis
Doctor Berry: Scott Cooper

"ANNA CHRISTIE"

First produced by Arthur Hopkins, November 2, 1921, at the Vanderbilt Theatre, New York City.

Direction: Arthur Hopkins
Design: Robert Edmond Jones

"Johnny-the-Priest": James C.
  Mack
First Longshoreman: G. O.
  Taylor
Second Longshoreman: John
  Hanley
A Postman: William Augustin

Chris. Christopherson: George
  Marion
Marthy Owen: Eugenie Blair
Anna Christopherson: Pauline Lord
Three Men of a Steamer's Crew:
  Messrs. Reilly, Hansen, and
  Kennedy
Mat Burke: Frank Shannon
Johnson: Ole Anderson

961.39–962.2   "My . . . tchee-tchee."]   See note to 802.38–40.

THE EMPEROR JONES

First produced by The Provincetown Players, November 1, 1920, at The Play-wrights' Theatre, New York City.

Direction: George Cram Cook
Design: Cleon Throckmorton

Brutus Jones: Charles S. Gilpin
Henry Smithers: Jasper Deeter
An Old Native Woman:
  Christine Ell
Lem: Charles Ellis
Soldiers: S.I. Thompson,
  Lawrence Vail, Leo
  Richman, James Martin, and
  Owen White
Jeff: S. I. Thompson
The Negro Convicts: Leo
  Richman, Lawrence Vail, S.
  I. Thompson, and Owen
  White

The Prison Guard: James Martin
Planters: Frank Schwartz, C. I.
  Martin, and W. D. Slager
Spectators: Jeannie Begg and
  Charlotte Grauert
Auctioneer: Frederick Ward Roege
Slaves: James Martin, S. I.
  Thompson, Leo Richman,
  Owen White, and Lawrence
  Vail
Congo Witch-Doctor: S. I.
  Thompson

1043.32   'im what's what!]   In the first book publication, *The Emperor Jones, Diff'rent, The Straw* (New York: Boni & Liveright, 1921), the passage continues: [*Then putting business before the pleasure of this thought, looking around him with cupidity.*] A bloke ought to find a 'ole lot in this palace that'd go for a bit of cash. Let's take a look, 'Arry, me lad. [*He starts for the doorway on right as . . .*

1061.28   o' style, any'ow!]   The Boni & Liveright edition (1921) continues: [LEM *makes a motion to the soldiers to carry the body out left.* SMITHERS *speaks to him sneeringly.*]

SMITHERS—And I s'pose you think it's yer bleedin' charms and yer silly beatin' the drum that made 'im run in a circle when 'e'd lost 'imself, don't yer? [*But* LEM *makes no reply, does not seem to hear the question, walks out left after his men.* SMITHERS *looks after him with contemptuous scorn.*] Stupid as 'ogs, the lot of 'em! Blarsted niggers!

CATALOGING INFORMATION

O'Neill, Eugene Gladstone, 1888–1953.
    Complete plays 1913–1920.

    (The Library of America ; 40)
    Edited by Travis Bogard.
    Contents (v. 1): Wife for a life — Web — Thirst — Recklessness —
Warnings — Fog — Bread and butter — Bound east for Cardiff —
Abortion — Movie man — Servitude — Sniper — Personal equation —
Before breakfast — Now I ask you — In the zone — Ile — Long voyage
home — Moon of Caribbees — Rope — Beyond the horizon — Shell
shock — Dreamy kid — Where cross is made — Straw — Chris
Christophersen — Gold — Anna Christie — Emperor Jones.
    1. Theater—American—20th century. I. Title. II. Series.
PS3529.N5   1988   812'52   88-50685

ISBN 0–940450–48–8 (v. 1)

This book is set in 10 point Linotron Galliard,
a face designed for photocomposition by Matthew Carter
and based on the sixteenth-century face Granjon. The paper
is acid-free Ecusta Nyalite and meets the requirements for perma-
nence of the American National Standards Institute. The binding
material is Brillianta, a 100% woven rayon cloth made by
Van Heek-Scholco Textielfabrieken, Holland. The com-
position is by Haddon Craftsmen, Inc., and The
Clarinda Company. Printing and binding
by R. R. Donnelley & Sons Company.
Designed by Bruce Campbell.

PS 3529 .N5 1988 v.1
O'Neill, Eugene, 1888-1953.
Complete plays

DATE DUE

NOV 0 3 1997			
NOV 2 4 1997			
DEC 0 9 1998			
JAN 0 3 1999			
SEP 3 0 2000			

CONCORDIA COLLEGE LIBRARY
2811 N. E. HOLMAN ST.
PORTLAND, OREGON 97211